٢

Real Estate Principles

A Value Approach

Fifth Edition

Finance Series Page, c 2018 (spring)

The McGraw-Hill/Irwin Series in Finance, Insurance, and Real Estate

Stephen A. Ross,
Franco Modigliani Professor of Finance and
Economics,
Sloan School of Management,
Massachusetts Institute of Technology,
Consulting Editor

FINANCIAL MANAGEMENT

Block, Hirt, and Danielsen
Foundations of Financial Management
Sixteenth Edition

Brealey, Myers, and Allen
Principles of Corporate Finance
Twelfth Edition

Brealey, Myers, and Allen
Principles of Corporate Finance, Concise
Second Edition

Brealey, Myers, and Marcus
Fundamentals of Corporate Finance
Ninth Edition

Brooks
FinGame Online 5.0

Bruner
Case Studies in Finance: Managing for
Corporate Value Creation
Eighth Edition

Cornett, Adair, and Nofsinger
Finance: Applications and Theory
Fourth Edition

Cornett, Adair, and Nofsinger
M: Finance
Third Edition

DeMello
Cases in Finance
Third Edition

Grinblatt (editor)
Stephen A. Ross, Mentor: Influence
through Generations

Grinblatt and Titman
Financial Markets and Corporate Strategy
Second Edition

Higgins
Analysis for Financial Management
Eleventh Edition

Ross, Westerfield, and Jaffe
Corporate Finance
Eleventh Edition

Ross, Westerfield, Jaffe, and Jordan
Corporate Finance: Core Principles
and Applications
Fifth Edition

Ross, Westerfield, and Jordan
Essentials of Corporate Finance
Ninth Edition

Ross, Westerfield, and Jordan
Fundamentals of Corporate Finance
Eleventh Edition

Shefrin
Behavioral Corporate Finance:
Decisions that Create Value
Second Edition

INVESTMENTS

Bodie, Kane, and Marcus
Essentials of Investments
Tenth Edition

Bodie, Kane, and Marcus
Investments
Tenth Edition

Hirt and Block
Fundamentals of Investment Management
Tenth Edition

Jordan, Miller, and Dolvin
Fundamentals of Investments: Valuation
and Management
Eighth Edition

Stewart, Piros, and Heisler
Running Money: Professional Portfolio
Management
First Edition

Sundaram and Das
Derivatives: Principles and Practice
Second Edition

FINANCIAL INSTITUTIONS
AND MARKETS

Rose and Hudgins
Bank Management and Financial Services
Ninth Edition

Rose and Marquis
Financial Institutions and Markets
Eleventh Edition

Saunders and Cornett
Financial Institutions Management: A Risk
Management Approach
Ninth Edition

Saunders and Cornett
Financial Markets and Institutions
Sixth Edition

INTERNATIONAL FINANCE

Eun and Resnick
International Financial Management
Eighth Edition

REAL ESTATE

Brueggeman and Fisher
Real Estate Finance and Investments
Fifteenth Edition

Ling and Archer
Real Estate Principles: A Value Approach
Fifth Edition

FINANCIAL PLANNING AND
INSURANCE

Allen, Melone, Rosenbloom, and Mahoney
Retirement Plans: 401(k)s, IRAs, and
Other Deferred Compensation Approaches
Eleventh Edition

Altfest
Personal Financial Planning
Second Edition

Harrington and Niehaus
Risk Management and Insurance
Second Edition

Kapoor, Dlabay, Hughes, and Hart
Focus on Personal Finance: An Active
Approach to Help You Achieve Financial
Literacy
Fifth Edition

Kapoor, Dlabay, Hughes, and Hart
Personal Finance
Eleventh Edition

Walker and Walker
Personal Finance: Building Your Future
Second Edition

Real Estate Principles

A Value Approach

Fifth Edition

David C. Ling
University of Florida

Wayne R. Archer
University of Florida

Mc
Graw
Hill
Education

REAL ESTATE PRINCIPLES: A VALUE APPROACH, FIFTH EDITION

Published by McGraw-Hill Education, 2 Penn Plaza, New York, NY 10121. Copyright © 2018 by McGraw-Hill Education. All rights reserved. Printed in the United States of America. Previous editions © 2013, 2010, 2008, and 2005. No part of this publication may be reproduced or distributed in any form or by any means, or stored in a database or retrieval system, without the prior written consent of McGraw-Hill Education, including, but not limited to, in any network or other electronic storage or transmission, or broadcast for distance learning.

Some ancillaries, including electronic and print components, may not be available to customers outside the United States.

This book is printed on acid-free paper.

1 2 3 4 5 6 7 8 9 LWI 21 20 19 18 17

ISBN 978-0-07-783636-8
MHID 0-07-783636-7

Chief Product Officer, SVP Products & Markets: *G. Scott Virkler*
Vice President, General Manager, Products & Markets: *Marty Lange*
Managing Director: *James Heine*
Executive Brand Manager: *Charles Synovec*
Director, Product Development: *Rose Koos*
Lead Product Developer: *Michele Janicek*
Product Developer: *Jennifer Upton*
Digital Product Developer: *Tobi Philips*
Director of Digital Content: *Douglas Ruby*
Digital Product Analyst: *Kevin Shanahan*
Marketing Manager: *Melissa Caughlin*
Director, Content Design & Delivery: *Linda Avenarius*
Program Manager: *Mark Christianson*
Content Project Managers: *Jeni McAtee, Bruce Gin, Karen Jozefowicz*
Buyer: *Jennifer Pickel*
Content Licensing Specialists: *Melisa Seegmiller, text; Melissa Homer, image*
Cover Image: *Photographs in the Carol M. Highsmith Archive, Library of Congress, Prints & Photographs Division*
Compositor: *Aptara, Inc.*
Printer: *LSC Communications*

All credits appearing on page or at the end of the book are considered to be an extension of the copyright page.

Library of Congress Cataloging-in-Publication Data

Names: Ling, David C., author. | Archer, Wayne R., author.
Title: Real estate principles : a value approach / David C. Ling, University of Florida, Wayne R. Archer, University of Florida.
Description: Fifth Edition. | Dubuque, IA : McGraw-Hill Education, [2016] | Revised edition of the authors' Real estate principles, c2012.
Identifiers: LCCN 2016047076| ISBN 9780077836368 (alk. paper) | ISBN 0077836367 (alk. paper)
Subjects: LCSH: Real estate business—United States.
Classification: LCC HD255 .L56 2016 | DDC 333.33/2—dc23 LC record available at https://lccn.loc.gov/2016047076

The Internet addresses listed in the text were accurate at the time of publication. The inclusion of a website does not indicate an endorsement by the authors or McGraw-Hill Education, and McGraw-Hill Education does not guarantee the accuracy of the information presented at these sites.

Dedications

To my wife, Lucy, for her continued patience and understanding during this latest revision of the book and to our children, Alex, Sarah, and Rebecca, who have really tried to understand why Dad spends so many nights and weekends working in his home office.

—DCL

To my wife, Penny, who has always matched our efforts in this book with an equal measure of her devotion, support, and assistance; to our children Stephen, John, and Jennifer, who generously supported me with enthusiasm for the task; and to my mother and Penny's mother, who always kept the faith that I would do something useful with my "typewriter."

—WRA

About the Authors

DAVID C. LING

David C. Ling is the McGurn Professor of Real Estate at the University of Florida. Professor Ling received an MBA (1977) in finance and a Ph.D. (1984) in real estate and economics from The Ohio State University. His academic and professional publications have included articles on housing policy and economics, mortgage markets and pricing, private commercial real estate investments, publicly traded real estate companies, and performance evaluation.

During 2000 Professor Ling served as President of the American Real Estate and Urban Economics Association (AREUEA). From 2000 to 2005, he also served as editor of *Real Estate Economics*. Professor Ling serves on numerous journal editorial boards including *Real Estate Economics,* the *Journal of Real Estate Finance and Economics,* the *Journal of Housing Economics,* and *The Journal of Real Estate Research.* In 2011, Professor Ling was the recipient of the George Bloom Award, which is presented annually by the Directors of the American Real Estate and Urban Economics Association for "outstanding contributions to the field of real estate academics." In 2010, he was awarded the David Ricardo Medal by the American Real Estate Society, which is ARES's highest honor "in recognition of research productivity and influence over a twenty year period."

Professor Ling has provided research and consulting services to several state and national organizations including the Federal National Mortgage Association, the National Association of Home Builders, the National Association of Realtors, the Florida Association of Realtors, and the CCIM Institute. He is a Fellow of the Homer Hoyt Institute, a faculty member of the Weimer School of Advanced Studies in Real Estate, a board member and Fellow of the Real Estate Research Institute, a member of the National Association of Real Estate Investment Trusts's Research Council, and a Fellow of the Royal Institution of Chartered Surveyors (FRICS).

Additional information on Professor Ling is available at http://warrington.ufl.edu/departments/fire.

WAYNE R. ARCHER

Wayne R. Archer is the William D. Hussey Professor at the Warrington College of Business, University of Florida. He is Executive Director of the Bergstrom Center for Real Estate Studies. He received a Masters in economics from Wichita State University (1968) and a Ph.D. in economics from Indiana University (1974). He has been a faculty member at the University of Florida since 1971. From 1979 through 1981, he served as a visiting researcher at the Federal Home Loan Bank Board and Federal Savings and Loan Insurance Corporation. His research publications include articles on office markets, house price indices, mortgage prepayment, mortgage pricing, and mortgage default risk.

Professor Archer is a member of the American Real Estate and Urban Economics Association, where he has served on the board of directors, and also is a member of the American Real Estate Society. He served on the editorial board of *Real Estate Economics.* He is a Fellow of the Homer Hoyt Institute.

Professor Archer has worked in industry education throughout his academic career, including service as the educational consultant to the Florida Real Estate Commission from 1985 to 1999. Among additional roles, he served as a regular faculty member in programs of the Mortgage Bankers Association of America, in the Institute of Financial Education affiliated with the U.S. League of Savings and Loan Associations, and, more recently, with Freddie Mac. In addition, he has provided consulting services to industry and government from time to time throughout his career.

Additional information on Professor Archer is available at http://warrington.ufl.edu/departments/fire.

Brief Table of Contents

Preface

The study and practice of real estate draws on a multitude of disciplines including architecture, urban and regional planning, building construction, urban economics, law, and finance. This diversity of perspectives presents a challenge to the instructor of a real estate principles course. Depending on their backgrounds and training and on the interests of the students, some instructors may choose to emphasize the legal concepts that define and limit the potential value of real estate. Other instructors may focus more on licensing and brokerage issues (popular topics with many students) or on the investment decision-making process. Still others may feel that real estate market and feasibility analysis should be the core topics in a principles class. In short, one of the difficulties in teaching an introductory real estate course is that there appear to be too many "principles." The critical question thus becomes: What framework should be used to teach these principles?

Although the subject of real estate can be studied from many perspectives, we have adopted the value perspective as our unifying theme. Why? Because value is central to virtually all real estate decision making including whether and how to lease, buy, or mortgage a property acquisition; whether to renovate, refinance, demolish, or expand a property; and when and how to divest (sell, trade, or abandon) a property. Thus, whether a person enters the business of real estate in a direct way (e.g., development and ownership), becomes involved in a real estate service business (e.g., brokerage, property management, consulting, appraisal), or simply owns a home, he or she must continually make investment valuation decisions or advise others on their decisions. The key to making sound investment decisions is to understand how property values are created, maintained, increased, or destroyed.

Once value is established as the central theme, all other concepts and principles of real estate analysis can be built around it. Legal considerations, financing requirements and alternatives, income and property tax considerations, and local market conditions all are important primarily in the context of how they affect the value of the property. For example, in Part 2 students will study growth management and land use regulations. Although these concepts have great interest from a political and public policy perspective, they are important from a real estate view primarily because of their potential effects on property rents and values. Similarly, the "imperfections" in real estate markets discussed in Part 3—such as the lack of adequate data, the large dollar value of properties, and the immobility of land and structures—are of interest primarily because of their effects on market values. Our objective is to provide the reader with a framework and a set of valuation and decision-making tools that can be used in a variety of situations.

The Fifth Edition

Since the publication of *Real Estate Principles: A Value Approach,* Fourth Edition, continued changes have come upon the world of real estate. This is true in transactions and brokerage with continued advancement of electronic marketing and the arrival of completely new forms and procedures for most real estate transactions, it is true in valuation with the expansion of automated valuation systems, a new version of the Uniform Residential Appraisal Report, and of new residential and commercial property data sources, and it is true in development and construction with the shift to "green" building. But it is still more true in real estate finance and capital sources where the dramatic advancement of internet lending and the implementation of the "Dodd-Frank" Act have displaced traditional practices, procedures and players, in mortgage finance. For investment property, the new players tend to be neither debt nor equity, but integrated entities who create a "capital structure," and even the ownership structure, for the property. In addition, there continues to be change with profound and far-reaching implications in a world where we now understand that both residential and commercial property values can go down as well as up. This realization colors the demand for home ownership as well as every aspect of real estate investment, finance, and transactions for the foreseeable future.

Changes in This Edition

- The Test Bank has been expanded by 5-10 questions per chapter.
- *Industry Issues* are updated throughout the text to reflect current issues and concerns in the real estate industry.
- All web links and web search exercises are revised and updated.
- Data, charts, and graphs have been updated wherever possible throughout the text.
- Chapter 1: The discussion of the role of government and the production of real estate assets is updated.
- Chapter 2: Numerous clarifications and updates have been made throughout the chapter. New material on condominiums has been added along with a related new Industry Issue.
- Chapter 3: All content is updated.
- Chapter 4: All content is updated, along with numerous clarifications. In addition, new topics are added, including form based zoning, and a summary overview of restrictions on real property.
- Chapter 5: The effect of the Great Recession is incorporated. References are expanded and updated. The use of aerial photos to depict changing urban patterns is refined.
- Chapter 6: All content is updated. New tools of market analysis are examined, including the use if exclusion analysis, use of proxy variables and use of analogy.
- Chapter 7: The chapter is updated to reflect recent changes in Uniform Standards for Professional Appraisal Practice (USPAP) that governs the appraisal process. The latest version of the Uniform Residential Appraisal Report (URAR) is included.
- Chapter 8: The Centre Point office building example is updated to reflect current mortgage rates and other market conditions. Additional practice problems on direct capitalization are added to the end-of-chapter problems.
- Chapter 9: All charts are updated. Discussion of foreclosure is expanded along with owner choices in case of a financially "underwater" residence, including the process of a short sale. Discusson of the Dodd-Frank Wall Street Reform and Consumer Protection Act is expanded, along with the Consumer Financial Protection Bureau and new forms and procedures required for home mortgage loans.
- Chapter 10: All the data and examples are updated. All FHA, VA, and conventional prime residential loan requirements and lender guidelines are updated. New topics include expanded discussion of "piggyback" mortgages and Qualified Mortgages.
- Chapter 11: Numerous topics have been clarified and all tables, charts, and examples have been updated. The terminology is updated to reflect current industry usage. Discussion of mortgage banking has been updated to reflect changes in the nature of that industry. A new industry issues topic has been added on the rent vs buy decision. Finally discussion is added on the new public policy focus in home mortgage lending: ability to pay.
- Chapter 12: A new *Industry Issues* insert is included on the question of who should use a broker. The example listing agreement form has been replaced with an updated version. All information and examples are updated and discussions are expanded or clarified.
- Chapter 13: The Dodd-Frank Act has resulted in complete change in the forms and procedures for home mortgage lending and for virtually all home sale closings. These changes have been fully incorporated in the chapter. Also, a new section has been added on the increasingly common practice of escrow and electronic closings.

- Chapter 15: The discussion of the trade-off between discount points and contract mortgage rates has been expanded.
- Chapter 16: Revisions reflect ongoing changes in the typical permanent loan origination process, recourse versus nonrecourse loans, the level of available commercial mortgage rates, and other typical loan terms. The discussion of alternative capital structures has been expanded. A discussion of participating mortgages has been added.
- Chapter 17: There is expanded discussion of private equity funds to reflect their surge in importance in recent years. The section on real estate investment trusts (REITs), including their recent return performance, has been completely updated. Updated data support the revised discussion of the sources of commercial real estate debt and equity.
- Chapters 18 and 19: The Centre Point office building example is updated, as are the data on capitalization rates.
- Chapter 20: All tax rates and data are updated. A brief discussion of the impact of the 2012 American Taxpayer Relief Act on real estate taxation is added. The Centre Point office building example is updated.
- Chapter 22: The discussion of lease terms and conditions is updated to reflect recent changes and industry standards. There is expanded discussion of nonmonetary lease clauses and terms.
- Chapter 23: All data and information have been updated. New discussion is added concerning appropriate criteria in development decisions.

Intended Audience

Real Estate Principles is designed for use in an introductory real estate course at both the undergraduate and graduate levels, though some chapters may be used by instructors teaching courses focused on real estate market analysis, finance, and investment. In terms of background or prerequisites, some familiarity with basic economics and business finance principles is helpful and will allow the instructor to move more quickly through some of the material (especially Parts 1, 3, 6, and 7). However, the book is designed to be largely self-contained. As a result, students with different backgrounds will find the text accessible. In particular, the direct use of discounting and other time-value-of-money techniques is limited to Parts 6–8, allowing the text to be used by students with little or no background in time-value-of-money techniques.

Organization

Part 1 of the book provides an overview of real estate and real estate markets. In Part 2, we provide an overview of the legal foundations of value and discuss the significant influence that federal, state, and local governments and agencies have on real estate decision making and property values. In Part 3, we discuss the market determinants of value, how the benefits and costs of ownership can be forecasted, and how real estate appraisers convert these estimates of future cash flows and expenses into estimates of current market value.

Part 4 discusses the financing of home ownership, including the law that underlies residential mortgage contracts, the most common types of mortgages used to finance home ownership, and the lenders and other capital market investors that provide funds for residential mortgage loans. In addition to financing their real estate acquisitions, owners must navigate the often time-consuming and complex waters associated with acquiring and disposing of real property. The brokering and closing of real property transactions is presented in Part 5.

Parts 1–5 (Chapters 1–13) do not require knowledge of discounting and time-value-of-money techniques; thus, these chapters are accessible to students with limited or no background in finance and economics. Although basic time-value concepts are at the heart of this book, not every student studies them before encountering a real estate course. We have separated the formal application (though not the underlying ideas) of time-value into one section (Part 6). This enables the instructor to choose when and how these concepts will be put before the student—whether before, parallel with, or after the student is introduced to the real estate content. Indeed, one option is for the student to complete Chapters 1–13 without interjection of formal time-value instruction. Further, this nontechnical approach can be extended to Chapters 16–18, as noted below.

In Part 6, we introduce the formal applications of compound interest and present value that are often key to a deeper understanding of mortgage calculations and the valuation of income-producing properties, such as office buildings and shopping centers. For students who have had basic economics and business finance courses, Chapters 14 and 15 of Part 6 may contain substantial review. For others, these chapters contain new concepts that will require study and practice to master. Instructors wishing to bypass Part 6 can move directly from Part 5 to Chapters 16–18. However, instructors wishing to dig more deeply into commercial real estate financing and investing should review or cover in detail Chapters 14 and 15 before proceeding with coverage of Part 7. We note that the three chapters contained in Part 8 also do not assume knowledge of time-value-of-money techniques.

Although we recommend the material be covered in the order presented in the text, Parts 2 through 8 can generally be covered in any order, depending on the preferences of the instructor and the primary focus of the course. For example, instructors who prefer to cover the investment material first may elect to move directly to Parts 6 and 7 immediately after Part 1.

Regardless of the emphasis placed on the various chapters and materials, we believe strongly that an introductory course in real estate should be as substantive and challenging as beginning courses in fields such as accounting, economics, and finance. The course should go beyond definitions and the discussion of current professional practice. Moreover, its focus should be on real estate principles and decision tools, not simply the current rules and practice for transactions that are so important to real estate sales licensing and brokerage.

David C. Ling

Wayne R. Archer

We have included many pedagogical features in this book that will be valuable learning tools for your students. This overview walks through some of the most important elements.

LEARNING OBJECTIVES

After reading this chapter you will be able to:

1 Explain the role of transportation modes and natural resources in the location and evolution of cities.

2 Define economic base activities, distinguish them from secondary activities, and explain the role of both in the growth or decline of a city.

OUTLINE

Introduction
Market Misjudgments in Real Estate
Minimizing Market Errors
The Creation, Growth, and Decline of Cities
Where Cities Occur
The Economic Base of a City
Resources of a City: The Supply Side of Urban Growth
The Shape of a City
Demand for Proximity and Bid-Rent Curves
Bid-Rent Curves, Urban Land Uses, and Land Value Contours
Changing Transportation, Changing Technology, and Changing Urban Form

Introduction

Most of the real property in the United States is privately owned. If real estate markets worked well, this should allow market forces to determine land uses quite effectively. Unregulated competitive bidding would bring about the most productive use of each parcel, and the price paid for the parcel would exactly reflect its usefulness, much as described in Chapter 5. But this does not completely happen for several reasons. One of the reasons is because of **externalities:** the unintended and unaccounted for consequences of one land user upon others. For example, the creation of a shopping center on a site may cause harm to neighbors through increased traffic delays, noise, increased storm runoff across neighboring land, "light pollution," or other visual or environmental deterioration. Another problem that arises is that buyers of property suffer from incomplete information. Once a structure is built

Learning Objectives

Each chapter begins with a summary of the objectives of the chapter and describes the material to be covered, providing students with an overview of the concepts they should understand after reading the chapter.

Chapter Outlines

A chapter outline is featured among each chapter opener. Each outline lists the chapter headings and subheadings for a quick reference for both professors and students.

Chapter Introductions

The first section of each chapter describes the purpose of reading each chapter, and provides links between the different concepts.

Main Features

Key Terms

Key terms are indicated in bold within the text for easy reference. A list of key terms from each chapter plus page references can be found in the end-of-chapter material. The glossary contains the definitions of all key terms.

Market Value, Investment Value, and Transaction Prices

Before discussing the framework for estimating the market value of real estate, it is important to distinguish among the concepts of market value, investment value, and transaction price. Real estate appraisers generally define the **market value** of a property as its most probable selling price, assuming "normal" sale conditions.[1] Alternatively, it can be viewed as the value the typical (imaginary) participant would place on a property. The concept of market value rests upon the presence of willing buyers and sellers freely bidding in competition with one another. It is the result of the interacting forces of supply and demand. If real estate markets were perfectly competitive, market value would equal the most recent transaction price.

Industry Issues

These boxes, located in almost all chapters, feature current and interesting real-world applications of the concepts discussed in the chapters.

1-2 INDUSTRY *ISSUES*

Selling Real Estate on eBay

eBay Real Estate is not quite an auction. Because of the wide variety of laws governing the sale of real estate, eBay auctions of real property are not legally binding offers to buy and sell. When a real estate auction ends, neither party is obligated (as they are in other eBay auctions) to complete the transaction. The buyer and seller must get together to consummate the deal.

Nonetheless, eBay Real Estate sales are popular, and the gross sales are growing by leaps and bounds. You do not have to be a professional real estate agent to use this category, although that kind of pro experience may help when it comes to closing the deal. If you know land and your local real estate laws, eBay gives you the perfect venue to subdivide those 160 acres in Wyoming that Uncle Regis left you in his will.

For less than the cost of a newspaper ad, you can sell your home, condo, land, or even timeshare on eBay Real Estate in the auction format.

More information on real estate auctions is provided by the National Association of Realtors: www.realtor.org/auction/the-basics-benefits.

Source: Collier, Marsha, *Starting an eBay Business for Dummies* 4e. John Wiley 2011.

Real Estate Applications

These boxes, located in select chapters, offer case applications of key topics.

6. **SELLER OBLIGATIONS:** In consideration of the obligation of BROKER, SELLER agrees to:

(A) Cooperate with BROKER in carrying out the purpose of this Agreement, including referring immediately to BROKER all inquiries regarding the Property's transfer, whether by purchase or any other means of transfer;
(B) Provide BROKER with keys to the Property and make the Property available to BROKER to show during reasonable times;
(C) Inform BROKER prior to leasing, mortgaging or otherwise encumbering the Property;
(D) Indemnify BROKER and hold BROKER harmless from losses, damages, costs and expenses of any nature, including attorney's fees, and from liability to any person, that BROKER incurs because of (1) SELLER's negligence, representations, misrepresentations, actions or inactions, (2) the use of a lock box, **(3) the existence of undisclosed material facts about the property. This clause will survive BROKER'S performance and the transfer of title;**
(E) Perform any act reasonably necessary to comply with FIRPTA (Internal Revenue Code Section 1445);
(F) Make all legally required disclosures. SELLER represents that the Property has no known latent defects and SELLER knows of no facts materially affecting the value or desirability of the Property which are not readily observable except the following (Please check) ☐ SELLER's property disclosure form or ☒ **None**

Subsequent to the execution of this agreement SELLER will immediately disclose in writing to BROKER any new material facts that have arisen that might affect the value or desirability of the property. (Note: failure to fully disclose may expose the SELLER to claims for damages and/or other legal remedies); and,
(G) To, in the sole determination of SELLER, consult appropriate professionals for related legal, tax, property condition, environmental, foreign reporting requirements and other specialized advice.

7. **INTERNET DISPLAYS:** I understand and acknowledge that, if I have elected under option "(A)" to withhold authorization to display the listed Property on the Internet, consumers who conduct searches for listings on the Internet will not see information about the listed Property in response to their search.

(A) _____ _____ (Initial) The Broker ☒ is or ☐ is not authorized to display the listed Property on the Internet. (If Broker is not authorized to display listed Property on the Internet then (B), (C), and (D) do not apply.)

Career Focus

These boxed readings provide students with valuable information on the many different career options available to them, and what those positions entail.

CAREER *FOCUS*

Urban and Regional Planners

Planners develop land use plans to provide for growth and revitalization of communities, while helping local officials make decisions ranging from broad urban problems to new community infrastructure. They may participate in decisions on alternative public transportation system plans, resource development, and protection of ecologically sensitive regions. Planners also may be involved with drafting legislation concerning local community issues.

Urban and regional planners often confer with land developers, civic leaders, and public officials. They may function as mediators in community disputes and present alternatives acceptable to opposing parties. Planners may prepare material for community relations programs, speak at civic meetings, and appear before legislative committees and elected officials to explain and defend their proposals. Planners rely heavily on sophisticated computer-based databases and analytical tools, including geographical information systems (GISs).

Most entry-level jobs in federal, state, and local government agencies require a master's degree in urban or regional planning, urban design, geography, or a similar course of study. Planners must be able to think in terms of spatial relationships and visualize the effects of their plans and designs. They should be flexible and able to reconcile different viewpoints and to make constructive policy recommendations. The ability to communicate effectively, both orally and in writing, is necessary for anyone interested in this field.

In 2015 80 percent of planners earned between about $43,000 and $102,000, with a median of $68,220.

Source: Summarized from The Occupational Outlook Handbook, U.S. Department of Labor.

**www.houstontx.gov/
legal/deed.html**

An unusually descriptive local government explanation of deed restrictions, their use and enforcement in Texas, where deed restrictions can replace zoning.

Website Annotations

Websites are called out in the margins in every chapter and include a notation of what can be found by visiting them.

✓ **Concept Check**

7.2   Assume a house is listed for sale for which you would be willing to pay up to $200,000. The seller has put the property on the market with an asking price of $180,000. List some possible reasons why your investment value exceeds that of the seller. Is the price you pay likely to be closer to $200,000 or $180,000? Explain.

Concept Check

Every major section contains one or more questions for review. This feature helps students test their understanding of the material before moving on to the next section. Solutions to each Concept Check are provided at the end of each chapter so students can check their answers.

year-end deposits. What is the relationship between the standard future the annuity due result? Note that the $5,801.91 annuity due solution ca multiplying the solution to the regular annuity problem by 1 plus the peri [i.e., $5,801.91 = $5,525.63 \times (1 + 0.05)$].

Calculator Keystrokes

Found in applicable chapters, calculator keys are shown with values to help guide students through numerical calculations.

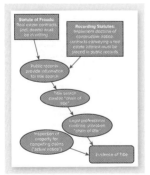

Exhibit 3-2   Creating Evidence of Title

Figures & Tables

This text makes extensive use of real data and presents them in various exhibits. Explanations in the narrative, examples, and end-of-chapter problems will refer to many of these exhibits.

Exhibit 6-10   Where People Work in Orlando

Chapter Summary

Each chapter ends with a short section that highlights the important points of the chapter. This provides a handy study tool for students when they review the chapter.

Summary

This chapter surveys three basic powers of government: its right to regulate land use, its right to take private property for public use, and its right to tax property. The power of federal, state, and local governments to regulate land use through planning, zoning, building codes, and other means is vested in their police power. Communities use these tools to limit the negative effects of market failures such as monopolies, externalities, and incomplete structure information, thus attempting to increase market efficiency and equity.

Planning is the process of developing guidelines for controlling growth and development. Zoning assigns specific permitted uses to individual parcels of land to carry out the comprehensive plan. States and local jurisdictions experiencing rapid growth have adopted a wide variety of measures to manage such growth. Some states pass laws requiring cities and counties to develop comprehensive plans, require economic and environmental impact statements in large development proposals, prohibit new development unless concurrency provisions are met, and require an allocation of affordable housing in new residential developments. Additionally, some states give local communities the right to establish urban service areas, or to plan and control urban development outside their boundaries. Though lawsuits have challenged zoning and growth management from a variety of standpoints, courts generally have upheld its validity when it is reasonable, nonexclusionary, and comprehensive.

Environmental hazards have become an important consideration in land use regulation in recent years. Asbestos, fiberglass, LUSTs, lead paint, radon gas, and mold are some of the most common threats. Real estate investors face large risks from these hazards because owners can be required to clean them up. They must protect themselves by having environmental inspections and by requiring written statements of indemnification from developers and previous owners.

The power of government to acquire private property for public use in exchange for just compensation is referred to as eminent domain. Courts have interpreted the term *public use* broadly to include property taken for a public purpose. Just compensation is the market value of the property. Courts have generally ruled that regulations imposing limits on property rights do not need to be compensated; however, if regulation goes "too far" it will be recognized as a taking and subject to compensation.

Test Problems

Because solving problems is so critical to a student's learning, approximately 10 multiple-choice problems are provided per chapter to help students master important chapter concepts.

Test Problems

Answer the following multiple-choice problems:

1. The final price for each comparable property reached after all adjustments have been made is termed the:
   a. Final estimate of value.
   b. Final adjusted sale price.
   c. Market value.
   d. Weighted price.
2. Which of the following is not included in accrued depreciation when applying the cost approach to valuation?
   a. Physical obsolescence.
   b. Functional obsolescence.
   c. External obsolescence.
   d. Tax depreciation.
3. In the sales comparison approach, the value obtained after reconciliation of the final adjusted sale prices from the comparable sales is termed the:
   a. Adjusted price.
   b. Final adjusted sale price.

   c. Market value.
   d. Indicated opinion of value.
4. A new house in good condition that has a poor floor plan would suffer from which type of accrued depreciation?
   a. Short-lived curable physical deterioration.
   b. Long-lived incurable physical deterioration.
   c. Curable functional obsolescence.
   d. Incurable functional obsolescence.
   e. External obsolescence.
5. To reflect a change in market conditions between the date on which a comparable property sold and the date of appraisal of a subject property, an adjustment must be made for which of the following?
   a. Conditions of sale.
   b. Market conditions.
   c. Location.
   d. Financing terms.
   e. None of the above.

Study Questions

Each chapter contains 10–20 study questions that ask students to apply the concepts they have learned to real situations and problems to reinforce chapter concepts.

Study Questions

1. List five major economic base activities for your city of residence.
2. Find the historical population figures for your community for the 20th century. Create a chart with 10-year intervals. Determine the most rapid periods of growth, and try to discover what caused them. (One source of the necessary population numbers is the U.S. Census home page, www.census.gov. Look for *QuickFacts*, and select your state. At the top of the large table of current information that appears select your county or city. Then click on "Browse more datasets"—the magnifying glass symbol beside the heading—and look down the page for the heading "Historical Population Counts."
3. On the U.S. Census website, use the approach shown in Explore the Web (next page) to access the American Community Survey. For your county and for your state find the distribution of income for all households. Graph the distributions using percentage for each income interval. Which is higher, county or state?

4. Identify at least five locational attributes that you believe are important in the location of a fast-food restaurant. Compare notes with someone in the industry such as a local restaurant manager or owner.
5. Perfect Population Projections Inc. (PPP) has entered into a contract with the city of Popular, Pennsylvania, to project the future population of the city. In recent years, Popular has become a desirable place to live and work, as indicated by the table on the next page.

   The contract states that PPP must project Popular's population for the year 2018 using both a simple linear method and an economic base analysis. The ratio of population to total employment is 2.0833.

   Your help is needed!

End-of-Chapter Features

Explore the Web

These boxes contain Internet activities that weave the Web, real data, and practical applications with concepts found in the chapters.

Solutions to Concept Checks

1. Three features of real property that introduce special challenges for the orderly transfer of ownership are:
   a. Real property interests can be very complex.
   b. Ownership has a very long history.
   c. All real property is bounded by other properties, so description errors always matter.
2. In a normal contract all parties must be legally competent, whereas in a deed only the grantor must be legally competent.
3. The three covenants that distinguish the "quality" of deeds are:
   a. Seizin, which promises that the grantor actually holds title.
   b. No encumbrances, which promises that there are no undisclosed encumbrances.
   c. Quiet enjoyment, which promises that no superior claim to title will appear.
4. Any property interest not being conveyed to the grantee is stated in the exceptions and reservations clause.
5. The highest-quality deed is the general warranty deed. A deed that businesses often use to convey real estate is the bargain and sale deed. A deed used to relinquish ambiguous or conflicting claims is the quitclaim deed.
6. When property is conveyed to heirs in accordance with a will, it is said to be conveyed testate or by devise, whereas when property is conveyed to heirs without a will it is said to be conveyed intestate or by descent.

7. Four events that can cause an owner to convey real property involuntarily through some type of deed are condemnation, bankruptcy, foreclosure, and divorce.
8. Two types of easements that are created without a deed, but with the knowledge of the grantor, are an implied easement and an easement by estoppel.
9. Real property can convey to a new owner without a deed, and without the consent or knowledge of the original owner. A fee simple interest being conveyed in this manner is said to convey by adverse possession, while an easement is said to convey by prescription.
10. All persons are presumed to be informed of legal documents placed in public records according to the doctrine of constructive notice.
11. Two types of legal notice that can provide evidence of a real property interest are constructive notice and actual notice.
12. The objective of a title search is to construct a chain of title.
13. The two main forms of evidence of title are abstract with attorney's opinion and a title insurance commitment.
14. A metes and bounds land description can be summarized or described as a point of beginning and a series of directed distances.
15. The oldest form of the three main land descriptions is metes and bounds. The most common form of urban land description is subdivision plat lot and block number. The most common rural land description in most states is the government rectangular.

Solutions to Concept Checks

Located at the end of each chapter, answers to each Concept Check question are provided to help the student understand the concepts and the reasoning behind them.

Additional Readings

The following books contain expanded examples and discussions of real estate valuation and appraisal:

Appraisal Institute. *The Appraisal of Real Estate*, 14th ed. Chicago: American Institute of Real Estate Appraisers, 2013.
Appraisal Institute. *2014–2015 Uniform Standards of Professional Practice*, Chicago: Appraisal Institute, 2014.
Betts, R. M. *Basic Real Estate Appraisal*, 6th ed. Florence, Ky: Cengage Learning, Inc., 2013.
Carr, D. H., J. A. Lawson, and J. C. Schultz, Jr. *Mastering Real Estate Appraisal*, Chicago: Dearborn Financial Publishing, Inc., 2003.

Fanning, S. F. *Market Analysis for Real Estate*. Chicago: Appraisal Institute, 2014.
Kane, M. S., M. R. Linne, and J. A. Johnson. *Practical Applications in Appraisal Valuation Modeling: Statistical Methods for Real Estate Practitioners*. Chicago: Appraisal Institute, 2004.
Lusht, Kenneth L. *Real Estate Valuation: Principles and Applications*. New York: McGraw-Hill, 1997.
Smith, H. C., L. C. Root, and J. D. Belloit. *Real Estate Appraisal*, 3rd ed. Upper Saddle River, NJ: Prentice Hall, 1995.

Additional Readings & Websites

Each chapter is followed by a list of books and articles to which interested students can refer for additional information and research.

Required=Results

McGraw-Hill Connect®
Learn Without Limits

Connect is a teaching and learning platform that is proven to deliver better results for students and instructors.

Connect empowers students by continually adapting to deliver precisely what they need, when they need it, and how they need it, so your class time is more engaging and effective.

Connect's Impact on Retention Rates, Pass Rates, and Average Exam Scores

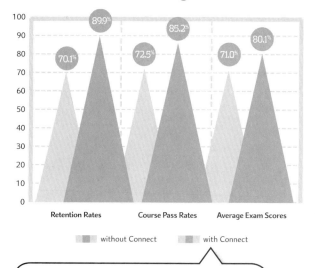

without Connect   with Connect

> **73% of instructors who use Connect require it; instructor satisfaction increases by 28% when Connect is required.**

> Using **Connect** improves retention rates by **19.8%**, passing rates by **12.7%**, and exam scores by **9.1%**.

Analytics

Connect Insight®

Connect Insight is Connect's new one-of-a-kind visual analytics dashboard—now available for both instructors and students—that provides at-a-glance information regarding student performance, which is immediately actionable. By presenting assignment, assessment, and topical performance results together with a time metric that is easily visible for aggregate or individual results, Connect Insight gives the user the ability to take a just-in-time approach to teaching and learning, which was never before available. Connect Insight presents data that empowers students and helps instructors improve class performance in a way that is efficient and effective.

Impact on Final Course Grade Distribution

without Connect		with Connect
22.9%	A	31.0%
27.4%	B	34.3%
22.9%	C	18.7%
11.5%	D	6.1%
15.4%	F	9.9%

> Students can view their results for any **Connect** course.

Mobile

Connect's new, intuitive mobile interface gives students and instructors flexible and convenient, anytime–anywhere access to all components of the Connect platform.

Adaptive

THE **ADAPTIVE** **READING EXPERIENCE** DESIGNED TO TRANSFORM THE WAY STUDENTS READ

More students earn **A's** and **B's** when they use McGraw-Hill Education **Adaptive** products.

SmartBook®

Proven to help students improve grades and study more efficiently, SmartBook contains the same content within the print book, but actively tailors that content to the needs of the individual. SmartBook's adaptive technology provides precise, personalized instruction on what the student should do next, guiding the student to master and remember key concepts, targeting gaps in knowledge and offering customized feedback, and driving the student toward comprehension and retention of the subject matter. Available on tablets, SmartBook puts learning at the student's fingertips—anywhere, anytime.

Over **8 billion questions** have been answered, making McGraw-Hill Education products more intelligent, reliable, and precise.

STUDENTS WANT

SMARTBOOK®

95% of students reported **SmartBook** to be a more effective way of reading material.

100% of students want to use the Practice Quiz feature available within **SmartBook** to help them study.

100% of students reported having reliable access to off-campus wifi.

90% of students say they would purchase **SmartBook** over print alone.

95% of students reported that **SmartBook** would impact their study skills in a positive way.

McGraw Hill Education

*Findings based on 2015 focus group results administered by McGraw-Hill Education

www.mheducation.com

Supplements

Instructor supplement files for this edition are available in *Connect*.

Instructor's Manual, *prepared by Benjamin Scheick, Villanova University*
Developed to clearly outline the chapter material as well as provide extra teaching support, the instructor's manual contains a number of valuable resources. Sections include: a chapter overview, a listing of chapter concepts, presentation strategies, and presentation outlines that reference the accompanying PowerPoint slides for easy classroom integration.

Solutions Manual, *prepared by Wayne R. Archer and David C. Ling, University of Florida*
This manual provides detailed answers to the end-of-chapter problems.

Test Bank, *prepared by Benjamin Scheick, Villanova University*
With hundreds of multiple-choice questions in Microsoft Word format, this Test Bank provides a variety of questions to meet any instructor's testing needs.

PowerPoint Presentation, *prepared by Wayne R. Archer and David C. Ling, University of Florida*
Prepared by the authors, more than 500 full-color slides of images and tables from the text, lecture outlines, and additional examples are available with this product.

Acknowledgments

We take this opportunity to thank those individuals who helped us prepare this fifth edition of *Real Estate Principles.* A special debt of gratitude goes to Dr. Halbert Smith, Professor Emeritus at the University of Florida. Professor Smith has been a long-time mentor and colleague to us both. His book *Real Estate and Urban Development* (Irwin 1981), coauthored with Tschappat and Racster, significantly influenced our approach to the teaching of real estate principles over the last 30 years. Many of the ideas first put forth in *Real Estate and Urban Development* can be found in this text. Dr. Smith served as Contributing Editor on the first edition of this book, providing detailed comments and suggestions during each phase of the book's original development.

Our good friend and colleague, Dean Gatzlaff, was to have joined us in the creation of this book, but found it to be infeasible. We are grateful to him for his substantial contribution in providing initial drafts of Chapters 1, 4, 7 and 8. We would also like to thank Jay Hartzell (University of Texas-Austin) for providing some of the ideas and material for the revision of Chapter 17.

We are grateful to the following individuals for their thoughtful reviews and suggestions for this text:

Paul Asabere,
  Temple University
Candy Bianco,
  Bentley University
Donald Bleich,
  California State University—Northridge
Steven Bourassa,
  Florida Atlantic University
Jay Butler,
  Arizona State University
Steve Caples,
  McNeese University

Charles Corcoran,
  University of Wisconsin—River Falls
Barbara Corvette,
  National Defense University
Dan Broxterman
  Florida State University
John Crockett,
  George Mason University
Jon Crunkleton,
  Old Dominion University
Charles Delaney,
  Baylor University
David Downs,
  Virginia Commonwealth University

Richard Ghidella,
Citrus College

Paul Goebel,
Texas Tech University

W. Michael Gough,
De Anza College

Chris Grover,
Victor Valley Community College

Daniel Ham,
California State University—Long Beach

Tom Hamilton,
Roosevelt University

Dana Harrell,
Bentley University

Michael H. Harrity,
Babson College

Darren Hayunga,
University of Georgia

Don Johnson,
Western Illinois University

Michael LaCour-Little
California State University-Fullerton

Han Bin Kang,
Illinois State University

George Lentz,
Cal Poly University—Pomona

Danielle Lewis,
Southeastern Louisiana University

Walt Nelson,
Missouri State University

Thomas Ortell,
Milwaukee Area Technical College-West

Steven Ott,
University of North Carolina—Charlotte

Ed Prill,
Colorado State University

Sid Rosenberg,
University of North Florida

Jeff Rymaszewski,
University of Wisconsin—Milwaukee

Marion Sillah,
South Carolina State University

David Sinow,
University of Illinois—Champaign

Carlos Slawson,
Louisiana State University

Brent Smith,
Virginia Commonwealth University

Bruce Southstone,
Cabrillo College

James Thorson,
Southern Connecticut State University

Neil Waller,
Clemson University

John Wiley,

Alex Wilson,

Alan Ziobrowski,
Georgia State University

In addition to the helpful suggestions and detailed reviews we have received from the academic community, we are extremely grateful for the interest, help, and guidance we have received from dozens of industry professionals. In particular, we would like to thank Steve Mench, Mench Real Estate Capital; Andy Hogshead, The Collier Companies; T.J. Ownby, Tavernier Capital Partners, LLC; Steve Deutsch, Frank, Weinberg & Black; Stumpy Harris, Harris, Harris, Bauerle & Sharma; Andrew Davidson, Andrew Davidson & Company; Don Emerson, Emerson Appraisal; Ralph Conti, Ra Co Real Estate Advisors, LLC; Michael Giliberto, Giliberto-Levy Index; Todd Jones, RealAdvice Valuation & Advisory Services; Carl Velie, Velie Appraisal; Amy Crews Cutts, Equifax; and Michael Kitchens, Melissa Murphy, Attorneys' Title Fund Services, LLC. David Ginn, retired mortgage banker; David Arnold, Crosland; Larry Furlong, Old Republic National Title Insurance Company, Dirk Aulabaugh, Green Street Advisors; Steve DeRose, Starwood Mortgage Capital; Angel Arroyo, Banyan Realty Advisors; Michael White, Harbert Management Corporation; Ted Starkey, Wells Fargo Real Estate Banking Group; Robert Klein, Monday Properties; and John Ebenger, Berkowitz Dick Pollack & Brant. Thanks also to the Gainesville, Alachua County Association of Realtors for providing the listing agreement in Chapter 12. Also we thank the Florida Association of Realtors for granting use of the exemplary "FAR-BAR" sales contract form in Chapter 13. In addition, thanks are due to Jeffrey Conn, Hallmark Partners, Inc. and to Dr. Wayne W. Wood, retired, for extremely valuable assistance with Jacksonville aerial photo information used in Chapter 5.

Special thanks go to Penny Archer for extensive Internet research leading to many of the photos and material used in the Industry Issues. We would also like to thank our graduate and undergraduate students who provided numerous suggestions and corrections through the first two editions.

We would especially like to thank Dr. Ben Scheick, Villanova University, for revising the Instructor's Manual and expanding the Test Bank. Dr. Kent Malone, University of Florida, contributed to previous versions of the test bank and has provided numerous helpful suggestions for improving the content and readability of the text. Carol Bosshart, Kim Bosshart and Lem Purcell of Bosshart Realty and J. Parrish and Michael Kitchens of Coldwell Banker M.M. Parrish, Realtors all have made special contributions to Chapters 12 and 13 over various editions of the book. Jeff Siegel, local realtor and friend, also contributed to Chapters 12 and 13. Nicholas Kastanias and Ben Scheick contributed significantly to the development of the glossary and to the solutions for the end-of-chapter problems. We are confident that users of the book will find these ancillary materials to be first rate.

Finally, we are grateful to the late Steve Patterson for encouraging us to undertake this project and for his help in developing the book's theme and target market.

We are also grateful to the talented staff at McGraw-Hill who worked on the book: Tara Slagle, Development Editor; Charles Synovec, Director; Jennifer Upton, Senior Product Developer; Jeni McAtee, Project Manager; Dave O'Donnell, Marketing Specialist; Natalie King, Marketing Director; Bruce Gin, Assessment Project Manager; and Karen Jozefowicz, Content Project Manager.

David C. Ling

Wayne R. Archer

Contents

PART ONE

Chapter 1

The Nature of Real Estate *and* Real Estate Markets

Wealth is not without its advantages and the case to the contrary, although it has often been made, has never proved widely persuasive.

—Galbraith, John Kenneth, "The Affluent Society" Houghton Mifflin

LEARNING OBJECTIVES

After reading this chapter you will be able to:

1 Provide three alternative definitions for the term *real estate*.

2 Discuss the distribution of U.S. land among the various uses to which it is put (e.g., developed land, federal land, forest land).

3 Discuss the value and importance of U.S. real estate compared with the values of other asset classes such as stocks and bonds.

4 Describe the role real estate plays in the portfolios of U.S. households.

5 Discuss the primary ways that real estate markets are different from the markets for assets that trade in well-developed public markets.

OUTLINE

Introduction
Real Estate: Some Basic Definitions
    Real Estate: A Tangible Asset
    Real Estate: A Bundle of Rights
    Real Estate: An Industry and Profession
Real Estate and the Economy
    Land Use in the United States
    Real Estate and U.S. Wealth
Real Estate Markets and Participants
    User, Capital, and Property Markets
    The Role of Government
    The Interaction of Three Value-Determining Sectors
    The Production of Real Estate Assets
Characteristics of Real Estate Markets
    Heterogeneous Products
    Immobile Products
    Localized Markets
    Segmented Markets
    Privately Negotiated Transactions with High Transaction Costs

Introduction

Real estate is the single largest component of wealth in our society. Because of its magnitude, it plays a key role in shaping the economic condition of individuals, families, and firms. It can substantially influence a family's ability to finance its education, health care, and other important needs. Changes in the value of real estate can dramatically affect the wealth of businesses and their capacity to grow.

Similarly, real estate resources can greatly affect a community's ability to attract and support profitable business activities, as well as to provide secure, convenient, and affordable living environments for its citizens. The adequacy of the housing stock, as well as the public infrastructure, including roads, bridges, dams, airports, schools, and parks, all affect the quality of life in a region.

Real estate, excluding primary residences, has been estimated to represent approximately 25 percent of the world's total economic wealth.[1] In addition, it is often viewed as an important symbol of strength, stability, and independence. Consider, for example, the symbolic importance of structures such as Saint Peter's Basilica in Rome to the Roman Catholic Church, the buildings of the Forbidden City in Beijing to the Chinese people, or the Burj Khalifa Tower, the tallest building in the world, to the citizens of the United Arab Emirates (see also Industry Issues 1-1). It is not surprising that real estate has been at the center of many regional disputes. It has been, and continues to be, a vital resource.

The prominence of real estate means that decisions about it also are important. For the individual, the firm, and the region, better decisions about the creation and use of real estate assets will bring greater productivity, greater wealth, and a better set of choices for life.

This book is about making informed decisions concerning real estate. We will show that virtually all decisions about the acquisition, disposition, or improvement of real estate depend on some assessment of the real estate's value. These decisions, which we refer to as investment decisions, involve comparing the resulting value of an action with its immediate cost. If the value exceeds the cost, the action should be pursued. The breadth and importance of these investment decisions in real estate are hard to overstate.

As a beginning, we first look at the different uses of the term *real estate*. This is followed by a discussion of land use in the United States and real estate's contribution to U.S. and household wealth. The chapter finishes with a discussion of the real estate market, its participants, and the characteristics that make real estate assets unique.

Real Estate: Some Basic Definitions

It is important at the outset that we define the term *real estate,* as well as some closely related terms used throughout this book. When people think of real estate, they often think of the homes in their community or the business of buying and selling houses. This is probably because the personal investment that most households make in their home represents their primary involvement in the real estate market. Of course, real estate includes not only our homes, but also our places of work, commerce, worship, government, education, recreation, and entertainment—our physical environments, natural and built. In addition, it includes a wide range of business and institutional activities associated with the development, purchase, use, and sale of land and buildings.

Real estate is property. The term **property** refers to anything that can be owned or possessed. Property can be a tangible asset or an intangible asset. **Tangible assets** are *physical* things, such as automobiles, clothing, land, or buildings. **Intangible assets** are *nonphysical* and include contractual rights (e.g., mortgage and lease agreements), financial claims (e.g., stocks and bonds), interests, patents, or trademarks.

The term *real estate* is used in three fundamental ways. First, its most common use is to identify the tangible assets of land and buildings. Second, it is used to denote the "bundle" of rights associated with the ownership and use of the physical assets. Finally, the term real estate may be used when referring to the industry or business activities related to the acquisition, operation, and disposition of the physical assets.

Real Estate: A Tangible Asset

When viewed purely as a tangible asset, **real estate** can be defined as the land and its permanent improvements. **Improvements *on* the land** include any fixed structures such as buildings, fences, walls, and decks. **Improvements *to* the land** include the components necessary to make the land suitable for building construction or other uses. These

---

1. *World Wealth Report 2014*, Capgemini Consulting, p. 19 (www.worldwealthrreport.com).

More than a dozen super-tall buildings have been completed in the last decade (see listing below). They are in cities such as Hong Kong and Shanghai in China and Dubai on the Arabian Peninsula. Currently, the world's tallest building—Burj Khalifa at 2,717 feet—is in Dubai, UAE. Tall structures are as old as civilization, from the Pyramids in Egypt to the cathedrals of medieval Europe. Historians attribute this phenomenon in part to religious and spiritual motives—the desire to build to the sky. In modern times, however, the motive has been largely economic. The skyscraper era began in the United States in the late 19th century when the technology of steel-framed construction and safe elevators made it possible. It started in Chicago, although New York evolved into the leading skyscraper city during the 20th century. However, only six of the world's 40 tallest buildings are now located in the United States.

Skyscrapers: A Shift in Development Trends

World's Tallest Buildings: 2014

2015 Rank	Building	City, Country	Height (feet)	Year Completed
1	Burj Khalifa	Dubai, UAE	2,717	2010
2	Shanghai Tower	Shanghai, China	2,074	2014
3	Makkah Clock Royal Tower	Makkah, Saudi Arabia	1,972	2012
4	One World Trade Center	New York City, US	1,776	2014
5	CTF Finance Centre	Guangzhou, China	1,739	2016
6	Taipei 101	Taipei, Taiwan	1,671	2004
7	Shanghai World Financial Center	Shanghai, China	1,614	2008
8	International Commerce Centre	Hong Kong, China	1,588	2010
9	Petronas Tower I	Kuala Lumpur, Malaysia	1,483	1998
10	Petronas Tower II	Kuala Lumpur, Malaysia	1,483	1998
11	Zifeng Tower	Nanjing, China	1,476	2009
12	Willis Tower	Chicago, US	1,450	1974
13	KK100	Shenzhen, China	1,449	2011
14	Guangzhou International Finance Center	Guangzhou, China	1,435	2010
15	Panyu Commercial Exhibition Center	Guangzhou, China	1,430	2001
16	432 Park Avenue	New York City, US	1,398	2015
17	Trump International Hotel and Tower	Chicago, US	1,388	2009
18	Jin Mao Tower	Shanghai, China	1,380	1998
19	Princess Tower	Dubai, UAE	1,356	2012
20	Two Int'l Fin. Ctr.	Hong Kong, China	1,352	2003
28	Empire State Bldg.	New York City, US	1,250	1931

Note: The Twin Towers of the World Trade Center in New York were 1,368 feet high when they were destroyed in 2001.

The rising value of land in densely settled cities has been the economic incentive to build up rather than out. The shift of skyscraper development to the Far East, however, has been a reflection of other trends, especially that region's emergence onto the global economic scene. The region's spectacular buildings are symbols of pride among nations that see themselves with new roles in the 21st century. A return on investment is less of an impediment in nations not wedded to market economics, such as China.

Source data: Emporis.com

improvements are often referred to as infrastructure and consist of the streets, walkways, storm water drainage systems, and other systems such as water, sewer, electric, and telephone utilities that may be required for land use. Subject to legal and practical limits, it should be noted that real estate includes not only the surface of the earth but also the area above and below the surface.

In practice the term **land** may include more than simply the earth; it may also include the improvements *to* the land. For example, the term *land* is often used to refer to a building site, or lot, and includes the infrastructure but not any structures. In contrast, land is also commonly used to refer to a larger area that does not include *any* improvements. These areas are sometimes identified as **raw land.** These distinctions become especially important when the value of land is considered.

Tangible assets include both real property and personal property. In professional practice and throughout this book, the terms **real property** and real estate are treated as interchangeable. **Personal property** refers to things that are movable and not permanently affixed to the land or structure. For example, a motor home is personal property, while a custom "site-built" house is real property. A mobile home may be real or personal property, depending on how it is secured to the land and legally recognized by the jurisdiction (e.g., city, county, or state) in which it is located.

> ### ✓ Concept Check
>
> **1.1** What distinguishes real property from personal property?

Real Estate: A Bundle of Rights

Although real estate is a tangible asset, it can also be viewed as a "bundle" of intangible rights associated with the ownership and use of the site and improvements. These rights are to the *services,* or benefits, that real estate provides its users. For example, real property provides owners with the rights to shelter, security, and privacy, as well as a location that facilitates business or residential activities. This concept of real property as a bundle of rights is extremely important to understanding real estate, and it is the subject of Chapter 2.

The bundle of property rights may be limited in numerous ways. It typically is reduced by state and local land use restrictions (see Chapter 4). Also, the rights can be divided and distributed among multiple owners and nonowners. For example, an apartment owner divides his or her full interest in the property when he or she leases an apartment unit and grants to a tenant the right to occupy and control access to the unit. Similarly, the tenant may be able to divide his or her interests by subleasing the apartment to another. As another example, an owner may purchase a property that has a utility access granted through a portion of the property. Thus, real estate can also be viewed as a bundle of rights inherent in the ownership of real property.

The value of a bundle of rights is a function of the property's physical, locational, and legal characteristics. The physical characteristics include the age, size, design, and construction quality of the structure, as well as the size, shape, and other natural features of the land. For residential property, the locational characteristics include convenience and access to places of employment, schools, shopping, health care facilities, and other places important to households. The location characteristics of commercial properties may involve visibility, access to customers, suppliers, and employees, or the availability of reliable data and communications infrastructure. The physical and location characteristics required to provide valuable real estate services vary significantly by property type.

> ### ✓ Concept Check
>
> **1.2** What is the difference between tangible and intangible assets? Does the ownership of "real estate" involve tangible assets, intangible assets, or both?

One of the exciting things about pursuing a career in real estate is that many options are available. Career paths can accommodate white-collar executives working for corporations, banks, advisory firms, or in the mortgage industry; analytical personality types working in real estate appraisal or consulting jobs; salespeople working in brokerage, leasing, or property management; or entrepreneurs interested in developing new properties or renovating historical buildings. Career opportunities also exist in the public sector with employers like the Department of Housing and Urban Development (HUD), the General Service Administration (GSA),

the Bureau of Reclamation, and numerous county property tax assessors, to name just a few.

As you familiarize yourself with the material presented in this book, the type of work associated with the job opportunities listed above will become increasingly clear. However, it is important that you begin to read some of the real estate articles that appear in newspapers, magazines, and journals. You should also begin searching for and bookmarking interesting real estate websites. To get started, we suggest you examine the career information available on the website of the University of Cincinnati's Real Estate Program (www.business.uc.edu/

realestate/careerpaths). The National Association of Realtors also maintains an informative site on real estate careers (www.realtor.org/realtor.org.nsf/pages/careers). You should also visit www.real-jobs.com, where you can post your resume, search for real estate jobs, and read descriptions of available job opportunities—all free of charge.

Career Opportunities in Real Estate

Real Estate: An Industry and Profession

The term *real estate* frequently is also used to refer to the industry activities associated with evaluating, producing, acquiring, managing, and selling real property assets. Real estate professions vary widely and include (1) real estate brokerage, leasing, and property management services; (2) appraisal and consulting services; (3) site selection, acquisition, and property development; (4) construction; (5) mortgage finance and securitization; (6) corporate and institutional real estate investment; and (7) government activities such as planning, land use regulation, environmental protection, and property taxation.

Real estate business opportunities in areas such as brokerage, leasing, appraisal, construction, and consulting often offer entrepreneurial-minded individuals the ability to observe and understand local real estate markets in addition to receiving above average compensation. These types of positions allow individuals the opportunity to have their fingers on the "pulse" of the market, often enabling them to directly participate in real estate investment activities.

Real estate professionals involved in a wide range of activities can be found in consulting firms, insurance companies, financial institutions, real estate investment firms, pension fund advisory firms, and non-real estate firms that use real estate in their business. Companies such as restaurant groups and retailers seeking to expand often require the services of "in-house" site acquisition analysts, construction managers, and facility managers.

Finally, the activities of state and federal government units, such as departments of transportation, commerce, planning, housing, and environmental protection, and local government agencies such as planning and property tax offices necessitate the employment of real estate research analysts and professionals.

www.realtor.org

Website of the National Association of Realtors; provides information about brokerage as well as other real estate professions.

Real Estate and the Economy

www.census.gov

Numerous construction statistics.

www.nahb.org

Website of the National Association of Home Builders; contains extensive information on the housing industry.

Real estate typically generates over 25 percent of U.S. gross domestic product (GDP), creates jobs for nearly 9 million Americans, and is the source of nearly 70 percent of local government revenues.[2] The total contribution of the housing sector alone averages 17 to 18 percent of GDP.[3] Because of the significant influence of real estate on the nation's

2. Statistics about the real estate industry, Real Estate Roundtable, www.rer.org.
3. Robert Dietz, "Housing's Share of GDP: 15.5% for the Second Quarter," *Eye on Housing*, National Association of Homebuilders, September 26, 2014.

economy, investors on Wall Street closely monitor real estate construction, construction permit activity, and real estate sales figures. Housing starts and sales are widely viewed as leading economic indicators.

Land Use in the United States

The United States represents about 6 percent of the Earth's land area, or approximately 2.3 billion acres (3.5 million square miles). To give a sense of scale to an acre, a football field, not including the end zone areas, is slightly more than one acre (1.1 acres). More precisely, an **acre** is defined as 43,560 square feet; there are 640 acres in one square mile. The size of a single-family residential lot is typically between one-fifth and four-fifths of an acre.

It is estimated that the contiguous 48 states comprise 1.9 billion acres and that 71 percent of this acreage is in nonfederal, rural land uses. According to the 2010 National Resources Inventory Report, developed land represents approximately 6 percent of the land in the continental United States (see Exhibit 1-1). Developed land consists of residential, industrial, commercial, and institutional land uses, including roads, railways, rights-of-ways, construction sites, utility sites, sanitary landfills, and other land uses of similar purpose. Much of the undeveloped land in the United States is divided in approximately equal shares among water areas and federal lands (23 percent), crop land and Conservation Reserve Program (CRP) land (20 percent), range land (21 percent), and forest land (21 percent).[4] Pastureland and other rural land comprise 6 percent and 3 percent, respectively, of the 1.9 billion acres.

Overall, land use changes from 1982 to 2010 have been relatively minor. Most notable, however, is the increase of developed land from 73 million acres in 1982 to 113 million acres in 2010. Although only a small portion of the total land area in the United States, the amount of developed land has increased 55 percent since 1982.

Real Estate and U.S. Wealth

It is hard to overstate the size and variety of capital commitments to real estate. We estimate that the total market value of real estate was approximately $30.8 trillion in the fourth quarter of 2015. This estimate includes owner-occupied housing, investible commercial real estate, and land, but excludes real estate held by non-real estate corporations

www.nrcs.usda.gov

U.S. Department of Agriculture resources include comprehensive information on trends for land use and development.

Exhibit 1-1   Land Use and Land Use Changes in the United States

Land Use	1982 Land use (mil. of acres)	% of Total	2010 Land use (mil. of acres)	% of Total
Developed land	73	4	113	6
Water areas and federal land	448	23	453	23
Crop land	420	22	361	19
CRP land			27	1
Pasture land	131	7	120	6
Range land	416	21	409	21
Forest land	403	21	409	21
Other rural land	48	2	51	3
Totals	1,938	100	1,943	100

Source of data: 2010 U.S. Department of Agriculture

4. CRP land is a federal program established under the Food Security Act of 1985 to assist private landowners in converting highly erodible crop land to vegetative cover.

Exhibit 1-2   Aggregate Market Values of Selected Asset Categories
(in $Trillions)—2015Q4

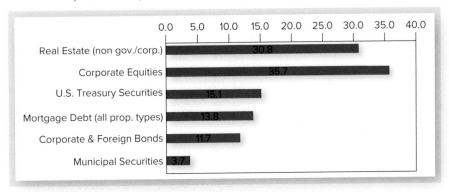

Note: Real estate (nongovernment) includes developed land. It does not include farmland, water areas, and other rural
lands. It also does not include real estate owned by non-real estate corporations.
Source of data: 2016 U.S. Federal Reserve and 2011 CBRE. Flow of Funds Accounts of the United States, Federal Reserve
(March 10, September 2016 various tables). The value of nongovernment and noncorporate real estate is equal to the
value of owner-occupied housing from the Fed Flow of Funds Accounts, plus the value of investible commercial real estate
from CBRE Global.

(such as McDonald's and Ford) and real estate owned by various governmental agencies.
Real estate constitutes the second largest asset class in the United States, as shown in
Exhibit 1-2. In comparison, the total value of publicly traded (listed) corporate equities (i.e.,
stocks) in late 2015 was approximately $35.7 trillion; the value of outstanding real estate
mortgage debt was approximately $13.8 trillion. This is larger than the value of corporate and
foreign bonds and just slightly less than the outstanding value of U.S. Treasury securities.

As reported by the U.S. Federal Reserve Board, housing represents the single largest
asset category in the net worth portfolios of households (see Exhibit 1-3). On average, it
represents approximately 22 percent of U.S. household wealth. This is similar to household
holdings of corporate stock and mutual fund shares. Housing's 22 percent share in the typical household's portfolio dominates deposits and money market funds (11 percent) and
equity invested in noncorporate businesses (11 percent). Moreover, the 22 percent housing
share understates the importance of real estate for some households, because direct investments in private commercial real estate assets (e.g., apartments, office buildings) are not
included as household assets in Exhibit 1-3. Finally, note that 65 percent of household liabilities are home mortgages.

By the fourth quarter of 2015, U.S. households had approximately $12.5 trillion in
housing equity (market value minus mortgage debt). This represents, on average, about
57 percent of the value of their real estate and about 14 percent of their net worth. As a
percentage of total household wealth, housing increased slightly during the early 2000s as
corporate stock values declined. Although the stock market performed better during the
2003 to 2005 period, the housing sector continued to outperform stocks and bonds. This
trend can be seen in Exhibit 1-4. However, in 2006 U.S. housing prices began a precipitous
decline, which reduced the value of housing assets as a percentage of total household
assets. Since 2010 housing has represented about 21 percent of total household assets.

Real Estate Markets and Participants

In the United States and many other countries, market competition serves to distribute most
resources (i.e., goods, services, and capital) among the various users. The market's forces of
demand and supply interact within the economy to determine the price at which goods, capital,
and services are exchanged and to whom they are allocated. Real estate resources are allocated
among its various users—individuals, households, businesses, and institutions—in the real

Exhibit 1-3   U.S. Household Wealth*

Asset/Liability category	2015Q4 ($ in billions)	% of Total
Tangible assets		
Housing	$22,029	22
Consumer durables	5,240	5
Nonprofit tangible assets	3,709	4
Financial assets		
Deposits & money market funds	10,693	11
Government & corporate bonds	3,231	3
Stocks & mutual fund shares	21,430	21
Pension assets (excluding stocks)	20,972	21
Other securities	3,262	3
Noncorporate business equity	10,739	11
Total assets	101,306	
Home mortgages (including lines of credit)	9,491	65
Other debt	5,019	35
Total liabilities	14,510	100
Net worth	$86,796	
Owner's equity in real estate	$12,539	
Owner's equity as a percent of housing and net worth	57%	14%

*This sector consists of individual households and nonprofit organizations. Nonprofits account for about 6 percent of the sector's financial assets.

Source of data: 2016 U.S. Federal Reserve. Flow of Funds Accounts of the United States, Federal Reserve (March 10, 2016, Table B.100 and L.100) www.federalreserve.gov.

Exhibit 1-4   Selected Household Assets as a Percentage of Total Assets

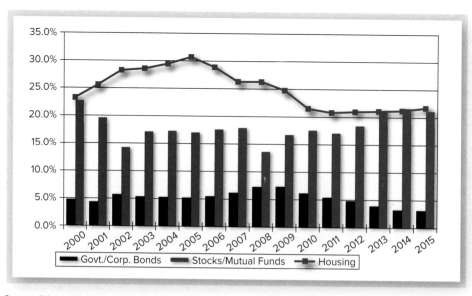

Source of data: U.S. Federal Reserve

✓ **Concept Check**

1.3 According to Exhibit 1-3, U.S. households own $16.1 trillion in housing assets. Assume this amount does not include rental real estate. On average, what percent of the value of the U.S. housing stock is financed with home mortgage debt?

estate market. Real estate values derive from the interaction of three different sectors, or markets, in the economy: local user markets (the "real world"), capital markets (the "financial world"), and property markets. A brief discussion of each of these sectors is presented below.

User, Capital, and Property Markets

Real estate **user markets** are characterized by competition among users for physical locations and space. As we will explain in Chapter 5, this competition determines who gains the use of each parcel of land and how much they must bid for its use. The primary participants in user markets are the potential occupants, both owner occupants and tenants, or renters. Ultimately, the demand for real estate derives from the need that these individuals, firms, and institutions have for convenient access to other locations, as well as for shelter to accommodate their activities. Based on the financial positions of households and firms and their wants and needs, they decide either to own and occupy property or to lease property from others. About two-thirds of U.S. households own their home, and many businesses own their real estate, while most commercial real estate located in the central business districts of U.S. cities is leased.

www.bloomberg.com

Private firm that provides data on interest rates and bond yields.

The **capital markets** serve to allocate financial resources among households and firms requiring funds. Participants in the capital markets invest in stocks, bonds, mutual funds, private business enterprises, mortgage contracts, real estate, and other opportunities with the expectation of receiving a financial return on their investment. Funds flow from investors to the investment opportunities yielding the highest expected return (i.e., the greatest benefit), considering risk. Thus, real estate competes for scarce investment capital with a diverse menu of other investment opportunities available in the capital market.

The capital markets can be divided into two broad categories: equity interests and debt interests. We commonly view the equity participants as the "owners of the real estate." Equity investors in real estate expect to receive a return on their investment through the collection of rent and through price appreciation.[5] The debt participants, the "lenders," hold claims to the interest on borrowed funds that are secured by individuals, businesses, and property. The equity and debt interests can each be divided further into private and public market components. The primary participants in each of the four capital market categories—private equity, public equity, private debt, and public debt—are outlined in Exhibit 1-5. (The capital sources of real estate finance are discussed further in Chapters 11 and 17.)

Finally, **property markets** determine the required property-specific investment returns, property values, capitalization rates, and construction feasibility. The **capitalization rate**, or the ratio of a property's annual net income from rental operations to its value, is a fundamental pricing metric in commercial real estate markets.

✓ **Concept Check**

1.4 Investible assets based on real estate are traded in each of the four capital market quadrants. List the four quadrants and at least one real estate asset that trades in each.

5. Investors who occupy their own properties "receive" the rent they would have paid to others had the property been leased from another investor. This is termed "implicit" rent.

e Bay Real Estate is not quite an auction. Because of the wide variety of laws governing the sale of real estate, eBay auctions of real property are not legally binding offers to buy and sell. When a real estate auction ends, neither party is obligated (as they are in other eBay auctions) to complete the transaction. The buyer and seller must get together to consummate the deal.

Selling Real Estate on eBay

Nonetheless, eBay Real Estate sales are popular, and the gross sales are growing by leaps and bounds. You do not have to be a professional real estate agent to use this category, although that kind of pro experience may help when it comes to closing the deal. If you know land and your local real estate laws, eBay gives you the perfect venue to subdivide those 160 acres in Wyoming that Uncle Regis left you in his will.

For less than the cost of a newspaper ad, you can sell your home, condo, land, or even timeshare on eBay Real Estate in the auction format.

More information on real estate auctions is provided by the National Association of Realtors: www.realtor.org/auction/the-basics-benefits.

Source: Collier, Marsha, *Starting an eBay Business for Dummies* 4e. John Wiley 2011.

Exhibit 1-5 The Four Quadrants of Real Estate Capital Market Participants for Income Property

	Private Markets	**Public Markets**
Equity/owners	Individuals, partnerships, limited liability corporations, private equity funds	Public real estate investment trusts (REITs) and real estate operating companies
Debt/lenders	Banks, insurance companies, finance companies, private lenders	Commercial mortgage-backed securities (CMBS) and mortgage REITs

The Role of Government

Government affects real estate markets, and therefore values, in a host of ways. Local government has perhaps the largest influence on real estate. It affects the supply and cost of real estate through zoning codes and other land use regulations, fees on new land development, and building codes that restrict methods of construction. Further, local government affects rental rates in user markets through property taxes. Finally, it profoundly affects the supply and quality of real estate by its provision of roads, bridges, mass transit, utilities, flood control, schools, social services, and other infrastructure of the community. (The influence of local government on real estate values through land use controls, property tax policy, and services is expanded upon in Chapter 4.)

State government has perhaps the least effect on real estate values, although it still is important. Through the licensing of professionals and agents, states constrain entry into real estate–related occupations. (See Chapter 12.) Through statewide building codes, they can affect building design and cost. Through disclosure laws and fair housing laws, states affect the operation of housing markets. In addition, states typically set the basic framework of requirements for local government land use controls, and even intervene in the realm of land use controls for special purposes such as protection of environmentally sensitive lands. Finally, states affect the provision of public services important to a community, including schools, transportation systems, social services, law enforcement, and others.

The national government influences real estate in many ways. Income tax policy can greatly affect the value of real estate and therefore the incentive to invest in it. (The extensive effect of income taxes on real estate value is detailed in Chapter 20.) Housing subsidy programs can have enormous effects on the level and type of housing construction. Federal flood insurance programs can influence development in coastal and wetlands regions. Federal financial reporting and disclosure requirements, and government-related financial agencies such as the Federal Reserve System and the Federal Deposit Insurance Corporation (FDIC) all have profound effects on the operation of the real estate capital markets. (See Chapter 11 for details of the government's role in mortgage markets.) Further, consumer protection laws affect few aspects of household activity more than they impact housing purchases and financing. (See Chapters 9 and 13.) In addition, laws protecting the environment and endangered species have significantly affected the use of real estate. Finally, national fair housing laws and other civil rights legislation are very important influences on housing markets.

www.uli.org

The Urban Land Institute is an influential U.S. organization for those engaged in development and land use planning.

The Interaction of Three Value-Determining Sectors

The interaction of the three value-determining sectors is illustrated in Exhibit 1-6. In local user markets, households and firms compete for the currently available supply of locations and space (left-hand side of Exhibit 1-6). This competition for space, coupled with the existing supply of leasable space, determines current rental rates (let's call this a space market equilibrium) and current cash flows (net operating incomes) of a property. The riskiness of the future cash flows depends on the degree of uncertainty about future space demand, future space supply, and the resulting future space market equilibriums.

Capital markets provide the financial resources (debt and equity) necessary for the development and acquisition of real estate assets (right-hand side of Exhibit 1-6). Within the capital markets, the returns investors require for a broad range of available investment opportunities, including real estate, are determined. Required investment returns equal the risk-free rate in the economy (i.e., the return available on a Treasury security), plus a risk premium that reflects how reliable or uncertain the forecasted net operating incomes are. Finally, in the interaction between user and capital markets, the expected stream of rental operating income for a particular property is capitalized into value through "discounting," which is the process of converting expected future cash flows into present value. Discounting incorporates the opportunity cost of waiting for the uncertain cash flows (center panel of Exhibit 1-6). (Discounting is the subject of Chapter 14.) Each market participant bids for properties based on his or her individual assessment of value. The prices current owners are willing to accept reflect each seller's assessment of value. This continuous bidding process determines market values and transaction prices in local property markets. As noted above, government influences on this value-determining process are numerous, ranging from local government land use controls and property taxes to federal income tax policy.

Our view is that sound decision making requires an understanding of how real estate values in local property markets are determined. Thus, value is the unifying theme of this book. This allows for an integrated framework for the study of real estate because all of the concepts and principles discussed in this text—such as legal considerations, local market conditions, interest rates, and local land use controls and regulations—are important primarily in the context of how they affect real estate values.

The Production of Real Estate Assets

If rental rates and their riskiness are determined in the space market, and required risk premiums are largely determined in the general capital markets, what role do local property (asset) markets play? First, local property markets allocate available property investments

Exhibit 1-6   User Markets, Capital Markets, and Property Markets

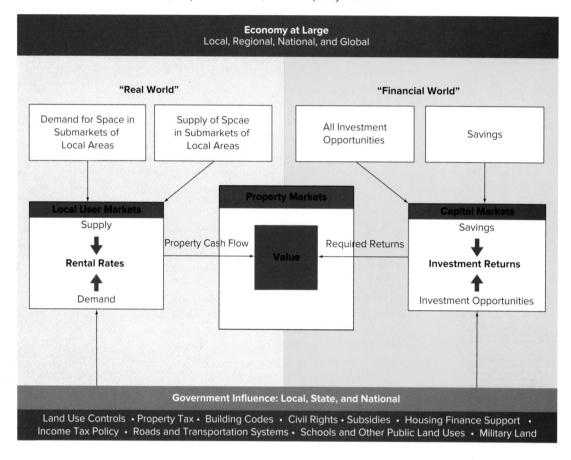

among competing investors. Second, local property markets determine the pace of new construction. A primary determinant of the feasibility of new construction is the relationship between the current level of property prices and the cost of new construction. If current property values are greater than the cost of new construction—including land costs and a fair developer profit—developers and investors have an incentive to add new space to the existing stock in an attempt to capture excess profits. Ultimately, the expansion of supply causes rents in the space market (and therefore values in the property market) to decrease toward the level of current construction costs.

If current property values are below construction costs, as in an overbuilt market, a combination of reduced construction, normal growth in demand for space, and the steady obsolescence of the existing stock is required to push market rents and property values to their required levels. Only then will developers find new construction projects profitable once more.

Real estate construction historically has been a volatile process because real estate prices and costs tend to be volatile. Thus, building booms and slumps often characterize real estate production, as discussed in Chapter 6. To compound the volatility further, real estate values also can be affected by shocks to the capital markets. For example, if interest rates rise, property values will generally fall, again rendering construction less profitable. Finally, construction costs can be very volatile. Organized labor disputes in cities such as New York or Boston, or unexpected events causing shortages in lumber, steel, or other building materials, can severely damage the financial viability of both small and large real estate development. (Real estate development is treated further in Chapter 23.)

Characteristics of Real Estate Markets

Real estate assets and markets are unique when compared to other goods. The two primary characteristics of real estate assets are their heterogeneity and immobility. Because of these two factors, the market for buying, selling, and leasing real estate tends to be illiquid, localized, and highly segmented, with privately negotiated transactions and high transaction costs.

www.marshallswift.com

Private firm that tracks construction costs.

Heterogeneous Products

Real estate tends to be heterogeneous, meaning that each property has unique features. An example of a relatively homogeneous product is gasoline. Although it is possible to purchase different grades of gasoline (e.g., octane levels), a gallon of gasoline received from a particular pump cannot be distinguished from the next gallon.

For real estate, however, age, building design, and especially location combine to give each property distinctive characteristics. Even in residential neighborhoods with very similar houses, the locations differ. Corner lots have different locational features than interior lots; their access to parks and transportation routes may differ, and the traffic patterns within the neighborhood create differences. The most influential site and structural attributes of a home are typically observable and amenable to valuation (e.g., pools, bedrooms, and garages). However, information about a property's location attributes is much more difficult to observe and value because numerous external effects (positive and negative) act upon a land parcel at a given location, and these effects are reflected in the parcel's value. Said differently, each parcel of land has a unique location-value signature (LVS) and differences in LVSs create variation in property values.[6] Locational differences are particularly critical for retail properties. Significant value differences may result between retail properties on different sides of the same street, depending on whether the property is on the "going-home" or the "going-to-work" side. Most food outlets, drugstores, clothing stores, and service centers prefer to be on the going-home side of the street. Even within a single shopping center, there are important differences in location for a retail establishment depending on the need of the establishment for exposure to shoppers.

Immobile Products

Real estate is immobile. Although it is sometimes physically possible to move a building from one location to another, this is generally not financially feasible. The vast majority of structures removed from the land are demolished rather than moved.

Another term for location is access. For households it is access to school, shopping, entertainment, and places of employment. For commercial properties it may be access to customers, the labor force, or suppliers. The nuances of access are fundamental to real estate value, as we discuss in Chapter 5.

Localized Markets

Real estate markets tend to be localized. By this we mean that the potential users of a property, and competing sites, generally lie within a short distance of each other. For example, competing apartment properties may lie within 15 minutes, or less, in driving time from each other, while competing properties of single-family residences may tend to be within a

6. The term *location-value signature* is attributable to "Modeling Spatial Variation in House Prices: A Variable Interaction Approach." Timothy J. Fik, David C. Ling, and Gordon F. Mulligan, *Real Estate Economics,* vol. 31, no. 4, 2004.

...school district or even within a small number of similar subdivisions. ... neighborhood shopping center is very localized. Such centers usu-...ustomers from within a five-mile radius, or less. For a par-

Segmented

www.prea.org

Pension Real Estate Association.

Real estate markets ... products. Households that s... ally not consider other residential product types such as an attached townhouse unit or condominium. In addition, real estate is segmented by product price. The same holds true, although to a lesser extent, in the commercial property market. Commercial property markets are segmented by both users and investors. Larger, more valuable commercial properties, generally well over $10 million, are often referred to as **investment-grade properties** or **institutional-grade real estate.** This is the segment of the property market targeted by institutional investors such as pension funds, publicly traded real estate companies, and real estate private equity funds. Individual private investors typically do not compete directly with institutional investors for properties.

The localized nature of real estate markets also contributes to segmentation and explains why rents and prices for otherwise similar property can vary significantly across metropolitan markets and even submarkets within a given metropolitan area.

Privately Negotiated Transactions with High Transaction Costs

www.costar.com

www.loopnet.com

Private firms with information on a large number of commercial properties for sale.

A final distinctive feature of real estate is the complexity of property and transactions. As we discuss in Chapter 2, real estate is a uniquely complex "bundle of rights." The property interest to be conveyed cannot be standardized and therefore must be carefully assessed to determine what rights it actually contains. Further, because real estate has a history of ownership, the current claims of ownership must be confirmed by examining the past history of the property. Finally, property parcels are contiguous, so the problem of accurate description requires unique and elaborate systems of delineation. All these special issues in real estate are sufficient to compel unique laws, institutions, and procedures for the conveyance of real estate. Moreover, real estate agents, mortgage lenders, attorneys, appraisers, property inspectors, and others are usually involved in the transaction. The negotiation process between buyers and sellers can be lengthy, and the final transaction price and other important details such as lease terms are not usually observable. Thus, in almost every transaction involving real estate, there are time requirements and costs not present in most non-real estate transactions. These special challenges in virtually any transaction involving real estate can affect real estate values and risks and must be recognized by investors. It is important to note that the use of auctions to sell real estate has increased in recent years (see Industry Issues 1-2). The growing popularity and use of auctions is a response by some market participants to the costs and delays associated with privately negotiated transactions. It will be interesting to see if this trend continues.

www.auction.com

Founded in 2007, this is one of the nation's leading online real estate marketplace.

One final note on the uniqueness of real estate: Investors and lenders seem to get into trouble most commonly when they lose sight of these unique characteristics of real estate. The latest, graphic example of this is the subprime mortgage meltdown that occurred in the late 2000s. Such mortgages were used mostly by borrowers with weak credit or by borrowers who wanted to use more debt to purchase their homes than could be obtained with a "prime" mortgage. The creation and dissemination of subprime mortgage investments became detached from any thoughtful assessment of the underlying borrowers, housing values, or market depth. When average housing prices declined dramatically from 2006 to 2010, the cost of this short-sightedness was felt in every corner of the United States.

www.mhhe.com/lingarcher5e

✓ **Concept Check**

1.6 Identify four ways in which real estate markets differ from the market for publicly traded stocks.

Summary

We began this chapter by looking at the different uses of the term *real estate*. This was followed by a discussion of land use in the United States and the contribution of real estate to U.S. and household wealth, and then a discussion of the real estate market.

The term *real estate* is used in three fundamental ways: (1) to identify the tangible assets of land and buildings; (2) to denote the "bundle" of rights associated with the ownership and use of the physical assets; and (3) to refer to the industry, or business activities, related to the acquisition, operation, and disposition of the physical assets. Viewed as a tangible asset, real estate constitutes the physical components of location and space. In this context, real estate is defined as the land and any improvements permanently affixed on, or to, the land. The bundle of intangible rights, or interests, associated with the ownership and use of the physical characteristics of space and location constitutes the services that real estate provides to its users. It is the services/benefits that result from the use of the property that create value. Said differently, tracts of dirt do not have any intrinsic value. It is the uses to which the dirt can be put that create value.

Real estate typically generates over 25 percent of U.S. gross domestic product (GDP), creates jobs for nearly 9 million Americans, and is the source of nearly 70 percent of local government revenues. The total contribution of the housing sector alone approaches 20 percent of GDP. Real estate construction, construction permit activity, and real estate sales figures are closely watched by investors on Wall Street and across the world because of the effect real estate has on the nation's economy. Real estate also represents a significant share of our accumulated national wealth. The total value of owner-occupied housing and investible commercial real estate in the United States is estimated to be $30.8 trillion. Approximately $22.0 trillion of this represents the value of owner-occupied housing. Housing alone represents approximately 22 percent of U.S. household wealth and is the single largest asset category owned by households.

Real estate market activity is influenced by the activities and conditions that take place in three sectors of a market economy: (1) the user market, (2) the financial or capital market, and (3) the government sector. Real estate users compete in the market for location and space. Among the users of space are both renters and owners. The financial resources to acquire real estate assets are allocated in the capital market; hence, equity investors and investors in mortgage debt (lenders) are capital market participants. Local and state governments, as well as the federal government, influence the activities of each of the participant groups through regulations, provisions of services and infrastructure, taxes, and various subsidies.

Two primary characteristics of real estate assets distinguish them from others: heterogeneity and immobility. Because of these two factors, the market for evaluating, producing, buying, selling, leasing, and managing real estate tends to be illiquid, localized, and highly segmented, and it usually involves privately negotiated transactions with relatively high transaction costs.

Key Terms

Acre 6
Capital markets 9
Capitalization rate 9
Improvements on the land 2
Improvements to the land 2
Institutional-grade real estate 14

Intangible assets 2
Investment-grade properties 14
Land 4
Personal property 4
Property 2
Property markets 9

Raw land 4
Real estate 2
Real property 4
Tangible assets 2
User markets 9

Test Problems

Answer the following multiple-choice problems:

1. A market where tenants negotiate rent and other terms with property owners or their managers is referred to as a:
   a. Property market.
   b. User market.
   c. Housing market.
   d. Capital market.

2. The market in which required rates of return on available investment opportunities are determined is referred to as the:
   a. Property market.
   b. User market.
   c. Housing market.
   d. Capital market.

3. The actions of local, state, and federal governments affect real estate values:
   a. Primarily through user markets.
   b. Primarily through the capital market.
   c. Primarily through their taxation policies.
   d. Through all of the above.

4. What portion of households owns their house?
   a. Approximately one-third.
   b. Approximately two-thirds.
   c. Approximately one-half.
   d. Approximately one-quarter.

5. Of the following asset categories, which has the greatest aggregate market value?
   a. Corporate equities.
   b. Mortgage debt.
   c. Government debt.
   d. Nongovernment real estate.

6. Storm water drainage systems are best described as:
   a. Tangible assets.
   b. Improvements to the land.
   c. Intangible assets.
   d. Improvements on the land.

7. What is the single largest asset category in the portfolio of a typical U.S. household?
   a. Housing.
   b. Consumer durables.
   c. Stocks.
   d. Bonds.

8. Real estate markets differ from other asset classes by having all of the following characteristics except:
   a. Local market.
   b. High transaction costs.
   c. Segmented market.
   d. Homogeneous product.

9. Which of the following is *not* important to the location of commercial properties?
   a. Access to customers.
   b. Visibility.
   c. Access to schools.
   d. Availability of communications infrastructure.

10. Which of the following attributes of a home are the most difficult to observe and value?
    a. Land/site attributes.
    b. Structural attributes.
    c. Location attributes.
    d. Financing attributes.

Study Questions

1. The term *real estate* can be used in three fundamental ways. List these three alternative uses or definitions.

2. The United States represents about 6 percent of the Earth's land surface, or approximately 2.3 billion acres. Who owns this land? What is the distribution of this land among the various uses (e.g., developed land, federal land, forest land)?

3. Describe the value of U.S. real estate by comparing it to the values of other asset classes (e.g., stocks, bonds).

4. How much of the wealth of a typical U.S. household is tied up in housing? How does this compare to the role that assets and investments play in the portfolios of U.S. households?

5. Real estate assets and markets are unique when compared with other assets or markets. Discuss the primary ways that real estate markets are different from the markets for other assets that trade in well-developed public markets.

6. Explain the role of government in real estate at the federal, state, and local levels. Which has the most significant impact on real estate markets?

7. Identify and describe the interaction of the three economic sectors that affect real estate value.

8. Real estate construction is a volatile process determined by the interaction of the user, capital, and property markets. What signals do real estate producers (i.e., developers) use to manage this process? What other factors affect the volatility of real estate production?

Solutions to Concept Checks

1. A major determinant between real and personal property is whether or not the property is movable or permanently affixed to the land or structure.

2. Tangible assets are physical assets such as land, automobiles, and buildings. Intangible assets are nonphysical, including patents, financial claims, or contractual agreements. Real estate is a tangible asset, but a bundle of intangible rights is also associated with the ownership and use of the property.

3. About 61 percent of the U.S. housing stock is financed with home mortgage debt. ($9.8 trillion in mortgage debt divided by $16.1 trillion in housing value.)

4. The four capital market quadrants include private equity, private debt, public equity, and public debt. The private equity market includes transactions of real property between individuals, firms, and institutions. Private debt includes the trading of home mortgages. Investors trade real estate companies

such as equity REITs in the public equity market. Mortgage-backed securities are traded in the public debt markets.

5. Commercial real estate rental rates are determined in local user (space) markets, while property values are determined largely in the local property market.

6. First, real estate is a heterogeneous product distinguished by its age, building design, and location. Second, real estate is immobile, and therefore location and its accessibility are important. Third, real estate is a localized, segmented market due to local competition and the heterogeneous nature of the product. Finally, real estate transactions have high transfer costs, and most deals are privately negotiated.

EXPLORE THE WEB

The government affects real estate in many ways. At the federal level, many housing programs exist. Go to the Department of Housing and Urban Development's website, www.hud.gov, click on the "Topic Areas" tab at the top of the page, and explore the resources available to households looking to avoid foreclose, buy a home, make home improvements, and obtain rental assistance, to name a few.

Additional Readings

Appraisal Institute. *Dictionary of Real Estate Appraisal,* 5th ed. Chicago: Appraisal Institute, 2002.

Archer, W. R. and D. C. Ling. "The Three Dimensions of Real Estate Markets: Linking Space, Capital, and Property Markets," *Real Estate Finance* (Fall 1997).

Edwards, K. W. *Your Successful Real Estate Career,* 5th ed. New York: AMACOM, 2007.

Evans, M., and R. Mendenhall. *Opportunities in Real Estate Careers,* Rev. 2nd ed. New York: McGraw-Hill/Contemporary Books, March 27, 2002.

Friedman, J. P., J. C. Harris, and B. Diskin. *Real Estate Handbook,* 7th ed. Hauppauge, NY: Barron's Educational Series, 2009.

Geltner, D. M., N. G. Miller, J. Clayton, and P. Eichholtz. *Commercial Real Estate Analysis and Investments*, 3rd ed. Mason, OH: OnCourse Learning, 2014.

Jacobus, C. J. *Real Estate: An Introduction to the Profession,* 11th ed. Mason, OH: Cengage Learning, 2009.

Ling, D. C. and A. Naranjo, "The Integration of Commercial Real Estate Markets and Stock Markets," *Real Estate Economics* 27, no. 3 (Fall 1999).

Rowh, M. *Careers in Real Estate.* New York: McGraw-Hill/ Contemporary Books, 2003.

Vault Career Guide to Real Estate. New York: Vault Reports, 2003.

PART TWO

Chapter 2

Legal Foundations *to* Value

LEARNING OBJECTIVES

After reading this chapter you will be able to:

1 List three characteristics of rights that distinguish them from permission and power, list three components of property rights, distinguish between real and personal property, and define a fixture.

2 State the distinguishing characteristic of an estate, list three types of freehold estates, and distinguish a freehold estate from a leasehold.

3 Define an easement, distinguish it from a license, distinguish two basic types of easements, and identify four examples of each.

4 Define a restrictive covenant, state who can enforce it and how, and list five ways that restrictive covenants can become unenforceable.

5 List one type of general lien and three types of specific liens, list two factors that determine priority among liens, and state the significance of priority.

6 List the features that distinguish these forms of ownership: tenancy in common, joint tenancy, tenancy by the entireties, condominium, and cooperative.

7 Distinguish among the provisions of dower, elective share, and community property for the distribution of property between husband and wife.

8 List three common levels of timeshare claims, and identify what is most important to evaluate in a timeshare plan.

OUTLINE

Introduction

When we purchase real estate, it is not so much the ground and bricks that we acquire but rights to do certain things with them. This understanding opens the window to a wealth of questions and possibilities. The diversity of the possible claims (rights) to land is rich, with important implications for value. In fact, no estimate of value is meaningful until we know what rights are involved. This chapter provides a tour of these possible claims on real estate, to some of their uses, and to some of the resulting effects on value.

Several concepts are necessary to understand the nature of real property. The very concept of rights is the beginning point. Next, the difference between personal rights and property rights is important. Finally, we must distinguish between personal property and real property.

The bundle of property rights can range from complete ownership down to little more than the "squatter's rights" of an unintended tenant. A variety of nonpossessory rights also can affect the value of real property, including restrictive covenants, easements, and liens. Ownership of the bundle can be by multiple persons. These co-ownership claims can arise both from traditional law and from laws enacted by states, and they can occur in a variety of forms. A special source of co-ownership claims is marriage, and it is important to understand the variations in joint property rights that automatically arise from that union. Real property also can be divided in time through a variety of "interval ownership" arrangements. Real property often involves bodies of water and the use of groundwater. It is important to understand the issues involved with water rights. Finally, an important part of land is rights to minerals, including oil and gas.

The Nature of Property

The notion of property is anything but simple, having more to do with society's rules or patterns of behavior than with actual physical objects. Three fundamental distinctions are important in understanding property:

- What do we mean by rights?
- What is the difference between personal rights and property rights?
- What is the difference between personal property and real property?

The Nature of Rights

A principal definition of real estate is "rights to land and its permanent structures." But what do we mean by rights? First, rights are claims or demands that our government is obligated to enforce. For example, ownership of a car gives us the right to possess it. If someone steals it, we can expect law enforcement to try to reclaim it for us and punish the offender. This is in contrast to claims that are enforced only by force or threat. For example, a street gang may claim part of a street by intimidation, but government will not honor and support its claim.

A second characteristic of rights is that they are nonrevocable. We can contrast this, for example, with the typical office space usage: Employees may have an office in which they have considerable privacy; have liberty to arrange, equip, and decorate with discretion; and can come and go freely. But the employees understand that this is not ownership. They have this access by permission of the employer and it is revocable. Property rights are not revocable. The ownership claims to a residence or other real estate cannot be canceled, ignored, or otherwise lessened by any other private citizen. While they may be diminished significantly by action of government in the interest of public health, safety, and welfare, there is a limit to the restriction. At some point it becomes excessive, and is regarded as a "taking." The government must then acquire the property through due process of law, and with just compensation.[1]

---

1. The power of government to take private property is called eminent domain. It, and the related legal procedure, condemnation, are discussed in Chapter 4.

The nonrevocable nature of rights suggests a third aspect of property rights: They are enduring. They do not fade away with time. The government is obligated to defend them in subsequent generations just as now, and it does not have the power to abandon that obligation.

✓ Concept Check

2.1   How do rights to an object differ from attaining it by force or intimidation? What distinguishes rights from permission?

Society is concerned with two kinds of rights: personal rights and property rights (see Exhibit 2-1). In the United States, **personal rights** (personal freedoms) derive primarily from the Bill of Rights and other amendments and clauses of the U.S. Constitution. **Property rights,** rights to things both tangible and intangible, derive from ancient times, and are as old as the notion of law itself. The principal rights in property include (exclusive) possession, use (enjoyment), and disposition. If we own a computer, for example, we have the right to:

1. Prevent others from using it.
2. Enjoy the use or benefit of it for ourselves.
3. Get rid of it as we see fit (but without harm to others).

✓ Concept Check

2.2   List three components of property rights.

As suggested by Exhibit 2-1, the two kinds of rights abut each other, and can conflict in important ways. (See Industry Issues 2-1.) For example, the right of a shopping mall owner to require behavior and attire that enhances the shopping environment—and thus the value of the property—can conflict with what patrons regard as their personal rights of expression and assembly in a "public" place.

Property is divided into two classes, real and personal. **Real property** is defined as rights in land and its permanent structures. **Personal property** is the rest; that is, it is simply rights in any other kind of object, including intellectual matters.

Exhibit 2-1   Rights in Our Society

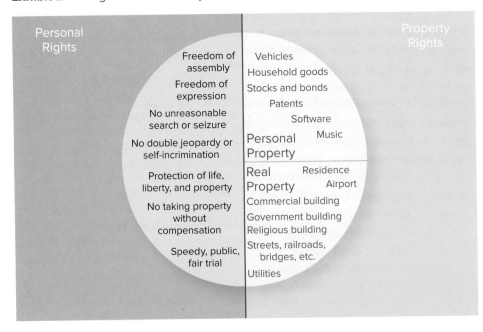

Exhibit 2-2 Real Property: Rights in Three Dimensions

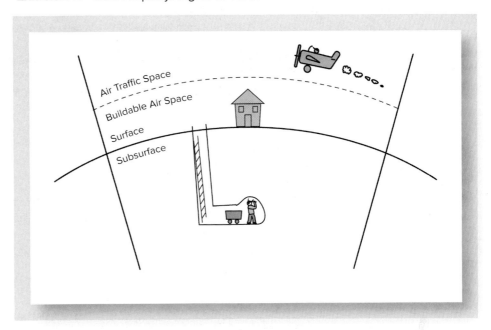

Real property is rights in land, but what is land? It is the surface of the earth, of course, but, as shown in Exhibit 2-2, it also includes rights to air space above the land either up to the height it is technologically feasible to erect structures or to the level where airspace becomes reserved for air traffic. Also, it includes rights to the subsurface down to the center of the earth, and to the minerals, including oil and gas, contained therein.[2] Rights to the subsurface and to airspace can be an extremely valuable part of real estate. In large cities many prominent structures are built on air rights alone, as exemplified in Exhibit 2-3.

Exhibit 2-3 "Groundless" Building Stories: The Use of Air Rights

© Felix Lipov/123RF

In New York City the MetLife Building towers 59 floors above the railroad right-of-ways entering Grand Central Station.

© Ron Rovtar Photography/ Alamy Stock Photo

In Chicago the "New East Side" is a cluster of world-class buildings built on air rights above a former railroad yard.

2. Oil, gas, and mineral rights are discussed briefly at the end of this chapter.

Tree protester sued for trespassing

SANTA CLARITA, California (AP)—A developer trying to get a 400-year-old oak tree out of the way of a road-widening project turned up the heat on tree-sitter, John Quigley, trying to protect it, charging him with trespassing and shooing away his supporters. . . . Supporters sleeping below the tree were ordered to clear the area, and a chain-link fence and "No Trespassing" signs went up around the oak.

Which of these poses a greater challenge to property rights?

Bill Rattazzi, president of the Los Angeles division of John Laing Homes, said no attempt was made to remove or arrest Quigley. "These actions were taken to stabilize the situation and allow the issue to be decided in the courts in an orderly manner," he said.

Laing, which owns the property on which the tree grows, wants it out of the way to widen a road that would serve the proposed 21,600-home Newhall Ranch development north of Los Angeles. Quigley's response: "You have this irreplaceable natural resource . . . for our lifetimes and the lifetimes of maybe 10 generations. We can't replace that." . . .

Update: The resolution was that "Old Glory" was moved to a nearby park in possibly the most ambitious tree relocation ever. Thirteen years later, it is reported to be surviving quite well.

Endangered species act restricts use of vast areas in the United States

The Endangered Species Act (1973), intended to conserve ecosystems vital to troubled plants and animals, has encountered troubles of its own through controversy about protected critical habitats. Early warning of the problem came in 1977 when threat to the habitat of the snail darter, a three-inch fish, held up construction of the Tennessee Valley Authority's Tellico Dam. Protection of spawning grounds for salmon in the Pacific Northwest is a recent issue, pitting protection of salmon against irrigation demands. Yet another skirmish involves a tiny bird, the southwest willow flycatcher. In seven southwestern states protecting its habitat along streams has threatened to end centuries-old cattle grazing. But the premier controversy stirred by the law concerns the northern spotted owl. In the Pacific Northwest, millions of acres of mature forest were restricted from logging to protect the owl's habitat. Loggers bitterly opposed this as a threat to their industry. To date, the habitat protection has been less effective than advocates hoped, while the economic damage may be less than its critics feared.

In 2010, a new chapter in the ESA was opened. The law prompted the Sage Grouse Initiative, a voluntary private and public effort to preserve the Sage Grouse habitat in 11 western states through such tools as conservation easements. By 2015 1,129 ranches and 4.4 million acres had been enrolled in the program.

Source: CNN.com/us, January 10, 2003, with updates. SCTV interview with Leon Wardon, January 26, 2004.

© Paul Harris Atticusimages/Newscom

Erie Foraman/Courtesy USGS

The distinction between personal rights and property rights is far from simple (see Industry Issues 2-1). However, this issue is beyond the scope of the current chapter. (It is discussed at length in Chapter 4.) We instead focus our attention on the distinction between personal property and real property.

Real Property and Personal Property: The Problem of Fixtures

A **fixture** is an object that formerly was personal property but has become real property. This special class of real property is an enduring problem in real estate. Consider these examples: On a construction site, when do building materials cease to be the personal property of the contractor and become part of the "land and its permanent structures" (real property)? If a valuable antique chandelier is hung in a new home, is it then part of the real property? Are custom draperies real property? What about removable shutters or storm windows? What about a kitchen range or refrigerator? This ambiguity between personal property and real property has long been recognized, and rules have evolved in the common law tradition to help sort it out.[3]

Specifically, these four rules help to determine whether an object has become a fixture:

1. **The manner of attachment:** The question in this rule is whether removal of the object results in damage to the property. Clearly, for example, removal of vinyl floor covering would damage a building. But a court may regard removal of wire connecting a dwelling to cable service as being damage as well.[4]

2. **The character of the article and manner of adaptation:** Under this rule, items that have been custom designed or custom fitted tend to be regarded as fixtures. Examples might include window screens, storm windows, church pews, custom bookshelves, custom draperies, or custom security systems.

3. **The intention of the parties:** This rule refers not to the private intention of the parties but to the facts of the situation and the intention that an observer familiar with customary practice would conclude from them. A major example would be kitchen appliances: If a kitchen range or refrigerator is in a single-family residence being sold, it normally is expected to remain with the seller. On the other hand, if the appliances are furnishings in a rental apartment building, they normally would be expected to remain with the building. Thus, the rule of intention would treat the appliances as personal property in the single-family residence, but as fixtures in the apartment.

4. **Relation of the parties:** For landlord and tenant relationships, special versions of the rule of intention have evolved in determining fixtures:

   a. **Trade fixtures,** which are items installed by a commercial tenant to conduct its business, are always considered personal property of the tenant unless they are abandoned at termination of the lease. Thus, despite the fact that wall treatments, wall display cases, floor display cases, and so forth are usually custom fitted, and usually "injure" the facility when removed, they still are regarded as property of the tenant.

   b. **Agriculture fixtures,** such as fences, also are considered property of the tenant. Anything that is installed by the tenant remains personal property.

   c. **Residential tenants** also tend to be given the same protection. Any item installed in the residence by the tenant is regarded as the tenant's personal property, at least until it is abandoned.

The rule of intention is the most recent, and dominant, rule. That is, if there is conflict among the rules, the rule of intention generally will prevail.

There is a very practical importance to the fixture issue for property value. A contract for the sale of real estate applies only to real property unless personal property involved is explicitly included. Frequently when property is purchased, including personal residences, there are items on the property that may or may not be fixtures. Thus, who owns them after sale of the property may not be clear. In any real estate transaction, it is important for both parties involved to carefully review the property with this issue in mind, and to draw up the contract so that there is no ambiguity regarding disposition of these items.

The Real Property Bundle of Rights

The owner of real property holds a bundle of rights that is complex. As noted above, this bundle is some combination of the right of exclusive possession, use (enjoyment), and disposition. But this bundle can be dismantled in many ways, creating lesser bundles, held by different individuals. These bundles of rights are referred to as **interests.** The value of

---

3. Common law is the body of traditional law derived from the ancient courts of England, constantly evolving through new court rulings or case law.

4. *T-V Transmission, Inc. v. County Board of Equalization,* 338 N.W. 2nd 752 (Neb. 1983).

the property will tend to vary with the completeness of the interest. Below, we examine the possible variation in the bundle.

> ### ✓ Concept Check
>
> **2.3** Is a fixture real or personal property? What is the dominant rule for determining whether something is a fixture? Under the "rule of intention," identify two possible results for the example of kitchen appliances.

Possessory Interests (Estates)

Interests in real property that include possession are called **estates.** These can range from the complete bundle of rights (fee simple absolute) to a claim that is little more than "squatter's rights" (tenancy at sufferance). In between are a variety of bundles, differing by the combination of other rights included. The range of estates is displayed in Exhibit 2-4. The most complete estate, the fee simple absolute, is singled out, as are the weakest, tenancy at will and tenancy at sufferance. Each possible estate is discussed below.

> ### ✓ Concept Check
>
> **2.4** When is a real property interest an estate?

Exhibit 2-4 Estates

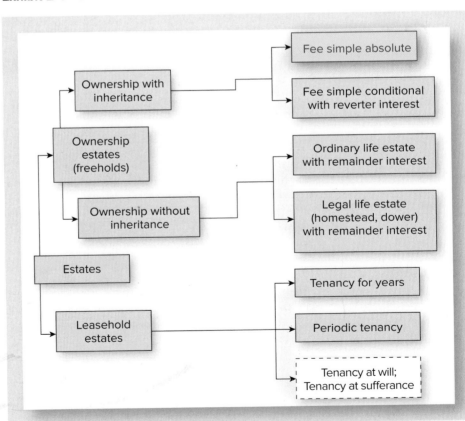

Ownership Estates (Freeholds or Titled Interests).   The more substantial or complete estates are those that are indefinite in length. These are the titled interests we commonly think of as ownership. In the common law term, they are **freeholds.** They can differ by variations in the right of disposition.

Fee Simple Absolute.   **Fee simple absolute** is the most complete bundle of rights possible, and has the greatest value. Subject to the limitations imposed by government or by prior owners, all possible rights of exclusive possession, use and enjoyment, and disposition are possessed by the owner. This is the traditional concept of landownership. It is this interest that is intended when persons of the real estate world refer to owning or holding the "fee."

Fee Simple Conditional.   In a **fee simple conditional,** ownership is subject to a condition or trigger event. In this case the owner's bundle of rights is complete unless the trigger event occurs, which may cause ownership to revert to a previous owner (or his or her heirs). This uncertain interest held by the previous owner (or heirs) is called a **reverter** interest. For example, an owner could convey a small apartment building to a university but require that the property be used for a scholarship dormitory for women students. As long as the university uses the property for this purpose, it may enjoy all the rights of a fee simple owner. However, if it ever allows men students to occupy the house, the previous owner or the owner's heirs can bring suit to recover the property. The resulting uncertainty that this kind of condition creates can, of course, greatly reduce the value of ownership.

Ordinary Life Estate and Remainder.   In an **ordinary life estate** the rights of disposition of the fee simple absolute are unbundled and separated completely. For example, suppose an older homeowner lives adjacent to an expanding university, and the university would like to acquire her residence for future university use. Suppose also that she is willing to sell, but is not interested in moving. A possible solution is for the university to purchase a **remainder estate** while the owner retains a life estate. In this arrangement the homeowner retains all rights of exclusive possession, use, and enjoyment for her lifetime while the university gains the right of disposition. The owner is compensated either through cash payment or a tax deduction (if the remainder is donated) and simplifies the eventual settlement of her estate, while assuring the continued right to occupy her home. At the time of her death the life estate and remainder estate are rejoined, becoming a complete fee simple absolute owned by the university.[5]

Legal Life Estate.   **Legal life estates** are created by the action of law. In Florida, for example, a family residence that is declared a homestead carries the possibility of becoming subject to a life estate. If a family having minor children occupies a homestead residence, and if one spouse dies, Florida's homestead law gives the surviving spouse a life estate and gives the children "vested remainder" interests in the residence. While intended to protect the surviving family, this law can create as many problems as it solves. If the surviving spouse needs to sell the residence to relocate, a trustee must be created to act on behalf of the minor children to convey their interests in the sale. Thus, additional legal costs and delays are likely to result.[6]

Other Life Estates.   Life estates also can arise out of a marriage. In the English common law tradition a right known as dower automatically gave a widow a life estate in one-third of the real property of her decedent husband. Today, however, dower generally has been displaced, as discussed later in this chapter.

---

5. While rare, and normally inadvisable, the life estate could be tied to the life of someone other than the owner.

6. For this reason, families in Florida are advised to acquire their primary personal residence by the special joint ownership known as tenancy by the entirety (discussed later in this chapter).

Leasehold (Nonownership or Non-freehold) Estates. **Leasehold** interests are possessory interests and are therefore estates. They differ from freehold estates in three respects: (1) They are limited in time. (2) The right of disposition is diminished because the property ultimately reverts to the landlord. (3) They are not titled interests. Essentially, they are a temporary conveyance of the rights of exclusive possession, use and enjoyment, but not the right of disposition.

Tenancy for Years (Estate for Years). A **tenancy for years** is a leasehold interest for a specific period of time. It may be for a few days, or for hundreds of years, state law permitting. Until recently the relationship between landlord and tenant was governed entirely by the terms of the lease. However, as explained below, a shift from rural to urban society and changing social needs have altered this. While all leases should be put in writing, this is especially true for the lease conveying a tenancy for years because the lease may be the only tangible evidence of the landlord–tenant understanding. If the term is for more than one year (a year and a day, or more) the lease *must* be in writing to be enforceable. (This requirement results from the Statute of Frauds, discussed in Chapter 3.)

Periodic Tenancy. Any lease that has no definite term at the start is a **periodic tenancy.** In sharp contrast to the tenancy for years, the lease conveying the periodic tenancy often is oral and, hence, is rather informal. While simpler and quicker, this arrangement carries more risk of landlord and tenant misunderstanding. The length of the period is implied by the payment period. Every state has specified requirements for notification prior to terminating a periodic tenancy, with both landlord and tenant subject to the same requirements. Generally, the minimum notice period is one-half the payment period, and begins the day after actual notification, running to the end of the last day of the rental period.[7] While periodic tenancy conveyed by an oral lease is common between individual landlords and tenants, it is less common where the landlord has multiple tenants. The use of written rental contracts is a superior practice that reduces risk for both parties, thus adding to the value of the property.

Tenancy at Will. Sometimes at the end of a lease there is a short period of time when it suits both landlord and tenant for occupancy to continue. For example, this might occur if the building is being sold or renovated in the near future. If there is agreement that the tenant will stay until either landlord or tenant gives notice, the tenancy is known as a **tenancy at will.**[8]

Tenancy at Sufferance. A **tenancy at sufferance** occurs when a tenant that is supposed to vacate does not. This tenancy, at least until the landlord accepts a rental payment, differs from trespassing only in that the tenant previously occupied the property under a legitimate leasehold interest.

Changing Leasehold Concepts. Dramatic change has occurred in leasehold law in recent decades. Until around 1970, the law of leasehold estates had evolved little from the English common law tradition of rural leaseholds. In that setting, the obligation of the landlord was little more than to get off the land and leave the tenant alone. In an urban setting of residential apartments, this treatment of landlord–tenant relations was woefully inadequate. As a result, states have enacted elaborate residential landlord–tenant laws that take great strides in defining the rights and obligations of both parties under a residential lease. The laws address such matters as obligations for care and repair of the premises, rights of entry, handling of deposits, notification requirements, and many other matters. In short,

---

7. In Florida, for example, the periods for notification are as follows: for year-to-year, three months; for a quarterly period, 45 days; for a monthly period, 15 days; for a weekly period, 7 days.

8. The use of the term here is derived from common law usage. In some states, such as Florida, "tenancy at will" has been redefined to be any periodic tenancy.

www.nolo.com/legal-encyclopedia/state-landlord-tenant-laws

Summarizes residential landlord and tenant legal issues by topic, by state.

"Google" Legal Information Institute. Then choose "Law by Source: State," then "Business and Finance Laws," then "Residential Landlord and Tenant Act."

Widely respected academic source of legal information with links to important kinds of state laws, including residential landlord and tenant law for about 40 states.

something of a revolution has taken place in residential leasehold law. During the last few decades it has gone from the common law tradition of simple agrarian relationships found in preindustrial England to the idea that an urban residential tenant is receiving shelter services from the landlord that must meet certain standards. (More about modern statutory landlord–tenant relationships is available on the websites in the margin, and in Chapter 21.)

Nonpossessory Interests

Bundles of real property rights that do not include possession are particularly varied and can affect the value of real estate significantly. Below, we consider three quite different classes of nonpossessory interests: easements, restrictive covenants, and liens.

Easements. An **easement** is the right to use land for a specific and limited purpose. The purpose can range from very passive, such as access to a view, to virtually exclusive possession of the land, such as a street right-of-way or railroad right-of-way. A rich variation of applications lies between these extremes, as we show below.

✓ **Concept Check**

2.5 What is the basic definition of an easement?

Easements Appurtenant. **Easements appurtenant** have two distinguishing features. First, the easement appurtenant involves a relationship between two adjacent parcels of land. The **dominant parcel** benefits from the easement while the **servient parcel** is constrained or diminished by the easement. Second, the easement appurtenant "runs with the land"; that is, it becomes a permanent and inseparable feature of both parcels involved. (See Exhibit 2-5.)

Easements appurtenant are of two types: affirmative and negative. The examples below clarify this difference.

Exhibit 2-5 An Easement Appurtenant Involves a Dominant Parcel and a Servient Parcel

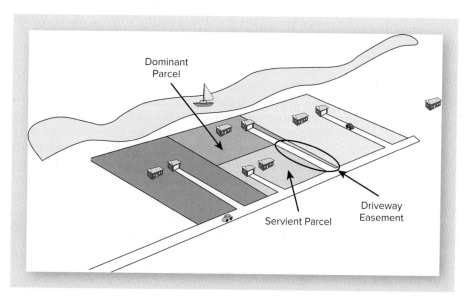

Affirmative Easements Appurtenant. Affirmative easements give the dominant parcel some intrusive use of the servient parcel. There are many examples:

1. A driveway easement across one parcel to another.
2. A drainage easement for storm water from one parcel across another.
3. Access across a parcel for sewer service.
4. A common wall easement requiring the wall of one townhouse to support the floors, roof, and structure of an adjacent one.
5. A common drive easement where owners of adjoining lots must permit each other to use a driveway lying on their shared property line.
6. Reciprocal parking easements among separately owned parcels in a shopping center.

Negative Easements Appurtenant. Negative easements allow no intrusion onto the servient parcel. One example of a negative easement appurtenant is a sunlight easement that restricts the configuration of adjacent buildings so as to assure access to direct sunlight. Another example, the scenic easement, has been used to restrict construction on adjacent parcels so as to preserve a valued view.

www.nature.org/about-us/private-lands-conservation/conservation-easements

Conservation easements as described by the nature conservancy.

Easements in Gross. An **easement in gross** is the right to use land for a specific, limited purpose unrelated to any adjacent parcel. While there is one or more servient parcels, there is no dominant parcel. Further, the easement in gross, unlike the easement appurtenant, is transferable to another owner without transfer of any parcel of land. Examples of easements in gross can include rights-of-way for roads, railroads, irrigation water, communication and electrical cables, gas lines, or billboards; and access for timber or crop harvesting, or for mineral or oil extraction. Not surprisingly, easements in gross are sometimes referred to as commercial easements, although noncommercial versions also exist. Noncommercial examples might be access for recreation purposes—fishing, hunting, boating, or snowmobiling—granted by a landowner to friends or family members. More recently, conservation easements have become an important tool to preserve wetlands or open spaces and well fields for a community's water supply.

One significant issue with a commercial easement in gross is whether it is exclusive or nonexclusive. The owner of an exclusive easement in gross holds all the easement rights, in effect, and can extend them to others, thus giving additional persons access to the easement and potentially increasing the usage burden on the servient land. If the easement is not exclusive, the owner of the easement cannot extend his rights to others. This prevents proliferation in use of the easement and preserves more of the value of the servient parcel.

Implications of Easements. In any locality, urban or rural, a variety of easements usually are present. As suggested above, the extent of the resulting restriction on the landowner's estate can range from minimal to nearly total. This adds challenges to the task of determining what bundle of rights is available to an owner of the land and what value the property has. This problem is highlighted in Exhibit 2-6. Examine the diagram and see if you can identify at least seven potential easements in the picture.

We began the discussion of easements with the notion that they are a non-possessory interest carved out of the freehold estate. What does this mean? The answer is suggested in Exhibit 2-7. The easement does not claim the right of exclusive possession (though it reduces the freeholder's right of exclusion). The easement claims part of the rights of use and enjoyment. For the right of disposition there are two cases: with an easement appurtenant all rights of disposition remain with the freehold estate; with an easement in gross the right of disposition of the easement is claimed as part of the easement.

✓ Concept Check
2.6 What is the major difference between an easement appurtenant and an easement in gross?

Exhibit 2-6 How Many Easements Are In This Scene?

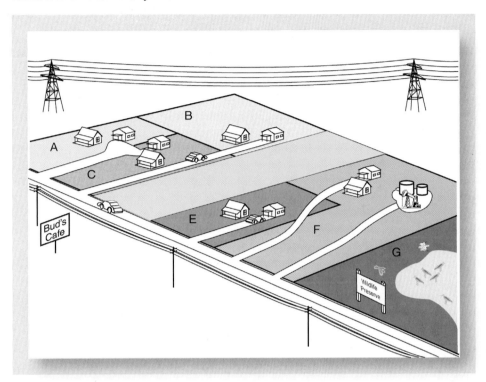

The easements suggested in this exhibit include the following: On parcels A and C is a common driveway easement. On parcel C is an implied easement of access in favor of parcel B. Parcel E appears to have an involuntary driveway easement known as an easement by prescription (see Chapter 3). On parcel F is an implied easement of access to extract oil. Associated with the power lines and the roadside electric lines are easements to permit the installation and maintenance of the lines. With the road sign is an easement to permit installation and maintenance of the sign. Finally, the wildlife preserve on parcel G may be protected by a conservation easement.

Exhibit 2-7 Rights Included in Various Real Property Interests

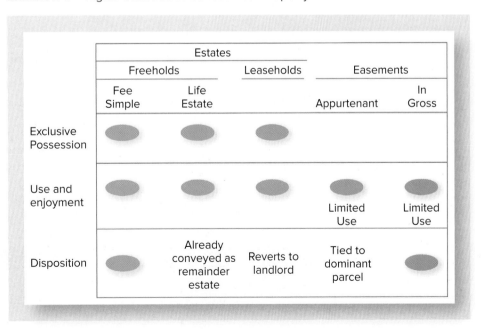

	Estates				
	Freeholds		Leaseholds	Easements	
	Fee Simple	Life Estate		Appurtenant	In Gross
Exclusive Possession	●	●	●		
Use and enjoyment	●	●	●	● Limited Use	● Limited Use
Disposition	●	Already conveyed as remainder estate	Reverts to landlord	Tied to dominant parcel	●

License. An important distinction both practically and conceptually is the difference between an easement and a **license.** Whereas an easement is the *right* to use another's land for a specific and limited purpose, a license is *permission* to do so. Unlike an easement, the license is revocable by the grantor. A license to use land is not uncommon. Examples might be permission for the various recreational uses of land noted above. A license is regarded as terminated if the land is sold or if the grantor dies. Licenses can be *granted orally,* whereas easements, being an interest in land, cannot.

Restrictive Covenants (Deed Restrictions).   **Restrictive covenants** impose limits on the uses of land. As their name suggests, they can be created when land is conveyed to a new owner by placing a restrictive clause in the deed that conveys the property. (Deeds are discussed in Chapter 3.) For example, it was not uncommon in the past to place a restriction in a deed prohibiting the new owner from certain activities on the property, such as the sale of alcoholic beverages. A much more common use of the restrictive covenant today is to control the character of land use in an entire subdivision. At the creation of a residential subdivision, a developer usually records a **declaration of covenants**, containing a series of restrictions on the use of the lots in order to improve the perceived quality, stability, and value of the lots. (Recorded documents are also discussed in Chapter 3.) Examples of residential subdivision restrictions include:

> Setback line and/or height restriction for houses.
> Minimum floor area.
> No freestanding garage.
> No freestanding utility building.
> No chain-link fences.
> No recreational vehicles or boats parked in view of the street.
> No garage door facing the street.
> Required architectural review of new structures or major additions.
> No external antennae, satellite dishes, or clotheslines.
> No habitual parking of cars in the driveway.
> Requirement to use professional lawn service.

www.houstontx.gov/ legal/deed.html

An unusually descriptive local government explanation of deed restrictions, their use and enforcement in Texas, where deed restrictions can replace zoning.

Traditionally, restrictive covenants are strictly private; that is, they can be enforced only by those who hold a legal interest in the property.[9] In the case of an isolated **deed restriction,** the owner who created the restriction or that owner's heirs are the only persons who can enforce the restriction. They would do so by suing for an injunction against a violation. Such individual restrictions usually must be enforced promptly. For example, if a seller of property created a restriction that the property must be used for residential purposes, and the seller seeks to enforce the restriction only after a commercial establishment has been created and is operating, the courts may be unwilling to uphold the restriction.[10] Court decisions concerning enforcement seem to reflect the common law tradition that property should be productive, with less restriction being better. When restrictions are ambiguous, the court is likely to interpret in favor of the current owner.

Enforcement of subdivisionwide restrictions is similar to enforcement of an isolated deed restriction. However, by a doctrine of rights known as "equitable servitude," subdivisionwide restrictions are deemed to serve the interest of all owners present and future in the subdivision lots, as well as others with interests in the land, such as mortgage lenders, and even renters. Any of these "parties at interest" can sue for injunction against violation of a restriction.

Whether the restriction is in an isolated deed or part of a general set of subdivision restrictions, the courts have been reluctant to maintain them for an unreasonably long time. Even in states where no time limit exists, courts may refuse to enforce restrictions due to changing neighborhood character, abandonment (neglect of enforcement, sometimes called

---

9. The strictly private character of deed restrictions can be blurred. In Texas, where deed restrictions have been used in place of public land use controls, state law has been enacted to allow local government to enforce certain deed restrictions (see Industry Issues 4-1). The action still is by civil suit, through the courts.

10. This culpable negligence in delaying enforcement is formally known as *laches.*

waiver), and changing public policy. In most states it is difficult to maintain individual restrictive covenants for more than a few decades, and several states have enacted time limits of 20 years or so.[11]

✓ Concept Check

2.7 Who can enforce a restrictive covenant? How is it done?

Liens. A **lien** is an interest in real property that serves as security for an obligation. It is useful to think of two types: general liens and specific liens. A **general lien** arises out of actions unrelated to ownership of the property. A **specific lien** derives directly from events related to a property. Specific liens include property tax and assessment liens, CDD liens (see below), mortgages, and mechanics' liens.

General Liens. The most prominent example of a general lien arises from a court judgment. If a property owner is successfully sued for damages for any reason, the court, in awarding the damages, normally will **attach** (place a lien on) available real property of the defendant as security for payment of the damage award. A second source of general liens is from unpaid federal taxes. The lien is imposed after the taxpayer has been billed for the back taxes and fails to pay.

Property Tax and Property Assessment Liens. Every real property owner is subject to property tax as a primary means of supporting local government. Since local government services are a benefit to property owners, the governments are able to exercise an automatic **property tax lien** on the benefiting properties to assure payment. Similarly, when a local government makes improvements in a neighborhood, such as street paving or utility installations, adjacent properties that receive the primary benefit will be charged a "fair share" assessment, usually based on the street frontage (front footage of each lot), though it sometimes is based on building or lot size. Typically, the property owners must pay the assessment in even amounts over 10 or 20 years. This fair share assessment is secured with an automatic **assessment lien.** One of the important aspects of the property tax liens and assessment liens is their priority; they automatically have senior priority among liens.

Community Development District Liens. A **community development district (CDD) lien** secures bonds issued to finance improvements within a private community. It attaches only to the properties within that community. CDDs are a recent creation that has grown rapidly among large residential developments. The CDD lien can secure financing for storm water management systems, other water systems, streets, recreation facilities, golf courses, and the like. This lien is a hybrid, in that it is not a government lien like the property tax or assessment lien, but it enjoys the same priority as if it were. Further, the financing it secures commonly is treated under income tax law as tax-exempt debt, as if it were local government debt.

Mortgages. A **mortgage** is an interest in property as security for a debt. Mortgage liens exist for a high percentage of all properties. Because of their central importance in real estate, they are discussed at length in Chapter 9. A property can have multiple mortgages, which are ordered in priority by the date of their recording. (This order can be changed by use of a subordination agreement, discussed in Chapter 9.) Later mortgages are referred to

---

11. Restrictive covenants, in effect, are a removal of some of the rights of use and enjoyment from property. Whether these covenants actually are real property interests has been questioned; that they tend to be more fragile and less durable than other real property interests may give credence to this question. Nevertheless, for some years after their creation, it is practical to regard restrictive covenants as amounting to negative property interests that cannot be altered.

as junior mortgages, or they are identified by order of creation as a second mortgage, third mortgage, and so forth.[12]

Mechanics' Liens.   **Mechanics' liens** arise from construction and other improvements to real estate. If a property owner defaults on a construction contract, it is not practical for the contractor to recover the materials and services used to improve the real estate. The solution is the mechanics' lien. Following completion of a contract, a contractor has a period of time (determined by each state) to establish a lien on the property improved. Since the priority of private liens depends upon when they were created, a major question with mechanics' liens is when they are deemed to be created. The answer varies, with some states treating the date that construction starts as the beginning of the lien, while other states use the date the construction contract was signed.

Mortgage lenders must be very attentive to the potential for mechanics' liens. They must carefully account for any possible mechanics' lien and assure that it is resolved with a waiver so that it does not preempt the priority of the mortgage.

Homeowner Association and Condo Association Liens.   Every homeowners association (HOA) or condo association has expenses, and imposes regular assessments on the owners. The association has the power to place a lien on an owner's property in case the owner fails to pay. But the status of this lien varies with state law and with the covenants and rules of the particular property. The effective date of the lien can be as early as when the covenants and rules are initially recorded, or when the assessment becomes due, depending on the property documents. Frequently, there are provisions in the covenants automatically subordinating the HOA lien to a first mortgage. State law also frequently makes the HOA lien subordinate to a first mortgage, but many states have a partial reverse, elevating at least part of delinquent HOA assessments (the first, say, six to nine months) to a "super lien" status, superior to all other chronological liens. Commonly, state law also may set a minimum number of delinquent months or amounts due before the HOA can exercise a lien against a homeowner.

traditionssoftware.com

Information on mechanics liens for all 50 states, with current developments. Under "State Lien Laws," select a state of interest.

✓ **Concept Check**

2.8   What is generally the determinant of lien priority? What lien always preempts this order?

Priority of Liens.   Several aspects of liens need to be clear. First, in case of default any lien can lead to sale of the property to compensate the creditor holding the lien. The priority, after property tax, assessment and CD liens, is by chronology among all other liens; the traditional expression of this is "first in time, first in right." Lien priority is significant because of the "all or nothing" treatment of creditors in the event of a property sale. Creditors receive no relief until all liens senior to theirs have been fully satisfied. A consequence of this ordering is that a lienholder who forces sale has no concern with liens below, but must satisfy all lienors that are senior.

The difference between general and specific liens is important in most states. Designation of a principal residence as a homestead usually creates automatic protection of the residence from general liens (except Federal tax liens), up to some limit.[13] So, while the homestead is subject to all other liens, it is protected from a judgment awarded for general debts.[14]

www.nolo.com/legal-encyclopedia/hoa-foreclosures

Links to numerous articles about HOAs, HOA assessments, and HOA liens.

---

12. In many states a deed of trust substitutes for a mortgage as security for a debt. The deed of trust, explained in Chapter 9, is a temporary conditional conveyance of ownership rather than a lien.

13. The amount of homestead value protected is unlimited for Florida, Texas, Iowa, Kansas, Oklahoma, and South Dakota. It ranges in most states from a few thousand dollars to $100 thousand, while there is no exemption in Pennsylvania, Maryland, or New Jersey. For more details see the adjacent websites.

14. In years past the homestead exemption was used notoriously in Texas and Florida to shelter wealth from bankruptcy. Notable modern cases included Kenneth Lay of Enron (Texas) and Scott Sullivan of WorldCom (Florida). The Bankruptcy Abuse Prevention and Consumer Protection Act (2005) imposed restrictions on the property eligible for such protection. Primarily, the law set a limit of $125,000 on the assets that receive homestead protection unless they have been held for 40 months prior to bankruptcy. Assets fraudulently acquired are not protected at all.

Exhibit 2-8 Levels of Liens on a Personal Residence

1st
Property Tax Liens,
Assessment Liens and CDD Liens
(*Always first priority*)

2nd
Priority by chronology
(first in time, first in right)

Mortgages, Mechanics Liens,
Federal Tax Judgment Liens and
HOA/Condo Association Liens*

Other Judgment Liens
(May be nullified by homestead, or by
a tenancy by the entirety if suit is
against only one spouse)

*HOA and Condo Association Liens are widely affected by state law and by property covenants. In some states they are partially superior to other chronological liens, in others, automatically subordinate to a first mortgage. Often, property covenants subordinate them to the first mortgage.

Similarly, a personal residence owned by husband and wife as a tenancy by the entirety (discussed below) is protected from judgment liens due to debt of one spouse alone. The priority of liens for a personal residence is summarized in Exhibit 2-8.[15]

Forms of Co-Ownership

Real estate often is owned by a group of persons; that is, more than one person holds precisely the same "bundle of rights," and the interests of the owners cannot be physically or otherwise separated. Imagine, for example, three unrelated persons who jointly purchase an ordinary house to live in, making equal contributions to the purchase price (the contributions would not need to be equal). While each may have an appointed bedroom, in large measure all must share the same space and rights of use. This indivisibility is the nature of true co-ownership that we are focusing on here; only if the owners vacate the house and rent it out can they truly divide up the "fruits" of the property by dividing up the rental income. Co-ownership can occur in a variety of ways, with significant variation in how the bundle of rights is jointly held. Exhibit 2-9 displays the variety of co-ownership forms, and each form is discussed on the following pages.

Indirect Co-Ownership through a Single Entity

In Chapter 17 we will present several business entities through which multiple persons can form a business organization: partnership, limited partnership, limited liability company, Subchapter S corporation, standard C corporation, and real estate investment trust (REIT). Any of these business entities can acquire real estate, acting as a single artificial "person." It is this artificial entity that owns the property rather than the individuals themselves. The owners have personal property ownership in the entity holding the real property. In these cases the co-ownership, in legal substance, is no different than a true single-person owner.

15. A numerical demonstration of the effect of priority among multiple liens is discussed in Chapter 9, under foreclosure.

texaspolitics.utexas.edu/educational-resources/comparing-homestead-exemption-states

Table summarizes homestead protections for all states. *Caution:* States change their homestead limits from time to time, and no Web source appears to be completely up to date. The complexity of homestead law causes a simple summary sometimes to be misleading. A helpful, more detailed source may be http://www.nolo.com/legal-encyclopedia/bankruptcy-information-your-state.

Exhibit 2-9 Forms of Co-Ownership

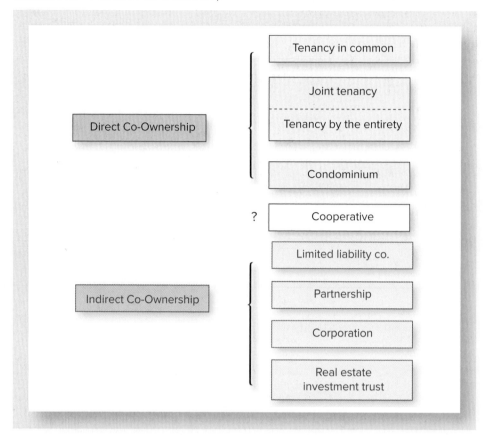

Direct Co-Ownership

In contrast to single entity ownership are several forms of direct co-ownership. Unlike ownership through a business organization that holds title to property, each direct co-owner holds a titled interest in the property. In effect, each owner holds a freehold estate, but without exclusive possession with respect to the other co-owners. The forms of direct co-ownership differ in how they can be created, and the rights of disposition each provides.

Tenancy in Common.   The **tenancy in common** is the "normal" form of direct co-ownership and is as close to the fee simple absolute estate as is possible. Each co-owner retains full rights of disposition and is free to mortgage, or to convey his or her ownership share to a new owner (in whole or in part), who receives exactly the same set of shared rights. While the owners' interests may differ in relative size, they are otherwise indistinguishable. No owner can use the property in a way that preempts the ability of the other owners to similarly enjoy the property. Tenancy in common is the "default" form of co-ownership, in that it results unless there is explicit provision for another form or the property is being acquired by a husband and wife. A common occurrence of this form of ownership is in the disposition of an estate to the heirs.

Tenancy in Common as a Business Ownership Form.   Tenancy in common sometimes arises, perhaps by default, as a co-ownership form for income-producing property. As a business ownership form it generally is inferior to other business entities. First, all co-owners may bear personal liability in judgments against the property, unless each co-owner is a limited liability entity. Second, spousal interests in the property (discussed below) will be governed by the state where the property is located rather than the state or states of residence of the co-owners. Third, tax and legal implications of tenancy in common may be less widely understood than for standard business entities. Fourth, the resulting "committee" of owners is ill-constituted to take action in a crisis.

Despite these concerns, a new use of tenancy in common has emerged in recent years related to real estate investment. Under U.S. income tax law (Internal Revenue code), investors can reduce the effect of income taxation by exchanging rather than selling an investment property outright. Tenancy in common can enable multiple investors to exchange into a large investment property thereby making exchange more feasible. Such "TIC" investments have received considerable attention in the real estate investment industry. (See Chapters 17 and 20.)

Joint Tenancy.   The distinctive feature of a **joint tenancy** is the **right of survivorship.** By this ancient common law concept the interest of a decedent co-owner divides equally among the surviving co-owners, and nothing passes the heirs of the decedent. Joint tenancy was important in feudal society to keep land holdings intact. In modern times it can have attraction as a simple and economical means of conveying property at death, particularly between a husband and wife in states that do not support tenancy by the entirety (below).

Requirements to create a joint tenancy are quite restrictive: it requires presence of the "four unities" of time, title, interest, and possession. That is, it must occur in a single conveyance, giving each recipient an identical and equal share, along with identical rights of possession. A joint tenant can convey his or her interest to another party, but the portion of the property conveyed becomes a tenancy in common for the new owner, leaving one fewer joint tenants.[16] Joint tenancy is limited in some states. However, the right of survivorship is very important in modern marital property law. (See both tenancy by the entirety and community property.)

Tenancy by the Entirety.   **Tenancy by the entirety** is a form of joint tenancy for husband and wife. In some states it occurs automatically when property is conveyed to a husband and wife jointly. In other states it must be created explicitly. As with joint tenancy, at the death of a spouse, tenancy by the entirety can reduce probate costs and complications since no disposition of property occurs in the eyes of the law. The concept is of special interest in states with homestead rights, especially in Florida.[17]

Tenancy by the entirety, in most states, offers some protection from judgment liens not related to taxes. In general, neither husband nor wife alone can pledge the property held in tenancy by the entirety. It follows that the property cannot be foreclosed in the event of default on an obligation of only one spouse or the other, nor can it be attached in non-tax-related judgment against one spouse alone.

en.wikipedia.org/wiki/ concurrent_estates

Additional detail on several co-ownership forms. The quality of Wikipedia as an authoritative source is debated. For definitional material, it has proven quite convenient and reliable for the authors.

✓ **Concept Check**

2.9   The most common and least specialized form of direct co-ownership is _____.

Condominium.   **Condominium** is a form of ownership combining single person ownership with tenancy in common. Specifically, the owner holds a fee simple interest, as an individual owner, to a certain space (such as an apartment). Joint, and inseparable, with this estate, the owner is a tenant in common in the "community" elements (e.g., building shell, floors, halls, elevators, stairwells, driveways, and other common areas) of the property.[18]

Condominium is an ancient concept but became enabled in the United States only as recently as the 1960s when every state adopted condominium laws. Condominium ownership is most common in apartment buildings, but also is used for townhouses, cluster homes, parking lots, recreational vehicle camping sites, marinas, offices, and even hotels. An important feature of a condominium is that each owner can mortgage his or her interest independently of other owners.

16. Some states have sought to restrict the use of joint tenancy, likely because of high potential for misunderstandings by owners or possibly due to what is regarded as unfair treatment of heirs.

17. In Florida a homestead automatically implies, at the death of one spouse, that a surviving spouse will share ownership with any surviving minor children. The surviving spouse receives a life estate in the homestead while minor children share vested remainder interests. However, if the homestead residence is held as a tenancy by the entirety, the law recognizes no event at the death of one spouse, and the survivor obtains a single-owner fee simple. Thus, it is possible to dispose of the property as needed without additional delays and legal expense.

18. In modern condominium law an important, arguably defining feature of condominium is that the interest in an individual unit and the accompanying shared interest in common elements cannot be separated. Thus a developer cannot retain the common elements and hold the unit owners hostage with an unconscionable lease for their use. (See Aalbert, *Real Estate Law*, 9th ed., pp 590–591.)

Condominium ownership is well established and is rapidly increasing in use with a rising population and urban density. However, those purchasing a condominium must realize that it entails a cost in ownership complexity and restrictions on owner discretion that follows from living in close proximity to others. Even the simplest condominium necessitates the creation and management of an owner association. This association is a minigovernment that must maintain all common areas and structures, make and enforce **condominium bylaws,** and levy and collect owner assessments. There must be an effective transfer of control from the original developer to the owner association. There also must be orderly and fair procedures for association meetings, elections, a budgeting process, and revision of bylaws pertaining to such matters as pets, parking, guests, exterior decorating, noise, and use of common facilities. The association must assure a program of property and liability insurance that is adequate for both the common facilities and for unit owners. There also must be adequate accounting, control, and reporting systems.

The condominium is created through a master deed or **condominium declaration.** In this document are three-dimensional descriptions of the space occupied by each unit, a description of the common facilities and areas, a determination of the proportion of common areas associated with each unit, provision for expansion of the property, if needed, and numerous fundamental rules. These basic rules may include restrictions on the presence of minor children or other age restrictions. They will define basic rights, procedures, and restrictions in leasing units, and in dealing with destruction of the facilities. Most importantly, they will set the framework to create and enforce bylaws, and to levy and collect assessments.

It is very important in considering the purchase of a condominium to carefully examine the declaration and bylaws. Condominiums have an unfortunate history of owners failing to understand the restrictions involved. All too often, this gives rise to conflicts among owners and to litigation, as exemplified in Industry Issues 2-2.

✓ Concept Check

2.10   The organization and rules of a condominium are very important because it serves as a small-scale _____. What are the two most important documents for a condominium?

Cooperative.   A **cooperative** actually is not a form of true direct co-ownership but rather is a proprietary corporation. Just as with a partnership, limited liability company (LLC), or standard corporation, the cooperative owns real estate as a single owner. The unique aspect is that each owner of the corporation holds a "proprietary lease" for some designated space.[19] Historically, this form of ownership has been used for apartment buildings, with each of the co-owners having a proprietary lease to one apartment unit. Before states adopted laws enabling condominiums, the cooperative enabled individuals to own their residence where it might otherwise not have been possible, such as in high-density cities like New York City. The arrangement has at least one major limitation: Because the corporation owns the property, occupants cannot obtain mortgage financing without placing all other owners at risk for the debt. By contrast, owners in a condominium can mortgage their property without putting other owners at risk. Perhaps due to this difference, the cooperative has been much less widely used than the condominium in recent decades.

Ownership Interests from Marriage.   All of the legal traditions that have descended to the United States—English common law, the French Napoleonic code (Louisiana), and Spanish traditional law—provide for spousal rights to property in a marriage. While these rights have carried to the United States, virtually every state has modified them to better fit our modern, nonagricultural society.

---

19. A proprietary lease is of indefinite length and requires the owner-tenant to make contributions for maintenance expenses, but does not require rent payments.

f you want to buy a home nowadays there are good reasons for considering a condo: valuable amenities such as a pool, exercise room, club room, etc.; escape from yard work; greater sense of security both when you are at home and when you lock it and leave; attractive location; lower price threshold.

But these attractions come with added risks because you enter into a new proximity to neighbors, and a whole new level of government.

So what new risks are there? First is the matter of design and construction. Enemy one is noise. Balconies or patios might not be well buffered from each other. Walls and, especially, floors can be more conduits than insulators of TV, loud music, raised voices, dogs barking, infants crying, and even just footsteps. So always a first question is how well designed and built the units are for privacy and sound control. Parking and storage also become heightened concerns in the more crowded environment.

More subtle are regulatory and governance risks. The condo will have rules not encountered in other kinds of homes. These rules hopefully are intended to maintain harmony and the value of the units. But almost by definition they will interfere with the lifestyle of some. What can you place on your balcony or patio? What kind of curtains can you hang? What kind of guests can you host, and for how long? Under what conditions can you rent your unit, or even sell it? You must examine these regulations carefully and be sure you can live with them or hope to change them.

There also are new kinds of financial risks. The governing board (all volunteers) controls the community "taxing and spending." Imprudent board decisions will lead either to property decline or excessive costs of operation. In the extreme, the board could be financially reckless—failing to maintain adequate insurance, failing to collect adequate reserves—or they even could be dishonest. (Arguably, a professional management contract is a prerequisite for a well-managed condo.) Bad performance of the board can "spook" lenders and finally render your unit difficult to refinance, or to sell. So you want to know the signals that lenders are sensitive to, and how your condo stacks up.

You can find discussions of these concerns and others by searching "condo risks" on the Web. If you find the issues raised to be daunting, you will want some help in trying to evaluate a condo for purchase. You can get help by hiring a knowledgeable construction expert to evaluate the physical state of the condo for you, and you can retain a knowledgeable real estate buyer's agent (see Chapter 12), or an attorney, to act for you in evaluating the financial and governmental aspects of the condo. For your evaluation, you also will want to obtain from the seller the condo declaration and bylaws as well as the latest financial report, minutes of recent board meetings, a summary of any pending legal actions, and the budget of the condo association.

The Condo Adventure

Dower/Curtesy.   The common law provision of **dower** gave a wife a one-third life estate in all of the real property of a decedent husband that was ever owned by him during the marriage, provided that the wife did not join in conveying the property to a new owner. Curtesy was a similar common law provision for husbands. Dower and curtesy are poor solutions to the needs of surviving spouses in an industrial, mobile society because they ignore personal property wealth (stocks and bonds), and because they created only a (nonmarketable) life estate. From the concept, only the notion of a one-third spousal share survives in most states, frequently blended with elements of the more progressive concepts discussed below.

Elective Share.   Recognizing the limitations of dower and curtesy, most states in the United States have replaced them with a modern substitute. The most common provision, adopted by more than 25 states, is **elective share,** which gives a surviving spouse a share of most of the wealth of the decedent. A common share is one-third, though up to 50 percent in some cases. The surviving spouse must elect to take the share within some time limit, usually no later than nine months after the death or six months after the conclusion of probate, whichever is later.[20] Elective share applies to both real and personal property of the decedent, though not all elective share laws have been effective in actually encompassing the bulk of the decedent's wealth.[21]

www.uniformlaws.org

Uniform Law Commission has created and disseminated a host of uniform laws for state adaptation and adoption, including The "Uniform Probate Code," the model for elective share, and the "Marital Property Act," which sets out a modern variant of community property.

20. Probate is the legal process of authenticating the will and administering distribution of the estate in accordance with it.

21. The most recent version of elective share is represented by the Uniform Probate Code (UPC). This model law has been adopted (and adapted), in whole or in part, by a growing minority of states. The UPC version of elective share represents a very extensive effort to apply elective share to all wealth of a decedent, whether real or personal, movable or immovable. UPC is an historic model, based on the notion of marriage as a mutual enterprise, and aims to move the rights of wives to greater equity, similar to community property. The details and progress of the Uniform Probate Code can be monitored on a variety of legal-oriented websites

Community Property.   In 10 states, mainly of Spanish tradition, the automatic right of husband and wife in property of each other is known as **community property.**[22] Community property gives a spouse a fifty percent claim on all property acquired "from the fruits of the marriage." Thus, if either spouse should independently acquire property during the marriage, it is likely to be regarded by courts as community property. Excluded from this is property that the husband or wife acquired prior to the marriage, or gifts or inheritance received during the marriage, all of which is **separate property.** In some states, community property also includes any rents, royalties, or profits from separate property.[23] Some community property states, including Alaska, Arizona, California, Nevada, Texas, and Wisconsin have advanced the traditional concept by adding a right of survivorship. As with tenancy by the entirety, at the death of one spouse, the survivor automatically becomes the sole owner of all community property, without probate and tax complications.

The notion of community property is widely regarded as more equitable than the marital property tradition of English common law and appears to be influencing marital property law in an increasing number of states.[24]

Implications of Ownership from Marriage.   Two main forms of marital property rights—elective share and community property—are summarized in Exhibit 2-10. All of the special property rights created from marriage have a clear implication for real estate transactions. A purchaser of real estate always must be sure that any current or previous spouse of a seller joins in the conveyance of a property. Otherwise, there is high risk that the spouse will have latent ownership claims that are not conveyed to the buyer.

Timeshare

In **timesharing,** multiple individuals have use of property but, unlike traditional forms of co-ownership, the interests are not simultaneous. Rather, the estate is divided into separate time intervals. This concept has been used almost exclusively for resorts. Commonly the time interval is in weekly units per year, although it can be for other periods. The term *timesharing* covers a variety of legal arrangements with varying levels of property rights and varying degrees of user flexibility or options.

Timeshare Rights.   A timeshare contract may convey any level of real property interest. The buyer may acquire a "slice" of a true fee simple interest (usually as a partial condominium owner). However, the buyer often acquires a leasehold interest for a fixed number of years (tenancy for years). Thus, at the end of the term the buyer's interest is extinguished. Finally, it is possible that the buyer only acquires a license for partial use. In this case, the

Exhibit 2-10   Two Main Forms of Marital Property Rights

	Elective Share	**Community Property**
Mainly used in:	English heritage states	Spanish/French heritage states
Spousal share:	At least one-third	One-half
How triggered:	Explicit declaration	Automatic
Wealth coverage:	Varies up to all wealth	All wealth created in the marriage
Number of states:	About 25	10 states, with influence on more

22. Community property states include Alaska, Arizona, California, Idaho, Louisiana, Nevada, New Mexico, Texas, Washington, and Wisconsin. In the French civil law tradition of Louisiana, the community property tradition exists, approximately, under the term *usufruct.* In Wisconsin, community property was created when the state adopted a model law in 1986 known as the Uniform Marital Property Act. In Alaska, since 1998, community property status is elective.

23. These states include Idaho, Louisiana, and Texas.

24. A central force in promulgating the notions of community property is the Uniform Marital Property Act, 1983. See Uniform Law Commission website on previous page.

buyer may not be able to transfer the license. Moreover, it is revocable. Thus, the buyers of a timeshare need to examine carefully what legal interest they are getting.

✓ **Concept Check**

2.11 Two types of modern co-ownership interest between spouses that occur automatically for any marriage are _____ or _____ depending on the state.

Timeshare Plans.   A very common form of timeshare plan involves "floating time intervals" (spanning a period of perhaps three or four months) and multiple resort properties. A buyer purchases a certain quantity of "points," which are used annually to bid for a particular site and time unit within the set of resorts and the designated floating time interval.

✓ **Concept Check**

2.12 What are three levels (qualities) of property rights found in timeshare arrangements?

History of Timeshare.   While timeshare began in the 1960s in the French Alps, and is found in many international resort locations, the predominant single market is in the United States. The largest concentrations of timeshare properties are beach resorts, followed by mountain and lake resorts. Not surprisingly, timeshare properties in the United States are concentrated in Florida, Hawaii, California, Colorado, North Carolina, Arizona, and Nevada, in roughly that order.[25]

The early history of timeshare in the United States was tainted by misrepresentations and failures to perform. Two major changes may have altered the industry in more recent times. First, Florida and other states have enacted laws regulating the industry and requiring extensive and strict disclosures for the sale of timeshares. Second, the industry appears to have become more concentrated in larger, more experienced, and financially stronger hospitality companies.

Nevertheless, even industry representatives offer cautions to those interested in purchasing a timeshare. First, it should never be considered a financial investment. (The strict financial yield on a timeshare has rarely, if ever, been positive.) Rather, it should be regarded as a purchase of long-term resort services. This implies another critical point. What a timeshare buyer really is purchasing is the ability of the management company to deliver the expected resort services. Thus, it is the capacity of that company to perform and endure that the buyer must evaluate foremost.

www.consumer.ftc.gov/ articles/0073-timeshares- and-acation-plans

A U.S. Government consumer's guide to evaluating timeshares and vacation club ownership.

www.arda.org

An industry information source for interval ownership resorts.

Rights Related to Water

As population and economic expansion exert ever-growing demands on the water supply, rights to water become increasingly important. Rights to water are a component of real property, and a particularly complex one. To sort them out, several questions must be considered:

1. Who owns the land under a body of water? (This is especially important for mineral, oil, and gas rights that may be involved.)

---

25. An industry trade organization for timeshare, American Resort Development Association, provides descriptive information about the industry and its offerings. See website in the margin.

Santa Claus may have come to the United States recently in the form of unexpected "clean" fossil fuel. Just when the United States faced 9-11 and a dark outlook for relying on oil from the Middle East, Texas oil engineers were changing the petroleum game. They were bringing together a spectacular convergence of three things: horizontal drilling, high-pressure fracturing ("fracking") to release embedded gas and oil, and the vast shale gas reserves of North America. (See map.) In 2000, only 1 percent of U.S. natural gas was extracted from shale. Ten years later, it was 25 percent, and rising.

Shale Gas Leases: Could Santa's Bag Contain a Lump of Coal?

North American shale plays (as of May 2011)

Source: U.S. Energy Information Administration based on data from various published studies. Canada and Mexico from ARI. Updated: May 9, 2011.

The impact of shale gas extraction has been both dramatic and, at times, traumatic. It has transformed shale gas regions (called "plays") from bucolic to beleaguered. Many of the areas impacted have been lifted from economic doldrums only to confront threats to land, environment, and lifestyle. Therein lies a major real estate issue: the meaning of gas leases.

From the Marcellus shale region of Pennsylvania come stories of overnight riches for those able to have wells drilled on their land. But they also are encountering disruptions and risks that were unknown before. For example, the right of the driller lessee to pursue the gas implies the right to operate on the property 24/7. And it also implies easements to bring heavy, disruptive, toxic industrial activity onto the property to complete and operate wells, and may require the lessor to fund easement improvements such as roadways and well pad construction. Furthermore, leases commonly give the driller the right to use millions of gallons of the land owner's water.

Legal risks are yet another threat. If fracking causes degradation of neighboring groundwater, as has frequently been reported, the lessor may be liable for the damage, with no recourse to the driller. Where the property has a residential mortgage still other troubles loom. Fracking likely violates prohibitions in the mortgage against industrial activity on the property or the presence of hazardous materials. So the mortgage may be in default, and the prospects for a subsequent residential mortgage may be dim, rendering the property, among other things, much less valuable. Moreover, homeowner's insurance generally does not cover the industrial risks that are created by the fracking operation, nor does the gas lease. And if the land is agricultural, and supported by government assistance programs, the presence of the lease could jeopardize that support. In addition, the leases may deny the landowner access to courts in favor of arbitration if there is an owner-driller dispute.

One message in all this is that land owners should never agree to a fracking lease without knowledgeable legal assistance. As experience with fracking mounts, the inherent risks and costs may be better understood and better managed. But in the near term, the presence of extractable shale oil may be a great gift to the nation, but to some property owners, it could be the proverbial lump of coal.

legal-dictionary. thefreedictionary.com/ Water+Rights

A long, but informed and lucid overview of rights in the United States to flowing surface water and ground water.

2. Who controls use of land under a body of water?
3. Who has the right to use the surface of a body of water?
4. Who has the right to use the water itself (to alter the character of the water by consumption, degradation, use in irrigation, and so on)?
5. Who has the right to use groundwater?

In addition, questions arise concerning ownership of coastal shorelines. Especially interesting are questions of ownership of the massive amount of coastal tidewater estuaries since some are extremely rich in petroleum and other mineral resources. Since an orderly

en.wikipedia.org/wiki/
Oil_and_gas_law_in_the_
United_States

geology.com/articles/
mineral-rights.shtml

Informational sites for oil and gas
extraction

www.mineralweb.com/
owners-guide/lease-
proposals/oil-and-gas-
leases-10-common-
mistakes-during-mineral-
lease-negotiation/

Thoughts about negotiating oil and
gas leases

answer to these issues may be beyond the scope of this book, further discussion is deferred to the appendix to this chapter.

Rights to Oil, Gas, and Minerals

Rights to the subsurface include rights to minerals. **Mineral rights,** including, oil, gas, coal, and other substances that are mined, can be separated from land ownership. When this occurs, the owner of the mineral rights also receives an implied easement to retrieve the minerals, which implies the right to disturb the surface as necessary (e.g., building roads, erecting mining equipment, opening mine shafts, drilling wells, creating storage tanks, and other drastic alterations of the terrain). States differ on several aspects of mineral rights. For example, in some states mining companies are deemed to own not only the minerals but the space the minerals occupied before they were removed. Regarding oil and gas rights, some states deem oil and gas to be owned just like any other mineral. These states are referred to as ownership states. But other states, recognizing that oil and gas can flow due to drilling, hold that the substance is not owned until it is removed from the earth. These states are known as "law of capture" states. Traditionally, all states followed a **rule of capture** whereby the owner of an oil or gas well could claim all that is pumped from it, regardless of whether the oil or gas migrated from adjacent property. However, because methods of so-called secondary recovery have enabled well owners today to recover oil and gas from such an extensive surrounding area, the law of capture has been curtailed in some states. Today every oil-producing state has evolved its own considerable statutory law pertaining to oil and gas rights.

Summary

Owning real property is a matter of having rights. These can include the rights of exclusive possession, of use (enjoyment), and of disposition. Rights are claims that organized government is obligated to enforce; they are nonrevocable and they are enduring. Real property is rights in land and its permanent structures, while personal property is rights to any other object or to intellectual matters. Government can reduce the bundle of rights called real property through its police power. However, if the exercise of police power goes too far, it becomes a "taking," which requires just compensation.

Bundles of real property that include the right of exclusive possession are called estates. Estates are either titled (freehold) or untitled (leasehold) interests. Freeholds are indefinite in length, allowing the right of disposition, while leaseholds have a definite ending, thus no right of disposition. The most complete estate is the fee simple absolute, which is the common notion of ownership.

Three important nonpossessory interests in real property are restrictive covenants, easements, and liens. Restrictive covenants are created in a deed or in subdivision declarations, and can impose a wide variety of restrictions on land use. An easement is the right to use land for a specific, limited purpose. The easement appurtenant involves the relationship between a dominant parcel and a servient parcel, and "runs with the land." The easement in gross often involves a right-of-way (e.g., road, pipeline, power line) and can be conveyed separately from the landownership. A lien is an interest in property as security for an obligation.

Co-ownership is the simultaneous ownership of essentially the same set of rights by multiple persons. The most flexible and robust co-ownership is tenancy in common, which has rights of disposition the same as individual ownership. A joint tenancy gives no rights of inheritance to any but the last surviving co-owner. A tenancy by the entirety is a marital form of joint tenancy. Condominium combines individual ownership of a space (unit) with tenancy in common ownership of the related common facilities. Cooperative is a special form of corporation, which gives each shareholder a "proprietary" (indefinite) lease to one unit in the structure (usually an apartment). Marriage usually creates automatic co-ownership interests. The most important of these are elective share and community property. In recent years, property also has been conveyed to multiple owners through timeshare interests, which range from true ownership to no more than a license.

Key Terms

Assessment lien   31

Attach   31

Community development district (CDD) lien   31

Community property   38

Condominium   35

Condominium bylaws   36

Condominium declaration   36

Cooperative   36

Declaration of covenants   30

Deed restriction   30

Dominant parcel   27

Dower   37

Easement   27

Easement appurtenant   27

Easement in gross   28

Elective share   37

Estate   24

Fee simple absolute   25

Fee simple conditional   25

Fixture   22

Freehold   25

General lien   31

Interest   23

Joint tenancy   35

Leasehold   26

Legal life estate   25

License   30

Lien   31

Mechanics' lien   32

Mineral rights   41

Mortgage   31

Ordinary life estate   25

Periodic tenancy   26

Personal property   20

Personal rights   20

Property rights   20

Property tax lien   31

Real property   20

Remainder estate   25

Restrictive covenants   30

Reverter   25

Right of survivorship   35

Rule of capture   41

Separate property   38

Servient parcel   27

Specific lien   31

Tenancy at sufferance   26

Tenancy at will   26

Tenancy by the entirety   35

Tenancy for years   26

Tenancy in common   34

Timesharing   38

Test Problems

Answer the following multiple-choice problems:

1. Which of the following is *not* a form of property right?
   a. Lien.
   b. Easement.
   c. Leasehold.
   d. License.
   e. Mineral rights.

2. Which of these easements is most likely to be an easement in gross?
   a. Common wall easement.
   b. Driveway easement.
   c. Drainage easement.
   d. Power line easement.
   e. Sunlight easement.

3. Rules used by courts to determine whether something is a fixture include all *except:*
   a. Intention of the parties.
   b. Manner of attachment.
   c. Law of capture.
   d. Character of the article and manner of adaptation.
   e. Relation of the parties.

4. Which of these is a titled estate?
   a. Fee simple absolute.
   b. Fee simple conditional.

   c. Conventional life estate.
   d. Legal life estate.
   e. All of these.

5. Which of these forms of co-ownership could best be described as "normal ownership," except that multiple owners share identically in one bundle of rights?
   a. Tenancy in common.
   b. Joint tenancy.
   c. Tenancy by the entirety.
   d. Condominium.
   e. Estate in severalty.

6. Which of these marriage-related forms of co-ownership gives each spouse a one-half interest in any property that is "fruits of the marriage"?
   a. Dower.
   b. Curtesy.
   c. Community property.
   d. Elective share.
   e. Tenancy by the entirety.

7. Which of these liens has the highest priority?
   a. First mortgage lien.
   b. Mechanics' lien.
   c. Property tax lien.

   d. Second mortgage lien.

   e. Unable to say because it depends strictly on which was created first.

8. Restrictive covenants for a subdivision usually can be enforced by:

   a. Subdivision residents.

   b. Lenders with mortgage loans in the subdivision.

   c. Local government.

   d. *a* and *b*, but not *c*.

   e. All three: *a*, *b*, and *c*.

9. Timeshare programs can involve which of the following claims or interests?

   a. Fee simple ownership.

   b. Leasehold interest.

   c. License.

   d. Condominium.

   e. All of these are possible.

10. Every condominium buyer needs to know the details of which document(s):

   a. Condominium declaration.

   b. Bylaws.

   c. Proprietary lease.

   d. *a* and *b*, but not *c*.

   e. All three: *a*, *b*, and *c*.

Study Questions

1. Explain how rights differ from power or force, and from permission.

2. A developer of a subdivision wants to preserve the open space and natural habitat that runs along the back portion of a series of large lots in the proposed subdivision. He is debating whether to use restrictive covenants to accomplish this or to create a habitat easement on the same space. What are the pros and cons of each choice?

3. Why are restrictive covenants a good idea for a subdivision? Can they have any detrimental effects on the subdivision or its residents? For example, are there any listed in the chapter that might have questionable effects on the value of a residence?

4. The traditional common law concept of the landlord–tenant relationship was that the landlord's obligation was simply to stay off the property and the tenant's obligation was to pay the rent. Explain why this is an obsolete arrangement for apartment residents in an urban society.

5. A friend has an elderly mother who lives in a house adjacent to her church. The church is growing, and would welcome the opportunity to obtain her house for its use. She would like to support the needs of her church, but she doesn't want to move and feels strongly about owning her own home. On the other hand, your friend knows that she will not be able to remain in the house many more years, and will be faced with moving and selling within a few years. What options can you suggest as possible plans to explore?

6. A friend has owned and operated a small recreational vehicle camp on a lake in Daytona Beach, Florida. It is close to the ocean and close to the Daytona Speedway, home of the Daytona 500 and a host of other prominent races. The occupants are very loyal, making reservations far in advance, and returning year after year. She is asking your thoughts on whether to continue the camp as a short-term rental operation, to convert it and sell the parking spaces as condominium parking spaces, or to convert to condominium timeshare lots. What thoughts would you offer?

7. In the United States the bundle of rights called real property seems to have gotten smaller in recent decades. Explain what has caused this. Why is it good? Why is it bad?

EXPLORE THE WEB

Choose two states of interest to you. Using your favorite search engine enter "*your state* statutes." The statutes of virtually all states are online and searchable, although all have different search formats. For the two states you have chosen, compare and contrast the statutes on issues such as:

1. Timeshare laws.
2. Laws pertaining to property obtained during marriage.
3. Laws regarding tenant–landlord relationships.
4. When mechanics' liens become effective (at contract signing? start of construction?).

Solutions to Concept Checks

1. Rights are claims or demands that government is obligated to enforce, whereas claims that are obtained by threat or force are not honored or supported by the government. Rights differ from permission in that rights are nonrevocable and permission is revocable. Finally, rights are enduring. They do not end.

2. The three components of property rights are exclusive possession, use (enjoyment), and disposition.

3. A fixture is defined as an object that formerly was personal property but has converted to real property. Although there are four rules used to determine whether something is a

fixture, the dominant rule is the intention of the parties. For example, a kitchen appliance in a single-family residence is expected to remain with the seller when the residence is sold. On the other hand, if the appliances are furnishings in a rental apartment building, they normally would be expected to remain with the building. Thus, the rule of intention would treat the appliances as personal property in the single-family residence case and as fixtures in the apartment case.

4. Real property interests that include exclusive possession are called estates.

5. An easement is the right to use land for a specific and limited purpose.

6. The major difference between the easement appurtenant and an easement in gross is that the easement appurtenant involves a dominant parcel constraining an adjacent servient parcel, and is an inseparable feature of both parcels. By contrast, an easement in gross involves only servient parcels. Also, the easement appurtenant "runs with the land" and the easement in gross can be transferred without the transfer of any parcel.

7. Restrictive covenants are strictly private and can only be enforced by those holding a legal interest in the property. They would be enforced by filing suit for an injunction against a violation.

8. The lien priority is generally determined by the order in which they were created. However, property tax, assessment liens, and CDD liens are always superior to any other liens.

9. The most common and least specialized form of direct co-ownership is tenancy in common.

10. Organization and rules are very important to a condominium because it serves as a small-scale government. The two most important documents for a condominium are the declaration and bylaws.

11. Two types of modern co-ownership between spouses, depending on the state, are elective share and community property.

12. The three levels of property rights in timeshare arrangements are a part of a fee simple interest, a leasehold interest for a tenancy for years, or a license for partial use of the timeshare.

Additional Readings

The following real estate law texts offer excellent additional material on many of the subjects in this chapter:

Aalberts, Robert J. *Real Estate Law,* 9th ed. Stamford, CT South-Western Cengage Learning, 2015.

Evans, Denise L. *How to Buy a Condominium or Townhouse.* Naperville, IL: Sphinx Publishing, 2006.

Jennings, Marianne. *Real Estate Law,* 10th ed., Stamford, CT: South-Western Cengage Learning, 2014.

Poliakoff, Gary A., and Ryan Poliakoff. *New Neighborhoods: The Consumer's Guide to Condominium, Co-op, and HOA Living.* Austin, TX: Emerald Book Company, 2009.

Portman, J., and M. Stewart. *Renter's Rights: Basics,* 8th ed. Berkeley, CA: Nolo Press, 2015.

Werner, Raymond J. *Real Estate Law,* 11th ed. Cincinnati, OH: Southwestern, 2002.

APPENDIX: Property Rights Relating To Water

To access the appendix for this chapter, please visit the book's website at

www.mhhe.com/lingarcher5e

Chapter 3

Conveying Real Property Interests

LEARNING OBJECTIVES

After reading this chapter you will be able to:

1 State three ways that a deed differs from normal business contracts.

2 Distinguish these clauses of a deed: words of conveyance, habendum clause, and exceptions and reservations; and state the importance of "delivery."

3 Distinguish between these deeds by the covenants they contain and when each deed is used: general warranty, special warranty, bargain and sale, quitclaim.

4 List four examples of involuntary conveyance of property with a deed.

5 List two voluntary and two involuntary transfers of property without a deed.

6 State the effect of the Statute of Frauds, of recording statutes, of constructive notice, and actual notice on conveyance of real estate.

7 State two reasons why determining title in real estate requires a title search.

8 Identify and distinguish two forms of evidence of title.

9 List and distinguish three "legal" descriptions of land, and be able to identify and interpret each.

OUTLINE

Introduction
Deeds
    Requirements of a Deed
    Types of Deeds
Modes of Conveyance of Real Property
    Voluntary Conveyance by a Deed
    Involuntary Conveyance by a Deed
    Voluntary Conveyance without a Deed
    Involuntary Conveyance without a Deed
Real Property Complexity and Public Records
    The Doctrine of Constructive Notice
    Statute of Frauds
    Recording Statutes
    Actual Notice
    Title
    Title Search, Title Abstract, and Chain of Title
    Evidence of Title
Land Descriptions
    Metes and Bounds
    Subdivision Plat Lot and Block Number
    Government Rectangular Survey

Introduction

The conveyance of real estate interests is uniquely complicated for three reasons:

1. Real property is a complex bundle of rights, as we have observed in Chapter 2, and the interests must be described with care.
2. Since land and rights to land are enduring, transactions long ago affect the bundle of rights conveyable to a buyer today.
3. Since all land parcels adjoin other parcels, any error in the description of land represents a loss to some owner. Therefore, methods of describing land must be very accurate.

Much is at stake in real property conveyance. If the transfer is flawed by being unclear or uncertain, the property can lose much of its value because buyers cannot be sure what they would get. This risk of defective transfer has compelled our legal system to create unique arrangements for the conveyance of real property. It has evolved special concepts, special documents, special legal procedures, and even special government institutions to address the unique challenges involved. In this chapter we tour the distinctive aspects of real property conveyance.

> ✓ **Concept Check**
>
> **3.1**   List the three features of real property that introduce special challenges for the orderly transfer of ownership.

Deeds are the primary means of conveying interests in real property. They are a special form of contract, distinguished by a group of clauses that determine the exact property interest being conveyed. Deeds vary in "quality" by the strength of covenants (i.e., promises) they contain. Under some circumstances, however, property can transfer to a new owner without a deed and even with no explicit document at all.

No deed or other document can convey rights that a person does not have. So a buyer must be able to learn what rights a seller can deliver. For this reason recording statutes have created a system of publicly recorded documents that provide "constructive notice" of real property transfers. From these documents, and from inspection of the property, "evidence of title" can be derived. An important element of all property records is an accurate description of the land. Only three methods of description are acceptable in modern practice for this purpose.

Deeds

A **deed** is a special form of written contract used to convey a permanent interest in real property. It had its origin in England in 1677, when Parliament passed the "Statute for the Prevention of Frauds and Perjuries," which required, for the first time, that conveyances of title to real property be in writing.

A deed can convey a wide variety of permanent real property interests. Depending on its wording, it can convey the full fee simple absolute or a lesser interest such as a life estate, a conditional fee, or an easement (see Chapter 2). Through restrictive clauses called deed restrictions, the deed also may "carve out" reductions in the rights conveyed. Similarly, the deed also can carve out easements. For example, the deed can withhold mineral rights, timber rights, or water rights, implying an easement of access to pursue these claims. Other easements that may be retained could be for access to adjacent property of the seller, or an easement in gross for a variety of commercial uses.

Requirements of a Deed

While deeds are not restricted to a particular physical form, all deeds contain a number of elements:

1. Grantor (with signature) and grantee.
2. Recital of consideration.
3. Words of conveyance.
4. Covenants.
5. Habendum clause.
6. Exceptions and reservations clause (if any).
7. Description of land.
8. Acknowledgment.
9. Delivery.

Grantor and Grantee.   The person or entity conveying the real property interest is the **grantor,** while the recipient is the **grantee.** Unlike most contracts in which both parties must be legally competent and of legal majority age, only the grantor must meet these conditions for a deed. In principle, the grantee would not even need to exist at the time of conveyance. For example, a grantor technically could convey property to a firstborn grandchild. As long as there is no ambiguity about the arrival of the child, the deed should be effective (if inadvisable).

✓ **Concept Check**

3.2   In a normal contract ——————— must be legally competent, whereas in a deed ——————— must be legally competent.

Recital of Consideration.   Unlike normal contracts where both parties have made promises to perform, only the grantor performs with a deed, and it is done immediately. So consideration is not important to a valid deed. When a grantor conveys property, the event is done, and details of the grantee's financial obligation to the grantor are spelled out elsewhere. Still, it is traditional to have a statement of consideration in deeds, and some states actually require it. However, it is not necessary to state the true consideration. A statement such as "for ten dollars and other good and valuable consideration" is often used.

Words of Conveyance.   Early in the deed will be words such as "does hereby grant, bargain, sell, and convey unto . . ." These **words of conveyance** serve two main purposes. First, they assure that the grantor clearly intends to convey an interest in real property. Second, they indicate the type of deed offered by the grantor. For example, either the words above or the words "convey and warrant" generally are taken to indicate a general warranty deed, while the words "convey and quitclaim" indicate a quitclaim deed. (See the discussion of types of deeds in the next section.) The practical message from these subtleties is that words of conveyance should be prepared by a competent legal professional.

Covenants.   The covenants in a deed are the most important differences among types of deeds, as discussed below. **Covenants** are legally binding promises for which the grantor becomes liable; that is, if the promises prove to be false, the grantee can sue for damages. The three normal covenants are:[1]

1. **Covenant of seizin**—a promise that the grantor truly has good title and the right to convey it.

---

1. The common law tradition provided for six covenants. In modern practice, they have been reduced to the three discussed.

2. **Covenant against encumbrances**—a promise that the property is not encumbered with liens, easements, or other such limitations except as noted in the deed.
3. **Covenant of quiet enjoyment**—a promise that the property will not be claimed by someone with a better claim to title.

✓ **Concept Check**

3.3   What are the three covenants that distinguish the "quality" of deeds? What does each promise?

Habendum Clause.   The **habendum clause** defines or limits the type of interest being conveyed. The legal tradition recognizes certain words and phrases as signals of various real property interests. For example, in the wording "to John Smith and to his heirs and assigns forever," the words "to his heirs and assigns forever" are regarded as distinguishing a fee simple interest from a life estate. Similarly, the words "to John Smith for use in growing timber" may be interpreted as conveyance of a timber easement rather than a fee simple absolute interest. Adding the words "so long as" is likely to be interpreted in a court as a reverter clause, and the estate conveyed as a conditional fee (see Chapter 2 for conditional fee and reverter). Since the court must interpret what is written rather than what the grantor later claims he or she intended, it is again critical that this wording be drafted under supervision of a competent legal professional.

Exceptions and Reservations Clause.   An **exceptions and reservations clause** can contain a wide variety of limits on the property interest conveyed. This clause may contain any "deed restriction" the grantor wishes to impose on the use of the property. Here the grantor may carve out mineral rights, timber rights, water rights, or a variety of easements.

Description of Land.   The important requirement for the land description is that it be unambiguous. Some traditional methods of property description are ill-advised at best, even though they may work in most cases. Street addresses, for example, can be ambiguous in older, transitional, or nonresidential urban neighborhoods where the use of an address may have subtly changed over time. A tax parcel number is convenient, but can be erroneous. A very old method of land description is by monuments, or prominent features of the land, such as reference to bends in rivers, large rocks, ridges, and forks in roads. But over a long period of time even prominent features of the land can change. In modern practice, three methods have been deemed sufficiently accurate and durable to be accorded special favor for use in legal documents. These "legal descriptions" are metes and bounds, subdivision plat lot and block number, and government rectangular survey. They are explained later in the chapter.

✓ **Concept Check**

3.4   Any property interest not being conveyed to the grantee is stated in what clause?

Acknowledgment.   The purpose of **acknowledgment** is to confirm that the deed is, in fact, the intention and action of the grantor. It is accomplished by having the grantor's signature notarized, or the equivalent. In some states, witnesses also must sign the deed, attesting to the grantor's signature. While acknowledgment is not always required to make a deed valid (i.e., enforceable), it is required for a deed to be placed in public records.

Delivery. A deed must be "delivered" to be valid. **Delivery** refers to an observable, verifiable intent that the deed is to be given to the grantee. Normally, this is accomplished when the grantor hands the deed to the grantee at closing. However, it also may occur through third parties, such as the attorney of either party. Delivery may fail to occur even if a deed is handed to the person named as grantee. For example, suppose the owner of real property prepares a deed and places it in a safe-deposit box (or desk drawer). Then someone, perhaps a relative, finds the deed and hands it to the person named as grantee. Or suppose an owner prepares a deed and gives it to his or her attorney, without instructions to deliver it, but the attorney gives it to the named grantee. In neither of these cases did legal delivery take place, and neither deed is valid.

Types of Deeds

No deed can convey what a grantor does not possess. There are several ways that a deed can be "empty." Property identified in a current deed might have been conveyed by the grantor to someone else at an earlier time by intention, making the current deed fraudulent. Also, the property may have been conveyed by mistake, or by one of several involuntary conveyances that we discuss below. Further, the grantor may unwittingly have failed to receive the rights to begin with, perhaps through a deed that was never successfully delivered. In all of these cases, it is beyond the power of the would-be grantor to convey the property anew. Someone else now holds the rights who is not bound to give them up.

Although deeds can only deliver what a grantor actually owns, they still can vary in "quality." Below are five types of deeds that appear in common practice. The main difference between them is the number of covenants for which the grantor is liable if the title turns out to be defective. Additional differences are in the prevailing usage of each type, and how that affects presumptions about title.

General Warranty Deed. The **general warranty deed** includes the full set of legal promises the grantor can make (see the covenants above). Effectively, it warrants against any and all competing claims that may arise from the chain of title that are not spelled out in the deed, or from unidentified physical conflicts such as easements or **encroachments** (intrusions on the property by structures from adjacent land). Thus, it is considered the "highest-quality" deed and affords the maximum basis for suit by the grantee in case the title is defective.

Special Warranty Deed. The **special warranty deed** is identical to the general warranty deed, except that it limits the time of the grantor's warranties to her time of ownership. That is, the grantor asserts only that she has created no undisclosed encumbrances during ownership, but asserts nothing about encumbrances from previous owners. Conveying title using a special warranty deed does not imply questions about the validity of the deed. In that sense, the special warranty deed is a "quality" deed. In California and some other states, the predominant form of deed is a **grant deed.** This type of deed is regarded as roughly equivalent to the special warranty deed.

Quitclaim Deed. The **quitclaim deed** has none of the covenants of the warranty deed. Also, its words of conveyance read something like "I . . . hereby quitclaim . . ." as opposed to "I . . . hereby grant or convey . . ." Thus, a quitclaim deed is worded to imply no claim to title, only to convey what interest the grantor actually has, if any. Courts therefore may regard a quitclaim deed as a questionable conveyance of title. Its very use may create a "cloud" on the title that must be cleared in order to obtain a fully **marketable title**—one that is free of reasonable doubt.[2]

2. More specifically, marketable title is a claim to title that "reasonable persons," knowing the evidence of ownership, would regard as free from reasonable doubt.

One use of a quitclaim deed is within a family, to add a spouse to title or remove a divorcing spouse. Another use is to extinguish ambiguous interests in a property as a means of removing clouds or threats to a marketable title. The title to a property may be clouded, for example, by a defective release of dower or elective share rights, or it may be clouded by disputes stemming from divorce proceedings. In such cases, restoring a marketable or clear title may require negotiating with the person possessing the questionable claim to relinquish it through a quitclaim deed. The quitclaim deed also may be used by a land-owner, perhaps a developer, to convey certain lands of a subdivision to the local government through dedication (discussed later in this chapter).

Deed of Bargain and Sale. The **deed of bargain and sale**, like the quitclaim deed, has none of the covenants of a warranty deed. But unlike the quitclaim deed, it purports to convey the real property and appears to imply claim to ownership. It commonly is used by businesses to convey property because, while implying ownership, it commits the business to no additional covenants, which are sources of liability.[3]

Judicial Deeds and Trustee's Deeds. The **judicial deed,** sometimes called an *officer's deed* or *sheriff's deed,* is one issued as a result of court-ordered proceedings. It may include deeds issued by administrators of condemnation proceedings or administrators of foreclo-sure sales. A **trustee's deed** is issued by the trustee in a court-supervised disposition of property—for example, by an executor and administrator of an estate, a guardian of a minor, a bankruptcy trustee, or an attorney in divorce proceedings. The quality of all these deeds may depend on the proceeding involved. In foreclosure sales, particularly, there are complex and demanding notification requirements to assure that all parties with a legal interest in the property are given the opportunity to defend their interest. It is not infrequent that the notification process is flawed, leaving some latent claim to the title "alive" follow-ing the sale and issuance of a deed.

The array of deeds has implications for real estate investment and transactions. When a property can be acquired only through a relatively weak deed such as a quitclaim deed or judicial deed from foreclosure, the grantee may need to gain additional assurance that the property title is safe. In many conveyances with a trustee's deed, the circumstances proba-bly imply an especially strong need for title insurance (discussed in a later section) as both buyer protection and assurance of good title.[4] Title insurance will defend and indemnify the grantee against attack on the title. In addition, if a question arises concerning marketable title at subsequent sale of the property, the insurance normally will compensate for any legal costs in curing the problem.

✓ **Concept Check**

3.5   What is the highest-quality deed?

What deed do businesses often use to convey real estate?

What deed is used to relinquish ambiguous or conflicting claims?

Modes of Conveyance of Real Property

While the vast majority of conveyances of real property are private grants through a deed, there are other modes of transfer. Some of these, as suggested before, may result in a less than marketable title. Some conveyances occur in the absence of any kind of document.

---

3. The definition of deed of bargain and sale seems to be as nebulous as the concept itself. Some see it as little different from a quitclaim deed while other sources describe it as similar to a special warranty deed.

4. A commitment from a title insurer has two benefits. It implies that the insurer regards the title as having low risk, and it provides indemnification should a threat to title actually occur.

Exhibit 3-1 Modes of Conveying Real Property

	With a Deed	Without a Deed
Voluntary	• "Normal" transaction • Patent	• Implied easement • Easement by estoppel • Dedication
Involuntary	• Probate • Bankruptcy • Divorce • Condemnation • Foreclosure	• Easement by prescription • Title by adverse possession • Action of water

The variation in possible modes of conveyance is summarized in Exhibit 3-1. In this section, we examine each mode.

Voluntary Conveyance by a Deed

The great majority of real property conveyances are voluntary. Among these, most are private transfers from one owner to another. The transfer may result from a sale and purchase, a gift, or an exchange. In these cases the transfer usually is by a warranty, special warranty, or bargain and sale deed. One exception is voluntary conveyance of public property by a government to a private citizen. This kind of conveyance is accomplished by a document known as a **patent,** and the interest conveyed also is referred to as a patent. An important point about all of these voluntary conveyances is that, typically, they are legally simple, especially when the deed is a "quality deed," and there is little risk of the title becoming clouded (i.e., unmarketable) by the transfer.

Involuntary Conveyance by a Deed

Several kinds of conveyances result from events beyond control of the grantor. These include probate proceedings to settle the grantor's estate, sale of property in bankruptcy proceedings, divorce settlement, condemnation proceedings, and foreclosure. We review each of these below:

Probate. At the death of a property owner, the property will convey in one of two modes: **testate**—in accordance with a will, or **intestate**—without a will. Either way, state laws of **probate** where the property is located will govern the disposition procedure. The final conveyance of property in the probate process is by either a judicial deed or a trustee's deed. An increasing number of states have adopted some version of the Uniform Probate Code (UPC), thus providing increasingly uniform terminology and standards for probate. Under the UPC, the decedent will have a "personal representative" who is responsible for administration of the procedure. If a will dictates the distribution of the decedent's real property, the property is said to be **devised,** or conveyed by devise. If there is no will, the property is conveyed by the **law of descent.** The law of descent for the state containing the property determines its distribution among the heirs, and these laws vary significantly among the states. An important implication is that any real property owner should draw up an explicit will rather than leave the distribution of the estate to intestate surprise.

**www.uniformlaws.org/
Acts.aspx**

Source of the Uniform Probate Code (and other model laws); a "Google" search of numerous websites can give a sense of what the UPC is about. It is a major streamlining of very old statutes.

3.6 When property is conveyed to heirs in accordance with a will, it is said to be conveyed ——————— or conveyed by ———————, whereas when property is conveyed to heirs without a will it is said to be conveyed ——————— or conveyed by ———————.

Bankruptcy. In a bankruptcy proceeding, real property of the debtor, unless preempted by a defaulted mortgage, may be included in other assets to be liquidated on behalf of the creditors. The court will appoint a trustee to conduct the liquidation, and the property will be conveyed by a trustee's deed. If the trustee follows requisite procedures, including obtaining permission of the court, sale of the property can be straightforward. However, since more things can go wrong than in a voluntary conveyance, the buyer has at least some additional risk, which is best alleviated through title insurance (discussed later in this chapter).

Divorce Settlement. In a divorce settlement, real property may transfer by a "final judgment of dissolution," instead of a deed. Often the disposition will be directed by a "property settlement agreement." It may award the property directly through the final judgment, or it may call for a trustee's deed. If the settlement agreement awards the property to one spouse, but awards the other spouse some compensation from the property, then the latter spouse retains what amounts to a lien on the property until the compensation requirement is fulfilled.

Condemnation. By the power of *eminent domain,* government can take private property for public purpose through due process, and with just compensation. The process of exercising this power is known as *condemnation.* (Eminent domain and condemnation are discussed in Chapter 4.)

Foreclosure. As discussed in Chapter 9, foreclosure can be either judicial or power of sale (nonjudicial). In both cases the foreclosed property, with few exceptions, is disposed of by public sale.[5] In judicial foreclosure, however, the process is administered by a court. Under power of sale, the process is administered by a trustee, subject to state law that specifies the procedure, particularly for advertising and notification. Title will convey by a deed from the court or from a trustee. Foreclosure is a complicated procedure, typically arising from legally messy circumstances. Therefore, the title obtained at foreclosure sale usually has significantly more risks than normal.

3.7 Name four events that can result in the conveyance of real property involuntarily through some type of deed.

Voluntary Conveyance without a Deed

There are multiple ways an easement can arise incidental to a voluntary conveyance of property. These include variations of implied easements and easement by estoppel.

---

5. The exceptions are in Connecticut and Vermont, where a lender may be able to take title of the foreclosed property directly through a court supervised process known as strict foreclosure.

Implied Easements.   An **implied easement** is not created by an explicit deed or an explicit clause in a deed. It often is created when a subdivision map is placed in the public records. On the map will be utility easements and possibly easements of access such as bike paths or footpaths that do not appear in any specific deed. While they are in the public records for all to see, the prospective grantee must realize that they may only be detectable by examination of the map or by careful inspection of the property.

An easement by prior use and an easement of necessity both arise when a landowner subdivides land, conveying part of it in a way that causes a parcel to be landlocked. By common law tradition, land is to be useful, and therefore must be accessible. An owner cannot convey land in a manner that makes it inaccessible. When a path of access across part of the property to a now landlocked parcel preexists, and if the sale leaves that path as the only access and egress, then the path becomes an implied **easement by prior use.** If the landlocked parcel has no prior path of access and egress, then an implied **easement of necessity** is automatically created.

Trouble can arise with these implied easements when the servient parcel bearing the easement subsequently passes to a new owner. There will be no indication of the easement in public records, even though it must exist.

Easement by Estoppel.   **Easement by estoppel** can occur if a landowner gives an adjacent landowner permission to depend on her land. For example, suppose a landowner gives a neighbor permission to rely on sewer access or drainage across his or her land. Courts may subsequently enforce that claim against the landowner (estop any attempt to deny access), or against subsequent purchasers of the burdened land, acting on behalf of the benefiting (dominant) parcel.

Dedication.   When a developer creates a subdivision, it is common to dedicate (convey to the local government) the street rights-of-way and perhaps open spaces such as parks, school sites, or retention ponds. Frequently, this is done simply through statements in a subdivision plat map (discussed later in this chapter), and no deed is involved. While the **dedication** commonly is accepted by official vote of the local government, even this action may not always occur.

> **✓ Concept Check**
>
> **3.8**   What are two types of easements that are created without a deed, but with the knowledge of the grantor?

Involuntary Conveyance without a Deed

An owner of land may involuntarily and unknowingly give up rights to land. The interest sacrificed can be either an easement, called an **easement by prescription,** or title to the land, called title by **adverse possession.**[6] This can occur if others use the property and their use meets five conditions, which must be:

1. *Hostile to the owner's interests,* and under claim of right (i.e., without the owner's permission and acting like an owner).
2. *Actual*—the land must be employed in some natural or normal use. (This may be only seasonal or occasional when appropriate to the use.)
3. *Open and notorious*—there can be no effort to disguise or hide the use from the owner or neighbors.

---

6. Adverse possession and prescription derive from the ancient notion that land is to be used. If the property has been effectively abandoned, these two modes of conveyance provide a mechanism for the land to be returned to productivity.

4. *Continuous*—possession must be uninterrupted by a period specified by state law; this period can be as short as 5 years or as long as 20 years.
5. *Exclusive*—the claimant cannot share possession with the owner, neighbors, or others.

These requirements generally apply both to title by adverse possession and to easement by prescription, although the requirement of exclusive possession may be interpreted less strictly for an easement by prescription. In addition to these requirements, some states require under adverse possession that the claimant has paid property taxes on the property for a period of time before acquiring title.

✓ **Concept Check**

3.9   Real property can convey to a new owner without a deed, and without the consent or knowledge of the original owner. A fee simple interest being conveyed in this manner is said to convey by ——————, while an easement is said to convey by ——————.

An owner also can involuntarily gain rights to land through the action of water bordering the property. By means of **accretion,** water may deposit soil, which can become the property of the owner. By **reliction,** subsiding water may leave additional land as property of the owner.

Real Property Complexity and Public Records

In Chapter 2 we saw the diversity of the "bundles of rights" in real property. In this chapter we have reviewed the multitude of ways that these rights can be conveyed from one owner to the next over many generations. Clearly, therefore, within the property rights system that we have described, the only way to be certain what rights are obtainable for a parcel of land, and from whom, is to be able to account for the complete legal history of the property.[7] Thus, our society has established a framework of laws, public record systems, and procedures to preserve this real property history. We describe this system in the sections below.

The Doctrine of Constructive Notice

The common law tradition is that a person cannot be bound by claims or rules he or she has no means of knowing. The corollary is that once a person is capable of knowing about a claim or rule, he or she can be bound by it. This is the **doctrine of constructive notice.** The importance of the doctrine here is that the public need not actually be *aware* of contracts conveying interests in real property for the contracts to be valid and enforceable. The public merely has to be *able* to know about the contracts.

Statute of Frauds

Every state has adopted some form of the original **Statute of Frauds** (1677) by enacting a law requiring any contract conveying a real property interest to be in writing. Thus, deeds, leases with a term of more than one year, and mortgages must be in writing to be enforceable.

Recording Statutes

Every state also has implemented the doctrine of constructive notice through the enactment of **recording statutes.** These laws require that a document conveying an interest in real

---

7. The property system we have described is common to countries with an English tradition. In other traditions, much less emphasis is placed on property history and more on a system of registration.

property must be placed in the public records if it is to achieve constructive notice. Once in the public records, the document is binding on everyone, whether or not they make an effort to learn of it. Thus, deeds, mortgages, mechanics' liens, attachments from court judgments, and other instruments that convey real property interests must be placed in local public records to be enforceable.[8] This recording process is maintained at the county level (parish or township where counties do not exist) and is an important function of the traditional county courthouse. A registrar of deeds, clerk of the court, or similar officer is charged with the responsibility of maintaining the property recording system.

✓ **Concept Check**

3.10 All persons are presumed to be informed of legal documents placed in public records according to the doctrine of ——————.

When a grantee receives a deed, or when a lender receives a mortgage, it is important to record it as soon as possible since priority of real property claims generally is by chronology of recording (see Chapter 9). If a mortgage, for example, is not recorded, an unscrupulous borrower could immediately issue a second, competing mortgage. If the second one issued is recorded first, it gains first priority, regardless of the original understanding with the borrower, and the aggrieved lender is powerless to correct the problem. Similarly, if an unscrupulous owner sells a parcel of land twice, the grantees recording their deed first become the true owners of the property.

Actual Notice

Unfortunately, recording statutes cannot assure complete knowledge of real property interests. Earlier in this chapter we noted that real property could be conveyed through adverse possession, prescription, implied easements, and estoppel easements. In addition, the property may be subject to a lease. None of these conveyances appears in recorded documents, but each is enforceable on the basis of actual notice. If the asserted claim is open, continuous, and apparent to all who examine the property, it meets the requirements for **actual notice** and is considered to have the same force as constructive notice. The obvious implication of actual notice is that property should never be acquired until it has been inspected. By the same token, when the validity of title is being examined, as discussed below, part of the process must be to inspect the property.

✓ **Concept Check**

3.11 Name two types of legal notice that can provide evidence of a real property interest.

Title

It is clear from the complexity and length of ownership history that no single document can prove ownership of land; that is, there is no single document that we can meaningfully refer to as the "title." Rather, title must be a *collection* of evidence. This evidence must point to some person (or entity) as the holder of the fee (titled) interest. From the discussion above, two kinds of evidence are pertinent: constructive notice and actual notice. In

---

8. Long-term leases generally are enforceable on the basis of actual notice.

short, the problem of establishing title is one of searching the public records for pertinent evidence, and then examining the property for any additional evidence from current occupancy and use.

Title Search, Title Abstract, and Chain of Title

The task of examining the evidence in the public records is called a **title search.** The object is to construct a **chain of title**—a set of deeds and other documents that traces the conveyance of the fee, and any interests that could limit it—from the earliest recorded time for the particular property to the current owner. If no breaks in this chain are discovered (i.e., no paths lead away from the current owner) then a complete chain is established. Events that must be accounted for in this process may include sales, gifts, marriages, estate settlements, divorces, mortgages, foreclosures, condemnations, and others.

Traditionally, each relevant document was summarized, and the document summaries were compiled into a chronological volume called a **title abstract.** Since the relevant public records might be housed in multiple offices and since each county historically has created its own system of public records, the title search process must be carried out by a knowledgeable person with local expertise. Further, since many of the documents can be subject to interpretation, only a competent legal expert can draw final conclusions about the chain of title. Thus, the title abstract was constructed and then given to an attorney for final interpretation. With electronic document storage and retrieval, the customary title abstract has largely been replaced by electronic equivalents. Exhibit 3-2 summarizes the laws and processes that combine to establish evidence of title.

Exhibit 3-2 Creating Evidence of Title

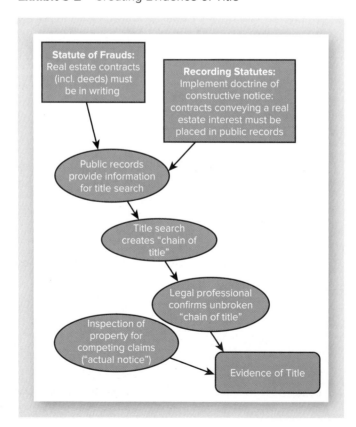

✓ **Concept Check**

3.12 What is the object of a title search?

Evidence of Title

Demonstrating a good title is a central part of any real estate transaction. A contract for sale of real estate usually calls for the seller/grantor to provide **evidence of title** as a requisite to completing the sale. The seller traditionally can meet this requirement in one of two ways:

1. Title abstract, together with an attorney's opinion of title. (Note that the abstract alone is not sufficient.)
2. Title insurance commitment.

Title Abstract and Attorney's Opinion. The **title abstract with attorney's opinion** is the traditional evidence of title. Its logic follows closely from the nature of the title search described above.

Title Insurance Commitment. A **title insurance commitment** is deemed equivalent to the traditional abstract and opinion of title. The logic of relying on a title insurance commitment as evidence of title is that the insurer would not make a commitment before conducting a title search and assuring a good title beyond reasonable doubt. **Title insurance** protects a grantee (or mortgage lender) against the legal costs of defending the title and against loss of the property in case of an unsuccessful defense. Therefore, the insurer will refuse to commit if good title is in doubt.

Title insurance has become the predominant type of evidence of title because the tradition of abstract with attorney's opinion, even if executed perfectly, cannot guard against certain risks. Among these are defective deeds (e.g., those improperly delivered), forgeries, flaws due to incorrect marital status (e.g., failure to reveal a marriage), and incapacity of a grantor due to insanity or minority age. Title insurance provides indemnification against these risks, among others. Litigation may be necessary to defend even a good title, and title insurance covers this cost.

There are important limits to title insurance. First, it is not hazard insurance; that is, it does not protect the owner from the threat of physical damage to the property. It only protects against legal attack on the owner's title arising from either a competing claim to title by someone else or a claim that diminishes the owner's rights of use. Restrictions on use may arise from easements on the property, from government restrictions affecting the property (discussed in Chapter 4), or from encroachments; that is, intrusions on the property by structures on adjacent land. But even for these legal challenges title insurance has limits. For example, title insurance typically excepts from coverage any restrictions that a survey of the property reveals, or that the owner would know by inspection of the property. In addition, title insurance normally does not insure against claim of title through eminent domain, or limitations on the property placed by government through the exercise of police power: that is, zoning, building codes, environmental laws, etc. Also, title insurance typically limits protection relating to mineral rights and the effect of extracting minerals. As a final example, title insurance often has exceptions concerning land adjacent to a body of water or coastline. Frequently, the boundaries of "waterfront" property are faulty, and some portion of the land is subject to potential government claim of ownership. But title insurance seldom protects against these claims.

To the credit of the title insurance industry, its association, the American Land Title Association, has recently improved title policy forms, adopting a new Owner's Policy of Title Insurance in 2006 and a new Homeowner's Policy of Title Insurance in 2008. These policy forms are now used in the vast majority of states. These forms are a notable improvement for purchaser understanding, and the Homeowner's Policy appears to offer broader

www.alta.org

American Land Title Association is the umbrella organization of the title insurance industry—a very rich site for information about title insurance and the industry.

Title Insurance: Robber Barons?

Are title insurers the last of the robber barons? Like the feudal lords along the Rhine River who held up shippers for ransom in an earlier era, title insurers have become the gatekeepers for home purchases. Since title insurance is required for most home mortgage loans, it has grown as the choice for evidence of title as well. But not without controversy. In Colorado, California, Florida, New York, and other states, regulators and class action suits have accused the industry of providing the buyers less than they pay for. While evidence seems sketchy, it has been reported that less than 10 cents of the typical title insurance dollar is paid out in claims, in contrast to automobile insurance, for example, where something like 90 percent is paid out. Much of the rest of the premium, some critics report, goes to

lavish marketing efforts to the real estate industry. Moreover, some studies have indicated that about half of the claims paid out result from errors or oversights in conducting the title examination that is being insured.

Title insurance defenders counter that the premium covers not just insurance but the cost of maintaining the "title plant" or record base and for closing-related services, which the homebuyer would need to pay for anyway. The pricing of closing services remains murky, and thus the merit of this argument is not clear. However, perhaps some indication of the pricing of title insurance is found from the state of Iowa. There, a division of the Iowa Finance Authority, a state agency, provides the only title insurance issued within Iowa. Insurance (called a Title Guaranty Certificate) is $110 up to a purchase price of $500,000, plus the cost of title search, attorney's certification and closing expense, a grand total of maybe $600. Compare this to 1/2 to 1 percent of value for private insurers. So the $250,000 home that costs about $600 to insure in Iowa costs at least $1,250 to

insure with private insurance. The controversy over the cost of title insurance continues, perhaps described best in the GAO Title Insurance Report, April 2007 (Google the title).

What are homebuyers to do? Shop! The core source of the problem is lack of competition, which in today's world is mitigated by some progress in regulations and the Internet revolution. It turns out that you can compare prices of providers, and should do so as soon as title insurance is on your horizon. Further, if the property was previously insured in the last three years or so, you may be able to go back to the most recent insurer and negotiate a lower "update" premium. Start by checking industry websites such as these for rate calculators:

First American Title (www.firstam.com)

Fidelity National Title (www.fntic.com)

entitledirect.com

onetitle.com

Old Republic National Title
(www.oldrepublictitle.com)

---

coverage than before for risks that could limit use of the property. Key in all of these policy forms is a section called Schedule B. This section, unique for every policy, spells out exceptions pertaining to the specific property being insured. One should always examine this part of the insurance policy to understand those specific limits.

Torrens Certificate. A third, rarely used means of providing evidence of title is through a Torrens certificate introduced by Sir Robert Torrens in Australia in 1858. A property is first converted to the Torrens system by going through a careful title search and examination. Then a **Torrens certificate** is issued that is accepted as evidence of good title. From that point on, no mortgage, deed, or other conveyance is binding until presented to the Torrens office where it is noted in an updated Torrens certificate. The intent is to simplify title conveyance. However, time has not been favorable to the system. Though it has been used in a handful of U.S. cities, including Boston, New York, Minneapolis–St. Paul, and Chicago, it seldom appears today.

✓ **Concept Check**

3.13 List the two main forms of evidence of title.

Marketable Title Laws. The past history of a property, once constructed, remains the same, and only recent conveyances alter the status of title. Recognizing this, an increasing number of states have sought to simplify title search and title risk through **marketable title**

Title researchers examine and analyze past deeds and other records that are on file with state and county registry offices. Many title insurance companies also maintain their own files for title research. Examiners check deeds, mortgages, court documents, and other records affecting property conveyance, and examine surveys of the property to assure that there is no dispute over the boundary lines. They also may check the property in person to be certain that there are no buildings, power lines, or other constructions encroaching on the property. In addition, they will check tax records to be sure all payments have been made. Basic skills and knowledge involved include:

- Considerable knowledge of forms and terminology as applied to real estate.

- Considerable knowledge of sources and procedures pertaining to title abstracts.
- Ability to search title records and to provide concise, accurate reports of findings.
- Ability to make routine decisions in accordance with regulations and procedures.
- Ability to establish and maintain effective working relationships with associates, property owners, appraisers, and the public.

If the examiner finds defects in the title, he or she will contact the necessary parties to determine the best means of correction, and assist in resolving the problem. Finally, the examiner will prepare a report.

Some companies hire high school graduates (normally with experience) and train them. Other companies prefer college graduates with courses in accounting, business, prelaw, and real estate. Title examiners may work for state, county, or local governments and may focus on condemnation cases. Also, they may work for utility companies or private title companies. They commonly are salaried employees with full fringe benefits. Entry positions start at around $25,000, whereas senior, supervisory positions as examiners can pay well over $50,000.

Title Researcher and Examiner

Source: US Dept. of Labor, *Occupational Outlook Handbook*

---

laws. These laws set limits on how far back a title search must go. Consequently, certain types of claims, including restrictive covenants and even easements in some cases, may cease to be binding if they do not *reappear* in recorded documents that postdate a so-called root of title. (Presumably, actual notice of easements is not affected.) The "root of title" conveyance is the last conveyance of the property that is at least a certain number of years old (typically 30 to 40 years). With some exceptions, a title that is good back to the root of title may be regarded as fully marketable.[9] Thus, the marketable title act provides, with some exceptions, a statute of limitations on title search.

Land Descriptions

At the outset of the chapter, we noted three aspects of real property transactions that make them uniquely complicated: the complexity of real property "bundles of rights," the long history of property ownership, and the need for precise descriptions. Since land parcels are defined on a continuous surface, adjacent everywhere to other land parcels, description is challenging. It cannot be accomplished, for example, by a bar code. Errors in a land description must imply a loss to some landowner that could be substantial.

While the basic requirement of a land description is to be unambiguous, only the three methods presented below are recognized as reliably clear for use in legal documents.[10]

Metes and Bounds

The method of **metes and bounds** is the oldest of the three major forms of land description. In ancient practice, *metes* referred to measures, and *bounds* referred to the identifiable boundaries of surrounding parcels of land. Without systematic reference points such as the longitude and latitude we use today, there was no simple place to begin a survey. The point of beginning, always critical, had to be defined in terms of any existing reference points

---

9. The most important "exception" concerns mineral rights. States adopting the marketable title act have divided on whether a separation (severance) of mineral rights preceding the root of title survives.

10. Historically, street addresses, tax parcel numbers, and prominent features of the land (monuments) have been used to identify parcels. These methods, however, produce too many failures to be acceptable in modern practice.

available. Thus, the best the surveyor could do was to make good use of trees, large rocks, and identifiable boundaries of neighboring properties. (See Industry Issues 3-2.)

In its modern version, metes and bounds is a very precise, GPS (Global Positioning System) and compass-directed walk around the boundary of a parcel. The boundary is defined by a point of beginning and a sequence of directed distances (metes, in Old English) that eventually lead back to the point of beginning. The point of beginning is a marker or monument that is presumed to be permanent. In early times the point of beginning might be a notable feature of the land, such as a large oak tree or a boulder. However, because such "permanent" features of land have a way of changing through time, modern practice is to install a steel or concrete marker as the point of beginning.

A metes and bounds description is the most flexible of descriptions, and is capable of describing even the most irregular of parcels. However, it should neither be created nor interpreted except by a trained surveyor. An example of a very simple metes and bounds description is shown in Exhibit 3-3. Notice that the four sides of the Glowing Hills Subdivision are defined in a clockwise sequence by pairs of precise compass headings and distances. Each compass heading has three elements. First is a reference direction (N, E, S, or W). Next are the degrees, minutes, and seconds of rotation from that direction. Third is the direction of rotation. Thus, the first compass heading gives a rotation of 89 degrees, 36 minutes and 01 seconds away from north, rotating to the west. The distance in that direction is 1,274.03 feet.

✓ **Concept Check**

3.14   A metes and bounds land description can be summarized or described as a —————— and a series of ——————.

Exhibit 3-3   Metes and Bounds Description: Glowing Hills Subdivision

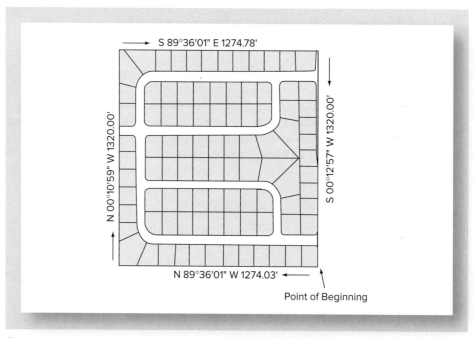

(From the point of beginning, north 89° 36 minutes and 01 seconds west 1,274.03 feet, thence north 00° 10 minutes and 59 seconds west 1,320.00 feet, thence south 89° 36 minutes and 01 seconds east 1,274.78 feet, thence south 00° 12 minutes and 57 seconds 1,320.00 feet to the point of beginning.)

In about 20 states the basic property description system is by metes and bounds. These include the original 13 colonies, along with Vermont, Maine, West Virginia, Texas, and parts of Ohio, Kentucky, and Tennessee. Some of these systems have more meat than others! In Kentucky and Tennessee, for example the system has been referred to as "indiscriminant metes and bounds," and had to describe land without the assistance of a compass, and with few systematic points of beginning. For example, read the description of a property in Mercer County, Kentucky:

Beginning at the mouth of a branch at an ash stump thence up the creek south 20 poles to 2 beech, thence east 41 poles to a small walnut in Arnett's line, thence north 50 east 80 poles to a linn hickory dogwood in said line, thence north 38 poles to an ash, thence west 296 poles

Source: © Hemera Technologies/Getty Images

with Potts's line till it intersects with Tolly's line, thence south 30 west 80 poles to a whiteoak and sugar, thence east 223 poles to beginning.

Often, descriptions followed creeks or rivers, and used the term "meander" to describe a boundary that simply followed the streambed. In this system distance is measured in 16 1/2 foot lengths, which are interchangeably known as poles, rods, or perches. A common device in measuring for these early descriptions was the "chain" (shown above†) which was 66 feet in length,

or 4 perches. An acre, which contains 43,560 square feet, derives from an area measuring 1 chain by 10 chains.

*Information obtained from a helpful, but unsigned Web source: www.outfitters. com/genealogy/land/metesbounds.html

†Another enjoyable site on early surveying in Tennessee is www.tngenweb.org/ tnland/terms.htm. The chain illustration is from that website.

Metes and Bounds: The Surveyor's Bread and Butter

Subdivision Plat Lot and Block Number

Most urban property is part of a platted subdivision. When a platted residential or other subdivision is created, a surveyed map of the subdivision is placed in the public records with each parcel identified by **plat lot and block number.** Since the original survey is contained in the recorded plat map, the lot and block number on that map provide an unambiguous description of the property.

The recorded plat map contains other important information as well. It usually shows the location of various easements such as utilities, drainage, storm water retention, and bicycle paths. In addition, it may contain a list of restrictive covenants, though it is more common in current practice to record the restrictions in an associated declaration.

Exhibit 3-4 shows a simple subdivision plat map based on an actual subdivision. It contains four blocks, each with lots numbered beginning with 1. Note that Block 1 extends around three sides of the subdivision, with lots running from 1 to 32. Though the subdivision is quite simple, it nevertheless contains numerous easements. A utility easement borders every lot. In addition, drainage easements for storm sewers affect six lots. Finally, a common path cuts through all four blocks leading to an adjacent elementary school and park. Often such a path is an easement across some of the lots. In this case, however, the path is the common property of all owners in the subdivision.

Government Rectangular Survey

A large portion of the United States, after the 13 colonies and the earliest post-Revolutionary new states, was originally described by government rectangular survey. This process of survey began with the Old Northwest Territory (Ohio, Indiana, Illinois, and Michigan) in 1789. As shown in Exhibit 3-5, numerous different regions were surveyed separately. For each region a **baseline,** running east and west, and a **principal meridian,** running north and south, were established as reference lines. From these lines a grid system was surveyed involving **checks** (24 miles square), **townships** (6 miles square), and **sections** (1 mile square).

Exhibit 3-4 Subdivision Plat Map with Lot and Block Number

Exhibit 3-5 Principal Meridians of the Federal System of Rectangular Surveys

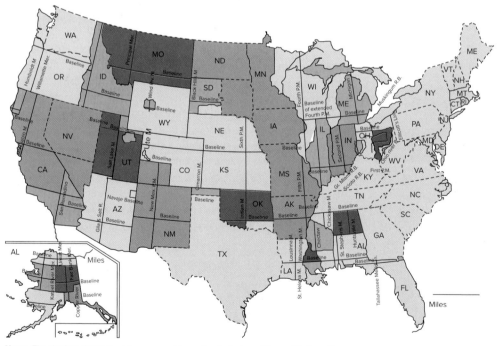

Note: The shading shows the area governed by each principal meridian and its base line.

Source data: U.S Department of the Interior, Bureau of Land Management. Smith, Tschappat, and Racster, *Real Estate and Urban Development* (Homeward, IL: Richard D. Irwin) 1981

Exhibit 3-6 Township Identification

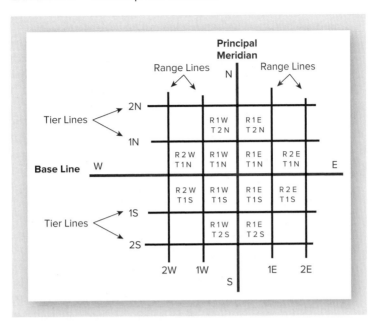

A government rectangular description relies on townships and section numbers as the essential units of identification. Townships are numbered east or west from the principal meridian. They are separated, east and west, by **range lines,** six miles apart, which parallel the principal meridian. They are numbered south or north from the baseline by **tier lines** (sometimes referred to as township lines), also six miles apart, which parallel the baseline. Exhibit 3-6 shows how this scheme uniquely identifies each six mile by six mile township.

Each six mile by six mile township is subdivided into 36 numbered sections, laid out (with rare exceptions) in the pattern shown in Exhibit 3-7. The numbering begins in the northeast

Exhibit 3-7 One Township, with Numbered Sections: Tier 24 South, Range 27 East

Range 26 E					Range 27 E
6	5	4	3	2	1
7	8	9	10	11	12
18	17	16	15	14	13
19	20	21	22	23	24
30	29	28	27	26	25
31	32	33	34	35	36

Tier 23 S (top left), Tier 24 S (bottom left)

corner of the township and ends in the southeast corner, going back and forth horizontally in between. Note that a section is not simply any one-square-mile area. It is a specifically surveyed and identified square mile within the framework of the rectangular survey system.

A section (which contains 640 acres) is subdivided, as necessary, according to a set of simple rules. It typically is quartered (160 acres), and each quarter section can again be quartered (40 acres), and so on. Sections can be halved without ambiguity (e.g., north one-half, west one-half), but a description never uses the term "middle" because it is ambiguous. Exhibit 3-8 displays a number of sample subdivisions for a typical section. Note that halves and quarters can be combined to form L-shaped or other block-like properties.

Clearly, the **acre** is an important measure in rectangular survey descriptions and in land measure generally. It is a measure of land area, with no specific configuration, containing 43,560 square feet. Note that this implies that a square lot of slightly over 200 feet on a side constitutes an acre. Ninety yards of the standard American football field constitutes approximately an acre.

Exhibit 3-9 shows the government rectangular description for a familiar Florida location (shown in the aerial photo). The property is located in the 27th north-south range of townships east of the Tallahassee principal meridian and in the 24th east-west tier of townships south of the baseline. (The principal meridian and baseline intersect near Florida's state capitol building.) The section is number 11, which always is in the second row from the top of the township, one removed from the right-hand boundary. The parcel of interest is in the northeast quarter of section 11, and within that quarter it lies in the northwest quarter. We leave it to the reader to figure out what the property is.

✓ Concept Check

3.15   What is the oldest form of the three main land descriptions?

What is the most common form of urban land description?

What is the most common rural land description in most states?

Exhibit 3-8   Subdividing a Section

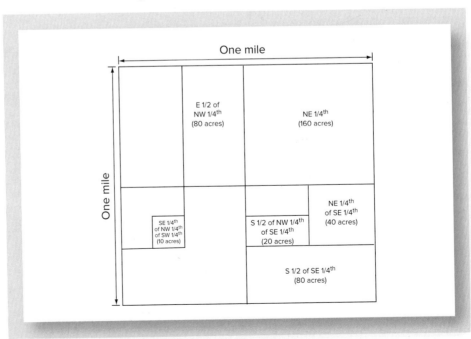

Exhibit 3-9   Government Rectangular Survey Description
of a Familiar Florida Site

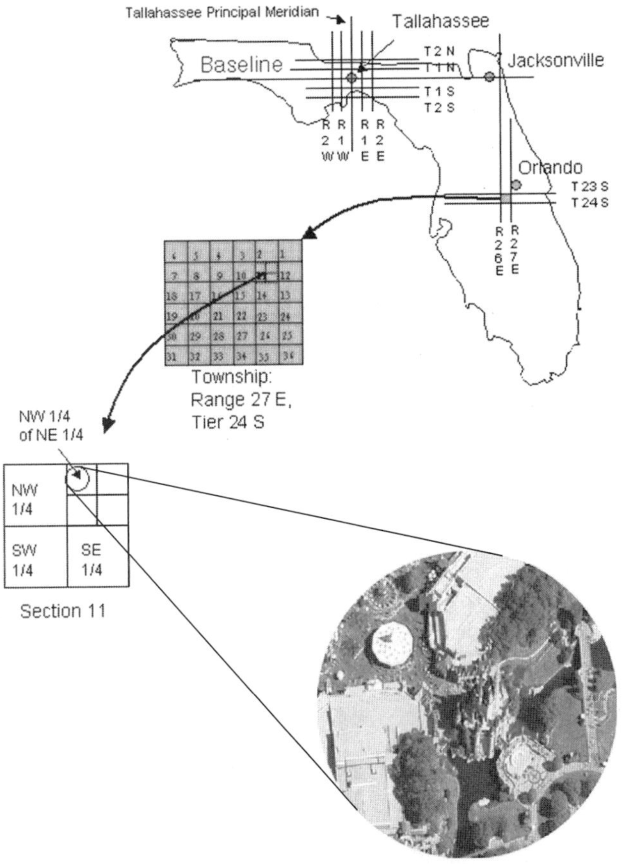

Township:
Range 27 E,
Tier 24 S

NW 1/4
of NE 1/4

Section 11

© LING

Summary

Conveyance of real property is complicated by three characteristics. First, real property interests can be complex. Second, because land is enduring, the history of real property ownership is very long. Third, describing land is critical because all land parcels adjoin other parcels; any errors in description inevitably favor one owner and hurt another.

Deeds are the principal means of conveying title or other interests in real property. They are a special form of contract. They differ from a normal business contract by not requiring a legally competent grantee, by not requiring explicit consideration, and by the requirement that they must be in writing. Deeds contain a number of specialized clauses necessary to define the bundle of rights and the precise location being conveyed. Deeds vary in "quality" in accordance with the number of covenants they contain. Finally, a deed is valid only if it has been "delivered" from the grantor to the grantee.

Transfers of property also can occur without a deed or any other explicit document. This can occur through an easement by implication, an easement by estoppel, by adverse possession, or by prescription. In these cases, an easement or the possession of the property, in whole or in part, is not recorded in the public records. However, the existence of the claim is often visibly detectable. Thus, actual inspection of property is always important.

www.mhhe.com/lingarcher5e

The complexity of real property interests, together with their long history, makes it challenging to determine what rights to a parcel are available today. The Statute of Frauds provides an essential first step by requiring every conveyance of real property to be in writing. Recording statutes require that deeds and other conveyances of real property interests must be placed in public records to be enforceable. Finally, the doctrine of constructive notice holds that all persons must honor any valid deed or other conveyance thus recorded and available for examination. However, it does not relieve a grantee from directly inspecting the property for "actual notice" of unrecorded claims to the land.

The resulting real property record systems make it possible to create "evidence of title" for a parcel of land. The first step is to construct a "chain of title" tracing ownership back through the record system for as long as it is deemed necessary. A qualified legal expert examines the conveyances in the chain to assure that they imply an unbroken transfer of the property interest in question down to the grantor. The substance of this search and evaluation can result in two main types of evidence of title. The most traditional form is title abstract with attorney's opinion. A more modern form is a title insurance commitment, which also offers the advantage of financial protection against title challenges.

In the sensitive issue of land description, three methods of legal descriptions are accepted for public records: metes and bounds, subdivision plat lot and block number, and government rectangular survey.

Key Terms

Accretion 54
Acknowledgment 48
Acre 64
Actual notice 55
Adverse possession 53
Baseline 61
Chain of title 56
Checks 61
Covenants 47
Covenant against
    encumbrances 48
Covenant of quiet enjoyment 48
Covenant of seizin 47
Dedication 53
Deed 46
Deed of bargain and sale 50
Delivery 49
Devise 51
Doctrine of constructive
    notice 54
Easement by estoppel 53
Easement by prescription 53

Easement by prior use 53
Easement of necessity 53
Encroachment 49
Evidence of title 57
Exceptions and reservations
    clause 48
General warranty deed 49
Grant deed 49
Grantee 47
Grantor 47
Habendum clause 48
Implied easement 53
Intestate 51
Judicial deed 50
Law of descent 51
Marketable title 50
Marketable title laws 58
Metes and bounds 59
Patent 51
Plat lot and block number 61
Principal meridian 61
Probate 51

Quitclaim deed 50
Range line 63
Recording statutes 54
Reliction 54
Section 61
Special warranty deed 49
Statute of Frauds 54
Testate 51
Tier line 63
Title abstract 56
Title abstract with attorney's
    opinion 57
Title insurance 57
Title insurance commitment 57
Title search 56
Torrens certificate 58
Township 61
Trustee's deed 50
Words of conveyance 47

Test Problems

Answer the following multiple-choice problems:
1. Which of these is *not* a requirement of a valid deed?
   a. Competent grantor.
   b. Competent grantee.

c. In writing.
d. Habendum clause.
e. Delivery.

2. The interest being conveyed by a deed is specified in the:
   a. Words of conveyance.
   b. Habendum clause.
   c. Property description.
   d. Exceptions and reservations clause.
   e. Covenant of seizin.

3. The "highest-quality" form of deed is the:
   a. General warranty deed.
   b. Special warranty deed.
   c. Deed of bargain and sale.
   d. Quitclaim deed.
   e. Judicial deed.

4. A deed used mainly to clear up possible "clouds" or encumbrances to title (conflicting interests) is the:
   a. General warranty deed.
   b. Special warranty deed.
   c. Deed of bargain and sale.
   d. Quitclaim deed.
   e. Judicial deed.

5. If a landowner sells the front part of a parcel of land, retaining the back portion as a "landlocked" parcel, and if there is an existing informal path across the front parcel to the back one, the seller is likely to retain the path as a(n):
   a. Easement in gross.
   b. Joint driveway easement.
   c. Implied easement by prior use.
   d. Easement by estoppel.
   e. Prescriptive easement.

6. If a neighboring landowner drives across a person's land openly and consistently for a number of years, the neighbor may acquire an easement by:
   a. Estoppel.
   b. Implication.
   c. Accretion.
   d. Prescription.
   e. Necessity.

7. If documents conveying interests in real property are properly recorded in the public records, they are binding or enforceable on all persons, regardless of whether those persons are aware of the documents, by the:
   a. Statute of Frauds.
   b. Recording statutes.
   c. Doctrine of constructive notice.
   d. Doctrine of actual notice.
   e. Evidence of title acts.

8. Which of these is a widely used form of "evidence of title"?
   a. Abstract of title.
   b. Title insurance commitment.
   c. Torrens certificate.
   d. Title certificate.
   e. General warranty deed.

9. The most common form of legal description for urban residential property is the:
   a. Street address.
   b. Tax parcel number.
   c. Plat lot and block number.
   d. Metes and bounds description.
   e. Government rectangular survey.

10. Factors that make it uniquely difficult to establish clear title in real estate compared to most personal property items include:
    a. Size of real estate.
    b. Length of the ownership history in real estate.
    c. Value of real estate.
    d. Land use controls.
    e. Serious deficiencies of property law in the United States.

Study Questions

1. Explain how title insurance works. What risks does it cover? Who pays for the insurance, and when? What common exceptions does it make?

2. If a grantee obtains title insurance, what value, if any, is there in the covenant of seizin in a warranty deed?

3. The use of Torrens certificates, never large in the United States, has diminished in recent years. Explain how marketable title laws, recently adopted in many states, might have made Torrens certificates less interesting and useful.

4. Name at least six adverse (conflicting) claims to property or other title defects that will not be evident from a search of property records but which might be detected by inspection of the property and its occupants.

5. Why might it be advisable to require a survey in purchasing a 20-year-old home in an urban subdivision?

6. Describe the shaded property in the diagram by government rectangular survey.

7. Some people in the real estate industry have suggested that it is good to require a title insurance commitment as evidence of title for rural property, but that it is satisfactory to use the less costly abstract with attorney's opinion as evidence of title for a residence in an urban subdivision. Discuss the merits or risks of this policy.

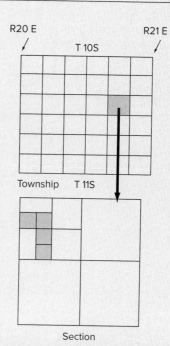

R20 E   T 10S   R21 E

Township   T 11S

Section

EXPLORE THE WEB

Most local government property appraisers (or assessors) have made their records and maps available today on the Internet. Find the website of your local property appraiser. Select a property of interest to you and see what information is available for it. Find the property description. Does the site give the area of the parcel? Is there a map of the parcel? Does the site also provide aerial photos?

Solutions to Concept Checks

1. Three features of real property that introduce special challenges for the orderly transfer of ownership are:
   a. Real property interests can be very complex.
   b. Ownership has a very long history.
   c. All real property is bounded by other properties, so description errors always matter.
2. In a normal contract all parties must be legally competent, whereas in a deed only the grantor must be legally competent.
3. The three covenants that distinguish the "quality" of deeds are:
   a. Seizin, which promises that the grantor actually holds title.
   b. No encumbrances, which promises that there are no undisclosed encumbrances.
   c. Quiet enjoyment, which promises that no superior claim to title will appear.
4. Any property interest not being conveyed to the grantee is stated in the exceptions and reservations clause.
5. The highest-quality deed is the general warranty deed. A deed that businesses often use to convey real estate is the bargain and sale deed. A deed used to relinquish ambiguous or conflicting claims is the quitclaim deed.
6. When property is conveyed to heirs in accordance with a will, it is said to be conveyed testate or by devise, whereas when property is conveyed to heirs without a will it is said to be conveyed intestate or by descent.
7. Four events that can cause an owner to convey real property involuntarily through some type of deed are condemnation, bankruptcy, foreclosure, and divorce.
8. Two types of easements that are created without a deed, but with the knowledge of the grantor, are an implied easement and an easement by estoppel.
9. Real property can convey to a new owner without a deed, and without the consent or knowledge of the original owner. A fee simple interest being conveyed in this manner is said to convey by adverse possession, while an easement is said to convey by prescription.
10. All persons are presumed to be informed of legal documents placed in public records according to the doctrine of constructive notice.
11. Two types of legal notice that can provide evidence of a real property interest are constructive notice and actual notice.
12. The objective of a title search is to construct a chain of title.
13. The two main forms of evidence of title are abstract with attorney's opinion and a title insurance commitment.
14. A metes and bounds land description can be summarized or described as a point of beginning and a series of directed distances.
15. The oldest form of the three main land descriptions is metes and bounds. The most common form of urban land description is subdivision plat lot and block number. The most common rural land description in most states is the government rectangular.

Additional Readings

The following real estate law texts offer excellent additional material on many of the subjects in this chapter:

Aalberts, Robert J. *Real Estate Law,* 9th ed. Stamford, CT: South-Western Cengage Learning, 2015.

Jennings, Marianne. *Real Estate Law,* 10th ed. Stamford, CT: South-Western Cengage Learning, 2014.

Werner, Raymond J. *Real Estate Law,* 11th ed. Cincinnati, OH: Southwestern Publishing, 2002.

Chapter 4

Government Controls *and* Real Estate Markets

LEARNING OBJECTIVES

After reading this chapter you will be able to:

1 Cite three reasons why the market system may not operate to maximize the net social benefits of land use.

2 Identify the principal provisions typically contained in state planning and growth management legislation.

3 Describe eight elements of traditional zoning and identify other traditional local land use controls.

4 Identify three possible adverse effects of traditional zoning.

5 Explain the "revolution" in scope, focus, and extent of land use controls that occurred during the 1970s.

6 Identify four tools of land use control widely adopted since 1970, and contrast *new urbanism* with traditional land use.

7 Identify the major types of environmental hazards and the steps real estate investors should take to protect against them.

8 Describe eminent domain and explain the current concern with its use for *public purpose.*

9 Explain how property tax is computed. Discuss three possible deficiencies with the property tax system.

OUTLINE

Introduction

Most of the real property in the United States is privately owned. If real estate markets worked well, this should allow market forces to determine land uses quite effectively. Unregulated competitive bidding would bring about the most productive use of each parcel, and the price paid for the parcel would exactly reflect its usefulness, much as described in Chapter 5. But this does not completely happen for several reasons. One of the reasons is because of **externalities:** the unintended and unaccounted for consequences of one land user upon others. For example, the creation of a shopping center on a site may cause harm to neighbors through increased traffic delays, noise, increased storm runoff across neighboring land, "light pollution," or other visual or environmental deterioration. Another problem that arises is that buyers of property suffer from incomplete information. Once a structure is built it is very difficult, and often impossible, to determine the sturdiness and safety of the structure, a problem that all too frequently has led to tragic fires or building collapses in places where building regulation is weak. Still another kind of problem that arises in a totally private land market is locational monopoly. For example, when land is needed for a road, certain specific parcels are required, for which there is no substitute. The owner of these critical parcels, in effect, has a monopoly on the supply and can extract unreasonable prices from other tax-paying citizens.

In summary, an unregulated private market for land would be fraught with problems resulting from externalities, from incomplete information, and from locational monopolies. These kinds of problems have persuaded most persons that government must intervene in the use of land.

In this chapter we survey three basic powers of government that limit private property use and affect property value. We first discuss the government's right to regulate land use and set minimum standards for safe construction through its broad police powers. Second, we look at the power of government to acquire private property for the benefit of the public using its power of eminent domain. Finally, we examine the right of government to tax property. All of these government interventions can have profound effects on the value of private property.

The Power of Government to Regulate Land Use

The authority of state and local governments to regulate land use and enforce development and construction standards is vested in its police power.[1] This power establishes the right of government to enact laws to protect the general health, welfare, and safety of the public. In the United States, almost all county and city governments use some combination of planning, **zoning,** building codes, and other restrictions to regulate the use of land and set development and construction standards within their jurisdiction.

> ✓ **Concept Check**
>
> **4.1** What constitutional power enables state and local government to regulate land use?

Monopolies, Externalities, and Other Market Distortions

Monopolies. Monopolies misallocate resources by overpricing goods and services and producing less output than is efficient from society's view. Monopoly pricing in the real estate market by owners is less common than often perceived since most land uses have

---

1. Police power is largely reserved to the states, and derives from the Constitution and the U.S. Supreme Court interpretations of it.

near-substitutes that effectively offer competition. However, city water, sewer, and other utility systems represent natural monopolies because it would be costly to establish competition. Competitive systems would require the duplication of costly capital investments (e.g., electrical grid, water distribution, and gas distribution lines). It is generally in the interest of the community to either regulate these services as monopolies or own them outright.

Another form of potential land monopoly is the holdout. For example, land must be acquired for most large public projects such as roads. When assembly of multiple private parcels is involved, one or more landholders can "hold hostage" the entire project by refusing to sell at a reasonable price, thus extracting wealth from other citizens. Thus, it is deemed necessary for governments to be able to take land from private owners at a reasonable price. This power of eminent domain is discussed below.

✓ **Concept Check**

4.2   Name two examples of monopoly affecting local land use.

Externalities.   Externalities can be either positive or negative. Examples of positive externalities are the beneficial effects on property value from exceptional vistas, nearby parks and recreation facilities, quality neighborhood schools, quality architecture in the neighborhood, attractive commercial areas, well-kept landscapes, and so forth. In a strictly private market the producers of these community benefits may be unrewarded for their value to other property owners, and therefore provide less than is desirable from the viewpoint of the community as a whole. Underprovision of positive externalities is an argument for government intervention to encourage more. Negative externalities, unaccounted negative effects of a land use on the value of surrounding properties, have the opposite result. The perpetrator of the externalities has too little incentive to curtail the offending activity, and produces an excess from the perspective of the community as a whole. This overproduction of negative externalities is an argument for government intervention to reduce their output.

There are many examples of *negative* externalities in land use: A factory may spew smoke or other emissions on surrounding properties; shopping centers and other businesses frequently generate a wide range of externalities, as noted above; building additional housing units in an area often brings increased traffic congestion, crowding of schools, and hastening of the disappearance of natural areas; public assistance facilities such as homeless shelters are regarded apprehensively by neighbors; increased neighborhood crime can result from poorly managed low-income apartments; and student housing may foster excessive cars and loud parties, producing unwanted noise for neighbors. While each of these land uses produces a good or service that benefits some, the property values of others may be diminished. In an unregulated private market the "victims" of these effects are likely to have no voice in the builder's or developer's decisions, no way to call the "perpetrator" to account for the damage, and are never "made whole" for the harm they suffer.

Congestion.   Congestion is a pervasive form of externality in urban life. It occurs when an individual uses any system (such as roads) near capacity and slows the performance of the entire system for all users. For example, when drivers enter a congested freeway they are well aware of the delay for themselves, but they usually feel little guilt for incrementally slowing down many other drivers on the freeway. We generally think of congestion in terms of highway traffic, but it can be present in many other services such as parks, social services, the court system, and public schools.

Urban Sprawl.   Externalities are a major argument cited by critics of "urban sprawl." If one defines urban sprawl as development taking place in rural areas well beyond the urban fringe ("leapfrog" development), then the argument is as follows. Such development can enable builders to offer lower prices than buyers can obtain within developed areas, but only because the builder is not bearing the full cost of development. Typically, the cost of extending community services—road improvements, new schools or more school buses, additional utilities, extended police and fire protection—are not accounted for in the prices or property taxes paid by the developers and homebuyers. Thus, the costs are shared by the entire community and, it is argued, other taxpayers must subsidize the leapfrog development at the urban fringe.

The costs and benefits of sprawl and congestion are controversial and require careful thought. There are reasons to doubt that government planning always improves these problems. For example, it is unlikely that planners and officials can accurately anticipate the market and forecast the most efficient locations for future land use. Government regulations may go beyond correcting misallocations, resulting in new misallocations and inequities. Rebuilding utilities and streets and assembling parcels of land for central city redevelopment can be more costly than providing services to suburban development.

Despite the risks of errors in the efforts, it is generally conceded that development must be managed by the community. Providing adequate services such as streets, parks, storm drainage, water, and waste treatment represents substantial investments of the community. The cost of expanding these systems is greatly affected by the degree to which it can be accomplished in an orderly and compact fashion. Therefore, government planning and regulation seem justified to increase market efficiencies.

> ### ✓ Concept Check
>
> **4.3** List three examples of negative externalities in local land use.

Incomplete Information. After a structure is built, it is impractical even for a building expert, let alone others, to fully assess the quality of the construction and the safety hazards it may harbor. This problem was broadly recognized by the early 20th century, and building codes were widely adopted as a remedy. Building codes remain an important protection against safety hazards. In similar fashion, subdivision regulations ensure minimum street design standards for traffic safety, adequate provision for fire hydrants and firefighting access, and other matters of safety and health.

Uncertainty and Value Stability. Homes are the largest single asset of most households, as we noted in Chapter 1. Uncertainty in the value of the home could pose a significant risk. In unregulated real estate markets, homeowners may become apprehensive about possible adverse changes in nearby land uses, and the apprehension alone could adversely affect values. Thus, homeowners may be willing to accept the constraints of land use regulation to reduce the risk of unexpected, harmful changes in surrounding land use. It has been argued that the main motivation for traditional residential zoning was precisely to attain such value stability.

Counterarguments to Land Use Controls. While the arguments presented earlier about market distortions are widely recognized, their acceptance is not universal. The value of zoning, in particular, as a corrective to market distortions has been questioned by many who examine the experience of Houston, Texas, where zoning does not exist. (See Industry Issues 4-1.) There, land use control is largely through private means, including restrictive covenants, easements, and owner associations (all discussed in Chapter 2).

Some critics of land use controls conclude that whatever market distortions exist in land use are outweighed by the detrimental effects of zoning. For zoning may restrict the supply of modestly priced housing. At the same time, excessively low zoning density may contribute to urban sprawl. Further, if a zoning plan conflicts with the natural economic land use pattern, it can cause inefficient distortions in land use. For example, it may force household services such as grocery stores, delicatessens, coffee shops, or hair salons to be excessively distant from residential neighborhoods they serve.

"**Z**oning goes down for third time" read the morning head-line of the *Houston Post* on November 3, 1994. As they had in 1948 and 1962, Houstonians voted once more to remain America's largest city without a zoning ordinance . . . Hispanics and low-income blacks voted overwhelmingly, 58 percent and 71 percent, against a measure touted as the way to "save" their neighbor-hoods. In a low-turnout referendum, only 10 percent of the city's registered voters gave their nod to zoning . . .

Exaggerated Risks

[Zoning] supporters said that homes unpro-tected by zoning risk a loss in property value if a business or apartment locates nearby . . . [but] within Houston are two small, independent cities, Bellaire and West University, with zoning. Between 1970 and 1980 home prices in Bellaire and West University climbed more slowly than in many Houston communities, including those lacking private neighborhood restric-tions against businesses and apartments . . . [Another concern] is that single-family neighborhoods without zoning are likely to be overrun by businesses and apartments. In the Houston Heights, a centuryold neigh-borhood of 300 blocks, only about 5 per-cent of the residential blocks have private restrictions . . . Yet single-family homes occupy almost 86 percent of the lots on interior streets. Businesses take up 7 per-cent; industrial uses, less than 2 percent; apartments, less than 2 percent; churches and schools, 4 percent . . .

The Houston Way

Under the Houston system, heavy industry voluntarily locates on large tracts near rail lines or highways; apartments and stores seek thoroughfares; gas stations vie for busy intersections . . . Businesses that thrive amidst homes often serve strong local demand. "Shade-tree" mechanics appear in low-income neighborhoods to service old cars owners cannot afford to replace. "Mom and pop" grocery stores supply those who have no cars . . . In loca-tions with stable demand for single-family homes, healthy real estate values are likely to prohibit many "noxious" uses—like junk-yards and machine repair shops—that want cheap land. Without realizing it, the home-owners have "zoned out" such uses through their own free choices. As zoning expert Bernard Siegan says, "The most effective of restrictions [is] competition." . . . Even without zoning, homebuyers wanting control over the development of land in their neighborhood have a choice called "deed restrictions." . . . most homes in Houston built since World War II have such renewable restrictions.

The Houston Advantage

Without zoning, Houston ranks consistently as the leader among major American cities for housing affordability. "It's more afford-able here than any other large city in the nation," said University of Houston econo-mist Barton Smith. According to Smith, one reason for this affordability is Houston's lack of zoning. And a federal report in 1991 cited zoning as a leading cause for the shortage of affordable housing in America.

The greatest beneficiaries of Houston's abstention from zoning are not the rich, greedy developers as zoning proponents would claim . . . As one Houston reporter recalls: "Because there were a handful of neighborhoods where there were no signifi-cant barriers to home businesses, the bust [of the 1980s] became an opportunity instead of a devastation. Time and time again I saw the unemployed become entrepreneurs." Time and time again in Houston's Hispanic neighborhoods, entre-preneurs also emerge from homes.

Update

During the housing boom and bust of the last few years, Hous-ton's lack of zoning may have paid new dividends. Some observ-ers, including an economist from the Dallas Federal Reserve, Robert Gilmer, point to the lack of zoning as one reason that Houston largely escaped the housing price shocks experienced elsewhere. The story of Houston's non-zoning continues to evolve. A now famous Ashby high-rise case, a 2007 proposed 23-story apart-ment in a single-family neighborhood has birthed the use of nuisance lawsuits to threaten proposed developments in Houston.

Houston Says No to Zoning

Source: Adapted from an essay by James D. Saltzman, "Houston Says No to Zoning", originally published on FEE.org. This article is licensed under a Creative Commons Attribution 4.0 Inter-national License. https://creativecommons.org/licenses/by/4.0/

Source: Adapted from Gilmer, Robert, "Neither Boom Nor Bust: How Houston's Housing Market Differs from Nation's," *Houston Business: A Per-spective on the Houston Economy,* Federal Reserve Bank of Dallas, Houston Branch, April 2008.

Source: Adapted from Mulvaney, Erin Mulvaney; "lawsuit by luxury condo owners targets senior living facility developer," *Houston Chronicle,* March 18, 2015.

Public Planning for Land Use Control

www.planning.org/

Website of the umbrella organiza-tion for urban planners, the American Planning Association.

The theory of public planning is that directing land uses from a community perspective is the best means of correcting market failure. Incompatible land uses are more efficiently separated; both congestion and environmental effects are more completely incorporated into the land use and development decision process; and buyers are best protected from incomplete information about structural inadequacies, flooding, or other threats.

Comprehensive Planning

A **comprehensive plan** is a general guide to a community's future growth and development. In its most complete form, it involves projecting a community's future population growth; its requirements for water and other natural resources; its physical characteristics (e.g., existing development and soil conditions); its need for public services (e.g., schools and utilities); and its need for various types of land use (e.g., single-family residential and office). Many communities and some states have developed detailed plans to "manage" growth, particularly those communities and states experiencing rapid growth. An enormous variety of material concerning planning methods, resources, and issues is on the Internet. (See Explore the Web.)

Growth management laws at the state level may require local jurisdictions to plan for and meet certain requirements.[2] In their most extensive form these laws may require that:

1. Local jurisdictions (counties and cities) must have comprehensive plans submitted and approved by a state agency.
2. Proposals for large-scale developments must be accompanied by **economic and environmental impact statements** (studies) that analyze the project's effect on surrounding areas. They usually must show that existing infrastructure will handle the added burdens or demonstrate how the burdens will be accommodated. They must also show that the environment will not be significantly degraded.
3. Further development at the local level must be prohibited unless adequate infrastructure, schools, police and fire protection, and social services are in place when development commences (sometimes termed a **concurrency** requirement).
4. Local governments must include an **affordable housing allocation** in their comprehensive plans. This type of requirement means local governments must encourage or mandate a "reasonable and fair" component of new housing construction for lower-income families.

Additionally, state laws may provide for the following techniques to manage growth and new development:

1. Establish **urban service areas.** For these areas, boundaries are delineated around a community within which the local government plans to provide public services and facilities, and beyond which urban development is discouraged or prohibited. Boundaries are usually designed to accommodate growth for 10 to 20 years with the intended result that the community can provide more efficient services and that rural land and natural resources will be protected from development.
2. Establish **extraterritorial jurisdiction.** Some states give local governments the power to plan and control urban development outside their boundaries until annexation can occur.

✓ **Concept Check**

4.4   In a sentence, explain these terms:
1. Economic and environmental impact statement.
2. Concurrency.
3. Affordable housing allocation.
4. Urban service area.
5. Extraterritorial jurisdiction.

---

2. At least 25 U.S. states have enacted laws requiring some form of land use planning at the local government level. Summary of State Land-Use Planning Laws, 2008. (Tampa, FL: Institute for Business and Home Safety). www.disastersafety.org

Challenges in Public Land Use Planning

Public land use planning faces serious challenges on a number of fronts. The entire concept of modern land use planning is extremely new, being the outgrowth of what some have called the revolution in land use controls since about 1970. Thus, planning has little data to work from concerning the true extent of various externalities or the effect of various remedies. Further, the very notion of what constitutes "best practice" in land use remains in evolution.

The "Revolution in Land Use Controls." As late as the mid-1960s public interest in land use controls was minimal. While land use plans existed, virtually none had the force of law. While building codes were well established for public safety, the zoning laws that existed had the limited purpose of protecting the value and stability of single-family subdivisions. Laws protecting the environment or water quality were virtually nonexistent.

This perspective was radically changed with the arrival of the environmental movement of the late 1960s. There was growing recognition of environmental disasters. *The Silent Spring* reported species being eliminated through insecticides.[3] This was followed by such stories as the Love Canal (see Industry Issues 4-3), all of which led to a radical change in the conception of the world at large. Perceptions of the environment as an endless and costless resource were replaced almost overnight by the notion of "spaceship earth," a closed system with limited space, air, water, or other resources.

> ✓ **Concept Check**
>
> **4.5** Explain what launched the "revolution in land use controls" about 1970.

Conflicting Notions of Best Practice. While land use planning gained enormous momentum with the birth of the environmental movement, it was compelled to go forward with only rudimentary intellectual foundation. Even basic notions of what constitutes best practice in land use planning are debated. For example, in basic street layouts, many U.S. planners of recent decades had favored hierarchies built around cul-de-sacs.[4] Many of these same planners favored complete "containment" of nonresidential land uses in designated centers. More recently, however, both of these tenets have been challenged.

A growing number of urban planners believe the social problems plaguing urban areas (e.g., crime, poverty, isolation, congestion) have resulted, at least in part, from incorrect assumptions about the way people want to live and relate to work, recreation, and other people. They contend that neighbors have become isolated because the layout and design of newer neighborhoods and homes do not foster interpersonal contact.

These planners have termed their package of remedies **smart growth.** As summarized on the smart growth website shown in the margin, the components include:

www.smartgrowth.org

A site hosted by a coalition of government and nonprofit organizations regarding "smart growth" and new urbanism.

1. Mixed land uses.
2. Compact building design.
3. Housing opportunities and choices for a range of household types, family size, and incomes.
4. Walkable neighborhoods.
5. Distinctive, attractive communities with a strong sense of place.
6. Preservation of open space, farmland, natural beauty, and critical environmental areas.
7. Reinvestment in and strengthening of existing communities, and balanced regional development.

---

3. Rachel Carson, *The Silent Spring* (Boston: Houghton Mifflin, 1962; Mariner Books, 2002).
4. Reid Ewing, *Best Development Practices* (Chicago: Planners Press, American Planning Association, 1996).

Exhibit 4-1   New Urbanism Integrates Multiple Types of Land Uses and Restores Spaces for Community Life

Traditional   New Urban

© Thinkstock/Superstock RF   Courtesy of Author

8. Provision for a variety of transportation choices.
9. Predictable, fair, and cost-effective development decisions.
10. Citizen and stakeholder participation in development decisions.

www.walkscore.com

An index to indicate the "walkability" of localities in the United States.

A closely related planning movement is **new urbanism.** (See Exhibit 4-1.) It subscribes to the smart growth components but adds certain focuses. It is more explicit in advocating a traditional grid pattern of development designed to give pedestrian life priority over motor vehicles. (This includes narrowed streets with houses close to the streets and garages accessed through alleys.) In general, new urbanism strongly advocates replacement of the car with walking, biking, and mass transportation. There may also be a stronger emphasis on preautomobile urban architectural style. While advocates point to positive results for new urbanism, a careful analysis and judgment as to the efficacy of the movement will take considerably more time, perhaps 10 to 20 years.

✓ Concept Check

4.6   Identify two divergent views in recent planning theory concerning the best practice in street layouts and in the relationship between residential and commercial land use.

Zoning and Other Tools of Public Land Use Control

www.newurbanism.org

A site that explains and advocates new urbanist planning. Rich with references and resources.

The comprehensive plan is a community vision. Its implementation must be through specific land use regulations. As noted before, these regulations grow out of the police powers of government to make laws to assure the health, safety, and welfare of citizens. In this section we look at the conventional kinds of land use regulations, which remain the "workhorses" of land use control. These include building codes, zoning, and subdivision regulations. We also consider the administration of these regulations through appointed commissions and site plan review.

Building Codes

Building codes were the earliest use of police power to regulate land use. By the turn of the 20th century it was well accepted that, in the urban environment, design and materials of structures were an important concern for public safety. Several mass urban fires had made this clear. Most famous was the Chicago fire of 1871, which destroyed about one-third of the value of the city and left some 100,000 persons homeless.

Modern building codes set standards for numerous aspects of construction. Specifications for fire safety are paramount. Minimum specifications for structural strength and integrity also are important. Structural standards have continued to be elevated in recent years in coastal states due to the devastating sequence of hurricanes beginning with Hurricane Andrew in 1992, which destroyed over 25,000 homes in south Florida and Louisiana, and continuing with the even more destructive effects of Katrina and other hurricanes in the beginning of the new century.

Building codes also address standards for safety, health, and sanitation. They require designs of stairways, elevators, and other aspects of the structure to be safe for normal use, and they require water pipes, fixtures, and sanitary plumbing to meet minimum requirements of integrity and durability. Similarly, codes set standards for ventilating and air-conditioning systems to maintain healthy air quality and energy efficiency. Because of the need for standardization in construction to control costs, building codes generally have been applied at the state, and even regional level (such as the Southern Standard Building Code adopted in many states of the South), though local areas sometimes exercise the right to impose still stricter standards.

Building codes respond to changing technology and to changing priorities of society. The most recent trend is to incorporate "green" standards for energy efficiency and sustainability. (See Industry Issues 23-3.) For example, the state of California has adopted statewide energy efficiency standards for all types of buildings, and numerous local governments around the nation have taken similar actions. In addition, many state and local governments have committed to making all new or rehabilitated government buildings "green."

www.usgbc.org

The U.S. Green Building Council is the umbrella organization for creating and promulgating "green" building standards. This organization created the Leadership in Energy and Environmental Design (LEED) rating system.

Zoning

Zoning ordinances have been the main approach to land use regulation in the United States since the 1920s. A zoning ordinance contains several important elements:

1. A land use classification list, with such categories as single family residential, multi-family residential, commercial, and industrial. Each of these categories is subdivided into multiple subcategories according to local needs. For example, single-family classifications are differentiated by minimum lot size, while multifamily classifications are differentiated by maximum residential units per acre.
2. A map showing the zoning classification of all areas within the municipality or county involved.
3. Minimum front, rear, and side setback requirements from the boundaries of a lot.
4. Building bulk limits, including size, height, "footprint," and placement on the lot. (For office buildings, maximum floor/area ratios often limit the floor space per square foot of lot.)
5. Minimum lot dimensions (depth and width).
6. Provision for special use districts (discussed below).
7. A zoning board or commission appointed to oversee the administration of the ordinance and to make recommendations regarding rezoning requests or proposed changes in the ordinance offered by the zoning and planning staff.
8. A zoning board of adjustment appointed to review hardship cases.

Historically, there has been a definite hierarchy in the classifications of zoning with the lowest density single family being at the top. Early approaches to zoning used *cumulative* classifications of land uses where the highest order classification (single-family homes) could be placed in any lower order, but not vice versa. However, this is a questionable approach to zoning since it permits, for example, residential areas adjacent to oil refineries or chemical plants with potentially dire consequences in case of fire or explosion. Thus, the trend in more modern practice has been to require *exclusive* categories where there is complete separation between at least some of the classifications.

A number of land uses are classified in the zoning ordinance but have no predesignated locations on the zoning map. Instead, a landowner must petition to be granted one of these *special use* classifications, and the petition is then considered in a public hearing. If the site meets the appropriate criteria stated in the ordinance the petition is granted. These special uses may include service stations, churches, hospitals, private schools, cemeteries, or clubs.

Usually when a zoning ordinance is revised some existing land uses then fall outside the new zoning classification. These are called **nonconforming uses;** they may continue to exist, despite the change in classification, provided that they never are discontinued (temporary interruption is tolerated) and the structure is not destroyed or substantially altered. (It can be repaired but not expanded or replaced.) Some courts will allow certain nonconforming uses to be "amortized" away over a period of years. For example, a zoning authority can require a billboard that is a nonconforming use to be discontinued after, say, five years.

A zoning ordinance must provide some relief mechanism for cases where the regulations impose exceptional hardship and loss of value. This relief is called a **variance.** For example if setback requirements render a lot too narrow to build on, it may be reasonable to waive a setback line by a small amount in order to make the land usable and restore its value. Variances are to be used only if three conditions are met:

1. The owner must show true hardship in terms of inability to use the lot as zoned.
2. The condition must be unique to the lot and not a condition common to other parcels in the vicinity.
3. The variance must not materially change the character of the neighborhood.

Most local ordinances are now available online. It is very informative to locate and browse the ordinance for your local government. (See the Web reference in the margin.)

> **www.municode.com**
>
> Most zoning ordinances are online. For example, at this website are the zoning codes for hundreds of local governments throughout the United States.

✓ **Concept Check**

4.7 List three aspects of land use typically restricted by zoning, in addition to the type of land use.

Legality of Zoning.   As mentioned earlier, zoning is an exercise of police power—the right of a government to enact and enforce laws to protect the health and welfare of its citizens. Increasingly, numerous and severe land use regulations have led some observers to contend that land is becoming more of a public resource than private property. For this reason, both zoning laws and their specific applications have been attacked as confiscation of property without compensation—an act prohibited by the U.S. Constitution (see Industry Issues 4-2).

Although some zoning laws have been declared unconstitutional, most have survived legal challenge, and zoning as a general practice has been legally acceptable in the United States for close to a century. The general thrust of court decisions is that zoning is constitutional and will be upheld if the ordinance is reasonable, is based on a comprehensive plan, and provides for all types of housing. Courts have overturned zoning ordinances that tend to exclude lower income groups by large lot size, or that do not adequately provide low- and moderate-income housing. This is termed **exclusionary zoning.**

The Ambler Realty Company intended to sell the 68-acre tract of land it owned in the village of Euclid, Ohio, to an industrial developer. However, in 1922 Euclid enacted a land use–zoning ordinance that set aside part of this tract for residential development, ostensibly reducing its value by 75 percent. Ambler Realty sued Euclid, claiming the ordinance resulted in a "taking" of Ambler's property without payment of just compensation, as prescribed by the U.S. Constitution.

The District Court agreed with Ambler Realty, but in a landmark decision, the U.S. Supreme Court ruled that Euclid was not taking any part of the tract for a public purpose and that this ordinance was a legitimate use of the village's police power to control land uses.

This Supreme Court ruling has withstood the test of time in that it has served as an important precedent in virtually all subsequent disputes involving the question of a "taking." The ruling legitimized both land use controls as a police power exercise and the separation of land uses into districts and zones for land use control.

Source: *Village of Euclid, Ohio v. Ambler Realty Co.* 272 U.S. 365, 47S. Ct. 1/4, 71 L. Ed. 303 (1926).

The Landmark Decision on the Legality of Land Use and Zoning Regulations

---

✓ Concept Check

4.8   List three requirements of the courts for zoning to be a legitimate use of police powers.

Subdivision Regulations

Along with zoning, virtually every local government has adopted regulations that govern the creation of subdivisions. The purpose of these regulations is to promote the proper arrangement and coordination of streets in relation to existing or planned streets and to assure coordination of subdivisions with the local comprehensive plan. The regulations provide guidelines for the layout of lots, for adequate and convenient provision of open spaces, utilities, recreation, and access for service and emergency vehicles. The standards imposed by the ordinance also assure adequate provision of water, drainage, sewer, and other sanitary facilities.

The developer who is subdividing will present a preliminary subdivision site plan in a public meeting where local officials, including utility officials, emergency service officials, school officials, transportation officials, and others have the opportunity to comment on the plan and challenge any aspects of it that concern them. One very practical reason for the review by a variety of officials is that roadways and utilities in subdivisions usually are **dedicated** to the local government, meaning that they become the property and responsibility of the local government to maintain.

Zoning and Planning Administration

Property owners frequently wish to have the zoning classification of their property changed. A developer, for example, may want to construct a residential subdivision on land currently zoned for agriculture, or an apartment building owner may wish to increase the allowed density of the project to accommodate more units. These requests will go before a special advisory board commonly called the planning or zoning commission. This commission is appointed by the elected governing body to oversee implementation of the zoning or subdivision ordinance. The commission will review requested changes and forward a recommendation to the elected governing body for final action.

In considering rezoning requests, they will use the following criteria:

1. Will the new zoning be compatible with the comprehensive plan?
2. Should the comprehensive plan be modified?
3. What effect will the new zoning have on surrounding land uses and on the larger community?

A request for rezoning is more likely to be approved if it is consistent with the comprehensive plan. If the request is inconsistent with the plan, the question becomes whether the comprehensive plan should be modified, and the planning and zoning commission, with staff, must turn to the third question: How does the proposal affect the larger community? They will form a recommendation on the zoning and any related change on the comprehensive plan. Both of these will go before the elected governing body for final action.

A second appointed board for administration of the zoning ordinance is the **board of adjustment.** This board is charged with reviewing petitions for variances. They must determine whether the three conditions for relief, noted above, are met. If so, they will grant the variance. Unlike the zoning and planning commission that makes recommendations to the elected governing body, determinations of the board of adjustment are final, and can only be appealed in court.

Site Plan Review.   Another advisory group is a site plan review board. Site plans arise both from proposed subdivisions and from proposed apartment, commercial, and industrial projects. As noted above with subdivision regulation, site plan reviews necessarily involve a diversity of views, interests, and voices, including the general public. It is a particularly complex and uncertain process from a developer's point of view, as discussed at length in Chapter 23. It typically is an open and informal process, thus leaving ample room for the unexpected, for misunderstandings and clashes in views. Developers often point to the site plan review process as one of the riskiest points in the development process.

✓ **Concept Check**

4.9   In a sentence, define each of these:
1. Nonconforming use.
2. Variance.
3. Exclusionary zoning.

Modern Tools of Land Use Control

Planned Unit Developments.   Traditional zoning has been criticized on several fronts. It has been accused of being oblivious to the effect of land use on traffic and environmental systems. At the same time it is accused of being far too rigid, forcing uniform types and density of development where variation would be much better. The planned unit development concept has emerged to address these concerns. In the **planned unit development (PUD),** traditional requirements, such as setback requirements (distance of buildings from lot lines) and apartment densities (units per acre), are allowed to vary in some areas in exchange for enhancements such as larger areas of open space and nature preservation, public facilities, and neighborhood strengthening designs. PUDs allow residential density to range from singlefamily detached to multifamily, and often include supporting commercial development. The developer of a property of qualified size can draw up a detailed site plan for the property and present it to authorities. If it is accepted, the plan replaces conventional zoning and becomes binding on the developer.

www.law.cornell.edu/ wex/land_use

Website for land use law.

✓ **Concept Check**

4.10   Identify four differences between a PUD and traditional zoning.

The role of land planners is to create actual site plans for subdivision development. In that capacity they must account for the characteristics of the site, including topography, soils, drainage and floodplains, possible environmental hazards, possible endangered species, and other natural factors. In addition, they must have a thorough knowledge of all land use and development regulations affecting the site. Finally, they must understand the requirements of the target market to which the final product is being directed as well as the goals, schedule, and budget requirements of the client. They must be able to integrate the character of the site, the pertinent regulatory guidelines and constraints, and the demands of the market into a creative and attractive site solution—and still fit the time and budgetary requirements of the client. Further, the planner often will need to represent the client in meetings with public officials, lenders, and others.

Usually working as a private consultant, the land planner commonly has a civil engineering, urban planning, or landscape architecture degree, but not always. Specific tools of value to the site planner include a strong capacity in geographic information systems, computer-aided design and drafting (CADD), and presentation graphics software.

Land Planner

Performance Standards.   Traditional zoning fails to address concerns for urban systems such as traffic, watershed, green space, air quality, or other aspects of the environment. A **performance standard** can fill this void. For example, storm runoff can be controlled by requiring that runoff from a parcel of land be no greater after development than before. Tree canopy can be preserved by requiring permits to remove trees of a certain size or character. Local emission and noise limits can be adopted for industrial and commercial activity. Further, traffic generation limits can be made a part of the development permission process. An important attraction of performance standards is their ability to offer a more flexible substitute to the traditional separation of land uses. Thus, rather than prohibiting industrial use in a commercial area or commercial use in a residential area, the use may be allowed if it meets acceptable performance standards.

www.realtor.org/field-guides/field-guide-to-development-impact-fees

Extensive references and material on impact fees.

www.impactfees.com

Reports surveys on impact fee usage.

www.epa.gov/epahome/state.htm

An overview of all major U.S. environmental laws.

formbasedcodes.org

Form-based Codes Institute examines videos and slide presentations under "Resources."

Impact Fees.   The primary means that economists advocate to "internalize" externalities is by charging compensating fees. Thus, if development imposes externality costs on the community at large, the developer should pay an **impact fee** commensurate with the externalities. This concept is growing in acceptance and a wide range of development impact fees can be found. Whether an impact fee improves economic efficiency depends on the size of the fee relative to the externality being addressed. Unfortunately, there generally has been little attempt to measure the externality involved. Rather, local governments appear to have treated impact fees primarily as a source of revenue.

Form-based Zoning Codes.   The most recent approach to land use control completely redefines zoning. Rather than creating a map by segregation of land uses—single family, apartments, retail, office—**form-based zoning** creates a map by segregation of building shapes. Several different models—packages of building designs and street/public space designs—are formulated. A sequence of these models will range from low-density semi-rural (large blocks, two-lane roads, large lots, casual parking, small free-standing structures with pitched roofs, large setbacks, mixed tree clusters, etc.), to high-density central urban (small blocks, multilane streets, small lots, zero setbacks, structured parking, high-rise buildings, aligned trees, and vegetation, etc.). Each model will extensively prescribe aspects of building character such as range in number of floors, minimum of street-side windows and entrances, other façade and roof characteristics, parking arrangements, etc. Similarly, each model will prescribe block size, street design, open spaces, and other public features. These models largely displace separation by type of use, with only a few broad use classifications remaining. Uses within a given form-based model will be limited simply by the features of the model rather than by explicit restrictions. Thus, most office activities or retail activities, for example, would be free to locate in any area where the "model" works for the business. As a result, each area would contain a mixture of uses that is natural to the area's model.

Advocates of form-based zoning share many goals with neo-traditional or "new urban" planning. Design of the form-based models places high priority on walkability, mixed use, developing a sense of place, sustainability, open spaces, subordination of vehicle traffic, etc. Interest in form-based zoning has grown explosively in the last decade, and many local planning agencies now are experimenting with it. Googling "form-based zoning" will reveal a large and growing number of websites and examples. A good place to begin exploring the approach is the website shown in the margin: Form-Based Code Institute.

Environmental Hazards

State and federal control of land uses has increased greatly over the past 40 years due in part to an increased awareness of environmental hazards. The following is a partial list of federal environmental control laws:

Clean Air Act, 1970	Gave EPA authority to set National Ambient Air Quality Standards.
Clean Water Act, 1972–1977	Gave EPA authority to control discharges of pollutants into waters of the United States.
Safe Drinking Water Act, 1974	Gave EPA authority to implement quality standards for drinking water.
Resource Conservation and Recovery Act, 1976	Gave EPA "cradle-to-grave" authority over handling of hazardous waste.
Toxic Substances Control Act, 1976	Gave EPA authority to monitor and control 75,000 industrial chemicals, and new ones that are created.
Comprehensive Environmental Response Compensation and Liability Act (CERCLA), 1980	Established the "Superfund," and gave EPA authority to clean up abandoned or uncontrolled toxic sites.

Environmental hazards are regulated by federal, state, and local agencies such as the federal Environmental Protection Agency (EPA), the U.S. Department of Housing and Urban Development, state environmental protection agencies, and local departments of environmental quality. In addition, oversight of these regulations falls partly to local building and fire departments, property lenders, and loan insurers.

Among the most far-reaching environmental acts has been the Clean Water Act, which, among other effects, has imposed permitting requirements on millions of acres of wetlands. This highly contested effect has reached the U.S. Supreme Court. (See Industry Issues 4-4.)

The Clean Water Act, CERCLA, and the Endangered Species Act (see Industry Issues 2-1) all reflect the modern perception of the planet as "spaceship earth." But this new view does not displace the spirit of entrepreneurship. See Industry Issues 4-5.

Types of Hazardous Materials

Several types of hazardous materials can be present in properties, and these materials are a major concern of property owners, prospective buyers, lenders, and the public. These hazardous materials, sometimes termed **toxic waste,** can include: asbestos, fiberglass, leaking underground storage tanks (LUSTs), radon, and the most recent culprit, mold.

n 1978 President Carter declared a state of emergency for the Love Canal area of Niagara Falls, New York, when toxic materials migrated to the surface through contaminated groundwater. The scope of the problem and its national attention ultimately led to the passage of the Comprehensive Environmental Response, Compensation, and Liability Act (CERCLA) in 1980. The act established the "Superfund" to finance emergency responses and cleanups of abandoned and unregulated waste dumps.

William Love began excavation on a canal in 1892 to divert water from the Niagara River for a hydroelectric power project that was never completed. Beginning in 1942 the partially completed canal was used as a landfill by Hooker Chemicals and Plastics (now Occidental Chemical Corporation) for the disposal of over 21,000 tons of various chemicals. Dumping ceased in 1952,

and in 1953 the landfill was covered and deeded to the Niagara Falls Board of Education. Subsequently, the area near the covered landfill was extensively developed, including the construction of an elementary school and numerous homes. Problems with odors and residues, first reported in the 1960s, increased during the 1970s as the water table rose, bringing contaminated groundwater to the surface. In 1976 chemicals were found to be leaking at the site.

More than 900 families were evacuated from affected areas and over 200 homes closest to the canal demolished. In 1988 some areas near the site were declared habitable for residential use. Since 1995 Occidental Corp. has paid over $250-million to the state and federal governments to reimburse cleanup costs and natural resource damages, and to property owners. In compliance with a 1991 order from the U.S. Environmental Protection Agency, the

company is required to manage and prevent the spread of pollution from the site.

Update

In 2004 the Love Canal site was released from the Superfund list. Except for a fenced-in, 70-acre containment area, the entire site was declared clean, at a cost approaching $400 million, and returned to private ownership for a combination of residential and light industrial uses.

Love Canal and the Establishment of the EPA Superfund

Source: Data from U.S. Environmental Protection Agency. Fact Sheet, EPA ID # NYD000606947; *New York Times,* July 20, 1999, section B, p. 7.

Implications for Real Estate Investors

Purchasers, owners, and lenders must be aware of potential environmental hazards in real estate. To protect themselves, both legally and economically, prospective buyers and lenders should require environmental risk assessments from qualified environmental consultants. Also, buyers of new properties should require confirmation from the developer that there are no toxic wastes that could be harmful to the property.

The initial standard environmental assessment is known as a *Phase I EVA* (Environmental Value Assessment). It is based largely on a sampling of air and water sources, a search of property records, and a visual inspection of the property. It determines whether there is a reasonable basis to suspect the presence of an environmental risk in the use of the property.[5] If evidence of toxicity is found, more invasive and costly studies will be necessary.

This report, together with written representation from the developer or current owner, constitutes a set of documentary protections for investors. They are particularly necessary because liability insurance to cover toxic wastes cannot be purchased. The risk can only be minimized or shifted to the seller through documentary provisions.

www.epa.gov/asbestos/

U.S. Environmental Protection Agency coverage of asbestos issues.

www.epa.gov/ust

U.S. Environmental Protection Agency coverage of leaking underground storage tanks (LUSTs)

www.epa.gov/radon

Consumer guide to radon.

www.construction.com/mold/

Provides current events concerning mold affecting buildings.

The Government's Power of Eminent Domain

Eminent domain is the right of government to acquire private property, without the owner's consent, for public use in exchange for just compensation. The legal procedure involved is called **condemnation.** The right of eminent domain arises from practical necessity of governments to provide basic public services. Federal, state, and local government agencies generally use their rights to take title to real property, or portions of real property, when constructing highways, schools, fire and police stations, and other public facilities.[6]

5. Albert R. Wilson, "The Environmental Opinion: Basis for an Impaired Value Opinion," *Appraisal Journal* 62, no. 3 (July 1994), pp. 410–23.

6. While the Fifth Amendment addresses the federal government's right to "take" private property with just compensation and due process, the right is also affirmed to states by the Fourteenth Amendment and confirmed in state constitutions and statutes. Governments may also delegate their power of eminent domain to nongovernmental agencies such as public utilities.

By the late 1960s United States waterways had reached devastating levels of pollution. Symbolic of the plight was that the Cuyahoga River in Cleveland had caught fire multiple times up to 1969. In 1972 the Congress drastically overhauled a 1948 law regulating the waters of the United States in order to restore them from the unbridled pollution. The concept for this "Clean Water Act" (CWA) is that all discharges into the "waters of the United States" are unlawful, unless specifically authorized by a permit, the act's primary enforcement tool. The act allows for a wide range of punishments, civil, criminal and administrative, for violations.

The Swampy Issue of Wetlands Regulation

The effect of the CWA has been, in many respects, one of the great success stories of modern times. But at the heart of the Clean Water Act is a difficult question: what are the waters of the United States? This issue was brought to center stage with a complicated decision by the United States Supreme Court in Rapanos/Carabell (2006). This case had two separate Michigan developers challenging whether their wetlands were appropriately classified as waters of the United States, and therefore subject to regulation. The views on this classification issue can differ radically. A conservative extreme would be that unless there is a continuous surface flow from wetlands to navigable waters the wetlands are not part of the "waters of the United States." The opposite extreme view is that any wetlands–or sometimes wetlands–feeding even occasionally into flowing steams, hence into navigable waters are "waters of the United States," and subject to the law. The difference in the extent of regulated land is enormous.

The range for regulatory debate lies somewhere between these extreme notions, but where? The search continues for clarification. In the years following the Rapanos decision the Environmental Protection Agency (EPA) and the U.S. Army Corps of

© Jeff Ripple

© John Moran

Engineers jointly initiated thousands of scientific investigations, exhaustive legal preparation and public comment leading to a new Clean Water Rule that became effective in August of 2015, but was soon blocked by a federal court pending further review.

The new Clean Water Rule was intended to create a classification system that minimized the wetlands situations requiring costly and time consuming case-specific investigations. But the complexity of the problem frustrates this goal. So the efforts and debates continue, and vast numbers of shallow depressions with no natural drainage remain in regulatory limbo throughout the United States. The Congress has seen several laws proposed to address the issue, but the future of the problem remains unclear.

Principal sources: EPA website, U.S. Fish and Wildlife Service website, Various reports of the Congressional Research Service on water quality issues, including R30030, R43455, R43867.

As awareness of wetlands and natural habitats grows, so does the challenge of developing land having both a valuable location and environmental sensitivity. There seem to be three unwelcome options for the developer when business location and environment clash:

- Give up and move on, sacrificing the benefits of development for all concerned in favor of environmental preservation.
- Develop so as to preserve the sensitive areas, but often at great cost and with limited success in preservation, and with continuing maintenance cost and liability.
- Offset the damage to the sensitive land by restoring damaged habitat elsewhere, at the risk of failure due to lack of experience and expertise, or uncontrolled conditions like weather, and, again, with continuing maintenance cost and liability.

Enter the mitigation banking entrepreneur. This is one who, anticipating the need for mitigation, has prepared to act in lieu of the developer. The banker will prepare for "business" through these steps:

1. Acquire a large tract of environmentally damaged land as a mitigation bank.
2. Negotiate agreement with regulators to allow mitigation of the bank land as replacement for sensitive land damaged through development elsewhere. Create a permanent conservation easement for the bank lands.
3. Assemble the resources and expertise to successfully mitigate the bank lands.
4. On terms of exchange determined by the regulators, offer mitigation on behalf of developers through mitigation of the bank lands. This may include transfer to the bank lands of protected species such as gopher tortoises and scrub jays or other birds.
5. Charge developers a fee per unit of mitigation that is sufficient to

accomplish the mitigation and generate a profit.

6. In due time, as the bank land is completely mitigated, either gift it to the government or sell it to someone who wants to own large tracts of conservation land for personal recreation, pride, or conscience.

The mitigation bank typically will be strictly conservation land, allowing only improvements essential for the maintenance of the habitat or wetlands that have been restored. Since habitats and wetlands grow in success with size, the use of a large mitigation bank to replace smaller, isolated wetlands and habitats is a compelling ecological advantage offered by the creation of mitigation land banks.

Mitigation Land Banking: Entrepreneurship Meets "Spaceship Earth"

Public Use or Public Purpose

recenter.tamu.edu

The website of the Texas A&M Real Estate Center, provides numerous articles about the effect of mold on real estate. Search under "mold."

Courts have interpreted the term *public use* broadly, and successful challenges to whether a taking is for a valid public use are rare.[7] Contrary to much recent public discussion, the exercise of eminent domain is not limited to narrow **public use** (public facilities only). Rather, it has long been recognized by the U.S. Supreme Court as applicable to broader **public purpose** (any purpose of clear public benefit). Thus, property intended for civic and convention centers, cultural centers, trade facilities, hotels, and sports facilities may be eligible, even if it ends up in new private ownership (sometimes called a "private-to-private" taking). In a 1954 ruling, the U.S. Supreme Court upheld the use of condemnation for private-to-private takings to remove community blight.[8] The Michigan Supreme Court later ruled (1981) that the government's power of eminent domain could be used to acquire property to revitalize the manufacturing facilities of the General Motors Corporation on the theory that it provided substantial economic benefit to the public.[9] These cases seem to open the door to a considerable array of arguable uses and apparent abuses as local governments seek to replace low-value land uses with higher-value uses producing greater tax revenue.[10]

7. Most successful challenges to the government's exercise of its eminent domain rights occur due to technical violations (e.g., improper notification).

8. See *Berman v. Parker,* 348 U.S. 26, 75S. Ct. 98, 99 L. Ed. 27 (1954). This case also was important in affirming the power through eminent domain to take property from one private owner and convey it to another private owner for "public purpose."

9. See *Poletown Neighborhood Council v. City of Detroit,* 410 Mich. 616, 304N.W. 2d 455 (1981).

10. The 1981 *Poletown* decision was overturned in 2004 by the Michigan Supreme Court. The court found that the Michigan Constitution required a narrow, traditional interpretation of "public use." See *County of Wayne v. Edward Hathcock,* 684N.W. 2nd 765 (Mich. 2004).

Using the principles of biology and chemistry, environmental engineers develop methods to solve problems related to the environment. They are involved in water and air pollution control, recycling, waste disposal, and public health issues. Environmental engineers conduct hazardous-waste management studies, evaluate the significance of the hazard, offer analysis on

Environmental Engineer

treatment and containment, and develop regulations to prevent mishaps. They design municipal sewage and industrial wastewater systems. They analyze scientific data, research controversial projects, and perform quality-control checks.

Environmental engineers are concerned with local and worldwide environmental issues. They study and attempt to minimize the effects of acid rain, global warming, automobile emissions, and ozone depletion. They also are involved in the protection of wildlife.

Many environmental engineers work as consultants, helping their clients comply with regulations and cleanup of hazardous sites, including brownfields, which are abandoned urban or industrial sites that may contain environmental hazards.

More than one-third work in engineering and management services and another third are employed in federal, state, and local government agencies. Most of the rest work in various manufacturing industries.

---

web.law.duke.edu/ voices/kelo#

A video interview with Susette Kelo regarding the historic case: Kelo v. City of New London

Controversy over abuse of the "public purpose" argument was inflamed further in 2005 by the decision of the U.S. Supreme Court in *Kelo v. New London, Connecticut*. The Court upheld the right of the city to condemn the well-kept residences of Kelo and six other homeowners in order to create a mixed-use complex supporting the new global research facility of the drug giant, Pfizer, next door. The Court determined that the city's goal of economic redevelopment was within the constitutional meaning of "public use." However, the Court left open that laws could be enacted to restrict such use of eminent domain. Congress and many states reacted immediately. The U.S. House of Representatives passed a bill (376 to 38) to withhold economic development funds from any government taking private property and conveying it to another private owner, though the bill did not survive. Some 44 states also took up legislation or constitutional amendments restricting the use of eminent domain in urban renewal. Just over half of them finally enacted some restrictions. (See Industry Issues 4-6.)

> ✓ **Concept Check**
>
> **4.11** Explain what change has occurred since 1950 in the use of eminent domain.

Just Compensation

Just compensation is the market value of the property, if completely taken, or the total value of all financial loss if partially taken. The value of a property is based on its highest and best use at the time it is condemned, not necessarily its current use. Just compensation is the amount that restores the property owner to a financial position equivalent to that existing before the property was taken. This compensation includes not only the value of the property taken but also the diminution in value of any property remaining.

Inverse Condemnation and Regulatory Takings

At times, government activities may result in "taking" a portion of an owner's property rights without using condemnation. New public projects or regulatory actions may substantially restrict the use of private property and diminish its value. In these cases, a property

On June 23, 2005, the U.S. Supreme Court refused to overturn the case of *Susette Kelo v. City of New London, Connecticut,* thus affirming that a local government engaged in a definite plan of revitalization could take property through eminent domain even in the absence of "blight."

New London had been crumbling for decades. It had lost tens of thousands of jobs. Its unemployment rate was twice that of the rest of the state. But in the late 1990s, it saw a ray of hope when the Navy closed its harbor facilities and turned over 32 acres of land to the city. At the same time, Pfizer decided to build a $300 million research facility next door to the newly acquired land, and the state pledged $7 million to open the riverfront to the public for the first time, fill in the flood plain, and clean up the area long zoned industrial and plagued with environmental hazards.

The "Little Pink House" of Susette Kelo, before removal (© Jack Sauer/AP Images)

The redevelopment plan designed by the city called for marinas, parks, private office complexes, condominiums, and a hotel. It was approved by the city council and state agencies but ran into trouble when seven of the 90 homeowners on the land, including Susette Kelo, refused to sell. So the city resorted to eminent domain.

Some of the residents lived in houses built by their parents, grandparents, and great-grandparents. Matt Dery gardened the same property that his great-grandmother gardened. Said Dery, "The Constitution does allow the taking of private property for public use, but (private) redevelopment," he argued, "is not a public use." The U.S. Supreme Court disagreed. Writing for the five-member court majority, Justice John Paul Stevens stated, "Promoting development is a traditional and long accepted function of government. Certainly, the city could not take property from one private owner and just transfer it to another." Stevens said the federal Constitution has long been interpreted broadly to allow the taking of private property for all manner of purposes: building railroads, stadiums, and highways, to facilitate mining, and eradicate slums. Stevens did not minimize what he called the hardship on the homeowners in this and similar cases, but he said it is the state legislatures that can limit such takings, not the federal courts.

Initial reaction to the *Kelo* decision was wide and swift in legislative halls, both state and national. However, the hunger of local governments for ways to pursue economic redevelopment seems to have dampened the reaction to *Kelo.* Only half of the 44 states initially reacting finally created enforceable prohibitions against "Kelo-like" takings where unblighted private property is taken and conveyed to another private owner.

While the Kelo decision ignited a political firestorm, it does not seem to have altered the meaning of property rights as has been widely claimed. More accurately, it simply dramatized the direction of court decisions for eminent domain since early in the 20th century. The events leading to *Kelo v. City of New London* reached print in a book by Jeff Benedict, *Little Pink House* (Grand Central Publishing).

How Far Can Eminent Domain Go?: Susette Kelo v. City of New London, Connecticut

Sources: Totenberg, Nina, Morning Edition, June 24, 2005. Nolon, R. John, "The Mighty Myths of Kelo," *Pace Law Faculty Publications* (2007). digitalcommons.pace.edu/lawfaculty/395

---

owner may seek compensation under a concept called inverse condemnation. **Inverse condemnation** is an action, initiated by a property owner against the government, to recover the loss in property value attributed to government activity. Since 1922 an opinion of the U.S. Supreme Court has influenced cases in which the right of compensation for property owners, resulting from zoning and other regulations, has been questioned. In ruling that restrictions on coal mining where surface subsidence could threaten dwellings did not constitute a taking, the Court stated, "The general rule at least is, that while property may be regulated to a certain extent, if regulation goes too far it will be recognized as a taking."[11] This is referred to as a **regulatory taking.** Nevertheless, a 1987 study pointed out that the limitation of property rights by zoning must be severe before the courts grant compensation to property owners. The authors concluded that in eminent domain takings, compensation is almost always expected and required; yet courts usually have refused to compensate owners whose rights have been limited or taken by zoning laws.[12] More recent

11. See *Pennsylvania Coal Company v. Mahon,* 260 U.S. 393, 43S. Ct. 158, 67 L. Ed. 322 (1922).
12. Jerry T. Ferguson and Robert H. Plattner, "Can Property Owners Get Compensation for 'Takings' by Zoning Laws?" *Real Estate Review* 16, no. 4 (Winter 1987), pp. 72–75.

When Does Regulation Become Inverse Condemnation? Lucas v. South Carolina Coastal Council

In June 1992, the U.S. Supreme Court had an opportunity to revisit (the issue of inverse condemnation) in the case of *Lucas v. South Carolina Coastal Council,* 112 S. Ct. 2886 (1992). In that case, developer David Lucas purchased two vacant lots in the Wild Dunes subdivision on the Isle of Palms, a barrier island near Charleston, South Carolina. . . . Between 1957 and 1963, the property was under water. During Hurricane Hugo, the lots were covered by four feet of water.

In July 1988, South Carolina enacted the Beachfront Management Act in response to the requirements of the 1980 amendments to the federal Coastal Zone Management Act. To regulate development, the South Carolina legislature established "baselines" back from the sand dunes. Most construction or rebuilding of damaged structures seaward of the baseline was prohibited by the act. Lucas, whose lots fell between the baseline and the sea, sued the state for "taking" the use and value of his property, claiming that the regulation constituted a compensable taking under the Fifth Amendment to the U.S. Constitution. The trial court awarded Lucas $1.2 million for the lots. On appeal, the state supreme court ruled that Lucas could not be compensated because building on the lots would be hazardous to the public and the environment. Lucas appealed the decision to the U.S. Supreme Court.

On June 29, 1992, the U.S. Supreme Court reversed the decision by the state supreme court and sent the case back to the South Carolina courts to determine whether the state statute deprived Lucas of his Fifth Amendment right to compensation. The Supreme Court held, by a six to three vote, that regulations that deny a property owner all economic use of land—regardless of the public interest in prevention of harm to the public health, safety, and welfare—violate a property owner's right to compensation under the Fifth Amendment. Thus, when government regulations prohibit previously legal land uses that have the effect of extinguishing all economic value of the property, compensation is owed.

Update: Before the state supreme court could rule on the case again, the legislature amended the Beachfront Management Act in a manner that now permitted building on Lucas's lots. The state purchased the lots from Lucas for $1.575 million, subsequently sold them, and large houses now stand on both lots.

Source: Excerpt from the National Conference of State Legislature's *State Legislative Report* 18, no. 9 by C Carolynne, J D White, and Gerald G. Alberts, M.A. (Sept. 1993)

---

decisions by the U.S. Supreme Court, however, have shifted the legal doctrine more toward the side of property owners.[13] (See Industry Issues 4-7.)

✓ Concept Check

4.12   Explain the difference between condemnation and inverse condemnation.

The Power of Government to Tax Real Property

web.law.duke.edu/
voices/lucas

Video of David Lucas telling the story of Lucas v. South Carolina Coastal Council in his own words.

In the previous sections of this chapter, we first discussed the power of government to regulate property use through planning, zoning, and building code administration. We then looked at the government's power to acquire private property for public benefit through eminent domain. In this section, we look at the power of government to tax real property owners.

Real estate taxes are a primary source of revenue for most local goverment entities. This includes counties, cities, school districts, and other special taxing jurisdictions, such as urban service districts, transit authorities, and water management districts. Most property taxes are **ad valorem taxes;** they are applied in relation to the value of the

---

13. See *First English Evangelical Lutheran Church of Glendale v. County of Los Angeles,* 482 U.S. 304, 107 S. Ct. 2378, 96 L. Ed. 2d 250 (1987); *Lucas v. South Carolina Coastal Council,* No. 505 U.S. 1003, 112 S. Ct. 2886 (1992); and *Dolan v. City of Tigard,* 854 P. 2d 437 (Ore. 1993), reversed, 114 S. Ct. 2309 (1994).

property.[14] Ad valorem property taxes are charged to property owners by each taxing jurisdiction in which the property is located. Although ad valorem property tax rates vary, they typically are levied at rates between 1.0 and 4.0 percent of a property's market value.[15]

In general, property tax revenues are used by governments to finance the public services they provide. For example, tax revenues pay for police and fire protection, schools, streets, curbs, sewers, street lighting, parks, and a number of social services. The value of the services provided is capitalized (i.e., captured) in the prices buyers are willing to pay for the properties served. In other words, properties that are occupied by users benefiting from the public services are worth more than they would be without the services. Unfortunately, property taxes may be levied unequally or the revenues misallocated.

Mechanics of the Property Tax

Although property taxes are typically collected through a single county office, several tax jurisdictions within the county where the property is located may levy taxes. A property owner, for example, may pay property taxes to support the budgets of a county, a city, a school district, and a special taxing district (e.g., a downtown redevelopment area). Estimating a particular property owner's total tax liability requires a general understanding of how tax rates are determined.

Determining a Jurisdiction's Budget and Tax Rate

A jurisdiction's **tax rate** depends on both its budget and the value of its **tax base.** The budget of each jurisdiction with taxing authority is determined by estimating all proposed expenditures of each unit within the jurisdiction. For example, police and fire services, judicial services, public works and engineering, various social service departments, and a host of other items may be included in the budget of a single municipality. The jurisdiction's administrative staff reviews and aggregates the budgets of the individual units and then estimates revenues to be obtained from *nontax* sources. These include license fees, inspection fees, garbage removal fees, fines, intergovernmental transfers (e.g., when a city sells fire protection services to the county), and profits from subsidiary operations (e.g., when a city owns a utility company that earns a profit).

The proposed budget, including projected expenditures and nontax revenues, is then presented to the elected governing board of the jurisdiction (e.g., a city council, a county a commission, or a school board) for approval. Since the tax base—which consists of the taxable value of all the jurisdiction's properties—is known, budget approval implies the adoption of a tax rate sufficient to support the budget.

The basic formula for determining the tax rate is

$$R_T = (E_B - I_O) \div (V_T - V_X)$$

where R_T denotes the tax rate; E_B, the budgeted expenditures; I_O, the income from sources other than property tax; V_T, the total assessed value of all properties; and V_X, the value of property exemptions.

As an example, consider a community's budget, which forecasts expenditures for the coming year of $65 million. Tax revenue from nonproperty sources is forecast to be $25 million, and the community contains properties with a total assessed value of $2.5 billion.

14. The Latin term *ad valorem* is defined as "according, or in proportion, to value."

15. Property tax rates vary considerably due to the number and types of taxing authorities, the different costs of services, and the statutory tax policies of each jurisdiction. While all properties in a single jurisdiction are generally taxed at the same rate, some jurisdictions tax properties of different types, classes, and values at different rates.

The total value of properties exempt from the property tax is $500 million. Thus, the tax base is $2.0 billion. The tax rate would be established by the following calculation:

$$R_T = (\$65,000,000 - \$25,000,000) \div (\$2,500,000,000 - \$500,000,000)$$
$$R_T = 0.020, \text{ or } 2.0 \text{ percent}$$

In other words, 2 percent of the taxable value of all properties in the community is required in taxes to pay for the community's expenditures during the coming year. Instead of percentages, however, tax rates are usually stated in **mills,** or dollars per $1,000 of value. Converted to mills, the tax rate, or **millage rate,** for the above community would be 20 mills (i.e., $20 of tax per $1,000 of value).

✓ **Concept Check**

4.13   With the following information, compute the property tax rate for the community. Total budget expenditures: $40 million, Total non-property tax income: $5 million, Total taxable value: $1 billion, Total exemptions: $250 million.

Tax-Exempt Properties

Most communities contain a number of **tax-exempt properties.** These include government-owned properties and others exempted by state law or the state constitution. This category typically includes universities, schools, hospitals, places of worship, and other property of religious organizations. Exempt properties lower the tax base of the community, thus raising the taxes of other property owners.

Homestead and Other Exemptions

Some states allow property owners to deduct a specified amount from their assessed valuations before calculating their property tax bills. The largest of these deductions is the **homestead exemption.** In homestead states, if the property owner occupies a home as the family's principal residence and has claimed residency within the state, the property may be regarded as the family's homestead. In Florida, for example, homeowners may apply for the homestead tax exemption on their principal residences.[16] If they qualify, up to $50,000 will be deducted from the assessed valuation before their taxes are calculated. Many states also allow property tax exemptions for agricultural and historical property, and for disabled persons, veterans, widows, and the blind. The value of all such exemptions must be subtracted from the total assessed value of properties in calculating a community's tax base.

Calculating Tax Liability

The **tax assessor** (or county property appraiser) appraises all taxable properties in a jurisdiction for property tax assessment. The value for taxation, or **assessed value,** is always related to market value; some states specify that the assessed value must be calculated as a certain percentage of market value, such as 50 percent or 80 percent. Today, however, many states require that assessed values be 100 percent of market values as defined in the law or as interpreted by a state agency, such as the department of revenue. For example, assessed value may be defined or interpreted as market value less the costs of making a property

---

16. To qualify for a homestead exemption in Florida, the law requires applicants to have legal and equitable title to the property and be residing on the property as of January 1 of the tax year the exemption is to apply. Proof of residency may be offered in the form of a Florida driver's license, a voter registration, or a vehicle registration and a tag number. For computational details, see dor.myflorida.com/dor/property/taxpayers/exemptions.html.

ready for sale, less a normal real estate commission. Thus, the assessed value, while nominally representing 100 percent of market value, may be perhaps 85 or 90 percent of market value, assuming that the market value is estimated accurately in the property tax valuation. After the property value for tax purposes is determined, the tax rate is multiplied by the **taxable value,** the assessed value less any applicable exemptions, to determine the amount of tax owed.

For example, consider a property appraised for $150,000 in a state that requires tax assessments to be 90 percent of market value. Assume the owner qualifies for a $25,000 homestead exemption. Thus, the taxable value is found to be $110,000.

Market value	$150,000
Assessed value	$135,000 = (0.90 × MV)
Less: Exemptions	−25,000
Taxable value	$110,000

Now assume the taxing authorities in the jurisdiction where the property is located have established their tax rates to be the following:

	Property Tax Calculation	
Taxing Authority	**Millage Rate**	**Taxes Levied**
County	8.58	$ 943.80
City	3.20	$ 352.00
School district	9.86	$1,084.60
Water management district	0.05	$ 5.50
Total	21.69	$2,385.90

The property owner's tax bill would be $110,000 × 0.02169 = $2,385.90, or $110 × 21.69 mills. If the property owner did not qualify for the homestead exemption, the tax liability would be $135,000 × 0.02169 = $2,928.15. Thus, the value of the homestead exemption in terms of property taxes saved is $2,928.15 − $2,385.90 = $542.25, or 0.02169 × $25,000 = $542.25.

A property owner's **effective tax rate** is an important calculation for comparison purposes. It is defined as the amount of tax paid (or owed) divided by the market value of the property. The effective tax rate for this property is 1.59 percent ($2,385.90 ÷ $150,000). Because assessment ratios and millage rates can vary, taxes among properties and among taxing jurisdictions are best compared on an effective rate basis.

✓ **Concept Check**

4.14 Given the following data, compute taxable value: Market value: 100,000. Assessment percentage: 85 percent. Exemption: 10,000.

(1) With a tax rate of 25 mills, what is the amount of the property tax?

(2) What is the effective property tax rate?

Special Assessments

In contrast to ad valorem property taxes levied to finance services that benefit the general community, **special assessments** are levied to pay for specific improvements that benefit a particular group of properties. They are commonly used to finance streets, storm water systems, sidewalks, and other area improvements. Special assessments are applied as pro rata charges, not ad valorem, to cover the cost of the improvement, and are levied directly

In the face of hyper-growth in recent decades, Sunbelt communities confronted a common problem: There was unprecedented demand for new infrastructure. Developers were desperate for streets, utilities, schools, parks and recreational facilities, drainage control, and all the other essentials for new residential neighborhoods. This demand was coupled with growing discontent about local taxation levels, seen by existing residents as subsidies to the new arrivals. Thus were local officials caught in a painful squeeze between obstructing local growth and stirring trouble with voters over high taxes. But some states coaxed a genie out of the bottle that appeared to resolve the dilemma as if by magic. The magic was variously called Community Development Districts (Florida), Municipal Utility Districts (Texas), or Community Service Districts (California).

Community Development Districts: Panacea or Pandora's Box?

These were special taxing districts on steroids. In contrast to more conventional special districts, operated by government officials and constrained to focus on a single narrow function—water management, transportation, waste disposal, and so forth—these new creatures could do it all . . . and on their own. Once sanctioned by the local government, a private developer could create a "CDD" for a proposed development. The CDD would be controlled completely by the developer at the outset, and eventually by a board of properly appointed land owners from within the development. Despite being essentially private (though with public disclosure requirements), the CDD was allowed to issue tax-exempt bonds funded by assessments on the properties involved. There was little that the CDD could not do, as witnessed by The Villages, in Florida, a private retirement community of over 100,000 persons with no municipal government. Rather, it simply consists of a dozen CDDs.

Have CDDs magically solved the growth–high taxes dilemma? To some extent, yes. In Houston, some observers believe that recourse to MUDs, together with Houston's absence of zoning (see Industry Issues 4-1), are the reasons that Houston has always been able to achieve a remarkably low cost of housing. And in places such as The Villages, explosive growth has been accommodated without burdening the host county governments.

But the story has two sides. The freedom and lack of review that developers have enjoyed have allowed them to inflate costs, to their own benefit. Moreover, because numerous CDDs—including The Villages— have built private clubs and golf courses that require costly memberships, the IRS is challenging the use of tax-exempt bonds for nonpublic facilities. But worst of all is the outcome for many a property owner in the recent housing crash. Over one-fourth of the more than 600 CDDs in Florida are reported to have defaulted on bond issues, because there are not enough lot owners to carry the bond debt service. And many hapless owners are learning that CDD assessments impose a lien on their property that is effectively a property tax lien. If they cannot negotiate a solution, they have no protection against the loss of their property through a tax foreclosure. For CDDs, it seems that panacea too often should be spelled "P-A-N-D-O-R-A."

on the properties benefited. For example, the cost of constructing new sidewalks in a subdivision may be shared equally by all the parcels located in the subdivision, or perhaps relative to the size of their lot frontages. In many areas, the use of special assessments has become a popular tool of elected officials to pay for community services and capital improvements while holding down the more politically sensitive tax rates. An important outgrowth of the assessment concept is the community development district, which has been used in most growth states as a means of funding infrastructure for large new residential developments. See Industry Issues 4-8.

Nonpayment of Property Taxes

Foreclosure for nonpayment of property taxes takes several forms among the states. Typically, lists of delinquent taxpayers are published in a newspaper of general circulation, and the delinquents are given a grace period to pay the taxes plus interest and penalties. If the taxes are not paid, the properties eventually may be sold at public auction, with the proceeds first used to pay back taxes.[17]

17. Nearly half of all states use the sale of tax lien certificates to manage defaulted property taxes. The certificates are auctioned to the public at a discount from the face value of the property taxes due. Thus, the taxing authority gets paid immediately. If and when the property owner pays the taxes, the certificate owner is then repaid the face value of the certificate. Failure to pay the taxes finally leads to foreclosure sale after, say, two years. Speculators appear to have made a lucrative business, at times, out of tax certificate purchases, but the risk of nonpayment can be great.

✓ **Concept Check**

4.15 In a sentence, explain each of these terms:
1. Ad valorem.
2. Pro rata.
3. Special assessments.
4. Exemption.

Criticisms of the Property Tax

For local government, the property tax is a very attractive and steady source of revenue, and it is easy to enforce. However, it is subject to three major criticisms: (1) It is regressive; (2) It varies among geographic areas; (3) It is poorly administered.[18]

Property Taxation Is Regressive. This criticism holds that the property tax of lower-income households is higher than that of higher-income households, *as a percentage of their respective incomes.* This is because the value of household residences tends not to increase proportionately with household income. For example, households with $75,000 annual incomes might own houses averaging $225,000 in value (three times the size of their incomes), whereas $500,000 income households might have houses averaging $1 million in value (two times their incomes). Thus, the lower-income households would pay property taxes at a higher rate as a percentage of their respective incomes. However, whether this really constitutes a regressive economic burden on households depends on how the resulting public services are distributed across income levels. "Regressive" property taxes may be fair if, as evidence indicates, lower-income households use more police protection, fire protection, public schools, and public health services.[19]

Property Tax Rates Are Uneven Across Geographic Areas and Property Types. Because of the local nature of the property tax and its administration, the incidence of the tax may vary from property to property, county to county, and state to state. To reduce inconsistency among counties, most states have undertaken programs to equalize the percentage of tax appraisals to market value. In these states, the tax rolls for each county must be submitted to a state agency for testing and approval. A number of states have enacted constitutional provisions or laws to limit property taxes. The most famous of these (because it was the first) was Proposition 13, adopted in 1978 in California, which limited the property tax rate to 1 percent of property values.

Even within an area property tax rates can differ across property types. Two of the most notorious examples are California's Proposition 13 and Florida's Save Our Homes Amendment. Both of these constitutional amendments limit the growth of property taxes for owner-occupied residences. As the years of ownership increase, this can create an increasingly large tax break for the homeowner, which forces other kinds of properties to bear more of the property tax burden. The advantage of this preference to homeowners can grow to be a barrier to selling long-occupied homes.

---

18. A fourth, more general criticism often directed at the property tax is that it imposes an extra tax on real property relative to other investment. To this extent, it creates a bias against improvement of real property. While this argument is not disputed, no single form of tax appears to be a viable, preferred replacement. The esteemed property tax expert, Dick Netzer, has argued for greater reliance on a mix of site taxation, user charges, and taxes on land value increments (at sale). See D. Netzer, *Economics of the Property Tax* (Washington, DC: Brookings Institution, 1966), Chapter 8.

19. D. Netzer, op. cit., pp. 45–62.

The Property Tax Is Poorly Administered.   In many states, county tax assessors or appraisers are elected officials. Special qualifications are not required; therefore the *quality* and *uniformity* of assessing procedures can be less than ideal. The property tax on large properties can be in the hundreds of thousands of dollars, thus giving owners high motivation to seek relief from the taxing authorities. So owners of higher value property may be able to submit more sophisticated appeals, and political supporters and large financial contributors may try to exert considerable influence for favorable appraisals.

To promote education and competence in tax assessing, the International Association of Assessing Officials (IAAO) sponsors courses and other educational programs for members. Many assessors also take courses and seminars sponsored by the leading professional appraisal organizations. And state departments of revenue require that assessors follow prescribed procedures and adhere to minimum appraisal standards.

✓ **Concept Check**

4.16   List three criticisms of the property tax.

Overview of Restrictions on Real Property Ownership

In Chapters 2 through 4 you saw the concept of real property as a bundle of rights. You also saw that the meaning of ownership is complicated by a host of possible "sub-bundles" that can be removed from the ownership rights.

In Exhibit 4-2 we review the range of these possible limitations to ownership. First, we see again that limits on ownership can be from both private claims and government claims. Restrictions on use can come from private deed restrictions, or from the rules of homeowner associations (HOAs) or condo associations. They also can come from the police power of government, exercised through land use controls. In the private realm, use can be separated from ownership. It can be conveyed temporarily through a lease, or permanently, but partially, through easements. An owner's rights also can be fully removed. From the private realm this is possible with a defaulted lien. In the government realm it can occur through eminent domain. Finally, government always has the right to share in the value of property through the power of property taxation.

In short, there never exists "pure" or total ownership of real property. So in considering acquisition of real property the question always is what limits exist on that property, both private and governmental in nature.

Exhibit 4-2   Limits on Real Property Ownership

	Restrictions on Use	Separation of Use or Possession	Complete Removal	Share of Value
Private	Deed Restrictions/HOA or Condo Bylaws	Easements & Leases	Liens (In default)	——
Government	Regulation through Police Power	——	Eminent Domain	Taxation

Summary

This chapter surveys three basic powers of government: its right to regulate land use, its right to take private property for public use, and its right to tax property. The power of federal, state, and local governments to regulate land use through planning, zoning, building codes, and other means is vested in their police power. Communities use these tools to limit the negative effects of market failures such as monopolies, externalities, and incomplete structure information, thus attempting to increase market efficiency and equity.

Planning is the process of developing guidelines for controlling growth and development. Zoning assigns specific permitted uses to individual parcels of land to carry out the comprehensive plan. States and local jurisdictions experiencing rapid growth have adopted a wide variety of measures to manage such growth. Some states pass laws requiring cities and counties to develop comprehensive plans, require economic and environmental impact statements in large development proposals, prohibit new development unless concurrency provisions are met, and require an allocation of affordable housing in new residential developments. Additionally, some states give local communities the right to establish urban service areas, or to plan and control urban development outside their boundaries. Though lawsuits have challenged zoning and growth management from a variety of standpoints, courts generally have upheld its validity when it is reasonable, nonexclusionary, and comprehensive.

Environmental hazards have become an important consideration in land use regulation in recent years. Asbestos, fiberglass, LUSTs, lead paint, radon gas, and mold are some of the most common threats. Real estate investors face large risks from these hazards because owners can be required to clean them up. They must protect themselves by having environmental inspections and by requiring written statements of indemnification from developers and previous owners.

The power of government to acquire private property for public use in exchange for just compensation is referred to as eminent domain. Courts have interpreted the term *public use* broadly to include property taken for a public purpose. Just compensation is the market value of the property. Courts have generally ruled that regulations imposing limits on property rights do not need to be compensated; however, if regulation goes "too far" it will be recognized as a taking and subject to compensation.

The power of government to tax real property owners is a major source of revenue for local governments. The tax is levied on the value of all property in the taxing jurisdiction, less exempt property. A property's value for tax purposes is usually equal to, or a direct function of, its market value.

Key Terms

Ad valorem taxes 89
Affordable housing allocation 74
Assessed value 91
Board of adjustment 80
Comprehensive plan 74
Concurrency 74
Condemnation 86
Dedicated (property) 79
Economic and environmental impact statements 74
Effective tax rate 92
Eminent domain 86
Exclusionary zoning 78
Externalities 70

Extraterritorial jurisdiction 74
Form-based zoning 81
Homestead exemption 91
Impact fee 81
Inverse condemnation 88
Just compensation 88
Millage rate 91
Mills 91
New urbanism 76
Nonconforming use 78
Performance standard 81
Planned unit development (PUD) 80
Public purpose 86

Public use 86
Regulatory taking 88
Smart growth 75
Special assessments 92
Taxable value 92
Tax assessor 91
Tax base 90
Tax-exempt properties 91
Tax rate 90
Toxic waste 82
Urban service area 74
Variance 78
Zoning 70

Test Problems

Answer the following multiple-choice problems:

1. Zoning is an exercise of which type of general limitation on property rights?
   a. Eminent domain.
   b. Taxation.
   c. Police power.
   d. Escheat.
   e. All of the above.

2. A comprehensive plan usually deals with which of the following elements?
   a. Land uses.
   b. Population.
   c. Public services.
   d. Natural resources.
   e. All of the above.

3. Property taxes are a major source of revenue for:
   a. The federal government.
   b. School districts.
   c. Local governments.
   d. State governments.
   e. Both local governments and school districts.

4. The authority for approving site plans for large projects ultimately rests with the:
   a. Elected governing commission or council.
   b. Mayor or city manager.
   c. Planning board or commission.
   d. Planning board or commission staff.
   e. Zoning review board.

5. The most accurate conclusion about the regressivity of the property tax is that it is:
   a. Regressive.
   b. Not regressive.
   c. Based on ability to pay.
   d. Regressive, but when benefits are considered, the net result may be fair.
   e. Not regressive until the benefits are considered.

6. Traditional land use controls (pre-1970) include:
   a. Zoning.
   b. Building codes.
   c. Subdivision regulations.
   d. *a* and *b,* but not *c.*
   e. All three: *a, b,* and *c.*

7. A new form of land use control that replaces zoning by land uses with separation of building/development types is:
   a. Form-based zoning.
   b. PUD.
   c. Performance requirements.
   d. Impact fees.
   e. Urban planning.

8. *New urbanism* is a term used to describe:
   a. Growth management laws enacted by state governments.
   b. Improvement of transportation systems to encourage dispersion of a city's population.
   c. The requirement that infrastructure be available concurrently with new development.
   d. The theory that residential and commercial uses should be integrated, streets and parking should discourage through traffic, and neighborhoods should be pedestrian oriented.
   e. The trend for the construction of self-sufficient "new towns."

9. Elements of traditional zoning include all *except:*
   a. Performance standards.
   b. Setback requirements.
   c. Bulk limits.
   d. Land use categories.
   e. Provision for special use districts.

10. Externalities in land use include all *except:*
    a. Leap-frog development.
    b. Increase storm runoff from paving.
    c. Traffic congestion.
    d. Inability to judge the quality of a structure, once built.
    e. Noise created by a land use.

Study Questions

1. Assume that you own a small apartment building close to a major commercial street and a service station. You learn that there has been a major leak of underground storage tanks from the service station, and the gasoline has spread onto and below the surface of your property. Discuss sources of value loss to your property from the contamination.

2. A local businessman has applied for a permit to construct a bar that will feature "adult dancing" in a commercially zoned area in view of the entrance to your residential subdivision. As an owner of a $350,000 house within the subdivision, would you favor or oppose this development? What effect do you think it could have on the value of your property? If you were opposed, how could you fight approval of the permit?

3. A medium-size city has proposed to build a "greenway" along a creek that flows through the center of the city. The city wants to clear a strip about 50 feet wide and construct a paved path for bicycles and foot traffic (walkers and joggers). Proponents claim that it would be a highly desirable recreational facility for the community, while a very vocal and insistent group of opponents claims that it would degrade the environment and open properties along the creek to undesirable users and influences.

   Identify some specific positive and negative aspects of the proposal. Would you be in favor of the proposal, if you lived in the city? Would it make a difference if you lived along the creek?

4. The main argument traditionally advanced in favor of zoning is that it protects property values. Do you believe this contention? If so, how does zoning protect property values? If you do not believe the contention, why not?

5. Do you believe that the owners of properties contaminated by events that occur on another property (e.g., gasoline leakage or spills) should be responsible for cleaning up their properties? Why or why not? If not, who should pay for the cleanup?

6. The property tax has been criticized as an unfair basis for financing public schools. Areas that have high property

values are able to pay for better schools than areas having lower property values. Thus, there is an inequality of educational opportunities that tends to perpetuate educational and social disadvantages for those who live in low-income areas.
a. Do you agree or disagree?

b. How could school financing be modified to provide more equal funding among all regions of a state?

7. A property owner who owes 8 mills in school taxes, 10 mills in city taxes, and 5 mills in county taxes and who qualifies for a $25,000 homestead exemption would owe how much tax on a property assessed at $80,000?

EXPLORE THE WEB

1. Go to Smart Growth Online wwwsmartgrowth.org. Locate an explanation of smart growth, and of each of its principles.

2. Select a city or a county of interest to you. Use municode.com to locate the zoning ordinance and determine how many zoning classifications are on the zoning map. What are some uses that do not appear on the map, but are granted through a request for special permit?

3. Go to your county's Internet home page. Locate your county's comprehensive plan and summarize one of its basic elements.

Solutions to Concept Checks

1. State and local governments are granted police power by the Constitution to regulate land use.

2. Examples of monopolies that affect local land use are electrical, water, and gas line systems.

3. Examples of negative externalities that affect local land use are excessive smoke, congestion, debris, noise, and excessive storm runoff.

4. Economic and environmental impact statements analyze a development project's effect on the surrounding areas. Concurrency is the requirement that infrastructure be available in an area before development takes place. Affordable housing allocation is a requirement that encourages or mandates a "reasonable and fair" component of new housing construction for lower-income families. An urban service area delineates a boundary around a community where local government plans are set to provide for public services while urban development is discouraged outside the urban service area. Extraterritorial jurisdiction allows local governments to plan and control urban development outside their boundaries until annexation can occur.

5. An environmental revolution in the late 1960s launched the revolution in land use controls about 1970. Environmental events such as publication of *Silent Spring,* the Love Canal incident, and the concept of spaceship earth all contributed to the land use control revolution.

6. Traditional planning of street layout is built through a hierarchy of cul-de-sacs. Additionally, traditional planning favors complete containment of nonresidential land uses in designated areas. On the other hand, the new urbanism planning allows for grid pattern, narrow streets, and a mix of land uses within the same area.

7. In addition to type of land use, zoning typically imposes setback requirements, building height limits, minimum lot dimensions, and building floor area limits as a ratio to land area.

8. Three requirements for zoning to be a legitimate use of police power are that the ordinances are reasonable, based on a comprehensive plan, and provide for all types of housing.

9. Nonconforming land use is one that has previously been allowed on a parcel of land but which would no longer be permitted due to a change in the zoning ordinance. A variance is an exception to the requirements of an existing zoning ordinance due to a hardship condition. Exclusionary zoning tends to exclude housing for lower-income groups.

10. A PUD can differ from traditional zoning by allowing mixed uses, not imposing uniform setbacks, allowing variable density, and incorporating open spaces and nature preservation along with structures.

11. Since 1950, the use of eminent domain has come to include public benefit as a public use. Therefore, the public does not need to use the property, but only to benefit from its taking.

12. Condemnation is the legal procedure of the government taking private property through eminent domain. Inverse condemnation is an action, initiated by property owners against the government, to recover the loss in their property's value, arguing that restrictions imposed on the property constitute a "taking."

13. The tax rate is 4.67 percent.

14. The amount of property tax equals $1,875. The effective tax rate is 1.875 percent.

15. Ad valorem taxes are based upon the value of the property. Pro rata charges are used for special assessments, where owners pay a fair share for the assessment, usually based on street front footage. Special assessments are taxes specifically levied for a certain purpose that benefits a limited area. Exemptions are a specified deduction from a property's assessed value before calculating property tax bills.

16. Criticisms of property taxes include that they can be regressive, the rates can be uneven by geographical area and property type, and it frequently has been poorly administered.

Additional Readings

The following books contain expanded examples and discussions of government regulation and real estate markets:

Collier, Nathan S., Coutland A. Collier, and Don A. Halperin. *Construction Funding: The Process of Real Estate Development, Appraisal, and Finance,* 4th ed. New York: John Wiley, 2008.

Downs, A. *Urban Affairs and Urban Policy.* Cheltenham U.K.: Edward Elgar Publication, 1998.

Gitelman, Mortan, and Robert R. Wright. *Land Use in a Nutshell,* 4th ed. St. Paul, MN: West Group, 2000.

Miles, Mike E., Laurence Netherton, and Adrienne Schmitz. *Real Estate Development: Principles and Practices,* 5th ed. Washington, DC: Urban Land Institute, 2015.

Russ, Thomas H. *Redeveloping Brownfields: Landscape Architects, Planners, Developers.* New York: McGraw-Hill, 2000.

Schiffman, Irving. *Alternative Techniques for Managing Growth,* 2nd ed. Berkeley: University of California, Institute of Governmental Studies Press, 1999.

Schilling, Joseph M., Christine Gaspar, and Nadejda Mishkovsky. *Beyond Fences: Brownfields and the Challenges of Land Use Controls.* Washington, DC: International City/County Management Association, 2000.

The following text is an excellent introduction to the field of urban planning:

Levy, John M. *Contemporary Urban Planning,* 10th ed. Upper Saddle River, NJ: Pearson Prentice Hall, 2013.

The following newsletter of the Lincoln Institute of Land Policy provides news, articles, and summaries of studies undertaken by the institute. Most of the articles and studies pertain to topics covered in this chapter.

Lincoln Institute of Land Policy. *Land Lines* (newsletter). 113 Brattle Street, Cambridge, MA 02138-3400. www.lincoln-inst.edu.

Market Determinants *of* Value

LEARNING OBJECTIVES

After reading this chapter you will be able to:

1 Explain the role of transportation modes and natural resources in the location and evolution of cities.

2 Define economic base activities, distinguish them from secondary activities, and explain the role of both in the growth or decline of a city.

3 Identify supply factors influencing the growth of a city.

4 Demonstrate how demand for access influences the value of urban land and determines the patterns of location of activities within a city.

5 Explain what effects evolving transportation technology, evolving communications technology, and changing production and retailing methods have had on urban form.

6 Distinguish between "convenience goods" and "comparison goods" in their urban location patterns.

7 Define industry economies of scale and agglomeration economies of scale, and offer examples of each.

OUTLINE

Introduction

To determine the value of a property, the most difficult and critical task is to evaluate the market for the property in order to estimate its future cash flows. Some stories from real estate experience help to make this case.

Market Misjudgments in Real Estate

In the early 1970s most downtowns of the United States witnessed the completion of office buildings that set new records in size, height, and cost. Unfortunately, many of the very buildings that defined new skylines for U.S. cities also defined new levels of financial loss because they fell far short in occupancy. In Atlanta, Miami, Minneapolis, and many other cities, the largest building on the downtown skyline was also the largest economic disaster. What is most intriguing about this office market disaster of the mid-1970s was its repetition in even larger terms little more than a decade later. By the end of the 1980s the average occupancy of major office buildings across the United States was falling toward a devastating 80 percent after a new building boom added more than 30 percent to an already ample supply.

The problem of market misjudgment is not limited to office buildings. In St. Louis the Pruitt-Igoe public housing project was completed in 1954 and heralded worldwide as a model for a generation of postwar public housing projects that followed. Unfortunately, this 33-building complex for 10,000 occupants was found to be ill-designed for the needs of the occupants and uninhabitable, setting a pattern for similar projects in the years that followed when it was completely demolished and replaced. In 1962 Robert Simon launched the new community of Reston, Virginia, in suburban Washington, D.C., which was heralded by architects and planners of the Western world as a model example of a new town. By 1967 he had lost control of the struggling community due to inadequate prospects for cash flow. About the same time, the residential condominium was discovered in Florida and elsewhere. In the first half of the 1970s, close to a quarter million condominium units were launched. But the market turned out to want far fewer than that number. Thousands of units were either never completed or, in some cases, torn down shortly after being constructed to make the land available for more viable uses. But this bitter experience didn't keep builders from more than tripling the condo supply of downtown Miami between the years 2003 and 2008, resulting in a three- to five-year oversupply.

These stories are only some of the more spectacular examples of individual market misjudgments in real estate. Virtually every community has its album of stories of landowners, large and small, who built their dream project, only to have it die financially for lack of an adequate market. Frequently, the developer disappears from the industry and little attention is ever again paid to the failure.

Most recently has come a global test of real estate viability with the great recession of 2007. The recession began with real estate but quickly engulfed the U.S. economy and the world. What is interesting is the reverse of the stories above: In a sea of real estate failures and falling values, most properties still survived. Certain types of properties—such as apartments and self-storage facilities—generally thrived, while other types—such as non-grocery local retail stores—suffered severely. But even this pattern varied from city to city, with some cities experiencing much less wreckage than others. In Nevada, California, Arizona, Florida, and Hawaii, many cities (though not all) experienced extreme real estate booms and busts. But in most cities of the central United States, real estate went through much less adversity. The lesson from this traumatic economic period is similar to that of earlier years: The experience of a property depends on its market context.

Market misjudgments in real estate too often are enduring and disastrous because the commitment is large, permanent, and immobile. Further, many developers have learned through bitter and financially devastating experience that if the market they had counted on is not there when their project is completed, it is beyond their power to create it.

Minimizing Market Errors

How, as a real estate investor, does one prevent market disaster? As with any business venture, there rarely is a sure protection against market misjudgment; this risk simply "comes with the territory." However, there are important ways to manage the market risk in real estate. One way is to avoid real estate investments that have a high market risk. For example, one can avoid any kind of land development where the end user is not already "locked in." And one can avoid any investment where there is a prospect of major change in the users or tenants of the property. More generally, however, investors in real estate must become students of urban land use and urban real estate markets. Most properties will need new tenants or users from time to time, and the investor wants to be reasonably sure they will appear. This assurance depends, first of all, on the property being in a supportive market environment. Lacking this, little or nothing can save most real estate investments.

What does a real estate investor need to know about urban markets? First, it is valuable to recognize the fundamental forces that create these markets, which are the same forces that create and shape cities. In addition, it is valuable to understand what brings change to the shape of cities. Finally, it is important to understand how land use types differ in their locational needs, something we will refer to as their **linkages.**

In this chapter we first consider why cities exist, and examine the demand for access as the "gravity" that holds a city together. Then we consider factors that cause change in this demand for access, thereby changing the shape and character of a city and its real estate markets. Next, we see how various land uses may compete for locations in the city, and how the result determines the topography of value for urban land. But there are important variations among land use types in how they need to arrange themselves across the urban landscape—some clustering close together, for example, and others dispersing evenly. We examine the causes and the variation in these patterns. Further, there are hierarchies in the resulting network of land uses, which we explore.

✓ **Concept Check**

5.1   The demand for access between one urban activity and others is referred to as the activity's _____.

Probably the best-known adage in real estate is that the three most important things about real estate are location, location, and location. The old saying survives because there is more than a little truth in it. But what does it really mean? This chapter might be thought of, in large part, as studying the many meanings of urban location.

The Creation, Growth, and Decline of Cities

Economic activity—production and exchange—brings people together. Traveling to the location of production or exchange requires time and cost whether it is commuting to work at a factory, traveling to a management meeting, calling on a customer, going shopping, or going to a show, concert, or sporting event. And time is valuable. Therefore, it is no surprise that human settlement has long tended to cluster so that people can gather more quickly and efficiently.[1]

Where Cities Occur

The interesting question is where did these clusters occur, and economists have noted several answers. The most compelling locations for cities were the intersections of different modes of transportation. Thus, many of the oldest cities were seaports where land travel and ocean travel interfaced. Still other great cities developed at the mouth of rivers where

---

1. A forceful, thought-provoking tribute to the importance of cities in human society is presented by Edward Glaeser in *Triumph of the City*.... (See the end-of-chapter bibliography for the full publication details.)

river transit intersected with oceans, such as New Orleans at the mouth of the Mississippi. Yet other cities emerged at the intersection of rivers or trails, such as St. Louis, Missouri, at the confluence of the Ohio, Missouri, and Mississippi rivers. In the industrial age, the intersection of rail transportation with seaports or with other rail lines became locations for cities, as with Chicago. Historical changes in transportation modes have brought changing fortunes to many cities. New Orleans and Baltimore, for example, were equal in size, and second only to New York City in 1840. But their relative fortunes faded with the coming of the railroad, and New Orleans idled for most of a century before the discovery of oil nearby, the "rebirth" of the South, and other factors gave it new momentum.

> ✓ **Concept Check**
>
> **5.2**   The "gravity" that draws economic activity into forming cities is the need for _____.

Still other cities were born of mining and resource extraction. A number of American cities, for example, were propelled by coal and iron ore extraction, and then became efficient centers for heavy manufacturing. Other cities were propelled by the extraction of oil and gas. Thus, Houston and neighboring cities stretching as far east as New Orleans have become the world's largest concentration of petrochemical industries. The latest chapter in the story of resource-based cities is likely to come from shale oil and gas extraction.

> ✓ **Concept Check**
>
> **5.3**   Historically, cities tended to form at the intersection of _____.

In many cases the driving activity for a city has changed through time. Many of the great modern cities result from the good fortune of being in a location that became important for a chain of functions, or core activities, through time. Often, as one core activity declined, another emerged, sustaining the growth of the city from one era to another. Hence, Minneapolis, Chicago, and other major cities of the middle United States evolved core functions far beyond the agriculture-based economy that first brought them to maturity: Detroit went from fur and agricultural trade to iron industry and manufacturing, and then to automobiles; Pittsburgh, Pennsylvania, transcended its original role as a river trade center with the birth of the iron and steel industries, which it then transcended to become a much more diversified center of commerce, manufacturing, research, and health care.

Other cities struggled with the erosion of their economic base in recent decades. Duluth, Minnesota, has mitigated the decline of its historic iron ore base through growth in tourism, general commerce, and more diversified Great Lakes shipping. Youngstown, Ohio, awaits new direction after the devastating loss of its coal and steel mill base, and the city of Detroit similarly searches for its new directions after the decline of its central city automobile plants.

The Economic Base of a City

The birth of every city resulted from some function that it served for the economic world at large. The great trade cities, for example, provided an interface among multiple continents. In the industrial world, both manufacturing cities and resource extraction cities frequently ship to worldwide markets. University cities and medical cities serve far more than the needs of a local population. Recognizing this, economists focus on the **economic base** of a city to understand it. The economic base is that set of economic activities that a city provides for the world beyond its boundaries (thus, often called its export base). The economic base of a city determines its growth or decline.

The Economic Base Multiplier.   The concept of economic base is extremely useful. As one better understands the economic base of a city and therefore what it offers, or can offer, to the larger world, one has a better basis to understand its potential for future growth or decline. Thus, for example, many cities heavily oriented toward Cold War defense production faced a time of stagnation following the fall of the Berlin Wall, and cities centered on supporting agriculture have faced decline for many decades as farms and farm populations have diminished in number. On the other hand, cities oriented to medical services such as Chapel Hill and Durham, North Carolina, or Rochester, Minnesota, have seen strong growth in recent decades due to increased demand for medical services as average real household income rises with economic growth, as medical advancements occur, and as the population ages. Similarly, many university cities have experienced strong growth due to the expansion of university age population and the growing importance in modern economies of higher education. In short, it is imperative for persons considering real estate investments or real estate careers to be aware of the economic base of cities they are contemplating. This gives them a much better chance to understand the city's real estate character, and its potential for the future.

A city's economic base drives local economic activity and land use through a multiplier process. As suggested in Exhibit 5-1, base (export) activities and services bring money into a city, which then is respent and recirculated within the city. Since most of this recirculation occurs through paychecks or commissions, employment is a particularly important measure of multiplier impact.

Several factors affect the size or power of the base multiplier. For example, as cities become larger, they tend to "take in more of their own linen"; that is, they tend to provide more of their own local goods and services. Thus, for example, a small town seldom will

Exhibit 5-1   The Economic Base Multiplier

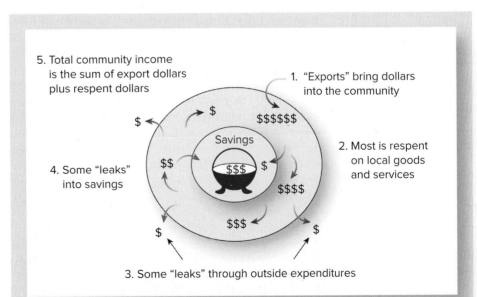

have a large regional shopping mall, and will have a limited array of furniture stores, automobile dealerships, medical specialists, and business services. Therefore, residents will tend to make frequent trips to the "big city" for shopping and other services, spending income outside of their local community. However, as cities grow, they become capable of supporting a larger share of household and business services locally. Further, more isolated cities tend to recirculate more base income locally. As the cost of traveling to alternative cities is greater, residents become more willing to accept the goods and services available locally. As base firms and households respend a larger share of their initial income, their impact on the local community is greater. But as more of the money "leaks" out through expenditures elsewhere, the impact is less. Thus, for example, tourism in cities such as Orlando, Florida, or Las Vegas, Nevada, is a rather high-impact or high-multiplier economic base activity. It is very labor intensive, and a large share of the money brought into a community through tourism goes to food and hospitality services that must be locally produced, by local labor. Even some of the ubiquitous screen-printed T-shirts may be created locally in the tourist city! On the other hand, most of the other necessary souvenirs are likely to come from China or another low-wage country, creating a "leakage" in the local tourism multiplier.

Another relatively high-multiplier activity may be retirement. In Florida and other Sun Belt states, persons who have retired from colder climates bring their retirement income to the locality, purchasing local housing and a wide range of local services. In contrast to tourism and retirement, computer assembly may have a lower economic base multiplier. For example, U.S.-bound computers tend to be manufactured in the Third World, then shipped to a U.S. city for final distribution. Thus, many of the dollars that might flow to the city of final distribution actually bypass it to flow elsewhere in the world. In short, economic base activities are those that bring money into a city to recirculate, producing additional income and employment. The impact of a base activity, per dollar of base income, varies, depending on how much of the base income finally recirculates within the local economy.

✓ **Concept Check**

5.5   The size of an economic base multiplier depends on the amount of "_____" from the local economy.

Base and Local Economic Activity.   In contrast to base activities are **local economic activities** (sometimes called *secondary activities*). Activities in a city that serve the local businesses and households are recirculating the income derived through base activities. Most urban land use is for local activities—retail centers, government and public land uses, medical offices, business service establishments, restaurants, automotive services, and so forth. The importance of this is that the creation of a new secondary activity facility, such as a new neighborhood shopping center, adds little to the economic activity of a city (except temporarily, through construction). Rather, it will compete with existing facilities for the total business derived from export activity. On the other hand, a new regional office center, a new manufacturing center, a new state government office center, or other new export activity will bring a true increase in export derived dollars, adding still more to secondary activity through the multiplier process.

In summary, persons involved in real estate need to be aware of the economic base in any community of interest. They must learn not only what the current economic base of the community is, but understand any important future economic base activity that may emerge. Then they can better judge the long-term prospects of the city for economic growth and business opportunities. Further, they will understand better how to assess the near-term impact of changes, either positive or negative, as businesses open or close in the community.

On the northeast border of Texas is the proud town of Marshall, population 24,000, in a county of about 60,000, and one of the oldest cities in the state. For a century its life revolved around the Texas and Pacific Railroad, and cotton production, followed later by oil and lumber. A center for production of fine railcars a century ago, it also is a town of well-built historic homes. But in the mid-1990s Marshall, like so many small cities in the United States, found itself with a struggling local economy. Its orientation to oil production and lumber gave it a ticket on the train of high unemployment and slow growth. Symptomatic of the economic challenges was the town's shopping center, the Marshall Mall, a 195,000-square-foot center built in 1980. By 1995 the anchor tenant, Kmart, occupying one-third of the space, had closed, leaving 61,000 feet of darkness. The unemployment rate in the county was over 8 percent at that time, and the Marshall Mall, owned by a major life insurance company, was for sale for a small fraction of replacement cost.

Enter a thoughtful and enterprising development group. They learned about the mall, and also found that Blue Cross/Blue Shield of Texas was undertaking a program of regional decentralization. While working with the local economic development agency and submitting a proposal to BCBS

Source: © Marshall, Texas Chamber of Commerce

for a regional processing center, the development group acquired the mall and set about to allow Kmart to buy out its lease. It worked. Kmart moved out, BCBS moved in. The mall came back to life, and rents began to flow. Since 2006 the Marshall Mall has been generating over three times as much net cash flow, and has increased its value probably fourfold. But Marshall Mall's

recovery may be the minor story. BCBS has brought over 500 new jobs to the economic base of Marshall, along with a healthy economic base multiplier effect that may easily have doubled the number of new jobs. BCBS remains in 2016 the city of Marshall's third largest private employer. Marshall's unemployment rate relative to the rest of Texas is the best it has been in years, and many more people are able to find jobs in their hometown.

A Redevelopment Where Everybody Wins

Source: © Marshall, Texas Chamber of Commerce

---

www.statsamerica.org

An excellent example of a quick access data source for a state and its counties. For other states, all U.S. counties, and metro areas, select the pages called States IN Profile, Counties IN Profile, and County/Metro Side-by-Side, respectively.

Indicators of the Economic Base. To quickly examine a local economic base, a growing number of information sources is available. Always important are data from a local chamber of commerce or government agency concerning the major employers, what they produce, and how many persons they employ locally. The most useful economic summary data on local economies are increasingly available on websites. For example, at www.statsamerica.org one can obtain a large portion of the available summary data on local population, income, and employment for any county in the United States.[2] Other types of local data are available through the Census Quickfacts website. (See the margin.) A review of employer and summary economic data puts one in a position to ask informed questions about the local economic base and its future. In addition, most cities have public economic development authorities whose officials can respond to questions about the local economic base. Thus, with a modest amount of time and effort, one can gain an understanding of a city and its future opportunities for economic growth, new business opportunities, and real estate investments.

www.census.gov/quickfacts

Portal to summary data from the U.S. Census of Population and Housing and other U.S. data for states, counties, cities and zip codes.

2. This website sets high standards for accessibility of data at the county level. Not only does it provide data from most available standard sources but it allows the user to specify a variety of useful display formats. For summary employment and population reports at the county level, few other sites should be necessary.

One quick indicator of a community's economic base is called a **location quotient.** The underlying idea is that a community has some normal pattern of employment distribution, and excessive concentrations of employment in a particular industry must indicate that the industry is producing surpluses for export. The location quotient is intended to identify such concentrations, and works as follows:

1. Compute the percentage of total employment in a given industry—for example, education—for the local community. Suppose this is 20 percent.
2. Compute the percentage in education employment for a reference population (often percentage employment for the entire United States is used). Suppose this is 9 percent.
3. Compute the location quotient, the ratio of the local to reference percentage. $(20 \div 9 = 2.22)$

In this case the 2.2 indicates that the concentration of education employment in the local community is 2.2 times normal, suggesting that education must be an export industry. By calculating location quotients for all industries, one can gain quick clues about the economic base of a local community. The primary database for these computations is the U.S. Census, which is readily available on the Web as noted above, and in Explore the Web, at the end of the chapter.

Resources of a City: The Supply Side of Urban Growth

The analysis of a city's economic base is largely preoccupied with what the external world wants from the city, which is largely a question of external demand. The other side of the question is: What can a city offer to the world? This is a supply-side question. It is a longer-run issue because, while world markets for a city's base output can vary quite rapidly in the short run, a city's mix of output capacities changes slowly.

Labor Force Characteristics.   The supply potential of a city depends on a diversity of factors. Certainly the nature of its available labor force is important. For example, when commercial aviation was born during the 1920s, Wichita, Kansas, was a small agricultural and oil city, not unlike many others across the Great Plains of the United States. A handful of local business leaders recognized the future of the aviation industry and that the small, often struggling farms of the region offered an abundant source of highly skilled, well-educated mechanics with a strong work ethic. They encouraged and financially supported the birth of several aircraft manufacturers, including two "barnstorming" aircraft designers of the era, Clyde Cessna and Walter Beech. In the next 70 years, Beech Aircraft, Cessna Aircraft, and other aircraft companies were born and prospered in the area. Wichita became recognized as the world's leading center for light commercial aviation production. Legions of other plant and company location decisions attest to the importance that companies give to the character of the available labor force in selecting a location.

Quality of Life and Leadership.   The existing labor force is not the only factor in the local growth equation. Increasingly, knowledge-intensive firms are sensitive to quality of life issues. They want to be where the characteristics of the community can provide their employees an enriching and satisfying lifestyle. Further, companies are concerned with the business leadership and environment. Sophisticated firms recognize that their "cost of doing business" can depend on the support of local leadership and government in assuring, for example, roads, utilities, effective airport service, reasonable taxation, and compatible land use controls. The aircraft story in Wichita attests to the importance of business leadership. Central to the story was the support of the core business leaders who staked large amounts of money on the aircraft industry.

✓ **Concept Check**

5.6   The customary analysis of a city's economic base tends to focus on _____, which tends to be a short-term phenomenon.

Planners develop land use plans to provide for growth and revitalization of communities, while helping local officials make decisions ranging from broad urban problems to new community infrastructure. They may participate in decisions on alternative public transportation system plans, resource development, and protection of ecologically sensitive regions. Planners also may be involved with drafting legislation concerning local community issues.

Urban and regional planners often confer with land developers, civic leaders, and public officials. They may function as mediators in community disputes and present alternatives acceptable to opposing parties. Planners may prepare material for community relations programs, speak at civic meetings, and appear before legislative committees and elected officials to explain and defend their proposals. Planners rely heavily on sophisticated computer-based databases and analytical tools, including geographical information systems (GISs).

Most entry-level jobs in federal, state, and local government agencies require a master's degree in urban or regional planning, urban design, geography, or a similar course of study. Planners must be able to think in terms of spatial relationships and visualize the effects of their plans and designs. They should be flexible and able to reconcile different viewpoints and to make constructive policy recommendations. The ability to communicate effectively, both orally and in writing, is necessary for anyone interested in this field.

In 2015 80 percent of planners earned between about $43,000 and $102,000, with a median of $68,220.

Source: Summarized from *The Occupational Outlook Handbook.* U.S. Department of Labor.

Urban and Regional Planners

Industry Economies of Scale.   Economists have long recognized that the growth of an industry within a city can create special resources and cost advantages for that industry. This phenomenon is called **industry economies of scale.** In Wichita, for example, the establishment of Beech and Cessna created an infrastructure of management and production knowledge, parts vendors, a strong aeronautical engineering program at the local university, and other resources. Such resulting resources apparently were material in attracting other aircraft companies to the city. Thus, formerly Seattle-based Boeing placed its largest plant outside the state of Washington in Wichita, and Lear Jet was launched in the city several decades after the beginning of Beech and Cessna. More familiar examples of where industry economies of scale have propelled city growth include the automobile industry in Detroit, the motion picture industry in the Los Angeles area, the petrochemical industry in the Houston area, and, more recently, the computer and software industry in "Silicon Valley" in the San Francisco–San Jose region of California, music in Nashville, and the computer industry in Austin, Texas.

Agglomeration Economies.   As cities grow, they develop a larger array of resources. Important examples include improved transportation terminals such as airline service and shipping terminals, specialized nonfinancial business services (e.g., in communications, technical support, and advertising), and more specialized financial services. For example, cities with a Federal Reserve Bank may have a level of advancement and specialization in the field of financial services that other cities find difficult to match. These cities tend to host a diverse range of financial information providers and financial consulting firms such as money management firms that are much less common in other cities. The emergence of specialized resources in response to demand from multiple industries is referred to as **agglomeration economies.** This phenomenon is perhaps the distinctive economic feature of very large cities. New York, for example, has served historically as a birthplace for complex industries, hosting the creation of a wide array of innovations in electronics, publications, communications, finance, and other fields. This birthing role has been possible because highly specialized resources necessary for development of innovations are readily available in the region, sustained by the occasional needs of a vast array of different industries.[3]

3. Ray, Vernon, *Metropolis 1985.* (Garden City, NY: Doubleday, 1963), pp. 99–118.

An important effect of agglomeration economies in real estate is upon market risk. Both for real estate investments and for real estate careers, it may be that larger cities, with greater diversity of the economic base, and more advanced development of agglomeration economies, have greater capacity to withstand industry downturns. An example might be Los Angeles following the end of the Cold War. While Los Angeles was a major production center for military electronics, aircraft, and other material, and felt the severe effects of reduced military production, it has rebounded, riding the tide of other industries. One particular effect of agglomeration economies in real estate is that it causes institutional investors to favor real estate investments in large urban markets. This appears to be due to better transportation and information access for these cities, and the greater likelihood of successful retenanting if the current tenants are lost. Thus, perceived agglomeration economies directly impact the investment policies of major real estate investors and the value they place on properties.

✓ Concept Check

5.7   Cost efficiencies that arise in a city due to concentration of an industry are called _____ whereas cost efficiencies arising from the concentration of multiple industries are called _____.

The Shape of a City

We have said that the central force creating cities is the demand for proximity. The cost of distance works as an "economic gravity," forever offering gains in efficiency for production and exchange through proximity, and forever shaping urban form. While we will consider a variety of other influences that differentiate the tapestry of urban land use, all are subject to this demand for proximity.

Demand for Proximity and Bid-Rent Curves

To explore the effects of demand for proximity, it is helpful to construct a logical model. Known as a **bid-rent model** by land economists and geographers, this simplified story of how land users bid for location is remarkably helpful in revealing the influences on the way density of land use is determined, how competing urban land uses sort out their locations, how urban land value is determined, and why land use change occurs.

Imagine a one-dimensional world that exists along a single street, as in Exhibit 5-2. Suppose that all employment and exchange takes place at point zero, the central business district (CBD), and that each household must select a place to live along the street, where all housing spaces have identical physical features. For convenience, we will assume that each residential lot is 100 feet wide and that, initially, households live in what amount to identical motor homes (large recreational vehicles, or "RVs") that can be moved costlessly from one lot to another. (Thus, we only need to be concerned with paying rent for the lot, rather than for a lot and house.) Further, we will assume the lots are not owned by households, so that households must pay rent for a space. We will allow households to live on both sides of our simple street.

Suppose that each household contains one person, who is employed and completes one round-trip daily to the downtown. Suppose further that each person earns $20 an hour, and assume initially that all transportation is by car, at an average speed of 20 miles per hour. Finally, suppose that there are 318 households working downtown and seeking housing locations and they all make competitive bids for locations up to the amount that leaves them indifferent between winning and losing.

The principal question is this: What will households bid for the various residential lots in this simple world? The answer lies in recognizing that by living closer to the downtown, households reduce their time cost of commuting. The idea is that time saved from

Exhibit 5-2 A Simple Bid-Rent Curve

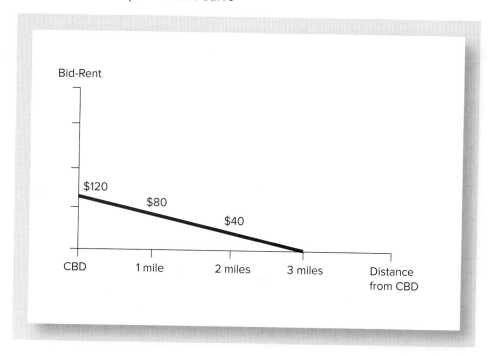

commuting can be used to earn money. From our assumptions, then, we can compute the cost of daily travel as $1.00 per mile ($20 per hour ÷ 20 miles per hour). Thus, a one-mile round-trip commute costs $2.00 per day in time given up. If each person works five days a week, 48 weeks a year, then he or she will commute on average, 20 days a month.

Using our assumptions, we now can consider how much households will bid for various locations on our urban street. With 318 households located on lots on both sides of the street, the farthest household from downtown commutes exactly three miles.[4] The cost of commuting from this lot will be $120 a month ($1 per mile × 3 miles × 2 directions × 20 days per month). Thus, this household will be willing to pay $120 per month more in rent to live downtown. (Remember, for simplicity, we assume there are no lifestyle or environmental differences in the two locations.) More generally, consider the choices of any commuter on any of the lots. By the logic above, we conclude that each commuter will be willing to bid $40 per month per mile to move closer to downtown than he or she currently lives.

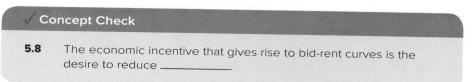

Concept Check

5.8 The economic incentive that gives rise to bid-rent curves is the desire to reduce _____.

Notice that our simple model of land rent implies several things about the patterns of rent in our city. First, beginning from the edge of settlement, rent for lots increases at a rate of $40 per mile as one moves closer to downtown. As shown in Exhibit 5-2, we can think of this rent level as forming a line (or curve) that runs from zero at the border of the city to $120 downtown. But we also can see what might change this "bid-rent" curve. If individuals earn more than $20 an hour, then they have a higher time cost. This means that they will bid still more per month per mile to be closer to the central business district (CBD). If, for example, they earn $30 an hour, then commuting costs $1.50 per mile, workers will pay

4. A mile is 5,280 feet. The midpoint of the most remote lot is located 50 + 158 × 100 = 15,850 feet from the center of downtown, whereas three miles is 15,840 feet.

$60 per month per mile to move closer to the CBD ($1.50 × 2 directions × 20 days), and the most remote commuter will pay $180 to move downtown. On the other hand, suppose that average travel speed increases from 20 miles per hour to 30. Then less time is required to commute one mile, and being closer is less valuable. At 30 miles per hour, our commuter will only bid $26.67 per month per mile to move closer to downtown ($20 per hour ÷ 30 miles per hour × 2 directions × 20 days per month), and the most remote commuter will pay only $80 to move downtown. Finally, if more households arrive, this growth will push the edge of settlement farther out, causing bidding to begin at a greater distance from the CBD. This raises the bid-rent curve at every point.

Bid-Rent Curves with Multiple Types of Households.   The simple bid-rent model enables us to think systematically about the factors that affect land value in a city, but it also can reveal how various land uses compete for space and sort themselves out on the urban map. Suppose that 106 of the households in our simple model are without cars, and people must walk to work. Suppose further they can walk, on average, at three miles an hour. From these assumptions, the cost of commuting for a walker is $266.67 per mile per month ($20 per hour ÷ 3 miles per hour × 2 directions × 20 days). In our original model, a driver living one mile from downtown is willing to bid $80 to be at that location rather than at the edge of the city. However, a walker is willing to bid far more, and will preempt the location. Since every walker will outbid every driver, all of the walkers will live in the first mile adjacent to the CBD. The most remote walker will simply outbid drivers, paying $80 per month in rent. But, just as drivers compete with each other, the walkers will bid against each other to live still closer. Since they are willing to pay $266.67 more to move the last mile to downtown, the bid-rent at the city center, determined by the walkers, is $346.67 ($80 + $266.67). The case with both walkers and drivers reveals how two different land uses with different intensities of need for access will get sorted out on the urban map. The workers with more costly commutes will command the closer locations and will bid against each other to set a higher level of rent. The resulting rent topography, or rent gradient, is shown in Exhibit 5-3.

Exhibit 5-3   Rent Gradient with Drivers and Walkers

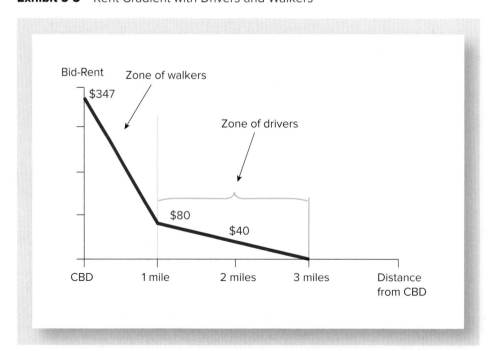

To further illustrate the model, suppose 26 of the households are medical doctors with incomes of $200 per hour. Assume the doctors have their offices in their homes and commute by car to a CBD hospital. Commuting to the hospital then costs each doctor $400 per month per mile ($200 ÷ 20 miles per hour × 2 directions × 20 days). Thus, all of the doctors will outbid every other household for the closest lots, and the closest lots to the CBD become medical office/residences rather than strictly residences. Bid-rent for the closest lot to downtown now becomes approximately $380.[5]

From this example, it is apparent how land users with the highest cost of commuting to downtown will bid the closest land away from other users, followed by the group having the second highest cost of commuting, and so forth. Thus, different land uses occupy different "zones" along the distance from the center, with rent at any point determined by the combined bidding of all current and lower intensity (i.e., lower commuting cost) land users. The resulting rent gradient for our three example groups is shown in Exhibit 5-4.

Exhibit 5-4 Rent Gradient with Drivers, Walkers, and Medical Offices

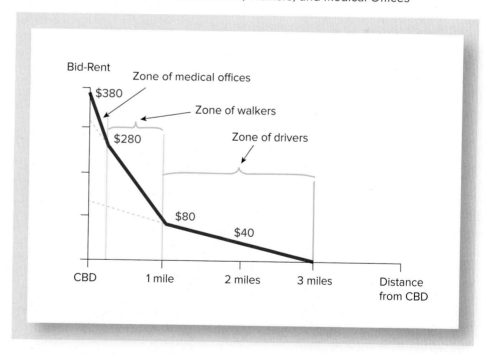

5. This assumes that there now are 26 doctors and 292 other commuters, of which 80 walk and 212 drive. Drivers, starting from three miles from downtown, bid rents up from zero to $80. Walkers dominate bids for the next three-quarters of a mile (40 lots ÷ 52.8 lots per mile), bidding rent from just over $80 up to $282.00 (approximately ($266.67 ÷ 52.8 lots per mile × 40 lots) + $80). Finally, doctors dominate the closest quarter-mile, bidding rent from just over $282 to about $380 for the first lot adjacent to the downtown.

Effect on Development Intensity. Not only does the bidding among various groups of commuters establish a rent gradient and sort out different zones of users along the curve; it also affects the density of land use. Since the locational rent increases with proximity to the CBD, so also does the incentive to build upward on the lot to allow multiple tenants. Even though the cost of building structures increases with density (structure height), higher locational rent justifies the additional cost per unit in order to capture multiple tenants. The effect rapidly becomes too complex for a simple numerical example. However, note that the profits from capturing multiple tenants increase as the lot is closer to the CBD. Thus, higher construction costs per unit are justified, and density of land use, through smaller lots and higher buildings, tends to increase with proximity to the downtown.

Multiple City Centers. Modern cities have multiple centers, with different core activities. We can expand our bid-rent model to represent this. Suppose our city has both a central business district and a medical center, including related physicians' offices and support services (e.g., laboratories, equipment vendors), located just over a mile from the downtown. For simplicity, we assume that all nonmedical activities are in the CBD, while all medical-related activities are centered around the hospital. In this case, the pattern of rent gradients and land use zones would be as shown in Exhibit 5-5. As before, the rent gradient will extend from the downtown to the perimeter of land use, with multiple zones of land use differentiated by cost of commuting. But preempting part of this curve will be curves extending in either direction from the hospital. These curves also will have multiple segments representing the bidding of hospital-oriented groups with different costs of commuting. Presumably, physicians' offices will have the highest cost of commuting to the hospital due to high opportunity cost and frequent needs to commute. The supporting laboratories, medical equipment vendors, and other medical services probably will be second while the residences of persons employed at the medical center might be third. To the extent the households commuting to the medical center have higher wages (opportunity cost of time) or they commute more frequently than commuters to the downtown, they will bid residential space away from CBD-oriented commuters. Thus, the pattern of Exhibit 5-5 results. At every location on our line, the land use is determined by bidding among multiple potential land users. The highest bidder at each location determines both the land use and, through interaction with all other bidders, the level and slope of the rent gradient.

Exhibit 5-5 Rent Gradient with Medical Center

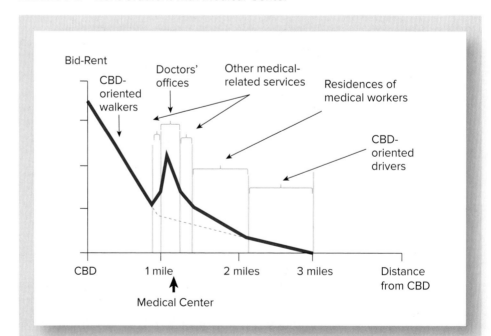

The bid-rent model also helps to understand land use changes. As a particular center grows, it generates more bidders for proximity. So, at the perimeter of the center, land is bid away from land uses oriented to elsewhere in the city.

Bid-Rent Curves, Urban Land Uses, and Land Value Contours

While bid-rent curves give a powerful means of understanding the forces determining urban land uses and land values, they cannot capture all of the influences on land use. Whereas bid-rent curves are based on one dimension of access need (the single-person commute), both households and businesses have multiple needs for access. Real estate analysts often refer to such needs for access as linkages, the important spatial connections between one urban land use and others. Restated, then, the problem with our bid-rent model is that it is based on only one linkage, the commuting linkage, whereas urban land uses involve many linkages. For example, a household may involve two or more working persons, each with different commuting linkages. In addition, the household has linkages to schools, friends, shopping, and other points of destination. In reality, all of these linkages enter into the household's bid for a location. In short, the bid-rent "equation" for a household or business may be more complex than can be accounted for in a simple graphical model. But the bid-rent model still reveals how demand for access—the urban economic "gravity"—creates, shapes, and sustains cities.

Changing Transportation, Changing Technology, and Changing Urban Form

Analysts have long recognized that cities are made up of a tapestry of different land uses. Through bid-rent curves we have seen the dynamics of how this tapestry is composed and how it can change. But transportation modes and production technology are the dominant factors in determining the number and location of nuclei within a city. As transportation modes and production technology have changed, so has our notion of urban form.

Concentric Ring Model of Urban Form.   In 1925 E. W. Burgess offered a **concentric ring model** of urban form, as depicted in Exhibit 5-6, panel A.[6] In the center circle is the CBD. Adjacent to it is a zone of transition that contains warehousing and other industrial land uses. This is followed by a ring of lower-income residential land use, followed by a ring of middle- and upper-income land use. In broad terms, it is easy to see a correspondence between this early model of land use and the notion of bid-rent curves. Each ring represents a different level of commuting cost to the CBD. The only puzzling aspect of the model is why lower-income residential land use is closer to the CBD than higher-income land use. Economists have long contemplated this apparent anomaly. They have offered as an explanation that higher-income households want sufficiently larger residential lots so that as they move closer to the city the rise in land prices more than offsets their savings in travel cost. There probably are dynamic reasons as well for the closer-in location of lower-income housing. Rapidly changing transportation systems and technology may cause housing design to change, rendering older housing obsolete. Then higher-income households will tend to leave older houses, allowing them to "filter down" to lower-income households. Meanwhile, the most available locations to build new housing are at the perimeter of the city, causing higher-income households to move farther from the CBD.

While the concentric ring model of urban form seems inappropriate today, it can be largely explained by the transportation and production technologies of its day. In 1923 less than half of U.S. households had acquired Ford's miraculous Model-T (the only affordable car), and most of these had been purchased within the last five years. Railroads were at their zenith in the economy and were the primary means of transportation. Chicago, where

---

6. E. W. Burgess, "The Growth of the City: An Introduction to a Research Project," in *The City*, ed. R. E. Park et al. (Chicago: University of Chicago Press, 1925).

Exhibit 5-6   Early 20th-Century Models of Urban Form

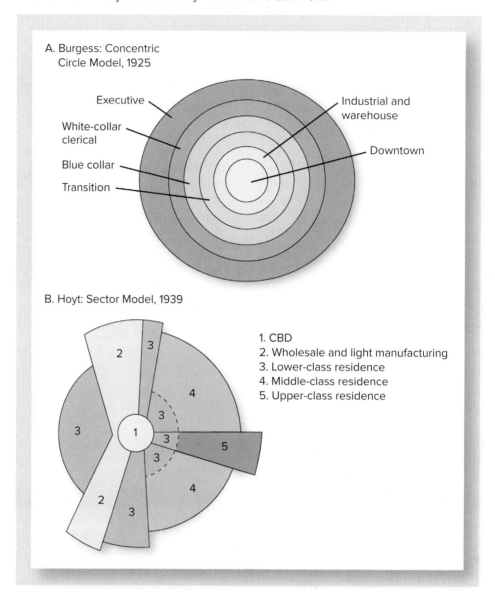

A. Burgess: Concentric Circle Model, 1925

Executive
White-collar clerical
Blue collar
Transition
Industrial and warehouse
Downtown

B. Hoyt: Sector Model, 1939

1. CBD
2. Wholesale and light manufacturing
3. Lower-class residence
4. Middle-class residence
5. Upper-class residence

Burgess formulated the concentric model, was centered on the main railroad station, Union Station (see Exhibit 5-7). Large parts of the downtown, including most of the modern-day park areas and lakeside office building complexes of the city, were railroad switchyards. Business communication was limited to few and rudimentary telephone systems, with no ability to transmit documents or graphical information except by physical means. Thus, for transportation and communication reasons, production, management offices, and rail stations had to be in close proximity. The elevator, made practical by Elisha Otis in the mid-19th century, became the means of facilitating the necessary close proximity. Management offices, production facilities, and warehousing were constructed vertically, packed close together in the center of the city around the railroad facilities.

Sector Model of Urban Form.   Roughly a decade after the concentric ring model of Burgess was published, Homer Hoyt studied data on residential rents from 1878 to 1928 for 142 cities in the United States.[7] He found a seemingly different pattern, shown in panel B of Exhibit 5-6, characterized by radial corridors or wedges, particularly for higher-income residential land use. In addition, he found that middle-income housing tended to be in wedges adjacent to the high-income corridors. Low-income housing, on the other hand, tended to be in areas opposite the CBD from the high-income corridor, typically adjacent to industrial areas. This is known as the **sector model** of urban form.

The difference between the Burgess concentric ring model and the Hoyt sector model tends to be overstated. A close examination of the diagrams from the two researchers shows some apparent evidence corresponding to the alternate theory in both cases. However, there is little question about the sector patterns reported by Hoyt. Furthermore, inspections of residential rental rate patterns during the 1990s in Moscow, Russia, for example, show a very strong pattern of wedges or corridors that strongly coincide with the Hoyt model. Thus, the sector pattern appears to span a wide range of time and cultures, probably shaped by the nature of the prevailing urban transportation system.[8]

✓ Concept Check

5.11   The Burgess concentric model of urban form was conceived in an era when the dominant form of transportation was by _____ and the principal method of moving goods within factories was by _____.

In American cities, it is generally conceded that the sector model was a good characterization of urban patterns when Hoyt did his analysis using pre-1930 data. However, it also is accepted that this model is no longer as valid. Two trends, at least, have served to weaken the sector pattern. First, in the last 70 years heavy manufacturing and industrial pollution have diminished, reducing the environmental differential across areas of the city and dependence on rail access. Second, the motor vehicle rapidly replaced fixed rail transit in intraurban use after 1920.

A Multinuclei City.   By 1945 departure from a single-center city was clear. In that year Harris and Ullman, in a landmark study, coined the term **multinuclei city.**[9] The motor vehicle, combined with new technologies of production, had released the city from its absolute ties to the CBD. Since 1945 continued advances in motor vehicles, along with waves of other technological innovations, have continued to propel urban activity away from the CBD, as we describe below.

✓ Concept Check

5.12   The radial or "pie slice" pattern in the Hoyt sector model of urban form probably can be explained by the dominance of _____ for intraurban transportation at the time the model was formulated.

Technological Change in the 20th Century.   Since 1930 technological changes have occurred on numerous fronts to propel employment centers out of the CBD. First, of course, was the transportation revolution, which was accompanied by a revolution in

---

7. Homer Hoyt, *The Structure and Growth of Residential Neighborhoods in American Cities* (Washington DC, Federal Housing Administration, 1939).

8. Until the dissolution of the USSR in 1991, there were few automobiles in Moscow. Automobile transportation was probably similar to that of the United States in the early 1920s. Urban commuting and other personal travel was by bus or by the highly developed subway system.

9. C. D. Harris and E. L. Ullman, "The Nature of Cities," *Annals, American Academy of Political and Social Science* 242 (1945), pp. 7–17.

Exhibit 5-7   The Transformation of American Downtown: Jacksonville, Florida 1955

In 1955, Jacksonville remained a classic monocentric city. Port activity on the St. Johns River intersected with the main coastal highway, U.S. 1, and with the large Union Station railroad depot—the "gateway to Florida."—just off to the left of the picture. Virtually every type of urban activity, including industrial, government, retail, business office, professional, theater and arts, medical, houses of worship, hotels, and hospitality, remained concentrated in the center of the city.

Source: © AERO-PIC PHOTOGRAPHY, JACKSONVILLE, FL. USA

Exhibit 5-7 The Transformation of American Downtown: Jacksonville, Florida 1985

Thirty years later, motor vehicles, air conditioning, and other technical innovations have worked their transformation on Jacksonville. All of the port and industrial activity has moved elsewhere around truck terminals. The Union Station closed. Most retail has gone to suburban shopping centers. Only specialty retail remains downtown, and a few very limited hotels. Most of the old structures have given way to parking or high-rise office buildings. Now the downtown is dominated by government, business administrative offices, banking, and finance uses. Symbolic of the change, Interstate 95 now can be seen stretching across the upper left corner of the picture.

Source: © AERO-PIC PHOTOGRAPHY, JACKSONVILLE, FL. USA

manufacturing organization and products, propelled especially by World War II. In the years following the war modern air-conditioning and fluorescent lighting were introduced, enabling new forms of urban structures. This was accompanied by the rapid evolution of self-service retailing technology that resulted in the emergence of modern shopping facilities. Finally, the most recent chapter of change has been the revolution in data processing, electronic communication, and the Internet.

The Urban Transportation Revolution.   The most obvious aspect of the transportation revolution was the rise of the automobile. As late as 1920 there was roughly one car for every 13 persons, and few highways. But 10 years later there was approximately one car for every five persons, approaching one per household. Further, by 1930 numerous state and federal laws had been enacted to support construction of roads for automobiles, including gasoline taxes to fund construction. By 1940 nearly half of the roads and highways in the United States had hard surfaces of some sort to support motor vehicle usage.

The emergence of the truck and bus has been at least as important as the car for the effect on urban form. The bus enabled the creation of lateral as well as radial passenger routes, with flexibility of routes to accommodate change. In the truck-oriented world of today, it is perhaps hard to appreciate the growth, not only in the number of trucks since 1920, but also in their design and capacity. Whereas the passenger capacity of cars has changed relatively little since 1920, the capacity and variety of trucks have grown manyfold. In short, the transformation of the United States into a motor vehicle society largely took place in the period from 1920 to 1940. It continued to accelerate after World War II with the increase in the number of vehicles and the construction of the Interstate Highway System, tollways, and other express highways. The impact on future urban form was profoundly affected by both the car and the truck, and continues to respond to the completion of new roadway systems in recent decades.

The Production Revolution.   Simultaneous with, and driven by, the motor vehicle revolution came the emergence of assembly lines. Increasingly, the efficient layout of assembly lines was horizontal, particularly as automation advanced. Thus, the older factories of the central city became obsolete. With trucks, cars, and highways, it now was possible to relocate production away from central railroad yards to areas where horizontal buildings and large parking lots were feasible. In numerous cities the movement of manufacturing to the suburbs was accelerated by the emergence of new industries such as the aircraft industry, especially during World War II. In the postwar era, flexibility in location was further advanced by the trend in the economy away from heavy manufacturing and toward services. Thus, there was increasing recognition of the growth of "footloose" industries that were not tied to rail lines, ports, or natural resources. This trend is demonstrated in the extreme with the AllianceTexas industrial community in Ft. Worth Texas, a 17,000 acre industrial and mixed use "inland port" built around its own industrial airport.

> ### ✓ Concept Check
>
> **5.13**   One of the most profound forces bringing about urban change in the United States is that whereas cars were a novelty in 1915, most households owned one by about _____.

Air-Conditioning, Lighting, and New Forms of Retailing and Offices.   Parallel with advances in production technology came changes that altered retailing and offices. First, during the 1930s fluorescent lighting became effective, enabling both retail facilities and office buildings to operate for the first time without direct sunlight. Coupled with this was the emergence of air-conditioning, making it possible to eliminate window ventilation.

For both retailing and office facilities, these technological advances propelled radical changes toward much larger floor plans for structures, hastening the obsolescence of traditional downtown structures and enabling the creation of modern, horizontal retailing facilities. Thus, the technology became available for the supermarket and the modern shopping center, adding another large thrust to the migration of employment to suburban nuclei following World War II.

Advances in Data Processing and Communications. One challenge that was posed by the migration of production out of the central city was separation of management from the production processes for the first time. When production was downtown, management could be at the production site and still maintain the necessary interface with banks and other external sources of financing, as well as other contacts important to the firm. This challenge was mitigated, first by the evolution of reliable and efficient telephone service, then by the emergence of high-speed data processing and reporting, then further by the growth of electronic data and document transmission, and in the present by wireless technology. As a result, it has become increasingly feasible to separate production processes from central management, further weakening a vast array of traditional intrafirm linkages and further enabling new spatial arrangements of production. Web-based information systems, e-mail, and cellular phones may have reduced the cost of distance still further in recent years, with effects that are not yet clear.

✓ **Concept Check**

5.14 The demand for space for horizontal factories was greatly accelerated in the 1920s by the development of _____ production.

Combined Effects on Urban Form. The transportation and technology changes of the last 90 years obviously have had profound effects on urban form. Not the least of these is that most urban employment is now outside the CBD. Whereas, in 1920, the largest percentage of all types of employment was in the CBD, today even the most centralized remaining function—office employment—is largely outside the CBD. In Houston, for example, with a relatively strong central city remaining, only about 20 percent of major office space is located in the CBD. Every other kind of urban activity is even less concentrated downtown. An important point about this is that it is easy to underestimate how long it takes the urban environment to adapt to new transportation and technology. For example, many downtown streets were laid out in the preautomobile era, and office buildings still exist that were built during the 1930s. While the process of adaptation in central cities has been greatly accelerated in many places by urban renewal programs, many aspects of the process are slow. The full impact of opening a new interstate highway can take decades, and its effect can be so gradual that naïve observers perceive existing arrangements to be a steady state when, in fact, they are being impacted by slow but inexorable change.

✓ **Concept Check**

5.15 Modern office structures and retail facilities were not possible before the development of _____ and _____.

The dramatic change in North American cities during the 20th century is shown by two photos of Jacksonville, Florida in Exhibit 5-7. In the 1955 view, virtually every type of urban land use—hotels, manufacturing, shipping, offices, retail, religious, governmental, medical, arts and entertainment—is concentrated downtown. Just out of view to the left is a major cause of this scene, the large Florida East Coast Railroad Depot. By 1985, however, only office functions, government, and some arts and entertainment remain. By then, the (out of view) railroad station also is out of service. In the upper left corner of the 1985 photo is Interstate 95, both symbol and cause of downtown's decline.

Since 1985, Jacksonville's downtown is experiencing the same cautious reawakening as many cities. Some professionals and many Millennials are moving into the urban center. Numerous luxury high-rise residences, with supporting activity, are appearing at the edges of Jacksonville's old center city.

Differing Location Patterns of Urban Land Uses

The models of urban form that we have considered recognize the qualitatively different types of land uses—residential, industrial, educational, medical, and other. Within some of these types of land use there are polar patterns of location among competitors. On one extreme are so-called central place activities. The other extreme is agglomeration activity.

Convenience "Goods" and Central Place Patterns

Some types of urban services and products are **convenience activities,** meaning that users seek to obtain the good or service from the closest available source. Examples typically include bakeries, delicatessens, hair salons and barbershops, supermarkets, fast-food restaurants, copy shops, dry cleaners, coffee boutiques, and many others. Providers of this type of "good" are compelled to disperse fairly evenly across the urban landscape.

The logic works as follows. Consider, for example, a convenience-type grocery store (a "quickshop") serving surrounding single-family residential areas. As a customer moves farther away from the store, the customer will patronize it less, perhaps tending to make a few, planned trips to a full-line supermarket instead of many, spontaneous trips to the quickshop. If there are multiple virtually identical quickshops at the same location, they will compete for the same available market. So, even if the market at that location were large enough to support multiple quickshops, the profit-maximizing strategy for each competitor is to separate from the others in order to capture a larger share of the market. In summary, the nature of "convenience" shopping creates the tendency for competitors to disperse over the region of potential customer units (households) to the point where each establishment is equidistant from any other, and they are separated by the minimum distance that allows sufficient customers to support each establishment.

The resulting pattern of establishment locations is suggested in Exhibit 5-8 and is known by geographers as a **central place pattern.** If the influence of transportation routes and constraints such as left-turn barriers were ignored, and if the density of customers were even, the resulting pattern of locations and markets would be a "honeycomb" of hexagonal markets with an establishment at the center of each cell in the honeycomb. Naturally, this pattern is distorted by variations in customer concentrations, travel routes, turning limitations, and variation in travel times, but the basic idea remains compelling.

At some level of geography most urban goods and services have a central place pattern. For example, even though regional shopping malls are driven by a phenomenon that is the polar opposite of convenience shopping, a large metropolitan area will have numerous regional malls. In relation to each other, they tend to locate in a central place pattern.

Geographers have studied central place patterns extensively, and have noted that there are hierarchies among them. Within a large city, regional malls and large discount stores may represent a relatively high-level central place function, while sandwich shops or hair salons may represent low-level ones. The difference in hierarchy is by area or population required for

Exhibit 5-8 Idealized Location Pattern of Convenience Goods and Services

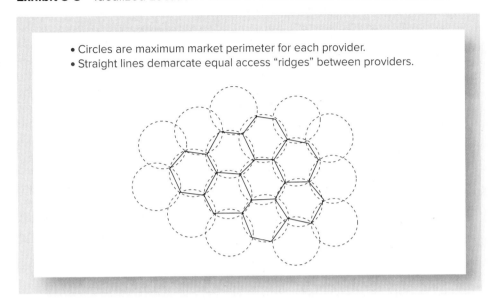

- Circles are maximum market perimeter for each provider.
- Straight lines demarcate equal access "ridges" between providers.

a viable market. The important features of all central place activities are that they tend to be evenly dispersed, and serve some minimum population as a threshold market.

> ✓ **Concept Check**
>
> **5.16** The essential feature of a convenience good or central place activity is that households, in acquiring it, go to the _____ source.

Comparison Goods and Clustering

The opposite of central place location patterns is clustering. In retailing this occurs with shopping or **comparison activities** ("goods"). Examples include apparel stores like those within a regional mall, car dealers, club districts, and other types of businesses where customers typically wish to go from one competitor to another in the course of a single trip. For these types of goods and services, the optimal location pattern is to cluster, and shopping malls are a major example of the phenomenon.[10]

Industry Economies of Scale and Clustering

In addition to the comparison behavior of customers, other forms of clustering also result from the industry economies of scale discussed earlier; that is, by clustering, firms engaged in the same kind of activity may create mutual efficiencies. For example, clustered suburban office buildings have been attractive to many office tenants. One reason for this may be the supporting services that tend to result when many offices cluster in the same location. These can include car rentals, office supplies, computer services and support, restaurants, health clubs, day care, and many other kinds of business and employee services. In addition, a highly visible and well-planned cluster of buildings may afford office tenants an attractive setting that has image or advertising value, or value as a pleasant environment for employees.

10. Regional malls and so-called festival and lifestyle shopping centers exemplify the comparison activity. In contrast, neighborhood shopping centers anchored by a supermarket, and "power centers" anchored by discount stores are primarily convenience good centers.

Where Have All the Factories Gone?

It is common knowledge that the factories which built and characterized many U.S. cities in earlier generations are now silent, or missing. So where have they gone? The answer may be the Pearl River Delta of China. That region, two-thirds the size of West Virginia, now has the greatest agglomeration of manufacturing that the world has ever known. In this area, guarded by Hong Kong on one side of the river outlet and by Macao on the other, the factory employment is thought to exceed the entire factory employment in the United States. In 2007 another standard shipping container of goods was launched from the region every second, continuously. Nearly 5 percent of the world's goods now are produced in this region.

Is it only low wages that fuel the explosive growth of this 30-year-young industrial colossus? Observers say no. Another component of its success is

Key Cities of the Pearl River Delta (01/05/2003)

Pearl River Delta Region

Source: © The Hong Kong Trader

production speed and flexibility. The region has become a manufacturing example of agglomeration economies in which the concentration of factories, materials, component inventories, and labor enables it to launch new production within days. The same product that would require automated production in the United States, with prolonged scheduling of existing assembly line equipment, plus time for setup, testing, and arranging supply sources, can get into production sometimes within hours.

Does this rapid response work for all manner of goods? No. But for a vast array of household electronics goods, toys, and similar items made of standard components, and where final assembly does not require super-high precision, where markets develop and fade quickly, and where modern packing and shipping can assure safe passage, the Pearl River Delta alternative appears to dominate.

Does the meteoric growth of Pearl River manufacturing imply doom for more U.S. manufacturing plants and cities? Probably some, but apparently not all. For goods that involve unorthodox or high-precision assembly, so that robot production is needed, or for goods where steady production demand enables high levels of automation, the labor-intensive mode of the Pearl River Delta may not be the competitive choice.

Will the rapid growth of 3-D printing (additive manufacturing) since about 2013 affect the Pearl River phenomenon? Apparently not much. While it promises to transform some areas of manufacturing, this is mainly in the high-precision, prototype, and unique parts manufacturing that already is in the United States today. What may put a greater damper on the growth of the Pearl River phenomenon is rising labor costs in China.

Source: Partially based on James Fallows, *Atlantic Monthly*, July/August 2007.

✓ Concept Check

5.17 The location tendency of comparison activities is to _____ whereas the location tendency of convenience activities is to _____.

Another interesting example of industry economies of scale is the typical large research university. Most graduate school and research-oriented universities have many different colleges, with separate administrations, separate students, separate curricula, and separate facilities. Thus, it may be less than obvious why the university exists as a total unit. Indeed, it is not uncommon for political leaders to suggest that various professional schools be pulled away from a major state university and relocated to their favorite urban center.

The explanation for the multicollege university lies in industry economies of scale. For example, even schools as diverse as medicine, engineering, and law share a multitude of common supporting services that are enhanced and refined through joint utilization by multiple schools. These include advanced library services, advanced technical and computer expertise, administrative support services, classroom and pedagogical support services, and editorial and publishing services. A second aspect of industry economies within the university is in advanced education curricula. Many degree programs depend on courses provided by one or more other schools because it is too costly, or even impossible, to

Community Development Specialist

Community development is the economic, physical, and social revitalization of a community led by the people who live in that community. Community developers work in community-based organizations; banks; city, state, and federal government; foundations; real estate development companies; social service agencies; job training and placement organizations; investment firms; and think tanks. Community developers do things with, not to or for, the community.

They transform a brownfield into a neighborhood shopping center, creatively finance low-cost mortgages, shape public policy, develop community health centers, build housing to shelter battered women and their families, train residents for well-paying jobs, start new local businesses, organize tenants to convert their apartments to cooperative ownership, create a joint venture with developers to develop a local supermarket, counsel families to move off welfare, assist farm workers to build their own houses, create new enterprises with community youth.[*]

Community development specialist describes a very diverse range of roles and settings, ranging from large central cities, to rural United States, to developing countries. The common thread is that such positions are needed anywhere that development by the private sector is less than what the community needs. Jobs in this emerging field appear to require at least an undergraduate degree. Many require business and real estate training, though many more seem primarily to demand organizational and communication skills.

[*]Brophy, Paul and Shabecoff, Alice *A Guide to Careers in Community Development* Island Press. © 2001 Island Press.

---

maintain the expertise for the needed courses internally. A third form of agglomeration comes in interdisciplinary research and development. In many universities, for example, engineering schools have joined with medical schools to produce an amazing array of materials suitable to replace or supplement components of the human body, as well as to produce equipment for medical and rehabilitative needs. Similar interactions also exist between medicine and biochemistry.

The university, like other activities in the economy, has felt the recent dramatic advancements in electronic communication and document transmission. But while this has reduced the need for proximity in some ways, it has enhanced it in others. For example, as electronic-based distance learning has grown, so has the need for common studios, equipment, software systems, and expertise necessary for delivering such programs. Further, internationalization has created additional common needs among schools of the university relating to foreign languages and translation, international travel arrangements, and provisions for international students and visitors. Thus, as some multicollege "industry economies" diminish, others seem to evolve.

The Role of Urban Analysis in Real Estate Decisions

It is reasonable to ask how the broad ideas about urban land use we have presented in this chapter really help with particular real estate decisions. In answer, it is the larger urban relationships that give meaning to the notion of location—that is, the most important meaning of location is location within a matrix of urban activities. Several points follow from this proposition. First, the location of a parcel is about its linkages or access to various nodes within the urban matrix. Second, the nature of this location depends on the type of land use being considered. For example, a weak location for a central place or convenience activity may be a strong location for a comparison shopping activity. Similarly, a weak location for a retail activity may be a strong location for warehouses. And a good location for student apartments may be a poor location for residential condominiums because of differences in linkage needs between the types of occupants.

Another point is that cities do not grow evenly. Rather, some nodes of activity grow faster, while some may decline. So the growth potential for a site, and the appreciation potential of a site, depends on where it is with respect to growing and declining nodes within the city. In short, the location quality of a particular site cannot be evaluated except as part of the larger urban matrix.[11]

Finally, the story of urban evolution recounted here punctuates the importance of urban change. In real estate analysis one must look not only to the current urban matrix but also to where changes in technology, transportation systems, and the economic base are leading this network of relationships in the future. The good location of one decade can become the declining location of the next as new arterials, new intersections, new employment centers, and new forms of retailing emerge.

11. To look at urban form and composition, few media are more useful than aerial photos. The websites shown in the margin are particularly interesting sources. They enable one to select a location, zoom in on it, and then navigate in any direction around that point.

Summary

History is replete with real estate ventures that failed due to an inadequate market for the project. While market risk is inherent in any business, many real estate failures could have been avoided through more thoughtful and careful assessment of market potential for the intended project.

To understand real estate markets requires an understanding of the urban economies that generate those markets. One must understand the economic base of a city—those activities that bring income into a city—and what is happening to it. One also must understand the subsectors or clusters within a city to be able to distinguish areas of high growth from areas of slow growth or decline. Further, one must understand differing locational needs among urban land uses, such as the need of convenience "goods" for dispersed locations as opposed to the need of "comparison" goods to cluster. One must be aware of the importance of industry and agglomeration economies as factors that strengthen and stabilize urban markets, or leave less stable markets in their absence.

Urban form and urban real estate markets have never ceased to be impacted by change. It is important to recognize the dominant patterns of change and the steady, yet profound, pressures they exert on land use. The real estate analyst must understand the long periods over which such changes occur, and must understand which land uses are favored and which are diminished by the forces of change. Especially important has been change in transportation systems, causing whole areas of cities to expand or decline drastically. But also important are changes in production and distribution technology, bringing the need for new kinds of structures and real estate developments. Finally, the revolutions in communications technology have been loosening spatial bonds through much of the 20th century and undoubtedly will continue to impact urban form for years to come.

Within the urban matrix are diverse types of activities with different locational needs with respect to competitors. Convenience activities seek to disperse uniformly over the urban landscape while comparison activities seek to cluster with competitors. Industry economies of scale may draw a cluster of complementary activities together at a single urban node, such as a medical center or major university.

Key Terms

Agglomeration economies　107	Convenience activities　120	Location quotient　105
Bid-rent model　108	Economic base　102	Multinuclei city　117
Central place pattern　120	Industry economies of scale　107	Sector model　117
Comparison activities　121	Linkages　101	
Concentric ring model　113	Local economic activities　104	

Test Problems

Answer the following multiple-choice problems:

1. The "gravity" that draws economic activity into clusters is:
   a. Common laws and regulations.
   b. Common language.
   c. Demand for access or proximity.
   d. Cost of land.
   e. Streets.

2. Spatial or distance relationships that are important to a land use are called its:
   a. Linkages.
   b. Agglomerations.
   c. Facets.
   d. Dimensions.
   e. Attractions.

3. Cities have tended to grow where:
   a. Transportation modes intersect or change.
   b. Transportation is uninterrupted.
   c. People are concentrated.
   d. There is ample land and energy.
   e. There is demand for economic goods.

4. The economic base multiplier of a city tends to be greater if the city is:
   a. Larger.
   b. Older.
   c. Less isolated from other cities.
   d. Newer.
   e. Less diversified.

5. The best example of a base economic activity would be a:
   a. Supermarket.
   b. Department store.
   c. Fire department.
   d. Large apartment complex.
   e. Regional sales office.

6. Important supply factors affecting a city's growth or growth potential include all of the following *except* the:
   a. Unemployment rate.
   b. Business leadership.
   c. Presence of any industry economies of scale.
   d. Labor force characteristics.
   e. Education system.

7. Which of these are true about agglomeration economies?
   a. They result from demand created by multiple industries.
   b. They create a readily available supply of highly specialized goods and labor.
   c. They tend to reduce risks in real estate.
   d. They occur in larger cities.
   e. All of the above.

8. Which of these influences will decrease the level of a bid-rent curve at the center of the city?
   a. Faster travel time.
   b. Higher average wage rate.
   c. Increased number of trips per household.
   d. Larger number of households bidding.
   e. None of these.

9. In a system of bid-rent curves, assuming that households are identical except for the feature noted, which of these prospective bidders will bid successfully for the sites nearest to the CBD?
   a. Households with the greatest number of commuting workers.
   b. Households with the lowest income.
   c. Households with superior means of transportation.
   d. Households that arrive in the city last.
   e. Households requiring more land.

10. A large university is an example of what kind of economic phenomenon?
    a. Convenience activity.
    b. Comparison activity.
    c. Industry economies of scale.
    d. Secondary or local economic activity.
    e. Quality of life activity.

Study Questions

1. List five major economic base activities for your city of residence.

2. Find the historical population figures for your community for the 20th century. Create a chart with 10-year intervals. Determine the most rapid periods of growth, and try to discover what caused them. (One source of the necessary population numbers is the U.S. Census home page, www.census.gov. Look for *QuickFacts,* and select your state. At the top of the large table of current information that appears select your county or city. Then click on "Browse more datasets"—the magnifying glass symbol beside the heading—and look down the page for the heading "Historical Population Counts."

3. On the U.S. Census website, use the approach shown in Explore the Web (next page) to access the American Community Survey. For your county and for your state find the distribution of income for all households. Graph the distributions using percentage for each income interval. Which is higher, county or state?

4. Identify at least five locational attributes that you believe are important in the location of a fast-food restaurant. Compare notes with someone in the industry such as a local restaurant manager or owner.

5. Perfect Population Projections Inc. (PPP) has entered into a contract with the city of Popular, Pennsylvania, to project the future population of the city. In recent years, Popular has become a desirable place to live and work, as indicated by the table on the next page.

   The contract states that PPP must project Popular's population for the year 2018 using both a simple linear method and an economic base analysis. The ratio of population to total employment is 2.0833.

   Your help is needed!

Year	Total Population	Total Employment	Basic Employment	Nonbasic Employment
2013	50,000	25,000	6,250	18,750
2014	53,000	26,500	6,625	19,875
2015	57,000	28,500	7,125	21,375
2016	65,000	32,500	8,125	24,375
2017	70,000	35,000	8,750	26,250
2018	?	?	9,000[*]	?

*Estimated from surveys.

EXPLORE THE WEB

American FactFinder: Electronic Gateway to the United States Census Bureau

One result of the Internet revolution is an amazing availability of government data about our society. Virtually all data collected by the U.S. Government now are readily available online in some aggregate form, where it can be viewed, downloaded, or mapped. Particularly valuable is the American Community Survey, which largely replaces the U.S. Census of Population for detailed information and provides fresh social and economic data every year. Many household characteristics are available at the national, state, metro, county, city, and even the census tract and ZIP code levels.[i] A principal gateway to these data is the American Fact-Finder of the U.S. Census Bureau. Google "American Factfinder." Explore the use of American FactFinder through this "treasure hunt."

Under Community Facts, select a county and a state of your choice. Then select the following sequence of topics:

1. To get an overview of your county, simply enter the county name in *state, county or place*, leave *topic* blank, and click GO. You see multiple data categories—population, age, business, industry, etc.—and you see sources of data, such as 2010 Census, latest available American Community Survey, etc. Select "Population," and the latest Census "General Population and Housing Characteristics."

   a. What percentage of the population is 65 years of age or older?
   b. How many total households are there?
   c. What percentage are families?
   d. What percentage are families with children?
   e. What is the average household size in owner-occupied housing units? In renter units?

2. In the top menu bar click ADVANCED SEARCH. Now in the left margin select "Topics," and "People," and "Income & Earnings," and "Households." (Be sure you still have the correct geography.) Open the latest ACS 5-year table titled "Selected Economic Characteristics."

   a. What is the median household income?
   b. What is the mean household income?
   c. What is the largest industry of employment other than retail?

3. At the top right, click on BACK TO ADVANCED SEARCH. In the top left box delete your current topic. Then in the box labeled *Refine your search* enter "migration (previous residence)" and click GO. A new list of tables will appear; select and view the latest table showing geographical mobility by selected characteristics. (You may need to scroll down to find it.)

   a. What percentage of the population lived in a household that was in the same house a year earlier? (You will need to deduce this percentage from the data reported.)
   b. How much does this percentage differ between owner and rental households?

4. Again, click BACK TO ADVANCED SEARCH. In the upper left, delete your current topic and confirm your geography selection. Then, in Topics, select Housing/Basic Counts/Housing Units. Then open Selected Housing Characteristics, ACS 5-year.

   a. How many occupied housing units are there?
   b. What percentage of occupied housing units are owner occupied?

c. What percentage of owner occupied housing units have a mortgage?

d. What percentage of housing units were built in 2000 or later?

e. What percentage are detached?

f. What percentage of owner households have a monthly housing cost that is 35 percent of income or greater?

g. What percentage of renter households have a monthly gross rent that is 35 percent of income or greater?

5. Again, click on BACK TO ADVANCED SEARCH. In the upper left, delete your current topic and verify your geography choice. Now, from Topics, select Housing/ Financial Characteristics/Mortgages and Status. Open the latest ACS 5-year table titled "Financial Characteristics for Housing Units with a Mortgage"

a. What is the median value of owner occupied housing units with a mortgage?

b. Examine the monthly housing cost by income. At each level of household income shown, what percent of the households have housing costs of 30 percent or more?

6. Go to American FactFinder Help and click on *Tutorials*. American FactFinder is the gateway to hundreds of tables for any area and level of geography. To get a better idea of the possibilities, run the short video tutorials on Topic Search and Search for Geographies.... Also note that you can download tables, modify them extensively, and map your data as well.

i. census tract is an explicit, relatively permanent, census subdivision containing roughly 1,500 to 8,000 persons.

ii. For the American Community Survey, each locality is divided by the Census Bureau into five equivalent sampling "sub-frames," one of which is sampled each year in rotation. The five-year estimates combine results from all five sampling sub-frames, and represent the largest overall sample.

Solutions to Concept Checks

1. The demand for access between one urban activity and others is referred to as the activity's linkages.

2. The "gravity" that draws economic activity into forming cities is the need for access.

3. Historically, cities tended to form at the intersection of different modes of transportation.

4. The theory underlying the concept of economic base is that cities exist to serve the economic world at large.

5. The size of an economic base multiplier depends on the amount of "leakage" from the local economy.

6. The customary analysis of a city's economic base tends to focus on external demand, which tends to be a short-term phenomenon.

7. Cost efficiencies that arise in a city due to concentration of an industry are called industry economies of scale, whereas cost efficiencies arising from the concentration of multiple industries are called agglomeration economies.

8. The economic incentive that gives rise to bid-rent curves is the desire to reduce commuting or travel time.

9. Faster travel results in less value to be close to the CBD, and a lesser slope of the bid-rent curve. More trips make being close to the CBD more valuable, and a steeper slope. More commuters will cause a higher curve with the same slope. Higher density housing means more trips from a given site or lot. Thus, it tends to increase the slope of the bid-rent curve. A higher hourly wage will cause the proximity to the CBD to be more valuable, thus an increase in the slope.

10. A person who commutes on foot will always outbid a person who commutes by car for space near downtown because the pedestrian commuter's time cost of traveling is far greater.

11. The Burgess concentric model of urban form was conceived in an era when the dominant form of transportation was by railway and the principal method of moving goods within factories was by elevator.

12. The radial or "pie slice" pattern in the Hoyt sector model of urban form probably can be explained by the dominance of the streetcar (fixed-rail transit) for intraurban transportation at the time the model was formulated.

13. One of the most profound forces bringing change in urban form in the United States is the automobile. Whereas cars were a novelty in 1915, most households owned one by about 1930.

14. The demand for space for horizontal factories was greatly accelerated in the 1920s by the development of assembly-line production.

15. Modern office structures and retail facilities were not possible before the development of air-conditioning and fluorescent lighting.

16. The essential feature of a convenience good or central place activity is that households, in acquiring it, go to the closest source.

17. The location tendency of comparison activities is to cluster, whereas the location tendency of convenience activities is to disperse.

Additional Readings

Books on real estate markets include the following:

Clapp, John M. *Handbook for Real Estate Market Analysis.* Upper Saddle River, NJ: Prentice Hall, 1987.

DiPasquale, Denise, and William C. Wheaton. *Urban Economics and Real Estate Markets.* Upper Saddle River, NJ: Prentice Hall, 1996.

Geltner, David, Norman G. Miller, Jim Clayton, and Piet Eichholz. *Commercial Real Estate Analysis and Investments.* Mason, OH: OnCourse Learning, 2014.

Glaeser, Edward. *Triumph of the City: How Our Greatest Invention Makes Us Richer, Smarter, Greener, Healthier and Happier.* New York: The Penguin Press, 2011.

Kelly, Hugh F. *24 Hour Cities: Real Investment Performance, Not Just Promises.* London and New York: Routledge, 2016.

Kibert, C. J., and A. Wilson. *Reshaping the Built Environment: Ecology, Ethics, and Economics.* Washington, DC: Island Press, 1999.

Thrall, Grant I. *Business Geography and New Real Estate Market Analysis.* New York: Oxford University Press, 2002.

For exposure to geographic information systems in many variations and levels, visit the website of ESRI: www.esri.com (ESRI is a principal provider of GIS systems).

www.mhhe.com/lingarcher5e

Chapter 6

Forecasting Ownership Benefits *and* Value: Market Research

LEARNING OBJECTIVES

After reading this chapter you will be able to:

1 Define market segmentation and give three examples for real estate markets.

2 Identify the sequence of steps in the cycle of real estate market research.

3 Identify five questions for writing a "market-defining story."

4 Locate data sources on the Internet for county, MSA, and census tract level household demographics, detailed local employment, and the composition of business by county.

5 Identify at least two applications in real estate market research for geographic information systems.

6 Explain what role psychographics can have in real estate market research.

7 Identify at least two possible applications of survey research in real estate market research.

OUTLINE

Introduction

In Chapter 5 we examined cities and the influences that cause their decline or growth. Further, we examined the forces that determine a city's shape and texture. It remains, however, to relate this urban matrix to the value of a specific property. This chapter is about bridging that gap through real estate market research. The objective here is to construct a plausible relationship between the urban matrix and the cash flows to an individual property that give value to its owner.

We first note a crucial element of real estate market research: market segmentation. Unfortunately, the challenge of market research is complicated by market segmentation because the segments are often less than obvious and less than stable. This leaves little to rely on as constant. For this reason real estate market research must be understood not as a form but as a process. We outline that process and demonstrate it through three cases. Then we consider the challenge that real estate market cycles pose for market research. Finally, we discuss three tools applicable to real estate market research: geographical information systems (GIS), psychographics, and survey research.

Market Research: Slipperiest Step in Real Estate Valuation

Chapter 5 opened with numerous examples of real estate market "disasters." The message of that chapter is that one cannot value real estate without understanding its urban context. This context certainly includes the urban "linkages" discussed in Chapter 5, as well as land use controls that may constrain the use of a site or dampen or accentuate the effects of economic forces.

But there is still more to the puzzle of market research. Not only do land uses vary by the set of linkages important to them, but they vary by nonlocational requirements as well. For example, the features required of a residence depend heavily upon the income level and makeup of the target household. Single persons or working couples certainly have different housing preferences than families with children, and retired households have different preferences than working households. Adding to the difficulty is that preferences appear to vary with time, prosperity, and context. For example, the portion of renter households that will accept a third-story apartment varies from one community to another, and the portion of homebuyers who insist on a three-car garage has varied with time and community.

In nonresidential realms, nonlocational needs among firms can become even more important. For example, some analysts believe that markets of neighborhood shopping centers and "power centers" have a winner-take-all character that enables only shopping facilities with a market-dominating anchor tenant to have long-term viability.[1] If so, the value of a center with a "winning" anchor tenant is likely to reflect that advantage. In the hotel industry each of the major chains, such as Marriott, Hilton, or Intercontinental Hotel Group (owner of Holiday Inn), offers a lengthy menu of hotel names with differing price levels, room designs, supporting facilities, and services, targeting different types of customers. (See the link in the margin on hotel groups.) Office buildings have their own set of nonlocational features that differentiate properties, including floor plate size, amount and character of parking, provisions for electronics and communications systems, adequacy of common areas, available amenities and services, nature of existing tenants, and other factors.

https://en.wikipedia.org/ wiki/List_of_chained- brand_hotels

A convenient list of the various hotel brands owned by each major hotel group.

> ✓ **Concept Check**
>
> **6.1**   List three kinds of factors that affect the value of an urban property.

1. "Power centers" are shopping centers dominated by such "big box" retailers as discount stores, or "category killers" such as Best Buy, Lowes, or Home Depot.

Our conclusion is that real estate market research must always be thoughtful and flexible. Rather than having a fixed procedure, the research must depend on the problem, and adapt to unfolding discoveries as the research goes forward. In short, rather than a formula, real estate market research is a process, which we try to illuminate here.

Market Segmentation

The nuances in the preferences or needs of market subgroups are generally termed **market segmentation.** The importance of market segmentation is this: To the extent that it exists in a market, market analysis should focus on the relevant market segments for the property involved. A common error, for example, has been the failure to recognize the differences between residential condominium markets and traditional, single-family home markets. But data on market conditions for single-family homes can be a very poor indicator of market conditions for nearby condominiums. Too often, information about condominium markets has been scarce. The challenge thus has been to cut through the easily available single-family data and create effective indicators about condo markets. It is not far off the mark to say that *effective real estate market research is often a matter of excluding the irrelevant.*[2]

> ✓ **Concept Check**
>
> **6.2**   Before effective real estate market research can be achieved, relevant _____ must be examined.

> ✓ **Concept Check**
>
> **6.3**   The presence of market segmentation in real estate gives rise to a valuable guide in sorting through available market and property data, which is _____.

Real Estate Market Research as Storytelling

The thoughtful real estate analyst realizes that market analysis cannot be simply facts. Market behavior, after all, is as complicated as the sum of all the economic decisions of all the persons potentially participating in a market. No data set—even "big data"—will ever account for all of the decisions that ultimately add up to market behavior. So what is a market analysis if not facts? It is opinion, based on the analyst's "model," or simplified assumptions and logic, about how the market works. We will call this the analyst's *story.* This view of market research as creating a story arguably makes it the most creative and challenging aspect of real estate analysis. The process is suggested in Exhibit 6-1. It begins by tentatively defining the market "story" involved. This is followed by collection of *relevant* data to examine the market and test the initial definitions. Then comes an initial evaluation of results, or market assessment. Frequently this may be followed by the refinement of the market definitions and further collection of *relevant* data. Sometimes at this point, very specifically focused survey research may become important. This iterative process may continue through multiple rounds until further refinements will yield no additional useful information.

> ✓ **Concept Check**
>
> **6.4**   Rather than approaching real estate market research as a form or formula, the conditional nature of the task makes it a _____.

2. This was a point frequently made by the brilliant real estate academic and analyst James Graaskamp. (See footnote 14.)

Exhibit 6-1   The Cycle of Market Research

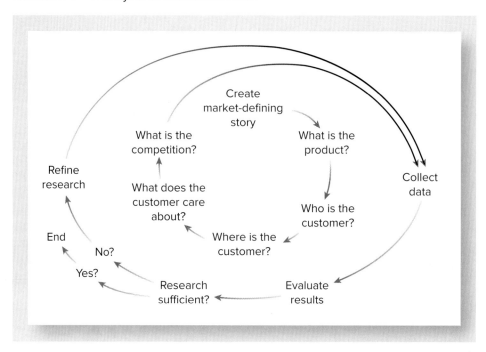

The Beginning Point: A Market-Defining Story

The beginning point of the market research process is to construct a market defining "story." This story needs to answer the following questions:

1. What is the real estate product under consideration?
2. Who are the customers (target market)?
3. Where are the customers? (What is the market area?)
4. What do the customers care about? (What aspects of the product?)
5. Who are the competitors?

We argue that an important beginning of any real estate market analysis should be to actually *write* a page or more story of this nature. The discipline of writing it cannot help but clarify the researcher's understanding of the market involved. Further, because market research is, after all, the researcher's story of what is happening and will happen, it is important to the ultimate user to understand the writer's underlying assumptions. The more difficult it is to write this story, the more important it is to do it. Below, we will show examples of such stories.

Important help in writing a market-defining story can come from industry literature. Clues about potential market segmentation can come from information on various types of properties and their characteristics. A particularly rich source is the list of publications from the Urban Land Institute.[3] Other good sources are listed at the end of this chapter.[4]

---

3. More recent examples of ULI publications include Adrienne Schmitz and Deborah L. Brett, *Real Estate Market Analysis: A Case Study Approach,* 2nd ed. (2015) and Richard Peiser and Anne B. Frej, *Professional Real Estate Development: The ULI Guide to the Business,* 2nd ed. (2003). Many older publications of ULI are excellent as well.

4. In addition to descriptive information, the literature mentioned contains a voluminous amount of material on methods and formats for market research in real estate. While we agree with the potential value of much of this material, we simply caution that its relevance depends altogether on the nature of the case involved—hence our focus on defining the market at the outset.

Initial Collection of Data

The market-defining story should serve to identify the needed data in the analysis. It also should identify as irrelevant a vast amount of commonly available data. However, little can be said in advance about which is which. For this reason we simply show examples of what data are relevant in the three "stories" that follow, and what data are at hand in each case.

First Analysis

With initial data in hand, one makes a first attempt to draw conclusions about the market questions. Commonly the critical questions will be about **market parameters,** that is, key numbers that characterize the current condition and trend in the market. For rental markets these typically include current occupancy rate, future occupancy rates, and rental rate growth. For buyer markets they include current and projected sales rates. Thus, one will ask what range of these critical parameters appears to be consistent with the data that have been assembled. For example, with subdivision or condominium projects, the critical question will concern how many units will sell (at a given price) in each month, quarter, or year of the study horizon, that is, the period covered by the study. For an operating property such as apartments, rental offices, or rental retail, the critical questions will be about projected occupancy level and rental rate growth over the study horizon. If the initial efforts have been successful, the analyst will be able to identify boundaries (never a single number) for these critical parameters.

Refining the Research

In some cases, the initial projections will answer the question at hand, and the analysis is complete. However, if the "story" is unconvincing or the range of projected parameters is too wide to answer the question at hand, the analysis will need to be refined.

After the first analysis, the analyst will better understand what factors are important to the market projections. He or she may need to modify the research accordingly. However, it may also become clear that additional research will not help. This would suggest that the property is highly risky, with very uncertain value.

A Reverse to Conventional Market Research

An important point about the "story" approach to market research is that it starts at the property and moves outward—that is, the initial step is to characterize the property and its specific market, whereas the conventional approach to market analysis has been to move from general to specific. While conventional market analysis starts with national or world conditions and works down by steps to the property, the story approach first seeks to define the property and its market in order to identify a stronger bridge outward to the macro conditions. This can give a clearer picture of what macro factors actually drive the target market.

Three Important Techniques in Market Analysis

How does one get from a market defining story to a completed market analysis? Three valuable techniques to accomplish this are:

- Excluding the irrelevant
- Finding proxy variables
- Using analogy

**www.esri.com & www.
esri.com/software/bao**

ESRI is the dominant provider and
supporter of GIS software. Of
special interest for common real
estate market analysis is Business
Analyst Online (and an adapted
version known as STDB). Among its
capabilities is to report estimates of
employment by a large number of
categories within an arbitrarily
chosen area.

We comment on each technique and then illustrate its possible role through a simple example.

Excluding the Irrelevant. We already have stressed this theme, but its central importance justifies more focus. Almost all data we can obtain about real estate markets were generated for some other purpose and encompassed more than the relevant people or properties. An extremely productive step in market analysis—sometimes all that is needed—is to try to exclude the portion of these data that are irrelevant.

Finding proxy variables. Frequently the data we really want for an analysis aren't available. Examples may be the occupancy rate for a certain size or type of apartment, or the number of student-oriented apartments in an area. For the occupancy rate we might turn to an overall occupancy rate as a proxy, trusting that there is high correlation in occupancy across apartment sizes. For a proxy of student apartments we might try to identify all apartment properties that offer individual bedroom leases, trusting that a high percentage of the student-oriented properties offer this type of lease. Note that the alternative to using a proxy variable sometimes is to do good field work. A rough proxy indicator often is a weak second choice to calling on site managers, visiting with them and asking the right questions.

Using Analogy. When you are evaluating the prospects for a project that is new in your setting you have no actual relevant market performance data. How can you proceed? One recourse is to find parallel situations elsewhere with a similar project in a similar context, and examine their experience. Once you have constructed your market defining story you should be able to determine the essential features of your project and your market context, and use them to identify analogous properties.

An example. Consider an example that involves all three of the techniques above. You are asked to evaluate the initial market potential for a 100 unit non-student luxury five-floor (mid-rise) apartment project in a mixed student and downtown neighborhood of a university city. The minimum monthly rent will be $1,200. There are many student apartments in the neighborhood, but no luxury non-student apartments. Your first question is how many households might be interested and can afford the proposed apartments. Your market defining story depicts the potential tenants as working households with professional jobs and with no children at home. You also have decided that job location is the main determinant of where these households locate.

For your analysis you start with your assumption that jobs drive the residential location of this market. Using a GIS subscription service (see margin) you are able to estimate all the jobs located within five minutes of your site, by job type. With this data you can narrow the focus to "professional" jobs in your five minute zone. But how do you get from jobs to apartments? For lack of more precise data, you use a proxy measure: you assume that employees holding the "professional" jobs in your target zone own or rent in the same proportions as non-student households in the community as a whole. This lets you narrow your estimated total to the renting professionals. Similarly, you assume that the metropolitan distribution of gross monthly rent households pay (from the ACS/American FactFinder) proxies for the distribution of your available rental households. With this proxy for ability to pay, you are able to exclude the households below your rent threshold.

Suppose by your analysis you find that 800 households remain in your set of "eligible" households for the project. Then you must ask how many can your project capture, and this will depend on the competitiveness of the project. How can you evaluate your competitiveness? This is where analogy plays a part. Using Internet search or other means (a subscription service such as CoStar is by far the most powerful) you can find similar existing projects elsewhere with similar context, and examine the experience of these properties. You can contact the persons involved, visit the analogous projects, etc. to determine what clues they hold as to how you can maximize the competitiveness of your project.

Below, we apply this story approach, along with the techniques discussed, to three diverse cases. The first two dramatically illustrate the significance of recognizing market segmentation, revealing real cases where a small amount of exclusion analysis could have prevented unmitigated real estate disasters. The final case is cast as a narrative to convey the quality of the market research process. It is an application to an apartment feasibility problem, and is a more standard example. Even so, it illustrates that seemingly standard real estate market analysis can have surprising twists that lead to much more revealing analysis.

✓ Concept Check

6.6 Whereas real estate market research traditionally starts with a _____ perspective, the approach argued here begins with _____.

Three Examples of Market Research

Market Research Example 1: Elysian Forest, a Planned Unit Development

Some years ago in a small college community, University City, the first planned unit development, Elysian Forest, was introduced by a large national developer.[5] As discussed in Chapter 4 a planned unit development (PUD) is a residential development that differs from traditional residential subdivisions in several respects. First, it allows for variable density, encompassing some blend of detached single family, attached single family, townhouses, and apartments. Second, it typically has smaller individual lots, often without side-yards, but includes a variety of common areas and recreation facilities. Elysian Forest was a bold, innovative, and sophisticated project for the city, and with 900 units, was of unprecedented scale.

In Exhibit 6-2 are basic dimensions of the local housing market and of Elysian Forest. Features that distinguished the houses of Elysian Forest include the following:

1. The lots of Elysian Forest averaged less than half the size of typical single family lots prevailing for University City housing at the time, with most of the lots planned for zero-lot-line cluster homes or townhouses. (See Exhibits 6-3 and Exhibit 6-4.)
2. The housing units of Elysian Forest were in a price range between the 70th and 92nd percentile of the University City sales distribution. (That is, only 30 percent of all

Exhibit 6-2 Characteristics of Elysian Forest and the University City Housing Market

	Projected Sales of Elysian Forest				
Year	**1**	**2**	**3**	**4**	**5**
Patio Homes, Townhouses, Condos, and Small-lot Single Family	88	212	236	260	104
	Estimated Sales in the University City Housing Market				
Year	**1**	**2**	**3**	**4**	**5**
All Sales	1,500	1,500	1,550	1,600	1,700
New Units	500	600	850	900	1,100

5. We ignore the actual times of the three cases that follow because the stories are essentially timeless.

Exhibit 6-3   Elysian Forest and Its Competition

(Elysian Forest: Two cluster homes with common wall)

(The competitive standard: Two "Parade of Homes" of the time)

Exhibit 6-4 Example Patio Home Cluster of Elysian Forest

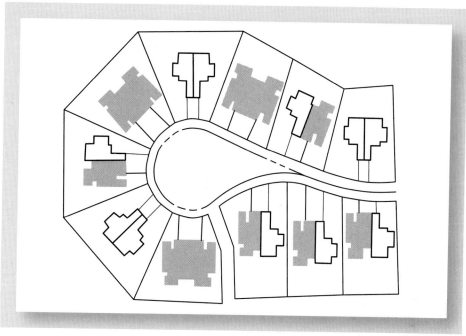

(Typical cluster plan)

local sales were at prices above the Elysian Forest minimum price, while 8 percent of all local sales were at prices still higher than those of Elysian Forest.)[6]

3. As a planned unit development, 15 to 20 percent of the land in Elysian Forest was reserved for open space and recreation areas.

4. The site and location were very typical of the area, with no outstanding visual or locational advantages.

The Market-Defining Story. Since Elysian Forest was very different from the customary housing stock of University City at the time of its introduction, careful attention to the market-defining story seems important. We approach the story using the five questions listed earlier:

1. *What is the product?* We have noted that it is mostly cluster homes and townhouses built at relatively high density. The project is relatively "high end" since the lowest-price unit is higher than 70 percent of the house prices transacted in the University City market. The prices projected for Elysian Forest were in a range with about 22 percent of the residences being sold at the time in University City.

2. *Who are the customers?* We must ask about the buyer income range, and about the types of households likely to be interested in Elysian Forest. Remembering that the units are relatively small, with a high cost per square foot of floor space, it becomes clear that a buyer can get much more house and yard by purchasing from the more conventional stock of houses in University City, such as shown in Exhibit 6-3. Further, the city is relatively small, with low density, and has a tradition of large private yards and houses. As a tentative story, we assume that families with children and pets are likely to prefer the more conventional residences where they can obtain more space and more distance from neighbors for the money. Adopting this assumption for the moment, we conclude that the primary market segment for Elysian Forest is an upper income range representing

---

6. One of the most valuable types of information about local housing markets is the volume of sales, by price. Unfortunately, in too many cases, neither local real estate organizations nor local governments bother to report these data, even though they are easily compiled from property transaction records.

Exhibit 6-5 Core Market Segment for Elysian Forest

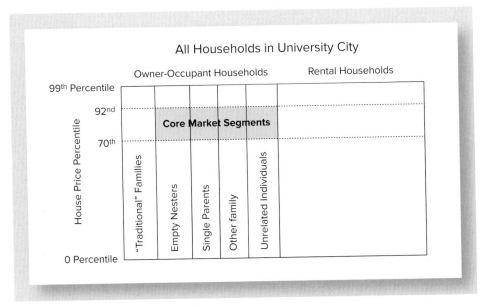

22 percent of the housing market in terms of price, and is comprised of households that are not traditional "full-nest" families.[7] Thus, the market might include childless couples, "empty nesters," retired couples, single adults, and possibly single parents.

3. *Where are the customers?* There are multiple possible market segments. With University City's fairly young population, most retirement buyers are likely to come from outside the city. In contrast, another market segment, empty nesters, is likely to come mainly from within the city because the city is predominantly a university and medical economy where most persons moving into the city for employment at higher-income levels are young faculty or medical residents rather than empty nesters. The remainder of market segments involved could come from either outside or inside the city.

4. *What do the customers care about in Elysian Forest?* We adopt the story that buyers want good access to employment, if employed, good recreation and social facilities, and distinctive, modern design.

5. *What is the competition?* At the time, there was no other project in the community comparable to Elysian Forest. The closest competition might be the homes offered by local builders in the annual "Parade of Homes" (see Exhibit 6-3) since many of those homes tended to be relatively upscale, with "state-of-the-art" special features.

Initial "Story."   What "story" does this initial tour through the market-defining questions give us? In summary, we tentatively assume that the primary market includes ownership households buying in the top 30 percent of the housing price range, but excluding the highest 8 percent. The main market segments are households other than traditional families with children at home. Finally, other than retirement households, the market is mainly local. Thus, we need to try to see how large the prospective market segments might be in University City.

Exhibit 6-5 suggests our "story." Out of the entire set of households in University City, we want to know what portion are in the Elysian Forest price range and also are in one of the target nontraditional family household types. If we start with the entire set of households and then exclude renters and traditional families, and finally exclude those households outside the target price range, we will have isolated the core market segments. We will turn to data of the U.S. Census for this purpose.

---

7. Families with husband, wife, and children at home.

Exhibit 6-6 Critical Numbers for Computing Elysian Forest "Market Share"

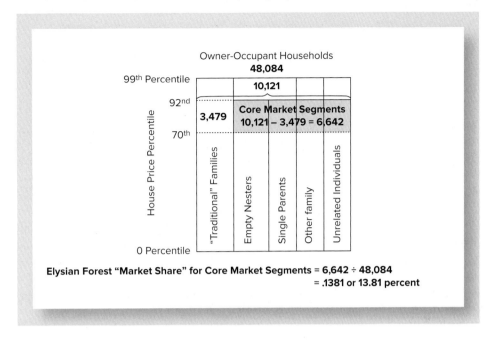

Elysian Forest "Market Share" for Core Market Segments = 6,642 ÷ 48,084
= .1381 or 13.81 percent

Initial Collection of Data. To estimate the size of the core market segments identified above, we need information about the composition of owner-occupant households in University City. We can find help in U.S. Census, which we can access through the Internet. On the U.S. Census website, in the dropdown menu "Data," select American FactFinder.[8] In the middle section of the main American FactFinder page, we can specify a *topic* and our county for the geography, then conduct a search of available tables. We will use this procedure.[9]

With the census data at hand, we are ready to attempt a first evaluation. We will do it in four steps:

1. *Determine the number of households in the core market segments.* We want a table showing the distribution of house prices by household type for owner-occupied homes. But, as is common in real estate research, the data do not speak directly to our questions, and we must tease out answers. We attempt different possible topics for our county and quickly realize that no census table is going to relate housing prices to household types. The closest we can get are tables showing the number of owner households by income (using the search topic: *tenure by income*) and showing family income by family type (using the search topic: *family type by income*). This will have to do. We find a table that reveals the income distribution of owner households, enabling us to compute the income boundaries for the 74th percentile and the 95th percentile.[10] We will take this 21 percent of owner households as a rough approximation of the households that might be a market for Elysian Forest. However, this includes all owner households in that income range, and we want to exclude traditional families. Searching further, we find that by incorporating information from another table we can estimate the traditional families that are owners and in our income range.[11] Then we subtract that group from our 21 percent of owner households, and we have an approximation of our core market segments. The resulting numbers are shown in Exhibit 6-6.

8. This is the same procedure demonstrated in greater detail at the end of Chapter 5, *Explore the Web*. The main Census URL is www.census.gov.
9. Geography options include state, metro area, county, zip code, and others.
10. Table B25118 Tenure by Household Income in the past 12 months.
11. Table B19131 Family Type by Presence of Own Children Under 18 Years by Family Income in the past 12 months.

Exhibit 6-7 Comparison of Target Sales for Elysian Forest with Total Potential Market Segment

Year	1	2	3	4	5
Total Target Sales	88	212	236	260	104
Total Market Segment Potential (Projected total market sales × 13.81%)	207	207	214	221	235
Projected Sales at Capture Rate of 20 Percent	41	41	43	44	47

www.census.gov

The source of virtually all detailed data on local household demographics. Click on QUICKFACTS for information of common interest for the United States, a state or local area.

Google American FactFinder

The primary search platform for U.S. Census data. See Explore the Web in Chapter 5.

2. *Determine the market share of the core market segments.* We divide the result from Step 1 by all owner households (from our census tables, once more) to get our core segment market share, 13.81 percent, as shown in Exhibit 6-6.

3. *From local market information, project the total housing unit sales for University City housing markets for the next five years.* For this projection we will rely on historic volumes of sales, tempered with judgment. We might obtain the data from the local real estate Multiple Listing Service (MLS), from local appraisers, or from the local property tax appraiser's office.

4. *For each year, estimate the sales to the core market segments of Elysian Forest.* We simply multiply market share for our core market segments (13.81 percent) by the projected sales of all housing units for each year. This gives us the volume of homebuyers by year that *could* be interested in Elysian Forest. The results appear in Exhibit 6-7.

✓ **Concept Check**

6.7 The primary data source for information on household characteristics is the _____.

Experienced real estate marketers know that in a normal community where there is competition among developers, builders, and sellers of existing homes, a single project rarely can capture more than a small percentage of a given market segment. We will assume a "capture rate" of 20 percent, which normally would be optimistic. The resulting projected sales for Elysian Forest are shown on the bottom line of Exhibit 6-7. Comparing the expected sales with target sales we see that the project appears to be far from feasible. The resulting forecast of sales is so low that the analysis can stop at this point. The project simply has no hope of success.

In fact, the project was undertaken without the benefit of this simple analysis, even though the computations required less than a day. The company built 20 speculative units, but never sold any. Despite sophisticated and expensive marketing efforts, once the taint of failure became attached to the development, no buyer was interested in it. Not only did the project fall into financial disaster, but the once prominent national company went bankrupt as well.

Market Research Example 2: Palm Grove Office Complex

A second market analysis example illustrates the importance of a market-defining story in a nonresidential context. Again in University City, a developer proposed the Palm Grove office complex, an innovative project for the city in both scale and type of buildings. The project proposed two four-floor "glass blocks," each with 40,000 square feet of space, or 10,000-square-foot floor plates. While a few buildings of similar magnitude existed in the city, they were built by and for the users, and no office building of the scale proposed ever had been built on a speculative basis.[12]

While the location is on a major arterial, the site poses some concerns. It is surrounded by housing, a car dealer, a high school, and a few small "strip" offices. It is distant from any other office centers.

The Market-Defining Story.   Once again we construct our market-defining story as answers to the series of questions identified previously:

1. *What is the product?* The structures are general-purpose office space, modern, but of modest quality (i.e., they lack distinguishing architecture, landscaping, or other notable features), in a location lacking strong positive supporting amenities and where the average distance to employee parking is approximately 75 yards. The structures are not designed with special facilities that might serve laboratories or medical offices.

2. *Who is the customer?* As a starting point in identifying the Palm Grove market segment, it is useful to compare the building design to the predominant stock of office buildings in University City. A drive down any of the main arteries of the city reveals that, apart from some medical offices near hospitals and some government offices, the typical office buildings are smaller than the proposed complex—say, 1,200 to 4,000 square feet, with two floors at most—with very close access to surface parking, and usually with high visibility from the street. This stock contrasts with Palm Grove where the floors are 10,000 square feet, parking is up to several hundred feet from the office, and three floors require an elevator ride. The design suggests that the proposed buildings are best suited to organizations that require the larger floor plates. If we suppose that office firms typically want 150 square feet of space per employee, then firms with, say, 25 or more employees would be the best candidates for the proposed office buildings. (The prevailing style of buildings should be preferable to firms that are any smaller.)

    For general-purpose office buildings such as proposed for Palm Grove, likely categories of firms include the following:

    - Finance and insurance, except depository institutions such as banks and credit unions.
    - Nonresidential real estate brokerage and management firms.
    - Engineering and consulting.
    - Accounting.
    - Computer services and programming.
    - Management consulting.
    - Market and public opinion research.

    Types of office firms unlikely to be interested in Palm Grove would include medical offices because of the distance from hospitals and the absence of special plumbing. Law offices also would have little interest due to the distance from the courtrooms (five miles away). Residential real estate firms do not concentrate their employees in a large single office, and they want maximum street access. Social service organizations might use the larger floor plates, but they might reduce the attractiveness of the property for nonsocial service businesses, and would not pay premium rents. Thus, they would be last-resort tenants in the view of the owner.

3. *Where are the customers?* The market could possibly be among firms relocating to University City, but the flow of such firms with 25 or more employees is small and quite uncertain. Thus, we assume that most of the prospective tenants are local.

4. *What do the customers (tenants) care about for Palm Grove?* The general business community of University City is small and local in character. Mostly, it provides services to households and other small businesses. The linkages of the site appear satisfactory for many of these users except for the isolation of the site from any comparable offices. In addition, several building features, which we already have alluded to, appear to be concerns for local service tenants.

---

12. Speculative building is constructing for unknown buyers or tenants.

5. *Who is the competition?* For occupants needing space of, say, 4,000 square feet or less (those with under 25 employees), existing single-floor office buildings and "build-to-suit" space is very competitive. Because of visual exposure, convenient access, and parking, the competitive space appears to hold significant advantages for most of these firms.

Initial "Story."   The outcome of our tour through the market-defining questions is this: We are looking for general-purpose office tenants with 25 or more employees. We believe that they must already be within the city.

Initial Data Collection.   In assessing the market potential for the building, one approach might be to canvass the business community in search of office-based businesses that have 25 or more employees. Lists of chamber of commerce members or lists of firms from a local economic development authority usually include the number of employees, and would assist with this effort. A virtue of this approach to market research is that it also could serve to actually market the buildings since the firms identified are the most likely tenants. However, as a preliminary approach, we can examine published data on local business patterns. Such information is instantly available over the Internet from the U.S. Bureau of the Census in *County Business Patterns,* an annual county-level survey of firms by industry and number of employees.

www.census.gov/econ/cbp

County Business Patterns

Initial Analysis.   Examination of *County Business Patterns* reveals the number of firms by size for detailed categories of all of the prospective market segment groups listed. The important result is that at the actual launch of the project in University City, the total number of firms in the office categories identified with more than 20 employees was less than 10. In short, University City is revealed to be a city of predominantly very small office firms, and there was little prospect of finding enough tenants from a total of less than 10 candidates to successfully fill the buildings.

The history of the project is that only one of the two buildings was built, and it has spent much of its life more than half vacant. Obviously, it was a financial disaster that could have been predicted with a few minutes of thoughtful examination of the relevant market segments and the use of freely available government data.

> **✓ Concept Check**
>
> **6.8**   A local source for local employers and their size usually is from the _____ or _____. A national source for county level data on firms and their size is _____.

www.google.com/earth

Provides aerial photo coverage for most areas of the United States.

Market Research Example 3: Plane Vista Apartments

Our third market research case is a narrative. While it was an actual case, and the data and sources (not the names) were actual, we fictionalize our presentation. This enables us to better capture the sequence of discovery that is inherent in the market research process.

REAL ESTATE APPLICATION:

The New Job

As Alex eased his off-lease Escape into the office parking lot, he sipped on his morning coffee and thought to himself, Great new truck! Cool apartment! Great city! Great new job! How lucky can I get! But, then, he had worked for it, spending over a year getting a specialty real estate masters degree so that he could land the kind of job he wanted in real estate consulting.

Exhibit 6-8 The Location of Plane Vista Orlando, Florida[13]

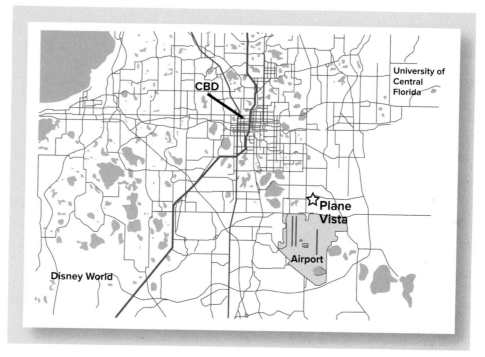

Source: Data from KeyInSites of Orlando

This was his second week on the job at KeyInSites, and he knew his boss, Ed, was waiting for him upstairs with his first major assignment. He was excited! He parked, walked briskly across the parking lot into the lobby, and was soon stepping out of the elevator into his "home" on the seventh floor. There were Sarah, who had joined the firm recently as a geographic information specialist, and Rebecca, the energetic college intern. "Did you get your truck?" they inquired excitedly. "Sure did. It's awesome. I'll have to give you a ride later." "How about taking Rebecca and me to lunch?" Sarah tossed. "Deal!" he replied, setting his bag down at his desk and heading for Ed's office.

Ed was busy loading the digital picture frame on his credenza with the latest pictures of the Swamp Monsters, the little league baseball team he managed, not that anyone could see the picture frame behind the stacks of papers. "Good morning, Alex. How was your weekend?"

"Crazy, but good," Alex replied. "I unpacked some more stuff, and found out I do have some pots and pans. My mother must have slipped them in, like she thinks I'd know what to do with them . . . . And then I picked up my truck!" They chatted enthusiastically for several minutes about the virtues of various SUVs. Finally, Ed said, "Well, are you ready?" "Bring it on," Alex replied eagerly.

"Just north of the airport is an apartment complex called Plane Vista. It currently has 500 units, and the owners are contemplating an addition of 400 more units. They want us to tell them if the market will support the addition at this time." Ed handed Alex a GIS generated map of the location (Exhibit 6-8). Just then the phone rang, and Ed stopped to answer.

Alex's mind kicked in as he gazed at the map. He had been trained at school in using all kinds of housing and population data, and here was his first chance to "bury" Ed and the clients with numbers. He would get with Sarah and have her generate maps and graphics that could make ESPN take notice. He'd have maps of existing apartments, of projected new ones, and tables about vacancy, rental growth . . . everything you would want to know. When Ed hung up Alex asked, "When do they want the report?" "End of the week," replied Ed.

13. All GIS maps were provided by KeyInSites of Orlando, Florida.

Reality Hits

Alex was silent. Maybe he wouldn't bring ESPN into the report this time after all. His mind raced faster. He knew that even with such a short horizon, Sarah could give him some good maps and graphics. He'd start out by getting a map of the current stock of apartments and other housing and use expected employment growth for Orlando to project needed housing increases. He'd use Sarah's GIS skills to allocate the growth over Orlando in proportion to newly built housing and come up with some pretty impressive looking results. Most importantly, this would give him an estimate of the additional apartment units for the neighborhood of Plane Vista.

Ed interrupted his brainstorming, "I assume you want to know about the existing apartments." Oh, yeah, Alex thought. That's right. In his studies, he had been hammered with the idea that real estate markets are segmented, meaning that there are different kinds of apartments, with different markets.

"I was just going to ask." Alex quickly replied. "Uh, tell me about them." "The owners are very experienced with apartments. They are good managers and have evolved design specifications that seem to work well in the market. I suppose you would describe Plane Vista as high-quality, semi-luxury. Data from Charles Wayne Associates, the local apartment gurus, indicate that Plane Vista has rental rates in the top 30 percent of the market. It has an unusually wide variety of apartment sizes and layouts and the full menu of standard amenities, so it can appeal to a wide mix of residents. It is not specialized to military, student, or retirement, and obviously, it is not specialized to low income. One feature that sets Plane Vista apart a bit is a really big gym. I'm told it has a full basketball court. That might give the place some special appeal to the basketball and volleyball crowds. I understand the proposed addition to Plane Vista will simply extend and refine the current formula."

"OK! I'm on it! What if I work on it today, and we meet first thing in the morning to go over it?"

"Good. Good luck!"

Sorting Out the Task

Alex hurried to his desk and set about to tackle his first project. Ed's comments had reminded him that he needed to be mindful of market segmentation. And he remembered that his graduate training in real estate market analysis stressed the need to narrow the scope of the problem—to carve away as much of the irrelevant as possible. This brought back to him some questions that could help refine the problem: What is the product? Who is the customer, that is, the renter or buyer? Where is the customer? What does the customer care about? What is the competition? He would see what tentative answers he could put down for the questions. Grabbing his computer, he started typing:

- *The product:* High-quality, general-purpose apartments. Varied sizes and designs. Well equipped with amenities. Especially large gym.
- *The customer (renter):* Not tourists. Not students (too far from the colleges and universities). Not retirees (they can go to more attractive, and maybe cheaper, areas). Not military (no bases nearby). Mainly people with jobs who need a place to live. (The location is not the most scenic in Orlando, so you wouldn't go there unless something "tied" you to the area.)
- *The location of customers:* Probably people working in south and east Orlando (again, if you worked in the central, north, or west part of the city, there are more lakes and trees, and less airplane noise elsewhere, and easier commutes.)
- *What customers care about:* Punt on this one. From Ed's comments, the owners know what they are doing, and whatever customers care about, Plane Vista will provide it as well as any place can.
- *The competition:* Other fairly new, semi-luxury apartments in the area.

Alex felt like he had made some progress. In short, he thought, the demand is from singles, couples, and roommates who have pretty solid jobs but who still want to rent or can't yet afford to buy. And, their jobs are in south or east Orlando. My competition is other quality apartment complexes that are relatively new, or are in the pipeline, he concluded.

The Beginning

OK, he thought, now what? First, he would ask Sarah to create a map from the Charles Wayne Associates data showing the location of recently built apartments (last 10 years). Stepping to her desk, he showed her the map Ed gave him, and asked, "Sarah, can you generate something like this with apartments built in the last 10 years using the Charles Wayne data?"

"If I get it to you before lunch are you buying as well as driving?" replied Sarah. "I'll go for that! Thanks!" said Alex. Sarah retorted, "You're a good sport, but I won't hold you to buying. I'll have it in a couple of hours."

We're making progress, Alex thought. Now what? Suddenly it occurred to him, he had just decided a few minutes ago that the main source of "customers" for Plane Vista was jobs. He should look at what is happening to jobs in south and east Orlando. But how? He could not remember any standard data source showing the location of jobs within a city. I'd be smart to run this one by Ed, he decided. As he walked to Ed's office, he mused over his first reaction about what he was going to do. Recognizing the idea of market segmentation and then attempting market refinement seems to have brought him a long way fast. Suddenly, he is looking at one very specific factor as the driver for Plane Vista demand, jobs. This seemed a lot more productive than simply trying to extrapolate demand by looking only at where apartments are being built.

Alex knocked on the door frame, "Do you have time for a few more questions about Plane Vista?" "Sure! Come in," replied Ed. Alex explained how he had decided that job growth in south and east Orlando was the dominating factor in demand for Plane Vista. And then raised his question, "But where can I find data on job locations in Orlando?"

"Well," Ed replied. "I like your theory about demand for Plane Vista, though you must always remember that no theory so simple is going to be entirely correct. Still, you should pursue it. The only problem is, the reason you can't think of any job location data is because there aren't any that we can get. I've heard that some researchers for the Department of Transportation have had access to that kind of data, through the IRS, I think. But if they let you see it, the price is that they have to kill you before you use it. So, unfortunately, though job locations might be important for a lot of real estate analysis, we can't get that data."

www.bls.gov

Source of virtually all detailed employment data for the United States, for states, counties, and MSAs. Also the source of household expenditure information. See *Explore the Web* at the end of this chapter. For Consumer Expenditure Survey Google the title.

A little stunned and frustrated, Alex walked slowly back to his desk. In today's world of electronic data, he wondered, how could something so useful be unavailable? Do I have to create the data, or what? Suddenly, an idea began to churn in his head. He quickened his step and headed toward Sarah's desk. "Sarah, I've got another GIS problem for you."

"Wow! Maybe I should hold you to paying for lunch," she chuckled as she handed him a map (Exhibit 6-9). "You finished the apartment map!" Alex declared appreciatively. "You *are* good!" "That's why they have me here. It keeps the rest of the staff humble! Now, tell me about your next problem."

✓ Concept Check

6.9   The location pattern of jobs in a city can be approximated by examining the location patterns of _____.

Alex explained the importance of job locations for the Plane Vista analysis, and that there were no data available. Then he proceeded to lay out an idea for a solution. "You have the county database for property parcels, structure size and detailed classification of use, right?"

"Yes."

"We also can download data from the Bureau of Labor Statistics on employment for the county by detailed industry, right?"

Exhibit 6-9 Locations of Recently Built Apartments[14]

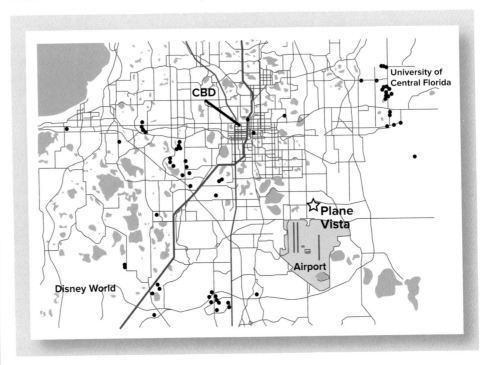

Source: Data from Charles Wayne Consulting Inc., Orlando, Florida

"Yes"

"Well, if we can pretty well match the employment industry categories with the property use classifications, and if we assume that jobs are concentrated proportionate with the amount of building space of the same category, can't we construct an approximation of where jobs are located? It would be crude, but crude strikes me as a lot better than total ignorance."

"Now you *are* buying lunch! Let me see what the data sets look like and print out the two classification lists involved. If you can look over them this morning, then, after we get back from a *nice* lunch, I can look at it with you. I've got other things in the queue, but I've got some flexibility, and you clearly need help, mister! Meanwhile, look over the map I've just made for you. It looks kind of interesting to me."

A Hidden Island?

"Hey! Thanks very much. I'm really impressed!" Alex said, and started back to his desk with the apartment map. As he glanced at it, he stopped. "What is this?" he exclaimed out loud. "Why are all the new apartments in Orlando concentrated in just three little clusters?" Not only were there only three clusters, they were all very distant from Plane Vista. It was like Plane Vista was in its own little world. As he sat down at his desk, still staring at the map, Sarah appeared with the property and employment classification lists. "Thanks. How about 11:30 if we are going someplace nice?"

"Sounds good. I'll tell Rebecca."

Baffled by the map of recent apartments, Alex turned his attention for the rest of the morning to cross-matching the two classification lists and then reviewing aerial photos of the Plane Vista area to look for clues about the clustered apartment construction.

About 1:00 they returned from a nice lunch, on Alex. Sarah enlisted the help of Rebecca to reconcile the employment data with the property use classifications, following notes that Alex had given her just before lunch. By mid-afternoon she and Rebecca had

14. All Orlando apartment data used here are courtesy of Charles Wayne Consulting Inc., Orlando, Florida.

Exhibit 6-10   Where People Work in Orlando

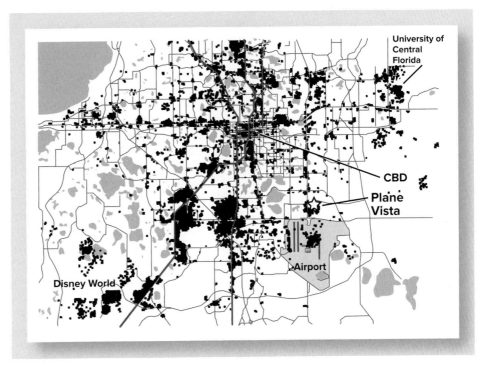

allocated the county employment across property parcels in the corresponding industry using the percent of the industry's total building space at each parcel. From this, Sarah was able to create a map approximating where people work in Orlando (Exhibit 6-10). Sarah walked up to Alex with the map in hand. "This ought to be worth dinner."

"Incredible! Thanks!" He was immediately engrossed in the map. Now the apartment clusters began to make some sense because jobs were tremendously concentrated just as the apartments were. One apartment cluster seemed to be just northwest of downtown, apparently serving the downtown employment. Another corresponded exactly with the apparent concentrations of jobs in south Orlando, and the third clustered around the exploding, and already huge University of Central Florida (UCF). But another amazing result was the isolation of the Plane Vista area. It was a job cluster of its own, set well away from south Orlando, from downtown, and from UCF. Obviously the dominating employment was at the airport, the 14th busiest in the United States, and one of the fastest growing in recent years. Instead of Plane Vista being part of a uniform Orlando landscape, it was part of an employment cluster quite set apart from most of the city, apparently driven by the airport. It was almost on an "airport island," Alex thought. As he looked further at aerial photos of the area, he realized that a combination of lakes, older residential areas, and industrial warehouse areas isolated the Plane Vista neighborhood from the employment centers to the west, single-family residential areas largely separated the area from other job centers to the north, the airport itself was a barrier on the south, and the land was undeveloped to the east. Plane Vista was on an island! This means, he mused, that Plane Vista and its neighboring apartments may be in a pretty weak position to compete for renters working elsewhere in Orlando. If the Orlando apartment market ever goes soft, without strong employment at the airport, they could get killed!

As Goes the Airport . . .

The next morning, when Alex arrived at Ed's office, he had organized his maps and his thoughts to tell his "airport island" story. Ed seemed appreciative. "So, where do you go from here?" he asked Alex.

"I think the main thing is that the future of the apartment market at Plane Vista is driven by employment on the 'island,' which means, primarily, employment at the airport. So, I need to focus on what apartments are being built on the 'island,' and what the employment growth looks like for the airport."

"Good work! See where it takes you. The client will have to be impressed with your analysis, however it comes out."

Encouraged, Alex hastened back to his desk to begin the next round. Now he had to project the market situation on "airport island." For starters, he thought, he ought to find out more about the role and future of the airport. Is airport employment really as dominant as it looks? Are there any other important components of jobs in the area? What changes are taking place? He suddenly realized he could get an approximation of the overall "airport island" employment the same way they had come up with the total Orlando jobs pattern. He would ask Sarah for one more GIS map of "airport island" jobs, and have her system give him a count. At the same time he would get on the telephone, contacting sources of information about employment and employment change on "airport island."

But first to Sarah. Alex stepped over to her desk. "OK, Ms. Spectacular, am I good for another map?" She looked up with a mischievous smile. "You know, before I think about that, I've got to get my new printer stand set up" "I can fix that!" said Alex. "And I can get you another map!" replied Sarah. "Cool. Thanks. Here's what I need." And he showed her his plan.

Back at his desk, Alex began his phone calls. First, he attacked the question of airport employment. After several calls and referrals he ended up in an intriguing conversation with the director of airport personnel, who said that the airport currently had 15,000 badges issued to all on-site workers. As the conversation moved on, Alex learned that the total had increased 2,000 in the last three years, and that the airport had fully recovered from a slump five years ago. In fact, it was again one of the fastest growing airports in the world, with almost a 10 percent increase in traffic in the last year. He also learned that steady expansion of the facilities was continuing. It seemed safe to conclude that employment will continue to grow at least as strongly as the last three years.

What Else Is Out There?

Next, Alex went after information about other employment on the "island." At Ed's suggestion, he called Frank at the metropolitan economic development agency. Frank regularly exchanged information and tips with Ed, and seemed happy to respond to Alex's questions about new jobs in the airport area. Frank knew of two firms planning to relocate into the neighborhood. One was a medical equipment firm, serving a national market, and expected to employ 450. The other was more local, and expected to employ 100.

Meanwhile, Sarah already had appeared with the new map (Exhibit 6-11). With it was a note that her GIS system estimated "airport island" to have a total of 25,000 jobs. Alex thought to himself, it looks like the airport will generate at least 750 new jobs per year, and new firms moving are adding 550 jobs to the area, for a total of 1,300. That's over 5 percent of the 25,000 base. But would this continue if Orlando is not growing in general? At Ed's suggestion, he turned to the city planning department website, and found a growth projections report for the area. It projected over 3.5 percent annual employment growth for the next five years. This gave reassurance that the growth of "airport island" would not be undermined by a stagnate citywide economy.[15]

The Meaning for Apartments?

So, Alex wondered, how should he translate job growth into apartment unit demand? He decided to look at the experience of Orlando as a whole. He knew that interest rates had been low for several years, prompting an unprecedented number of renter households to elect home ownership. Could this mean that apartment demand was growing more slowly

---

15. How did the "great recession" affect these projections? This area, now known as the Lake Nona area, has become one of the fastest growing urban subareas in all of Central Florida, driven by both airport-related growth and the creation of several medical centers just after Alex did his analysis.

Exhibit 6-11 "Airport Island" Job Locations

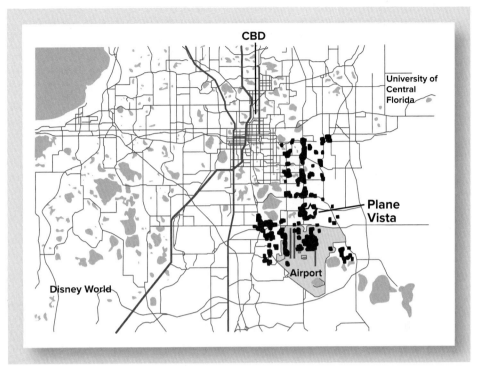

than job growth? He returned to the planning office growth projections and found that Orlando job growth had been around 2.5 percent for the last few years. But, from the Charles Wayne apartment data, he found that absorption of new apartments had been at a rate of 4.5 percent per year over the same time period. It looked like he didn't need to worry about apartment absorption being less than job growth!

But how big was the "airport island" market for quality apartments? From the Charles Wayne data, again, Alex could find the apartment properties on the "island" that were in the quality and age range of Plane Vista. He found 3,500 units, including Plane Vista's 500.

It was coming together in Alex's mind. If job growth on the "island" is at 5 percent over the next few years, and if apartment absorption is equal or almost double the job growth, then, from a base of 3,500 units, he could reasonably project apartment absorption of 150 to 300 units per year, and feel very safe. He would go with that.

Competitors?

Now to the question of competitors. From his training, Alex knew to contact the local building and planning authority to get information on any projects in the pipeline. He reached Herold, who was an experienced staff member of the permitting office. After a short, cordial conversation, Alex came away convinced that there were no significant apartment projects on the horizon for "airport island." That made his work simpler.

The final problem was to project rental rates. He decided to chat with Ed about this one since it is a complex judgment call. Their discussion led him to the conclusion that if occupancy rates are below 90 percent, rental rates would not increase. Between 90 and 95 percent occupancy they would move toward increasing at the rate of inflation. Above that, they would increase faster than the rate of inflation. He would go with this rule.

The Bottom Line?

Now Alex could put it all together! He boiled all his research down to a simple three-row table showing, for the next five years, the total number of units at Plane Vista, the occupancy rate, and the rental rate growth (Exhibit 6-12).

Exhibit 6-12   Projections of Rental Rate Growth and Occupancy for Plane Vista, Phases I and II

(Projection Date: January, Year 1)					
	Year 1	**Year 2**	**Year 3**[*]	**Year 4**	**Year 5**
Total units	500	500	900	900	900
Occupancy	90%	91–93%	90–93%	91–95%	92–95%[†]
Rental rate growth	0%	1–2%	2–3%	2–4%	2–4%[‡]

[*]Initial Year of Phase II

[†]Occupancy projections assume that demand growth is 150 to 300 units per year, with an initial base demand of 3,500 units in the relevant market segments.

[‡]It is assumed that continued strong growth of employment will bring a new supply of apartments into the market, limiting further occupancy and rental rate gains.

    As he looked over his results, a word that had been thrown at him time after time in school came to mind: risk. He knew that any estimates like his were, ultimately, merely assumptions about the future. He thought of one of his professors quoting a guy named Graaskamp that when you buy real estate you are buying a set of assumptions about the future. And all assumptions can be wrong. So what were the vulnerabilities in this set of assumptions? Well, the idea that renters on "airport island" mostly work on airport island was pretty crucial here. He mused that the client could test this fairly easily with a simple survey of their residents about where they work. In fact, Plane Vista's management probably could glean that information from their own records. Another crucial assumption is about airport employment growth. More careful assessment about the airport growth might be a wise investment. But he would get back to the risks later.

    Alex felt great! With Sarah's and Rebecca's help, he had made great progress in a day and a half. Now he just needed to write up how he got to his conclusions—probably 10 to 15 pages, plus tables, he guessed—and he was ready to convert the rental rate and occupancy projections into cash flow projections for the new units.

    He glanced at his watch. Wow! Time had flown! Noon was approaching. Suddenly an idea hit him. He hadn't adhered to the first rule of real estate analysis: Inspect the property. But he had his "truck," it was a beautiful day, and he thought he had noticed a Friday's near Plane Vista . . . . "Sarah! Rebecca!" he called. "Got lunch plans?"

A Perspective on the Plane Vista Story.   It is important to understand the role of projections such as in Exhibit 6-12. The late James Graaskamp often asserted that when one buys real estate, what one is buying is a set of assumptions about the future.[16] The projections in Exhibit 6-12 are an example of such assumptions. When translated into cash flow projections they will determine the estimated value of the property. The process of turning assumptions about the future of a property into cash flow projections and estimates of value is developed in detail beginning with Chapter 8. The subject continues through much of the remainder of the book.

    16. Professor Graaskamp was a revered teacher at the University of Wisconsin and an acclaimed industry guru. Few have offered more insightful observation on real estate analysis.

Some Final Notes on the Process of Market Research

By the approach that we advocate for market research, the format, organization, and content of the presentation will always be somewhat unique. (There still may be many common elements.) Further, the same assignment will be executed somewhat differently by different analysts. This will occur, in part, because different analysts will form different market-defining stories. Is one analysis the correct one? In short—not that we will ever know. There will always be more than one answer to questions as complex as those involved in market research. Some answers will be more compelling than others, but no human will know the "correct" one. It is always in the nature of business and markets that decision makers are dealing with uncertainty. Successful market research is a dialogue between researcher and client that serves to articulate and reduce this uncertainty but never to eliminate it.

Improving One's Capacity in Real Estate Market Research

Real estate market research is a blend of knowledge, skill, and inspiration. There are ways to increase one's effectiveness in the task. First, an effective real estate analyst needs to study real estate firsthand. There probably is no substitute for the habit of observing real estate persistently. This includes looking for what is successful, and asking why, but perhaps more importantly it includes finding the unsuccessful ventures, and asking why. Discussing both extremes with "experts" or other thoughtful observers can be revealing about the actual properties as well as how views ("stories") can differ among experts.

Another means of improving real estate market analysis is careful observation of a subject property. One very successful real estate expert suggested the following exercise in studying any urban property: Go to the property of interest in time for the morning commuting hour and find a place on or near it where you can remain for some time. Then observe the traffic coming to the property and to surrounding properties for perhaps 30 minutes to an hour. Ask yourself whether any surrounding properties interact, or should interact, with the subject property. Finally, peruse the neighborhood around the site. It can be remarkable what insights you can take away from that effort concerning the market context of the property. A closely related suggestion in evaluating a property is to stand at the site and look away from it in all directions. Consider what clues that perspective yields about what the property can (and cannot) be used for.

Market Projections and Real Estate Cycles

www.ngkf.com

See various kinds of regional and local research reports.

A major challenge in forecasting real estate market parameters, and therefore in predicting value, is the presence of real estate cycles. For example, Exhibit 6-13 portrays apartment vacancy rates for the Orlando MSA and for the United States. In the national vacancy pattern since 1987, note the peaks in 1988, 2004, and 2009. Notice that Orlando vacancy patterns have tended to follow movements of the national vacancy level, but with far greater amplitude. A graph of vacancy cycles for office, retail, and hotel/motel properties would show that they are even more extreme.

www.cbre.com/research

CB Richard Ellis office and industrial market vacancy reports.

If real estate markets were perfectly correcting, cycles would not occur. Indeed, an incentive for self-correction exists. Builders and developers watch real estate values, and when the market value of their product exceeds its construction cost, it is profitable for them to build. The resulting increase in supply eventually causes occupancy levels to decline, therefore causing real rental rates to decline, lowering market values. Thus, the market value of the product eventually falls below construction cost, causing further building to become unprofitable, so builders cease to build. With supply thus curtailed, the market value of the product will begin to rise once more, and the cycle continues.

If this natural correction process were instantaneous, there would be no cycles, but it is not. Development of subdivisions, apartments, offices, or other commercial structures can have a lead time of two years or more. Note in Exhibit 6-13 that the local Orlando vacancy

Exhibit 6-13   Apartment Vacancy Rates

Source: *Current Population Survey/Housing Vacancy,* Series H-111, U.S. Bureau of the Census.

rate frequently has changed radically within a two-year interval. Thus, what appears to be a favorable market when the builder commits to build may turn out quite differently, particularly if numerous builders make the same decision at the same time. In general, the longer the construction lead time, the greater the amplitude of real estate cycles. But there is another contributor to cycles as well. Real estate cycles might eventually fade out, except for the presence of business cycles. The economy has never been without ups and downs in employment and in business income, and therefore in demand for real estate.

✓ **Concept Check**

6.10   The amplitude or volatility of the real estate cycle tends to be
          greater for a property type, as its _____ is _____.

The sobering implication of real estate cycles is that effective market forecasts must account for them. Unfortunately, it is not easy to do so. Generally, the best that can be done is to monitor good information about the business outlook and be well informed about the construction "pipeline." Knowing about all relevant building permits issued reveals the maximum amount of building that can occur during the immediate construction "-gestation" period (some permits will not be used). But it does not reveal what additional permits will be issued in the days ahead. Thus, the investigation of the construction pipeline ideally goes beyond existing permits to judgments about probable additional projects seeking permits.

An important aspect of assessing a real estate project is how vulnerable it will be to future cycles. For example, an all-too-common pattern with new apartments is that the project built at the "end of the line" in commuting distance is the most vulnerable to vacancy in a down cycle. Further, some types of real estate historically have been more cyclically sensitive than others. Office and hospitality, for example, have historically tended to be more cyclical than industrial and apartments.

✓ **Concept Check**

6.11   A key indicator in attempting to evaluate where a property is in the
          real estate cycle is to carefully assess _____.

M ost real estate development projects and many real estate appraisal assignments require supporting market research. Development projects usually also require an economic and financial feasibility analysis. This type of research may be offered by a variety of firms, including sophisticated appraisal firms, accounting/consulting firms, or firms devoted exclusively to market research and market consulting. While the type of firm can vary, the qualifications of the researchers will be similar. They usually will have a degree in economic geography, economics, or a closely related field. Often they will have an **MBA** or master's degree in economics, real estate, or geography. With the exception of the real estate practices of large accounting firms, the firms providing market research and feasibility analysis are structured similarly to appraisal firms and tend to be compensated in the same manner. They will be paid on a fee basis rather than a commission. Real estate researchers may need to be familiar with several kinds of quantitative tools, including a general knowledge of computers, geographical information systems (GIS), multivariate statistical analysis, and database management. Like all real estate consulting and advisory services, the typical market researcher works out of the office a substantial portion of the time, in contact with other persons of the real estate industry.

Market and Feasibility Analysis for Real Estate

Some Tools of Market Research

Numerous skills, data, and technologies can be useful in real estate market research. Geographical information systems technology (GIS) is becoming increasingly recognized for its extreme power to process and display spatial (location-specific) data. Another tool of value in real estate is psychographics, a high-tech approach to analysis of market segmentation. Finally, a tool that can be very valuable in many contexts is survey research.

Geographical Information Systems (GIS)

www.stdb.com Select "Samples"

STDB (Site to Do Business) is an increasingly extensive, increasingly recognized real estate industry application of GIS services. Developed and sponsored by the CCIM organization. Among the powerful capacities of STDB is that it can provide estimates of employment, by category, for almost any arbitrarily defined market area.

Geographical information systems (GIS) are computer software systems that enable one to manipulate and "map" information with great flexibility and speed. GIS offers benefits at several levels in real estate research. Most obviously, it can produce quality maps and displays with unprecedented efficiency. But more importantly, it can make feasible new avenues of real estate market research. Note that without GIS tools, our analysis of the market for Plane Vista would have been impossible. Our effort to approximate job locations required us to identify and obtain data from more than 43,000 specific parcels of land in central Orlando from a total of several hundred thousand parcels in Orange County, Florida.

GIS can be a powerful facilitator in identifying market opportunities. If researchers can translate market segmentation features to a geographically coded database, then they can use GIS to quickly determine the locational patterns of that market segment, and compare them with the locational patterns of competitors. Thus, they can conduct a sophisticated form of "gap" analysis, searching for untapped market opportunities. This is far more difficult, if not infeasible, using conventional tables and charts.

www.nielsen.com/us/en/solutions/segmentation.html

Scroll down to find "Prizm Premier" Nielson PRIZM is a prominent example of "psychographic" market segmentation, with 66 reported separate segment groups.

For example, suppose a major grocery chain is considering a site for a shopping center (with a grocery store and other retail uses) in Columbia, South Carolina. Exhibit 6-14 shows a GIS map of the metropolitan area with the selected site, Dentsville Square Shopping Center. The map depicts highways, population density by census tract, and existing grocery stores in the Columbia area. By selecting any given grocery store, detailed data can be available about its size, owner, and volume of business. Additionally, the GIS can be used to calculate detailed information for a market area (such as a two-mile or five-mile radius) around Dentsville Square. This information might include the number of persons, number of households, median household income, estimated annual retail expenditures, daily traffic counts, and the total and vacant square footage of other retail properties. Thus, by having a GIS program and the appropriate data, an analyst can quickly and easily determine whether the site meets basic criteria and should be investigated further.

Exhibit 6-14 Population Density and Grocery Stores: Columbia, South Carolina

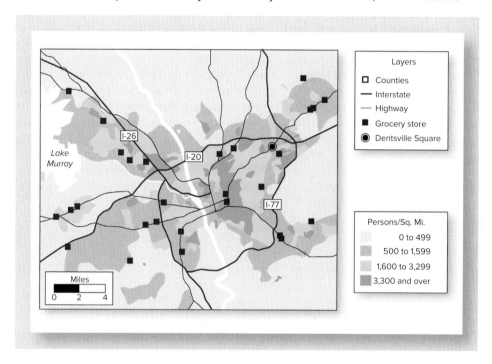

Psychographics

Psychographics is a tool for sophisticated determination of market segmentation. One description of psychographics is that it "seeks to describe the human characteristics of consumers that may have bearing on their response to products, packaging, advertising, and public relations efforts. Such variables may span a spectrum from self-concept and lifestyle to attitudes, interests, and opinions, as well as perceptions of product attributes."[17] The idea of psychographics is to relate a consumer's activities, interests, opinions, and values—especially as they relate to product choices—to a consumer's demographics. Through the application of complex multivariate statistical analysis, an analyst seeks to develop one or more equations that can use observable demographics, (e.g., as in the census data used in this chapter) to distinguish various market segments. Firms providing this kind of research claim to identify several dozen market segments for consumer behavior. In real estate, psychographics has been applied primarily to retailing and consumer services. Both Industry Issues features of this chapter demonstrate settings where psychographics could apply.

> ✓ **Concept Check**
>
> **6.12** GIS is a uniquely powerful tool for assisting retailers or service providers in the task of _____.

> ✓ **Concept Check**
>
> **6.13** Psychographics are of potential interest to real estate market researchers to refine the identification and use of _____.

17. B. Gunter and A. Furnham, *Consumer Profiles: An Introduction to Psychographics.* (New York: Routledge, 1992).

What do Blockbuster Video, Movie Gallery, Hollywood Video, and Borders Books/Waldenbooks have in common? One answer is bankruptcy. But a more sobering answer for owners of retail real estate is that they all were victims of the Internet. Altogether the failures of these firms led to the closing of nearly 10,000 stores in North America. And these failures essentially occurred before the accelerated growth of online commerce that has happened very recently. In 2016 the share of e-commerce retailing has grown eight percent—with such sources as Amazon.com, Staples, Apple, Dell, Office Depot, Walmart, and Sears among those leading the way.[1] This seems like a modest portion of retail sales, but it has thus far been concentrated in a fairly narrow range of merchandise types, making the impact on traditional retailers in those categories far more

RIP

Source: © Andrew Resek/McGraw-Hill Education

significant. And, as Zappos.com and other e-commerce retailers demonstrate, shoes and clothing can be successfully sold through the Internet, raising questions about where the limits are.

Virtually every major retailer now has an online presence and their e-commerce business is growing apace with that of exclusive online retailers. The big question is, What will this do to their "bricks-and-mortar" or on-site business? Will the traditional store be reduced to a pickup and return site? Will it become an unintended showroom for exclusively online competitors, as Target and Best Buy seem to have detected in their stores in late 2011? Or will traditional retailers find creative ways to make the Internet their ally?

The question for retail property landlords is, What kind of retail space is going to be in demand in an Internet-adjusted world?

RIP

Source: © Ron Heflin/AP Images

Numerous retailers are experimenting with departures from their traditional store formats, some going to smaller, "bare essentials," stores but with greater proximity to the customer. Efforts to attain more flexible and efficient inventory management may also reduce space needs. In contrast, Amazon.com has announced plans in late 2015 to open some 400 bricks-and-mortar "bookstores," that are expected to serve as "fulfillment centers," for a wide range of their sales.[2] The retail industry appears to be focusing heavily on understanding customers better, so as to offer them a more attractive, valuable in-store shopping experience. This effort hopefully would be the basis for building customer trust and loyalty. But what does this mean for the market for retail space? It is not yet clear.

The Internet: A Threat to Retail Real Estate?

1. U.S. Census Bureau News, CB16-138.
2. Miriam Gottfried, "Amazon Stores: Why All Retailers Should Be Afraid," *Wall Street Journal,* February 3, 2016.

Survey Research

Survey research has been applied to real estate markets at many levels. Perhaps one of the most useful is at the project design level. For example, a development team for a coastal condominium arranged for some of their sales staff to contact and interview owners of existing condominiums in the target area concerning what they liked and disliked about their units. From these interviews, the developers were able to identify some design features that enabled them to create a project distinctly more successful than others in the area. One of the authors conducted a survey of restaurant preferences among students, which succeeded in identifying a very promising chain of restaurants not represented in the local area. The chain subsequently entered the community successfully. Builders often use interviews or questionnaires to obtain helpful clues in designing for a local market. For this purpose, the opinions of those rejecting a builder's product are frequently the most informative. Another potential use of survey research is to identify target markets for advertising and market assessment. In the case of Plane Vista, for example, a survey of where residents work could help confirm our assumptions concerning where the demand for Plane Vista comes from, and it also could help identify effective project marketing channels.

In a time when many suburban retail centers are ringing hollow with vacancies, are there still retail markets untapped? The answer appears to be yes. So says the Initiative for a Competitive Inner City (ICIC), a sophisticated non-profit organization. The ICIC estimates a $40 billion untapped retail market in the inner-city neighborhoods of the United States, suggesting the possibility of thousands of new stores.* The ICIC also argues that coordinated efforts by local government, private funding, and retailers can produce high-return retail ventures, if the ventures are well designed and the markets are well selected. While the inner-city households have much lower income than

Untapped urban Retail Markets?

suburban households, they are much more concentrated, tend to spend more of their income on groceries and retail, and can be a captive market due to their transportation costs. Adding to the attraction, the employees can be local, and loyal, since they have few distracting options.

What kind of stores are good prospects for inner-city markets? A first option seems to be groceries. There remain large areas of older cities where the modern supermarket format is irrelevant due to space requirements.

Who is pursuing the inner-city retail frontier? Several major grocery chains are experimenting with "urban formats" but only on an isolated basis. One of the most intriguing possibilities for urban stores is the rise of the "dollar" store. In recent years Dollar General, Dollar Tree, and Family Dollar (which merged with Dollar Tree in early 2016) have evolved the dollar store concept from little more than a permanent flea market into a sophisticated, attractive,

and efficient operation with higher quality merchandise. And the concept has become the most rapidly expanding retail type of recent years, now with some 30,000 in total. Several aspects of these stores are interesting for the inner-city environment: First, the dollar store has a much smaller scale than the urban format grocery stores—8,000 to 10,000 square feet, as opposed to something three to four times larger. Second, the dollar stores have figured out how to merchandise to a wide range of income levels. Thus, dollar stores may suggest the kind of small, adaptable, well-operated format that can penetrate the promise of the inner-city retail market.

The inner-city market has obvious economic and social challenges. The ICIC (icic.org) has focused on these issues since 1994.

*Deirdre M. Coyle, Jr. "Realizing the Inner City Retail Opportunity: Progress and New Directions," *Economic Development Journal*, 6:1, Winter, 2007.

A word of caution regarding survey research: While simple survey research is not difficult, it can be fraught with abortive errors. Thus, it is wise to prepare carefully and to pretest any questionnaire at least one time. If possible, obtain the guidance of an experienced survey researcher. A little advice in formulating questions, designing a questionnaire format, selecting a sampling method, and administering the survey can reduce time and cost enormously, and can avoid the all-to-common misfortune of getting uninterpretable results.

✓ **Concept Check**

6.14 Survey research can be especially valuable in real estate during project _____.

Summary

Real estate market research seeks to derive the cash flow prospects of a property from the economic and social forces of its urban context. It must account for the effects of the urban economic matrix, but also the effect of land use controls. It must recognize both locational and nonlocational market segmentation.

Because of market segmentation and the variation in property context, little can be said, in general, about the form of effective real estate market research. It is a process rather than a formula. We have presented it as a process of constructing, verifying, and quantifying a story. The process begins with constructing the market-defining story. This is followed by initial data collection and then initial analysis or evaluation. From that point, one determines whether a conclusion can be reached or whether the research should be refined. The goal of the research is to determine a plausible range for critical cash flow parameters for the subject property. For rental property these parameters are projected rental rate growth and vacancy rates. For a subdivision or condominium project the critical parameters are prices and sales rates.

A market analysis never will explain its conclusions completely. The number of variables involved in determining the projection of occupancy and rental rate growth parameters is beyond any formal analysis. Thus, at some point the analyst makes a judgment leap to the final projections. The objective of market analysis is to make that leap as controlled and understandable as is reasonably possible. It should be spelled out to the point that other reasonably knowledgeable analysts know whether they agree or disagree with the final leap of judgment.

Key Terms

Geographical information systems (GIS) 153

Market parameters 133
Market segmentation 131

Psychographics 154

Test Problems

Answer the following multiple-choice problems:

1. Factors that affect housing market segmentation include all *except:*
   a. Household income.
   b. Household age.
   c. Household size.
   d. Household unemployment status.
   e. Household lifestyle.

2. The process of creating a market-defining story includes all of these questions *except:*
   a. What is the product?
   b. Who is the customer?
   c. Where is the customer?
   d. What is the price?
   e. What is the competition?

3. The cycle of real estate market research starts with:
   a. Creating a market-defining story.
   b. Assessing the national market.
   c. Collecting market data.
   d. Posing preliminary conclusions.
   e. Testing the current market condition.

4. Features of an office building that may be important to one market segment or another include:
   a. Floor plate size.
   b. Character and amount of parking.
   c. Nature of other tenants.
   d. Provision for electronics and communication systems.
   e. All of the above.

5. A strong assertion about the large amount of data seemingly available for real estate market research is that most of it is:
   a. Inaccurate.
   b. Too costly.
   c. Irrelevant to a given analysis.
   d. Too detailed.
   e. Too old.

6. The approach to real estate market research advocated in this chapter starts with the:
   a. National economy.
   b. Local economy.

   c. Relevant industry market.
   d. Region.
   e. Nature of the property.

7. A powerful tool for managing, manipulating, and displaying location-specific data is:
   a. Statistical regression analysis.
   b. Development cash flow software.
   c. Psychographics.
   d. Geographical information systems.
   e. Database management software.

8. A very sophisticated, data intensive, and statistically intensive method of examining market segmentation is known as:
   a. Regression analysis.
   b. Discriminant analysis.
   c. Survey research.
   d. Psychographic research.
   e. Cluster analysis.

9. Causes of real estate cycles include:
   a. Business cycles.
   b. Long real estate "gestation" periods.
   c. Weather cycles.
   d. Both *a* and *b,* but not *c.*
   e. All three: *a, b,* and *c.*

10. Data used in the market research cases in this chapter that are publicly available over the Internet include all of the following *except:*
    a. Detailed data of the U.S. decennial census.
    b. Data from *County Business Patterns* (U.S. Bureau of the Census).
    c. National apartment vacancy rates from the U.S. *Current Population Survey.*
    d. Data on job location from the National Transportation Board.
    e. Data from the U.S. Bureau of Labor Statistics.

Study Questions

1. On the U.S. Census website, use the approach shown in Explore the Web, Chapter 5, to access the latest American Community Survey. For your county, find the distribution of reported house values for owner-occupied residences.

2. If you were looking for an apartment at this time, what are six nonlocational requirements that you would consider important?

3. Select a site in your city that is in a mixed-use or nonresidential area, and either is vacant or appears to be ready for change (e.g., structure partially used or vacant, or in need of refurbishing). Go to the site during the morning commuting period of a business day. Situate yourself at or near the site and observe the activity at and around the site. Pay particular attention to why people pass the site—where they are coming from and where they are going. Note any nearby land uses or pedestrian flows that could potentially involve the site. Then explore the area around the site for a block or so in each direction, and record on a simple map the main patterns of traffic flow and the broad variations in land uses. Finally, after at least one observation session of 30 minutes, record your main impressions and thoughts concerning the potential use of the site. (*Hint:* A good way to select a site might be to go to a commercial real estate/broker or appraiser and ask him or her about a site this professional finds intriguing. This will give you an interesting industry contact, and another perspective on the problem.)

4. Select a property of interest to you or to an industry contact, and one for which market research would be interesting. Examine the property and collect available information about it. Then write a market-defining story for the property using the questions from the chapter as a guide.

5. University City is a town of more than 200,000 persons, with over 50,000 university and community college students. It has over 30,000 apartment units which, with one or two exceptions, are garden apartments with a maximum of three floors. Except for buildings within or immediately adjacent to the university medical center, the football stadium, and two graduate student dorms, only two other buildings in University City exceed five floors. A developer proposes to introduce two 24-story apartment buildings halfway between the downtown and the university, which are about 1.5 miles apart. One tower would be targeted to undergraduate students and the other to graduate students. The downtown consists of little more than government offices, mostly local and county. What questions should the developer ask in order to create a "market-defining story" for the twin towers?

EXPLORE THE WEB

Tapping the Master Sources of Employment Data

1. Go to the U.S. Bureau of Labor Statistics (www.bls.gov).
   - Once there, click on the tab *Databases & Tables (or Data Tools)*.
   - Next, from "On This Page:", *select Employment*.
   - Then under *Monthly*, go to *Employment, Hours, and Earnings-State and Metro Area* and select the icon for one-screen data search.
   - From the sequence of menus, (1) Select a state. (2) Select a city (MSA) of interest to you. (3) Select *Total Nonfarm Employment*. [For this exercise you skip Step 4] (5) For Data Type, select *All Employees, In Thousands*. (6) Check both *Seasonally Adjusted* and *Not Seasonally Adjusted*. (7) Add to your selection and click on *Get Data*.
   - What is the latest annual count? How much has it changed from the previous year?
   - How far back does the data series go?
2. Now return to the list of databases under *Employment*.
   - Read down the menu under *Quarterly to State and County Employment . . .*
   - Again select the icon for one-screen data search.
   - For a county within your MSA of interest, find the employment in residential property management and nonresidential property management (North American Industry Classification System, or NAICS, codes 531311 and 531312)
   - Find the employment in two other industry categories that interest you.

Solutions to Concept Checks

1. Three kinds of factors affecting the value of an urban property are locational characteristics, land use controls, and nonlocational characteristics.

2. Before effective real estate market research can be achieved, relevant market segmentation must be examined.

3. The presence of market segmentation in real estate gives rise to valuable advice in sorting through available market and property data: *Exclude the irrelevant.*

4. Rather than approaching real estate market research as a form or formula, the conditional nature of the task makes it a process of discovery.

5. It is recommended that the first step in evaluating any property is to write a market-defining story.

6. Whereas real estate market research traditionally starts with a national or global perspective, the approach argued here begins with the property.

7. The primary data source for information on household characteristics is the American Community Survey.

8. A local source for local employers and their size is usually the chamber of commerce or a local economic development agency. A national source for county-level data on firms and their size is *County Business Patterns.*

9. The location pattern of jobs in a city can be approximated by examining the location patterns of nonresidential buildings.

10. The amplitude or volatility of the real estate cycle tends to be greater for a property type, as its "gestation" or construction lead-time is longer.

11. A key indicator in attempting to evaluate the place of a property in the real estate cycle is to carefully assess relevant building permits.

12. GIS is a uniquely powerful tool for assisting retailers or service providers in the task of site selection.

13. Psychographics are of potential interest to real estate market researchers to refine the identification and use of market segmentation.

14. Survey research can be especially valuable in real estate during project design.

Additional Readings

Books on real estate markets and market analysis include the following:

Brett, Deborah L. and Adrienne Schmitz. *Real Estate Market Analysis: A Case Study Approach,* 2nd ed. Washington DC: Urban Land Institute, 2015.

Clapp, John M. *Handbook for Real Estate Market Analysis.* Upper Saddle River, NJ: Prentice Hall, 1987.

DiPasquale, Denise, and William C. Wheaton. *Urban Economics and Real Estate Markets.* Upper Saddle River, NJ: Prentice Hall, 1996.

Fanning, Stephen F. *Market Analysis for Real Estate.* Chicago: Appraisal Institute, 2005.

Geltner, David, Norman G. Miller, Jim Clayton, and Piet Eichholz. *Commercial Real Estate Analysis and Investments,* 2nd ed. Mason, OH: OnCourse Learning, 2014. (See Part II.)

Miles, Mike, Laurence Netherton and Adrienne Schmitz. *Real Estate Development Principles and Process,* 5th ed. Washington, D.C.: Urban Land Institute, 2015. (See Part VI.)

Thrall, Grant I. *Business Geography and New Real Estate Market Analysis.* New York: Oxford University Press, 2002.

The article below is a position paper adopted by the Joint Valuation/Research Subcommittees of the National Council of Real Estate Investment Fiduciaries (NCREIF) on the role, purpose, and procedures for market analysis in appraisals:

Wincott, D. Richard, and Glenn R. Mueller. "Market Analysis in the Appraisal Process." *Appraisal Journal 63,* no. 1 (January 1995), pp. 27–32.

The following article presents a structure for market analysis. It also suggests nine specific improvements to the customary practice of real estate market analysis:

Malizia, Emil E., and Robin A Howarth. "Clarifying the Structure and Advancing the Practice of Real Estate Market Analysis." *Appraisal Journal 63,* no 1. (January 1995), pp. 60–68.

For exposure to geographic information systems in many variations and levels, visit the website of ESRI: www.esri.com. (ESRI is a principal provider of GIS systems.)

Chapter 7

Valuation Using the Sales Comparison *and* Cost Approaches

LEARNING OBJECTIVES

After reading this chapter you will be able to:

1 Explain why the sales comparison and cost approaches are important methods of property appraisal.

2 Explain the steps involved in applying the sales comparison approach to valuation.

3 Make adjustments to sale prices in the proper sequence in the sales comparison approach.

4 Explain the steps involved in applying the cost approach to valuation.

5 Define the three primary types of accrued depreciation.

6 Reconcile three or more final adjusted sale prices in the sales comparison approach into an indicated value, or two or more indicated values into a final estimate of value.

Introduction

This chapter and the one immediately following are focused on estimating the market value of real estate. Understanding the market value of a property is vital to potential purchasers and sellers, to owners contemplating renovations and improvements, to a judge attempting to determine the appropriate division of assets in a divorce, to lenders contemplating a mortgage loan on a property, to government officials when estimating the costs of acquiring the right-of-way to construct a highway, or to anyone needing an objective estimate of current market value.

Why must the market value of real estate be estimated? Cannot values simply be observed in the marketplace? Consider the value of Simon Property Group (SPG), a retail real estate company that trades on the New York Stock Exchange (NYSE). At the close of trading on August 17, 2015, SPG was selling for $191.69 a share. There may have been some investors who felt that SPG was worth more, or less, than $191.69 a share at that time, but the consensus among those actively buying and selling SPG was that $191.69 was a fair price.

What are some of the characteristics of the NYSE that permit us to conclude that $191.69 was the fair market value of a share of SPG stock at the closing of the exchange on August 17, 2015? First, there are many active buyers and sellers of SPG on the NYSE, and the trading activities of any one buyer or seller are not likely to affect SPG's stock price. Second, many transactions of SPG occur each hour; thus, market prices are revealed almost instantaneously and continuously during a trading day. Third, each share of SPG's common stock is *exactly* alike; thus, any one share is a perfect substitute for another. In addition, shares of SPG's stock can be taken anywhere—unlike real estate assets. Thus, the location of the seller or the share offered for sale has no bearing on the price that potential buyers are willing to pay.

Contrast these characteristics of the New York Stock Exchange to a typical real estate market. First, unlike stocks, no two properties are exactly alike. Even if the physical attributes of two properties are similar, their different locations render them less than perfect substitutes. Second, transactions of similar properties occur infrequently, resulting in a scarcity of comparable price data. The physical immobility of real estate also has important implications for the valuation of real estate. Since a parcel of real estate cannot be moved from its location, its value is subject to the effects of economic, social, or political developments emanating from the regional, community, and neighborhood levels; that is, real estate markets are decidedly local in nature.

The unique characteristics of real estate markets, including those discussed above, significantly complicate the estimation of market value. Nevertheless, for many real estate decisions it is sufficient to rely on *informal* methods of appraising the value of real estate assets. Informal appraisal is a common part of our lives. Whenever we make purchases of goods or services, we generally perform an informal appraisal to determine if the prices are reasonable. We do this by comparing one product and its price to competing products.

Informal appraisal methods also are used frequently in real estate. These informal methods include discussions with neighbors, friends, and local real estate sales professionals, as well as the collection of readily available data (e.g., newspaper articles and websites). However, the complexity and large dollar value of many real estate decisions dictate that homeowners, lenders, judges, and other decision makers often base their valuation decisions on a *formal* appraisal, which is an estimate of value reached by the methodical collection and analysis of relevant market data.

www.trulia.com

Compare prices of similar homes across the United States.

✓ **Concept Check**

7.1 List several types of real estate decisions that often require formal real estate appraisals.

---

www.appraisalinstitute .org

The Appraisal Institute is the primary industry professional organization for real estate appraisers in the United States.

The focus of this chapter is on the formal approaches to real estate valuation used by trained and state licensed professionals who are in the business of providing opinions of value for a fee. An **appraisal** is an unbiased written estimate of the market value of a property, usually referred to as the **subject property,** at a particular time. The **appraisal report** is the document the appraiser submits to the client and contains the appraiser's final estimate of value, the data upon which the estimate is based, and the reasoning and calculations used to arrive at the estimate. The licensing and certification of real estate appraisers is the subject of this chapter's Career Focus.

Real Estate Appraisers

Real estate appraisal practices are typically focused on either residential or nonresidential appraisal. Residential appraisers focus on single-family homes and small residential rental properties. Much of this work deals with appraisals for mortgage lending purposes or for corporate relocation firms.

National appraisal standards are established by the Appraisal Foundation. The Appraisal Foundation was established by Congress to regulate the appraisal industry and establish uniform appraisal standards and educational requirements on a national basis. The Appraisal Qualifications Board (AQB) establishes the minimum educational requirements for state-certified residential and general appraisers. The Appraisal Standards Board (ASB) promulgates the Uniform Standards of Professorial Appraisal Practice (USPAP), establishing the minimum ethical requirements and standards of practice on an industry-wide basis. All 50 states require real estate appraisers to be licensed or certified and the standards set by the AQB represent the minimum requirements each state must implement for individuals applying for a real estate appraiser license or certification.

Certification is at two levels, residential and general, and is based on a combination of education, tests, and experience. For example, effective January 1, 2008, the prior experience requirement for a certified general appraiser is 3,000 hours of appraising, half of which must be with nonresidential property. The certified general appraiser must also complete 300 hours of classroom instruction, including a required core curriculum, have a bachelors degree or higher from an accredited college or university, and pass a required state exam. There is also a continuing education requirement (see www.appraisal foundation.org for more information).

Many appraisers go beyond certification to obtain trade association designations. These designations signal to potential clients that the appraiser has obtained even more education and/or professional experience in the field than is required for state certification. The Appraisal Institute (www.appraisalinstitute.org) offers the residential Senior Residential Appraiser (SRA) designation and the prestigious Member of the Appraisal Institute (MAI) designation for commercial appraisers.

The outlook for appraisers involved in specialized commercial appraisal and consulting, such as site analysis, buy versus lease decisions, property tax appeals, portfolio revaluation, and investment analysis, is quite promising. The outlook for residential appraisal is being greatly influenced by the introduction of new technology. Opportunities abound for real estate professionals to revolutionize the residential sector, and residential appraisal firms that do not embrace new technology may become extinct.

Source: Real Estate Career Paths, University of Cincinnati, business.uc.edu/academics/centers/real-estate.html; the Appraisal Institute, www.appraisalinstitute.org; and the Appraisal Foundation, www.appraisalfoundation.org.

---

www.rics.org

The Royal Institute of Chartered Surveyors is the largest professional association of appraisers (valuers) outside the United States.

We next discuss the relationships among market value, investment value, and transaction prices. This is followed by an overview of the real estate appraisal process, including the three conventional approaches used to estimate the market value of real estate. We then focus on the two methods (approaches) that provide a means for estimating a property's market value without directly considering the property's income-producing potential: the sales comparison approach and the cost approach. The income approach to valuation is the focus of Chapter 8.

www.iaao.org

International Association of Assessing Officers. A nonprofit, educational, and research association.

Market Value, Investment Value, and Transaction Prices

Before discussing the framework for estimating the market value of real estate, it is important to distinguish among the concepts of market value, investment value, and transaction price. Real estate appraisers generally define the **market value** of a property as its most probable selling price, assuming "normal" sale conditions.[1] Alternatively, it can be viewed as the value the typical (imaginary) participant would place on a property. The concept of market value rests upon the presence of willing buyers and sellers freely bidding in competition with one another. It is the result of the interacting forces of supply and demand. If real estate markets were perfectly competitive, market value would equal the most recent transaction price.

---

1. In professional appraisal practice, market value definitions may vary as to the precise motivations, terms, and conditions specified.

There would be no need for value estimates.[2] As discussed above, the problem of market value estimation arises because of the existence of imperfections in the real estate market.

In contrast to market value, **investment value** is the value a *particular* investor places on a property. Investment value, discussed in detail in Chapters 18 and 19, is useful to buyers and sellers for making investment decisions. It is based on the unique expectations of the individual investor, not the market in general. It may differ between a buyer and a seller. A buyer's investment value is the *maximum* that he or she would be willing to pay for a particular property. The seller's investment value is the *minimum* he or she would be willing to accept. Investment values generally differ from market values because individual investors have different expectations regarding the future desirability of a property, different capabilities for obtaining financing, different tax situations, and different return requirements. Although the methods used to estimate investment value and market value are similar, analysts who determine investment value apply the expectations, requirements, and assumptions of a particular investor, not the market.

Finally, **transaction prices** are the prices we observe on sold properties. They are different, but related, to the concepts of market value and investment value. We observe a transaction only when the investment value of the buyer exceeds the investment value of the seller. Real estate appraisers and analysts observe transaction prices and use them to estimate the market value of similar properties. However, there is no guarantee that an observed transaction price is equal to the (unobservable) true market value of the property. It simply represents the price agreed upon by one willing buyer and one willing seller.

In summary, market value is an estimate of the most probable selling price in a competitive market. Market value can be estimated from observed transaction prices of similar properties. These transaction prices are negotiated in an imperfect market between buyers and sellers, each having his or her own investment value of the property. Investment value and market value thus are linked through the competitive market process that determines transaction prices.[3]

> ✓ **Concept Check**
>
> **7.2**   Assume a house is listed for sale for which you would be willing to pay up to $200,000. The seller has put the property on the market with an asking price of $180,000. List some possible reasons why your investment value exceeds that of the seller. Is the price you pay likely to be closer to $200,000 or $180,000? Explain.

---

www
.appraisalfoundation.org

Contains links to USPAP information.

The Appraisal Process[4]

How do real estate appraisers do their job? Professional appraisal groups have long supported strict standards of ethics and practice among their members. In 1987 nine leading appraisal groups jointly promulgated uniform appraisal standards, now recognized by professional appraisal organizations throughout North America. Maintained by the Appraisal Foundation, the **Uniform Standards of Professional Appraisal Practice (USPAP)** are required and followed by all states and federal regulatory agencies. USPAP imposes both ethical obligations and minimum appraisal standards that must be followed by all professional appraisers. At present, USPAP is updated biannually.

---

2. Students of economics may note that the definition of market value adopted by appraisers is similar, but not identical, to the definition of value under perfect competition.

3. Market and investment values are but two kinds of value of concern to the real estate analyst. Other values that sometimes must be estimated include the assessed value, the value assigned to the property for property tax calculations; insurable value, the value of the insurable portion under the provisions of an insurance contract; going-concern value, the value of a property that includes the value of the associated businesses occupying the property; use value, the value of a property for a specific use; and others.

4. This section draws from Chapter 4 of *The Appraisal of Real Estate,* 14th ed. (2013).

Exhibit 7-1　The Valuation Process

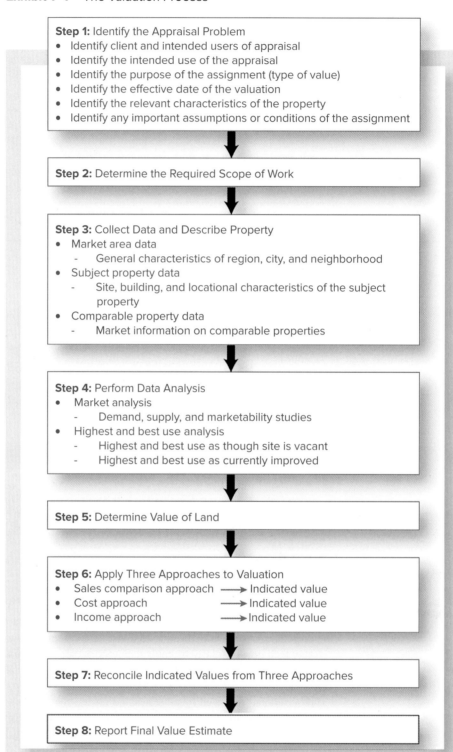

Step 1: Identify the Appraisal Problem
- Identify client and intended users of appraisal
- Identify the intended use of the appraisal
- Identify the purpose of the assignment (type of value)
- Identify the effective date of the valuation
- Identify the relevant characteristics of the property
- Identify any important assumptions or conditions of the assignment

Step 2: Determine the Required Scope of Work

Step 3: Collect Data and Describe Property
- Market area data
  - General characteristics of region, city, and neighborhood
- Subject property data
  - Site, building, and locational characteristics of the subject property
- Comparable property data
  - Market information on comparable properties

Step 4: Perform Data Analysis
- Market analysis
  - Demand, supply, and marketability studies
- Highest and best use analysis
  - Highest and best use as though site is vacant
  - Highest and best use as currently improved

Step 5: Determine Value of Land

Step 6: Apply Three Approaches to Valuation
- Sales comparison approach ⟶ Indicated value
- Cost approach ⟶ Indicated value
- Income approach ⟶ Indicated value

Step 7: Reconcile Indicated Values from Three Approaches

Step 8: Report Final Value Estimate

To comply with USPAP, certified fee appraisers must follow an established framework, or process. As outlined in Exhibit 7-1, this process consists of (1) identifying the appraisal problem; (2) determining the required scope of work; (3) collecting data and describing property; (4) data analysis, including market analysis and highest and best use analysis; (5) determining the value of the land; (6) applying the valuation approaches; (7) reconciling the indicated values that result from the multiple approaches to valuation; and (8) preparing the appraisal report for submission to the client. Although the details of each of these steps are beyond the scope of this text, a brief description follows.

Identify the Problem

In the first step, identification of the appraisal problem, the appraiser must discuss the following: the intended use of the appraisal; the purpose of the assignment (i.e., type of value to be estimated); the effective date of the valuation, the relevant characteristics of the property, and any important assumptions, conditions, or limitations of the appraisal assignment. Most appraisal assignments focus on estimating the current market value of a property under the assumption that the owner(s) will hold full (i.e., fee simple) title to the property. (The various forms of ownership, or estates, in real estate, including fee simple absolute ownership, are discussed in detail in Chapter 2.) However, lesser interests (estates) in property can be the subject of an appraisal. Moreover, a large portion of commercial property appraisals are completed subject to the leasehold interests of current tenants, as we will show in Chapter 8. Other appraisal problems may involve retrospective or prospective value estimates required for insurance, property taxation, lending, or other purposes.

Determine the Scope of Work

The appraiser is responsible for determining the appropriate scope of work for the appraisal assignment. The work performed must be consistent with the work that a typical appraiser would perform in conducting a similar assignment. The scope of work must be clearly described, and any deviations from a standard approach to valuation must be carefully explained. Time and personnel requirements must be clearly identified. Finally, the data and procedures used to complete each task, should be provided.

Collect Data and Describe Property

Data must be gathered concerning the market context of the "subject" property. These data include information on economic, demographic, regulatory, and geographic factors that may influence value. This information often includes such items as the expected rates of return on alternative investments (i.e., stocks, bonds, and real estate), population and employment trends, existing and future land use data, and flood zone data. Additionally, property-specific data must be gathered for the subject. This normally includes information on the physical and locational characteristics of the subject property. Similar information, along with transaction prices, must be collected for comparable properties.

Perform Data Analysis

Once the required market, subject, and comparable data are identified, collected, and reviewed for accuracy, the process of data analysis begins. Data analysis, in turn, has two components: market analysis and highest and best use analysis. As discussed in detail in Chapters 5 and 6, to understand a real estate market, one must understand the economic base of a city, the various submarkets sectors or clusters within a city, and the differing locational needs among land uses within the city, such as the tendency of convenience activities (e.g., bank branches, drug stores) to disperse uniformly over the urban landscape while comparison activities (e.g., discount clothing stores) tend to cluster. We argue that market analysis and research is a process rather than a formula. Nevertheless, the goal of market analysis is to develop market-specific knowledge about the factors that affect the demand and supply of properties similar to the subject and to use that knowledge to forecast how real estate values are likely to change over time.

The concept of highest and best use is central to the estimation of market value, primarily because it serves as the foundation for identifying comparable properties. The

highest and best use of a property is defined as that use found to be (1) legally permissible, (2) physically possible, (3) financially feasible, and (4) maximally productive (i.e., yielding the greatest benefit to an owner). The principal idea is that the market value of a property is a function of its most productive use. In most appraisal assignments, property is valued at its highest and best use, which may include consideration of both the highest and best use of the land, assuming the site is vacant, and the highest and best use of a property as currently improved.

Highest and Best Use as Though Site Is Vacant.   Land, vacant or not, is always valued as though vacant and available for development to its highest and best use. The value attributed to the land is the total estimated value of the property, assuming its highest and best (ideal) use, less the estimated value of the anticipated improvements (e.g., the building). Identification of the highest and best use of land as though vacant helps the analyst identify the appropriate comparable data with which to value the land. Market analysis drives highest and best use analysis; highest and best use conclusions drive market value conclusions.

Highest and Best Use of the Property as Improved.   When a separate estimate of the value of the land is not necessary, the appraiser focuses on the highest and best use of the property as it is currently developed. Again, this analysis helps the appraiser identify the appropriate comparable data to select in valuing the property. In addition, it may help to determine whether the existing improvement should be retained, modified, or demolished. The appraiser must decide whether the value estimate should be reached under the assumption that the improvement will remain, or with the assumption that the improvements are torn down, or put to another use.

In summary, market value is determined by the highest and best use of the property, which in turn can be determined only by a well-designed and executed market analysis.

√ Concept Check

7.3   You estimate that the value of an existing single-family home is $450,000. However, local zoning regulations would permit a four-unit rental housing structure to be built and demand supports the need for more rental housing. The estimated value of the rental structure is $600,000 upon completion, but the construction costs total $300,000, including the demolition costs of the existing house. What is the property's highest and best use?

Determine Land Value

Although most appraisal assignments involve the valuation of properties with extensive improvements to the land, appraisers often develop a separate opinion regarding the value of the land. Several techniques can be used to obtain an indication of land value. However, the most reliable approach is by sales comparison.[5]

Apply Conventional Approaches to Estimate Market Value

There are three conventional approaches used to estimate the market value of real estate: the income approach, the sales comparison approach, and the cost approach. Generally, all three approaches are used in a formal appraisal. Although we discuss the approaches

---

5. Although beyond the scope of this book, these alternative land valuation techniques are discussed in detail in Chapter 17 of *The Appraisal of Real Estate,* 14th ed. (2013).

separately in this and the following chapter, each approach is, when properly developed, related to the other two. The three approaches can be regarded as different methods of seeking the same final objective: a defensible and reliable estimate of value.

The sales comparison approach is applicable to almost all one- to four-family residential properties and even to some types of income-producing properties where enough comparable sales are available. This approach has the advantage of being easily understood by buyers and sellers, who can follow the valuation procedures and check the data to determine whether they agree with the appraiser's value estimate.

The income approach, presented in Chapter 8, is the dominant approach when estimating the value of income-producing property. It assumes a property's value is determined by its expected future cash flows. Thus, the income approach is less appropriate as the value of a property depends more on nonmonetary future benefits, as with owner-occupied homes.

The cost approach to valuation involves estimating the cost of replacing the property new, and then subtracting the loss in value due to physical, functional, and external obsolescence. The sum of these three effects is termed *accrued depreciation.* As the subject structure ages, the amount of accrued depreciation increases. This renders the estimate of market value by the cost approach increasingly uncertain because, as discussed below, estimating accrued depreciation is very difficult.

The cost approach is relied on more when reliable comparable sales or income data are absent. It is the approach most relied upon for valuing specialty properties such as education facilities, places of worship, or special-purpose government properties—parks, monuments, bridges, or courthouses, for example. There are usually few sales of comparable properties that can be used to value such specialty properties using the sales comparison approach; moreover, they generally do not produce an income stream.

There is a clear order of preference for methods of appraisal. An appraiser generally prefers to estimate value directly from the market, that is, from the actual sales of comparable properties. That way the appraiser can rely on the value judgments of actual buyers and sellers, whereas other valuation methods only simulate these judgments. Often, however, adequate sales comparables are not available. In this case, an appraiser simulates market judgment for income-producing properties through an income capitalization approach. If there are no comparable sales and there is no income to measure and value, as a last resort the appraiser must turn to the cost method. Which appraisal method is the most preferred for the appraisal of each property in Exhibit 7-2?

Exhibit 7-2   Which Appraisal Method Should Be Used to Value Each of These?

Source: © LING.

Reconcile Indicated Values from Three Approaches

Whenever possible, each of the three approaches is applied to establish alternative "indicators" of market value. For example, all three may be applied in estimating the value of a rented single-family home. In this case, the appraisal process will result in three value indicators. In assigning a final (single) estimate of market value, the appraiser weighs the relative reliability of value indicators for the property being valued—a procedure referred to as **reconciliation.** A simple average of the indicated values is seldom applied. Rather, more weight is generally given the most applicable method and most reliable data. When applying this last step, the appraiser needs to understand and clearly explain the relationship among the three approaches and be able to discern and articulate which approach is most appropriate in a given situation.

Report Final Value Estimate

The eighth and final step in the formal appraisal process is reporting the appraisal opinion or conclusion. Appraisers spend a significant portion of their time preparing written appraisal conclusions, and experienced appraisers understand that report writing is one of the most important functions they perform.

The content of an appraisal document must meet the requirements of one of the two reporting options available under USPAP: (1) appraisal report and (2) restricted appraisal report. When producing an **appraisal report,** it is the appraiser's responsibility to determine the amount of detail and explanation that is required based on the intended use of the appraisal and the intended user of the report. Appraisal reports are typically "form" reports or longer, "narrative" reports. The narrative appraisal report is the longest and most formal format for reporting and explaining appraisal conclusions and contains a step-by-step description of the facts and methods used to determine value. In that sense, narrative reports are self-contained. Narrative appraisal reports are typically used in appraisals of income-producing properties.

Most appraisals of single-family homes are summary reports that use the form reporting option. Forms reports are much shorter than narrative reports and their frequent standardization creates efficiency and convenience. Form reports are generally required by mortgage lenders when households are purchasing or refinancing a single-family home. In fact, the most common appraisal report is the Uniform Residential Appraisal Report (URAR) Form 1004. This form report has been developed by the mortgage industry to standardize the appraisal of single-family homes.

A **restricted appraisal report** provides a minimal discussion of the appraisal with large numbers of references to internal file documentation. If the client just wants to know what the property is worth and does not intend to provide the appraisal to anyone for their use or reference, a restricted report may be sufficient.[6]

Traditional Sales Comparison Approach

The sales comparison approach is a general method for appraising all types of properties and involves comparing the subject property with **comparable properties** (i.e., similar properties) that have sold recently. The economic principle of substitution implies that the value of the subject property is determined by the price that market participants would pay to acquire a substitute property of similar quality, utility, and desirability. Theoretically, no adjustments to the sale prices of the comparable properties would be needed if the site, building, and location characteristics of the comparable properties were *identical* to the

---

6. Prior to January 1, 2014, three reporting options were available: (1) self-contained report, (2) summary appraisal report, and (3) restricted use appraisal report. Beginning January 1st, the 2014 USPAP guidelines reduce the number of reporting options to two: (1) appraisal report and (2) restricted appraisal report. The appraisal report replaced the previous self-contained and summary reports, while the restricted appraisal report replaced the previous restricted use appraisal report.

Exhibit 7-3 Steps in the Sales Comparison Approach

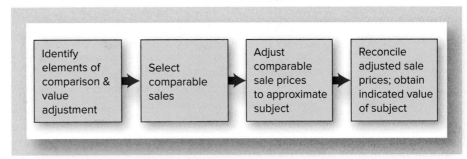

subject property, and if the transactional details were the same. The real estate market, however, is imperfect; no two properties are exactly alike, and various aspects of transactions may vary greatly. Therefore, to estimate the market value of the subject property, appraisers make explicit adjustments—additions and subtractions—to and from the sale prices of comparable properties. The appraiser then evaluates and reconciles the final adjusted sale prices of the comparable properties into a single **indicated value** for the subject property. The fundamental steps of the sales comparison approach are outlined in Exhibit 7-3.

Comparable Sales Data

The selection of appropriate sales data is crucial to the sales comparison approach. The appraiser's objective is to identify property sales that are similar to the subject property and reflect the general pricing preferences (values) of the *typical* buyer in the market. When appraising detached single-family homes and attached townhomes and condominiums, an appraiser will often begin by identifying recent sales located in the subject property's immediate neighborhood. Such properties are generally influenced by common economic, demographic, geographic, and regulatory factors. However, seldom are there enough comparable sales transactions in the subject's neighborhood. This forces the appraiser to expand the search both geographically and backwards in time. When appraising commercial real estate, it is almost always necessary to search beyond the immediate area for comparable sale transactions. In doing so, an appraiser must take care to ensure that selected comparables truly compete with the subject property for buyers or tenants. This is where real estate appraisal is "more art than science"; identifying truly comparable (i.e., substitute) properties is a subjective process that requires skill, experience, and extensive knowledge of the area's real estate market and submarkets.

In addition to determining whether the comparable sales are truly close substitutes for the subject property, it is important that the sales represent **arm's-length transactions;** that is, a fairly negotiated transaction that occurred under typical market conditions. Properties that are sold under unusual conditions (e.g., as part of estate auctions, foreclosure proceedings, special low-interest financing programs, or commingled business transactions) should not typically be used as comparables. Assuming the transactions are representative, the comparable properties are selected to be as physically similar to the subject property as possible, to minimize the number and size of any necessary price adjustments.

www.reis.com

www.rcanalytics.com

www.costar.com

Subscription-based services that provide comparable sales information for commercial properties.

> ✓ **Concept Check**
>
> **7.4**   Assume you are appraising a single-family home. Recently, a home directly across the street was sold by the owners to their daughter. Why should the appraiser exclude this transaction from the set of comparable sales? If included, what kind of adjustment probably needs to be made to the sale price of the comparable?

Once the comparable sales have been investigated and verified, the next step is to collect the required data on each comparable transaction. Generally, information on the property's physical characteristics, legal status, and exact location are required.

There is no specific number of comparables that is adequate for every appraisal assignment. If the comparables sales are very similar, three sales are considered adequate for most appraisal assignments. However, if the sales are less comparable or the appraiser has concerns about the reliability of the information obtained about the comparable sales, a larger number is usually desirable.

Sources of Market Data

The appraiser generally must search a variety of sources to obtain the necessary information on the subject and comparable properties. These sources include public records, multiple listing services, and private companies.

Public Records.   Many agencies in the federal government are rich with statistical information useful for appraisal assignments (three widely used federal statistics agencies are referenced in the margin). At the local level, the public records collected by cities and counties include copies of most local deeds that transfer the ownership or other interests in real estate. (Deeds and other issues associated with acquiring and disposing of ownership interest in real estate are discussed in Chapter 3.) The local (usually county) property tax assessor is also a major source of information, including records of sale prices, for appraisers. In addition to showing the assessed value (for property tax purposes) of the subject and comparable properties, the assessor's records also show the name(s) and address of the current owner(s) and the properties most recent, and in some cases the second most recent, sale price. The tax assessor's office or planning commission may also be able to provide maps and information on permitted uses, wetlands, and other use restrictions for every parcel of real estate in the county.

Multiple Listing Services.   The local board of Realtors usually sponsors and maintains a multiple listing service (MLS). All properties listed for sale by MLS members are combined and listed in this easily accessible and searchable database. When listed properties are sold, the sale price is added to the record. Thus, MLSs are a potential rich source of current price trends in a local market.

Private Data Services.   In recent years, the number of private, for profit, data vendors has increased dramatically. Some vendors specialize in only one geographic market, some have regional or even national platforms. Local appraisers are also excellent sources of data. Title insurance companies are another potential source of valuable data. Regardless of the source, most of these data can be delivered electronically to the appraiser's computer, tablet, or phone. The days of appraisers searching for papers and documents in physical locations have given way to electronic distribution except, perhaps, in rural markets.

Adjustments to Comparable Property Transaction Prices

Appraisers must consider numerous **adjustments** when employing the sales comparison approach. These adjustments are divided into two major categories: transactional adjustments and property adjustments. The goal of these adjustments is to convert each comparable sale transaction into a closer approximation of the subject property. Therefore, if the comparable property is inferior to the subject property with respect to valuable characteristics, the comparable property's sale price would be adjusted upward. Conversely, if the comparable property is superior to the subject property along any important dimension, the

www.bea.gov

Bureau of Economic Analysis U.S. Department of Commerce.

www.bls.gov

Bureau of Labor Statistics U.S. Department of Labor.

www.census.gov

U.S. Census Bureau.

www.economy.com

A leading provider of economic, financial, and industry data and research.

www.stdb.com

The CCIM Institute's site to do business provides aerials, demographic data, consumer expenditure reports, and more.

www.yahoo.com/ realestate

Provides sale price information for specific properties as well as aggregate data for the industry.

www.zillow.com

Find homes for sale, sell real estate, check home values.

comparable property's sale price would be adjusted downward. The most common required sale price adjustments are listed below.

Transactional Adjustments	Property Adjustments
1. Property rights conveyed	6. Location
2. Financing terms	7. Physical characteristics
3. Conditions of sale	8. Economic characteristics
4. Expenditures made immediately after purchase	9. Use
5. Market conditions	10. Nonrealty items (personal property)

The first five, labeled **transactional adjustments,** concern the nature and terms of the deal. These potential influences on the bargaining position or motivation of the buyer, seller, or both can affect the negotiated price, regardless of the physical, economic, and locational characteristics of the property. The five **property adjustments** recognize that the locational, physical, and economic differences between properties, plus the ways in which the properties are used and the presence or absence of personal property, all can add or subtract incrementally to a base value, much like the effect of options on the price of a car. Each of these types of adjustments to the sale price of each of the comparable properties is briefly explained below.

Real Property Rights Conveyed.   Potentially, a sale price adjustment must be made if the legal estate, or bundle of rights, of a comparable property differs from those of the subject property. (Legal estates are discussed in Chapter 2.) In reality, however, the amount of the required adjustment is almost impossible to measure from the market. Thus, a property having a legal estate different than that of the subject property should generally be eliminated as a comparable, even if physically very similar.

✓ Concept Check

7.5   Assume the interest conveyed from seller to buyer is a fee simple estate. A similar property in the neighborhood that recently sold conveyed title under the condition that the property not be sold for three years. What adjustment is required to the sale price of the comparable property?

Financing Terms.   Occasionally, properties are sold with nonmarket financing. For example, a lender may participate in a government-sponsored low-income (or first-time) homebuyer program and grant below-market interest rate loans to buyers. Favorable mortgage financing may allow buyers to pay a somewhat higher purchase price. Thus, the possibility of nonmarket financing must always be considered. When detected, we recommend that the property not be used as a comparable sale. However, if the number of comparable sale transactions is extremely limited, compelling the appraiser to include the transaction, the transaction price of the comparable property must be adjusted downward when such favorable financing occurs.

Conditions of Sale.   A forced sale or a desperation purchase can cause unequal bargaining power between buyers and sellers. More commonly, personal relationships may cause a transaction price to be lower than true market value, as when a parent "sells" real estate to a son or daughter. Appraisal analysts must check each comparable sale to ensure that it truly was an arm's-length transaction between buyers and sellers who had relatively equal bargaining power. Normally, a non-arm's-length transaction should not be included as a comparable. Thus, this information is used more as a screening device than as a basis for a comparable sale price adjustment.

Homebuyers are willing to pay more for homes with solar photovoltaic (PV) energy systems, according to a report by the U.S. Department of Energy's Lawrence Berkeley National Laboratory. The study, "Selling into the Sun: Price Premium Analysis of a Multi-State Data-set of Solar

Solar Sells

Homes," found that buyers were willing to pay an average of about $4 per watt of PV installed—across various states, housing and PV markets, and home types. This equates to a premium of about $15,000 for a typical 3.75 kW PV system.

The research team analyzed almost 22,000 sales of homes—nearly 4,000 of which contained PV systems, in eight states

from 2012–2013–producing an authoritative estimate of price premiums for homes with PV systems. The study can be downloaded at emp.lbl.gov/publications/selling-sun-price-premiums.

Source: Adapted from the appraisalinstitute.org, "Solar Sells: Homebuyers Willing to Pay More for Solar" *Valuation*, First Quarter, 2015, p. 5.

Expenditures Made Immediately after Purchase. Buyers usually estimate expenditures that will have to be made after the property is acquired. Because the buyer is often able to negotiate price concessions from the seller, the expected cost of the expenditures must be added to the observed transaction price if, in fact, the expenditures were made after the acquisition. Such expenditures should be verified by the appraiser before an upward adjustment is made to the sale price of the comparable sale.

Market Conditions. Transactions of selected comparable properties may have taken place yesterday, last month, or even several years ago, although "old" comparable sales should be avoided if at all possible. In using transaction data to determine the *current* value of the subject property, it is therefore important to recognize that general market conditions may have changed since the transaction occurred. Changes in **market conditions** may result from general inflation (or deflation) in the economy or changes in local supply and demand conditions.

The value movements attributed to changes in market conditions are best estimated by tracking the prices of individual properties as they sell repeatedly over time. This method is known as **repeat-sale analysis.** For example, consider three comparable properties that all sold recently (assumed to be today) and also at some time during the past 24 months (see Exhibit 7-4). By dividing the average monthly price increase of each property by its respective initial sale price (SP_1), it is determined that transaction prices of comparable properties have increased, on average, about 0.32 percent per month.[7]

Appraisers can use this rate to adjust the sale prices of comparable properties for the number of months since they were sold. For example, if a comparable property sold 10 months ago for $100,000, assuming an arm's-length transaction under normal financing conditions, the adjustment would be $100,000 × (0.0032 × 10) = $3,200, and the market-adjusted sale price would equal $103,200. If sufficient repeat-sale data are not available, the appraiser may rely on other information to infer recent price changes, such as recent changes in the median sale prices of comparable properties in the market.

www.fhfa.gov/DataTools

The Federal Housing Finance Agency produces house prices indices for all 50 states and all metropolitan areas based on repeated sales.

---

7. Students may note that this is not the compounded monthly rate of increase, but rather a linear rate of increase. This rate is commonly used in practice to estimate changes over short time periods.

Exhibit 7-4 Repeat-Sale Analysis for Market Conditions Adjustment

Property	Date of Previous Sale	Price at Previous Sale (SP_1)	Price Today (SP_2)	Change per Month ($SP_2 - SP_1$)/mos.	Monthly Rate of Increase (% of SP_1)
A	12 mos. ago	$191,000	$197,900	$575	0.30%
B	18 mos. ago	158,600	167,000	467	0.29
C	24 mos. ago	148,900	162,000	546	0.37
				Average monthly rate of increase =	0.32%

✓ Concept Check

7.6 Assume an analysis of recent sale prices indicates that properties in the subject's market have declined, on average, ¼ of a percent each month over the last two years. If the comparable property sold 12 months ago, what adjustment is required?

Location. The importance of location in real estate valuation is discussed extensively in Chapters 5 and 6. A location adjustment is required when the location of a comparable property is either superior or inferior to the location of the subject property, which is almost always the case. When the subject and comparable properties are located in different neighborhoods, an appraiser must quantify the required location adjustment by somehow comparing the prices of similar properties, some of which are in the subject property's neighborhood and some in the comparable property's neighborhood. These location adjustments require skill and expert knowledge of the local housing market.

Physical Characteristics. Adjustments for physical characteristics are intended to capture the dimensions in which a comparable property differs physically from the subject property. These include differences such as lot size, structure size, desirability of the floor plan, architectural style, condition, type of construction, materials, and the presence or absence of various features such as a garage, fireplace, built-in appliances, bookshelves, carpet, swimming pool, or patio. Exhibit 7-5 depicts several physical adjustments required of the comparable properties. Again, these numerical adjustments require expert skill and knowledge.

Economic Characteristics. This element of comparison is usually not applied to personal residences. In income-producing property, important economic characteristics may include operating expenses, management quality, lease terms, and tenant mix. Great care must be taken when making these adjustments.

Use. Two properties located in the same market can be physically similar, but their *uses* may differ, requiring either an adjustment or elimination of the property as a comparable. For example, an appraiser may be valuing an older single-family residence near the center of a medium-size city. One of the comparable properties is a similar house next door that is used for law offices. Although existing zoning (see Chapter 4) permits the subject to be used as an office building, its value depends on its anticipated highest and best use. If the appraiser believes the highest and best use is as a single-family residence, he should not use the law offices as a comparable sale. Note that the decision to use or exclude the

Exhibit 7-5 Object of Adjustments: Adjust Each "Comp" to Approximate the Subject

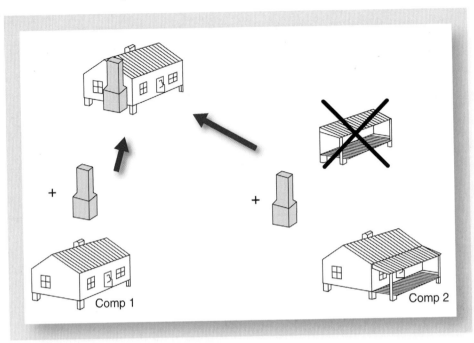

comparable sale depends on the *anticipated* use of the subject at its highest and best use, not its historic or current use.

Nonrealty Items. The sale price of one of the comparable properties may contain items of personal property, such as furniture, equipment, rugs, and built-in TVs. The price of the comparable must therefore be adjusted downward to reflect the presence of these **nonrealty items** when estimating the real estate value of the subject property. In doing so, it is the current market value of these items that is used as the adjustment, not their original cost.

Types of Adjustments

Appraisers use two types of quantitative sale price adjustments: dollars and percentages. If a dollar adjustment is estimated, the appraiser simply adds it to, or subtracts it from, the adjusted price of the comparable property. Some adjustments (e.g., financing and physical characteristics) are often made in dollars, whereas adjustments for market conditions and location are more typically made in percentage terms.

Sequence of Adjustments

The sequence of adjustments to the sale prices of the comparable properties can vary with the availability and reliability of comparable sales information. However, the transactional adjustments are generally applied first and in the order listed in Exhibit 7-6. The property adjustments are next applied, but in no particular order.[8] Note that each adjustment is made to the adjusted price of the comparable property, not the sale price of the comparable.

---

8. For a more detailed discussion, see Chapter 18 in *The Appraisal of Real Estate,* 14th ed. (2013).

Exhibit 7-6 Sequence of Adjustments to Sale Price of Comparable

Sale price of comparable	
Transaction adjustments:	
Adjustment for property rights conveyed	+/ −
Adjusted price	
Adjustment for financing terms	+/ −
Adjusted price	
Adjustment for conditions of sale	+/ −
Adjusted price	
Adjustment for expenditures immediately after purchase	+/ −
Adjusted price	
Adjustment for market conditions	+/ −
Adjusted price	
Property Adjustments for	
Location	+/ −
Physical characteristics	+/ −
Economics characteristics	+/ −
Use	+/ −
Nonrealty components	−
Final adjusted sale price	

Nevertheless, the sequence would make no difference if all adjustments were dollar adjustments. However, if percentage adjustments are involved, the sequence does matter.

> ✓ **Concept Check**
>
> **7.7** Assume a comparable property sold three months ago for $350,000. Immediately after the property was purchased, the buyer replaced the roof at a cost of $20,000, which was equal to the cost expected by the buyer before purchase. Market values in the comparable's neighborhood have increased a total of 1.5 percent during the three months since the sale (0.50 percent per month). Assume no adjustments for property rights conveyed, financing, or conditions of sale are required. What is the adjusted price of the comparable if the adjustment for the $20,000 roof expenditure is first? What is the adjusted price if changes in market conditions/ values is made first?

EXAMPLE 7-1   2380 APPLETREE COURT

To illustrate the sales comparison approach, assume transaction data from three comparable properties are used in valuing the subject property—a modest single-family residence located at 2380 Appletree Court, in the Parkway Estates neighborhood.

Jacob Jones has signed a contract to purchase the home from Blaine Strickland for $163,000. Mr. Jones has applied for a $122,250 mortgage loan from the Bank of Florida. The relevant characteristics, termed the **elements of comparison,** used to compare and adjust the property prices, are summarized in Exhibit 7-7, the market data grid.

We can see from the location line on the market data grid that the comparable properties are located in the subject property's neighborhood. Two sold within the last three months, while the third sold four months ago. Their prices range from $157,100 to $169,900. Note that the property rights conveyed, conditions of sale, financing terms, use, and several of the physical features of the subject are identical to the comparable properties. Thus, no adjustment will be necessary for these elements. However, adjustments are necessary for differences in several characteristics that, in the opinion of the appraiser, materially affected the comparable transaction prices. The amount of the adjustment for each item has been estimated by the appraiser and is shown in the list below:

- Market conditions: 0.3 percent per month (values have increased in neighborhood).
- Lot size: $100,000 per acre.
- Construction quality: No adjustment if all siding. $1,500 adjustment if brick front with remainder siding; $3,000 adjustment if all brick.
- Effective age: $1,250 per year.
- Living area: $48.00 per square foot.
- Porch, patio, deck area: $16.00 per square foot.
- Pool area: $7,000.
- Bath: $4,000 per bath.

The individual adjustments are shown in Exhibit 7-8. For example, Comparable Sales 2 and 3 require an upward adjustment for market conditions because they sold in earlier months and prices in the market have been increasing. The adjustment for Comparable 2 is calculated as $167,200 × 0.003 per mo. × 3 mos. = $1,504.80, and Comparable 3 as $157,100 × 0.003 per mo. × 4 mos. = $1,885.20. However, these estimates suggest a degree of precision in the estimate that is unintended and the adjustments are rounded to $1,500 and $1,900.

The individual adjustments for the various differences in physical characteristics are shown next. For example, the subject does not have a pool although Comparable Sales 2 and 3 do. Therefore, the estimated value of the pool in this market ($7,000) is *subtracted* from the sale price of the comparable sales 2 and 3. Adjustments are made for all items that differ, resulting in a final adjusted sale price for each of the comparable properties.

It is extremely important to emphasize that making required adjustments, such as those detailed in Exhibit 7-8, requires significant experience as well as constant attention to market transactions, trends, and conditions. Note that if the comparable properties are identical to the subject with respect to an element of comparison, that element can be deleted from the adjustment grid.

Exhibit 7-7 Sales Comparison Approach: Market Data Grid for 2380 Appletree Court

Elements of Comparison	Subject	Comp Sale 1	Comp Sale 2	Comp Sale 3
Sale price of comparable		$169,900	$167,200	$157,100
Transaction characteristics				
Property rights conveyed	Fee simple	Same	Same	Same
Financing terms	Conventional	Same	Same	Same
Conditions of sale	Arm's length	Same	Same	Same
Expenditures immed. after purchase		None	None	None
Market conditions	Today	This month	3 mos. ago	4 mos. ago
Property characteristics				
Location	Parkway Estates	Same	Same	Same

Exhibit 7-7 Continued Sales Comparison Approach: Market Data Grid for 2380 Appletree Court

Elements of Comparison	Subject	Comp Sale 1	Comp Sale 2	Comp Sale 3
Physical characteristics:				
Site/lot size	0.50 acres	0.50 acres	0.45 acres	0.48 acres
Construction quality	Siding	Siding/brick	Siding	Brick
Effective age	3 years	6 years	10 years	15 years
Living area	1,960 sq. ft.	2,060 sq. ft.	2,077 sq. ft.	1,818 sq. ft.
Number of baths	2.5 baths	2.5 baths	2.5 baths	3.0 baths
Garage spaces	2-car	2-car	2-car	2-car
Porch, patio, deck	None	None	None	200 sq. ft.
Fence, pool, etc.	None	None	Pool	Pool
Economics characteristics	N.A.	N.A.	N.A.	N.A.
Use	Single-family	Same	Same	Same
Nonrealty components	None	None	None	None

Exhibit 7-8 Sales Comparison Approach: Adjustment Grid for 2380 Appletree Court

Elements of Comparison	Subject	Comp Sale 1	Comp Sale 2	Comp Sale 3
Sale price of comparable		$169,900	$167,200	$157,100
Transaction adjustments				
Adj. for property rights conveyed	Fee simple	0	0	0
Adjusted price		$169,900	$167,200	$157,100
Adjustment for financing terms	Conventional	0	0	0
Adjusted price		$169,900	$167,200	$157,100
Adjustment for conditions of sale	Arm's length	0	0	0
Adjusted price		$169,900	$167,200	$157,100
Adj. for expend. immed. after purchase		0	0	0
Adjusted price		$169,900	$167,200	$157,100
Adjustment for market conditions	Today	0	1,500	1,900
Adjusted price		$169,900	$168,700	$159,000
Property Adjustments for				
Location	Suburban	0	0	0
Physical characteristics:				
Site	0.50 acres	0	5,000	2,000
Construction quality	Siding/good	(1,500)	0	(3,000)
Effective age	3 years	3,750	8,750	15,000
Living area	1,960 sq. ft.	(4,800)	(5,600)	6,800
Baths	2.5	0	0	(2,000)
Porch, patio, deck	None	0	0	(3,200)
Fence, pool, etc.	None	0	(7,000)	(7,000)
Total adj. for physical characteristics		(2,550)	1,150	8,600
Economics characteristics		0	0	0
Use	Single-family	0	0	0
Nonrealty components	None	0	0	0
Final adjusted sale price		$167,350	$169,850	$167,600

Exhibit 7-9   Reconciliation of Final Adjusted Sale Prices

Source	Final Adjusted Sale Price		Weight (%)		Weighted Price
Comparable Sale 1	167,350	×	60%	=	$100,410
Comparable Sale 2	169,850	×	20	=	33,970
Comparable Sale 3	167,600	×	20	=	33,520
Indicated Opinion of Value (using the sales comparison approach)				=	$167,900

✓ **Concept Check**

7.8   Explain why adjustments are made to the sale prices of the comparable properties instead of to the value of the subject property.

A Note on the Selection of Comparables and Adjustments

The steps of the sales comparison approach involve both the selection of comparables and the calculation of adjustments to the comparable sale prices. While both steps can be important in the procedure, the authors have observed that more and greater errors in appraisal have resulted from careless selection of comparables than from poor adjustments. Unless the adjustments are unusually large, say, greater than 10 percent of a sale price, the first order of investigation in evaluating an appraisal is to assure that the comparables used are reasonable.

Reconciliation to an Indicated Value Estimate

The final step in obtaining an indicated opinion of value of the subject property from the sales comparison approach is to reconcile the final adjusted sale prices of the comparable properties. In this step an appraiser considers which, if any, of the comparable properties are better indicators of the subject property's value. More complete data, fewer and smaller adjustments, and more recent transactions probably would cause the appraiser to consider the adjusted sale prices of some comparable properties to be better indicators of the value of the subject than others. In this case, Comparable 1 was weighted more heavily (60 percent) than the other two (20 percent each) because the appraiser believed that Comparable 1 was very similar to the subject property, required few adjustments, and represented the best indicator of value. As shown in Exhibit 7-9, reconciliation is a weighting process. The weighted average price (*indicated opinion of value*) from the sales comparison approach is $167,900.

In professional practice, appraisers do not explicitly identify the weights given to each comparable. They apply the weights implicitly in rendering their professional opinion of value. The weights are detailed here only to describe the process.

The Cost Approach

When the total cost to construct a property is less than its expected market value upon completion, developers have an incentive to build additional competing properties, which tends to reduce market values.[9] When the cost to produce a property exceeds its expected market value, developers have the incentive to stop or slow construction,

---

9. The costs, as described here, include all outlays required to acquire the land, develop it, and construct the building improvements. The all-in costs include the direct material and labor costs, as well as all indirect overhead, design, permit, financing, marketing, and a reasonable builder's profit.

Exhibit 7-10 Summary of Cost Approach

	Estimated cost to construct structure today
−	Estimated accrued depreciation
=	Depreciated cost of building improvements
+	Estimated value of land
=	Indicated market value by the cost approach

which tends to increase the market value of competing properties. Thus, construction costs and market values differ, but are always pressured toward each other by the actions of market participants.

The cost approach to valuation is based on the economic principle of substitution and assumes the market value of a *new* building is similar to the cost of constructing it today. For an older property, the appraiser identifies and measures reductions in the value from today's construction cost. These reductions are termed *accrued depreciation.* After the appraiser has estimated the building's current value by subtracting all elements of accrued depreciation from the building's construction cost, the value of the land (and permanent improvements to the land) is estimated separately and added to the depreciated construction cost of the building. The general steps of the cost approach are outlined in Exhibit 7-10.

Estimating Cost

For appraisal purposes, there are two types of construction cost estimates: reproduction costs and replacement costs. The **reproduction cost** of an existing building is the expenditure required to construct the building today, replicating it in exact detail. This includes any outdated functional aspects of the building such as a poor interior design, inadequate equipment, or an outdated heating and air conditioning system. It also includes the cost of constructing the building using outdated materials such as surface wiring, steel window frames, and steel plumbing.

www.marshallswift.com

Leading cost estimator for the appraisal industry.

In contrast, **replacement cost** is the expenditure needed to construct a building of *equal utility* to the existing building.[10] This cost estimate incorporates the use of modern construction techniques, materials, and design and represents the cost of a building for which some or all outdated aspects are eliminated.

The theoretical basis for the cost approach to valuation is reproduction cost. However, reproduction cost is often difficult, if not impossible, to estimate because the building may contain construction methods and materials that are no longer available or no longer permitted by current construction standards and building codes. The requirements in some local markets that new or significantly renovated buildings meet new environmental ("green") standards also eliminates the use of reproduction cost in some appraisals. As a result, replacement cost is most often used, because it is typically easier to obtain than reproduction cost.

www.rsmeans.com

Provider of cost estimation services.

In estimating current construction costs, appraisers may rely on cost-per-square-foot or cost-per-cubic-foot data available from builders and construction cost estimating firms. In addition, several companies, such as Marshall and Swift and R.S. Means are in the business of providing detailed construction cost estimates.

✓ Concept Check

7.9 Distinguish between reproduction cost and replacement cost. Which would generally be higher, assuming both could be estimated?

---

10. The term *utility* means satisfaction. Therefore, a building of equal utility is a building that provides satisfaction to its users equal to that of the building being appraised as if it were new.

Accrued Depreciation

Accrued depreciation is the difference between the current market value of a building (or improvement) and the total cost to construct it new.[11] This difference generally increases with building age and is attributed to three elements: physical deterioration, functional obsolescence, and external obsolescence.

Physical deterioration represents the loss in value of a building over time associated with the aging and decay of its physical condition. This occurs in both short-lived items (e.g., carpeting, roofing materials, appliances) and long-lived items (e.g., roof framing, windows, doors, stairs, foundation). Simply stated, older buildings are worth less than otherwise equivalent newer structures.

Functional obsolescence is a loss in the value of a structure due to changes in tastes, preferences, technical building innovations, or market standards. Similar to physical deterioration, functional obsolescence tends to be associated with the passage of time. Newer building materials, construction techniques, and designs, coupled with changing consumer tastes and preferences, generally make older buildings less desirable to tenants and thus not as valuable as newer buildings. However, newer buildings can suffer from functional obsolescence. For example, a new home without a large master bathroom suite is functionally obsolete in many markets today. Examples of curable functional obsolescence include outdated fixtures, too few electrical outlets, lack of bookcases, too-high ceilings, and lack of insulation. Examples of functional obsolescence that are often incurable include a poor exterior design or interior floor plan. Note that the use of replacement cost, rather than reproduction cost, eliminates the need to estimate some forms of functional obsolescence.

Finally, **external obsolescence** reflects the loss in market value due to influences *external to the site*. Simply stated, external obsolescence results from a deterioration in the subject property's neighborhood. Noxious odors, unpleasant sights, and increased traffic due to more intensive uses (e.g., commercial and industrial) introduced into a residential neighborhood are examples of this external obsolescence.

EXAMPLE 7-2   2380 APPLETREE COURT

To estimate the value of 2380 Appletree Court using the cost approach, an appraiser estimates the current cost of the building improvements, the total accrued depreciation, and the value of the site (and any site improvements). The appraiser's estimates are shown in Exhibit 7-11.

The reproduction cost estimates are based on information supplied by a private cost estimating firm and data obtained from local building contractors. The living area of the dwelling is estimated to cost $121,520 to replace new (1,960 sq. ft. × $62 per sq. ft.). The cost of the garage ($8,800) and appliances ($2,400) is added, resulting in total estimated construction costs of $132,720. Physical depreciation of the existing property is estimated at 5 percent of the total replacement costs ($6,636 = $132,720 × 0.05). The appraiser concludes that the property has not suffered any functional or external obsolescence. This results in a depreciated value of $126,084 ($132,720 − $6,636). The site value is estimated to be $40,000. Landscaping and other miscellaneous site improvements are estimated to have a current value of $4,000. Thus, the indicated value of the subject property using the

---

11. It is important to note that the appraisal concept of depreciation differs substantially from the accounting concept used for income tax calculation. The appraisal term is associated with *actual* reductions in market value, while the term used in calculating taxable income deals with *allowable* reductions to a property's book value, or depreciable basis (see Chapter 20).

"Automated valuation models" or AVMs are computer programs that try to replicate work done by human real estate appraisers. This is accomplished by combining a home's physical and locational characteristics and nearby sales trends into a computer-generated estimate of market value. AVMs use sophisticated multiple regression techniques and a database of thousands—or millions—of sale transactions to determine the market value of the subject home's physical and locational attributes and therefore its predicted price/value. This value estimate can then be reviewed by an appraiser, or the appraisal process can be deemed complete.

Traditional appraisals provided by licensed real estate appraisers cost $300–$400 a home. Appraisals generated by AVMs are one-tenth the cost—or less. Plus, automated models are quick, making large-scale reviews of numerous home values financially feasible.

However, several limitations affect the potential accuracy of AVMs, including the complexity and variation of homes and their locations as well as inaccurate data about the subject and comparable properties. A home's value isn't simply the by-product of a traceable mix of lot sizes, bedroom counts, comparable sales prices, and other factors. Even the deepest real estate database can't effectively juggle the intangibles altering a home's value, from its condition inside and out to the quality of the view. For example, AVMs can't detect serious structural problems, termite damage, or hazardous wiring. This can lead to an overstated value for a property in bad condition or an understated value for a home in superior condition with many upgrades. Furthermore, AVMs are largely dependent on public record databases, and if those databases have incorrect or outdated information, the statistical model will return an inaccurate valuation. Also, AVMs may not distinguish between various sale types, such as foreclosures and traditional sales. For example, it could compare a well-kept traditional sale to a severely damaged foreclosed property sale.

As a result, many lenders prefer to have an appraiser involved, but at a lower cost than a traditional appraisal. Some industry analysts are therefore predicting an increased use of a hybrid methodology that combines AVM technology and the use of an appraiser (i.e., actual "boots on the ground") to verify data and the validity of assumptions.

Do Prices Compute? Using Statistical Models to Estimate Home Values

---

cost approach is $170,084, rounded to $170,100. Declines in market value associated with accrued depreciation are difficult to estimate in practice. This explains why the other methods of valuation are relied upon more in most appraisal assignments.

Exhibit 7-11   2380 Appletree Court: Cost Approach Summary

Reproduction cost of improvement		
Living area (conditioned space)	$121,520	
Garage area	8,800	
Appliances, porch, patio areas	2,400	$132,720
Less: Depreciation of improvement		
Physical deterioration	6,636	
Functional obsolescence	0	
External obsolescence	0	−6,636
Depreciated value of improvements		$126,084
Plus: Value of the site		40,000
Plus: Depreciated Value of site improvement		4,000
Indicated value by cost approach (rounded)		$170,100

✓ Concept Check

7.10   Of the three basic steps in the cost approach to valuation—estimate replacement cost, estimate accrued depreciation, and estimate site value—which is generally the most difficult and why?

Final Reconciliation

In determining the final estimate of the subject's market value, an appraiser considers and weighs the reliability of the indicated values from different approaches, and the relevance of the approaches to the valuation of the subject property. In the Appletree Court example, the appraiser has produced estimated market values using the sales comparison approach and the cost approach of $167,900, and $170,100, respectively. The appraiser has determined that owing to the reliability of the comparable sales data and the applicability of the approach to residential properties, the sales comparison approach yields the most reliable indicator of value. Therefore, all weight is placed on this approach in reconciling the value indicators. Thus, the final estimate of value of the residence located at 2380 Appletree Court is $167,900.

The appraisal of a residence, as described using the Appletree Court example, is generally required to obtain financing when purchasing a property. Lenders usually ask appraisers to submit their independent value opinion for a home by completing a Uniform Residential Appraisal Report (URAR) form. A sample URAR is shown for the Appletree Court property in Exhibit 7-12.

EXPLORE THE WEB

The Emergence of Online Appraisal Tools

Numerous private firms are now offering online automated valuation models (AVMs) and/or comparable sales reports for borrowers, lenders, and other participants in the single-family residential market interested in homes values. Real Data (www.realdata.com/ls/online-real-estate-valuation-services-compared.shtml), a provider of real estate investment software, compiles a list of companies that have developed online valuation resources, including AVMs based on multiple regression analysis (MRA). One of the authors paid $29.95 to have his home appraised online by the *Electronic Appraiser* (www.electronic appraiser.com). Just prior to this, the author's home had been appraised by a traditional fee appraiser for the purposes of a mortgage refinancing. The online AVM returned a value estimate 7 percent greater than the traditional appraiser's estimate.

Search the provided by Real Data for an AVM model available for use free of charge. Use this website to obtain an estimate of market value for a relative's (or your) home. We recommend that you visit www.zillow.com for a free, instant valuation of many U.S. homes. Type in the address for your parent's home or one of your neighbors and surprise them with your market knowledge.

Exhibit 7-12 Sample Uniform Residential Appraisal Report

Uniform Residential Appraisal Report
File No. R2003-100

The purpose of this summary appraisal report is to provide the lender/client with an accurate, and adequately supported, opinion of the market value of the subject property.

Property Address 2380 Appletree Court	City Orlando	State FL Zip Code 32855
Borrower Jacob Jones	Owner of Public Record Blaine Strickland	County Orange

Legal Description Lot 10, Block B, Parkway Estates, Plat Book 245, Page 34

Assessor's Parcel # T34SR26E-59-B-0100	Tax Year 2002	R.E. Taxes $ 2,520.00
Neighborhood Name Parkway Estates	Map Reference 34-26	Census Tract 38.04

Occupant [X] Owner ☐ Tenant ☐ Vacant   Special Assessments $ 0.00   ☐ PUD HOA $ 30.00 ☐ per year [X] per month

Property Rights Appraised [X] Fee Simple ☐ Leasehold ☐ Other (describe)

Assignment Type [X] Purchase Transaction ☐ Refinance Transaction ☐ Other (describe)

Lender/Client Bank of Florida   Address 15760 N. Main, Orlando, FL

Is the subject property currently offered for sale or has it been offered for sale in the twelve months prior to the effective date of this appraisal? [X] Yes ☐ No

Report data source(s) used, offering price(s), and date(s).   The house was listed for $165,000 in the local MLS on July 20, 2016.

I [X] did ☐ did not analyze the contract for sale for the subject purchase transaction. Explain the results of the analysis of the contract for sale or why the analysis was not performed. Sale is an arms-length transaction.

Contract Price $ 163,000   Date of Contract 9/1/2016   Is the property seller the owner of public record? [X] Yes ☐ No   Data Source(s) Tax Assessor

Is there any financial assistance (loan charges, sale concessions, gift or downpayment assistance, etc.) to be paid by any party on behalf of the borrower? ☐ Yes [X] No

If Yes, report the total dollar amount and describe the items to be paid.

Note: Race and the racial composition of the neighborhood are not appraisal factors.

Neighborhood Characteristics	One-Unit Housing Trends	One-Unit Housing		Present Land Use %	
Location ☐ Urban [X] Suburban ☐ Rural	Property Values [X] Increasing ☐ Stable ☐ Declining	PRICE $(000)	AGE (yrs)	One-Unit	80% %
Built-Up [X] Over 75% ☐ 25-75% ☐ Under 25%	Demand/Supply ☐ Shortage [X] In Balance ☐ Over Supply	100 Low	New	2-4 Unit	5% %
Growth ☐ Rapid [X] Stable ☐ Slow	Marketing Time ☐ Under 3 mths [X] 3-6 mths ☐ Over 6 mths	220 High	30	Multi-Family	5% %

Neighborhood Boundaries The subject neighborhood is bounded to the north by Red Lake Road, to the east by Shamrock Way, to the south by Dodd Road, and to the west by Aloma Avenue.

140-160 Pred. 10 Commercial 5% %   Other Vacant 5% %

Neighborhood Description The subject is located approximately 10 miles NE of the Orlando downtown and is comprised primarily of owner occupied, single-family, detached homes. The subject is located close to centers of employment and public schools. Shopping, banking and restaurants are also located nearby.

Market Conditions (including support for the above conclusions) This is an established residential area. The area appears to be stable with moderately increasing property values. Most homes in the area, when placed on the market, sell within six months. Market interest rates are at competitive levels. Sales and financing concessions are uncommon.

Dimensions 110 x 180 x 98 x 210	Area 21,345 +/- square feet	Shape Rectangular	View Residential properties

Specific Zoning Classification R-1   Zoning Description Residential

Zoning Compliance [X] Legal ☐ Legal Nonconforming (Grandfathered Use) ☐ No Zoning ☐ Illegal (describe)

Is the highest and best use of the subject property as improved (or as proposed per plans and specifications) the present use? [X] Yes ☐ No If No, describe.

Utilities	Public	Other (describe)		Public	Other (describe)	Off-site Improvements—Type	Public	Private
Electricity	[X]		Water	[X]		Street Asphalt	[X]	
Gas			Sanitary Sewer	[X]		Alley None		

FEMA Special Flood Hazard Area ☐ Yes [X] No FEMA Flood Zone C FEMA Map # 12077-C-0400-E FEMA Map Date 11/19/99

Are the utilities and off-site improvements typical for the market area? [X] Yes ☐ No If No, describe.

Are there any adverse site conditions or external factors (easements, encroachments, environmental conditions, land uses, etc.)? ☐ Yes [X] No If Yes, describe.

GENERAL DESCRIPTION	FOUNDATION	EXTERIOR DESCRIPTION materials/condition	INTERIOR materials/condition
Units [X] One ☐ One with Accessory Unit	[X] Concrete Slab ☐ Crawl Space	Foundation Walls Concrete	Floors Car/Vinyl/Good
# of Stories One	☐ Full Basement ☐ Partial Basement	Exterior Walls Siding (Hardy)	Walls Drywall/Good
Type [X] Det. ☐ Att. ☐ S-Det./End Unit	Basement Area N/A sq. ft.	Roof Surface Comp shingle	Trim/Finish Wood/Good
[X] Existing ☐ Proposed ☐ Under Const.	Basement Finish N/A %	Gutters & Downspouts None	Bath Floor Ceramic/Good
Design (Style) Traditional	☐ Outside Entry/Exit ☐ Sump Pump	Window Type Alum/thermal	Bath Wainscot Ceramic/Good
Year Built 2000	Evidence of ☐ Infestation	Storm Sash/Insulated None	Car Storage ☐ None
Effective Age (Yrs) 3	☐ Dampness ☐ Settlement	Screens Screens	Driveway # of Cars
Attic ☐ None	Heating [X] FWA ☐ HWBB ☐ Radiant	Amenities ☐ WoodStove(s) #	Driveway Surface Concrete
[X] Drop Stair ☐ Stairs	☐ Other Fuel Electric	[X] Fireplace(s) # 1 ☐ Fence None	[X] Garage # of Cars 2
☐ Floor [X] Scuttle	Cooling [X] Central Air Conditioning	☐ Patio/Deck ☐ Porch None	☐ Carport # of Cars
☐ Finished ☐ Heated	☐ Individual ☐ Other	☐ Pool No Pool ☐ Other	☐ Att. ☐ Det. ☐ Built-in

Appliances [X] Refrigerator [X] Range/Oven [X] Dishwasher [X] Disposal [X] Microwave [X] Washer/Dryer [X] Other (describe) Fan/Hood

Finished area above grade contains: 7 Rooms   3 Bedrooms   2.5 Bath(s)   1,960 Square Feet of Gross Living Area Above Grade

Additional features (special energy efficient items, etc.).   The additional features include crown molding, 9-foot ceilings, and a bay window.

Describe the condition of the property (including needed repairs, deterioration, renovations, remodeling, etc.).   The subject appears to be in good to excellent condition. The subject has been well maintained and there are no apparent signs of deferred maintenance. No elements of functional or external obsolescence were observed at inspection.

Are there any physical deficiencies or adverse conditions that affect the livability, soundness, or structural integrity of the property? ☐ Yes [X] No If Yes, describe.

Does the property generally conform to the neighborhood (functional utility, style, condition, use, construction, etc.)? [X] Yes ☐ No If No, describe.

Exhibit 7-12   **Continued**   Sample Uniform Residential Appraisal Report

Uniform Residential Appraisal Report   File No. R2003-100

There are **2** comparable properties currently offered for sale in the subject neighborhood ranging in price from $ **156,000** to $ **170,500**

There are _____ comparable sales in the subject neighborhood within the past twelve months ranging in sale price from $ _____ to $ _____

FEATURE	SUBJECT	COMPARABLE SALE NO. 1		COMPARABLE SALE NO. 2		COMPARABLE SALE NO. 3	
Address	2380 Appletree Court Orlando	2043 Appletree Court Orlando		4207 E. Park Trail Orlando		4470 E. Park Trail Orlando	
Proximity to Subject		Approx. 3 blocks south		Approx. 1 block east		Approx. 3 blocks east	
Sale Price	$ 163,000	$ 169,900		$ 167,200		$ 157,100	
Sale Price/Gross Liv. Area	$ 83.16 sq. ft.	$ 82.48 sq. ft.		$ 80.50 sq. ft.		$ 86.41 sq. ft.	
Data Source(s)	Inspection	MLS & Public Records		MLS & Public Records		MLS & Public Records	
Verification Source(s)							
VALUE ADJUSTMENTS	DESCRIPTION	DESCRIPTION	+(-) $ Adjustment	DESCRIPTION	+(-) $ Adjustment	DESCRIPTION	+(-) $ Adjustment
Sale or Financing Concessions	Refinance	Conventional Typical		Conventional Typical		Conventional Typical	
Date of Sale/Time	9/1/2016	09/16		06/16	+1,500	05/16	+1,900
Location	Suburban/Avg	Suburban/Avg		Suburban/Avg		Suburban/Avg	
Leasehold/Fee Simple	Fee Simple	Fee Simple		Fee Simple		Fee Simple	
Site	.5 Acres +/-	.5 Acres +/-		.45 Acres +/-	+5,000	.4 Acres +/-	+2,000
View	Residential/Avg	Residential/Avg		Residential/Avg		Residential/Avg	
Design (Style)	Traditional	Traditional		Traditional		Traditional	
Quality of Construction	Wood Siding	Brick - 1 side	-1,500	Wood Siding		Brick - 1 side	-3,000
Actual Age	9+/- Years	A6/E6	+3,750	A15/E10	+8,750	A15/E15	+15,000
Condition	Good-Excellent	Good-Excellent		Good-Excellent		Good-Excellent	
Above Grade Room Count	Total 7 / Bdrms. 3 / Baths 2.5	Total 6 / Bdrms. 3 / Baths 2.5		Total 7 / Bdrms. 4 / Baths 2.5		Total 7 / Bdrms. 3 / Baths 3	-2,000
Gross Living Area	1,960 sq. ft.	2,060 sq. ft.	-4,800	2,077 sq. ft.	-5,600	1,818 sq. ft.	+6,800
Basement & Finished	None	None		None		None	
Rooms Below Grade	None	None		None		None	
Functional Utility	Average	Average		Average		Average	
Heating/Cooling	FWA C/Air	Central		Central		Central	
Energy Efficient Items	Average	Average		Average		Average	
Garage/Carport	2 Car Garage	Garage (2)		Garage (2)		Garage (2)	
Porch/Patio/Deck						Porch, Deck	-3,200
	1 F/P	1 F/P		1 F/P		1 F/P	
	No Pool	No Pool		Pool	-7,000	Pool	-7,000
Net Adjustment (Total)		[ ] + [X] - $	2,550	[X] + [ ] -	2,650	[X] + [ ] - $	10,500
Adjusted Sale Price of Comparables		Net Adj. -1.5% % Gross Adj. 5.9% % $	167,350	Net Adj. 1.6% % Gross Adj. 16.7% % $	169,850	Net Adj. 6.7% % Gross Adj. 26.0% % $	167,600

I [X] did [ ] did not research the sale or transfer history of the subject property and comparable sales. If not, explain _____

My research [ ] did [X] did not reveal any prior sales or transfers of the subject property for the three years prior to the effective date of this appraisal.
Data source(s) _____

My research [ ] did [X] did not reveal any prior sales or transfers of the comparable sales for the year prior to the date of sale of the comparable sale.
Data source(s) _____

Report the results of the research and analysis of the prior sale or transfer history of the subject property and comparable sales (report additional prior sales on page 3).

ITEM	SUBJECT	COMPARABLE SALE NO. 1	COMPARABLE SALE NO. 2	COMPARABLE SALE NO. 3
Date of Prior Sale/Transfer	N/A	N/A	N/A	N/A
Price of Prior Sale/Transfer				
Data Source(s)				
Effective Date of Data Source(s)				

Analysis of prior sale or transfer history of the subject property and comparable sales   Prior sales of the comparable properties selected occurred more than one year ago. The subject property was not listed for sale.

Summary of Sales Comparison Approach.   The sample of comparable sales is taken from the subject's general area. Other sales were reviewed, and the sample data selected is comparable in terms of size, location, age, and condition. All sales occurred within the last three months.

Indicated Value by Sales Comparison Approach $ 167,900

Indicated Value by: Sales Comparison Approach $ 167,900   Cost Approach (if developed) $ 170,100   Income Approach (if developed) $ 0

The value estimate is supported by the sales comparison approach and the cost approach. However, the sales comparison approach best reflects the preferences of the buyers and sellers. Homes in the subject neighborhood are not typically leased; therefore, the income approach is not relevant to our analysis.

This appraisal is made [X] "as is," [ ] subject to completion per plans and specifications on the basis of a hypothetical condition that the improvements have been completed, [ ] subject to the following repairs or alterations on the basis of a hypothetical condition that the repairs or alterations have been completed, or [ ] subject to the following required inspection based on the extraordinary assumption that the condition or deficiency does not require alteration or repair:

Based on a complete visual inspection of the interior and exterior areas of the subject property, defined scope of work, statement of assumptions and limiting conditions, and appraiser's certification, my (our) opinion of the market value, as defined, of the real property that is the subject of this report is $ 167,900 as of **September 15, 2009**, which is the date of inspection and the effective date of this appraisal.

Freddie Mac Form 70 March 2005   Produced using ACI software, 800.234.8727 www.aciweb.com   Page 2 of 6   Fannie Mae Form 1004 March 2005 1004_05 062906

Velie Appraisal Services

Exhibit 7-12 Continued Sample Uniform Residential Appraisal Report

Uniform Residential Appraisal Report   File No. R2003-100

ADDITIONAL COMMENTS

COST APPROACH TO VALUE (not required by Fannie Mae)

Provide adequate information for the lender/client to replicate the below cost figures and calculations.

Support for the opinion of site value (summary of comparable land sales or other methods for estimating site value) _____

ESTIMATED	[X] REPRODUCTION OR	[ ] REPLACEMENT COST NEW	OPINION OF SITE VALUE .... = $	40,000
Source of cost data			Dwelling 1,960 Sq. Ft. @ $ 62.00 .... = $	121,520
Quality rating from cost service	Effective date of cost data		_____ Sq. Ft. @ $ .... = $	
Comments on Cost Approach (gross living area calculations, depreciation, etc.)			Appliances	2,400
See Attached Addendum.			Garage/Carport 440 Sq. Ft. @ $ 20.00 .... = $	8,800
			Total Estimate of Cost-New .... = $	132,720
			Less Physical Functional External	
			Depreciation $6,636	= $ (6,636)
			Depreciated Cost of Improvements .... = $	126,084
			"As-is" Value of Site Improvements .... = $	4,000
Estimated Remaining Economic Life (HUD and VA only)	Years		INDICATED VALUE BY COST APPROACH .... = $	170,100

INCOME APPROACH TO VALUE (not required by Fannie Mae)

Estimated Monthly Market Rent $ N/A X Gross Rent Multiplier   N/A = $ 0   Indicated Value by Income Approach

Summary of Income Approach (including support for market rent and GRM) N/A

PROJECT INFORMATION FOR PUDs (if applicable)

Is the developer/builder in control of the Homeowners' Association (HOA)? [ ] Yes [X] No Unit type(s) [ ] Detached [ ] Attached

Provide the following information for PUDs ONLY if the developer/builder is in control of the HOA and the subject property is an attached dwelling unit.

Legal name of project N/A

Total number of phases N/A   Total number of units N/A   Total number of units sold N/A

Total number of units rented N/A   Total number of units for sale N/A   Data source(s) N/A

Was the project created by the conversion of an existing building(s) into a PUD? [ ] Yes [ ] No If Yes, date of conversion. N/A

Does the project contain any multi-dwelling units? [ ] Yes [ ] No Data source(s) N/A

Are the units, common elements, and recreation facilities complete? [ ] Yes [ ] No If No, describe the status of completion. N/A

Are the common elements leased to or by the Homeowners' Association? [ ] Yes [ ] No If Yes, describe the rental terms and options. N/A

Describe common elements and recreational facilities. N/A

Freddie Mac Form 70 March 2005   Produced using ACI software, 800.234.8727 www.aciweb.com   Fannie Mae Form 1004 March 2005
                                                              Page 3 of 6   1004_05 062906

Summary

Appraisal is the process of developing an opinion of the value of real estate. The process involves the systematic comparison of the sale prices of a subject property and several comparable properties. Professional appraisers use three general methods, or approaches: sales comparison, cost, and income (the topic of Chapter 8).

Appraising one- to four-family residential properties has been an important activity for many appraisers, and the most applicable method for these appraisals is generally the traditional sales comparison approach. However, the appraisal of small residential properties is becoming increasingly computerized, and the traditional sales comparison approach is being augmented, if not replaced, by computer-aided statistical analyses. Nevertheless, the sales comparison approach will continue to be important in the appraisal of residential properties. Appraisers using the sales comparison approach adjust the sale price of each comparable property to reflect differences between it and the subject property for each element. They follow a sequence of adjustments calculated either as percentages or dollar amounts. The proper selection of comparable sales is essential to the successful implementation of the sales comparison approach.

In the cost approach, the appraiser subtracts the building's estimated accrued depreciation from the cost to construct the property today. Three types of accrued depreciation may exist: physical deterioration, functional obsolescence, and external obsolescence. The cost to construct the building today less accrued depreciation equals the building's indicated value. The estimated site value (plus the current value of site improvements) is then added to obtain the indicated property value by the cost approach.

Key Terms

Accrued depreciation   180
Adjustments   170
Appraisal   161
Appraisal report   161
Arm's-length transaction   169
Comparable properties   168
Elements of comparison   175
External obsolescence   180
Functional obsolescence   180
Highest and best use   166

Indicated value   169
Investment value   163
Market conditions   172
Market value   162
Nonrealty items   174
Physical deterioration   180
Property adjustments   171
Reconciliation   168
Repeat-sale analysis   172
Replacement cost   179

Reproduction cost   179
Restricted appraisal report   168
Subject property   161
Transactional adjustments   171
Transaction price   163
Uniform Standards of Professional Appraisal Practice (USPAP)   163

Test Problems

Answer the following multiple-choice problems:

1. The final price for each comparable property reached after all adjustments have been made is termed the:
   a. Final estimate of value.
   b. Final adjusted sale price.
   c. Market value.
   d. Weighted price.

2. Which of the following is not included in accrued depreciation when applying the cost approach to valuation?
   a. Physical obsolescence.
   b. Functional obsolescence.
   c. External obsolescence.
   d. Tax depreciation.

3. In the sales comparison approach, the value obtained after reconciliation of the final adjusted sale prices from the comparable sales is termed the:
   a. Adjusted price.
   b. Final adjusted sale price.

   c. Market value.
   d. Indicated opinion of value.

4. A new house in good condition that has a poor floor plan would suffer from which type of accrued depreciation?
   a. Short-lived curable physical deterioration.
   b. Long-lived incurable physical deterioration.
   c. Curable functional obsolescence.
   d. Incurable functional obsolescence.
   e. External obsolescence.

5. To reflect a change in market conditions between the date on which a comparable property sold and the date of appraisal of a subject property, an adjustment must be made for which of the following?
   a. Conditions of sale.
   b. Market conditions.
   c. Location.
   d. Financing terms.
   e. None of the above.

6. Under the cost approach to appraisal, the expenditure required to construct a building with equal utility as the one being appraised is termed the _____.
   a. Reproduction cost
   b. Replacement cost
   c. Normal sale price
   d. Market-adjusted normal sale price

7. You find two properties that have sold twice within the last two years. Property A sold 22 months ago for $98,500; it sold last week for $108,000. Property B sold 20 months ago for $105,000; it sold yesterday for $113,500. Assuming no compounding, what is the average monthly rate of change in sale prices?
   a. 0.40%.
   b. 4.20%.
   c. 5.04%.
   d. 0.42%.

8. A comparable property sold 10 months ago for $98,500. If the appropriate adjustment for market conditions is 0.30% per month (with compounding), what would be the adjusted price of the comparable property?
   a. $95,504.
   b. $101,455.
   c. $95,545.
   d. $101,495.

9. A comparable property sold six months ago for $150,000. The adjustments for the various elements of comparison have been calculated as follows:
   Location: −5 percent.
   Market conditions: +8 percent.
   Physical characteristics: +$12,500.
   Financing terms: −$2,600.
   Conditions of sale: None.
   Property rights conveyed: None.
   Use: None.
   Nonrealty items: −$3,000.
   Making the adjustments in the order suggested in Exhibit 7-6, what is the comparable property's final adjusted sale price?
   a. $160,732.
   b. $164,400.

c. $169,600.
d. $162,500.
e. $163,232.

10. A property comparable to the single-family home you are appraising sold three months ago for $450,700. You have determined that the adjustments required for differences in the comparable and subject property are as follows:

Elements of Comparison	Required Adjustment
Transaction characteristics	
Property rights conveyed	None
Financing terms	None
Conditions of sale	None
Expenditures immed. after purchase	+$3,000
Market conditions	+0.50%/month, Not compounded
Property characteristics	
Location	+3%
Physical characteristics:	−5%
Economics characteristics	N.A.
Use	None
Nonrealty components found in comparable	−$5,000

Making the adjustments in the order suggested by Exhibit 7-6, what is the final adjusted sale price of the comparable?
   a. $455,605.
   b. $445,605.
   c. $432,286.
   d. $455,638.
   e. None of the above is within $10 of the correct answer.

Study Questions

1. What is the theoretical basis for the direct sales comparison approach to market valuation?
2. What main difficulty would you foresee in attempting to estimate the value of a 30-year-old property by means of the cost approach?
3. The cost approach to market valuation does not work well in markets that are overbuilt. Explain why.
4. What is meant by functional obsolescence? Could a new building suffer from functional obsolescence?
5. Why is an estimate of the developer's fair market profit included in the cost estimate?
6. Replacement costs have been estimated as $350,000 for a property with a 70-year economic life. The current effective age of the property is 15 years. The value of the land is estimated to be $55,000. What is the estimated market value of

the property using the cost approach, assuming no external or functional obsolescence?
7. What is a self-contained appraisal report?
8. What is the difference between market value and investment value?
9. Contrast self-contained appraisal reports, summary appraisal reports, and restricted appraisal reports.
10. How would you go about estimating the current market value of a publicly traded common stock? Would it take more or less time than most real estate appraisals?
11. Define the highest and best use of a property.
12. In the sales comparison approach, if the comparable property is superior to the subject property in some way, is an upward or downward adjustment to the sale price of the comparable required? Explain.

www.mhhe.com/lingarcher5e

13. A comparable property sold recently for $250,000. The comparable contained an estimated $3,000 in nonrealty items. In addition, the appraiser estimates that market values (conditions) have increased a total of 2 percent since the sale of the comparable. What is the adjusted price of the comparable if the dollar adjustment for nonrealty items is made before the market conditions adjustment? What is the adjusted price of the comparable if the percentage adjustment for market conditions is made before the adjustment for nonrealty items?

14. You are appraising a single-family residence located in the Huntington neighborhood at 4632 NW 56th Drive. The property is being acquired by a mortgage applicant and you have been asked to appraise the property by the lender. Seven potential comparable sales were initially identified. However, three of these seven were highly similar to the subject property in their transactional, physical, and locational characteristics. You therefore decided to exclude the other four transactions from the comparable set.

The elements of comparison you used to compare and adjust the sale prices of the comparable properties are listed in the market data grid below. The property rights being conveyed in the acquisition of the subject property are fee-simple absolute. Conventional mortgage financing will be used by the purchaser and the acquisition appears to be an arm's-length transaction. Thus, no adjustments need to be made to the sale prices of the comparable properties for the type of property rights conveyed, financing terms, or conditions of sale. However, the buyer of Comparable 2 was aware that she would have to replace one of the air-conditioning units immediately after acquiring the property (which she did); thus, she was able to negotiate a $3,000 price reduction from the seller.

Elements of Comparison	Subject	Comp Sale 1	Comp Sale 2	Comp Sale 3
Sale price of comparable		$510,000	$525,000	$499,000
Transaction characteristics				
Property rights conveyed	Fee simple	Same	Same	Same
Financing terms	Conventional	Same	Same	Same
Conditions of sale	Arm's length	Same	Same	Same
Expenditures immed. after purchase		None	$3,000	None
Market conditions	Today	3 mos. ago: add 2% total	6 mos. ago: add 4% total	6 mos. ago: add 4% total
Property characteristics				
Location	Huntington	Huntington	Kensington	Millhoper
Physical characteristics:				
Site/lot size	6,662 sq.ft.	6,700 sq. ft.	6,800 sq. ft	6,600 sq.ft
Construction quality	Typical	Typical	Typical	Typical
Condition	Average	Average	Average	Average
Effective age	5.5 years	7 years	8 years	10 years
Living area	3,473 sq. ft.	3,920 sq. ft.	3,985 sq. ft.	3,835 sq. ft.
Number of baths	3.0 baths	3.5 baths	3.0 baths	2.0 baths
Garage Spaces	2-car	2-car	2-car	1-car
Porch, patio, deck	Cov. porch/wood deck	Cov. Porch	Cov. Porch	Cov. Porch
Fence, pool, etc.	None	None	Pool	Pool
Economics characteristics	N.A.	N.A.	N.A.	N.A.
Use	Single-family	Same	Same	Same
Nonrealty components	None	None	None	None

Comparable 1 sold three months ago, while Comparables 2 and 3 sold six months ago. Based on your knowledge of recent price appreciation in this market, you have decided that Comparable 1 would sell for 2 percent more if sold today and that Comparables 2 and 3 would sell for 4 percent more if sold today. The subject property is located in Huntington, as is Comparable 1. However, Comparables 2 and 3 are located in Kensington and Millhoper, respectively. Although Huntington is a high-end neighborhood, both Kensington and Millhoper are generally considered to be slightly more desirable. In fact, homes in these two neighborhoods generally sell for about a 3 percent price premium relative to similar homes in Huntington.

In these neighborhoods, an incremental square foot of lot size or living area is worth about $20 per square foot and $80 per square foot, respectively. Each year of effective age reduces the value of properties in this market by about $3,000 per year. Your experience suggests that each additional half-bath is worth $500; each additional full bath $1,000. Additional garage spaces, wood decks, and pools in these neighborhoods are worth $8,000, $1,000, and $12,000, respectively. No significant nonrealty items were included in the comparable transactions.

Based on the above discussion of the elements of comparison, complete an adjustment grid for the three comparable properties. What is the final adjusted sale price for Comparables 1, 2, and 3?

15. Assume the market value of the subject site (land only) is $120,000. You estimate that the cost to construct the improvements to the subject property would be $428,000 today. In addition, you estimate that accrued depreciation on the subject is $60,000. What is the indicated value of the subject using the cost approach?

Solutions to Concept Checks

1. A few examples of real estate decisions that require a formal appraisal include a judge attempting to determine the appropriate division of assets in a divorce, lenders contemplating a mortgage loan on a property, government officials estimating the costs of acquiring the right-of-way to construct roadways, or local tax officials determining the appropriate property tax on a property.

2. A potential purchaser may place a higher value on the property than the seller because individuals have different expectations regarding the future desirability of a property, different capabilities for obtaining financing, different tax situations, and different return requirements. The price paid for the home should be closer to $180,000. Although an investor may be willing to pay $200,000, this house and, presumably other close substitutes, are available at $180,000. Although willing, investors should not generally pay more than market value.

3. The highest and best use of the property as though vacant is the four-unit rental housing structure, which is valued at $600,000 compared with $450,000 for the single-family home. However, the highest and best use of the property as improved is the single-family home. After subtracting the demolition and construction costs, the four-unit rental structure's value is only $300,000, which is less than the single-family home value of $450,000.

4. Under these circumstances, an appraiser would typically exclude the sale because the sale was not at arm's length. More than likely, the daughter paid a price below market value. If included, an upward adjustment of the comparable sale price would likely be required, though such an adjustment would be difficult to quantify.

5. Although a similar property in the neighborhood sold recently, it is very difficult to measure the impact on value of the condition that the property not be sold for three years. Therefore, this property should be dropped as a comparable. If retained, an upward adjustment would need to be made to the comparable sale price.

6. The comparable sale price should be adjusted downward by three percent (0.25×12) to find the value of the subject property.

7. If the adjustment for the roof replacement comes first, the adjusted sale price of the comparable is:

$ 350,000
+ 20,000 Expected cost of roof replacement
─────────
$ 370,000
+   5,550 Adjustment from changes in market conditions
─────────
$ 375,550 Adjusted sale price

If the 1.5 percent adjustment for changes in market conditions is computed first, the adjusted sale price is:

$ 350,000
+   5,250 Adjustment for changes in market conditions
─────────
$ 355,250
+ 20,000 Expected cost of roof replacement
─────────
$ 375,250

Thus, when using percentage adjustments, the order matters.

8. Because the value of the subject property is unknown, adjustments are made to the observed transaction prices of the comparables to adjust for how they vary from the subject.

9. The reproduction cost of a building is the cost to construct the building today, replicating it in exact detail. The replacement cost is the money required to construct a building of equal utility. The reproduction cost estimate is generally greater than the replacement cost.

10. Estimating accrued depreciation is generally the most difficult step in the cost approach to valuation because it is very difficult to quantify the dollar value of physical depreciation and often even more difficult to quantify the dollar value of functional and external obsolescence.

Additional Readings

The following books contain expanded examples and discussions of real estate valuation and appraisal:

Appraisal Institute. *The Appraisal of Real Estate,* 14th ed. Chicago: American Institute of Real Estate Appraisers, 2013.

Appraisal Institute. *2014–2015 Uniform Standards of Professional Practice,* Chicago: Appraisal Institute, 2014.

Betts, R. M. *Basic Real Estate Appraisal,* 6th ed. Florence, Ky: Cengage Learning, Inc., 2013.

Carr, D. H., J. A. Lawson, and J. C. Schultz, Jr. *Mastering Real Estate Appraisal,* Chicago: Dearborn Financial Publishing, Inc., 2003.

Fanning, S. F. *Market Analysis for Real Estate.* Chicago: Appraisal Institute, 2014.

Kane, M. S., M. R. Linne, and J. A. Johnson. *Practical Applications in Appraisal Valuation Modeling: Statistical Methods for Real Estate Practitioners.* Chicago: Appraisal Institute, 2004.

Lusht, Kenneth L. *Real Estate Valuation: Principles and Applications.* New York: McGraw-Hill, 1997.

Smith, H. C., L. C. Root, and J. D. Belloit. *Real Estate Appraisal,* 3rd ed. Upper Saddle River, NJ: Prentice Hall, 1995.

Ventola, W. L, and M. R. Williams, *Fundamentals of Real Estate Appraisal,* 12th ed. Chicago: Dearborn Real Estate Education, 2015.

The following journals contain numerous articles on real estate valuation and appraisal:

Valuation, published quarterly by the Appraisal Institute, Chicago.

The Appraisal Journal, published quarterly by the Appraisal Institute, Chicago.

Real Estate Review, published quarterly by Warren, Gorham and Lamont, Boston.

Real Estate Issues, published three times annually by the American Society of Real Estate Counselors, Chicago.

APPENDIX: Multivariate Regression Analysis

To access the appendix for this chapter, please visit the book's website at

www.mhhe.com/lingarcher5e

Chapter 8

Valuation Using *the* Income Approach

LEARNING OBJECTIVES

After reading this chapter you will be able to:

1 Explain the difference between direct capitalization and discounted cash flow (DCF) models of property valuation.

2 Distinguish between operating expenses and capital expenditures.

3 Explain the general relationship between discount rates and capitalization rates.

4 Calculate the overall capitalization rate by direct market extraction given appropriate data.

5 Describe an effective gross income multiplier (*EGIM*) approach to valuation and demonstrate its use, given appropriate data.

6 Develop a five-year net cash flow forecast (pro forma), including the expected cash flows from sale, given appropriate data.

7 Estimate an indicated market value by DCF analysis.

OUTLINE

Introduction

In Chapter 7 we introduced the formal appraisal process, including the three conventional approaches to estimating the market value of real estate assets: the sales comparison approach, the cost approach, and the income approach. The chapter then focused on the two approaches—the sales comparison and cost approaches—that provide a method for estimating a property's current market value without directly considering the property's income-producing potential.

In this chapter we turn our attention to the income approach to valuation. The rationale for the income approach is straightforward: Common among commercial property owners is the anticipation that they will receive cash flows from the property in the form of income from rental operations and price appreciation. The current value of a property is therefore a function of the income stream it is expected to produce. Although the sales comparison and cost approaches to valuation discussed in Chapter 7 are used to estimate the value of commercial property, they are most applicable to the valuation of non-income-producing property.

Because the income approach is based on the premise that a property's market value is a function of the income it is expected to produce, appraisers first estimate the net income that a typical investor would be forecasting today for the subject property over the expected **holding period.** Said differently, it is not the appraiser's job to forecast future cash flows based on *her* expectations. Rather, her job is to emulate the thinking and behavior of market participants. As long as the appraiser properly identifies what the typical investor would expect to occur, the value estimate for the subject property will be credible.[1]

The measure of income generally sought by property valuers is annual **net operating income** (*NOI*), which is equal to expected rental income over the next 12 months, net of vacancies, minus annual operating and capital expenses. In most cases, the property owner or investor does not pocket the full amount of NOI. Why? Because if the owner has made use of borrowed funds to help finance the investment, a portion of the NOI will be payable, usually on a monthly basis, to the mortgage lender(s). In addition, the U.S. government (and most states) will collect a portion of the property's annual NOI in the form of income taxes. Nevertheless, because NOI measures the overall income-producing ability of a property, it is considered the fundamental determinant of market value.[2]

✓ **Concept Check**

8.1   If a commercial property is performing well, what other parties, in addition to the owner(s), also benefit from this performance?

The second step in the income approach is to convert the *NOI* forecast into an estimate of property value. This is sometimes referred to as **income capitalization.** There are many models or techniques available to the appraiser for income capitalization. However, these models can be divided into two categories: (1) direct capitalization models and (2) discounted cash flow models.[3]

Direct Capitalization versus Discounted Cash Flow

With direct capitalization models, value estimates are based on a ratio or multiple of expected *NOI* over the next 12 months. It is essential that the ratios used to value the subject property are based on data from sales of comparable properties. Direct capitalization is analogous to the use of price-earnings (PE) ratios to value common stocks. For example, if publicly traded retail REITs (real estate investment trusts) are, on average, currently trading at 20 times expected earning over the next 12 months, this PE ratio can be multiplied by the expected earnings of the subject REIT to approximate its market value. For example, if Simon Property Group, a retail REIT, is expected to produce earnings of $9.60 per share during the next 12 months, then a defensible estimate of Simon's stock market value is $192 ($9.60 × 20) per share, assuming Simon is very similar to other retail REITs. Similarly, if properties comparable to the subject property are, on average, currently selling for

---

1. This point is emphasized in an article by David C. Lennhoff: "Direct Capitalization: It Might Be Simple But it Isn't Easy," *The Appraisal Journal,* Winter 2011, pp. 66–73.

2. For students of finance, it is worth noting that *NOI* is similar to EBIDTA (earnings before deductions for interest, depreciation, income taxes, and amortization), a commonly used metric of cash flow in the corporate world.

3. Some real estate appraisers refer to discounted cash flow models of valuation as "yield capitalization" models.

7 times first-year *NOI,* then a reasonable estimate of the subject's market value is obtained by multiplying the subject's expected first-year *NOI* times 7.

Discounted cash flow (DCF) valuation models differ from direct capitalization models in several important ways. First, the appraiser must identify the investment holding period that is typical of investors who might purchase the subject property. Second, the appraiser must convert the expectations of typical investors into explicit forecasts of the property's NOI for each year of the expected holding period, not just a single year. This forecast must include the net income produced by a hypothetical sale of the property at the end of the expected holding period. Third, the appraiser must select the appropriate yield rate, or required internal rate of return, at which to discount all future cash flows. The requirements of DCF analysis place a greater analytical burden on the appraiser because forecasts of future cash flows cannot be explicitly abstracted from past sales of comparable properties. Critics of DCF models argue that future cash flow projections not supported by market evidence can result in flawed value estimates.

The chapter proceeds as follows. First, we discuss how the appraiser estimates the expected annualized net operating income of the subject property—either for a single year or for each year of an expected holding period. We then discuss, in turn, direct capitalization models and discounted cash flow models of market value.

> ✓ **Concept Check**
>
> **8.2**   List three important ways in which DCF valuation models differ from direct capitalization models.

Estimating Net Operating Income

Net operating income (*NOI*) is calculated by deducting from the property's estimated rental income all expenses associated with operating and maintaining the property. As discussed above, *NOI* focuses on the income produced by the property after operating expenses, but before mortgage payments and the payment of income taxes. These latter expenses are personal and unique to each owner and not directly related to the property's basic income-producing ability. Although, as we shall see in Chapters 18, 19, and 20, mortgage financing and income taxes are important considerations in investment decisions.

Exhibit 8-1 Reconstructed Operating Statement

	PGI	Potential gross income
−	VC	Vacancy & collection loss
+	MI	Miscellaneous income
=	EGI	Effective gross income
−	OE	Operating expenses
−	CAPX	Capital expenditures*
=	NOI	Net operating income

*Traditionally, appraisers have included in their estimates of *NOI* a "reserve for replacement" of capital items. However, in the real estate investment community, expected capital expenditures are increasingly referred to in cash flow forecasts as "capital expenditures" or "capital costs." To be consistent with the current treatment in the investment community, and to avoid changing terminology as we progress through the text, we will refer to these anticipated expenses as capital expenditures or "CAPX."

In estimating the expected *NOI* of an existing property, appraisers and analysts rely on (1) the experience of similar properties in the market and (2) the historic experience of the subject property. The current owners may not be renting the subject property at the going market rate, and its current expenses may differ from market averages. Thus, an appraiser must evaluate all income and expense items in terms of current market conditions. These items are then placed in a **reconstructed operating statement** format (see Exhibit 8-1). It is important to emphasize that the appraiser is basing her estimates of future operating cash flows on what she believes the typical market participant is expecting, not what she expects.

> **✓ Concept Check**
>
> **8.3**   What is "stabilized" net income? Why must the appraiser base her cash flow forecasts on what she believes the typical market participant is expecting?

To show how the analyst estimates the cash flows from owning an existing commercial property, assume the appraiser's assignment is to determine the market value of a small suburban office building, called Centre Point. The appraiser's forecasts for Centre Point are listed in Exhibit 8-2.[4] Unfamiliar terms are discussed below.

Potential Gross Income

The starting point in calculating *NOI* is to estimate **potential gross income (*PGI*).** *PGI* is the total annual rental income the property would produce assuming 100 percent occupancy and no collection losses (in other words, assuming tenants always pay their full rent on time). Although rents are generally received from tenants on a monthly basis and operating expenses are incurred during each month, as a matter of practice most appraisers and investment analysts estimate property cash flows on an annual basis.[5] *PGI* is the estimated rent per unit (or per square foot) for each year multiplied by the number of units (or square

4. The remainder of this chapter focuses on the analysis of existing commercial properties. Existing properties provide analysts with historical information on rents and operating expenses to evaluate. Market rents and expenses are established by evaluating the rents and operating expenses of the subject property and comparable properties. The valuation of proposed properties (i.e., new development) is the focus of Chapter 23.

5. To the degree that appraisers replicate the decision making practice of investment analysts, this method produces valid estimates of market value.

Exhibit 8-2 Forecasts for Centre Point Office Building

- Property consists of 8 office suites, 3 on the first floor and 5 on the second.
- Contract rents: 2 suites at $1,800 per month, 1 at $3,600 per month, and 5 at $1,560 per month.
- Annual market rent increases: 3% per year
- Vacancy and collection losses: 10% per year
- Operating expenses: 40% of effective gross income each year
- Capital expenditures: 5% of effective gross income each year
- Expected holding period: 5 years

feet) available for rent. Appraisers estimate *PGI* by carefully examining current market conditions and by examining the terms of any existing leases and the present tenant(s), if any. From this examination they decide whether to estimate *PGI* based on contract rents or market rents. **Market rent** is the rental income the property would most probably command if placed for lease on the open market as of the effective date of the appraisal. **Contract rent** refers to the actual rent being paid under contractual commitments between owners and tenants. Generally, if the property is subject to long-term leases to financially reliable tenants at rates above or below market, the estimation of *PGI* will include the contract rent of these leases.[6]

✓ Concept Check

8.4 Distinguish between contract rent and market rent.

---

www.reis.com

REIS, a for-profit firm, provides trends and forecasts of rents and vacancies for hundreds of metropolitan areas.

It should be noted that office, retail, and industrial tenants often occupy their space under leases ranging from three to five years. However, tenants of more specialized properties such as restaurants, department stores, and freestanding drugstores often sign leases of 10 years or more. An additional complication is that appraisers encounter numerous lease types. The flat lease is one in which the monthly rent remains fixed over the entire lease term. The step-up (or "graduated") lease establishes a schedule of rental rate increases over the term of the lease. In some retail leases the total rent collected is a function of the sales of the tenant's business. Clearly, the existing lease structure of the subject and comparable properties can significantly complicate the appraisal, as can the creditworthiness of tenants. An extended discussion of commercial leases and leasing strategies is provided in Chapter 22.

Effective Gross Income

It is nearly impossible for an owner to realize a property's full potential income. Even if there is no excess supply of space for lease in the market, there will often be a few premature vacancies, some rental income will be lost when tenants vacate space that then must be refurbished and released, and not all rent will be paid in a. timely fashion. Furthermore, owners often choose to hold a small inventory of space off the market to have available to show prospective tenants. The **natural vacancy rate** is the proportion of potential gross income not

---

6. However, if the appraiser is valuing the property using direct capitalization, her reconstructed operating statement may be based on her estimate of stabilized income and expenses. By "stabilized," we mean under current economic conditions, but adjusted to show current market rents, average vacancy and collection losses, and normal operating and capital expenses for this type of property in this location and market. If the property is not at, or near, stabilized rent, occupancy, and expense levels, it may not be realistic to assume that stabilization of the NOI could occur in the first year of operations. In such cases, the use of a DCF valuation model may be preferable to direct capitalization, because more gradual changes in rents, occupancy, and expenses can be explicitly incorporated into a multi-year DCF forecast.

EXAMPLE 8-1   CENTRE POINT

The Centre Point Office Building has two 1,000-square-foot, first-floor suites, each renting for $1,800 per month, or $1.80 per square foot. The first floor also contains a 2,000-square-foot suite renting for $3,600 per month. The second floor contains five 800-square-foot suites, all of which currently rent for $1,560 per month ($1.95 per square foot). All eight tenants are operating under short-term leases. Potential gross income in the first year of operations is estimated to be $180,000, calculated as follows:

First Floor	
1,000 sq. ft. suites: 2 × $1,800 × 12 months	$ 43,200
2,000 sq. ft. suite: 1 × $3,600 × 12 months	$ 43,200
Second Floor	
800 sq. ft. suites: 5 × $1,560 × 12 months	$ 93,600
Potential gross income (*PGI*) =	$180,000

The analyst should gather rental data on similar properties in the same market to judge whether the subject property's contract rents are similar to market rents. For example, to determine market rental rates for the second-floor units of Centre Point, the analyst should obtain data on second-floor units in similar buildings. This market rent survey should be limited to properties of the same general age, design, services, location, and amenities as the subject property. If the comparable rents obtained from the survey are as shown in Exhibit 8-3, current market rents of the 800 square-foot, second-floor units are estimated as:

$$\$1.94 \times 800 \text{ sq.ft.} \times 5 \text{ units} = \$7,760 \text{ per month, and}$$

$$\$7,760 \times 12 \text{ mos.} = \$93,120 \text{ per year}$$

Exhibit 8-3   Market Rents for Comparable Second-Floor Units

	Comparable			
	1	2	3	Average
Rent per month	$1,620	$1,540	$1,680	
Sq. ft. per unit	790	810	900	833
Rent per sq. ft. per month	$2.05	$ 1.90	$ 1.87	$1.94

In this case, data from the comparable properties imply that the indicated market rent of $93,120 for the second-floor units is very similar to the current contract rents of $93,600. Because of the assumed short-term nature of the subject property's leases, normal rent increases tied to changes in market rents should be expected in the future.

collected—even when supply equals demand in the rental market.[7] Of course, if there is an excess supply of leasable space, the actual amount of vacancy and collection losses will exceed the natural rate. Therefore, the second step in projecting *NOI* is to estimate the expected vacancy and collection (*VC*) losses for the property, consistent with market expectations. Again, appraisers should estimate these losses on the basis of (1) the historical experience of the subject property, (2) actual current vacancies, and (3) the experiences of competing properties. The normal range for vacancy and collection losses for apartment, office, and retail properties is 5 to 15 percent of *PGI,* although vacancies well in excess of 15 percent have occurred in overbuilt markets.[8] The expected vacancy and collection loss is subtracted from *PGI.*

In addition to basic rental income, there may be miscellaneous revenue from sources such as garage rentals, parking fees, laundry machines, and vending machines. Expected miscellaneous income should be added to the potential gross income. The net effect of subtracting the vacancy allowance and adding miscellaneous income is **effective gross income (EGI).**[9]

EXAMPLE 8-2   CENTRE POINT

Using current contract rents, vacancy and collection losses of 10 percent, and no miscellaneous income, the projected first year *EGI* for the Centre Point Office Building is:

	Potential gross income (*PGI*)	$180,000	
−	Vacancy & collection loss (*VC*)	18,000	(0.10 × $180,000)
=	Effective gross income (*EGI*)	$162,000	

Operating Expenses

www.boma.org

Association of Building Owners and Managers website provides detailed operating expense information for numerous property types and U.S. cities.

www.irem.org

Institute of Real Estate Management provides detailed historical operating expense information for multiple property types and regions of the country.

The typical expenses owners incur in maintaining and operating rental properties are termed **operating expenses (OE).** Operating expenses include the ordinary and necessary expenditures incurred during the year (including incidental repairs) that do not materially add value, but keep the property operating and competitive in its local market. They are generally divided into two categories: fixed and variable expenses. Fixed expenses do not vary directly with the level of operation (i.e., occupancy) of the property, at least in the short run. Common fixed expenses are local property taxes and hazard and fire insurance; owners must pay them whether the property is vacant or fully occupied. Variable expenses, as the name implies, increase as the level of occupancy rises and decrease when occupancy is reduced. Variable expenses include items such as utilities, maintenance, repairs, supplies, and property management. The annual operating expense estimate is based on the historical experience of the subject property in comparison with competing properties, the appraiser's knowledge of typical expense levels, and any property-specific characteristics.

---

7. The natural vacancy rate is sometimes referred to as *frictional vacancy,* implying that normal market frictions will cause a portion of *PGI* not to be collected even in stable markets.

8. Vacancy and collection loss rates in a reconstructed operating statement reflect the income lost as a percentage of the *PGI.* This is referred to as the *economic vacancy rate* and, although similar, it may differ from the percentage of space vacant.

9. Many commercial property leases require tenants to reimburse the owner for some, or all, of a property's operating expenses. For example, "expense stops" place an upper limit on the amount of operating expenses that owners must pay. Operating expenses in excess of the "stop" amount are paid by the tenant. Shopping center leases typically require tenants to reimburse the owner for their fair share of all common area maintenance, property taxes, insurance, and other operating expenses—not just those in excess of a stop amount. All of these payments from the tenant are typically displayed in the pro forma as "expense reimbursement revenue" and are added in, along with miscellaneous income, in the calculation of effective gross income. For simplicity, we ignore expense reimbursement income in our cash flow estimates. These issues are further discussed in Chapters 18 and 22.

In addition to comparing owner-reported expenses for the subject property to similar properties in the market, comparisons to industry averages are also available. Published expense reports that show typical expense levels are available from the Institute of Real Estate Management, the Building Owners and Managers Association, the International Council of Shopping Centers, and the Urban Land Institute.

Capital Expenditures

Appraisal analysts commonly include in the reconstructed operating statement an annual "allowance" to recognize the capital expenditures typically required to replace building components as they age and deteriorate. In contrast to operating expenses, **capital expenditures (CAPX)** are replacements and alterations to a building that materially prolong its economic life and therefore increase its value. Market participants may refer to this item as a reserve for replacement, replacement allowance, capital costs, or another similar term. Examples of such expenditures may include roof replacements, additions, floor coverings, kitchen equipment, heating and air-conditioning equipment, electrical and plumbing fixtures, and parking surfaces. In addition, the costs owners incur to make the space suitable for the needs of a particular tenant (i.e., "tenant improvements") are generally included as part of *CAPX,* or as an additional line item in the operating statement.[10]

✓ **Concept Check**

8.5   How is an operating expense distinguishable from a capital expenditure?

In practice, *CAPX* is often estimated as the expected cost to replace each item, or all items, allocated as a constant annual "expenditure" over the item's expected life. For example, if the cost of replacing a roof is expected to be $47,000 in 15 years (its expected life), the required annual set-aside—often called a reserve—is $1,731, assuming the annual deposits would earn interest at a rate of 8.0 percent.[11] In other words, if an owner puts $1,731 into an account or investment that each year yields 8.0 percent, he or she would have a $47,000 reserve balance for roof replacement at the end of 15 years. For simplicity, the *CAPX* shown in Exhibit 8-4 for the Centre Point example is assumed to total 5 percent of the *EGI.*

The recognition of capital expenditures in the estimation of annual net operating income varies in practice. Many appraisers include a reserve for expected capital expenditures annually, as demonstrated above. Others, though, may attempt to estimate the actual capital expenditure in the period it is anticipated to occur. As noted later, the treatment of *CAPX* generally reflects the valuation method applied. The use of direct capitalization requires an annualized estimate (reserve) for capital expenditures—given that cash flows beyond the next year are not explicitly considered. In contrast, multiyear DCF valuation models permit the appraiser to be specific about the expected timing of future capital expenditures.

To further complicate matters, where the estimated *CAPX* appears in the reconstructed cash flow statement is not consistent in the commercial real estate industry. Many appraisers subtract *CAPX* in the calculation of *NOI.* This is referred to as an "above-line" treatment where the "line" is *NOI.* Other market participants, more typically investment analysts, often treat *CAPX* as a "below-the-line" expenditure—subtracting it from *NOI* to obtain

---

10. Leasing commissions paid by some property owners to brokers who are responsible for finding tenants are not technically capital expenditures, and should be budgeted for separately when appropriate.

11. The calculator keystrokes are $N = 15$, $I = 8\%$, $PV = 0$, $PMT = ?$, and $FV = 47,000$. Compounding and discounting calculations are discussed in detail in Chapter 14.

Exhibit 8-4   Centre Point Office Building: Reconstructed Operating Statement

Potential gross income (*PGI*)			$180,000
Less: Vacancy and collection losses (*VC*)			18,000
Effective gross income (*EGI*)			162,000
Less: Operating expenses (*OE*)			
Fixed expenses			
Real estate taxes	$15,900		
Insurance	9,200	$25,100	
Variable expenses			
Utilities	$12,800		
Garbage collection	1,000		
Supplies	3,000		
Repairs	5,200		
Maintenance	10,500		
Management	7,200	$39,700	
Total operating expenses			$ 64,800
Less: Reserve for capital expenditures			
Roof and other exterior expenditures	$ 4,900		
Tenant improvements to be paid by owner	3,200		
Total reserves for capital expenditures			8,100
Net operating income (*NOI*)			$ 89,100

what may be defined as the property's "net cash flow." We will subtract capital expenditures above the line in this chapter. However, it is important for analysts (1) to determine how the *CAPX* is reported in the property and survey data they review, (2) to consistently apply the estimate of *CAPX* to the subject property and all comparable properties, and (3) to value the appropriate measure of estimated net operating income.

> ✓ **Concept Check**
>
> **8.6**   If capital expenditures are subtracted from revenues in the calculation of *NOI*, is this an above-line or a below-line treatment?

Net Operating Income

Appraisers obtain the final estimate of *NOI* for the first year of property operations after acquisition by subtracting all operating expenses and capital expenditures from *EGI*. With the assumed operating expenses and capital expenditures for the Centre Point Office Building, Exhibit 8-4 shows the *NOI* in a reconstructed operating statement. In the example, total operating expenses are estimated at $64,800 (40 percent of *EGI*) and total capital expenditures are $8,100 (5 percent of *EGI*). Thus, estimated net operating income over the next 12 months is $89,100.

Using Direct Capitalization for Valuation

Direct capitalization, as typically practiced, is the process of estimating a property's market value by dividing a single-year *NOI* by a "capitalization" rate. The general relationship between estimated market value and operating income is expressed in the basic income capitalization equation:

$$V = \frac{NOI_1}{R_o} \qquad \text{(8-1)}$$

where V is current value, NOI_1 is the projected income over the next 12 months, and R_o is the capitalization rate. We begin the discussion of direct capitalization by first explaining how capitalization rates for valuation can be obtained from the market and how the basic capitalization equation (8-1) can be applied to the subject property's operating income to produce an estimate of market value. We then develop some intuition about what a cap rate is, and is not, and discuss the important linkage between cap rates and required total rates of return.

Abstracting Cap Rates from the Market

Appraisers rely on recently completed transactions of similar properties to guide their selection of the cap rate to be used to value the subject property. The basic capitalization formula can be rearranged so that:

$$R_o = \frac{NOI_1}{V_o}, \text{ or } R_o = \frac{NOI_1}{\text{Sale price}} \qquad \text{(8-2)}$$

This allows R_o to be estimated from comparable property sales if the sale price and first-year NOIs for the comparables are known or can be estimated. This method of estimating the appropriate valuation cap rate is called **direct market extraction**.[12] The estimated R_o can then be applied, using equation (8-1), to capitalize the estimated first-year NOI of the subject property into an estimate of market value.

For example, in evaluating the Centre Point Office Building, assume the appraiser found five comparable properties that sold recently. Comparability is as important here as in the sales comparison approach discussed in Chapter 7. Location, size, age and condition, and intensity of land use must be similar to the subject property. The selected comparables should then be screened to ensure that only recent open market sales are used. Unusual financing terms must be analyzed. If the appropriate adjustment can be quantified, the comparable may be used; if not, it must be excluded. Although space limitations do not permit a detailed discussion here, many appraisers argue that the selection and use of comparable sales is the most important, and difficult, component of the appraisal process.

For each comparable property, the appraiser estimates expected first-year NOI, making sure that all appropriate operating expenses and capital expenditures have been deducted. The NOI of each comparable is then divided by the sale price of the property. This calculation provides an indicated capitalization rate ($NOI \div$ sale price) for each comparable sale, as displayed in Exhibit 8-5. Assume each of the five selected comparable sales in this example are equally similar to the subject and therefore deserve equal weight. The simple average of the five comparable capitalization rates (R_o) is 8.4 percent. Dividing the subject property's expected NOI of $89,100 by 8.4 percent (or 0.084) produces an indicated value for the subject property of $1,060,714 ($89,100 ÷ 0.084), which we round to $1,061,000.

✓ **Concept Check**

8.7 Assume the estimated first-year *NOI* of the subject property is $400,000. Also assume that data from the sale of comparable properties indicates the appropriate cap rate is 9 percent. What is the indicated value of the subject property?

---

12. This technique is also referred to as the direct comparison method and the comparable sales method.

F or some appraisers, the ability to capture data and leverage it has always been part of their efforts to stay competitive. "As early as 1985, we were very successful in capturing business because our data was so fresh," says Alan Hummel, senior vice president and chief appraiser for Forsythe Appraisals LLC. "We had staff posted in court houses and runners going back and forth between tax assessors' offices and our office." Much of that same data that Hummel's staff collected and maintained is now accessible on appraisers' desktops 24/7. "For the most part, in the past, data has been available to us in bits and pieces," Hummel says. "Now they're getting closer to having all the data available at my desktop." In addition to local tax assessors, a variety of companies, industry associations, and government entities offer economic research, real estate market reports, and databases full of property

information. The increasing accessibility of information is revolutionizing the appraisal industry.

Not only is there an ever increasing amount of data to track, but better data management software and analysis tools also are available to appraisers. According to Mark R. Linne, executive vice president, education and analytics, for Appraisal World, appraisers just need to make more of a connection between the two—and do it soon. "The future appraiser will be a data gatherer and analyst," Linne predicts. "Unless you're actively developing new skills in using software, you're going to become obsolete." Adds an appraiser, "Data are becoming ubiquitous. The challenge is not finding quality data, but evaluating the data that are available and interpreting what the data mean."

Some observers predict that some people will emerge from the current pool of

appraisers as "data analysts" and others will be the "feet on the street," needed to verify data and determine the true condition of a property. If so, the appraisal industry may end up with fewer but better trained appraisers.

Source: Adapted from Mark R. Linne, "Thriving in the valuation 2.0 world: more data, advanced analytics and an industry in need of solutions offer appraisers opportunities to provide greater value," *Valuation Insights and Perspectives,* June 22, 2008; Apryl Motley, "Reining in the Data," *Valuation,* 3d Quarter, 2010

Booming Information Age Continues to Revolutionize How Appraisers Operate

In addition to abstracting cap rates directly from comparable sales transactions, appraisers and other market participants may also look to published survey results for evidence on required cap rates. The Real Estate Research Corporation (RERC) regularly surveys the cap rate expectations of institutional investors in the United States. These survey results are published quarterly in the *Real Estate Report* (www.rerc.com). RealtyRates.com (www.realtyrates.com), Real Capital Analytics (www.rcanalytics.com), REIS (www.reis.com), and numerous other firms provide similar information—generally for the price of a subscription. Cap rate information is also available from many brokerage firms and other local research companies and data providers.

Three points are worth emphasizing at this stage. First, in most states the sale prices of the comparable properties are publicly recorded and therefore easily obtainable. However, the comparable *NOI*s are not publicly available; thus, the appraiser must typically contact the buyer and/or seller of each comparable property, or a broker involved in the transaction, for revenue and expense information. These data must generally be adjusted and supplemented by the appraiser because, for example, the seller is generally too optimistic about the *NOI* forecast for the property. Second, R_o is a "rate" that is used to convert the first-year *NOI* (the property's overall cash flow) into an estimate of current market value. Thus, R_o is referred to as the **overall capitalization rate,** or the **going-in cap rate.** Third, R_o is *not* a discount rate

Exhibit 8-5 Direct Market Extraction of the Overall Capitalization Rate, R_o

Comparable	First-year *NOI*		Sale Price		R_o
A	$ 80,000	÷	$ 919,540	=	0.087
B	114,000	÷	1,390,244	=	0.082
C	100,000	÷	1,250,000	=	0.080
D	72,000	÷	808,989	=	0.089
E	90,000	÷	1,097,561	=	0.082
				Average	=	0.084

that can be used to value future cash flows. It is simply the ratio of the first year's annual income to the overall value of the property. Finally, note that the reciprocal of R_o is $1 \div 0.084$, or 11.905. Thus, another way of looking at the relationship between income and value is to observe that office buildings similar to the subject property sell for 11.905 times their estimated first-year *NOI*s. Thus, the $1,061,000 market value estimate may also be obtained by multiplying the subject's expected *NOI* times the abstracted price/income multiple—that is, $89,100 \times 11.905 = \$1,060,736$, which rounds to $1,061,000.

The direct capitalization approach to estimating value does not require an appraiser to estimate cash flows beyond the next 12 months. It is assumed that the investors who purchased the comparable properties had *already done so*—their future cash flow estimates are reflected in the negotiated sale price of each comparable property and therefore embedded in the abstracted capitalization rates. In contrast to the discounted cash flow approach to valuation, the market value estimate produced by this short-cut method, which relies on prices paid by investors for similar properties, may be *more* reliable for the purpose of estimating a property's market value. Why? Because the short-cut requires fewer *explicit* forecasts and judgments than are necessary if the appraiser is constructing a 5- or 10-year discounted cash flow analysis. In effect, the appraiser relies on the decisions and valuations made by other market participants to help "read" what the market is forecasting for rent growth and price appreciation.

Understanding Capitalization Rates

We have just seen that cap rates can be used to convert a one-year forecast of *NOI* into an estimate of market value. What else can be said about the cap rates we observe in the market? First, the cap rate is a measure of the relationship between a property's current income stream and its price or value. It is not an interest rate, discount rate, or internal rate of return. It does not measure total investment return because it ignores future cash flows from operations and expected appreciation (or depreciation) in the market value of the property. In this sense, the cap rate is analogous to the dividend yield on a common stock, defined as the company's projected annual dividend, divided by the current stock price. All else being the same, investors prefer stocks (and commercial properties) with the highest dividend yield (cap rate).

But all else is usually not the same when comparing the investment desirability of stocks and real estate. Cash flows beyond year 1 and changes in the value of the asset can significantly affect total rates of return. Consider again the Centre Point Office Building. If the property is purchased by an investor for the asking price of $1,056,000, and the estimated first-year *NOI* is $89,100, the investor's going-in capitalization rate (dividend yield) is 8.44 percent. If the property is expected to increase in value to $1,077,120 by the end of year 1, the expected total rate of return, y_o, assuming a one-year holding period and no transaction costs, is 10.44 percent, calculated as follows:

$$y_o = R_o + g = \frac{\$89,100}{\$1,056,000} + \frac{\$1,077,120 - \$1,056,000}{\$1,056,000}$$

$$= 0.0844 + 0.0200 = 0.1044, \text{ or } 10.44\%$$

where

$$R_o = \frac{NOI_1}{Price} \text{ and}$$

$$g = \frac{P_1 - P_o}{Price}$$

The expected total rate of return, y_o, is often referred to by investors as the **internal rate of return *(IRR)*** on the investment.[13] Note that the y_o for a one-year holding period is comprised

---

13. Appraisers traditionally have referred to the estimated total (internal) rate of return as the investment's "yield rate." To be consistent with the investment perspective developed in Chapters 18-22, we refer to the total return as the internal rate of return.

of two parts: the 8.44 percent overall cap rate (or "current" yield in year 1), and the 2.00 percent rate of price appreciation.

This formulation clearly shows that the investor's total rate of return is expected to be obtained from two sources:

1. The property's annual dividend (i.e., *NOI*).
2. Annual appreciation (or depreciation) in the value of the property.

If a larger portion of y_o is expected to be obtained from annualized price appreciation (g), then a smaller portion of y_o must be provided in the form of current yield (i.e., cap rates can be lower). This helps explain why cap rates often vary significantly across property types and across the markets; expected appreciation rates can be very different.

Although the relation between required total returns, capitalization rates, and expected price appreciation can be written as $y_o = R_o + g$, it is important to recognize which way causality runs. In competitive capital markets, y_o is a function of the rates of return available on competing investments of similar risk, including stocks, bonds, and other financial assets. Thus, capitalization rates are a function of available returns on other assets of similar risk and the expected appreciation of the subject property; that is, $R_o = y_o - g$. Thus, required total rates of return, along with expected growth rates, determine market values and, therefore, cap rates.

The point is that y_o, in conjunction with expected appreciation and current rental income, determines the maximum amount investors are willing to bid for a property, which in turn determines actual transaction prices, and thus R_o. Therefore, cap rates do not actually determine values; cap rates react to changes in cash flow projections and/or changes in returns required on competing investment alternatives. Note that this integration of real estate markets with general capital markets can cause a variation in local real estate values and therefore in observed cap rates when, for example, returns on risky corporate bonds change.

✓ **Concept Check**

8.8 If new information suggests that rents in a market are going to increase at a faster rate than what had been projected, what will happen to the cap rates that appraisers abstract from this market after this new information becomes known to market participants?

Income Multipliers

For some smaller income-producing properties, appraisers may use a variant of the direct income capitalization method known as the income multiplier approach as an additional indicator of value. For example, the **effective gross income multiplier (*EGIM*)** of a comparable property is defined as the ratio of the property's selling price to its effective gross income.

$$EGIM = \frac{\text{Sale Price}}{EGI} \tag{8-3}$$

While income capitalization methods generally use income after expenses (i.e., *NOI*), the *EGIM* analysis uses the effective gross income of the subject and comparable properties. Hence, it can be estimated by acquiring recent sale price, rent, and vacancy information. The resulting *EGIM*s of the comparable properties are reconciled and subsequently applied to the income of the subject property to produce an indicated value ($V_o = EGI \times EGIM$), where *EGIM* is the reconciled multiple from comparable sales data.[14]

As shown in Exhibit 8-6, a defensible *EGIM* for the Centre Point Office Building, based on the sale prices and estimated EGIs of three comparable properties, is 6.49. Multiplying the effective gross income of Centre Point, $162,000, by the abstracted *EGIM* results in an indicated value of $1,051,380 ($162,000 × 6.49), rounded to $1,051,000.

---

14. Estimation of income multipliers varies in practice. Some appraisers and analysts may estimate the gross income multiplier (GIM), which uses potential gross income, rather than effective gross income. Analysts and appraisers should take care to note this distinction when interpreting or applying income multipliers.

Exhibit 8-6   *EGIM* Analysis for Centre Point Office Building

	Comparable		
	A	**B**	**C**
Recent sale price	$1,044,120	$1,151,720	$904,050
Effective gross income (*EGI*)	$ 158,200	$ 175,300	$143,500
EGIM (sale price ÷ *EGI*)	6.60	6.57	6.30
		Average *EGIM* =	6.49

Several crucial assumptions are implicit in the use of income multipliers to value the subject property. First, it is assumed that the operating expense percentage and the capital expenditure percentage of the subject and comparable properties are equal. Thus, adjustments to the abstracted EGIMs may be required to account for differences in OEs and CAPXs between the comparable properties and the subject property. For example, if a comparable property's effective gross income includes operating expense payments (e.g., utility fees), but the subject property does not, the expenses would be subtracted from the comparable property's income.

Gross income multiplier analysis also assumes the subject and comparable properties are collecting market rents. In particular, the application of *EGIM* analysis is especially tenuous when the subject and/or comparable properties are subject to long-term leases at rates above or below current market rents. For example, assume the rents of the comparable office properties are at market. In contrast, however, the subject office property is 50 percent leased at rates 25 percent below market. Moreover, the tenants' original 10-year leases have remaining terms of 5 years or more; thus, it will be at least 5 years before the entire property can be leased at market rates. Intuitively, the subject property should sell at a lower multiple of current rents than the comparable office properties because the subject's rental income will grow more slowly. Therefore, using, say, the average *EGIM* of the comparables would place too high a value on the subject property.

For this reason, it is frequently argued that an income multiplier approach to valuation is more appropriate for apartment buildings than for most office, industrial, and retail properties. Why? Because apartment leases seldom exceed one-year terms. This allows contract rents to track movements in market rents more closely. In addition, there is generally less variation in the operating expenses of comparable apartment properties than the variation often observed in other types of commercial property. Moreover, there is generally little variation across apartment properties in the proportion of operating expenses paid by tenants. In contrast, tenants in office and retail properties often reimburse the owner for a significant portion of the property's operating expenses. These reimbursements, however, can vary significantly across properties and even across tenants in a single property. In short, the typical lease structure of apartment properties permits the use of income multipliers more readily than the lease structures of other commercial property types.

✓ **Concept Check**

8.9   If an appraiser concludes that the rents of a subject property will grow faster than the rents of comparable properties, how would the appraiser adjust for this when reconciling the *EGIM*s abstracted from the comparable sales? How would this adjustment affect the estimate of value for the subject?

Using Discounted Cash Flow Analysis for Valuation

The previous sections of this chapter have been devoted to direct capitalization—a valuation process that involves the use of rates or ratios to convert a single, first-year cash flow forecast into an estimate of current market value. Because direct capitalization relies heavily on data from comparable sales, its effective use requires a high degree of comparability between the subject property and the comparable sale transactions. However, such comparability is often difficult for an appraiser to obtain. Recall that, with the possible exception of apartments and motels, commercial properties are often subject to long-term leases. These in-place leases may carry rental rates above or below the current market rate. In fact, multitenant properties can be subject to numerous leases, all with different rental rates, remaining terms, and rent escalation clauses. There also can be a significant variation between the owner and the tenant in the percentage of operating expenses that each pays.

In addition to the heterogeneous nature of commercial leases, the increasing complexity of many transactions also requires adjustments to comparable sale prices that are difficult to quantify. For these many reasons, the use of DCF valuation models is often a necessity. Moreover, DCF analysis has become the main financial tool used by investors to evaluate the merits of commercial real estate investments. Because appraisers typically are paid to estimate the most probable selling price of a subject property, it may be beneficial for them to use the valuation framework employed by most investors.

The term *discounted cash flow (DCF) analysis* refers to the process and procedures for estimating (1) future annual cash flows from property operations, (2) the net cash flow from disposition of the property at the end of the assumed investment holding period, (3) the appropriate holding period, and (4) the required total rate of return, and then using these inputs to generate an indicated value for the subject property.

To demonstrate the DCF valuation process, we turn again to our Centre Point example. The assumptions in Exhibit 8-2 were used to generate a reconstructed operating statement and an estimate of *NOI* for the first year of operations after acquisition (see Exhibit 8-4). However, the appraiser has determined that the typical expected holding period for investors in properties comparable to Centre Point is five years. Thus, the appraiser must prepare a five-year cash flow forecast, often referred to as a **pro forma.**[15]

Exhibit 8-7 contains these estimates. Given the assumptions in Exhibit 8-2—*PGI* increasing 3 percent per year, 10 percent annual vacancy and collection losses, operating expenses at 40 percent of *EGI,* and capital expenditures at 5 percent of *EGI—NOI* is expected to increase from $89,100 in year 1 to $100,283 in year 5.

www.cbre-ea.com

CBRE Econometric Advisors provides analytical tools and advisory services.

www.cushmanwakefield.us

Provides both free and fee-based data and analysis on real estate trends.

www.colliers.com

Brokerage firm that provides data on real estate trends.

---

15. The most typical holding period assumed in DCF analyses of commercial real estate assets is 10 years, although, to our knowledge, an adequate explanation of this assumption has never been offered. We have chosen a 5-year holding period to simplify and reduce the number of required assumptions and calculations.

Exhibit 8-7   Centre Point Office Building: Five Year Pro Forma *NOI*

Year	1	2	3	4	5	6
Potential gross income (*PGI*)	$180,000	$185,400	$190,962	$196,691	$202,592	$208,669
− Vacancy & collection loss (*VC*)	18,000	18,540	19,096	19,669	20,259	20,867
= Effective gross income (*EGI*)	162,000	166,860	171,866	177,022	182,332*	187,802
− Operating expenses (*OE*)	64,800	66,744	68,746	70,809	72,933	75,121
− Capital expenditures (*CAPX*)	8,100	8,343	8,593	8,851	9,117*	9,390
= Net operating income (*NOI*)	$ 89,100	$ 91,773	$ 94,526*	$ 97,362	$100,283*	$103,291

*Subtraction discrepancy due to rounding.

A Word of Caution

As Chapters 2 through 6 clearly demonstrate, many qualitative and difficult to predict economic, social, and legal factors influence real estate cash flows and values. Thus, the usefulness of quantitative valuation tools and techniques, such as discounted cash flow analysis, depends on the quality of the cash flow assumptions employed. How does one learn to develop relevant and realistic cash flow projections? Certainly, familiarity with the material in prior chapters will provide a solid foundation. However, directly related work experience and in-depth knowledge of the local market in which the subject property is located are required for a successful implementation of DCF analysis. Although recent college graduates often hold analytical (i.e. "number crunching") positions within real estate firms, the input assumptions they employ in their analyses should be guided by seasoned professionals.

Estimating Future Sale Proceeds

The second major source of expected property cash flows comes from the disposition (typically, the sale) of the ownership interest in a property at the end of the holding period. With a sale, the invested capital "reverts" to the owner; hence, the proceeds from the sale are frequently referred to as the **reversion.** Because income properties are usually held for a limited time period, the net cash flow from the eventual sale of the property must be estimated in addition to the cash flows from annual operations.

There are numerous methods available for estimating the sale price at the end of the expected holding period—commonly termed the **terminal value (V_t),** or reversion value. For example, an appraiser may simply assume a resale price or assume that the value of the subject property will grow at some compound annual rate. However, direct capitalization is the most common method used to estimate terminal value. This is because estimating the sale price at the end of an expected five-year holding period is analogous to estimating the current value of the property at the beginning of year 6. If the estimated NOI in year 6 is $103,291 and a **terminal capitalization rate (R_t),** or **going-out cap rate,** of 8.75 percent (0.0875) is deemed appropriate for determining the future sale price (terminal value) of Centre Point, then the estimated sale price at the end of year 5 is:

$$V_5 = \frac{NOI_6}{R_t} = \frac{\$103,291}{0.0875} = \$1,180,469.$$

Note that DCF analysis, as commonly employed, uses a combination of DCF and direct capitalization (to find terminal value).

www.economy.com

This subscription service provides market reports for major metropolitan areas.

For fully leased, stabilized properties in normal markets, the going-out cap rate is usually assumed to be approximately 1/4 to 3/4 percentage points higher than the going-in cap rate—and higher cap rates produce lower value estimates. The higher going-out cap rate at termination usually reflects the assumption that the income-producing ability of properties (i.e., their productivity) declines over time as the property ages, all else being equal. Thus, investors generally pay less per dollar of current NOI for older properties than newer properties, all else equal.

www.nreionline.com

Online version of National Real Estate Investor—a comprehensive source of industry news and data.

The **net sale proceeds (*NSP*)** at the end of the expected holding period are obtained by subtracting estimated **selling expenses (*SE*)** from the expected selling price. Selling expenses include brokerage fees, lawyer's fees, and other costs associated with the sale of the property. Selling expenses in our example are forecasted to be $47,219, or 4 percent of the expected sale price. When deducted from the estimated selling price, this leaves an expected *NSP* of $1,133,250.

Sale price (*SP*)	$1,180,469
−Selling expenses (*SE*)	47,219
=Net sale proceeds (*NSP*)	$1,133,250

✓ **Concept Check**

8.10 Explain why DCF analysis, as commonly used in market valuation, is really a combination of DCF and direct capitalization.

Valuing Future Cash Flows

Implementation of DCF valuation requires that future cash flow estimates be converted into present values. This conversion process is often referred to as *discounting*. Why must future cash flows be discounted (reduced) into a present value? Because a dollar to be received in, say, one year is not as valuable as having the dollar in hand today. If the dollar were in the possession of the investor today, it could be invested at some positive rate. To adjust for the fact that future dollars are not as valuable as current dollars, we must discount them to reflect the lost investment opportunity. Discounting is discussed in detail in Chapter 14. For now it is important to stress that, in addition to well-researched and reasonable

---

EXAMPLE 8-3 CENTRE POINT

Assume an appraiser has evaluated the estimates of *NOI* and net sale proceeds previously constructed for Centre Point and now listed in Exhibit 8-8, and has determined they reasonably represent the market's expectations. In addition, assume the appraiser concludes that the overall *market* discount rate (y_o) for the property is 10.00 percent; that is, 10.00 percent is the return typical investors could earn on an alternative investment of similar risk. The discounted *NOI*s and net sale proceeds are shown in the last column of Exhibit 8-8. Summing these present estimates produces an estimate of market value of $1,060,291, or $1,060,000 when rounded to the nearest $1,000.

Exhibit 8-8 Centre Point Office Building: Present Value of Future Cash Flows

Year	*NOI*	Net Sale Proceeds	Total Cash Flow	Present Value 10.00%
1	$ 89,100		$ 89,100	$ 81,000
2	91,773		91,773	75,845
3	94,526		94,526	71,019
4	97,362		97,362	66,500
5	100,283	$1,133,250	1,233,531	$ 765,927
			Present value =	$1,060,291

Send in the Drones

"John," a Dallas-based appraiser, wanted to add something special to his appraisals of several industrial properties, and he decided that video footage of the properties shot from an aerial drone perfectly fit the bill. He used the unmanned aircraft system to take videos of the structures and their surroundings, which he included in his reports. The drone provides a unique inspection experience." "It allows us to get up higher, get a better view of the roof and rotate 360 degrees above the property to provide a view of the surrounding properties. We could not provide that footage without using the drone. A picture is worth a thousand words and video is worth 10,000 words. The client loved the technology." Many appraisers see a considerable range of commercial uses for aerial drone technology, including marketing of appraisal services, examining difficult-to-reach points on a structure or property and making remote structural measurements.

But in late 2016, their use by FAA-approved operators for photographing and videotaping real estate has been strictly limited by the FAA to just the "line-of-sight" of the operator. That is, the person remote controlling the drone needs to be able to see the drone doing its work.

Of course, there are other issues as well. Can something as important as an inspection for an appraisal reasonably be delegated to a toy helicopter with a Go-Pro® camera mounted to it? What about privacy issues? It is one thing to allow a stranger to walk through your house taking notes and a few pictures as she does. It may be much harder for a homeowner to wrap their minds around a robot flying through each room shooting video. What about liability when the drone crashes into the vase holding the remains of Great Aunt Matilda?

Source: Adapted from David Tobenkin, "Send in the Drones," *Valuation*, First quarter, 2015 and The Appraiser Coach, "Drones Doing Appraisal Inspections" https://theappraisercoach.com.

estimates of future cash flows, selection of the appropriate discount rate is also of critical importance. In the appraisal process, where the purpose is to estimate the property's current market value (V_O), the rate used to discount the expected future cash flows (*NOI*s and *NSP*) is the typical investor's required rate of return on comparable properties. We refer to this discount rate as y_o. As discussed in Chapter 14, discount rates typically are determined by examining data on comparable property sales, evaluating the required returns on alternative investments of similar risk, talking to market participants, and reviewing investor survey information.

Other Approaches

Other approaches and methods may be also used to determine the market value of an income producing property. In applying the income approach, alternative methods may be used to determine the overall capitalization rates for application in the direct capitalization approach (see the appendix to this chapter). In addition, an indicated value using the cost approach generally is reported. However, appraisers usually rely less on the cost approach for income properties because of the difficulties in measuring accrued depreciation, as discussed in Chapter 7. Also, variations of the sales comparison approach may be applied; again, less reliance typically is placed on those methods. Income is the most important characteristic for which commercial real estate is purchased, and the greatest reliance thus is placed on the approach that converts future income into present value.

Final Reconciliation

Proper application by the appraiser of each of the several income approaches to valuation discussed in this chapter would, in theory, produce identical estimates of market value for Centre Point. Market value is determined by demand and supply conditions, not the methodology chosen by the appraiser to measure it. In practice, of course, we would be surprised if the values obtained by use of two or more methods were identical. The realities of the imperfect markets that provide valuation inputs, such as market rents, typical expenses,

Exhibit 8-9 Centre Point Office Building: Reconciliation of Value Indicators

Approach	Indicated V_O	Weight (%)	Weighted V_O
Indicated values from income approach			
DCF analysis (NOIs)	$1,060,000	60%	$ 636,000
Direct capitalization	1,061,000	30	318,300
$EGIM$ analysis	1,051,000	5	52,550 .
Indicated value from cost approach	1,075,000	5	53,750
Indicated value from sales comparison approach	Not applied	0	0
	Weighted V_O added to yield final estimate of value:		$1,060,600
	Rounded to:		$1,061,000

sale prices, and loan terms, will result in discrepancies among market value estimates. Thus, the reconciliation process requires informed judgment and expert opinion; it is not a simple averaging of divergent data.

Exhibit 8-9 summarizes the various indications of market value for the Centre Point Office Building obtained so far. Appraisers obtain a final estimate of value by reconciliation of these indications into a final estimate of value. Relevance and reliability serve as the criteria for determining the weight assigned to the *values* indicated by each approach.

For income-producing properties, the most reliable methods are usually DCF analysis and direct capitalization. Recall that DCF analysis employed market inputs—that is, market-derived rents, expenses, and discount rate. The DCF analysis and direct capitalization should produce similar results, with generally no more than a 10 percent difference. In this example, the DCF method and the direct capitalization method are weighted 60 percent and 30 percent, respectively. The *EGIM* analysis and the cost approach (not demonstrated here, but assumed to result in an indicated value of $1,075,000) are each weighted only 5 percent, indicating the lower level of confidence placed on these methods for this particular type of property.

The final estimate of market value, 1,061,000, is the weighted average of all of the value indications shown in Exhibit 8-9. It reflects the appraiser's best estimate of the current market value of the property, using the valuation methods believed relevant and reliable.

It should be noted that, in practice, appraisers seldom explicitly identify the weights given each method. Rather, they apply the weights implicitly in rendering their professional opinion of value. In this example, the weights are identified to describe the reconciliation process.

Valuing Partial and Other Interests

Alternative capitalization rates are often applied when valuing partial interests (and future interests) of the entire property. For example, the "property" valued may be any legal interest in real estate such as a **fee simple estate** (complete ownership of a property without regard to any leases) or a **leased fee estate** (ownership subject to leases on the property). The value of other estates, such as those in the land only, the building only, leasehold estates, and other partial interests, may also be estimated.

Whenever a specific property, or a component of, or interest in, the property, is appraised, the income associated with that particular component or interest must be estimated, and the appropriate rate applied using direct capitalization or DCF procedures similar to those employed when estimating overall market value. A detailed description of the valuation of partial interests is beyond the scope of this book; however, examples of some of the capitalization rates (and their symbols) are listed in Exhibit 8-10.

Exhibit 8-10   Capitalization Rates, Income, and Value Components

Overall cap rate (R_o)	$= NOI_1$	$\div$ Current property value (V_o)
Terminal cap rate (R_t)	$= NOI_{n+1}$	$\div$ Terminal property value (V_n)
Building cap rate (R_b)	$=$ Building income	$\div$ Value of the building (V_b)
Land cap rate (R_L)	$=$ Land income	$\div$ Value of the land (V_L)

Summary

This chapter focuses on the third approach to market valuation—the income approach. The income approach includes the valuation of income-producing properties by discounted cash flow (DCF) analysis, direct capitalization, and effective gross income multiples (EGIMs). The mechanics of DCF analysis are the same whether the analysis is used for the purpose of making investment decisions or for valuation. For valuation purposes, however, the viewpoint is different; consequently, the data employed may differ from those used in investment analysis for the same property. To estimate the market value of a property using DCF analysis, an appraiser must use market-derived data. Thus, for appraisal purposes, market data are the inputs, and an estimate of market value is the output.

Direct capitalization involves dividing projected net operating income over the next 12 months by a capitalization rate to estimate market value. The income and cap rate could be for any interest in real estate: the fee simple interest, leased fee interest, leasehold interest, land only, or building only. The only requirement is that the cap rate is obtained for whatever interest produces the income. In most situations, the value of the fee simple interest in a property is estimated, so the relevant income is net operating income (NOI) and the relevant cap rate is an overall cap rate (R_o). Once an R_o is selected, it is used to convert an annual income estimate into an estimate of current market value. In straightforward appraisal situations, direct capitalization can be more accurate and reliable than DCF analysis because the appraiser can rely on the decisions of other investors represented in the sale prices and incomes of comparable properties. It is not necessary to explicitly estimate cash flows over an expected holding period.

The sales comparison and cost approach to market valuation should also be applied when reliable data are available. However, these approaches to commercial property valuation are usually not considered as reliable as the income approach and are usually weighted less in the final estimate of market value of income-producing properties.

Key Terms

Capital expenditures (*CAPX*)   198
Contract rent   195
Direct capitalization   199
Direct market extraction   200
Effective gross income (*EGI*)   197
Effective gross income multiplier (*EGIM*)   203
Fee simple estate   209
Going-in cap rate (R_o)   201
Going-out cap rate (R_t)   206

holding period   192
Income capitalization   192
Internal rate of return (*IRR*)   202
Leased fee estate   209
Market rent   195
Natural vacancy rate   195
Net operating income (*NOI*)   192
Net sale proceeds (*NSP*)   207
Operating expenses (*OE*)   197
Overall capitalization rate (R_o)   201

Potential gross income (*PGI*)   194
Pro forma   205
Reconstructed operating statement   194
Reversion   206
Selling expenses (*SE*)   207
Terminal capitalization rate (R_t)   206
Terminal value (V_t)   206

Test Problems

Answer the following multiple-choice problems:

1. Which of the following expenses is not an operating expense?
   a. Utilities.
   b. Property taxes.
   c. Management.
   d. Mortgage payment.
   e. Advertising.

2. An overall capitalization rate (R_o) is divided into which type of income or cash flow to obtain an indicated market value?
   a. Net operating income (*NOI*).
   b. Effective gross income (*EGI*).
   c. Before-tax cash flow (*BTCF*).
   d. After-tax cash flow (*ATCF*).
   e. Potential gross income (*PGI*).

3. Which of the following types of properties probably would not be appropriate for income capitalization?
   a. Apartment building.
   b. Shopping center.
   c. Farm.
   d. Warehouse.
   e. Public school.

4. Estimated capital expenditures
   a. generally reflect ongoing (recurring) expenditures on the property.
   b. are generally easier to forecast than operating expenses.
   c. are subtracted to compute NOI in an above-line treatment.
   d. are subtracted to compute NOI in a below-line treatment.

5. An appraiser estimates that a property will produce *NOI* of $25,000 in perpetuity, y_o is 11 percent, and the constant annual growth rate in *NOI* is 2.0 percent. What is the estimated property value?
   a. $277,778.
   b. $227,273.
   c. $323,762.
   d. $243,762.
   e. $231,580.

6. If a comparable property sells for $1,200,000 and the effective gross income of the property is $12,000 per month, the effective gross income multiplier (EGIM) is:
   a. 0.12
   b. 8.33
   c. 100
   d. 0.01
   e. 10

7. Which of the following statements regarding capitalization rates on commercial real estate investments is the most correct?
   a. Cap rates vary inversely with the perceived risk of the investment.
   b. Cap rates vary positively with the perceived risk of the investment.
   c. Cap rates tend to decrease when yields on long-term Treasury securities increase.
   d. Cap rates tend to increase when the expected growth rate in net rental income increases.

8. The methodology of appraisal differs from that of investment analysis primarily regarding:
   a. Use of DCF analysis.
   b. Use of direct capitalization.
   c. Length of holding period analyzed.
   d. Type of debt assumed in the analysis.
   e. Point of view.

Use the following information to answer questions 9 and 10. You have just completed the appraisal of an office building and have concluded that the market value of the property is $2,500,000. You expect potential gross income (PGI) in the first year of operations to be $450,000; vacancy and collection losses to be 9 percent of PGI; operating expenses to be 38 percent of effective gross income (EGI); and capital expenditures to be 4 percent of EGI.

9. What is the implied going-in capitalization rate?
   a. 9.5 percent
   b. 10.0 percent
   c. 10.5 percent
   d. 11.0 percent
   e. 16.4 percent.

10. What is the effective gross income multiplier *(EGIM)*?
    a. 5.56
    b. 6.11
    c. 10.53
    d. 16.38
    e. 18.00

Study Questions

1. Data for five comparable income properties that sold recently are shown in the accompanying table.

Property	NOI	Sale Price	Overall Rate
A	$57,800	$566,600	0.1020
B	49,200	496,900	0.0990
C	63,000	630,000	0.1000
D	56,000	538,500	0.1040
E	58,500	600,000	0.0975

What is the indicated overall cap rate (R_o)?

2. Why is the market value of real estate determined partly by the lender's requirements and partly by the requirements of equity investors?

3. Assume a reserve for nonrecurring capital expenditures is to be included in the pro forma for the subject property. Explain how an above-line treatment of this expenditure would differ from a below-line treatment.

4. Use the following property data:

Cash flow from operations:

Year	1	2	3	4	5
NOI	$150,000	$150,000	$150,000	$150,000	$150,000
Debt service	$125,000	$125,000	$125,000	$125,000	$125,000

Cash flow at sale:

Sale price:	$2,000,000
Cost of sale:	$ 125,000
Mortgage balance:	$1,500,000

a. Assuming the going-in capitalization rate is 8 percent, compute a value for the property using direct capitalization.

b. Assuming the required return on unlevered cash flows is 10 percent, and that the property will be held by a buyer for five years, compute the value of the property based on discounting unlevered cash flows.

c. Assuming the relevant required return on levered cash flows is 15 percent, and that the property will be held by a buyer for five years, what is the present value of the levered cash flows?

5. Given the following owner's income and expense estimates for an apartment property, formulate a reconstructed operating statement. The building consists of 10 units that could rent for $550 per month each.

Owner's Income Statement

Rental income (last year)	$60,000
Less: Operating & Capital Expenses	
Power	$ 2,200
Heat	1,700
Janitor	4,600
Water	3,700
Maintenance	4,800
Capital Expenditures	2,800
Management	3,000
Depreciation (tax)	5,000
Mortgage payments	6,300

Estimating vacancy and collection losses at 5 percent of potential gross income, reconstruct the operating statement to obtain an estimate of *NOI*. Assume an above-line treatment of CAPX. Remember, there may be items in the owner's statement that should not be included in the reconstructed operating statement. Using the *NOI* and an R_o of 11.0 percent, calculate the property's indicated market value. Round your final answer to the nearest $1,000.

6. You have been asked to estimate the market value of an apartment complex that is producing annual net operating income of $44,500. Four highly similar and competitive apartment properties within two blocks of the subject property have sold in the past three months. All four offer essentially the same amenities and services as the subject. All were open-market transactions with similar terms of sale. All were financed with 30-year fixed-rate mortgages using 70 percent debt and 30 percent equity. The sale prices and estimated first year net operating incomes were as follows:

Comparable 1: Sales price $500,000; *NOI* $55,000
Comparable 2: Sales price $420,000; *NOI* $50,400
Comparable 3: Sales price $475,000; *NOI* $53,400
Comparable 4: Sales price $600,000; *NOI* $69,000

What is the indicated value of the subject property using direct capitalization?

7. You are estimating the market value of a small office building. Suppose the estimated *NOI* for the first year of operations is $100,000.

a. If you expect that *NOI* will remain constant at $100,000 over the next 50 years and that the office building will have no value at the end of 50 years, what is the present value of the building assuming a 12.2% discount rate? If you pay this amount, what is the indicated initial cap rate?

b. If you expect that *NOI* will remain constant at $100,000 forever, what is the value of the building assuming a 12.2% discount rate? If you pay this amount, what is the indicated initial cap rate?

c. If you expect that the initial $100,000 *NOI* will grow forever at a 3% annual rate, what is the value of the building assuming a 12.2% discount rate? If you pay this amount, what is the indicated initial cap rate?

8. Describe the conditions under which the use of gross income multipliers to value the subject property is appropriate.

9. In what situations or for which types of properties might discounted cash flow analysis be preferred to direct capitalization?

10. What is the difference between a fee simple estate and a leased fee estate?

11. What is the difference between contract rent and market rent? Why is the distinction more important for investors purchasing existing office buildings than for investors purchasing existing apartment complexes?

12. Estimate the market value of the following small office building. The property has 10,500 sq. ft. of leasable space that was leased to a single tenant on January 1, four years ago. Terms of the lease call for rent payments of $9,525 per month for the first five years, and rent payments of $11,325 per month for the next five years. The tenant must pay all operating expenses.

During the remaining term of the lease there will be no vacancy and collection losses; however, upon termination of the lease it is expected that the property will be vacant for three months. When the property is released under short-term leases, with tenants paying all expenses, a vacancy and collection loss allowance of 8 percent per year is anticipated.

The current market rental for properties of this type under triple net leases is $11 per sq. ft., and this rate has been increasing at a rate of 3 percent per year. The market discount rate for similar properties is about 11 percent, the "going-in" cap rate is about 9 percent, and terminal cap rates are typically 1 percentage point above going-in cap rates.

Prepare a spreadsheet showing the rental income, expense reimbursements, *NOI*s, and net proceeds from sale of the property at the end of an eight-year holding period. Then use the information provided to estimate the market value of the property.

EXPLORE THE WEB

The CoStar Group offers an online data service called CoStar COMPS Professional®. Users have access to a comprehensive commercial real estate database that contains over 1 million verified sales records across all property types. Because of CoStar COMPS Professional and other competing data providers, due diligence no longer requires hours of digging through records, microfiche, and news sources for information and the dozens of subsequent verification calls. CoStar COMPS® employs hundreds of researchers who follow a standardized process to compile and confirm 200 + data fields on a single property. Thousands of transactions are added every month and data are updated daily, making CoStar COMPS Professional® a real-time sales transaction database.

Go to www.costar.com. After browsing the home page, click on the *Product Solutions* tab at the top of the page and then select CoStar *COMPS* from the menu of individual offerings. Take the short visual tour of the website.

Solutions to Concept Checks

1. When a commercial asset is performing well, there is sufficient cash being generated to both service the debt (i.e., make the mortgage payment) and pay all state and federal income taxes. So, both the lender and the income tax collector(s) benefit from good property performance.

2. Direct capitalization models require an estimate of income for one year. DCF models require estimates of net cash flows over the entire expected holding period. In addition, the cash flow forecast must include the net cash flow expected to be produced by the sale of the property at the end of the expected holding period. Finally, the appraiser must select the appropriate investment yield (required return) at which to discount all future cash flows.

3. The appraiser is generally tasked with estimating market value. Thus, it is the expectations of the market that are relevant, not the appraiser's personal opinion about where the market is heading. Stabilized income means under current market conditions, but adjusted to reflect market rents (not contract rents), "normal" vacancy and collection losses (not current if they are higher than normal), and normal operating expenses and capital expenditures. For example, sometimes an investor feels the current owner is not managing the property well in that rents are lower than the market will bear and expenses are higher than they need be. In putting together the reconstructed operating statement, the appraiser values the property under the assumption that the owner will quickly stabilize the property (i.e., bring revenues and expenses to market levels).

4. Contract rent is the actual rent being paid under the terms of the lease(s). A listing of these contract rental rates is sometimes called the property's "rent roll." Market rent is the income the property is capable of producing if leased at current market rates.

5. Operating expenses include the ordinary and necessary expenditures associated with operating an income producing property. They keep the property competitive in its market, but they do not prolong the useful life of the asset or increase its market value. In contrast, capital expenditures are replacements, alterations, or additions significant enough to prolong life and increase value.

6. When capital expenditures are subtracted (i.e., taken out) in the calculation of *NOI*, this is referred to as an "above-line" treatment of capital expenditures.

7. The indicated value is $4,444,444 ($400,000 / 0.09).

8. If new information suggests that rents are going to increase at a faster rate, but y_o (the required total rate of return) has not changed, then capitalization rates will fall because $R_o = y_o - g$. Said differently, if a larger portion of the required total return is going to come in the form of future rent growth and price appreciation, then a smaller portion of the total return needs to be obtained from the current cash flow.

9. If the appraiser believes that the subject's rents will grow faster than the rents of the comparable properties, then an investor can justify paying a higher price per dollar of current rental income. Thus, the appraiser should adjust upward the *EGIM* abstracted from the market, which would imply a higher estimated value for the subject property.

10. DCF analysis requires an estimate of the value of the property at the end of the assumed holding period. The most common method used to estimate the market value of the property at the end of, say, 10 years, is to capitalize the *NOI* estimate in year 11 into an end-of-year 10 value. Thus, DCF is a combination of DCF analysis and direct capitalization.

Additional Readings

The following books contain expanded examples and discussions of real estate valuation and appraisal:

Appraisal Institute. *The Appraisal of Real Estate,* 14th ed., Chicago: Appraisal Institute, 2013.

Appraisal Institute. *Dictionary of Real Estate Appraisal,* 4th ed. Chicago: 2002.

Betts, Richard M. *Basic Real Estate Appraisal,* 6th ed., Mason, OH: Thomson Southwest, 2013.

Carr, D. H., J. A. Lawson, and J. C. Schultz, Jr. *Mastering Real Estate Appraisal,* Chicago: Dearborn Financial Publishing, Inc., 2003.

Collier, N. S., C. A. Collier, and D. A. Halperin. *Construction Funding: The Process of Real Estate Development, Appraisal, and Finance.* 4th ed. New York: John Wiley & Sons, 2008.

Fanning, S. F. *Market Analysis for Real Estate.*: Chicago: Appraisal Institute, 2014.

Fisher, J. D., and R. S. Martin. *Income Property Appraisal.* 3rd ed. Chicago: Dearborn Real Estate, 2007.

Lennhoff, D. C., "Direct Capitalization: It Might Be Simple But It Isn't That Easy," *The Appraisal Journal*, Winter 2011, pp. 68–73.

Linne, M. R., M. S. Kane, and G. Dell. *Guide to Appraisal Valuation Modeling.* Chicago: Appraisal Institute, 2000.

Lusht, Kenneth L. *Real Estate Valuation: Principles and Applications*, Burr Ridge, Il: McGraw-Hill/Irwin, 1997.

Ratterman, M. R. *The Student Handbook to the Appraisal of Real Estate* 13th ed. Chicago: Appraisal Institute, 2009.

Smith, Halbert C., Linda Crawford Root, and Jerry D. Belloit. *Real Estate Appraisal*, 3rd ed., Upper Saddle River, NJ: Gorsuch Scare Brock Publishers, 1995.

Ventola, W. L., and M. R. Williams, *Fundamentals of Real Estate Appraisal*, 12th ed. Chicago: Dearborn Real Estate Education, 2015.

The following journals contain numerous articles on real estate valuation and appraisal:

The Appraisal Journal, published quarterly by the Appraisal Institute, Chicago, Il.

Real Estate Review, published quarterly by Warren, Gorham and Lamont, Boston, MA.

Real Estate Issues, published quarterly by the American Society of Real Estate Counselors, Chicago, Il.

The Real Estate Appraiser, published monthly by the Society of Real Estate Appraisers, Chicago, Il.

APPENDIX: Other Methods of Estimating Cap Rates

When adequate reliable market data are available, appraisers often prefer to estimate overall cap rates directly from recent transactions of similar income properties using direct market extraction. Often, however, estimates of *NOI* for the comparable properties may not be available or reliable, and the sale prices may reflect special considerations such as favorable financing or an unusual income tax situation. Thus, appraisers must sometimes rely on alternative methods for estimating the R_o to be applied to a subject property's net operating income. The Centre Point Office Building example is used to illustrate two of these alternative methods: (1) mortgage-equity rate analysis and (2) application of the general constant-growth model formula.

Mortgage-Equity Rate Analysis

Mortgage-equity rate analysis recognizes that the *NOI* produced by a property represents the initial return on the total acquisition price of the property. However, the acquisition is usually financed with a combination of equity (cash) and mortgage debt. Mortgage-equity rate analysis assumes the investor's minimum required cap rate is a weighted average of the required cap rate on debt financing and the required cap rate on equity financing. Thus, appraisers must determine the one-year cap rate on both debt and equity capital. Appraisers then weight these capital costs by the proportion of each part to the total property value. They then add the two weighted rates to obtain R_o.

The cap rate on mortgage financing, R_m, is easily obtained by observing current lending terms for the type and amount of mortgage financing the typical investor would use if acquiring the subject property. The cap rate on equity financing should reflect the dividend rate investors could earn on alternative investments of equal risk. The *equity dividend rate* (R_e) is estimated by dividing the before-tax cash flow (*BTCF*) available on alternative investments by the typical amount of equity (V_e) investors use to finance similar investments. *BTCF* is equal to the *NOI* minus the expected mortgage payment; *equity* is the difference between the value (sale price) of the property and the value of the mortgage (the mortgage amount). The equity dividend rate (*EDR*) is thus defined as

$$R_e = \frac{BTCF_1}{V_e}$$

Investors view the equity dividend rate as the one-year (before-tax) income return (i.e., dividend) they could earn on their equity investments in properties similar to the subject property. The appropriate going-in cap rate, R_o, is a weighted average of R_m and R_e, or

$$R_o = mR_m + (1 - m)R_e$$

where R_o denotes the overall capitalization rate; m, the loan-to-value ratio; R_m, the mortgage capitalization rate; $(1 - m)$, the equity-to-value ratio; and R_e, the equity capitalization rate (equity dividend rate). Mortgage-equity rate analysis is sometimes also referred to as *band-of-investment analysis*.

EXAMPLE A-1   CENTRE POINT

The appraiser has determined that the typical investor can obtain mortgage financing at 75 percent of value for the Centre Point Office Building. The typical cap rate on this debt financing, R_m, is 8.0 percent. The equity dividend rate available on comparable properties is estimated to be 10.0 percent, which was obtained from reviewing market investor surveys and the estimated *BTCF*s of similar recently sold properties. The indicated R_o is calculated as follows:

$$R_o = (0.75)(0.080) + (0.25)(0.100) = 0.085$$

The overall capitalization rate of 0.085 is a weighted average of the cost of debt and the equity dividend rate (the opportunity cost of equity).

Applying the General Constant-Growth Formula

A third approach to determining the appropriate capitalization rate is to apply the constant-growth formula. Recall that the capitalization rate is composed of a required return on equity and an income growth rate: $R_o = y_o - g$. In the Centre Point Office example, the appraiser has determined the overall market discount rate is 10.0 percent. If the appraiser expects the property's *NOI*s and market value to grow, on average, by 2.0 percent per year into perpetuity, then $R_o = (0.100 - 0.0200) = 0.080$.

Reconciling Cap Rates and Estimating an Indicated Value

We have discussed three methods for estimating the going-in cap rate, R_o, for a particular property in a given market: market extraction, mortgage-equity rate analysis, and the general constant-growth formula. The questions that naturally arise are: Which one is correct? or which should I use? All are correct, of course; they are simply different methods of analyzing market data to estimate the value of a property. Even so, the methods will not produce the same numerical results. Real estate markets are not totally efficient, and different methods of analysis will not yield the same conclusions. Nevertheless, if accurate, reliable data are available for the various methods, the resulting going-in cap rates should be quite close because there is only one true "market value."

The appraiser's choice of method(s) depends on data availability and reliability. The preferred method—if reliable price, income, and expense data are available for at least three (and preferably more) comparable properties—is the direct market extraction of R_o. Remember, however, that observed transaction prices should not reflect any nonmarket considerations such as unusual financing or other concessions. Also, income, operating expense, and capital expenditure data must be consistently placed in a reconstructed operating statement format. In other words, direct market extraction requires the same availability, reliability, and consistency of data and analysis for the comparable properties as for the subject property.

Exhibit A-1   Reconciliation of the Indicated R_os

Source	Indicated R_o		Weight (%)		Weighted R_o
Direct market extraction	0.084	×	60%	=	0.0504
Mortgage-equity rate analysis	0.085	×	20	=	0.0170
General constant growth formula	0.080	×	20	=	0.0160
Final R_o: (calculated by summing the weighted R_os)				=	0.0834

Mortgage-equity rate analysis and the general constant-growth formula are substitute methods for deriving R_o. They are often used because appraisers cannot obtain accurate, reliable data for direct market extraction. At times, however, appraisers are able to obtain typical mortgage financing data and equity dividend rates on comparable properties. In these situations, the mortgage equity method may be preferred to direct market extraction.

Exhibit A-1 shows how the three indicated cap rates for our example property are reconciled. *Reconciliation* is accomplished by using weights to reflect the degree of confidence the appraiser has in each estimate of R_o. This confidence is usually based on the quantity and reliability of the data used to produce the alternative estimates. In this case the appraiser would weight the R_o obtained by direct market extraction twice as heavily as each of the other estimates because he or she has high-quality data for five very comparable properties. The data for the other two methods were acceptable, but the methods are not as directly applicable as direct market extraction. Using this final R_o to capitalize the *NOI* of the subject property produces the following *indicated value* from the direct income capitalization approach:

$$V_o = \frac{\$89,100}{0.0834} = \$1,068,345, \text{ rounded to } \$1,068,000$$

PART FOUR

Chapter 9

Real Estate Finance: *The* Laws *and* Contracts

LEARNING OBJECTIVES

After reading this chapter you will be able to:

1 Correctly use these terms concerning an adjustable interest rate: *index, margin, periodic cap, overall cap, payment cap, adjustment period,* and *teaser rate.*

2 With respect to a note, state the meaning of *personal liability, exculpatory clause, demand clause,* and *default.*

3 State the effect of these clauses in a mortgage: insurance clause, escrow clause, acceleration clause, and due-on-sale clause.

4 Contrast a mortgage, a deed of trust, and a contract for deed.

5 List four alternative actions to foreclosure that a lender can take as a remedy for default.

6 State the function of foreclosure, and the role of the following: equity of redemption, statutory redemption, deficiency judgment, and judicial versus power-of-sale foreclosure.

7 Distinguish three types of bankruptcy and what effect each has upon foreclosure.

8 Distinguish acquiring a property "subject to" a mortgage from assuming the mortgage.

9 Identify at least four major national laws affecting home mortgage lending, and state at least three provisions of each.

OUTLINE

Introduction

Most real estate transactions involve debt financing. Most homebuyers lack the cash to purchase their residence outright, most businesses want their cash available in their core business rather than tied up in real estate, and most investors want to "leverage" their investment to increase equity returns or acquire more assets for greater diversification. In addition, many homeowners find that their best source of financing for household needs is a credit line loan secured by their house. As a result, mortgage debt financing is a major aspect of real estate decisions, and mortgage lending is a major industry in the United States and many other countries.

To understand mortgage financing requires some knowledge of law, which is presented in this chapter. In effect, this chapter provides the "rules of the game" for mortgage finance.

In a mortgage loan the borrower always creates two documents: a note and a mortgage (or deed of trust).[1] The note details the financial rights and obligations between borrower and lender. The mortgage pledges the property as security for the debt.

Several aspects of a mortgage note are important for a borrower to understand. These include computation of the interest rate (if adjustable), whether a loan can be paid off early (and at what cost), whether there is personal liability for a mortgage, what fees can be charged for late payments, and whether the loan must be repaid upon sale of the property. Finally, a borrower should know whether the lender has the right to terminate the loan, calling it due.

In case of default on a mortgage, a lender's ultimate recourse is foreclosure. But foreclosure is costly to implement. The lender needs to know what the alternatives to foreclosure are, and their risks. Bankruptcy frequently accompanies default and can have serious adverse consequences that a lender must understand.

When property is purchased, new mortgage debt is not the only means of financing the purchase. Existing debt may be preserved, in which case the seller and buyer must understand his or her liability. Further, a contract for deed may substitute for mortgage financing. Finally, whenever residential mortgage debt is created both borrower and lender need to understand several federal laws governing the process.

> ✓ **Concept Check**
>
> **9.1**   What two contracts are always involved in a mortgage loan?

The Note

The **note** defines the exact terms and conditions of the loan. Both the large size of a real estate loan and the long maturity compel the note to be very explicit to prevent misunderstandings between the borrower and lender. The complexity of loan terms can vary with its size and the risks involved. In this section we discuss the major elements common to most mortgage notes.

Interest Rate and Interest Charges

Interest rates can be fixed or variable. Either way, virtually all small- to medium-size real estate loans from standard lenders follow the same conventions for interest rate computation and interest charges.[2] The actual interest charged per month is the annual stated

---

1. Roughly an equal number of states use a mortgage and a deed of trust. Since, under equivalent circumstances, the two contracts differ only in one major point (explained later) we will use "mortgage" to refer to both types of contracts.

2. Standard lenders are banks, savings and loan associations, savings banks, credit unions, mortgage bankers, and mortgage brokers. These are discussed in Chapter 11.

contract interest rate divided by 12, multiplied by the beginning-of-month balance. The payment is due on the first day of the following month. For example, if the contract interest rate on a home loan is 6.00 percent, and the balance on the first day of the month is $100,000, then interest for the month is 0.5 percent (0.06 ÷ 12) × 100,000, or $500, payable on the first day of the next month.[3]

✓ Concept Check

9.2   What is the monthly interest rate for a mortgage loan with a 12 percent annual rate?

Adjustable Rates

Many mortgage loans use an adjustable interest rate. This is common in commercial real estate loans and in many home loans where the loan is known as an **adjustable rate mortgage (ARM).** Finally, adjustable interest rates are used in virtually all home equity credit line mortgage loans (discussed in Chapter 10). The computation of an adjustable interest rate opens several questions not present when the interest rate is fixed. A number of components must be defined in the note, including the index, margin, method of computing the index, adjustment period, date of change in the interest rate, and determination of any "caps" or limits on interest rate changes. These components are explained below.

www.fhfa.gov

Look under: Research & Analysis/ Market Data/Monthly Interest rate Survey/Historical Summary Tables/. See Table 12 for fixed rate mortgages, and see Tables 23-25 for ARM.

Index.   The **index rate** is a market determined interest rate that is the "moving part" in the adjustable interest rate. In principle, it could be any regularly reported market interest rate that cannot be influenced by either borrower or lender. In practice, a relatively small number of choices are used. With ARM home loans, for example, the most common index rates include U.S. Treasury **constant maturity rates** (most commonly one year in maturity, although longer maturities are used as well), and a **cost-of-funds index** for depository lenders.[4] Occasionally, a home mortgage index rate may be used as well, such as the national average rate for new loans on existing homes. Home equity credit line loans, commonly offered by banks, rely on the commercial bank "prime rate" as published regularly in *The Wall Street Journal.* Finally, a common index is a **LIBOR** rate, especially for loans on income-producing property.[5]

Not only must an adjustable rate note specify the index, but it must state how it is used at each adjustment period. For example, when the rate is recomputed at the **change date,** the new index value may be the latest published value, a value from a certain number of days earlier, or an average of a recent period.[6] Generally, home mortgage lenders must notify borrowers of interest rate changes at least 30 days in advance.

---

3. For large mortgage loans on income-producing property the most common computation of interest is by the actual 360 method. By this method monthly interest is computed as the annual interest rate divided by 360, multiplied by the actual number of days in the month, multiplied by the beginning-of-month balance. This results in higher interest payments than for the standard computation above.

4. Treasury constant maturity interest rates are computed by the Federal Reserve Board as follows: The one year constant maturity rate, for example, is the average of the market yield, found by survey, on all outstanding U.S. Treasury debt having exactly one year remaining to final repayment, regardless of what the original maturity of the debt was. The Federal Reserve regularly reports several maturities of constant maturity rates.

A cost-of-funds index for depository lenders is a weighted average of all the rates of interest paid on all types of funds deposited with thrift institutions (savings and loan associations, credit unions, and savings banks) and banks. The most common cost-of-funds index used is based on West Coast member depository institutions of the Federal Home Loan Bank system (District 12).

5. LIBOR (London Interbank Offering Rate) refers to a short-term interest rate for U.S. dollar denominated loans among foreign banks based in London.

6. A common choice is to use the latest weekly average available a certain number of days (e.g., 45) before the change date.

Exhibit 9-1 The Most Common ARM Index Rate: One-Year Constant Maturity Treasury Rate

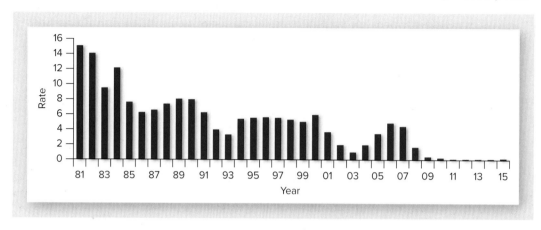

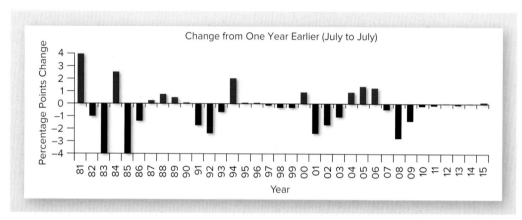

The one-year constant maturity Treasury rate is displayed in Exhibit 9-1 for the earliest available day in July from 1981 through 2015. Its behavior is representative of other index rates. First, the enormous range in the value of the rate is apparent. Also evident is the downward trend over the last two decades, which is interlaced with numerous significant upward reversals. The year-to-year effect is most evident in the second panel, showing changes in the Constant Maturity Treasury (CMT) rate from one year earlier. It reveals that borrowers have experienced more years of declining rates than rising rates. If one regards any increase of less than 1/2 of 1 percent as a win, the borrower has won 26 of 35 years from 1981 through 2015. Still, many borrowers may not be comfortable with the very apparent possibility of occasional large rate increases. For this reason, most home borrowers prefer caps on changes in the ARM rate, as discussed below.

www.federalreserve. gov/releases/h15/update

Reports latest Constant Maturity Treasury rates.

Margin. Added to the index of the adjustable rate is a **margin,** which is the lender's "markup." The margin is determined by the individual lender and can vary with competitive conditions and with the risk of the loan. It normally is constant throughout the life of the loan. For standard ARM home loans, the average industry margin has been very stable at around 275 basis points (2.75 percentage points). Margins frequently are lower for home equity loans made by banks.

www.freddiemac.com/ pmms/pmmsarm.htm

One-year ARM rates and margins.

✓ **Concept Check**

9.3 What are four sources of index interest rates for use in adjustable interest rates?

Rate Caps. Any change to an ARM adjustable rate commonly is restricted by two kinds of limits, or *caps*: periodic caps and overall caps. **Periodic caps** limit change in the interest rate from one change date to the next. **Overall caps** limit change over the life of the loan. Typically, the caps are binding for both increases and decreases in the index.

Teaser Rates. Most ARM home loans have been marketed with a temporarily reduced interest rate known as a **teaser rate.** This reduction, which may be a percentage point or two below the sum of index plus margin, usually applies for a short time, perhaps one year. The presence of a teaser rate creates a question about how the periodic cap works: Does the cap apply to the teaser rate, or does it apply only to the index plus margin? For example, suppose the periodic cap is 1 percent (100 basis points), the initial index plus margin implies a starting rate of 5.0 percent, but a teaser rate of 3.5 percent applies in the first year.

At the start of year 2, is the new interest rate limited to 4.5 percent (3.5 + 1.0) or to 6.0 percent (5.0 + 1.0)? The answer depends on how the note is written, and the borrower must examine the wording of the note to find the answer. A detailed computation of ARM interest rates and payments, demonstrating the interaction of the teaser rate and caps, is shown in Chapter 15.

Payment Caps. Some lenders offer ARM home loans with caps on payments rather than on the interest rate. For example, while the actual interest rate may be allowed to adjust without limit, the payment may be capped at increases of no more than 5 percent in a single year. Thus, if the payment in the initial year of a loan with annual payment adjustments is $1,000 and there is a 5 percent payment cap, then the maximum payment in year 2 is $1,050 regardless of how much the interest rate (index plus margin) increases. The **payment cap** enables the lender to enjoy the advantage of unconstrained interest rate adjustments while protecting the borrower against the shock of large payment changes. However, it can become very complicated. It is possible for interest charges to increase more than the payment cap will allow. The unpaid interest must be added to the original balance, causing the loan balance to increase, a result that is known as **negative amortization.**

✓ **Concept Check**

9.4 The two most common types of caps in an adjustable rate mortgage are: _____.

Payments

Payments on standard mortgage loans are almost always monthly. Further, most standard, fixed rate home loans are level payment and fully amortizing.[7] That is, they have the same monthly payment throughout, and the payment is just sufficient to cover interest due plus enough principal reduction to bring about full repayment of the outstanding balance at exactly the end of the term. Exhibit 9-2 shows the pattern of interest and principal payments on a fixed rate, 30-year, level payment, fully amortizing loan. Notice that the payment is largely interest for about the first half of the loan life before it begins to decline. This pattern is very similar for all level payment, long-term loans, although the actual interest share of the payment depends on the interest rate and term.

Not every loan is fully amortizing. A loan may be **partially amortizing,** as noted in the next paragraph; that is, it may pay down partially over a certain number of years, but may require an additional (large) payment of principal with the last scheduled payment. Loans also may be **nonamortizing,** that is, they require interest but no regularly scheduled

---

7. Amortizing refers to repayment through a series of scheduled balance reductions.

Exhibit 9-2   Interest and Principal on a Level-Payment Loan

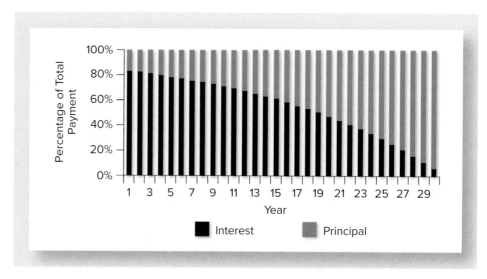

principal payment prior to the last payment. Finally, some loans may contain negative amortization. As noted before, this means that their scheduled payment is insufficient to pay all of the accumulating interest, causing some interest to be added to the outstanding balance after each payment shortfall, increasing the loan amount.

> ✓ **Concept Check**
>
> **9.5**   What happens to the balance of a loan with negative amortization?

Term

Most real estate loans have a definite term to maturity, usually stated in years. For example, home loans typically have a term to maturity between 15 and 30 years. If a loan is not fully amortizing, it will have two terms. The first is a **term for amortization** that determines the payment, and the schedule of interest and principal payments, just like a fully amortized loan. The second is a **term to maturity** that is shorter. This determines when the entire remaining balance on the loan must be paid in full. This type of loan often is called a **balloon loan.** Until recently, balloon loans were used infrequently as primary home loans but, as explained in Chapter 10, they have become more common. They are the dominant form of mortgage loan for income-producing property.

> ✓ **Concept Check**
>
> **9.6**   What is a balloon loan?

Right of Prepayment

There is important variation in the **right of prepayment** on a mortgage loan, and several situations are possible. First, the note may be silent on the matter. In this case, the right of prepayment will depend on the law of the state where the property is located. Under the traditional law of mortgages, which derives from English common law, there is no right to prepay a mortgage before its term, unless explicitly stated. However, most states have altered this common law tradition; that is, by statute, usually for residential first mortgages only, they now prohibit prepayment restrictions, or they limit the time or amount of a prepayment penalty, or they require that the prepayment restriction be explicitly stated to be enforceable.[8]

A simpler case is where the note is explicit on the right of prepayment. In this case the provisions of the note will prevail. Most standard home loans give the borrower the right to prepay any time, without penalty.[9] However, in recent years prepayment penalties have become more common in larger home loans. In addition, they frequently occurred in subprime home mortgage loans. (Subprime loans are discussed further at the end of this chapter and in Chapter 11.) **Subprime loans,** made to homeowners who do not qualify for standard home loans, commonly had very costly prepayment penalties that "locked in" the borrower to a very high interest rate.

Prepayment Penalties

For most mortgage loans on commercial real estate, the right of prepayment is constrained through a **prepayment penalty.** This penalty usually is very severe for the first few years of the loan, but declines in the latter half of the loan term. Three types of prepayment penalties have been used. Earlier generation income-property loans often specified a prepayment penalty as a percentage of the remaining balance at the time of prepayment. More recent practice has been to specify a **yield maintenance prepayment penalty.** In this approach, a borrower wishing to prepay must pay the balance, plus a lump sum representing the value (as defined in the note) of the interest income that will be lost by the lender due to prepayment. Still more recently, an even more demanding prepayment barrier has been used. This is a **defeasance requirement,** where a borrower wishing to prepay must usually provide the lender with some combination of U.S. Treasury securities producing interest income that replaces the cash flows of the loan being paid off.

✓ **Concept Check**

9.7 Of these types of loans, which typically have prepayment restrictions or penalties? a. Standard home loan. b. Large home loan. c. Subprime loan. d. Commercial property mortgage loan.

Late Fees

Late fees are a significant issue on debt contracts. Many credit card users discover the hard way that late fees are a major source of revenue for credit card lenders. Late fees on standard home loans typically are around 4 to 5 percent of the late monthly payment. Almost universally, they are assessed for standard home loans on payments received after the 15th of the month the payment is due. On subprime loans, and on nonstandard loans in general, late fees can be larger.

Personal Liability

When borrowers sign a note, they assume **personal liability,** in general, for fulfillment of the contract; that is, if the borrowers fail to meet the terms of the note, they are in a condition of **default,** and can be sued. Because the lender has this legal recourse against the mortgagor in

---

8. The variation in state statutes concerning prepayment restrictions on residential mortgages is very complex. See, for example, Connecticut General Assembly Office of Legislative Research, State Mortgage Prepayment Penalty Laws, October 7, 1996.

9. The right of prepayment without penalty is required in the note for standard home loans purchased by Freddie Mac or by Fannie Mae, and for Federal Housing Administration (FHA) and Veterans Affairs (VA) home loans. However, loans not eligible for FHA or VA, and loans too large to be eligible for purchase by Freddie Mac or Fannie Mae (generally over $424,100 in 2017) frequently have prepayment penalties.

A home loan originator (loan officer or broker) is the sales arm of the home financing industry. An effective loan originator is one who can help to make a home purchase happen. He or she assists brokers and buyers in overcoming the single largest obstacle to completing a successful home purchase: obtaining financing. "Loan officers" work directly for a lending institution. "Brokers" are agents for various lending institutions. Loan originators spend most of their day calling on industry salespersons or meeting with them and their clients. They are active in a variety of industry and community affairs both because they are "people oriented" and because the resulting interactions are the seedbed of their business opportunities. Much of their work occurs in the hours when households are buying homes, which often includes evenings and weekends. Originators have a wide range of educational and experience backgrounds. Most have an undergraduate college degree, frequently in business. Compensation for originators can be good.

For brokers it is achieved primarily through transaction-based commissions, though some firms may provide a "draw" against future earnings or a modest salary at the outset. Loan officers, in contrast, are primarily salaried, with more modest upside potential. Residential lending is a blend of sales work and technical expertise. While the broker and loan officer must have a solid knowledge of their products and of complex loan application and closing processes, their core business remains understanding, assisting, and influencing clients.

case of default, these loans often are called **recourse loans.** Recourse is less commonly available with loans on commercial real estate. For commercial loans, the note is often written so as to avoid personal liability on the part of the mortgagor, or borrower. Equivalently, an **exculpatory clause** is negotiated in the note that releases the borrower from liability for fulfillment of the contract. These loans are referred to as **nonrecourse loans.** While they relieve the borrower of personal liability, they do not release the property as collateral for the loan. In practice, most standard home loans and income-property mortgage loans from commercial banks have personal liability while most nonbank income-property mortgage loans do not.

Demand Clause

A **demand clause** permits a lender, from time to time, to demand prepayment of the loan. This clause is common with loans from commercial banks. If the bank determines after periodic review that the borrower's creditworthiness has deteriorated, the bank may exercise a demand clause. While a demand clause is rare in fixed-term, standard home loans (it is prohibited in many), it is quite common in "home equity" credit line loans from commercial banks.

> ✓ **Concept Check**
>
> **9.8**   What does a demand clause permit a lender to do?

Inclusion of Mortgage Covenants by Reference

The note usually will, by reference, add to its clauses all of the covenants (i.e., legally binding provisions) of the mortgage. In addition, it commonly reiterates some of the important mortgage covenants. Among these is likely to be a so-called due-on-sale clause, and an acceleration clause, which are discussed below.

The Mortgage or Deed of Trust

We have said that a mortgage loan involves two contracts: a note and a mortgage (or deed of trust). In this section we examine elements of the mortgage or deed of trust. However, we will simply refer to a mortgage since the two types of contracts generally have identical elements except for one provision, called *power of sale.* We explain that difference last.

The **mortgage** is a special contract by which the borrower conveys to the lender a security interest in the mortgaged property. Because the property is being pledged by the action of the borrower, the borrower is referred to as the **mortgagor,** or grantor of the mortgage claim. The lender, who receives the mortgage claim, is known as the **mortgagee.** Under traditional English common law, a mortgage temporarily conveyed title of the property to the mortgagee/lender. This **title theory** tradition has been largely replaced by the more modern **lien theory.**[10] Under the lien theory, the mortgage gives the lender the right to rely on the property as security for the debt obligation defined in the note, but this right only can be exercised in the event of default on the note.[11]

Because the mortgage conveys a complex claim for a long period of time, it must anticipate numerous possible future complications. Most of the clauses in a mortgage are for this purpose. Below is a sample of major clauses in a standard home loan mortgage.

Description of the Property

The mortgaged property must be described unambiguously. Three methods of property description generally are considered acceptable for this purpose (see Chapter 3). These are description by metes and bounds, by government rectangular survey, or by recorded subdivision plat lot and block number. Tax parcel number or street address are insufficient if used alone, since they can be erroneous or ambiguous.

Insurance Clause

An **insurance clause** requires a borrower/mortgagor to maintain property casualty insurance (e.g., fire, windstorm) acceptable to the lender, giving the lender joint control in the use of the proceeds in case of major damage to the property.

Escrow Clause

The **escrow clause,** or impound clause, requires a borrower to make monthly deposits into an **escrow account** of money to pay such obligations as property taxes, community development district (CDD) obligations, casualty insurance premiums, or community association fees. The lender can use these escrowed funds only for the purpose of paying the expected obligations on behalf of the borrower. Note that the obligations involved in some manner affect the ability of the lender to rely on the mortgaged property as security for the debt. The insurance must be paid to protect the value of the property against loss due to physical damage. The property tax, CDD obligation, and association dues must be paid because all are secured by superior claims to the property, as explained below.[12]

✓ **Concept Check**
9.9   Why does a mortgage lender want to be able to pay the property taxes on behalf of a mortgage borrower?

10. The pure lien theory is found, generally, in states west of the Mississippi, while title theory states include Alabama, Maryland, and Tennessee. Many states have a mixture of the traditions.

11. The difference between lien theory and title theory, now largely erased through state laws, is in the time that a mortgagee (lender) has claim to possession and rents of a property. Upon default, according to the pure title theory, a lender has claims extending back to the date the mortgage was created. But by the most extreme interpretation of lien theory, a lender has claim to no income or possession until a statutory redemption period (discussed later) has expired. While state laws have largely limited a lender's claims to those of a lien, state variations remain. The practical implication is that only a knowledgeable attorney should ever attempt to write or interpret a mortgage.

12. Lenders are not required under U.S. law to pay interest on mortgage escrow accounts, though they are by some states. The effect of such a requirement is debated. Lenders argue that in the highly competitive environment of mortgage lending there are no excess profits, and interest paid to borrowers on escrow accounts simply raises other fees charged to the borrower.

Acceleration Clause

In the event a borrower defaults on the loan obligation, an **acceleration clause** enables the lender to declare the entire loan balance due and payable. If this were not so, the default would apply only to the amount overdue. As a result, the cost of legal action against the borrower would almost always exceed what could be recovered. It would never pay to sue in case of default, and the mortgage would be meaningless.

Due-on-Sale Clause

If a property is sold, either in fact or in substance (for example, through a lease with an option to buy), a **due-on-sale clause** gives the lender the right to "accelerate" the loan, requiring the borrower to pay it off. This right can be waived at the lender's option, of course. It protects the lender from degradation in the quality or reliability of the person(s) paying the loan. This clause became extremely important in the early 1980s when interest rates were very high relative to rates on existing loans. Mortgagors selling their homes had a powerful incentive to preserve old, low interest rate loans that would be attractive to buyers, whereas the lender had an equally powerful incentive to terminate the old loans as soon as possible. The issue reached the U.S. Supreme Court in 1982 in *Fidelity Federal Savings and Loan v. De la Cuesta*. The court upheld the right of federally regulated lenders to enforce the clause despite actions in several states to restrict it.

The presence or absence of a due-on-sale clause is a major distinguishing feature between basic classes of home mortgage loans. So-called conventional home loans (see Chapter 10) almost always contain a due-on-sale clause, giving the lender the right to terminate the loan at sale of the property. By contrast, Federal Housing Administration (FHA) and Veterans Affairs (VA) loans are assumable, as long as the buyer can qualify for the loan. An **assumable loan** means that the buyer can preserve the existing loan by signing the note, and thus assuming the obligation.

Hazardous Substances Clause and Preservation and Maintenance Clause

A lender wants to protect the loan security from damage due to negligence or excessive risk taking by the borrower. Therefore, the borrower is prohibited from using or storing any kind of toxic, explosive, or other "hazardous substance" on the property beyond ordinary, normal use of such substances.[13] In addition, the borrower is required to maintain the property in essentially its original condition. Failure to meet either of these provisions constitutes default.

✓ **Concept Check**

9.10   What types of standard home loans are assumable?

Deed of Trust

In over 20 states, a **deed of trust** commonly is used in place of a mortgage. This arrangement works as follows: As shown in Exhibit 9-3, the borrower conveys a deed of trust to a **trustee,** who holds the deed on behalf of both borrower and lender. If the loan obligation is paid off in accordance with the note, the trustee returns the deed to the borrower. But if the borrower defaults, the trustee usually can exercise the power of sale (discussed later in "Judicial Foreclosure versus Power of Sale") to dispose of the property on behalf of the

---

13. A recent application of this clause is to illegal "meth" labs.

Exhibit 9-3   Mortgage versus Deed of Trust

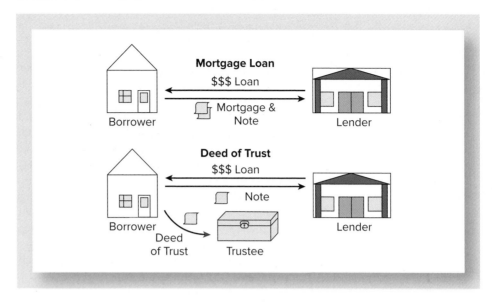

lender. Compared to a mortgage, the power of sale process offers significant advantages to a lender, as we will explain later in the next section.[14]

When Things Go Wrong

Only when something goes wrong does the meaning of the note and mortgage become clear. Below we review the main possibilities when this happens.

Default

Failure to meet the requirements of the note (and, by reference, the mortgage) constitutes *default*. Clearly, however, defaults can range in degree of seriousness. Violations of the note that do not disrupt the payments on the loan tend to be viewed as "technical" defaults. While these violations may require some administrative response, they do not compel legal action. For example, if for some reason hazard insurance were to lapse, the borrower must restore it, but that problem alone would not warrant legal action. When payments are missed (typically for 90 days), however, the lender normally treats the default as serious. In this case, the ultimate response is the process of *foreclosure*. Foreclosure is a costly and time-consuming action for all concerned, and traditionally it was a last resort, used sparingly.[15] But in the housing bust since 2006, foreclosures reached levels not seen since the Great Depression. In this historic crisis, critics pointed to the new phenomenon of mortgage securitization as frustrating default management and resulting in more foreclosures. (We discuss securitization in Chapter 11.) But thoughtful research has suggested otherwise.[16] The rate of foreclosure was little different between securitized and nonsecuritized loans of the same type, suggesting the nature of default remains largely unchanged. For that

14. The deed of trust is used exclusively rather than a mortgage in at least 9 states, and is used predominantly in as many as 15 more. The most important effect of the deed of trust is in those states where it is associated with power of sale, rather than judicial foreclosure. (See discussion later in this chapter.) However, power of sale is not dependent on use of the deed of trust. Some "deed of trust" states use judicial foreclosure while many "mortgage" states allow power of sale. The most important question is which states allow power of sale. This is shown in Exhibit 9-4.

15. For higher quality, "prime" first mortgages, as discussed in Chapter 10, foreclosure historically occurred with less than one-half of 1 percent of all loans.

16. See Manuel Adelino, Kristopher Gerardi, and Paul S. Willlen, "Why Don't Lenders Renegotiate More Home Mortgages? Redefaults, Self-cures and Securitization." *Journal of Monetary Economics* 60, 2013, pp. 835--53.

reason, we choose the much simpler and more transparent scenario of a single lender and a single borrower to explore default below.

Nonforeclosure Responses to Default

Sometimes when a homeowner misses a mortgage payment, the problem can be mitigated by improved household financial management. In this case, credit counseling, together with possible reorganization of consumer credit obligations, may be a far more constructive and less costly solution than legal action for both borrower and lender.

A more definite response to missed payments may be to allow a temporary reduction of payments. As long as some regular payment is being made, the lender might also allow a missed payment to be deferred. However, there are practical and legal risks in this response. If it is clear that the household will not be able to rectify its financial problem, the solution will only allow losses to compound. Further, any agreement to change the payment schedule on the loan may be interpreted by a court as a "recasting" of the loan. Theoretically, this can then be interpreted by a court as the creation of a new, replacement mortgage. Since the determination of priority among liens (i.e., security claims) generally is by date of creation, this could have disastrous consequences to the lender, as explained below.

✓ **Concept Check**

9.11 In practice, lenders commonly define default as occurring when a loan is _____ days overdue.

If a homeowner in mortgage distress owes more than the value of the home and is unable to make the loan manageable by refinancing or modifying the mortgage, the next recourse often is a **short sale.** The owner gives a letter of appeal to the lender, with whatever documentation the lender requires, establishing the case of distress. If the lender accepts the appeal, the owner must obtain a contractual offer from a buyer. If the lender decides that the offer is acceptably close to fair market value, the buyer pays the lender, and the seller is relieved of some or all of the outstanding balance on the mortgage. This does not relieve the seller of any other outstanding obligations on the home, such as owner association fees or a second mortgage. So the owner must either satisfy those obligations or negotiate separately for a resolution that is acceptable to the creditor. The short sale solution has several attractions: It usually enables a better sale price and a faster sale than foreclosure, and it is more likely to provide the lender a clean end to the case than foreclosure or deed in lieu of foreclosure. Legal costs also should be lower. It thus benefits both borrower and lender. In addition, it is less damaging to the borrower's credit, allowing him/her to be eligible for another mortgage loan sooner, as discussed below.

knowyouroptions .com/ avoid-foreclosure/ options-to-leave-your-home/short-sale

Fannie Mae website explaining short sales and deed in lieu.

If a short sale is not feasible, another option is a **deed in lieu of foreclosure;** that is, the lender may allow the borrower simply to convey the property to the lender. This solution is less favorable to the lender than a short sale, but still it has several attractions. It is faster than foreclosure, less costly, and—of special value for loans on commercial property—creates less public attention to the event. Public perception of the property may be especially important for retail and hospitality properties, for which adverse publicity may taint the tenants and damage their business.

But accepting a deed in lieu of foreclosure has significant risks since financial problems tend to travel in packs. The mortgagor is likely to have other financial problems apart from the property, but which can generate additional liens. Whatever liens have been imposed on the property subsequent to the creation of the mortgage will remain with the property. The lender has no choice but to accept the property subject to these liens.

The worst risk in accepting a deed in lieu of foreclosure is bankruptcy. The same conditions of distress that caused default on the mortgage may well lead the borrower finally to declare bankruptcy. If this occurs within a year after conveyance of the deed in lieu of foreclosure, the courts can treat the conveyance as an improper disposition of assets, deeming it unfair to other creditors. But the deed in lieu of foreclosure will erase the lender's priority claim to the property as security for the debt. So, when the bankruptcy court reclaims the property, the lender ends up as simply one more in the line of creditors seeking relief through the court.

✓ Concept Check

9.12   Give two reasons a lender might be ill-advised to accept a deed in lieu of foreclosure for a distressed property.

Foreclosure

Foreclosure is the ultimate recourse of the lender. It is a court-supervised process of terminating all claims of ownership by the borrower, and all liens inferior to the foreclosing lien. This can enable the lender to bring about free and clear sale of the property to recover the outstanding indebtedness. It is a delicate process because only those claimants who are properly notified and engaged in the foreclosure suit can lose their claims to the property. Thus, there is risk that persons with a claim on the property will remain undiscovered or will be improperly treated in the process. This would result in a defect in the title at a foreclosure sale.

Another concern in foreclosure is the presence of superior liens. In general, liens have priority according to their date of creation, with earlier liens being superior. In addition, government liens are automatically superior to any private lien. Foreclosure cannot extinguish a superior lien. Therefore, the foreclosing lender must be sure that obligations secured by superior liens—property taxes, assessments, community development district obligations, earlier mortgages—are met.[17] Otherwise, the lender can become subject to a subsequent foreclosure initiated by the holder of the superior lien.

✓ Concept Check

9.13   What liens would have priority over the mortgage of a lender?

Lien priority is a major concern to a lender because the highest priority lien receives all net proceeds from the foreclosure sale until that obligation is fully satisfied. Only then does the second lien claimant receive any satisfaction. For example, if a property with a first mortgage loan of $100,000 and a second mortgage loan of $30,000 brings net proceeds of $110,000 from a foreclosure sale, the first mortgagee would receive full satisfaction of $100,000 while the second mortgagee would receive only $10,000. More commonly, net proceeds from foreclosure are less than the amount of the first mortgage, and the second mortgagee receives nothing. Thus, a second mortgage is significantly less secure than the superior mortgage. Subsequent liens are progressively even less secure.

The start of a foreclosure suit does not necessarily spell the end of ownership for the mortgagor. By a legal tradition long part of the English law of equity, the mortgagor has a right, known as the **equity of redemption,** to stop the foreclosure process by producing the amount due and paying the costs of the foreclosure process.[18] This right traditionally

---

17. Technically, liens other than property tax, assessment and CDD liens have priority according to when they are recorded. See Chapter 3 for the process of recording. See Chapter 2 for a discussion of the various liens.

18. In some states the amount due includes the entire mortgage balance. In other states it is limited to the defaulted payments, plus certain expenses.

**www.alllaw.com/articles/
nolo/foreclosure/right-of-
redemption.html**

Information about statutory right of
redemption, by state.

extends up to the time of actual sale of the property. In over 20 states the right of redemption has been extended further, to some time beyond the sale of the foreclosed property. This period of **statutory right of redemption** varies among states, typically between six months and a year. However, it can range from a few days to as much as three years.

Foreclosure is a costly process to all involved. First, the legal search and notification process can be costly, time consuming, and risky in that it may be difficult to identify all claimants to the property. Second, the sale of the property typically is a distressed sale for a number of reasons: The property often suffers deterioration or abuse, it tends to be tainted and less marketable, normal market exposure of the property is not feasible, the title may be questionable so debt financing is not available, and, in many cases, the mortgagor may still have the statutory right of redemption. Consequently, the price received at a foreclosure sale tends to be low. Finally, the negative public exposure and the time involved must be counted as a cost for all parties involved. The net recovery by a lender from a foreclosed loan seldom is higher than 80 percent of the outstanding loan balance and commonly is much less.[19] As a result, mortgage lenders traditionally have had a strong incentive to avoid loans with high foreclosure risk.

Deficiency Judgment

Because a mortgage loan involves both a note and a mortgage, the lender may have the option, in addition to foreclosure, of simply suing the defaulting borrower on the note. This right of recourse exists, at least under some conditions, for 40 states and the District of Columbia.[20] In principle, funds not recovered through foreclosure can be recovered through a **deficiency judgment.** In practice, however, this seldom happens. Many loans on income-producing properties are nonrecourse, as discussed earlier in the chapter, placing the borrower beyond legal reach. Further, lenders recognize that a defaulted borrower usually has extensive financial problems and does not possess the net worth to compensate the lender beyond what is recoverable from sale of the property.

The Effect of Default on the Borrower

**www.nolo.com/legal-
encyclopedia/when-can-
i-get-mortgage-after-
foreclosure.html**

**www.nolo.com/legal-
encyclopedia/when-can-i-
get-mortgage-after-short-
sale.html**

Overview of consequences of
default on credit and eligibility for a
home mortgage. For consequences
of default on FHA and VA mortgages, google the subject.

What happens to the borrower who gets in trouble with a home mortgage? The answer is not simple. In most cases, there is damage to the borrower's credit. If a default goes into the borrower's records it remains for seven years. A borrower can see his credit score reduced by possibly 100 to 150 points, or more. Recovery is gradual, based on good performance, but can take as long as the full seven years.

A major question is how long before the defaulted borrower can qualify for another mortgage. The answer depends on both the nature of the default and the type of new loan. At one extreme is a borrower who suffered foreclosure or a short sale with a large deficiency and who wants a loan that will be purchased by Fannie Mae or Freddie Mac. The penalty waiting period could be a full seven years. At the other extreme is a new FHA or VA loan, where the waiting period could be three or two years, respectively. But if the default was beyond the control of the borrower, and the borrower's credit record is otherwise good enough, the waiting period could be much shorter in all these cases. All of the agencies mentioned have programs to help mitigate the problems of a borrower in distress. A troubled borrower should expect, under modern consumer information requirements of

---

19. Laurie Goodman and Jun Zhu, "Loss Severity on Residential Mortgages," February 2015, Urban Institute Housing Finance Policy Center.

20. In some "power of sale" states the lender is prohibited from both exercising the power of sale and seeking a deficiency judgment. Because of the typical circumstances of financial distress when a borrower defaults, the lender will virtually always elect the power of sale. For rights of recourse by state, see Andra Ghent and Marianna Kudlyak, "Recourse and Residential Mortgage Default..." WP09-10R, Working paper, Federal Reserve Bank of Richmond.

Exhibit 9-4 States Having Power of Sale for Residential Mortgages

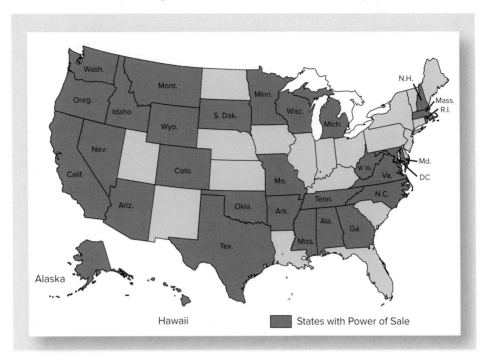

States with Power of Sale

the Consumer Financial Protection Bureau, to receive full information from his loan servicer about any programs that might apply.[21]

Judicial Foreclosure versus Power of Sale

There are two leading procedures among states of the United States in the treatment of defaulted mortgages, and the difference is significant. In states requiring **judicial foreclosure,** the sale of the foreclosed property must be through a court-administered public auction. In contrast to this are states having the **power of sale,** sometimes referred to as **nonjudicial foreclosure,** which are shown in Exhibit 9-4. In these states either the mortgagee (lender) or the trustee (for a deed of trust) conducts sale of the property. In using this power, the mortgagee or trustee must abide by statutory guidelines that protect the borrower: Typically, they must give proper legal notice to the borrower, advertise the sale properly, and allow a required passage of time before the sale.

The power of sale is advantageous to the lender for several reasons. In almost all cases it is faster and cheaper than a court-supervised auction. Further, with a deed of trust the borrower has no statutory right of redemption. This further shortens the process, ending it with finality at sale of the property. The difference between judicial foreclosure and power of sale is so significant that lenders may favor power of sale states in making some types of more risky loans.

The difference between judicial foreclosure and power of sale only partially captures the diversity in foreclosure law among states. There is significant variation within both groups, with many states having completely unique provisions. (See the websites shown for foreclosure law by state.) Texas and Iowa suggest the extremes in variation. In Texas, a power of sale state, there is only a 20-day period for a homeowner to cure a default, and notice of sale requires only another 21 days, making the process unusually quick and easy

www.nolo.com/legal-encyclopedia/state-foreclosure-laws

Foreclosure laws for each state.

---

21. Credit scores are discussed in Chapter 11 under the section titled "Modern Home Mortgage Underwriting." FHA and VA loans are discussed in Chapter 10.

Real Estate Attorney

Real estate attorneys play important roles in real estate and real estate finance, including drafting documents, assisting with the contracts of individual financings, and handling the complex problem of default. The following excerpt describes their broad role in the industry:

Real estate lawyers act as advisers to those who are buying or selling property, or to those involved in other matters related to real estate. They help process much of the paperwork involved in land transfers or other real estate transactions. Attorneys provide counsel to clients regarding their legal rights and obligations, and may suggest specific courses of action in buying or selling property or handling related matters. In this role, they research the intent of relevant laws and judicial decisions, and then apply the law to their client's specific circumstances and needs . . . Real estate lawyers spend the majority of their time outside the courtroom. They conduct research, meet with clients, process documents, and assess the legal positions of their clients in terms of the situation at hand . . . While some attorneys specialize entirely in real estate, others make it a segment of their practice. In both cases, further specialization is possible . . . Real estate attorneys work with a great variety of people . . . They . . . interact with other professionals involved in the real estate business including appraisers, real estate agents and brokers, mortgage loan officers, tax attorneys, and other specialists.[*]

Like all attorneys, those who practice in real estate must have the requisite law school training, and must be admitted to the bar in the states where they practice.

Source: Excerpted from Rowh, Mark, *Careers in Real Estate*, [pp. 99–101] New York, McGraw-Hill Education, © 2003 McGraw-Hill Education

for the lender. In Iowa, which allows power of sale, but only by voluntary agreement, judicial foreclosure dominates. Further, for farms, there is a redemption period of five years during which the lender can be forced to rent the property to the owner. After five years, the owner still can buy the property back from the lender.

> ✓ **Concept Check**
>
> **9.14**   Depending on the state, the process of foreclosure sale is either by _____ or by _____ . The method most favorable to a lender is _____ .

Bankruptcy and Foreclosure

The risk of **bankruptcy** tends to travel with the risk of foreclosure since both can result from financial distress. When a firm or individual has fewer total assets than total liabilities, bankruptcy is a possibility. While traditional bankruptcy has little effect on foreclosure, more modern forms can interfere significantly. Three types of bankruptcy must be distinguished, known by their section in the Federal Bankruptcy Code: Chapter 7, liquidation; Chapter 11, court supervised "workout"; Chapter 13, "wage earner's proceedings."

Chapter 7 Bankruptcy.   **Chapter 7 bankruptcy** is the traditional form of bankruptcy wherein the court simply liquidates the assets of the debtor and distributes the proceeds to creditors in proportion to their share of the total claims. So, if total assets sum to 50 percent of total claims, each creditor receives one-half of his or her claim. Because Chapter 7 involves a quick liquidation of assets, it does not disturb liens, and the power to foreclose remains. In short, a Chapter 7 proceeding typically will not seriously threaten the security interest of a mortgagee.

Chapter 11 Bankruptcy.   **Chapter 11 bankruptcy** is a court-supervised workout for a troubled business.[22] Once a court accepts the petition of a debtor firm, creditors are suspended from pursuing legal action against the assets of the firm. This follows the view that

---

22. The business can be of any legal form: corporation, partnership, proprietorship, or other.

competition among creditors likely will dismantle an otherwise viable business, which would benefit all the creditors if left intact. Under supervision of the court, the debtor will propose a workout plan, which is presented to creditors for acceptance. If the creditors cannot agree on the plan, a major concern is that the court will then impose a plan on the creditors that is even less acceptable. As part of the workout plan, the court is likely to forestall the possibility of foreclosure on defaulted real estate. The resulting delay can affect the defaulted lender in numerous adverse ways, the principal one being a delay in any possible recovery of funds. Also, the period in which payments are lost is extended, and the value of the property may deteriorate due to neglect.

Chapter 13 Bankruptcy.   **Chapter 13 bankruptcy** is similar to Chapter 11, but applies to a household. It allows the petitioner to propose a repayment plan to the court. In principle, the plan may not interfere with the claims of a mortgagee upon the debtor's principal residence, but it is likely to forestall any foreclosure proceeding and to allow any arrearages on the loan at the time of the bankruptcy filing to be paid back as part of the debtor's rehabilitation plan. Thus, the lender suffers delay in recovery, if not worse.[23]

> ### ✓ Concept Check
>
> **9.15**   Which form of bankruptcy is least harmful to a lender's mortgage interest?

Acquiring a Property with an Existing Debt

Sometimes in a property sale the parties agree to preserve an existing mortgage. In this case the question of personal liability arises. As long as the buyer does not add his or her signature to the note, the buyer takes on no personal liability, although the property still serves as security for the loan and can be foreclosed in the event of default. In this case the buyer is said to purchase the property **"subject to"** the existing loan. The seller remains personally liable for the debt and is said to "stand in surety" for the obligation. This means that in case of default, a lender who fails to obtain satisfaction from the current owner or from the property can go "up the line" to the original borrower. The seller or original borrower may not be comfortable with this contingent liability from the loan. A solution is to have the buyer sign the original note, and obtain from the lender a **release of liability** from the note. In this case the buyer is said to *assume* the old loan, that is, to **assume liability** for the note.

An important characteristic of a loan is whether or not a subsequent owner of the property can preserve it. This feature is commonly referred to as **assumability.** As we noted in the discussion of the due-on-sale clause, it is a major distinguishing feature between the broad types of home loans.

> ### ✓ Concept Check
>
> **9.16**   When a purchaser of mortgaged real estate accepts personal liability for an existing mortgage loan on the property, the borrower is said to _____.

---

23. The Congress, in the Bankruptcy Abuse Prevention and Consumer Protection Act of 2005, made it more difficult for defaulting home mortgage borrowers to elect Chapter 7 bankruptcy, compelling more to use Chapter 13. In the spring of 2009, the Congress considered giving judges power to alter the terms of home mortgage loans in default, but did not enact it.

The tradition of family members assisting each other is no doubt as old as the human race. In today's world of home buying, over a third of first-time home buyers received help from friends or relatives—most of them through gifts and about 7 percent through loans—according to a report of the National Association of Realtors for 2011.

Many observers believe these figures understate the true amount of such assistance, since parents often make gifts to children well in advance of their actual home purchase. In the years leading up to the "Great Recession" this parental assistance with home purchases no doubt was driven by the skyrocketing prices of homes. Post-recession, it is more likely to be driven by the extreme reluctance of lenders to qualify first-time home buyers.

But should parents go so far as to finance a first home for a child? The answer doubtless depends on the circumstances of both the parents and the child. However, there is wide agreement on one point: If parental financing is to be done, it is usually wise to approach it through a formal legal arrangement that includes a mortgage. This can go far to avoid painful stresses and misunderstandings that can arise in divorce, or settlement of an estate, since the loan is a clear matter of record. Recognizing this, there have been efforts from time to time to create assistance with intrafamily mortgages. The latest entrant in this service is National Family Mortgage (nationalfamily-mortgage.com), launched by Tim Burke in 2010. As of February 2016, National Family Mortgage reports having arranged family mortgage loans in excess of $380 million dollars.

What does National Family Mortgage provide? First, once the parents and children have settled on the amount and terms of the financing, NFM uses the information to generate a note and mortgage appropriate to the location and property. After all documents have been completed and signed NFM records the mortgage with the appropriate authorities. They also can provide ongoing collection of payments, mailing of statements and reminders, property tax and insurance escrow service, and appropriate annual reports for income tax records.

The attractions of "home to home" financing are numerous. First is the obvious; through higher loan-to-value ratio, lower interest rate, and lower closing costs, it can provide the children with financing that is otherwise unobtainable, and thus home ownership that is otherwise unachievable. At the same time it can provide the parents with an interest return that is not otherwise available in a severely "quantitative eased" (low interest) world, or it can facilitate their wish to transfer wealth to their children. Moreover, having the financing immediately available to the children may enable them to pursue a quick bid on a foreclosed home or other special purchase opportunity that would be unapproachable if they had to go through the normal process of mortgage loan qualification.

So what are factors that should be weighed in considering "home to home" financing? First, it should be considered only for the children who are a good risk, not already in financial difficulty. Otherwise, it is likely to sink two households. But even with financially strong children, the parents should be sure that they can tolerate some loss of principal should financial disaster befall their children. If the parents have a strong inclination to direct the lives of their children the loan may be unwise. It may amplify that inclination, resulting in something less than gratitude for the parents' generosity.

Home Mortgages in More Ways Than One

Real Estate Debt without a Mortgage

It is possible to have a secured real estate loan without a mortgage through the use of a **contract for deed,** or land contract. As the name suggests, this is a contract for sale of a property with the special provision that the actual delivery of a deed conveying ownership will occur well after the buyer takes possession of the property. The idea of the contract for deed is that a seller can finance the sale through installment payments and, by retaining title, have recourse in case of default. As shown in Exhibit 9-5, this arrangement contrasts with the standard real estate sale where both conveyance of possession and conveyance of title occur at the closing. With the contract for deed, the deed is conveyed only after the bulk of the installment payments have been made.

With a contract for deed, the effect of default varies. In the most favorable case for a seller, they can simply evict the would-be buyer and have full recovery of the property. However, this is by no means the typical case. Many courts have given greater recognition to the claims of buyers under contracts for deeds, especially when a personal residence is involved. Then the court may require that a defaulted contract for deed be treated as a mortgage, requiring a foreclosure proceeding. In general, the rights, obligations, and recourses of the parties in a contract for deed depend significantly on the jurisdiction and the nature of the property involved.

Exhibit 9-5   Standard Sale Timeline versus Contract for Deed Timeline

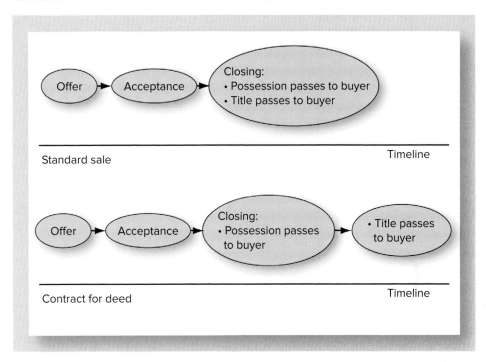

The contract for deed has served a number of purposes in real estate, some controversial. On the positive side, it can facilitate financing in situations deemed too risky for standard mortgage financing. For example, it can secure payments by a "speculator" interested in holding land for potential conversion from agricultural use to urban development. A farmer can sell the land on a contract for deed. In case of default, the farmer still has title to the land, and may be able to easily reclaim it outright. Another significant use of the contract for deed is in financing marginal housing; that is, there is some evidence that the land contract is a major means of financing for home purchases in which neither the dwelling nor the borrower can qualify for normal mortgage financing.

There can be a negative side to the contract for deed as well. Because it can be created hastily, there are often few, if any, protections or standards built into the arrangement. It frequently involves unsophisticated buyers who tend to overlook the need for legal and financial advice. Too often the transaction will go forward without a title search (see Chapter 3), and without sufficient legal guidance, leading to serious misunderstandings and grief later. Without a title search, the buyer has no way to know whether the seller can actually deliver clear title. Further, unless the contract is recorded in public records, there is little to prevent the seller from subsequently mortgaging the property to someone else, placing the buyer at risk.

In this situation an unprincipled seller can easily exploit a naïve and uninformed buyer. One example of this is shown in the history of interstate land sales, which affected large areas of the rural South and southwestern United States prior to about 1980. In this activity, it was common to sell land to distant buyers for future retirement homes, at unreasonable prices, expecting the buyer eventually to abandon the purchase. Sales commonly were made through contracts for deed, allowing the seller to easily reclaim the abandoned property for eventual resale to another victim. In the current use of the contract for deed in the sale of marginal homes, there again is little to prevent sellers from exploiting the lack of knowledge and experience of marginal homebuyers.

✓ **Concept Check**

9.17   How does a sale by contract for deed differ from a normal real estate sale? What does the contract for deed accomplish?

Regulation of Home Mortgage Lending

Few business are regulated more extensively than home mortgage lending. Five laws are particularly important because they determine criteria for evaluating home loan applicants and stipulate extensive disclosures in the origination of home loans: the Equal Credit Opportunity Act of 1974, the Consumer Credit Protection Act of 1968 (Truth-in-Lending Act), the Real Estate Settlement Procedures Act of 1974, the Home Ownership and Equity Protection Act of 1994, and the Dodd-Frank Wall Street Reform and Consumer Protection Act of 2010. In addition, two laws require monitoring of home mortgage lending to reveal discrimination: The Home Mortgage Disclosure Act of 1975 and the Community Reinvestment Act of 1977.

Equal Credit Opportunity Act

Because of what Congress perceived to be a long history of both deliberate and unconscious discriminatory practices in home mortgage lending, in 1974 it enacted the **Equal Credit Opportunity Act (ECOA)**.[24] This act prohibits discrimination in lending practices on the basis of race, color, religion, national origin, sex, marital status, age, familial status, disability, or because all or part of an applicant's income derives from a public assistance program. The law now also requires that the lender provide the applicant with any available estimates of value for the property involved. Numerous kinds of information are restricted from consideration in evaluating a loan application, including the childbearing plans of a female applicant, and whether income is from part-time or full-time employment. Further, the lender cannot ask for information about a spouse who is not part of the loan application.

✓ **Concept Check**

9.18 What law prohibits discrimination in lending by race, sex, religion, and national origin? What types of income discrimination does it prohibit?

Truth-in-Lending Act

The **Truth-in-Lending Act (TILA)** is Title 1 of the Consumer Credit Protection Act of 1968. It requires important disclosures concerning the cost of consumer credit. Perhaps the best known of its provisions is the required computation of the annual percentage rate (APR) for most consumer loans, including home mortgage loans. (APR is examined closely in Chapters 10 and 15.) In addition, the law requires disclosure of numerous other aspects of a home mortgage loan, including the following:

- Whether the loan contains a "demand feature."
- Whether the loan can be assumed.
- Whether the loan has a variable rate.
- Whether property hazard insurance is a required condition of the loan.
- Whether there are late charge provisions.
- Whether the loan has a prepayment charge (penalty).

Finally, under TILA the borrower has the right to **rescind** certain types of loans secured by his or her principal residence for three days following consummation of the loan. That is, the borrower can cancel the loan contract completely. This applies as long as the loan is not for purchasing or constructing a principal residence, is not for a business purpose, and is not to refinance a prior loan for these purposes from the same lender.

---

24. The detailed implementation of ECOA is through Federal Reserve Regulation B, often referred to in real estate finance circles.

9.19　Under the Truth-in-Lending Act, for how many days after closing does a borrower have the right to rescind a mortgage loan agreement?

Real Estate Settlement Procedures Act

The **Real Estate Settlement Procedures Act (RESPA),** enacted initially in 1974, was a response to the confusion and potential for exploitation of homebuyers applying for home financing. The experience of obtaining a home mortgage loan is the most complex business process most households ever experience and many are relatively unprepared for the numerous forms and fees involved. As a consequence, would-be homebuyers are vulnerable to exploitation. Further, it is not difficult for careless or unscrupulous lenders to create forms and procedures that few persons, if any, can understand. Through RESPA, Congress sought to "level the playing field" in home mortgage lending. The law applies if a buyer obtains a new first mortgage home loan from a lender having deposit insurance from the U.S. government (including virtually all banks, savings and loan associations, and credit unions), if the loan is insured by the FHA or guaranteed by the VA, or if the loan will be sold in the secondary market to Fannie Mae or Freddie Mac. As revised after 2013, requirements include:

- A standard format closing statement for most home mortgage loan closings (the Closing Disclosure form demonstrated in Chapter 13).
- Presentation of a document explaining closing fees and the Closing Disclosure form.
- A good-faith estimate of closing costs, specifically, the Loan Estimate form, to be provided within three business days of the loan application.
- The opportunity to examine the Closing Disclosure at least three days in advance of the loan closing.
- Prohibition of "kickbacks" and referral fees between the lender and providers of services in connection with the loan closing.

Among the services subject to the prohibition against kickbacks are appraisals, property inspections, document preparation, surveys, hazard insurance, mortgage insurance, and title insurance. (Title insurance is explained in Chapter 3; mortgage insurance is explained in Chapter 10.) In addition, RESPA prohibits a lender from specifying the source of title insurance to be used for the loan.

Finally, RESPA limits escrow deposits for interest, property taxes, hazard insurance, community association dues, or other items. First, it limits the deposits at closing. Second, it limits the regular monthly deposit that follows. Property taxes serve as an example of how these limits work: The maximum deposit that can be required at closing for property taxes has two parts. First, the initial deposit is limited to the amount that would have been in the account at the time of closing if monthly deposits had been made since the previous payment of property taxes. Second, any additional "cushion" is limited to one-sixth of the estimated annual obligation (two additional monthly deposits). Thus, if a loan will be closed on September 1 and property taxes are paid on November 1, there would have been 10 monthly deposits from the last property tax payment up to the time of closing. So if estimated property taxes are $2,400, the lender would be allowed to require a deposit at closing in the amount of $2,000 (10 × $200) plus a $400 "cushion," for a total of $2,400. The monthly escrow deposit is limited to one-twelfth of the estimated annual obligation. So the maximum monthly deposit for property taxes would be $200. While RESPA does not require payment of interest on these escrow deposits, roughly one-third of states have laws that do require interest payment.

9.20　List five requirements of RESPA for a standard first mortgage home loan.

One of the most damaging developments in home mortgage lending in recent years was predatory lending. It prompted the Congress to enact HOEPA, however ineffective it was. Enormously amplified by the explosion of subprime and Alt A lending, described in Chapter 11, abusive home mortgage loans appear to have taken a very heavy toll in our society in the first decade of the new century. We can hope that the creation of the Consumer Financial Protection Bureau will go far to prevent another epidemic of predatory lending, but it is unlikely that the disease is eradicated. So, from a variety of industry and government reports, here are the symptoms to guard against:

The Bad Old Days of Predatory Lending

- *Financing excess fees into loans.* Borrowers were routinely charged fees of just under 8 percent of the loan amount, compared to the average 1 to 2 percent assessed by banks to originate loans.
- *Charging higher interest rates than a borrower's credit warrants.* Borrowers with perfect credit were often charged interest rates 3 to 6 percentage points higher than the market rates.
- *Making loans without regard to the borrower's ability to pay.* Some predatory lenders made loans on a home-owner's equity, even when homeowners clearly would not be able to afford their payments. . . .
- *Prepayment penalties.* Over two-thirds of subprime loans reportedly had prepayment penalties, compared to less than 2 percent of normal prime loans—often as much as six months' interest.
- *Loans in excess of 100 percent of value.* Some lenders regularly made loans for more than a borrower's home is worth with the intent of trapping them as customers for an extended period.
- *Home improvement scams.* Some home improvement contractors targeted lower-income neighborhoods where owners were unable to pay for needed repairs. The contractor, in collusion with a predatory lender, pressures the owner into financing the work.
- *Single premium credit insurance.* Credit insurance pays off a particular debt if the borrower cannot pay because of sickness, death, or loss of job. Rarely promoted in the "A" lending world, it has been aggressively and deceptively sold in "single premium" form in connection with higher cost loans, and then financed into the home loans.
- *Negative amortization.* Predatory lenders used negative amortization to sell the borrower on the low payment, without revealing that the principal will rise rather than fall.
- *Loan flipping.* Some lenders intentionally started borrowers with a loan at a higher interest rate, so that the lender could then refinance the loan to a slightly lower rate and charge additional fees to the borrower.
- *Aggressive and deceptive marketing—the use of live checks in the mail.* One of the methods used routinely and successfully by predatory lenders was the practice of sending "live checks" in the mail to target homeowners. The checks were usually for several thousand dollars and the cashing or depositing of the check bound the borrower to a loan agreement with the lender.

Source: Data from www.treasury.gov/press-center/press-releases/Documents/treasrpt.pdf

---

Home Ownership and Equity Protection Act

www.consumerfinance .gov

Website of the Consumer Financial Protection Bureau.

In 1994 Congress enacted the **Home Ownership and Equity Protection Act (HOEPA).** This law was passed out of concern for abusive, predatory practices in subprime lending—that is, in lending to homebuyers with limited financial knowledge and inability to qualify for standard mortgage financing. About all that can be said for HOEPA is that in its first dozen years it was woefully ineffective in limiting the abuse it was intended to control. Now under the umbrella of the CFPB (see below), one hopes it will accomplish more. (See Industry Issues 9-2.)

The Dodd-Frank Wall Street Reform and Consumer Protection Act of 2010

The **Dodd-Frank Wall Street Reform and Consumer Protection Act** is impacting home mortgage lending on at least two fronts. First, it is altering the character of home loans by imposing a standard of "ability to repay" and by rewarding an even stronger standard called Qualified Mortgages. (We discuss both in the next two chapters.) These two steps should significantly curtail the kinds of loans most prone to default during the Great Recession.

The second action of "Dodd-Frank" was to drastically alter regulation of home mortgage lending by creating the **Consumer Financial Protection Bureau (CFPB).**

Previously this regulation was balkanized into a host of federal and state authorities. But now the CFPB has been given responsibility to oversee and enforce federal consumer financial protection laws; enforce antidiscrimination laws in consumer finance; restrict unfair, deceptive, or abusive acts or practices; receive consumer complaints; promote financial education; and watch for emerging financial risks for consumers. This mandate gives the CFPB control over all of the previous laws discussed and integrates, for the first time, the federal regulation of home mortgage lending into one authority. A first undertaking of CFPB was to redesign documents central to home mortgage closings. (We present the new documents in Chapter 13.) The CFPB mortgage website (see left margin) takes you to a wide range of consumer assistance information, including two very helpful summary documents on borrower protections.

Other Laws Regulating Discrimination in Home Mortgage Lending

Additional laws have been created that affect the practice of home mortgage lending at a community or neighborhood level. Through the **Home Mortgage Disclosure Act (HMDA)** of 1975 and the **Community Reinvestment Act (CRA)** of 1977 Congress has required home mortgage lenders to maintain a record of home loans granted and home loans denied by applicant income level, neighborhood income level, loan purpose (e.g., investment, home improvement, refinancings), applicant gender, and neighborhood area (e.g., census tract). The latter is to address the issue of **redlining** where lenders may tend to avoid certain neighborhoods without regard to the merits of the individual loan applications. This record is publicly available and frequently has been used to exert public pressure on banks, credit unions, and savings associations for more equitable community lending. It has been particularly prominent as a consideration in the evaluation of merger applications by banks and other financial institutions.

Summary

A mortgage loan involves two contracts: a note and a mortgage. The note specifies details of the financial obligation, while the mortgage conveys to the lender an interest in the property as security for the debt. The borrower is the mortgagor, who conveys the security interest to the recipient lender, the mortgagee.

Mortgage clauses important to a borrower include the due-on-sale clause and the escrow clause. The escrow clause allows the lender to collect monthly deposits for property taxes, hazard insurance, and other recurring owner obligations. Rights of prepayment for a mortgage loan differ by state and type of property. Under the common law tradition, a mortgagor had no right of prepayment unless it was explicitly granted in the mortgage. It is common today, however, for state statutes to give the right to prepay unless it is explicitly prohibited in the loan. Most standard home loans allow prepayment, but most commercial mortgage loans impose severe penalties for prepayment.

Adjustable rate mortgages are more complex than fixed rate. The ARM borrower needs to be aware of teaser rates, index rate, margin, caps, and change date. When a borrower defaults on a loan, the lender may pursue foreclosure, but first may try less drastic strategies ranging from credit counseling to accepting a deed in lieu of foreclosure. Foreclosure terminates other claims to the security property in order to sell it to recover the debt. The lender is very sensitive to lien priorities because they affect the value of the lender's *security position.* Numerous aspects of state law affect the cost and effectiveness of foreclosure, including the equity of redemption, the statutory right of redemption, and whether the state provides for judicial foreclosure or power of sale. Bankruptcy can jeopardize a lender's ability to foreclose on a loan, particularly if it leads to a court-supervised workout.

The buyers of real property can secure financing through a contract for deed instead of a mortgage. The contract for deed provides for transfer of possession to a buyer, but delays transfer of title until a schedule of installment payments is largely completed.

The home mortgage lending process is heavily regulated. The Truth-in-Lending Act requires disclosure of the annual percentage rate (APR) and numerous disclosures about late fees, prepayment penalties, and other matters. The Equal Credit Opportunity Act (ECOA) prohibits unequal treatment in mortgage lending on the basis of race, color, religion, national origin, sex, marital status, age, familial status, disability, or because all or part of an applicant's income derives from a public assistance program. The Real Estate Settlement Procedures Act (RESPA) requires numerous disclosures for most standard home mortgage originations, and requires the use of a standard closing statement, the Closing Disclosure Form. It also prohibits kickbacks from vendors of services provided in connection with the loan and sale.

The Home Ownership and Equity Protection Act (HOEPA) seeks to curtail abusive practices in the origination of subprime loans. Finally, the Home Mortgage Disclosure Act (HMDA) and the Community Reinvestment Act (CRA) establish public monitoring of potential discriminatory lending. The Dodd-Frank Wall Street Reform and Consumer Protection Act centralized regulation and oversight of home mortgage lending under the Consumer Financial Protection Bureau.

Key Terms

Test Problems

Answer the following multiple-choice problems:

1. The element of an adjustable interest rate that is the "moving part" is the:
   a. Teaser rate.
   b. Index.
   c. Margin.
   d. Adjustment period.
   e. None of these.

2. Which of these aspects of a mortgage loan will be addressed in the note rather than in the mortgage?
   a. Late fee.
   b. Escrow requirement.
   c. Takings.
   d. Acceleration.
   e. Maintenance of property.

3. A lender may reserve the right to require prepayment of a loan at any time they see fit through a(n):
   a. Taking clause.
   b. Acceleration clause.
   c. Demand clause.
   d. Due-on-sale clause.
   e. Escrow clause.

4. When a buyer of a property with an existing mortgage loan acquires the property without signing the note for the existing loan, the buyer is acquiring the property:
   a. By assumption.
   b. By contract for deed.
   c. By deed of trust.
   d. By default.
   e. Subject to the mortgage.

5. Which of these points in a mortgage loan would be addressed in the mortgage (possibly in the note as well)?
   a. Loan amount.
   b. Interest rate.
   c. Late fees.
   d. Escrows.
   e. Loan term.

6. To finance purchase of a property where the borrower, the property, or both fail to qualify for standard mortgage financing, a traditional *nonmortgage* solution is through the:
   a. Subprime loan.
   b. Deed of trust.
   c. Unsecured loan.
   d. Contract for deed.
   e. Balloon loan.

7. Ways that a lender may respond to a defaulted loan without resorting to foreclosure include all of the following *except:*
   a. Offer credit counseling.
   b. Allow short sale to a third party.
   c. Defer or forgive some of the past-due payments.
   d. Accelerate the debt.
   e. Accept a deed in lieu of foreclosure.

8. If the lender in a standard first mortgage wishes to foreclose cost effectively, it is crucial to have which clause in the mortgage?
   a. Acceleration clause.
   b. Exculpatory clause.
   c. Demand clause.

   d. Defeasance clause.
   e. Taking clause.

9. A common risk that frequently interferes with a lender's efforts to work out a defaulted loan through either nonforeclosure means or foreclosure is:
   a. Equity of redemption.
   b. Statutory right of redemption.
   c. Exculpatory clauses.
   d. Bankruptcy.
   e. Deficiency judgment.

10. The characteristics of a borrower that can be considered by a lender in a mortgage loan application are limited by the:
    a. Truth-in-Lending Act.
    b. Real Estate Settlement Procedures Act.
    c. Equal Credit Opportunity Act.
    d. Home Ownership and Equity Protection Act.
    e. Community Reinvestment Act.

11. The Real Estate Settlement Procedures Act does which of these:
    a. Requires the use of a standard settlement statement for a mortgage loan closing.
    b. Prohibits kickbacks between vendors of closing-related services and lenders.
    c. Requires that a borrower receive a good-faith estimate of closing costs shortly after a loan application.
    d. Requires that the borrower be able to inspect the closing statement a day before the actual closing.
    e. All of the above.

12. Foreclosure tends to be quickest in states that:
    a. Are title theory states.
    b. Are lien theory states.
    c. Have judicial foreclosure.
    d. Have power of sale.
    e. Have statutory redemption.

13. From a home mortgage lender's perspective, which statement is true about the effect of bankruptcy upon foreclosure?
    a. Chapter 7 bankruptcy is the most "lender friendly" form.
    b. Chapter 11 bankruptcy is the most "lender friendly" form.
    c. Chapter 13 bankruptcy is the most "lender friendly" form.
    d. All forms of bankruptcy are equally devastating to a lender's efforts to foreclose.
    e. No form of bankruptcy causes serious problems for a lender seeking to foreclose a mortgage.

14. The most internationally oriented index rate for adjustable rate mortgages is:
    a. Federal Home Loan Bank cost-of-funds index.
    b. Treasury constant maturity rate.
    c. A LIBOR rate.
    d. A home mortgage loan interest rate index.
    e. *The Wall Street Journal* prime rate.

15. A type of loan that occurred in recent years, which raised concerns about predatory lending practices, was the:
    a. Adjustable rate mortgage.
    b. Contract for deed.
    c. Purchase money mortgage.

   d. Subprime mortgage.
   e. Power of sale mortgage.
16. A partially amortizing loan always will have:
   a. Caps.
   b. Only one stated term.
   c. A balloon payment.
   d. A prepayment penalty.
   e. Recourse.
17. Which of these statements is true about mortgage loans for income-producing real estate?
   a. They usually are partially amortizing loans.
   b. They often have a prepayment penalty.
   c. They often are nonrecourse loans.
   d. They can be interest-only loans.
   e. All of the above.
18. With what type of loan security arrangement is the deed held by a neutral third party and returned upon payment of the mortgage in full?
   a. Contract for deed.
   b. Mortgage.
   c. Deed of trust.
   d. Nonrecourse loan.
   e. Recourse loan.

19. The Truth-in-Lending Act gives some mortgage borrowers how long to rescind a mortgage loan?
   a. 24 hours.
   b. Two days.
   c. Three days.
   d. A week.
   e. A month.
20. Which statement is correct about the right of prepayment of a home mortgage loan?
   a. All home mortgage loans have the right of prepayment without charge.
   b. Most home mortgage loans have the right of prepayment without charge, but not all, and the borrower should check the loan carefully.
   c. Home mortgage loans give the right of prepayment without charge only in some states.
   d. Home mortgage loans never have the right of prepayment without charge unless it is explicitly stated.
   e. Home mortgage loans never have the right of prepayment without charge.

Study Questions

1. Mortgage law is as clear, consistent, and enforceable in the United States as in any place in the world, and far more so than in many countries. Why is this a vital element of an efficient real estate finance system?
2. The Congress has adopted changes in bankruptcy law that make Chapter 7 bankruptcy more difficult for households, requiring greater use of Chapter 13, thus providing greater protection to unsecured credit card companies. As a mortgage lender, do you care about this? If so, what would be your position?
3. Residential mortgage terms and rates have become increasingly uniform as the mortgage market has become more national and efficient. Is there any downside to this for the homeowner?
4. Most lenders making adjustable rate mortgage (ARM) loans offer a "teaser rate." Is this a good policy or is it misrepresentation?
5. Home mortgage lending is heavily regulated by federal laws. Is this a result of congressional pandering to consumer groups, or are there good reasons why home mortgage lending should be regulated more than, say, automobile financing?
6. For your own state, determine whether:
   a. It is a judicial or nonjudicial foreclosure state.
   b. The standard home loan is based on a deed of trust or a mortgage.
   c. There is a statutory right of redemption and, if so, how long.
   d. Deficiency judgments are allowed against defaulted homeowners.
   Based on this information, can you judge whether your state is relatively lender friendly or borrower friendly? For this exercise use the websites noted in the text.
7. Download one mortgage and one deed of trust from the Freddie Mac website (see Explore the Web). Compare them to see what differences you can find in their clauses.

EXPLORE THE WEB

Go to the Freddie Mac website (www.freddiemac.com). In the drop-down menu (upper left), select *Single-Family*. There, select *The Guide and Forms*. Then, in the middle of the page, select *Uniform Instruments*.

1. Scroll down to *Security Instruments*. There, under First Lien Security Instruments, you see a mortgage or deed of trust for each state. Select and download the security instrument for the state of your choice. Answer these questions:

   a. How many states have deeds of trust rather than mortgages?
   b. In your chosen security instrument, what circumstances will a lender not enforce a due-on-sale clause? (Usually section 18.)
   c. What actions must a borrower take to reinstate the loan in good standing after acceleration? (Usually section 19.)
   d. Can a borrower store any toxic or hazardous substances on the mortgaged property? (Usually section 21.)
   e. What points must a lender cover in a notice of acceleration? (Usually section 22.)

EXPLORE THE WEB—CONTINUED

2. Find and download a one-year Treasury adjustable rate residential mortgage note form appropriate to your state.

   a. What is the index rate?
   b. How is the adjustment computed?
   c. What is the periodic cap?
   d. Does it apply to both increases and decreases?
   e. Does the cap apply to the first interest rate change?
   f. What must a buyer of the property do to have the loan continue after purchase?

Solutions to Concept Checks

1. A borrower always conveys a mortgage and a note to the lender in a mortgage loan.
2. The monthly interest rate for an annual interest rate of 12 percent is 1 percent.
3. The U.S. Treasury constant maturity rate, the cost of funds index rate, the commercial bank "prime rate," the mortgage loan index rate, and the LIBOR rate are all sources for index interest rates for adjustable interest rates.
4. The two most common types of caps in an adjustable rate mortgage are periodic caps and overall caps.
5. A loan balance with negative amortization will increase because the scheduled payment is insufficient to cover the accumulated interest.
6. A balloon loan has an amortization term that determines interest and principal payments as if it were a fully amortized loan and a shorter term for maturity at which the remaining loan balance must be paid in full.
7. Prepayment penalties occur mainly in large home loans, subprime loans, and commercial mortgage loans.
8. A demand clause permits a lender, from time to time, to demand prepayment of the loan.
9. The mortgage lender wants to be able to pay the property taxes on behalf of the borrower because the property tax lien is superior to the mortgage and can preempt it in default.
10. FHA and VA loans are assumable, subject to the buyer's ability to qualify for the loan.
11. In practice, lenders commonly define default as occurring when a loan is 90 days overdue.
12. Lenders may be ill-advised to accept a deed in lieu of foreclosure because liens may remain with the property even after it is conveyed back to the lender. Also, if the borrower claims bankruptcy, the lender may ultimately lose its priority claim to the property.
13. Property taxes, property assessments, community development district obligations, and previous mortgages have priority over the mortgage of a lender.
14. Depending on the state, the process of foreclosure sale is either by judicial foreclosure or by power of sale. The method most favorable to a lender is power of sale.
15. Chapter 7 bankruptcy is the least harmful type of bankruptcy to a lender's mortgage interest.
16. When a purchaser of mortgaged real estate accepts personal liability for an existing mortgage loan on a property, the borrower is said to assume the loan.
17. A sale by contract for deed differs from a normal real estate sale in that the actual delivery of the deed conveying ownership will not occur until well after the buyer takes possession of the property. This allows the seller to finance the sale through installment payments and to have recourse in case of default.
18. The Equal Credit Opportunity Act prohibits discrimination in lending by race, sex, religion, and national origin. It also prohibits discrimination because an applicant receives income from a public assistance program.
19. Under the Truth-in-Lending Act, some borrowers have three days to rescind a non-purchase mortgage loan agreement.
20. Five requirements of the Real Estate Settlement Procedures Act (RESPA) for a standard home mortgage loan are (1) a standard format closing statement Closing Disclosure, (2) presentation of a document explaining closing fees and the Closing Disclosure, (3) good-faith estimate of closing costs, to be provided within three business days of the loan application, (4) opportunity to examine the Closing Disclosure at least three days in advance of the loan closing, and (5) prohibition of kickbacks and referral fees between the lender and providers of services in connection with the loan closing.

Additional Readings

Aalberts Robert J. *Real Estate Law,* 9th ed. Stamford, CT: Cengage Learning, 2015.

Brueggeman, William B., and Jeffrey B. Fisher. *Real Estate Finance and Investments,* 15th ed. New York: McGraw-Hill/Irwin, 2016.

Geltner, David M., Norman G. Miller, Jim Clayton, and Piet Eichholz. *Commercial Real Estate Analysis and Investments,* 3rd ed. Mason, OH: OnCourse Learning, 2014.

Jennings, Marianne. *Real Estate Law,* 10th ed. Stamford, CT: Cengage Learning, 2014.

The Mortgage Bankers Association of America, www.mbaa.org. See this site for information about current regulatory issues in home mortgage lending.

Chapter 10

Residential Mortgage Types *and* Borrower Decisions

LEARNING OBJECTIVES

After reading this chapter you will be able to:

1   List two secondary mortgage market institutions and four types of primary mortgage market lenders, and state two effects of the secondary mortgage market upon home mortgage lending.

2   State the distinguishing characteristics of conventional loans, conforming and nonconforming conventional loans, and "jumbo" conventional loans.

3   Define private mortgage insurance, state what it accomplishes, and why it is important to borrowers.

4   State the special purposes served by purchase-money mortgages, package mortgages, and reverse mortgages, and name two borrower advantages of a home equity credit line mortgage over unsecured consumer loans.

5   Determine whether refinancing is financially desirable given the terms and amount of an existing loan, the terms of a new loan, the expected life of the existing loan, and the costs of refinancing.

6   State two factors that commonly influence the likelihood that a home borrower will default on a home mortgage loan.

OUTLINE

Introduction

Most people dream of owning a home. But it is the largest single purchase they will ever make, and they usually must borrow the necessary funds. Therefore, a system of mortgage lending has developed in which people with excess funds lend them to people who need money to buy houses. With mortgage credit available, households can purchase homes now and pay for them, with interest, over 10, 20, or 30 years.

Even many households that could put more cash into a home purchase choose to borrow instead because the interest rates and terms of mortgage borrowing are so favorable. They can put the funds from the mortgage borrowing to a variety of uses more productive than the cost of the resulting mortgage debt. This strategy, discussed in Chapter 16, is known as *positive financial leverage.* The use of borrowed funds also allows households to better diversify their portfolios of investments. If home purchasers needed to pay all cash, many household portfolios would be even more overweighted in housing than they are currently. For these reasons—lack of funds, the possibility of positive financial leverage, and a better diversified portfolio—most homebuyers borrow at least a portion of the needed funds.[1]

This chapter introduces the various types and forms of mortgage loans commonly available to homeowners and the types of decisions to be made about them. In addition to selecting a mortgage type and form, homeowners must evaluate the various costs associated with the loan and their desired loan-to-value (LTV) ratio or leverage. After obtaining the mortgage funds, borrowers usually have the option to refinance the mortgage, as well as the option to default. Good decisions regarding the financing of real estate can improve the value of the property, and add to the owner's wealth. This chapter demonstrates effective approaches to these numerous borrower decisions.

The many types and forms of available residential loans can be thought of as the **mortgage menu.** What determines the items on a lender's mortgage menu? Similar to restaurant food and other consumer products, lenders in the highly competitive residential mortgage market offer only those mortgage products for which there is a profitable market. In recent years residential lenders across the United States have added many different products to their mortgage menus. The majority of these added mortgage products have been dropped, either because borrowers did not "order" them or because lenders could not profit sufficiently by offering them. For example, U.S. housing economists have long argued that payments on residential mortgages should be tied (i.e., indexed) to inflation. However, despite the sound economic rationale for indexed mortgages and the willingness of numerous lenders to originate them, they have never caught on with borrowers and therefore remain absent from lenders' mortgage menus.

The Primary and Secondary Mortgage Markets

www.freddiemac.com
www.fanniemae.com

The two entities, Freddie Mac and Fannie Mae, that are the foundation of the modern secondary mortgage market.

The market for home mortgage loans can be divided into the primary mortgage market and the secondary mortgage market. The **primary mortgage market** is the loan origination market, in which borrowers and lenders come together. Numerous institutions supply money to borrowers in the primary mortgage market, including savings and loan associations, commercial banks, credit unions, and mortgage banking companies. Increasingly, this lending has been done through a mortgage broker. These direct sources of home mortgage funds are discussed in detail in Chapter 11.

Mortgage originators can either hold the loans in their portfolios or sell them in the **secondary mortgage market**. The largest purchasers of residential mortgages in the secondary mortgage market are **Fannie Mae and Freddie Mac.** These **government-sponsored enterprises (GSEs),** also discussed in Chapter 11, were created by acts of Congress to promote an active secondary market for home mortgages by purchasing mortgages from

---

1. The American Housing Survey of the U.S. Bureau of Census indicates, in 2013, that the total loan-to-value ratio for owner occupied homes averaged 70 percent. However, 36 percent of owner occupied residences had no debt at all (2013 Housing Profile: United States, American Housing Survey Factsheets, May 2015 (AHS/13-1)).

local originators.[2] The existence of a well-functioning secondary market makes the primary mortgage market more efficient. Mortgage originators are able to sell their mortgage investments quickly and obtain funds to originate more loans in the primary market. The GSEs have played a leading role in this process. In fact, the menu of loans that the GSEs are willing to buy has heavily influenced the menu of loans that lenders are willing to originate. However, since 2007 Fannie Mae, Freddie Mac, and the character of the mortgage secondary market have seen drastic change. We will recount the dramatic events and transitions in Chapter 11.

✓ **Concept Check**

10.1 The difference between the mortgage primary market and secondary market is _____.

Prime Conventional Mortgage Loans

The most common type of home loan is a **conventional mortgage loan.** This refers to any standard home loan that is not insured or guaranteed by an agency of the U.S. government.[3] Thus, it includes all standard home loans except those known as FHA (Federal Housing Administration) and VA (Veterans Affairs) loans, which we discuss later in this chapter. In recent years there have been two polar types of conventional home loans: prime and subprime, with an intermediate group of loans known as "alt-A." We will first discuss the prime conventional loans, which one might think of as the classical type home mortgage loan. Once we have examined the history, features, and practice with prime loans, we will be able to contrast these with the other types. Prime conventional home loans preceded FHA and VA loans historically, but, as we will observe later, derived their modern form from the influence of these "government" mortgages.

✓ **Concept Check**

10.2 What is a conventional home mortgage loan?

Google Housing Finance at a Glance: a Monthly Chartbook.

This is a new, unprecedented compilation of housing and housing finance data produced monthly by the Urban Institute.

Forms of Prime Conventional Mortgages

The predominant form of prime conventional mortgage remains the (fixed-rate) level-payment mortgage (LPM). For example, in the first three-quarters of 2016 something over 90 percent of all conventional loans appear to have been fixed-rate LPMs.[4] The fixed-rate conventional home loan has evolved dramatically in its forms twice in modern history. The first time was the 1940s, a decade that saw the birth of the LPM, though on much more limited terms than today. The evolution of the conventional LPM was enormously accelerated following World War II by the birth of private mortgage insurance (PMI), discussed below. Only after the introduction of PMI did lenders view it feasible to offer conventional LPMs for maturities much longer than 15 years, or for loan-to-value ratios exceeding 80 percent.

---

2. We will refer to Fannie Mae and Freddie Mac as "GSEs," though in September of 2008 they were placed under U.S. government conservatorship and may transition to a new form in the future.

3. By standard home loan we refer to loans from such "third-party" lenders as banks, savings and loan associations, credit unions, mortgage bankers, or brokers arranging similar mortgages. This excludes purchase money mortgages between seller and buyer, or similar personal loans.

4. "Housing Finance at a Glance: A Monthly Chartbook," January 2016. Housing Policy Group, Urban Institute. Washington, DC.

In the new millennium the once conservative residential finance industry became a swirl of new kinds of mortgages, touted to hopeful homebuyers as the "easy" solution to getting the home they wished they could afford. There were buy downs, and hybrids, and option-type ARMs. There were "Low-Docs" and "No-Docs" and I-O balloons. Then there were 100 percent HELOCs and skip-a-payment loans, and piggybacks and sponsorings for the down payment poor.

This loan party was hosted by glittering names like Countrywide, World Savings, Washington Mutual, IndyMac, and Wells Fargo, all apparently bent on demonstrating what competitive capitalism really meant. And the effect was dramatic! Though house prices soared, so did home ownership, to the highest level on modern record, pushing 70 percent. But innovativeness and competitiveness did not assure a successful business or a successful result, at least to the firm and community. While individuals may have profited richly from this housing and mortgage party, at the larger level, it became a drag. The party was fueled by uninterrupted home appreciation. When unsustainable appreciation began to sag, the results became painfully evident to the partiers, and then to everyone else who had to fear for their job.

So what of these party hosts and their party favor mortgages? Of the top 20 I-O and option ARM lenders in the nation in 2006, 8 survived to 2012, 7 by 2015. The remainder have disappeared involuntarily through forced sale, bankruptcy, or closure by FDIC. Four of the top five have disappeared, including Countrywide, WaMu, Wachovia/World Savings, and IndyMac.

What of the "party" mortgages? Several of these "innovations" may have been "born to abuse," such as the option ARM and the "No-Doc" (no documentation loan), I-O balloons (interest-only with balloon payment), and the 100 percent (or more) HELOC (home equity line of credit). But many of the others, including I-O reset (interest-only with option to refinance), the piggyback (pairing a small second mortgage with a maximum 80 percent LTV first mortgage to avoid required mortgage insurance), and the hybrid (initially a fixed interest rate, then changing to an ARM), if used prudently, are useful additions to the tools of residential real estate finance. We examine most of them in this chapter. In time, after the partiers recover, some of the party favors actually will be worth keeping.

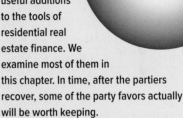

The Party Has Ended

A second important period of change in the conventional home loan is the post-2000 years. The dramatic changes in the structure of home lending, including rapid concentration of the industry and the growing strength and influence of Fannie Mae and Freddie Mac, brought about a dazzling evolution in the variety of conventional home loans being offered, particularly for groups in our society with special home financing needs. (See Industry Issues 10-1.) So, while the 80 to 90 percent loan-to-value, 30-year LPM remains the predominant form of conventional loan, there was rapid growth in alternatives. We discuss several of these new forms later in the chapter. Sadly, as we detail more in Chapter 11, along with this rapid growth of alternative mortgages came the growth of reckless lending processes and securitization processes that brought very bad outcomes for many homes, for the well-being of many households, and for our economy.

An important distinction among prime conventional mortgage loans is the difference between conforming and nonconforming. A **conforming conventional loan** is one that meets the standards required for purchase by Fannie Mae or Freddie Mac. Although both of these government-sponsored enterprises (GSEs) were privately owned and issued stock, they remained subject to government oversight, and Congress sets the maximum size of home mortgages they can purchase from originating lenders. To conform to the underwriting standards of the GSEs, a loan must use standard GSE documentation, including the application form, mortgage note, and appraisal form. It must not exceed a certain percentage of the property's value, monthly payments on the loan must not exceed a certain percentage of the borrower's income, and the loan must not exceed starting in 2017 at $424,100 on single-family homes in most localities.[5] Loans that fail one or more of these underwriting standards are termed **nonconforming conventional loans**. Loans that generally conform, but exceed the dollar limit, are called **jumbo loans.** Jumbo loans have averaged almost a

www.freddiemac.com/ singlefamily/mortgages/

Provides links to over 40 different types of home mortgages purchased by Freddie Mac.

www.fanniemae.com/ singlefamily/ mortgage-products

A similar set of links to the types of mortgages that Fannie Mae purchases.

---

5. The limits increased annually until 2006, and can change again in the future. Higher dollar limits apply in Alaska, Hawaii, Guam, and the U.S. Virgin Islands. High-cost limits up to fifty percent above the standard limit apply in localities with high house prices. The current limits are available from the websites of Fannie Mae and Freddie Mac.

248

www.fhfa.gov/DataTools/
Downloads/Pages/
Conforming-Loan-Limits
.aspx

"GSE" loan limits for every county in
the United States.

fifth of total single-family mortgage originations since 1990.[6] Because conforming loans can be much more readily bought and sold in the secondary mortgage market (i.e., they are more liquid), they carry a lower contract interest rate than otherwise comparable nonconforming loans. Over the last several years, this interest rate advantage averaged approximately 0.25 percentage points. However, following disruptions in the non-GSE secondary mortgage market about mid-2007, this spread increased to over 1.50 percentage points. Thus, on a $500,000 loan, this could translate into monthly payments that are larger by as much as $625. In addition, quoted rates and fees on nonconforming loans are much less uniform from lender to lender and region to region.

Adjustable Rate Mortgages

Especially important in the evolution of conventional loans was the rise of the adjustable rate mortgage (ARM). Fixed-rate, level-payment mortgages serve lenders and borrowers well when mortgage interest rates are relatively low and stable. Unfortunately, during the late 1970s and early 1980s, interest rates on LPMs increased dramatically, averaging 14.4 percent from 1979 through 1982. Beginning in the mid-1970s, mortgage rates also became more volatile (i.e., less predictable). This increase in the level and volatility of mortgage rates caused two major problems. First, the higher required monthly payments on a LPM made housing less affordable. Second, the increased volatility of mortgage rates made lenders nervous. Why? Savings and loans (S&Ls) and other depository institutions were in the business of making long-term LPMs using short-term deposits and savings. When interest rates, both short term and long term, accelerated in the late 1970s and early 1980s, the average spread that many LPM lenders were earning on their fixed-rate mortgage investments actually became *negative*. As related in Chapter 11, this negative spread contributed to the eventual failure of many S&Ls.

> ✓ **Concept Check**
>
> **10.3** What were three major events in the evolution of conventional mortgages since the 1930s?

In financial management terms, funding long-term LPMs with short-term deposits and savings creates a severe **maturity imbalance problem** for depository institutions because their assets (e.g., mortgages) are very long term, whereas their liabilities (e.g., savings deposits and certificates of deposit) are short term. To address the maturity imbalance problem and to avoid or reduce their exposure to the interest rate risk associated with making LPMs, many lenders began searching for alternatives to the LPM. For depository lenders, the most compelling alternative home mortgage is the *adjustable rate mortgage (ARM)*. Not only has it become a core product for their business, but ARMs have evolved significantly in recent years to make them more attractive to home borrowers, as we discuss later in the chapter. (Again, see Industry Issues 10-1.)

Private Mortgage Insurance

Private mortgage insurance (PMI) protects a lender against losses due to default on the loan. It gives no other protection; that is, it does not protect against legal threat to the lender's mortgage claim, nor does it protect against physical hazards. It indemnifies the lender, but not the borrower. Lenders generally require private mortgage insurance for conventional loans over 80 percent of the value of the security property. Private mortgage insurance companies provide such insurance, which usually covers the top 25 to 35 percent of loans. In other words, if a borrower defaults and the property is foreclosed and sold for

www.mgic.com

Website of the original mortgage
insurance company. Contains
extensive information on programs
and pricing.

6. Federal Housing Finance Agency: Originations of Single-Family Mortgages, 1990–2011 Q2, page 14, "Mortgage Market Statistical Annual—2015 Yearbook," Inside Mortgage Finance Publications, Inc., Bethesda, MD.

less than the amount of the loan, the PMI will reimburse the lender for a loss up to the stated percentage of the loan amount. Thus, the net effect of PMI from the lender's perspective is to reduce default risk.[7] This reduction of default risk was sufficient to make LPMs a viable risk for lenders where they had never been before.

✓ Concept Check

10.4   Whom does private mortgage insurance protect? Against what?

EXAMPLE 10-1   HOW PMI WORKS

Assume a borrower purchased a $200,000 home with 5 percent cash and a $190,000 loan. The initial LTV ratio is quite high (95 percent), so mortgage insurance is required. We will assume it covers $57,000—30 percent of the loan. Suppose the borrower defaults after the loan has been paid down to $188,000. Suppose further the market value of the property falls and the property is sold for $180,000. The lender then looks to the mortgage insurer for compensation for the $8,000 loss.

Mortgage insurance companies have generally followed the practice of reimbursing the lender in full should a foreclosure become necessary. In this example, this option provides a zero net loss for the lender and an $8,000 loss for the insurance company. The outcomes of this option are summarized as follows:

Lender's position:

Payment from insurer	$188,000
Loss of mortgage asset	(188,000)
Net loss	$0

Insurance company position:

Takes ownership of property	$180,000
Pays remaining balance to lender	(188,000)
Net loss	$(8,000)[8]

✓ Concept Check

10.5   Lenders usually require mortgage insurance for loans in excess of_____.

Typical Terms of Private Mortgage Insurance.   Premiums on PMI can be paid by the borrower in a lump sum at the time of loan origination or in monthly installments added to the mortgage interest rate. For example, a one-time premium equal to 2.5 percent of the loan amount may be required at closing. For our example, this would mean a premium payment at closing of $4,750 (0.025 × $190,000). Alternatively, a monthly premium payment

---

7. Another type of insurance, sometimes confused with PMI, is mortgage life insurance. It provides for the continuing payment of the mortgage after the death of the insured borrower. This special form of life insurance enables the survivors of the deceased to continue living in the house. Mortgage life insurance has sometimes been criticized because it is no different, in substance, from other life insurance, but often has been relatively expensive.

8. The above discussion ignores the transaction costs that the insurer would incur in the process of taking title to a property and subsequently selling it in the open market. These costs increase the net loss associated with taking title to the property.

equal to, say, 0.0417 percent (0.5 percent annually) of the remaining loan balance may be included in the monthly mortgage payment and passed on by the lender to the insurance company. Thus, the first month's premium in our example would be $79.23 (0.000417 × $190,000). The premium would decline as the balance of the loan is amortized.

Mortgage insurance rates vary with the perceived riskiness of the loan: Higher loan-to-value ratio, longer loan term, and weaker credit record of the borrower all result in a higher mortgage insurance premium. Also premiums on loans for second homes or for investment property are higher than owner-occupied residences, while premiums on loans due to corporate relocation are lower. Finally, a "cash-out" refinancing loan (i.e., one that is larger than the loan it replaces) requires a higher insurance premium. These effects are readily apparent, for example, in the MGIC (Mortgage Guarantee Insurance Corporation) rate summaries found in the MGIC Web reference.

Cancellation of PMI coverage may be allowed if the borrower has a record of timely payments and the remaining loan balance is less than 80 percent of the *current* market value of the home. A new appraisal, paid for by the borrower, is typically required as proof of the increase in the value of the property. Under the Homeowners Protection Act of 1998, a borrower with a good payment record has the right to terminate PMI when the loan reaches 80 percent of the original value of the residence. The PMI company is *required* to terminate insurance when the loan reaches 78 percent of the original value of the residence.

Government-Sponsored Mortgage Programs

Housing experts have argued that inadequate housing production would occur if government policies and programs did not help middle- and lower-middle-income households finance the purchase of homes.[9] The quest for fairness in housing and mortgage finance markets is viewed as a legitimate and ongoing concern of governments, and was adopted as national policy of the United States in the National Housing Act of 1949.[10]

With some exceptions, the predominant approach to making better housing available has been through intervention in the private mortgage markets. This approach is thought to capitalize on the efficiencies of private industry in supplying the funds and managing the risks of the housing finance system.

Some government programs make loans directly to homebuyers in the primary market. Examples at the federal level include certain home loan programs of the United States Department of Agriculture's Rural Housing Services. In addition, state governments issue tax-exempt debt to support loans with below-market interest rates for first-time homebuyers. Many state and local housing agencies also offer low-interest loan programs to low- and moderate-income households. The most prominent national government-sponsored housing finance programs that operate in the primary market at the national level are the **Federal Housing Administration (FHA)** default insurance program and the **Veterans Affairs (VA)** program that provides guarantees on loans made by private lenders to qualified veterans.

✓ **Concept Check**

10.6   Name two government agencies that provide direct financing assistance to selected eligible households.

---

9. This view has come under question in recent years. The severe housing shortage that prevailed in the post-World War II years has evolved in more recent decades into an era of relative housing affluence, for *most* American households. See, for example, Dwight Jaffee, "How to Privatize the Mortgage Market," *The Wall Street Journal,* October 25, 2010.

10. Among the national goals expressed in the National Housing Act was "a decent home and a suitable living environment for every American family."

portal.hud.gov/hudportal/ HUD?src=/program_ offices/housing/sfh/ fharesourcectr

Main website of the Federal Housing Administration (FHA).

portal.hud.gov/ hudportal/HUD?src=/ federal_housing_ administration

A versatile starting point from which to probe questions about FHA loans.

FHA-Insured Loans

The FHA is a U.S. government agency that insures loans made by private lenders that meet FHA's property and credit-risk standards. The insurance is paid by the borrower and protects the FHA-approved lender against loss due to borrower default. Unlike private mortgage insurance, which protects the lender against only part of the loan loss, **FHA mortgage insurance** covers any lender loss. It then transfers title of the property to the U.S. Department of Housing and Urban Development (HUD) for public sale.

FHA targets loans to borrowers in slightly weaker financial circumstances than the typical prime conventional borrower, including first-time homebuyers and other households with moderate income. FHA allows a high loan-to-value ratio, requiring only that the borrower contribute 3.5 percent of the lesser of actual sale price or appraised value as a cash down payment for an owner-occupied residence. This is in contrast to 10 percent or more that typically is required for prime conventional loans. Similarly, FHA allows more tolerant qualifying debt-to-income ratios (discussed in Chapter 11) and slightly lower credit scores than are needed for prime conventional loans. Finally, FHA is more forgiving of past financial failures of loan applicants, generally requiring no more than two years (rather than four) to elapse after the borrower declares bankruptcy and three years (rather than up to seven) after the borrower goes through foreclosure.

The main limitations of FHA loans are their higher insurance premiums and limits on their maximum size. Higher premiums are a natural result of the higher risks that are accepted by FHA. It follows that borrowers presenting lower risk may find a conventional insured loan preferable. The loan limit, for most areas in the United States, is 65 percent of the loan limit for conforming conventional loans ($424,100 in 2017). As with limits on conforming conventional loans, the FHA limit is higher for higher cost areas. (The current loan limits for FHA and conforming conventional loans can be quickly found for any place in the United States at entp.hud.gov/idapp/html/hicostlook.cfm.)

FHA insurance requires two premiums: the UFMIP (upfront mortgage insurance premium) and the annual **mortgage insurance premium (MIP)**. As of January 2015, the UFMIP is 1.75 percent of the loan for normal loans used to purchase a personal residence. For example, on a 30-year, 6.0 percent loan of $150,000 the UFMIP would be $2,625. The UFMIP normally is financed, that is, included in the loan. Thus, for the example the total loan amount would be $152,625. The monthly payment on this loan would be $915.06, including $15.74 to cover the UFMIP.[11]

In addition to the UFMIP, the owner-occupant borrower normally will pay an annual MIP that depends on the loan-to-value ratio and the term of the loan. As of January 2015, for loans with maturity longer than 15 years, the MIP is 0.85 percent of the average annual loan balance if the loan is more than 95 percent of appraised value, and 0.80 percent if the loan is no more than 95 percent of appraised value. For loans of 15 years or less the MIP is 0.70 percent if the loan exceeds 90 percent of appraised value and 0.45 percent if the loan does not exceed 90 percent. This annual premium is based on the average outstanding balance of the loan during the year. The monthly premium payment is simply the annual premium divided by 12. Thus, for the example above, the first-year average loan balance is $151,775.27. So, assuming the appropriate annual premium is 0.85 percent, the first-year monthly premium would be $107.51 ($151,775.27 × 0.0085 ÷ 12). This premium decreases each year as the outstanding balance decreases.

✓ Concept Check

10.7 What is the upfront fee for FHA insurance? What is the MIP for a 30-year loan with a 97.5 percent LTV?

---

11. The calculator keystrokes are $N = 360$, $I = 6.0\% ÷ 12$, $PV = 152,625$, $PMT = ?$, and $FV = 0$.

The premiums are automatically canceled when the loan-to-original value reaches 78 percent.[12] In no case does this automatic cancelation of the MIP cause discontinuation of insurance coverage. FHA is required each year to advise the borrower of these cancelation provisions. The monthly premiums paid by borrowers are deposited by FHA into the Mutual Mortgage Insurance Fund, which reimburses lenders in case of foreclosure. As with private mortgage insurance, FHA insurance increases the borrower's cost of the mortgage.[13]

> ✓ **Concept Check**
>
> **10.8** At a certain loan-to-value ratio, PMI must be canceled by the provider. For FHA insurance, MIP payments must be terminated. What is this "trigger" LTV ratio?

The FHA insures mortgages for various types of properties. Some of the programs, for example, insure loans for low-income housing, nursing homes, cooperative apartments, and condominiums. The most widely used FHA program insures single-family home mortgages and is authorized by Title II, Section 203(b) of the National Housing Act. Thus, the insured loans are often called **Section 203 loans.** FHA loans are available from a variety of lenders, including banks, savings and loan associations, mortgage companies, and credit unions. FHA insurance terms are in a state of historic transition. The reader will need to monitor FHA news to ascertain what additional changes may occur. (See HUD-FHA mortgagee letters, www.hud.gov/offices/adm/hudclips/letters/mortgagee/.)

Importance of the Federal Housing Administration. It would be hard to overstate the importance of the FHA in the history of housing finance. Before the FHA was established in 1934, the typical home loan was relatively short term (5 to 15 years) and required

EXAMPLE 10-2 DETERMINING THE AMOUNT OF AN FHA LOAN, THE UFMIP, THE MONTHLY PAYMENT, AND MIP

Consider the purchase of a house with an appraised value of $200,000, an actual sale price of $203,000, and loan terms of 30 years at 6.0 percent. We need to know how much can be borrowed in total, and what portion of that must go to pay the UFMIP. The maximum FHA loan, excluding the UFMIP, cannot be greater than 96.5 percent of $200,000, or $193,000. Find the loan amount, loan payment, and MIP premiums as follows:

$$\text{Base loan} = \$193,000\ ((1 - 0.035) \times \$200,000)$$

$$\text{UFMIP} = \$3,377.50\ (0.0175 \times 193,000)$$

$$\text{Total loan} = \$196,377.50\ (\$193,000 + \$3,377.50)$$

The payment on the $196,377.50 loan is $1,177.38. (See footnote 11 in this chapter for calculation method.)

The average balance on the loan during the first year is $195,284.15. Thus, the MIP is $138.33 ($195,284.15 × 0.0085 ÷ 12), and the total first-year monthly payment is $1,315.71 ($138.33 + $1,177.38).[14] (Note that the amount of the UFMIP will be paid to FHA, and is not available to pay the seller. Only the base loan amount is available to put toward the purchase.)

12. The 78 percent rule for cancelation is consistent with requirements of the Home Owner's Protection Act of 1998, which Congress enacted to limit excessive terms for PMI.
13. In Chapter 15 we show how to compute the exact effect of mortgage insurance on borrowing cost.
14. The reader familiar with past calculations for an FHA down payment will appreciate that the calculation has been simplified significantly.

principal repayment in full at the end of the term of the loan—that is, loans were nonamortizing. The FHA was organized to demonstrate the feasibility of home lending with long-term amortized loans through insurance protection for lenders. In short, the FHA program created the single most important financial instrument in modern U.S. housing finance, the level-payment, fully amortizing loan. Further, through its power to approve or deny loans, the FHA heavily influenced housing and subdivision design standards throughout the United States during the middle of the 20th century. Today, FHA mortgage insurance is still an important tool through which the federal government expands home ownership opportunities for first-time homebuyers and other borrowers who would not otherwise qualify for conventional loans at affordable terms. It continues to play a potentially important role in housing finance innovation with its nascent home equity conversion mortgage (HECM) program, discussed later in the chapter.

FHA's market presence faded beginning in the mid-1990s due to innovative competition from high loan-to-value prime conventional loans, and even more so, from subprime lenders. Its market share fell from around 15 percent in the early 1990s to barely 2 percent by 2006. However, with the collapse of subprime lending in 2007, FHA has emerged once again as a mainstay to residential finance in the United States. In 2015 it accounted for almost 23 percent of single-family mortgage loan originations.

> ✓ **Concept Check**
>
> **10.9** What was the greatest historic contribution of the FHA?

VA-Guaranteed Loans

www.benefits.va.gov/ homeloans

Main website for the VA home loan program.

The Department of Veterans Affairs (VA) is a cabinet-level government department whose purpose is to help veterans readjust to civilian life. **VA-guaranteed loans** help veterans obtain home mortgage loans with favorable terms for which they might not otherwise qualify. For a private lender making a loan to a qualified veteran, the VA guarantee protects against default loss up to a maximum percentage of the loan amount. This guarantee begins at 50 percent of the amount of the loan for loans up to $45,000 and declines in steps to 25 percent for loans in excess of $144,000.[15] Thus, for a loan of $144,000 the guarantee is $36,000. The maximum guarantee is specified as one-fourth of the maximum allowable loan purchased by Freddie Mac and Fannie Mae ($424,100 in 2017 for most localities of the United States). Since lenders are reluctant to have the guarantee be less than 25 percent of the loan amount, this effectively sets the maximum VA loan equal to the maximum current loan amount for the two GSEs.

www.benefits.va.gov/ homeloans/

Details for VA loans.

The VA will guarantee loans to eligible veterans up to 100 percent of a property's value. For this, the VA charges a funding fee that is a percentage of the loan, with the percentage based on the down payment and the service classification of the veteran.[16] The funding fee can be added to the loan amount but closing costs cannot be included in the amount of the loan. Since 2000 the VA has guaranteed about 275,000 home loans per year but has surged to nearly double that volume since 2013. In areas where eligible veterans cannot obtain loans from approved VA lenders, the VA can make direct loans to them.

---

15. Note that the guarantee is unrelated to the loan-to-value ratio. This maximum loss amount was effective beginning December 27, 2001.

16. For first-time loans with no down payment, the funding fee is 2.15 percent for veterans of active duty and 2.4 percent for those with Reserve or National Guard duty only. For loans with a down payment of 5 percent up to 10 percent, the funding fees are 1.5 percent and 1.75 percent, respectively. For loans with a down payment of 10 percent or greater, the funding fees are 1.25 percent and 1.5 percent, respectively. Fees are higher for repeat users. These fees were effective through at least September 30, 2016.

Mortgage Broker

A mortgage broker is an independent agent who specializes in the origination of residential and/or commercial mortgages. Mortgage brokers normally defer the actual funding and servicing of loans to capital sources who act as loan "wholesalers." Since the mid-1990s their role in home mortgage lending in the United States has grown explosively to where over 20,000 brokers were originating over half of all home mortgage loans by the time of the Great Recession.

A mortgage broker is an independent contractor working, on average, with 40 wholesale lenders at any one time. By combining professional expertise with direct access to hundreds of loan products, a broker provides consumers the most efficient and cost-effective method of offering suitable financing options tailored to the consumer's specific financial goals. The wholesale lender underwrites and funds the home loan, may service the loan payments, and ensures the loan's compliance with underwriting guidelines. The broker, on the other hand, originates the loan. A detailed application process, financial and creditworthiness investigation, and extensive disclosure requirements must be completed for a wholesale lender to evaluate a consumer's home loan request. The broker simplifies this process for the borrower and wholesale lender, counseling consumers on their loan package choices, and enabling them to select the right loan for their homebuying needs.

Mortgage brokers have a national industry association, NAMB The Association of Mortgage Professionals (www.namb.org). An important service of NAMB is to provide information and training relating to the complex laws and regulations pertinent to home mortgage lending. The association provides two certifications for members: Certified Mortgage Consultant and Certified Residential Mortgage Specialist. Both are attained through a combination of education and experience requirements. Brokers normally are compensated primarily through fees and commissions. They often combine mortgage brokerage with some closely related real estate occupation. Brokers must be licensed in the state where they practice.

A major threat to the mortgage brokerage industry has been its open, lightly regulated entry. While it became the dominant avenue for home mortgage lending, it allowed highly competent and reputable industry members to be joined by far too many incompetents and criminals. (See *Miami Herald*, "Borrowers Betrayed," July 19, 2008.) The Secure and Fair Enforcement for Mortgage Licensing Act of 2008 set in motion national oversight of broker registration and licensing. The Dodd-Frank Wall Street Reform and Consumer Financial Protection Act of 2010 created a host of restrictions to prevent abusive home mortgage lending and created the Consumer Financial Protection Bureau as an all-inclusive watchdog for abuses and misleading practices in home mortgage lending. Both acts should do much to fix this mortgage brokerage breakdown.

Source: Information partially excerpted from www.namb.org, The Association of Mortgage Professionals.

✓ Concept Check

10.10 What is the maximum loan-to-value ratio for a VA loan?

Other Mortgage Types and Uses

Some mortgages on real property are known by their unique roles. These include purchase money mortgages, "piggyback" mortgages, reverse annuity mortgages, and home equity loans.

Purchase-Money Mortgage

Whenever a mortgage is created simultaneously with the conveyance of title, it is a **purchase-money mortgage (PMM).** Thus, technically, any mortgage granted from any source for purchase of property is a purchase-money mortgage, and government statistical reports use the term this way. However, in the real estate brokerage industry the term usually is restricted to a mortgage from a buyer to a seller. Most frequently this is a second mortgage. The primary function is to provide the buyer with a higher loan-to-value ratio than they are able or willing to obtain from a traditional mortgage lender, to provide the buyer with a lower cost of financing than is generally available, or to provide both.

EXAMPLE 10-3   A PURCHASE-MONEY MORTGAGE

Suppose the Browns want to sell their home for $150,000. The Greens want to buy it, but can pay only $15,000 in cash. They can borrow $120,000 with a first mortgage from Third Federal Savings and Loan, but they are still short of $15,000. The Browns agree to lend them $15,000 with a second mortgage—a PMM. In effect, the Browns are "taking paper" in lieu of $15,000 in cash at closing. The second mortgage will have a position inferior to the first mortgage in the event of default.

Usage.   Purchase-money mortgages are used to finance all kinds of property. For example, landowners often partially finance the sale of large tracts for development with a PMM. They take cash for a portion of the sale price but finance the remainder themselves. The PMM is paid off from the proceeds of lots as they are developed and sold. The landowner, in effect, is a partner of the developer.

Piggyback Mortgages.   An important purchase-money mortgage in recent years has been the "piggyback." Conventional home mortgage loans exceeding 80 percent of value generally require private mortgage insurance, so there is incentive to keep the loan within that limit. But many buyers cannot pay 20 percent down. During the boom years following 2000, second mortgage lenders responded with the **piggyback loan,** a second mortgage created simultaneously with the first mortgage for 10 percent of value or more. Thus, the borrower could obtain 90 percent financing or greater while avoiding the cost of private mortgage insurance. The piggyback could be fixed or adjustable rate, with a relatively high interest rate and a term much shorter than the term of the underlying first mortgage. The percentage of all home purchase mortgage loans with piggybacks was around 15 percent in 2004, over 28 percent by 2006, but has fallen below 2 percent since 2009.[17] The use of the piggyback has drastically diminished, but it still can be a reasonable alternative to private mortgage insurance, depending on the costs of both choices.

> ✓ **Concept Check**
>
> **10.11**   What is a purchase-money mortgage?

Home Equity Loan

The **home equity loan** has become quite popular in recent decades. A form of second mortgage, home equity loans owe their popularity to lower interest rates, longer terms than other consumer debt, tax-favored status, and easy availability, not to mention aggressive marketing by lenders. Although traditionally used to finance home improvements, home equity loans have become all-purpose loans.

Forms of Loans.   Banks and savings institutions dominate home equity lending, but credit unions, finance companies, brokerage houses, and insurance companies also offer these loans. The loans come in two forms:

1. *Closed-end loan*—a fixed amount is borrowed all at once and repaid in monthly installments over a set period, such as 10 years.
2. *Open-end line of credit*—money is borrowed as it is needed, drawn against a maximum amount that is established when the account is opened. Interest is paid on the balance due, just as with a credit card. This type of credit commonly requires a minimum monthly

---

17. Computations based on data from HMDA National Aggregate Report Table A1, 2004--2014. See https://www.ffiec.gov/hmda/.

payment equal to a percentage (e.g., 1.5 percent) of the outstanding balance. This gives the debt a much longer term than consumer debt. Normally, the interest rate is adjustable, most commonly based on the prime rate published in *The Wall Street Journal,* plus a margin ranging from zero to perhaps 1.5 percent. Open-end lenders frequently provide a book of special checks that allows the borrower to tap the line of credit as if it were a checking account. This form of loan commonly is referred to as a HELOC (home equity line of credit).

How much can one borrow? The limit is set by a total mortgage loan-to-value (LTV) ratio such as 75 percent or 80 percent. The maximum home equity loan is the amount that increases total mortgage debt up to that LTV limit. If a house is appraised at $200,000, has a $100,000 mortgage balance, and the lender sets a 75 percent LTV ratio, a homeowner could borrow $150,000, minus the $100,000 existing debt, or an additional $50,000.

Tax Advantages.   Interest on consumer debt, such as loans to finance the acquisition of automobiles, college tuition, and household appliances and electronics, is *not* tax deductible. But interest is 100 percent deductible on the sum of home mortgage loans, including a home equity loan, up to a total of $100,000 for federal and many state tax returns.[18]

✓ **Concept Check**

10.12   Give three reasons why homeowners might be interested in a home equity loan rather than a consumer loan.

---

www.reversemortgage.org

National Reverse Mortgage Lenders Association, a primary reverse mortgage trade organization.

www.aarp.org

A search of the AARP website produces over 150 links to reverse mortgage articles.

Reverse Mortgage

Many older, retired households suffer from constrained income and a resulting reduction in their quality of life. Over 80 percent of older households are homeowners, often with little or no mortgage debt on their residence. But even when income is constrained, they remain unwilling to sell their homes for many reasons. In short, a very significant percentage of older households are "house poor," with little income, but substantial illiquid wealth in their home. A **reverse mortgage** is designed to mitigate this problem. It offers additional monthly income to these homeowners through various loan disbursement plans, using the home as security for the accumulating loan. Essentially, a reverse mortgage allows homeowners to liquify a portion of their housing equity without having to sell the house and move.

✓ **Concept Check**

10.13   For whom is a reverse mortgage intended? What problem does it address?

EXAMPLE 10-4   A SIMPLE FIXED-TERM REVERSE MORTGAGE

In a fixed-term, level-payment reverse mortgage, sometimes called a *reverse annuity mortgage,* or RAM, a lender agrees to pay the homeowner a monthly payment, or annuity, and to be repaid from the homeowner's equity when he or she sells the home or obtains other financing to pay off the RAM. A fixed-term RAM provides a fixed payment for a certain period of time, say, 10 years. For example, consider a household that owns a $100,000 home free and clear of mortgage debt. The RAM lender agrees to a $70,000 RAM for 10 years at 6 percent. Assume payments are made *annually,* at the beginning of each year, to the homeowner. The annual payment on this RAM would be $5,010.15.[19] The annual payment, accrued interest, and accumulated loan balance are displayed in Exhibit 10-1.

---

18. This limit excludes money borrowed to buy, build, or improve one's residence.
19. The calculator inputs to compute this payment are as follows: $N = 10$, $I = 6$, $PV = 0$, $FV -70,000$. Note that the calculator must be in *begin* mode because the payment is at the beginning of each year.

Exhibit 10-1 Fixed-Term Reverse Annuity Mortgage*

Year	Beginning Balance	Payment	Ending Interest	Ending Balance
1	$ 5,010	$5,010	$ 301†	$ 5,311‡
2	$10,321	$5,010	$ 619	$10,940
3	$15,950	$5,010	$ 957	$16,907
4	$21,917	$5,010	$1,315	$23,233
5	$28,243	$5,010	$1,695	$29,937
6	$34,947	$5,010	$2,097	$37,044
7	$42,054	$5,010	$2,523	$44,578
8	$49,588	$5,010	$2,975	$52,563
9	$57,573	$5,010	$3,454	$61,028
10	$66,038	$5,010	$3,962	$70,000

*$70,000, 6.0 percent, 10-year loan.

†6 percent of beginning balance.

‡Beginning balance, plus payment, plus interest.

Note that the disbursement and loan payment pattern on a RAM is not at all like a typical mortgage from which the borrower receives the entire loan proceeds at closing and then immediately begins to make monthly payments of interest and principal. With our RAM example, the loan proceeds are distributed to the borrower in periodic amounts. Interest on the loan disbursements begins to accumulate immediately. However, no payments of any kind are made on the loan until the borrowers, or their heirs, pay off the loan with proceeds from the sale of the house (or other assets from the borrower's estate).

"Mortality" Risk. The main risk of a reverse mortgage is that the outstanding balance ultimately will exceed the value of the property. If the property is sold or the homeowner dies prior to the end of the loan term, the loan is designed so that the sales proceeds should be sufficient to pay off the accumulated balance. However, if the owner is still living and occupying the residence at the end of the loan term, then default is likely. But to foreclose would cause distress for the homeowner (commonly an elderly widow) and severe negative publicity for the lender. So foreclosure is not a practical option. To address this "mortality risk," several departures from the fixed-payment, fixed-term RAM have emerged. In one, the payments to the homeowner cease at the end of the loan term, but the owner is allowed to stay in the house as long as he or she wishes. Interest on the unpaid mortgage balance simply continues to accrue at the contract rate, ultimately raising the specter of the loan balance exceeding the value of the property. The lender must either limit the initial loan to an overly conservative amount to minimize this risk or find another way to manage the risk, such as insurance. This is where FHA becomes crucial to reverse mortgage lending.

✓ **Concept Check**

10.14 What is the unique risk of a reverse mortgage? How is it mitigated?

Role of FHA. A vital step in the development of reverse mortgages was the creation of reverse mortgage insurance. In 1987 Congress created the FHA Home Equity Conversion Mortgage (HECM) program to provide insurance for reverse mortgages. This program set the framework, in large part, for acceptable forms of the mortgage. It provides guidelines for maximum loans that depend on the age of householders and the value of the residence. It provides for a variety of acceptable disbursement plans, including lump sum, annuity

portal.hud.gov/hudportal/
HUD?src=/program_
offices/housing/sfh/hecm/
hecmhome

HUD's reverse mortgage website.

Help from a Reverse Mortgage

Charles and Joan H., aged 79 and 77, respectively, have 26 miniature flags in their downstairs living room. Each represents the country of a foreign exchange student they have befriended. Although the couple are no longer a host family, they've kept in close contact with many of their former exchange students. Three of them—Christine from France, Gabrielle from Mexico, and Carlos from Brazil—had wedding plans. Charles and Joan were invited to attend all three weddings, which were held in their friends' native countries.

To raise the money to attend the weddings, they decided to get a reverse mortgage. "We got the reverse mortgage, so that we could go to France and Brazil," explained Joan. "Later we were invited to Gabrielle's wedding in Mexico. Getting the reverse mortgage was a smart move, because we didn't have to dip into our savings."

Their four bedroom ranch-style home, where they've lived for 50 years, was appraised at $130,000. They obtained a $72,000 reverse mortgage, after payment of closing costs. The loan was closed and the couple took out an initial draw of $10,500 to pay for the first two trips, and left the balance in a line of credit.

In addition to paying for their travel, Charles and Joan also used the funds from their reverse mortgage to buy a computer. The computer, Joan said, "opened up a whole new world for us." The couple now uses e-mail to keep in touch with their children and other friends. "I used the Internet to purchase our plane tickets, reserve hotel rooms, and make other travel arrangements," she noted. "I doubt we could have done any of this without our reverse mortgage, which is why we're advising our friends to get one, too."

Note: (Dollar amounts are adjusted to 2016 equivalents.)

Source: Excerpt from website of National Reverse Mortgage Lenders Association. www.reversemortgage.org

(level payment), and credit line. It provides mortgage insurance for reverse mortgages originated by FHA-approved lenders. More specifically, if the proceeds from the sale of the home are not sufficient to pay the amount owed, HUD will pay the lender the amount of the shortfall. After the origination of the HECM program in 1989, there was slowly growing acceptance of the reverse mortgage concept but with only about 50,000 loans created in the following decade. However, as shown in Exhibit 10-2, the rate of growth in reverse mortgages insured under FHA's HECM program increased dramatically after 2001. Many analysts predict the demand for these loans will grow as the baby-boom generation continues to age. Indeed, even with the depressed condition of the housing market since 2007, the volume of HECM loans has remained much greater than in the early years of the decade.

The Economic and Housing Recovery Act of 2008 enacted several changes that may bolster the growth of HECMs. It raised the loan limits to correspond with GSE loan limits, starting at $424,100 in 2017. It also limited upfront fees and prohibited lender tie-in contracts for other financial services.

Exhibit 10-2   Reverse (HECM) Mortgages Insured by FHA

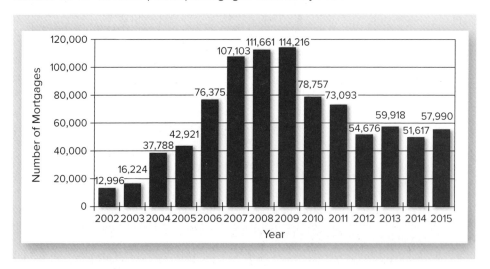

Source: FHA Annual Management Report, selected years.

Recent Mortgage Forms

It is hard to overstate the degree of change in home mortgages since the mid-1990s. New names of mortgages that have become common include interest-only, hybrid ARMs, and option ARMs, with extensive variation in each form. In this section we explain some of these mortgages. Unfortunately, in recent years a number of factors in our economy led to a serious breakdown in risk control for residential mortgage lending. This allowed reckless use of many of these new mortgage forms, exacerbating a "housing bubble," and tainting even the most promising new mortgage forms. In Exhibit 10-3 we compare the payment patterns and balances over time for the main mortgages we discuss.

Interest-Only (I-O) and Balloon Mortgages

The **interest-only mortgage** (I-O) home mortgage is not totally new, having been a mainstay of home finance prior to the arrival of FHA in 1934. What *is* new is the variety of forms of the I-O. And what is remarkable was its comeback from near oblivion in home finance. The true I-O mortgage requires no monthly principal payment, and the balance remains at the original amount. So, the borrower must pay off the loan after five to seven years with a "**balloon**" payment equal to the original balance. The I-O balloon can have a fixed or adjustable interest rate.

In contrast to the true I-O mortgage is a variety of **interest-only amortizing mortgages and partially amortizing mortgages.** With one form there is a period of up to 15 years of interest-only payments at a fixed interest rate. Then the payment is reset to fully amortize the loan over the remaining term. During the amortizing period the interest rate may be either fixed or adjustable. A second variant is a partially amortizing loan—set to amortize over 30 years, but ballooning in five or seven years. Since the loan is shorter term than a fully amortized mortgage, the rate will be lower. As a safety measure, Freddie Mac and Fannie Mae, when they supported these loans, required that the borrower be able to refinance at maturity into a standard level payment loan at the then market interest rate.

Why did I-O and balloon home loans suddenly reappear after some 70 years of near extinction? As we show in Exhibit 10-3, they can offer payment advantages in a world where affordability is of paramount concern. Despite the attractions of I-O loans their default record obscured any benefits they offered, and they no longer are supported by Fannie Mae and Freddie Mac.

Hybrid ARM

In the 1970s traditional home lenders turned to adjustable rate mortgages for protection from increasingly turbulent interest rates.[20] This was a near perfect solution to their asset-liability (mortgage loan-savings deposit) imbalance problem. However, it was a rather unattractive solution for the typical homebuyer, who then faced the threat of increasing payments if interest rates rose. After nearly 20 years lenders finally found an effective compromise in the **hybrid ARM.** It begins with a fixed interest rate, but converts to a standard ARM. It differs from an I-O mortgage in that the payment is always set to amortize the loan over the remaining term, so it always includes principal payment. With a "3/1" hybrid ARM, the interest rate charged is fixed for three years, then adjusts each year thereafter. The hybrid ARM has been offered with fixed interest for 2, 3, 5, 7, or 10 years. Not surprisingly, the interest rate charged during the initial interval usually is higher as the fixed-rate period is longer.

The hybrid ARM is a remarkably simple solution to a far-reaching financial need. Since the late 1970s, the two main forms of home mortgage loans were fixed rate and a standard one-year ARM. This put the borrower and lender in a "zero-sum" contest where the lender's gain in risk reduction through creating ARMs was the home borrower's loss.

---

20. The story of traditional home lenders' disastrous experience with interest rate risk is related in Chapter 11.

Exhibit 10-3   Payment and Balance with Alternate Loans

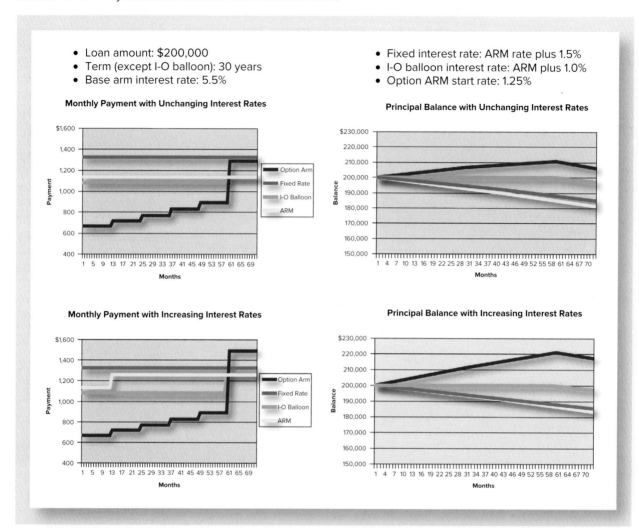

- Loan amount: $200,000
- Term (except I-O balloon): 30 years
- Base arm interest rate: 5.5%
- Fixed interest rate: ARM rate plus 1.5%
- I-O balloon interest rate: ARM plus 1.0%
- Option ARM start rate: 1.25%

By contrast, the hybrid ARM offers more of a win–win solution. The borrower has a fixed payment during the early years of homeownership when financial vulnerability is greatest while the lender retains, in large part, the ability to have the loan's interest rate rise if market rates go up. Further, this arrangement comes to the borrower with the advantage that the initial fixed interest rate is significantly lower than the standard fixed rate because it is for a much shorter time than 30 years.

Unfortunately, hybrid ARMs got off to a bad start. In 2006 the hybrid arm became the tool of choice for subprime loans and predatory lending, most commonly in the form known then as a 2-28 (two years fixed rate and 28 years adjustable rate). But the strength of the concept prevailed. Despite a terrible first impression, both lenders and borrowers have embraced the hybrid ARM to the point that by 2016 5/1 and 7/1 hybrid ARMs have effectively replaced the standard one-year ARM.[21]

Option ARM

The most radical, and controversial, home mortgage form of recent years was the **option ARM.** Consistent with its name, the loan allowed the borrower to switch among a variety of

21. One reason lenders have switched to 5/1 and 7/1 hybrid ARMs is because they can more easily become Qualified Mortgages, discussed later in this chapter.

payment arrangements. One common form allowed the borrower to select from a fully amortizing payment, interest-only, or a minimum payment. It is the minimum payment that distinguishes the loan, and is the one that most borrowers are reported to have selected. The minimum payment was based on an extremely low interest rate, say, 1.25 percent, well below the actual rate charged. The payment would increase in yearly steps, but unpaid interest would cause the balance to grow. After around five years, the payment would adjust to a fully amortizing level to pay off the new, larger balance. This final payment increase typically was severe, and often unmanageable for the borrower, compelling her to refinance.

This minimum payment scheme is of interest to mortgage experts for what it does and does not accomplish. Several decades ago the Nobel Prize financial economist Franco Modigliani proposed a mortgage form similar in important respects to the minimum payment described above.[22] He and others argued that it would be far superior to the fixed-rate, level-payment mortgage in simultaneously meeting the needs of lenders and borrowers in a time of high interest rate risk and high inflation. Ironically, the mortgage form became mainstream in an era of neither high interest rate risk nor high inflation. Rather, it emerged in a time when the dominant problem was housing price increases. Does it help borrowers in that context, or simply create a deferred payment trauma? It appears that the minimum payment choice of an option ARM had an intoxicating attraction that was allowed to do much more harm than good.

Subprime and Alt-A Loans

In 2006 over 20 percent of all loans created were called subprime, and over 13 percent were called Alt-A. But what do these terms mean? Both terms refer to a diverse class of conventional loans, consisting of variations on the types of loans discussed above. Subprime and Alt-A were more about the lending practices and borrower circumstances than about the loan designs, and we discuss this "lending climate" in Chapter 11. Still, there are some distinguishing features of the loans in each group, which we discuss below.

Subprime Loans

Most **subprime loans** were adjustable rate mortgages, with a very large percentage being 2-28 hybrid, interest-only, or option ARM. Whichever loan design was involved, a common characteristic was an initial payment that was sufficiently low to cause negative amortization, and, at some point, a payment increase so severe as to compel the borrower to seek refinancing. In short, subprime loans were generally designed to be refinanced in order to avoid a sharply increased payment. Since the typical borrower had weak credit, the replacement was likely to be another subprime loan. Because all of these loans bore a relatively high interest rate, the negative amortization could be severe, exacerbating the payment spike problem inherent in the loans, and tending to perpetuate a high loan-to-value ratio. Since the loan-to-value ratio typically started quite high, with negative amortization the ability to refinance depended on significant appreciation of the property.

Alt-A Loans

Alt-A loans generally were more "standard" in their terms than subprime loans with notably less of the forced refinancing character. They tended to be standard conventional loans with one or more borrower requirements relaxed, such as allowing a very high loan-to-value ratio (97 percent or higher), allowing lower than normal cash down payment, allowing weaker than normal borrower credit scores, or, most frequently, requiring little or no documentation of the borrower's financial circumstances. In short, Alt-A loans differed

22. Franco Modigliani, "The Inflation-proof Mortgage: The Mortgage for the Young." *Collected Papers of Franco Modigliani, Vol. 5, Savings, Deficits, Inflation and Financial Theory.* Cambridge: MIT Press, 1989. pp. 350–68.

from prime conventional loans almost entirely by the use of more relaxed borrower requirements. (In Chapter 11 we will refer to these requirements as underwriting standards.) Not surprisingly, the loans also were characterized by a higher interest rate as well.

Qualified Mortgages

www.fdic.gov/
regulations/resources/
director/technical/atr.
html#two

The Dodd-Frank Wall Street Reform and Consumer Protection Act of 2010 created an important new class of home mortgages, the **Qualified Mortgage**. The QM class facilitates mortgage lenders in implementing a broad new requirement imposed by the law: an "ability-to-repay" standard for *every* "dwelling-secured consumer credit transaction, including vacation homes and home equity loans" (though not home equity lines of credit). QM status meets this ability-to-repay standard with a minimum of underwriting tests, and, for most loans, affords a special "safe harbor" shield to the lender against legal defense by the borrower in case of default.[23]

What makes a Qualified Mortgage? There are both loan feature and underwriting elements. Generally, QMs exclude loans that are not fully amortizing, that is, do not have substantially level payments (though balloon payments after five years will be allowed for some rural lenders). The QM cannot exceed 30 years, or have fees in excess of three percent (if the loan is over $100,000). In underwriting requirements, the loan cannot have a debt-to-income ratio, or total debt ratio (see Chapter 11), exceeding 43 percent. If it is an ARM the loan must be underwritten to the highest possible rate in the first five years of the loan. Underwriting information must be verified using reasonably reliable third-party records (no "no-doc" or "low-doc" loans, for example). Generally, the so-called ability-to-repay guidelines must be followed.

Qualified mortgages initially include three groups: (1) any mortgage meeting the specifications above; (2) any conforming conventional mortgage eligible for purchase by Fannie Mae or Freddie Mac, plus any "government" mortgage, including FHA, VA, and home mortgages under Rural Housing Services or other programs of the U.S. Department of Agriculture; (3) "small creditor" home loans—loans meeting the ability-to-pay standard, made by small, usually rural lenders that make less than 500 first mortgage home loans per year and hold them in portfolio.

Altogether, the QM class is expected to encompass perhaps 85 percent of first-lien home mortgages. Any nonqualified mortgage will be more risky for the lender, providing a strong incentive to follow QM guidelines in lending.

The Borrower's Mortgage Loan Decisions

Once a household has selected a home to purchase, it faces a number of financing decisions. First, the buyer must choose a mortgage from the mortgage menu. This is a very complex decision, often requiring the borrower to make trade-offs concerning several features of loans: Are the payments to be fixed, or can they vary? Will the payments start low and increase, or be level? How soon must the loan be paid off? How much down payment is manageable? How costly is the loan? The dominating questions will vary, and the best solution depends on the particular case.

Once the borrower has selected a mortgage form, there are likely to be multiple choices in the combination of fees and interest rate. We discuss annual percentage rate (APR) as an important tool to compare these choices, but we note important limitations of APR that compel more sophisticated analysis.

After the mortgage has been originated, the household usually has the option to prepay the mortgage (in whole or in part) and the option to default. Borrowers typically do not give serious consideration to default unless the value of the property has fallen well below the

---

23. Underwriting is the lender's process of determining whether a loan is a prudent risk. We discuss this at length in Chapter 11, including the Dodd-Frank "ability-to-repay" requirements.

remaining mortgage balance, and they are facing some kind of severe financial distress. Prepayment may result from a household's decision to move, to refinance for a lower interest rate, or to obtain a larger mortgage, drawing some of the household's equity out of the property.

Mortgage Choice

As we have noted, mortgage choice is a particularly complex problem. Even the important questions will vary with the circumstances of the buyer. For example, the buyer's capacity for a down payment and the buyer's tolerance for payment uncertainty usually increase through their life cycle, all things equal. But all things are not equal from city to city, for example, and the burden of home buying can be much greater in high-cost areas, forcing much more severe trade-offs for the buyer. What is important in each mortgage choice decision is to recognize the viable alternatives and to sort through the relevant costs and benefits of each.

Comparing the Cost of Mortgage Choices.　When buyers of single-family homes seek financing, they discover that mortgages have two kinds of costs: upfront fees and continuing regular interest. The problem is that the mix of the two charges varies from one loan to another, and the borrower must find a way to compare trade-offs between the two. So, how can a borrower reduce multiple cost aspects to a single measure in order to compare mortgages? Fortunately, a partial solution to this problem is available and widely used: namely, annual percentage rate (APR). The approach of annual percentage rate is to convert upfront expenses into an equivalent increment to the regular interest charges. For example, suppose a loan has a contract interest rate of 7 percent, but also has upfront expenses amounting to 4 percent of the loan. We cannot simply add the two expenses together. Rather, we restate the 4 percent, one-time expense as if it were spread over the life of the loan. We might determine that the 4 percent upfront fee is equivalent to paying an extra 0.5 percent interest each year over the life of the loan. Then we would add 7 percent and 0.5 percent to obtain an APR of 7.5 percent. In Chapter 15 we show how this equivalency is actually obtained.

As an example of using APR, suppose we are considering two possible fixed-rate, level payment loans, as shown in Exhibit 10-4. Despite the difference in the contract interest rates of 6.5 and 6.25 percent, after the upfront fees and mortgage insurance are accounted for, the APRs on the two loans are virtually identical, suggesting that the borrower would be indifferent between the loans.

While APR is a valuable tool in comparing the cost of mortgages, it usually understates the true cost of borrowing. The main reason is that APR assumes the loan always goes to maturity even though, for many reasons, almost every home loan is prepaid well before maturity. Effectively, APR assumes that upfront fees are "buying" financing for the entire maturity of the loan, whereas, in reality, they buy a shorter financing period—the *actual* life of the loan. So a shorter actual life means that the upfront fees must be accounted for more rapidly, and the effective interest cost is accordingly higher. As a result, the earlier that prepayment comes in the life of the loan, the greater APR understates the true cost of

Exhibit 10-4　Mortgage Comparison Using Annual Percentage Rate (APR)

	Loan A	Loan B
Loan amount	$200,000	$200,000
Maturity	30 years	30 years
Contract interest rate	6.5 percent	6.25 percent
Upfront fees	1.5 percent	4.0 percent
Upfront mortgage insurance fee	1.0 percent	1.0 percent
APR	6.75 percent	6.74 percent

upfront expenses. As an example, if the loans in Exhibit 10-4 are paid off early, then, despite having equivalent APRs their true cost will be higher, and Loan B, with larger upfront expenses, will be the more costly of the two. We will show in Chapter 15 a better tool for comparing mortgage costs that accounts for this prepayment distortion, namely, the effective borrowing cost (EBC).[24]

Loan Size

A borrower must consider several factors in determining how much debt to obtain. First, the use of mortgage debt depends on the relative costs of debt and equity financing.

> √ **Concept Check**
>
> **10.15** In comparing alternative mortgage choices, what is the principal tool of comparison?

Consider a household that has agreed to purchase a home for $200,000. Assume that the household currently owns several other assets, including $200,000 in corporate bonds. This household has two basic financing options: (1) sell the $200,000 in bonds and put its own money into the house or (2) debt finance a portion of the purchase price. If the household chooses the first option, it is, in effect, lending the money to itself. What is the cost of this self-financing? It is the rate of return that the household could have earned from keeping the bonds. If the risk-adjusted bond yield is *equal* to the borrowing cost of the mortgage financing, the borrower is indifferent between the two options from a financial perspective. However, if the bond yield exceeds the mortgage borrowing cost, the household has an incentive to finance some, if not all, of the purchase with mortgage debt. A second consideration is the interaction of loan-to-value ratio and borrowing cost. Due mainly to the cost of mortgage insurance, a higher LTV ratio results in a higher borrowing cost.

The Refinancing Decision

Because of frequent declines in mortgage interest rates, most home mortgage borrowers have had opportunities to refinance, and thereby significantly improve their financial situation. But there are significant costs involved. So it is important to recognize when you really are better off from refinancing, and when you are not.

Refinancing is an investment problem. So the core question is whether the benefit, the value of the future loan payment reductions, exceeds the cost of refinancing. That is, we need to determine whether the net benefit of refinancing is positive, where the net benefit is:

$$\text{Net benefit} = \text{Benefit of loan payment reductions} - \text{Cost of refinancing}$$

The most complete way to view this problem is as a question of net present value (NPV). In the appendix to this chapter, we present that view of refinancing. However, since many homebuyers are unfamiliar with NPV, our discussion here takes a more approximative, but simpler approach. (In Chapters 14 and 15 we provide the background in time-value analysis to be able to use NPV analysis.)

To implement the Net Benefit equation, we need to define the benefit and cost. The benefit is the reduced interest expense resulting from the lower interest rate. So we will approximate that by simply recomputing our loan payment with the new interest rate, holding ALL OTHER aspects of the loan unchanged. This way, the difference between the actual and the recomputed payment will approximate our monthly interest reduction, and we can simply multiply it by the number of months involved. For example, suppose a homeowner has an existing mortgage loan with a remaining term of 17 years and 5 months, a remaining balance

---

24. We defer discussion of EBC until Chapter 15 because it requires knowledge of time-value math, presented in Chapter 14.

of $100,000, and an interest rate of 7 percent per year. The monthly payment on this loan would be $829.22.[25] But suppose a new loan is available at an interest rate of 5.5 percent. Then the payment on the existing loan with the new interest rate would be $744.69.[26] Thus, the reduction in payment, due strictly to the interest rate reduction, would be $84.53 per month. Suppose that the homeowner expects to sell or refinance again by the end of six more years. This would mean that the payment reduction would occur for 6 years, or 72 months, resulting in a cumulative reduction of payments of $6,086 (rounded to the nearest dollar). This gives us our first approximation of the benefit of interest expense reductions.

The second part of the net benefit equation is the cost of refinancing. Commonly, refinancing costs can run between 4 percent and 9 percent of the loan amount. Suppose our costs are 5 percent of the loan, or $5,000.

With both benefits and costs of refinancing estimated, we are ready to compute the net benefit of refinancing:

$$\text{Net benefit} = \text{Benefit of loan payment reductions} - \text{Cost of refinancing}$$
$$= \$6,086 - \$5,000$$
$$= \$1,086$$

This indicates that the homeowner is better off by approximately $1,086 from refinancing. So, barring intervening considerations, the borrower should refinance.

One word of caution in using the foregoing net benefit analysis: In recomputing the payment, remember that it is important to change only the interest rate from the original loan terms. Otherwise, irrelevant amortization effects confuse the outcome. A little experimentation can demonstrate this.

Other Considerations: Personal Costs and Income Taxes.   But what intervening considerations might be missing from the net benefit equation? First, it is important that the borrower consider all the costs of refinancing, including his or her own time and stress. These costs tend to be left out of estimates of refinancing cost such as we have mentioned above.

A second missing factor is income taxes. Tax deductions for mortgage interest can reduce the interest cost of mortgage debt. For example, suppose the homeowner currently pays taxes of $0.25 for every dollar of additional income. (We call this the taxpayer's marginal income tax rate.) Then each dollar of interest deducted reduces taxable income by a dollar, thus reducing taxes by $0.25. The net result is that the after-tax cost of deductible interest is reduced 25 cents on the dollar, making it only 75 percent of the contract interest rate. For example, 6 percent interest that is deductible would cost only 4.5 percent $((1 - .25) \times 6.0)$.

There is a simple adjustment for this tax effect in the net benefit equation. Since the benefit component of the equation is the interest saved by refinancing, if it is all deductible then we can simply multiply the benefit component by the appropriate adjustment factor, which, for our example, is 75 percent, or 0.75 $(1 - .25)$. Thus, the after-tax net benefit equation would be:

$$\text{After-tax net benefit} = \text{Benefit of loan payment reductions} \times \text{Tax adjustment}$$
$$- \text{Cost of refinancing}$$
$$= \$6,086 \times 0.75 - \$5,000$$
$$= \$4,564.50 - \$5,000$$
$$= (\$564.50)$$

The result now indicates that refinancing has negative benefits, and should not be pursued.

Though this after-tax computation is often overlooked, it is apparent from the example that it can be important. However, there is a very important caution. It only applies to U.S. homeowners if they itemize their tax deductions rather than using the standard deduction. Further, if the homeowner has no other deductions, then only interest in excess of the

25. On a financial calculator the payment can be found as follows: With the calculator set for monthly payments and set for end of period payments, then set $N = 209$, $I = 7.0$, $PV = 100,000$, $FV = 0$. Then solve for *PMT*.

26. The new payment can be found as follows: With the calculator set as before, $N = 209$, $I = 5.5$, $PV = 100,000$, $FV = 0$. Again, solve for *PMT*.

standard deduction amount should be regarded as reducing taxable income, and thus reducing the cost of the interest. Thus, which of the net benefit equations the borrower should use, tax adjusted or not tax adjusted, depends altogether on the income tax situation of the borrower.

✓ **Concept Check**

10.16   In the refinancing decision, the benefit of refinancing can be approximated by multiplying the _____ by the _____.

Refinancing Rules of Thumb.   There are several "rules of thumb" widely referred to in news media as refinancing guides. Probably the most common has been a rule of interest rate spread; that is, the borrower should refinance when the interest rate spread between the existing loan and a new loan reaches 2 percentage points or some other level. However, a "spread" rule of thumb cannot cover the important variations in the benefits. We see from the net benefit equation above that the benefits will be approximately proportional to the time one keeps the new loan, as well as to the interest rate spread. Moreover, the net benefit will change if the costs of refinancing change, and it also depends on the borrower's income tax situation. In short, any interest rate spread rule of thumb is unable to account for a variation in refinancing benefits due to cost, holding period, or income tax differences. It offers a one-dimensional solution to address a problem of at least three dimensions.

www.mtgprofessor.com/
ArticleLists/
BorrowersRefinancing
ToLowerCosts.html

A second refinancing rule of thumb concerns a form of payback period. This approach divides the total cost of refinancing by the monthly payment reduction. In our example above, we would divide the refinancing cost, $5,000, by the monthly payment reduction of $81.75, resulting in a payback period of 61.16 months. That is, in 62 months the sum of payment reductions will exceed the cost of refinancing. Notice that the information used for the payback period is the same information used for our net benefit calculation. So it should not be surprising that the payback period and our net benefit approach are completely consistent with each other. Choosing between them is really a matter of which is most useful in the context.

Because home mortgage refinancing is a major financial decision that affects virtually all homeowners, many refinancing guides have appeared on the Internet. In our opinion these Web-based financial tools should be state of the art, which means for refinancing analysis that they should use the time-value concepts we present in Chapters 14 and 15. Unfortunately, many do not. One of the better examples appears in Explore the Web at the end of the chapter. Even more sophisticated refinance calculators appear in the "mortgage professor" website shown in the margin.

✓ **Concept Check**

10.17   Which rule of thumb has a better chance of giving a valid result: interest rate spread rule or payback period?

Implicit Opportunity Cost of Refinancing.   Refinancing involves an additional implicit cost. Suppose you refinance, and then loan interest rates decline. You have incurred the opportunity cost of missing the better deal. This cost is limited by the fact that if rates fall sufficiently, you always can simply incur the cost of refinancing again and obtain the new rate.[27] We offer two observations on this risk of "jumping too early." Most financial economists argue that we never know whether interest rates will go up or down from where they currently are. Thus, the chance of rates falling further is 50 percent. This means that the expected value of the risk of jumping too early can never be greater than half the cost of refinancing again. We suspect it is a good bit less.

---

27. Note that if refinancing were costless, this problem would not exist.

Due to the risk of lost opportunity, a borrower would require a greater decline in interest rates before refinancing is beneficial. Specifically, the borrower might increase the estimated cost of refinancing by, say, 25 to 35 percent, but less than 50 percent, to account for this potential lost opportunity. Then the borrower would repeat the net benefit analysis just as we did before.

The Effect of Income Taxes, Implicit Opportunity Cost, and Borrower's Effort on the Refinancing Decision.   We have three reasons why a borrower may regard our quantitative analysis of the refinancing decision as overstating the benefits. First, income tax deductions may reduce the benefit of refinancing. Second, rates may fall subsequent to refinancing, providing an even more beneficial opportunity. Third, the experience of refinancing may be time-consuming and stressful for many homeowners. It is not possible to fully quantify all of these factors influencing the refinance decision. Thus, the net benefit computations above are "upper bounds" on the benefit of refinancing. Since the net benefit of refinancing decreases dollar for dollar with increased costs of refinancing, an easy robustness test might be the following: Double the estimated cash cost of refinancing and see whether the before-tax net benefit remains positive.

Refinancing Decisions with a Debt Increase.   Many times a homeowner is interested in replacing an old mortgage loan with a larger loan, thus drawing out some of his or her equity from the home. These "cash-out" refinancings often are to replace high-cost consumer debt such as credit card debt, a car loan, or a personal credit line loan. The analysis of a "cash-out" decision is analytically no different from our analysis above. The only changes are in the amounts to be used for the old loan balance and payments. The old loan amount becomes the total of all the existing debt to be replaced. Similarly, the payments on the old loan include the payments on all of the old debt. Thus, instead of finding the payment reduction of one old loan, you find the payment reduction for all the existing loans to be replaced, and sum the results.

The Default Decision

When default occurs, the lender must either renegotiate the terms of the mortgage with the borrower or take action to obtain title to the property. From the lender's perspective, the degree of default risk is related (1) to the probability that the market value of the home will fall below the remaining loan balance (plus the cost of foreclosure) and (2) to the risk that the lender will not be able to take possession of the home from the borrower in a timely fashion.

Before 2007 default was a very infrequent occurrence for home mortgage loans. For example, according to the Mortgage Bankers Association the past due delinquency rate for all home loans averaged 4.30 percent from 1986 to 2006, and the rate of foreclosure averaged only 0.36 percent of outstanding single-family loans. Since then, default became so extensive that in some localities the local housing market was dominated by sales of foreclosed homes. In the second quarter of 2010, nationwide delinquencies had risen to 10 percent for all loans, and nearly 30 percent for subprime ARMs. Further, serious delinquencies had risen to nearly 5 percent for all loans and to 18 percent for subprime ARMs.[28]

Why do borrowers default? One might reason that when the value of the property is less than the remaining loan obligation—that is, when equity is negative—the borrower is likely to default. But further reflection should challenge this idea. Consider, for example, that most car loans, at some point, exceed the value of the car, but most car owners don't abandon their vehicle. Why? A major reason is the value of the services provided by the car

---

28. National Delinquency Survey, Mortgage Bankers Association of America. Serious delinquency is 90 days or more.

When do you renege on a financial obligation? NPR's Yuki Noguchi reported the situation of Grace Chen and her husband Antonis Orphanou in Mountain View California.[1] The home they purchased three years earlier for $1,000,000 had fallen in value by $200,000. At that point their mortgage probably was "underwater." Both Grace and Antonis had jobs, and they had never missed a payment on their home mortgage. Grace had been trying for a year to discuss a reduction in interest rate with the lender (mortgage rates had declined sharply by then). However, the bank had not responded. Meanwhile, they believed they could abandon their house and rent a similar one nearby for a third of their mortgage payment.

Strategic Default: The Dilemma of Walking Away from a Mortgage

During the Great Recession, an unprecedented number of home owners faced this default question when their home mortgage was "underwater," or larger than the value of their house. Those who had lost their income to unemployment likely had little choice but to default, while, at the other extreme, persons more fortunate were able to mitigate the problem by renegotiating their loan to a lower interest rate, or even to a lower balance.[2] But for many, like Grace and Antonis, it seems that the problem was more complex.

So why shouldn't the couple default? For one thing, Grace, a CPA, was concerned that a foreclosure could stain her professional record, harming her career opportunities. But on the other hand, it seemed that every dollar paid on the mortgage "simply evaporated." Part of the problem was that banks had bet, right along with home buyers, that house values could not fall, and they were too quick to make high loan-to-value loans that depended on that bet. So the bank shared some of the guilt, and one could ask why it refused to share the loss by negotiating a friendlier loan. After all, under normal conditions Grace and Antonis could simply have refinanced the existing mortgage into a new, lower interest rate loan and gained a lot of relief. In other words, the bank arguably was exploiting them by refusing to refinance. Meanwhile, as reported by Noguchi, the executive vice-president of the American Bankers Association, a spokesman for the banking industry, commented on the plight of Grace and Antonis by simply saying: "We believe people should meet their contractual obligations when they have the ability to meet them." Was he right?

1. NPR Morning Edition, October 28, 2010.
2. Through the government sponsored programs, Home Affordable Modification Program (HAMP) and Home Affordable Refinance Program (HARP) between 3 and 4 million households with troubled mortgages have been able to restructure their mortgage if it was owned by either Fannie Mae or Freddie Mac.

Source: Adapted from Noguchi, Yukl, "The Dilemma of Walking Away from a Mortgage," 2010, NPR.

---

exceeds the monthly payment that must be made to keep it. Similarly, as long as the value of housing services exceeds the mortgage payment, the home borrower is likely to make the payment. In addition, there are likely to be "transactions costs" or economic penalties to default, including damaged credit, household disruption, relocation costs, and perhaps stigma, that will deter default even when the benefits of home-ownership no longer equal the debt payments. In fact, best evidence is that homeowners rarely default unless they have negative equity. But even in case of negative equity, they rarely default unless they encounter a "trigger event," a seriously disruptive household event such as unemployment, serious illness or death in the family, or divorce.[29] A new kind of "trigger" event with the arrival of the subprime binge appears to be the refinancing crisis when the subprime payment spikes and the borrower no longer can refinance to a lower payment. It may be remarkable that such a small percentage of subprime borrowers facing this crisis elected to default considering that house prices fell approximately 33 percent from mid-2006 to the end of 2011![30] Evidently the value of housing services for even most of these households remains greater than their mortgage payment.

Concept Check

10.18 What two conditions typically must be present to result in home mortgage default?

---

29. For recent analysis of residential default behavior, see, for example, Christopher L. Foote, Kristopher Gerardi, and Paul S. Willen, *Negative Equity and Foreclosure: Theory and Evidence,* Public Policy Discussion Papers, No. 08-3, Federal Reserve Bank of Boston, 2008.

30. See S&P/Case-Shiller Home Price Indices, www2.standardandpoors.com.

Summary

Prospective homebuyers are confronted with many choices when deciding what type of mortgage financing to obtain. Conventional loans (i.e., those that do not enjoy some form of government support) are clearly the dominant choice, accounting for at least 75 percent of all single-family home loans. If these loans conform to standards of Freddie Mac and Fannie Mae, they are eligible for purchase, and therefore tend to have a lower interest rate. These secondary market purchases have become a dominant influence on the types and terms of home mortgage loans, especially for fixed rate level payment loans. Major alternatives to conventional loans are FHA and VA loans. Especially for income constrained households (including most first-time home-buyers) these types of loans can offer more feasible requirements and terms.

Conventional versus government-guaranteed financing is not the only mortgage choice potential borrowers face. They must also select a payment schedule that matches their risk tolerance and affordability concerns. Thirty-year fixed-rate mortgages remain the most popular alternative, though adjustable rate mortgages are common as well. Fifteen-year fixed-rate mortgages still account for a sizable fraction of the market, while other options such as interest-only loans partially amortized mortgages have sometimes been available.

Homebuyers who borrow more than 80 percent of the purchase price are required to purchase private mortgage insurance (PMI). PMI typically insures the lender against default loss of 25 to 35 percent of the loan amount. If the lender must foreclose, the insurer will generally reimburse the lender for the remaining loan balance, take title to the property, and sell the asset for its current market value. PMI can be paid either as a lump sum or in monthly installments. After the loan has been paid down sufficiently, borrowers are permitted to cancel their mortgage insurance.

Potential buyers should be aware of many alternative mortgage instruments that can alter the required payment schedule. For example, sellers may issue purchase-money mortgages to alleviate buyer affordability problems. Reverse mortgages allow older homeowners to draw equity out of their residence. Interest-only mortgages and option ARMs became widespread as a solution to growing affordability problems, too often with unfortunate results. Also, hybrid ARMs have emerged, mitigating the problem of interest rate risk for ARM borrowers. Finally, the home equity loan, a form of second mortgage, is also very popular.

Borrowers should consider APR in selecting the appropriate mortgage type. The borrower should refinance when the value of the payment savings exceeds the costs associated with the refinancing. In actuality, an additional potential cost to refinancing today is the resulting inability to refinance at even lower rates tomorrow. Further, the benefits of refinancing depend on whether the borrower expects to treat mortgage interest as an itemized (i.e., explicit) deduction for taxes. As for default, naive financial theory again indicates that the borrower should default if and when the current market value of the property falls below the value of the outstanding mortgage. In reality, many homeowners with negative equity continue to make their monthly payments, perhaps because of the personal costs of default or because the house is providing services that have value greater than the mortgage payment. In addition, there is the possibility that changed market conditions could bring improved value to the residence.

Key Terms

Alt-A loan   261
Balloon   259
Conforming conventional loan   247
Conventional mortgage loan   246
Fannie Mae   245
Federal Housing Administration (FHA)   250

FHA mortgage insurance   251
Freddie Mac   245
Government-sponsored enterprise (GSE)   245
Home equity loans   255
Hybrid ARM   259

Interest-only amortizing mortgage   259
Interest-only mortgage   259
Jumbo loans   247
Maturity imbalance problem   248
Mortgage insurance premium (MIP)   251

Test Problems

Answer the following multiple-choice problems:

1. Private mortgage insurance (PMI) is usually required on _____ loans with loan-to-value ratios greater than _____ percent.
   a. Home, 80 percent.
   b. Home, 60 percent.
   c. Income property, 75 percent.
   d. Income property, 80 percent.

2. The type of mortgage loan that best fits the asset-liability mix of most depository institutions is a(an):
   a. Fixed-payment, fully amortized mortgage.
   b. Adjustable rate mortgage.
   c. Purchase-money mortgage.
   d. Interest-only, fixed-rate mortgage.

3. Which of the following mortgage types has the most default risk, assuming the initial loan-to-value ratio, contract interest rate, and all other loan terms are identical?
   a. Interest-only loans.
   b. Fully amortizing loans.
   c. Partially amortized loans.
   d. There is no difference in the default risk of these loans.

4. A mortgage that is intended to enable older households to "liquify" the equity in their home is the:
   a. Graduated payment mortgage (GPM).
   b. Adjustable rate mortgage (ARM).
   c. Purchase-money mortgage (PMM).
   d. Reverse annuity mortgage (RAM).

5. A jumbo loan is:
   a. A conventional loan that is large enough to be purchased by Fannie Mae or Freddie Mac.
   b. A conventional loan that is too large to be purchased by Fannie Mae or Freddie Mac.
   c. A multiproperty loan.
   d. A VA loan that exceeds the normal limits.

6. The maximum loan-to-value ratio for an FHA loan is approximately:
   a. 90 percent.
   b. 97 percent.
   c. 99 percent.
   d. 100 percent.

7. The maximum loan-to-value ratio on a VA-guaranteed loan is:
   a. 90 percent.
   b. 98 percent.
   c. 99 percent.
   d. 100 percent.

8. Conforming conventional loans are loans that:
   a. Are eligible for FHA insurance.
   b. Are eligible for VA guarantee.
   c. Are eligible for purchase by Fannie Mae and Freddie Mac.
   d. Meet federal Truth-in-Lending standards.

9. Home equity loans typically:
   a. Are fixed-rate, fixed-term loans.
   b. Are first mortgage loans.
   c. Are originated by mortgage bankers.
   d. Have tax-deductible interest charges.

10. A simple but durable method of determining whether to refinance is to use:
    a. Net benefit analysis.
    b. Cost of borrowing.
    c. An interest rate spread rule.
    d. APR.

11. Probably the greatest contribution of FHA to home mortgage lending was to:
    a. Establish the use of the level-payment home mortgage.
    b. Create mortgage insurance for conventional loans.
    c. Create the adjustable rate mortgage.
    d. Create the home equity loan.

Study Questions

1. On an adjustable rate mortgage, do borrowers always prefer smaller (i.e., tighter) rate caps that limit the amount the contract interest rate can increase in any given year or over the life of the loan? Explain why or why not.

2. Explain why a home equity mortgage loan can be a better source of funds for household needs than other types of consumer debt.

3. Distinguish between conforming and nonconforming residential mortgage loans and explain the importance of the difference.

4. Discuss the role and importance of private mortgage insurance in the residential mortgage market.

5. Explain the maturity imbalance problem faced by savings and loan associations that hold fixed-payment home mortgages as assets.

6. Suppose a homeowner has an existing mortgage loan with these terms: Remaining balance of $150,000, interest rate of 8 percent, and remaining term of 10 years (monthly payments). This loan can be replaced by a loan at an interest rate of 6 percent, at a cost of 8 percent of the outstanding loan amount. Should the homeowner refinance? What difference would it make if the homeowner expects to be in the home for only 5 more years rather than 10?

7. *Assume an elderly couple owns a $140,000 home that is free and clear of mortgage debt. A reverse annuity mortgage (RAM) lender has agreed to a $100,000 RAM. The loan term is 12 years, the contract interest rate is 9.25 percent, and payments will be made at the end of each month.
   a. What is the monthly payment on this RAM?
   b. Fill in the following partial loan amortization table:

Month	Beginning Balance	Monthly Payment	Interest	Ending Balance
1	____	____	____	____
2	____	____	____	____
3	____	____	____	____
4	____	____	____	____
5	____	____	____	____

*Optional question, using concepts from Chapter 15

   c. What will be the loan balance at the end of the 12-year term?
   d. What portion of the loan balance at the end of year 12 represents principal? What portion represents interest?

8. *Eight years ago you borrowed $200,000 to finance the purchase of a $240,000 home. The interest rate on the old mortgage loan is 6 percent. Payments are being made *monthly* to amortize the loan over 30 years. You have found another lender who will refinance the current outstanding loan balance at 4 percent with monthly payments for 30 years. The new lender will charge two discount points on the loan. Other refinancing costs will equal $6,000. There are no prepayment penalties associated with either loan. You feel the appropriate opportunity cost to apply to this refinancing decision is 4 percent.
   a. What is the payment on the old loan?
   b. What is the current loan balance on the old loan (five years after origination)?
   c. What would be the monthly payment on the new loan?
   d. Should you refinance today if the new loan is expected to be outstanding for five years?

9. You are offered two choices for financing your house, valued at $200,000, as follows:
   a. A 90 percent LTV fixed-rate 30-year mortgage at 6.00 percent. It will require private mortgage insurance for nine years (until the loan is reduced to 78 percent of value), effectively increasing the payment as if the loan were a 6.75 percent loan for nine years.
   b. An 80 percent LTV first mortgage, fixed rate, 30 years at 6.00 percent. (No mortgage insurance is required because the loan is 80 percent of value.) A "piggyback" second mortgage for 10 percent of value of the house, with an effective borrowing cost of 8.00 percent, and a maturity of nine years is required too.

   You expect for the financing to be in place for seven years. If there is no difference in the upfront cost of the two arrangements, which would be the better choice financially? Why?

EXPLORE THE WEB

Mortgage Professor's Mortgage Refinance Calculator

Go to www.mtgprofessor.com/calculators. Select Mortgage Refinance Calculator 3a and use it to solve the problem below.

Assume that on a home valued at $270,000 you have the following existing mortgage: $200,000, 6 percent, 30 years, with 25 years remaining (current balance of $186,108.71) and with current payment of $1,199.10. You can replace it with a 5 percent loan for 25 years. Also assume that the costs of refinancing include the following: Points (1 percent), other ($4,000). Finally, assume that your marginal tax rate is 25 percent, you earn zero interest on savings, you are not paying mortgage insurance on either mortgage (they are below 80 percent LTV), and you will be in the home for 8 more years. See if the result that you get from this calculation corresponds to your results using net benefit analysis. That is, does a net benefit analysis break even in about the same length of time as with Mortgage Professor Refinance Calculator 3a?

Solutions to Concept Checks

1. The difference between the mortgage primary market and secondary market is that in the primary market, new loans are created by borrowers and lenders; in the secondary market, existing loans are sold by one investor to another.

2. A conventional home mortgage loan is simply any standard home mortgage loan not insured or guaranteed by the U.S. government.

3. Three major developments in the history of conventional mortgage loans since the 1930s were (1) introduction of the LPM, assisted by private mortgage insurance; (2) introduction of adjustable mortgage loans; and (3) introduction of numerous alternatives to the standard 80–90 percent LPM beginning in the late 1990s.

4. Private mortgage insurance protects the lender from losses due to default. It indirectly aids the borrower by making the LPM a viable investment for lenders.

5. Lenders usually require mortgage insurance for loans in excess of 80 percent of value.

6. Two government agencies that provide direct housing assistance are the Rural Housing Services and sometimes the Department of Veterans Affairs.

www.mhhe.com/lingarcher5e

7. The upfront MIP for FHA mortgage insurance is 1.75 percent of the loan. It can be added to the loan amount. The annual MIP for an FHA loan of 30 years, 97.5 percent LTV, is 0.85 percent of the average outstanding balance.

8. When the loan balance is below 78 percent of original value, both PMI and MIP must be discontinued.

9. The greatest historic contribution of the FHA was to introduce the level-payment mortgage and to demonstrate its viability.

10. The maximum loan-to-value for a VA loan is 100 percent.

11. A purchase-money mortgage is a mortgage loan created simultaneously with the transfer of a property between buyer and seller. It can be by the buyer to the seller, but can be from a third party as well. It often is a second mortgage loan.

12. Three attractions of a home equity mortgage loan include (1) a better interest rate than found with consumer loans, (2) longer term, and (3) tax deductibility of the interest.

13. Reverse mortgages are for older households who need more cash flow and who have substantial wealth accumulated in their residence.

14. The unique risk of a reverse mortgage is that the mortgage will "outgrow" the value of the securing residence. Special mortgage insurance has been created by the FHA to indemnify the lender in case this occurs, without causing the borrower to lose the home.

15. In comparing alternative mortgage choices, the principal tool is APR. A better one is effective borrowing cost.

16. In the refinance decision, the benefit of refinancing can be approximated by multiplying the reduction in monthly payment by the number of months the borrower will keep the new loan.

17. The payback period rule of thumb is equivalent to the net benefit computation for refinancing. Therefore, it is superior to the spread rule.

18. Typically, a homeowner does not default unless the loan exceeds the value of the residence, and the household has experienced some traumatic economic event such as death, unemployment, or divorce.

Additional Readings

Brueggeman, William B., and Jeffrey D. Fisher. *Real Estate Finance and Investments,* 15th ed. New York: McGraw-Hill/Irwin, 2016.

Clauretie, T. M., and G. S. Sirmans. *Real Estate Finance: Theory and Practice,* 7th ed. Cincinnati, OH: South-Western Publishing, 2014.

Pinkowish, Thomas J. *Residential Mortgage Lending: Principles and Practices,* 6th ed. Mason, OH: Cengage Learning, 2012.

Wiedemer, John P., and J. Keith Baker. *Real Estate Finance,* 9th ed. Mason, OH: Cengage Learning, 2013.

APPENDIX: Refinancing as a Problem of Net Present Value

To access the appendix for this chapter, please visit the book's website at

www.mhhe.com/lingarcher5e

Chapter 11

Sources *of* Funds *for* Residential Mortgages

LEARNING OBJECTIVES

After reading this chapter, you will be able to:

1 Contrast the traditional pre-1980 system of home mortgage lending with the modern system in terms of lenders and methods of doing business.

2 Distinguish four channels of modern home mortgage lending by types of loans, major participants, and methods of funding.

3 List the three major functions of mortgage banking, identify a major risk to be managed in each function, and identify how it is managed.

4 List critical aspects of mortgage lending for which Fannie Mae and Freddie Mac have created uniformity, and state how this has improved mortgage markets.

5 State what home mortgage underwriting is, list the "three Cs" of traditional underwriting, and list what has changed or is changing with each "C" in the evolution of "automated underwriting."

6 List three reasons that automated underwriting is replacing traditional methods.

7 Identify three "deficiencies" of home loan applicants that can make them candidates for a "subprime" home mortgage loan.

8 Identify three factors that contributed to the "subprime meltdown" of 2006–08.

OUTLINE

Introduction

This chapter continues our examination of the residential mortgage market. In Chapter 10 we discussed the most common types of mortgage instruments available to homeowners, ranging from the fixed-rate, level payment mortgage to ARMs, to more exotic types of loans such as I-Os, hybrids, and option ARMs. We also contrasted conventional conforming loans with conventional nonconforming loans, and with FHA and VA loans. But what we did not consider was where to obtain a loan, and what factors influence the availability and terms of home loans. These questions are the subject of this chapter.

We first recount the extremely dynamic nature of home mortgage lending, and the virtual revolution that it has experienced during the last generation, changing from a world of local depository lenders to a world dominated by securitization and international capital markets. We explain what forces have brought about the extreme change and what its implications are for home mortgage lending today. We will explain that the legacy of this transformation includes a more reliable and less expensive supply of mortgage funds, but that it also has brought new risks to both the borrower and the lender. We will consider the various ways that loans reach the home borrower, and note the trade-offs to the borrower in relying on the different sources. As part of this, we will explain how the lender underwrites home mortgage loans (assesses borrower risk), and how this process has evolved as part of the changing home mortgage world. In addition, we will review briefly how and why the process of home mortgage lending spun out of control in recent years, with devastating consequences for many homeowners and for our economy.

Do the availability and terms of home mortgage financing affect the value of homes? The experience of housing markets from 2001 to 2006 makes the answer clear. This was a period of unprecedented mortgage funds availability, on excessively friendly terms. The result was to bring about the highest rate of home ownership in modern history, and an often frenetic demand for homes that drove prices far beyond a sustainable level.

The Market for Home Mortgage Loans

Mortgage borrowers must compete to borrow funds in the credit markets. They must bid against other home borrowers, businesses worldwide, and governments and their agencies of all kinds. Total mortgage debt outstanding at the end of 2011 approached $13.7 trillion. Exhibit 11-1 identifies the four major types of mortgage debt. Residential (home) mortgage debt was almost $10 trillion and accounted for 73 percent of total outstanding mortgage debt. Loans for acquisition of apartment (multifamily) buildings represented 8 percent of the total, and loans to fund commercial real estate investments (e.g., office buildings, shopping centers, and warehouses) accounted for 18 percent of the total.

Exhibit 11-1 Mortgage Debt Outstanding by Type of Loan
(Third Quarter, 2015 in Billions of Dollars)

Loan Type	Amount	Percent of Total
Residential (1–4 family)	$9,952	72.7
Apartment (multifamily)	1,059	7.7
Commercial	2,483	18.1
Farm	207	1.5
Total	$13,701	100%

Source: 2015 U.S. Federal Reserve Board of Governors System Data Releases.

How large is the nearly $10 trillion in outstanding residential debt? By way of comparison, the marketable debt of the U.S. government was approximately $10.1 trillion near the end of 2015. The $10 trillion also is more than twice as large as the value of all outstanding corporate bonds and almost three times as large as the amount of outstanding consumer credit.[1]

The Revolution in Home Mortgage Finance

Home mortgage lending in the United States is a story of transformation. The change is suggested in Exhibits 11-2 and 11-3. Exhibit 11-2 contrasts an old world and a new world in type of lender and source of funds. Entering the 1970s, the financial system of the United States was localized to a degree difficult to imagine today. Home mortgage lenders were predominantly local depository institutions, taking in local savings deposits and using them to make local mortgage loans. As shown in Exhibit 11-2, these lenders were predominantly savings associations—we will call them **thrifts**—and local banks.[2] In the 1970s thrifts held almost 60 percent of all home mortgage loans, with local banks holding around 15 percent, and other lenders, mainly life insurance companies (LICs), holding the rest. Thus, home mortgage lending was completely dominated by local depository lenders. Exhibit 11-3 shows this arrangement beginning to change in the early 1980s and giving way almost completely by 2010 to a new regime. Even the seemingly stable share of home mortgages for banks masks a drastic shift from small local banks making simple home loans to megabanks making a combination of standard home mortgages and home equity loans. Where

Exhibit 11-2   Traditional and Modern Housing Finance

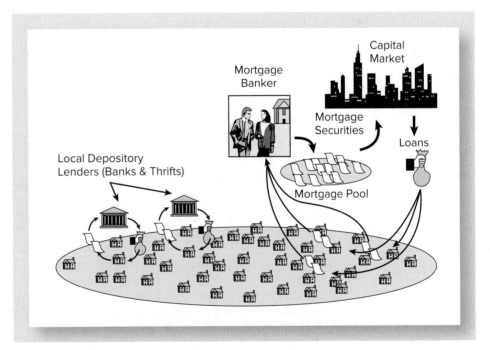

---

1. Source: *Flows of Funds Accounts of the United States,* Federal Reserve Statistical Release, December 10, 2015, B.101 and B.103.

2. The savings associations (thrifts) were mostly savings and loan associations ("S&Ls"). S&Ls were uniquely American, growing out of mutual savings societies to facilitate home ownership. In New England, however, there were savings banks, a slightly different type of thrift that grew out of efforts to foster factory-worker thrift. The savings banks were less completely focused on home ownership and tended to have a somewhat more diversified portfolio of assets than S&Ls.

Exhibit 11-3   The Revolution in Home Mortgage Finance:
From Savings Associations to Securities

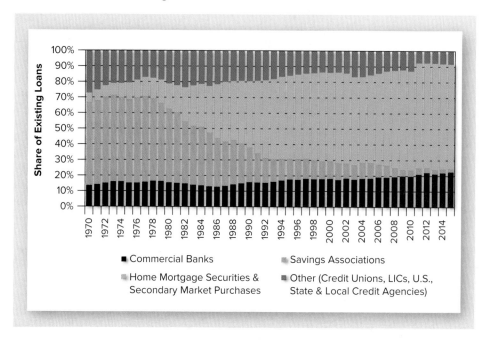

Source: U.S. Federal Reserve Board of Governors of the Federal Reserve System, Statistical Releases: Table 1.54 Mortgage Debt Outstanding, Historical Data.

no bank held more than a tiny fraction of the total share in 1970, five banks—Wells Fargo, Bank of America, JPMorgan Chase, Citigroup, and US Bancorp—held half of the total share of bank home loans in 2015.[3] Today's home mortgage story is predominantly about a combination of megabanks, the secondary mortgage market and securitization. A central element of the story is the process historically known as mortgage banking (now often called "originating to distribute").

How did this revolution come about? We recount the story to show how the arrangements of home mortgage lending are shaped by forces in the larger economy.

The Rise of a World Economy and The Demise of the Thrifts

The system of thrifts had worked exceedingly well in the years following World War II to finance the post-war exodus of households from the central cities to their dream homes in the suburbs. Despite a fatal vulnerability, an asset–liability maturity mismatch, the world of thrifts was rosy because interest rates remained low and stable.

But the thrifts became victims of their own system. When Congress created deposit insurance in 1933 and 1934 to save depository institutions from the financial panic of the Great Depression, in return for this salvation it also cocooned them in a vast array of regulations to ensure their "safety and soundness." These regulations, which fiercely protected the local thrifts and banks, also preserved the localized system of real estate finance into the late 1970s.

However, the economic world changed dramatically during the 1970s. Names like Sony, Toshiba, Honda, Toyota, and others largely unrecognized in the United States became household words. Suddenly the U.S. economy and financial system were far more

3. Source: Federal Deposit Insurance Corporation, Statistics on Depository Institutions (SDI), www2.FDIC .gov/sdi. Selected custom reports for commercial banks.

international than Congress, financial regulators, or even depository managers had ever conceived. This brought tides in the flows of capital funds never before seen, and interest rate volatility previously unknown. This change converged with an overheated economy in the late 1970s that began to fuel the fires of inflation. Meanwhile, as housing demand boomed—What better way to hedge inflation than to buy a bigger house?—thrifts were creating record numbers of 30-year, fixed-rate home loans, funded by short-term local deposits. Throughout the thrift industry the "good times rolled" as never before. The only problem was to find attractive-enough toasters, golf bags, and other premiums to attract savings deposits that were earning less than the rate of inflation.

But the party music turned to an ominous tone in the late 1970s when money market funds were born and savers suddenly could get a decent return on their short-term savings from Wall Street. **Disintermediation** raged as huge blocks of savings were diverted from thrifts to Wall Street.[4] Then, in 1979 the good times collapsed. The Federal Reserve saw fit to "declare war" on inflation by restricting the growth of the money supply, and the result was catastrophic to the old housing finance system in the United States. Suddenly thrifts, gorged with new 30-year fixed-rate home loans, saw the cost of their deposits rise above the yield on their loan portfolios. In substance, a large percentage of thrifts were permanently crippled or dead at that point. For the next decade, thrifts went through an inexorable and turbulent demise. As they fell, they created widespread "collateral damage" to overwhelmed regulators, to pressured members of Congress, and to taxpayers who were faced with a thrift "bailout" of (in 2015 dollars) $95 billion. Ultimately, some 1,300 thrifts failed.

> **✓ Concept Check**
>
> **11.1**   The basic financial vulnerability of thrifts was _____.

www.fdic.gov/bank/historical/history/index.html

A Federal Deposit Insurance Corporation (FDIC) site with extremely rich documentation and discussion of the story of thrift and bank struggles since 1980.

Responding to the chaos, in 1989 Congress enacted the Financial Institutions Reform, Recovery and Enforcement Act (FIRREA), which took major steps to establish depository institution accountability. The act finally created long-called-for risk-based capital standards for depository institutions requiring them to hold more capital as they hold riskier assets. Its goal was to supplant the conventional regulatory approach of attempting to suppress risky behavior through restrictions—an approach that was always one step behind the actions of bank or thrift managers, and that ignored the incentives to engage in the risky behavior. As a result of the closing of weak thrifts and the strengthening of capital requirements, the dominating thrift industry of the late 1970s shrank drastically.[5] By the end of 2008 its share of home loan originations had fallen from over half to 5 percent, and continued to decline.

> **✓ Concept Check**
>
> **11.2**   A major new regulatory approach for thrifts introduced by the FIRREA was to impose _____ capital standards.

The experience of the thrifts dramatizes the interdependency of housing finance systems and the larger economic environment. Thrifts were a product of a pre-World War II era in which economic life was extremely local; most people had grown up without a car, air travel was virtually nonexistent, and technology and communication were rudimentary by today's standards. By the 1970s thrifts were dinosaurs, preserved artificially by archaic regulatory structures. Later, we will consider the most recent catastrophe in housing finance

---

4. *Disintermediation*, a horror word to depository institutions, refers to conditions when the growth of deposits becomes negative, due to other, more attractive, direct investment opportunities.

5. Source: Federal Deposit Insurance Corporation, *Statistics on Depository Institutions*, www2.FDIC.gov/sdi/main.asp.

and note that both technical change and lagging regulatory structure are, again, contributing factors to the latest crisis in home mortgage lending.

The Transformation of Commercial Banks

What happened to commercial banks during the demise of the thrifts? For several reasons the fortunes of banks were quite different, enabling them ultimately to emerge as a dominant, central player in the "postrevolutionary" world of home mortgage lending. The core business of **commercial banks** always has been to make short-term loans to businesses for inventory financing and other working capital needs. Mortgage lending was simply an important adjunct of this business in order to meet the real estate finance needs of business customers, including financing their homes. While many banks expanded their home mortgage lending beyond business customers, rarely did they make it a dominant element of their business.

Larger commercial banks have traditionally provided funds for real estate finance in two other ways besides home mortgages. First, they make short-term construction loans that provide funds for the construction of multifamily, commercial, and industrial buildings. The timing and risks of construction lending are not unlike business inventory lending, and therefore tend to be natural for banks. Thus, they have traditionally dominated the commercial construction lending business. Second, some large commercial banks also have specialized in providing short-term funds to mortgage banking companies (which will be discussed later) to enable them to originate mortgage loans and hold the loans until the mortgage banking company can sell them in the secondary mortgage market. This type of financing is termed **warehousing** because the mortgage bankers put up the originated loans as security for the bank financing and the loans are "stored" (at the bank or with a trustee) for a relatively short time.

We return to the question of how banks flourished while thrifts died: First, banks were better able to survive the asset–liability mismatch that ravaged the thrifts. They always were more diversified due to the nature of their business, and note that many of their real estate assets were of much shorter maturity than the dangerously long-lived fixed-rate home mortgage loans.

But a second major help to banks during this time was deregulation and resulting bank consolidation. Legislation in 1980 intended partly to give thrifts more freedom to find ways to survive also permitted depositories to begin merging. Powers that banks had lost by the reforms of the early 1930s slowly were regained through a complex sequence of state and Federal changes in law. This transformation in their governing framework was essentially completed in 1994.[6] In the process, banks regained powers to engage in insurance and securities businesses, in real estate investment and development, and gained the ability to engage in interstate branching, acquisitions, and mergers. In mortgage lending, it seems that these new powers set banks up to get themselves into deep distress 10 years later.

Parallel to the broadening of bank powers came significant changes in the workings of bank regulation. Historically, the regulatory framework of banking was labyrinthine. State chartered banks generally were regulated by their state, the Federal Deposit Insurance Corporation (FDIC), and the Federal Reserve System (Fed). Federally chartered banks were regulated by the Office of the Controller of the Currency, by the FDIC, and by the Fed. This system was replete with duplication of requirements and conflicting rules. Thus, a crucial part of the transformation was elimination of much of the duplication and inefficiency in regulation, permitting larger, more complex, multistate operations. Out of this transformation in bank powers and bank regulation, completed in the mid-1990s, came the megabanks of today hungry for aggressive new ventures.

---

6. Congress enacted the Riegle Community Development and Regulatory Improvement Act of 1994, which addressed, among other issues, simplification and efficiency of regulation; and the Riegle-Neal Interstate Banking and Branching Efficiency Act of 1994, which provided for the possibility of full interstate branching, acquisitions, and mergers by 1997. The latter law effectively finished a process that already had become far advanced. State legislation enabling reciprocal interstate banking through bank holding companies was well advanced by the early 1990s.

> ✓ **Concept Check**
>
> **11.3** Name three ways that banks traditionally have served mortgage lending.

The birth of megabanks had major implications for home mortgage lending. Several megabanks identified megascale residential mortgage banking as a business opportunity of choice. Wells Fargo, Bank of America, J. P. Morgan Chase & Co., Citigroup, and other banking groups devoured or created mortgage banking subsidiaries that now are among the largest mortgage lenders in the country, and have reached unprecedented levels of market share. This phenomenon is discussed further later.

> ✓ **Concept Check**
>
> **11.4** Today, the largest market share in home mortgage lending among depository lenders is held by _____.

Mortgage Banking and Mortgage Brokerage

The rise of mortgage securities propelled mortgage banking and mortgage brokers onto the center stage of home mortgage lending. These activities differ fundamentally from thrifts and banks. Where thrifts and banks are **portfolio lenders** that use savings deposits to fund and hold mortgage loans as investments, mortgage companies neither collect deposits nor hold mortgages as investments. Instead, their business is mortgage creation. **Mortgage banking** originates mortgages, providing the origination services and initial funding, and then sells them as quickly as possible. As noted previously, this process is frequently referred to as "originating to distribute." **Mortgage brokers** simply bring borrowers and lenders together, but never own the resulting loans nor fund them. With the rise of securitization, mortgage banking became the natural method for doing mortgage lending: The mortgage banker would originate loans and sell them by pooling them into securities. To find lending opportunities, mortgage bankers frequently turned to mortgage brokers. Because of the importance of their process in modern mortgage lending, we will examine mortgage banking more closely, and contrast it with the companion function of mortgage brokering.

> ✓ **Concept Check**
>
> **11.5** Name two ways that mortgage brokers differ from a typical mortgage banker.

Mortgage Banking

What is mortgage banking? Rather than a particular type of firm, it is a process. It is a sequence of:

1. Committing to borrowers to make mortgage loans;
2. Creating and funding the loans;
3. Collecting them into "pools";
4. Securitizing the pools and selling the securities;
5. "Servicing" the loans for as long as they exist.

These steps may all be within a single firm, but commonly they are unbundled in a sequence of firms. Even if they are in a single firm, it can have several forms. It may be an

www.mba.org

Home page of the most important industry trade group involved in non-portfolio home mortgage lending.

independent business, or part of a bank, either as a subsidiary or simply as one of the bank's internal units. For simplicity, we will discuss the process as if it is a single firm conducting the entire series of steps. The process is depicted in Exhibit 11-4.

Loan Commitment. In the first step, the mortgage banker makes a commitment to a prospective borrower who has qualified for a loan. Generally, the commitment will be for a Qualified Mortgage (see Chapter 10)—that is, an FHA, VA, conventional conforming loan to be sold to Fannie Mae or Freddie Mac, or a prime jumbo loan. The loan is commonly fixed rate.

Creating and Funding. The second step is creating (called the "loan closing") and funding the loan. If the mortgage banker is an independent firm, it will fund the loan almost entirely from borrowed money, commonly using a "warehouse credit line" from a large bank that specializes in this process.[7] These independent mortgage bankers are extremely highly leveraged; their equity capital is only a small fraction of the amount they must borrow to fund their loan commitments. This leverage makes the mortgage banker highly vulnerable to the so-called pipeline risk.

Pipeline Risk. **Pipeline risk** refers to a pair of companion risks that the mortgage banker bears between loan commitment and final sale of a loan. The first is **fallout risk**: The loan commitment is an option given to the prospective borrower, and if market interest rates decline after the loan commitment, the borrower can turn away to a better deal, leaving the mortgage banker without a loan. But if interest rates rise after the commitment, the mortgage banker faces **interest rate risk**: The borrower becomes more likely to "take down" the loan commitment, forcing the mortgage banker to own a below-market rate loan that must be sold at a loss. In short, if interest rates fall after commitment, the mortgage banker loses business. But if interest rates rise, the mortgage banker loses money on loans created.

These two sides of the pipeline risk coin can be quite challenging to manage, making pipeline risk a dominating factor in mortgage banking that has destroyed many firms overnight due to a sudden rise in interest rates when the firm was not adequately hedged.

---

7. The largest mortgage bankers also issue commercial paper, very short-term, high-grade, marketable debt, as a way to finance their "pipeline" of loans.

Exhibit 11-4 The Mortgage Banking Process Creates Two Financial Assets: A Loan and Servicing

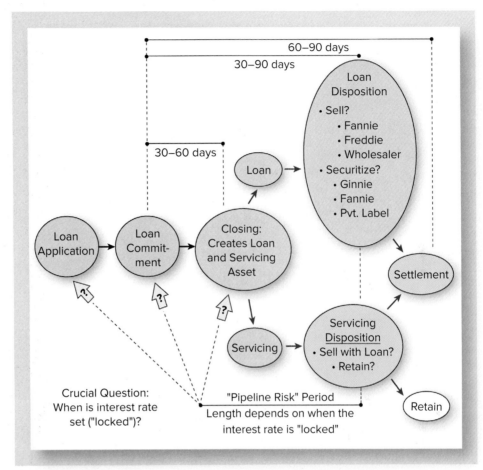

Therefore, a critical requirement of a successful mortgage banking operation is to have adequate pipeline hedging.

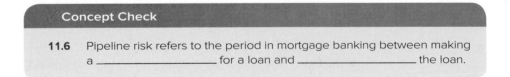

✓ **Concept Check**

11.6 Pipeline risk refers to the period in mortgage banking between making a _____ for a loan and _____ the loan.

Pooling and Securitizing Loans. The mortgage banker making conforming conventional loans has a simple procedure. It can simply sell them as "whole loans" to the GSEs, Fannie Mae, or Freddie Mac. It can either retain the servicing rights (see below) or sell them to a servicing oriented firm. The GSE buying the loans will pool them into one of its "agency" securities.

For FHA, VA, or prime jumbo loans, the choices are different. The mortgage banker might simply sell the loan to a larger "wholesale" mortgage banker in a manner similar to selling conforming loans to the GSEs. But a larger mortgage banker may want to do its own securitizing. For FHA or VA loans, the mortgage banker will create Ginnie Mae securities. (See Exhibits 11-6 and 11-9.) For jumbo conventional loans, the mortgage banker will create "private label" mortgage securities. It will then sell either kind in the "over-the-counter" securities market.

Servicing the Loans.   The profit in mortgage banking is in servicing the loans created. When the mortgage banker originates a home loan, it actually creates two assets: the loan and the servicing rights. It will always sell the loan but can either retain the servicing, if its servicing portfolio is sufficiently large to be profitable, or it can sell it to a servicing oriented firm. Either way, creating the loan servicing rights has been the true goal of mortgage banking, even to the extent that lenders accept losses in the origination process to get the servicing rights.

Servicing includes collecting the monthly payment from the borrower and remitting principal and interest payments to the security investors. It also includes ensuring that the borrower's monthly escrow payments for hazard insurance, property taxes, and other obligations with preemptive liens are sufficient to pay these obligations for the borrower when they are due. Servicers also are responsible for managing delinquent payments, default, and even foreclosure, should it arise. For these efforts the mortgage banker earns a fee, paid as part of the loan interest, ranging from 0.19 to 0.44 percent annually (referred to as 19–44 basis points). For example, if the outstanding balance of a loan at the beginning of a month is $100,000, and the annual servicing fee is 0.375 percent, then the servicer's fee for that month would be $31.25 ($0.00375 \div 12 \times \$100,000$). If the borrower's monthly mortgage payment is $750, the servicer would keep $31.25 and pass $718.75 on to the secondary market investors who own the loan.

The Mortgage Banking Cycle.   Thus goes the sequence of mortgage banking. It is a perpetual cycle through the five steps. The profit center of servicing naturally diminishes through loan amortization and prepayments, and the challenge of the business is to generate enough new loans to replenish the servicing portfolio. All the while, the mortgage banker must maintain sufficient loan quality through effective underwriting so that delinquencies and foreclosures do not destroy the profit center of servicing.

✓ **Concept Check**

11.7   The two components of pipeline risk are _____ and _____.

✓ **Concept Check**

11.8   The primary source of mortgage banking profit is from _____.

Megamortgage Banking.   The birth of megabanking and the explosion of cybercommunication have converged to drastically reshape home mortgage lending, especially mortgage banking. Unprecedented economies of scale now are possible in mortgage banking, given enough capital and potential volume of business. As mentioned above, the new megabanks seized this opportunity. They acquired mortgage banking subsidiaries and wedded the mortgage banking process with cyberspace. The result was a transformation in borrower interface and scale of operation. The megamortgage bankers can operate in any of four modes: traditional "face-to-face" (retail) lending, wholesale purchases of loans from smaller mortgage bankers and smaller banks (called *correspondent banks*), lending through mortgage brokers and, increasingly, Internet lending. Some large nonbank mortgage banking firms now have no retail operations, turning primarily to wholesale, broker operations, or the Internet for their business.

The effect of bank consolidation and the explosion of cybertechnology in the mortgage banking industry were transformational. There occured an unprecedented rise in industry concentration, shown in Exhibit 11-5. In 1989 the top 20 originators of home mortgages accounted for 23 percent of all first-lien home mortgage originations. By 2011 the top 20

Exhibit 11-5 Consolidation in the Top 20 Home Mortgage Lenders

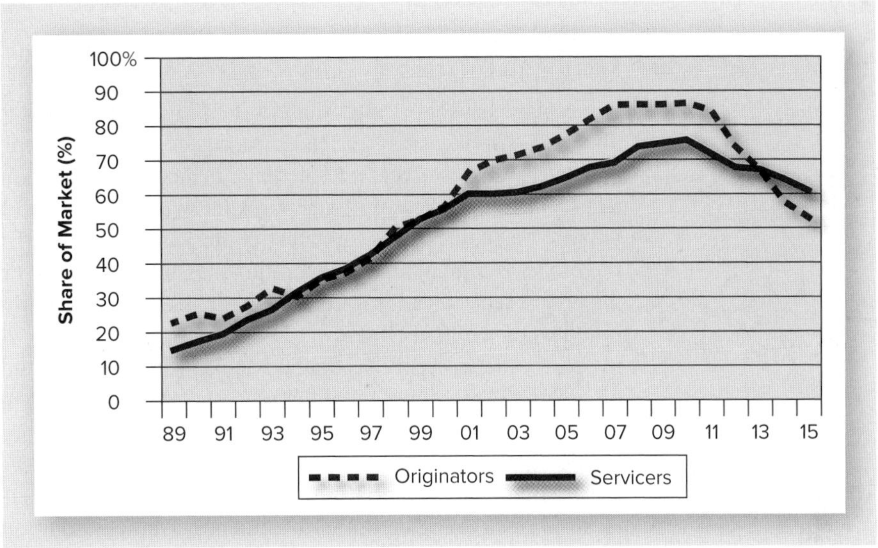

Source: Various editions of *The Mortgage Market Statistical Annual*. Inside Mortgage Finance Publications Inc. Bethesda, MD.

originators accounted for over 87 percent of these originations. As can be seen from Exhibit 11-5, the concentration of home mortgage servicing has been just as dramatic. By then, five banks (Wells Fargo, Bank of America, Chase, GMAC/Ally, and Citigroup) accounted for nearly two-thirds of all home mortgage originations and about 58 percent of all home mortgage servicing.[8]

But it seems that, unlike the thrifts, independent mortgage bankers do not disappear so easily. As Exhibit 11-5 hints, since 2011 they have resurged. Seizing on a sudden and dramatic withdrawal from home mortgage lending by the megabanks, mortgage banking firms—now referred to as "non-bank lenders"—have reappeared across the mortgage landscape, and, along with smaller banks, have taken back market share from the mega-players.

What happened to the megabanks? Factors driving this dramatic reversal are numerous. They seem to include improved access to bank warehouse financing for mortgage bankers as the economy stabilized, a resurgence of FHA/VA lending traditionally done by independent mortgage bankers, more equitable fees for small firms doing business with the GSEs, and new limits on bank holdings of mortgage servicing assets under Basel III banking regulation standards. Also the massive commitment of big banks to home mortgage lending appears to have been a disappointing experience due to a high incidence of troublesome loans leading to foreclosures, huge fines, and forced "buybacks" from the GSEs. These problems grew, in part, out of a heavy commitment to gathering loans through the use of brokers when the mortgage brokerage industry was out of control (as discussed below). Finally, it may be for regulatory and organizational reasons that a fresh non-bank can adopt new technology with greater efficiency and success than can an existing bank organization, as suggested, for example, by the meteoric rise of the purely online mortgage bankers, Quicken Loans and PennyMac.

What, then, is the tapestry of mortgage banking in 2016? It is radically different from the small firms of 1989, but also different from 2011. In short, the big banks still are prominent but are on the defensive from resurging small independent mortgage bankers and smaller banks on one side and non-bank, massive electronic platforms on the other.

8. See the 2011 and 2015 editions of *The Mortgage Market Statistical Annual,* Inside Mortgage Finance Publications, Inc., Bethesda, MD, 2011.

Mortgage banking continues to adapt constantly to changing technology, changing regulation, and changing market conditions.

Mortgage Brokers

A mortgage broker operates quite differently from a mortgage banker in that a broker does not actually make loans. Instead, a mortgage broker is simply an intermediary between the borrower (the customer) and the lender (the client). Many mortgage brokers serve as correspondents for large mortgage bankers who desire to do business in an area where the volume of business does not justify the expense of staffing a local office. Frequently, the broker is a small, or even medium-size, bank, thrift, or **credit union.** As compensation, the broker receives a fee for taking the loan application and a portion of the origination fee if and when the loan closes.[9]

As home mortgage lending advanced further into securitization, it relied increasingly on brokers as the front line of the process. In too many cases, this proved to be unfortunate. There were concerns early on that licensure for mortgage brokerage required too few qualifications and had perverse incentives. Unfortunately, the worst of nightmares in this concern seem to have materialized. In an exposé of brokerage the *Miami Herald* revealed that lack of effective regulatory enforcement permitted thousands of criminals to obtain mortgage broker licenses.[10] Further, the requirements for licensure, even if enforced, were inadequate to ensure a reasonable threshold of competence. At least as troublesome, the incentive system was prone to encourage irresponsible behavior because fees were all paid at the front end, leaving to the borrower no recourse for misdeeds or errors discovered later. Moreover, the practice tended to encourage abusive lending because larger fees often were given to brokers to push more costly loans, and the fees were hidden (see footnote 9). As noted in Career Focus, Chapter 10, Congress has enacted legislation requiring more extensive broker licensing requirements (Secure and Fair Enforcement for Mortgage Licensing Act of 2008). The most important change affecting mortgage brokerage is likely to be the Dodd-Frank Wall Street Reform and Consumer Protection Act of 2010. The key element is this act's creation of the Consumer Financial Protection Bureau, with apparently strong power to regulate mortgage brokerage. It is likely that brokerage will be a continuing part of securitized home mortgage lending, and only time will reveal whether the necessary changes have been accomplished to ensure more responsible business behavior.

www.namb.org

Website of NAMB The Association of Mortgage Professionals, the main industry organization of mortgage brokers.

> ✓ **Concept Check**
>
> **11.9** Why might there be more concern about moral hazard in mortgage brokerage than with mortgage banking or depository mortgage lenders?

The Secondary Market for Residential Mortgages

During the era of traditional portfolio lending, it was difficult for a lender to resell existing home loans. The secondary market for residential mortgages before government involvement in the early 1970s was, to state it kindly, informal. About the only secondary market for mortgages involved lenders, usually mortgage bankers, loading bundles of FHA loans

---

9. A practice in recent years has been for the brokerage fees to be incorporated into the loan as a higher interest rate. This "yield-spread premium" reduces the front-end cash payment for the borrower, but it also can be used by lenders as an incentive to encourage brokers to steer naive borrowers toward higher interest rate loans. This controversial practice was prohibited by rules of the Federal Reserve, implemented in April 2011.

10. "Borrowers Betrayed." *Miami Herald,* July 20, 2008.

in a suitcase and carrying them up to northeastern states to "peddle" them to insurance companies or savings banks that had a shortage of local loan investment opportunities.[11]

The reasons for a weak private secondary mortgage market were abundant. There was variation from state to state in mortgage documents, variation in appraisal practices, and variation in the properties serving as collateral. Further, there was variation in underwriting practices of lending institutions (i.e., the process and policies for evaluating the risks of mortgage loan default). This lack of standardization made it extremely difficult for purchasers in the secondary mortgage market to analyze the risk and return characteristics of mortgage investments, which in turn increased the return (or yield) they required on mortgage investments—if they were willing to invest at all. The originating lenders then passed on these higher required yields to mortgage borrowers in the form of higher mortgage rates.

The absence of an effective secondary market created liquidity problems for mortgage originators because loans could not be quickly and easily sold. This resulted in fewer loans and higher mortgage interest rates for homebuyers. The problem had two main facets: First, it created sizable home mortgage interest rate differentials between growth areas of the United States, such as California and Florida, and the more mature areas of the Northeast and Midwest. Second, in periods of increased interest rates, disintermediation would restrict flows of savings into thrifts, leaving local mortgage lenders without funds to lend and unable to sell the loans they already had originated. As a result, horror stories were not uncommon in the late 1960s and early 1970s of lenders simply "shutting the credit window" and bringing otherwise active local housing markets to a standstill.

The lack of a well-functioning secondary market for residential mortgages was addressed in 1968 by Congress. It spun *Fannie Mae* (then, the Federal National Mortgage Association, or FNMA) out of the Department of Housing and Urban Development to establish it as a separate, quasi-private corporation to act as a buyer of FHA and VA loans. In the same act Congress created the **Government National Mortgage Association (GNMA),** popularly known as Ginnie Mae, as a unit within HUD. Among its intended roles was to guarantee mortgage-backed securities based on pools of FHA, VA, and loans from certain U.S. Department of Agriculture residential loan programs. Two years later, recognizing the need for a secondary market for conventional loans, Congress also created *Freddie Mac* (then known as the Federal Home Loan Mortgage Corporation). These steps laid the groundwork for a revolutionary system of housing finance which, out of the wreckage of the thrift-based system, would burst forth a decade later.

Mortgage-Backed Securities

The most important innovation that occurred in residential mortgage markets since World War II was the creation of mortgage-backed securities (MBSs). This process for the GNMA MBS is depicted in Exhibit 11-6. Pass-through MBSs are created by pooling a group of similar mortgages. The owner then uses the mortgage pool as collateral to issue a new security—the MBS. For example, a mortgage banker assembles a $10 million pool of 4.5 percent, 30-year, level-payment mortgages. The mortgage banker then sells an undivided interest, or participation, in the mortgage pool to many investors who are promised a 4 percent rate of interest on their invested capital. The issuer continues to service the underlying mortgages, collecting payments from borrowers and "passing through" to each security holder (1) its pro rata (proportionate) share of any principal repayments on the underlying mortgages and (2) 4 percent interest on its share of the remaining outstanding principal balance. The difference between the 4.5 percent rate on the underlying mortgages and the 4 percent rate paid to investors is kept by the MBS issuer. This "spread" must cover the issuance and servicing costs, and the cost of absorbing the default risk in the pool of mortgages. When a mortgage is used as collateral for the issuance of an MBS, the underlying

---

11. As described by a veteran mortgage banker, Mr. David Ginn.

Exhibit 11-6   The GNMA Mortgage-Backed Security Process

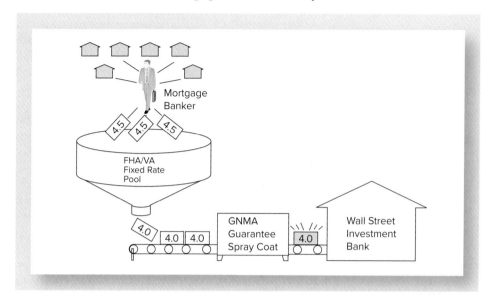

mortgage is said to be "securitized." Agencies and private companies that pool mortgages and sell MBSs are sometimes called **conduits.**

As high as 90 percent of conventional conforming and FHA or VA mortgage loans originated in the United States are now sold into the secondary mortgage market and used as collateral for the issuance of mortgage-backed securities.[12] This securitization has greatly increased the liquidity and efficiency of the mortgage market. By attracting nontraditional investors, such as pension funds, life insurance companies, mutual funds, and foreign institutional investors, MBSs have brought many new sources of investment capital into housing finance. The dramatic change that securitization represents in home mortgage lending is indicated in Exhibit 11-7. In 1980 just over 10 percent of all existing home

Exhibit 11-7   Percentage of All Home Loans Securitized*

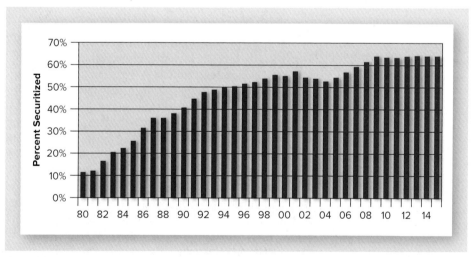

* First-lien home mortgage loans

Source: *Mortgage Market Statistical Annual,* 2013 and 2016. (Bethesda, MD. Inside Mortgage Finance Publications Inc.)

12. *Mortgage Market Statistical Annual,* 2016. (Bethesda, MD: Inside Mortgage Finance Publications, Inc., 2016), p. 72.

mortgages were securitized. At the beginning of 2015, about 65 percent had been securitized and sold in the secondary market.

✓ **Concept Check**

11.10   The three main government-related entities involved in creation or support of residential mortgage-backed securities are _____.

Purchasers of Residential Mortgages in the Secondary Market

Through the formative decades of the home mortgage secondary market, up to about 2000, the story of the market was the story of Ginnie Mae and the two government-sponsored enterprises (GSEs), Fannie Mae, and Freddie Mac. To be sure, other entities played significant and productive roles, including private conduits and state government housing agencies. But it was in the game defined by "Ginnie," "Fannie," and "Freddie" that the others played. More recently the role of Ginnie Mae had diminished with the eclipse of FHA/VA lending, while private conduits burgeoned into a major component of the secondary market. Now both of these trends are dramatically reversed in the wake of the "subprime meltdown." Subprime lending and securitization have virtually disappeared, while FHA–Ginnie Mae business is resurgent. A closer look at these players follows.

Ginnie Mae (GNMA)

www.ginniemae.gov

Website of Ginnie Mae. Information for homebuyers, issuers, and investors.

Ginnie Mae is the popular name for the Government National Mortgage Association (GNMA), a government-owned and financed corporation. In modern times Ginnie Mae's dominant activity is as a guarantor of mortgage-backed securities. Early on in securitization the Ginnie Mae MBS became the definitive mortgage "pass-through" security. Through its first 20 or more years, it remained the most liquid and widely held single type of MBS. Further, it was the security that introduced much of the investment community to MBSs. In this program, Ginnie Mae does not issue, buy, or sell mortgages or MBSs. Rather, as suggested in Exhibit 11-6, its role is to guarantee the timely payment of principal and interest on MBSs issued by private lenders. Ginnie Mae primarily guarantees MBSs backed by pools of FHA-insured or VA-guaranteed fixed-rate mortgages. These securities carry the full faith and credit of the U.S. government. Ginnie Mae mortgage-backed securities are thus free of default risk—just like Treasury securities—and therefore trade at relatively low yields. By linking housing and mortgage markets to the capital markets, this tremendously successful program has channeled vast sums of investment capital into the residential mortgage market. In recent years the market share of Ginnie Mae securities had diminished sharply. At the end of 2008, $599 billion in MBSs guaranteed by Ginnie Mae were outstanding, or about 5.4 percent of all outstanding mortgage debt; just half of Ginnie Mae's share seven years earlier. However, with the mortgage lending crisis of 2007–08 Ginnie Mae security issuance rebounded strongly to a double digit percentage of all securitization by December of 2014.[13] (See Exhibit 11-8.)

✓ **Concept Check**

11.11   GNMA's role in residential mortgage-backed securities is to guarantee _____ to the investors in the securities.

---

13. *The 2015 Mortgage Market Statistical Annual,* (Bethesda, MD: Inside Mortgage Finance Publications, Inc., 2015), p. 11.

Exhibit 11-8 Holders of Outstanding One- to Four-Family Residential Mortgage Debt

(4th Qtr. 2014, in billions of dollars)

All Depository Financial Institutions*			$ 2,422	(25)%
Fannie Mae	$ 212**	(2)%		
Freddie Mac	77**	(<1)%		
Other federal agencies	100	(<1)%		
Total federal agencies			$ 389	(4)%
MBSs guaranteed by Fannie Mae	$2,637**	(27)%		
MBSs guaranteed by Freddie Mac	1,572**	(16)%		
MBSs guaranteed by Ginnie Mae	1,452	(15)%		
Private MBS pools	704	(7)%		
Total MBS pools			$ 6,365	(64)%
Individuals and others†			$ 705	(7)%
All holders			$ 9,881	(100)%

*Depository institutions include commercial banks, thrifts, and credit unions.

**Estimate: GSE mortgages in portfolio no longer are reported separately from mortgages securitized. Estimates are made using data from SIFMA: http://www.sifma.org/research/statistics.aspx

† Others include mortgage companies, REITs, noninsured pension funds, finance companies, and state and local housing credit agencies.

Source: U.S. Federal Reserve Board of Governors of the Federal Reserve System, Statistical Releases: Table 1.54 Mortgage Debt Outstanding, Historical Data.

Fannie Mae

Fannie Mae was created as the Federal National Mortgage Association in 1938 to provide a secondary market for FHA-insured mortgages and, later, VA-guaranteed loans. Originally a U.S. Government agency, in 1968 Fannie Mae became a private, self-supporting company with publicly traded stock. In 1970 Fannie Mae was authorized to purchase conventional mortgages in addition to FHA-insured and VA-guaranteed loans, but it remained focused on FHA and VA loans throughout the 1970s. Fannie Mae does not lend money directly to homebuyers. Rather, it is charged to ensure that mortgage funds are consistently available and affordable by buying mortgages from qualified lenders who are making home loans.

Fannie Mae now has well-developed programs for the purchase of both conventional and government-underwritten residential mortgages. It purchases from mortgage bankers, commercial banks, thrifts, and other approved lenders. The majority of these acquired mortgages are combined into packages or mortgage pools, mortgage-backed securities are issued based on the pools, and the MBSs are then sold to investors.

Fannie Mae's history as a stock-issuing company ended in September 2008, when the U.S. government placed both GSEs into conservatorship. What its form will be for the future remains to be determined, but it appears far from extinction in 2016. (See Industry Issues 11-1.)

✓ Concept Check

11.12 Whereas Fannie Mae was created to purchase _____ and _____ mortgages, it now also buys _____ mortgages.

www.fanniemae.com

Under "Funding the Market," select "Mortgage-Backed Securities," explore MBS programs.

At the end of 2015 Fannie Mae held $2.83 trillion in its single-family residential loan portfolio and in residential MBS. Because the MBS investors are the actual owners of the mortgage pools used as collateral for the MBSs, these mortgages are not Fannie Mae assets but they are a contingent obligation since Fannie Mae fully guarantees timely payment of interest and principal to the investors. The MBSs issued and guaranteed by Fannie Mae, along with their portfolio of owned mortgages, accounted for 29 percent of outstanding residential mortgages.

Freddie Mac

www.freddiemac.com/ singlefamily

Freddie Mac, single-family loan business page. Explore various aspects of their loan purchase programs.

Freddie Mac was originally designed to create an active secondary market for mortgages originated by savings and loan associations. S&Ls primarily originated conventional loans and Fannie Mae was not authorized to purchase conventional loans until 1970. Like Fannie Mae, Freddie Mac was chartered by Congress, with obligations to support housing and home ownership. It eventually issued publicly traded stock, but its private ownership days ended along with Fannie Mae's when they were placed into conservatorship in September 2008. Freddie Mac currently buys almost exclusively conventional loans, purchasing from all types of lenders. It pools the majority of these loans and uses them as collateral for the issuance of MBSs. Freddie Mac and Fannie Mae have become operationally quite similar. Freddie Mac, however, has put greater emphasis on issuing MBSs; in 2015 Freddie Mac's combined portfolio of owned home loans and residential MBS issued was $1.65 trillion, representing 17 percent of all outstanding home loans.

www.freddiemac.com/ mbs

The entry page to Freddie Mac's mortgage security programs.

> **✓ Concept Check**
>
> **11.13** In 2015 the share of all residential mortgage loans either owned or securitized by Fannie Mae and Freddie Mac, together, was _____ percent.

The Importance and Status of Fannie Mae and Freddie Mac

Beginning in the 1970s, by making a standing commitment to purchase conforming conventional loans, Fannie Mae and Freddie Mac created the first real secondary market for conventional loans ever. This central accomplishment also brought about numerous landmark changes in the creation of conventional mortgage loans. First, the GSEs jointly fostered uniformity of mortgage notes, mortgages/trust deeds, appraisal forms, and loan application forms. Virtually all **"prime"** home mortgage loans came to be originated using these standard contract forms or close variants.[14] Further, these two GSEs set underwriting standards and practices that have been widely accepted as benchmarks for prudent lending. In addition, they used their unprecedented base of home mortgage information to research and develop new underwriting practices (discussed later in this chapter) that both reduced default risk and broadened the reach of conventional home lending, and they developed new electronic automated underwriting procedures that helped accelerate the loan application process from weeks to hours, or even minutes. In addition, Freddie Mac pioneered and implemented the use of reliable **automated valuation models** (see Chapter 7) as a substitute for standard appraisals for most home financings.

---

14. *Prime* is a casual term used in recent years referring, roughly, to conforming conventional home loans and "jumbo" loans written to similar underwriting quality. Sometimes it refers to borrowers with FICO scores over 660 (see later in this chapter), and sometimes it refers more to the type of lender. Some use the term to include FHA and VA loans as well.

What Will Become of Fannie Mae and Freddie Mac?

The story of Fannie Mae and Freddie Mac, told in this chapter, is one of "white knights" bringing great innovations to home mortgage lending and leading the industry out of the darkness of a preelectronic, preinternational world to become a model home financing system around the globe. But there is a dark side. The success of the GSEs led to their massive growth to where they became the largest single "private" financial obligation on the face of the earth, and the largest systemic risk to our financial system. At the end of 2008, their combined mortgage exposure through mortgages owned or mortgage securities guaranteed had grown to 87 percent of all U.S. Treasury marketable debt, or 78 percent of all nonfinancial corporate debt in the United States.[1] That was fine, in the minds of all but a few "prophets of doom," because house prices, the underlying bet, never go down: that is, until they did go down, and the net worth of Fannie and Freddie began to disappear.

It became clear in September of 2008 when the U.S. Government placed Fannie and Freddie under conservatorship, that our magnificent housing finance machine was broken and would never be the same. Its distinguishing character was being a pair of *private* companies with a *public* obligation: to assure liquidity and efficiency in housing finance. In return for this charter obligation, the GSEs had a U.S. Treasury credit-line backstop and, despite official denials, an implicit Treasury guarantee of its obligations.

So as Fannie and Freddie struggle forward under U.S. Government supervision, the question is: What now? Despite their vehement detractors, Fannie and Freddie are extremely good at what they do. They were not the cause of the financial collapse,

as some assert. And their management of home mortgage lending remains the best of the business, in terms of default rates and cost of borrowing. Complicating the debate further is that the GSEs technically have more than paid back any losses to the government and taxpayers in the years since their takeover, and have become something of a revenue machine for the US government.

So what are the options for the GSEs? Here are some that have been suggested:

- We could junk the machine—disassembling its parts, dissolving its portfolio of mortgage investments, and turning over its securitization functions to the private sector. A problem with that is that Fannie and Freddie have tremendous economies of scale that could be lost by this strategy, and they would no longer be able to serve as the backstop to a housing finance system in crisis as they did after 2007. (Since 2007 they have funded more than 60 percent of all first mortgage loans made, and about 94 percent of conforming mortgages.[2]) In this scenario, banks would play a much bigger mortgage role. Since junking the machine would raise the cost of housing finance, it is likely to be attractive only to those who believe that there already are too many subsidies to home ownership in our economy.
- We could fully nationalize the machine, possibly combining the two GSEs. But it is hard to find an example of a machine that works efficiently when political interests can get their hands on it; and housing is among the most politically sensitive issues in our society. (Perhaps the most compelling justification for privatizing the GSEs in the first place was that they would be somewhat insulated from political influence by their obligation to investors.)
- The GSEs could become regulated utilities. They would remain private, thus preserving the separation from direct government management. They would

answer to a regulatory commission for certain key aspects of their business such as fees and risk-taking levels. A possible risk in this choice is the one that haunts regulation of any utility, namely, determining reasonable costs and a fair profit.

- We could replace Fannie and Freddie with a cooperative. The cooperative would issue and guarantee mortgage securities for its members, who would contribute initial capital and pay user fees in proportion to their share of securities issued. The capital and fees would back the securities issued, but there would be protections both in front, through down payment requirements and PMI, and behind the guarantee, through U.S. government catastrophe insurance. This insurance would be paid for by the cooperative. The affordable housing objectives of Freddie and Fannie would be transferred to FHA or another government agency. The mutual nature of the entity could go far in providing the right incentives for competitiveness, efficiency, and safety, and the U.S. catastrophe insurance would assure market acceptance. There are many precedents for a financial cooperative, including the Federal Home Loan Bank System described in this chapter.

For further discussion of the future of Fannie and Freddie, look for statements by the Federal Reserve chairman and the secretary of Treasury. For a comprehensive collection of the thinking, through 2011, about the future of the U.S. home mortgage system, see the Wachter and Smith volume listed in the chapter "Additional Reading."

1. *Flows of Funds Accounts of the United States,* Federal Reserve Statistical Release, March 12, 2009, L.1 Credit Market Debt Outstanding.

2. *The Mortgage Market Statistical Annual,* Bethesda, MD: Inside Mortgage Finance Publications, Inc. 2015), p. 141.

✓ **Concept Check**

11.14   Fannie Mae and Freddie Mac jointly brought about uniform
_____ , _____ , _____ and _____
documents for home mortgage loans, and the use among lenders
of uniform _____ standards.

These changes enabled the growth of an extremely successful national (and world) secondary market for conforming conventional loans. As a result, the previously described problems of cross-national differentials in mortgage interest rates and an unreliable supply of mortgage funds were virtually eliminated. Further, as we noted in the previous chapter, MBSs based on conforming conventional loans have become so widely accepted by investors that the borrower's cost of a conforming conventional loan is significantly lower than that for nonconforming loans.

Recently, the GSEs experienced hard times. Their growth in size and activities was aggressively criticized before the Congress, especially by the megabanks. More recently, the GSEs suffered severe losses in the 2007–08 financial crisis, which led them into conservatorship of the U.S. Government. There are widely disparate views as to their role in the crisis. While a few suggest that they caused the crisis by investing in poor quality loans, others argue that in the midst of runaway lending, the GSEs remained the only prudent investors active in the secondary market.[15] In any case, there seems to be agreement that the business model under which they grew—issuing privately held stock but being chartered with a public mission to "support liquidity, stability, and affordability to the housing market"—is not viable.[16] Thus, change in the character of the two agencies appears inevitable. (See Industry Issues 11-1.)

✓ **Concept Check**

11.15   A central accomplishment of Fannie Mae and Freddie Mac is to
_____ .

Private Conduits

In recent years the most rapidly growing source of residential mortgage-backed securities was private conduits. These were created by the megabanks and megamortgage banking organizations as well as large finance companies and investment banking houses. Altogether, issuances of home mortgage MBS by private conduits more than tripled from 2002 to their peak at the end of 2007. Since then they have declined from $2.16 trillion, nearly 20 percent of home loans outstanding, to $0.7 trillion at the end of 2015, or 7 percent of home loans outstanding. (See Exhibit 11-8.) Embedded in this explosive growth and decline is the story of the subprime growth and "meltdown," which we discuss later in the chapter.

Federal Home Loan Banks

The system of 12 Federal Home Loan Banks was created to provide liquidity to savings and loan associations. They are privately owned by their members (originally, thrift institutions) and, like the GSEs, borrow as if they were backed by the U.S. government. Thus, they enjoy a low cost of funds. Moreover, since their stock is not publicly traded, they do not need the same level of earnings that the GSEs did. As the savings and loan industry receded, the FHLB system was reconstituted to serve as the "wholesale" lender (i.e., provider of liquidity) to all

---

15. As of the end of 2008, when the transition to conservatorship occurred, home mortgage delinquency data, as reported in the National Delinquency Survey of the Mortgage Bankers Association of America, seemed to support the latter view. The rate of "serious delinquency" (90 days late or in foreclosure) on "prime" fixed-rate home mortgages (90 percent of what the GSEs purchase) was 2.25 percent, as compared with 6.98 percent for all FHA loans, 10.45 percent for prime ARMs (most of what banks and thrifts originate to keep), and 23.1 percent for all subprime loans.

16. See mission statements on the respective websites.

thrifts, any banks that elect to become members, insurance companies, and credit unions. They make loans, called *advances*, secured by mortgage loans as collateral, and they have been an important source of liquidity for smaller mortgage lending institutions.

Other Secondary Market Purchasers

In addition to Fannie Mae, Freddie Mac, and Ginnie Mae, there are federal credit agencies that support the primary and secondary mortgage market for rural housing. The primary rural housing finance program in recent years has been the U.S. Department of Agriculture's Rural Housing Service.

State and local housing finance agencies also are a significant source of mortgage financing for first-time homebuyers and for those engaged in developing low- and moderate-income housing. The key to the success of these state and local programs has been the ability to finance their activities by issuing bonds exempt from federal taxation. Because investors in these bonds do not pay federal taxes on the interest they receive, the bonds can be issued with interest rates that are only 70–80 percent of the rates on typical bonds paying interest that is taxable to the investor.

The Big Picture of Home Mortgage Lending: Four Different Channels

In today's world of home mortgage lending there are four ways, or channels, by which first mortgage home loans are created. First, traditional direct (portfolio) lending is still present, if diminished from earlier decades. But in addition, there now are three channels involving securitization, explained later. Traditional portfolio lending accounted for over half of all loans created as late as 1989. Its share had fallen to 13 percent by 2010, but rebounded to nearly 25 percent by 2015 with growth in jumbo, non-conforming loans. A special aspect of portfolio lending is that it has a very high concentration of ARMs, as high as 40 percent. By contrast, the securitization channels generally have a very small percentage of ARM loans, around 5 percent.[17] This ARM concentration is not surprising since depository lenders must constantly balance the interest rate maturity of their assets against the rather short interest rate maturity of their liabilities; ARMs help since they have short-term interest rates.

Exhibit 11-9 summarizes the variation in the securitization channels of home mortgage lending. There are three different types of home loans being securitized: FHA/VA (including Rural Housing Service loans), conforming conventional, and nonconforming conventional (including jumbos, Alt-A, and, formerly, subprimes). Each of the three securitization channels has different players and different structure. The FHA/VA–Ginnie Mae securitization channel involves mortgage bankers and banks that pool the loans and also issue the securities, relying on GNMA's U.S. government credit guarantee to attract investors. It involves a credit guarantee external to the process. The conforming conventional loan–GSE securitization involves banks and mortgage bankers again, but they sell the loans to the GSE, which then pools the loans, issues the securities, and issues its own guarantee against default risk for the investors. In this case, the credit guarantee is internal to the issuer. The third channel, for nonconforming conventional loans, is still different. The securitizer can be a large bank (or its mortgage subsidiary), a large finance company, or a Wall Street investment bank. The securitizer obtains loans (mainly from brokers), pools the loans, and creates a senior—subordinate security structure. The securitizer then sells the senior securities, keeping the subordinate share, which absorbs all losses that result from

---

17. For statistics on bank and thrift ARM loans, see FDIC Statistics on Depository Institutions (SDI) Reports on the FDIC website. Important exceptions to the predominance of fixed-rate loans in securitized home loans were Alt-A and subprime loans. Alt-A loans were 60–70 percent ARMs, while subprimes were 80–90 percent ARMs. (See Amy Crews Cutts and William A Merrill, *Interventions in Mortgage Default: Policies and Practices to Prevent Home Loss and Lower Costs.* Freddie Mac Working Paper #08-01. Table 3. Available on Freddie Mac website.)

Exhibit 11-9 The Three Securitization Channels in U.S. Home Mortgage Lending: *Different Loans, Different Players, Different Investor Protections*

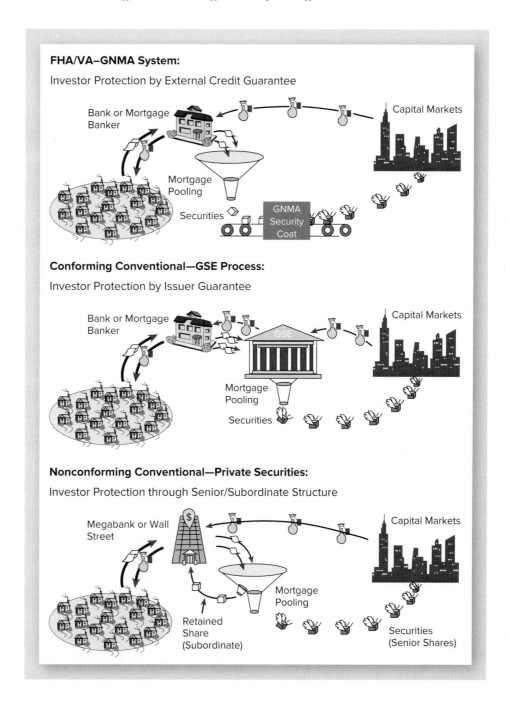

defaulted loans in the pool.[18] In this case the investor's protection against losses depends strictly on the mortgage pool.

The market share for each of the four channels from 1989 through 2014 is shown in Exhibit 11-10. While the traditional portfolio lending channel has given way over time, the change has been very uneven, probably reflecting the rise and fall in demand for ARM

18. If total loan losses in the pool exceed the percentage of the subordinated share, then the senior investors will experience losses as well. In a manner of speaking, this has been the case with many subprime securities.

Exhibit 11-10 Market Share for Four Channels of Home Mortgage Creation*

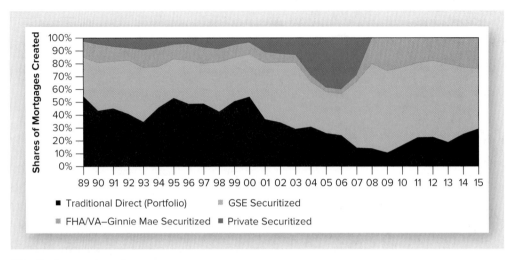

*First-lien home mortgage loans.

Source: *Mortgage Market Statistical Annual,* various editions "Secruitization Rates for Home Mortgages." (Bethesda, MD. Inside Mortgage Finance Publications Inc.)

loans and jumbo loans. And while the three securitization channels have grown in aggregate, it is apparent that their individual market shares have been anything but steady over time. The latest surge of private securitization after 2003, and then its total collapse, represents the subprime boom and meltdown. At its peak, in 2006, private securitization actually exceeded GSE securitization. The subsequent resurgence of the FHA/VA and conforming loan channels represents the reaction to the meltdown.

Where Does a Borrower Find a Home Loan?

The retail source of yore for home mortgage loans, the local thrift or bank, has given way to a complex and confusing array of home loan vendors. Retail sources now range from branches of the megabanks to local banks or credit unions, to mortgage bankers, to brokers, to web-based lenders.

When the source of a home mortgage can range from the branch of a megabank to the mother of one's real estate agent, to a web-based lender, how does one select? Because the business is fluid and subject to change, few simple conclusions are possible. However, one immediate conclusion is to shop aggressively. That said, one might expect this tendency among mortgage lenders: The more direct the lending source, the lower the cost for the borrower. That is, a bank that creates loans for its own portfolio should (all else equal) offer the lowest rates because there are fewer fees to be paid in between borrower and ultimate lender. So the shorter the lending chain, the lower should be the cost. Offsetting this is that the more direct lender may have a higher cost of funds for the loan or a less efficient mortgage operation. So shop! But even if this direct lender effect is true, there seems to be a trade-off. If brokers are to earn a fee, they may try to offer something that makes them competitive with the direct lender, namely service and loan terms. It is generally recognized that brokers tend to be available nights and weekends, in contrast to the customary practice of depository lenders. Further, the broker appears more likely to arrange a lower down payment, and to finance fees (including its own fee) by incorporating them in the quoted interest rate.[19] In summary, the broker may tend to offer more flexible and convenient service, and lower front-end costs, but at a higher interest rate. Is this always true? Apparently not. So shop!

19. The common arrangement of embedding the broker's fee in the loan interest rate has been referred to in recent years as a "yield-spread premium." (See footnote 9.)

A major real estate decision is whether to rent your residence or to buy. The answer depends heavily on lifestyle factors—Do you have economic stability in your life? How soon might you need or want to move? Do you have or expect children? Do you have or want a dog? Do you enjoy fixing up or keeping up your residence and yard? Do you enjoy the privacy that a yard can afford? What kind of surroundings appeal to you? Urban? Suburban?

But there also is a major financial side to the rent or buy decision, and it is complex enough to be either intriguing or befuddling. In principle, the choice is an investment decision: are you financially better off by buying? In later chapters of this book, you will learn about such decisions in detail for income producing property investments, but it also looms large for a home purchase. There are numerous online calculators for the rent or buy question, but one the best is

the *New York Times* Rent or Buy Calculator. To find it, simply google the name. You can run the calculator with as little information as the price of a purchased home and how long you plan to stay. But you can refine the analysis by adding any of this information:

- Mortgage rate, terms, and amount.
- Home price growth rate, rent growth rate, and inflation rate.
- Future return on savings and investments.
- Basic income tax situation.
- Expenses for buying and selling a home.
- Owner expenses such as maintenance, insurance, utilities, and common fees.
- Additional renting costs: security deposit, broker's fee, and renter's insurance.

The analysis tells you the most you would want to pay in rent. Any higher

means buying is the best financial choice. Three things make this calculator attractive: First, it is very easy to use and the results are easy to understand. Second, it incorporates more of the relevant factors than most calculators. Third, it uses net present value as its foundation for analysis, as we present in later chapters of this book. In other words, it recognizes the opportunity cost of tying up your wealth in a house rather than investing or using the money elsewhere.

Rent or Buy

Source: http://www.nytimes.com/interactive /2014/upshot/buy-rent-calculator.html?_r=2

Is It Better to Rent or Buy?

Home Price

A very important factor, but not the only one. Our estimate will improve as you enter more details below.

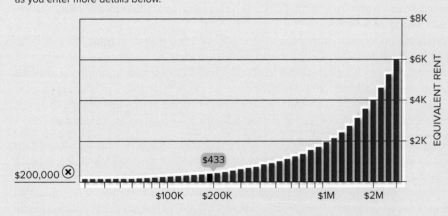

If you can rent a similar home for less than ...

$433 PER MONTH

... then renting is better.

Costs after 10 years	Rent	Buy
Initial costs	$1,110	$72,000
Recurring costs	$59,041	$210,151
Opportunity costs	−$14,135	−$83,156
Net proceeds	−$433	−$153,413
Total	$45,582	$45,582

How Long Do You Plan to Stay?

Buying tends to be better the longer you stay because the upfront fees are spread out over many years.

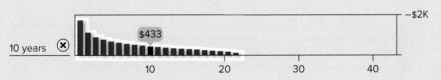

How to Read the Charts Charts that are relatively flat indicate factors that are not particularly important to the outcome. Conversely, the factors that have steep slopes have a large Impact.

A final aspect of the home lending pattern is the difference between fixed-rate mortgages and ARMs. Any lender is likely to offer both fixed-rate and ARM loans today. However, ARM loans are the most "natural" type of loan for a bank or thrift while fixed-rate is more marketable for mortgage banking. Thus, the borrower interested in an ARM loan would want to be sure to include banks or thrifts in their search, while the fixed-rate borrower would want to include lenders who sell their loans. A very positive result of the modern age is that an increasing number of lenders are offering their menu of loans on their website, together with detailed closing expenses. Specifically, with their list of loans they are making available Loan Estimates as required by the Consumer Financial Protection Bureau and described in Chapter 13.

The Lender's Mortgage Loan Decisions

The lender's process of determining whether to make a mortgage loan is called **loan underwriting.** It is a matter of determining whether the risks of the loan are acceptable. The process has undergone dramatic change since the mid-1990s, with traditional manual methods giving way to automated methods.

Traditional Home Mortgage Underwriting

Traditional home mortgage underwriting is said to rest on three elements, like a three-legged stool. The legs are collateral (the house), creditworthiness (willingness to pay), and capacity (income). These are often referred to as the "three Cs" of mortgage underwriting.

Collateral. To evaluate the loan **collateral,** an appraisal of the residence is required. The Uniform Residential Appraisal Report, created jointly by Fannie Mae, Freddie Mac and the primary appraisal associations, became virtually the universal document format for this purpose (see Exhibit 7-12).

The appraisal is important because the loan-to-value ratio always has been recognized as an important factor in mortgage loan risk. For example, studies of loans bought by Freddie Mac from the 1975–83 period revealed a decade later that loans with a loan-to-value ratio above 90 percent were 25 times more likely to default than loans originated with a loan-to-value ratio less than 70 percent, and the severity of loss from default was over twice as great.[20] More recent research confirms that high loan-to-value ratio is the characteristic most strongly associated with default.[21]

Despite the importance of the loan-to-value relationship in underwriting, the role of an appraisal has been reduced. Because appraisal is a costly and time-consuming part of underwriting, the search for substitutes has been active. For example, to simply refinancing of an existing loan—already paid down for some years—it is arguable that an appraisal is not needed. More generally, substantial progress has occurred in developing long-distance, electronic appraisal substitutes, called *automated valuation models* (see Chapter 7).

Creditworthiness. Until the 1990s, evaluation of borrower creditworthiness was perhaps the most complex and uncertain element in underwriting. It involved obtaining a credit report for the applicant and then examining the pattern of balances and payment punctuality. Consistent and reliable rules of interpretation were difficult to define, so considerable judgment could be necessary to evaluate a report. This process began to be replaced by the use of statistical **credit scoring** during the mid-1990s, as explained later. This set the stage for a virtual revolution in loan underwriting.

Capacity (Ability to Pay). From the beginning of the FHA and conventional lending, two payment burden ratios were important elements of underwriting.[22] The first,

20. Robert B. Avery, Raphael W. Bostic, Paul S. Calem, and Glenn B. Canner, "Credit Risk, Credit Scoring, and the Performance of Home Mortgages," *Federal Reserve Bulletin,* July 1996.

21. Wayne R. Archer and Brent C. Smith, "Residential Mortgage Default: The Roles of House Price Volatility, Euphoria and the Borrower's Put Option," *Journal of Real Estate Finance and Economics,* July 2011. See their findings and bibliography for references to other default studies.

22. VA underwriting originally used a different approach, which computed the amount of income available for a housing payment. FHA adopted the versions of the ratios presented here in the early 1990s.

commonly known as the **housing expense ratio,** or "front-end" ratio, is defined as:

$$\text{Housing expense ratio} = \text{PITI} \div \text{GMI}$$

PITI is the monthly payment of principal and interest on the loan plus monthly payments into an escrow account toward property taxes and hazard insurance. GMI is the borrower's gross monthly income. For conventional loans, a standard maximum for this ratio was 28 percent by the mid-1990s. For FHA loans it was 29 percent (now 31 percent), reflective of slightly more tolerant standards.

The second underwriting ratio, now called the **Debt-to-income ratio,** or "back-end" ratio, is defined as:

$$\text{Debt-to-income ratio} = (\text{PITI} + \text{LTO}) \div \text{GMI}$$

LTO (long-term obligations) is the sum of payments for other repeating obligations that extended for more than, say, 10 months, including such obligations as car lease payments and child support. For conventional loans, a standard maximum for the debt-to-income ratio came to be 36 percent by the mid-1990s. The maximum for FHA was 41 percent, again reflecting more tolerant standards. A profound change, discussed later, is that these two ratios no longer serve as cutoffs for mortgage underwriting to the extent that they did in the past. On the other hand, an important use of the total-debt-ratio now is with Qualified Mortgages. As discussed in Chapter 10, one standard for QMs is a debt-to-income ratio no greater than 43 percent.

✓ **Concept Check**

11.16   The housing expense ratio is computed as _____.

Since gross monthly income is the denominator in all of the expense ratios, how it is determined is important. Often computing the "quantity and quality" of GMI involves much more than taking a single number from a paycheck stub. Rather, there may be multiple jobs, multiple borrowers, and uncertain employment situations to consider. Because of the many judgments involved, biases and abuses can result. As a result, this step has become the most carefully regulated part of the underwriting process. As explained in Chapter 9, the Equal Credit Opportunity Act (ECOA) regulates extensively what information can be used and what income can be excluded from the process.

✓ **Concept Check**

11.17   The "three Cs" of home loan underwriting are _____.

Modern Home Mortgage Underwriting

In the middle 1990s, radical change began to occur in the process of home loan underwriting with the introduction of credit scoring. The use of individual credit reports in loan applications was largely replaced in a very short time by the FICO score, a product by the Fair Isaac Corporation. So, on the FICO scale that ranges from 300 to 850, it became the prevailing practice to regard applicants with a FICO score above 660 as high quality (prime) whereas an applicant whose FICO score was less than 620 was "risky."[23] The credit scoring methodology rapidly evolved to **automated underwriting** and has virtually replaced the traditional approach. The modern approach relies on a statistically derived equation to determine the level of default risk

23. *Automated Underwriting: Making Mortgage Lending Simpler and Fairer for America's Families,* Freddie Mac, 1996.

with a loan application. This approach exploits the combination of cybertechnology and the vast lending experience embedded in the giant loan portfolios of Freddie Mac, Fannie Mae, and of the new megamortgage lenders. Applying multivariate statistics to past loans, researchers build an equation (index) to predict default from the data of the loan application "package." The equation can then be used to evaluate almost instantly a new application submitted electronically by a lender for a prospective borrower. The system classifies the loan application according to its computed risk index. If the index is favorable, the loan application is classified as accepted, and the loan, if originated, will be accepted for purchase without further question. At some lower index value, the loan must be underwritten manually before it can be considered for purchase. At some still poorer index value, the loan application is likely not to be acceptable for purchase unless underlying problems in the application are solved.

Automated underwriting now is used in virtually all home mortgage lending. Lenders not selling to "Freddie" or "Fannie" still can "rent" the use of their systems.[24] Further, these systems have been adapted for use with FHA and VA loan applications. Finally, several of the giant mortgage lenders of today have evolved their own proprietary automated underwriting systems.

✓ Concept Check

11.18   In modern automated underwriting, a critical difference from the traditional approach is that credit evaluation is accomplished through a _____.

This technology has proved to dominate manual traditional underwriting in many important ways. First, it is capable of being virtually instantaneous whereas traditional underwriting could require days, or more. Second, its use is totally electronic and thus has much lower marginal cost per loan than manual underwriting. Most importantly, it has proved to be much "smarter," on average, than manual methods. Its success in identifying risky loans has made it a critical enabling factor for Fannie Mae, Freddie Mac, and the giant lenders to safely undertake "affordable housing" loan programs that would be prohibitively risky otherwise. Thus, through underwriting cost reductions and improved risk discrimination, automated underwriting has made home ownership available to large numbers of households for whom it previously was inaccessible.[25]

Ability-to-Repay Standard

The Dodd-Frank Act has brought a new standard for home mortgage underwriting. To ensure "ability-to-repay," the lender must consider at least the following eight factors in borrower risk: (1) current or reasonable income or assets; (2) current employment status; (3) the monthly payment on the loan; (4) the monthly payment for any simultaneous loan; (5) the monthly payment for mortgage-related obligations; (6) current debt obligations, alimony, and child support; (7) monthly debt-to-income ratio; and (8) credit history. The specific details of these eight points are not defined. So it is left to the lender to implement them in a reasonable manner. However, the ability-to-repay standard is now required of any lender underwriting any home mortgage loan.

---

24. Freddie Mac's automated underwriting system is called Loan Product Advisor, while Fannie Mae's is called Desktop Underwriting.

25. If automated underwriting (AU) is so good, why are there now so many defaulted loans? Answer: There are two dimensions to the default risk involved. First is relative risk, or risk ranking among borrowers. Automated underwriting addresses this risk, and is clearly superior to alternatives in evaluating it. The second is the general level of default risk due to changing economic conditions—especially employment—that affects every borrower's risk of default at once. No underwriting method is effective in predicting changes in that risk, but it has dominated in the Great Recession. For research on the effectiveness of AU, see references by Freddie Mac and by Avery, et al. in the end-of-chapter references.

Cash Down Payment Requirement

In both traditional and modern home loan underwriting, a standard practice has been to require some portion of the down payment to be in cash. As noted in Chapter 10, this is a minimum of 3.5 percent of the house value for FHA loans. For conventional loans it usually was greater. Some economists have argued that this requirement is questionable since true equity is not what one puts into a house, but what one can recover from it. Others explain the requirement as a signal. Putting cash into the purchase indicates that the borrower believes in the purchase and intends to stay with it. As discussed later, an important aspect of some recent affordable housing loan programs was to remove the cash down payment requirement.

Recent Underwriting Failures

Since 2007 many dramatic stories have hit the news about the failure of underwriting and of outright fraud in home mortgage origination. How does this relate to the automated underwriting described above? A partial answer is in footnote 25. More generally, the underwriting standards presented here were too often cast aside. New lenders and private securitization channels made it possible to avoid traditional mortgage underwriting. The worst failures appear to have been with subprime loans, where it appears that underwriting was widely suppressed by higher-level management in the securitizing firms. In one report, for example, the portion of subprime borrowers who did not fully document their income or assets was as high 50 percent, and still higher for Alt-A.[26] A large portion of these loans likely were the now infamous "no-doc" loans that came to be called "liar loans."[27]

✓ **Concept Check**

11.19   Two important advantages of automated underwriting are that it is _____ and it enables lenders to more safely make _____ loans.

Home Financing for Marginal Borrowers

The creation of the long-term, level-payment loan, the creation of mortgage insurance, and the evolution of modern residential lending institutions since World War II went far to make home ownership available to mainstream American households. But some groups in the society still have found this dream chronically difficult to achieve. Among these are minority households, lower-income households, and even some moderate-income households lacking accumulated wealth. The barrier to home ownership had two aspects: qualifying for a loan and making a down payment. Three developments brought relief to this problem. The first was automated underwriting, discussed in the previous section. The other two were new kinds of lending programs: affordable housing loans and nonprime loans.

Affordable Housing Loans

**www.loanprospector
.com**

Website for Freddie's Loan Product Advisor automated underwriting.

In the mid-1990s a powerful convergence of GSE capability and Congressional interest led to a harvest of **affordable housing loan** programs. The general strategy of affordable housing loans adopted by the GSEs was to allow unusual flexibility in one of the "three Cs" of underwriting while maintaining the other two at more normal standards. For example, a loan program might allow the down payment to go less than 3 percent while maintaining

---

26. See Amy Crews Cutts and William A. Merrill, op.cit. (in footnote 16), Table 3.

27. No-doc loans were loans that did not require the borrower to document their stated income or assets. The idea was to enable self-employed persons to obtain home financing, which was sometimes arduous, if not impossible, because of the difficulty in documenting self-employment income. The idea quickly ran out of control in the years up to 2006.

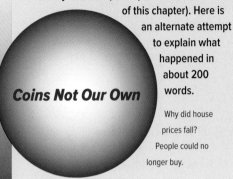

What was that thunderous crash?

A defining event of our age was the housing crash that started the Great Recession. Its complex causes have been the subject of many volumes (see a partial list at the end of this chapter). Here is an alternate attempt to explain what happened in about 200 words.

Coins Not Our Own

Why did house prices fall?

People could no longer buy.

Why could they no longer buy?

They owed too much debt to add more.

Why did they owe too much debt?

From loans in excess with equity nil,

With payments too small and certain to grow,

So refi or sale at increasing price

Was all that could keep the borrower whole.

Why did people think this could work?

Because it had worked before.

Why did they have no worry of loss?

They gambled with coins not their own.

Why did lenders make loans in excess?

Prices kept rising to bail out the loans,

And money became too easy to get,

So they gambled with coins not their own.

Why was money too easy to get?

To salve 9-11 the Fed lowered rates,

While Congress presumed we should own our own home,

And surplus world savings were hungry for yield,

And "Laissez Faire" reigned in financial controls,

But prices seemed always to reach a new high.

So Wall Street could dare to create "magic bonds"...

Change home loans to gold with no risk to the eye!

But why would we gamble that prices would rise?

Because they had always risen before,

And easy money would drive them up more,

And we thought we'd bet coins not our own.

So, why did house prices start to fall?

People could no longer buy.

---

standard payment burden ratios and minimum credit score. So did the GSE underwriting approach to affordable lending work? While direct evidence is not available, the programs have not been cited for special problems as Alt-A and subprime have.

> ✓ **Concept Check**
>
> **11.20** In recent years the combination of GSE underwriting and risk management capability, together with increased congressional interest, brought about an unprecedented variety in the types of _____ loans.

Subprime Lending

Most "affordable" housing loans still permitted only slightly deficient credit quality. This left a significant population of households unable to qualify, even for affordable home loans. In addition, some creditworthy borrowers sought refinancing at extremely high loan-to-value levels (in excess of 100 percent). Often they did so in the hope of replacing high-interest, high-payment consumer debt with more favorable mortgage debt. Still others were creditworthy and sought a conventional loan-to-value ratio, but lacked adequate income documentation to qualify for prime financing. These three types of borrowers—those with weak credit, those who seek 100 percent financing and more, and those who cannot document their income—were the original clientele for *subprime loans.* Subprime loans were at a substantially higher interest rate than prime loans (200–600 basis points higher), carried greater fees, and often included prepayment penalties. Despite the more difficult terms, these types of loans increased exponentially from the early 1990s to exceed 25 percent of all loans originated in 2005 and 2006.[28]

> ✓ **Concept Check**
>
> **11.21** The three original clienteles for subprime loans included households that _____, _____, or _____.

28. Source: "Mortgage Originations by Product," *The Mortgage Market Statistical Annual* (Bethesda, MD: Inside Mortgage Finance Publications, Inc.) 2015.

Subprime lending was always the subject of major controversy. Defenders of the industry argue that the terms of the subprime loan typically are better than credit card and personal loans that the household would be forced to depend on otherwise. But others pointed to horror stories of "predatory" lending practices in this largely unregulated industry.[29] (See Industry Issues 9-2.)

Whatever the arguments for and against subprime lending, it is apparent that something went terribly wrong. The details of the "subprime meltdown" have been recounted in countless newspaper and periodical articles, on TV and radio, and in numerous books.[30] Virtually every participant in residential finance has been blamed, from "greedy" lenders and investment bankers to "greedy" homebuyers, to the Congress for failing to regulate, to then-Federal Reserve Chairman Alan Greenspan for keeping interest rates too low following "9-11." Sorting out the causes will keep pundits and researchers busy for a very long time. In any case it is clear that the "subprime mess" reached far beyond the almost 14 percent of home mortgage loans classified as subprime in 2006.[31] It appears to include, among other factors, a systemic disregard for the kind of mortgage underwriting described above. It also involved overproduction of housing and a financial system that was allowed to invent almost incomprehensible techniques of leveraging a bet that housing prices would continue to rise. For better or for worse, that story is beyond the scope of this book, though at the end of this chapter we list several of the more compelling books addressing the crisis.

archives.hud.gov/ reports/treasrpt.pdf

HUD-Treasury reports on predatory lending.

29. Congress addressed the predatory lending problem by enacting the Home Owners Equity Protection Act of 1999. It is discussed in Chapter 9.

30. An example of newspaper coverage is a series of *Wall Street Journal* articles under the theme "Debt Bomb," May 30, 2007; June 27, 2007; July 5, 2007; and August 7, 2007, all on page A-1. Other interesting articles include "How Ratings Firms' Calls Fueled Subprime Mess," *The Wall Street Journal,* August 15, 2007, page A-1; and "One family's Journey into a Subprime Trap," *The Wall Street Journal,* August 16, 2007, page A-1. A television video production that is especially effective in telling the "meltdown" story is CNBC's "House of Cards," released in February of 2009. It can be purchased as a DVD or watched from secondary sources on the Web.

31. Estimated from data of the Mortgage Bankers Association *National Delinquency Survey,* various editions.

Summary

The home mortgage lending system of the United States has gone through an extreme transformation since the 1970s from a very localized system dominated by local thrifts to a national and international system dominated by megabanks, megamortgage bankers, and securitization. Mortgage bankers originate home mortgages, owning them for only long enough to sell them in the secondary market. They may sell the mortgages as part of a mortgage-backed security (MBS) that they have issued, or they may sell the mortgages to someone else to securitize. That buyer may be another lender (large bank or mortgage banker), or it may be one of the GSEs, Fannie Mae or Freddie Mac. The mortgage banker makes its profits from the rights to service the loans it has created and sold.

In contrast to a mortgage banker, a mortgage broker simply brings borrowers and lenders together, for a fee, but never owns or services the loans created. Mortgage brokerage has encountered controversy, resulting from the ease of entry to the business, and an incentive structure based on single, up-front fees. Recent scandals have prompted more control of entry and fee practices.

MBSs involve creating a pool of similar mortgage loans, putting them into a trust, and then issuing securities that are prorated claims on the cash flows from the pool. To be accepted by investors, these MBSs must be guaranteed against investor losses due to default. The issuer can do this several ways: Use an external guarantee (the GNMA approach); use its own guarantee (the GSE approach); or create a senior-subordinate structure of claims within the MBS so that the subordinate interest absorbs any loss (the private security approach).

In developing a secondary market in residential mortgages, Fannie Mae and Freddie Mac have brought about standardization of mortgages, mortgage notes, appraisals, loan applications, and loan underwriting practices. Because of this standardization, there is an economy-wide mortgage market, and investors are much better able to buy and sell mortgages and MBSs since the risk-return characteristics of these securities are more easily analyzed. The increased standardization and liquidity provided by the GSEs have greatly improved mortgage market efficiency.

The current home mortgage delivery system of the United States involves four different channels for mortgage money flows. These include traditional portfolio lending of thrifts and banks, plus three securitization systems: FHA/VA–GNMA, conforming conventional loans–GSE, and nonconforming conventional loans–private securitization. Each channel tends to have somewhat different lenders, different financial structure, and deals with different kinds of loans. The market share of each channel is sensitive to the relative demand for different types of loans and to investor perceptions.

When underwriting home loans—that is, when deciding whether to extend credit—lenders traditionally have examined the "three Cs" of a borrower: creditworthiness, collateral (appraised value), and capacity (income). Although the same issues are examined today, the approach has changed radically through the use of credit scores, appraisal substitutes, and automated underwriting. Because of the advances in lending operations and in underwriting, and because of increased awareness and support of minority interest, new loan programs have been developed that are designed to extend credit to marginal home borrowers who do not meet traditional standards.

The housing boom and bust of the last few years is severely testing the home finance system of the United States. Among the most dramatic effects so far are the explosive growth and then disappearance of subprime lending, the possible end of Fannie Mae and Freddie Mac, at least in their current form, and unprecedented rates of home foreclosure. Every financial and economic crisis seems to leave the home mortgage finance system changed, and the current one has every prospect of doing so again.

Key Terms

Affordable housing loan 299	Debt-to-income ratio 297	Mortgage banking 279
Automated underwriting 297	Disintermediation 277	Mortgage brokers 279
Automated valuation models 289	Fallout risk 280	Pipeline risk 280
Collateral 296	Government National Mortgage	PITI 297
Commercial banks 278	Association (GNMA) 285	Portfolio lenders 279
Conduits 286	Housing expense ratio 297	Prime 289
Credit scoring 296	Interest rate risk 280	Thrifts 275
Credit unions 284	Loan underwriting 296	Warehousing 278

Test Problems

Answer the following multiple-choice problems:

1. Mortgage banking companies:
   a. Collect monthly payments and forward them to the mortgage investor.
   b. Arrange home loan originations, but do not make the actual loans.
   c. Make home loans and fund them permanently.
   d. None of the above.

2. In the last 20 years, the mortgage banking industry has experienced:
   a. Nearly complete obsolesence.
   b. Decentralization.
   c. Limited consolidation.
   d. Rapid consolidation.

3. Currently, which type of financial institution in the primary mortgage market provides the most funds for the residential (owner-occupied) housing market?
   a. Life insurance companies.
   b. Thrifts
   c. Credit unions.
   d. Commercial banks

4. For conforming conventional home loans, the standard payment ratios for underwriting are:
   a. 28 percent and 36 percent.
   b. 25 percent and 33 percent.
   c. 29 percent and 41 percent.
   d. 33 percent and 56 percent.

5. The numerator of the standard housing expense (front-end) ratio in home loan underwriting includes:
   a. Monthly principal and interest.
   b. Monthly principal, interest, and property taxes.
   c. Monthly principal, interest, property taxes, and hazard insurance.
   d. All of these plus monthly obligations extending 10 months or more.

6. The most profitable activity of residential mortgage bankers normally is:
   a. Loan origination.
   b. Loan servicing.
   c. Loan sales in the secondary market.
   d. Loan brokerage activities.

7. Potential justifiable subprime borrowers include persons who:
   a. Are creditworthy but want a 100 percent or higher LTV loan.
   b. Are credit-impaired.
   c. Persons with no documentation of their income.
   d. All of these.

8. The normal securitization channel for jumbo conventional loans is:
   a. GNMA.
   b. GSEs.

   c. Private conduits.
   d. FDIC.

9. Over the last two decades the reduced importance of certain institutions in the primary mortgage market has been largely offset by an expanded role for others. Which has diminished, and which has expanded?
   a. Commercial bankers; thrifts.
   b. Mortgage banking; commercial banks.
   c. Commercial banks; mortgage banking.
   d. Thrifts; mortgage banking and commercial banks.

10. *Warehousing* in home mortgage lending refers to:
    a. Short-term loans made by mortgage bankers to commercial banks.
    b. Short-term loans made by commercial banks to mortgage bankers.
    c. Long-term loans made by commercial banks to mortgage bankers.
    d. Short-term loans to finance the construction of builder warehouses.

Study Questions

1. What is the primary purpose of the risk-based capital requirements that Congress enacted as part of the Financial Institutions Reform, Recovery, and Enforcement Act (FIRREA)?
2. Explain what "pipeline risk" is in mortgage banking and why it is such a dominating risk to mortgage banking.
3. Describe the basic activities of Fannie Mae in the secondary mortgage market. How are these activities financed?
4. Explain the importance of Fannie Mae and Freddie Mac to the housing finance system in the United States.
5. What went wrong with mortgage brokerage? Is it being fixed?
6. Describe the mechanics of warehouse financing in mortgage banking.
7. Explain how affordable housing loans differ from standard home loans.

8. List three "clients" for subprime home mortgage loans.
9. You have just signed a contract to purchase your dream house. The price is $120,000 and you have applied for a $100,000, 30-year, 5.5 percent loan. Annual property taxes are expected to be $2,000. Hazard insurance will cost $400 per year. Your car payment is $400, with 36 months left. Your monthly gross income is $5,000. Calculate:
   a. The monthly payment of principal and interest (PI).
   b. One-twelfth of annual property tax payments and hazard insurance payments.
   c. Monthly PITI (principal, interest, taxes, and insurance).
   d. The housing expense (front-end) ratio.
   e. The debt-to-income (back-end) ratio.
10. Contrast automated underwriting with the traditional "three Cs" approach.

EXPLORE THE WEB

1. In home mortgage lending today, automated underwriting based on a single statistical risk equation has largely replaced the traditional method of risk evaluation through separate examinations of the "three Cs": collateral, creditworthiness, and income capacity. Central to the automated risk equation is the borrower's credit score (FICO score). Go to the FICO score website: www.myfico.com and read about the use of FICO scores. You may want to pay the modest fee required to obtain your FICO score, plus an analysis of factors that could improve it.

2. Go to the websites of Freddie Mac and Fannie Mae and find their affordable housing loan products. Compare their offerings.

3. Go to the website of one of the megabanks (Wells Fargo, Bank of America, J. P. Morgan Chase, Citibank). See if you can obtain an array of home mortgage loan rate quotes. Does it provide a downloadable Loan Estimate?

Solutions to Concept Checks

1. The vulnerability of thrifts was asset–liability maturity mismatch.

2. A major new regulatory approach for thrifts introduced by the FIRREA was to impose risk-based capital standards.

3. Three ways that commercial banks have served mortgage lending is by making mortgage loans to its regular customers, by providing "warehouse" lines of credit to mortgage bankers, and through construction lending.

4. Today, the largest market share in home mortgage lending among depository lenders is held by commercial banks.

5. Mortgage brokers differ from mortgage bankers in that they neither fund mortgage loans nor service them.

6. *Pipeline risk* refers to the risks in mortgage banking between making a commitment for a loan and selling the loan.

7. The two components of pipeline risk are fallout risk (falling rates cause prospective borrowers to go elsewhere) and interest rate risk (rising rates diminish the value of existing loans).

8. The primary source of profits in mortgage banking is fees for servicing mortgage loans on behalf of the mortgage investors.

9. There might be more concern about moral hazard among mortgage brokers than among mortgage bankers or depository mortgage lenders because brokers have no continuing involvement with the loan or borrower after the loan is made.

10. The three main government-related entities involved in creation or support of residential mortgage-backed securities are Ginnie Mae, Fannie Mae, and Freddie Mac.

11. Ginnie Mae's role in residential mortgage-backed securities is to guarantee timely payment of interest and principal to the investors in the securities.

12. Whereas Fannie Mae was created to purchase FHA and VA mortgages, it now also buys conventional mortgages.

13. In 2015, the share of all residential mortgage loans either owned or securitized by Fannie Mae and Freddie Mac together was about 46 percent.

14. Fannie Mae and Freddie Mac jointly brought about uniform application, mortgage, note, and appraisal documents for home mortgage loans, and the use among lenders of uniform underwriting standards.

15. A central accomplishment of Fannie Mae and Freddie Mac is to create a market to buy conforming conventional loans.

16. The housing expense ratio is computed as PITI/GMI, or monthly principal, interest, taxes, and insurance divided by gross monthly income.

17. "Three Cs" of home loan underwriting are collateral, creditworthiness, and capacity.

18. A critical difference in modern automated underwriting from the traditional approach is that credit evaluation is accomplished through a credit score.

19. Two important advantages of automated underwriting are that it is faster and it enables lenders to more safely make affordable housing loans.

20. In recent years the combination of GSE underwriting and risk management capability, together with renewed congressional interest, brought about an unprecedented variety in the types of affordable housing loans.

21. The three original clients for subprime loans included households that had weak credit, wanted 100 percent financing, or could not document their income.

Additional Readings

Substantial portions of the following books are devoted to residential mortgage financing:

Avery, Robert B., Raphael W. Bostic, Paul Calem, and Glenn B. Conner. "Credit Risk, Credit Scoring, and the Performance of Home Mortgages," *Federal Reserve Bulletin*, July 1996.

Brueggeman, William B., and Jeffrey D. Fisher. *Real Estate Finance and Investments,* 15th ed. New York: McGraw-Hill/Irwin, 2016.

Clauretie, T. M., and G. S. Sirmans. *Real Estate Finance: Theory and Practice,* 6th ed. Mason, OH: Cengage Learning, 2010.

Lewis, Michael. *The Big Short: Inside the Doomsday Machine.* New York: W.W. Norton & Company, 2010.

Mahoney, Peter E. and Peter M. Zorn, *Automated Underwriting: Making Mortgage Lending Simpler and Fairer for America's Families.* McLean, VA: Freddie Mac, 1996. Out of print. Variants can be found through Google.

McLean, Bethany, and Joe Nocera. *All the Devils Are Here.* New York: Penguin Group, 2010.

Rajan, Raghuram G. *Fault Lines.* Princeton, NJ: Princeton University Press, 2010.

Shiller, Robert J. *The Subprime Solution: How Today's Global Financial Crisis Happened, and What to Do About It.* Princeton, NJ: Princeton University Press, 2008.

Wachter, Susan M., and Marvin M. Smith. *The American Mortgage System Crisis and Reform.* Philadelphia, PA: University of Pennsylvania Press, 2011.

Chapter 12

PART FIVE

Real Estate Brokerage *and* Listing Contracts

LEARNING OBJECTIVES

After reading this chapter, you will be able to:

1 Describe the brokerage function.

2 State three reasons sellers use brokers.

3 Explain the real estate licensing process.

4 Explain the difference between licensing and industry designations.

5 Explain how commission rates are determined.

6 List and describe three types of listing contracts.

7 Describe three types of agency relationships in real estate brokerage.

8 List at least three protective provisions each for a property owner and broker that should be included in a listing contract.

9 List the ways that a listing contract can be terminated.

OUTLINE

Introduction: Brokerage—The Best-Known Type of Real Estate Business

Many people think of real estate brokerage as *the* real estate business. Although we take a much broader view of real estate, we agree that brokerage is one of the largest and most visible parts of the real estate business. Also, most people are more apt to come in contact with real estate brokers or salespeople than other real estate professionals.

Real estate brokerage also tends to be better known than other real estate businesses because it is easier to enter. Educational requirements are not extensive, and capital requirements are not as high as in other businesses; a small office, a telephone, a computer, and a car may be the only requirements. Although many people enter the business, many also leave it; turnover is high.

Yet real estate brokerage is a demanding occupation for those who would succeed. It requires a great deal of knowledge, skill, and effort. It also can be quite rewarding monetarily and personally. As with any other business or profession, however, the price of success is preparation, dedication to the welfare of customers, and hard work.

> ### ✓ Concept Check
>
> **12.1** Name three conditions that represent the "price of success" in real estate brokerage.

Real Estate Brokers as Market Facilitators

www.realtor.org

Home page of the National Association of Realtors (NAR), the umbrella organization for the real estate brokerage industry, and more.

Real estate brokers are intermediaries. They are the catalysts of real estate transactions; they help make markets work by bringing buyers and sellers together physically and emotionally to create sales and purchases. Without their services, it would be more difficult and costly to buy and sell properties, and real estate values—at least in some markets—would undoubtedly be lower. The buyers who value the property most would be less likely to find it.

For this service, brokers are paid a fee, usually called a **commission.** Commissions are typically paid by sellers, but they may be paid by buyers or—in some unusual situations—by both sellers and buyers.

> ### ✓ Concept Check
>
> **12.2** Without real estate brokers, real estate values would be lower. Explain this statement.

Commissions usually are determined as a percentage of the gross sale price, though other arrangements are possible. For example, an owner and a broker may agree to a **net listing,** whereby the seller is assured a certain fixed net price for the property and the broker is allowed to retain any amount of the actual sales price above that figure.[1]

Economic Rationale for Employing a Broker

Brokers are employed to sell properties because they can offer expertise and efficiency. Brokers have specialized knowledge of the real estate market and have developed expertise in selling properties. Furthermore, they spend time and effort in finding buyers for listed properties. Successful brokers have knowledge in the following areas:

- Prices and terms of recent market transactions for similar properties.
- Marketing procedures that have been successful in the past.

---

1. Because the net listing agreement encourages the broker to be less than candid to the seller, it is viewed by some as unethical, and may be prohibited in some places.

- Legal obligations of buyers and sellers.
- Similar properties, prices, and terms currently listed for sale.
- Needs of prospective buyers who seek out brokerage firms as sources of properties.
- Procedures that buyers and sellers should follow in consummating a transaction (e.g., how to obtain a title search, financing, insurance, utility services, and the like).

While some property owners attempt to sell their properties themselves to avoid a brokerage commission, they often find they are ill equipped for this task, and they may end up with less cash than if they had employed a broker. Consider the two alternative transactions in Exhibit 12-1 for the same property—one without and the other with a broker. The gain to the owner by using a broker is the result of a number of factors. While some owners may believe otherwise, buyers tend to negotiate prices downward by at least a portion of the commission when they know a broker is not involved. Furthermore, the asking price may be lower to begin with because a seller who does not employ a broker has access to fewer prospective buyers. And sellers may waste time with unqualified buyers. In other words, an owner-seller must usually rely on a "thinner" market than a broker, and the selling time may be longer.

✓ **Concept Check**

12.3   Name five areas in which an expert real estate broker has special knowledge.

Careful readers of Exhibit 12-1 may agree with these points, but may also realize that by ignoring his or her time in the calculation, the owner would be ahead not to use a broker. But even though the owner's time is not a cash cost, it normally should be counted, since he or she must typically take time off from a job or give up other valuable or pleasurable activities. Owners also subject themselves to greater legal risks, financial risks, and potential frustration because they are less aware of the pitfalls of selling property than brokers who specialize in this activity.

The net result is that sellers who employ brokers often end up better economically than sellers who do not employ brokers. If this were not so, most owners would not use brokers, and the number of brokerage firms would decline dramatically.

✓ **Concept Check**

12.4   What is a cost of selling a property that tends to be overlooked by prospective "for-sale-by-owners"?

Exhibit 12-1   Transactions with and without a Real Estate Broker

		Without Broker	**With Broker**
Price		$190,000	$200,000
Owner's marketing costs	$1,500		—
Time of owner (60 hrs. @ $50 per hr.)	3,000	4,500	—
Commission (6 1/2%)		—	13,000
Proceeds to owner		$185,500	$188,000

Law of Agency

Real estate brokers and salespersons traditionally have operated under the **law of agency,** which gives a broker or salesperson the right to act for a **principal** in trying to buy or sell a property. In acting for another person, brokers automatically fell into the category of agents, which means the broker must "stand in the shoes" of the principal. Thus, a broker must look out for the best interests of the principal and can do nothing to compromise a principal's interests, position, or bargaining power. In most states, statutory law has intervened recently to alter the agency status of brokers, as we explain later. To understand the changes, it is necessary to first understand agency.

> ✓ **Concept Check**
>
> **12.5**   An agent's relationship to a principal is characterized by what phrase?

Types of Agents

In general, agency relationships can have three different breadths. The broadest scope of authority is the **universal agent,** to whom a principal delegates the power to act in *all* matters that can be delegated in place of the principal. A **general agent** is delegated by the principal to act within the confines of a business or employment relationship. An insurance agent, for example, may be a general agent of the insurance company if the agent can sign contracts that bind the company, supervise employees of the company, and in other ways carry out the business of the company. Similarly, a property manager is a general agent if he or she can rent apartments, collect rents, handle tenant relations, supervise maintenance, and perform accounting functions, but is not an employee of the property owner. Further, as discussed later, a salesperson in a real estate brokerage firm is a general agent of the firm's owning broker. A **special agent** is authorized by the principal to handle only a specific business transaction or to perform only a specific function. Under traditional agency, the real estate broker acts in the capacity of a special agent in representing the buyer or the seller to purchase or dispose of a property.

Fiduciary Responsibilities

Agents have a **fiduciary relationship** with their principals. This relationship, by legal tradition, carries several special responsibilities. As fiduciaries, agents must observe the following duties:

1. *Confidentiality*—Never betray confidential information about their principals, their financial status, or their motivations.
2. *Obedience*—Follow the instructions of their principal to the limits of what is legal. If agents regard the orders of the principal to be legal but unethical, they should withdraw from the relationship rather than disobey.
3. *Accounting*—Keep the principal informed about financial aspects of their assignment.
4. *Loyalty*—Never subordinate the best interest of their principal to the interests of others.
5. *Disclosure*—Be completely open and honest with their principals.
6. *Skill and Care*—Represent the interests of their principals to the best of their ability—in the same way they would represent themselves, acquiring and applying the necessary skills, knowledge, and information about relevant laws and regulations, the market, and subject property.[2]

---

2. It may be helpful to note that the first letter of the duties spell "COALDS."

A principal in a fiduciary relationship also has duties. These are to be open, honest, and fair with the agent. This implies also that the principal will cooperate with the agent in providing information about the property (e.g., repair and expense records and defects) when requested by the agent. When the agent has successfully completed the task assigned (the sale of the property), the agent is entitled to prompt payment for services rendered.

✓ Concept Check

12.6   The broker traditionally has what kind of relationship to the principal? What are the six duties owed the principal?

Real Estate Agents

**www.realtor.org/
mempolweb.nsf/pages/
code**

NAR code of ethics.

An *agency relationship* traditionally was created between a seller and a broker when both parties agreed to a **listing contract.** Such a contract may be written or oral, and it establishes the rights and duties of each party. In most listing contracts the sellers agree to make the properties available for purchase at a specified price for a specified period of time (e.g., four months). They also agree to pay the broker a specified fee or a certain percentage of the selling price when the broker finds a buyer who is "ready, willing, and able" to purchase the property, or upon closing of the transaction. Brokers usually agree to use their best efforts to try to sell the property on terms acceptable to the sellers. (A detailed listing contract, Exhibit 12-6, is discussed later.)

✓ Concept Check

12.7   What are the three basic types of agency relationships? Which of these refers to a broker's relationship to a principal?

An agency relationship also can exist between a buyer and a broker. In a **buyer agency agreement** a broker agrees to use his or her best efforts to find properties meeting the requirements of the buyer. The buyer agrees to pay the broker a commission or a fee upon consummating a purchase or, more commonly, to permit the broker to share a commission paid to the seller's broker.

Salespersons must be affiliated with a broker, from whom they derive their agency status. As general agents of their broker, they assume all of the special agency obligations that the broker has created, thus becoming special agents to any of the broker's principals. This type of agency, whether with a seller or a buyer, has come to be called *single agency.*

Subagency.   Modern real estate brokerage normally relies on a **multiple listing service (MLS)** through which brokers have access to each other's listings. Brokers who are members of the MLS can make their listings available to be sold by other broker members, and the commission is split between them. If the listing broker is an agent, then it becomes a **subagency** arrangement, and the chain of agency becomes rather long, but clear. The listing salesperson represents the listing broker, and both become special agents to the seller-principal. A selling broker and any affiliated salespersons traditionally become subagents of the listing broker and thus are special agents of the seller as well. So every person in this chain is a special agent to the seller, and owes the same level of loyalty, confidentiality, trust, obedience, disclosure, accounting, care, skill, and due diligence to the seller-principal.

Dual Agency.   Another agency relationship allowable in some states is dual agency. In these situations the broker is an agent of both a seller and a buyer, and the broker owes equal loyalty to both. A **dual agency** must be disclosed to all parties in the transaction, and both principals must give their informed written consent. While the broker owes equal loyalty to both parties, it cannot be *undivided* loyalty. For example, a dual agency broker cannot inform the seller that the buyer will pay more than the price stated in the written offer or that the seller or buyer will accept financing terms other than those offered. Similarly, the broker cannot reveal to the buyer that the seller will accept a price lower than the listing price, unless instructed in writing to do so. Dual agency is inherently problematic because of the divided loyalty, and views on it are polar. While California, for example, embraces it, Florida, on the other hand, prohibits it.

> ✓ **Concept Check**
>
> **12.8**   What is the name of a very complicated agency relationship that arises when one firm represents both seller and buyer?

Comparison of Traditional Agency Relationships.   A variety of agency relationships for real estate brokerage are compared in Exhibit 12-2. The first case, traditional brokerage, involves a seller-principal listing with a broker (through a salesperson). Through MLS and subagency, the resulting special agency relationship runs through the seller-broker all the way to the salesperson in direct contact with the buyer. However, the relationship between that salesperson and the buyer is "arm's length." Thus, the buyer is simply a customer of the seller-broker firm rather than a client.

In the second case, where there is both a seller agency and a buyer agency, two special agency relationships confront each other at the interface between the brokers. The two brokerage firms can deal at arm's length in the transaction. Until recently, however, transactions involving both seller-principal and buyer-principal had special difficulties. MLS membership generally required subagency. Therefore, the buyer's broker dealing with an MLS listing was, by contract, also a subagent of the seller and unavoidably a dual agent (the third case in Exhibit 12-2). To avoid this problem, the requirement of subagency generally has been dropped from MLS membership.

> ✓ **Concept Check**
>
> **12.9**   In traditional MLS property listings, the broker selling a listing traditionally was an agent of the seller, in spite of all appearances otherwise, by virtue of what kind of required agency relationship?

The fourth case represents the basic example of dual agency. A single broker has both the listing contract with the seller and a buyer agency agreement with the purchaser. As noted later, this is a common situation, often treated through the use of designated agents, one for the buyer and one for the seller.

The fifth case, transaction brokerage, represents recent widespread efforts to replace the classical agency relationship. Some background on the problems of agency is helpful to understand it.

> ✓ **Concept Check**
>
> **12.10**   Brokerage firms are increasingly faced with an unintended internal dual agency problem because of the increase in what practice?

Problems in Real Estate Agency Relationships and Disclosures

The nature of the real estate brokerage business tends to confuse and stress the traditional agency relationships described above. For example, many thoughtful observers have questioned whether it is possible for a broker serving as a dual agent to simultaneously "stand in the shoes" of both a buyer and a seller. Yet the occurrence of this conflict is

Exhibit 12-2 Types of Brokerage Relationships

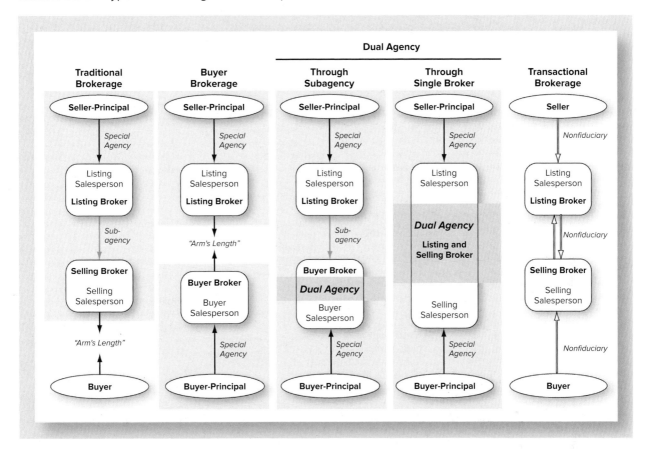

inherent with the practice of buyer brokerage. To mitigate the concern about dual agency, virtually every state has imposed strict requirements of disclosure and written consent for the buyers and a sellers involved. Many observers still question whether this is sufficient protection since the nature of the problem is subtle and challenging to understand. One solution that a number of states have resorted to in dual agency is to allow **designated agents.** When a brokerage firm is serving both a buyer and a seller as clients, the broker appoints a separate salesperson to represent each client. These persons are charged to maintain an "arm's-length" relationship within the firm, though the broker remains privy to the affairs of both clients. There is debate whether any such device is sufficient to solve the dual agent conflict. Meanwhile, numerous legal challenges to dual agency have emerged.

Probably the most common problem in real estate brokerage relationships is *unintended* dual agency. As noted above and depicted in Exhibit 12-3, the normal brokerage practice of today depends on MLS systems, with a salesperson working with the buyer as a subagent of the seller. Yet that salesperson typically "represents" numerous listings, has no direct contact with the seller, and meanwhile is actively engaged in fostering a personal relationship with the buyer. Under these conditions, it is no surprise that a 1984 study found 74.2 percent of buyers believed that the selling agent represented them rather than the seller.[3] Unfortunately, though states have universally enacted agency disclosure laws since that study, more recent survey evidence suggests little improvement in the

---

3. Federal Trade Commission Staff Report: "The Residential Real Estate Brokerage Industry," Vols. 1 and 2, 1984.

Exhibit 12-3 The Problem of Unintentional Dual Agency

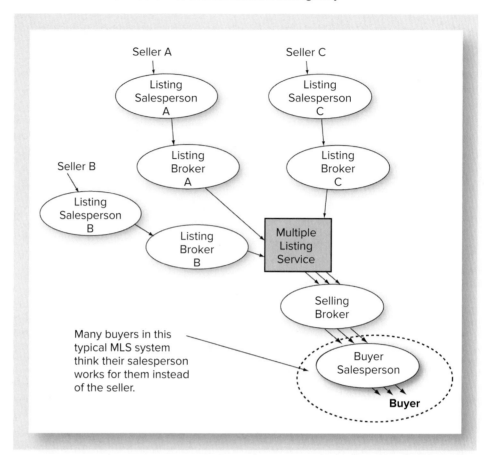

buyer understanding.[4] Some states now have gone so far as to enact laws stipulating that a salesperson showing a house to a prospective buyer automatically becomes the agent of the buyer unless the salesperson declares otherwise in writing at the outset of the dealings.[5]

> ### ✓ Concept Check
>
> **12.11** What might a broker do to mitigate the dual agency problem occurring within the firm due to the firm's being both a listing broker and a buyer broker?

Transaction Brokers

The inherent tendency for real estate brokerage to result in dual agency has prompted nearly half of all states to create a new type of brokerage relationship known as a **transaction broker** or *facilitating or intermediary broker* (shown as the fifth case in Exhibit 12-2). In this relationship a broker assists with a transaction between a buyer and a seller, but the broker does not represent either party. Transaction brokers are required to exercise skill, care, and diligence in dealing with the parties, and they must deal honestly and fairly with both parties.

---

4. Jonathan A. Wiley and Leonard V. Zumpano, "Questioning the Effectiveness of Mandatory Agency Disclosure Statutes," Journal of Housing Research: 2004, Vol. 15, No 2, pp. 161–174.

5. See, for example, Illinois, Maryland, and Washington.

In other words, they owe both parties the standard business characteristics of competence and fair dealing, but they are not bound by the strict fiduciary requirements of agents. As a rough approximation, the obligations of the transaction type broker are the traditional fiduciary duties, minus the obligations of loyalty and obedience and with only limited confidentiality. A transaction broker's status must also be disclosed in writing to all relevant parties.[6]

Agency problems within real estate brokerage remain difficult to fully solve, and no proposed solution is perfect. Therefore, wise practice in use of brokerage services includes two steps: First, be sure that you clearly understand whom a broker represents. Second, unless the broker is clearly a single agent representing you alone, provide information to the broker strictly on a need-to-know basis. That is, do not impart any more information about your income, motivations for sale, financing alternatives, or other financial matters than is clearly pertinent to the transaction, and don't rely on the broker's word alone as a basis for critical decisions.

> ### ✓ Concept Check
>
> **12.12**   What type of broker represents neither buyer nor seller?

Licensing of Real Estate Brokers and Salespersons

All 50 states and the District of Columbia have **licensing laws** that regulate persons and companies that engage in the brokerage business. In all of these jurisdictions, a license is required to conduct real estate brokerage activities, which include the purchase, sale, renting, leasing, auctioning, and managing of real estate for others.

State licensing laws generally prescribe two levels of real estate brokerage licensing—the broker license and the salesperson license.[7] The most complete license is the **broker license,** because only a broker is permitted to own and operate a real estate brokerage business. Brokers are responsible for the completion of documents used in sales and leases negotiated by people in their business, for handling money held in trust for clients (e.g., earnest money deposits or rent collected), and for the actions of their employees. Each real estate sales office, therefore, must have at least one licensed broker.

To enter the brokerage business, one usually must first obtain a **salesperson license.**[8] The salesperson can be an employee of a broker, but more commonly is an independent contractor of the brokerage firm. The salesperson may perform business activities, such as negotiating listing contracts or contracts for sale, but must perform them in the name of the broker. Also, laws and regulations usually strictly forbid salespersons from holding client moneys; these funds must be delivered to an appropriate broker's trust account shortly after receiving them.

Many states (over 35) allow some form of reciprocity with other states for real estate licensees. However, the terms of reciprocity and the number of states for which it is permitted are quite varied.

www .mortgagenews-daily .com/real_estate_license

Summarizes real estate license requirements for all states. For state-by-state government real estate license sites, Google *state name* "real estate license law."

> ### ✓ Concept Check
>
> **12.13**   List five real estate services that require licensing to be performed for others.

---

6. The adoption of designated agency and of transaction or facilitating brokerage by states is detailed in periodic surveys of the Association of Real Estate License Law Officials (ARELLO). The most recent is 2015.

7. Colorado, New Mexico, North Carolina, Oregon, and Tennessee have only a broker's license, but each state still requires experience or additional education to qualify as an independently operating broker.

8. A number of states allow equivalencies for education and experience requirements for the salesperson license, the broker's license, or both.

Exhibit 12-4   Organizational Structure for Administering Real Estate
Licensing Laws

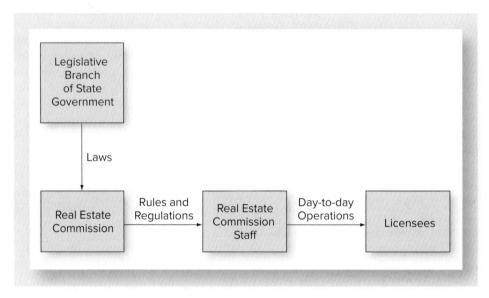

Brokerage Licensing Administration

As shown in Exhibit 12-4 the line of authority for real estate brokerage licensing begins with the legislative branch of state government, which originates licensing laws and amendments. Interpretations of state licensing laws take the form of rules and regulations set by the state's **real estate commission.** The commission is usually composed of prominent brokers and nonbroker (i.e., public interest) members. In some states, the commission is part of the department of state government responsible for licensing many occupations (e.g., appraisers, barbers, contractors, and morticians).

The real estate commission has several functions. First, it specifies educational requirements for applicants and licensees. Second, it is responsible for creating and administering examinations to qualify prospective licensees. Finally, the commission enforces the license law and regulations implementing the law. It must hold hearings for licensees accused of violating state licensing laws and has the right to reprimand licensees and to suspend or revoke their licenses.

The commission staff carries out the day-to-day business of administering the license law. The chief administrative officer is responsible to the commission for developing educational materials, record keeping, collecting license fees, and researching complaints against licensees.

How to Obtain a Real Estate License

Unlike a driver's license, a real estate license obtained in one state does not necessarily qualify one to practice real estate brokerage in another state. Nevertheless, the requirements for obtaining brokerage licenses generally have become more uniform among the states in recent years. A greater degree of reciprocity exists today than in the past, especially with respect to education and examination requirements. To answer the question of how to obtain a broker's license, we examine the various licensing requirements, which include exemptions, general requirements, education, examinations, and experience.

Exemptions.   Some persons who buy, sell, rent, or lease real estate for others are exempt from licensing laws. Usually attorneys, because of their extensive legal training, are exempt. Other exempt categories may include resident managers, government employees (e.g., state transportation department employees), trustees, executors, and those with the power of attorney. These exemptions involve either public employees or persons who have a special relationship with the parties for whom they perform brokerage services.

General Requirements.   Anyone interested in obtaining a salesperson license generally must apply to take a salesperson license examination. On the application, individuals must demonstrate that they have satisfied a set of general requirements, such as minimum age (usually 18 years for a salesperson license but occasionally 21 years for a broker license), general education (usually a high school diploma or GED), and a good reputation. Some states require references. Finally, the applicant must satisfy any specified prelicensing education requirements of the state. On average, the required prelicensing education is about 70 classroom hours of prescribed material, though it ranges from 24 hours in Massachusetts to 180 hours in Texas.

Once applicants satisfy these general and educational requirements and pay a fee, they may sit for the state examination. If they earn a passing grade, applicants may receive or apply for a license from the state real estate commission. Applicants for a license usually must specify a broker (i.e., a sponsor) with whom the license will be placed.

Traditionally, applicants for brokerage licenses had to demonstrate their financial capacity to cover damage judgments brought against them by clients. Some states now, however, have established a **recovery fund** with moneys from license fees. Payments from this fund can be used to pay some types of judgments against licensees. Other states require licensees to purchase **errors and omission insurance** to cover damages arising from professional mistakes.

Experience Requirements.   Generally, states do not impose a brokerage experience requirement (i.e., an apprenticeship) for obtaining salesperson licenses. For a brokerage license, however, an applicant usually must have actual experience as a salesperson in addition to taking further course work in real estate. This experience requirement involves at least one year and, more commonly, two to three years.

License Law Infractions

www.arello.com

State licensing laws prescribe behavioral requirements with which licensees must comply to keep their licenses. Most laws specify that licensees must not behave in an unethical, fraudulent, or dishonest manner toward their clients and prospective buyers. License laws generally seek to prevent the following activities:

- *Mishandling trust money,* including practices such as commingling trust money with personal funds and accepting noncash payments in trust.
- *Improper handling of fees,* including paying commissions to licensees not in the broker's employ and paying commissions to unlicensed persons.
- *Failure to provide required information,* including failure to provide copies of contracts to all relevant parties and failure to inform buyers of closing costs.
- *Misrepresentation and fraud,* including taking kickbacks without the employer's knowledge, false advertising, and intentionally misleading clients or prospective buyers.
- *Improper business practices,* including offering property at terms other than those specified by clients or failure to submit all offers to clients.

Designations in Sales and Brokerage

There are a number of designation programs in real estate brokerage. Practitioners voluntarily seek designations and certificates from trade or professional organizations because they want to differentiate themselves from those with less training, experience, and professionalism. With these credentials they expect to obtain more customers or be able to charge higher fees. Various institutes, societies, and councils affiliated with the **National Association of Realtors** (NAR) offer designations in specialty fields of the real estate brokerage business. In addition, minority brokers may seek designations through the National Association of Real Estate

Brokers. Some of these designations are primary signaling devices within a particular segment of the real estate business (e.g., property management, industrial and office properties, and real estate counseling).

Brokerage and salesperson licensees may choose to become affiliated with a local Board of Realtors, which is associated with the NAR, as a Realtor (broker) or Realtor-Associate (salesperson).[9] Salespersons working under a broker member of a Board of Realtors are also required to belong to the board. Such affiliations are secondary signals to the public that licensees abide by the NAR code of ethics, in addition to the primary signaling device of state licensing.

www.realtor.org

Select "Business Specialties" for a very large set of links to NAR specialty affiliates and other sites.

The Marketing Function

Market Segmentation and Specialization and Service

Real estate brokerage firms, like most firms that have a marketing function, practice **market segmentation;** that is, they attempt to identify **submarkets** in which they can specialize and concentrate. Some brokers specialize by property type; they serve sellers and buyers of commercial, industrial, residential, agricultural, office, or recreational properties. Sometimes, brokers limit their activities to a particular section of a city. In contrast, brokers who specialize in large commercial or industrial properties may operate over a wide geographic area, sometimes even nationally or internationally.

In all cases, however, successful brokers are able to relate to the needs of buyers and sellers and help them solve their problems. Thus, the broker's role is to facilitate the transaction process and guide the client successfully through the steps of the process. As marketing and transaction specialists, real estate brokers know that they have only one thing to sell—their service.

www.sior.com

Home page of a leading professional organization for commercial property brokers and other professionals.

Commercial Brokerage

Although the function of commercial brokerage is the same as that of residential brokerage—facilitating transactions between buyers and sellers—the activities of commercial brokers usually differ considerably from those of residential brokers. Almost all types of properties except one- to four-family residential properties, public properties (e.g., schools, municipal buildings, courthouses), and churches can be included in the catch-all commercial category. In reality, it includes almost all income-producing properties.

Relative to residential transactions, commercial transactions are larger and the parties are more knowledgeable. Thus, brokers often seek to match potential buyers with the owners of specific properties and then "get out of the way." Even in these cases, however, potential buyers will want important information about the property and perhaps competing properties. They will want a multiyear record of past income and expenses; detailed information about current leases, together with summary information about the implications of the leases for projected income, expenses, and tenant turnover; and information on major repairs, additions, or renovations. In short, they will want a complete and detailed cash flow analysis as discussed in Chapters 18 and 19. In addition, they will want certifications of inspections and compliance with all relevant laws and regulations. Buyers also may want inspections to detect the presence of any hazardous wastes on the property. The broker often must work with the seller in obtaining and providing all requested information. Thus, an important part of the broker's service is to put together a printed marketing information package for a listed property and reports to enable a prospective buyer to complete "due diligence" for the property. This can include a detailed description of the property, adequate market information to evaluate the market context of the property, descriptions of competitive properties, details of current leases and tenants, one or more cash flow "pro

---

9. The term Realtor® is a federally registered collective trademark. Only active brokers who are members of local and state Boards of Realtors affiliated with NAR are permitted to use this trademark.

Real estate brokers and salespersons are people oriented. They are persons who can understand the instructions, requests, and feelings of others. Moreover, they are comfortable guiding and persuading others to make decisions. Finally, they are positive persons who are basically optimistic, enthusiastic, and self-motivated. About 80 percent of brokers and salespersons are involved in residential sales. However, within that sphere are a wide variety of products, clients, and firms. Though there are very large brokerage organizations, the typical residential firm is small, with 88 percent of firms having no more than four persons. Few occupations see more diversity in the background of the persons involved. About 95 percent of brokers and salespersons come to real estate from another career, and their backgrounds virtually span the spectrum of service occupations from accounting to zookeeping. While the educational level of persons in brokerage and sales is varied, almost three-fourths of salespersons have a college degree.

A strong attraction for many who pursue real estate brokerage is the opportunity to be self-employed. By the same token, it is a field offering little income security. While the potential is good, the income can be uncertain and volatile. The 2014 median incomes for brokers and salespersons, are, before expenses, $65,300 and $45,800 respectively. It is notable, however that the top 13 percent of salespersons, and the top 20 percent of brokers earned over $150,000. Work hours for brokers and salespersons are relatively long. Fifty-nine percent of the industry are full-time workers, and these persons typically work around 50 hours a week. In addition, the hours regularly involve evenings and weekends.

Residential Real Estate Brokerage

Sources: County Business Patterns, U.S. Department of Commerce and National Association of Realtors 2015 Member Profile

formas" or cash flow projection displays, and other items. The broker must be capable of collecting this information and assembling it into an effective professional "sales package."

Commercial brokers also must negotiate compromises between buyers and sellers when they reach an impasse over a particular issue. Often a major obstacle is the price; brokers often find it in their best interest to suggest a compromise, which might involve creatively placing nonreal estate consideration on the negotiating table as well. Not infrequently, the broker is required to lower the commission in order to bring the asking and bid prices into line.

✓ **Concept Check**

12.14 Two important functions of a commercial real estate broker are to provide the prospective buyer with _____, and to negotiate _____.

Residential Brokerage

Almost all brokers in a community have the same inventory (e.g., the list of MLS properties), and buyers could learn about many of these properties through online advertising. Therefore, a broker's property inventory is not the main reason buyers and sellers use brokers or choose one brokerage firm over others. Rather, it is the service the firm is expected to provide.

Potential customers usually choose a brokerage firm on the basis of the firm's reputation in the community, personal acquaintance with the broker or a salesperson, or recommendation by a satisfied customer. Some customers may also rely on the reputation or general image of a brokerage franchise operation such as RE/MAX, Century 21, Berkshire Hathaway, Keller Williams, or Coldwell Banker.

The service provided by a brokerage firm is to help clients make a decision and then to help them implement that decision. For example, buyers will usually need information about alternative choices of properties in the market, their prices, and how they may meet the buyer's needs. The broker or salesperson can obtain information about such matters as

CAREER *FOCUS*

Commercial Real Estate Brokerage

Commercial property brokerage involves the sale and leasing of income-producing properties. These include all manner of rental and owner-occupied properties of businesses or other entities. The types of properties span office buildings, hotels, restaurants, apartments, retail stores, shopping centers, industrial plants, and a host of specialty properties. Most commercial brokers and salespersons will specialize in one or a few of these, sometimes becoming established as an expert for a type of specialty property at the national or international level.

Commercial real estate brokers, unlike residential brokers, deal with two separate clienteles. On the one hand, they are involved with actual occupants, that is, as a leasing agent or tenant representative. On the other hand, they are dealing with income property investors. They must market the space to the first group and ownership of the properties to the second. Most of the large commercial brokerage companies in the United States provide a great deal of local market data and research so they can service a cadre of sophisticated clients who are making multimillion dollar investment decisions. Several trade organizations represent the various commercial real estate subspecialties, including the American Industrial Real Estate Association, the Hotel and Motel Brokers of America, the National Association of Industrial and Office Properties, the Real Estate Exchange—a forum for women in commercial real estate, the International Council of Shopping Centers, and the Society of Industrial and Office Realtors. The latter organization sponsors an important industry designation, the SIOR. The CCIM

Institute also provides a well-established industry designation, Certified Commercial Investment Member (CCIM), and a supporting education program for the designation.

About 6 percent of real estate brokers are involved with commercial real estate. In general, commercial brokers and salespersons work on a straight commission basis, though newer members in the profession may be given a draw or salary since deals often require many months to consummate. Commissions on commercial sales can range between 2 and 10 percent, while leasing commissions may be 4–7 percent of the total lease payments involved. Where the median residential broker, before expenses, earned $65,300 per year in 2014, the median commercial broker earned around $146,200, and significantly more for those with an industry designation.*

*Sources: National Association of Realtors 2015 Member Profile and 2015 Commercial Member Profile.

utility expenses, taxes, maintenance, and legal issues regarding alternative properties. The broker or salesperson can also suggest ways of modifying or using the property in particular ways needed by the buyer. Finally, the broker or salesperson can help the buyer find and compare financing alternatives. Overall, the objective of a broker or salesperson should be to help the client (buyer or seller) to analyze the proposed purchase or sale and to guide the client to a decision with which he or she is comfortable.

Experienced brokers might point out that before a broker can offer much service to clients they must first obtain listings. This point is sometimes bluntly stated, "If you don't list, you don't last." But note that the quality of service still is important if one considers how a broker obtains good listings. Over any length of time, we believe the dominant factor in successfully obtaining listings is reputation, which is primarily derived in the real estate business by word of mouth from previous customers and clients. Thus, the quality of brokers' service follows them in their search for new business.

Concept Check

12.15 Name three factors that might influence a customer's choice of brokerage firm.

Discrimination Prohibited. Federal and state laws prohibit **discrimination in housing** on the bases of race, color, religion, national origin, sex, familial status, and handicap. The main federal law prohibiting discrimination is Title VIII of the Civil Rights Act of 1968, commonly called the Fair Housing Act. This law declares the following acts to be illegal:

1. Refusing to sell, rent, or deal with any person.
2. Offering terms and conditions that differ among buyers or renters, influenced by the prohibited characteristics.

A recent case* alleging housing discrimination decided in June 1999 by a U.S. District Court demonstrates that agents and brokerage firms cannot be held liable when they follow the law and act in good faith, in spite of comments that might suggest otherwise. In *Ileka v. Lyons,* the African-American plaintiffs argued initially that the white defendant, Mary Lyons, refused to sell them a house after they had made an offer in July 1997, and that the listing agent (Mary Small) and her brokerage firm (Erickson Realty and Management Co.) had aided and abetted in the discrimination. The seller claimed health reasons and the inability to find suitable alternative housing, and not racial prejudice, had caused her to refuse the offer.

Subsequently, in July 1998, the Ilekas bought the house from the seller, leaving only the agent and brokerage company as defendants in the case alleging violations of the U.S. Fair Housing and Civil Rights Acts.

In spite of a comment by the agent to the seller when she listed the property and agreed to place the listing in the MLS that "the blacks will come," the court found that the company and agent did not refuse to deal with the buyers. Rather, the agent Mary Small had placed the property in an MLS accessible to African-American buyers. Furthermore, she had tried to find suitable alternative housing for the seller, Mary Lyons, which would have facilitated the sale. The court also found no evidence that the agent had attempted to sell the house

to white buyers and concluded that there had been no "coercion, intimidation, threat, or interference" by the defendants against either the seller or the buyers.

*Ileka, Ileka, and Leadership Council for Metropolitan Open Communities, Inc. v. Mary Lyons, Michael Lyons, Kevin Lyons, James P. Heywood, Mary Small, and Vincent R. Innocenti, d/b/a Erickson Realty and Management Co., No. 98C 986, U.S. District Court for the Northern District of Illinois, Eastern Division.

Actions Are More Important than Words in Deciding Whether Discrimination Occurred

3. Advertising housing as available only to certain buyers.
4. Denying that housing is available for sale or rental when it is actually available.
5. Persuading someone to sell housing by telling him or her that minority groups are moving into the neighborhood, a practice commonly called "blockbusting."
6. Denying home loans or varying home loan terms on the basis of prohibited characteristics.
7. Denying or limiting the use of real estate services to anyone on the basis of prohibited characteristics.
8. Coercing, intimidating, or interfering with any person in the exercise or enjoyment of these federal rights.

An important exemption to the Fair Housing Act is for owner-occupants living in a unit of a residential building serving four or fewer households, including single-family homes. In other words, by the exemption to this law, owners of such units may discriminate on the prohibited bases, provided they do not employ the services of a broker or an agent. For *racial* discrimination, however, the one- to four-unit exemption is overridden by another federal law. In June 1968 the U.S. Supreme Court in the case of *Jones v. Mayer Co.* held that the Civil Rights Act of 1866, barring "all racial discrimination, private as well as public, in the sale or rental of property," preempts the 1968 law.[10]

Concept Check

12.16 What are the seven factors on which discrimination is prohibited under the fair housing laws?

Another exemption pertains to discrimination against "familial status." In multifamily residential facilities operated for "elderly" persons, defined to be individuals 62 years and over, the owners or management can refuse to sell or rent to persons under 62 years, or to families having children.[11] State laws generally mirror the Fair Housing Act.

10. See *Fred v. Kokinokos,* D.C. Ill. 1973, 381 F. Supp. 165. In 1868 the substance of the Civil Rights Act of 1866 was incorporated into the 14th Amendment to the Constitution of the United States.
11. The age limit is dropped to 55 when at least 80 percent of the units are occupied by at least one person 55 years or older.

The Internet has brought new levels of access to residential real estate listings, and a recent survey reports that 89 percent of home shoppers rely, in part, on Internet search.* But, how much has it truly altered the basic face-to-face nature of the business? The answer seems to be "significantly."

Enter the era of Internet data exchange (IDX) and, beginning in 2009, virtual office websites (VOWs). These are ways of doing residential brokerage business, offered through the National Association of Realtors. For both systems the entire initial search by the house hunter can be conducted on the Web, with no face-to-face contact until the searcher wants to view a property live. Core to these modes of business is access to the local

It's an IDX! It's a VOW! . . . It's a Realtor© in Cyberspace!

Realtors' MLS nonconfidential database. MLS data goes beyond the information earlier networks typically have offered to home searchers, potentially making available more properties, and more detail about them. This can enable the prospective customer to engage in a more complete search and evaluation of available properties than she could through earlier Internet systems or an assisting broker.

Here is how the systems work. With IDX, the house hunter goes to a specific Realtor's website and finds a limited version of the MLS database as if it were offered by that Realtor. Access to the IDX is completely open to Internet searchers—no sign-in or passwords needed. In contrast, VOWs work the same way, but with access control; the user must sign in and give some contact information. Why would the house hunter want to sign in? VOWs can offer additional information not available though IDX. This can include all of the information available from MLS, together with valuation service or blogs and viewer comments, among

other items. Each firm offering IDX or a VOW effectively will also have an active licensed local broker, a Realtor, capable of carrying out house visits and a transaction when the house hunter is ready.

The evolution of cyberspace home marketing continues. Where IDX and VOW systems may have daily or less frequent data updates, some firms now are developing close to real-time access to MLS listings so that a prospective buyer can see new listings or sold properties almost immediately.

The result so far? There is some indication that the front-end efficiency of these systems already has encouraged lower total brokerage fees, and Realtors report that cyberspace listings are now integral to their way of doing business. From increasing sources, one hears firms reporting that the majority of their business now starts with cyberspace inquiries.

*National Association of Realtors, *2015 Profile of Home Buyers and Sellers.*

The federal and state fair housing laws apply equally to property owners and their agents. In other words, discrimination on any of the specified bases by anyone involved in a housing transaction is prohibited, unless covered by an exemption. (See Industry Issues 12-1 for an example of how the courts determine whether discrimination may have occurred.)

> ### ✓ Concept Check
>
> **12.17** Name the 1968 case in which the U.S. Supreme Court ruled that discrimination by race is absolutely prohibited in any form or at any level.

Internet Marketing. The Internet is increasingly central to marketing properties. From the website of the National Association of Realtors (www.realtor.com), buyers can find residential properties listed by Realtors all across the country.

Commercial properties are also marketed over the Internet. The CCIM Institute (www.ccim.com), for example, has an Internet listing service called CCIM/Net (ccim.net). Both Co-Star (www.costar.com) and LoopNet (www.loopnet.com) provide online listing, trading, and information for commercial real estate professionals. They have raised the amount of market information available for commercial property markets by an order of magnitude. By all indications, the **Internet marketing** of real properties will continue to grow. Additional examples of sites with Internet marketing of homes and related services are:

www.cre.org

Under "Related Sites," provides links to the organizations whose websites are shown in the text, and to other real estate websites.

www.century21.com
www.homegain.com
www.zillow.com
www.Redfin.com
www.trulia.com

International Aspects of Brokerage

World economies have become increasingly intertwined, compelling real estate markets to become internationalized. Many U.S. companies and investors have purchased real estate in foreign countries, and many foreign companies and investors have purchased U.S. real estate.

Although most foreign investors speak English or have English-speaking staff, most U.S. brokers must work through cooperative arrangements with local brokers in non-English-speaking countries. Brokers who deal with foreigners must be sensitive to the cultures, customs, and mores of other countries. Speaking a foreign language can facilitate communication with a client and also increase a broker's sensitivity to other cultures. To deal in international real estate, U.S. brokers must think increasingly in terms of a global market and be prepared to deal with foreign investors on their own terms.

Listing Contracts

Central to the brokerage business is the listing contract. A listing contract is an agreement between the owner of real estate and a real estate broker or brokerage firm that allows the broker to attempt to sell the property. If the broker finds a buyer, the agreement states what the owner must pay the broker. The broker's fee or commission is usually calculated as a percentage of the selling price (e.g., a commission of 6 percent on a selling price of $100,000 is $6,000). If the broker is unsuccessful in selling the property, the agreement lapses after a specified time period (or reasonable time period if a time period is not specifically stated), and neither party has any further obligation.

As discussed previously in this chapter, the broker, if an agent, has a fiduciary relationship with the principal and therefore cannot do anything that would not be in the best interests of the principal. For example, the broker may not purchase the property for himself or herself secretly through a third party. The broker could, of course, purchase the property openly and directly from the principal, provided the complete identity of the broker and his or her relationship to the principal is known by the principal. Furthermore, the broker-agent cannot withhold information from the principal. In general, the broker must present every offer to purchase the property to the principal, even if the agent considers an offer too low, since it may be in the principal's best interest to sell the property quickly, no matter how low the offer.

Additionally, the broker-agent may not attempt to frighten the principal into accepting a low offer or suggest to a prospective buyer that the seller will accept a price lower than the listed price, unless the principal has specifically instructed him to convey such information to a prospective buyer. (A broker can, of course, state the obvious fact that the seller *might* accept a lower price and that he or she is obligated to present every offer to the seller.)

Critical to any listing contract is the question of when the broker becomes entitled to a commission. Traditionally, the broker is entitled to a commission upon finding a buyer who is ready, willing, and able to purchase the property at the price and terms specified in the listing contract. Of course, if the seller accepts (signs) an offer with different terms and conditions, then the broker also is entitled to the commission. A number of situations can cause a seller to refuse an offer, as shown in Industry Issues 12-3. If the seller refuses to sell upon being presented with an offer meeting the original terms and conditions, or cannot deliver the property for any reason due to his or her fault, the broker is entitled to the full commission, and has grounds for suit. If both buyer and seller sign a contract but then agree to cancel it, the broker still is entitled to a commission. If a contract is contingent upon the buyer obtaining financing, or upon any other condition, then the broker generally is not entitled to a commission until the condition has been fulfilled. Recourse for the broker, seller, and buyer, in the event of failure to perform by one of the parties, is discussed in Chapter 13.

> ✓ **Concept Check**
>
> **12.18**   What must a broker do to be entitled to a commission under a listing contract?

A Ready, Willing, and Able Buyer

Lloyd and Edna Evans desired to sell their property. They employed the services of Fleming Realty and Insurance, Inc., a corporation engaged in providing real estate brokerage services. These parties entered into a listing agreement containing the usual provision that required the Evanses to pay a commission if Fleming obtained a ready, willing, and able purchaser. The broker located Neal Hasselbach, who signed a standard purchase agreement offering to buy the Evans property on the terms specified in the listing agreement. In essence, in this document Mr. Hasselbach offered to pay the asking price to the Evanses. Based on their fears that Mr. Hasselbach was not financially able to purchase their property, Mr. and Mrs. Evans refused to sign a sales contract with this buyer.

Issue: Did Fleming Realty and Insurance procure a ready, willing, and able buyer, and was it therefore entitled to the agreed-upon commission?

Decision: Yes.

Reasons: The evidence at the trial court showed that Hasselbach had a net worth, in cash and property, in excess of $250,000. The proposed contract for the Evanses' land totaled $155,840, to be paid in a down payment of $35,000 and 10 annual installments of $12,184 each. The jury's conclusion that Hasselbach was financially able to perform this sale contract was reasonable. Since the buyer fulfilled the requirements of the listing agreement's procuring clause, the broker was entitled to collect the commission established even though the sale was not closed.

Source: *Fleming and Insurance Inc. v Evans,* 259 NW 2d 604 9NEG. 1977.

Types of Listing Contracts

There are three basic types of listing contracts, although only two—the *open listing* and the *exclusive right of sale listing*—are used with much frequency. Another term, *multiple listing,* is sometimes confused as a type of listing; however, multiple listing is actually a cooperative arrangement among brokerage firms to share their listings. It is not a basic type of listing contract between a seller and a broker.

Open Listing

The **open listing** is a contract between a property owner and a broker that gives the broker the right to market the property. The distinguishing characteristic of the open listing is its lack of exclusivity. The property owners are not precluded from listing the property with other brokers. If they do list the property with two or more brokers, only the broker who procures a buyer will be owed a commission. If the owners sell the property themselves, none of the brokers will be owed a commission.

The open listing is sometimes used with large, special-purpose, or otherwise difficult-to-sell properties. The owners may not be willing to tie up the property with one broker. A single brokerage firm may not operate in a wide enough geographic area or have sufficient expertise, so the owners may list with several brokers to obtain a wider market for their property. A broker may be willing to accept such a listing because he or she already has identified a prospective buyer and needs the listing contract to qualify for a commission.

Exclusive Agency Listing

This type of listing contract requires the sellers to pay a commission to the broker if the property is sold by anyone other than the owners. The owners, however, retain the right to sell the property without incurring liability for a commission.

This type of listing is used infrequently. Since the owner can sell the property and avoid paying a commission, the **exclusive agency listing** provides far less protection to the broker than the exclusive right of sale listing discussed later. Thus, brokers are usually less willing to spend time and effort to market properties listed under the exclusive agency arrangement.

Exclusive Right of Sale Listing

For the **exclusive right of sale listing** contract, the sellers list their property with one broker and agree to pay that broker a commission if the property is sold within a certain time. Thus, the broker will be owed a commission if any other broker *or even the owner* sells the property during the contract period. A typical exclusive right of sale listing contract form is shown at the end of the chapter in Exhibit 12-6. Note the operative words in provision 1, "seller gives broker the exclusive right to sell the real and personal property . . . described below . . . "

For several reasons, the exclusive right of sale feature is included in the vast majority of brokerage arrangements. Although one might think at first that such a feature would create an unfair burden on sellers, the exclusivity provision has produced faster sales. With the exclusive right of sale, brokers are more willing to commit their firms to engage in thorough marketing programs for properties and to spend whatever time is necessary to sell them. Under this arrangement, brokers usually advertise in public media, prepare photographs and brochures about listed properties, and work long hours to obtain buyers.

Second, brokers have realized that to justify their best efforts, they must have the protection provided by the exclusive right of sale provision. Thus, most brokers require sellers to accept this feature. Owners may, of course, refuse and attempt to find a broker who will accept an open or exclusive agency listing, but most do not.

Finally, a multiple listing service (MLS) accepts only exclusive right of sale listings. Other types of listings would undermine the workings of an MLS. For example, if an MLS property were sold by an owner or a broker who was not a member of the MLS, the MLS broker would probably lose the commission. It would not take many such sales to put the MLS out of business. Thus, to obtain the advantages of having their properties listed by an MLS, owners must agree to an exclusive right of sale listing contract with their broker.

Innovations in Brokerage

Because real estate brokerage firms are small and numerous, it is not surprising that there is constant experimentation with new approaches to the business. This tendency has been intensified in recent years by a confluence of events. First, the problems with agency relationships discussed earlier in this chapter have propelled interest in new forms of representation, including buyer brokerage. Second, a rapid rise in house prices threw the traditional commission arrangement out of balance. Third, the Internet explosion opened up a host of new possibilities in ways to conduct brokerage business.

Buyer Brokerage

Traditionally, virtually all residential real estate brokers represented sellers. The industry was, in large part, organized around this arrangement, as reflected in customary multiple listing services with subagency, as shown, for example, in Exhibit 12-3. But in 1996 the National Association of Realtors recognized a new approach to brokerage by establishing a designation for buyer representatives. As of 2014 a fairly steady 9 percent of all NAR members were exclusively buyer representatives, with 38 percent sometimes serving as a buyer representative.[12] In this role, the broker serves as an agent of the buyer.[12] As we noted earlier, the buyer agent may be compensated either by a fixed fee from the buyer, or, more commonly, by splitting a commission with the listing broker.[13] The services of the buyer representative can range from initial search and evaluation of prospective residences to negotiation of a contract, to assistance at the closing.

New Listing Services and "Discount" Brokerage

In years past, listing brokers were almost always compensated by a fairly stable fixed percentage commission.[14] This was unsurprising as long as house prices increased from year to

---

12. Source: National Association of Realtors® 2015 Member Profile.

13. The practice of a buyer representative splitting the customary commission has been criticized because it results in the buyer representative being rewarded for negotiating a higher price.

14. The commission percentage has been so stable that it has regularly prompted critics to accuse the industry of engaging in price fixing. But economists have pointed out that the industry has extremely low entry barriers, which should assure competitive pricing despite any efforts within the industry to influence commission rates.

year at approximately the rate of inflation; business expenses probably grew proportionately, keeping net compensation stable. But when house prices grow much faster than inflation, then the normal fixed rate commission begins to exceed the cost of doing business, and brokerage attracts new competition. In recent times this condition has arisen simultaneously with growth of the Internet, creating strong motivation and rich possibilities for new approaches to residential brokerage. Brokers have widely experimented with the "unbundling" of brokerage services, offering home sellers services ranging from minimal administrative and document services for a fee of a few hundred dollars to nearly a complete "package" of services. Most of these unbundled services involve the Internet. As part of this movement, there has been an emergence of Internet-based services for FSBO properties (for sale by owner).[15] There are other approaches to "discount" brokerage services as well (see Industry Issues 12-4). The emergence of discount brokerage has had an effect, though apparently modest, on the price of brokerage services. Where the average commission had been close to 6 percent in the past, it appeared to have fallen closer to 5 percent on average by 2005.

The ultimate effect of the Internet on real estate brokerage appears to be transformation rather than displacement. The purely informational aspects of the buying and selling process are dramatically altered; the inventory of properties on the market is now readily accessible on the web, complete with photos and "virtual tours." But this has not lessened the frequency of broker involvement in transactions. A 2015 survey of the National Association of Realtors reported that brokers were involved in the highest percentage of home sales since the survey began in 1981, and purchases directly from an owner had declined from 15 percent in 2001 to 5 percent in 2015.[16] Many observers point out that real estate is an extremely complex good, with many nonfinancial characteristics. As a result, an important part of brokerage is counseling: informing, educating, guiding, and assisting both buyers and sellers through the transaction process. Apparently the value of this service is not diminished by the presence of the Internet.

> ### ✓ Concept Check
>
> **12.19**   When is a broker entitled to a commission in an open listing? Exclusive agency listing? Exclusive right-of-sale listing?

Listing Contract Provisions

Listing contracts are central to real estate brokerage. While most residential brokers use standard, preprinted listing contract forms (see Exhibit 12-6) and most property owners are willing to sign such forms, both parties to such a contract should be certain that their interests are protected. For example, when signing a listing contract, sellers may want to assure themselves that the brokerage firm will try diligently to sell the property by advertising in various media, that the property will be put in the local MLS, that the listing agreement is limited to a reasonable period, and that the firm will provide regular reports to the seller about the progress (or lack of it) being made.

The brokerage firm, on the other hand, will want to assure itself that the duration of the listing agreement is long enough to give the firm reasonable time to sell the property; that the seller understands that a commission will be owed when the firm has found a buyer who is ready, willing, and able to pay the purchase price; that the sales personnel will have access to the property at all reasonable times; and that the firm is protected for a reasonable time after the listing expires—that is, if a buyer learns about the property through the broker's efforts, but then purchases the property after expiration of the listing, the seller still owes the broker a commission.

Also, the listing contract should specify any items of personal property that are included with the real estate and any items whose status as real estate is questionable (e.g., fireplace tools, drapes, carpets, crystal chandeliers, art objects that are built in).

---

15. The U.S. Department of Justice appears to have facilitated further growth of Internet-based innovation. In the Spring of 2005 it acted to prevent the National Association of Realtors from implementing MLS restrictions keeping Internet-oriented brokers from showing MLS-listed properties.

16. National Association of Realtors, 2015 Profile of Home Buyers and Sellers.

EXAMPLE 12-1 DERIVING A GROSS SELLING PRICE TO ACHIEVE A TARGET NET PRICE

Often a seller has a target net price in mind, and the listing broker needs to know what gross price will achieve the seller's target after payment of the commission. As an example, if the seller's target price is $200,000, and the broker's commission is 6 percent, then the broker can derive the gross price as follows:

$$\text{Target net price} = \text{Gross price} - \text{Commission rate} \times \text{Gross price}$$
$$= (1 - \text{Commision rate}) \times \text{Gross price}$$

So,

$$\text{Gross price} = \frac{\text{Target net price}}{(1 - \text{Commission rate})}$$

For the example,

$$\text{Gross price} = \$200,000/(1 - .06)$$
$$= \$212,766$$

Often, in the negotiation of a listing contract the seller will wish to achieve some target net price, and the broker must understand what gross sale price is necessary to achieve that target. The necessary computation is shown in Example 12-1.

Concept Check

12.20 What are five issues on which a seller should be clear before signing a listing agreement?

Termination of a Listing Contract

A listing contract terminates under any of three business circumstances: the specified period expires, the property is sold, or one of the parties abrogates the terms of the contract. The first two courses of termination are straightforward, and there is usually little question about the result.[17] Abrogation of terms is less clear and usually more difficult to prove. A seller may refuse to show the property, or refuse to a sign contract from a bona fide buyer. A broker may make insufficient effort to market the property.

Splitting the Commission

The commission paid by a seller upon consummation of a transaction can be divided between the listing and selling broker in any way they agree. In most communities, however, members of the Board of Realtors agree to a specified percentage of the total commission that the listing brokerage firm and the selling brokerage firm receive. In many communities this percentage is 50 percent to each, but occasionally it is 60–40 percent (in either direction).

Within each firm the policy may differ as to the percentage the salesperson who obtained the listing and the salesperson who found the buyer receive, but again, 50 percent

17. The listing contract also terminates in the event the property is destroyed or either party dies.

The Puzzle of Real Estate Agents: Use Them or Not?

Suppose you want to sell your house (or buy one). Should you use an agent? How do you select one? How do you work most effectively with her?

Almost everyone contemplating a home purchase faces these questions at some point, and they can be uncomfortable. The material in this chapter can help with these questions, but here also are some points from thoughtful industry sources.

First, should you use an agent? Tara Struyk, writing for Forbes,* sees five reasons to do so, which we expand upon. Even with more services available (like the Internet) to assist persons in buying or selling for themselves, here are reasons why most persons will be happier using an agent:

- **Convenience and market access are important**–An experienced agent is prepared to search efficiently for the properties of interest to you and obtain the maximum of information about them. Similarly, the experienced agent is prepared to respond quickly and effectively to any inquiries if you are selling your home. Handling these matters yourself can be a powerful learning experience, but typically is time consuming and disruptive, at best.
- **Negotiating is tricky business**–Home purchase transactions involve emotional dimensions as well as information—a seller's memories can clash with a buyer's dreams. The combination often contributes to a delicate exchange where an experienced intermediary can facilitate reaching a successful conclusion.
- **Contracts can be complicated**—The experienced agent is familiar with the contract in use, with all the issues involved. She can understand which issues in it are most important for you, and can help you identify your options.
- **Real estate agents "can't lie"**—Sort of! Because of the agency aspects of the relationship, and licensing law, she is obligated to be honest. Moreover, she understands that most of her business comes from referrals.
- **Eliminating the agent doesn't assure saving money**—As noted in the chapter, there are costs to using yourself as your agent: your time and hassle, access to fewer properties or buyers, expectations by the opposite party that you will share any savings.

So, if you do elect to use an agent: Who? How do you work with her?

Most advise you to find the agents already working in your neighborhood: Use recommendations of friends and relatives; watch for the names on yard signs; use Internet sources to see who is active in your area.

When you identify a possible agent, be quick to inquire about her experience: How many transactions? Where? (In your area?) What kind? (Condo? Single family?) If you are looking for a buyer agent, has she done this before and how does she get compensated? Among other things, her response to these questions may help you determine if you are comfortable working with her?

Teresa Mears, writing for *U.S. News & World Report:* Money,** has these thoughts about "red flags" from prospective agents. She suggests you should pause if the agent:

- Suggests a price higher than any other agent proposes.
- Is a part-timer in real estate.
- Is your relative.
- Is not active with properties in your neighborhood.
- Charges a lower commission.
- Is pictured on online listings. (Not an assurance of their expertise).
- Usually deals with other types of property. (For example, detached housing rather than condominiums)
- Usually works in another price range. (You don't want your property to be too small to have her attention.)

As you interact with the prospective agent, you want to assess whether she can handle the necessary negotiations, how committed she is, and how organized she will be: What kind of marketing efforts? What kind of reports to you? How frequent? How quickly will she respond to messages?

*http://www.forbes.com/2010/05/25/why-you-need-real-estate-agent-personal-finance-commission.html
**http://money.usnews.com/money/personal-finance/articles/2014/11/07/9-red-flags-to-watch-for-when-picking-a-real-estate-agent

each is typical. The split between the salespersons and their broker is more complex. The broker hires most salespersons as independent contractors rather than employees to avoid the responsibility of income tax withholdings, and contributions for workers, compensation, unemployment insurance, Social Security, and other benefits. But the broker is responsible for the office expenses and needs to be reimbursed by the salespersons who use it. The most common solution is for the salespersons to split their commission with the broker. Though the split is entirely negotiable, frequently it will give over half to the broker with less--experienced salespersons but favors the salesperson more as he or she has more experience. An alternative approach is called a 100 percent commission arrangement; the salesperson gets his or her full commission but is billed by the broker for a share of office expenses plus a fixed management fee. Exhibit 12-5 shows a typical commission split in a transaction involving different listing and selling brokerage firms.

Exhibit 12-5 Typical Commission Split

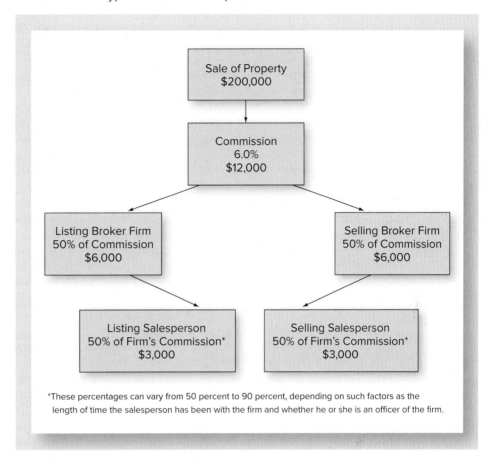

*These percentages can vary from 50 percent to 90 percent, depending on such factors as the length of time the salesperson has been with the firm and whether he or she is an officer of the firm.

REAL ESTATE APPLICATIONS

A Listing Situation

Robert and Penelope Jordan decide to sell their home in Gainesville, Florida, because Robert's firm has transferred him to Fort Myers. They contact Ben Park, a Realtor with Baden Associates Realty, who sold them the house five years ago. They like Ben—he was courteous and efficient when he helped them find a home, and he has stayed in touch with them since.

On May 1, 2017, Ben comes to the Jordans' home, which is located in Spring Meadow Estates. The Jordans remind Ben that they paid $240,000 for the house five years ago, and, they believe the house is now worth around $270,000. Ben points out some recent sales of similar houses in the neighborhood ranging from $253,000 to $272,000, and he tells them that the house realistically will not sell for more than $265,000. (He suspects this is high and that it will ultimately sell between $255,000 and 265,000 but feels he should give the benefit of the doubt to the client.) After some discussion about the advantages and disadvantages of their house relative to others in the neighborhood, the Jordans agree the listing price should be $268,000, which will include the kitchen range and refrigerator, and a patio table and chairs as well as the real estate.

The property is free of encumbrances except for an existing mortgage with a remaining balance of $204,072. The Jordans prefer not to give a second mortgage or other financing terms. The existing mortgage has a due-on-sale clause—that is, it cannot be *assumed* (taken over) by the buyer without agreement of the lender.

The house has four bedrooms, two baths, a living room, dining room, screened porch, double garage, and an outside storage room. It has central heating and central air conditioning and was built in 1976 with concrete block and stucco (CBS)-on-slab construction. Like other houses in the neighborhood, it lacks modern windows and wall insulation that are necessary for energy efficiency. This lowers its value significantly below comparable newer homes. The entire house, except for the kitchen, was carpeted about eight years ago. The house is in a reasonably good condition, although the interior and exterior paint is beginning to look dull and the carpet is becoming worn in heavy traffic areas. The lot is approximately one-fourth acre and is modestly landscaped. The neighborhood contains similar generally well-maintained houses, and property values are increasing after several years of decline. According to the Jordans' deed in the Alachua County Courthouse, the property description is "Parcel No. 3, Block 2 of Spring Meadow Estates, recorded in Plat Book 12, page 28." Ben and the Jordans agree on a commission rate of 6 percent.

Exhibit 12-6 shows the completed listing form for the Jordans' property. Several clauses in the listing contract should be noted: Clause 1 states that it is an exclusive right of sale agreement, covering the real property plus personal property as listed. In Clause 2 the question of fixtures appears. The default treatment of the contract includes all carpets and all "permanently installed equipment." Clause 4F delineates the seller's responsibility for closing expense items, including responsibility to purchase a title insurance commitment for the prospective buyer. Section 5 states the performance obligations of the broker to bring about a sale. Clause 5F gives the broker the right to incur expenses on behalf of the seller as needed to effect the closing of a sale. Clause 5G states the agency status of the broker. Clause 6D holds the seller liable for any seller misrepresentations, failures to disclose material facts, or failures to perform the requirements of the contract. Clause 6F addresses the question of latent defects. The seller is held fully responsible for known but undisclosed defects, and the broker is explicitly absolved of any liability for such defects. Section 8 details the compensation to the broker under several outcomes, including sale, securing an option to purchase, or renting. Clause 9 details the broker's compensation in case the seller wants to terminate the listing. Clause 12 details the disposition of the buyer's deposit if the buyer defaults and the seller elects the recourse of liquidated damages. Section 15 states that this contract replaces any oral agreements between the seller and the broker, and can only be modified in writing.

An issue of growing prominence in residential brokerage is the latent defects problem addressed in clause 6F of the following exhibit. States generally have adopted laws holding the sellers of a residence, and *sometimes their* agent, liable for any material defects not plainly evident (e.g., a deteriorated roof or plumbing) if the seller knows about the defects and does not disclose them. In short, the doctrine of caveat emptor (buyer beware) has been almost entirely reversed.

Exhibit 12-6 An Exclusive Right of Sale Listing Agreement

GAINESVILLE MULTIPLE LISTING, INC
Exclusive Right of Sale Listing Agreement
Transaction Broker

In consideration of this Exclusive Right to Sell Listing Agreement ("Agreement") contained here, the sufficiency of which is hereby cknowledged by ___Baden Associates Realty_____

ereinafter called BROKER, and ___Robert and Penelope Jordan_____

ereinafter called SELLER, we hereby jointly agree to the following:

1. **AUTHORITY TO SELL PROPERTY**: SELLER gives BROKER the EXCLUSIVE RIGHT TO SELL the real and personal property (collectively "Property") described below, at the price and terms described below, beginning the ___first___ day of ___May___, 20_17_, and terminating at 11:59 p.m. the ___thirtieth___ day of ___October___, 20_17_ (If left blank then the termination date shall be ___ days from execution by SELLERS ("Termination Date")). Upon full execution of a contract for sale and purchase of the Property, all rights and obligations of this Agreement will automatically extend through the date of the actual closing of the contract for sale and purchase. **SELLER certifies and represents that he/she/it is legally entitled to convey the Property and all improvements. This Property will be offered to any person without regard to race, color, religion, sex, handicap, familial status, national origin or any other factor protected by federal, state or local law.**

2. **DESCRIPTION OF PROPERTY:**

   (A) Real Property Street Address: ___1822 NW 40th Avenue, Gainesville, FL___

   (B) Legal Description: ___Parcel No. 3 Block 2 of Spring Meadow Estates PB 12 Pg 28 (Tax Parcel #### ### ###)___

   (C) Personal Property: Unless excluded in Paragraph 2(D) or by other terms of this Agreement, the following items which are owned by Seller and existing on the Property as of the date of the initial offer are included in the purchase: range(s)/oven(s), refrigerator(s), dishwasher(s), disposal, ceiling fan(s), intercom, light fixture(s), drapery rods and draperies, blinds, window treatments, permanently installed carpeting, smoke detector(s), garage door opener(s), security gate and other access devices, and storm shutters/panels ("Personal Property").
   Other Personal Property items included in this purchase are: ___patio table and chairs___

   Personal Property also includes all plants and shrubbery now installed on the Property.
   Personal Property is included in the Purchase Price, has no contributory value, and shall be left for the Buyer.

   (D) The following items are excluded from the purchase: ___Backyard copper fountain and birdbath___

3. **OCCUPANCY/POSSESSION:**

   (A) Occupancy: The Property ☐ is ☒ is not currently occupied by a tenant. If occupied, the lease term expires: _____

   (B) Buyer shall take possession at the date and time of closing unless otherwise stipulated in a deposit receipt and purchase and sale agreement ("Purchase Agreement") or an addendum to the Purchase Agreement.

4. **PRICE AND TERMS**: The Property is offered for sale on the following terms, or on other terms acceptable to SELLER.

   (A) **PRICE**: $ ___$268,000.00___

   (B) ☐ **AUCTION LISTING:** The Property subject to this Listing Agreement is to be sold at auction, and the Price represents the "reserve price" for the Property at the time of the auction.

   (C) **FINANCING TERMS:** ☒ Cash ☐ Conventional ☐ VA ☐ FHA ☐ Other: _____
   (VA AND FHA MAY REQUIRE SELLER TO PAY A CERTAIN AMOUNT OF BUYER'S CLOSING COSTS)

SELLER [RJ] [PJ] [ ] acknowledge receipt of this page, which is Page 1 of 6

Listing Agreement/Transaction Broker   Rev. 06/14

Gainesville Multiple Listing, Inc. - All Rights Reserved

Exhibit 12-6 Continued An Exclusive Right of Sale Listing Agreement

(D) ☐ **SELLER FINANCING**: SELLER will consider a purchase money mortgage in the amount of $_____, bearing interest rate of _____% per annum, for a term of _____years. Other: _____

Notice to SELLER: Extensive regulations affect SELLER financed transactions. It is beyond the scope of a real estate licensee's authority to determine whether the terms of your SELLER financing agreement comply with all applicable laws or whether you must be registered and/or licensed as a loan originator before offering SELLER financing. You are advised to consult with a legal or mortgage professional to make this determination.

(E) ☐ **ASSUMPTION OF EXISTING MORTGAGE:** Buyer may assume existing mortgage for $_____ plus an assumption fee of $_____. The mortgage has an approximate remaining term of _____ years at an interest rate of _____% ☐ fixed ☐ variable (described) _____.
Lender approval of assumption ☐ is required ☐ is not required ☐ unknown. **Notice to SELLER:** You may remain liable for an assumed mortgage for a number of years after the Property is sold. Check with your lender to determine the extent of your liability. SELLER will insure that all mortgage payments and required escrow deposits are current at the time of closing and will transfer the escrow deposits to the Buyer at closing.

(F) **CLOSING COSTS:** SELLER agrees, at SELLER'S expense, to pay for (1) preparation of and delivery to Buyer of a statutory warranty, trustee, personal representative or guardian deed, as appropriate to the status of SELLER. (2) title search, municipal lien search, if any, and closing services (collectively, "Owner's Title Insurance Policy and related Charges") (3) state documentary stamps on the deed; (4) SELLER's attorney's fee; (5) recording fees for satisfaction of the liens of record, if same are to be paid off; (6) SELLER will pay, on Buyer's behalf, mortgage discount or other closing costs not to exceed $ ___$0.00_____ or _____0.0____% of the purchase price; inclusive of any FHA/VA required fees; and (7) any other expenses including but not limited to home warranty costs and repair expenses as provided for under a Purchase Agreement.

(G) **PRORATIONS:** All taxes for the current year, rentals, monthly insurance premiums, hazard insurance premiums, Homeowners and/or Condo Association fees, and interest on existing mortgages (if any) shall be prorated as of the date of closing.

(H) **TITLE INSURANCE**: SELLER shall provide to BUYER at Closing an Owner's Title Insurance Policy insuring that the title to the property is marketable, subject only to the Standard Exceptions of the title insurance policy, taxes for the year of closing, public utilities and subdivision restrictions that do not effect marketability of title, and encumbrances of record that are to be assumed by BUYER as part of the Purchase Price.

5. **BROKER OBLIGATIONS AND/OR AUTHORITY:** BROKER agrees to make diligent and continued efforts to sell the Property until a sales contract is pending on the Property. SELLER authorizes BROKER to:

(A) Advertise the Property as BROKER deems advisable in newspapers, publications, the Internet and other media, place appropriate transaction signs on the Property, including "For Sale" signs, "Pending" and/or "Sold" signs (once SELLER signs a sales contract); and use SELLER's name in connection with marketing or advertising the Property;
(B) Obtain information relating to the present mortgage(s) on the Property;
(C) Place the property in a multiple listing service(s) "(MLS)". **Placing the Property in a MLS is beneficial to SELLER because the Property will be exposed to a large number of potential buyers. As a MLS participant, BROKER is obligated to, within 24 hours, deliver this listing to the MLS. This listing will be promptly published in the MLS unless SELLER directs BROKER otherwise in writing.** SELLER authorizes BROKER to report to the MLS/Association of REALTORS this listing information and price, terms and financing information on any resulting sale. SELLER authorizes BROKER, the MLS and/or Association of REALTORS to use, license or sell the active listing and sold data;
(D) Provide objective comparative market analysis information to potential Buyers;
(E) (Check if applicable)
    (1) Lock Box: ☒ Use a Lock Box System to show and access the Property. A lock box does not ensure the Property's security; SELLER is advised to secure or remove valuables. SELLER agrees that the lock box is for SELLER's benefit and releases BROKER, persons working through BROKER and BROKER's local Association of REALTORS from all liability and responsibility in connection with any possible loss that may occur;
    (2) Offers: ☒ Withhold verbal offers.
             ☒ Withhold all offers once SELLER accepts a sales contract for the Property.
             ☒ SELLER authorizes BROKER to disclose the existence of offers on the Property in response to inquires from buyers or cooperating Brokers.
(F) At BROKER's discretion, order and obtain on behalf of SELLER all items necessary to consummate a closing on the Property, such as, but not limited to, pest control report, title search and municipal lien search, if any, title insurance, covenant and deed restrictions, survey, and any other materials or services as may be agreed to by SELLER, by verbal or written communication. SELLER agrees to reimburse BROKER for any cost incurred in ordering and obtaining such information; and,
(G) Act as a transaction broker unless otherwise agreed upon by the parties in writing. SELLER acknowledges receipt of Broker disclosure notices set forth on page six (6) of this Agreement.

SELLER [signature] acknowledge receipt of this page, which is Page 2 of 6

Exhibit 12-6 Continued An Exclusive Right of Sale Listing Agreement

6. **SELLER OBLIGATIONS**: In consideration of the obligation of BROKER, SELLER agrees to:

(A) Cooperate with BROKER in carrying out the purpose of this Agreement, including referring immediately to BROKER all inquiries regarding the Property's transfer, whether by purchase or any other means of transfer;
(B) Provide BROKER with keys to the Property and make the Property available to BROKER to show during reasonable times;
(C) Inform BROKER prior to leasing, mortgaging or otherwise encumbering the Property;
(D) Indemnify BROKER and hold BROKER harmless from losses, damages, costs and expenses of any nature, including attorney's fees, and from liability to any person, that BROKER incurs because of (1) SELLER's negligence, representations, misrepresentations, actions or inactions, (2) the use of a lock box, **(3) the existence of undisclosed material facts about the property. This clause will survive BROKER'S performance and the transfer of title;**
(E) Perform any act reasonably necessary to comply with FIRPTA (Internal Revenue Code Section 1445);
(F) Make all legally required disclosures. SELLER represents that the Property has no known latent defects and SELLER knows of no facts materially affecting the value or desirability of the Property which are not readily observable except the following (Please check) ☐ SELLER's property disclosure form or ☒ **None**

Subsequent to the execution of this agreement SELLER will immediately disclose in writing to BROKER any new material facts that have arisen that might affect the value or desirability of the property. (Note: failure to fully disclose may expose the SELLER to claims for damages and/or other legal remedies); and,

(G) To, in the sole determination of SELLER, consult appropriate professionals for related legal, tax, property condition, environmental, foreign reporting requirements and other specialized advice.

7. **INTERNET DISPLAYS**: I understand and acknowledge that, if I have elected under option "(A)" to withhold authorization to display the listed Property on the Internet, consumers who conduct searches for listings on the Internet will not see information about the listed Property in response to their search.

(A) **(Initial)** The Broker ☒ is or ☐ is not authorized to display the listed Property on the Internet. (If Broker is not authorized to display listed Property on the Internet, then (B), (C), and (D) do not apply.)
(B) **(Initial)** The Broker ☐ is or ☒ is not authorized to have the address of the listed Property displayed on the Internet.
(C) **(Initial)** The Broker ☒ is or ☐ is not authorized to have the automated value of the listed Property displayed on a Broker's Virtual Office Website (VOW) or Broker's IDX displays. SELLER acknowledges BROKER does not have control or authority over Third Party Websites that may contain automated valuations.
(D) **(Initial)** The Broker ☒ is or ☐ is not authorized to have blogging of the listed Property displayed on a Broker's Virtual Office Website (VOW) or Broker's IDX displays.

8. **COMPENSATION**: SELLER will compensate BROKER as specified below for procuring a Buyer who is ready, willing and able to purchase the Property or any interest in the Property on the terms of this Agreement or on any other terms acceptable to SELLER. SELLER will pay BROKER as follows (plus applicable sales tax, if any):

(A) ___6.0___ % of the total purchase price OR $_____, no later than the date of closing specified in the Purchase Agreement. However, closing is not a prerequisite for BROKER's fee being earned.
(B) ___10.0___ % of the consideration paid for an option OR $_____ at the time an option is created. If the option is exercised, SELLER will pay BROKER the paragraph 8(a) fee, less the amount BROKER received under this subparagraph.
(C) ___10.0___ % of the gross lease value as a leasing fee, OR $_____ on the date SELLER enters into a lease or agreement to lease, whichever is earlier. This fee shall be paid in the event the Property is rented or leased by SELLER in lieu of sale or in connection with a lease option agreement. Upon exercise of an option to purchase, SELLER will pay BROKER additional compensation as set forth in paragraph 8(a) above.
(D) BROKER's fee is due in the following circumstances: (1) if any interest in the Property is transferred, whether by sale, lease, exchange, governmental action, bankruptcy or any other means of transfer, regardless of whether a Buyer is secured by BROKER, SELLER or any other person; (2) if SELLER refuses or fails to sign an offer at the price and terms stated in this Agreement, defaults on an executed sales contract or colludes with a Buyer to cancel an executed sales contract. (3) if, within ___90___ days after the Termination Date ("Protection Period"), SELLER transfers or contracts to transfer the Property or any interest in the Property to any prospects with whom SELLER, BROKER or any real estate licensee communicated regarding the Property prior to the Termination Date. However, no fee will be due BROKER if the Property is relisted after the Termination Date and sold through another BROKER.
(E) Other: _____

9. **CONDITIONAL TERMINATION**: At SELLER's request, BROKER may agree to conditionally terminate this Agreement. If BROKER agrees to a conditional termination, SELLER must sign a conditional termination agreement, reimburse BROKER for all direct expenses incurred in marketing the Property and pay a cancellation fee of $ _2,000.00_ plus applicable sales tax. BROKER may void this conditional termination and SELLER will pay the fee stated in paragraph 8(a) less the cancellation fee if SELLER transfers or contracts to transfer the Property or any interest in the Property during the time period from the date of conditional termination to Termination Date and Protection Period, if applicable. However, no fee will be due BROKER if the Property is relisted after the Termination Date and sold through another BROKER.

SELLER [_____] acknowledge receipt of this page, which is Page 3 of 6

Listing Agreement/Transaction Broker

Rev. 06/14

Gainesville Multiple Listing, Inc. - All Rights Reserved

Exhibit 12-6 Continued An Exclusive Right of Sale Listing Agreement

10. **COOPERATION WITH OTHER REALTORS**: BROKER's office policy is to cooperate with all other REALTORS. Cooperation is defined as providing access to and information about the Property. SELLER authorizes BROKER to cooperate with selling REALTORS who operate in the following brokerage relationship capacities: (check all that apply)

☒ Buyer's Agents ☒ Nonrepresentative Brokers ☒ Transaction Brokers ☐ None of the foregoing.
(If "NONE" is checked, the Property cannot be placed in the Gainesville Multiple Listing database)

11. **COMPENSATION TO OTHER BROKERS**: BROKER agrees, unless precluded by previous notice between Brokers, to offer compensation per the following, to other Gainesville Multiple Listing, Inc. ("GML") Brokers and those the GML has reciprocal arrangements with:

☒ offer compensation in the amount of _____3.0_ % of the purchase price or $_____ to Buyer's Agents, who represent the interest of the Buyers, and not the interest of SELLER in a transaction;
☒ and to offer compensation in the amount of _____3.0_ % of the purchase price or $_____ to a broker who has no brokerage relationship with the Buyer or SELLER;
☒ and to offer compensation in the amount of _____3.0_ % of the purchase price or $_____ to Transaction brokers for the Buyer;
☐ None of the above (if "NONE" is checked, the Property cannot be placed in the Gainesville Multiple Listing database)

12. **ESCROW DEPOSITS / FORFEITURE / BUYER DEFAULT**: SELLER authorizes BROKER or selling BROKER to accept in escrow and hold all money paid or deposited as a binder on the Property and if such deposit is later forfeited by the Buyer, to disburse the deposit as follows: 1) all unpaid fees and costs incurred by the BROKER or any third party on behalf of either the Buyer or the SELLER shall be paid to BROKER, and BROKER will pay said sums to unpaid vendors; 2) one-half of the remaining net deposit, or total commission the BROKER would have received, whichever is less, shall be disbursed to the BROKER as compensation for BROKER services and marketing expenses; 3) the remainder of the deposit, if any, shall be disbursed to the SELLER as liquidated damages. In the disbursement of any escrowed fund, the BROKER shall be governed and shall comply with the provisions of Chapter 475, Florida Statutes.

13. **DISPUTE RESOLUTION**: In the event any litigation arises out of this Agreement, the prevailing party shall be entitled to recover reasonable attorney's fees and costs.

14. **WITHDRAWAL**: SELLER and BROKER acknowledge that this listing shall be withdrawn from the GML, upon BROKER's withdrawal, suspension or termination from the GML.

15. **MISCELLANEOUS**: This Agreement is binding on BROKER's and SELLER's heirs, personal representatives, administrators, successors and assigns. BROKER may assign this Agreement to another listing office. Signatures, initials and modifications communicated by facsimile, digital or electronic signatures will be considered as originals. The term "Buyer" as used in this Agreement includes Buyers, tenants, exchangors, optionees and other categories of potential or actual transferees. SELLER and BROKER acknowledge that there are no other agreements, promises or understandings either expressed or implied between them other than specifically set forth herein and that there can be no alterations or changes to this Agreement except in writing and signed by each of them. They also agree that this Agreement supersedes any prior agreement regarding the marketing of the Property. IF THIS AGREEMENT IS NOT FULLY UNDERSTOOD, SELLER SHOULD SEEK COMPETENT LEGAL ADVICE.

16. ADDITIONAL TERMS:

SELLER _____ acknowledge receipt of this page, which is Page 4 of 6

Listing Agreement/Transaction Broker

Rev. 06/14

Exhibit 12-6 Continued An Exclusive Right of Sale Listing Agreement

17. SELLER AND BROKER ACKNOWLEDGE THAT THIS AGREEMENT DOES NOT GUARANTEE A SALE.

Seller's Signature: _Robert Jordan_

Home Telephone: (###) ###-#### Work Telephone: (###) ###-#### Facsimile: _____

Address: 1822 NW 40th Avenue, Gainesville, FL

Email Address: _____

Seller's Signature: _Penelope Jordan_

Home Telephone: (###) ###-#### Work Telephone: _____ Facsimile: _____

Address: 1822 NW 40th Avenue, Gainesville, FL

Email Address: _____

Seller's Signature: _____

Home Telephone: _____ Work Telephone: _____ Facsimile: _____

Address: _____

Email Address: _____

Authorized Sales Associate or Broker: Ben Park _Ben Park_

Brokerage Firm Name: Baden Associates Realty _____ Telephone: _____

Address: _____

SELLER _____ acknowledge receipt of this page, which is Page 5 of 6

Listing Agreement/Transaction Broker

Gainesville Multiple Listing, Inc. - All Rights Reserved

Rev. 06/14

Exhibit 12-6 Continued An Exclusive Right of Sale Listing Agreement

---

TRANSACTION BROKER NOTICE

As a transaction broker, ___Baden Associates Realty___
(insert name of Real Estate entity) and its Associates provides to you a limited form of representation that includes the following duties:

1. Dealing honestly and fairly;
2. Accounting for all funds;
3. Using skill, care and diligence in the transaction;
4. Disclosing all known facts that materially affect the value of residential real property and are not readily observable to the buyer;
5. Presenting all offers and counteroffers in a timely manner, unless a party has previously directed the licensee otherwise in writing;
6. Limited confidentiality, unless waived in writing by a party. This limited confidentiality will prevent disclosure that the seller will accept a price less than the asking or listed price, that the buyer will pay a price greater than the price submitted in a written offer, of the motivation of any party for selling or buying property, that a seller or buyer will agree to financing terms other than those offered, or of any other information requested by a party to remain confidential; and
7. Any additional duties that are entered into by this or by separate written agreement.

Limited representation means that a buyer or seller is not responsible for the acts of the licensee. Additionally, parties are giving up their rights to the undivided loyalty of the licensee. This aspect of limited representation allows a licensee to facilitate a real estate transaction by assisting both the buyer and the seller, but a licensee will not work to represent one party to the detriment of the other party when acting as a transaction broker to both parties.

Robert Jordan	5-01-2017
Signature	Date
Penelope Jordan	5-01-2017
Signature	Date
Signature	Date

SELLER [☑] [☑] [ ] acknowledge receipt of this page, which is Page 6 of 6

Listing Agreement/Transaction Broker

Rev. 06/14

Gainesville Multiple Listing, Inc. - All Rights Reserved

Summary

Real estate brokerage is an important type of real estate business dealing with marketing. Brokers provide a service for sellers and buyers of properties that involves finding available properties, finding potential buyers, helping buyers identify needs and set priorities, negotiating between buyers and sellers, providing advice about other needs and specialists (e.g., financing, attorneys, architects), making certain all relevant federal and state laws are followed (e.g., those regarding discrimination and disclosure), and arranging for the closing of the transaction. Probably the most important of these functions is helping buyers and sellers determine their needs and enabling them to meet those needs in the best possible manner.

Listing contracts create an agency relationship between a real estate broker and the owners of real estate. This is a fiduciary relationship, binding the broker to a commitment of confidentiality, obedience, accounting, loyalty, disclosure, and skill and care. It requires of the principal a commitment of honesty, openness, and cooperation.

Several forms of special agency relationships arise in real estate brokerage, including listing agent, buying agent, and dual agent. Of particular concern is unintended dual agency. This risk has prompted widespread legislation to either require more extensive disclosures of agency relationships or to prohibit dual agency altogether. Laws have been enacted to create alternative brokerage relationships such as transaction or facilitating brokerage where the broker does not represent either buyer or seller.

There are three types of listing contracts: open, exclusive agency, and exclusive right of sale. The exclusive right of sale listing is the predominant type of contract, especially for residential properties. This contract is required when the property is to be filed with a multiple listing service. A multiple listing service is a cooperative arrangement among brokerage firms in which all member firms pool their listings. All sales personnel of the member firms can then attempt to sell the listed property. When the property is sold, the commission is split between the listing and selling firms according to a predetermined schedule.

In signing a listing contract, both broker and owner obtain rights and responsibilities. The brokerage firm has the right to collect a commission if the property is sold within a specified or reasonable period and agrees to exert its best efforts to sell the property; the owner can expect the firm to try to sell the property through a marketing program. The owner can also expect an MLS member firm to file the listing with the multiple listing service and for sales personnel of other member firms to work on the sale. The owner is obligated not to impede the selling effort and to pay a commission if the property is sold.

Key Terms

Broker license 313
Buyer agency agreement 309
Commission 306
Designated agent 311
Discrimination in housing 318
Dual agency 309
Errors and omission insurance 315
Exclusive agency listing 322
Exclusive right of sale listing 322
Fiduciary relationship 308

General agent 308
Internet marketing 320
Law of agency 308
Licensing laws 313
Listing contract 309
Market segmentation 316
Multiple listing service (MLS) 309
National Association of
   Realtors 315
Net listing 306

Open listing 322
Principal 308
Real estate commission 314
Recovery fund 315
Salesperson license 313
Special agent 308
Subagency 309
Submarket 316
Transaction broker 312
Universal agent 308

www.mhhe.com/lingarcher5e

Test Problems

Answer the following multiple-choice questions:

1. A down payment deposit from a potential buyer must be held in:
   a. The seller's bank account.
   b. The salesperson's own bank account.
   c. The broker's escrow trust account.
   d. Long-term government bonds.
   e. The broker's own bank account.

2. One of the most effective ways that salespersons or brokers can distinguish themselves as a preferred agent in a particular specialization of real estate brokerage is to:
   a. Obtain a license to practice.
   b. Take related courses.
   c. Read related books.
   d. Engage in personal advertising.
   e. Obtain a related industry designation.

3. All of the following are duties that a broker would have to the seller in a single agency listing contract, **EXCEPT**:
   a. Skill and care.
   b. Obedience.
   c. Loyalty.
   d. Knowledge.
   e. Disclosure.

4. Real estate salespersons can lose their licenses for:
   a. Using aggressive sales techniques.
   b. Not showing buyers all available properties in an area.
   c. Commingling escrow (trust) money with personal funds.
   d. Not using modern sales methods.
   e. All of the above.

5. The state real estate commission is responsible for:
   a. Setting fees for brokerage services.
   b. Marketing data on real estate transactions.
   c. Establishing education requirements for licensees.
   d. Overseeing the activities of mortgage lenders.
   e. Setting up multiple listing systems.

6. Real estate brokers are paid commissions primarily for:
   a. Having an inventory of properties.
   b. Having many contacts.
   c. Providing a service.
   d. Knowing how to close a transaction.
   e. Having specialized education.

7. Traditionally, a real estate broker is what type of agent for his or her principal?
   a. General agent.
   b. Special agent.
   c. Limited agent.
   d. Designated agent.
   e. All of the above.

8. The subagency relationship that traditionally has characterized multiple listing services has tended to result in the widespread danger of:
   a. Monopoly.
   b. Deliberate dual agency.
   c. Unintended dual agency.
   d. Discrimination.
   e. Price wars.

9. How are commission rates that real estate brokers charge determined?
   a. By agreement among local Realtors.
   b. By rule of the local Board of Realtors.
   c. By state real estate commissions.
   d. By agreement between broker and principal.
   e. By state law.

10. According to most listing contracts, a broker has earned a commission when:
    a. A contract for sale is signed by the buyer.
    b. The transaction closes.
    c. The broker finds a buyer who is ready, willing, and able to buy on the terms specified in the listing contract.
    d. The seller signs a listing contract.
    e. The broker sends a bill for services rendered to the principal (usually the seller).

Study Questions

1. Ted Richardson owns a large industrial building in your city that he wishes to sell. As a real estate broker, you would be delighted to obtain the listing on this property. You have worked with Richardson on two other transactions in which he was the buyer; therefore, you approach Richardson to request that he consider listing his property with you. Richardson agrees to do so, but indicates that he will not give you an exclusive right of sale listing, because he wants to retain the right to sell the property himself without owing a real estate commission. He will, however, give you an exclusive agency listing.
   a. What should you do? Should you accept such a listing from Richardson?
   b. What provisions, if any, would you include in the listing contract to give yourself some protection?

2. You are a real estate salesperson working for Good Earth Realtors, Inc. You receive 50 percent of all commissions received by the firm (net of MLS fees) for which you were either the listing agent or the selling agent. The firm receives 40 percent of commissions for sales of properties it lists and 45 percent of commissions for sales of properties it sells in cooperation with other firms. Fifteen percent of all commissions for properties sold through the multiple listing service must be paid to the MLS. If you are both the listing and selling agent in a transaction, you receive 60 percent of the firm's proceeds. If you are either the listing agent or the selling agent for a transaction in which another member of Good Earth is the selling agent or the listing agent, your split remains the same as when another firm cooperates in the transaction. Recently, you were the selling agent for a property that was sold for $127,250. Another salesperson associated with Good Earth had listed the property two months previously for $135,000. The property was in the MLS, and the commission rate was 6 percent.
   a. How much in total commission, net of the MLS fee, will your firm receive?
   b. What will be your split of the commission?

3. If you owned your own real estate brokerage firm, how could you establish a niche in the market for your firm? How could you set your firm apart from other brokerage firms and create a unique image for your firm?

4. Explain why there occurred numerous experimental or innovative approaches to residential real estate brokerage in the United States in the years following 2000.

5. A friend of yours, Cindy Malvern, is moving to your town to begin a new job. Cindy has decided to buy a condominium, and because you are taking a real estate course, she asks you how to proceed.

    You first "Google" condominiums for your city and notice that a number of existing condominiums are for sale. Most of them are advertised by brokers, but some are advertised by the owners. You also notice ads by some local builders for new condominiums. You ask Cindy whether she prefers to buy a previously owned condominium or a new one. She says she doesn't know; it depends on the condominium, the location, the price, and so on.

    Next, using Google once more, you find a list of local area real estate brokers. You have heard of three or four of the firms, but you have had no direct contact or dealings with any of them.

    a. How would you advise Cindy to proceed? Should she call a real estate brokerage firm? Why or why not?

    b. If Cindy decides to call a real estate broker, how should she select the broker? What criteria should she use?

    c. If Cindy decides to work through a real estate broker, can she look at new condominiums for sale by builders? If she buys a new condominium while working with a broker, would she or the builder have to pay a commission to the broker?

6. You decide to open a real estate office in your community, but you know you would face stiff competition from established firms. You believe that one method of drawing attention to your firm and obtaining clients who would otherwise go to the established brokers is to advertise that you will sell any house in town and charge a commission of only $2,000. Do you believe such a marketing tactic would be successful? Why or why not?

EXPLORE THE WEB

1. On the Web, go to www.realtor.org. Click on the link *About NAR,* and then look at *Affiliated Organizations.*

    a. How many societies, institutes, and councils are affiliated with the National Association of Realtors?
    b. Identify each affiliate, and briefly describe its area of specialization.
    c. List the designations offered by each affiliate. What do these designations indicate?

2. Google the association of Realtors for a state of interest to you. Find out what services they offer to: members; home buyers; and consumers.

3. Go to www.realtors.org. Under the "Education" tab, select "Designations & Certifications." Select the type of certification that seems most interesting and answer these questions: Who would use the designation? What are the qualifying requirements?

4. Go to zillow.com. Use zillow to get a "zestimate" of the value of a house that interests you.

5. Go to www.realtor.com. Select a zip code of interest to you. Determine how many residential listings are available for that zip code. Determine the price range of the listings. Determine how many of the listings have video tours available.

Solutions to Concept Checks

1. The "price of success" in real estate brokerage is preparation, dedication to the welfare of customers, and hard work.

2. Without real estate brokers, the buyer that values the property most would be less likely to find it.

3. Areas of special knowledge of an expert real estate broker include current prices and terms, successful marketing procedures, legal obligations of all parties of the transaction, knowledge of properties in the market, needs of prospective buyers, and procedures for a transaction.

4. A cost of selling a property that tends to be overlooked by prospective for-sale-by-owners is the time, inconvenience, and risks of handling the sale.

5. A phrase that characterizes an agent's relationship to a principal is that the agent must "stand in the shoes" of the principal.

6. A broker has a fiduciary relationship with the principal and owes the principal the six duties of confidentiality, obedience, accounting, loyalty, disclosure, skill, and care.

7. The three basic types of agency relationship are universal, general, and special. A broker is a special agent of the principal (buyer or seller).

8. A very complicated agency relationship that arises when one firm represents both seller and buyer is dual agency.

9. In MLS property listings, the broker selling a listing traditionally was an agent of the seller, in spite of all appearances, by virtue of a required agency relationship called subagency.

10. Brokerage firms are increasingly faced with an unintended internal dual agency problem as they are more likely to be representing both the buyer and the seller.

11. One attempt to mitigate the dual agency problem occurring within a firm that is both the listing broker and buyer broker is for the broker to appoint designated agents.

12. A broker who represents neither buyer nor seller is called a transaction, facilitating, or intermediary broker.

13. Five real estate services that require licensing to be performed for others are buying, auctioning, renting, managing, and selling.

14. Two important functions of a commercial real estate broker are to provide the prospective buyer with information about the property and to negotiate compromises.

15. Three reasons influencing a customer's choice of brokerage firm include the broker's reputation in the community, recommendations of friends, and familiarity with the broker.

16. Fair housing laws prohibit discrimination on the basis of race, color, religion, age, sex, familial status, and handicap.

17. Discrimination by race is absolutely prohibited in any form or at any level by a 1968 U.S. Supreme Court ruling in the case of *Jones v. Mayer.*

18. Under a listing contract, a broker is entitled to a commission if he or she produces a ready, willing, and able buyer.

19. In an open listing, the broker is entitled to a commission only if the broker procures a ready, willing, and able buyer. In an exclusive agency listing, the broker is entitled to a commission if any broker procures a buyer. In an exclusive right-of-sale listing, the broker is entitled to a commission if any broker or the seller procures a buyer.

20. Five issues on which a seller should be clear before signing a listing agreement are:
    a. What advertising program will be used?
    b. Will the property be placed in the MLS?
    c. How long is the term of the listing?
    d. What progress reports will the broker provide?
    e. What personal property is being listed?

Additional Readings

Reilly, John. *Agency Relationships in Real Estate,* 2nd ed. Chicago: Real Estate Education Company, 1994.

Wilson, Ray. *Bought, Not Sold.* Greenfield, MA: CognaBooks, 1998. An exposé-like treatment of real estate agency relationships.

The following periodical is the monthly journal of the National Association of Realtors. It contains articles on both residential and commercial brokerage and runs several special features.

Realtor Magazine (monthly), National Association of Realtors, 430 North Michigan Avenue, Chicago, IL 60611–4049. An online version of the magazine is available through www.realtor.org.

Additionally, several of the affiliates of NAR publish professional journals in specialized areas of brokerage, and many state Boards of Realtors publish monthly magazines containing articles and news features about brokerage issues in those states. You may find information about the publications of the NAR affiliates by using the links on the home page of NAR at www.realtor.org select *About NAR* and then *Affiliated Organizations.*

On the same website, under the headings "Products and Services," then "Real Estate Publications," then "Realtor VIP Publications" are listed a variety of publications concerning the real estate brokerage industry.

Chapter 13

Contracts *for* Sale *and* Closing

LEARNING OBJECTIVES

After reading this chapter you will be able to:

1. List the seven requirements for a valid contract for the sale of real estate.

2. Write a simple contract that contains the seven requirements.

3. Complete a standard form contract, given the facts of a property transaction.

4. Identify five expenses typically paid by the seller and five expenses typically paid by the buyer.

5. List three remedies for nonperformance by a buyer and three remedies for nonperformance by a seller.

6. List the steps that must be taken before closing a real estate transaction.

7. Describe the activities that occur at closing.

8. Explain the principal provisions of the Real Estate Settlement Procedures Act (RESPA).

9. Complete a Closing Disclosure form.

OUTLINE

Introduction: The Most Important Document in Real Estate

A poorly executed conveyance of real estate can harm its value. Success of the transfer depends on a well-formed **contract for sale** since the contract dictates the rights and type of deed involved, and choreographs the entire transaction. The principal provisions of a contract for sale require the seller to deliver a deed for the property to the buyer in exchange for payment of the purchase price to the seller. The contract is signed when a buyer and seller decide to commit themselves to the transaction under terms and conditions worked out between them. **Contract terms** refer to the arrangements agreed to by the parties, such as price and date of closing, whereas **contract conditions** refer to the circumstances that must prevail, such as mechanical equipment being in good condition and title being unencumbered. Thus, real estate transactions differ from personal property transactions in that realty sales almost always involve a two-step process. The parties reach agreement first; sometime later, perhaps a month or more, they complete the sale at a meeting called the **closing.** In a personal property transaction, the parties usually close the transaction at the same time they reach agreement.

Like any contract, a contract for sale of real estate is a legal, enforceable document. If its provisions are not carried out, financial penalties (i.e., damages) may be imposed on the party unwilling or unable to fulfill the contract. Because it determines virtually all the important aspects of the transaction—price and other terms, property interest conveyed, grantee(s), conditions of the transaction—a contract for sale is the *most important document* in a real estate transaction. Whereas most contracts are legal and enforceable whether they are written or oral, the laws (called statutes of fraud) of every state require that contracts for the sale and purchase of real estate be *in writing* to be enforceable. The many provisions in such a contract leave too much room for both legitimate misunderstandings and purposeful disagreements (fraud) when the agreements are oral. Although disagreements also may arise with written contracts, these contracts contain definite language that the courts can interpret and enforce.

Rights and Obligations of Sellers and Buyers

A contract for the sale of real estate creates certain rights and obligations for both sellers and buyers. Sellers, for example, have the right to receive the sale price on the terms specified in the contract. They are obligated to deliver clear and marketable title to the property to the buyers at closing, to maintain the property in good repair until closing, to allow the buyers to inspect the property just prior to closing, and to pay the agreed upon brokerage commission.

Buyers have the right to obtain clear and marketable title at closing, to receive the property and appliances in the same condition they were when the contract was signed, and usually to back out of the transaction if the property is substantially damaged or destroyed before closing. They are obligated, of course, to pay the price on the terms specified in the contract at closing.

Requirements of a Contract for Sale

A legally binding contract for sale can take many forms. It can be a short handwritten note, a preprinted form containing several standard paragraphs, or a lengthy document prepared by attorneys to cover many points in a complex transaction. Whatever the form, any contract, whether it be for the sale of real estate or for some other purpose (such as a mortgage), must contain the following elements:

1. Competent parties.
2. Legal objective.
3. Offer and acceptance.
4. Consideration.
5. No defects to mutual assent.

Two additional requirements must be part of any contract for the sale of real estate:

1. Written form.
2. Proper description of the property.

✓ **Concept Check**

13.1 List five essential elements of any valid contract. Name two additional essential elements of a valid contract for sale of real estate.

Competency of the Parties to Act

The principal parties to a transaction must be legally *competent.* In the case of individuals, such parties must have reached a minimum age (18 years in most states) and be of sound mind. Although minors may be legally competent to participate in real estate transactions, a contract with a minor generally is *voidable:* The minor may legally declare the contract invalid and refuse to carry out its provisions. A contract also may be voidable if one party is under the influence of drugs or alcohol, or is insane at the time the contract is signed. However, the incapacitation must be sufficient that the party is incapable of understanding the nature of the contract. Frequently when an elder parent suffers failing health and mental capacity, a child who is caring for the parent may obtain a deed for their home or other real estate, to the exclusion of other sons or daughters. The child may regard the conveyance as compensation for providing care to the parent. However, a court may find the parent incapable of making contracts under the circumstances and set aside the deed.

In the case of corporations, a party acting on behalf of the corporation must be legally empowered to do so. For example, if a corporation sells property, its president or some other officer must be authorized by a resolution of the board of directors or a corporation bylaw to act in this capacity. Similarly, personal representatives (e.g., executors, administrators, agents, and attorneys-in-fact) and trustees must be authorized to act on behalf of their principals by a legal instrument or order, such as a *power of attorney.* Their powers are defined and limited by the instrument. Real estate purchasers or professionals should always assure themselves that personal representatives and trustees have legal authority to sell properties.

✓ **Concept Check**

13.2 List three aspects of legal competency.

Lawful Intent of the Parties

The objective of a contract must not be illegal or against public policy. For example, a contract to commit a crime for payment is not enforceable in the courts. Similarly, a contract to sell property for the purpose of growing illegal marijuana or for storing illegal weapons is legally invalid. A contract to sell property to members of a certain race, or to exclude members of a certain race, would be counter to public policy against racial discrimination and would be void.

An Offer and an Acceptance

An offer and acceptance indicate that the parties to a contract have a meeting of the minds, or *mutual assent.* The contract binds the parties to specified actions in the future: the seller to deliver *marketable* legal title to the buyer and the buyer to pay the stipulated price for a property. In a real estate contract for sale, the buyer normally offers a specified price under specific terms for specific property rights. The seller has three options: to reject the offer outright, to accept the offer outright, or, as frequently occurs, to reject the offer and present a *counteroffer.* A series of offers and counteroffers often will ensue until an agreement is reached—a successful offer and acceptance—or one party rejects an offer outright.

The basic agreement ultimately reached between buyer and seller may be simple and straightforward. However, it usually creates many other issues on which agreement must be reached, including the closing date, prorating of expenses, type of title evidence, liability for property damage, and condition of the property. The purpose of a contract for sale is to specify these agreements and to make them legally binding.

> ✓ **Concept Check**
>
> **13.3**   What kind of title does a seller implicitly agree to deliver in a contract for sale?

Consideration

The value given up, or promise made, by each party to a contract is the **consideration.** Both parties to a valid and enforceable contract must provide consideration. In a contract for the sale and purchase of real estate, the seller's consideration is the property to be given up. The buyer's consideration is the money or other goods that constitute the purchase price. Mere promise of consideration by one party does not constitute a contract and cannot be enforced. For example, Bill Rich promises to deed a property to his friend B. Weiser, and even writes this promise on a piece of paper. Such a promise cannot be enforced because Mr. Weiser did not promise anything in return. Mutual obligations of the parties are necessary to create a legally binding contract.

No Defects to Mutual Assent

In certain circumstances, mutual assent—the meeting of the minds—between the contracting parties may be broken, thus invalidating the contract. The following constitute defects to mutual assent:

1. One party attempts to perpetrate a fraud on the other party or makes a misrepresentation.[1]
2. A substantial error is made (e.g., the name of a party to the contract is incorrect).
3. One of the parties is under duress, undue influence, or menace.[2]

In addition to the elements for any contract described above, an enforceable contract for the sale of real estate must fulfill two additional requirements.

> ✓ **Concept Check**
>
> **13.4**   Name three possible defects to mutual assent.

A Written Real Estate Contract

The Statute of Frauds, the old English law that serves as the basis for contract law in most states, imposed the requirement of writing on some types of contracts in order for them to

---

1. *Fraud* is intentional misrepresentation, whereas a *misrepresentation* per se is unintentional. However, both have the same effect.

2. *Undue influence* involves an abuse of the influence that one person (often a relative) has over another. *Duress* involves compelling a person to act by the use of force, and *menace* is the use of the threat of force to compel a person to act.

be enforceable.[3] Many agreements involving real estate are subject to this requirement, including contracts for sale, installment sales contracts, option contracts, exchange contracts, and, in many states, leases, listing contracts, and mortgage contracts.[4] In most states, the *parol* evidence rule is in effect, which prohibits the admission of oral evidence in disputes involving written contracts.

As noted, most real estate contracts contain many technicalities and points of agreement. Legitimate misunderstandings could easily arise over any of these points in an oral contract. Even more important, unscrupulous parties to an oral contract could gain an unfair advantage by later claiming they did not agree to protective provisions. For example, most written contracts contain a provision that allows a buyer to back out of a transaction if the building is destroyed by fire or by other hazard before the closing. A seller could easily claim such a provision was not part of an oral contract; it would be his or her word against the buyer's.

To satisfy the writing requirement, the contract usually must include adequate identification of the parties, the subject matter, and the terms of agreement, as well as the signatures of the parties or their legally empowered agents. It is essential that both principal parties to a transaction—buyers and sellers—sign the contract. The signatures are legal evidence that the parties understand and agree to the provisions in the contract. They cannot later claim they did not agree to a provision in the contract or did not understand its meaning.

In addition to the principals' signatures, the statute of frauds may require a spouse's signature to release his or her marital rights such as homestead rights, dower rights, or community property rights. Technically, a spouse's signature on a contract indicates his or her agreement to sign the deed, where these rights are actually waived. Also, as noted, legal written authorization must accompany a contract that is signed by an agent, personal representative, or trustee.

Proper Description of the Property

It is essential that the property be properly described so that a court can resolve any controversies about it. If the property is inadequately described, the validity of the contract may be destroyed. Methods for describing property are discussed in Chapter 3, and include the recorded subdivision plat method, the metes and bounds method, and the government rectangular survey system.

Legal Title versus Equitable Title

Legal title means the ownership of a freehold estate. In contrast, **equitable title** is the right to obtain legal title. The importance of this distinction is that when a contract for sale is signed, the buyers immediately obtain equitable title, and the sellers cannot sell the property to someone else. (They could, however, sell the property contingent upon the possibility that the buyers might fail to close the transaction.) In addition, the creation of equitable title gives the buyer a real property interest while converting the seller's interest to personal property. Thus, if the buyer dies the heirs receive the property as part of his or her estate. Also the buyer bears the risk of changing property value before the conveyance of legal title.

> ✓ **Concept Check**
>
> **13.5** What is legal title? What is equitable title? When does equitable title arise?

3. The *statute of frauds* was intended to prevent fraudulent practices in contracting; thus, the writing requirement was imposed for situations where substantial sums of money would normally be involved.

4. Leases for less than one year normally are not required to be in writing to be enforceable.

The Form of the Contract for Sale

While the contract for sale may take a variety of forms, the important question to be answered is whether all essential ingredients of a valid and enforceable contract for sale are present. Most transactions today, especially residential transactions, are completed with the use of standard forms, which force the parties to consider all of the necessary elements.

Simple Contract

The following statement constitutes a simple real estate contract:

> *I, Ben Byer, agree to buy and pay $20,000, and I, Cecil Celler, agree to sell the parcel of real estate at 1013 NE Seventh Road in North Platte, Nebraska.*
>
> *Signed: Ben Byer*   *Signed: Cecil Celler*

For most transactions, such a brief contract would not be sufficient; however, it contains the seven essential elements, and therefore it could be enforceable. Mr. Byer and Mr. Celler presumably are competent. Mr. Byer offers $20,000, and Mr. Celler accepts by agreeing to sell. Consideration is stated for both: $20,000 for the buyer and the property for the seller. The objective is legal, the property is identified, and there are no apparent defects to mutual assent. The contract is written and is signed by both parties.

But several important points are omitted. These could be subject to disagreement later, and they could cause the transaction to be delayed or even aborted. The missing points include:

- Date of the contract.
- Date and place of closing.
- The marital status of the parties.
- Financing terms, if any.
- Prorating of costs and expenses.
- Inspections of the property for termites, radon, or needed repairs.
- Condition of any buildings, subsystems, and appliances.
- Assurance of good and marketable title.
- Right of occupancy (or rents) until closing.
- Liability for major damage to buildings before closing.
- Remedies by each party for breach of contract by the other party.
- Exact dimensions and location of the property.
- Brokerage commission, if any.
- Earnest money deposit.

www.fool.com/

Select Guides/Personal Finance/ Home & Real Estate The Motley Fool is a good source of ideas in financial and personal planning, and has a rich section on homebuying/financing as well.

Since these points are not covered in the contract, misunderstandings and severe losses for both parties can result. For example, the seller may need the money and count on closing within two weeks. The buyer, however, may be in no hurry and not want to close for three months. Since the contract does not specify the date of closing, the courts will interpret the time between contract and closing as a reasonable time—which could easily be three months. As another example, consider the buyer's problem if the building burns down before closing. Without the contract specifying otherwise, the buyer must complete the transaction even if the building is destroyed. For these reasons, a longer contract form is usually used.

Standard Form Contracts

Since the issues in many transactions are similar, brokers often use standard preprinted contract forms. For most straightforward transactions, these work well. All or most of the normal issues requiring agreement are addressed in a way that protects both buyers and sellers. They are not inherently biased toward one party or the other, as can be the case

A new marketing professor, Dr. David Dennis, was hired by a large midwestern university. After looking at a number of houses, he and his wife, Marie, decided to purchase a large, older home in a pleasant section of town. When they looked at the house, Marie noted that the master bedroom was carpeted, with the carpet fastened to the floor. After the transaction was closed and they began moving in, however, they discovered the carpet in the master bedroom had been removed.

The Dennises immediately protested to the broker who had sold them the house,

Ms. Jan Dancy. She contacted the former owners, Mr. and Mrs. Jim Rockledge, who had moved several hundred miles to another city, to inquire why they had removed the carpet. They told Jan they had every right to remove the carpet. It was not part of the house, since it was not tacked to the floor.

When told that Marie had noticed the carpet was fastened to the floor, Mrs. Rockledge replied that the carpet had been tacked down only at the doorway to prevent its being kicked up. It was not fastened down in any other place and was not

permanently installed. The contract did not mention the carpet, and it was not intended to be sold as part of the house.

The Dennises were deprived of carpet they believed should have belonged to them, the Rockledges refused to pay, and the broker suffered customer dissatisfaction. To keep their goodwill, Jan bought the Dennises a new bedroom carpet.

Contract for Sale

www.freddiemac.com

See "My Home by Freddie Mac." An exceptionally good array of helps, including a rent versus buy calculator.

www.fanniemae.com

Under "Homeowners & Communities," see "KnowYourOptions.com."

www.homeloan learningcenter.com

This is the Mortgage Bankers–sponsored site for homeowners strong information on obtaining financing.

with contracts drawn up by one of the parties to a transaction. These forms contain ready-made provisions to address issues such as prorations, closing, financing terms, liability for property damage, easements, condition of fixtures and appliances, real estate commission, and so on.

Generally, the best standard form contracts are those prepared and approved by local Associations of Realtors.[5] These usually are superior to a generic contract form obtained from, for example, an office supply firm or a Web source of forms because they are customized for issues that are especially important in that particular community. For example, they may highlight floodplain risk, radon inspection, insulation quality, water supply, or other matters of special concern for the local climate and environment. Also, they frequently address local legal and regulatory issues such as state disclosure requirements for real estate transactions, state law concerning evidence of title, or special state or local taxes on real estate transactions.

A standard form real estate contract can be disadvantageous if it is misused. If, for example, parties to the sale of a small commercial or multifamily rental property attempt to adapt a standard residential contract form to the transaction, there is risk that important issues can be overlooked. For example, the standard residential contract form is not likely to clarify rights of the buyer relative to existing tenants of the property, or even to provide for inspection of existing leases, verification and transfer of tenant deposits, or for other landlord and tenant concerns. The same kind of problem could arise in trying to adapt a standard residential contract form to a sale of land for future building or for conversion to another use. The contract form is likely to give inadequate attention to the examination of public land-use controls, private restrictions, or easements that could affect the future use of the property. Local Associations of Realtors, recognizing this risk of the standard contract form, often design a set of different contract forms, each appropriate to one common type of real estate transaction.

Even with standard contract forms and straightforward transactions, buyers and sellers should examine the contract carefully; once they sign a contract, they can be held to its provisions, no matter how deleterious to their interests. Both parties can achieve maximum protection by having a competent attorney examine the document *before* signing. Having

---

5. Because contract forms are central to member business, and because members understand that they will do business with persons more than once, as both seller and buyer, local associations are motivated to maintain both up-to-date and fair contract forms.

www.HUD.gov

Select "Buying a Home." Especially informative on housing assistance and home buyer protections.

an attorney examine a contract after it has been signed is like locking the barn door after the horse has run away. While many buyers and sellers of single-family homes do not hire an attorney to draft or examine the contract and do not suffer severe financial losses, small disagreements and losses are relatively common (see Industry Issues 13-1).

✓ **Concept Check**

13.6   Name two advantages and one disadvantage of a standard form contract for the sale of real estate.

Contracts for the purchase and sale of larger, more complex, income-producing properties are usually drafted by attorneys. Typically, the sellers or buyers will have their attorneys draft the instrument, sign it, and then submit it to the other parties and their attorneys. The instrument tends to protect the parties that have drafted the instrument, to the detriment of the other side. Thus, it is rare to encounter acceptance of the first draft of a contract drawn by the other parties' attorneys. Usually, objections will be raised, new drafts will be prepared, and a bargaining process will occur before a contract is acceptable to both sides.

A standard form contract for the purchase and sale of real estate is presented in Exhibit 13-1 showing the purchase and sale agreement between the Jordans and the buyers, the Lees, from our example in Chapter 12. This form, developed jointly by the Florida Realtors and the Florida Bar Association, is relatively comprehensive and fair to both parties.[6] Although our example contract contains all the elements common to purchase and sale agreements, it is important to emphasize that such contracts can vary significantly in form across cities and states within the United States.

Components of a Form Contract

The example contract form is typical in many respects. It has two distinct parts. The first part is comprised of sections 1-9, with items to be filled in. These concern issues most likely to depend on the specific property and transaction, and thus need to be "customized" or negotiated. The second part, comprised of sections 10-18, includes the following subjects: "Disclosures," "Property Maintenance, Condition, Inspection and Examinations," "Escrow Agent and Broker," "Default and Dispute Resolution," and "Standards for Real Estate Transactions." These are all topics thought to be less dependent on the specific transaction, and thus are routine. However, these points are no less a part of the contract, no less binding on the parties, and no less negotiable, if the case requires it. An important example of this is clause 18F, concerning time. In the example form, the "standard" is that "time is of the essence." This means that the slightest breach of a specified time limit constitutes "drop-dead" default on the contract, and the aggrieved party can take immediate action. In contrast, other contract forms do not include the "time is of the essence" standard, meaning that deadlines must be honored only within a "reasonable time."

✓ **Concept Check**

13.7   Distinguish between the two main parts in a standard form contract for the sale of real estate.

Notice that the form contract in Exhibit 13-1 contains the elements of any valid contract. The parties to the transaction are identified at the top of the form. There is an offer

---

6. Many state Realtor associations and state bar associations have similarly cooperated to create model contracts for sale. Frequently the resulting contracts can be found by "googling" for model real estate contract forms.

Exhibit 13-1 Example of a Standard Form Contract for Sale and Purchase of Real Estate

"AS IS" Residential Contract For Sale And Purchase
THIS FORM HAS BEEN APPROVED BY THE FLORIDA REALTORS AND THE FLORIDA BAR

FloridaRealtors

1* **PARTIES:**_____ Robert and Penelope Jordan _____ ("Seller"),
2* and _____ Nicolas and Katie Lee _____ ("Buyer"),
3   agree that Seller shall sell and Buyer shall buy the following described Real Property and Personal Property
4   (collectively "Property") pursuant to the terms and conditions of this AS IS Residential Contract For Sale And
5   Purchase and any riders and addenda ("Contract"):
6   **1. PROPERTY DESCRIPTION:**
7*   (a) Street address, city, zip:_____ 1822 N.W. 40th Avenue, Gainesville, FL _____
8*   (b) Property is located in: __Alachua__ County, Florida. Real Property Tax ID No.:_____
9*   (c) Real Property: The legal description is__ Parcel No. 3 Block 2 of Spring Meadow Estates PB 12 Pg. 28
10 _____
11 _____
12   together with all existing improvements and fixtures, including built-in appliances, built-in furnishings and
13   attached wall-to-wall carpeting and flooring ("Real Property") unless specifically excluded in Paragraph 1(e) or
14   by other terms of this Contract.
15   (d) Personal Property: Unless excluded in Paragraph 1(e) or by other terms of this Contract, the following items
16   which are owned by Seller and existing on the Property as of the date of the initial offer are included in the
17   purchase: range(s)/oven(s), refrigerator(s), dishwasher(s), disposal, ceiling fan(s), intercom, light fixture(s),
18   drapery rods and draperies, blinds, window treatments, smoke detector(s), garage door opener(s), security
19   gate and other access devices, and storm shutters/panels ("Personal Property").
20*   Other Personal Property items included in this purchase are:_Patio table and chairs (as observed on 5/14/2017)
21 _____
22   Personal Property is included in the Purchase Price, has no contributory value, and shall be left for the Buyer.
23*   (e) The following items are excluded from the purchase:_Backyard copper fountain/birdbath
24 _____

25 **PURCHASE PRICE AND CLOSING**

26* **2. PURCHASE PRICE** (U.S. currency): ....$____250,000.00
27*   (a) Initial deposit to be held in escrow in the amount of **(checks subject to COLLECTION)** ......$____12,000.00
28   The initial deposit made payable and delivered to "Escrow Agent" named below
29*   **(CHECK ONE):** (i) ☒ accompanies offer or (ii) ☐ is to be made within _____ (if left
30   blank, then 3) days after Effective Date. IF NEITHER BOX IS CHECKED, THEN
31   OPTION (ii) SHALL BE DEEMED SELECTED.
32*   Escrow Agent Information: Name:__Seminole Title_____
33*   Address:__75 East First Street, Gainesville, FL 32601_____
34*   Phone:_(352) 373-5555__ E-mail:_info@semtitle.com__ Fax:_(352) 373-0555_
35*   (b) Additional deposit to be delivered to Escrow Agent within _____ (if left blank, then 10)
36*   days after Effective Date ....$_____
37   (All deposits paid or agreed to be paid, are collectively referred to as the "Deposit")
38*   (c) Financing: Express as a dollar amount or percentage ("Loan Amount") see Paragraph 8......$__200,000.00
39*   (d) Other:_____ ....$_____
40   (e) Balance to close (not including Buyer's closing costs, prepaids and prorations) by wire
41*   transfer or other **COLLECTED** funds..........................$____38,000.00
42   **NOTE: For the definition of "COLLECTION" or "COLLECTED" see STANDARD S.**
43 **3. TIME FOR ACCEPTANCE OF OFFER AND COUNTER-OFFERS; EFFECTIVE DATE:**
44   (a) If not signed by Buyer and Seller, and an executed copy delivered to all parties on or before
45*   _____, this offer shall be deemed withdrawn and the Deposit, if any, shall be returned
46   to Buyer. Unless otherwise stated, time for acceptance of any counter-offers shall be within 2 days after the
47   day the counter-offer is delivered.
48   (b) The effective date of this Contract shall be the date when the last one of the Buyer and Seller has signed or
49   initialed and delivered this offer or final counter-offer ("Effective Date").
50 **4. CLOSING DATE:** Unless modified by other provisions of this Contract, the closing of this transaction shall occur
51   and the closing documents required to be furnished by each party pursuant to this Contract shall be delivered
52*   ("Closing") on _____7/01/2017_____ ("Closing Date"), at the time established by the Closing Agent.

Buyer's Initials _____   Page 1 of **12**   Seller's Initials _____

Exhibit 13-1   Continued Example of a Standard Form Contract for Sale and Purchase of Real Estate

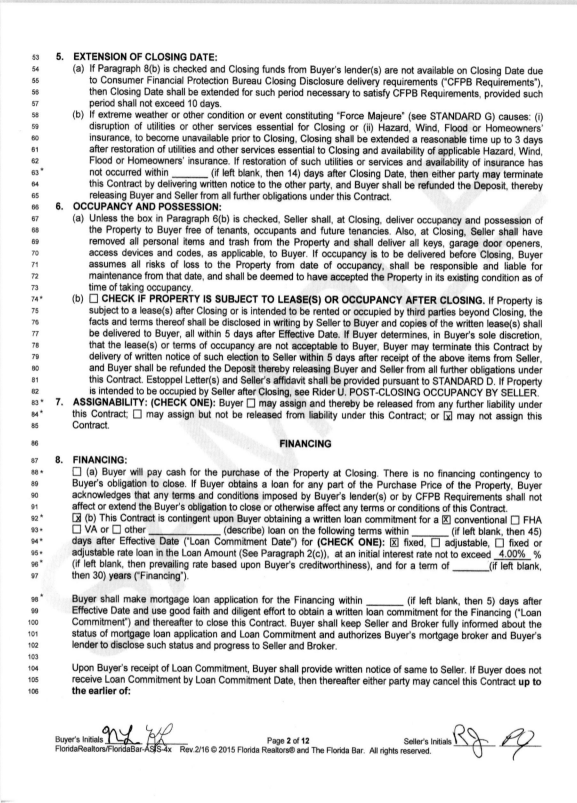

53 **5. EXTENSION OF CLOSING DATE:**
54   (a) If Paragraph 8(b) is checked and Closing funds from Buyer's lender(s) are not available on Closing Date due
55   to Consumer Financial Protection Bureau Closing Disclosure delivery requirements ("CFPB Requirements"),
56   then Closing Date shall be extended for such period necessary to satisfy CFPB Requirements, provided such
57   period shall not exceed 10 days.
58   (b) If extreme weather or other condition or event constituting "Force Majeure" (see STANDARD G) causes: (i)
59   disruption of utilities or other services essential for Closing or (ii) Hazard, Wind, Flood or Homeowners'
60   insurance, to become unavailable prior to Closing, Closing shall be extended a reasonable time up to 3 days
61   after restoration of utilities and other services essential to Closing and availability of applicable Hazard, Wind,
62   Flood or Homeowners' insurance. If restoration of such utilities or services and availability of insurance has
63 *   not occurred within _____ (if left blank, then 14) days after Closing Date, then either party may terminate
64   this Contract by delivering written notice to the other party, and Buyer shall be refunded the Deposit, thereby
65   releasing Buyer and Seller from all further obligations under this Contract.
66 **6. OCCUPANCY AND POSSESSION:**
67   (a) Unless the box in Paragraph 6(b) is checked, Seller shall, at Closing, deliver occupancy and possession of
68   the Property to Buyer free of tenants, occupants and future tenancies. Also, at Closing, Seller shall have
69   removed all personal items and trash from the Property and shall deliver all keys, garage door openers,
70   access devices and codes, as applicable, to Buyer. If occupancy is to be delivered before Closing, Buyer
71   assumes all risks of loss to the Property from date of occupancy, shall be responsible and liable for
72   maintenance from that date, and shall be deemed to have accepted the Property in its existing condition as of
73   time of taking occupancy.
74 *   (b) ☐ **CHECK IF PROPERTY IS SUBJECT TO LEASE(S) OR OCCUPANCY AFTER CLOSING.** If Property is
75   subject to a lease(s) after Closing or is intended to be rented or occupied by third parties beyond Closing, the
76   facts and terms thereof shall be disclosed in writing by Seller to Buyer and copies of the written lease(s) shall
77   be delivered to Buyer, all within 5 days after Effective Date. If Buyer determines, in Buyer's sole discretion,
78   that the lease(s) or terms of occupancy are not acceptable to Buyer, Buyer may terminate this Contract by
79   delivery of written notice of such election to Seller within 5 days after receipt of the above items from Seller,
80   and Buyer shall be refunded the Deposit thereby releasing Buyer and Seller from all further obligations under
81   this Contract. Estoppel Letter(s) and Seller's affidavit shall be provided pursuant to STANDARD D. If Property
82   is intended to be occupied by Seller after Closing, see Rider U. POST-CLOSING OCCUPANCY BY SELLER.
83 * **7. ASSIGNABILITY: (CHECK ONE):** Buyer ☐ may assign and thereby be released from any further liability under
84 *   this Contract; ☐ may assign but not be released from liability under this Contract; or ☒ may not assign this
85   Contract.

86   **FINANCING**

87 **8. FINANCING:**
88 *   ☐ (a) Buyer will pay cash for the purchase of the Property at Closing. There is no financing contingency to
89   Buyer's obligation to close. If Buyer obtains a loan for any part of the Purchase Price of the Property, Buyer
90   acknowledges that any terms and conditions imposed by Buyer's lender(s) or by CFPB Requirements shall not
91   affect or extend the Buyer's obligation to close or otherwise affect any terms or conditions of this Contract.
92 *   ☒ (b) This Contract is contingent upon Buyer obtaining a written loan commitment for a ☒ conventional ☐ FHA
93 *   ☐ VA or ☐ other _____ (describe) loan on the following terms within _____ (if left blank, then 45)
94 *   days after Effective Date ("Loan Commitment Date") for **(CHECK ONE):** ☒ fixed, ☐ adjustable, ☐ fixed or
95 *   adjustable rate loan in the Loan Amount (See Paragraph 2(c)), at an initial interest rate not to exceed __4.00%__ %
96 *   (if left blank, then prevailing rate based upon Buyer's creditworthiness), and for a term of _____(if left blank,
97   then 30) years ("Financing").

98 *   Buyer shall make mortgage loan application for the Financing within _____ (if left blank, then 5) days after
99   Effective Date and use good faith and diligent effort to obtain a written loan commitment for the Financing ("Loan
100   Commitment") and thereafter to close this Contract. Buyer shall keep Seller and Broker fully informed about the
101   status of mortgage loan application and Loan Commitment and authorizes Buyer's mortgage broker and Buyer's
102   lender to disclose such status and progress to Seller and Broker.
103
104   Upon Buyer's receipt of Loan Commitment, Buyer shall provide written notice of same to Seller. If Buyer does not
105   receive Loan Commitment by Loan Commitment Date, then thereafter either party may cancel this Contract **up to**
106   **the earlier of:**

Exhibit 13-1 Continued Example of a Standard Form Contract for Sale and Purchase of Real Estate

107	(i.) Buyer's delivery of written notice to Seller that Buyer has either received Loan Commitment or elected
108	to waive the financing contingency of this Contract; or
109	(ii.) 7 days prior to the Closing Date specified in Paragraph 4, which date, for purposes of this Paragraph
110	8(b) (ii), shall not be modified by Paragraph 5(a).
111	If either party timely cancels this Contract pursuant to this Paragraph 8 and Buyer is not in default under the terms
112	of this Contract, Buyer shall be refunded the Deposit thereby releasing Buyer and Seller from all further
113	obligations under this Contract. If neither party has timely canceled this Contract pursuant to this Paragraph 8,
114	then this financing contingency shall be deemed waived by Buyer.
115	If Buyer delivers written notice of receipt of Loan Commitment to Seller and this Contract does not thereafter
116	close, the Deposit shall be paid to Seller unless failure to close is due to: (1) Seller's default; (2) Property related
117	conditions of the Loan Commitment have not been met (except when such conditions are waived by other
118	provisions of this Contract); (3) appraisal of the Property obtained by Buyer's lender is insufficient to meet terms
119	of the Loan Commitment; or (4) the loan is not funded due to financial failure of Buyer's lender, in which event(s)
120	the Deposit shall be returned to Buyer, thereby releasing Buyer and Seller from all further obligations under this
121	Contract.
122*	☐ (c) Assumption of existing mortgage (see rider for terms).
123*	☐ (d) Purchase money note and mortgage to Seller (see riders; addenda; or special clauses for terms).

CLOSING COSTS, FEES AND CHARGES

124

125 **9. CLOSING COSTS; TITLE INSURANCE; SURVEY; HOME WARRANTY; SPECIAL ASSESSMENTS:**

126   (a) **COSTS TO BE PAID BY SELLER:**

127 • Documentary stamp taxes and surtax on deed, if any   • HOA/Condominium Association estoppel fees

128 • Owner's Policy and Charges (if Paragraph 9(c) (i) is checked)   • Recording and other fees needed to cure title

129 • Title search charges (if Paragraph 9(c) (iii) is checked)   • Seller's attorneys' fees

130* • Municipal lien search (if Paragraph 9(c) (i) or (iii) is checked)   • Other:_____

131   If, prior to Closing, Seller is unable to meet the AS IS Maintenance Requirement as required by Paragraph 11

132   a sum equal to 125% of estimated costs to meet the AS IS Maintenance Requirement shall be escrowed at

133   Closing. If actual costs to meet the AS IS Maintenance Requirement exceed escrowed amount, Seller shall

134   pay such actual costs. Any unused portion of escrowed amount(s) shall be returned to Seller.

135   (b) **COSTS TO BE PAID BY BUYER:**

136 • Taxes and recording fees on notes and mortgages   • Loan expenses

137 • Recording fees for deed and financing statements   • Appraisal fees

138 • Owner's Policy and Charges (if Paragraph 9(c)(ii) is checked)   • Buyer's Inspections

139 • Survey (and elevation certification, if required)   • Buyer's attorneys' fees

140 • Lender's title policy and endorsements   • All property related insurance

141 • HOA/Condominium Association application/transfer fees   • Owner's Policy Premium (if Paragraph

142 • Municipal lien search (if Paragraph 9(c) (ii) is checked)   9 (c) (iii) is checked.)

143* • Other:_____

144*   (c) **TITLE EVIDENCE AND INSURANCE:** At least _____ (if left blank, then 15, or if Paragraph 8(a) is checked,

145   then 5) days prior to Closing Date ("Title Evidence Deadline"), a title insurance commitment issued by a

146   Florida licensed title insurer, with legible copies of instruments listed as exceptions attached thereto ("Title

147   Commitment") and, after Closing, an owner's policy of title insurance (see STANDARD A for terms) shall be

148   obtained and delivered to Buyer. If Seller has an owner's policy of title insurance covering the Real Property,

149   a copy shall be furnished to Buyer and Closing Agent within 5 days after Effective Date. The owner's title

150   policy premium, title search and closing services (collectively, "Owner's Policy and Charges") shall be paid, as

151   set forth below. The title insurance premium charges for the owner's policy and any lender's policy will be

152   calculated and allocated in accordance with Florida law, but may be reported differently on certain federally

153   mandated closing disclosures and other closing documents.

154   **(CHECK ONE):**

155*   ☒ (i) Seller shall designate Closing Agent and pay for Owner's Policy and Charges, and Buyer shall pay the

156   premium for Buyer's lender's policy and charges for closing services related to the lender's policy,

157   endorsements and loan closing, which amounts shall be paid by Buyer to Closing Agent or such other

158   provider(s) as Buyer may select; or

159*   ☐ (ii) Buyer shall designate Closing Agent and pay for Owner's Policy and Charges and charges for closing

160   services related to Buyer's lender's policy, endorsements and loan closing; or

161*   ☐ (iii) **[MIAMI-DADE/BROWARD REGIONAL PROVISION]:** Seller shall furnish a copy of a prior owner's

162   policy of title insurance or other evidence of title and pay fees for: (A) a continuation or update of such title

Exhibit 13-1 **Continued** Example of a Standard Form Contract for Sale and Purchase of Real Estate

163 evidence, which is acceptable to Buyer's title insurance underwriter for reissue of coverage; (B) tax search;
164 and (C) municipal lien search. Buyer shall obtain and pay for post-Closing continuation and premium for
165 Buyer's owner's policy, and if applicable, Buyer's lender's policy. Seller shall not be obligated to pay more
166 * than $ _____ (if left blank, then $200.00) for abstract continuation or title search ordered or
167 performed by Closing Agent.
168 (d) **SURVEY:** On or before Title Evidence Deadline, Buyer may, at Buyer's expense, have the Real Property
169 surveyed and certified by a registered Florida surveyor ("Survey"). If Seller has a survey covering the Real
170 Property, a copy shall be furnished to Buyer and Closing Agent within 5 days after Effective Date.
171 * (e) **HOME WARRANTY:** At Closing, ☐ Buyer ☐ Seller ☒ N/A shall pay for a home warranty plan issued by
172 * _____ at a cost not to exceed $_____. A home
173 warranty plan provides for repair or replacement of many of a home's mechanical systems and major built-in
174 appliances in the event of breakdown due to normal wear and tear during the agreement's warranty period.
175 (f) **SPECIAL ASSESSMENTS:** At Closing, Seller shall pay: (i) the full amount of liens imposed by a public body
176 ("public body" does not include a Condominium or Homeowner's Association) that are certified, confirmed and
177 ratified before Closing; and (ii) the amount of the public body's most recent estimate or assessment for an
178 improvement which is substantially complete as of Effective Date, but that has not resulted in a lien being
179 imposed on the Property before Closing. Buyer shall pay all other assessments. If special assessments may
180 be paid in installments (**CHECK ONE**):
181 * ☐ (a) Seller shall pay installments due prior to Closing and Buyer shall pay installments due after Closing.
182 Installments prepaid or due for the year of Closing shall be prorated.
183 * ☒ (b) Seller shall pay the assessment(s) in full prior to or at the time of Closing.
184 IF NEITHER BOX IS CHECKED, THEN OPTION (a) SHALL BE DEEMED SELECTED.
185 This Paragraph 9(f) shall not apply to a special benefit tax lien imposed by a community development district
186 (CDD) pursuant to Chapter 190, F.S., which lien shall be prorated pursuant to STANDARD K.

DISCLOSURES

188 **10. DISCLOSURES:**
189 (a) **RADON GAS:** Radon is a naturally occurring radioactive gas that, when it is accumulated in a building in
190 sufficient quantities, may present health risks to persons who are exposed to it over time. Levels of radon that
191 exceed federal and state guidelines have been found in buildings in Florida. Additional information regarding
192 radon and radon testing may be obtained from your county health department.
193 (b) **PERMITS DISCLOSURE:** Except as may have been disclosed by Seller to Buyer in a written disclosure,
194 Seller does not know of any improvements made to the Property which were made without required permits
195 or made pursuant to permits which have not been properly closed.
196 (c) **MOLD:** Mold is naturally occurring and may cause health risks or damage to property. If Buyer is concerned
197 or desires additional information regarding mold, Buyer should contact an appropriate professional.
198 (d) **FLOOD ZONE; ELEVATION CERTIFICATION:** Buyer is advised to verify by elevation certificate which flood
199 zone the Property is in, whether flood insurance is required by Buyer's lender, and what restrictions apply to
200 improving the Property and rebuilding in the event of casualty. If Property is in a "Special Flood Hazard Area"
201 or "Coastal Barrier Resources Act" designated area or otherwise protected area identified by the U.S. Fish
202 and Wildlife Service under the Coastal Barrier Resources Act and the lowest floor elevation for the building(s)
203 and /or flood insurance rating purposes is below minimum flood elevation or is ineligible for flood insurance
204 coverage through the National Flood Insurance Program or private flood insurance as defined in 42 U.S.C.
205 * §4012a, Buyer may terminate this Contract by delivering written notice to Seller within _____ (if left blank,
206 then 20) days after Effective Date, and Buyer shall be refunded the Deposit thereby releasing Buyer and
207 Seller from all further obligations under this Contract, failing which Buyer accepts existing elevation of
208 buildings and flood zone designation of Property. The National Flood Insurance Program may assess
209 additional fees or adjust premiums for pre-Flood Insurance Rate Map (pre-FIRM) non-primary structures
210 (residential structures in which the insured or spouse does not reside for at least 50% of the year) and an
211 elevation certificate may be required for actuarial rating.
212 (e) **ENERGY BROCHURE:** Buyer acknowledges receipt of Florida Energy-Efficiency Rating Information
213 Brochure required by Section 553.996, F.S.
214 (f) **LEAD-BASED PAINT:** If Property includes pre-1978 residential housing, a lead-based paint disclosure is
215 mandatory.
216 (g) **HOMEOWNERS' ASSOCIATION/COMMUNITY DISCLOSURE: BUYER SHOULD NOT EXECUTE THIS**
217 **CONTRACT UNTIL BUYER HAS RECEIVED AND READ THE HOMEOWNERS'**
218 **ASSOCIATION/COMMUNITY DISCLOSURE, IF APPLICABLE.**

Exhibit 13-1 Continued Example of a Standard Form Contract for Sale and Purchase of Real Estate

(h) **PROPERTY TAX DISCLOSURE SUMMARY:** BUYER SHOULD NOT RELY ON THE SELLER'S CURRENT PROPERTY TAXES AS THE AMOUNT OF PROPERTY TAXES THAT THE BUYER MAY BE OBLIGATED TO PAY IN THE YEAR SUBSEQUENT TO PURCHASE. A CHANGE OF OWNERSHIP OR PROPERTY IMPROVEMENTS TRIGGERS REASSESSMENTS OF THE PROPERTY THAT COULD RESULT IN HIGHER PROPERTY TAXES. IF YOU HAVE ANY QUESTIONS CONCERNING VALUATION, CONTACT THE COUNTY PROPERTY APPRAISER'S OFFICE FOR INFORMATION.

(i) **FIRPTA TAX WITHHOLDING:** Seller shall inform Buyer in writing if Seller is a "foreign person" as defined by the Foreign Investment in Real Property Tax Act ("FIRPTA"). Buyer and Seller shall comply with FIRPTA, which may require Seller to provide additional cash at Closing. If Seller is not a "foreign person", Seller can provide Buyer, at or prior to Closing, a certification of non-foreign status, under penalties of perjury, to inform Buyer and Closing Agent that no withholding is required. See STANDARD V for further information pertaining to FIRPTA. Buyer and Seller are advised to seek legal counsel and tax advice regarding their respective rights, obligations, reporting and withholding requirements pursuant to FIRPTA.

(j) **SELLER DISCLOSURE:** Seller knows of no facts materially affecting the value of the Real Property which are not readily observable and which have not been disclosed to Buyer. Except as provided for in the preceding sentence, Seller extends and intends no warranty and makes no representation of any type, either express or implied, as to the physical condition or history of the Property. Except as otherwise disclosed in writing Seller has received no written or verbal notice from any governmental entity or agency as to a currently uncorrected building, environmental or safety code violation.

PROPERTY MAINTENANCE, CONDITION, INSPECTIONS AND EXAMINATIONS

11. PROPERTY MAINTENANCE: Except for ordinary wear and tear and Casualty Loss, Seller shall maintain the Property, including, but not limited to, lawn, shrubbery, and pool, in the condition existing as of Effective Date ("AS IS Maintenance Requirement").

12. PROPERTY INSPECTION; RIGHT TO CANCEL:

(a) *PROPERTY INSPECTIONS AND RIGHT TO CANCEL: Buyer shall have ___10___ (if left blank, then 15) days after Effective Date ("Inspection Period") within which to have such inspections of the Property performed as Buyer shall desire during the Inspection Period. If Buyer determines, in Buyer's sole discretion, that the Property is not acceptable to Buyer, Buyer may terminate this Contract by delivering written notice of such election to Seller prior to expiration of Inspection Period. If Buyer timely terminates this Contract, the Deposit paid shall be returned to Buyer, thereupon, Buyer and Seller shall be released of all further obligations under this Contract; however, Buyer shall be responsible for prompt payment for such inspections, for repair of damage to, and restoration of, the Property resulting from such inspections, and shall provide Seller with paid receipts for all work done on the Property (the preceding provision shall survive termination of this Contract). Unless Buyer exercises the right to terminate granted herein, Buyer accepts the physical condition of the Property and any violation of governmental, building, environmental, and safety codes, restrictions, or requirements, but subject to Seller's continuing AS IS Maintenance Requirement, and Buyer shall be responsible for any and all repairs and improvements required by Buyer's lender.*

(b) **WALK-THROUGH INSPECTION/RE-INSPECTION:** On the day prior to Closing Date, or on Closing Date prior to time of Closing, as specified by Buyer, Buyer or Buyer's representative may perform a walk-through (and follow-up walk-through, if necessary) inspection of the Property solely to confirm that all items of Personal Property are on the Property and to verify that Seller has maintained the Property as required by the AS IS Maintenance Requirement and has met all other contractual obligations.

(c) **SELLER ASSISTANCE AND COOPERATION IN CLOSE-OUT OF BUILDING PERMITS:** If Buyer's inspection of the Property identifies open or needed building permits, then Seller shall promptly deliver to Buyer all plans, written documentation or other information in Seller's possession, knowledge, or control relating to improvements to the Property which are the subject of such open or needed Permits, and shall promptly cooperate in good faith with Buyer's efforts to obtain estimates of repairs or other work necessary to resolve such Permit issues. Seller's obligation to cooperate shall include Seller's execution of necessary authorizations, consents, or other documents necessary for Buyer to conduct inspections and have estimates of such repairs or work prepared, but in fulfilling such obligation, Seller shall not be required to expend, or become obligated to expend, any money.

Exhibit 13-1 Continued Example of a Standard Form Contract for Sale and Purchase of Real Estate

271   (d) **ASSIGNMENT OF REPAIR AND TREATMENT CONTRACTS AND WARRANTIES:** At Buyer's option and
272   cost, Seller will, at Closing, assign all assignable repair, treatment and maintenance contracts and warranties
273   to Buyer.

274   **ESCROW AGENT AND BROKER**

275 **13. ESCROW AGENT:** Any Closing Agent or Escrow Agent (collectively "Agent") receiving the Deposit, other funds
276   and other items is authorized, and agrees by acceptance of them, to deposit them promptly, hold same in escrow
277   within the State of Florida and, subject to **COLLECTION**, disburse them in accordance with terms and conditions
278   of this Contract. Failure of funds to become **COLLECTED** shall not excuse Buyer's performance. When conflicting
279   demands for the Deposit are received, or Agent has a good faith doubt as to entitlement to the Deposit, Agent
280   may take such actions permitted by this Paragraph 13, as Agent deems advisable. If in doubt as to Agent's duties
281   or liabilities under this Contract, Agent may, at Agent's option, continue to hold the subject matter of the escrow
282   until the parties agree to its disbursement or until a final judgment of a court of competent jurisdiction shall
283   determine the rights of the parties, or Agent may deposit same with the clerk of the circuit court having jurisdiction
284   of the dispute. An attorney who represents a party and also acts as Agent may represent such party in such
285   action. Upon notifying all parties concerned of such action, all liability on the part of Agent shall fully terminate,
286   except to the extent of accounting for any items previously delivered out of escrow. If a licensed real estate
287   broker, Agent will comply with provisions of Chapter 475, F.S., as amended and FREC rules to timely resolve
288   escrow disputes through mediation, arbitration, interpleader or an escrow disbursement order.
289   Any proceeding between Buyer and Seller wherein Agent is made a party because of acting as Agent hereunder,
290   or in any proceeding where Agent interpleads the subject matter of the escrow, Agent shall recover reasonable
291   attorney's fees and costs incurred, to be paid pursuant to court order out of the escrowed funds or equivalent.
292   Agent shall not be liable to any party or person for mis-delivery of any escrowed items, unless such mis-delivery is
293   due to Agent's willful breach of this Contract or Agent's gross negligence. This Paragraph 13 shall survive Closing
294   or termination of this Contract.
295 **14. PROFESSIONAL ADVICE; BROKER LIABILITY:** Broker advises Buyer and Seller to verify Property condition,
296   square footage, and all other facts and representations made pursuant to this Contract and to consult appropriate
297   professionals for legal, tax, environmental, and other specialized advice concerning matters affecting the Property
298   and the transaction contemplated by this Contract. Broker represents to Buyer that Broker does not reside on the
299   Property and that all representations (oral, written or otherwise) by Broker are based on Seller representations or
300   public records. **BUYER AGREES TO RELY SOLELY ON SELLER, PROFESSIONAL INSPECTORS AND**
301   **GOVERNMENTAL AGENCIES FOR VERIFICATION OF PROPERTY CONDITION, SQUARE FOOTAGE AND**
302   **FACTS THAT MATERIALLY AFFECT PROPERTY VALUE AND NOT ON THE REPRESENTATIONS (ORAL,**
303   **WRITTEN OR OTHERWISE) OF BROKER.** Buyer and Seller (individually, the "Indemnifying Party") each
304   individually indemnifies, holds harmless, and releases Broker and Broker's officers, directors, agents and
305   employees from all liability for loss or damage, including all costs and expenses, and reasonable attorney's fees
306   at all levels, suffered or incurred by Broker and Broker's officers, directors, agents and employees in connection
307   with or arising from claims, demands or causes of action instituted by Buyer or Seller based on: (i) inaccuracy of
308   information provided by the Indemnifying Party or from public records; (ii) Indemnifying Party's misstatement(s) or
309   failure to perform contractual obligations; (iii) Broker's performance, at Indemnifying Party's request, of any task
310   beyond the scope of services regulated by Chapter 475, F.S., as amended, including Broker's referral,
311   recommendation or retention of any vendor for, or on behalf of Indemnifying Party; (iv) products or services
312   provided by any such vendor for, or on behalf of, Indemnifying Party; and (v) expenses incurred by any such
313   vendor. Buyer and Seller each assumes full responsibility for selecting and compensating their respective vendors
314   and paying their other costs under this Contract whether or not this transaction closes. This Paragraph 14 will not
315   relieve Broker of statutory obligations under Chapter 475, F.S., as amended. For purposes of this Paragraph 14,
316   Broker will be treated as a party to this Contract. This Paragraph 14 shall survive Closing or termination of this
317   Contract.

318   **DEFAULT AND DISPUTE RESOLUTION**

319 **15. DEFAULT:**
320   (a) **BUYER DEFAULT:** If Buyer fails, neglects or refuses to perform Buyer's obligations under this Contract,
321   including payment of the Deposit, within the time(s) specified, Seller may elect to recover and retain the
322   Deposit for the account of Seller as agreed upon liquidated damages, consideration for execution of this
323   Contract, and in full settlement of any claims, whereupon Buyer and Seller shall be relieved from all further
324   obligations under this Contract, or Seller, at Seller's option, may, pursuant to Paragraph 16, proceed in equity
325   to enforce Seller's rights under this Contract. The portion of the Deposit, if any, paid to Listing Broker upon

Buyer's Initials _____ _____   Page 6 of 12   Seller's Initials _____ _____

Exhibit 13-1 Continued Example of a Standard Form Contract for Sale and Purchase of Real Estate

326 default by Buyer, shall be split equally between Listing Broker and Cooperating Broker; provided however,
327 Cooperating Broker's share shall not be greater than the commission amount Listing Broker had agreed to
328 pay to Cooperating Broker.

329 (b) **SELLER DEFAULT:** If for any reason other than failure of Seller to make Seller's title marketable after
330 reasonable diligent effort, Seller fails, neglects or refuses to perform Seller's obligations under this Contract,
331 Buyer may elect to receive return of Buyer's Deposit without thereby waiving any action for damages resulting
332 from Seller's breach, and, pursuant to Paragraph 16, may seek to recover such damages or seek specific
333 performance.

334 This Paragraph 15 shall survive Closing or termination of this Contract.

335 **16. DISPUTE RESOLUTION:** Unresolved controversies, claims and other matters in question between Buyer and
336 Seller arising out of, or relating to, this Contract or its breach, enforcement or interpretation ("Dispute") will be
337 settled as follows:

338 (a) Buyer and Seller will have 10 days after the date conflicting demands for the Deposit are made to attempt to
339 resolve such Dispute, failing which, Buyer and Seller shall submit such Dispute to mediation under Paragraph
340 16(b).

341 (b) Buyer and Seller shall attempt to settle Disputes in an amicable manner through mediation pursuant to Florida
342 Rules for Certified and Court-Appointed Mediators and Chapter 44, F.S., as amended (the "Mediation Rules").
343 The mediator must be certified or must have experience in the real estate industry. Injunctive relief may be
344 sought without first complying with this Paragraph 16(b). Disputes not settled pursuant to this Paragraph 16
345 may be resolved by instituting action in the appropriate court having jurisdiction of the matter. This Paragraph
346 16 shall survive Closing or termination of this Contract.

347 **17. ATTORNEY'S FEES; COSTS:** The parties will split equally any mediation fee incurred in any mediation permitted
348 by this Contract, and each party will pay their own costs, expenses and fees, including attorney's fees, incurred in
349 conducting the mediation. In any litigation permitted by this Contract, the prevailing party shall be entitled to
350 recover from the non-prevailing party costs and fees, including reasonable attorney's fees, incurred in conducting
351 the litigation. This Paragraph 17 shall survive Closing or termination of this Contract.

352 **STANDARDS FOR REAL ESTATE TRANSACTIONS ("STANDARDS")**

353 **18. STANDARDS:**

354 **A. TITLE:**

355 (i) **TITLE EVIDENCE; RESTRICTIONS; EASEMENTS; LIMITATIONS:** Within the time period provided in
356 Paragraph 9(c), the Title Commitment, with legible copies of instruments listed as exceptions attached thereto,
357 shall be issued and delivered to Buyer. The Title Commitment shall set forth those matters to be discharged by
358 Seller at or before Closing and shall provide that, upon recording of the deed to Buyer, an owner's policy of title
359 insurance in the amount of the Purchase Price, shall be issued to Buyer insuring Buyer's marketable title to the
360 Real Property, subject only to the following matters: (a) comprehensive land use plans, zoning, and other land
361 use restrictions, prohibitions and requirements imposed by governmental authority; (b) restrictions and matters
362 appearing on the Plat or otherwise common to the subdivision; (c) outstanding oil, gas and mineral rights of
363 record without right of entry; (d) unplatted public utility easements of record (located contiguous to real property
364 lines and not more than 10 feet in width as to rear or front lines and 7 1/2 feet in width as to side lines); (e) taxes
365 for year of Closing and subsequent years; and (f) assumed mortgages and purchase money mortgages, if any (if
366 additional items, attach addendum); provided, that, none prevent use of Property for **RESIDENTIAL PURPOSES.**
367 If there exists at Closing any violation of items identified in (b) – (f) above, then the same shall be deemed a title
368 defect. Marketable title shall be determined according to applicable Title Standards adopted by authority of The
369 Florida Bar and in accordance with law.

370 (ii) **TITLE EXAMINATION:** Buyer shall have 5 days after receipt of Title Commitment to examine it and notify
371 Seller in writing specifying defect(s), if any, that render title unmarketable. If Seller provides Title Commitment and
372 it is delivered to Buyer less than 5 days prior to Closing Date, Buyer may extend Closing for up to 5 days after
373 date of receipt to examine same in accordance with this STANDARD A. Seller shall have 30 days ("Cure Period")
374 after receipt of Buyer's notice to take reasonable diligent efforts to remove defects. If Buyer fails to so notify
375 Seller, Buyer shall be deemed to have accepted title as it then is. If Seller cures defects within Cure Period, Seller
376 will deliver written notice to Buyer (with proof of cure acceptable to Buyer and Buyer's attorney) and the parties
377 will close this Contract on Closing Date (or if Closing Date has passed, within 10 days after Buyer's receipt of
378 Seller's notice). If Seller is unable to cure defects within Cure Period, then Buyer may, within 5 days after
379 expiration of Cure Period, deliver written notice to Seller: (a) extending Cure Period for a specified period not to
380 exceed 120 days within which Seller shall continue to use reasonable diligent effort to remove or cure the defects
381 ("Extended Cure Period"); or (b) electing to accept title with existing defects and close this Contract on Closing

Exhibit 13-1 **Continued** Example of a Standard Form Contract for Sale and Purchase of Real Estate

STANDARDS FOR REAL ESTATE TRANSACTIONS ("STANDARDS") CONTINUED

382   Date (or if Closing Date has passed, within the earlier of 10 days after end of Extended Cure Period or Buyer's
383   receipt of Seller's notice), or (c) electing to terminate this Contract and receive a refund of the Deposit, thereby
384   releasing Buyer and Seller from all further obligations under this Contract. If after reasonable diligent effort, Seller
385   is unable to timely cure defects, and Buyer does not waive the defects, this Contract shall terminate, and Buyer
386   shall receive a refund of the Deposit, thereby releasing Buyer and Seller from all further obligations under this
387   Contract.

388   **B. SURVEY:** If Survey discloses encroachments on the Real Property or that improvements located thereon
389   encroach on setback lines, easements, or lands of others, or violate any restrictions, covenants, or applicable
390   governmental regulations described in STANDARD A (i)(a), (b) or (d) above, Buyer shall deliver written notice of
391   such matters, together with a copy of Survey, to Seller within 5 days after Buyer's receipt of Survey, but no later
392   than Closing. If Buyer timely delivers such notice and Survey to Seller, such matters identified in the notice and
393   Survey shall constitute a title defect, subject to cure obligations of STANDARD A above. If Seller has delivered a
394   prior survey, Seller shall, at Buyer's request, execute an affidavit of "no change" to the Real Property since the
395   preparation of such prior survey, to the extent the affirmations therein are true and correct.

396   **C. INGRESS AND EGRESS:** Seller represents that there is ingress and egress to the Real Property and title to
397   the Real Property is insurable in accordance with STANDARD A without exception for lack of legal right of
398   access.

399   **D. LEASE INFORMATION:** Seller shall, at least 10 days prior to Closing, furnish to Buyer estoppel letters from
400   tenant(s)/occupant(s) specifying nature and duration of occupancy, rental rates, advanced rent and security
401   deposits paid by tenant(s) or occupant(s)("Estoppel Letter(s)"). If Seller is unable to obtain such Estoppel Letter(s)
402   the same information shall be furnished by Seller to Buyer within that time period in the form of a Seller's affidavit
403   and Buyer may thereafter contact tenant(s) or occupant(s) to confirm such information. If Estoppel Letter(s) or
404   Seller's affidavit, if any, differ materially from Seller's representations and lease(s) provided pursuant to
405   Paragraph 6, or if tenant(s)/occupant(s) fail or refuse to confirm Seller's affidavit, Buyer may deliver written notice
406   to Seller within 5 days after receipt of such information, but no later than 5 days prior to Closing Date, terminating
407   this Contract and receive a refund of the Deposit, thereby releasing Buyer and Seller from all further obligations
408   under this Contract. Seller shall, at Closing, deliver and assign all leases to Buyer who shall assume Seller's
409   obligations thereunder.

410   **E. LIENS:** Seller shall furnish to Buyer at Closing an affidavit attesting (i) to the absence of any financing
411   statement, claims of lien or potential lienors known to Seller and (ii) that there have been no improvements or
412   repairs to the Real Property for 90 days immediately preceding Closing Date. If the Real Property has been
413   improved or repaired within that time, Seller shall deliver releases or waivers of construction liens executed by all
414   general contractors, subcontractors, suppliers and materialmen in addition to Seller's lien affidavit setting forth
415   names of all such general contractors, subcontractors, suppliers and materialmen, further affirming that all
416   charges for improvements or repairs which could serve as a basis for a construction lien or a claim for damages
417   have been paid or will be paid at Closing.

418   **F. TIME:** Calendar days shall be used in computing time periods. **Time is of the essence in this Contract.**
419   Other than time for acceptance and Effective Date as set forth in Paragraph 3, any time periods provided for or
420   dates specified in this Contract, whether preprinted, handwritten, typewritten or inserted herein, which shall end or
421   occur on a Saturday, Sunday, or a national legal holiday (see 5 U.S.C. 6103) shall extend to 5:00 p.m. (where the
422   Property is located) of the next business day.

423   **G. FORCE MAJEURE:** Buyer or Seller shall not be required to perform any obligation under this Contract or be
424   liable to each other for damages so long as performance or non-performance of the obligation is delayed, caused
425   or prevented by Force Majeure. "Force Majeure" means: hurricanes, earthquakes, floods, fire, acts of God,
426   unusual transportation delays, wars, insurrections, and acts of terrorism, and which, by exercise of reasonable
427   diligent effort, the non-performing party is unable in whole or in part to prevent or overcome. All time periods,
428   including Closing Date, will be extended for the period that the Force Majeure prevents performance under this
429   Contract, provided, however, if such Force Majeure continues to prevent performance under this Contract more
430   than 14 days beyond Closing Date, then either party may terminate this Contract by delivering written notice to
431   the other and the Deposit shall be refunded to Buyer, thereby releasing Buyer and Seller from all further
432   obligations under this Contract.

433   **H. CONVEYANCE:** Seller shall convey marketable title to the Real Property by statutory warranty, trustee's,
434   personal representative's, or guardian's deed, as appropriate to the status of Seller, subject only to matters
435   described in STANDARD A and those accepted by Buyer. Personal Property shall, at request of Buyer, be
436   transferred by absolute bill of sale with warranty of title, subject only to such matters as may be provided for in
437   this Contract.

438   **I. CLOSING LOCATION; DOCUMENTS; AND PROCEDURE:**

Buyer's Initials _____ _____   Page **8** of **12**   Seller's Initials _____ _____

Exhibit 13-1 Continued Example of a Standard Form Contract for Sale and Purchase of Real Estate

STANDARDS FOR REAL ESTATE TRANSACTIONS ("STANDARDS") CONTINUED

(i) **LOCATION:** Closing will take place in the county where the Real Property is located at the office of the attorney or other closing agent ("Closing Agent") designated by the party paying for the owner's policy of title insurance, or, if no title insurance, designated by Seller. Closing may be conducted by mail or electronic means.

(ii) **CLOSING DOCUMENTS:** Seller shall at or prior to Closing, execute and deliver, as applicable, deed, bill of sale, certificate(s) of title or other documents necessary to transfer title to the Property, construction lien affidavit(s), owner's possession and no lien affidavit(s), and assignment(s) of leases. Seller shall provide Buyer with paid receipts for all work done on the Property pursuant to this Contract. Buyer shall furnish and pay for, as applicable the survey, flood elevation certification, and documents required by Buyer's lender.

(iii) **PROCEDURE:** The deed shall be recorded upon **COLLECTION** of all closing funds. If the Title Commitment provides insurance against adverse matters pursuant to Section 627.7841, F.S., as amended, the escrow closing procedure required by STANDARD J shall be waived, and Closing Agent shall, **subject to COLLECTION of all closing funds**, disburse at Closing the brokerage fees to Broker and the net sale proceeds to Seller.

J. ESCROW CLOSING PROCEDURE: If Title Commitment issued pursuant to Paragraph 9(c) does not provide for insurance against adverse matters as permitted under Section 627.7841, F.S., as amended, the following escrow and closing procedures shall apply: (1) all Closing proceeds shall be held in escrow by the Closing Agent for a period of not more than 10 days after Closing; (2) if Seller's title is rendered unmarketable, through no fault of Buyer, Buyer shall, within the 10 day period, notify Seller in writing of the defect and Seller shall have 30 days from date of receipt of such notification to cure the defect; (3) if Seller fails to timely cure the defect, the Deposit and all Closing funds paid by Buyer shall, within 5 days after written demand by Buyer, be refunded to Buyer and, simultaneously with such repayment, Buyer shall return the Personal Property, vacate the Real Property and re-convey the Property to Seller by special warranty deed and bill of sale; and (4) if Buyer fails to make timely demand for refund of the Deposit, Buyer shall take title as is, waiving all rights against Seller as to any intervening defect except as may be available to Buyer by virtue of warranties contained in the deed or bill of sale.

K. PRORATIONS; CREDITS: The following recurring items will be made current (if applicable) and prorated as of the day prior to Closing Date, or date of occupancy if occupancy occurs before Closing Date: real estate taxes (including special benefit tax assessments imposed by a CDD), interest, bonds, association fees, insurance, rents and other expenses of Property. Buyer shall have option of taking over existing policies of insurance, if assumable, in which event premiums shall be prorated. Cash at Closing shall be increased or decreased as may be required by prorations to be made through day prior to Closing. Advance rent and security deposits, if any, will be credited to Buyer. Escrow deposits held by Seller's mortgagee will be paid to Seller. Taxes shall be prorated based on current year's tax with due allowance made for maximum allowable discount, homestead and other exemptions. If Closing occurs on a date when current year's millage is not fixed but current year's assessment is available, taxes will be prorated based upon such assessment and prior year's millage. If current year's assessment is not available, then taxes will be prorated on prior year's tax. If there are completed improvements on the Real Property by January 1st of year of Closing, which improvements were not in existence on January 1st of prior year, then taxes shall be prorated based upon prior year's millage and at an equitable assessment to be agreed upon between the parties, failing which, request shall be made to the County Property Appraiser for an informal assessment taking into account available exemptions. A tax proration based on an estimate shall, at either party's request, be readjusted upon receipt of current year's tax bill. This STANDARD K shall survive Closing.

L. ACCESS TO PROPERTY TO CONDUCT APPRAISALS, INSPECTIONS, AND WALK-THROUGH: Seller shall, upon reasonable notice, provide utilities service and access to Property for appraisals and inspections, including a walk-through (or follow-up walk-through if necessary) prior to Closing.

M. RISK OF LOSS: If, after Effective Date, but before Closing, Property is damaged by fire or other casualty ("Casualty Loss") and cost of restoration (which shall include cost of pruning or removing damaged trees) does not exceed 1.5% of Purchase Price, cost of restoration shall be an obligation of Seller and Closing shall proceed pursuant to terms of this Contract. If restoration is not completed as of Closing, a sum equal to 125% of estimated cost to complete restoration (not to exceed 1.5% of Purchase Price), will be escrowed at Closing. If actual cost of restoration exceeds escrowed amount, Seller shall pay such actual costs (but, not in excess of 1.5% of Purchase Price). Any unused portion of escrowed amount shall be returned to Seller. If cost of restoration exceeds 1.5% of Purchase Price, Buyer shall elect to either take Property "as is" together with the 1.5%, or receive a refund of the Deposit, thereby releasing Buyer and Seller from all further obligations under this Contract. Seller's sole obligation with respect to tree damage by casualty or other natural occurrence shall be cost of pruning or removal.

N. 1031 EXCHANGE: If either Seller or Buyer wish to enter into a like-kind exchange (either simultaneously with Closing or deferred) under Section 1031 of the Internal Revenue Code ("Exchange"), the other party shall cooperate in all reasonable respects to effectuate the Exchange, including execution of documents; provided,

Buyer's Initials _____ _____   Page **9** of **12**   Seller's Initials _____ _____

Exhibit 13-1 Continued Example of a Standard Form Contract for Sale and Purchase of Real Estate

STANDARDS FOR REAL ESTATE TRANSACTIONS ("STANDARDS") CONTINUED

495 however, cooperating party shall incur no liability or expense related to the Exchange, and Closing shall not be
496 contingent upon, nor extended or delayed by, such Exchange.
497 **O. CONTRACT NOT RECORDABLE; PERSONS BOUND; NOTICE; DELIVERY; COPIES; CONTRACT**
498 **EXECUTION:** Neither this Contract nor any notice of it shall be recorded in any public records. This Contract shall
499 be binding on, and inure to the benefit of, the parties and their respective heirs or successors in interest.
500 Whenever the context permits, singular shall include plural and one gender shall include all. Notice and delivery
501 given by or to the attorney or broker (including such broker's real estate licensee) representing any party shall be
502 as effective as if given by or to that party. All notices must be in writing and may be made by mail, personal
503 delivery or electronic (including "pdf") media. A facsimile or electronic (including "pdf") copy of this Contract and
504 any signatures hereon shall be considered for all purposes as an original. This Contract may be executed by use
505 of electronic signatures, as determined by Florida's Electronic Signature Act and other applicable laws.
506 **P. INTEGRATION; MODIFICATION:** This Contract contains the full and complete understanding and agreement
507 of Buyer and Seller with respect to the transaction contemplated by this Contract and no prior agreements or
508 representations shall be binding upon Buyer or Seller unless included in this Contract. No modification to or
509 change in this Contract shall be valid or binding upon Buyer or Seller unless in writing and executed by the parties
510 intended to be bound by it.
511 **Q. WAIVER:** Failure of Buyer or Seller to insist on compliance with, or strict performance of, any provision of this
512 Contract, or to take advantage of any right under this Contract, shall not constitute a waiver of other provisions or
513 rights.
514 **R. RIDERS; ADDENDA; TYPEWRITTEN OR HANDWRITTEN PROVISIONS:** Riders, addenda, and typewritten
515 or handwritten provisions shall control all printed provisions of this Contract in conflict with them.
516 **S. COLLECTION or COLLECTED: "COLLECTION" or "COLLECTED" means any checks tendered or**
517 **received, including Deposits, have become actually and finally collected and deposited in the account of**
518 **Escrow Agent or Closing Agent. Closing and disbursement of funds and delivery of closing documents**
519 **may be delayed by Closing Agent until such amounts have been COLLECTED in Closing Agent's**
520 **accounts.**
521 **T. LOAN COMMITMENT:** "Loan Commitment" means a statement by the lender setting forth the terms and
522 conditions upon which the lender is willing to make a particular mortgage loan to a particular borrower. Neither a
523 pre-approval letter nor a prequalification letter shall be deemed a Loan Commitment for purposes of this Contract.
524 **U. APPLICABLE LAW AND VENUE:** This Contract shall be construed in accordance with the laws of the State
525 of Florida and venue for resolution of all disputes, whether by mediation, arbitration or litigation, shall lie in the
526 county where the Real Property is located.
527 **V. FOREIGN INVESTMENT IN REAL PROPERTY TAX ACT ("FIRPTA"):** If a seller of U.S. real property is a
528 "foreign person" as defined by FIRPTA, Section 1445 of the Internal Revenue Code requires the buyer of the real
529 property to withhold up to 15% of the amount realized by the seller on the transfer and remit the withheld amount
530 to the Internal Revenue Service (IRS) unless an exemption to the required withholding applies or the seller has
531 obtained a Withholding Certificate from the IRS authorizing a reduced amount of withholding. Due to the
532 complexity and potential risks of FIRPTA, Buyer and Seller should seek legal and tax advice regarding
533 compliance, particularly if an "exemption" is claimed on the sale of residential property for $300,000 or less.
534 (i) No withholding is required under Section 1445 if the Seller is not a "foreign person," provided Buyer accepts
535 proof of same from Seller, which may include Buyer's receipt of certification of non-foreign status from Seller,
536 signed under penalties of perjury, stating that Seller is not a foreign person and containing Seller's name, U.S.
537 taxpayer identification number and home address (or office address, in the case of an entity), as provided for in
538 26 CFR 1.1445-2(b). Otherwise, Buyer shall withhold the applicable percentage of the amount realized by Seller
539 on the transfer and timely remit said funds to the IRS.
540 (ii) If Seller has received a Withholding Certificate from the IRS which provides for reduced or eliminated
541 withholding in this transaction and provides same to Buyer by Closing, then Buyer shall withhold the reduced
542 sum, if any required, and timely remit said funds to the IRS.
543 (iii) If prior to Closing Seller has submitted a completed application to the IRS for a Withholding Certificate and
544 has provided to Buyer the notice required by 26 CFR 1.1445-1(c) (2)(i)(B) but no Withholding Certificate has been
545 received as of Closing, Buyer shall, at Closing, withhold the applicable percentage of the amount realized by
546 Seller on the transfer and, at Buyer's option, either (a) timely remit the withheld funds to the IRS or (b) place the
547 funds in escrow, at Seller's expense, with an escrow agent selected by Buyer and pursuant to terms negotiated
548 by the parties, to be subsequently disbursed in accordance with the Withholding Certificate issued by the IRS or
549 remitted directly to the IRS if the Seller's application is rejected or upon terms set forth in the escrow agreement.
550 (iv) In the event the net proceeds due Seller are not sufficient to meet the withholding requirement(s) in this
551 transaction, Seller shall deliver to Buyer, at Closing, the additional COLLECTED funds necessary to satisfy the

Buyer's Initials _____ _____ Page **10** of **12** Seller's Initials _____ _____
FloridaRealtors/FloridaBar-ASIS-4x Rev.2/16 © 2015 Florida Realtors® and The Florida Bar. All rights reserved.

Exhibit 13-1 Continued Example of a Standard Form Contract for Sale and Purchase of Real Estate

STANDARDS FOR REAL ESTATE TRANSACTIONS ("STANDARDS") CONTINUED

552 applicable requirement and thereafter Buyer shall timely remit said funds to the IRS or escrow the funds for
553 disbursement in accordance with the final determination of the IRS, as applicable.
554 (v) Upon remitting funds to the IRS pursuant to this STANDARD, Buyer shall provide Seller copies of IRS Forms
555 8288 and 8288-A, as filed.
556 **W. RESERVED**
557 **X. BUYER WAIVER OF CLAIMS:** *To the extent permitted by law, Buyer waives any claims against Seller*
558 *and against any real estate licensee involved in the negotiation of this Contract for any damage or*
559 *defects pertaining to the physical condition of the Property that may exist at Closing of this Contract and*
560 *be subsequently discovered by the Buyer or anyone claiming* by, through, under or against the Buyer.
561 *This provision does not relieve Seller's obligation to comply with Paragraph 10(j). This Standard X shall*
562 *survive Closing.*

ADDENDA AND ADDITIONAL TERMS

563
564 * **19. ADDENDA:** The following additional terms are included in the attached addenda or riders and incorporated into
565 this Contract (**Check if applicable**):

☐ A. Condominium Rider	☐ K. RESERVED	☐ T. Pre-Closing Occupancy
☐ B. Homeowners' Assn.	☐ L. RESERVED	☐ U. Post-Closing Occupancy
☐ C. Seller Financing	☐ M. Defective Drywall	☐ V. Sale of Buyer's Property
☐ D. Mortgage Assumption	☐ N. Coastal Construction Control Line	☐ W. Back-up Contract
☐ E. FHA/VA Financing	☐ O. Insulation Disclosure	☒ X. Kick-out Clause
☐ F. Appraisal Contingency	☐ P. Lead Paint Disclosure (Pre-1978)	☐ Y. Seller's Attorney Approval
☐ G. Short Sale	☐ Q. Housing for Older Persons	☐ Z. Buyer's Attorney Approval
☐ H. Homeowners/Flood Ins.	☐ R. Rezoning	☐ AA. Licensee Property Interest
☐ J. Interest-Bearing Acct.	☐ S. Lease Purchase/ Lease Option	☐ BB. Binding Arbitration

566 * **20. ADDITIONAL TERMS:**_____
567 _____
568 _____
569 _____
570 _____
571 _____
572 _____
573 _____
574 _____
575 _____
576 _____
577 _____
578 _____
579 _____
580 _____
581 _____
582 _____

COUNTER-OFFER/REJECTION

583
584 * ☒ Seller counters Buyer's offer (to accept the counter-offer, Buyer must sign or initial the counter-offered terms and
585 deliver a copy of the acceptance to Seller).
586 * ☐ Seller rejects Buyer's offer.

587 **THIS IS INTENDED TO BE A LEGALLY BINDING CONTRACT. IF NOT FULLY UNDERSTOOD, SEEK THE**
588 **ADVICE OF AN ATTORNEY PRIOR TO SIGNING.**

589 **THIS FORM HAS BEEN APPROVED BY THE FLORIDA REALTORS AND THE FLORIDA BAR.**

590 *Approval of this form by the Florida Realtors and The Florida Bar does not constitute an opinion that any of the terms*
591 *and conditions in this Contract should be accepted by the parties in a particular transaction. Terms and conditions*

Exhibit 13-1   **Continued**   Example of a Standard Form Contract for Sale and Purchase of Real Estate

592   *should be negotiated based upon the respective interests, objectives and bargaining positions of all interested*
593   *persons.*

594   AN ASTERISK (*) FOLLOWING A LINE NUMBER IN THE MARGIN INDICATES THE LINE CONTAINS A BLANK TO
595   BE COMPLETED.

596
597*   Buyer: _Nicolas Loo_____   Date: _5/15/17_
598
599*   Buyer: _Katie Lee_____   Date: _5/15/17_
600
601*   Seller: _____   Date: _____
602
603*   Seller: _____   Date: _____
604
605   Buyer's address for purposes of notice   Seller's address for purposes of notice
606*   _____   _____
607*   _____   _____
608

609   **BROKER:** Listing and Cooperating Brokers, if any, named below (collectively, "Broker"), are the only Brokers entitled
610   to compensation in connection with this Contract. Instruction to Closing Agent: Seller and Buyer direct Closing Agent
611   to disburse at Closing the full amount of the brokerage fees as specified in separate brokerage agreements with the
612   parties and cooperative agreements between the Brokers, except to the extent Broker has retained such fees from the
613   escrowed funds. This Contract shall not modify any MLS or other offer of compensation made by Seller or Listing
614   Broker to Cooperating Brokers.

                                         Ben Park
615*   _____   _____
616   **Cooperating Sales Associate, if any**   **Listing Sales Associate**

                                         Baden Associates Realty
617*   _____   _____
618   **Cooperating Broker, if any**   **Listing Broker**

Buyer's Initials _____ _____   Page **12** of **12**   Seller's Initials _____ _____
FloridaRealtors/FloridaBar-ASIS-4x   Rev.2/16 © 2015 Florida Realtors® and The Florida Bar. All rights reserved.

Exhibit 13-1 Example of a Standard Form Contract for Sale and Purchase of Real Estate

Counter Offer
FLORIDA ASSOCIATION OF REALTORS

1. REJECTION OF OFFER : ☒Seller ☐Buyer rejects the offer to purchase/sell dated the __15th__ day of __May__, __2017__ (" Offer ") for the property described as follows (legal description):

2. TERMS: This counter offer consists of all terms of the Offer with modifications to particular clauses as follows:

Clause	Counter Offer Term
2 (Pur. Price)	$260,000.00
2c (Fin. Amt.)	$208,000.00
2e(Bal. Pay.)	$40,000.00

3. **ACCEPTANCE AND EXPIRATION OF COUNTER OFFER:** This counter offer must be signed **and** delivered back to ☒**Seller** or **Seller's** licensee ☐**Buyer** or **Buyer's** licensee within __48__ hours from (time) __5:00__ ☐a.m. ☒p.m. the __16th__ day of __May__, __2017__ or it will expire.

4. RIGHT TO WITHDRAW COUNTER OFFER: The party making this counter offer reserves the right to withdraw the counter offer at any time prior to acceptance by the other party.

CO-2 Revised 10/97   ©1997 Florida Association of REALTORS ®   All Rights Reserved

formsimplicity
forms. made simple. finally.

Exhibit 13-1 Continued Example of a Standard Form Contract for Sale and Purchase of Real Estate

Signatures of Parties Making Counter Offer:

Robert Jordan

5 - 15 - 2017
Date

Penelope Jordan

5 - 15 - 2017
Date

Signatures of Parties Accepting Counter Offer:

Nicolas Lee

5/18/17
Date

Katie Lee

5/18/17
Date

Acceptance Received by (initial): _B P_ Date: _5/18/17_ Time: _4:37_ ☐ a.m. ☒ p.m.

CO-2 Revised 10/97   ©1997 Florida Association of REALTORS®   All Rights Reserved

formsimplicity
forms. made simple. finally.

and acceptance, stated as an agreement that the seller shall sell and the buyer shall buy. Consideration is stated as the purchase price for the buyer and the property for the seller. The conveyance of title to the property is the legal objective, and the property is identified adequately. The contract is in writing, and the buyers and sellers sign in the spaces provided on page 12 of the form.

In addition to these elements, the contract form also covers other matters. Beginning on page 7, it explicitly incorporates the Standards for Real Estate Transactions, many of which clarify the first set of contract provisions, and are thereby agreed to by the parties. The contract also includes a space on page 1 to specify items of personal property and questionable items (e.g., the carpet matter from Industry Issues 13-1) as property to which title is being conveyed. The purchase price and form of payment are listed in section 2 and a financing contingency clause is provided in Clause 8B. Buyers normally pay a deposit—known variously as escrow money, earnest money, or a binder—at the time they make an offer to show they are serious and to indemnify the sellers in the event they, the buyers, fail to perform. The broker holds the deposit in a segregated account called an *escrow account* until closing or until other arrangements are made for its disposition.

The contract form also covers type of title evidence (section 9); time for acceptance by the parties (3); closing date (4); restrictions, easements, and limitations (18A); occupancy date (6); assignability (7); liens (18E); marketable title (18H); special assessments (9(f)); expenses (9(a),9(b)); inspections, repair, and maintenance (11,12); inspection period (12 (a)); and flood zone contingency (10(d)). Spaces are provided for signatures of the principals and the representative of the real estate firm.

Contracts with Contingencies

Contracts for sale may contain sections that cause implementation of the contract to depend on the successful completion of some prior action or condition. These are known as **contracts with contingencies.** Examples are financing contingencies in which the buyer can back out of the transaction if financing cannot be obtained on specified terms, engineering contingencies in which the buyer can back out if an inspection shows the property is physically deficient, and the flood zone contingency noted in the previous paragraph. Contingencies appear most often in contracts for properties that are difficult to sell. Unless contingency clauses are worded with great care they can bring unpleasant surprises to either the buyer or the seller. They should be written carefully, perhaps with legal guidance, and reviewed with care.

Assignment

In general, most contracts—including real estate contracts—can be assigned. **Assignment** means that one party's contractual rights and obligations are transferred to someone else. If buyers of real estate assign the contract, new buyers, in effect, take their place. The new buyers may pay the agreed upon price and obtain title to the property.

But any type of **personal performance** contracted by one party cannot be assigned without that party's permission. For example, if a seller has agreed to take a purchase money mortgage as part of the payment for the property, the buyer cannot assign this right to someone else unless he or she remains personally liable to the seller for payment of the loan. Similarly, land (installment sale) contracts are not assignable without the owner's permission. In these situations, the seller relies on the buyer's qualifications, and the assignee may not be as well qualified.

Although buyers may assign their rights to someone else, they do not escape liability under the contract. They are still obligated to the seller and, should the assignees not fulfill the requirements of the contract, the seller can look to the assignors for satisfaction. In effect, assignment is an agreement by the assignee to carry out the obligations of the assignor; the assignor's contract with the other party is not affected.

Of course, the seller can agree to an assignment and relieve the assignor of all obligations. When this occurs, a contract is created between the seller and the assignee that absolves the assignor of further responsibility under the contract.

A contract can also prohibit assignment. Such a prohibition would be contained in an *assignment clause*. In the purchase and sale agreement displayed in Exhibit 13-1, section 7 states explicitly that the agreement between the parties to this contract—the Lees and the Jordans—is not assignable by either party.

✓ **Concept Check**

13.8 What is assignment of a contract? Who is liable for a contract that has been assigned?

Remedies for Nonperformance

Buyers and sellers sometimes fail to live up to the provisions of a contract. They may change their minds for a number of reasons. For example, if one spouse dies, the other may not want to move. Or, if their financial circumstances change, they may decide they cannot afford a new home.

When a party fails to perform (e.g., breach of contract, nonperformance, or default), the other party has a variety of remedies. An aggrieved seller may (1) sue for damages, (2) retain the earnest money deposit as liquidated damages, or (3) agree to **rescission** of the contract (agree to return both parties to their precontract status). An aggrieved buyer may (1) sue for damages, (2) agree to rescission of the contract, or (3) sue for **specific performance** (i.e., appeal to the court to force the defaulting seller to carry out the contract). The suit for specific performance is generally unique to real estate. It derives from the early English law of equity, rather than the common law, and rests on two notions about land. First, a parcel of land is unique, and irreplaceable, so that nothing except that parcel can make an aggrieved buyer whole. Second, because the value of land often is uncertain, the damages due to a seller's default could be difficult to measure. As long as the buyer's claim is not deemed "unfair (inequitable) by the court, the court may grant specific performance. In some states, a buyer also has an automatic right of cancellation if the property is destroyed.

Escrow

To lessen the chances for nonperformance, real estate contracts are often placed in **escrow.** An **escrow agent** is a third party who is instructed to carry out the provisions of the contract by means of a separate escrow agreement. The escrow agent must be impartial and may not benefit from the provisions of the purchase and sale contract. The escrow agent is allowed, of course, to collect a fee for services rendered.

✓ **Concept Check**

13.9 What are three standard remedies to a defaulted contract for sale of real estate for a seller? For a buyer?

Escrow agents are usually attorneys, financial institutions, or title companies, although in some states they may be separate individuals or companies. They hold the documents and funds relevant to a transaction and distribute them according to the written instructions at the time of closing. For example, a buyer would give a deposit or full purchase price to the escrow agent, while the seller would deliver a deed and evidence of title (e.g., an abstract or a title insurance policy) to the escrow agent. Insurance policies, mortgage financing information, and any other documents would also be provided. When all the documents have been assembled, title has been searched, funds have been obtained, and all other conditions met, the escrow agent delivers the deed to the buyer and the funds to the seller.

When escrow agents are not used, attorneys, title companies, or financial institutions still frequently provide closing services. Although they assemble the necessary documents and arrange for the title search and evidence of title, the real estate broker may hold the earnest money deposit until closing. The broker, however, must hold the deposit for the benefit of the principal, cannot commingle deposits with personal funds, and must not disburse deposits except as provided in the contract.

Closing and Closing Statements

The first step in a real estate transaction is negotiating and completing the contract for sale. The final step is the closing. Real estate closings, including the roles of the various parties and the documents that are prepared and signed at closing, are the topic of this section.

Role of the Brokers

The selling broker's role may be simply as moral support and facilitator once the contract for sale is signed (if the selling broker is different from the listing broker). The selling broker frequently is not an agent of the buyer but, rather, a subagent of the listing broker. Once the contract is signed, therefore, the selling broker has no further *legal* role with the buyers or the listing broker. It is, however, wise business practice and arguably the responsibility of the selling broker to the seller, to assist the buyers toward a smooth and successful closing.

The listing broker's role at closing can vary widely from state to state and community to community. Because real estate brokers are not permitted to give legal advice in many parts of the country, their strictly legal role is largely finished when the contract for sale is signed. Nevertheless, like the selling broker, the wise listing broker continues to counsel the sellers about steps to take before closing. Moreover, as part of the broker's obligation of diligence, the broker is bound to take reasonable steps to assure that the sale is not delayed or aborted due to logistical problems. Therefore, the broker may take care of details such as arranging for title evidence, surveys, termite inspections, and agreed upon repairs. It is in the listing broker's best interest to make certain the closing actually occurs at the time specified in the contract for sale.

Although attorneys, lending institutions, and title companies normally take over a transaction after the contract for sale is signed, the listing broker continues to have *legal* responsibility to the sellers through the closing. In some transactions not financed by a financial institution, the listing broker might actually conduct the closing. Although someone else may prepare the closing statement, the broker is also responsible to the sellers for its accuracy. Thus, real estate brokers must know what happens at closings, as well as all other aspects of a transaction.

> ✓ **Concept Check**
>
> **13.10**   In most closings, who is responsible to see that the closing is completed successfully?

Role of the Lenders

Lenders must protect their security interest in a property involved in a transaction. They want to be certain that the buyer is obtaining marketable title to the property.

Also, they want to assure that the tax and insurance payments are current so that a tax lien cannot preempt the mortgage lien and that insurance proceeds will cover the property if it is damaged or destroyed. Lenders normally participate in the closing of a real estate transaction by having an attorney present who often conducts the proceedings. The lender normally requires the buyers to have a fire and hazard insurance policy and a title insurance policy, with the lender as the beneficiary. The lender also usually wants an appraisal, a survey, a termite inspection, a certificate of occupancy (for a new building), and establishment of an escrow account for payment of hazard insurance and local property taxes.

RESPA, TILA, and the Dodd-Frank Act

www.consumerfinance.gov

The Consumer Financial Protection Bureau: The new portal to regulation, disclosure, and consumer assistance for home finance and other consumer financial matters. For home finance, select "Consumer Tools," then "Owning a Home."

Two federal laws that shape home mortgage lending are the Real Estate Settlement Procedures Act of 1974 (RESPA) and the Federal Truth-in-Lending Act of 1968 (TILA). These laws were placed by the Dodd-Frank Act of 2010 under the umbrella of the newly created Consumer Financial Protection Bureau, which was mandated to integrate their oversite and enforcement. To this end, the CFPB has reshaped the procedures and documents emanating from the laws, merging their requirements into a completely new set of documents and new procedures for home mortgage lending. These apply, as with RESPA before, to all home mortgage transactions involving "federally related" home loans—those made by a federally insured bank or thrift, all FHA or VA loans, and loans purchased by Fannie Mae or Freddie Mac. If the experience under RESPA is an indication, the new resulting documents and procedures will be used almost universally in home sale transactions, even when "federally related" debt is not involved. What does this mean for home transactions? The same requirements that were in RESPA and TILA will remain for federally related transactions, but with CFPB enhancements:

1. An information booklet concerning home mortgage borrowing must be presented to a loan applicant. The CFPB version of this is titled "Your home loan toolkit: A step-by-step guide" and is available from the CFPB website.

2. An estimate of loan costs must be provided to the borrower within three days of application, now combined with TILA-required disclosures and blended into a new document called the **Loan Estimate**. (See Exhibit 13-3.)

3. The lender must disclose (in the Loan Estimate) whether it plans to continue servicing the loan.

4. A standard settlement statement must be used for the closing, now called the **Closing Disclosure**. (See Exhibit 13-4.) This closing statement must state in detail all charges caused by the loan for the buyer/borrower. It also determines the exact amount of cash at closing due to or from both the buyer and seller. Finally, it contains additional disclosures about the cost and terms of borrowing, as required by TILA, including the APR, whether the loan is assumable, what late fees may apply, whether there is negative amortization, and whether there is a prepayment penalty. This document must be accurate to a high degree, and must be made available, in complete form, to the borrower three business days before the date of closing. (Adjustments at closing are allowed for minor expense items.)

5. Kickbacks are prohibited, per RESPA. The extensive number of supporting services in a home loan transaction—insurance, inspections, surveys, and so on—create opportunities for service vendors to arrange in advance for lenders to direct the borrower to them in return for a share of the fee charged. Such arrangements are prohibited.

6. Escrow payments required by the lender are limited, per RESPA. Roughly speaking, the amount that the borrower must deposit into escrow for, say, future property taxes, is limited to one-sixth (two months of ongoing escrow contributions) beyond the amount necessary to assure that the accumulated escrow balance will cover the property tax payment when it is due. (See Chapter 9 for an extended example.

Preparation of Closing Statements

Normally, when a buyer signs an offer to purchase, the broker receives **earnest money** from the purchaser amounting to 5 or 10 percent of the purchase price. This amount should immediately be placed in an account with a title company or financial institution. Most states have laws requiring brokers to maintain a separate account (an escrow account) for earnest money deposits and be able to account for all such moneys at any time. Failure to do so may result in a broker's license being suspended or revoked.

The seller must sign the offer to signify acceptance. The accepted offer is then a contract for sale (and purchase). Expenses incurred by the closing agent for the buyer and seller must be strictly accounted for and accurately disclosed in separate statements prepared for the buyer and seller at closing. The broker must also keep a copy of the closing statement and a summary of receipts and disbursements of all moneys involved in the transaction.

Exhibit 13-2 lists some common expenses paid by the buyer or seller, or prorated between the two. Responsibility for the payment of closing expenses should be governed by the contract for sale; if they are not covered by the contract, local custom should be followed in charging and crediting each expense to the buyer and seller.

Buyers and sellers can (and often do) negotiate which party will pay various closing expenses. In soft markets, buyers can often insist sellers pay all or part of the expenses that would normally be the buyers' responsibility. Substantial amounts can be saved through

Exhibit 13-2   Common Closing Expenses and Allocation of Responsibility between Buyer and Seller

Item	Comment
1. Purchase price	Paid from buyer's funds
2. Earnest money deposit	Prepaid by buyer, who requires a credit at closing
3. First mortgage balance (when assumed by buyer)	Assumption is a form of payment to the seller
4. Second mortgage (to seller)	Seller accepts mortgage in lieu of a portion of the sale price
Prorations and prepayments:	
5. Interest on mortgage (existing mortgage)	Paid later by buyer, who is credited at closing
6. Insurance (for unexpired term)	Prepaid by seller, who receives credit at closing
7. Property taxes	Paid after closing by buyer, who receives credit at closing
Expenses:	
8. Title insurance	
Owner's policy	Premium paid by seller
Lender's policy	Premium paid by buyer/borrower
9. Attorney's fee (buyer)	
10. Attorney's fee (seller)	
11. State documentary stamp tax on new mortgage and note	Paid by buyer at closing
12. State documentary stamp tax on deed	Generally paid by seller at closing
13. State intangible tax on new mortgage and note	Paid by buyer at closing
14. Recording of new mortgage	Cost paid by buyer at closing
15. Recording of deed	Cost paid by buyer at closing
16. Brokerage commission	Generally paid by seller at closing

such negotiations. An explanation of each closing expense listed in Exhibit 13-2 and its allocation between the buyer and seller follows:

1. The purchase price is the principal charge paid from the buyer's funds at closing. It is the ultimate closing cost; without its payment there would be no closing.

2. The earnest money deposit has already been paid by the buyer before the closing. Thus, the amount of cash required from the buyer at closing is reduced by the previously paid earnest money.

3, 4. An assumed first mortgage or a second mortgage provided by the seller are obligations taken on by the buyer that reduce the amount of cash the buyer must pay the seller at closing. So buyer is credited at closing for assuming these obligations.

5. Interest on a mortgage is generally paid at the end of each month. Thus, the buyer will make a payment on an assumed mortgage, part of which represents the seller's ownership period and part of which represents the new owner's period. The portion of the buyer's end-of-month payment that represents the period of time during which the seller occupied the house will be credited to the buyer. That is, it will reduce the amount the buyer must pay to the seller at closing.

6. Hazard insurance premiums are typically paid annually. While it is rare for a buyer to continue the existing insurance policy on a residence, it is instructive to consider how that would be accomplished. The seller would have paid for the entire year. Thus, at closing the buyer would need to pay the seller an amount proportionate to the time the buyer will use the insurance.

7. Property taxes are paid in arrears (i.e., after the tax year). Thus, the seller will not have paid the property taxes for the year before transferring ownership to the buyer. As a result, the buyer will be required to pay the entire tax bill at the end of the year. Therefore, the estimated tax bill must be allocated in proportion to the time the property is owned by the respective parties. The buyer receives a credit at closing for the amount the buyer will pay on behalf of the seller's ownership period.

8. The seller must provide assurance of good title to the new owner. Thus, sellers are usually required to pay the full premium at closing for an "owner's" title insurance policy. Lenders also demand assurance of good title and indemnification in the event the title is not good. The borrower generally purchases this title insurance protection on behalf of the lender.

9. Buyers should hire an attorney to examine the seller's evidence of title and to represent them at the closing. These fees are generally paid at closing.

10. Sellers usually hire an attorney to prepare the deed and represent them at closing.

11. A state documentary stamp tax on mortgages, notes, and contracts may be required on any new loans used to finance the transaction. This tax is paid by the buyer at closing.

12. A state documentary stamp tax on deeds also may be required. It is considered an expense of delivering title to the buyer and is therefore paid by the seller, unless there is an agreement to the contrary.

13. A state intangible tax on mortgages and notes may be imposed. Since the buyers are obtaining such mortgages to finance the purchase, the tax is usually charged to them.

14, 15. Recording of both the mortgage and the deed is usually the buyer's burden. Recording of the deed is necessary to protect the buyer's interest, whereas the lender requires the borrower (buyer) to pay the mortgage recording charges.

16. Usually the seller has hired the broker and therefore must pay the commission.

✓ Concept Check

13.12   Name two methods of determining which party will be responsible for the various costs of closing.

The procedures for **prorating** should reflect the actual number of days in the period, the number of days during the period the property was owned by the seller, and the number of days it will be owned by the buyer. The date for dividing the financial responsibilities of buyers and sellers is subject to agreement between the parties. Usually the day of closing is said to "belong to the buyer," that is, counted as a day of buyer ownership. However, this convention is negotiable. If the contract does not cover this matter, local custom will prevail.

For example, if a transaction is scheduled to close on May 14 of a 365-day year, taxes for the year would be allocated between buyers and sellers as shown below (the day of closing belongs to the buyer):

Jan. 1		May 14		Dec. 31
	Sellers		Buyers	
	133 days		232 days	

If the estimated tax for the year is $500, the sellers would be responsible for $182.19 [(133 ÷ 365) × $500)]. The buyers would be credited with this amount, since they will pay the entire amount of the tax at year-end.

As another example, consider the hazard insurance proration for a transaction scheduled to close on March 16 of a 365-day year. The premium in the amount of $450 was paid by the sellers for the policy commencing December 15 of the previous year and ending December 14 at midnight of the current year. The premium is prorated between buyers and sellers as shown below, with the day of closing assumed to belong to the buyers:

Dec. 15		March 16		Dec. 14
	Sellers		Buyers	
	91 days		274 days	

www.alta.org/ consumer/index.cfm

American Land Title Association website with information for consumers on title insurance and home closings. Also has closing statement forms for sellers to complement the CFPB Closing Disclosure.

Since the sellers paid the premium prior to closing, they are credited with the portion of the policy period the buyers will own the property. Thus, the sellers will receive an additional $337.81 from the buyer at closing [(274 ÷ 365) × $450].

The Continuing Story of a Sale

Recall from Chapter 12 that Robert and Penelope Jordan have listed their house with Baden Associates Realty, through Ben Park, a Realtor with the firm. The listing price is $268,000. Another salesperson in the same company, Josh Hairston, shows the Jordan home to Nicolas and Katie Lee who are moving to Gainesville from Ohio.

The Lees like the house and believe it would suit their needs, but they note several maintenance and replacement items. They believe they would have to paint the interior and exterior, install new carpeting, and purchase drapes. Thus, they decide to make the following offer:

Price: $250,000
Financing: New 30-year fixed-rate mortgage at 4.00 percent
Closing date: July 1, 2017
Earnest money deposit: $12,000

Ben and Josh present the offer to the Jordans, who reject it and counter with a price of $260,000. The counteroffer is then presented to the Lees. They accept this offer contingent on their obtaining a 30-year, 80 percent fixed-rate loan commitment at an initial rate not to exceed 4.00 percent. They also want the sellers to furnish a title insurance policy and a termite inspection report, and they want to have the right to have radon and building inspections made at their own expense. This offer/counteroffer process is reflected in the purchase and sale contract form shown in Exhibit 13-1. The counter offer is displayed as the last page of the exhibit.

Loan Estimate

The laws of some states require that real estate brokers provide buyers and sellers with a list of **estimated closing costs** before signing a contract for sale. Also, as previously noted, current U.S. law, as implemented by the Consumer Financial Protection Bureau, requires a lender to provide an estimate of the settlement expenses that are likely to occur, using a form known as the Loan Estimate. The Loan Estimate must be provided when the borrower applies for a loan or within three business days. Exhibit 13-3 shows this document for the Lees' estimated closing expenses, provided by the lender, DownTrust Bank, on the sale of the Jordans' property.

The Lees are seeking a 30-year, 80 percent loan-to-value ratio, fixed-rate loan of $208,000, at an annual interest rate of 3.75 percent. There will be numerous closing costs, and these are shown in detail on page 2 of the Loan Estimate:

In section A on page 2 (Origination Charges) are the direct charges of the lender in creating the loan. These include one-half point of advanced interest ($1,040), a loan application fee ($200), a loan underwriting fee ($425), and a collection of small processing fees ($136). These charges are directly from the lender, and are strictly binding; by CFPB regulation, they cannot increase at closing from the amounts shown.

In section B (Services You Cannot Shop For) are charges necessary for the loan, but not from the lender. In this case they include an appraisal ($400), a credit report ($25), and a flood certification ($23). Since these charges are not completely under the control of the lender they generally are allowed by CFPB regulation to increase at closing from the amounts shown by as much as 10 percent.

In section C (Services You Can Shop For) are additional expenses necessary for the loan, but for services where the borrower can select the vendor. The lender is presumed to have no influence or control over the cost of these services, and they can vary at closing from the stated amount without limit. In this example these expenses include the borrower's attorney ($275), lender's title insurance ($650), a structure inspection ($250), and a survey ($375).

In section E (Taxes and Other Government Fees) are recording fees and mortgage taxes. The borrower will need to record both the deed and mortgage in the public records ($173). As discussed in Chapter 3, this gives constructive notice of the buyer's claim to title and the lender's mortgage claim. In addition, the borrower will pay taxes on the creation of the mortgage ($1,144). State tax stamps on the mortgage amount to $728, and intangibles tax is $416.

As is typical, DownTrust will require the Lees to prepay certain items at the time of settlement (July 1). These are shown in section F (Prepaids). In particular, the annual hazard insurance premium must be paid in advance for six months ($663). If the loan closing were on any day other than the first of the month—the first day in the monthly interest cycle—DownTrust would require the Lees to prepay interest for the days preceding the first full month of the loan. But since the loan is for all of July, the first regular payment, due August 1, will pay the July interest.

In section G (Initial Escrow Payment at Closing) are several more possible up-front payments. City and county property taxes represent a first lien on mortgaged property. That is, if the property owners fail to pay their taxes in a timely fashion, the local taxing jurisdictions can force a foreclosure sale of the property. Mortgage lenders do not want this to happen. So they usually require borrowers to add 1/12 of the borrower's estimated tax bill to their required monthly mortgage payments. These prepaid taxes are held in escrow accounts by the lender until the property tax payments are due, at which time the lender pays the taxes on behalf of the borrower. To help ensure that the property tax reserve account will have a sufficient balance to pay the borrower's taxes when due, lenders generally require that several months of property tax reserves be paid at closing. Similar to property taxes is hazard insurance, for which lenders often require borrowers to create reserves to pay future premiums. As noted before, RESPA prohibits the lender from

Exhibit 13-3 Loan Estimate

Save this Loan Estimate to compare with your Closing Disclosure.

Loan Estimate

DATE ISSUED	5/15/2017
APPLICANTS	Nicolas and Katie Lee
PROPERTY	1822 N.W. 40th Avenue Gainesville, FL 32611
SALE PRICE	$260,000

LOAN TERM	30 years
PURPOSE	Purchase
PRODUCT	Fixed rate
LOAN TYPE	☒ Conventional ☐ FHA ☐ VA ☐ _____
LOAN ID #	
RATE LOCK	☐ NO ☒ YES, until 7/16/2017 @ 5:00 PM EDT

Before closing, your interest rate, points, and lender credits can change unless you lock the interest rate. All other estimated closing costs expire on

Loan Terms

		Can this amount increase after closing?
Loan Amount	$208,000	NO
Interest Rate	3.75%	NO
Monthly Principal & Interest See Projected Payments below for your Estimated Total Monthly Payment	$963.28	NO
		Does the loan have these features?
Prepayment Penalty		NO
Balloon Payment		NO

Projected Payments

Payment Calculation		
Principal & Interest		$963.28
Mortgage Insurance	+	0
Estimated Escrow Amount can increase over time	+	$370.42
Estimated Total Monthly Payment		**$1,333.70**

Estimated Taxes, Insurance & Assessments Amount can increase over time	$370.42 a month	**This estimate includes** ☒ Property Taxes ☒ Homeowner's Insurance ☐ Other:	**In escrow?** YES YES

See Section G on page 2 for escrowed property costs. You must pay for other property costs separately.

Costs at Closing

Estimated Closing Costs	$8,600	Includes $3,799 in Loan Costs +$4,801 in Other Costs –in Lender Credits. *See page 2 for details.*
Estimated Cash to Close	$48,600	Includes Closing Costs. *See Calculating Cash to Close on page 2 for details.*

Visit **www.consumerfinance.gov/mortgage-estimate** for general information and tools.

LOAN ESTIMATE

PAGE 1 OF 3 · LOAN ID #

Exhibit 13-3 **Continued** Loan Estimate

Closing Cost Details

Loan Costs

A. Origination Charges	**$1,801**
0.5% of Loan Amount (Points)	$1,040
Application Fee	$ 200
Other Origination Costs	$ 136
Underwriting Fee	$ 425

B. Services You Cannot Shop For	**$ 448**
Appraisal	$ 400
Credit report	$ 25
Flood certification	$ 23

C. Services You Can Shop For	**$1,550**
Attorney	$ 275
Lender's Title Insurance	$ 650
Structure Inspection	$ 250
Survey	$ 375

D. TOTAL LOAN COSTS (A + B + C)	**$ 3,799**

Other Costs

E. Taxes and Other Government Fees	**$1,317**
Recording Fees and Other Taxes	$ 173
Transfer Taxes	$1,144

F. Prepaids	**$663**
Homeowner's Insurance Premium (6 months)	$663
Mortgage Insurance Premium (months)	
Prepaid Interest (per day for days @)	
Property Taxes (months)	

G. Initial Escrow Payment at Closing	**$2,821**
Homeowner's Insurance $110.42 per month for 2 mo.	$221
Mortgage Insurance per month for mo.	
Property Taxes $260.00 per month for 10 mo.	$2,600

H. Other

I. TOTAL OTHER COSTS (E + F + G + H)	**$4,801**

J. TOTAL CLOSING COSTS	**$8,600**
D + I	$8,600
Lender Credits	

Calculating Cash to Close

Total Closing Costs (J)	$ 8,600
Closing Costs Financed (Paid from your Loan Amount)	0
Down Payment/Funds from Borrower	$52,000
Deposit	- $12,000
Funds for Borrower	0
Seller Credits	0
Adjustments and Other Credits	0
Estimated Cash to Close	**$48,600**

Exhibit 13-3 Continued Loan Estimate

Additional Information About This Loan

LENDER	DownTrust Bank	MORTGAGE BROKER	
NMLS/___ LICENSE ID		NMLS/___ LICENSE ID	
LOAN OFFICER	Ellen Rich	LOAN OFFICER	
NMLS/___ LICENSE ID		NMLS/___ LICENSE ID	
EMAIL	e.rich@downtrust.com	EMAIL	
PHONE		PHONE	

Comparisons

Use these measures to compare this loan with other loans.

In 5 Years	$61,596	Total you will have paid in principal, interest, mortgage insurance, and loan costs.
	$20,639	Principal you will have paid off.
Annual Percentage Rate (APR)	3.821%	Your costs over the loan term expressed as a rate. This is not your interest rate.
Total Interest Percentage (TIP)	66.7%	The total amount of interest that you will pay over the loan term as a percentage of your loan amount.

Other Considerations

Appraisal
We may order an appraisal to determine the property's value and charge you for this appraisal. We will promptly give you a copy of any appraisal, even if your loan does not close. You can pay for an additional appraisal for your own use at your own cost.

Assumption
If you sell or transfer this property to another person, we
☐ will allow, under certain conditions, this person to assume this loan on the original terms.
☒ will not allow assumption of this loan on the original terms.

Homeowner's Insurance
This loan requires homeowner's insurance on the property, which you may obtain from a company of your choice that we find acceptable.

Late Payment
If your payment is more than _15_ days late, we will charge a late fee of _5% on the monthly principal and interest payment_

Refinance
Refinancing this loan will depend on your future financial situation, the property value, and market conditions. You may not be able to refinance this loan.

Servicing
We intend
☐ to service your loan. If so, you will make your payments to us.
☒ to transfer servicing of your loan.

Confirm Receipt

By signing, you are only confirming that you have received this form. You do not have to accept this loan because you have signed or received this form.

Nicolas Lee 5/15/17
Applicant Signature   Date

Katie Lee 5/15/17
Co-Applicant Signature   Date

LOAN ESTIMATE   PAGE 3 OF 3 · LOAN ID #

collecting more than a certain amount of reserves (i.e., escrow deposits) at closing (see Chapter 9). In brief, the lender cannot demand an escrow "cushion" of more that one-sixth of the total charges in the annual escrow cycle. Thus with estimated annual taxes of $3,120, the closing date of July 1, and expected payment of the taxes by mid-November, four future monthly payments are scheduled prior to the tax payment. So the lender can ask for an initial payment to escrow for future property taxes equal to eight monthly payments of $260 plus two additional months, giving the total of $2,600.

In summary, section D shows total loan costs as $3,799, while other costs at closing shown in section I sum to $4,801. The lender estimates that the borrower's costs at closing will total $8,600.

Steps before Closing

Recall that the contract for sale signed by the Jordans and Lees specifies that "The transaction shall be concluded on July 1, 2017, or such earlier date as may be mutually agreeable." (See section 6 in Exhibit 13-1.) It is now July 1, 2017. The Jordans, the sellers; the Lees, the buyers; the Jordans' attorney, James Henry; the listing agent, Ben Park; and the selling agent, Josh Hairston, arrive at the offices of Seminole Title Company, where closing is to take place. The Lees' application for a 3.75 percent, 30-year fixed-rate mortgage was approved by DownTrust. DownTrust's attorney, Joe Jenkins, is there to handle the closing.

After signing the contract for sale on May 15, 2017, and before arriving for closing July 1, 2017, the Lees and their attorney took the following steps:

1. Surveyed the property for possible encroachments.
2. Reviewed an abstract of documents in the public records to make certain there are no violations of private restrictions.
3. Reviewed the zoning ordinance to assure the property is used as legally permitted.
4. Examined the list of estimated closing costs as they appear in the Closing Disclosure to make certain that they are correct and reasonable (see Exhibit 13-4).
5. Ordered a lender's title insurance policy from the same company the sellers asked to issue an owner's title policy. When a title company issues a policy to both an owner and a mortgagee, it is termed a *simultaneous issue.*
6. Inspected the property to verify condition and vacancy for possession. (This step is so important that many buyers hire a professional property inspector.)
7. Reviewed the contract to make certain other terms and conditions have been met by the sellers, such as having the property inspected for termites.
8. Arranged to have hazard insurance coverage, utilities, telephone, and other services begin on the date of closing.[7]

As sellers, the Jordans also took some steps between the signing of the purchase and sale contract and the closing. In particular, they:

1. Ordered an owner's title insurance policy. If the contract for sale had specified that an abstract and attorney's opinion serve as the evidence of title, they would have (a) ordered the abstract brought up to date or (b) had the abstract delivered to the buyers' attorney, Mr. Henry, for examination.
2. Ordered a termite inspection and had the certificate showing the improvements to be free of active infestation or visible damage delivered to the Lees' attorney.
3. Ordered their hazard insurance coverage, utilities, and other services to be stopped on the closing date.

---

7. If the Lees were assuming any mortgages, the attorney would obtain an *estoppel certificate* (or letter) from the lender that would show the amount being assumed, interest rate, length of debt period, periodic payments, and frequency of amortization.

Lawyers (attorneys) serve multiple roles in real estate. Because of the complexity and value of real estate, the contracts that arise can be lengthy, complicated, and diverse, including leases, contracts for sale and purchase, deeds, mortgages, notes, listing agreements, investor agreements, and many others. Attorneys provide important guidance to the parties involved, assisting them in understanding the legal options available and the legal implications of the wording in documents. Attorneys help their clients translate their business goals and requirements into appropriate and effective contract language. Beyond this technical role, attorneys can serve as advisors to their clients on the choices available to them, and frequently represent their client in real estate negotiations.

Attorneys may practice in the area of real estate as part of a broader law practice. Others specialize in real estate, and even in specific aspects of the field such as land use controls, mortgage finance, investments, or a specific type of real estate such as commercial. Those attorneys specializing in real estate may work in various contexts. They may work for a large corporation, handling the corporation's real estate affairs, or they may set up an individual real estate law practice. Especially if they are in a private partnership or individual practice, they may be able to control their work hours. While most attorneys work longer than 40-hour weeks, as they reach retirement age, they often simply reduce the number of clients served, and the number of hours worked. Most of the work of attorneys is in offices. It is less common for them to be involved in public meetings or court proceedings unless they specialize in a field such as land use regulation.

To qualify as an attorney the aspirants generally must complete an undergraduate degree, a graduate law degree, and pass the bar exam in the state where they seek to practice. In 2012 salary websites reported salaries for real estate attorneys roughly similar to other attorneys in private practice. Salary.com, for example, reported that the middle half of real estate attorney salaries was approximately between $116,000 and $148,000.

Source: Based partly on information from Evans, Marlwyn *Real Estate Careers*, McGraw-Hill, New York; 2002, Chapter 7.

Real Estate Attorney

As closing agent and representative of DownTrust Bank, Mr. Jenkins has obtained or prepared the following documents and legal instruments:

1. General warranty deed in proper form, to be signed by the Jordans at closing.
2. Mortgage and note, to be signed by the Lees at closing.
3. Check from the lender made payable to the seller.
4. Closing Disclosure (Exhibit 13-4) showing the expenses and obligations incurred by both parties. Real estate taxes for 2017 as specified in the contract for sale are prorated between buyers and sellers as of the date of closing.
5. A *satisfaction of mortgage* from the Jordans' mortgage lender indicating that the remaining balance on their mortgage is $204,070.[8]

Steps at Closing and the Closing Disclosure

The Jordans, the Lees, Mr. Park, Mr. Hairston, Mr. Henry, and Mr. Jenkins go to a small conference room for the closing. They take seats around a rectangular table, with Mr. Jenkins sitting at the head of the table. He informs everyone that he is closing the transaction on behalf of DownTrust Bank and is also serving as the Lees' attorney. He introduces Mr. Henry as the Jordans' attorney. Mr. Jenkins states he has prepared all documents in accordance with the terms of the contract for sale, the loan application and approval, and applicable state and federal laws. He also states that he has coordinated title matters, inspections, and documents with Mr. Henry and Mr. Park.

Mr. Jenkins presents copies of the Closing Disclosure (CD) shown in Exhibit 13-4 to the Jordans and Lees and explains it as follows: Settlement charges to be paid by the Lees total $8,600 (CD, page 2, line J.00.), exactly the same as estimated by DownTrust Bank in the Loan Estimate they issued. As sellers, the Jordans will pay the $15,600(0.06 × $260,000) brokerage commission to Baden Associates Realty (CD, page 2, line H.04). Other major closing expenses to be paid by the sellers include a $1,381 owner's title insurance policy (page 2, line H.02) and $1,820 in state tax stamps to transfer the deed (page 2, line E.02).

8. If there had been any leases or assignments of interests transferred to the buyers, copies of these documents would also have been obtained.

Exhibit 13-4 Closing Disclosure

Closing Disclosure

This form is a statement of final loan terms and closing costs. Compare this document with your Loan Estimate.

Closing Information	Transaction Information	Loan Information
Date Issued July 1, 2017	**Borrower** Nicolas and Katie Lee	**Loan Term** 30 years
Closing Date July 1, 2017		**Purpose** Purchase
Disbursement Date July 1, 2017		**Product** Fixed Rate
Settlement Agent DownTrust Bank	**Seller** Robert and Penelope Jordan	
File #		**Loan Type** ☒ Conventional ☐ FHA
Property 1822 N.W. 40th Avenue		☐ VA ☐ _____
Gainesville, FL 32611	**Lender** DownTrust Bank	**Loan ID #**
Sale Price $260,000		**MIC #**

Loan Terms

		Can this amount increase after closing?
Loan Amount	$208,000	NO
Interest Rate	3.75%	NO
Monthly Principal & Interest *See Projected Payments below for your Estimated Total Monthly Payment*	$963.28	NO
		Does the loan have these features?
Prepayment Penalty		NO
Balloon Payment		NO

Projected Payments

Payment Calculation	
Principal & Interest	$963.28
Mortgage Insurance	+ 0
Estimated Escrow *Amount can increase over time*	+ $370.42
Estimated Total Monthly Payment	**$1,333.70**

Estimated Taxes, Insurance & Assessments *Amount can increase over time* *See page 4 for details*	**This estimate includes**	**In escrow?**
	☒ Property Taxes	YES
	☒ Homeowner's Insurance	YES
	☐ Other:	
	See Escrow Account on page 4 for details. You must pay for other property costs separately.	

Costs at Closing

Closing Costs	$8,600	Includes $3,799 in Loan Costs + $4,801 in Other Costs – in Lender Credits. *See page 2 for details.*
Cash to Close	$48,600	Includes Closing Costs. *See Calculating Cash to Close on page 3 for details.*

Exhibit 13-4 Continued Closing Disclosure

Closing Cost Details

Loan Costs	Borrower-Paid		Seller-Paid		Paid by Others
	At Closing	Before Closing	At Closing	Before Closing	
A. Origination Charges	$1,801				
01 0.5% of Loan Amount (Points)	$1,040				
02 Application Fee	$ 200				
03 Other Orignation Charges	$ 136				
04 Underwriting Fee	$ 425				
05					
06					
07					
08					
B. Services Borrower Did Not Shop For	$ 448				
01 Appraisal	$ 400				
02 Credit Report	$ 25				
03 Flood Certification	$ 23				
04					
05					
06					
07					
08					
09					
10					
C. Services Borrower Did Shop For	$1,550				
01 Survey	$ 275				
02 Attorney	$ 650				
03 Lender's Title Insurance	$ 250				
04 Structure Inspection	$ 375				
05					
06					
07					
08					
D. TOTAL LOAN COSTS (Borrower-Paid)	$3,799				
Loan Costs Subtotals (A + B + C)					

Other Costs					
E. Taxes and Other Government Fees	$1,317				
01 Recording Fees $ 173 Deed: Mortgage: $1,144	$1,317				
02 Transfer Tax			$1,820		
F. Prepaids	$ 663				
01 Homeowner's Insurance Premium (6 mo.)	$ 663				
02 Mortgage Insurance Premium (mo.)					
03 Prepaid Interest (per day from to)					
04 Property Taxes (mo.)					
05					
G. Initial Escrow Payment at Closing	$2,821				
01 Homeowner's Insurance $110.42 per month for 2 mo.	$ 221				
02 Mortgage Insurance per month for mo.					
03 Property Taxes $ 260.00 per month for 10 mo.	$2,600				
04					
05					
06					
07					
08 Aggregate Adjustment					
H. Other					
01 Deed Preparation			$ 400		
02 Owner's Title Insurance			$1,381		
03 Pest Inspection			$ 85		
04 Real Estate Commission			$15,600		
05 Recording of Mortgage Satisfaction			$ 6		
06 Title Services			$ 95		
07					
08					
I. TOTAL OTHER COSTS (Borrower-Paid)	$4,801				
Other Costs Subtotals (E + F + G + H)					
J. TOTAL CLOSING COSTS (Borrower-Paid)	$8,600				
Closing Costs Subtotals (D + I)	$8,600		$19,387		
Lender Credits					

Exhibit 13-4 **Continued** Closing Disclosure

Calculating Cash to Close

Use this table to see what has changed from your Loan Estimate.

	Loan Estimate	Final	Did this change?
Total Closing Costs (J)	$8,600	$8,600	NO
Closing Costs Paid Before Closing	0	0	NO
Closing Costs Financed (Paid from your Loan Amount)	0	0	NO
Down Payment/Funds from Borrower	$52,000	$52,000	NO
Deposit	- $12,000	- $12,000	NO
Funds for Borrower	0	0	NO
Seller Credits	0	0	NO
Adjustments and Other Credits	0	0	NO
Cash to Close	$48,600	$48,600	

Summaries of Transactions

Use this table to see a summary of your transaction.

BORROWER'S TRANSACTION

K. Due from Borrower at Closing	$268,600
01 Sale Price of Property	$260,000
02 Sale Price of Any Personal Property Included in Sale	
03 Closing Costs Paid at Closing (J)	$ 8,600
04	

Adjustments

05	
06	
07	

Adjustments for Items Paid by Seller in Advance

08 City/Town Taxes	to	
09 County Taxes	to	
10 Assessments	to	
11		
12		
13		
14		
15		

L. Paid Already by or on Behalf of Borrower at Closing	$221,547
01 Deposit	$12,000
02 Loan Amount	$208,000
03 Existing Loan(s) Assumed or Taken Subject to	
04	
05 Seller Credit	

Other Credits

| 06 | |
| 07 | |

Adjustments

08	
09	
10	
11	

Adjustments for Items Unpaid by Seller

12 City/Town Taxes	to	
13 County Taxes	1/1/17 to 6/30/17	$1,547
14 Assessments	to	
15		
16		
17		

CALCULATION

Total Due from Borrower at Closing (K)	$268,600
Total Paid Already by or on Behalf of Borrower at Closing (L)	$221,547
Cash to Close ☒ From ☐ To Borrower	$47,053

SELLER'S TRANSACTION

M. Due to Seller at Closing	$260,000
01 Sale Price of Property	$260,000
02 Sale Price of Any Personal Property Included in Sale	
03	
04	
05	
06	
07	
08	

Adjustments for Items Paid by Seller in Advance

09 City/Town Taxes	to	
10 County Taxes	to	
11 Assessments	to	
12		
13		
14		
15		
16		

N. Due from Seller at Closing	$225,004
01 Excess Deposit	
02 Closing Costs Paid at Closing (J)	$ 19,387
03 Existing Loan(s) Assumed or Taken Subject to	$204,070
04 Payoff of First Mortgage Loan	
05 Payoff of Second Mortgage Loan	
06	
07	
08 Seller Credit	
09	
10	
11	
12	
13	

Adjustments for Items Unpaid by Seller

14 City/Town Taxes	to	
15 County Taxes	1/1/17 to 6/30/17	$1,547
16 Assessments	to	
17		
18		
19		

CALCULATION

Total Due to Seller at Closing (M)	$260,000
Total Due from Seller at Closing (N)	$225,004
Cash ☐ From ☒ To Seller	$34,996

Exhibit 13-4 **Continued** Closing Disclosure

Additional Information About This Loan

Loan Disclosures

Assumption
If you sell or transfer this property to another person, your lender

☒ will allow, under certain conditions, this person to assume this loan on the original terms.

☐ will not allow assumption of this loan on the original terms.

Demand Feature
Your loan

☐ has a demand feature, which permits your lender to require early repayment of the loan. You should review your note for details.

☒ does not have a demand feature.

Late Payment
If your payment is more than __15__ days late, your lender will charge a late fee of ___5% of monthly principal and interest___

Negative Amortization (Increase in Loan Amount)
Under your loan terms, you

☐ are scheduled to make monthly payments that do not pay all of the interest due that month. As a result, your loan amount will increase (negatively amortize), and your loan amount will likely become larger than your original loan amount. Increases in your loan amount lower the equity you have in this property.

☐ may have monthly payments that do not pay all of the interest due that month. If you do, your loan amount will increase (negatively amortize), and, as a result, your loan amount may become larger than your original loan amount. Increases in your loan amount lower the equity you have in this property.

☒ do not have a negative amortization feature.

Partial Payments
Your lender

☒ may accept payments that are less than the full amount due (partial payments) and apply them to your loan.

☐ may hold them in a separate account until you pay the rest of the payment, and then apply the full payment to your loan.

☐ does not accept any partial payments.

If this loan is sold, your new lender may have a different policy.

Security Interest
You are granting a security interest in _____1822 N.W. 40th Avenue, Gainesville, FL 32611_____

You may lose this property if you do not make your payments or satisfy other obligations for this loan.

Escrow Account
For now, your loan

☒ will have an escrow account (also called an "impound" or "trust" account) to pay the property costs listed below. Without an escrow account, you would pay them directly, possibly in one or two large payments a year. Your lender may be liable for penalties and interest for failing to make a payment.

Escrow		
Escrowed Property Costs over Year 1	$4,445	Estimated total amount over year 1 for your escrowed property costs:
Non-Escrowed Property Costs over Year 1		Estimated total amount over year 1 for your non-escrowed property costs: You may have other property costs.
Initial Escrow Payment	$2,821	A cushion for the escrow account you pay at closing. See Section G on page 2.
Monthly Escrow Payment	$370.42	The amount included in your total monthly payment.

☐ will not have an escrow account because ☐ you declined it ☐ your lender does not offer one. You must directly pay your property costs, such as taxes and homeowner's insurance. Contact your lender to ask if your loan can have an escrow account.

No Escrow		
Estimated Property Costs over Year 1		Estimated total amount over year 1. You must pay these costs directly, possibly in one or two large payments a year.
Escrow Waiver Fee		

In the future,
Your property costs may change and, as a result, your escrow payment may change. You may be able to cancel your escrow account, but if you do, you must pay your property costs directly. If you fail to pay your property taxes, your state or local government may (1) impose fines and penalties or (2) place a tax lien on this property. If you fail to pay any of your property costs, your lender may (1) add the amounts to your loan balance, (2) add an escrow account to your loan, or (3) require you to pay for property insurance that the lender buys on your behalf, which likely would cost more and provide fewer benefits than what you could buy on your own.

Exhibit 13-4   **Continued**   Closing Disclosure

Loan Calculations

Total of Payments. Total you will have paid after you make all payments of principal, interest, mortgage insurance, and loan costs, as scheduled.	Omitted due to unclear instructions
Finance Charge. The dollar amount the loan will cost you.	Omitted due to unclear Instructions
Amount Financed. The loan amount available after paying your upfront finance charge.	$204,232
Annual Percentage Rate (APR). Your costs over the loan term expressed as a rate. This is not your interest rate.	3.821%
Total Interest Percentage (TIP). The total amount of interest that you will pay over the loan term as a percentage of your loan amount.	66.7%

Questions? If you have questions about the loan terms or costs on this form, use the contact information below. To get more information or make a complaint, contact the Consumer Financial Protection Bureau at **www.consumerfinance.gov/mortgage-closing**

Other Disclosures

Appraisal
If the property was appraised for your loan, your lender is required to give you a copy at no additional cost at least 3 days before closing. If you have not yet received it, please contact your lender at the information listed below.

Contract Details
See your note and security instrument for information about
- what happens if you fail to make your payments,
- what is a default on the loan,
- situations in which your lender can require early repayment of the loan, and
- the rules for making payments before they are due.

Liability after Foreclosure
If your lender forecloses on this property and the foreclosure does not cover the amount of unpaid balance on this loan,

☒ state law may protect you from liability for the unpaid balance. If you refinance or take on any additional debt on this property, you may lose this protection and have to pay any debt remaining even after foreclosure. You may want to consult a lawyer for more information.

☐ state law does not protect you from liability for the unpaid balance.

Refinance
Refinancing this loan will depend on your future financial situation, the property value, and market conditions. You may not be able to refinance this loan.

Tax Deductions
If you borrow more than this property is worth, the interest on the loan amount above this property's fair market value is not deductible from your federal income taxes. You should consult a tax advisor for more information.

Contact Information

	Lender	Mortgage Broker	Real Estate Broker (B)	Real Estate Broker (S)	Settlement Agent
Name	DownTrust Bank		Baden Assoc. Realty	Baden Assoc. Realty	DownTrust Bank
Address	147 Gale Lamerand Drive Gainesville, FL 32605				
NMLS ID					
__ License ID					
Contact	Ellen Rich		Josh Hairston	Ben Park	Joe Jenkins
Contact NMLS ID					
Contact __ License ID					
Email	e.rich@downtrust.com		j.hairston @badenrealty.com	b.park @badenrealty.com	j.jenkins @alllaw.com
Phone					

Confirm Receipt

By signing, you are only confirming that you have received this form. You do not have to accept this loan because you have signed or received this form.

Applicant Signature	Date	Co-Applicant Signature	Date

CLOSING DISCLOSURE   PAGE 5 OF 5 • LOAN ID #

Source: http://www.consumerfinance.gov/owning-a-home/closing-disclosure

The seller is also responsible for the $85 termite inspection (page 2, line H.03). Total settlement costs paid by the seller equal $19,387 (page 2, line J.01)

Moving to page 3 of the CD, under Summary of Transactions, we see in the right-hand column that the sellers are owed the total purchase price of $260,000 (line M.00). However, the $260,000 gross amount due the Jordans is reduced by the $19,387 closing costs (line N.02) and the $204,070 that is required to pay off the remaining mortgage balance on their loan (line N.03). In addition, because the buyers will be required to pay the entire property tax bill at the end of the year, they must be compensated by the sellers who will have occupied the home for six months. This compensation is accomplished by reducing the amount the buyer must pay the seller at closing by the amount of the sellers' unpaid property taxes (lines L.13 and N.15). Reductions in the amount due the sellers at closing total $225,004 (line N.00). Thus, the Jordans will walk away from closing with a $34,996 check ($260,000 − $225,004).

The left-hand column of page 3 summarizes the transaction from the buyers' perspective. In addition to the $260,000 purchase price (line K.01), the Lees are required to pay $8,600 in closing costs (line K.03). Thus, the gross amount due from the Lees is $268,600 (line K.00). However, the buyers are credited the $12,000 deposit of earnest money (line L.01) and the amount of the new mortgage they are obtaining from DownTrust Bank (line L.02). In effect, they are responsible for bringing these mortgage funds into the transaction and are committed to paying off the loan, with interest, over the next 30 years.

Property taxes are the only item *prorated* in this transaction. Since property taxes will be paid in arrears (after the period for which they are incurred), the *buyers* will have to pay the tax bill for the entire year of 2017 in November or December of 2017. Therefore, they are given credit for the amount of time the property was occupied by the sellers—181 out of 365 days. Item 18K in the Standards for Real Estate Transactions (see page 9 of Exhibit 13-1) indicates that the buyer pays for the day of closing. Since the total tax bill for 2017 is estimated to be $3120 (slightly higher than the previous year), the adjustment for unpaid property taxes (lines L.13 and N.15) is $1,547 [(181 ÷ 365) × $3,120].

Including the $1,547 credit for the seller's unpaid property taxes (line L.13), a total of $221,547 either is being paid by another party on behalf of the buyer or has already been paid by the buyer (line L.00). The total amount collected from the buyer at closing (bottom line, left) is $47,053 ($268,600 − $221,547). The buyers must write a personal check for this amount that, together with the escrow deposit, borrowed funds, and prorated tax credit, will cover all the amounts owed.

After explaining the various items on the closing statement, Mr. Jenkins asks the Lees to write a check to DownTrust Bank in the amount of $47,053 and to sign the note and mortgage. He asks the Jordans to sign the deed and to hand it to the Lees. He then hands a check for $34,996 to the Jordans and states that all of the expenses either have been paid or will be paid immediately. He gives to Mr. Park a check for $15,600 payable to Baden Associates Realty. The closing is now completed, and all parties in the room rise, shake hands, and leave. Baden Associates Realty will split the commission with Ben and Josh. While commission splits vary within the firm, its agreement with both Ben and Josh is that the firm gets half of any commission they generate. Thus, Ben and Josh will share the other half, receiving a $3,900 commission from the sale [0.50 × (0.50 × $15,600)].

Escrow Closings

The story of the Jordans and the Lees in this chapter details the process of a live closing event, which is the prevailing practice in much of the United States, but not everywhere. In a number of states, including California, escrow closings are the primary mode of real estate transaction. Further, the growing use of electronic transactions may favor this practice in general. Escrow closings accomplish the same results as live closings, but without the requirement of an actual gathering of the parties. Rather, a qualified escrow agent is given detailed instructions and authority to execute all the necessary steps to the transaction, carrying it through to the creation and final distribution of all signed documents, collection and distribution of funds, and distribution of the closing statement.

Who are escrow agents? In California, for example, there are independent escrow agents, licensed by the state to serve in that capacity. In addition, banks, thrifts, insurance companies, and, especially common, title companies can serve as escrow agents. Finally, attorneys and brokers may serve in the escrow role for transactions they are a part of.

What do escrow agents do? In areas where the escrow closing prevails, the contract for purchase and sale will identify an escrow agent to be used in the transaction. When the parties have reached agreement and fully executed the contract, it, and usually any earnest moneys will be given to the escrow agent, usually by the listing broker. A largely standard set of detailed instructions will have been incorporated in an agreement between the agent and the parties to the transaction that spells out the process. Typically the agent will undertake a wide range of tasks, as described in a California description of the escrow officer role:

> An escrow officer is responsible for the preparation and processing of a significant amount of paperwork. That paperwork includes, but it is not limited to, escrow instructions and amendments, grant deeds and quitclaim deeds, estimated and final closing statements … required by lending institutions. Escrow officers also facilitate the request, delivery, and signing of documents, not only for the benefit of the principals, but for the real estate brokers, and the applicable title company and lending institution. The escrow officer must also comply with local, county, State and federal requirements relative to required documentation and fees. If the buyer is obtaining financing, the escrow officer will work with the mortgage broker and/or lender to help move the loan approval and underwriting process along, satisfy the lender's conditions, and will likely coordinate the loan document sign-up. Additionally, escrow officers will request closing funds, authorize the release and recording of documents, and are the primary party responsible for all of the accounting of an escrow transaction and disbursement of funds held in the escrow. Another large part of an escrow officer's job is requesting payoff demands and lien releases, and working to ensure that free and clear title will be conveyed to the buyer and in compliance with the lender's instructions, if applicable. In some ways, the escrow officer has one of the most difficult jobs in a real estate transaction as he or she is the neutral party to which all buyers, sellers, borrowers, lenders, real estate brokers, and title companies look to for the proper, efficient and effective administration of an escrow.[9]

9. Wayne S. Bell and Summer B. Bakotich, "Surviving the Real Estate 'Escrow' Process in California: Important Things and Tips You Should Know, and Mistakes to Avoid." http://www.dre.ca.gov/files/pdf/Escrow_Info_Consumers.pdf.

Summary

The contract for sale is the most important document in real estate. It contains the rights and obligations to which the principals in a transaction—buyers and sellers—commit themselves. The contract governs all elements of a transaction; a court can enforce its provisions.

Contracts for sale can be simple or complex. They may be typed, handwritten, or prepared on preprinted forms. No matter what the form, however, an agreement is valid and enforceable if it contains the seven elements required of real estate contracts: (1) competent parties, (2) offer and acceptance, (3) consideration, (4) legal objective, (5) no defects to mutual assent, (6) written form, and (7) a proper description of the property.

Since a contract is a legally binding document, buyers and sellers can protect themselves by having a competent attorney examine the contract before signing; after the contract has been signed, it is too late and any changes would have to be agreed to by both parties.

When one party breaks the provisions of a contract, the other party may have one or more remedies. An aggrieved buyer may (1) agree to rescind the contract, (2) sue for specific performance, or (3) sue for damages. An aggrieved seller can (1) agree to rescind,

(2) sue for damages, or (3) retain all or a portion of any deposits if the buyer fails to complete the transaction. Escrow agents often assist in carrying out the provisions of a contract and lessen the chances of default by either party.

Closing is the consummation of a real estate transaction. At closing, title is conveyed and the purchase price is paid. Expenses are paid by each party and prorations between the parties are made. A document summarizing the financial flows that occur at closing is known as the closing (or settlement) statement; the prevailing form now is the Closing Disclosure. The closing statement includes a detailed itemization of the expenses that must be paid by the buyers and sellers at closing.

Prorating is required when an expense has been prepaid by the seller or will be paid subsequently by the buyer, and covers a time period during which both buyer and seller own the property. The procedure involves crediting the party that pays the expense with the proportionate amount covering the period during which the other party owns the property. Typical items to be prorated are prepaid rent, insurance, real estate taxes, mortgage interest (either prepaid or paid in arrears), and prepaid mortgage principal.

Key Terms

Assignment　361

Closing　340

Closing Disclosure (CD)　364

Consideration　342

Contract conditions　340

Contract for sale　339

Contract terms　340

Contracts with contingencies　361

Earnest money　365

Equitable title　343

Escrow　362

Escrow agent　362

Estimated closing costs　368

Legal title　343

Loan Estimate (LE)　364

Personal performance　361

Prorating　367

Rescission　362

Specific performance　362

Test Problems

Answer the following multiple-choice questions:

1. If a buyer defaults on a contract to purchase real property, which of the following is *not* a remedy the seller can pursue?
   a. Rescind the contract.
   b. Sue for damages.
   c. Sue for specific performance.
   d. Retain all or part of the binder deposit.

2. When contracts for the sale of real property are placed with a disinterested third party for executing and closing, they are said to be placed in:
   a. Safekeeping.
   b. A title company or financial institution.
   c. Option.
   d. Escrow.
   e. Assignment.

3. Which of the following conditions would be a defect to mutual assent in a contract for the sale of real property?
   a. One party attempts to perpetrate fraud on the other.
   b. The contract is in written form.
   c. The price is excessive.
   d. One of the parties is legally incompetent.
   e. The contract does not specify a time for closing.

4. Oral evidence in contract disputes is prohibited by:
   a. A parol contract.
   b. An executory contract.
   c. An inferred contract.
   d. An unspecified contract.
   e. The parol evidence rule.

5. Which of the following is one of the *terms* of a real estate contract?
   a. Mechanical equipment must be in good condition.
   b. Title must be marketable.
   c. Price to be paid.
   d. Property must be free of termites.
   e. All of the above items are terms.

6. Real estate transactions do not close at the same time the contract for sale is signed by both parties because:
   a. An inspection must be made.
   b. Financing must be arranged.
   c. Title must be checked.
   d. Documents must be prepared.
   e. All of the above.

7. An earnest money deposit is:
   a. A preliminary contract.
   b. A provision in a contract for sale.
   c. A payment of money by a buyer to evidence good faith.
   d. An escrow provision.
   e. A conveyance.

8. In most straightforward transactions involving houses or other relatively small properties, the contract is:
   a. Prepared by the seller's attorney.
   b. Prepared by the buyer's attorney.
   c. Prepared by the broker.
   d. A form, with blanks filled in by the broker.
   e. A form, with blanks filled in by buyer and seller.

www.mhhe.com/lingarcher5e

9. Equitable title to real estate is:
   a. Legal ownership of property.
   b. Legal title obtained in a court of equity.
   c. Title obtained by adverse possession.
   d. A legal interest in a property conveyed by a listing contract to a broker.
   e. The right to obtain legal title conveyed by the contract for sale.

10. The purpose of a closing statement is to:
   a. Determine who pays the brokerage commission.
   b. Allocate expenses and receipts of buyer and seller.
   c. Prorate expenses between buyer and seller.
   d. Account for moneys in a transaction.
   e. All but **a** above.

Study Questions

1. If a closing occurs on September 1 of a 365-day year, how will the year's property tax of $900 be prorated? (*Note:* The day of closing "belongs" to the buyer.)

   Use the following information to answer questions 2 to 5. Rosie Malone sold her house to D.M. Band. The contract was signed June 1, 2017, and closing was set for June 25, 2017. Rosie had prepaid her three-year hazard insurance policy in the amount of $ 1,825 on April 1, 2016, and D.M. agreed to assume it at closing. Water and sewer are paid the first of each month for the previous month. They are estimated to total $200 for June. D.M. also agrees to assume Rosie's mortgage, which will have a balance of $85,385 on date of closing. Monthly payments are $817.83 payable on the first of the month for the previous month. The seller is responsible for the day of closing.

2. How would the hazard insurance premium be prorated?

3. How would the water and sewer charges be prorated?

4. How will the mortgage assumption be entered?

5. How will the monthly mortgage payment be prorated?

6. The owner of a parcel of land containing approximately 25 acres contracted a debilitating disease and decided to sell his real estate as quickly as possible. Within a week, he received an offer of $320,250. The owner accepted this offer by signing a standard form contract that had been obtained and prepared by the buyer. Soon after, when the owner's family discovered the situation, they convinced him that he had sold the land at much too low a price and he should not complete the transaction.

   The owner commissioned an appraisal that showed the land to be worth $460,000, a difference of $5,590 per acre between the contract price and the property value. He then refused to attend the closing and to deliver title to the buyer. The buyer sued the owner for damages in the amount of the difference between the property value and the contract price ($139,750). The buyer contended he had a valid contract and he was damaged by the owner's unwillingness to complete the transaction. The seller contended he was not of sound mind when he signed the contract and the price was so ridiculously low, the contract should not be enforced.

   Identify the issues the court probably would consider in deciding whether or not to enforce the contract.

7. A couple decided to sell their house in Washington, DC, without the aid of a real estate broker. Their asking price was $425,000, which they believed was about $15,000 less than the price they would need to list the property with a broker. They realized they would probably have to accept an offer as low as $420,000. Another couple looked at the house, liked it, and offered to buy it for $423,500. The sellers were delighted and suggested that they fill in the blanks on a form sales contract used by many of the local real estate brokerage firms, and both parties could sign it. The buyers, however, objected, saying they preferred to write their own contract. The wife was an attorney who worked for the U.S. State Department, specializing in international law.

   What advice would you have given the sellers?

8. Given the following situation and facts, complete a closing settlement statement similar to that shown in Exhibit 13-4.

   On May 15, 2017, Eric Martin signed a contract to purchase a rental house for $195,000. Closing is to occur on June 8, 2017, with the day of closing to be counted as a day of ownership by the buyer. Eric can assume the seller's first mortgage, which will have a balance of $149,000 on June 8. The seller, Reuben Smith, has agreed to take a second mortgage of $30,000 as part of the payment at closing. Eric paid an escrow deposit of $10,000 when he signed the purchase contract. Other pertinent facts include:

   a. The monthly interest on the first mortgage is $745, which must be paid by the 20th day of the month.

   b. Reuben paid a hazard insurance policy for the calendar year 2017. The premium was $850, and Eric has agreed to purchase Reuben's interest in the policy.

   c. The monthly rental of $1,250 has been collected by Reuben for June.

   d. The total amount of property tax for 2017 is estimated to be $2,200. The tax will be paid by Eric at the end of the year.

   e. The broker will pay the following expenses for Reuben and will be reimbursed at the closing:

Abstract continuation	$ 85.00
Attorney's fee	$ 300.00
Deed stamps (tax)	$ 1,365.00
Brokerage commission (6%)	$11,700.00

   f. The broker will also pay the following expenses for Eric and will be reimbursed at the closing:

Attorney's fee	$250.00
Deed recording fee	$ 6.00
Mortgage recording fee	$ 10.00
Mortgage note stamps (tax)	$682.50
Intangible tax on mortgage	$390.00

EXPLORE THE WEB

Examine two or three of the homebuyer websites shown in the text: Motley Fool, HUD, Freddie Mac, Fannie Mae, CNNMoney, MSN Money, for example, or scout for others. Do they seem to agree on the circumstances in which one should, and should not, buy a home? Do they agree on the upfront costs of home purchase?

Solutions to Concept Checks

1. Essential elements of any contract are competent parties, legal objective, consideration, offer and acceptance, and no defects to mutual assent. Two additional essential elements to a contract for sale of real estate are unambiguous description and that the contract be in writing.
2. Three aspects of legal competency are attainment of legal age, not incapacitated, and having authority to enter into a contract.
3. In a contract for sale of real estate, the seller implicitly agrees to deliver marketable title.
4. Three possible defects to mutual assent are fraud, errors, and one party being under duress.
5. Legal title is ownership of a freehold estate. Equitable title is the right to receive legal title. Equitable title results from signing a contract for sale of real estate. It terminates when legal title is obtained by a deed or other means.
6. Two advantages of a standard form contract for the sale of real estate are that it is relatively easy to complete and that it is likely to be fair to both parties. A disadvantage is that it can fail to address issues important to a particular transaction.
7. Two sections of a standard form contract are the negotiated items that need to be "filled in," and the standard provisions that seldom need to be negotiated.

8. Assignment means to pass all of one's rights and obligations in a contract to a subsequent party. Both the assignor and the assignee are then liable for performance of the contract.
9. Three standard remedies for a buyer with a defaulted real estate contract are rescission, suit for damages, and suit for specific performance. Three standard remedies for a seller with a defaulted contract are rescission, suit for damages, and retaining the buyer's deposit as liquidated damages.
10. In most real estate closings, the listing broker is responsible for the successful completion of the closing.
11. Four effects of RESPA on most residential real estate closings, now part of CFPB requirements, are (1) requires a good-faith estimate of closing costs, (2) requires that the borrower/buyer receive a CFPB closing booklet, (3) requires the use of the CFPB Closing Disclosure form, and (4) prohibits kickbacks for transaction-related services. TILA requires disclosure of the following home mortgage features: the APR, whether the loan is assumable, what late fees may apply, whether there is negative amortization, and whether there is a prepayment penalty.
12. Two methods of allocating closing-related expenses between buyer and seller are by local custom and by negotiation.

Additional Readings

Aalberts, Robert J. *Real Estate Law,* 9th ed. Stamford, CT: South-Western Cengage Learning, 2015.

Jennings, Marianne. *Real Estate Law,* 10th ed. Stamford, CT: South-Western Cengage Learning, 2014.

This booklet provides an overview of the home buying and home financing process with helpful worksheets and references:

Consumer Financial Protection Bureau, *Your home loan toolkit: A step-by-step guide*

www.mhhe.com/lingarcher5e

Chapter 14

PART SIX

The Effects *of* Time *and* Risk *on* Value

LEARNING OBJECTIVES

After reading this chapter you will be able to:

1 Explain why future cash flows must be converted (discounted) into present values.

2 Perform basic compounding and discounting calculations using a financial calculator.

3 Explain the importance of risk in the cash flow valuation process.

4 Explain and use the internal rate of return decision rule.

5 Explain and use the net present value decision rule.

OUTLINE

Introduction
The Time Value of Money
    The Timeline
    Terminology
    Equations, Calculators, and Spreadsheets
    Compounding Operations
    Discounting Operations
    Yields and Internal Rates of Return
Value and Risk
Determining Required Returns
Comparing Investment Values to Acquisition Costs
Appendix: Solving Time-Value-of-Money Problems
Using Excel

Introduction

Any decision about real estate involves the commitment of resources over time, usually a number of years. For example, owners must repeatedly determine how much to spend on property maintenance and repair. Decisions also must be made periodically about rehabilitation, modernization, expansion, conversion of the property to another use, or demolition of the existing improvements. Further, an owner may repeatedly face the decision of whether to continue to hold the property or to sell. Even the decision to abandon real estate involves an investment decision.

Each of these decisions involves comparing the immediate cost of an action against the value of the future resulting benefits (usually quantified as cash flows). However, the valuation of future benefits is complicated by two factors. First, even if their timing and magnitude can be known with certainty, the future benefits of a proposed investment cannot simply be added up to determine their current value to investors because the present value of future benefits declines as the time the investor must wait for the future benefits increases.

Consider, for example, what happens when investors purchase real estate. Their balance of cash (or other valuables) is reduced by the required down payment on the property. Why will investors sacrifice assets to acquire property? Because they expect the present value of the benefits from future cash flows to exceed the burden of the initial down payment. Clearly, the timing of these future cash flows matters. For example, if investors must wait, say, 20 years, for a series of annual cash flows to begin, they would surely value them less than if the same series of cash flows were to begin immediately after the acquisition of the property. Thus, future cash flows must be "discounted" for time before they can be compared to current cash inflows and outflows.

The second complication associated with real estate decision making is that value assessments are generally based on *expected* cash flows, but what actually happens is seldom, if ever, exactly what the investor expected. **Risk** is the possibility that actual outcomes will vary from what was expected when the asset was purchased. Because most investors are risk averse, the relationship between risk and required return is positive: The more risk investors face when undertaking an investment, the greater the rate of return they should expect (require). When valuing real estate, adjusting for risk introduces an important complication.

This chapter discusses standard techniques for quantifying the effects of time and risk on value. These **time-value-of-money (TVM)** techniques are not unique to real estate valuation and decision making. They are widely used by finance professionals to calculate mortgage payments, determine values for stocks and bonds, calculate insurance premiums, and decide whether potential capital expenditures are profitable enough to commit investment capital. Nonfinance professionals also find an understanding of TVM concepts extremely beneficial. Armed with such an understanding, individuals can apply TVM procedures to compare costs on alternative loans, determine whether an existing mortgage loan should be refinanced, calculate the future value of a retirement fund (given estimates of annual contributions to the fund), decide whether a car leasing plan is preferred to a bank loan, and calculate the returns their investments have earned in the past. In short, an understanding of TVM techniques is necessary for informed valuation assessments and decision making.

The emphasis in the current chapter is on asset valuation techniques; we do not discuss the factors that actually contribute to the value of the real estate, such as location, building design, and the existing supply of competing properties. These determinants of expected future cash flows are discussed in detail in earlier chapters (see, especially, Chapters 2–6).

The Time Value of Money

Money is an economic good. Like other economic goods, such as televisions and automobiles, people prefer to have more, rather than less, money—that is, the magnitude of the cash flows matters. Moreover, investors prefer to have the money *now* rather than later. If money is received later, for example, next week instead of today, it isn't worth as much to those receiving it, and an adjustment is required. This adjustment is called *discounting*. Understanding how to adjust cash flows received at different times is the essence of time-value-of-money problems.

Assume an investor with $100 to invest is considering three alternatives, each covering 10 years. These alternatives are as follows:

Plan A: The investor receives $10 at the end of the first year, plus the original $100 at the end of year 10.

Plan B: The investor receives $1 at the end of each year for 10 years, plus the original $100 at the end of 10 years.

Plan C: The investor receives $10 at the end of the 10th year of the plan, plus the original $100.

Each plan returns the investor's $100, plus $10 of income over the 10-year period. Which plan should the investor prefer?

Answer: The investor should choose Plan A. Why? Because money can be put to one of two possible uses when it is received. First, the investor may spend the money, for example, by taking a friend to dinner. Second, the investor may invest the money. With Plan A, the investor has the greatest opportunity to spend the money or to earn interest on the money throughout the 10-year period by spending or reinvesting the $10 received at the end of year 1. Ten dollars invested for nine years will accumulate more interest than the 10 yearly investments of $1 each he or she would be able to make in Plan B. Therefore, investors who plan to reinvest their returns prefer earlier returns to later returns because of the opportunity to earn interest. Investors who consume their returns have the same time preferences for early returns. Would you want to wait 10 years to take your friend to dinner, as you would with Plan C?

The Timeline

Panel A of Exhibit 14-1 presents a timeline, which is simply an aid for visualizing the time pattern of money returns. The line is broken into time points and time intervals, or periods, beginning on the left with the present, time 0, and ending on the right with the terminal time point, N. Annual time periods are typically used in evaluating single-property investments, but sometimes monthly periods are appropriate (e.g., when analyzing mortgage or lease payments).

All money *inflows* are placed on top of the line, and all *outflows* of money (e.g., the time 0 investment) go beneath the line, corresponding to the time point at which they occur. The inflows and outflows from the investment decision involving the three alternative plans are shown in panel B of Exhibit 14-1. All future inflows and outflows are assumed to occur at the end of the period in which they are received or paid, respectively.

Exhibit 14-1 The Timeline

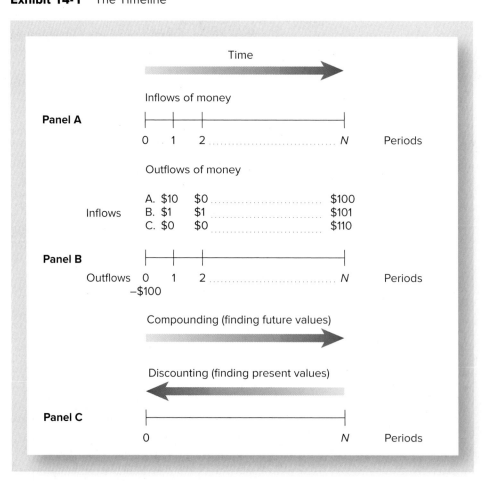

Terminology

The following are common terms used in applying time-value-of-money concepts:

Future value (*FV*)—the value of money in some period beyond time zero. "Calculating a future value" means converting cash invested in the current period (or some prior period) into what it will be worth at some future date.

Present value (*PV*)—the value of future cash flows at time zero. "Taking the present value of inflows" means converting future cash flows in present value (i.e., at time zero).

Lump sum—a one-time receipt or expenditure occurring in a given period. In panel B of Exhibit 14-1, the $10 received in year 1 under Plan A is an example of a lump sum, as is the $110 received in the 10th period under Plan C.

Ordinary annuity (*A*)—a fixed amount of money paid or received at the end of every period (i.e., a series of equal lump sums). The series of $1 annual cash flows under Plan B is an example of a 10-year annual annuity.

Compounding—calculation of future values, as shown in panel C of Exhibit 14-1.

Discounting—calculation of present values, as shown in panel C of Exhibit 14-1.

Equations, Calculators, and Spreadsheets

Various mathematical equations can be used to adjust for differences in the timing of cash flows. However, most analysts employ a financial calculator or use "spreadsheet" programs, such as Microsoft's Excel, that are loaded on their personal computers. Both calculators and spreadsheet software contain internal programs that provide solutions to common TVM calculations.

There are four basic time-value-of-money adjustments. Exhibit 14-2 lists these adjustments and their associated mathematical equations. In the equations for monthly adjustments, the annual interest rate is divided by 12 to obtain the monthly interest rate, and the number of years (*n*) is multiplied by 12 to obtain the total number of monthly periods. If interest on an investment is earned (compounded) daily, the annual interest rate is divided by 365 to obtain the daily interest rate, and the number of years (*n*) is multiplied by 365 to determine the number of daily periods.

Through the manipulation of the financial functions of handheld calculators, any problem that may be solved with a TVM equation may be solved with a calculator—and usually much faster. Financial calculators, which have the necessary formulas preprogrammed into their

Exhibit 14-2 Equations for Time-Value-of-Money Adjustments

Operation	Symbols	Equation for Annual Adjustment (n = number of years) (r = annual interest rate)	Equation for Monthly Adjustment (r = annual interest rate)
Future value of a lump sum	FV	$(1 + r)^n$	$(1 + r/12)^{12n}$
Future value of annuity	FV_A	$\dfrac{(1 + r)^n - 1}{r}$	$\dfrac{(1 + r/12)^{12n} - 1}{r/12}$
Present value of a lump sum	PV	$\dfrac{1}{(1 + r)^n}$	$\dfrac{1}{(1 + r/12)^{12n}}$
Present value of annuity	PV_A	$\dfrac{1 - [1/(1 + r)^n]}{r}$	$\dfrac{1 - [1/(1 + r/12)^{12n}]}{r/12}$

Real estate professionals must constantly update their knowledge and skill set. They must constantly strive to stay abreast of business trends, and think about issues—tax laws, new highway routes, technology, or existing and proposed zoning regulations—affecting their

Real Estate Careers

clients, business, and investments. Beyond a general knowledge of business, economics, and, increasingly, a global market perspective, employers often expect young real estate professionals to be computer literate and adept at using spreadsheets, database analysis, word processing, graphical analysis, and mapping software. Employers also expect new employees to

communicate well and to be comfortable making oral presentations. Negotiation skills are also an important aspect of the real estate industry.

Source: Adapted from http://business.uc.edu/ centers/real-estate/academics/career-paths.html.

---

computational algorithms, are merely a more efficient option than equations for making TVM adjustments. Although financial calculators vary, all have five basic keys (or registers):

N—the number of compounding (or discounting) periods. If the cash flows from a real estate investment are received, say, annually for five years, then $N = 5$. If they are received monthly for five years, then $N = 60$.

I—the periodic (usually monthly or annual) interest rate. If the cash flows are received or invested annually, I is the annual interest rate. If the cash flows occur at monthly intervals, I equals the annual rate divided by 12.

PV—the lump sum amount invested at time zero. In real estate, this is often the required cash down payment. PV may also be the discounted present value of future cash flows at time zero.

PMT—the periodic level payment or receipt (annuity). This may be a fixed monthly mortgage payment or a lease payment. The expected cash inflows on income-producing properties are generally not fixed-level amounts.

FV—the lump sum cash flow or the future value of an investment. In real estate, FV may be the net cash flow expected to be received from the sale of a property at the end of an N year holding period.

Once a student becomes comfortable with the basic operations of his or her calculator, the key to solving time-value-of-money problems is knowing what, if anything, to enter into each of these five registers. In the problems that follow, and throughout the text, the basic keystrokes needed to solve a TVM problem are identified without specifying the exact sequence of keystrokes necessary to solve the problem on a particular calculator.

Spreadsheet programs such as Microsoft Excel have significantly increased the use of personal computers in the analysis of real estate decisions. The Appendix discusses how to solve basic time-value-of-money problems using an Excel spreadsheet.

Compounding Operations

The first two time-value-of-money (TVM) operations are used for calculating future values resulting from the compounding of interest. Compound interest means the investor earns interest on the principal amount invested, plus interest on accumulated interest.

Future Value of a Lump Sum. Suppose an investor deposits $1,000 today in an interest-bearing account at a local bank. The account pays 5 percent interest compounded annually,

Exhibit 14-3 Timeline Demonstration for Compounding Problems

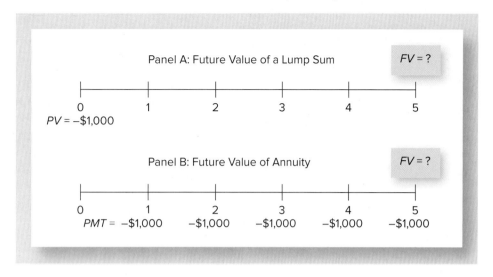

Panel A: Future Value of a Lump Sum   FV = ?

0   1   2   3   4   5
PV = −$1,000

Panel B: Future Value of Annuity   FV = ?

0   1   2   3   4   5
PMT = −$1,000 −$1,000 −$1,000 −$1,000 −$1,000

and the investor expects to withdraw the original principal, plus accumulated interest, at the end of five years. Panel A of Exhibit 14-3 provides a timeline demonstration of the cash inflows and outflows for this problem.

To solve this problem, the present value (*PV*) amount of $1,000 invested at time zero is converted to a future value (*FV*) at the end of five years. The conversion is made by multiplying the *PV* by the future value interest factor (*FVF*) for the specified interest rate and time period. Because the interest rate is 5 percent and the period is five years, the equation for conversion of a present value into a future value is

$$FV = PV \times FVF \text{ (5\%, five years)}$$
$$= \$1,000 \times 1.276282$$
$$= \$1,276.28$$

The *FVF* of 1.276282 is the solution to the future value of a lump sum equation in Exhibit 14-2, assuming $1 is invested at 5 percent for five years. It reveals that a dollar invested today at 5 percent for five years will grow (compound) to $1.276282 at the end of five years (assuming annual compounding). Therefore, $1,000 invested today will grow to $1,276.28 in five years. The calculator keystrokes required to solve this problem are

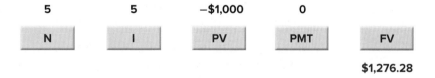

5	5	−$1,000	0	
N	I	PV	PMT	FV

$1,276.28

The $1,000 lump sum investment is entered as a negative number, consistent with its being an outflow (i.e., cash paid) from the perspective of the investor. Solving using a calculator requires the user to enter *N, I, PV,* and *PMT* (the "knowns"); pressing the *FV* key (the "unknown") produces the $1,276.28 solution. If the interest rate is 10 percent, then $1,000 invested today will grow to $1,610.51 in five years. The conversion equation and calculator keystrokes are

$$FV = PV \times FVF \text{ (10\%, five years)}$$
$$= \$1,000 \times 1.610510$$
$$= \$1,610.51$$

5	10	−$1,000	0	
N	I	PV	PMT	FV

$1,610.51

Note that if any four of the five required inputs are known, the fifth can be determined. For example, assume the future value of $1,610.51 is known and that I, the annual interest rate, is unknown. Entering $1,610.51 in the *FV* register (along with $N = 5$, $PV = -\$1,000$, and $PMT = 0$) and pressing the I key will produce a solution of 10 percent.

✓ **Concept Check**

14.1 You have agreed to purchase a small piece of real estate today for $15,000. You expect to hold the property for eight years and then sell it. You expect the property to increase in value 15 percent per year, compounded annually. For how much should you be able to sell the property in eight years?

A Note of Caution. It is important when learning TVM techniques that students be able to match their answers to those provided in the text or in other materials. Therefore, throughout this chapter we will generally provide answers that include both dollars and cents in order to avoid rounding errors that may be confusing. In practice, however, professionals rarely display digits to the right of the decimal. In fact, industry professionals often round TVM calculations to the nearest one hundred dollar amount or even to the nearest one thousand dollar amount. Why? Because although TVM calculations are mathematically precise, the outcomes are based on a set of assumptions that may not be accurate. Displaying results with digits to the right of the decimal point may convey a sense of accuracy that does not exist in many cases.

The Power of Compounding. To illustrate the power of compounding, we examine more closely the rate of growth in the above $1,000 investment. Exhibit 14-4 shows the amounts to which the lump sum investment will grow if interest is compounded (paid) annually and the investor does not withdraw any of the $1,000 initial investment or any of the interest earnings. With annual compounding, the value of the investment remains unchanged throughout the year. At the end of the year, the accumulated investment amount increases by the interest earned during the first year.

If the investor withdraws the investment after one year, the accumulated investment value will be $1,100, which represents the initial $1,000 investment plus $100 of interest

Exhibit 14-4 The Power of Compounding

	$1,000 Investment at 10 percent with Annual Compounding		
End of Year	Investment Value	Total Interest Earned	Average Annual Interest Earned
1	$1,100	$100	$100
5	1,611	611	122
10	2,594	1,594	159
20	6,727	5,727	286
30	17,449	16,449	548

income. If the investment is withdrawn after five years, the accumulated investment value will be $1,611, which is equal to the $1,000 investment plus $611 in interest income. By the end of year 30, the value of the investment will have grown to $17,449. Note that the average amount of interest earned increases as the length of time increases. This is because interest is being earned on an increasingly larger investment. Thus, the greater the length of time an investment is allowed to compound, the greater the power of compounding! The growth in the initial $1,000 investment with annual compounding at 10 percent is displayed graphically in Exhibit 14-5. Note that the slope of the curve increases as the length of the investment holding period increases.

This example assumes annual compounding of interest. However, banks and other borrowers often pay interest more frequently, such as monthly or even daily. Exhibit 14-6 compares accumulated investment values for the $1,000 investment, assuming monthly and daily compounding to accumulated values assuming annual compounding. For a five-year investment, a $1,000 investment will accumulate to $1,645 with monthly compounding compared with $1,611 with annual compounding. With daily compounding of interest, the investment value will grow to $1,649 in five years. Note that the effects of more frequent compounding are more pronounced as the investment time horizon increases. Unless otherwise specified, we will assume that the frequency of compounding equals the frequency

Exhibit 14-5 Power of Compounding

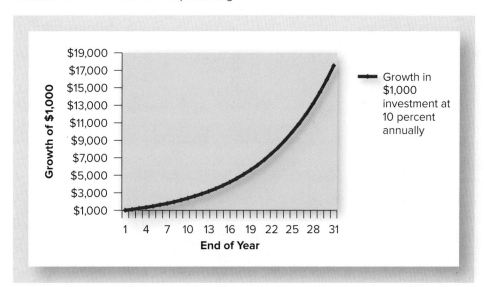

Exhibit 14-6 Accumulated Future Value of an Initial $1,000 Lump Sum Investment at 10 percent with Varying Compounding Periods

End of Year	Annual Compounding	Monthly Compounding	Daily Compounding
1	$1,100	$1,105	$1,105
5	1,611	1,645	1,649
10	2,594	2,707	2,718
20	6,727	7,328	7,387
30	17,449	19,837	20,077

with which the payments are made or received. Thus, for example, if cash flows are received annually, we will assume annual compounding.

✓ Concept Check

14.2 Assume $1,000 is invested for 10 years. The annual interest rate is 10 percent, but the interest will be compounded quarterly. What is *N*? What is the periodic (i.e., quarterly) interest rate? What will be the accumulated *FV* in 10 years?

Future Value of Annuity. Now assume the investor plans to deposit $1,000 at the end of *each* year in a 5 percent annually compounded account and wants to know how much these five deposits will be worth at the end of five years. As shown in panel B of Exhibit 14-3, solving this problem involves finding the future value of the annuity. Future value factors for annuities (FVF_A) are used to convert the $1,000 annuity (i.e., cash flows occurring at the end of each period) into future values. The conversion equation is

$$FV_A = \text{Annuity} \times FVF_A \ (5\%, \text{five years})$$
$$= \$1,000 \times 5.525631$$
$$= \$5,525.63$$

The FVF_A of 5.525631 is the solution to the future value of an annuity equation in Exhibit 14-2 at 5 percent for five years. It reveals that $1 invested at the end of each year for five years at 5 percent will compound to $5.52563 at the end of five years. Thus, $1,000 invested each year for five years will grow to $5,525.63. The calculator keystrokes are

5	5	0	−$1,000	
N	I	PV	PMT	FV

$5,525.63

Future value is again the unknown. Note that when finding the future value of a series of level payments (deposits), the level deposit amount is entered as a negative number in the *PMT* register and the *PV* register contains a zero amount (or is empty). This tells the calculator that the amount will be deposited *every* year for *N* years. Recall that when finding the future value of a lump sum, the one-time deposit is entered in the *PV* register—the *PMT* register contains a zero or is empty.

Finally, assume the investor is instead considering making monthly deposits of $83.33 ($1,000 ÷ 12) for five years. *N* in this case is 60 (5 × 12) and *I*, the monthly interest rate, is equal to 0.41667 percent (5 percent/12). The conversion equation is

$$FV_A = \text{Annuity} \times FVF_A \ (5\%/12, \ 60 \text{ months})$$
$$= \$83,33 \times 68.006083$$
$$= \$5,666.95$$

The corresponding keystrokes are

60	5 ÷ 12	0	−$83.33	
N	I	PV	PMT	FV

$5,666.95

In this example, the investor will deposit a total of $1,000 per year regardless of whether payments are made monthly or annually. However, if payments of $83.33 are made monthly, the investor will accumulate $5,666.95 at the end of five years compared with $5,525.63 with annual deposits. Why is there a $141.32 difference in future values if total deposits over the five-year period are the same with both strategies? Notice that the initial deposit occurs at the end of month 1 in the monthly compounding scenario, whereas it occurs at the end of *year* 1 in the annual case. Thus, the monthly deposits begin to accumulate interest 11 months earlier than the annual case.

✓ **Concept Check**

14.3   You purchase a parcel of land today for $50,000. For how much will you have to sell the property in 15 years to earn a 10 percent annual return on both your initial $50,000 outlay and the expected annual payment of $1,000 for property taxes and insurance? Assume these funds could be invested at comparable risk to earn a 10 percent annual return.

Future Value of an Annuity Due.   What if the investor plans to deposit $1,000 at the *beginning* of each year for five years? These situations are referred to as "future value of an annuity due" problems. Because the initial and subsequent $1,000 annual payments are shifted forward a year, the total amount of interest earned over the five-year period will increase. Financial calculators readily permit the user to specify that cash flows will be invested or received at the beginning of each period ("begin mode") instead of the end ("end mode"). The keystrokes otherwise remain the same. The future value of this annuity due is $5,801.91, or $276.28 greater than the $5,525.63 accumulated value assuming year-end deposits. What is the relationship between the standard future value result and the annuity due result? Note that the $5,801.91 annuity due solution can be obtained by multiplying the solution to the regular annuity problem by 1 plus the periodic interest rate [i.e., $5,801.91 = $5,525.63 × (1 + 0.05)].

✓ **Concept Check**

14.4   Assume the owner of a 10-unit apartment building will deposit $2,000 per year, or $200 per unit, in an interest-bearing reserve account. These funds will be used to refurbish the apartments at the end of five years. If the deposits are made at the beginning of each year and will earn 5 percent interest, compounded annually, what will be the accumulated value of the reserve account at the end of five years?

Discounting Operations

The third and fourth basic TVM operations are used to convert future cash flow amounts into present values. The concept underlying these operations is extremely important for investment analysis because converting future dollar amounts into present values is the cornerstone of property valuation.

Present Value of a Lump Sum.   This operation is used to calculate the present value of future lump sum (i.e., one-time) receipts. Consequently, it is useful for discounting future cash flows back to the present.

Assume the investor has been offered an investment opportunity that is expected to provide a $1,276.28 cash inflow at the end of five years, as shown in panel A of

Exhibit 14-7 Timeline Demonstration for Discounting Problems

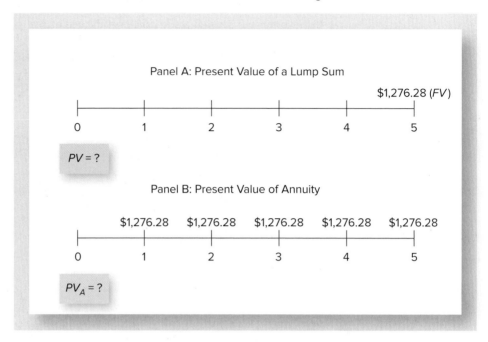

Exhibit 14-7. Assume also that the investor is able to earn 5 percent, compounded annually, on similar investments. More specifically, the 5 percent discount rate can be thought of as an **opportunity cost**—that is, the return the investor is forgoing on an alternative investment of equal risk in order to invest in the current opportunity.

How much can the investor pay today for this $1,276.28 future lump sum receipt and earn a 5 percent return on the investment? This problem calls for the conversion of a future lump sum receipt into a present value. The conversion equation is

$$PV = FV \times PVF \ (5\%, \text{five years})$$
$$= \$1,276.28 \times 0.783526$$
$$= \$1,000.00$$

The investor is willing to pay up to $1,000 today for the right to receive $1,276.28 in five years if he or she can earn a 5 percent annual return on similar investments. The corresponding calculator keystrokes are

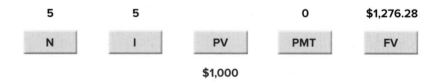

Your calculator should produce a result of −$1,000 with these inputs. Present values are displayed by the calculator as negative amounts (if the future value is entered as a positive amount) because calculators require a matching of inflows (+) with outflows (−) to perform TVM calculations.

Another interpretation of this result is that the investor is exactly indifferent between having $1,000 today and having (owning) the right to receive $1,276.28 five years from today. How can this be? Why doesn't the investor prefer the larger amount?

14.5   You are considering the purchase of some raw land. If the property is expected to be worth $50,000 in 15 years, what is the present value of this investment? Assume there will be no intermittent cash inflows or outflows and that the investor expects to earn a 10 percent annual return on such investments.

Present Value as a Point of Indifference.   To understand why investors are indifferent between having $1,000 today and having the right to receive $1,276.28 five years from today, recall the future value of a lump sum problem depicted in panel A of Exhibit 14-3. If they invest a lump sum of $1,000 at 5 percent they will accumulate $1,276.28 at the end of five years. Thus, investors can either (1) purchase today, for $1,000, the right to receive $1,276.28 at the end of five years or (2) invest the $1,000 elsewhere at 5 percent. The second option will also yield $1,276.28 in five years; thus, investors have a "take it or leave it" attitude toward the first option because they can replicate the $1,276.28 payoff in five years on their own by simply investing the $1,000 at 5 percent. The present value of the $1,000 is the only current value that makes investors indifferent between the two options, assuming a 5 percent required annual rate of return.

What if investors could purchase the right to receive $1,276.28 in five years for $900 today? Would they be happy to undertake this investment? Given that we know they are indifferent to the investment opportunity if the asking price is $1,000, clearly investors would be happy to invest at a price of $900. Why? If they were to invest the $900 at 5 percent annually, they would accumulate $1,148.65 at the end of five years, which is less than the promised payoff of $1,276.28. Because they cannot replicate the $1,276.28 payoff in year 5 by investing $900 in the alternative investment, they would be happy to pay $900 today for this investment opportunity. In fact, by paying $900 today for an investment worth $1,000 to them, investors' current wealth would increase by $100.

Why would investors not be willing to pay more than $1,000—say, $1,100—for the right to receive $1,276.28 in five years? Because if they were to invest the $1,100 at 5 percent, they would accumulate $1,403.91 by the end of five years. That is, they could do better with an alternative investment. Investors should reject this investment opportunity at any price greater than $1,000 because they could more than replicate the $1,276.28 payoff on their own.

The first discounting operation can be used to find the present value of multiple lump sums. For example, in the above problem, there may have been a lump sum of $2,000 at the end of year 7 in addition to the $1,276.28 at the end of year 5. The value of this additional lump sum is $1,421.36 and was found by entering $2,000 as *FV,* 7 as *N,* 5 as the interest rate, and then solving for *PV.* The result of this operation is added to the previous result (i.e., $1,000) to obtain a total value of $2,421.36 for the investment opportunity. Once individual future cash flow amounts are discounted (or "brought back") to time zero, they may be added or subtracted to determine the total present value of the investment package.

14.6   Assume the owner of an apartment complex follows a strict schedule for replacing carpeting. She currently projects she will spend $10,000 at the end of three years and $12,000 at the end of six years to replace the carpeting in all units. What is the total present value of these expected expenditures assuming a 7 percent annual rate of return?

Present Value of Annuity.   Now suppose investors are confronted with an opportunity to receive $1,276.28 at the end of *every* year for five years, as shown in Exhibit 14-7, panel B. Investors requiring a 5 percent return need to know the maximum amount they could pay for this annuity and still earn their required 5 percent return. Two options are available for converting the annuity into a present value. One is to find the present value of five separate lump sum amounts, one for each year, then sum the results. The less time-consuming option is to calculate the present value of an annuity (PV_A). The conversion equation and calculator keystrokes for this alternative operation are

$$PV_A = \text{Annuity} \times PVF_A \ (5\%, \text{five years})$$
$$= \$1,276.28 \times 4.329477$$
$$= \$5,525.62$$

5	5	$1,276.28		0
N	I	PV	PMT	FV

$5,525.62

Note that because the cash flows will be received *every* year over the five-year period, the annuity amount is entered into the *PMT* register. There is no lump sum (*FV*) amount.

What if the payments are to be received at the *beginning* of each year? The present value of this annuity due is $5,801.90 and is calculated by using your calculator's "begin mode" or by multiplying the present value of the regular annuity by an additional year's worth of interest [i.e., $5,801.90 = $5,525.62 × (1 + 0.05)].

✓ **Concept Check**

14.7   You have just purchased 100 shares of stock in a publicly traded real estate company that invests in apartment complexes throughout the United States. The company is expected to pay quarterly dividends of $1.50 per share. If you expect the stock will be worth $75 per share at the end of the five years, what is the value of the stock to you today if your required rate of return on an annual basis is 14 percent?

A Commercial Property Example.   The expected future cash flows from direct investments in commercial properties typically come from two sources:

1. Rental operations.
2. Eventual sale of the property.

Both cash flow components must generally be considered when calculating present value.

Consider a small warehouse building that is leased to a high-quality tenant on a long-term basis. The property is expected to produce $10,000 in net income from rental operations each year for five years. The expected sale of the property at the end of the fifth year will generate an additional (lump sum) net cash flow of $100,000. Assume the investor requires a 10 percent annual return on investments of similar risk. The equation to convert these uncertain future cash flows into a present value is

$$PV = \text{Annuity} \times PVF_A \ (10\%, \text{five years}) + FV \times PVF \ (10\%, \text{five years})$$
$$= (\$10,000 \times 3.790787) + (\$100,000 \times 0.620921)$$
$$= \$37,908 + \$62,092$$
$$= \$100,000$$

The first term on the right-hand side of the conversion equation represents the valuation of the annual net rental income (i.e., the annuity), while the second term represents the valuation of the future lump sum sale proceeds. The total present value of the cash flow components can also be determined with the following keystrokes:

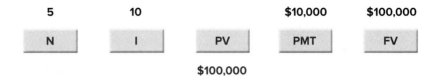

Note that the $10,000 annual annuity is entered into the *PMT* register and the lump sum sale proceeds are entered in the *FV* register. Also note that 62 percent of the total $100,000 present value is contributed by the expected cash flow from the sale of the property in five years. With longer expected holding periods, this percentage generally decreases. However, expected future property values are an extremely important determinant of current property values.

> ### Concept Check
>
> **14.8**   What is the maximum price you should pay today for the right to receive $10,000 per year for 20 years from a piece of rental real estate if the series of rental payments is discounted at a 10 percent annual rate? Assume the property will be worth $50,000 at the end of the 20-year period.

Uneven Cash Flows.   Typically, the periodic cash flows from owning and operating commercial real estate assets are not expected to be constant over time. Consider the following investment opportunity in a small four-unit apartment building named Lee Vista. The total net cash flow from owning and operating Lee Vista is estimated to be $48,000 in year 1, growing to $54,025 in year 5. The estimated selling price in year 5 is $560,000. These uncertain future cash flows must be converted into a lump sum present value. One approach to solving this problem is to find the present value of the separate annual cash flow amounts, then sum the results. This approach is depicted in Exhibit 14-8. The total present value of the potential investment is $464,480, assuming a 14 percent required annual return. The calculator keystrokes that would be used to solve for the present value of the cash flow in, say, year 3, which equals $34,372, are

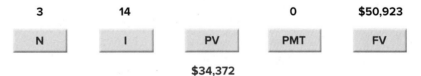

An alternative, and usually preferred, approach to solving present value problems when the periodic future cash flows are uneven is to use the cash flow ("CF $_j$") key available on most financial calculators. In this example, 0 would be entered as CF_0, 48,000 would be entered as CF_1, 49,440 as CF_2, 50,923 as CF_3, 52,451 as CF_4, and 614,025 as CF_5. The investor would then solve for present value by pressing the appropriate key (which, for example, is the shift "NPV" key on the Hewlett-Packard 10BII). The calculations that appear in Exhibit 14-8 can also be performed with Microsoft's Excel, as is demonstrated in the Appendix.

Two final points concerning discounting should be stressed. First, the present value of future cash flows is *inversely* related to the magnitude of the interest rate used

Exhibit 14-8 Present Value of Series of Uneven Cash Flows:
Lee Vista Apartments

Year	Annual CF	CF from Sale	Total CF	PVF @ 14%	Present Value
1	$48,000		$ 48,000	0.877193	$ 42,105
2	49,440		49,440	0.769468	38,042
3	50,923		50,923	0.674972	34,372
4	52,451		52,451	0.592080	31,055
5	54,025	$560,000	614,025	0.519369	318,905
				Total present value =	$464,480

Exhibit 14-9 *PV* of Future $1,000 Lump Sum Payment

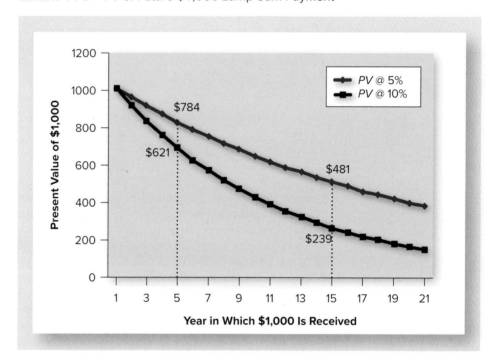

for discounting. This concept is reinforced by results displayed in Exhibit 14-9, which
show the present values of a lump sum receipt of $1,000 for periods that extend from 1
to 20 years and for two discount rates, 5 percent and 10 percent. When the discount rate
is 5 percent, the present value of the right to receive $1,000 in five years is $784.
However, if the interest rate (discount rate) increases to 10 percent, this present value
declines to $621, a reduction of $163.

If an investment is expected to produce a fixed set of cash flows, the only way the
expected return can change is if the market price (present value) on the investment changes.
For example, if a higher return is required by the investor, perhaps because of an increase
in perceived risk, the present value will decline. This inverse relation between discount
rates and present values explains, for example, why mortgage loan amounts move inversely
to changes in market interest rates. That is, the higher the interest rate, the smaller the mortgage the borrower can obtain, given the same monthly payments. Conversely, with lower
interest rates, borrowers can obtain larger mortgage loans with the same monthly
payments.

A second important concept is also revealed by examination of Exhibit 14-9. The present value of long-term cash flows is more sensitive to changes in discount rates than securities with shorter-term cash flows. Recall that the present value of $1,000 to be received in five years is $163 lower when a discount rate of 10 percent is used instead of 5 percent. Now consider the present values of $1,000 to be received in 15 years. When the discount rate is 5 percent, the present value equals $481, but if the discount rate increases to 10 percent, the present value falls to $239, a $242 decline (versus a $163 decline in year 5). The conclusion, of course, is that the present value of more distant cash flows is more sensitive to discount rate changes than nearer-term cash flows.

Yields and Internal Rates of Return

To this point we have explored (1) how to determine future values when the amounts to be invested are known (i.e., compounding) and (2) how to determine present values when the future values are known or assumed (i.e., discounting). These TVM concepts can also be used to calculate rates of return on real estate investments—an extremely important extension.

Consider the future value of a lump sum problem examined earlier in which we determined that if $1,000 is invested today for five years in an account that pays 5 percent interest, compounded annually, the balance of the account at the end of five years will be $1,276.28. Hence, making this investment is equivalent to earning a rate of return of 5 percent. This rate of return is usually referred to as the **investment yield** or the **internal rate of return (IRR).**

Recall also the present value of an annuity problem in which investors were presented with an opportunity to receive $1,276.28 at the end of every year for five years. If investors believe they should earn a 5 percent return on such investments, the present value of the future cash flows is $5,525.62. What yield or *IRR* will investors earn if they purchase this investment opportunity for $5,525.62? It should be clear that investors will earn a 5 percent internal rate of return on their $5,525.62 investment. The calculator keystrokes are

5.00%

If the periodic cash flows from owning and renting real estate assets are not expected to be constant over time, the above calculator solution procedure will not work. Instead, investors must use a spreadsheet program or use the cash flow ("CF $_j$") key on their financial calculators. For example, assume the Lee Vista investment opportunity depicted in Exhibit 14-8 is purchased by the investor for $464,480. Given the expected annual cash flows, what is the internal rate of return on this investment? To solve this problem, −464,480 would be entered as CF_0, 48,000 would be entered as CF_1, 49,440 as CF_2, 50,923 as CF_3, 52,451 as CF_4, and 614,025 as CF_5. The investor would then solve for the *IRR* by pushing the appropriate key (which is the "shift IRR/YR" key on a Hewlett-Packard 10BII). This would return a solution of 14 percent.

The internal rate of return is an indispensable tool widely used in real estate investment and finance. It captures the return on an investment, expressed as a compound rate of interest, over the entire investment holding period. The calculated (or "going-in") *IRR* can be compared to the investor's required *IRR* on similar projects of equivalent risk. If the going-in *IRR* exceeds the investor's required rate of return, the investment should be undertaken. If the going-in *IRR* is less than the investor's required rate of return, the investment should be forgone and other opportunities pursued.[1]

A Final Note on Terminology.   Throughout the book, we will use the terms *investment yield* and *internal rate of return* interchangeably. If the calculation is based on expected cash flows, we will use the terms *expected investment yield* or *going-in IRR* to differentiate the results from historical (i.e., realized) yields and *IRR*s. In the real estate appraisal business, the *IRR* is often referred to as the "total yield." This convention reflects the fact that income-producing properties generally provide a "current yield" in the form of current income relative to the required investment and an "appreciation yield" that results from appreciation in the market value of the asset. By referring to the return as a total yield, the investor is making it clear that the measured return includes current and future income and expected price appreciation.

✓ Concept Check

14.9   Assume a $400,000 investment in a small shopping center is expected to produce the following annual cash flows over a five-year holding period: CF_1, 37,000; CF_2, 38,100; CF_3, 39,253; CF_4, 40,431; and CF_5, 504,000. What is the going-in *IRR* on this investment?

Value and Risk

If there were no risk associated with costs and benefits, the determination of the required rate of return and investment valuations would be quite simple. Any accountant, financial analyst, or other person with training in basic present value analysis could find the correct answers to real estate investment questions. Sometimes real estate investment decisions do approach certainty. For example, suppose you are contemplating investing in a new state-of-the-art warehouse, fully occupied through a long-term lease by a high-quality company such as Microsoft. Moreover, Microsoft is responsible for paying all of the property's expenses. This type of lease is referred to as a "net" lease.[2] In this example, the net rental revenue to the owner is relatively certain, much like the income from a high-quality bond. If the cost of acquisition also is certain, then a simple comparison of the present value of the future cash flows to the cost of the investment is easily done and is a reliable guide to decisions.

But an investment with relatively certain cash flows is a rarity in real estate and in most other realms of business investment. As suggested in Exhibit 14-10, there is a wide spectrum of cash flow risk (uncertainty) in the investment world, ranging from very high quality bonds (e.g., U.S. Treasury bonds or private bonds rated AAA by a credit rating agency) to start-up technology stocks with extreme uncertainty. Real estate investments also present a range of risk possibilities, though perhaps not quite as broad as the entire investment spectrum. The lowest risk level in real estate may be investment in properties like the warehouse example, involving a financially strong tenant committed to a long-term net lease.

In no case is the uncertainty of future income greater than with investments in "raw" land held for development. To begin, the value of the land usually is dependent on future urban growth to create market potential that presently does not exist. But this risk historically has been amplified by the uncertainty of land use regulation. If, for example, the

---

1. The *IRR* has some inherent assumptions that make its use as an investment criterion problematic in some situations. These issues are discussed in Chapter 19.
2. Leases are discussed in more detail in later chapters (see, for example, Chapters 21 and 22).

Exhibit 14-10   The Spectrum of Risk in Investments

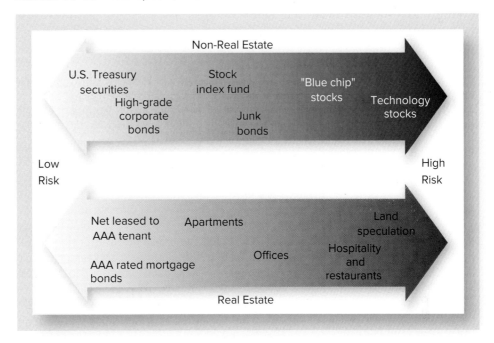

land is included within a designated "urban service boundary," the permits for development of the land are likely to be expedited by the local planning authority, and demand for the land will be enhanced.[3] If, on the other hand, the land is excluded from the urban service boundary, obtaining permits for development could be difficult or impossible, and the market potential would be diverted elsewhere. If an investor "wins" this uncertain bet, the value of the land involved can increase many fold. But the risks can be severe and unforgiving.

Uncertainty of cash flows also varies across existing properties. Many investors believe that high-quality **industrial property** (e.g., warehouses with long-term leases) tend to have relatively reliable cash flows. Others point to **multifamily property** (e.g., apartments) located in established markets as having relatively steady cash flows since every individual or household must live somewhere. Toward the other extreme, office property markets have generally been more cyclical, creating volatility in occupancy and rental rate growth. Near the top of the spectrum in cash flow uncertainty may be **hospitality property.** Hotels, motels, and many types of restaurants have experienced great volatility. Further, even in a stable market these types of properties seem inherently vulnerable to competition from new entrants in the market.

It is clear from the TVM problems above that the present value of an investment opportunity is a function of:

1. The magnitude of the expected future cash flows.
2. The timing of the expected future cash flows.
3. The interest (discount) rate used to convert the expected future cash flows into present value.

To complete our discussion of basic TVM calculations, we need to give some more attention to the discount rate used to convert uncertain future cash flows into a present value.

---

3. An urban service boundary designates an area within which local government gives priority in establishing development infrastructure such as roads, sewers, and utilities.

Fundamentally, the discount rate can be thought of as the investor's required internal rate of return (*IRR*).

Determining Required Returns

Consider again the expected cash flows from investing in the Lee Vista apartment complex displayed in Exhibit 14-8. When discounted at 14 percent, these uncertain cash flows have a total present value of $464,480 (see Exhibit 14-11). However, when discounted at 12 percent the value increases to $500,264, which is a 7.7 percent increase. If the required *IRR* is 10 percent, present value increases 16.2 percent to $539,841. When discounted at 16 percent and 18 percent, the present value falls 7.0 percent and 13.3 percent, respectively, relative to the use of 14 percent as the required yield. Clearly, even small changes in the assumed rate of discount can significantly affect the estimated present value of the risky future cash flows and, therefore, the ultimate decision.

So from where do required *IRR*s/yields come? A good place to begin is to recall that the discount rate is meant to reflect the investor's opportunity cost of investing in the subject investment. That is, the appropriate discount rate is the total return the investor would likely earn on other investments of *similar risk*. As "other investments" are traded in the capital market (see Exhibit 1–6), it should be clear that discount rates come primarily from the capital market where investors buy and sell real estate, stocks, bonds, and other assets.

But how, exactly, do investors determine the specific discount rate to use in a TVM calculation? To address this question, consider the following representation of an investor's required return:

$$E\ (IRR_j) = R_f + RP_j$$

where

- $E(IRR_j)$ is the expected or required *IRR* on the *j*th investment
- R_f is the current return available on a risk-free U.S. Treasury security of comparable maturity
- RP_j is the required risk premium

As an example, assume potential investors in downtown Chicago office buildings require an 11 percent going-in *IRR* on their expected 10-year investments. Also assume that U.S. Treasury bonds with remaining maturities of 10 years are priced to yield a 5 percent *IRR* to investors. The 11 percent expected yield on the office building is therefore composed of a 5 percent compensation for time, as measured by the 5 percent risk-free Treasury bond rate, and a 6 percent risk premium. Recall that risk is the possibility that actual returns will vary from what was expected at acquisition. Thus, the 6 percent risk premium reflects

Exhibit 14-11 The Effect of Discount Rates on Present Values

Year	Annual CF	Cash Flow from Resale	Total Cash Flow	PVF @ 10%	PVF @ 12%	PVF @ 14%	PVF @ 16%	PVF @ 18%
1	$48,000		$ 48,000	$ 43,636	$ 42,857	$ 42,105	$ 41,379	$ 40,678
2	49,440		49,440	40,860	39,413	38,042	36,742	35,507
3	50,923		50,923	38,259	36,246	34,372	32,624	30,993
4	52,451		52,451	35,825	33,334	31,055	28,968	27,054
5	54,025	$560,000	614,025	381,261	348,414	318,905	292,345	269,396
Total present value =				$539,841	$500,264	$464,480	$432,059	$402,628
% Change in *PV* from 14%				16.2%	7.7%		−7.0%	−13.3%

the extent to which investors in Chicago office buildings believe actual returns are likely to vary from expectations.

Investors struggling to determine their required investment yields on a potential investment frequently find themselves asking the following question: "What rate of return are other investors requiring on similar investments?" Although attitudes toward risk—and therefore required risk premiums—vary across investors, the ability to abstract this information from other investors is very useful in determining the investor's required risk premium and *IRR.*

The Real Estate Research Corporation (RERC: www.rerc.com) regularly surveys the real estate return expectations (on all cash investments) of a sample of institutional investors and managers. Published quarterly in the *Real Estate Report,* this survey provides insights into the required returns and risk adjustments used by institutional investors when making real estate acquisitions. As such, this and other similar surveys (both formal and informal) provide potentially valuable information to individual investors.

Portions of tables from various issues of the *Real Estate Report* are reproduced in Exhibit 14-12. The mean required return for first quarter 2015 investments in all property types was 7.9 percent. The spread over 10-year U.S. Treasury securities was 5.9 percentage points, or 590 basis points (one basis point equals 0.01 percent). Note that the required yield spread over 10-year Treasuries in the first quarter of 2007 was the lowest in the years sampled. Spreads over Treasuries during this period have varied from 3.7 percentage points in 2007 to a high of 7.3 percentage points in the first quarter of 2003.

Although useful in helping investors quantify required risk premiums and returns, it is important to understand that the RERC required yields reported above represent broad averages across many properties and local markets. Thus, they should not be directly applied to specific properties without adjustments for the physical and lease characteristics of the subject property and the specific market in which the subject property is located.

It is also important to emphasize that the going-in *IRR*s reported by RERC are for existing properties that are large (values in excess of $10 million), relatively new, located in major metropolitan areas, and fully or substantially leased. Such properties, often referred to as **investment-grade properties,** are among the lowest risk real estate investments available. Yet as can be seen in Exhibit 14-12, even investment-grade properties still require substantial risk premiums relative to risk-free Treasury securities. Generally, properties that are less than investment grade are even more risky because of their smaller size, advanced age, location in a small or transient market, lack of tenants or even improvements, or some combination of these and other shortcomings. In the end, however, determination of the required *IRR* is a subjective process that relies heavily on the experience and expertise of the investor.[4]

Exhibit 14-12   Required Returns on Investment-Grade Properties versus Comparable Treasury Securities, 1995–2011

	1Q99	1Q01	1Q03	1Q05	1Q07	1Q09	1Q11	1Q13	1Q15
Required real estate return	11.4%	11.5%	11.2%	9.6%	8.4%	10.1%	8.9%	8.6%	7.9%
Return on 10-year Treasuries	5.0	5.1	3.9	4.3	4.7	3.4	3.5	1.9	2.0
Spread over Treasuries	6.4	6.4	7.3	5.3	3.7	6.7	5.4	6.7	5.9

Source: Data from The *Real Estate Report,* various issues, Real Estate Research Corporation, Chicago

4. The subjectivity of the discount rate specification is perceived by some to be a weakness of real estate TVM valuation techniques. At a minimum, it has frequently left investors asking whether more objective quantitative models for specifying the discount rate are available. Formal asset pricing models, developed initially for the valuation of stocks, are able to quantify required risk premiums in a more objective fashion. Unfortunately, these techniques are difficult, if not impossible, to apply to the valuation of individual real estate properties.

Comparing Investment Values to Acquisition Costs

We have emphasized that real estate decision making fundamentally involves comparing the costs of various decisions, including the decision to purchase a property, to the benefits the decision is expected to produce. In this chapter, we show that benefits (cash flows) to be received in the future must be discounted (converted) into present values in order to make rational, wealth-enhancing investment decisions. These conversions of future cash flows into present values are simply direct applications of time-value-of-money concepts.

Take the case of a real estate investor who wants to purchase a small apartment building across the street from the local university to add to her portfolio at year-end 2015. Numerous potential investments have been screened and two four-unit properties have been identified as potentially worthy of acquisition. The first is Lee Vista, the property discussed earlier in the chapter. The second investment opportunity is known as Colony Park. The investor estimates the expected cash flows from annual operations for each property during the next five years. She also estimates the net proceeds from the sale of each complex at the end of the fifth year (2020). Exhibit 14-13 displays these cash flow estimates.

The investor estimates that her required *IRR* on investments of this type is 14 percent. The annual present value conversions are found in Exhibit 14-14. The present value of the Lee Vista investment opportunity is $464,480, while the present value of the Colony Park alternative is $510,875. Given its *PV* of $510,875, Colony Park may appear to be a superior

Exhibit 14-13 Cash Flows from Two Alternative Apartment Investment Opportunities

	Lee Vista		Colony Park	
Year-End	Estimated Cash Flows from Operations	Estimated Sale Proceeds	Estimated Cash Flows from Operations	Estimated Sale Proceeds
2016	$48,000		$56,000	
2017	49,440		57,400	
2018	50,923		58,835	
2019	52,451		60,306	
2020	54,025	$560,000	61,814	$597,000

Exhibit 14-14 Present Value Calculations for Alternative Apartment Investment Opportunities

		Lee Vista		Colony Park	
Year	PVF @ 14%	Total Cash Flows	Present Value	Total Cash Flows	Present Value
2016	0.877193	$ 48,000	$ 42,105	$ 56,000	$ 49,123
2017	0.769468	49,440	38,042	57,400	44,167
2018	0.674972	50,923	34,372	58,835	39,712
2019	0.592080	52,451	31,055	60,306	35,706
2020	0.519369	614,025	318,905	658,814	342,167
Total present value =			$464,480		$510,875

investment because of its higher present value. However, one important consideration has been omitted—the acquisition price of each property.

The **net present value** (**NPV**) of an investment alternative is defined as the difference between the present value of the cash inflows (PV_{in}) and the present value of the cash outflows (PV_{out}). In symbols,

$$NPV = PV_{in} - PV_{out}$$

If, for example, the year-end 2015 acquisition prices are $425,000 for Lee Vista and $540,000 for Colony Park, the *NPVs* of the two opportunities are

$$NPV \text{ (Lee Vista)} = \$464,480 - \$425,000 = \$39,480$$
$$NPV \text{ (Colony Park)} = \$510,875 - \$540,000 = -\$29,125$$

The *NPV* simply compares the costs (PV_{out}) with the benefits (PV_{in}) of investment opportunities. This measure is interpreted using the following very simple, but very important, decision rule: If the *NPV* is greater than zero, the property should be purchased, assuming the investor has adequate resources, because it increases the investor's wealth. If the calculated *NPV* is negative, the investment should be rejected. If the *NPV* equals zero, the investor is indifferent. A negative *NPV* means the investor expects to earn an *IRR* less than her required *IRR* for such an investment.

✓ Concept Check

14.10   Does a zero NPV imply that the investor's expected yield/IRR is equal to zero?

Now that the asking price of each has been incorporated into the analysis, a different picture emerges concerning the investor's two alternatives. Although the Colony Park cash flows from annual operations and from the sale of the property have a higher present value, the cost of the property is sufficiently high to make the *NPV* negative. Lee Vista is the only acceptable investment because of its positive *NPV*. The going-in *IRRs* for Lee Vista and Colony Park are 16.5 percent and 12.5 percent, respectively. Given a required yield of 14 percent, Lee Vista would be accepted, while Colony Park would be rejected. Note also that use of *IRR* as the decision-making criterion produces the same accept/reject decision as *NPV*.

Summary

Commercial real estate developers, investors, appraisers, and managers are continually making decisions about committing funds to real estate. These decisions typically involve significant upfront cash investments in exchange for uncertain future benefits. The costs and benefits frequently, although not always, assume the form of cash flows (i.e., money) to the investor/owner. The primary purpose of this chapter is to examine how the timing and riskiness of cash inflows and outflows affect the value of real estate assets and, thus, the decision-making process.

There are four fundamental time-value-of-money (TVM) calculations: (1) finding the future value of a current lump sum investment, (2) finding the future value of a series of level cash flows, (3) finding the present value of a future lump sum cash flow, and

(4) finding the present value of a series of future cash flows. This chapter introduces these basic TVM calculations and demonstrates how they are solved using handheld calculators (spreadsheet solutions using Excel are demonstrated in an Appendix).

TVM concepts are the cornerstone of real estate valuation techniques. The prices at which real estate assets and other securities trade are based on the discounted present value of each asset's future cash flows. This does not mean that all market participants make explicit present value calculations before they buy or sell an asset. Indeed, some investors have no knowledge of TVM calculations. But many investors, traders, and portfolio managers do have a good understanding of TVM and base their real estate decisions (e.g., buy, sell, and renovate) on a comparison of the costs and the present value of the asset's expected future cash flows when discounted at the appropriate (equivalent risk) opportunity cost.

Solving TVM problems can involve a significant amount of "number crunching." Although these quantitative valuation tools are of fundamental importance, decision makers should not put total reliance on the quantitative information—the "numbers"—provided by TVM calculations. Many real estate decisions involve costs and benefits that are difficult to quantify in terms of monetary cash flows. In such situations, the owner (or potential owner) must collect and rely upon, in whole or in part, qualitative information. This qualitative information, in the form of appraiser, lender, and investor interpretations and judgments, plays a significant role in real estate decision making. Therefore, quantitative information used in value estimation should be viewed in many situations as merely one important input into the real estate decision-making process. Judgment and interpretations also are important inputs.

Key Terms

Compounding 387	Investment-grade properties 403	Ordinary annuity 387
Discounting 387	Investment yield 399	Present value 387
Future value 387	Lump sum 387	Risk 385
Hospitality property 401	Multifamily property 401	Time value of money (TVM) 385
Industrial property 401	Net present value 405	
Internal rate of return 399	Opportunity cost 394	

Test Problems

Answer the following multiple-choice questions:

1. How much will a $50 deposit made today be worth in 20 years if interest is compounded annually at a rate of 10 percent?
   a. $150.00.
   b. $286.37.
   c. $309.59.
   d. $336.37.
   e. $2,863.75.

2. How much would you pay today for the right to receive $80 at the end of 10 years if you can earn 15 percent interest on alternative investments of similar risk?
   a. $19.15.
   b. $19.77.
   c. $38.48.
   d. $38.82.
   e. $70.65.

3. How much would you pay today to receive $50 in one year and $60 in the second year if you can earn 15 percent interest on alternative investments of similar risk?
   a. $88.85.
   b. $89.41.

   c. $98.43.
   d. $107.91.
   e. $110.00.

4. What amount invested at the end of each year at 10 percent annually will grow to $10,000 at the end of five years?
   a. $1,489.07.
   b. $1,637.97.
   c. $1,723.57.
   d. $1,809.75.
   e. $2,000.00.

5. How much would you pay today for the right to receive nothing for the next 10 years and $300 a year for the following 10 years if you can earn 15 percent interest on alternative investments of similar risk?
   a. $372.17.
   b. $427.99.
   c. $546.25.
   d. $600.88.
   e. $1,505.63.

6. What is the present value of $500 received at the end of each of the next three years and $1,000 received at the end of the fourth year, assuming a required rate of return of 15 percent?
   a. $900.51.
   b. $1,035.59.
   c. $1,713.37.
   d. $1,784.36.
   e. $2,049.06.

7. If a landowner purchased a vacant lot six years ago for $25,000, assuming no income or holding costs during the interim period, what price would the landowner need to receive today to yield a 10 percent annual return on the land investment?
   a. $40,262.75.
   b. $41,132.72.
   c. $44,289.03.
   d. $64,843.56.

8. What is the present value of the following series of cash flows discounted at 12 percent: $40,000 now, $50,000 at the end of the first year; $0 at the end of the second year; $60,000 at the end of the third year; and $70,000 at the end of the fourth year?
   a. $165,857.
   b. $167,534.
   c. $168,555.
   d. $171,836.

9. Assume an investment is priced at $5,000 and has the following income stream:

Year	Cash Flow
1	$1,000
2	−2,000
3	3,000
4	3,000

   Would an investor with a required rate of return of 15 percent be wise to invest at a price of $5,000?
   a. No, because the investment has a net present value of −$1,139.15.
   b. No, because the investment has a net present value of −$1,954.91.
   c. Yes, because the investment has a net present value of $1,069.66.
   d. Yes, because the investment has a net present value of $1,954.91.
   e. An investor would be indifferent between purchasing and not purchasing the above investment at the stated price.

10. As the level of perceived risk increases,
   a. Values and expected returns increase.
   b. Values and expected returns decrease.
   c. Values increase and expected returns decrease.
   d. Values decrease and expected returns increase.
   e. Values decrease but expected returns are unaffected.

Study Questions

1. Dr. Bob Jackson owns a parcel of land that a local farmer has offered to rent from Dr. Bob for the next 10 years. The farmer has offered to pay $20,000 today or an annuity of $3,200 at the end of each of the next 10 years. Which payment method should Dr. Jackson accept if his required rate of return is 10 percent?

2. You are able to buy an investment today for $1,000 that gives you the right to receive $438 in each of the next three years. What is the internal rate of return on this investment?

3. Calculate the present value of the income stream given below assuming a discount rate of 8 percent. What happens to present value if the discount rate increases to 20 percent?

Year	Income
1	$3,000
2	4,000
3	6,000
4	1,000

4. Calculate the *IRR* and the *NPV* for the following two investment opportunities. Assume a 16 percent discount rate for the *NPV* calculations.

Project 1		Project 2	
Year	Cash Flow	Year	Cash Flow
0	−$10,000	0	−$10,000
1	1,000	1	1,000
2	2,000	2	12,000
3	12,000	3	1,800

5. How much would you pay today for an investment that provides $1,000 at the end of the first year if your required rate of return is 10 percent? Now compute how much you would pay at 8 percent and 12 percent rates of return.

6. Your grandmother gives you $10,000 to be invested in one of three opportunities: real estate, regular bonds, or zero coupon bonds. If you invest the entire $10,000 in one of these opportunities with the expected cash flows shown below, which investment offers the highest *NPV*? Assume for simplicity that an 11 percent discount rate is appropriate for all three investments.

	Cash Inflows				
Investment	Year 1	Year 2	Year 3	Year 4	Year 5
Real estate	$1,300	$1,300	$1,300	$1,300	$ 9,000
Bond	1,000	1,000	1,000	1,000	11,000
Zero coupon	0	0	0	0	18,000

7. If you purchase a parcel of land today for $25,000, and you expect it to appreciate 10 percent per year in value, how much will your land be worth 10 years from now assuming annual compounding?

8. If you deposit $1 at the end of each of the next 10 years and these deposits earn interest at 10 percent compounded annually, what will the series of deposits be worth at the end of the 10th year?

9. If you deposit $50 per month in a bank account at 10 percent annual interest (compounded monthly), how much will you have in your account at the end of the 12th year?

www.mhhe.com/lingarcher5e

10. If your parents purchased an endowment policy of $10,000 for you and the policy will mature in 12 years, how much is it worth today, discounted at 15 percent annually?

11. A family trust will convey property to you in 15 years. If the property is expected to be worth $50,000 when you receive it, what is the present value of your interest, discounted at 10 percent annually?

12. You want to buy a house for which the owner is asking $625,000. The only problem is that the house is leased to someone else with five years remaining on the lease. However, you like the house and believe it will be a good investment. How much should you pay for the house today if you could strike a bargain with the owner under which she would continue receiving all rental payments until the end of the five-year leasehold, at which time you would obtain title and possession of the property? You believe the property will be worth the same in five years as it is worth today and that this future value should be discounted at a 10 percent annual rate.

13. If someone pays you $1 a year for 20 years, what is the present value of the series of future payments discounted at 10 percent annually?

14. You are at retirement age and one of your benefit options is to accept an annual annuity of $75,000 for 15 years. The first payment would be received one year from today. What lump sum settlement, if paid today, would have the same present value as the $75,000 annual annuity? Assume a 10 percent annual discount rate.

15. What *monthly* deposit is required to accumulate $10,000 in eight years if the deposits earn an annual rate of 8 percent compounded monthly?

16. You are thinking about purchasing some vacant land. You expect to be able to sell the land 10 years from now for $500,000. What is the most you can pay for the land today if your required rate of return is 15 percent? What is the expected (annualized) return on this investment over the 10-year holding period if you purchase the land for $170,000?

17. You are considering the purchase of a small income-producing property for $150,000 that is expected to produce the following net cash flows.

End of Year	Cash Flow
1	$50,000
2	50,000
3	50,000
4	50,000

Assume your required internal rate of return on similar investments is 11 percent. What is the net present value of this investment opportunity? What is the going-in internal rate of return on this investment? Should you make the investment?

18. Raw land at the edge of urban development that lacks the necessary permits for development is one of the most risky kinds of real estate investment. Defend or refute this assertion.

19. You are contemplating replacing your conventional hot water heater with a solar hot water heater system at a cost of $4,000. How should you define the potential benefits that you need to receive to justify the investment?

20. Solve for the unknown discount rate in each of the following:

Present Value	Years	Discount Rate	Future Value
$ 2,400	2		$ 2,970
3,600	10		10,800
390,000	15		1,853,820
382,610	30		5,316,180

21. Solve for the unknown number of years in each of the following:

Present Value	Years	Discount Rate	Future Value
$ 5,600		9%	$ 12,840
8,100		10	43,410
184,000		17	3,645,180
215,000		15	1,734,390

22. Assume the total cost of a college education will be $310,000 when your infant child enters college in 18 years. How much must you invest at the end of each month to accumulate the required $310,000 at the end of 18 years, if your monthly investments earn an annual interest rate of 5 percent, compounded monthly?

23. You are trying to accumulate a $40,000 down payment to purchase a home. You can afford to save $1,000 per quarter. If these quarterly investments earn an annual rate of 7 percent, how many quarters will it take to reach your goal?

24. You have signed a new lease today to rent office space for five years. The lease payments are fixed at $4,500 per month for the first two years, but rise to $5,500 per month in years 3–5. What is the present value of this lease obligation if the appropriate discount rate is 8 percent?

25. Suppose you are going to receive $10,000 per year for five years. The appropriate interest/discount rate is 11 percent.
   a. What is the present value of the payments if they are in the form of an ordinary annuity? What is the present value if the payments are an annuity due?
   b. Suppose you plan to invest the payments for five years. What is the future value if the payments are an ordinary annuity? What if the payments are an annuity due?

EXPLORE THE WEB

RealtyRates.com provides information on real estate investment and development news, trends, analytics, and market research. The RealtyRates.com quarterly *Investor Survey* includes national mortgage and equity return requirements, capitalization and discount rates, and financing rates and terms for a variety of

EXPLORE THE WEB—CONTINUED

income-producing property types. The RealtyRates. com quarterly *Developer Survey* includes actual and projected rates of return for numerous property types including subdivisions, PUDs, business and industrial parks, and residential and commercial condominiums and co-ops. Go to the RealtyRates.com home page and explore the types of available surveys and information. Click on the *Free Survey Data* link in the top right-hand corner of the home page. Scroll down to the information on the Developer Survey and click on the link to *Market Commentary*. What kinds of returns are developers projecting on subdivisions and planned unit developments? How do these compare with the returns of condominium developments? How do projected rates of return compare to historical returns?

Solutions to Concept Checks

1. $45,885.34 ($N = 8$; $I = 15.0/12$; $PV = 15,000$; $PMT = 0$; $FV = ?$).

2. $N = 40$ (4×10), $I = 2.5\%$ ($10\% \div 4$), the accumulated FV in 10 years is $2,685.06 ($N = 40$; $I = 2.5$; $PV = 1,000$; $PMT = 0$; $FV = ?$).

3. $240,634.89 ($N = 15$; $I = 10$; $PV = -50,000$; $PMT = -1,000$; $FV = ?$).

4. $11,603.83 ($N = 5$; $I = 5$; $PV = 0$; $PMT = -2,000$; $FV = ?$) use "BEGIN MODE."

5. $N = 15$; $I = 10$; $PMT = 0$; $FV = 50,000$; $PV = $11,969.60.

6. *PV* of $10,000 expenditure is $8,162.98 ($N = 3$; $I = 7$; $PV = ?$; $PMT = 0$; $FV = -10,000$). *PV* of $12,000 expenditure is $7,999.10 ($N = 6$; $I = 7$; $PV = ?$; $PMT = 0$; $FV = -12,000$). Total present value is $16,159.09.

7. $N = 20$; $I = 3.5\%$ ($14\% \div 4$); $PMT = 1.5$; $FV = 75$; $PV = $59.01 per share.

8. $N = 20$; $I = 10$; $PMT = 10,000$; $FV = 50,000$; $PV = $92,567.82.

9. −$400,000 is entered as CF_0. Pressing the "shift IRR/YR" key (on the HP 10B) will produce a going-in *IRR* of 12.20%.

10. A zero *NPV* does not mean the investor's yield/*IRR* is zero. What it does mean is the expected yield/*IRR* on the investment is equal to the investor's required yield/*IRR*.

Additional Readings

Burrell, J. *The Real Estate Math Handbook: Simplified Solutions for the Real Estate Investor.* Ocala, FL: Atlantic Publishing Company, 2007.

Gaines, G., D. Coleman, and L. L. Crawford. *Real Estate Math: What You Need to Know,* 6th ed. Chicago, IL: Dearborn Financial Publishing, 2005.

Gallinelli, F. *What Every Real Estate Investor Needs to Know,* 2nd ed. Chicago, IL: McGraw-Hill Companies, Inc., 2009.

Harvard Business Press. *The Time Value of Money: Calculating the Real Value of Your Investment.* Cambridge, MA: Harvard Business School Press, 2009.

Kahl, A. L., and W. F. Rentz. *Financial Mathematics with MS Excel: Time Value of Money.* Alfred L. Kahl and William F. Rentz, 2014.

Mooney, S. P. *Real Estate Math Demystified.* New York: McGraw-Hill, 2007.

Pattavina, J. *The Time Value of Money.* Leverage Business Group LLC, 2013.

Petersen, P., and F. J. Fabozzi. *Foundations and Applications of the Time Value of Money.* Hoboken, NJ: John Wiley & Sons, 2009.

Prakash, A. J., and D. K. Ghosh. *Financial, Commercial, and Mortgage Mathematics and Their Applications.* Santa Barbara, CA, 2014.

Tamper, R. *Mastering Real Estate Math,* 7th ed. Chicago, IL: Dearborn Publishing, 2002.

APPENDIX   Solving Time-Value-of-Money Problems Using Excel

To access the appendix for this chapter, please visit the book's website at

www.mhhe.com/lingarcher5e

Chapter 15

Mortgage Calculations *and* Decisions

LEARNING OBJECTIVES

After reading this chapter, you will be able to:

1 Compute the payment on a loan, and the balance with any number of remaining payments, given the original loan terms: maturity, interest rate, and amount.

2 Compare loan choices using either the lender's yield or the borrower's effective borrowing cost, accounting for the effect of prepayment and the amount of any initial loan fees or loan expenses.

3 State the distinguishing characteristics of an interest-only loan, a partially amortized loan, and an early payment loan.

4 Determine whether a 15-year loan or a 30-year loan is a better financial choice for a borrower, given the borrower's discount rate.

5 Define index, margin, caps, and adjustment periods on an adjustable rate mortgage, or ARM; state how the latter two features affect the distribution of interest rate risk between borrower and lender.

OUTLINE

Introduction

Chapter 9 introduced the laws and contracts of mortgages. Chapter 14 discusses standard time-value-of-money (TVM) techniques and their use in valuing investment alternatives. In this chapter we introduce the basic TVM analytics of mortgages. We focus first on level-payment mortgages since many mortgage loans either are, or descend from, a level-payment pattern. It is valuable to know how to find the payment on this type of loan as well as the remaining balance at any time during the life of the loan. Further, it is important to be able to compute the lender's expected internal rate of return (i.e., "yield") on the mortgage, the true cost to the borrower, and the current market value of the mortgage debt.

For choices involving mortgage loans, present value is the core criterion. In this chapter we show its application in choosing between different loan maturities. Since adjustable rate mortgages are an important option for borrowers, we also examine the computation of payments and balances on adjustable rate loans. Although the basic concepts discussed in this chapter are applicable to commercial mortgages, we focus on applications to residential (i.e., home mortgage) lending. Commercial mortgage types and decisions are the focus of Chapter 16.

Basic Computations

www.mortgageinvestments.com

800-plus pages of mortgage information and forms, financial calculators, and spreadsheets.

Five quantitative characteristics of a mortgage are vital to making informed decisions. First, we must know the amount and frequency of the payments involved and, since the majority of residential mortgage loans are paid off early, we must know the *loan balance* at any time as well. Knowing these two benchmark mortgage cash flows enables us to compute three results: the *lender's yield (IRR)*, the borrower's *effective borrowing cost*, and the present value of the debt payments. The analytics of a level-payment loan are a straightforward application of the time-value tools presented in Chapter 14. Below, we use time-value tools to compute these five vital characteristics of a loan.

> ✓ **Concept Check**
>
> **15.1** Name five important quantities or measures that are important to mortgage loan analytics.

Payments

www.mortgagecalculator.org

Provides loan payment calculation, amortization graphs and tables, and more.

Suppose you are a lender being asked to supply a loan with monthly payments of $1,000 for 30 years, or 360 months. Suppose also that you currently receive interest on loans of similar risk of 6 percent, or 0.5 percent per month. As a lender who understands time-value concepts, the maximum amount you should be willing to loan is the present value of the future payments that you expect to receive. Discounting the proposed payments at your opportunity cost of 0.5 percent per month, you calculate the present value, and therefore the maximum loan amount, to be $166,791.61. You can find this result on your calculator as follows:

360	6 ÷ 12		$1,000	0
n	i	PV	PMT	FV
		$166,791.61		

Now suppose another borrower wishes to obtain a similar risk, level-payment loan with a term of 30 years, and in the amount of $166,791.61. (Granted, the borrower is overly precise!) Again, you require an annual return of 6 percent on this type of loan. The question is: What payment would you require on this loan? If your answer is $1,000, you are on the way to being a successful lender. You have recognized that this prospective loan is the reverse of our starting example, so the payment you are solving for is the payment we started with in the first place.

This payment–loan relationship generalizes to all fixed-payment loans. The maximum amount the lender should be willing to distribute to the borrower at loan closing is the present value of the expected future payments, discounted at the loan's interest rate.[1] But since this is so, we always can reverse the logic to find the payment for that loan amount. That is, we simply need to find the fixed payment that has a present value equal to the prospective loan amount.

Suppose, for example, we want to find the required monthly payment on a level-payment loan of $100,000 for 15 years at an annual interest rate of 6 percent. The calculator keystrokes are:

180	6 ÷ 12	$100,000		0
n	**i**	**PV**	**PMT**	**FV**
			$843.86	

The monthly mortgage payment divided by the loan amount (843.86/100,000 = 0.0084386) is commonly known as the **monthly loan constant,** or the monthly payment per $1 of loan.

> ✓ **Concept Check**
>
> **15.2**   Find the monthly payment on this loan: $125,000, 15 years, 6.25 percent annual interest rate.

Loan Balance

Finding the **loan balance** at any point in time also is quite simple, once the logic is clear. Consider the following: We have just used the idea that the loan amount at origination is the present value of the future payments, discounted at the contract interest rate. This is true at the outset of the loan, but what about after payments have been made? With a bit of thought, you may conclude that it still must be true, and you would be correct!

Here is one way to confirm the point. Consider the 15-year loan in the example given earlier with a payment of $843.86. The interest charged for the first month is the monthly interest rate times the original balance (0.005 × 100,000), or $500. The remainder of the payment, $343.86, is loan balance reduction. When this payment is made on the last day of month 1, it also reduces the remaining number of scheduled payments by 1, to 179. Discounting the remaining 179 monthly payments of $843.86 at the contract interest rate of 6 percent results in a present value of $99,656.14, a reduction of exactly $343.86 from the original loan amount of $100,000. Thus, the present value of the remaining payments is reduced by exactly the amount of the first month's principal payment, making it again equal to the remaining principal balance. When each principal payment is made, the present value of the remaining payments decreases by exactly the amount of that principal payment. We leave it to the reader to repeat this experiment for the remaining 179 periods, or until you feel assured that it is true.

We have demonstrated that the remaining balance on a fixed-payment loan is the present value of the remaining payments, discounted at the contract interest rate. This result makes it easy to find the balance on any fixed-rate loan, at any point in its schedule. Suppose, for example, we want to know the balance at the end of five years (60 months) on the 15-year loan discussed earlier. All that we need to do is find the present value of the

www.nationalmortgage-news.com

Mortgage news and data, industry reports, and mortgage blogs.

---

1. Note that this relationship actually applies to any fixed rate loan, regardless of the payment pattern. That is, the maximum amount of a fixed-rate loan always must be the present value of its future payment stream, discounted at the loan's required interest rate. This relationship is the "gate to the kingdom" in analyzing fixed-rate loans.

payments remaining at that time. Thus, with 120 months remaining (180 − 60), we can solve as follows:

The present value of $76,009.38 is the loan balance at the end of year 5. Most financial calculators allow the user to solve for a remaining loan balance with a designated function or keystroke.

> ✓ **Concept Check**
>
> **15.3** Find the balance on this mortgage at the end of six years: $125,000 loan amount, 15 years, monthly payments, 6.25 percent annual interest rate.

Lender's Yield

Suppose we have a loan with payments of $1,000 per month, a term of 360 months, and an annual contract interest rate of 7 percent. We can determine the initial loan balance as before:

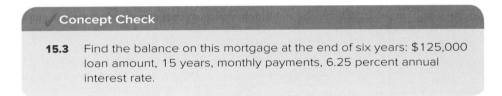

Thus, we obtain a loan amount of $150,307.57.

   Now we extend this present value relationship. Suppose we are making this loan, but we charge advance interest, called **discount points,** in an amount ($5,307.57) such that we really only pay out $145,000, net to the borrower, when we close the loan. We could then ask, to what loan interest rate is this deal equivalent? That is, if we were to make a new loan, what interest rate would result in $1,000 payments, given an initial investment of $145,000? Notice that we are simply asking what monthly discount rate causes our 360 payments of $1,000 to have a present value of $145,000. The computation is straightforward.

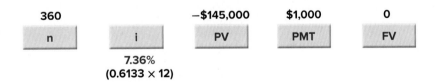

Recall from Chapter 14 that most calculators and spreadsheets will require either *PV* or *PMT* to be negative. The signs should be consistent with the direction of the cash flow; that is, expenditures negative and incomes positive.[2] The resulting equivalent interest rate is

---

2. A more analytically precise reason for the sign requirement is that you are solving the following equation for *i:*

$$0 = PV + PMT \sum_{j=1}^{n} \frac{1}{(1 + i)^j} + \frac{FV}{(1 + i)^n}$$

Note that the equation requires at least one of the cash flows to be negative, and at least one to be positive.

0.6133 percent per month, although your calculator may show it as an annual rate of 7.36 percent, which is the monthly rate multiplied by 12.

This notion of "equivalent interest rate" usually is referred to as the **lender's yield.** It is the internal rate of return, given all of the cash flows for the loan. Note that by changing the borrower advanced interest of $5,307.59, the lender is able to increase her yield (internal rate of return) from 7 percent to 7.36 percent.

> ✓ **Concept Check**
>
> **15.4** Find the lender's yield for this mortgage: $125,000 loan amount, 15 years, monthly payments, 6.25 percent, and lender "points" equal to $2,500. Assume no prepayment.

Effective Borrowing Cost (EBC)

Closely related to lender's yield is the borrower's **effective borrowing cost (EBC).** Mathematically, EBC does not differ from the lender's yield (it also is an *IRR*). The difference is in the cash flows used in the calculations. Normally, when a mortgage loan is created, the borrower must pay certain up-front expenses, all of which are not income to the lender. These include some **closing costs,** discussed below, such as title insurance, mortgage insurance, recording fees and taxes, an appraisal, and a survey. Since the borrower pays these costs but the lender does not receive them as income, the lender's cash flows from the loan are not the same as what the borrower pays out. EBC is simply the implied *IRR* (yield) from the borrower's perspective. For example, suppose our original 7 percent loan has total closing expenses of $8,000 ($5,307.57 in discount points, plus $2,692.43 in other closing expenses not paid to the lender). Therefore, the borrower will receive $150,307.57 (the "face" value of the loan) *less* $8,000, for net loan proceeds of $142,307.57, after paying all the up-front expenses. We can find the implied *IRR* for these cash flows as follows:

www.freddiemac.com/

Learn more about the mortgage process and the costs you can expect to pay at closing.

360		$142,307.57	−$1,000	0
n	i	PV	PMT	FV
	7.55%			

The solution is 7.55 (0.62924 × 12) percent, which is greater than the lender's annualized yield of 7.36 percent. That is, the expected cost of the loan to the borrower is greater than the expected yield (return) to the lender.

APR: A Special Application of EBC. An important special application of EBC is the **annual percentage rate (APR),** which is required by *Truth-in-Lending Act (TILA),* legislation to be reported by the lender to the borrower on virtually all U.S. home mortgage loans. The APR is computed under the assumption of no prepayment; that is, it is a yield to loan maturity. The items that must be accounted for include up-front expenses in the APR calculation, as governed by Federal Reserve Regulation Z, and are rather detailed. In brief, they include the following:

www.federalreserve .gov/bankinforeg/ reglisting.htm

A peek at Federal Reserve Regulation Z, itself. Click on the drop down menu and then choose "Reg Z Truth in Lending." Then browse, for example, the pages on finance charges, right of rescission, and determination of the APR.

- All finance charges in connection with the loan, including discount points and origination fees, underwriting fee, loan processing fee or document preparation fee, and required mortgage insurance.
- All compensation paid to the originating mortgage broker if one was used by the borrower.
- Other charges if the lender receives direct or indirect compensation in connection with the charge, if the charge is paid to an affiliate of the lender, or if the lender stipulates who is to provide the service. (Typically, this *excludes* items such as the appraisal

In 1968, when Congress enacted the Consumer Credit Protection Act, it took a big step toward rescuing consumer credit contracts from the jungles of confusion and deception. Better known as the Truth-in-Lending Act, this law created, among other things, the annual percentage rate (APR) which was to enable consumers to compare interest charges on alternative loans. APR has become part of the consumer language. But how far out of the jungle has APR really brought us? Well, most of the way. It turns out that there may be more credit costs associated with a mortgage loan than APR accounts for.

First, APR requires a lender to account for all finance charges . . . or does it? The way the implementing regulation, Federal Reserve Regulation Z, is written, some significant charges typically don't count. These can include appraisal fees, lender's title insurance paid for by the borrower, a survey of the mortgaged property, and state taxes on the mortgage. As long as these charges are from a source unrelated to the lender, the APR computation does not account for them. Worse, if they vary between loans, any chance to account for them in the comparison is lost. Finally, even if APR is computed correctly, it still

has a built-in bias. APR is a yield (cost) to maturity; however, few home loans are outstanding until maturity. And as the loan is paid off earlier in its life, the effect of front-end finance charges upon the true cost of financing is much greater. So APR systematically understates the impact of front-end finance fees on the true cost of home mortgage debt. Home-buyers beware, at least a little bit!

What Does APR Really Tell You?

fee, survey fee, state tax on the mortgage, possibly a lender's title insurance, and borrower's legal fees.)
- Premiums for required life, accident, health, or loss-of-income insurance or for debt cancellation coverage.

Although the annual percentage rate can be thought of as approximating the true effective borrowing cost, there are two potentially important differences. (See Industry Issues 15–1.) First, the expense items required to be included, though extensive, may still omit a few significant ones for a particular loan. Second, APR always is based on the assumption of no prepayment.

✓ **Concept Check**

15.5 Find the EBC for this mortgage: $125,000 loan amount, 15 years, monthly payments, 6.25 percent annual interest rate, lender "points" and origination fee: $2,500, plus other up-front costs of $3,500 paid by the borrower to third parties. Assume no prepayment.

Prepayment, Lender's Yield, and Effective Borrowing Cost.   We will consider one more example of both lender's yield (IRR) and effective borrowing cost (EBC), incorporating prepayment. A home mortgage loan rarely survives to maturity. Homeowners may move, or they may simply wish to take advantage of lower interest rates; therefore, they replace their current mortgage loan. Suppose that our example loan is expected to be paid off at the end of seven years. What does this prepayment do to the lender's yield and the EBC? The loan balance at the end of seven years, equal to the present value of the remaining 276 payments, is $137,001.46. So, if a lender originates this loan with a net disbursement to the borrower at closing of $145,000, the computation of lender's yield would be:

84		−$145,000	$1,000	$137,001.46
n	i	PV	PMT	FV

7.68%

with a resulting yield of 7.68 percent (0.63986 × 12). By contrast, if the borrower received net proceeds of $142,307.57 after including expenses paid to third parties, the keystrokes would be as follows:

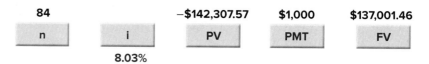

84   n   i   −$142,307.57 PV $1,000 PMT $137,001.46 FV

8.03%

with a resulting EBC of 8.03. In general, whenever a lender charges "up-front" points or other fees on a loan, the earlier the loan is paid off, the higher is the lender's yield. For the same reason, since a borrower virtually always encounters up-front expenses in obtaining a mortgage loan, the earlier the borrower pays off the loan, the higher is the EBC, all else equal.

✓ **Concept Check**

15.6   What assumption about prepayment is made in computing the annual percentage rate (APR)?

Up-front Costs, Holding Period, and Effective Borrowing Cost

Since almost every home mortgage loan is paid off before it is fully amortized, the computation of EBC with prepayment deserves more attention. Clearly the EBC depends on two aspects of the prepayment scenario: how large the up-front financing costs are and how long until the loan is prepaid (holding period). Before exploring the effect on EBC, as these two factors vary, we focus on the several elements of up-front financing costs.

Up-front Financing Costs.   Lenders charge discount points (prepaid interest) to increase the expected yield (IRR) on a loan. But there are other up-front loan fees as well that typically run between 3 percent and 5 percent of the loan amount. In addition to discount points, home borrowers must usually pay a loan origination fee, which is usually equal to 1 percent of the loan amount. Other borrower costs usually include loan application and document preparation fees ($200–$700), the cost of having the property appraised ($250–$400), credit check fee ($35–$75), title insurance (0.5–1.0 percent of the loan amount), mortgage insurance (over 2 percent of the loan amount if purchased with a single advanced premium), charges to transfer the deed and record the mortgage ($40–$200), survey costs ($200–$300), pest inspection ($25–$75), and attorneys' fees. Although many of these fees will occur with any mortgage loan, discount points and other terms can vary significantly across lenders and over time. Therefore, borrowers should shop around and compare more than just contract interest rates.

Multiple EBC Scenarios.   To consider the effect of up-front financing costs on the effective (or true) cost of borrowing, consider a 6.00 percent, 30-year, $200,000 level-payment mortgage with a monthly payment of $1,199.10. Assume up-front financing costs, including all costs paid to the lender and third parties except discount points, equal $3,000. Exhibit 15-1 displays the effective borrowing cost on this mortgage for different combinations of discount points and the number of years the loan remains outstanding. For example, if there are no discount points and the borrower repays the loan after two years, the effective borrowing cost is 6.81 percent (0.56782 × 12). The calculator keystrokes are:

24   n   i $197,000 PV   −$1,199.10 PMT   −$194,936.47 FV

6.81%

Exhibit 15-1 The Effect of Discount Points and Holding Period on Effective Borrowing Cost*

Discount Points	Number of Years Loan Is Outstanding					
	2 Yrs.	4 Yrs.	6 Yrs.	8 Yrs.	10 Yrs.	30 Yrs.
0.00	6.81%	6.44%	6.31%	6.25%	6.22%	6.14%
0.50	7.09	6.58	6.42	6.34	6.29	6.19
1.00	7.36	6.73	6.52	6.42	6.36	6.24
1.50	7.64	6.88	6.63	6.51	6.44	6.29
2.00	7.92	7.03	6.74	6.59	6.51	6.34
2.50	8.20	7.18	6.85	6.68	6.58	6.39

*30-year $200,000 fixed-payment mortgage with a contract rate of 6.0 percent and total up-front financing costs, excluding discount points, of $3,000.

where $194,936.47 is the loan balance after 24 monthly payments. The EBC of 6.81 percent is greater than the 6.00 percent contract rate because of the $3,000 in total up-front financing costs.

Holding the contract interest rate constant, adding discount points to the $3,000 in other up-front costs increases the EBC because it decreases the net loan proceeds *without* altering the scheduled monthly payment or remaining loan balance. One discount point (equal to $2,000 on a $200,000 loan) decreases the borrower's net loan proceeds to $195,000 and increases the EBC to 7.36 percent with a two-year holding period.[3] The payment of 2 1/2 discount points would increase the EBC to 8.20 percent. The effect of up-front financing costs on the EBC decreases as the holding period increases. For example, with 2 1/2 discount points the EBC decreases from 8.20 percent with a two-year holding period to 6.58 percent if the loan remains outstanding for 10 years. As the holding period increases toward 30 years, the EBC will approach, but not equal, the contract interest rate of 6.0 percent. Keep in mind that this example holds the contract interest rate constant to demonstrate the effect of discount points and holding periods on EBCs. In a competitive mortgage market, lenders must reduce the contract interest rate in exchange for more up-front discount points. Thus, in some situations the EBC could actually decrease with additional discount points if the corresponding reduction in the contract interest rate is large enough. This is a calculation all informed borrowers should perform.

✓ Concept Check

15.7 Find the lender's yield for this loan: $125,000, 15 years, 6.25 percent annual rate, monthly payments, lender "points" and origination fee: $2,500. (Assume prepayment after four years.)

www.freddiemac.com

Under the "About Homeownership" link, Freddie Mac provides a calculator for estimating how paying discount points might lower your mortgage rate.

Implications for Borrowers. Borrowers who *expect* they may have to move relatively soon should choose to pay few or no discount points and a slightly higher contract interest rate on their home loans. Conversely, borrowers who expect to keep the loan outstanding for a long period of time may consider paying discount points to *buy down* the interest rate. Why? The monthly savings from paying the discount points to reduce the contract rate will be greater the longer the loan remains outstanding. Note that because the length of time the loan will be outstanding is uncertain, the effective or true cost of each mortgage option can only be estimated at the time of loan origination.

The last column in Exhibit 15-1 is the EBC assuming no prepayment prior to maturity. Note that this, approximately, is APR. Thus, the table reveals how much error can result from comparing APRs between loans when the borrower expects to have the loan for just a

3. $195,000 = $200,000 − $3,000 − (0.01 × $200,000)

few years. EBC is much more sensitive to up-front costs for short holding periods, so "buying down" the contract interest rate through points is much more costly to the borrower for short holding periods.

> ✓ **Concept Check**
>
> **15.8** Find the EBC for this loan: $125,000, 15 years, 6.25 percent, monthly payments, lender points and origination fee: $2,500, plus other up-front costs of $3,500. Assume prepayment at the end of four years.

Some Final Notes on Estimating Closing Costs.   Under the Real Estate Settlement and Procedures Act (RESPA), discussed in Chapter 9, an estimate of closing costs is required to be furnished by the lender for virtually every standard home loan application.[4] However, as discussed in more detail in Chapter 13, the estimated closing expenses usually include both the cost of acquiring legal ownership of the property and the costs of obtaining the mortgage financing, if applicable. For the purposes of estimating EBC, only those up-front expenses associated with obtaining the mortgage should be included (e.g., discount points, loan origination fees, credit report, appraisal fee). In particular, those settlement costs associated with obtaining ownership of the property (e.g., buyer's title insurance, if required, and attorney fees) should not be included in the EBC calculation. A simple test should be applied to estimated closing expenses on a mortgage: If the expense would be incurred even if no mortgage financing were obtained, it is an expense associated with obtaining ownership and should not be included in the EBC calculation.

portal.hud.gov/hudportal/ HUD?src=/program_ offices/housing/rmra/res/ respa_hm

All about RESPA directly from HUD.

> ✓ **Concept Check**
>
> **15.9** Name an up-front expense in purchasing a home that should *not* be used in computing EBC for the loan involved.

Fixed-Rate Mortgages

When a loan's interest rate is fixed, time-value tools can illuminate numerous loan decisions through the application of present value. Below we demonstrate this by applying present value calculations to the choice of loan term.

Level-Payment, Fully Amortized Mortgages

Single-family mortgages can take any form negotiated between a borrower and a lender, as noted in Chapter 9. Historically, however, the most common form has been a fixed-rate, level-payment, fully amortized mortgage. Fully amortizing mortgages are paid off completely by periodic (virtually always monthly) payments. At maturity, the loan balance is zero. As the loan is amortized, the owner's equity in the property grows, so long as the property value does not decline.[5] When fully amortizing loans call for equal periodic payments, they are known as **level-payment mortgages (LPMs).** (A display of typical level-payment principal and interest payments appears in Exhibit 9-2.) With adjustable rate mortgages (discussed later), monthly payments can change as market interest rates vary.

The Choice of Loan Term: A Question of Present Value

A common loan term on an LPM is 30 years. However, 15-year mortgages are also popular, and 40-year mortgages are available from some lenders. Other maturities are often possible. There is, however, a common misconception about the choice of loan term. With, for

---

4. Commercial loans are not covered by RESPA. Residential mortgage loans are defined as those issued to finance the acquisition of one- to four-family homes, condominiums, and cooperatives.

5. Owners' equity at any point in time is equal to the current market value of the property minus the current remaining balance on any mortgage.

Exhibit 15-2   Total Interest Paid on 6 Percent LPM of $250,000

	30-Year	15-Year
Monthly payment	$1,498.88	$2,109.64
Total payments (loan term × monthly payment)	539,595	379,736
Minus: Principal amortization	250,000	250,000
Equals: Total interest	$289,595	$129,736

example, a 15-year loan, the borrower pays substantially less interest over the life of the loan than with an otherwise identical 30-year loan. For example, consider a 30-year $250,000 LPM with an annual interest rate of 6 percent. Assume for simplicity that the contract interest rate on an otherwise equivalent 15-year mortgage is also 6 percent. With 30-year amortization, the monthly payment is $1,498.88; with 15-year amortization, the payment is $2,109.64. As calculated in Exhibit 15-2, total interest paid over the life of the 30-year and 15-year mortgages would be $289,595 and $129,736, respectively.

At first glance, the 15-year mortgage appears to provide a total interest saving equal to $159,859 ($289,595 − $129,736). But does this make the 15-year loan better, as is often asserted? Instead of comparing the accumulated interest of the loans, our understanding of time-value compels us to compare their *present values.* Because in this case the loan payments represent cash *outflows,* borrowers should choose the option with the *lowest* present value. To reinforce this idea, remember, if we have money in hand now, we can put it to use at some productive return (even if this is simply to eliminate existing debt and interest costs). By this reasoning, money received later is less valuable due to lost use, but payments deferred are better because we retain the use of the payment money for a longer time. Since all of these points are captured in the concept of present value, the relevant question between the 15-year and 30-loan is: which has the smaller present value? The answer may not be obvious.

To compare the present values of the two loans, we need a discount rate. Recall that the discount rate represents our opportunity cost, that is, the return that we can get on alternative investments of similar risk. One use of available money is to lessen the amount of debt we owe, thereby escaping future interest payments. In this case, our opportunity cost equals the interest rate on the payments that we escape. But what result do we get in comparing the present values of the two example loans above, discounted at their interest rate of 6 percent? Do we really need to calculate to get the answer? Recall that both loans were originated at 6 percent. We know that the balance on a loan is the present value of its payments, discounted at the loan interest rate. Thus, discounting both loans at their contract interest rate of 6 percent will simply confirm that each loan is worth its original balance of $250,000, assuming no up-front financing costs. In present value, our true measure of worth (or cost), the loans are equivalent, regardless of the difference in total interest charges.

> ### ✓ Concept Check
>
> **15.10**   Under financially unconstrained circumstances, which of these monthly fixed-rate mortgage loans would a borrower prefer, and why? 15-year, 7 percent or 30-year, 7 percent. Assume no up-front financing costs. Explain your answer.

The earlier example assumes the contract interest rates on both the 15-year and 30-year mortgages are equal. However, 15-year mortgages typically are offered at a lower interest rate than 30-year mortgages. How does this affect the choice? Note that the logic we use remains the same.[6] That is, whichever loan we consider, an alternative use of available money is to lessen the amount of debt contemplated, thereby "earning" interest cost

---

6. We assume that both loans are competitively priced; that is, they have competitive interest rates for their terms and risk.

savings at the rate charged on the loan. Thus, the appropriate discount rate for each loan is its own interest rate. The result will be that each loan again has a present value equal to its principal amount. For example, if we are considering two $250,000 loans, with the 30-year loan at 6.0 percent and the 15-year loan at 5.5 percent, then we would discount the 30-year loan at 6.0 percent and the 15-year loan at 5.5 percent. The result is that each loan still would have a present value of $250,000.[7]

How popular are 15-year mortgages? Since 1994, approximately 10–20 percent of conventional single-family mortgage originations have been 15-year mortgages. (Conventional loans are the largest single class of home mortgage loans. They are discussed in Chapter 10.) The evidence also indicates that 15-year mortgages are more popular among mature households than among younger and first-time homebuyers who are likely to be financially constrained. Also, the use of 15-year mortgages is decidedly more pronounced among homeowners who are refinancing.

Alternative Amortization Schedules

Numerous alternatives to a fully amortizing loan are available, as noted in Chapter 9. For example, borrowers may arrange to pay only interest over the life of the loan, and to then pay off the loan completely in one repayment of principal at maturity. Alternatively, borrowers may partially amortize the loan over its maturity. In addition, borrowers may select, for example, a 30-year fully amortizing loan, and then make additional payments in some months to reduce principal more quickly than scheduled. These alternative patterns of amortization identify loans as *interest-only mortgages, partially amortized mortgages,* or *early payment mortgages,* respectively.

Interest-Only (Straight-Term) Mortgages. **Interest-only mortgages** are repaid in full with one payment on maturity of the loan. During the life of the loan, however, borrowers make only interest payments periodically (e.g., monthly). For example, assume the borrower and the lender agree to a $250,000, seven-year, interest-only loan at 6 percent. The monthly payment is $1,250 (0.06 ÷ 12 × $250,000). If the loan were to be fully amortized over 30 years, the monthly payment would equal $1,498.88.[8] The $248.88 difference is principal amortization. Unlike the amortizing mortgage, the loan balance on the interest-only loan would remain constant at $250,000.

During the house price boom of the early to mid-2000s, loans that allow borrowers to pay interest but no principal in the early years became popular with households with large ("Jumbo") loans. Interest-only mortgages are often used in commercial real estate financing and in land transactions. Developers often purchase land with interest-only loans, expecting to be able to repay the loans after the development and sale of lots.

Partially Amortizing Mortgages. *Partially amortizing mortgage loans* require periodic payments of principal, as well as interest, but they are not paid off completely over the loan's term to maturity. Instead, as noted in Chapter 9, the loan has an amortization term longer than the term to maturity. The balance at maturity is called a balloon and is satisfied with a *balloon payment.* For example, assume the $250,000, 6 percent loan would be amortized over 30 years, but the term to maturity is 7 years. The monthly payment is $1,498.88 and the remaining mortgage balance at the end of year 7 would equal $224,098.[9] The borrower at that time must either (1) negotiate a new $224,098 loan with the original lender at current rates, (2) negotiate a loan with a new lender and use the proceeds to pay off the original lender, or (3) sell the property and use the sale proceeds to pay off the original lender.

---

7. Students of finance will recognize that the difference in interest rates between the 15-year and 30-year loans corresponds to different maturities or durations on a yield curve. It follows that the two loans should be valued or discounted at different, appropriate rates from the yield curve.

8. The calculator keystrokes are: $N = 360$; $I = 6.00/12$; $PV = 250,000$; $PMT = ?$; and $FV = 0$.

9. The calculator keystrokes are: $N = 276$; $I = 6.00/12$; $PV = ?$; $PMT = \$1,498.88$; and $FV = 0$.

> ✓ **Concept Check**
>
> **15.11** Find the balloon payment on this mortgage loan: $100,000, 6.5 percent annual interest rate, monthly payments, 30-year amortization, but 7-year term to maturity.

www.mortgages.com

Common mortgage programs, forms, and mortgage calculators.

Early Payment Mortgages. With an **early payment mortgage (EPM),** principal payments may exceed the schedule of principal payments for an LPM. Most first mortgage home loans can become an EPM if the borrower chooses to make supplemental principal payments. The result is that the loan is paid off before the original maturity. As discussed in Chapter 9, most "prime" home loans give the borrower the right to prepay, in whole or in part. However, some loans do limit prepayment. Costless prepayment is generally not allowed on commercial loans.

Despite the freedom to pay down a home loan early, it may not be financially wise for a borrower to do so. The primary decision criterion in this case is the same one used to evaluate the desirability of a 15-year loan relative to a 30-year loan. If borrowers can invest the prospective prepayment amount in an alternate use at a higher risk adjusted return than the interest rate on the loan (e.g., by paying off expensive credit card debt), they would be ahead financially to elect the alternate use and not pay down the home loan. Simply put, there is a significant opportunity cost associated with paying down a loan early.

Adjustable Rate Mortgages

The most popular alternative to a level-payment mortgage in the home loan market is the *adjustable rate mortgage (ARM).* While the share of home borrowers electing ARM loans over LPMs is quite volatile, since 2010 it has ranged from 10 to 16 percent.

The Mechanics of Adjustable Rate Mortgages

The interest rate on ARMs originated by federally insured U.S. banks must be tied to a published index of interest rates that is beyond the control of the lender. As discussed in Chapter 9, the most common indexes are U.S. Treasury rates. At a predetermined *change date,* the loan interest rate will fall or rise as the index rate falls or rises.

When the ARM market first began to develop in the early 1980s in response to high and volatile interest rates, lenders and borrowers experimented with numerous ARM designs. Between 400 and 500 different types of ARM products were being offered in early 1984.[10] Over time, the terms of ARMs have become somewhat more uniform. One of the most popular has been a 1-year ARM based on a 30-year amortization, although the popularity of the 1-year ARM has declined in recent years. With a one-year ARM, the initial contract rate remains in effect for one year and adjusts annually thereafter based on movements in the yield on one-year Treasury securities.

EXAMPLE 15-1: ARM EXAMPLE WITHOUT CAPS

Consider a $100,000 ARM with a 30-year amortization schedule. The adjustment period is one year, the *index rate* is the one-year Treasury rate (see Chapter 9), and the *margin* is 2.75 percentage points (275 basis points). Also assume the current rate on one-year Treasury securities is 2.00 percent—which would seem to imply a 4.75 percent mortgage interest rate (2.00 + 2.75). However, assume the first-year contract interest rate is a *teaser rate,* set at 3.25 percent.

---

10. Jack M. Guttentag, "Recent Changes in the Primary Mortgage Market," *Housing Finance Review* (July 1984), pp. 221–55.

The first three years of the loan are summarized in Exhibit 15-3. The monthly payment in year 1, by our standard method of computation, is $435.21 and the remaining mortgage balance at the end of year 1 (beginning of year 2) is $97,997.88. If the interest rate on one-year Treasury securities is still 2.00 percent at the end of year 1, the contract interest rate in year 2 will equal the one-year Treasury rate plus the constant margin, or

$$= 2.00\% + 2.75\%$$
$$= 4.75\%$$

Thus, the monthly payment in year 2 will equal $519.22.[11]

Note that even though the Treasury index rate remained unchanged at 2.00 percent, the contract rate increased 1.50 percentage points to 4.75 percent on the first change date. This results in a significant increase in the monthly payment. In the third year the index rises from 2.00 percent to 2.25 percent. Thus, the Treasury index plus margin increases accordingly, or

$$= 2.25\% + 2.75\%$$
$$= 5.00\%$$

This results in a new payment of $533.58 for year 3, based on a beginning balance of $96,387.43.

Exhibit 15-3 Adjustable Rate Mortgage with Teaser Rate but No Caps

Loan Assumptions
  Initial amount: $100,000   Caps: None
  Term: 30 years (360 months)
  Margin: 2.75% (275 basis points)

	Beginning of Year		
	1	2	3
Index	2.00%	2.00%	2.25%
Teaser rate	3.25%		
Interest rate	3.25%	(2.00 + 2.75) 4.75%*	(2.25 + 2.75) 5.00%*
Loan balance	$100,000	$97,997.88	$96,387.43
Months remaining	360	348	336
Monthly payment	$435.21	$519.22	$533.58

*Interest rate equals (index + margin) after year 1.

✓ **Concept Check**

15.12 Given the following information for a 30-year $75,000 uncapped ARM loan, find the loan balance at the end of year 2: Margin, 2.75 percent; index for year 1, 2.50 percent; Index for year 2, 2.75 percent; teaser, 4.00 percent.

Initial Adjustment Periods

Despite the popularity of the one-year ARM, many borrowers prefer longer initial **adjustment periods.** For example, with a 3/1 ARM, the interest rate is fixed for three years and then adjusts annually thereafter. Many lenders also offer 5/1 ARMs, 7/1 ARMs, and a

11. The calculator keystrokes are: $N = 348$; $I = 4.75 \div 12$; $PV = \$97,997.88$; $PMT = ?$; and $FV = 0$.

10-year product. The longer-term alternatives allow ARM borrowers to defer the first payment adjustment for 3, 5, 7, or 10 years, respectively. Afterward, the payments start to reflect changes in the index to which the loan interest rate is tied.

Because ARM borrowers and lenders share the interest rate risk, ARM interest rates are typically lower than those on fixed-rate loans, all else equal. However, the less interest rate risk the borrower assumes, the higher the interest rate charged during the initial adjustment period. Thus, three-year ARMs typically have higher initial interest rates than standard one-year ARMs, five-year ARMs have higher rates than three-year ARMs, and so on.

Exhibit 15-4 displays the ARM share of conventional mortgage originations from 1996 through 2014. Over this time period, the ARM share has varied from 6 to 50 percent, and it has been positively correlated with the *level* of rates on 30-year LPMs.

Rate Caps

As noted in Chapter 9, ARM loans may have a *periodic cap,* an *overall cap,* or both. Assume our example one-year ARM has a 1 percent annual adjustment cap and a 5 percent overall cap. Exhibit 15-5 shows interest rates, payments, and loan balances for the first three years. We assume again that the yield on one-year Treasury securities at the end of year 1 remains unchanged at 2.00 percent. Then the contract rate in year 2 again would rise to 4.75 percent in the absence of an annual cap (2.00 + 2.75). But in our example it is constrained by the annual cap to move no more than 1.00 percent (100 basis points). Thus, the mortgage rate in year 2 will be:

$$= 3.25\% + 1.00\%$$
$$= 4.25\%$$

This results in a monthly payment of $490.36 in year 2.

Exhibit 15-4　Mortgage Rates and ARM Share of Total Originations

Year	Average Rate 30-Year Mortgages	Average Rate 1-Year ARMs	30-Year Rate Less 1-Year Rate	ARM Market Share (%)
1996	7.8	5.7	2.1	30
1997	7.6	5.6	1.0	26
1998	6.9	5.6	1.3	16
1999	7.4	6.0	1.4	24
2000	8.1	7.0	1.1	30
2001	7.0	5.8	1.2	16
2002	6.5	4.6	1.9	23
2003	5.8	3.8	2.0	26
2004	5.8	3.9	1.9	50
2005	5.9	4.5	1.4	48
2006	6.4	5.5	0.9	45
2007	6.3	5.6	0.7	30
2008	6.0	5.2	0.8	16
2009	5.0	4.7	1.3	6
2010	4.7	3.8	0.9	9
2011	4.5	3.0	1.5	13
2012	3.7	2.7	1.0	10
2013	4.0	2.6	1.4	10
2014	4.2	2.4	1.8	16
2015	3.8	2.5	1.7	n.a.

Source: Data from Freddie Mac Primary Mortgage Market Survey www.freddiemac.com/pmms: 2015, Mortgage Market Statistical Annual, Inside Mortgage Finance Publications.

Exhibit 15-5 Adjustable Rate Mortgage with Teaser Rate and Caps

Loan Assumptions			Caps		
Initial amount: $100,000			Periodic (annual): 1.00%		
Term: 30 years (360 months)			Overall: 5.00%		
Margin: 2.75% (275 basis points)					

	Beginning of Year		
	1	**2**	**3**
Index	2.00%	2.00%	2.25%
Teaser rate	3.25%		
Interest rate	3.25%	Lesser of: (2.00 + 2.75) or (3.25 + 1.00) 4.25%*	Lesser of: (2.25 + 2.75) or (4.25 + 1.00) 5.00%*
Loan balance	$100,000	$97,977.88	$96,244.61
Months remaining	360	348	336
Monthly payment	$435.21	$490.36	$532.79

Overall maximum interest rate: 8.25% (3.25 + 5.00).

*Assumes the periodic cap applies to the "teaser" rate.

It is important to note that not every loan will result in an interest rate of 4.25 percent in this situation. Whether the rate change from the first year to the second is constrained by the periodic cap depends on how the note is written. The question is whether the cap applies to the teaser rate, or whether it applies only to the index plus margin. ARM loans have been written with both arrangements.

In the third year, the interest rate is determined in the manner that will apply in all subsequent years. The rate change is the lesser of the change in the index or the periodic cap limit. Thus, for our loan, the change is the lesser of 1 percent or the index change. Normally, the cap applies for both positive and negative changes, although this again can depend on how the loan contract is written. For year 3 in our example the index change is 0.25 percent (25 basis points). Since this is less than the periodic cap, the interest rate rises to 5.00 percent on the change date for year 3. This results in a new payment of $532.79, based on a beginning-of-the-year balance of $96,244.61.

The use of rate caps in an ARM loan shifts the risk between the borrower and the lender. If interest rates rise in an LPM, the borrower's payments are unaffected, while the value of the lender's asset (the loan) falls because the market now discounts the loan's payment stream at a higher discount rate. If short-term Treasury rates rise in an unconstrained ARM, so does the borrower's payment, protecting the value of the lender's mortgage asset, at least to some extent. Thus, the LPM places the bulk of the interest rate risk of the loan on the lender, while an unconstrained ARM does much the opposite. Caps, on the other hand, reallocate interest rate risk someplace between these extremes.

The shift of interest rate risk back to the lender when tight caps are included is a cost to the lender. How do lenders balance the pricing of ARMs with rate caps relative to ARMs without such caps? They must, in some fashion, increase their *expected* return on the ARM with caps. Thus, borrowers who choose ARMs with rate caps can expect a higher initial contract interest rate, a higher margin, more up-front financing costs, or some combination of the three.

Many have observed that in this interest rate risk tug-of-war between borrower and lender, the lender has more knowledge and alternatives in managing interest rate risk than most households have. This suggests that an efficient market solution in designing home

Many entrepreneurs and existing firms are developing new tools to help homebuyers tackle one of the most confusing decisions they face: figuring out whether a mortgage is a fair deal.

Comparison shopping for mortgages is a difficult job—a world of "points," "ARMs," "balloons," insurance, FICO scores, and a long list of surprise fees. The problem for borrowers, according to some observers, is that lenders have a vested interest in making it tough to understand their loan and to compare rival offerings.

Some entrepreneurs and mortgage experts are stepping in to give consumers some much needed help. One of the most informative (and quirkiest) tools available is a website, www.mtgprofessor.com, by a maverick retired finance professor who has made a hobby of skewering mortgage lenders. The site is a compilation of tutorials, calculators, answers to frequently asked questions, a list of mistakes to avoid, and a comprehensive glossary of mortgage terms. It also has some tough words for many lenders from Jack M. Guttentag, the Wharton professor emeritus behind the site. Example: In one paragraph, he compares parts of the mortgage market with a camel bazaar—except that the chances of being fleeced by a camel dealer are smaller. The Mortgage Professor is also on Facebook.

Other companies such as FICO (www.fico.com), a provider of credit-rating scores, and Bankrate Inc (www.bankrate.com), a financial website operator, have been refining their own websites designed to demystify mortgage shopping.

Understanding Mortgages: Websites Help Borrowers

loans would place more of the interest rate risk with the lender. From this view, it is not surprising that many households still strongly prefer LPMs.

The three-year ARM, five-year ARM, and so forth are a creative truce in the interest rate risk tug-of-war. They allow a borrower to select an ARM where the payment is fixed for approximately the amount of time the borrower expects to keep the loan. For example, borrowers who expect to move or refinance within five years can select a five-year ARM, and their payment may never change before paying off the loan. Thus, borrowers are paying for only the protection against interest rate risk that is most valuable to them, while the lender's interest rate risk is much less than with a standard LPM.

Other Options

It should be apparent that ARMs contain a wide variety of features and provisions. When comparing a particular ARM to a fixed-payment mortgage or to other ARMs, a borrower should calculate the payments and effective borrowing cost (EBC) of the ARM under several different assumptions about changes in the index interest rate. Lenders disclose the payments that would occur if the interest rate increases to the limit of the caps. The borrower must then determine whether the resulting payment risk of the ARM is tolerable. This suggests that "ARM wrestling" requires the consideration and comparison of all of the following:

myhome.freddiemac .com/resources/ calculators.html

Additional resources for home buying, mortgage computations, and financing decisions.

- Initial interest rates.
- Initial adjustment period.
- Margins.
- Adjustment rate caps.
- Overall caps.
- Discount points.
- Other up-front financing costs.

✓ Concept Check

15.13 Given the following information for a 30-year, $75,000 capped ARM loan, find the interest rate and ending balance for year 2: Margin, 2.75 percent, index for year 1, 2.50 percent; Index for year 2, 2.75 percent; teaser, 4.00 percent; periodic cap, 1.00 percent, overall cap, 5.00 percent. Assume that the cap applies to the teaser rate.

Summary

To work with mortgage loan computations, one must be able to find the loan payment and the balance at any time over the life of the loan. These cash flows enable one to compute the lender's yield (internal rate of return) as well as the borrower's effective borrowing cost. Further, these cash flows are the requisite inputs to present value analysis, the central criterion for making mortgage-related decisions. Since almost every home mortgage loan is paid off before it is fully amortized, the computation of the lender's yield and the borrower's effective borrowing cost with prepayment is discussed in detail.

For fixed-rate loans, an important example of decision analysis is the choice of loan maturity (often a choice between a 15-year loan and a 30-year loan). Analysis with present value reveals that the most beneficial choice is not always the loan that has the lowest payment, nor is it always the loan with the least accumulated interest or the loan that pays off the fastest. The opportunity cost (discount rate) of the borrower, often measured by the cost of high-interest consumer debt, is a central determinant of the best loan choice. Another important decision facing the borrower is the rate at which the principal balance is amortized. Options include interest-only mortgages, partially amortized mortgages, and early payment mortgages.

Adjustable rate loans involve recomputation of the loan payment each time the interest rate changes. Careful attention is warranted in how to compute the new interest rate, particularly in the first few years where an artificially low "teaser" rate may interact with rate caps in different manners, depending on the provisions of the mortgage.

Key Terms

Adjustment period   422
Annual percentage rate (APR)   414
Closing costs   414
Discount points   413
Early payment mortgages (EPM)   421

Effective borrowing cost (EBC)   414
Interest-only mortgages   420
Lender's yield   414

Level-payment mortgage (LPM)   418
Loan balance   412
Monthly loan constant   412

Test Problems

Answer the following multiple-choice problems:

1. The most common adjustment interval on an adjustable rate mortgage (ARM) once the interest rate begins to change has been:
   a. Six months.
   b. One year.
   c. Three years.
   d. Ten years.
   e. None of the above.

2. A characteristic of a partially amortized loan is:
   a. No loan balance exists at the end of the loan term.
   b. A balloon payment is required at the end of the loan term.
   c. All have adjustable interest rates.
   d. All have a loan term of 15 years.
   e. None of the above.

3. If a mortgage is to mature (i.e., become due) at a certain future time without any reduction in the original principal balance, this is called:
   a. A second mortgage.
   b. An amortized mortgage.
   c. A limited reduction mortgage.
   d. An interest-only mortgage.
   e. An open-end mortgage.

4. The dominant loan type originated by most financial institutions is the:
   a. Fixed-payment, fully amortized mortgage.
   b. Adjustable rate mortgage.
   c. Purchase-money mortgage.
   d. FHA-insured mortgage.

5. Which of the following statements is true about 15- and 30-year fixed-payment mortgages?
   a. Thirty-year mortgages are more popular than 15-year mortgages among homeowners who are refinancing.
   b. Borrowers pay more total interest over the life of a 15-year mortgage than on a 30-year loan, all else being equal.
   c. The remaining balance on a 30-year loan declines more quickly than an otherwise equivalent 15-year mortgage.
   d. Assuming they can afford the payments on both mortgages, borrowers usually should choose a 30-year mortgage over an otherwise identical 15-year loan if their discount rate (opportunity cost) exceeds the mortgage rate.

6. Adjustable rate mortgages commonly have all the following *except:*
   a. A teaser rate.
   b. A margin.
   c. An index.
   d. A periodic interest rate cap.
   e. An inflation index.

7. The required calculation of annual percentage rate (APR) by the lender is a result of:
   a. The Truth-in-Lending Act of 1968.
   b. The Real Estate Settlement Procedures Act of 1974/1977.
   c. The Equal Credit Opportunity Act of 1974.
   d. State real estate licensing laws.
   e. Rules of the Federal Trade Commission.

8. On a level-payment loan with 12 years (144 payments) remaining, at an interest rate of 9 percent, and with a payment of $1,000, the current balance is:
   a. $144,000.
   b. $100,000.
   c. $87,871.
   d. $76,137.

9. On the following loan, what is the best estimate of the effective borrowing cost if the loan is prepaid six years after origination?

Loan amount:	$100,000
Interest rate:	7 percent
Term:	180 months
Up-front costs:	7 percent of the loan amount

   a. 8.2 percent.
   b. 8.4 percent.
   c. 8.5 percent.
   d. 8.7 percent.
   e. 9.0 percent.

10. Lender's yield differs from effective borrowing cost (EBC) because:
    a. Lender's yield is strictly a yield to loan maturity and EBC is not.
    b. EBC is strictly a yield to maturity and lender's yield is not.
    c. EBC accounts for additional third-party up-front expenses paid by the borrower that lender's yield does not account for.
    d. Lender's yield accounts for additional third-party up-front expenses that EBC does not.

Study Questions

1. Calculate the original loan size of a fixed-payment mortgage if the monthly payment is $1,581.59, the annual interest rate is 5.0 percent, and the original loan term is 15 years.

2. For a loan of $100,000, at 4 percent annual interest for 30 years, find the balance at the end of 4 years and 15 years assuming monthly payments.

3. On an adjustable rate mortgage, do borrowers always prefer smaller (tighter) rate caps that limit the amount the contract interest rate can increase in any given year or over the life of the loan? Explain why or why not.

4. Consider a $75,000 mortgage loan with an annual interest rate of 4 percent. The loan term is seven years, but monthly payments will be based on a 30-year amortization schedule. What is the monthly payment? What will be the required balloon payment at the end of the loan term?

5. A mortgage banker is originating a level-payment mortgage with the following terms:

Annual interest rate:	9.0 percent
Loan term:	15 years
Payment frequency:	Monthly
Loan amount:	$160,000
Total up-front financing costs (including discount points):	$4,000
Discount points to lender:	$2,000

   a. Calculate the annual percentage rate (APR) for Truth-in-Lending purposes.
   b. Calculate the lender's yield with no prepayment.
   c. Calculate the lender's yield with prepayment in five years.
   d. Calculate the effective borrowing cost with prepayment in five years.

6. Give some examples of up-front financing costs associated with residential mortgages. What rule can one apply to determine if a settlement (closing) cost should be included in the calculation of the effective borrowing cost?

7. A homeowner is attempting to decide between a 15-year mortgage loan at 3.5 percent and a 30-year loan at 4.0 percent. Assume the up-front financing costs of the two alternatives are equal. What would you advise? What would you advise if the borrower also has a large amount of credit card debt outstanding at a rate of 15 percent?

8. Suppose a one-year ARM loan has a margin of 2.75 percent, a teaser rate for the first year of 4.00 percent, and a cap of 1.00 percent. If the index rate is 3.00 percent at both the beginning and the end of the first year, what will be the interest rate on the loan in year 2? If there is more than one possible answer, what does the outcome depend on?

9. Assume the following for a one-year adjustable rate mortgage loan that is tied to the one-year Treasury rate:

Loan amount:	$150,000
Annual rate cap:	2%
Life-of-loan cap:	5%
Margin:	2.75%
First-year contract rate:	5.50%
One-year Treasury rate at end of year 1:	5.25%
One-year Treasury rate at end of year 2:	5.50%
Loan term in years:	30

   Given these assumptions, calculate the following:
   a. Initial monthly payment.
   b. Loan balance end of year 1.
   c. Year 2 contract rate.
   d. Year 2 monthly payment.
   e. Loan balance end of year 2.
   f. Year 3 contract rate.
   g. Year 3 payment.

10. Assume the following:

Loan Amount:	$100,000
Interest rate:	10 percent annually
Term:	15 years, monthly payments

a. What is the monthly payment?

b. What will be the loan balance at the end of nine years?

c. What is the effective borrowing cost on the loan if the lender charges 3 points at origination and the loan goes to maturity?

d. What is the effective borrowing cost on the loan if the lender charges 3 points at origination and the loan is pre-paid at the end of year 9?

11. For a 30-year loan with a face value of $150,000, 5 percent annual interest, and monthly payments, find the monthly payment and remaining mortgage balance at the end of years 5, 20, and 30.

12. Consider a 20-year loan with a monthly payment of $1,897.95 and an annual interest rate of 4.5 percent. What was the original loan size?

13. You are considering buying a $200,000 house with a 5 percent down payment, a 30-year mortgage, a fixed annual rate of 4.5 percent, and monthly payments. What is the monthly payment? What is the monthly payment times 12? What is the annual payment assuming payments are made annually instead of monthly?

14. Consider a $200,000 mortgage loan with an annual interest rate of 7 percent. The loan term is 8 years, but the monthly payment is based on a 25-year amortization period. Find the monthly payment and the balloon payment at the end of the loan term.

15. Assume a $175,000 mortgage loan and 10-year term. The lender is charging an annual interest rate of 6 percent and 4 discount points at origination. What is the monthly payment assuming that it is based on an amortization period of 30 years? What will be the required balloon payment at the end of the tenth year? What is the effective borrowing cost on the loan if it is held to maturity?

16. Assume that you have purchased a home and can qualify for a $200,000 loan. You have narrowed your mortgage search to the following two options:

Mortgage A
Loan term: 30 years
Annual interest rate: 6 percent
Monthly payments

Up-front financing costs: $5,000
Discount points: 3

Mortgage B
Loan term: 15-years
Annual interest rate: 5.5 percent
Monthly payments
Up-front financing costs: $7,000
Discount points: 3

Based on the effective borrowing cost, which loan would you choose?

17. Consider a 25-year loan with an annual interest rate of 7 percent and monthly payments of $1,201.53. The discount points charged by the lender at origination are 3 percent and the cost of borrower title insurance and mortgage insurance are, respectively, 0.5 percent and 2.0 percent of the loan amount. Additional fees paid to other third parties (i.e., not the lender) will equal $4,000. What is the loan amount? What is the lender's yield/IRR? What is the effective borrowing cost (EBC)?

18. Consider a one-year, $150,000 ARM with a 30-year amortization period. The index rate is currently 3.75 percent, and you estimate that it will increase by 25bp (0.25%) each year for the following 2 years. The fixed margin is 225bp (2.25%), but the lender is offering a teaser rate of 5 percent for the first year of the mortgage.

a. Calculate the contract rate, remaining loan balance, and monthly payment for each of the three years.

b. Suppose that the ARM has a 1 percent annual adjustment cap and a 6 percent overall cap. What is the loan balance and monthly payment for each of the three years?

19. Consider a $150,000 loan with an annual interest rate of 6.5 percent and a 30-year term. Discount points are equal to 2 percent. All other up-front financing costs to be paid by the borrower total $3,000. Compute the monthly payment and the loan balance at the end of months 1–6. What is the effective borrowing cost (EBC), assuming that the loan remains outstanding to maturity?

EXPLORE THE WEB

Freddie Mac: Mortgage Market Survey

Accurate and important interest rate information for residential mortgage markets is available online from Freddie Mac. Go to the Freddie Mac home page: www.freddiemac.com and click on the *About Freddie Mac* tab at the top of the page. Under the *Media Room* banner, click on the *Primary Mortgage Market Survey* link.

What was the average interest rate charged on 30-year fixed-rate residential mortgages last week?

What was the average 15-year fixed rate?

What was the one-year ARM rate?

Do these figures represent an increase or a decrease over the previous week's rates?

Solutions to Concept Checks

1. Five important measures that are important to mortgage loan analytics are (1) loan payment, (2) loan balance (at any time in the life of the loan), (3) lender's yield, (4) effective borrowing cost, and (5) present value.

2. The monthly payment for a loan of $125,000, 15 years, and 6.25 percent is $1,071.78 ($N = 180$; $I = 6.25/12$; $PV = 125,000$; $PMT = ?$; and $FV = 0$).

3. The balance after six years on the 6.25 percent, 15-year $125,000 loan is $88,359.45 ($N = 108$; $I = 6.25/12$; $PV = ?$; $PMT = 1,071.7786$; and $FV = 0$).

4. The lender's yield on the 6.25 percent, 15-year $125,000 loan, assuming no prepayment and assuming the lender charges $2,500 in discount points, is 6.57 percent ($N = 180$; $I = ?$; $PV = -122,500$; $PMT = 1,071.7786$; and $FV = 0$). Note: $6.75 = 0.5474 \times 12$.

5. The EBC on the 6.25 percent, 15-year $125,000 loan, assuming no prepayment and total up-front costs to the borrower of $2,500 in points and origination fee plus $3,500 in other up-front costs, is 7.03 percent ($N = 180$; $I = ?$; $PV = 119,000$; $PMT = 1,071.7786$; and $FV = 0$). Note: $7.03 = 0.58605 \times 12$.

6. In computing APR, it is assumed the loan remains outstanding to maturity (no prepayment).

7. If the 6.25 percent, 15-year, $125,000 loan is prepaid at the end of four years, and if points and origination fees sum to $2,500, the lender's yield is 6.87 percent. Balance of loan after four years is $102,123.28 ($N = 132$; $I = 6.25/12$; $PV = ?$; $PMT = 1,071.7786$; and $FV = 0$). Thus, the lender's yield is 6.87 percent ($N = 48$; $I = ?$; $PV = -122,500$; $PMT = 1,071.7786$; and $FV = 102,123.28$). Note: $6.87 = 0.5729 \times 12$.

8. If the 6.25 percent, 15-year, $125,000 loan is prepaid at the end of four years, and if total up-front costs to the borrower are $6,000, then the EBC is 7.77 percent ($N = 48$; $I = ?$; $PV = 119,000$; $PMT = 1,071.7786$; and $FV = 102,123.28$). Note: $7.77 = 0.6478 \times 12$.

9. An up-front expense in purchasing a house that should not be included in computing EBC is buyer's title insurance.

10. Under financially unconstrained circumstances, a home-buyer is likely indifferent between 15-year and 30-year loans at the same interest rate of 7 percent, because both have the same present value (cost).

11. The balance at the end of seven years on a 6.5 percent, 30-year, $100,000 loan would be $90,416.25. [Solution: Payment is equal to $632.068 ($N = 360$; $I = 6.5/12$; $PV = 100,000$; $PMT = ?$; $FV = 0$). Thus, the loan balance at end of year 7 is $90,416.25 ($N = 276$; $I = 6.5/12$; $PV = ?$; $PMT = 632.068$; $FV = 0$).]

12. For the uncapped ARM, the balance at the end of year 2 is $72,616.39. The initial payment, at 4 percent, is $358.06. The payment in year 2, at 5.5 percent, is $424.05. [Solution: First year payment is $358.0615. ($N = 360$; $I = 4.0/12$; $PV = 75,000$; $PMT = ?$; $FV = 0$). Thus, the loan balance at the end of year 1 is $73,679.22 ($N = 348$; $I = 4.0/12$; $PV = ?$; $PMT = 358.0615$; $FV = 0$). The interest rate in year 2 is 5.5 percent (2.75% index plus 2.75% margin). Thus, the payment in year 2 is $424.0549 ($N = 348$; $I = 5.5/12$; $PV = 73,679.22$; $PMT = ?$; $FV = 0$) and the loan balance at the end of year 2 is $72,616.39 ($N = 336$; $I = 5.5/12$; $PV = ?$; $PMT = 424.0549$; $FV = 0$).]

13. For the capped ARM, the balance at the end of year 2 is $72,519.46. The initial payment, at 4 percent, is $358.06. The payment in year 2, at 5 percent, is $401.45. [Solution: From Concept Check 12, we know the loan balance at the end of year 1 is 73,679.22. If the ARM was uncapped, the interest rate in year 2 would rise to 5.5 percent. However, the periodic cap of 1 percent will allow the interest rate to rise only to 5.00 percent (4.00 + 1.00). Thus, the payment in year 2 is $401.4488 ($N = 348$; $I = 5.0/12$; $PV = 73,679.22$; $PMT = ?$; $FV = 0$). Thus, the balance at the end of year 2 is $72,519.45 ($N = 336$; $I = 5.0/12$; $PV = ?$; $PMT = 401.4488$; $FV = 0$.]

Additional Readings

Brueggeman, W. B., and J. D. Fisher. *Real Estate Finance and Investments,* 15th ed. New York: McGraw-Hill/Irwin, 2015.

Clauretie, T. M., and G. S. Sirmans. *Real Estate Finance: Theory and Practice,* 7th ed. Mason, OH: Thomson South-Western Publishing, 2013.

Crawford, L. L., G. Gaines, and D. Coleman. *Real Estate Math: What You Need to Know,* 6th ed. New York: Kaplin Publishing, 2005.

Guitierrez, S. M. *Mortgage Matters: Demystifying the Loan Approval Maze.* RealWorks Press, 2015.

Guttentag, J. *The Mortgage Encyclopedia: The Authoritative Guide to Mortgage Programs, Practices, Prices, and Pitfalls,* 2nd ed. New York: McGraw-Hill Professional, 2010.

Kolbe, P. T., G. E. Greer, and H. G. Rudner III. *Real Estate Finance,* 2nd ed. Chicago: Dearborn Financial Publishing, 2008.

Sirota, D., and Doris Barrell. *Essentials of Real Estate Finance,* 14th ed. Chicago: Dearborn Financial Publishing, 2015.

Commercial Mortgage Types *and* Decisions

LEARNING OBJECTIVES

After reading this chapter, you will be able to:

1 Identify the most common types of long-term commercial mortgages and the most common provisions contained in these mortgages.

2 Identify and explain three alternative financing structures and explain their advantages and disadvantages from the borrower's perspective.

3 Define and explain positive and negative financial leverage and the risks to the borrower associated with the use of borrowed funds.

4 Identify and explain the items commonly included in a loan submission package.

5 Identify the characteristics of the loan application on which lenders focus when making their funding decisions.

Introduction

In this chapter we discuss the permanent financing of commercial real estate properties. Permanent financing refers to the long-term debt financing of existing properties that are operating and producing income. Permanent financing for commercial real estate is provided by a wide variety of lenders, including Fannie Mae and Freddie Mac, commercial banks, the Department of Housing and Urban Development (HUD), and life insurance companies, as well as by investors in commercial mortgage-backed securities. A detailed discussion of the role and importance of these lenders as sources of commercial mortgage credit is contained in Chapter 17.

We first discuss commercial loan documents and contract provisions. We then consider the most common types of long-term commercial mortgages. Unlike residential mortgage markets, 25- or 30-year mortgages are found infrequently, as mortgages with 3- to 10-year terms are the most common. Alternative financing arrangements, such as floating-rate loans and sale-leasebacks, are then considered. In addition to choosing a financing structure, commercial property investors also must determine, subject to lender restrictions, the size of the mortgage that is most advantageous to them. Here investors must carefully consider the cost of available mortgage financing, the cost of equity (or self-) financing, and the effect of debt (i.e., financial leverage) on investment risk and return.

We next discuss how prospective borrowers obtain financing from lenders, including the contents of a typical loan submission package and how the lender "underwrites" the loan—including the determination of the maximum allowable loan size. The chapter concludes with a brief overview of the various types of short-term (i.e., nonpermanent) mortgage debt often used to finance the development and construction of new properties, including land acquisition loans, land development loans, and construction loans.

Loan Documents and Provisions

Commercial and residential mortgage lenders use the same basic types of documents, and many of the same standard clauses apply. The primary ways in which commercial mortgage loan documents differ from residential loan documents (see Chapters 9 and 10) are briefly described in the remainder of this section.

The Note

As in residential mortgage financing, the *note* is the document used to create a legal debt. In residential property financing, the note is usually a relatively simple document. In commercial property financing, however, the note is usually quite lengthy. It contains the terms of the loan and the provisions agreed to by each party. It presents in detail the borrower's obligations in various situations. The provisions typically deal with such matters as these:

- Amounts and timing of periodic payments.
- Penalties for late payments.
- Record keeping.
- Hazard insurance requirements.
- Property maintenance.
- Default.

In most states, the note creates personal liability for residential borrowers; that is, home mortgage lenders have recourse (access) to other borrower assets in situations where the foreclosure sale price is less than the total amount owed to the lender.[1] However, recourse is less likely to be required in the case of mortgage loans obtained to finance the acquisition of existing commercial properties. To avoid personal liability for the equity investors, a separate legal entity is usually created by the sponsor/organizer of the investment opportunity, and it is that special entity that is actually named in the promissory note. This special-purpose entity generally has one asset: the mortgaged property. Thus, in the event of default, the only recourse the lender has is still the mortgaged property. This arrangement shields the actual investors from personal liability and, in the absence of borrower guarantees, makes the loan effectively nonrecourse.

---

1. Currently, however, first mortgage liens on personal residences in 12 states, including California, are explicitly nonrecourse.

An important function closely related to the commercial real estate industry is that of making loans. Commercial lending takes on many forms in today's complex and competitive world. Commercial real estate loans usually can be originated by a bank, by a commercial mortgage banker or broker, by a life insurance company or pension fund or by other lenders.

Commercial Mortgage Loan Officer

Banks generally hire their own loan originators and processors, as do some of the larger life insurance companies and pension funds. However, commercial mortgage brokers often represent smaller life insurance companies, pension funds, and other lenders that cannot efficiently originate their own commercial loans. Commercial mortgage brokers have also been an important source of mortgages for entities that package pools of commercial mortgages into securities (CMBS) that are sold to investors. Loan officers employed by banks usually earn a regular salary, with bonuses sometimes available. Lending officers who work for mortgage bankers or brokers generally work on a commission basis and are paid after successfully placing mortgage loans that meet the needs of the borrower (e.g., developer or investor) and lender (e.g., life insurance company or CMBS originator).

Commercial mortgage lending requires more business education and analytical skills than residential lending. Since mortgage brokers negotiate loans between borrowers and lenders, they must have strong communication skills.

Although nonrecourse loans tend to dominate the commercial mortgage lending practices of pension funds, life insurance companies, and commercial mortgage-backed security (CMBS) originators, banks are more likely to require some form of credit "enhancement." This enhancement is often provided in the form of a guarantee by the organizer/sponsor of the investment opportunity to make the lender whole in the event the lender suffers a loss on the loan. Most commercial mortgage lenders are also unwilling to relieve borrowers from personal liability in the event that borrower fraud, environmental problems, unpaid property tax obligations, or other willful acts of the borrower that are specifically prohibited by the loan documents cause a capital loss for the lender. Therefore, a non-recourse "carve-out" clause is usually included in the note. This "bad boy" clause pierces the single-purpose borrowing entity to hold the organizer/sponsor personally liable for lender losses caused by such problems.

From the perspective of the equity investor, nonrecourse financing can significantly reduce the downside risk associated with investing in commercial real estate. If rents and property values should fall, equity investors have the option to walk away from the property and mortgage, bearing no personal responsibility to repay the debt. Creditworthy borrowers are loath to exercise this option because they understand that nonrecourse does not mean "not responsible." Nevertheless, when nonrecourse financing is coupled with high loan-to-value ratios (LTVs), equity investors can limit their downside risk exposure without constraining their upside potential.

✓ **Concept Check**

16.1 Distinguish between recourse and nonrecourse loans. Which is the standard in commercial mortgage lending for the acquisition of existing properties?

www.mbaa.org

Mortgage Bankers Association.

www.namb.org

National Association of Mortgage Professionals.

The Mortgage

The commercial mortgage creates security for lenders. As in a residential mortgage, it states that lenders can foreclose and have the property sold to satisfy the debt if borrowers default on any of their obligations. Lenders must follow foreclosure proceedings, determined by state law, just as in residential foreclosures. To protect the lender's security interest in the mortgaged property, commercial mortgages may contain a due-on-sale clause. As in residential lending, this clause precludes the mortgage from being assumed by a subsequent purchaser of the collateralized property without permission of the lender. This protects the lender from a degradation of credit that may occur if a less creditworthy borrower was allowed to assume the loan. However, if the property is sold prior to the end of the loan term, some commercial mortgages allow a "one-time" transfer of the mortgage liability from the original borrower to the purchaser of the property. This transfer requires the approval of the lender and, generally, the payment of a fee equal to 1 percent of the remaining loan amount.

Common Types of Permanent Mortgages

Three main repayment mechanisms can be used for long-term commercial mortgages: fully amortizing loans, partially amortizing loans, and interest-only loans. Recall from Chapter 15 that on a fully amortized loan, the principal repayment portion of the periodic payment is large enough to reduce (i.e., amortize) the outstanding balance to zero over the term of the loan. On a partially amortized loan, the payments are based on an amortization schedule that is longer than the actual term of the loan. Thus, the outstanding balance is reduced, but not to zero, at loan maturity. This requires the borrower to refinance the remaining mortgage balance at loan maturity or pay off the remaining balance with a balloon payment.

> ### ✓ Concept Check
>
> **16.2** All else being the same, are fully amortizing or partially amortizing loans more risky for the lender?

Balloon Mortgages

The **balloon mortgage** is the most common instrument used to finance the acquisition of existing commercial property. Payments are typically based on a 25-year or 30-year amortization schedule, but the loan matures in 3, 5, 7, or 10 years.[2] Exhibit 16-1 contains typical loan terms on permanent fixed-rate financing in the second-quarter of 2016 from Wells Fargo Commercial Real Estate. The mortgage interest rate **spread** over 10-year Treasury securities or 10-year swap contracts (whichever is greater) in the second-quarter of 2016 was 2.75 percentage points (275 basis points). These rates apply to mortgages with a 30-year maximum amortization term and a loan-to-value ratio of 75 percent.[3] Assuming, for example, a 4.3 percent interest rate, a 30-year amortization schedule, and a $5 million mortgage, the monthly payment is $24,743.57 and the remaining mortgage balance at the end of 10 years (RMB_5) would be $3,978,676. The borrower must satisfy the $3,978,676 obligation by either selling the property at the end of the 10-year loan term or refinancing (perhaps with the original lender) at the then-current interest rate.

The 10-year loan term on a balloon mortgage reduces the lender's interest rate risk. If interest rates increase after the origination of a balloon mortgage, the value of the remaining payments, and therefore the value of the mortgage, falls less than if the loan could be outstanding 25 or 30 years. For example, if interest rates were to rise from 4.3 percent to

---

2. A bullet loan is often defined as an interest-only balloon loan.

3. An interest rate swap is an agreement between two parties where one stream of future interest payments is exchanged for another based on a specified principal amount. Interest rate swaps often involve an exchange of variable payments that are linked to a floating interest rate (often LIBOR) in exchange for a fixed rate/payment. The competitively determined rate to swap floating (variable) rate payments for fixed payments of the same duration are often used as a benchmark for fixed rate mortgages.

Exhibit 16-1 Typical Loan Terms on Permanent, Fixed-Rate Financing (2nd Quarter, 2016)

	Apartment	Industrial	Office	Retail
Spread over 10-year swap (or Treasury, whichever is greater)	2.75%	2.80%	2.85%	2.85%
Debt Service Coverage Ratio	1.20	1.25	1.25	1.25
Loan-to-value ratio	75%	75%	75%	75%
Amortization	30	30	30	30
Loan term	10	10	10	10
Capital Expenditure Reserve Requirements (Annual)	$250/unit	$0.10–$0.20 PSF	$0.20–$0.25 PSF	$0.20–$0.25 PSF

4.8 percent immediately after origination of the 10-year, 4.3 percent balloon mortgage, its market value would decline from $5,000,000 to $4,818,795, assuming the loan was expected to be held to its 10-year maturity.[4] However, if both the term of the loan and the amortization period were 30 years, the present value of the remaining payments, and therefore the value of the loan, would decline to $ 4,716,067.[5]

Although reducing the term of the mortgage to 10 years from 30 reduces the lender's exposure to interest rate risk, the 30-year amortization schedule keeps the payment low and therefore does not reduce the payment *affordability* of the mortgage relative to a 30-year mortgage. Generally, larger loans carry slightly lower interest rates, all else being equal. This is because the lender's fixed costs of making the loan are lower per dollar of loan principal and because there is generally more competition among lenders for larger loans.

The contract rates on commercial mortgages reported in Exhibit 16-1 are determined by the perceived riskiness of mortgage investments relative to a riskless alternative. Widely used benchmarks for the riskless alternative are the investment yields (going-in *IRRs*) available on U.S. Treasury securities of different maturities and the yields on swap contracts.[6] The average monthly interest rates on 10-year commercial mortgages and the yield to maturity on 10-year Treasury securities are plotted in Exhibit 16-2 for 1997 through March of 2016. The exhibit clearly demonstrates that commercial mortgages are priced in relation to comparable maturity Treasury securities; that is, monthly movements in mortgage rates are highly correlated with monthly changes in available returns on riskless Treasury securities. The correlation from 1997 through March of 2016 is 0.85. The yield spread (mortgage rate minus Treasury rate) required by mortgage lenders has averaged 210 basis points (or 2.10 percentage points) since 1997 and has ranged between 114 basis points and

4. The calculator keystrokes are $N = 120$; $I = 4.8 \div 12$; $PV = ?$; $PMT = 24,743.57$; and $FV = 3,978,676$. The future value of $ 3,978,676 is the remaining mortgage balance at the end of year 10 ($N = 240$; $I = 4.3$; $PV = ?$; $PMT = 24,743.57$; and $FV = 0$).

5. The calculator keystrokes are $N = 360$; $I = 4.8 \div 12$; $PV = ?$; $PMT = 24,743.57$; and $FV = 0$. If the lender did not expect the 4.3 percent below-market rate loan to be outstanding the full 30 years, the decline in value would be less.

6. U.S. Treasury securities that pay periodic interest are not, technically, risk free because investors are subject to reinvestment risk, which is the risk that interest rates will fall and the periodic payments will have to be reinvested at lower rates. Also, available yields on Treasury securities are stated in *nominal* terms. However, the *real* return earned by investors is uncertain because it depends on the rate of general inflation in the U.S. economy over the investment holding period. Despite these limitations, the nominal returns on interest-paying Treasury securities are common benchmarks used to measure the "riskless" rate of return available to investors in the U.S. economy.

Exhibit 16-2 10-Year Commercial Mortgage Rates versus 10-Year Treasury Yields
(1997 through 1st quarter of 2016)

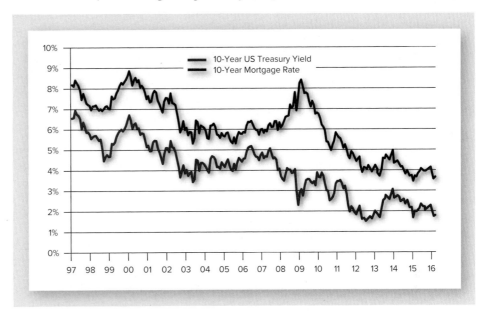

Source: The yields on 10-year Treasury securities are from the Federal Reserve Board's H-15 Report. The monthly mortgage rates are based on the Giliberto-Levy Commercial Mortgage Performance Index (www.jblevyco.com). The 10-year mortgage rate applies a fixed set of weights (40% for office/20% each for apartment, industrial and retail) to the individual property sector mortgage rates.

537 basis points. Nevertheless, the directions of change have followed "Treasuries" very closely. A prominent recent exception was late 2008 and early 2009 when spreads widened significantly during the onset of the financial crisis. It is important to note that the mortgage rates displayed in Exhibit 16-2 reflect low leverage loans on high-quality existing properties. Rates on riskier loans would be higher.

✓ **Concept Check**

16.3 When calculating present values, expected future cash flows must be adjusted for their magnitudes, timing, and risk. Which of these three is adjusted for when discounting at the riskless Treasury rate?

Restrictions on Prepayments

As discussed in Chapter 9, homeowners typically have the right to costlessly prepay the remaining loan balance on residential mortgages, which is often referred to as the **par value** of the mortgage. In sharp contrast, most fixed-rate commercial mortgages do not allow borrowers to freely prepay at par, as they contain a lockout provision, a prepayment penalty, or frequently both. A **lockout provision** prohibits prepayment of the mortgage for a period of time after its origination. For example, a commercial mortgage can have a 10-year loan term, a 25-year amortization schedule, and a 3-year lockout period. Lockout periods reduce the risk that lenders will have to reinvest the remaining loan balance at a lower rate when borrowers prepay mortgages with above-market rates. Thus, lockout provisions reduce lenders' **reinvestment risk,** all else being equal.

> ### ✓ Concept Check
>
> **16.4** Assume a 10-year, 5 percent, commercial mortgage loan with a $1,400,000 remaining balance is paid off by the borrower after 3 years. Assume interest rates have declined to 4 percent since origination. If the $1,400,000 is invested for the remaining 7 years at 4 percent, to what amount will the principal balance increase if interest is compounded monthly? What if the lump sum is invested at a 5 percent annual rate with monthly compounding?

Some commercial mortgages contain **prepayment penalties** instead of, or in addition to, lockout provisions. These penalties may be expressed as a fixed percentage of the remaining loan balance, say, 2–4 percent, or the percentage may decline as the loan ages. Prepayment penalties can significantly increase the cost of refinancing and, therefore, reduce the benefits to the borrower. An alternative form of prepayment penalty is a **yield-maintenance agreement.** With such an agreement, the penalty that borrowers pay depends on how far interest rates have declined since origination. Why tie the penalty to interest rate movements? When interest rates decline and borrowers prepay at par, lenders must reinvest the remaining loan balance at current (i.e., lower) rates. Effectively, lenders lose the present value of the difference between the payments on the old mortgage and the payments on a new mortgage at current rates. With a yield-maintenance agreement, the prepayment penalty can be set to approximate this lost present value, or some portion of it.

Finally, a **defeasance clause** is typically found in mortgages that are originated to become collateral for a commercial mortgage-backed security. With defeasance, a borrower who prepays must purchase for the lender a set of U.S. Treasury securities whose coupon payments replace the mortgage cash flows the lender will lose as a result of the early retirement of the mortgage. Thus, similar to yield maintenance agreements, defeasance clauses provide borrowers with the flexibility to prepay (assuming they are not locked out). However, the clauses are designed such that the borrower's cost of purchasing the Treasury securities for the lender effectively eliminates any interest savings associated with the mortgage prepayment. "Defeasing" a loan is more expensive for the borrower than providing yield maintenance.

www.defeasewithease .com

The website of Commercial Defeasance, LLC. provides an online calculator to estimate the total cost to defease a loan, including the cost to purchase the Treasury securities.

Alternative Financing Arrangements

Although the use of fixed-rate balloon mortgages from a third-party lender is common, alternative mortgage products and financing structures do exist for the acquisition of existing commercial properties. These alternatives are briefly discussed in the following section.

Floating-Rate Loans

Some commercial mortgages have adjustable, or floating, interest rates. The index on a **floating-rate mortgage,** to which the contract rate is tied, is typically the London Interbank Offer Rate—commonly referred to as LIBOR. Floating-rate loans decrease the lender's interest rate risk and are tied to short-term interest rates, both of which tend to reduce the rates on floating-rate loans relative to fixed-payment mortgages, all else being the same. However, floating-rate mortgages can increase the default risk of a mortgage because the borrower may not be able to continue to service the debt if payments on the loan increase significantly. Chapter 15 provides examples of how to calculate the revised payments on mortgages that have interest rates tied to a market index.

Commercial banks most commonly provide floating rate loans. For borrowers who prefer a fixed rate, an interest rate hedge (or swap) agreement can be obtained, which allows a borrower to swap floating rate payments for a fixed rate schedule. Another method for a borrower to hedge its risk on a floating rate loan, which is sometimes required by the lender, is to purchase for a fee an interest rate cap, which allows a borrower to make floating rate payments when the rate is below the capped rate and to pay the capped rate when the floating rate exceeds the cap.

Participation Mortgages

With a participation loan, the lender receives a specified portion of a property's net operating income and/or net sale proceeds. The interest rate is also generally higher. In exchange for participating in the cash flows generated by the property and the higher contract rate, the lender provides a larger loan amount, which is often attractive to borrowers.

Concept Check

16.5 If participation loans reduce the borrower's upside return potential, why do borrowers sometimes seek such a loan?

Sale-Leasebacks

Sale-leasebacks are an alternative vehicle for financing commercial property. With a *land* sale-leaseback, the borrower either currently owns or purchases the building(s) and other improvements. The other party to the transaction purchases the land and leases it back to the borrower. Usually, the investor also provides the long-term mortgage for the building if the land and structure are to be acquired. The investor's cash flow comes from (1) debt service on the mortgage note that has financed the building acquisition and (2) lease payments on the land. Because the investing entity has a long-term economic interest in the land, it benefits from any price appreciation. Although the borrower relinquishes his or her economic interest in the land, depreciation deductions on the building improvements are retained which, along with the lease payments on the land and the interest payments on the building mortgage, are generally fully deductible. (Income taxes are discussed in detail in Chapter 20.)

Investors sometimes negotiate the purchase of both the land and building of an existing property or underwrite the development and construction costs for a proposed new property. The property is then leased back to the user of the property, who becomes a rent-paying tenant (lessee). With such a complete sale-leaseback, the tenant obtains the use of a structure that is presumably well suited to its needs. The arrangement also allows funds not invested in the land and building to be invested in other assets or in other facets of the tenant's business. In most cases, the tenant's primary business is not real estate. Thus, it may make sense to *sell* the property to an investor who specializes in real estate and then lease the property back on a long-term basis. Proceeds from the sale can then be invested in the tenant's core business. This strategy is especially useful for a company that is looking at the expansion of its locations, yet suitable facilities do not exist. From the tenant's viewpoint, a complete sale-leaseback also carries the advantages of 100 percent financing and the deductibility of lease payments for tax purposes. However, appreciation in the value of the property accrues to the owner of the land and buildings, as do the depreciation deductions for tax purposes.

Concept Check

16.6 For a company whose primary business is not the development, ownership, or management of commercial real estate, what is the primary reason it may be better off leasing rather than owning its real estate?

Exhibit 16-3 Alternative Capital Structures for an Acquisition

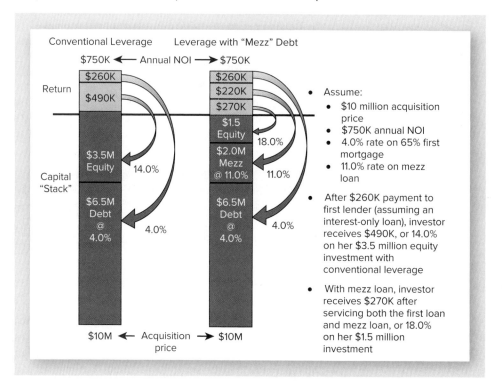

Second Mortgages and Mezzanine Financing

Some investors obtain more than one loan when acquiring properties, thereby substituting more debt financing for equity financing. Even if borrowers have the funds to increase their equity financing, they often prefer to minimize their use of equity capital. Doing so allows investors to take on a larger number of projects. In addition, increased leverage usually increases the investment's expected return on equity, as is discussed more fully later.

The first bar in Exhibit 16-3 depicts a conventional approach to financing a commercial property acquisition. Sixty-five percent of the $10 million acquisition price of the property is provided by a secured first mortgage that carries a 4.0 percent interest rate; the remaining 35 percent of the "capital stack" is supplied by the equity investor. Assume for simplicity that the first mortgage is an interest-only loan and that the $10 million investment will produce an annual net operating income of $750,000. After making the required $260,000 interest-only payment (0.04 × $6,500,000), the equity investor expects to receive $490,000 in before-tax cash flow from operations ($750,000 − $260,000), which is a 14.0 percent expected return on her equity investment.

One approach to increasing the amount of financial leverage is to obtain a second mortgage. A traditional **second mortgage** is secured by the borrower's pledge of the property as collateral. However, a second mortgage is subordinate to the first mortgage in the event of default and foreclosure; that is, the second mortgage lender is "second in line" to receive the sale proceeds from a foreclosure sale. Because the second mortgage lender is in a more risky position than the first lien holder, second mortgages carry higher interest rates.

The second bar in Exhibit 16-3 depicts a situation in which an 11 percent, $2 million second mortgage, equal to 20 percent of the required capital investment, replaces a portion of borrower equity in the capital stack. Although the second mortgage carries a higher interest rate than the first, the weighted average cost of the first and second mortgages is 5.65 percent, still below the unlevered property return (cap rate) of 7.5 percent.[7] Therefore,

---

7. 5.65% = [(2.0M/8.5M) × 11.0% + (6.5M/8.5M) × 4.0%].

the use of the second mortgagee is often attractive to the investor. Senior lenders, especially life insurance companies and pension funds, generally will not allow their loan security to be pledged again as collateral for a second mortgage, which could delay and complicate a foreclosure. Thus, the senior lender may preclude the borrower's use of a second mortgage.

However, some senior lenders may permit borrowers to add mezzanine debt on top of the first mortgage in the capital stack. **Mezzanine loans** are similar to second mortgages except that such loans are not secured by a lien on the property. Rather, mezzanine loans are secured by the equity interest in the borrower's company—which is usually a limited partnership (LP) or a limited liability company (LLC).[8] If the LP or LLC that owns the property fails to make payments, the mezzanine lender can foreclose on the "stock" of the company in a matter of weeks, compared to the 12–18 months it often takes to foreclose on a traditional commercial mortgage secured by real estate. By taking over ownership of the LP or LLC, the mezzanine lender effectively acquires control of the property.

How does the addition of mezzanine financing to the capital stack affect the borrower's expected return on equity in the first year of operations? After servicing both the first mortgage and the mezzanine loan, the equity investor will receive $270,000 in cash flow, which is an 18.0 percent expected return on her $1.5 million equity investment. Thus, adding a $2.0 million mezzanine loan to the capital stack increases the expected first year return on equity to 18 percent from 14 percent. This increase in expected return, however, comes with increased risk.[9]

Government-Sponsored Programs

www.cmalert.com

Commercial Mortgage Alert site delivers news, analysis, and statistics on all aspects of the commercial real estate finance business.

www.property.com

An established portal to news and information on the commercial mortgage market.

www.GlobeSt.com

Another portal to commercial real estate news and information.

The U.S. government provides multiple incentives to encourage the construction and ownership of affordable multifamily housing. Sponsoring and encouraging the construction of affordable rental housing meet the government's public policy goal of providing safe and affordable housing for all U.S. citizens. The Department of Housing and Urban Development (HUD) administers many of the federal government's multifamily initiatives, although certain tax credit programs are the responsibility of the Internal Revenue Service. As with the home loan mortgage market, HUD provides loan guarantees for multifamily mortgages through the Federal Housing Administration (FHA). HUD's initiatives include a program for the purchase and refinancing of existing, qualified, low-income properties that allows higher loan-to-value ratios (LTVs), a low-income program that targets new construction and substantial rehabilitation, as well as programs that finance rental housing for the elderly and subsidize the interest rates on multifamily properties targeted to low-income families. HUD also uses the "Section 8" program to allow local housing authorities to subsidize the rent payments of low-income households.[10]

Although Freddie Mac and Fannie Mae were placed into conservatorship by the federal government in 2008, they remain an important source of mortgage financing for multifamily housing. Freddie Mac offers a variety of multifamily loan types including affordable housing, housing for the elderly, construction and permanent loans, and refinancings. Fannie Mae is also an active participant in the multifamily mortgage market supplying a wide variety of loans targeted at housing for the elderly and low- and moderate-income households.[11] The future role these government entities, or their eventual successor(s), should play in the multifamily mortgage market continues to be a hotly debated topic.

---

8. Both limited partnership and limited liability companies are discussed in detail in Chapter 17.

9 The capital stack may also include preferred equity. Investors in preferred equity positions are higher in "pecking order" to receive the net cash flows produced by the underlying property than regular equity. Some argue that preferred equity is really a form of debt masked as equity.

10. For more information on HUD multifamily programs, visit the HUD website, www.hud.gov, and search the site for "Multifamily Housing."

11. For more information on Fannie Mae and Freddie Mac, visit the Fannie (www.fanniemae.com) or Freddie (www.freddiemac.com) websites.

The Benefits and Risks of Online CRE Lending

Over the past several years, the commercial real estate finance industry has seen increased regulatory oversight. The risk retention rules and increased reserve requirements, which went into effect at the end of 2016, put even more pressure on traditional lending sources, limiting their capability to provide clients with construction loans for new properties and refinancing of existing loans. Non-traditional lenders, including online marketplace lending platforms, will have an opportunity to fill the void and provide borrowers with access to alternative forms of capital.

A variety of online lending platforms have been developed for the purpose of funding commercial real estate deals, on both the debt and equity sides. Crowdfunding platforms fund deals online by raising varied amounts of money from many investors, pooling it to assemble the capital necessary to fund a deal. Marketplace lending, or peer-to-peer platforms, takes a different approach. On many of these platforms, borrowers and lenders are matched through online platforms. As a result, borrowers can often access funds more quickly and at better terms than by turning to many traditional lenders. Lenders on these platforms range from individuals to institutional investors who are looking for risk-adjusted returns on alternative forms of fixed income investing.

As this market continues to grow, it is important that platforms rely on the fundamentals of commercial real estate in their lending practices. Every commercial real estate loan is different. There are significant complexities in evaluating properties and understanding commercial real estate cycles. As companies' platforms continue to grow and fill the void in the marketplace, their teams will need to be made up of professionals with strong backgrounds in commercial real estate finance, ensuring that loans are originated and underwritten solidly. When executed correctly, online lending platforms are an effective and efficient way to fund commercial real estate loans, bringing capital sources traditionally unavailable to borrowers to the marketplace.

Source: Bechtel, Gary, "The Benefits and Risks of Online CRE Lending," nreionline.com/finance-investment/benefits-and-risks-online-cre-lending"
© 2016 Reprinted by permission of Gary Bechtel.

The Borrower's Decision-Making Process

Once investors have decided to purchase a commercial property, they are faced with a number of decisions. First, as discussed earlier, they must choose a financing structure. Do they use a standard balloon mortgage or a floating-rate loan, or do they pursue a more complicated structure such as a joint venture or sale-leaseback. Owners must also choose their desired amount of debt, although the maximum loan size is typically limited by the lender based on the income-producing ability and market value of the property.

Typical Loan Terms

Exhibit 16-1 contains typical loan terms on standard fixed-rate commercial mortgages as of the second-quarter of 2016. This information was obtained from Wells Fargo Commercial Real Estate (www.wellsfargo.com/com/financing/real-estate). The typical interest rate spread over 10-year Treasuries (or swaps) ranged from 2.75 percentage points (275 basis points) for apartment loans to 2.85 percent for loans on office and retail buildings. Although not reported in Exhibit 16-1, interest rate spreads are lower for floating-rate loans largely because borrowers, not lenders, are absorbing the interest rate risk. Thus, lenders must offer lower rates on floating-rate loans.

The **debt coverage ratio (DCR)** is defined as:

$$DCR = \frac{NOI}{DS}$$

where *NOI* is generally the net operating income estimated for the next 12 months of property operations and *DS* is the annual debt service. The *DCR* shows the extent to which *NOI* can decline from expectations before it is insufficient to service the mortgage debt. It therefore provides an indication of the safety associated with the use of borrowed funds. Recall from Chapter 8 that we are assuming capital expenditures are included in the calculation of *NOI* (an "above-line" treatment). If CAPX are not included in *NOI*, they should be subtracted from *NOI* when calculating the DCR. In early 2016, lenders were typically requiring *DCR*s of 1.20 to 1.25. However, their *DCR* requirements vary depending on the risk characteristics of the loan and competitive market pressures.

The loan-to-value ratio (*LTV*) measures the percentage of the price (or value) encumbered by the first mortgage. The higher the ratio, the less protection the lender has from loss of capital in the event of default and foreclosure (the *LTV* and *DCR* are discussed further in a later section). Maximum LTVs on first mortgagees typically range from 60 to 80 percent, depending on the lender and property type.

✓ Concept Check

16.7 What is the relation between the probability of default and the *LTV* and the *DCR*?

If the mortgage loan is going to be packaged with similar loans and then resold to investors as part of a commercial mortgage-backed security, the originating lender may rely more heavily on the debt yield ratio than the debt coverage ratio to determine the maximum amount they are willing to lend to the borrower. The **debt yield ratio** (*DYR*) is defined as the property's projected first year NOI divided by the amount of the first mortgage loan, or

$$DYR = \frac{NOI_1}{Loan\ Amount}$$

The *DYR* indicates the cash-on-cash return the lender would earn on its invested capital (i.e., the loan amount) if it had to foreclose on the mortgaged property immediately after originating the loan. Unlike the debt coverage ratio, the debt yield ratio is not affected by the interest rate or amortization period of the loan; the *DYR* is simply a measure of how large the *NOI* is relative to the loan amount. So what is an acceptable *DYR*? In 2016, *DYR*s ranged from 8 percent for high-quality multifamily or retail properties to 9 percent or more for other property types. Commercial banks and life insurance companies that intend to hold the loans they originate in their portfolios as long-term investments have not yet adopted the *DYR* as their primary metric for sizing loans.

The most common loan term on fixed-rate commercial mortgages is 10 years for all property types, though terms ranging from 5 to 40 years are available from some lenders. Lenders typically allow 30-year amortization periods.

Finally, apartment borrowers are typically required to set aside $250 a year for each apartment unit. The accumulated balances in these reserve accounts are used to fund nonrecurring capital costs, such as replacing carpeting, appliances, roofs, and heating and air-conditioning units. Industrial owners are typically required to set aside $0.10 to $0.20 per square foot per year for nonrecurring capital costs. On average, office and retail properties require slightly higher reserves.

✓ Concept Check

16.8 If $100,000 must be accumulated for a major roof repair that will be required at the end of four years, how much must be set aside at the end of each year if the annual deposits will earn 3 percent compounded annually?

We next discuss the borrower's choice of loan size, carefully considering the advantages and disadvantages of using financial leverage. The ongoing prepayment and default decisions borrowers face after origination are then considered.

Loan Size

Why do real estate investors and homeowners borrow funds—use financial leverage—for real estate investments? The first reason is limited financial resources. If an investor desires to purchase real estate but has insufficient wealth to pay cash for the property, then borrowing is a necessity. The second reason for the use of mortgage financing is that it alters the expected risk and return of real estate investments. In particular, the use of leverage amplifies the rate of return investors earn on their invested equity. This *magnification* of equity returns is known as positive (or negative) financial leverage; and may induce investors to at least partially debt-finance (use "other people's money") even if they have sufficient wealth to avoid borrowing.

When is the use of leverage favorable? The use of financial leverage will increase the internal rate of return (*IRR*) on equity when the cost of borrowing is less than the unlevered *IRR;* that is, the *IRR* calculated assuming the property is purchased with 100 percent equity financing. In other words, as long as each borrowed dollar is earning a greater return than it costs, the net difference goes to the owner, enhancing the equity return. Although the use of leverage may increase the investor's expected *IRR* on equity, it should be stressed that financial leverage also increases the riskiness of the equity investment by increasing the risk of default *and* by making the *realized* return on equity more sensitive to changes in rental rates and resale values. Thus, the increase in *expected* return from the use of debt may not be large enough to offset the corresponding increase in risk to the equity investor.

Financial Risk

Recall that mortgage lenders have a claim on operating cash flows that is superior to the claims of the equity investor. However, so long as the net operating income (*NOI*) from monthly operations exceeds the promised mortgage payment (i.e., the property is "cash flowing"), satisfying the lender's claim is not a problem. Increasing the amount of borrowed funds—and thus the promised mortgage payment—increases the probability that *NOI* will be insufficient to cover (service) the mortgage payment obligation. The risk that *NOI* will be less than debt service is often referred to as **financial risk.** Default risk is the risk that borrowers will cease to make timely payments of principal and interest, as required by the mortgage agreement. Such behavior could lead to lender foreclosure on the property if not cured by the borrower. As the amount of leverage increases beyond a critical level, it becomes increasingly likely that debt service will exceed the *NOI*. If the property is not cash flowing, the borrower will have to draw on money from other sources to avoid default.

✓ **Concept Check**

16.9   Define *financial risk*. From the lender's perspective, is it more closely linked to the risk of default or prepayment?

Increased Variability of Equity Returns from Leverage

The use of mortgage debt to help finance the acquisition of real estate is pervasive, and therefore its effect on risk and return should be clearly understood. Many market participants recommend extensive use of debt. Although increased financial leverage increases, in some cases substantially, the estimated *IRR*, financial leverage is a "double-edged sword." Its use enhances equity returns when the property is performing well. However, if the property performs poorly, the use of debt can make a bad situation worse, although the right to default can limit the amount of downside risk when nonrecourse financing is used. Think of it this way: Higher expected returns on equity can be "purchased" with additional leverage—but at the "price" of significantly increased variability in the return on equity. The acute sensitivity of investor returns to debt financing is demonstrated with a numerical example in Chapter 19.

The Prepayment and Default Decisions

As with residential mortgages, the most accurate guide to a commercial mortgage refinancing decision is net present value. This decision rule compares the present value of future payment reductions to the immediate costs of obtaining a new loan. The costs of refinancing an existing commercial mortgage are large and can vary depending upon the number of points and fees charged by the new lender. In addition, the up-front costs of commercial refinancing typically include a penalty for extinguishing the existing mortgage, as discussed earlier. Moreover, lockout provisions may preclude the borrower from refinancing. For these reasons, the risk to the commercial lender of a prepayment due to a decline in interest rates or a borrower move is generally small relative to residential mortgages.

What is the most significant risk faced by commercial mortgage lenders? The signature risk of commercial mortgage lending is default risk. Putting aside transaction costs and other considerations (including the borrower's credit rating), commercial borrowers with nonrecourse mortgages are more likely to default on their loans if the value of the property were to fall below the value of the remaining mortgage balance. However, the evidence indicates that commercial borrowers do not default as soon as the mortgage balance exceeds the value of the property. Many borrowers with negative equity continue to make payments because they expect the value of the property to increase. The propensity of commercial borrowers to default also is impeded by the costs of default. These costs include direct costs such as penalty fees or any recourse the lender holds to other assets of the borrower, and indirect costs such as greater difficulty or higher cost of obtaining mortgage financing subsequent to the default.

> ✓ **Concept Check**
>
> **16.10** Yield spreads on commercial mortgages since 1997 are displayed in Exhibit 16-2. What type of risk accounts for the majority of this spread over Treasury securities?

The Permanent Loan Application and Approval Process

Borrowers seeking to acquire or refinance an existing commercial property may submit loan requests directly to commercial banks, life insurance companies, or other direct lenders. These institutions have commercial property lending units that consider such requests. Informal discussions with loan officers in these firms inform would-be borrowers of the expected items in a loan submission package. Another channel for commercial loan requests is through mortgage bankers and brokers. Many of these intermediaries enjoy close business relationships with dozens of direct lenders. A business relationship in which a permanent lender agrees to purchase loans or to consider loan requests from a mortgage banker or broker is frequently termed a **correspondent relationship.** Many mortgage brokers specialize in seeking loan opportunities and putting together loan application packages that meet the requirements of both borrowers and lenders. In short, mortgage brokers help borrowers and lenders find each other. They also assist borrowers in assembling the loan submission package. For these services, commercial mortgage brokers receive a fee, generally from the borrower, at loan closing that may range from 1/2 to 1 percent of the loan amount.

Relative to home loans, the underwriting process for commercial loans is more complicated and focuses more on the property used as collateral for the loan. The primary reason for this difference in emphasis is the anticipated source of funds for loan repayment. Lenders expect that payments on residential loans will come from the personal income of the borrower. Payments on commercial real estate loans are expected to come from income generated by the property. As a result, the commercial loan underwriting process focuses on the property being pledged as collateral for the loan.

The process by which equity investors request and obtain permanent financing to acquire or refinance an existing commercial property varies by lender, by the type and quality of the property, and by any existing relationship the lender has with the borrower. However, we next discuss a possible sequence.

Loan Submission Package and Application

Borrowers, perhaps aided by a mortgage broker, submit a loan package to a lender (or lenders). The purpose of the loan submission package (executive summary) is to provide lenders with the information they need to quickly evaluate the borrower's request. The package typically contains information on the type, size, and location of the property, maps and photographs, when the property was built and most recently renovated, the purchase price of the property, the requested loan amount and other basic loan terms, the operating history of the property over the last several years, the current rent roll, and estimated potential gross income over the next 12 months.

Based on the information contained in the loan submission package and, in some cases, conversations with the borrower or borrower's mortgage broker, the lender either rejects the loan opportunity or issues a preliminary quote, which contains the basic terms of the proposed loan. This quote is sometimes referred to as a term sheet. The borrower will then choose to reject or accept the lender's quote or, in some cases, attempt to negotiate better loan terms. If the lender and the borrower are able to come to agreement on the basic terms of the loan, the lender will finalize the loan application to be signed by the borrower.

The length and details of the loan application vary with the size of the loan request, the type of property being used as collateral (e.g., office, apartment), and whether the loan will be held in the lender's portfolio or sold in the secondary market to be used as collateral for the issuance of a commercial mortgage-backed security. However, the loan application typically contains a great deal of the terms and language that will be included in the final promissory note and mortgage including: the contract interest rate or how the interest rate will be determined at closing if the rate is not locked at application, the repayment terms, the minimum debt coverage ratio, the maximum loan-to-value ratio, insurance requirements, restrictions on prepayments, restrictions on the borrower's ability to obtain a second mortgage, and situations under which the lender's recourse in the event of default will be against the property only, as well as situations and events that make the borrower personally liable for the loan, if applicable.

The loan application also details all of the items the borrower must provide directly to the lender subsequent to the loan application but before the loan commitment is issued. These items usually include proof of title insurance, a current survey, evidence of zoning and building code compliance, and certified operating statements and rent roll. The lender will typically order an appraisal of the property as well as environmental and engineering reports showing that all the improvements are in good condition and in compliance with all applicable regulations. The borrower must also agree to make all existing leases available to the lender for inspection.

When the loan application is signed, the borrower is typically required to pay a nonrefundable loan processing fee to cover actual expenses the lender has incurred to complete the loan application. These include the expenses incurred by the lender to travel to and inspect the property. The loan processing fee can range from $30,000 to more than $100,000 depending on the complexity of the property/transaction. The lender will also usually require a "good faith" deposit, which can be 1–2 percent of the loan amount. This deposit is required as the lender will now proceed to secure the loan funds, complete the loan underwriting process, and prepare for closing.

The good faith deposit is typically refunded to the borrower at loan closing. However, if the loan fails to close because the borrower does not act in good faith, the lender may keep the deposit. For example, consider a lender who issued a binding commitment to make a permanent loan to a borrower at an interest rate of 4.0 percent. The borrower signed the loan application and the lender incurred the considerable expense of fully underwriting the loan. However, just prior to the scheduled loan closing, mortgage rates on similar loans moved down to 3.75 percent from 4.0 percent and the borrower has received a quote from a second lender at the reduced rate. If the borrower walks away from her original commitment, the lender would be entitled to keep the good faith deposit.

Lenders may also require a deposit of $20,000 or more for legal fees and required third-party reports. This deposit is used by the lender to retain legal counsel to work on loan documents and to cover the costs of obtaining required third-party reports, such as the appraisal, mechanical system reports, roof reports, and environmental reports. The signed loan application authorizes the lender to order such reports and acknowledges that such deposits are nonrefundable to the extent the funds are used to retain legal counsel to draft loan documents and to obtain third-party reports, regardless of whether the lender ultimately issues a commitment that is acceptable to the borrower.

From Loan Application to Closing

www.LoopLender.com

Affiliated with LoopNet.com, this site provides information on current rates and permits an online mortgage search.

With the signed application, loan processing fee, good faith deposit, and deposit for legal fees and third-party reports in hand, the lender is confident the borrower intends to close the loan. It therefore makes sense for the lender to incur the additional expenses associated with moving the loan forward from signed application to loan closing.

The lender's required **due diligence** begins once the loan application is signed. The due diligence process typically includes ordering the fee appraisal, the title report, and a number of third-party inspection, compliance, and engineering reports. For example, the lender will require evidence that the property is in compliance with all zoning and building codes and that the borrower is up-to-date on property tax payments. This is also when the lender digs into an evaluation of the property's income-producing ability. In part, the lender performs due diligence to make sure the potential borrower did not misrepresent the property in any way in the original loan submission package. Thus, in addition to the rent roll that summarizes the individual leases on the property, the lender may perform a detailed analysis of some or all of the leases and lease amendments, including guarantees and subleases. The lender will also collect and analyze more information on the recent operating performance of the property, including capital expenditures, utilities, property taxes, and hazard and liability insurance. Finally, the lender will collect and examine more detailed information on the building, such as mechanical system reports, heating and air conditioning units, roof reports, geotechnical soil reports, and various environmental reports, including mold, radon gas, lead paint and asbestos reports.

If the lender's due diligence process uncovers an inconsistency or error in the information provided by the borrower in the loan submission package, or an undisclosed problem with the land, building, title, or borrower, the lender may choose to reduce the loan amount, alter other loan terms, or back out of the deal until the issue is addressed to the satisfaction of the lender's staff. If full resolution is obtained, the staff prepares a package that is presented to a committee of top executives for final approval. Once approved and issued to the borrower, the loan commitment is a binding agreement between the lender and the borrower. A typical permanent loan submission and approval process is summarized in Exhibit 16-4. It is important to remember, however, that this process can vary significantly by property type and size and across borrowers and lenders.

A typical commercial real estate loan may take 60 days from the signing of the purchase and sale contract until loan closing, but some loans are processed more quickly. Processing time depends on numerous factors such as the type and size of loan, the number and complexity of the existing leases, and whether the borrower and the lender are familiar with each other's requirements.

Mezzanine Financing on the Upswing as Industry Sees More Construction

Commercial real estate borrowers have a growing appetite for mezzanine loans that is fueled by redevelopment and refinancing activity, as well as the return of new construction. Mezzanine lenders are finding ample opportunities in a market where traditional lenders remain conservative in the amount of leverage they are willing to provide. Increased regulations have had a profound negative impact on banks' ability to lend against real estate, particularly against value-added real estate and new construction. That creates a greater opportunity for nonregulated, non-deposit private capital to step in and help to finance new construction, he says.

Many of the developers/sponsors need capital that goes beyond what a commercial bank construction loan will provide. Banks will typically provide 60 or 65 percent leverage on a property, while mezzanine lenders will go up to 75 or 80 percent with a non-recourse loan.

Mezz lenders also expect to see more business coming from the ongoing wave of loan maturities. Ten-year loans made at the peak of the market in 2005, 2006, and 2007 are coming due and will need to be refinanced. There will be opportunities for mezzanine lenders to provide additional leverage to some of those legacy loans as they are refinanced.

Source: Beth Mattson-Teig, "Mezzanine Financing on the Upswing as Industry Sees More Construction," nreionline.com/bridge-mezzanine-finance/mezzanine-financing-upswing-industry-sees-more-construction © 2015 Reprinted by permission of *National Real Estate Investor.*

Exhibit 16-4 The Loan Submission, Application, and Approval Process—An Illustration

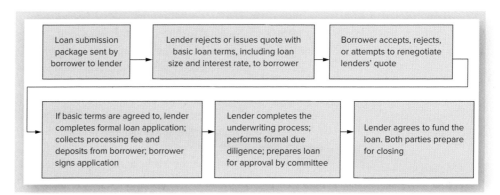

The lender may offer the borrower the opportunity to "lock in" the interest rate on the loan prior to closing. If the rate is not locked, the borrower and the lender will usually agree to a spread. For example, the lender may commit to close a 10-year apartment loan at a rate 250 basis points (2.50 percentage points) above the yield on 10-year Treasury securities. If the yield on 10-year Treasury securities increases after the loan commitment but before closing, the contract interest rate will increase. To protect against such increases, the borrower is often willing to pay a nonrefundable fee to obtain a **rate lock agreement** from the lender.

Maximum Loan Amount

Several factors may determine whether the borrower's requested loan amount is too high. First, lenders usually set limits on allowable loan-to-value ratios that often vary by property type and by the market in which the property is located. Second, the lender typically underwrites the property's first year *NOI* (net of capital expenditures and leasing commissions); that is, they estimate what they believe will be the net cash flow of the property. From this, the lender backs out a maximum loan amount—given an interest rate, amortization period, and minimum required debt coverage ratio.

Exhibit 16-5 Assumptions for a Loan on Gatorwood Apartment Complex

Input	Assumption
Number of units	296 units with average monthly rent of $534.91
Purchase price	$13,375,000
Vacancy and collection losses	6 percent per year
Operating expenses	$610,000 in year 1
Reserve for capital expenditures	$88,800 in year 1. Expenditures are reserved for in calculation of NOI (i.e., an above-line treatment)
Financing:	
Loan amount	$10,000,000 (equals 74.7664 percent of price)
Interest rate (annual)	5.25 percent
Amortization schedule	25 years, *monthly* payments
Loan term	10 years
Annual payment	$719,097 ($59,924.77 × 12)*

*The calculator keystrokes for finding the monthly payment are $N = 300$; $I/YR = 5.25/12$; $PV = 10,000,000$; $PMT = ?$; and $FV = 0$. Loan payment calculations are discussed in detail in Chapters 14 and 15.

To demonstrate the loan underwriting process, consider the example summarized in Exhibit 16-5. A lender is offering a $10 million fixed-payment mortgage with a 5.25 percent interest rate and monthly payments. With a loan term of 10 years and a 25-year amortization schedule, the annual payment is $719,097. The expected cash flow in the first year of rental operations implied by the assumptions in Exhibit 16-5 is contained in Exhibit 16-6.

The debt coverage ratio (*DCR*) for our Gatorwood Apartment example, assuming a $10 million loan, is:

$$DCR = \frac{Net\ operating\ income}{Debt\ service} = \frac{\$1,087,200}{\$719,097} = 1.51$$

Because *NOI* in the first year of operations is expected to be half again as large as the prospective mortgage payment, there appears to be sufficient protection against a decline in rental rates and net operating income.

If the lender feels that $1,087,200 is a reasonable estimate of first year *NOI* (net cash flow) the *DCR* can be used to calculate the maximum allowable loan, given the lender's

Exhibit 16-6 Gatorwood Apartment Complex Before-Tax Cash Flows from Annual Operations

Potential gross income (PGI)	$1,900,000
− Vacancy and collection loss (VC)	114,000
= Effective gross income (EGI)	1,786,000
− Operating expenses (OE)	610,000
− Capital expenditures (CAPX)	88,800
= Net operating income (NOI)	1,087,200
− Debt service (DS)	719,097
= Before-tax cash flow	$ 368,103

Construction Lenders

minimum acceptable *DCR*. For example, if a conservative lender requires the *DCR* to be 1.35 or greater, we can obtain the maximum debt service payment by rearranging the *DCR* formula as follows:

$$Maximum\ debt\ service = \frac{NOI}{Minimum\ DCR} = \frac{\$1,087,200}{1.35} = \$805,333$$

This implies a maximum fixed monthly payment of $67,111 ($805,333/12). This maximum monthly debt service, together with a 5.25 percent interest rate and a 25-year loan term, implies a maximum loan of $11,199,208 (an 83.7 percent *LTV*).[12] Although it appears that the property can support a $11,199,208 loan, the loan limit will be determined by the lender's maximum allowable *LTV* if it is less than 83.7 percent, which is likely. If the lender sizes the loan based on a minimum debt yield ratio *(DYR)* of 9.0 percent instead of a minimum *DCR* of 1.35, the maximum loan amount would be $12,080,000 ($NOI_1$ ÷ loan amount = $1,087,200 ÷ 0.09). However, the maximum loan amount may be dictated by the lender's maximum allowable LTV if it is less than the maximum loan size indicated by the debt yield ratio.

> ### ✓ Concept Check
>
> **16.11** You are analyzing the potential acquisition of a small apartment property. Some of the estimates from the first year pro forma are as follows: potential gross income, $185,000; vacancy and collection losses, $18,500; annual debt service, $72,643; operating expenses, $58,275; capital expenditures, $0. Calculate the *DCR*.

Land Acquisition, Development, and Construction Financing

The development, construction, and operation of large income properties take time and different types of effort. The developer may acquire land that must then be made ready (i.e., improved) for construction. The improved land may be sold as individual lots, which is typical with new home development, or it may be used as an industrial or office site, or as

---

12. The calculator keystrokes to find the maximum loan amount are $N = 300$; $I = 5.25/12$; $PV = ?$; $PMT = 67,111$; and $FV = 0$.

a site for some other form of income-producing property. Different financing requirements usually are involved in the various phases of a property's life, and lending arrangements have evolved to serve these needs. **Land acquisition loans** finance the purchase of the raw land: **Land development loans** finance the installation of the on-site and off-site improvements to the land (e.g., sewers, streets, and utilities) that are necessary to ready the land for construction. **Construction loans** are used to finance the costs associated with erecting the building or buildings (i.e., "going vertical").

Land acquisition loans are difficult to obtain and lenders offer these loans on an exception basis at low leverage (25–35 percent LTV) to their very best clients. For land development loans, lenders will typically require presale contracts with homebuilders or the ultimate buyers of the land and typically have leverage equal to 50–60 percent of the expected value of the property when eventually sold. Construction loans have LTVs equal to 65–75 percent of expected value of the completed property and often require significant preleasing with major tenants prior to the construction loan closing. For example, for a proposed shopping center the construction lender often requires preleases with the anchor tenants (i.e., Publix, Target, Walmart, etc.) and a portion of the local tenants, typically 50 percent of the total local space proposed. Terms on construction loans typically range from one to three years and allow for time to construct and lease up the project.

The land acquisition, development, and construction loans used by developers differ significantly from the "permanent" mortgages we have focused on in this chapter. Developers are always personally liable for such loans; non-recourse financing is simply not available. In addition, these development-oriented loans typically have floating interest rates tied to short-term interest rate indices and are interest-only. Finally, land acquisition, development, and construction loans are prepayable at any time without penalty.

Some lenders may be willing to make acquisition, development, and construction loans. In these loans, the same lender advances enough money for the developer to purchase the land and develop it to the point that it is ready for a building to be constructed on it. Then the lender advances additional funds for construction, with the developed land and partial construction serving as security for the construction loan. The existence of one lender and one set of loan documents simplifies the financing process and eliminates potential conflicts of interest between the various lenders in the development chain. In some cases, the developer may obtain a single, short-term permanent mortgage—or **miniperm loan**—from a lender that provides financing for the construction period, the lease-up period, and for several years beyond the lease-up stage. Developers may be attracted to miniperms, which enable them to proceed with construction without long-term financing, if they expect to sell the project or refinance into a permanent loan before the term of the miniperm loan expires. (Land acquisition, land development, and construction loans are discussed in more detail in Chapter 23.)

Ultimately, the success of land development and construction loans depends on the developer's ability to complete projects with market values in excess of development and construction costs. The developer's failure to create adequate value at any stage of the development process may result in default and foreclosure. Certainly, development and construction loans lie on the high end of the real estate risk spectrum.

Summary

Most commercial properties require debt financing tailored to meet the unique circumstances of the situation. Although some of the same institutions (e.g., commercial banks) that originate home loans also provide commercial property financing, the loan terms are considerably different. For example, commercial mortgages are typically shorter in term and limit or penalize prepayment.

The three main repayment mechanisms used in the market for long-term (permanent) commercial mortgages are fully amortizing loans, partially amortizing loans, and interest-only loans. Fixed-rate, partially amortizing mortgages with balloon payments are the most commonly used structure, although it is not uncommon for commercial mortgages to have adjustable, or floating, interest rates. Fixed-rate commercial mortgages do not typically allow borrowers to freely prepay at par because they contain a lockout provision, a prepayment penalty such as a yield-maintenance agreement or defeasance, or both. Floating-rate loans generally are prepayable at par without penalty. The availability of participation mortgages and sale-leaseback financing provides alternative financing structures for investors and property owners to consider.

After selecting the appropriate financing structure, investors must next choose their desired loan amount. Borrowed funds magnify the equity returns on a given project. By employing higher loan-to-value ratios—using more financial leverage—investors can generally increase their expected returns. By doing so, however, they also increase the variability of equity returns and the probability that net operating income will not be sufficient to cover the mortgage payment obligation. This latter concern is often referred to as *financial risk*. Other decisions facing commercial borrowers subsequent to loan origination include the decision to prepay and the decision to default. In both situations, net present value calculations should guide decision making, remembering of course that it is important to include all potential costs, such as a diminished ability to obtain financing in the future, when selecting the default option.

Borrowers seeking to acquire or refinance an existing commercial property may submit loan requests directly to commercial banks, life insurance companies, or other direct lenders. Another channel for commercial loan requests is through mortgage bankers and brokers, who specialize in putting together loan applications that meet the requirements of both borrowers and lenders. Relative to home loans, the underwriting process for commercial loans is more complicated and focuses more on the property used as collateral for the loan.

The process by which equity investors request and obtain permanent financing to acquire or refinance an existing commercial property varies by lender, by the type and quality of the property, and by any existing relationship the lender has with the borrower. Borrowers, perhaps aided by a mortgage broker, typically submit a loan package to a lender (or lenders). The purpose of the loan submission package is to provide lenders with the information they need to quickly evaluate the borrower's request. Based on the information contained in the loan submission package, the lender either rejects the loan opportunity or issues a preliminary quote, which contains the basic terms of the proposed loan. The borrower will then choose to reject or accept the lender's quote or, in some cases, attempt to negotiate better loan terms. If the lender and the borrower are able to come to agreement on the basic terms of the loan, the lender will finalize the loan application to be signed by the borrower.

The length and details of the loan application vary with the size of the loan request, the type of property being used as collateral (e.g., office, apartment), and whether the loan will be held in the lender's portfolio or sold in the secondary market where it will be used as collateral for the issuance of a commercial mortgage-backed security. When the loan application is signed, the borrower is typically required to pay a nonrefundable loan processing fee and one or more deposits including a "good faith" deposit, which can total 1–2 percent of the loan amount. The good faith deposit is typically refunded to the borrower at loan closing.

With the signed application, loan processing fee, and borrower deposits, the lender is confident the borrower intends to close the loan. The lender's required due diligence begins once the loan application is signed. In part, the lender performs due diligence to make sure the potential borrower did not misrepresent the property in any way in the original loan submission package. The lender will also collect and analyze more information on the building and the recent operating performance of the property. If the loan application survives the due diligence process, the lender must decide whether or not to finalize the loan and schedule a closing date.

Key Terms

Test Problems

Answer the following multiple-choice problems:

1. Due-on-sale clauses are included in commercial mortgages primarily to protect lenders from:
   a. Interest rate risk.
   b. Default risk.
   c. Reinvestment risk.
   d. Prepayment risk.

2. Consider a 30-year, 7 percent, fixed-rate, fully amortizing mortgage with a yield maintenance provision. Relative to this mortgage, a 10-year balloon mortgage with the same contract interest rate and yield maintenance provisions will primarily reduce the lender's:
   a. Interest rate risk.
   b. Default risk.
   c. Reinvestment risk.
   d. Prepayment risk.

3. An interest-only balloon mortgage loan is commonly referred to as a:
   a. Mini-perm loan.
   b. Mezzanine loan.
   c. Land acquisition loan.
   d. Bullet loan.

4. The acquisition price of a property is $380,000. The loan amount is $285,000. If the property's NOI is expected to be $22,560, operating expenses $12,250, and the annual debt service $19,987, the debt yield ratio (*DYR*) is approximately equal to:
   a. 0.059 or 5.9%.
   b. 0.079 or 7.9%.
   c. 0.0701 or 7.0%.
   d. 0.0526 or 5.3%.
   e. None of the above.

5. Which of the following statements is most accurate?
   a. Joint ventures usually increase the amount of equity capital the developer/borrower must invest in the project.
   b. Joint ventures usually decrease the amount of equity capital the developer/borrower must invest in the project.
   c. Joint ventures give the developer/borrower a priority claim on the property's cash flows.
   d. Joint ventures increase the developer/borrower's exposure to the risk of property price fluctuations.

6. Commercial mortgage borrowers may decide to prepay the principal on their loan even if they face prepayment penalties. One way that lenders protect themselves from prepayments in such circumstances is by requiring the borrower who prepays to purchase for the lender a set of U.S. Treasury securities whose coupon payments replicate the cash flows the lender will lose as a result of the early retirement of the mortgage. This process is referred to as:
   a. Lockout.
   b. Yield-maintenance.
   c. Defeasance.
   d. Curtailment.

7. Using financial leverage on a real estate investment can be for the purpose of all of the following *except:*
   a. Greater diversification.
   b. Greater expected return on equity.
   c. Being able to acquire the property.
   d. Reduction of financial risk for the leveraged investment.

8. Which of these ratios is an indicator of the financial risk for an income property?
   a. Debt coverage ratio.
   b. Loan-to-value ratio.
   c. Equity dividend rate.
   d. Both *a* and *b,* but not *c.*
   e. All three, *a, b,* and *c.*

9. The acquisition price of a property is $380,000. The loan amount is $285,000. If the property's *NOI* is expected to be $22,560, operating expenses $12,250, and the annual debt service $19,987, the debt coverage ratio (*DCR*) is approximately equal to:
   a. 0.89.
   b. 1.13.
   c. 1.84.
   d. 1.74.
   e. None of the above.

10. With a mezzanine loan:
    a. the mezzanine lender has a lien on the property that is subordinate to the senior lien holder's position.
    b. the borrower pledges the same property as collateral for the mezzanine loan that was pledged as collateral for the first mortgage.
    c. the borrower's promise to pay is secured by the equity interest in the borrower's limited partnership or limited liability company.
    d. the mezzanine lender has a more difficult time foreclosing than would be the case with a second mortgage.

Study Questions

1. Discuss several differences between long-term commercial mortgages and their residential counterparts.
2. Answer the following questions on financial leverage, value, and return:
   a. Define financial risk.
   b. Should the investor select the origination *LTV* that maximizes the expected return on equity? Explain why or why not.
3. Distinguish between recourse and nonrecourse financing.
4. Explain lockout provisions and yield-maintenance agreements. Does the inclusion of one or both of these provisions affect the borrower's cost of debt financing? Explain.
5. Assume the annual interest rate on a $500,000 seven-year balloon mortgage is 6 percent. Payments will be made monthly based on a 30-year amortization schedule.
   a. What will be the monthly payment?
   b. What will be the balance of the loan at the end of year 7?
   c. What will be the balance of the loan at the end of year 3?
   d. Assume that interest rates have fallen to 4.5 percent at the end of year 3. If the remaining mortgage balance at the end of year 3 is refinanced at the 4.5 percent annual rate, what would be the new monthly payment assuming a 27-year amortization schedule?
   e. What is the difference in the old 6 percent monthly payment and the new 4.5 percent payment?
   f. What will be the remaining mortgage balance on the new 4.5 percent loan at the end of year 7 (four years after refinancing)?
   g. What will be the difference in the remaining mortgage balances at the end of year 7 (four years after refinancing)?
   h. At the end of year 3 (beginning of year 4), what will be the present value of the difference in monthly payments in years 4–7, discounting at an annual rate of 4.5 percent?
   i. At the end of year 3 (beginning of year 4), what will be the present value of the difference in loan balances at the end of year 7, discounting at an annual rate of 4.5 percent?
   j. At the end of year 3 (beginning of year 4), what will be the total present value of lost payments in years 4–7 from the lender's perspective?
   k. If the mortgage contains a yield-maintenance agreement that requires the borrower to pay a lump sum prepayment penalty at the end of year 3 equal to the present value of the borrower's lost payments in years 4–7, what should that lump sum penalty be?
6. Consider the stand-alone corner locations favored by Walgreens for locating their drugstores. In most cases, Walgreens does not own these properties. Instead, they lease the properties on a long-term basis from institutional owners. What does Walgreens gain by leasing instead of owning? What do they lose?

7. Consider the following table of annual mortgage rates and yields on 10-year Treasury securities:

Year	Mortgage Rate (%)	10-Year U.S. Treasury Yield (%)
1990	9.98	8.48
1991	9.76	7.87
1992	9.01	7.02
1993	7.90	5.90
1994	8.66	6.97
1995	8.13	6.69
1996	7.79	6.39
1997	7.63	6.36
1998	6.85	5.23
1999	7.59	5.57
2000	8.18	6.07
2001	7.25	4.95
2002	6.65	4.64
2003	5.70	4.03
2004	5.67	4.31
2005	5.43	4.25

   a. What was the average annual spread on mortgage rates relative to 10-year Treasury securities over the 1990–2005 period?
   b. What was the correlation between annual mortgage rates and Treasury yields over the 1990–2005 period? (Use your financial calculator or the statistical functions in Excel.)
8. List and briefly describe the typical items included in a commercial mortgage loan submission package.
9. You have decided to purchase an industrial warehouse. The purchase price is $1 million and you expect to hold the property for five years. You have narrowed your choice of debt financing packages to the following two alternatives:
   • $700,000 loan, 6 percent interest rate, 30-year term, annual, interest-only payments (the annual payment will not include any amortization of principal), and $50,000 in up-front financing costs.
   • $750,000 loan, 6 percent interest rate, 30-year term, annual, interest-only payments. No up-front financing costs.
   What is the difference in the present value of these two loan alternatives? Assume the appropriate discount rate is 6 percent.
10. You are considering the purchase of an industrial warehouse. The purchase price is $1 million. You expect to hold the property for five years. You have decided to finance the acquisition with a $700,000 loan, 6 percent interest rate,

30-year term, and annual interest-only payments (i.e. the annual payment will not include any amortization of principal). There are $50,000 in up-front financing costs. You estimate the following cash flows for the first year of operations:

$135,000	Effective gross income
27,000	Operating expenses
$108,000	*NOI*

a. Calculate the overall rate of return (or "going-in cap rate").
b. Calculate the debt coverage ratio.
c. What is the largest loan that you can obtain (holding the other terms constant) if the lender requires a debt service coverage ratio of *at least* 1.2?

11. Distinguish among land acquisition loans, land development loans, and construction loans. How would you rank these three with respect to lender risk?

12. Discuss the potential advantages of a miniperm loan from the perspective of the developer/investor, relative to the separate financing of each stage of the development.

13. You are considering purchasing an office building for $2,500,000. You expect the potential gross income (*PGI*) in the first year to be $450,000; vacancy and collection losses to be 9 percent of *PGI*; and operating expenses and capital expenditures to be 42 percent of effective gross income (*EGI*). You will finance the acquisition with 25 percent equity and 75 percent debt. The annual interest rate on the debt financing will be 5.5 percent. Payment will be made monthly based on a 25-year amortization schedule.

a. What is the implied first year overall capitalization rate?
b. What is the expected debt coverage ratio in year 1 of operations?
c. If the lender requires the *DCR* to be 1.25 or greater, what is the maximum loan amount?
d. What is the debt yield ratio?

EXPLORE THE WEB

Looking for information on commercial real estate loans? Go to the homepage of Mortgage-Investment.com and click on the "Mortgage & Investment" tab at the top of the page. Then click on the "Learn About Commercial and Residential Mortgages" tab. Under Commercial Real Estate Financial Ratios, explore the definitions of common ratio used by lenders and investors.

Solutions to Concept Checks

1. With recourse loans, the borrower/investor has personal liability for the amount borrowed. This means that if default and foreclosure occur and the foreclosure sale proceeds are less than the amount due to the lender, the lender may come after other borrower assets to satisfy the lender's claim. With nonrecourse loans, the borrower/investor is not personally liable for the loan. Thus, the lender can look only to the property pledged as collateral for the loan to satisfy the debt. The industry standard for existing properties is a nonrecourse loan, although some lenders, especially commercial banks, may require recourse.

2. With a partially amortizing loan, the balance is not zero at the end of the loan term. This means the remaining loan balance must be paid off or refinanced when the loan matures. If the value of the property has fallen below the remaining loan balance, the borrower may simply choose to default. With a fully amortizing loan, the balance of the mortgage is zero at the end of the loan term. This reduces the probability of default throughout the life of the loan. Thus, partially amortizing loans are more risky for the lender, all else being equal.

3. When discounting at the riskless Treasury rate, investors are adjusting for the *timing* of the cash flows because the Treasury rate represents their opportunity cost of waiting for the future cash flows. To adjust for risk, an appropriate risk premium must be added to the riskless Treasury rate.

4. If the $1,400,000 principal balance is reinvested at 4 percent, compounded monthly, for the remaining seven years, the balance will increase to $1,851.519 ($N = 84$; $I/YR = 4.00/12$; $PV = 1,400,000$; $PMT = 0$; and $FV = ?$). If

invested at 5 percent, compounded monthly, for the remaining seven years, the principal balance will increase to $1,985,250. This illustrates why lenders do not want borrowers to prepay 5 percent mortgages in a 4 percent interest rate environment; lenders do not want to reinvest the loan balance at 4 percent when they are earning 5 percent on the mortgage.

5. Borrowers may be willing to give the lender a piece of the property's upside in order to obtain a larger mortgage.

6. Leasing allows funds not invested in the land and building to be invested in the tenant's core business. If they expect returns on capital invested in their primary business to exceed the returns on their real estate holdings, they may be better off leasing. In addition, leasing effectively provides 100 percent financing of the real estate and the entire lease payment is deductible for tax purposes.

7. Loans with higher *DCR*s and lower *LTV*s have lower probabilities of default, all else equal.

8. To accumulate $100,000 by the end of four years, $23,903 must be deposited annually at a 3 percent interest rate compounded annually ($N = 4$; $I/YR = 3.00$; $PV = 0$; $PMT = ?$; and $FV = 100,000$).

9. Financial risk is the risk that *NOI* will be less than debt service. From the lender's perspective, financial risk is more closely linked to default risk.

10. The majority of the spread of commercial mortgages over Treasuries is compensation to the lender for default risk.

11. The *DCR* is equal to *NOI* ÷ debt service = $108,225 ÷ $72,643 = 1.49.

Additional Readings

Berges, S. *The Complete Guide to Real Estate Finance for Investment Properties.* Hoboken, NJ: John Wiley and Sons, Inc., 2004.

Brueggeman, William B., and Jeffrey D. Fisher. *Real Estate Finance and Investment,* 15th ed. New York: McGraw-Hill Irwin, 2016.

Clauretie, T. M., and G. S. Sirmans. *Real Estate Finance: Theory and Practice,* 7th ed. Cincinnati, OH: Cengage Learning, 2013.

Collier, N. S., C. A. Collier, and D. A. Halperin. *Construction Funding: The Process of Real Estate Development, Appraisal, and Finance,* 4th ed. New York: John Wiley and Sons, 2008.

Geltner, D., N. G. Miller, Jim Clayton, and Piet Eichholtz. *Commercial Real Estate Analysis & Investment,* 3rd ed. Mason, OH: Thomson South-Western Publishing, 2014.

Kolbe, P. T., G. E. Greer, and B.D. Waller. *Real Estate Finance,* 3rd. Chicago, IL: Kaplan Publishing, 2012.

Linneman, P. *Real Estate Finance & Investments: Risk and Opportunities,* 3rd ed. Philadelphia, PA: Linneman Associates, 2011.

Sirota, D and D. Barrell. *Essentials of Real Estate Finance, 14th ed.* Chicago: Kaplan Publishing, Inc., 2015.

Wiedemer, John P., Joseph E. Goeters, and J. Edward Graham. *Real Estate Investment*, 7th ed. Mason, OH: South-Western Cengage Learning, 2011.

Wiedemer, John P., and J. Keith Baker. *Real Estate Finance*, 9th ed. Mason, OH: South-Western Cengage Learning, 2011.

Chapter 17

Sources *of* Commercial Debt *and* Equity Capital

LEARNING OBJECTIVES

After reading this chapter, you will be able to:

1 Describe the size of the U.S. commercial real estate market relative to alternative asset classes such as stocks and bonds.

2 Identify potential ownership structures for pooling private equity capital and explain the advantages and disadvantages of each.

3 Identify the advantages and disadvantages of investing in commercial real estate both directly and through intermediaries.

4 Identify the primary sources of public and private mortgage debt and discuss their relative importance.

5 Discuss the role private syndications play in commercial real estate markets.

6 Comment on the size and importance of the real estate investment trust (REIT) market.

7 Explain how REIT income is measured and how REITs are valued.

OUTLINE

Introduction

Several of the preceding chapters focus on building a framework for understanding how commercial real estate assets are valued. But little attention has been paid to the types of investors that actually acquire commercial real estate or to the forms of ownership (e.g., partnership, corporation) these investors employ when purchasing real estate. Similarly, Chapter 16 discusses the most common mortgage products used by equity investors to finance commercial real estate investments. Again, the emphasis in Chapter 16 is on the description of common commercial mortgage products and the decision-making processes of borrowers and lenders, not on the role and importance of each of the various lenders who provide mortgage credit.

In this chapter, we discuss the most common public and private equity investors and the ownership structures these investors use when purchasing commercial real estate. We then discuss the sources (i.e., long-term holders) of commercial mortgage debt. In short, it is time to answer the following question: Who owns and finances the existing stock of U.S. commercial real estate assets?

How Large Is the U.S. Commercial Real Estate Market?

Before discussing the roles and importance of the various real estate owners and lenders, it is important to emphasize that commercial real estate plays a significant role in the U.S. (and other) economies. The estimated market value of investible commercial real estate is $8.8 trillion.[1] To put this into perspective, this $8.8 trillion estimate is displayed in Exhibit 17-1 along with the market values of other asset classes in U.S. capital markets. In late 2015, owner-occupied housing had an estimated market value of $22.0 trillion. With a total stock market capitalization of $35.7 trillion, the listed corporate equity market was 62 percent more valuable than the owner-occupied housing stock. Corporate and foreign bonds provide investors with an additional $11.7 trillion in investible assets. At $8.8 trillion in market value, commercial real estate is smaller in size than the U.S. Treasury securities market. However, the commercial real estate market is a significant component of investible wealth in the United States.

A significant amount of commercial real estate is owned by corporations and other business entities that are not primarily in the commercial real estate business—for example, telephone and communications companies, publicly owned auto manufacturers, banks, and restaurant chains. This real estate cannot be invested in directly or in a securitized form and is therefore not included in the $8.8 trillion estimated value of investible U.S. commercial real estate. To illustrate, Bank of America (BOA), a large commercial bank, owns its office tower headquarters in Charlotte, North Carolina. However, should BOA decide to divest, this office tower would become part of the investible commercial real estate universe. The market value of U.S. real estate held by non–real estate corporations, including the BOA office tower, is difficult to measure but the Federal Reserve estimates its market value to be $12.5 trillion. The Federal Reserve also estimates that the market value of U.S.

Exhibit 17-1   Relative Size of Select Asset Categories

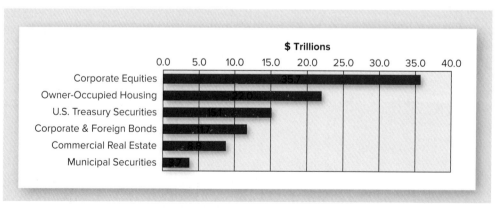

Source: Data from *Flow of Funds Accounts of the United States Federal Reserve*, March 10, 2016, various tables, www.federalreserve.gov. Estimate of investible commercial real estate is from CBRE Global Investors (www.cbreglobalinvestors.com).

1. This estimate comes from CBRE Global Investors (www.cbreglobalinvestors.com).

Exhibit 17-2 Value of U.S. Commercial Real Estate

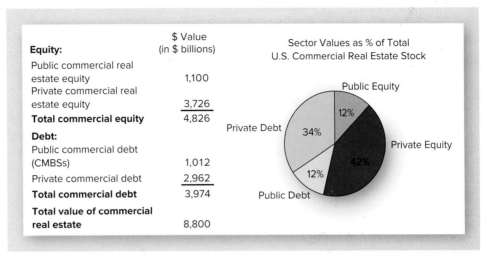

Equity:	$ Value (in $ billions)
Public commercial real estate equity	1,100
Private commercial real estate equity	3,726
Total commercial equity	4,826
Debt:	
Public commercial debt (CMBSs)	1,012
Private commercial debt	2,962
Total commercial debt	3,974
Total value of commercial real estate	8,800

Source: Data from CBRE Global Investors, Real Capital Analytics, ACLI Source Book 2015, Prequin, and *Flow of Funds Accounts of the United States Federal Reserve*, March 10, 2016, www.federalreserve.gov.

income-producing real estate owned by the federal government and state governments is an additional $11.1 trillion.[2]

As displayed in Exhibit 17-2, the $8.8 trillion total market value of commercial real estate can be broken into four quadrants: public equity capital, $1.1 trillion; privately held equity, $3.7 trillion; publicly traded mortgage debt, $1.0 trillion; and privately held mortgage debt, $3.0 trillion. We next turn our attention to the ownership structures investors use when purchasing commercial real estate.

✓ **Concept Check**

17.1 According to Exhibit 17-1, what is the total estimated market value of owner-occupied housing and commercial real estate? How much smaller than corporate stocks is the sum of commercial real estate and owner-occupied housing in percentage terms?

Forms of Ownership for Pooled Equity Investments

The choice of ownership form for a property or portfolio of properties to be owned by an investment entity is driven by trade-offs along multiple dimensions: (1) federal income tax issues, (2) the desire to avoid personal liability for the debts and obligations of the entity, (3) management control issues (including the potential for conflicts of interest to arise), (4) the ability to access debt and additional equity capital, (5) the ability to reduce return volatility and share the risk of the investment with other investors, (6) the ability of investors to dispose of their interests in the organization, and (7) the ability to distribute cash flows to investors based on percentages that differ from the percentage of equity capital contributed.

In this section, we consider alternative ownership forms for pooled equity investments. Thus, we do not discuss the simplest organizational form, the sole proprietorship, where there is no separation between the owner and the business (or investment). Due to the typical size of commercial real estate investments, the eventual owners of investment properties almost always pool their capital using some form of ownership, allowing them access

2. *Flow of Funds Accounts of the United States Federal Reserve,* March 10, 2016, Table B.103.

to a larger amount of equity to invest and more efficiently share the risk of the investment with others.

It is important to understand that there are two levels of organizations commonly at work in commercial real estate investments. A particular property might be owned through a certain form of ownership, while the ultimate owners of that organization may in turn have a different structure. For example, an office building may be owned by a general partnership whose partners are a private equity fund and a publicly traded real estate investment trust (REIT). We first discuss and compare alternative ownership structures for pooled equity investments, such as the general partnership in the example given earlier. Then, we turn our attention to the ultimate equity investors, from direct owners to intermediaries such as funds, REITs, and operating companies.

General Partnership

The simplest form of pooled ownership is a **general partnership.** One of the biggest advantages of this form is that general partnerships are treated as conduits for tax purposes; taxable income and losses flow through to the individual partners who pay the tax. Thus, investors who own commercial real estate through a general partnership do not face "double taxation," where the entity that owns the real estate pays tax first, followed by a second tax obligation at the investor level.

Other advantages of general partnerships are the ease with which one can be created, and the fact that the partners also make the operating decisions, such as how much money to borrow or when to dispose of an asset. Thus, there is no separation between the ownership and control of the organization, and conflicts of interest are lessened, although partners might disagree over some decisions, of course.

A partner's share of the cash flow produced by the investments is determined by the partnership agreement and may vary from item to item. In particular, if certain conditions are met, a partnership can allocate cash flow and tax liabilities in a manner different from each partner's ownership interest in the partnership. This ability to structure cash flow rights enables the creation of multiple classes of investors.

A major disadvantage of a general partnership is that all partners have unlimited liability. General partners are liable for *all* debts of the partnership, including contractual debts and debts arising from legal actions against the partnership. General partners are also liable for wrongful acts committed by other partners in the course of the partnership's business. Therefore, the personal assets of the general partners are subject to the claims of the partnership's creditors. For this reason, real estate general partnerships are fairly uncommon, and those that do exist tend to have only a few partners.

Limited Partnership

A **limited partnership** is created and taxed in the same way as a general partnership. However, a limited partnership (LP) introduces an important trade-off by creating two types of partners—"general" and "limited"—and a limited partnership must have at least one partner of each type. The advantage of this structure is that it allows the limited partners to cap their personal liability to an amount equal to their total investment in the partnership. The general partner still faces unlimited liability for the debts and other obligations of the partnership.

One disadvantage of this form of ownership is that in exchange for limited personal liability, the limited partners give up day-to-day control of the partnership and are prohibited from participating in management or policy making. They must rely on the general partner(s) to make decisions on their behalf. This is an example of a "principal–agent" relationship, where the agent (the general partner) makes decisions that ultimately affect the cash flows of the principals, the limited partners, who typically provide the majority of the equity capital. Situations are likely to arise where the interests of these two parties are in conflict—termed "agency problems"—potentially leading to a loss in the value of the investment, or "agency costs." Thus, it is important that limited partners understand the motives of the general partner(s) when they decide to cede control in exchange for more favorable liability exposure. The general partner, who is sometimes referred to as the "syndicator" or "sponsor" of the LP, creates the "partnership agreement" that details the operation and management of the LP.

The general partner(s) is frequently a knowledgeable real estate builder, broker, or investor and is typically the party who organized the partnership to make the investments. Note that the general partner can in turn have its own organizational structure, including one that creates limited liability for the ultimate owners. For example, the general partner may be a corporation. With regard to cash distributions and double taxation, limited partnerships are similar to general partnerships—double taxation does not exist.[3]

Ownership interests in a LP can be divided in any reasonable way, as in a general partnership. For example, with 21 partners, 20 limited partners each may have a 4.5 percent ownership share, for a total of 90 percent. The general partner would then have a 10 percent share. Often, the general partner receives a larger distribution of cash flows than her percentage equity investment would warrant. This disproportionate share of cash flows (sometimes referred to as a "special allocation") generated by the underlying property or properties provides the general partner with at least partial compensation for her efforts in organizing and structuring the limited partnership. The flow-through feature of a limited partnership coupled with limited liability for the limited partners largely explains why the LP form of ownership is an attractive option.

> ✓ **Concept Check**
>
> **17.2** What is the primary advantage of limited partnerships relative to general partnerships?

C Corporation

A **C corporation** constitutes a legal and taxable entity separate from the owners who are the shareholders in the corporation. Thus, a C corporation earns income and incurs tax liabilities. C corporations pay income taxes on taxable corporate income and have their own tax rate structure and rules. Dividends paid to shareholders are not deductible by the corporation and are taxable to the shareholders. Thus, one of the major disadvantages of using a C corporation to invest in commercial real estate is that the income from the underlying property or properties may be taxed twice. C corporation income is currently subject to federal tax rates as high as 35 percent and, in 2016, individuals can be taxed at federal rates as high as 39.6 percent. Thus, the effective tax rate on income from properties held by corporations can exceed 60 percent.[4]

www.irs.gov

Current tax rates for individuals and corporations can be found at the Internal Revenue website.

For shareholders, a C corporation provides limited liability for the obligations of the corporation. This limited liability includes liability from contractual obligations as well as obligations arising from tort actions brought against the corporation. This limited risk extends to all owners of the corporation, unlike general partnerships, where only the limited partners are afforded such protection.

Another similarity with general partnerships is the separation of ownership and control. In a C corporation, operating decisions are made by managers who may or may not own much of the firm and who act as agents on behalf of the principals, the stockholders. This separation allows for managerial expertise and helps resolve coordination problems

---

3. The ability of limited and general partners in a limited partnership to utilize losses is identical to the treatment afforded participants in a general partnership. However, all tax losses may be subject to a separate set of restrictions referred to as passive activity loss restrictions, which are discussed in Chapter 20.

4. This is calculated as $1 - [(1 - 0.35) \times (1 - 0.39.6)] = 0.61$. Note that the existence of a state income tax would push this effective tax rate even higher.

(imagine trying to get all of a large corporation's shareholders to agree on every operating decision) but comes at the cost of potential conflicts of interest.

C corporations are not generally a desirable structure for entities whose primary purpose is to acquire and own commercial real estate because there are alternative ownership structures that provide limited liability but avoid potential double taxation of income. Although C corporations are not typically used if the primary business of an ownership entity is to make long-term investments in commercial real estate, many regular C corporations do own a significant amount of real estate (e.g., General Motors, Microsoft, McDonald's).

✓ Concept Check

17.3 Why are C corporations seldom used by investors to purchase commercial real estate?

S Corporation

A **subchapter S corporation** possesses the same limited liability benefits for its shareholders as C corporations. Although an S corporation is a separate *legal* entity, it is not a separate *taxable* entity; that is, S corporations pay no income taxes, and taxable income is passed through to its stockholders who become liable for the tax at their individual tax rates.[5] A major drawback of S corporations for some investor groups is that they must not have more than 75 shareholders. Also, the S corporation's cash flow and taxable income must be allocated to each shareholder in proportion to his or her ownership of the corporation. Allocation of these items based on some other criteria—that is, special allocations— is not allowed. Although used in some cases by individuals and families to own real estate, the use of S corporations by real estate investment sponsors is uncommon since the advent of limited liability companies.

Limited Liability Company

A **limited liability company** (LLC) is a hybrid ownership structure that combines the corporate characteristics of limited liability for the owners with the tax characteristics of a partnership.[6] All 50 states have adopted LLC legislation. Compared with S corporations, LLCs offer greater flexibility in terms of the number of owners, types of owners, and ownership structure, as well as the inclusion of debt in the owner's tax basis. Relative to limited partnerships, LLCs permit all owners to participate in the management of the business entity and to have limited liability (so there is no need for a general partner who is subject to unlimited liability). In most states, a LLC is cheaper and easier to set up and run than a limited partnership.

To create a LLC, the "managing member" (i.e., the sponsor) files articles of organization with the state on behalf of all members (investors). The managing member also creates the "operating agreement" that explains the operation and management of the LLC.

Some have characterized LLCs as "super passthrough entities." In fact, LLCs have become the preferred ownership form for many private real estate investors. However,

---

5. Although tax losses of an S corporation flow through to its shareholders, the ability of the shareholders to utilize these tax losses is subject to several limitations. First, shareholders cannot utilize tax losses in excess of the amount they have invested, or their "at-risk" basis. The at-risk basis is generally equal to the amount paid for the stock, plus allocated taxable income, minus cash distributions received. The debts and liabilities of the S corporation do *not* increase the shareholder's at-risk basis in the stock. Thus, if the S corporation takes out a mortgage on property it owns, no part of the mortgage is included in the amount the individual shareholders have at risk. This could limit the amount of tax deductions that can be used by shareholders. Shareholder loans to the S corporation increase the shareholders' at-risk basis and therefore their ability to utilize tax losses.

6. Depending on state law, a LLC may be organized as a limited liability partnership or a limited liability corporation.

private real estate funds are typically set up as limited partnerships, not as LLCs. Perhaps it is more accurate to say that LLCs are generally used for small, local investments marketed to higher income, but noninstitutional, investors, whereas LPs are used by private funds that are trying to attract capital from very high net worth and institutional investors.

✓ **Concept Check**

17.4 List two ways in which limited liability companies differ from limited partnerships.

Tenancy-in-Common

As discussed in Chapter 2, limited partnerships and limited liability companies represent *indirect* forms of real estate ownership. This is because investors own a portion of the LP or LLC, which, in turn, holds title to the property or properties. A tenancy-in-common (TIC) constitutes *direct* ownership of the property. That is, each co-owner possesses an undivided ownership interest in the property as evidenced by the fact that each receives a separate deed. TIC investors share pro rata in the periodic cash flows, tax consequences, and price appreciation achieved by the property, and the number of investors cannot exceed 35.

TIC investments generally provide investors with many of the benefits associated with other forms of co-ownership, including access to more expensive properties, portfolio diversification, access to cheaper debt capital, and the services of real estate professionals in acquisitions, management, and dispositions.

However, TICs have substantial disadvantages. Some detractors note that TIC syndication fees and other up-front expenses may consume up to 25 percent of investor equity. Also, investors are subject to joint and several liability for the debts of the TIC; that is, their liability is not limited to the amount of their equity investment. Moreover, many decisions, including when to sell the property, require the unanimous approval of all investors. Unfortunately, the significant downturn in commercial real estate markets that began in 2008 and lasted until 2010 in most markets brought to light the many disadvantages of the TIC ownership structure.

So why the use of TICs in commercial real estate markets? The answer is income tax avoidance. Many investors with accumulated gains from appreciation attempt to make use of (Section 1031) tax-deferred exchanges when disposing of commercial real estate assets. Briefly, Section 1031 of the Internal Revenue Code permits investors to defer some or all of the taxable gain that would ordinarily be due on the sale of a property if they exchange for "like-kind" property. However, ownership interests in a limited partnership or limited liability company are not considered by the IRS to be like-kind. Thus, investors who dispose of commercial real estate they owned directly cannot use a tax-deferred exchange to acquire an ownership interest in a LP or LLC.

Under a revenue procedure released in 2002 by the IRS, taxpayers *can* exchange an interest in real property for a partial interest in a TIC investment. This led in just a few years to the creation of the TIC industry—entities engaged in the creation and sale of TIC investment vehicles for tax-motivated investors.

Optimal Ownership Form

When assessing which ownership form is optimal, it is useful to start by asking what we observe most frequently in practice, which should give us a strong indication of the preferred structure and the relative weights owners of commercial real estate place on the various factors discussed earlier. Limited partnerships and LLCs are the dominant

T he use of a tenancy-in-common (TIC) ownership form by a sponsor allows taxpayers to satisfy requirements for completing a Section 1031 like-kind exchange. However, as discussed in the text, TICs have serous disadvantages. Recently, a lesser-recognized strategy has attracted serious interest. This concept is known as a Delaware Statutory Trust or DST. Although DSTs are not a new

Is a Delaware Statutory Trust a Safe Real Investment?

creation, current tax laws have made Delaware Statutory Trusts an attractive investment vehicle for passive 1031 exchange investors. In 2004, the IRS blessed Delaware Statutory Trusts with an official Revenue Ruling that details how to structure a DST that will qualify as replacement property for investors/taxpayers seeking to purchase "real estate" to complete a delayed exchange.

The real estate firm sponsoring the DST simply acquires the property under the DST umbrella and opens up the trust for potential investors to purchase a beneficial interest. Exchange investors simply deposit their proceeds from the

disposition of the relinquished property into the DST.

Delaware Statutory Trust investors may benefit from a professionally managed, high-quality property. The underlying property could be a 500-unit apartment building, a 100,000 square-foot medical office property, or a shopping center leased to investment-grade tenants. The possibilities are endless.

Source: Adapted from Elizabeth Warren, June 13, 2016, homebuying.about.com/od/investmentproperties/a/120108_Delaware.htm.

---

ownership structures in the United States for private real estate investment vehicles, suggesting the combination of single taxation, limited liability for most, if not all, of the owners and the ability to provide special allocations of cash flows are of primary importance when investors structure commercial real estate investments.

In the next section, we turn our attention to the ultimate equity investors. As we mentioned earlier, these sources of capital do not necessarily match the ownership form just discussed. For example, a publicly traded C corporation may invest in commercial real estate through its pension fund to meet some of its future obligations to retirees. By doing so, the C corporation may own a share of a particular property through a limited partnership. Thus, while the C corporation structure meets the needs of a shareholder of an industrial company (such as General Electric), the corporation may hold commercial real estate through an alternative form of ownership.

Ultimate Equity Investors in Commercial Real Estate

Investors can purchase ownership (equity) positions in commercial real estate either directly or through **intermediaries.** For our purposes, an intermediary is an entity that invests in real estate and sells claims on those investments to the ultimate investors. Examples of such intermediaries include real estate limited partnerships and limited liability companies, a variety of private equity fund structures (e.g., closed- and open-ended funds) and real estate investment trusts (REITs). Much like the trade-offs inherent in choosing a form of ownership, the choice of direct investment versus investment through an intermediary involves trade-offs between control, access to managerial talent and expertise, liquidity, and risk sharing. In this section, we discuss the pros and cons of direct investment in commercial real estate, along with various alternatives for investing through an intermediary.

✓ **Concept Check**

17.5   What trade-offs are involved in the choice between investing directly in commercial real estate and investing through an intermediary?

Direct Investment in Commercial Real Estate

With direct private investment, individual and institutional investors purchase and hold title to the properties. They do not invest alongside others in an investment structure put together by a sponsor. Although purchasing directly, these investors will typically form a LP or LLC to acquire property to limit potential loss of capital. Purchasing individual properties directly in the private market gives investors complete control of the asset: who leases it, who manages it, how much debt financing is used, and when it is sold. In order to have such control, however, the investor must also supply the expertise. For a wealthy individual or family, the principal herself could provide this expertise, conducting the necessary analysis to make the many decisions involved or working with a local broker or other real estate professional. For a larger organization, such as an institutional investor (e.g., a pension fund), direct investment implies the fund must retain in-house experts (perhaps in conjunction with consultants and advisors) to manage the real estate portfolio. The liquidity of direct investment corresponds to the liquidity of the commercial real estate market as a whole. Thus, while direct investment implies the investor can decide when to sell a specific property, market conditions at a given point in time may make a timely sale at a reasonable price more or less likely. The limited liquidity of direct investments in private real estate markets has been a problem in declining markets, such as the commercial real estate downturn that began in 2008. More generally, by owning an asset directly, the investor bears the full risk of that investment.

These issues help explain observed patterns in direct ownership of commercial real estate. Direct ownership is a frequently used means of ownership for the largest institutional market participants and high net worth investors. As the size of an investor's portfolio increases, the economies of scale of retaining in-house real estate expertise, the ability to diversify risk, and the ability to generate liquidity across various asset classes (stocks, bonds, etc.) mitigate the primary cons of direct ownership. At the same time, these investors are able to take advantage of greater control over their real estate portfolios to tailor their construction and operation to meet their specific objectives.

Direct ownership is also prevalent at the smaller end of the investor spectrum. Examples of this include single-family rental homes and single-tenant office buildings occupied by family businesses. Depending on the magnitude of these real estate investments relative to the investor's total wealth, there may be a significant implicit cost of direct ownership in some cases due to inadequate diversification and/or liquidity. As a result, a smaller private investor who directly places much of her wealth in a small number of income-producing properties is placing a large weight on the value of control and/or her relative advantages versus the market (e.g., due to greater expertise or better information).

Turning back to the large investors in commercial real estate that tend to make direct investments, we are still left with the question, who are they? Many of them are institutional investors—pension funds, life insurance companies, foreign investors, and financial institutions. We discuss these groups in more detail below.

Pension Funds. **Pension funds** are an important participant in commercial real estate equity markets. They want reliable income from stable real estate investments to pay out retirement benefits to increasing numbers of retirees/beneficiaries. The total value of real estate owned by pension funds is estimated to be $225 billion (see Exhibit 17-3). This includes their indirect real estate investments through private real estate equity funds and joint ventures. Thus, pension funds account for less than 5 percent ($225 billion ÷ $4.8 trillion) of commercial real estate equity. Nevertheless, because of the capital they have to invest, pension funds and their advisors and consultants have an influence on commercial markets that is disproportionate to the relatively small percentage of assets they own.

Life Insurance Companies. Life insurance policies involve the payment of premiums by the insured in exchange for benefits to be paid upon the death of the insured. Using mortality tables, life insurers are able to predict the mortality rates of policyholder groups with a high degree of accuracy. As a result, the liabilities of life insurers can be characterized as both long term and fairly predictable. To match the maturity of their assets to the

www.rcanalytics.com

Real Capital Analytics produces monthly reports on trading volume, pricing, and the active buyers and sellers in private commercial real estate markets.

www.prea.org

Pension Real Estate Association.

www.ncreif.org

National Council of Real Estate Investment Fiduciaries. Industry leader in resolution of technical industry issues and producer of property performance indices.

Exhibit 17-3 Value of U.S. Commercial Real Estate Equity

Asset/Liability Category	$ Value (in $Billions)	Private Commercial RE Equity	$ Value (in $Billions)
Public Com. RE Equity	1,100	Pension Funds	225
Private Com. RE Equity	3,726	Foreign Investors	497
Total Commercial Equity	4,826	Life Insurance Companies	26
		Private Financial Institutions	15
Public Com. Debt	1,012	Other Institutional Investors	1,040
Private Com. Debt	2,962	Noninstitutional Investors–	
Total Commercial Debt	3,974	small properties	1,924
Total Value of Com. RE	8,800	**Total Privately Held Equity**	3,726

Source: Data from CBRE Global Investors, ACLI Fact Book 2016, *Flow of Funds Accounts of the United States Federal Reserve,* March 10, 2016, www.federalreserve.gov; Real Capital Analytics; National Council of Real Estate Investment Fiduciaries; National Association of Real Estate Investment Trusts.

maturity of their liabilities, it makes sense for life insurance companies to invest on a long-term basis. Moreover, it is not necessary that their assets be highly liquid; large unexpected payments to policyholders are unlikely. These characteristics make life insurance companies well suited for investment in commercial real estate markets, which are characterized by low liquidity and high transaction costs. And, indeed, life insurers have traditionally been a major source of commercial real estate capital. In late 2015, life insurers owned $26 billion of commercial real estate assets. As we shall see, however, they are much more active as suppliers of commercial mortgage debt.

www.irei.com

Institutional Real Estate, Inc., extensive news and information on the activities of institutional real estate investors.

Other Institutional Investors. Foreign investors often grab headlines for their active participation in U.S. real estate markets. In late 2015, foreign investors controlled approximately $497 billion in U.S. real estate.[7] Foreign investors tend to concentrate their acquisitions in major U.S. cities, acquiring mostly office and retail properties.

Exhibit 17-3 shows that commercial banks and other private financial institutions collectively own a modest $15 billion in commercial real estate equity. However, the majority of these real estate holdings are not the result of direct equity investments. Rather, these holdings often represent "real estate owned" (REO); that is, real estate obtained by the financial institution as a result of borrower default and foreclosure.

> ✓ **Concept Check**
>
> **17.6** What percentage of total private commercial real estate equity is held collectively by pension funds, foreign investors, life insurance companies, and financial institutions?

Investment in Commercial Real Estate through Intermediaries

A large amount of equity investment in commercial real estate takes place through intermediaries. Why is their role so significant? This goes back to the drawbacks of investing directly. Depending on the specific structure, intermediaries who sponsor investment opportunities can help mitigate the various cons of direct investment by supplying expertise (including better information), improving liquidity, and allowing the investor to more

---

7. This estimate comes from Real Capital Analytics (www.rcanalytics.com).

Source: Adapted from Real Estate - Institutional Real Estate Investment, University of Cincinnati, business.uc.edu/centers/real-estate/academics/career-paths/institutional-investment.html.

Many of today's large-scale real estate transactions ($10 million and up) involve institutional investors, such as real estate investment trusts (REITs), the larger life insurance companies, international investors, and pension funds. These institutional investors generally utilize commercial brokers in the local markets, but they also rely on internal staff to review and analyze proposed investments. When hiring, these institutions frequently look for a real estate background, strong analytical skills, the ability to manage portfolios, and excellent communication skills. Increasingly, they are also looking for a MBA degree or a specialized graduate degree, such as an MS in real estate, when staffing positions. Industry experience and advanced degrees are important because institutional investors must be knowledgeable about industry market trends, tax law trends, regulatory trends, geographically based economic trends, demographic trends, and global economic trends, in addition to property-specific issues.

Institutional Real Estate Investors

fully diversify and share risk. On the other hand, using an intermediary typically involves another layer of costs—the investor has to pay for expertise, for example—and shifts more control from the investor to the sponsor/intermediary. As we discussed earlier with forms of ownership that lead to principal–agent conflicts, the use of an intermediary can lead to conflicts of interest. Thus, creating proper incentives for the delegated managers to maximize the objectives of the investors is an important issue.

Generally, investments through intermediaries occur via real estate securities. **Securitized investments** pool money from multiple investors. Securitized investments are purchased and resold in either "public" or "private" markets. We define public markets as those in which securities are bought and sold on an exchange that is broadly accessible to investors, such as the New York Stock Exchange or the National Association of Securities Dealers (NASDAQ) system. Private markets are characterized by individually negotiated transactions that take place without the aid of a centralized market. Exchange-traded assets provide investors with a relatively high degree of liquidity and relatively low transaction costs. In contrast, private markets are generally characterized by high transaction costs and low liquidity.[8]

Securitized investments are the norm in commercial real estate, due to the advantages of investing through intermediaries discussed earlier, plus the sheer access to greater amounts of capital that commercial real estate investments typically require. Even modest office buildings, strip shopping centers, and apartment buildings often require more equity capital than individual investors are able or willing to contribute. The large capital requirements lead to the common practice of groups of private investors pooling their equity capital and purchasing commercial real estate through a sponsored vehicle.

The pooling of equity capital by investors to purchase real estate in the private market is often referred to as syndication. A **syndicate** is a group of persons or legal entities who come together to carry out a particular activity. A real estate syndicate, therefore, is a group organized to develop a parcel of land, buy an office building, purchase an entire portfolio of properties, make mortgage loans, or perform other real estate activities. Syndicates take place among both institutional and noninstitutional investors. For example, some sponsors of syndications market investment opportunities with high front-end fees to small "mom and pop" investors through Wall Street brokers and financial advisors. Wealthy investors often access the market by buying into small- to medium-size deals structured and sold by local developers/sponsors. And, institutional investors participate in a wide variety of pooled/syndicated structures. We discuss many types of pooled equity investment

8. A liquid market is one in which assets can be sold quickly for fair market value.

alternatives following an overview of single-investor ownership through intermediaries, termed separate accounts.

✓ **Concept Check**

17.7   What are real estate syndications and what do they do?

Separate Accounts.   Perhaps the closest alternative to direct ownership that still involves some degree of intermediation is the use of **separate accounts** with a dedicated real estate investment manager. For example, a large investment management company (e.g., AEW, Invesco) will buy, hold, and dispose of assets on behalf of investors, where each investor's assets are treated independently. This structure allows the investor to utilize the expertise of the investment manager (the intermediary), in exchange for fees. By maintaining separate accounts, the investment manager is better able to tailor the assets (and their expected returns and risks) to the needs and objectives of the ultimate investor. This structure provides an intermediate degree of liquidity; it may allow the ultimate investor to time the sale of assets by requesting or pushing the manager to do so, but the ability to execute sales still depends on the liquidity of the underlying commercial real estate market. Separate accounts also provide no additional aid in diversification or risk sharing relative to direct ownership.

Commingled Real Estate Funds.   **Commingled real estate funds** (CREFs) are offered by major banks, life insurance companies, investment banks, and real estate advisory firms to pension funds and other institutional investors for investment in real estate. Legally, they are organized as limited partnerships, LLCs, or private REITs. Because many pension funds do not have (or wish to acquire) the in-house expertise required for real estate investment, fund managers collect contributions from multiple pension funds and pool or "commingle" them to purchase properties. In addition to expertise, these structures allow for better diversification, as smaller institutions are able to own a portion of a bigger, better diversified portfolio than they would be able to afford on their own.

Commingled funds can be closed- or open-end. Closed-end funds have a finite life but offer very little to no liquidity before the fund begins to sell properties and distribute the proceeds to investors. Open-end funds have an infinite life but allow investors to redeem their interests. It should be noted that this "internal" liquidity solution has some drawbacks and risks. For example, many investors may want out of the fund in tough economic times, but it is at those times that it is difficult for the manager to sell properties quickly at fair value—and the properties in the fund that are the most liquid may be the "best" properties, ones that the manager and investors most want to retain. As a result, there may be a "redemption queue" of investors waiting for cash flows to exit the fund, and the notion of liquidity during real estate market downturns may be illusory.

The fee structure of commingled funds typically includes an ongoing asset management fee (e.g., 1–2 percent of the fund's assets per year). The manager may also receive front-end fees as compensation for putting the properties together (e.g., 1–2 percent) and back-end fees upon disposition of the properties (e.g., 5–6 percent for acting as the sale broker). The manager typically has limited or no ownership interest in the fund. These fee structures can cause incentive alignment issues. For example, the fund manager may have an incentive to hold properties (especially ones that have declined in value) to continue collecting fees, and some investors may prefer that the compensation to managers were more closely linked to investors' returns (which is more difficult to accomplish without management investing in the funds themselves).

Real Estate Private Equity Funds.   **Real estate private equity funds** originated in the early 1990s. These funds were created to address some of the perceived drawbacks of the CREF structure. The funds have a finite life, typically 7–10 years with an option for the fund manager or sponsor to extend the life by an additional year or two. Because of this finite life, the fund manager is forced to eventually dispose of the assets and return the investors' capital (mitigating the potential conflict of interest where the manager has the incentive to continue to hold assets). Unlike typical CREFs, real estate private equity funds typically have economically meaningful side-by-side investment by the fund sponsor/manager, aligning the manager's economic outcomes with those of the investors.

The fee structures are also usually richer and more complex, allowing more features that further align interests. The fund manager is the general partner (GP) of the fund, while the investors are LPs. The fund manager typically provides something like 1–5 percent of the fund's equity, with any further investment by the manager occurring as a LP, side-by-side with the other LPs (and thus experiencing the same returns on that capital). The LPs typically earn a preferred return, such as 8 percent, often before the GP receives any cash flow distributions. Once LP returns exceed this threshold, the GP receives a disproportionate share of the cash flows produced by the underlying properties, often 20 percent. This 20 percent is termed the GPs "carried interest." Note that the GP does not receive carried interest unless the fund performs well enough to provide the LPs with their preferred return. There are a number of variations to this theme, allowing the fund manager and LP investors to tailor the contract and incentives as they see fit (and as the market dictates at that point in time).

www.preqin.com

Preqin provides comprehensive data and research on real estate private equity funds.

While carried interest often constitutes the bulk of the GP's cash flow distributions— at least in well-performing funds—there are additional sources of GP compensation that vary from fund to fund. These include management fees (as a fraction of assets under management or funds committed), leasing commissions, acquisition fees, and disposition fees. Of course, the GP has to incur manpower and other costs to produce these fees. The size and other details of these fees vary from fund to fund and over time, depending on the fund manager's bargaining power relative to the investors', and current market norms.

From an investor's standpoint, it is important to understand the timing and structure of these funds. At the beginning, the investors commit capital to the fund. Those commitments are not collected in full by the fund manager until she acquires properties, which may take the first couple of years of the fund's life. However, the LPs usually begin paying the management fee on the dollar value of their commitments as soon as they become binding. In the middle years of the fund's life, the properties are held, operated, and possibly improved with the intent of eventual sale. Then, over the final years of the fund, the manager disposes of properties and returns the investors' capital (net of fees and the GP's carried interest).

Real estate private equity funds have been used to facilitate investment across the real estate spectrum. Real estate private equity funds specialize in all property types and within those property types, focus on anything from core "Class A" real estate to redevelopment in the urban core (termed "brownfield" development) to turnaround opportunities in distressed markets, to the acquisition of real estate securities and nonperforming loans. Often, these funds are placed along the risk–return spectrum with labels of "core," "value-added," and "opportunistic," though there are no strict cutoffs for each category. Core funds invest in high-quality properties that typically have strong leases in place and are located in major metropolitan areas. As a result, they offer lower expected returns in exchange for less risk. Value-added funds incur some additional risk in exchange for higher expected returns, and their investments might include a building with some lease-up risk or the need for moderate renovation and repositioning. Opportunistic funds have still greater risk, with even higher expected returns. Their investments may have a heavier development component and often involve riskier property types and locations (e.g., resort hotels overseas). It is worth noting that real estate private equity funds often employ significant leverage—adding more risk and more expected return—though there is substantial variation in leverage across funds.

✓ **Concept Check**

17.8   Distinguish between a core investment strategy and an opportunistic investment strategy.

Full Platform Operating Companies.   Another vehicle for commercial real estate investment is to own a **full platform operating company.** Rather than being a passive investor in commercial real estate by means of placing money with an investment advisor, real estate company, or fund, this strategy involves starting (or acquiring) and operating a real estate company itself. The company may then acquire real estate investments, develop properties, and/or act as a general partner in a variety of investments funds. Because the investment's ultimate cash flows derive from the profits of the operating company, which in turn typically stem from fees and speculative investments, this alternative is perhaps the highest risk/highest return one among the broad sets of investment vehicles discussed here. High net worth families have been common investors in full-platform companies, while more conservative pension funds have gravitated toward safer, more passive forms of investment.

Institutional versus Noninstitutional Equity Investors

Referring to Exhibit 17-3, we estimate the value of privately owned commercial real estate equity in late 2015 was $3.7 trillion, or 42 percent of the total value of investible U.S. commercial real estate. As can be seen in Exhibit 17-3, this $3.7 trillion in private equity market value includes direct investments totaling $763 billion by the following institutional investors: pension funds, foreign investors, life insurance companies, and financial institutions. We estimate that $1.04 trillion of the remaining $3.0 trillion is held by other institutional investors (hedge funds, endowment funds, etc.).

However, $1.9 trillion of equity capital is invested by noninstitutional investors in "small" properties. These properties are often owned by "local" real estate syndications organized as limited liability companies. It is common for these LLCs to own just one property. In addition, the required minimum equity investment may be as low as $50,000–$100,000; thus, these smaller, local, single property-investment opportunities are within the reach of a broader set of equity investors. Generally, the syndicator/sponsor has raised the equity capital needed for the LLC from investors that are known to him/her or connected to investors who have contributed equity capital to one of the syndicator/sponsor's prior investment opportunities. Some refer to this potential pool of equity capital as "country club money." However, a new form of raising equity capital, referred to as "crowdfunding," is now permitted and is expected by some to substantially alter fundraising for commercial real estate investments (see Industry Issues 17-1).

It is clear from Exhibit 17-3 and the discussion above that the majority of commercial real estate in the United States is owned by private investment vehicles. Nevertheless, $1.1 trillion of the existing commercial real estate stock is financed by the equity capital of publicly traded real estate companies. We next discuss the primary source of public capital—exchange traded (listed) real estate investment trusts.

✓ **Concept Check**

17.9   What percentage of privately owned and operated commercial real estate is held by noninstitutional investors?

Real Estate Investment Trusts

Real estate investment trusts (REITs) are a special type of corporation and a creature of the U.S. tax code. The growing importance of REITs can largely be attributed to their appealing features in terms of both liability and taxation. Shareholders receive the same

U ntil recently, no "general solicita-
tion" could be used to attract equity
capital for a project/fund. Sponsors
had to rely on friends, family, and business
associates with whom they had a preexisting relationship ("country-club" money). In
particular, advertising on websites, social
media sites, or newspapers was not
allowed, nor were e-mails to individuals
with whom you did not have a preexisting
relationship.

Prompted by the "JOBS" Act of 2012,
the Securities and Exchange Commission
(SEC) has made it easier to market and
solicit investments and opened the door for
small businesses to engage in so-called
"equity crowdfunding." Final rules for "Regulation Crowdfunding" were issued by the
SEC on October 30, 2015. Sponsors/issuers
can now market directly to investors.

After passage of the JOBS Act in 2012,
there was much talk about hedge funds
sponsoring Superbowl halftime shows and
mom-and-pop millionaires lining up on Main
Street to pour money into private equity or
venture capital funds. The rule was "the
most significant change to capital markets
since the 1930s," said business website
Quartz.

It has not happened so far. Investments
in nonregistered securities have risen
dramatically—in 2014, there were 33,429
offers raising a total of $1.3 trillion, up from
18,295 raising $595 billion in 2009. But
only about 2 percent of the 2014 offers
were solicited under the new JOBS Act
rules, according to the Securities and
Exchange Commission.

However, many in the commercial real
estate industry remain optimistic about the
future of crowdfunding. "When you bring
the internet and you're allowed to advertise
a private security, more investors do take
part," says cofounder and CEO Mat Dellorso
of WealthForge. His company has completed 150 private financing transactions,
bringing in 2,500 investors. "A traditional
investment bank might complete three or
five a year," he says. "It's a lot more volume
because it's more transparent and online
now. Normally these transactions take
weeks and months, but an investor can lit-
erally invest in a private placement on our
platform in a matter of minutes," he says.

Source: Adapted from Diana Britton, "Is There a
Crowd for Equity Crowdfunding?" *National Real
Estate Investor Online*, January 6, 2016;
nreionline.com/finance-investment/
there-crowd-equity-
crowdfunding.

**Is There a Crowd
for Equity
Crowdfunding?**

www.reit.com

National Association of Real Estate
Investment Trusts.

limited liability protection as shareholders in regular C corporations. Unlike a C corporation, however, REITs are not taxed at the entity level if they satisfy a set of restrictive conditions on an ongoing basis. The most important of these conditions are as follows.[9]

At least 100 investors must own a REIT's shares; to ensure diversified ownership, no
five investors can own more than 50 percent of a REIT's shares. A REIT must distribute
at least 90 percent of its taxable income to shareholders in the form of dividends, which
limits the ability of a REIT to retain earnings for future investments.[10] Fully 75 percent of
the value of a REIT's assets must consist of real estate assets, cash, and government securities. Real estate mortgages and mortgage-backed securities are considered real estate for
the purposes of this test. At least 75 percent of the REIT's gross income must be derived
from real estate assets. These last two requirements ensure that REITs invest primarily in
real estate. In exchange for meeting these and several other requirements, REITs, effectively, do not pay federal income taxes. This leaves more cash flow available to pay dividends to investors (who do pay taxes on the dividends).[11]

REITs can be segmented on the basis of the type of real estate investment they make,
and how they are traded. There are two major types of REITs. **Equity REITs** invest in and
operate commercial properties, whereas **mortgage REITs** purchase mortgage obligations
(both home loans and commercial loans, as well as mortgage-backed securities) and thus
become, effectively, real estate lenders. Independent of their investment focus, REITs can
be classified as publicly traded (i.e., listed), public but nontraded, and private. As of the

**www.avaloncommunities
.com**

An equity REIT that owns apartment
communities across the United
States.

9. On May 28, 2003, President George W. Bush signed the "Jobs and Growth" tax relief package. This bill
cut income tax rates on most dividends and capital gains received by individuals to a 15 percent maximum.
Because REITs generally do not pay taxes at the corporate level, the majority of REIT dividends will continue
to be taxed at the shareholder's ordinary income tax rate. For more information, visit the NAREIT website
(www.nareit.com).

10. Prior to 2001, this percentage was 95.

11. For a complete list of what a company must do to qualify as a REIT, go to www.reit.com, and click on
the "What's a REIT?" tab under "Investing."

end of 2015, the total equity market capitalization of listed REITs was $939 billion;[12] 82 percent of the 223 listed REITs were classified by the National Association of Real Estate Investment Trusts (NAREIT) as equity REITs. According to NAREIT, there were approximately 50 public, nonlisted REITs in 2016.

REITs have been described as mutual funds for real estate in that they afford the same advantages to investors: portfolio diversification and liquidity. Diversification comes from the large portfolios that a REIT can own on behalf of shareholders. For example, Simon Property Group, Inc. (www.simon.com; ticker symbol SPG), is a large REIT that, in 2016, owned or had an interest in more than 325 large shopping centers in North America and Asia. Each SPG shareholder owns an interest in these shopping centers. For publicly traded REITs, liquidity is achieved because shares of stock traded on a major stock exchange are more easily disposed of than the underlying properties that are traded in private markets.

The REIT market has grown significantly since the early 1990s, and REITs are now more broadly accepted by mutual funds and other institutional investors, especially pension funds. Further evidence of the rise in the size and stature of the REIT market is that in 2001 the first REIT was added to the S&P 500, a bellwether stock return index published by Standard & Poor's that includes 500 of the largest and most important U.S. corporations. As of May 2016, 27 REITs were included in the S&P 500. Other REITs are included in a broader set of REIT indicies. With the growth of investor interest in indexed mutual funds and exchange-traded funds (ETFs), the largest shareholders of many listed REITs are indexed funds and ETFs.

> ✓ **Concept Check**
>
> **17.10**   List several advantages of investing in listed REITs.

It is important to note that publicly traded REITs are not the only means of investing in commercial real estate through listed markets. There are many companies that operate in the real estate industry, such as professional service firms (e.g., CBRE, HFF, JLL) and large homebuilders (e.g., Toll Brothers). Because these firms are not "pure" long-term investment plays, their equity market capitalizations are not included in Exhibit 17-3.

The public, nonlisted REIT market has also grown significantly over the last several years. Shares in the majority of these companies are offered to individual investors via a network of broker-dealers. The structure of these firms is somewhat analogous to finite-lived real estate funds. Investors can buy shares of the REIT at a stated price until the REIT is fully subscribed. The REIT invests the money raised in properties and provides an "exit" for the investors—generally by selling the properties (e.g., as a portfolio). While these funds have come under scrutiny for their high fees and other governance concerns, they have been marketed to investors as providing a means for individuals to invest in a diversified portfolio of professionally managed commercial real estate, and by offering high dividend yields relative to alternative investments in recent times. In 2016, the number of public, nonlisted REITs totaled 47, according to NAREIT (www.reit.com).

Private REITs are forms of ownership that investment managers use to pool capital from investors such as institutions and high net worth individuals. For example, commingled funds can be structured as private REITs. Like listed REITs, this structure provides investors with access to a larger portfolio of assets and limited liability while avoiding double taxation. The market value of shares of stock in private REITs is unknown because they are private companies.

---

12. This does not include the market value of preferred shares.

August 31, 2016, was circled on the calendars of REIT professionals and dedicated REIT investors. However, what many consider the biggest development to hit the sector in 15 years may have a greater impact on those investors who previously overlooked REITs. After the market closed on that date, stock exchange-listed Equity REITs and other listed real estate companies were elevated to a new Real Estate Sector in the closely watched Global Industry Classification Standard (GICS), making it the 11th Headline-level Sector under GICS.

GICS serves as the de facto classification system for equities worldwide, providing an organizational framework for everything from performance analysis to product development. The move, which pulled listed Equity REITs and other real estate companies from their longtime home in the Financials Sector, might sound routine and wonky to the uninitiated, but it is far from it. This is the first time since the launch of GICS in 1999 that a new Headline Sector will be added. It shows just how prominent the real estate and, in particular, the listed Equity REIT space—praised for its handsome dividends, seasoned leadership, sound returns, and diversification benefits—have become.

This real estate classification revolution is fueling increased discussion about the real estate asset class that includes trillions of dollars' worth of holdings nationwide. Simply, listed Equity REITs and real estate companies are no longer a niche, but rather representative of a distinct real estate asset class. It is a "momentous event for the industry," says Michael Knott, director of U.S. REIT research for Green Street Advisors, a real estate research firm.

Source: Dawn Wotapka, "Effects of the Upcoming GICS Classification for the REIT Industry," May 24, 2016, www.reit.com/news/reit-magazine/may-june-2016/effects-upcoming-gics-classification-reit-industry.

Effects of the GICS Classification for the REIT Industry

Sources of Commercial Real Estate Debt

We now turn our attention to the providers of commercial mortgage debt who tend to hold the mortgages or mortgage-backed securities as long-term investment. Exhibit 17-4 displays the amount of outstanding mortgage debt by holder/investor as of late 2015. Of the $3.97 trillion in outstanding mortgage debt, $2.96 trillion (or 75 percent) is privately held by institutional and individual investors. Commercial banks and savings associations are the largest single source of private mortgage funds, holding $1.84 trillion (or 46 percent) of the total commercial mortgage debt outstanding. Life insurance companies are also major participants in the long-term commercial mortgage market, holding $368 billion, or 9 percent, of the total commercial mortgage debt outstanding. As previously discussed, the long-term nature of their liabilities encourages life insurance companies to seek long-term investments. The remaining privately held mortgage debt is owned by government-sponsored enterprises (Freddie Mac and Fannie Mae) (6 percent); federal, state, and local governments (5 percent); pension funds (<1 percent); private equity funds that investment in commercial real estate debt (2 percent); and "other" investors, such as finance companies. We also include the nonmortgage and noncorporate bond liabilities of equity REITs, as these liabilities represent financing used to acquire ownership positions in commercial real estate. The importance of private, noninstitutional lenders, including private equity funds that invest in debt, has grown in recent years as exploding regulatory constraints have impeded traditional bank lending. These private lenders are more active in providing shorter-term financing to investors and owners, including mezzanine loans (see Chapter 16).

Whereas residential MBS are issued against a pool of residential mortgages, CMBS are backed by a pool of commercial mortgages or, perhaps, a single large commercial loan. In 2005, a record $157 billion in domestic CMBS were issued. In 2006 and 2007, CMBS issuance soared to $184 billion and $230 billion, respectively. Investors found CMBS attractive because they offered premium yields over comparable Treasury securities and corporate bonds. In fact, CMBS had become a mainstream fixed-income investment product. On the supply side, originators of commercial mortgages feed the demand for CMBS by issuing CMBS themselves or by selling loans to CMBS issuers. By 2006,

www.mbaa.org

An extensive source of data and information on the commercial mortgage market.

www.trepp.com

Leading provider of information and analytics for the CMBS and commercial mortgage market.

Exhibit 17-4   The Value of U.S. Commercial Real Estate Debt

	$ Value (in $Billions)		$ Value (in $Billions)
		Public Commercial RE Debt	
		Agency & GSE-Backed CMBS	204
		Non-Government Backed CMBS	415
		REIT Unsecured Debt	393
Public Com. RE Equity	1,100	Total Publicly Traded Debt	1,012
Private Com. RE Equity	3,726		
Total Commercial Equity	4,826	**Private Commercial RE Debt**	
		Banks and Savings Associations	1,844
Public Com. Debt (CMBS)	1,012	Equity REITs (non-mortgage liabilites)	108
Private Com. Debt	2,962	Life Insurance Companies	368
Total Commercial Debt	3,974	Federal, State & Local Governments	191
		Govern. Sponsored Enterprises	257
Total Value of Com. RE	8,800	Pension Funds	24
		Private Equity Debt Funds	71
		Other	99
		Total Privately Held Debt	2,962

Source: Data from *Flow of Funds Accounts of the United States Federal Reserve*, March 10, 2016, various tables, www.federalreserve.gov.

approximately 75 percent of commercial loan originations were being securitized. The CMBS market revolutionized the U.S. commercial mortgage market by providing a source of liquidity for mortgage originators and bringing nontraditional investors into the mortgage market.

Then the wheels of the CMBS engine fell off. In 2008, CMBS issuance plummeted to $17 billion; in 2009, issuance fell to $5 billion. According to many, non-government-backed CMBS had morphed into murky investment bets with sliced and diced classes of mortgages combined in complex structures, which were highly leveraged and often hedged in complex swap agreements. Clearly, neither the rating agencies nor investors really understood how the (CMBS) "sausage" was being made. As default rates of commercial mortgages increased, the CMBS market shut down, forcing many borrowers to turn to alternative sources of loan funds. By 2011, however, the CMBS market had begun to recover with the issuance of approximately $31 billion. Issuance steadily increased, reaching $100 billion in 2015.

The outstanding principal balances of CMBS backed by the government-sponsored enterprises (GSEs, such as Fannie Mae and Freddie Mac) totaled $204 billion in late 2015. These GSE-backed CMBS consist entirely of multifamily mortgages (see Exhibit 17-4). The outstanding principal balances of "private label" CMBS securities (i.e., those not issued or backed by a government agency) totaled $415 billion. Thus, the total outstanding value of CMBS was $619 billion, which represents 16 percent of total commercial mortgage debt outstanding. The remaining $393 billion in publicly traded commercial debt represents unsecured corporate debt issued by listed REITs.

www.crefc.org

The CRE Finance Council (CREFC) is the trade association for the commercial real estate finance industry. More than 300 companies and 8,000 individuals are members of the CREFC.

> ✓ **Concept Check**
>
> **17.11**   What was the fastest-growing source of commercial mortgage funds from 2002 to 2007?

Development and Construction Lending

To this point we have concerned ourselves entirely with the originators and holders of long-term commercial mortgages. However, as discussed in Chapter 16, the development and construction of commercial properties generally are financed with short-term development and construction loans.

Development and construction lending can be extremely risky. The primary risk is that the developer will fail to complete the project in a timely manner or fail to complete it at all. Builders may experience cost overruns, poor weather, strikes, structural or design problems, or difficulties with subcontractors. The builder may simply be a bad manager. In addition, failure to pass various building code inspections may delay the ability of tenants to occupy the building (and pay rent). All of these risks are assumed by the construction lender. Thus, construction lenders must have specialized skills in monitoring and controlling the construction process.

✓ Concept Check

17.12 Why are so many long-term mortgage lenders not involved in construction lending?

Because the risks of development and construction financing are significant and much different in nature than the risks of long-term lending, the capital sources for short-term development and construction loans differ significantly from the providers of permanent financing displayed in Exhibit 17-4. Construction lenders generally require recourse to other borrower assets to protect their capital from potential losses. They may also require the borrower to obtain a "take-out" loan commitment from a long-term lender to pay off the construction loan once the project is built and stabilized. The construction loan market is dominated by commercial banks. The remainder of the construction market is served primarily by savings institutions, federal, state, and local credit agencies and, increasingly, private equity lenders/funds.

A Closer Look at Real Estate Investment Trusts

www.crewnetwork.org

Association of Commercial Real Estate Women (CREW).

This section traces the rapid growth and development of the U.S. REIT industry from 1991 to 2006, the significant contraction that occurred in 2007 and 2008, and the impressive rebound that occurred in 2009–2015. The management and investment strategies of REITs are then discussed. We then turn our attention to REIT valuation and the performance of REITs as an asset class.

The Importance of Public Real Estate Markets

One measure of the importance of a publicly traded asset class in the U.S. economy is its stock market capitalization. The market capitalization of an individual stock is equal to the number of publicly traded shares times the current price of the stock. At year-end 1991, the total market capitalization of all listed REITs was only $13 billion (see Exhibit 17-5).[13] During the entire 10-year period from 1982 to 1991, there were 116 initial public offerings (IPOs) of REIT stocks. These 116 IPOs raised $9.4 billion in equity capital. Another 133 secondary equity offerings raised an additional $5.2 billion in capital for publicly traded REITs during this 10-year period, while 103 secondary debt offerings raised $9.5 billion.

---

13. "Listed" means the shares are traded on the New York Stock Exchange or over the counter on the National Association of Securities Dealers Automated Quotation (NASDAQ) system.

Exhibit 17-5 Historical Stock Offerings and Total Equity Market Capitalization of Listed REITs

	Initial Equity Offerings		Secondary Equity Offerings		Secondary Debt Offerings		Year-End Market Capitalization
	No.	($ Mil.)	No.	($ Mil.)	No.	($ Mil.)	($ Mil.)
1982–1991	116	$9,384	133	$5,178	103	$9,495	12,968*
1992	8	919	24	1060	26	4,642	15,912
1993	50	9,335	50	3850	41	5,135	32,159
1994	45	7,176	52	3,940	49	3,651	44,306
1995	8	939	93	7,270	95	4,245	57,542
1996	6	1,107	139	11,200	76	4,754	88,776
1997	26	6,296	292	26,380	145	12,597	140,534
1998	17	2,129	297	19,370	160	16,874	138,301
1999	2	292	100	6,450	103	10,477	124,263
2000	0	0	42	2,830	72	7,542	138,715
2001	0	0	79	6,080	48	12,670	154,899
2002	3	608	110	7,770	74	11,383	161,937
2003	8	2,646	146	10,660	74	12,252	224,212
2004	29	7,980	140	13,200	97	17,306	305,025
2005	11	3,789	107	11,610	141	22,088	330,691
2006	5	2,271	114	19,920	85	26,812	438,071
2007	4	1,820	82	16,050	43	18,155	312,009
2008	2	491	69	12,320	11	5,173	191,651
2009	9	2,990	87	21,240	34	10,422	271,199
2010	9	1,975	108	26,246	56	19,230	389,295
2011	8	2,307	123	35,183	33	13,790	450,501
2012	8	1,822	177	45,774	69	24,730	603,415
2013	19	5,707	149	40,511	86	30,739	670,334
2014	5	3,984	126	28,724	87	30,934	907,428
2015	7	1,423	83	25,669	72	32,201	936,852

Source: Data from National Association of Real Estate Investment Trusts (www.reit.com).
*As of year-end 1991.

After 1991, the real estate investment trust market exploded with 95 initial public offerings in 1993–1994. Secondary equity offerings by REITs also increased significantly during the early- to mid-1990s. After 1994, the REIT IPO market cooled with just 62 issues coming to market over the 1995–2002 period. The REIT IPO market did show signs of life during the 2003–2005 period. Existing REITs have consistently tapped the secondary market for equity and debt. The total dollar value of debt and equity security offerings by publicly traded REITs is displayed graphically in Exhibit 17-6.

Not surprisingly, capital raised through debt and equity security offerings is primarily used by equity REITs to acquire properties. By 2016, the value of properties owned by REITs was approximately $1.6 billion. Over the 1991–2006 period, the total equity market capitalization of the REIT market increased from $13 billion to $438 billion. However, the REIT industry contracted significantly in 2007 and 2008. Total returns on the FTSE-NAREIT All Equity REITs Index were −16 percent in 2007 and −38 percent in 2008. Numerous REITs were taken private by hedge funds and other private buyers or merged with other public REITs. By year-end 2008, the number of listed REITs tracked by NAREIT had declined to 136 from 183 in 2006. The market capitalization of the industry plunged from $438 billion to $192 billion.

Exhibit 17-6 Securities Offerings by REITs
(in billions of U.S. dollars, 1990–2015)

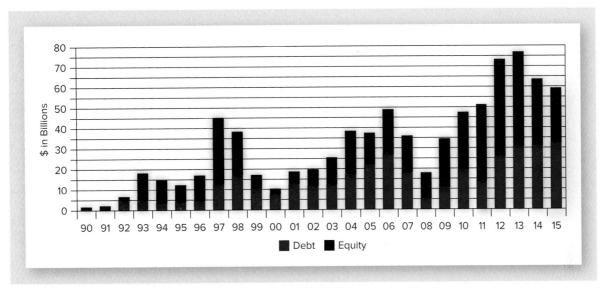

Source: Data from National Association of Real Estate Investment Trusts (www.reit.com).

However, over the 2009–2011 period, equity REITs produced an average annual total return of approximately 21 percent, and the market capitalization of the industry more than doubled to over $450 billion. From 2011 through 2015, the market capitalization of listed REITs increased to $939 billion. As can be seen in Exhibit 17-7, approximately 23 percent of this total market capitalization represented the market value of the 31 REITs that specialized in retail property investments. The representation of other property types includes apartments, 11 percent; office properties, 10 percent; and health care properties, 9 percent.

Exhibit 17-7 REITs by Property Type and Percent of Market Capitalization
(as of April 29, 2016)

Type of REIT	Number of Companies	% of Total Market Capitalization
Retail	31	23%
Apartments	15	11%
Office	26	10%
Health Care	17	9%
Infrastructure	5	8%
Self-Storage	5	6%
Mortgage REITs	38	5%
Industrial	11	5%
Data Centers	6	5%
Diversified	14	5%
Lodging/Resorts	17	4%
Speciality	8	3%
Timber	4	3%
Manufactured Homes	3	1%
Single-Family Homes	3	1%
Totals	203	100%

Source: Data from *REIT Watch*, May 2016, National Association of Real Estate Investment Trusts, www.reit.com.

REIT Management

Most REITs are actively managed operating companies. Property management is carried out either internally or by management that works solely for the benefit of the REIT shareholders. Property investments are generally focused by property type and/or geographic market because this specialization allows shareholders to benefit more fully from the specific expertise of the REIT management team.

Over the last decade, REITs have attracted significantly more institutional investors, which has been attributed to the growing acceptance of REITs among such investors as viable alternatives to direct investments in real estate and to the prospects of greater liquidity in the REIT market. Further evidence that the REIT market is attracting a wider range of investors can be found in the number of mutual funds that invest in REIT securities. By 2016, more than 120 dedicated REIT funds and exchange-traded funds were available to investors; there had been only a handful of such dedicated REIT funds in the early 1990s.

An important development in the REIT industry has been the creation of the **umbrella partnership REIT (UPREIT).** As an UPREIT, the REIT is a managing partner and typically majority owner in a single large umbrella partnership, which in turn owns all or part of individual property limited partnerships (LPs) or limited liability companies (LLCs). LPs and LLCs transferring their partnership or LLC interests into the umbrella partnership can receive umbrella partnership units or REIT shares in return for the original LP or LLC interests. Although the properties that made up the original LP or LLC have effectively been "sold" to the acquiring UPREIT, the exchange of LP or LLC units is *not* treated as a sale for federal income tax purposes. This is extremely important. Why? Because many of these property contributing LPs and LLCs, and therefore their investors, would face significant tax liabilities if they engaged in a "regular" taxable sale. As a result, the owner would be much less likely to agree to transfer the property or properties to the REIT. Because of this deferral of capital gain taxation, the UPREIT structure has played a critical role in the conversion of private ownership of real estate to public REIT ownership.[14]

Concept Check

17.13   You are the general partner in a limited partnership that owns a portfolio of five large apartment complexes. For various reasons, the partnership is to be dissolved and the properties disposed of. Both a large pension fund and an UPREIT have offered to acquire the portfolio at similar prices/values. What is the primary advantage of finalizing negotiations with the UPREIT?

Measuring REIT Income

According to generally accepted accounting principles (GAAP), a corporation's net income includes a tax deduction for the depreciation and amortization of certain financial and fixed assets. Tax depreciation, discussed in detail in Chapter 20, is the process whereby the cost of depreciable improvements is allocated (i.e., expensed) over the cost recovery period of the asset. Mechanically, depreciation and amortization expenses therefore reduce reported net accounting income. However, these expenses do not represent actual cash outflows. Thus, if a corporation's assets are primarily depreciable, as are most of the assets of an equity REIT, accounting income may understate the actual net cash flow available to distribute to investors as dividends.

---

14. It should be pointed out that the capital gain not taxed at the time the partnership or LLC units are exchanged is not excluded from future taxation. If the investor subsequently disposes of the partnership units or shares acquired from the UPREIT in the exchange, the capital gain that previously went untaxed will be added to the taxable gain reported by the contributing partner or LLC member on the sale of the UPREIT stock. Thus, the UPREIT structure does not eliminate accrued tax liabilities; rather, it allows them to be deferred, perhaps indefinitely.

The REIT industry's response to this issue was to create a supplemental earnings measure that adds back depreciation and other amortization expenses to GAAP net income. This measure is termed **funds from operations (FFO)** and is defined as

> FFO = net income (GAAP) excluding gains and losses on property sales
>   + Depreciation (real property)
>   + Amortization of leasing expenses
>   + Amortization of improvements made to tenants' space
>   − Gains (losses) from infrequent and unusual events

Similar to depreciation deductions, charges to amortize certain leasing expenses and the cost of tenant improvements paid for by the owner are added back to net accounting income when estimating the REIT's cash flow. Many industry analysts and observers argue that FFO is too easily manipulated by REITs, thus reducing its usefulness as an income measure. For example, what is an "infrequent" or "unusual" event? Nevertheless, FFO remains a widely used measure of a REIT's cash flow.[15]

✓ Concept Check

17.14 Why is GAAP net income not an appropriate metric of an equity REIT's ability to generate cash flow for investors?

REIT Valuation

REITs typically use income capitalization and discounted cash flow techniques (see Chapters 8 and 19) to make individual property acquisition and disposition decisions. That is, REITs seek to purchase properties that have positive net present values (*NPV*s) and internal rates of return (*IRR*s) in excess of the REIT's opportunity cost of capital. But how are the REITs themselves valued? Said differently, how do capital market investors determine the appropriate price to pay for a share of stock in a REIT, which in turn holds a portfolio of commercial properties or mortgages?

In general, REIT stocks are valued similarly to the stocks of other public companies; that is, investors attempt to forecast the stream of dividends the REIT will pay out over time. The projected dividend stream is, in turn, based on projections of future funds from operations. The projected dividend stream is then converted into a present value using a discounted cash flow model. In practice, however, long-term dividend projections are difficult to develop. Thus, investors also use other indicators of relative value in their REIT acquisition and disposition decisions.

One commonly employed approach to assessing the attractiveness of a REIT centers on the concept of **net asset value (NAV)**. *NAV* is equal to the estimated total market value of a REIT's underlying assets, less all liabilities having a prior claim to cash flow—including mortgages. To estimate the market value of the REIT's property holdings, analysts estimate the aggregate net operating income (*NOI*) of the REIT's property holdings. This aggregate *NOI* is then converted into an estimate of market value by capitalizing it at the appropriate (weighted average) cap rate for the portfolio. (Income capitalization is discussed in detail in Chapter 8.) The capitalization process uses information from the private real estate market to perform something resembling a mass appraisal of the REIT's properties. The ability to use information from the well-functioning private real estate market to

15. See NAREIT FFO "White Paper," National Association of Real Estate Investment Trusts, April 5, 2002. This article is available at the NAREIT website (www.reit.com). Adjusted funds from operations (AFFO) also are widely reported and used by REIT industry participants. AFFO is equal to FFO minus certain recurring capital expenses, principal amortization, and the difference between actual lease income and the "straight-line" lease income reported in the REIT's financial statement.

value shares of listed REITs is unique and distinguishes the REIT market from other industries where the assets are not separately traded in a private market.

How is the estimate of net asset value used to make acquisition decisions? If the per-share stock price of a REIT is greater than its per share *NAV,* the REIT is said to be selling at a premium to *NAV.* Although some of this premium may reflect the market's assessment of the ability of the REIT's management team to create value, a stock price in excess of per share *NAV* may indicate the REIT is overpriced relative to the value of the real estate assets currently in the portfolio. Conversely, REITs selling at discounts to net asset value may signal buying opportunities for investors or, perhaps, takeover opportunities for other management teams.

✓ Concept Check

17.15 In the *NAV* calculation, how is the value of the portfolio of properties estimated?

Analysts and potential REIT investors may also track and compare the ratio of a REIT's current stock price to estimated FFO per share. For example, if the stock of an office REIT is currently selling for $20 per share and analysts forecast that current year FFO per share will be $1, the current price–FFO multiple is 20. This multiple can then be compared to other similar office REITs. If the average office REIT has a current price–FFO multiple of, say, $22 per share, it *may* indicate that the stock of the office REIT in question is undervalued, although numerous other explanations are likely to exist. For example, the lower price–FFO multiple may indicate the market perceives the REIT to have lower-quality management and/or less FFO growth potential than similar REITs. Investors also consider the amount of financial leverage used by REITs when valuing individual companies. Investors tend to punish the stock prices of REITs that use more leverage than is typical.

www.reits.com

REITNet provides access to information and decision-making tools needed to evaluate REIT investments.

REIT Investment Performance

To obtain evidence on the return performance of listed REITs, we analyze data acquired from the National Association of Real Estate Investment Trusts. The FTSE-NAREIT All Equity REITs Index tracks total returns (income plus capital appreciation) on all listed equity REITs. For comparison purposes, we also report total returns on the S&P 500 and the Russell 2000. The Russell 2000 is a "small cap" stock index that tracks the performance of 2,000 publicly traded companies that rank 1,001–3,000 in U.S. stock market capitalization. Exhibit 17-8 presents annualized total returns for each index over selected holding periods.

Exhibit 17-8 Comparison of Historical Total Returns
(Annualized returns, as of April 29, 2016)

Holding Period (in years)	FTSE NAREIT All Equity REITs	S&P 500	Russell 2000
1	8.11%	1.21%	−5.94
3	6.97	11.26	7.53
5	10.05	11.02	6.98
10	6.72	6.91	5.42
15	11.23	5.48	7.22
20	10.94	7.92	7.48
30	10.35	9.99	8.59

Source: Data from *REIT Watch*, May 2016, National Association of Real Estate Investment Trusts, www.reit.com.

As a sector, equity REITs produced an average annual return of 22.9 percent from 2000 to 2006. The corresponding average return on the S&P 500 and Russell 2000 were 2.5 percent and 9.6 percent, respectively. This significant outperformance induced many investors to add REITs to their investment portfolios. In 2007 and 2008, however, equity REITs produced returns of −15.7 percent and −37.7 percent, respectively. This performance was even worse than the −32 percent two-year return produced by the S&P 500. Over the three-year period from May 2013 through April of 2016, the FTSE-NAREIT All Equity REITs Index returned 7.0 percent annually. The corresponding S&P 500 and Russell 2000 returns were 11.3 percent and 7.5 percent, respectively. When looking back 10 years from the end of April in 2016, equity REITs generated a 6.7 percent annualized return, slightly less than the returns earned by those who invested in the S&P 500 and 130 basis points per year more than the Russell 2000. Over longer periods, equity REITs have outperformed the two stock indices. When evaluating the historical performance of the three asset classes, it is important to recognize that Exhibit 17-8 contains only mean returns, unadjusted for risk. Rational investors should also consider the volatility of returns and their comovement with the returns on other asset classes when making investment decisions.

Summary

The market value of investible commercial real estate in the United States is approximately $8.8 trillion. In this chapter, we answer the following questions: Who owns these commercial real estate assets, what forms of ownership are used to develop and acquire properties, and who provides the mortgage financing that is so often used in conjunction with investors' equity to acquire and hold these assets?

Investors can own commercial real estate either through direct investment or by investing through intermediaries. With direct equity investment, individual and institutional investors choose an ownership form and then purchase and hold title to the properties without pooling their equity capital with other investors, thereby gaining complete control of the assets. Generally, investment through intermediaries occurs via real estate securities that allow individuals and institutions to pool their equity capital and invest in an ownership entity, which in turn purchases and holds title to the real estate.

Securitized equity investments can be purchased and resold in public markets or they can be privately owned. Publicly traded (i.e., "listed") securities, including many real estate investment trusts (REITs), are bought and sold on public stock exchanges, such as the New York Stock Exchange. These listed securities provide investors with a high degree of investment liquidity and relatively low transaction costs. Approximately 23 percent of commercial real estate equity is traded in public markets. The remaining 77 percent is privately owned. Approximately $763 billion of this 77 percent is owned by pension funds, foreign investors, life insurance companies, commercial banks, and savings associations. The remaining $3.0 trillion is held by other institutional investors, high net worth investors, and other "smaller" investors.

Who are the noninstitutional investors that own and control a significant amount of U.S. commercial real estate assets? High net worth investors account for a portion. More commonly, groups of private investors pool their equity capital when purchasing commercial real estate. A real estate syndicate is a group organized to develop a parcel of land, buy an office building, purchase an entire portfolio of properties, make mortgage loans, or perform other real estate activities. Examples of pooled ownership structures that purchase real estate directly in the private market include limited partnerships and limited liability companies. The relative advantages and disadvantages of each ownership structure are discussed with special attention given to the prominent role played by limited liability companies.

The chapter then covers the sources of commercial mortgage debt. Approximately 25 percent of outstanding commercial mortgage debt is publicly traded, primarily in the form of commercial mortgage-backed securities (CMBS). The remaining 75 percent of outstanding commercial mortgage debt is privately held by institutional and individual investors. Commercial banks are the largest single source of private mortgage funds. Life insurance companies and savings associations are also participants in the long-term commercial mortgage market. The remaining privately held mortgage debt is primarily owned by pension funds, private equity debt funds, and federal, state, and local credit agencies that supply mortgage funds for the acquisition of low- and moderate-income rental housing.

Finally, the chapter takes a closer look at REITs. In particular, we discuss the size and importance of the REIT market, how REIT income is measured, how REITs are valued, and how REITs as an asset class have performed relative to the investment returns of alternative stock investments.

Key Terms

C corporation   459
Commingled real estate funds   466
Equity REITs   469
Full platform operating
    company   468
Funds from operations (FFO)   477
General partnership   458
Intermediaries   462

Limited liability company
    (LLC)   460
Limited partnership   458
Mortgage REITs   469
Net asset value (*NAV*)   477
Pension funds   463
Real estate investment trusts
    (REITs)   468

Real estate private equity
    funds   466
Securitized investments   465
Separate accounts   466
Subchapter S corporation   460
Syndicate   465
Umbrella partnership REIT
    (UPREIT)   476

Test Problems

Answer the following multiple-choice problems:

1. Double taxation of the income produced by the underlying properties is most likely to occur if the commercial properties are held in the form of a(n):
   a. S corporation.
   b. Limited partnership.
   c. C corporation.
   d. Real estate investment trust.
   e. Limited liability company.

2. With regard to double taxation, distributions, and the treatment of the losses, general partnerships are *most* like:
   a. S corporations.
   b. C corporations.
   c. Limited partnerships.
   d. Real estate investment trusts.

3. Special allocations of income or loss are available if the form of ownership is a(n):
   a. S corporation.
   b. Real estate investment trust.
   c. Limited liability company.
   d. C corporation.

4. Small- to medium-sized real estate syndicates that develop or acquire property in a local market are most typically organized as:
   a. S corporations.
   b. C corporations.
   c. Limited liability companies.
   d. Real estate investment trusts.

5. A real estate investment trust generally:
   a. Must have fewer than 100 shareholders.
   b. Can only invest directly in income-producing properties.
   c. Can pass tax losses through to shareholders.
   d. None of the above.

6. Which of the following forms of ownership involve both limited *and* unlimited liability?
   a. Limited partnerships.
   b. Corporation.
   c. General partnership.
   d. Sole partnership.
   e. None of the above.

7. Which statement is *false* concerning the limited partnership form of ownership?
   a. The general partner has nearly complete control and is liable for debts and actions of the partnership.
   b. The limited partners have little management control and are not liable except to the amount of their investment.
   c. The limited partners cannot enjoy tax deduction benefits, but the general partners can.
   d. The partnership is not a taxable entity.
   e. None of the above.

8. Which of these lenders is most likely to provide a construction loan?
   a. Savings and loan association.
   b. Credit union.
   c. Commercial bank.
   d. Life insurance company.
   e. Real estate investment trust.

9. Which of these loans is a life insurance company most likely to invest in?
   a. Single-family home loan.
   b. Small commercial property loan (nonconstruction).
   c. Large office building loan (nonconstruction).
   d. Large construction loan.
   e. Small construction loan.

10. Which of these financial firms is the least likely to invest in a large, long-term mortgage loan on a shopping center?
    a. Commercial bank.
    b. Savings and loan association.
    c. Life insurance company.
    d. Mortgage broker.

Study Questions

1. For what debt in a general partnership is each of the general partners liable?
2. What are the potential advantages of investing in commercial real estate through intermediaries instead of direct investment? What are the potential disadvantages?
3. Discuss the role life insurance companies play in financing commercial real estate.
4. Approximately 52 percent of private commercial real estate equity (on a value-weighted basis) is owned by "noninstitutional" investors. Who are these investors?
5. Briefly describe a commingled real estate fund. Who are the investors in these funds and why do these investors use commingled funds for their purchases?
6. There are two primary considerations that affect the ownership form selected by equity investors to hold commercial real estate. List each and explain how they affect the choice of ownership form.
7. Explain what is meant by the double taxation of income.

8. What are the major restrictions that a REIT must meet on an ongoing basis in order to avoid taxation at the entity level?
9. Compare the tax advantages and disadvantages of holding income-producing property in the form of a REIT to the tax advantages and disadvantages of holding property in the form of a real estate limited partnership. Does either form of ownership dominate *from a tax perspective?*
10. Of the $4.0 trillion in outstanding U.S. commercial real estate debt, what percentage is traded in public markets? What percentage is traded in private markets? What institutions or entities are the long-term holders of private commercial real estate debt?
11. Distinguish between equity REITs and mortgage REITs.
12. Define funds from operations (FFO) and explain why this measure is often used instead of GAAP net income to quantify the income-producing ability of a real estate investment trust.
13. How have equity REITs, measured in terms of total returns, performed in recent years relative to alternative stock investments?

www.mhhe.com/lingarcher5e

EXPLORE THE WEB

Real estate investment trusts have become a popular vehicle for real estate investment. Investors can monitor the performance of REITs, as well as non-REIT stocks and bonds, using the Web page of the National Association of Real Estate Investment Trusts (NAREIT). Go to the NAREIT home page: www.reit.com. Download the latest REIT Watch performance report. In 500 words or less, analyze the recent performance of REITs and compare their returns to those realized on portfolios of stocks and bonds. Have REITs outperformed stocks and bonds over the last 12 months? Have equity or mortgage REITs exhibited the strongest recent performance?

Solutions to Concept Checks

1. The estimated value of the U.S. housing stock is $22.0 trillion; the estimated value of commercial real estate is $8.8 trillion. The sum of these two asset classes is $30.8 trillion. This is 14 percent less than the stock market.
2. The primary advantage of a limited partnership relative to a general partnership is that the passive limited partners can avoid unlimited liability for the debts and obligations of the partnership. In a general partnership, all partners must assume unlimited liability.
3. C corporations are seldom used by investors to purchase and hold commercial real estate, primarily because the structure does not permit the enterprise to avoid double taxation. Thus, for the purposes of making long-term investments in commercial real estate, this structure is dominated by

"flow-through" ownership forms such as limited liability companies and limited partnerships.
4. First, unlike limited partnerships, LLCs permit all owners to participate in the management of the business entity. The nature of their participation is detailed in the LLC's operating agreement. Second, LLCs permit all investors to have limited liability; thus, there is no need for a general partner who is potentially subject to unlimited liability.
5. When investing directly, the investor has complete control. When investing through an intermediary or sponsor, much of the control must be relinquished. However, in return, the investor obtains access to managerial talent and expertise and the ability to share the risk of the investment with other providers of equity capital.

6. In late 2015, pension funds, foreign investors, life insurance companies, and financial institutions held an estimated $763 billion in equity investments. This is 20 percent ($763 ÷ $3,726) of total private commercial real estate equity.

7. A real estate syndication is a group of investors or legal entities that is organized to develop or purchase real estate, often with the intention of holding the assets as long-term investments. The syndicate must choose a form of ownership to conduct its business, such as a limited partnership or a limited liability company.

8. Core investments are high-quality properties that typically have strong leases in place and are located in major metropolitan areas. They offer lower expected returns in exchange for less risk. Opportunistic investments have greater risk, with even higher expected returns. These investments may have a heavier development component and often involve riskier property types and locations.

9. In late 2015, the $3.7 trillion in commercial real estate equity owned by private entities included investments totaling $1.9 trillion by noninstitutional investors, or 52 percent.

10. REIT investors obtain more diversification by investing in REITs than they could obtain on their own. Also, shares of listed REITs are much more liquid (easier to sell) than the individual properties.

11. The fastest-growing source of commercial mortgage funds from 2002 to 2007 was commercial mortgage-backed securities.

12. Construction lending is a much different business than long-term lending and has significantly more risk for the lender. It is primarily short-term lending that requires significant knowledge of the development and construction business.

13. By "selling" the property to the UPREIT, the LP investors can avoid the immediate recognition of the accrued capital gain. There can be significant value associated with tax deferral.

14. GAAP net income understates the true ability of an equity REIT to generate cash flow because it includes deductions for noncash expenses, such as tax depreciation. These noncash deductions should be added back to get a true picture of the income-producing ability of the REIT.

15. To calculate the value of the portfolio of properties owned by the REIT, the net operating income (*NOI*) to be produced by all of the underlying properties is estimated and then aggregated. This total *NOI* is then converted into an estimate of the market value of the portfolio by capitalizing the aggregate *NOI* at the appropriate cap rate. This is akin to applying direct capitalization on an aggregate basis.

Additional Readings

Block, R. L. *Investing in REITS: Real Estate Investment Trusts,* 4th ed. Burlington, VT: Bloomberg Press, 2011.

Brueggeman, William B., and Jeffrey D. Fisher. *Real Estate Finance and Investment,* 15th ed. New York: McGraw-Hill/Irwin, 2016.

Chan, S. H., J. Erickson, and K. Wang. *Real Estate Investment Trusts: Structure, Performance, and Investment Opportunities.* New York: Oxford University Press, 2002.

Collier, N. S., C. A. Collier, and D. A. Halperin. *Construction Funding: The Process of Real Estate Development, Appraisal, and Finance,* 4th ed. Hoboken, NJ: John Wiley & Sons, Inc. 2008.

Geltner, D., N. G. Miller, Jim Clayton, and Piet Eichholtz. *Commercial Real Estate Analysis & Investment,* 3rd ed. Mason, OH: Thomson South-Western Publishing, 2014.

Imperiale, R. J. K. *Getting Started in Real Estate Investment Trusts.* New York: John Wiley and Sons, 2006.

Kolbe, P. T., and G. E. Greer. *Investment Analysis for Real Estate Decisions,* 6th ed. Chicago, IL: Kaplan Publishing, 2012.

Linneman, P. *Real Estate Finance & Investments: Risk and Opportunities,* 3rd ed. Philadelphia, PA: Linneman Associates, 2011.

Wiedemer, John P., Joseph E. Goeters, and J. Edward Graham. *Real Estate Investment*, 7th ed. Mason, OH: South-Western Cengage Learning, 2011.

Wiedemer, John P., and J. Keith Baker. *Real Estate Finance,* 9th ed. Mason, OH: South-Western Cengage Learning, 2011.

Chapter 18

Investment Decisions: Ratios

LEARNING OBJECTIVES

After reading this chapter you will be able to:

1 Calculate the effects of mortgage debt on the required initial investment, first year cash flows, and returns.

2 Calculate and interpret the basic cash flow multipliers, profitability ratios, and financial ratios that apply to real estate investment decisions.

3 Explain why real estate investors borrow money and calculate what effect financial leverage has on investment decisions, given assumptions about the mortgage.

4 Explain how income taxes affect property cash flows and initial returns.

5 Explain the advantages and disadvantages of using ratio analysis to make real estate investment decisions.

OUTLINE

Introduction

We examined the concept of market value and its measurement in Chapters 7 and 8. Professional real estate appraisers are often called upon to estimate the market value of real estate because market value is the basis for economic transactions. A buyer does not usually wish to pay more, nor the seller take less, than the market value of the property.

Nevertheless, for many purposes the market value estimate is not the whole story. Since most decisions that determine the role of real estate assets in shaping the future of neighborhoods and cities are made with an investment motive, it is our contention that the professional approach to the study of real estate must employ investment valuation as its base. Investment valuation calculations, whether implicit or explicit, are made whenever a property transaction is contemplated; when a maintenance or repair decision is made; when a structure is modernized, renovated, converted, abandoned, or demolished; and when a site is developed with a new set of improvements. In short, expected cash flows—and the property values they create—are at the center of investment decision making.

This chapter introduces the framework for making single-asset real estate investment decisions. The focus is on a set of widely used single-year return measures, ratios, and income multipliers. These returns, ratios, and multipliers have the advantage of being relatively easy to calculate and understand. They do not, however, explicitly incorporate cash inflows and outflows beyond the first year of the analysis—a potentially serious limitation in their use and interpretation given the long-lived nature of real estate assets. To overcome the shortcomings of single-year decision-making metrics, many investors also perform multiyear analyses of the income-producing ability of potential acquisitions. These multiyear discounted cash flow (DCF) valuation and decision-making methods, most notably net present value and the internal rate of return, are discussed in detail in Chapter 19.

A word of caution is in order before we begin our two-chapter tour of commonly used investment decision-making tools. The cash flows at the heart of investment valuation are, in the "real world," often estimated with significant uncertainty. In prior chapters, especially Chapters 2 to 6, we sought to explain and demonstrate the importance of the complex economic, social, political, and legal processes that affect real estate markets and, hence, the income-producing ability of commercial real estate. For example, in Chapter 4 we discussed growth management and local land use regulations. Why? Because these rules and regulations will likely affect the future income-producing ability, and therefore the value, of a property. Similarly, the numerous "imperfections" in real estate markets, such as a frequent lack of adequate market data and the immobility of land and structures, are all discussed in Chapter 5 because of their potential effect on rents and property values.

As these prior chapters clearly demonstrate, many qualitative and difficult-to-predict factors influence real estate cash flows. In this chapter, however, we largely assume the influences of these myriad factors have already been converted into assumptions and projections of rents, vacancies, and operating expenses. This allows us to focus in this chapter and the next on how these often tenuous assumptions are used by the industry to quantify the income-producing ability and investment value of commercial real estate. Despite the emphasis in this and the subsequent chapter on quantitative decision tools, students should not conclude that investment valuation and decision making is simply a matter of "getting the numbers to add up." Although quantitative valuation tools and techniques are widely used in commercial real estate markets, their usefulness is limited by the quality of the cash flow assumptions employed. Thus, most all of the concepts discussed in prior chapters should help form the investor's projections of rents, vacancies, operating expenses, and future sale prices. In short, the "garbage in, garbage out" maxim applies directly to real estate investment decision making.

Investment Decision Making

Investment decision making centers around the estimation of the net cash flows from annual rental operations. In Chapter 8, we discuss the mechanics of constructing cash flow projections for appraisal. In this section, we demonstrate and explain the mechanics of constructing cash flow projections for a particular investor.

Centre Point Office Building Example

To demonstrate how commercial real estate appraisers estimate the income-producing ability of an existing commercial property, Chapter 8 provided a detailed case example: the Centre Point Office Building. We now return to this example to demonstrate investment valuation and decision making. For convenience, the basic assumptions for this potential investment in a small office property are reproduced in Exhibit 18-1.

Exhibit 18-1 Assumptions for Centre Point Office Building

- Total acquisition price: $1,056,000.
- Property consists of eight office suites, three on the first floor and five on the second.
- Contract rents: two suites at $1,800 per month, one at $3,600 per month, and five at $1,560 per month.
- Annual market rent increases: 3 percent per year.
- Vacancy and collection losses: 10 percent per year.
- Operating expenses: 40 percent of effective gross income each year.
- Capital expenditures: 5 percent of effective gross income each year.
- Expected holding period: five years.

Potential gross income (*PGI*) over the next 12 months is estimated to be $180,000 and vacancy and collection losses are estimated at $18,000, resulting in an effective gross income (*EGI*) of $162,000.[1] Total operating expenses in the first year are estimated at $64,800 (40 percent of *EGI*) and capital expenditures are projected to be $8,100 (5 percent of *EGI*). As displayed in Exhibit 18-2, these assumptions produce an estimated net operating income (*NOI*) of $89,100 over the next 12 months. (Please see Chapter 8 for more discussion of these calculations.)

✓ **Concept Check**

18.1 Summarize the calculation of net operating income (*NOI*).

---

www.wellsref.com

Wells Real Estate Fund is a national investment firm that purchases existing Class A office and industrial properties.

The property's current and projected future *NOI* is the fundamental determinant of Centre Point's value. In an analogy to the stock market, *NOI* is the annual "dividend" expected to be produced by the property. It must be sufficient, given other attributes of the property, to provide the investor with an acceptable rate of return.

Treatment of Capital Expenditures

Many components of commercial properties wear out faster than the building itself; thus, owners can expect to replace them several times during the building's economic life. In addition, investors typically expect to incur "retenanting" expenses when leases expire and

Exhibit 18-2 Centre Point Office Building: First-Year Net Operating Income

Potential gross income (*PGI*)	$180,000
− Vacancy and collection loss (*VC*)	18,000
= Effective gross income (*EGI*)	162,000
− Operating expenses (*OE*)	64,800
− Capital expenditures (*CAPX*)	8,100
= Net operating income (*NOI*)	$ 89,100

---

1. The *PGI* of $180,000 is equal to $12 \times [(2 \times \$1,800) + (1 \times \$3,600) + (5 \times \$1,560)]$.

the vacant space must again be made ready for occupancy. These tenant improvements may be relatively minor. To re-lease an apartment, for example, owners may simply apply a fresh coat of paint and clean the carpet. However, in some situations these replacement and retenanting expenditures can be quite large but difficult to forecast. In a typical apartment acquisition, the investor uses assumptions in the pro forma acceptable to mortgage lenders. For example, the investor may forecast that replacement and retenanting expenses will be $0.15 per square foot per year or $300 per unit per year. The re-leasing of office space often requires that substantial changes be made to the space, such as removing or adding walls, raising ceilings, and altering electrical capacity. Most office leases provide a new tenant with a tenant improvement allowance, or "TI." This lease provision obligates the landlord to incur a prespecified dollar amount of expenditures, perhaps $5 to $10 per square foot for an existing structure, to improve the space to the tenant's specifications.[2]

Various terms are applied to nonrecurring capital expenses and tenant improvements in cash flow projections. Examples include "capital costs," "capital expenditures," and "reserve for capital expenditures." The tradition in real estate appraisal is to refer to the projected nonrecurring expenses as "reserves." The investment community increasingly refers to these items as capital expenditures. We adopt the latter convention here (and, for consistency, did so in Chapter 8).

In addition to inconsistent terminology, the placement of these nonrecurring capital expenditures in pro forma cash flow projections has not been standardized. In appraisal, capital expenditures (*CAPX*) have traditionally been treated as "above-line" expenses, meaning they are included in the calculation of *NOI*. More frequently, however, nonrecurring capital expenditures are treated as "below-line" expenses; that is, they are subtracted *from NOI*. The modern treatment of capital expenditures in investment analysis is to include nonrecurring expenses below line.

✓ Concept Check

18.2 What is the modern treatment of *CAPX* in investment analysis?

---

www.irs.gov/
publications/p535/
index.html

Read how the IRS distinguishes between operating expenses and capital expenditures.

Although many investors and analysts treat capital expenditures as below-line costs, we continue to use the above-line treatment depicted in Exhibit 18-2 to be consistent with our treatment of such costs in Chapter 8.

How does the investor distinguish between operating expenses and capital expenditures in historical data or in future projections? The key characteristic of an operating expense is that the expenditure is necessary to keep the property operating and competitive in its local market. An operating expense does not add to the market value of the property. For example, minor roof repairs are occasionally required on commercial properties, but they do not affect the market value of the property because they do not extend its useful life. In contrast, major roof replacements do affect the market value of the property and, as a result, are considered capital expenditures, not operating expenses.[3]

---

2. When new leases are signed on some types of commercial properties, the leasing agents are usually entitled to leasing commissions that typically range from 4 to 6 percent of the face value of the lease (monthly base rent times number of months in lease). Although leasing commissions are not technically capital expenditures, we do not differentiate such expenses in the examples and discussion that follows.

3. As we shall see in Chapter 20, the distinction between operating expenses and capital expenditures has significant income tax ramifications because operating expenses are fully deductible for tax purposes in the year in which they are paid. Although capital expenditures generally require an immediate cash outflow, they are not immediately deductible. Instead, they must be added to the property's tax basis and then expensed (i.e., recovered) over a legislatively determined period of time meant to approximate the economic life of the improvements. Thus, most taxable investors are motivated to classify expenditures as operating expenses to minimize current income tax liabilities.

Effects of Debt Financing on Cash Flows

Many investors make at least some use of debt financing—also called financial leverage—when acquiring real estate. The use of financial leverage affects the amount of cash (equity) required at acquisition, the net cash flows to the investor from rental operations, the net cash flow from the eventual sale of the property, and the riskiness of the return on invested equity capital.

Why Do Investors Borrow?

There are two primary reasons why real estate investors use financial leverage. The first is limited financial resources. If an investor desires to purchase real estate but does not have sufficient wealth to pay cash for the property, then borrowing is the only alternative. The price the investor/borrower must pay is the periodic interest rate on the borrowed funds.

The second reason for the use of mortgage financing is that it alters the expected risk *and* return of real estate investments. In particular, the use of financial leverage amplifies the rate of return investors earn on their invested equity. Positive *magnification* of equity returns is known as positive financial leverage, and it may induce investors to partially debt-finance (i.e., use "other people's money") even if they have sufficient accumulated wealth to avoid borrowing. As discussed in more detail in Chapter 19, however, financial leverage may magnify returns in a negative direction if the property underperforms. Thus, the use of leverage increases investment risk.

✓ Concept Check

18.3 Why might a real estate investor borrow to help finance an investment even if she could afford to pay 100 percent cash?

Effect on Initial Equity Investment

When a mortgage loan is obtained, the cash down payment (i.e., equity) required at property acquisition, E, is equal to

$$E = \text{Acquisition price} - \text{Net loan proceeds}$$

where the net loan proceeds equal the face (or stated) amount of the loan, minus total upfront financing costs paid by the borrower at closing to obtain the loan. Recall that upfront financing costs include any charges or fees the borrower pays to obtain the mortgage financing. Examples include attorney fees, loan origination fees, and costs associated with having the property surveyed or appraised. The effects of loan origination fees and costs on the cost of borrowed funds are discussed in detail in Chapter 15.

Assume the $1,056,000 Centre Point acquisition price is to be financed with a 30-year, 6.5 percent mortgage loan. The face amount of the loan will equal 75 percent of the purchase price, or $792,000. For simplicity, assume total upfront financing costs will equal 3 percent of the $792,000 loan amount, or $23,760. Thus, the investor's required equity down payment is

$$E = \$1,056,000 - (\$792,000 - \$23,760) = \$287,760$$

The net loan proceeds received by the investor at closing are equal to $768,240 ($792,000 − $23,760). The monthly mortgage payment, however, is based on $792,000, the face amount of the loan.

✓ Concept Check

18.4 Define net loan proceeds.

The CCIM Institute, an affiliate of the National Association of Realtors (NAR), confers the prestigious Certified Commercial Investment Member (CCIM) designation. A CCIM is a recognized expert in commercial real estate.

The CCIM curriculum consists of four core courses that incorporate the essential CCIM skill sets: financial analysis, market analysis, user (i.e., tenant)

The CCIM Designation

decision analysis, and investment analysis for commercial investment real estate. In addition, the education component of the designation includes an ethics course, negotiation training, and several elective courses.

Following the course work, candidates must submit a portfolio of qualifying activities, transactions, projects, or work products. After fulfilling these requirements, candidates must successfully complete a comprehensive examination to earn the CCIM designation. This designation process ensures that CCIMs are proficient not only in theory but also in

practice. The CCIM membership network mirrors the increasingly changing nature of the industry and includes brokers, leasing professionals, investment counselors, asset managers, appraisers, corporate real estate executives, property managers, developers, institutional investors, commercial lenders, attorneys, bankers, and other allied professionals. A CCIM is part of a global commercial real estate network with members in more than 30 countries.

Source: Adapted from www.ccim.com/about-ccim/

Effect on Cash Flows from Annual Operations

Before-tax cash flow from annual rental operations (*BTCF*) is defined as net operating income (*NOI*) minus the sum of the mortgage payments (debt service). *BTCF* is the expected cash flow left over from rental operations each year after paying all operating expenses, capital expenditures, and servicing the mortgage debt.

✓ **Concept Check**

18.5   Why is *BTCF* a better measure of investor cash flow than *NOI*?

Consider again the Centre Point Office Building example. The monthly payment on the $792,000 mortgage loan is $5,005.98; annual payments total $60,072 ($5,005.98 × 12).[4] The estimate of the *BTCF* for the first year of property operations after acquisition is $29,028 and is displayed in Exhibit 18-3. The *BTCF* is considered a "levered" cash flow because it represents cash flow to the equity investor *after* the effects of financial leverage (i.e., debt service) have been subtracted. In contrast, *NOI* is an unlevered cash flow because it represents the return on the entire investment (in this case $1,056,000), not just the return on the portion of the investment financed with equity capital.

Exhibit 18-3   Centre Point Office Building: Estimated Before-Tax Cash Flow

= Net operating income (*NOI*)	$89,100
− Debt service (*DS*)	60,072
= Before-tax cash flow (*BTCF*)	$29,028

4. The keystrokes for this calculation are $N = 360$; $PV = -792,000$; $PMT = ?$; $FV = 0$; and $I = 6.5 \div 12$. This series of keystrokes produces a monthly payment of $5,005.98. The calculation of mortgage payments is discussed in detail in Chapter 15.

Evaluating the Cash Flow Estimates

The key to meaningful cash flow analysis is to use defensible cash flow estimates. Therefore, investors should consider some important questions when estimating rents, vacancies, operating expenses, and capital expenditures. The answers to these questions will assist in the evaluation of the completeness and accuracy of the pro forma cash flow projections.

www.boma.org

Building Owners and Managers website provides detailed operating income and expense information for office properties numerous in U.S. cities.

www.icsc.org

International Council of Shopping Centers website provides operating income and expense information for U.S. shopping centers.

www.nmhc.org

Website of the National Multi Housing Council. Track the latest trends in apartment investing with this site.

www.reis.com

Detailed trend information on commercial rents and vacancies for over 200 metropolitan areas.

www.netronline.com

A public records and research information portal for U.S. public records, parcel maps, deed and mortgage copies, and tax records nationwide.

1. **Are the sources of income and expenses appropriate?** Investors should include only those sources of income and expenses that relate directly and entirely to the income-producing ability of the property. Operating expense estimates should not include financing costs and federal income taxes because these expenses are specific to the investor. Estimates of operating expenses also should exclude capital expenditures and business-related expenses not directly attributable to the operation of the property (e.g., unnecessary "business" lunches and club memberships).

2. **Have the trends for each revenue and expense item been considered?** Investors should avoid considering only recent events to the detriment of long-term trends. For example, current vacancy rates may be high relative to historic averages. Thus, current market conditions could easily bias upward an estimate of the future vacancy rates. No assumptions are more critical to investment decision making than rental growth rate and vacancy assumptions. The creditworthiness of tenants is also an important consideration.

3. **What about comparable properties?** Considering only the experience of the subject property, regardless of its current status, is too narrow a perspective. Similar to appraisers, investors should obtain information about revenue and expense items for comparable properties whenever possible. As an example, property tax trends for frequently reassessed comparable properties may be better for estimating property taxes of the subject property than its own past property tax trends. Obtaining this information on comparable properties requires that investors develop and maintain relationships with various market participants such as appraisers, brokers, lenders, and other investors.[5] Also, as discussed in detail in Chapters 7 and 8, numerous other sources of comparable data and information are available on the Internet and elsewhere.

4. **What are the prevailing social and legal environments?** Local zoning, land use, and environmental controls evolve continuously at both the state and the local level. Changes in these rules and regulations can have a dramatic effect on property values and returns. Accurately predicting such changes is a difficult task, especially given that many changes are based on political, not economic, considerations. An understanding, however, of current local controls and regulations is a prerequisite for successful real estate investing, even if changes are difficult to predict.

5. **How is the demand and the supply of properties similar to the subject property likely to change?** Especially in multiyear analyses, future demand/supply conditions are crucial considerations.

Partnerships and Other Direct Forms of Ownership

The before-tax cash flow (*BTCF*) associated with the Centre Point Office Building investment displayed in Exhibit 18-3 represents the expected *total* cash flow available for distribution to equity investors—after the payment of operating expenses, capital expenditures, and debt service. To this point, we have implicitly assumed there is one equity investor

---

5. A significant amount of historical information on typical operating expense levels is available, by property type, for the United States and major submarkets. See, for example, the following annual publications of the Institute of Real Estate Management (IREM): *Income/Expense Analysis: Office Buildings; Income/Expense Analysis: Shopping Centers;* and *Income/Expense Analysis: Conventional Apartments.* IREM's website is www.irem.org.

entitled to receive the cash flow. As emphasized in Chapter 17, however, the majority of commercial properties in the United States, both large and small, are held not by individuals but by multiple investors in the form of partnerships, limited liability companies, private equity funds, and other ownership entities. When investing through such entities, all cash flow and income tax consequences of real estate ownership "flow through" directly to the individual investors. There is no separate corporate entity that collects the cash flows, pays corporate income taxes, and distributes all or part of the net corporate cash flow to investors in the form of dividends.

How does investment through a partnership, limited liability company, or private equity fund affect investment decision making? Investment in real estate limited liability companies, for example, is governed by an operating agreement, which prescribes the percentage of the required equity capital that must be contributed by each investor, as well as the portion of the cash flows distributed to the various investors. In a few cases the operating agreement dictates that all investors receive their **pro rata share** of all cash flow distributions. For example, if an investor contributed 1/10 of the required equity investment she would receive 1/10 of all future cash flow distributions.

However, in most cases the operating agreement calls for certain classes of investors to receive a higher percentage of some future cash flows than their initial equity contribution would warrant. This is almost always the case for the sponsor (managing member in a limited liability company) of the investment opportunity, who usually contributes significant time and resources to create the investment opportunity and ownership entity. Thus, the sponsor needs to earn a higher *expected* return than the "passive" investors in order to be induced to organize and manage the venture. In short, it is important to understand that the estimate of property-level cash flows demonstrated in this chapter is just the first step in determining the cash flows and returns expected to be received by various investors in the ownership entity.

> ### Concept Check
>
> **18.6** Why is the estimation of property level cash inflows and outflows often just the first step in determining the cash flows and returns expected by various investors in the ownership entity?

Effects of Income Taxes

The direct ownership of commercial real estate is expected to produce cash flows from rental operations and cash flow from the eventual sale of the property. Recall, however, that mortgage lenders have a claim on property cash flows superior to the claim of the equity investor. Moreover, property cash flows are subject to federal, and potentially state, income taxation. Investors receive only the funds left after the lender(s) and the state and federal government collect their share of the cash flows. The claims of the state and federal government on property-level cash flows are substantial. Maximum statutory federal income tax rates on individuals (as of 2016) are 39.6 percent. Although some states do not have an income tax, many do and the maximum tax rate in some states exceeds 10 percent. Thus, many real estate investors face a combined state and federal tax rate in excess of 50 percent! Consequently, the measure of cash flow most relevant to investors is the **after-tax cash flow (*ATCF*)** from property operations. Although investors are not expected to be income tax experts—tax accountants and attorneys are readily available—wise investors should not make a commitment to purchase commercial real estate without a clear understanding of the income tax implications.

Unfortunately, the portion of the federal tax code pertaining to commercial real estate is extensive and complex. In particular, the income subject to taxation generally differs, often significantly, from the actual cash flow generated by the property because some expenditures that reduce net investor cash flows (e.g., capital expenditures and the principal portion of mortgage payments) are *not* tax deductible. Conversely, federal income tax law allows investors to claim tax deductions for several items that are not associated with a concurrent cash expense. In particular, capital expenditures are not immediately deductible for income tax purposes when paid. Rather, they are required to be expensed (i.e., depreciated) over time.

For example, if the Centre Point Office Building is purchased at a price equal to $1,056,000, this capital expenditure is *not* fully deductible in the year in which the investment is undertaken, as most investors would prefer. Rather, the nonland portion of the $1,056,000 expenditure must be written off—under current federal tax law—in equal amounts over 39 years. As we shall see in Chapter 20, the allowable annual deduction for our Centre Point property is $21,662. This deduction, referred to as depreciation, reduces the investor's taxable income by $21,662. However, it is extremely important to recognize that the investor does expend $21,662 in depreciation each year—the "check" for the purchase price was actually written when the property was purchased. Hence, the complication in income tax calculations: Allowable tax deductions in any year do not equal cash expenditures. Therefore, we cannot simply apply an assumed rate of income tax to our *BTCF* estimates to estimate annual tax liabilities.

> ### ✓ Concept Check
>
> **18.7** To calculate the expected income tax liability in a given year, why can't the analyst simply apply the investor's tax rate to the estimated *BTCF*?

So, what do we do? Because even an introductory treatment of real estate tax calculations requires considerable time and effort to work through, we simply report a projection of the first-year tax liability for our Centre Point example (see Exhibit 18-4). These calculations assume the investor faces a 30 percent tax rate on additional taxable income. The estimated tax liability in year 1 is $7,058, or 24.3 percent of *BTCF*. Interested readers are referred to Chapter 20 for detailed explanations of these calculations.

Two points are worth emphasizing. First, the estimated tax liability is a significant percentage of the before-tax cash flow. Thus, *BTCF* estimates overstate the amount of cash investors will actually net from the investment. Second, estimated tax liabilities are *not* calculated by applying the assumed tax rate to the before-tax cash flows. As we have stressed above, *cash flow is not the same as taxable income!*

Exhibit 18-4 Centre Point Office Building: After-Tax Cash Flows from Annual Operations

Net operating income (*NOI*)	$89,100
− Debt service (*DS*)	60,072
= Before-tax cash flow (*BTCF*)	$29,028
− Tax liability (*TAX*)	7,058
= After-tax cash flow (*ATCF*)	$21,970

Single-Year Investment Criteria

We now turn to a discussion of single-year return measures and ratios widely used by real estate investors and lenders to evaluate potential investments. These ratios—or *rules of thumb*—can be grouped into three categories: profitability ratios, multipliers, and financial risk ratios. These ratios work best when used to compare a "stabilized" property to other stabilized properties. Such properties have vacancy rates and rental rates that are at or near current market rates and do not require abnormal amounts of deferred maintenance or capital expenditures.

Profitability Ratios

The ultimate determination of an investment's desirability is its capacity to produce income in relation to the capital required to obtain that income. Two frequently used profitability ratios are discussed in this section: the capitalization rate and the equity dividend rate.

Capitalization Rate. The going-in capitalization rate on an acquired property—known as the overall cap rate—is defined as

$$R_o = \frac{NOI_1}{\text{Acquisition price}}$$

where NOI_1 is the estimated *NOI* over the next year (12 months).

R_o indicates the (first year) cash flow return on the total investment—that is, the return over the next 12 months on funds supplied by both equity investors and lenders. As such, it measures the *overall* income-producing ability of the property.[6] To illustrate, consider again the Centre Point Office Building, which has an acquisition price of $1,056,000 and an estimated first-year net operating income of $89,100. The going-in capitalization rate therefore is

$$R_o = \frac{\$89,100}{\$1,056,000} = 0.0844, \text{ or } 8.44\%$$

Is 8.44 percent an acceptable overall cap rate for the investor? This question can only be addressed by comparisons with cap rates on similar properties in the market. The Real Estate Research Corporation (RERC) regularly surveys the going-in cap rates currently observed in the market by a sample of institutional investors, lenders, appraisers, and consultants. Published quarterly in the *Real Estate Report,* this survey provides useful information on cap rate trends in the United States. Portions of several tables from the third quarter 2015 report are reproduced in Exhibit 18-5. All figures are for the South, one of four

Exhibit 18-5 Average Cap Rates by Property Type and Quality of Property: South Region of the United States. *(Third Quarter 2015)*

	Warehouse	Regional Mall	Neighborhood Shop. Center	Suburban Office	Apartment
First-tier properties	7.2%	7.2%	7.4%	7.4%	6.3%
Second-tier properties	7.8%	7.8%	8.0%	8.0%	6.9%
Third-tier properties	8.8%	8.9%	8.7%	8.7%	8.0%

Source: Data from Real Estate Research Corporation (www.rerc.com), third quarter 2015.

---

6. The role of the capitalization rate in commercial property appraisal is discussed in Chapter 8.

regions in the United States for which RERC reports separate results. First-tier properties are defined by RERC as new or newer quality construction in prime to good locations. Second-tier properties are defined as aging, formerly first-tier properties in good to average locations. Finally, third-tier properties are defined as older properties with functional inadequacies and/or marginal locations.

Exhibit 18-5 reveals several notable patterns. First, required going-in cap rates vary significantly by property quality. For example, cap rates for first-tier regional malls averaged 7.2 percent, whereas third-tier cap rates for malls averaged 8.9 percent. Third-tier properties typically have less predictable cash flows or are likely to produce less rent growth than first-tier and second-tier properties. Third-tier properties must therefore sell for a lower price *per dollar of current income,* which implies higher cap rates.

Exhibit 18-5 also reveals variation in cap rates by property type. Apartment cap rates are, on average, lower than other property types. Centre Point's going-in cap rate of 8.44 percent is above the 8.0 percent average cap rate for second-tier office properties located in suburban markets. If Centre Point is considered a second-tier property, it may suggest that Centre Point is underpriced relative to its current income, but additional analysis using local market data is certainly needed.

It is very important when comparing cap rates across properties to be consistent in the treatment of capital expenditures. If the estimated net operating income for the subject property does not include a deduction for estimated capital expenditures, the investor must take significant care to ensure that cap rates obtained from comparable properties do not include estimated capital costs in the *NOI,* which would lower the cash flow estimate and, therefore, the calculated capitalization rate of the comparable property.

✓ Concept Check

18.8 Why do second-tier properties sell at higher going-in cap rates than class A properties?

Equity Dividend Rate. Because many commercial property investments involve the use of mortgage funds and because the cost of mortgage debt may differ across investment opportunities, the use of the capitalization rate as a measure of profitability has potential limitations. Another profitability measure—**the equity dividend rate (*EDR*)**—is defined as

$$EDR = \frac{\text{Before-tax cash flow}}{\text{Equity investment}}$$

The equity dividend rate shows investors what percentage of their initial equity investment is expected to be returned to them in cash during the next 12 months (before income taxes). Note that the difference between the *EDR* and R_o is that the effects of mortgage financing have been subtracted from both the numerator and the denominator of the *EDR*. Thus, the cash flow in the numerator measures the amount received by the equity investor after paying all operating and capital expenses *and* after servicing the debt. This "residual" cash flow is then compared to the equity investors' cash investment. For this reason, the equity dividend rate is also referred to as the "cash-on-cash" return. The *EDR* for the Centre Point Office Building is

$$EDR = \frac{\$29,028}{\$287,760} = 0.1009, \text{ or } 10.1\%$$

The estimated *EDR* of 10.1 percent can be compared to other investments of similar risk to determine its relative magnitude. Note that the *EDR* for Centre Point exceeds R_o; thus, positive financial leverage is expected.

Multipliers

Several cash flow multipliers may be calculated by potential investors. Two examples are the net income multiplier and the (effective) gross income multiplier. The **net income multiplier (*NIM*)** is defined as

$$NIM = \frac{\text{Acquisition price}}{NOI_1}$$

Recall that the overall cap rate is equal to year 1 net operating income divided by the acquisition price. The *NIM* is, therefore, the reciprocal of the cap rate—properties with a relatively high cap rate (overall first-year return) sell for a lower multiple of *NOI*.

The effective gross income multiplier (*EGIM*) is defined as

$$EGIM = \frac{\text{Acquisition price}}{\text{Effective gross income}}$$

The effective gross income multiplier, also defined in Chapter 8, is employed more frequently than the net income multiplier; however, it must be used with great care. To compare gross income multipliers, the properties should be traded in the same market and should be similar in expense patterns, risk, location, physical attributes, time, and terms of sale.[7]

For Centre Point, the *EGIM* is

$$EGIM = \frac{\$1,056,000}{\$162,000} = 6.52$$

Income multipliers can be used to provide a quick assessment of whether a property is priced reasonably in relation to its gross or net income. For example, if the *EGIM* multipliers for similar office buildings in Centre Point's market average approximately 7.5, Centre Point's EGIM of 6.52 indicates that the seller's asking price may be low. Why? Because Centre Point's asking price is only 6.52 times current (effective gross) income. In comparison, similar properties are selling for 7.5 times EGI. Of course, other explanations for Centre Point's relatively low asking price likely exist.

Financial Risk Ratios

Financial risk ratios measure the income-producing ability of the property to meet operating and financial obligations. As we saw in Chapter 16, these ratios are helpful to lenders in assessing the risk of lending to investors on particular projects. Commercial lenders typically require borrowers to include estimates of these ratios in the loan application package submitted to lenders. Lenders are concerned whether the property will generate sufficient operating income to service the debt and, eventually, ensure the loan principal will be repaid. Several ratios widely used for this purpose are discussed below. Investors need to be able to calculate these ratios and to understand how their use by lenders may reduce the size of the loan they are able to obtain to acquire the property.

Operating Expense Ratio

This ratio expresses expected operating expenses over the next year as a percentage of effective gross income (*EGI*); thus the **operating expense ratio (*OER*)** is

$$OER = \frac{\text{Operating expenses}}{\text{Effective gross income}}$$

---

7. The gross income multiplier (*GIM*) is calculated using potential, instead of effective, gross income.

The *OER* in year 1 for Centre Point is calculated as

$$OER = \frac{\$64,800}{\$162,000} = 0.40, \text{ or } 40\%$$

The greater the *OER*, the larger the portion of effective rental income consumed by operating expenses. Knowledgeable market participants are aware of typical operating expense ratios; thus, this ratio may provide information to investors and lenders. For example, if the *OER* of a property is higher than average, it may signal that expenses are out of control or, perhaps, that rents are too low. This may indicate a "turnaround" opportunity for a buyer. However, investors should not simply seek properties with low *OER*s because the seller may be underreporting expenses in an effort to increase pro forma *NOI* and, therefore, the sale price. As discussed earlier, ratios are most useful as preliminary screening devices when evaluating stabilized properties.

Loan-to-Value Ratio

As previously discussed, this ratio measures the percentage of the acquisition price (or current market value) encumbered by mortgage debt. To protect their invested capital in the event that property values decline, lenders who provide mortgage financing for the acquisition of existing stabilized commercial properties generally require that the senior mortgage not exceed 65 to 80 percent of the acquisition price. For our Centre Point example, the initial *LTV* is

$$LTV = \frac{\$792,000}{\$1,056,000} = 0.75\%, \text{ or } 75\%$$

Note that a second mortgage would increase the borrower's overall *LTV*.

Debt Coverage Ratio

The debt coverage ratio (*DCR*) indicates the extent to which net operating income (*NOI*) can decline before it is insufficient to cover the debt service (*DS*). For Centre Point,

$$DCR = \frac{NOI}{DS} = \frac{\$89,100}{\$60,072} = 1.48$$

The *DCR* provides an indication of safety from potential borrower default in the event rental revenues fall and the mortgage payment is in jeopardy. Typically, lenders require this ratio to be *at least* 1.2 to 1.3. Thus, Centre Point's 1.48 coverage ratio would seem to provide the lender (and investor) with a satisfactory safety margin. Required *DCR*s, however, vary over time and location and across property types. For example, required *DCR*s for hotel properties often exceed 1.6.

Debt Yield Ratio

As discussed in Chapter 16, if the mortgage loan is going to be packaged with similar loans and then resold to investors as part of a commercial mortgage-backed security, the originating lender may rely more heavily on the debt yield ratio than the debt coverage ratio to determine the maximum amount he is willing to lend to the borrower. The debt yield ratio (*DYR*) is defined as the property's projected first-year *NOI* divided by the amount of the first mortgage loan. For our Centre Point example, the *DYR* is

$$DYR = \frac{\$89,100}{\$792,000} = 0.1125, \text{ or } 11.25\%$$

Exhibit 18-6   Common Ratios Used in Real Estate Investment Analysis

Ratio	Form	Use	Comment
Capitalization rate	$\dfrac{NOI}{\text{Acquisition price}}$	To indicate one-year return on total investment (including both lender and investor provided capital)	Also called overall or going-in cap rate; measures the initial overall income-producing ability of the property
Equity dividend rate	$\dfrac{BTCF}{\text{Equity investment}}$	To indicate the investor's one-period rate of return on invested equity	Ignores tax consequences, future year cash flows, and changes in property values
Net income multiplier	$\dfrac{\text{Acquisition price}}{NOI}$	To indicate relationship between total price and first-year NOI—measures price per current dollar of NOI	A quick method of comparing the price per dollar of net operating income of one property to others sold in the market
Effective gross income multiplier	$\dfrac{\text{Acquisition price}}{EGI}$	To indicate the relationship between total price and EGI—measures price per current dollar of EGI	A quick method of comparing the price per dollar of effective gross income of one property to others sold in the market
Operating expense ratio	$\dfrac{OE}{EGI}$	To indicate the portion of rental income consumed by operating expenses	Typical range is 25–50 percent of EGI, but varies significantly by property type
Loan-to-value ratio	$\dfrac{\text{Mortgage amount}}{\text{Property value}}$	To measure the degree of financial leverage	Maximum allowable on commercial property usually 65–80 percent at acquisition
Debt coverage ratio	$\dfrac{NOI}{\text{Debt Service}}$	To see how much NOI can decline before it will not cover debt service	Lenders usually seek a minimum DCR of 1.20–1.30, but may vary their requirements based on competition
Debt yield ratio	$\dfrac{NOI}{\text{Loan Amount}}$	To indicate the expected overall return on the loan proceeds	Lenders who rely on this ratio usually require a minimum DYR of 9–10 percent

This indicates the mortgage lender would earn an 11.25 percent cash-on-cash return on its invested capital (i.e., the loan amount) if it had to foreclose on the Centre Point property immediately after originating the loan. Unlike the debt coverage ratio, the debt yield ratio is not affected by the interest rate or amortization period of the loan; the *DYR* is simply a measure of how large the *NOI* is relative to the loan amount. Commercial banks who intend to hold the loans they originate in their portfolios as long-term investments, and most other commercial lenders, have not yet adopted the *DYR* as their primary metric for sizing acquisition loans. Common ratios used in the analysis of commercial real estate investments are summarized in Exhibit 18-6.

EXAMPLE 18-1

You are considering the purchase of a small existing office building for $1,975,000 today. Your expectations for this stabilized property include these: first-year gross potential income of $340,000; vacancy and collection losses equal to 15 percent of gross potential income; operating expenses equal to 40 percent of effective gross income; and capital expenditures equal to 5 percent of *EGI*. You have arranged a $1,481,250 first mortgage loan (75 percent initial *LTV*) with an annual interest rate of 7 percent. The loan will be amortized over 25 years with a monthly payment of $10,469.17. Total upfront financing cost will equal 2 percent of the loan amount, or $29,625. Therefore, the required equity investment is $523,375 [$1,975,000 – ($1,481,250 – $29,625)].

What is estimated net operating income (*NOI*) and before-tax cash flow (*BTCF*) for the *first* year of operations? Assume an above line treatment of capital expenditures.

Item	Amount
Potential gross income (*PGI*)	$340,000
− Vacancy & collection loss (*VC*)	51,000 (15% of PGI)
= Effective gross income (*EGI*)	289,000
− Operating expenses (*OE*)	115,600 (40% of EGI)
− Capital expenditures (*CAPX*)	14,450 (5% of EGI)
= Net operating income (*NOI*)	158,950
− Debt service (DS)	125,630 ($10,469.17 × 12)
= Before-tax cash flow (*BTCF*)	$ 33,320

Calculate the following for comparison to other similar properties: Going-in capitalization rate

$$R_o = \frac{\text{Net operating income}}{\text{Acquisition price}} = \frac{\$158,950}{\$1,975,000} = 0.080, \text{ or } 8.0\%$$

Equity dividend rate

$$EDR = \frac{\text{Before-tax cash flow}}{\text{Equity investment}} = \frac{\$33,320}{\$523,375} = 0.063, \text{ or } 6.3\%$$

Effective gross income multiplier

$$EGIM = \frac{\text{Acquisition price}}{\text{Effective gross income}} = \frac{\$1,975,000}{\$289,000} = 6.83$$

Operating expense ratio

$$OER = \frac{\text{Operating expenses}}{\text{Effective gross income}} = \frac{\$115,600}{\$289,000} = 0.40, \text{ or } 40\%$$

Debt coverage ratio

$$DCR = \frac{\text{Net operating income}}{\text{Debt servive}} = \frac{\$158,950}{\$125,630} = 1.27$$

Debt yield ratio

$$DYR = \frac{\text{Net operating income}}{\text{Loan amount}} = \frac{\$158,950}{\$1,481,250} = 0.107 \text{ or } 10.7\%$$

Limitations of Ratio Analysis

The use of ratios to make investment decisions is favored by some investors in some acquisitions over the use of discounted cash flow valuation methods (discussed in detail in Chapter 19). There are two basic arguments for using the single-year ratios and multipliers discussed in this chapter instead of multiyear discounted cash flow (DCF) valuation methods. First, ratios are easier to calculate and more widely understood than *NPV* and *IRR* (internal rate of return). Second, because DCF analysis requires estimation of net operating incomes, before-tax cash flows, and the before-tax cash flow from a subsequent (hypothetical) sale, some believe the numbers can be easily manipulated to achieve any result the analyst desires (again, the "garbage in, garbage out" problem).

In contrast, the basic shortcoming of multipliers and single period rate of return measures is that they do *not* consider future cash flows. For example, the estimated effective gross income multiplier (*EGIM*) of 6.52 for Centre Point may be low relative to similar properties. But does this necessarily imply the $1,056,000 asking price is low and that the property should be purchased? Perhaps, but the investor should consider alternative explanations for the apparently low multiplier. For example, it is possible that the current owner has not maintained the property well. This deferred maintenance would have to be taken care of shortly after purchase if the property is going to be competitive in the local office rental market. Given that potential investors anticipate substantial capital expenditures subsequent to the purchase, they are willing to pay less today for each dollar of current *income*. This implies a lower effective gross income multiplier as well as a higher going-in cap rate.

Another possible explanation for a relatively low *EGIM* (high cap rate) is that the property may be located in an office market that is declining relative to most office markets in the area. As a result, potential investors are forecasting less growth in future rental rates than in other markets. Given lower expected growth rates in rents, investors again are going to bid less today for each dollar of current *income*—thereby lowering the *EGIM*. If investors expect less growth in rental income and, therefore, appreciation in a particular market, they must be compensated in the form of a higher income return. However, differences in expected rental growth rates are ignored if investment decisions are based solely on comparisons of *EGIMs* or capitalization rates.

Although ratios have their place in real estate investment analysis, there are problems associated with their use. Ratios are generally single-year, before-tax measures and are void of formal decision rules. Their strength comes in isolating specific aspects of a property or investment and facilitating *comparisons* with similar investment opportunities. For example, an operating expense ratio of 60 percent says nothing about the acceptability of the investment, but when compared with similar properties having 40 percent operating ratios, it illuminates an undesirable feature or perhaps an opportunity associated with the investment.

In conclusion, both ratio analysis and discounted cash flow analysis have their place in real estate investment decisions. Ratios may provide quick signals to alert the investor to deviations between the subject property and "typical" properties. Ratios tend to be more informative for acquisitions of stabilized properties in stabilized markets. On the other hand, net present value and the internal rate of return provide a comprehensive evaluation of the property. These (DCF) methods, however, require considerable data, many assumptions, and much judgment, as we will see in Chapter 19.

✓ Concept Check

18.9   What is the major shortcoming of most ratios when they are used to make investment decisions?

Summary

Investment is one of the most interesting and important areas of study in the field of real estate. Whether the student is considering a career in a firm or institution that invests in real estate, or is seeking knowledge for personal investment reasons, numerous questions must be answered to make better-informed investment decisions.

This chapter introduces the framework for making single-property real estate investment decisions. The first step in the analysis of an existing income-producing property is the estimation of net operating income (*NOI*) in the first year of operations after acquisition. *NOI* is the "dividend" expected to be produced by the property over the next 12 months and is therefore the fundamental determinant of a property's value and investment desirability. However, most investors make some use of debt financing (i.e., "financial leverage") when acquiring real estate. It is therefore important to understand how the use of mortgage debt affects the amount of equity capital required at acquisition, the cash flows from annual rental operations, the cash flow from the eventual sale of the property, and the risk of the investment as well. The cash flows produced by real estate investments are also subject to taxation at the state and federal levels. This income taxation can significantly reduce the amount of spendable income investors actually net from their real estate investments.

After the standard industry approach to estimating cash flows from annual property operations is presented and discussed, the chapter turns its attention to a set of widely used single-year investment criteria. These returns, ratios, and multipliers are relatively easy to calculate and understand. In addition, some real estate professionals argue that these single-year investment criteria avoid many of the potential problems and errors associated with multi-year cash flow estimates.

Single-year decision-making metrics, however, are not without their limitations and detractors. First, the use of ratios works best for stabilized properties in stabilized markets. In addition, an often-cited advantage—that single-year metrics avoid the potential errors associated with multiyear projections—is also a disadvantage. Most real estate investments are expected to be held for multiple years. Therefore, to ignore cash flows beyond the first year of operations is a potentially serious limitation in their use and interpretation. To avoid these shortcomings, many investors also perform multiyear analyses of a property's income-producing ability. These multiyear discounted cash flow (DCF) valuation and decision-making methods are discussed in Chapter 19.

Key Terms

After-tax cash flow (*ATCF*) 490	Net income multiplier (*NIM*) 494	Pro rata share 490
Equity dividend rate (*EDR*) 493	Operating expense ratio (*OER*) 494	

Test Problems

Answer the following multiple-choice questions:

1. Income multipliers:
   a. Are useful as a preliminary analysis tool to weed out obviously unacceptable investment opportunities.
   b. Are adequate as the sole indication of a property's investment worth.
   c. Relate the property's price or value to after-tax cash flow.
   d. None of the above.

2. The overall capitalization rate calculated on a potential acquisition:
   a. Is the reciprocal of the net income multiplier.
   b. Explicitly incorporates the effects of expected future rent growth.
   c. Considers the risk associated with an investment opportunity.
   d. All of the above are true.

3. The operating expense ratio:
   a. Highlights the relationship between net operating income and operating expenses.
   b. Shows the percentage of potential gross income consumed by operating expenses.
   c. Expresses operating expenses as a percent of effective gross income.
   d. Should reflect the cost of mortgage financing.

4. The equity dividend rate:
   a. Incorporates income tax considerations.
   b. Expresses before-tax cash flow as a percent of the required equity capital investment.
   c. Expresses before-tax cash flow as a percent of the property's acquisition price.
   d. Expresses net operating income as a percent of the required equity capital investment.

5. Ratio analysis:
   a. Includes estimating the net present value of the investment opportunity.
   b. Is generally adequate to fully assess an investment's expected return.
   c. Requires cash flow estimates for the investment's entire expected holding period.
   d. Serves as an initial evaluation of the adequacy of an investment's expected cash flows.

6. Assume a retail shopping center can be purchased for $5.5 million. The center's first year *NOI* is expected to be $489,500. A $4,000,000 loan has been requested. The loan carries a 9.25 percent fixed contract rate, amortized monthly over 25 years with a 7-year term. What will be the property's (annual) debt coverage ratio in the first year of operations?
   a. 1.40.
   b. 1.19.
   c. 0.84.
   d. 0.08.

7. Which of the following is not an operating expense associated with income-producing (commercial) property?
   a. Debt service.
   b. Property taxes.
   c. Fire and casualty insurance.
   d. Janitorial services.

Use the following information to answer questions 8 and 9. You are considering purchasing an office building for $2,500,000. You expect the potential gross income (*PGI*) in the first year to be $450,000; vacancy and collection losses to be 9 percent of *PGI*; and operating expenses and capital expenditures to be 38 percent and 4 percent, respectively, of effective gross income (*EGI*).

8. What is the implied first-year overall capitalization rate?
   a. 9.5 percent.
   b. 10.0 percent.
   c. 10.5 percent.
   d. 11.0 percent.

9. What is the effective gross income multiplier?
   a. 5.56.
   b. 6.11.
   c. 16.38.
   d. 18.00.

10. Given the following information, what is the required equity down payment?
    - Acquisition price: $800,000
    - Loan-to-value ratio: 75%
    - Total upfront financing costs: 3%
    a. $118,000.
    b. $200,000.
    c. $218,000.
    d. $250,000.

Study Questions

Use the following information to answer questions 1–3.

You are considering the purchase of an office building for $1.5 million today. Your expectations include the following: first-year potential gross income of $340,000; vacancy and collection losses equal to 15 percent of potential gross income; operating expenses equal to 40 percent of effective gross income; and capital expenditures equal 5 percent of *EGI*.

1. What is estimated effective gross income (*EGI*) for the *first* year of operations?
2. What is estimated net operating income (*NOI*) for the *first* year of operations?
3. What is the estimated going-in cap rate (R_o) for the *first* year of operations?
4. An investment opportunity having a market price of $1,000,000 is available. You could obtain a $750,000, 25-year mortgage loan requiring equal monthly payments with interest at 7.0 percent. The following operating results are expected during the first year:

Effective gross income	$200,000
Less operating expenses and *CAPX*	$100,000
Net operating income	$100,000

For the first year only, determine the:
   a. Gross income multiplier.
   b. Operating expense ratio.
   c. Monthly and annual mortgage payment.
   d. Debt coverage ratio.
   e. Debt yield ratio.
   f. Overall capitalization rate.
   g. Equity dividend rate.

5. You are considering the purchase of a quadruplex apartment building. Effective gross income during the first year of operations is expected to be $33,600 ($700 per month per unit). First-year operating expenses are expected to be $13,440 (at 40 percent of *EGI*). Ignore capital expenditures. The purchase price of the quadruplex is $200,000. The acquisition will be financed with $60,000 in equity and a $140,000 standard fixed-rate mortgage. The interest rate on the debt financing is 8 percent and the loan term is 30 years. Assume, for simplicity, that payments will be made *annually* and that there are no upfront financing costs.

   a. What is the overall capitalization rate?
   b. What is the effective gross income multiplier?
   c. What is the equity dividend rate (the before-tax return on equity)?
   d. What is the debt coverage ratio?
   e. Assume the lender requires a minimum debt coverage ratio of 1.2. What is the largest loan that you could obtain if you decide that you want to borrow more than $140,000?

6. Why do Class B properties generally sell at higher going-in cap rates than Class A properties?

7. Why might a commercial real estate investor borrow to help finance an investment even if she could afford to pay 100 percent cash?

8. You are considering purchasing an office building for $2,500,000. You expect the potential gross income (*PGI*) in the first year of operations to be $450,000; vacancy and collection losses to be 9 percent of PGI; and operating expenses and capital expenditures to be 42 percent of effective gross income (*EGI*). What is the estimated *net operating income*? What is the implied first-year overall capitalization rate? What is the effective gross income multiplier?

9. What distinguishes an operating expense from a capital expenditure?

10. Explain why income property cash flow is not the same as taxable income.

11. What is the basic shortcoming of most ratios and rules of thumb used in commercial real estate investment decision making?

12. Using the following information, compute net operating income (*NOI*) for the first year of operations. Use an "above-line" treatment of capital expenditures.
    - Number of apartments: 10
    - Rent per month per apartment: $900.00
    - Expected vacancy and collection loss: 10 percent
    - Annual maintenance: $18,000
    - Property taxes: $9,000
    - Property insurance: $7,000
    - Management: $8,000
    - Capital expenditures: $5,000
    - Other operating expenses: $3,000
    - Annual mortgage debt payments: $35,000

EXPLORE THE WEB

The National Council of Real Estate Investment Fiduciaries (NCREIF) is an association of real estate investment professionals who share a common interest in their industry. They are investment managers, pension plan sponsors, academicians, consultants, appraisers, CPAs, and other service providers who have a significant involvement in institutional real estate investments. They come together to address vital industry issues and to promote research. Produced quarterly, the NCREIF Property Index (NPI) shows real estate performance returns using data submitted to NCREIF by its data contributing members. The NPI is used as an industry benchmark to compare an investor's returns against the industry average and against returns on stocks and bonds.

Go to the NCREIF home page (www.ncreif.org). Under *Data & Products,* select "NCREIF Property Index Returns," then go to the drop down menu and select "Apartment." Using your calculator or, preferably, a spreadsheet, calculate the average annual return on the U.S. apartment investments tracked by NCREIF since 2000. How does this return compare to the performance of other property types?

Solutions to Concept Checks

1. Effective gross income (*EGI*) is equal to potential gross income (*PGI*), minus vacancy and collection losses, plus miscellaneous income. Net operating income (*NOI*) is equal to *EGI* minus operating expenses (*OE*s) and capital expenditures (*CAPX*), although in a below-line treatment of *CAPX*, they would be subtracted from *NOI*.

2. The traditional treatment of nonrecurring capital expenditures in appraisal is to treat them above line with an estimated reserve for replacement. The modern treatment of nonrecurring capital expenditures in investment analysis is below (the *NOI*) line. Recall that before the advent of computers and spreadsheets, direct capitalization was the only feasible income approach to valuation. When capitalizing a single-year estimate of stabilized *NOI* into a value estimate, it is necessary for the analyst to deduct from rental income the expected annualized cost of nonrecurring capital expenditures. However, with the advent of spreadsheet programs and prepackaged software, the construction and estimation of multiperiod discounted cash flow models is straight forward. Thus, instead of estimating an annual reserve, analysts may choose to make explicit forecasts of future capital expenditures.

3. Borrowing—that is, the use of "other people's money"—is also referred to as the use of financial leverage. If the overall return on the property exceeds the cost of debt, the use of leverage can significantly increase the expected rate of return investors earn on their invested equity. This expected magnification of return often induces investors to partially debt-finance even if they have the accumulated wealth to pay all cash for the property.

4. Net loan proceeds to the borrower equal the face amount of the loan minus all costs associated with obtaining the mortgage that are paid to the lender or to a third party (such as the title insurer) at closing. It can be thought of as the actual cash the borrower nets from the loan at closing. Recall, however, that monthly mortgage payments are based on the face value of the loan, not the net loan proceeds.

5. The investor does not get to keep the net operating income of the property if the acquisition has been partially debt financed. Rather, the investor/borrower must pay the promised mortgage payment out of the property's *NOI*. Thus, *BTCF* better reflects the amount of cash the investor will net from the investment after servicing the debt, but before income taxes.

6. The majority of commercial properties in the United States are not purchased by individuals, but by multiple investors in the form of partnerships, limited liability companies, and other ownership entities. Thus, the property-level cash inflows and outflows must be allocated to the various investors in order to calculate a particular investor's cash distributions and returns.

7. The analyst cannot simply apply a tax rate to the estimated before-tax cash flows from rental operations to calculate income tax liability in a given year because some cash expenditures that reduce *BTCF*, such as capital expenditures and the principal portion of mortgage payments, are not deductible in the calculation of taxable income from property operations. On the other hand, tax law allows investors to take deductions for several items that are not associated with actual cash expenses. In short, taxable income from operations can vary significantly from *BTCF*, so the analyst cannot simply multiply the estimated *BTCF* by the investor's tax rate.

8. Relative to class A properties, class B properties are more risky and/or are expected to produce smaller rental rate increases over time. Both effects reduce the amount an informed investor is willing to pay today per dollar of current net operating income. When values/prices fall relative to current net operating income, cap rates increase.

9. A major shortcoming of using ratios to make investment decisions is that they generally ignore cash flows beyond the first year of rental operations. Thus, unlike *NPV* and *IRR*, simple ratios are not able to capture the magnitude and timing of all expected future cash inflows and outflows.

Additional Readings

Brueggeman, William B., and Jeffrey D. Fisher. *Real Estate Finance and Investments,* 15th ed. New York: McGraw-Hill, 2015.

Collier, N. S., C. A. Collier, and D. A. Halperin. *Construction Funding: The Process of Real Estate Development, Appraisal, and Finance,* 4th ed. Hoboken, NJ: John Wiley & Sons, Inc., 2008.

Eldred, Gary W. *Investing in Real Estate,* 7th ed. Hoboken, NJ: John Wiley and Sons, Inc., 2012.

Friedman, Jack P., and J. C. Harris. *Keys to Investing in Real Estate,* 4th ed. Hauppauge, NY: Barron's Educational Series, 2005.

Gallinelli, Frank. *Mastering Real Estate Investment: Examples, Metrics and Case Studies.* Southport, CT: RealData, Inc., 2008.

Geltner, David M., Norman G. Miller, Jim Clayton, and Piet Eichholtz. *Commercial Real Estate Analysis and Investments,* 3rd ed. Mason, Ohio, Oncourse Learning, Inc., 2014.

Linneman, P. *Real Estate Finance & Investments: Risk and Opportunities,* 3rd ed. Philadelphia, PA: Linneman Associates, 2013.

Sirota, D. *Essentials of Real Estate Investment,* 10th ed. Chicago, IL: Dearborn Financial Publishing, 2012.

Wiedemer, John P., Joseph E. Goeters, and J. Edward Graham. *Real Estate Investment,* 7th ed. Mason, OH: South-Western Cengage Learning, 2010.

Chapter 19

Investment Decisions: NPV *and* IRR

LEARNING OBJECTIVES

After reading this chapter you will be able to:

1   List the primary difference between market value and investment value.

2   List the three steps required in a discounted cash flow analysis of a potential commercial real estate investment.

3   Explain the difference between unlevered and levered cash flows.

4   Calculate the net present value and internal rate of return on a proposed investment, given assumptions about cash flows and required rates of return.

5   Calculate what effect financial leverage has on expected returns and risk, given assumptions about current and future cash flows.

6   Explain how income taxes affect discount rates, net present values, and internal rates of return.

OUTLINE

Introduction

A major theme of this book is that most real estate decisions are made with an investment motive and that the magnitude of expected future cash flows—and the property values they create—is at the center of investment decision making. In Chapter 18, we introduced the standard approach to estimating an existing property's net operating income (*NOI*) and the methods and metrics used to make valuation and investment decisions. The focus in Chapter 18 is on a set of widely used single-year return measures, ratios, and income multipliers, such as the capitalization rate (*NOI* ÷ acquisition price) and the gross income multiplier (acquisition price ÷ gross income). These investment criteria are relatively easy to calculate and understand—a decided advantage in the eyes of many industry professionals.

A limitation of these single-year return measures and ratios, however, is that they do not incorporate in any direct fashion the income-producing ability of the property beyond the first year of rental operations. Focusing only on cash flow magnitudes and ratios in the first year after acquisition may lead to suboptimal investment decisions. For example, a property being considered for purchase by an investor may have a higher first-year (i.e., "going-in") capitalization rate than several comparable investment alternatives. However, what if the relatively low price at which the property can be acquired—and, therefore, the high going-in cap rate—reflects the pressing need for significant capital expenditures (e.g., a roof replacement and a parking lot resurfacing) that have been deferred by the current owner? If the investor anticipates spending significantly more on capital improvements after acquisition than would be required on other properties, the seller must compensate the investor by lowering the price and, thereby, raising the capitalization rate. The higher cap rate, however, does not signal the property is a superior investment; rather, the higher cap rate may be required to compensate the investor, in whole or in part, for required capital expenditures (and potentially more risk) in the years subsequent to the acquisition.

To overcome the potential shortcomings of single-year decision-making metrics, many investors also perform multiyear analyses of the income-producing ability of potential acquisitions. These multiyear discounted cash flow (DCF) valuation and decision-making methods differ from single-year valuation metrics in several important ways. First, the investor must estimate how long she will hold the property. Second, the investor must make explicit forecasts of the property's net operating income for each year of the expected holding period, not just a single year. This forecast must include the net cash flow produced by the sale of the property at the end of the expected holding period. Third, the investor must select the appropriate required rate of return at which to discount all future cash flows.[1] The requirements of DCF analysis place a greater analytical burden on the investor because future cash flow projections not supported by market evidence can result in flawed valuations and decisions.

In the following section, we discuss the important difference between investment valuation and market valuation. We then proceed to a discussion of investment valuation and decision making using two DCF decision models: net present value and the internal rate of return.

Investment Valuation versus Market Valuation

Investment value was defined in Chapter 7 as the maximum the buyer would be willing to pay and the minimum the seller would be willing to accept. How is investment value calculated? The investment calculation begins where the market value calculation ends. The calculation of market value will have already taken into account the general, or average, investment conditions in the market. To the extent that a particular investor's situation is different, the price the investor is willing to pay will differ from market value. For example, investors may vary with respect to their expectations of future rental rates and vacancies. The amount and cost of both equity and debt financing also may vary somewhat across investors and these differences in the cost of capital may affect how much a particular investor is willing to pay for a property. Thus, explicit assumptions about how the acquisition is to be financed should generally be included in an investment valuation. Finally, expected income tax consequences are usually significant; thus, investors may choose to incorporate future income tax consequences into their analysis of a proposed investment.

> ✓ **Concept Check**
>
> **19.1**   How does investment value differ from market value?

---

1. Discounting is discussed in detail in Chapter 14.

Investment Valuation Using Discounted Cash Flow Models

Similar to the discounted cash flow (DCF) method used for market valuation in Chapter 8, the calculation of net present value and the internal rate of return for an existing property have three basic components: estimating net cash flows from annual operation; estimating cash proceeds from the eventual sale of the property; and converting these uncertain cash flow projections into present value.

Centre Point Office Building Example

To demonstrate how commercial real estate investors estimate the current and future cash flows from an existing commercial property, we return once again to our example investment opportunity: the Centre Point Office Building. The expanded set of assumptions for this potential investment is displayed in Exhibit 19-1.

As discussed in Chapters 8 and 18, these assumptions produce an estimated *NOI* of $89,100 in year 1. Although the expected cash flow in the first year of operation is a significant determinant of the property's investment value, pro forma cash flow projections over the expected investment horizon are required (10 years is the industry standard). This is because real property assets have long economic lives (50–100 years) and because investors tend to hold properties for long periods in order to recover the significant transaction costs associated with buying and selling commercial real estate. However, even if a particular investor expects to hold a property for only, say, three years, the market/resale value of the property after three years is a function of the expected ability of the property to generate cash flows *after* year 3. Therefore, an expected three-year holding period does not relieve the investor of the burden of forecasting the income-producing ability of the property in year 4 and beyond.

Another advantage of longer projection periods is that it forces the investor to consider all of the economic, social, political, and legal changes that could affect the long-term, income-producing ability of the property. Such an exercise does not guarantee accurate projections, but it does reduce the likelihood that key issues and variables will be overlooked.

> ✓ **Concept Check**
>
> **19.2** Ten years is the most commonly assumed holding period in commercial real estate appraisal and investment analysis. Any ideas why?

Exhibit 19-1 Assumptions for Centre Point Office Building

- Total acquisition price: $1,056,000.
- Property consists of eight office suites, three on the first floor and five on the second.
- Contract rents: two suites at $1,800 per month, one at $3,600 per month, and five at $1,560 per month.
- Annual market rent increases: 3 percent per year.
- Vacancy and collection losses: 10 percent per year.
- Operating expenses: 40 percent of effective gross income each year.
- Capital expenditures: 5 percent of effective gross income each year.
- Expected holding period: five years.
- Expected selling price in year 5: year 6 *NOI* capitalized at 8.75 percent.
- Selling expenses in year 5: 4 percent of the sale price.
- First mortgage loan: $792,000 (75 percent *LTV*).
- Annual mortgage interest rate: 6.5 percent.
- Loan term and amortization period: 30 years.
- Total upfront financing costs: 3 percent of loan amount.

Exhibit 19-2 Centre Point Office Building: Five-Year Operating Pro Forma

	1	2	3	4	5	6
Potential gross income (*PGI*)	$180,000	$185,400	$190,962	$196,691	$202,592	$208,669
− Vacancy and collection loss (*VC*)	18,000	18,540	19,096	19,669	20,259	20,867
= Effective gross income (*EGI*)	162,000	166,860	171,866	177,022	182,332	187,802
− Operating expenses (*OE*)	64,800	66,744	68,746	70,809	72,933	75,121
− Capital expenditures (*CAPX*)	8,100	8,343	8,593	8,851	9,117	9,390
= Net operating income (*NOI*)	$89,100	$ 91,773	$ 94,526*	$ 97,362	$100,283*	$103,291

*Subtraction discrepancy due to rounding.

Despite the prevalence of 10-year investment horizons, we assume for simplicity that the Centre Point Office Building will be sold five years after its acquisition. Exhibit 19-2 contains the projected operating cash flows for each year of the expected five-year holding period. Based on the assumptions in Exhibit 19-1, *NOI* is expected to increase from $89,100 in year 1 to $100,283 in year 5. Note that *PGI* is expected to grow at 3 percent per year, the assumed rate of growth in market rents. If the property to be purchased is subject to one or more leases with fixed rental rates for a period of time, these fixed contract rents would have to be incorporated into the projection of *PGI*.

As discussed in Chapter 8, there are numerous methods available for estimating the sale price, or terminal value, at the end of the expected holding period. However, direct capitalization is the most common. If a going-out (terminal) cap rate, R_t, of 8.75 percent (0.0875) is deemed appropriate for estimating the sale price of Centre Point at the end of year 5, then

$$V_5 = \frac{NOI_6}{R_t} = \frac{\$103,291}{0.0875} = \$1,180,469$$

Total selling expenses in our example are projected to be 4 percent of the expected sale price, or $47,219. When deducted from the estimated sale price, this leaves expected net sale proceeds (*NSP*) of $1,133,250 (see Exhibit 19-3).

www.mrofficespace.com

Mr. Office Space. Search for office space for free in 10 major commercial real estate markets.

Levered versus Unlevered Cash Flows

To this point, we have estimated annual operating cash flows net of vacancy and collection losses, operating expenses, and capital expenditures. But are the pro forma *NOI*s, if realized, the actual amounts the owner of Centre Point will have available each year to spend, save, or invest elsewhere? The answer is no. Why? Because in many cases, property owners use a combination of equity and mortgage debt to finance an acquisition such as Centre Point. Therefore, the investor's cash flows from rental operations will be reduced by any payments required to stay current on (i.e., "service") the mortgage. The use of mortgage debt to help finance an investment is commonly referred to as **leverage**. Thus, the expected annual stream of *NOI*s and the expected *NSP* are **unlevered cash flows** because they represent the income-producing ability of the property *before*

Exhibit 19-3 Centre Point Office Building: Reversion Cash Flow

Sale price (*SP*)	$1,180,469
− Selling expenses (*SE*)	47,219
= Net sale proceeds (*NSP*)	$1,133,250

subtracting the portion of the annual cash flows that must be paid to the lender to service or retire the debt. **Levered cash flows** measure the property's income *after* subtracting any payments due the lender.[2]

✓ **Concept Check**

19.3   Are levered cash flows from annual operations greater in magnitude than unlevered cash flows, all else equal?

Valuation of the cash flows to the equity investor is accomplished by discounting the expected **before-tax cash flows** (*BTCF*s), rather than the *NOI*s. The *BTCF* is calculated by subtracting the estimated annual mortgage payment from the *NOI*. Note that the equity investor(s) has a residual claim on the property's cash flow stream. The lender has the first claim on the cash flows generated by the property because it has been pledged as collateral for the mortgage loan.[3]

✓ **Concept Check**

19.4   Why is the owner's claim on the property's cash flows referred to as a *residual claim*?

In the Centre Point example, the $1,056,000 total acquisition price is to be financed with a 30-year, 6.5 percent mortgage loan. The face amount of the mortgage will equal 75 percent of the total acquisition price, or $792,000. Total upfront financing costs will equal 3 percent of the loan amount, or $23,760. Thus, the required equity down payment is $287,760 [$1,056,000 − ($792,000 − $23,760)]. The monthly payment on the mortgage loan is $5,005.98, or $60,072 annually.[4] Estimates of the *BTCF*s for the expected five-year investment holding period are displayed in Exhibit 19-4. The *BTCF* is $29,028 in year 1 and is expected to increase to $40,211 in year 5.

As discussed above, the *BTCF*s are considered levered cash flows because they represent cash flows to the equity investor *after* the effects of financial leverage (i.e., debt service) have been subtracted.

Effect of Leverage on Cash Flow from Sale

The before-tax equity reversion (*BTER*) is defined as the net selling price minus the remaining mortgage balance (*RMB*) at the time of sale. The loan balance in year 5 on the Centre

www.irei.com

Institutional real estate investment news. Sign up for *IREI Monthly*, a free electronic newsletter you can receive by e-mail.

Exhibit 19-4   Centre Point Office Building: Estimated Before-Tax Cash Flows

	1	2	3	4	5
Net operating income (*NOI*)	$89,100	$91,773	$94,526	$97,362	$100,283
− Debt service (*DS*)	60,072	60,072	60,072	60,072	60,072
= Before-tax cash flow (*BTCF*)	$29,028	$31,701	$34,454	$37,290	$ 40,211

---

2. In addition to ignoring the effects of mortgage debt, unlevered cash flows do not capture the effects of state and federal income taxes on investor cash flows.

3. The lender's legal interest in the property is a security interest rather than an ownership interest. See Chapter 9 for more details.

4. The calculation of mortgage payments is explained in Chapter 15. In this example, the calculator keystrokes are $N = 360$; $I = 6.5/12$; $PV = -792,000$; $PMT = ?$; and $FV = 0$.

The widespread adoption and use of spreadsheet programs such as Microsoft's Excel have greatly facilitated the quantitative analysis of real estate development and acquisition decisions. However, creating a spreadsheet capable of

Computer-Aided Discounted Cash Flow Analysis

analyzing, say, a large office property with 50 tenants and leases is a task generally too time consuming even for the most accomplished spreadsheet users. Fortunately, there are numerous ready-to-use software programs available to commercial real estate investors that are capable of handling even the most sophisticated analytical requirements

encountered in today's commercial leases and transactions. ARGUS Enterprise (www.argussoftware.com) is one widely used valuation tool. Competitors to ARGUS Enterprise include RealData (www.realdata.com), Real Cash-Flow (www.realcashflow.com), and planEASe (www.planease.com).

Exhibit 19-5   Centre Point Office Building: Before-Tax Equity Reversion

Sale price (*SP*)	$1,180,469
− Selling expenses (*SE*)	47,219
= Net sale proceeds (*NSP*)	1,133,250
− Remaining mortgage balance (*RMB*)	741,399
= Before-tax equity reversion (*BTER*)	391,851

Point mortgage will be $741,399.[5] Thus, the estimated *BTER* in year 5 is $391,851. A summary of this calculation is provided in Exhibit 19-5.

Discounted cash flow analysis has become the main financial analysis tool used to evaluate the investment desirability of commercial real estate. Although much of the effort in DCF analysis goes toward the estimation of future cash flows, net present value and the internal rate of return on equity are the bottom-line decision tools of investors. In the next two sections, we demonstrate the use of these two investment criteria.

Net Present Value

Real estate decision making fundamentally involves comparing the costs of various decisions, including the decision to purchase a property, to the benefits. The net present value (*NPV*) of an investment decision was defined in Chapter 14 as the difference between the present value of the expected cash inflows (PV_{in}) and the present value of the expected cash outflows (PV_{out}) or:

$$NPV = PV_{in} - PV_{out}$$

Net present value is interpreted using the following very simple, but very important, decision rule: If the *NPV* is greater than zero, the property should be purchased, assuming the investor has adequate capital resources, because it will increase the investor's wealth. If the calculated *NPV* is negative, the investment should be rejected because the investor expects

5. The calculator keystrokes are $N = 300$; $I = 6.5/12$; $PV = ?$; $PMT = 5005.98$; and $FV = 0$. The calculation of remaining mortgage balances is explained in more detail in Chapter 15.

Exhibit 19-6 Levered Cash Flows from Centre Point Office Building

Year	Annual *BTCF*	*BTER*	Total *CF*	*PV* @ 14%
1	$29,028		$ 29,028	$ 25,463
2	31,701		31,701	24,393
3	34,454		34,454	23,256
4	37,290		37,290	22,079
5	$40,211	$391,851	$432,062	$224,400

Total present value of levered cash flows = $319,591

Exhibit 19-7 Net Present Values of Levered Cash Flows from Centre Point Office Building at Different Discount Rates

Required Internal Rate of Return (y_e)	Net Present Value
10.00%	$ 84,461
12.00%	56,817
14.00%	31,831
16.00%	9,203
16.8727%	0
18.00%	(−11,330)
20.00%	(−29,997)

to earn a return less than his or her required rate of return for such an investment. If the *NPV* equals zero, the investor is indifferent.

To illustrate the calculation of *NPV* in an investment setting, consider again our Centre Point example with a required equity investment of $287,760. In exchange for this cash investment, the investor will acquire a set of property rights. These rights are expected to produce the annual *BTCF*s and *BTER* shown in Exhibits 19-4 and 19-5. Assume 14 percent is the levered discount rate currently being used by investors to value investments of similar risk and leverage to Centre Point. The projected cash flows and their individual present values are displayed in Exhibit 19-6.

The total present value of the levered cash flows is $319,591. Thus,

$$NPV = PV_{in} - PV_{out}$$
$$= \$319,591 - \$287,760$$
$$= \$31,831$$

Using our net present value decision rule, the levered Centre Point investment should be accepted because the investor's current wealth would be increased by $31,831 as a result of undertaking the investment.[6]

The *NPV*s at different discount rates can be calculated using either a handheld calculator or a spreadsheet program. Spreadsheet programs are ideally suited to solving such problems. The *NPV* calculations for a range of discount rates are presented in Exhibit 19-7.

6. The "*CFj*" key of most financial calculators can also be used to solve this problem. After entering the 14% discount rate in the "I" register, the annual cash flows are entered as follows: $CF_0 = -287,760$, $CF_1 = 29,028$, $CF_2 = 31,701$, $CF_3 = 34,454$, $CF_4 = 37,290$, and $CF_5 = 432,062$. To solve for *NPV* with the HP 10B II calculator, press "Shift NPV."

Note that as the required *IRR* increases, *NPV* declines. Also note that *NPV* equals zero only when the cash flows are discounted at *exactly* 16.8727 percent. At lower discount rates, *NPV* is positive, indicating an accept decision. When the discount rate exceeds 16.8727 percent, *NPV* is negative, indicating a reject decision.[7]

Internal Rate of Return

It often hinders comparisons to other investment alternatives when investment performance is expressed in dollar terms. For example, if the investor were to determine that the Centre Point Office Building before-tax *NPV* is $31,831, it may be difficult to evaluate how this expected performance compares to other investment opportunities such as stocks, bonds, and other real estate investments. If, however, the investor expects the Centre Point investment to provide, say, a 17 percent *IRR*, this facilitates more direct comparisons to available returns on other investment opportunities. Although certain technical problems are associated with its use, the internal rate of return (*IRR*) continues to be a widely used measure of investment returns in real estate and other business fields, such as corporate finance.

How is the *IRR* defined? The *IRR* on a proposed investment is the discount rate that makes the net present value of the investment equal to zero. The only method for calculating the *IRR* in the absence of a calculator or spreadsheet program is trial and error. Let's return to our Centre Point example. Suppose we select 14 percent as the equity discount rate. At this rate, the net present value of the levered before-tax cash inflows is $31,831. Thus, the *IRR* is not equal to 14 percent.

But is the *IRR* higher or lower than 14 percent? To answer this question, note that the present value (*PV*) at 14 percent is $31,831 greater than the required cash investment at acquisition. To decrease the net present value, we must increase the discount rate. With a 16 percent discount rate, the *NPV* of the cash flows is $9,203, still in excess of zero. However, at 18 percent, the *NPV* of the levered cash flows is −$11,330. Thus, an 18 percent discount rate is too high. This indicates the discount rate that makes the *NPV* equal to zero, the *IRR*, is somewhere between 16 and 18 percent. As shown in Exhibit 19-7, the discount rate that makes *NPV* equal to zero and, therefore, exactly solves the *IRR* equation is 16.8727 percent.[8]

Should the project be accepted or rejected? Because the investor requires a 14 percent return on levered equity invested in projects of similar risk, and the going-in *IRR* is nearly 17 percent, the project should be accepted. The decision rule for the internal rate of return method is, therefore,

If $r \geq y_e$, accept

If $r < y_e$, reject

where r is the calculated *IRR* and y_e is the required *IRR* on equity.

Comparing Net Present Value and the Internal Rate of Return

www.uli.org

Urban Land Institute produces an annual compendium of market studies for numerous metropolitan areas in North America as well as international markets.

When calculating Centre Point's *NPV*, we selected a discount rate (14 percent) and solved for present value. With *IRR*, we are *solving* for the discount rate that makes *NPV* = 0. Net present value and the internal rate of return use the same cash inflows and outflows in their calculations. Therefore, we would expect that investment decisions using the two DCF methods would be fairly consistent and, to a large extent, this is true. Both *NPV* and *IRR* produce the same accept/reject signal with respect to a particular investment opportunity— if a project's *NPV* is greater than zero, the *IRR* will exceed the required *IRR* (y_e).

---

7. The determination of appropriate discount rates is discussed in more detail in Chapter 14.

8. Financial calculators also allow the user to solve for the *IRR* of a stream of uneven cash flows by using the cash flow (*CFj*) key. In this example, −287,760 would be entered as CF_0, 29,028 as CF_1, 31,701 as CF_2, and 34,454, 37,290, and 432,062 (40,211 + 391,851) as CF_3, CF_4, and CF_5, respectively. Then solve for *I*.

However, the *IRR* has some inherent assumptions that make its use as an investment criterion problematic in some situations. For example, the *IRR* method does not discount cash flows at the investor's required rate of return (y_e). This is significant because both *NPV* and *IRR* (implicitly) assume that the cash flows from an investment will be reinvested. With the net present value method, cash flows are assumed to be reinvested at the investor's required rate of return. However, with the internal rate of return method, it is implicitly assumed that cash flows are reinvested at the *IRR,* not the actual rate investors expect to earn on reinvested cash flows.

A related problem with the use of the *IRR* as a decision criterion is that it will not necessarily result in wealth maximization for the investor. In particular, the *IRR* may produce a different ranking than *NPV* of alternative investment opportunities. If all positive *NPV* investments cannot be purchased by the investor—perhaps because of limited financial resources—the use of *IRR* instead of *NPV* may therefore lead to the selection of a project with a lower *NPV* than one of the rejected projects.

An additional difficulty with the *IRR* decision criterion is that multiple solutions are possible for investments where the sign (+ or −) of the cash flows changes more than once over the expected holding period. That is, more than one discount rate may equate the present value of future cash flows with the initial investment. In most commercial real estate investments in stabilized properties, an initial cash outflow (−) is followed by a series of expected cash inflows (+) from operations and sale of the property. It is possible, however, that the expected net cash flow from operations could be negative in some future year(s)—perhaps due to large capital expenditures. This additional "sign flip" could result in multiple *IRR*s. This is problematic because investors may not be aware that multiple *IRR* solutions to their investment problems exist, and it is not clear which *IRR* investors would choose even if they were aware of the existence of multiple solutions.

> ✓ **Concept Check**
>
> **19.5** List three technical problems potentially associated with the use of the internal rate of return as your final investment criterion.

Although the use of net present value (*NPV*) avoids the potential problems associated with the use of the *IRR*, the *IRR* is widely used for making comparisons across different investment opportunities.

The Impact of Leverage on Expected Returns

When will the increased use of financial leverage increase *NPV* and *IRR*, holding all other assumptions constant? To explore this question, consider Exhibit 19-8. If 75 percent of the acquisition price is borrowed, and upfront financing costs equal 3 percent of the loan amount, then increasing the leverage rate to 80 percent from 75 percent increases the calculated *NPV* (assuming y_e remains constant at 14 percent) to $43,627 from $31,831. The going-in *IRR* increases to 18.7 percent from 16.9 percent. Conversely, decreases in the leverage rate reduce *NPV*s and *IRR*s, all else constant. Thus, based on the given set of input assumptions, the Centre Point investment opportunity displays positive financial leverage.

How can these *NPV* and *IRR* results be explained? Note that the effective borrowing cost for the Centre Point Office Building is 7.24 percent, including the effect of upfront financing costs.[9] However, if the investor's required *IRR* remains 14 percent, he has an incentive to substitute additional debt for the more expensive equity financing. Put differently, if the investor can borrow an additional dollar at an effective rate of 7.24 percent,

---

9. The keystrokes for this calculation are $N = 60$; $PV = 768{,}240$; $PMT = -5{,}005.98$; $FV = -741{,}339$; and $I = ?$, where 768,240 equals the net loan proceeds ($792{,}000 - $23{,}760$). $FV = -741{,}339$ is the remaining mortgage balance at the end of year 5. Because the mortgage cash flows are monthly, the calculator produces a monthly *IRR* of 0.603 percent. This monthly *IRR* is annualized by multiplying by 12; that is, $7.24\% = 0.603 \times 12$. Effective borrowing costs are explained in detail in Chapter 15.

Exhibit 19-8 The Effects of Leverage on Centre Point *NPVs and IRRs*

Mortgage as a % of Acquisition Price	NPV: $y_e = 14\%$	IRR
0%	$(145,119)	10.1%
60%	(3,559)	13.8%
70%	20,034	15.6%
75%	31,831	16.9%
80%	43,627	18.7%
85%	55,424	21.3%
90%	$ 67,221	25.7%

then an additional dollar can be left invested in other assets (presumably of similar risk) that are expected to earn 14 percent—the investor's opportunity cost. The use of an additional dollar of leverage will increase the calculated *IRR* if the unlevered *IRR* (10.1 percent for Centre Point) exceeds the effective borrowing cost of the mortgage.

✓ Concept Check

19.6 When will the use of leverage increase the calculated *IRR*? The calculated *NPV*?

Despite the potential return-enhancing effects of leverage, financial leverage increases the riskiness of the equity investment by increasing the risk of default and by making the return on equity more sensitive to changes in actual *NOI*s from expected *NOI*s. This increased sensitivity occurs because a given amount of variation in *NOI* will have increasingly larger effects on the equity return as the use of debt increases (and the dollar amount of invested equity capital decreases). Thus, equity discount rates *should* increase as the amount of leverage increases, all else equal. As a result, the decision to substitute more debt financing for equity financing is complicated because the increase in *expected* return from the increased use of debt may not be large enough to offset the corresponding increase in risk and required return. Moreover, lenders may also increase the mortgage rate as the borrower's desired amount of leverage increases. This increase in borrowing costs reduces the marginal benefit of increased leverage. In fact, if the increase in the cost of debt is large enough, the marginal benefit of increased leverage may be negative.

The Impact of Leverage on Risk

To demonstrate the acute sensitivity of equity returns and risk to the use of debt financing, we return again to our Centre Point example. Recall that the base case assumptions contained in Exhibit 19-1 produce the levered cash flows from annual operations and from the eventual sale of the property contained in Exhibits 19-4 and 19-5. These cash flows, along with the initial equity investment of $287,760, produce an estimated before-tax *IRR* on equity of 16.9 percent.[10]

---

10. The calculator keystrokes are $I = ?$; $CF_0 = -287,760$; $CF_1 = 29,028$; $CF_2 = 31,701$; $CF_3 = 34,454$; $CF_4 = 37,290$; and $CF_5 = 432,062$. The total cash flow in year 5 is equal to the *BTCF* in year 5, $40,211 plus the *BTER* of $391,851.

Exhibit 19-9 The Effects of Leverage on Centre Point Cash Flows, *IRRs*, and Risk

Initial loan amount	$ 0	$633,600	$792,000	$950,400
Initial loan-to-value ratio	0%	60%	75%	90%
NOI in year 1	$ 89,100	$ 89,100	$ 89,100	$ 89,100
−Annual debt service	0	$ 48,057	$ 60,072	$ 72,086
=*BTCF*	$ 89,100	$ 41,043	$ 29,028	$ 17,014
Initial equity*	$1,056,000	$441,408	$287,760	$134,112
BTCF/initial equity	8.4%	9.3%	10.1%	12.7%
Growth rate in *PGI:*	*IRR*	*IRR*	*IRR*	*IRR*
−1% (5% probability)	6.2%	4.6%	3.0%	3.8%
+1% (20% probability)	8.1%	9.4%	10.6%	19.9%
+3% (50% probability)	10.1%	13.8%	16.9%	25.7%
+5% (20% probability)	12.1%	17.8%	22.4%	34.6%
+7% (5% probability)	14.0%	21.7%	27.4%	42.0%
Mean *IRR*	10.1%	13.6%	16.5%	26.0%
Standard deviation of *IRR*	1.8%	3.8%	5.4%	7.7%
Mean return/std. dev.	5.7	3.6	3.1	3.4

*The initial equity is equal to the total purchase price minus the net loan proceeds. The net loan proceeds equal the face amount of the loan minus upfront financing costs equal to 3 percent of the loan amount.

We now investigate the sensitivity of before-tax cash flows and equity *IRRs* to variations in the initial *LTV* and in the assumed annual rate of growth in potential gross income (*PGI*). These sensitivities, assuming a constant 6.5 percent mortgage rate, are displayed in Exhibit 19-9. The results in the first column were calculated with an Excel spreadsheet assuming a zero percent *LTV*. Columns 2 through 4 assume initial loans of $633,600, $792,000, and $950,400, respectively. First, note that estimated *NOI* is assumed to be unaffected by the *LTV*.[11] In the absence of financial leverage (column 1), the estimated *BTCF* equals the *NOI* of $89,100, and the required initial equity investment is equal to $1,056,000—the purchase price of the property. The equity dividend rate (*BTCF*/Equity) is 8.4 percent. Annual debt service with a $633,600 (60 percent) mortgage loan is $48,057. This results in a first-year *BTCF* of $41,043 and an equity investment of $441,408. The estimated *BTCF* continues to decrease as the *LTV* increases, but so does the required equity investment. It is important to note that the equity dividend rate increases as the amount of leverage increases. This positive relation between the equity dividend rate and the *LTV* will be observed whenever the annual mortgage constant (annual payment/loan amount) is *less* than the overall capitalization rate. The annual mortgage constant in this example is equal to 7.6 percent, and the going-in cap rate (*NOI*/price) is 8.4 percent.[12] Thus, holding the contract interest rate constant, increasing leverage increases the equity dividend rate in this example.

The middle section of Exhibit 19-9 displays the going-in *IRR* for annual growth rates in *PGI* ranging from −1 to +7 percent, all assuming a five-year holding period. The *assumed* probability of each growth rate scenario is listed in parentheses. With no leverage and a 1 percent annual decline in *PGI,* the *IRR* on equity is 6.2 percent. As noted above, the use of financial leverage will increase the estimated *IRR* on equity if the unlevered *IRR* exceeds the borrower's cost of debt.

11. In a simple world, the amount of debt financing (leverage) will not affect the income-producing ability of the property. However, if the incentives of the borrower and lender are not aligned, leverage may impact the operating decisions of the borrower, and thus *NOI.*

12. The monthly mortgage constant can be determined with the following keystroke sequence: $N = 360$, $I = 6.5/12$, $PV = -1$, $PMT = ?$, and $FV = 0$. This produces a monthly mortgage constant of 0.00632, or an annual constant of 0.07585.

Nathan S. Collier is the founder and chair of The Collier Companies and has been involved in multifamily acquisition, development, operation, and finance for most of his business life. Beginning with a single duplex purchased while he was in college, Collier has assembled a still growing portfolio of approximately 10,000 apartments— more than 18,000 bedrooms—in Gainesville, Ocala, Orlando, Tallahassee, Tampa, and other Florida locations, as well as in Norman, Oklahoma.

Regarding the importance of understanding real estate pro formas and *NPV* and *IRR*, Mr. Collier wrote the following in his blog:

NPV and *IRR are major ways in which investment decisions are evaluated. Each method has its strengths and weaknesses. Proper analysis of investment real estate requires a pro forma, an estimate of income and expenses over a period of time, usually 5 to 10 years. It is amazing how many people in real estate and finance have never created a pro forma from scratch and couldn't to save their lives. I've told my chief operating officer that the requirement to be a financial analyst for The Collier Companies should include the ability to at least create a rough pro forma from scratch solo. Otherwise, how can you truly understand what you are doing? I'm a big "back of the envelope" kind of guy. If the deal is so close that it does not pencil out on a napkin at the table, I'm pretty sure I don't want to go for it. But before we proceed we double and triple check our gut feeling by sifting the deal numbers through a great pro forma.*

The effective borrowing cost of the Centre Point mortgage is 7.24 percent. Thus, increasing the *LTV* will *decrease* the calculated *IRR* on equity if *PGI* decreases 1 percent per year because 6.2 percent (the unlevered *IRR*) is less than 7.24 percent (the cost of debt). With *PGI* growth rates of approximately 1 percent or higher, increasing the use of leverage increases the calculated *IRR* because the unlevered *IRR* for these growth rates is greater than the 7.24 percent cost of debt.

Although increased financial leverage increases, in some cases substantially, the calculated *IRR* when rental growth rates exceed approximately 1 percent per year, this benefit of financial leverage must be weighed against the cost of increased risk. Given the assumed probability distribution of *PGI* growth rates, the mean and standard deviation of the *IRR* assuming no leverage are 10.1 percent and 1.8 percent, respectively.[13] With a 60 percent *LTV*, the mean *IRR* on equity increases to 13.6 percent, holding constant all other assumptions. However, the standard deviation of the *IRR* increases to 3.8 percent. Thus, higher expected returns on equity can be "purchased" with additional leverage—but at the "price" of increased risk (standard deviation of return). In fact, the mean return per unit of risk (standard deviation) decreases from 5.7 to 3.6 as leverage increases from zero to 60 percent. With 90 percent leverage, the mean *IRR* jumps to 26.0 percent. However, the potential variation in the *IRR* also increases significantly. Why does the volatility (riskiness) of the return on equity increase at an increasing rate as leverage increases? As leverage increases, the "denominator" in the equity return equation decreases. The lower is the equity, the greater is the effect that a given change in *PGI* growth, and therefore *NOI* growth, will have on the return on equity.

The use of mortgage debt to help finance the acquisition of real estate is pervasive, and therefore its effect on risk and return should be clearly understood. Many market participants

---

✓ **Concept Check**

19.7 After watching a late night "get rich by investing in real estate" cable TV show, your roommate reports that the key ingredient to successful real estate investing is using "lots" of mortgage debt. What response would be appropriate and also allow you to contradict your roommate?

---

13. The mean *IRR* of 10.1 percent is equal to: $(0.05 \times 6.2\%) + (0.20 \times 8.1\%) + (0.50 \times 10.1\%) + (0.20 \times 12.1\%) + (0.05 \times 14.0\%)$. The standard deviation of 1.8 percent is equal to the square root of the sum of the squared deviations of calculated *IRR*s minus the mean *IRR*, where the squared deviations are weighted by the discrete probabilities of each *PGI* growth rate.

recommend extensive use of debt. In fact, one of the basic tenets of the numerous "get rich by investing in real estate schemes" is to make maximum use of "other people's money." The discussion and example above, however, demonstrate that leverage is a double-edged sword. Its use enhances equity returns when the property performs well. However, if the property performs poorly, the use of debt can make a bad situation worse, although the ability of the borrower to default can limit the amount of downside risk when nonrecourse financing is used.

Income Taxes and Investor Cash Flows

As briefly discussed in Chapter 18, the direct ownership of commercial real estate through a sole proprietorship, limited partnership, limited liability company, or private equity fund produces income that is subject to federal and state income taxation. Consequently, the cash flows most relevant to investors are the after-tax cash flows from annual operations and sale.

In Exhibit 19-10, we report estimates of annual tax liabilities and after-tax cash flows for our Centre Point example. These calculations assume the investor faces a 30 percent tax rate on taxable income from annual rental operations. The calculations also assume a 25 percent tax rate on depreciation recapture income, and a 15 percent tax rate on capital gain income. In Exhibit 19-11, we display the expected taxes due on the sale of Centre Point, and the resulting **after-tax equity reversion,** at the end of the expected five-year holding period. Interested readers are again referred to Chapter 20 for detailed explanations of these tax calculations.

Effect of Taxes on Discount Rates

Given the required equity investment of $287,760, the *ATCF*s from annual operations (Exhibit 19-10) and the *ATER* (Exhibit 19-11), we are now in a position to calculate the levered, after-tax, *NPV* and *IRR* for Centre Point. However, one additional decision is required: What is the appropriate discount rate to apply to the *after-tax* cash flows? Recall that we discounted the levered, *before-tax* cash flows from Centre Point at a 14 percent rate; we assumed that if the investor did not purchase Centre Point, he or she could invest in an alternative project, of similar risk, and earn a 14 percent pretax return. That is, we assumed y_e was equal to 14 percent. However, a taxable investor is not giving up a 14 percent *after-tax* return by acquiring Centre Point. Rather, by not investing in the alternative asset, the investor would be forgoing the expected 14 percent before-tax return minus the taxes that would be paid on that return. If the effective

Exhibit 19-10 Centre Point Office Building: After-Tax Cash Flows from Annual Operations

	1	2	3	4	5
Before-tax cash flow (*BTCF*)	$29,028	$31,701	$34,454	$37,290	$40,211
− Tax liability (*TAX*)	7,058	8,111	9,202	10,332	5,564
= After-tax cash flow (*ATCF*)	$21,970	$23,590	$25,253*	$26,958	$34,647

*Subtraction discrepancy due to rounding.

Exhibit 19-11 Centre Point Office Building: Estimated After-Tax Equity Reversion

Before-tax equity reversion (*BTER*)	$391,851
− Taxes due on sale (*TDS*)	32,214
= After-tax equity reversion	$359,637

Exhibit 19-12 After-Tax Cash Flows from Centre Point Office Building

Year	ATCFs	ATER	Total CFs	PV @ 9.8%
0	($287,760)		($287,760)	($287,760)
1	$21,970		$21,970	$ 20,009
2	23,590		23,590	19,567
3	25,253		25,253	19,077
4	26,958		26,958	18,547
5	$ 34,647	$359,637	$394,284	$247,057
			Net present value =	$ 36,498*
			Internal rate of return =	12.8%

*Addition discrepancy due to rounding.

Exhibit 19-13 Effect of Debt & Taxes on *IRRs* & *NPVs*: Centre Point Office Building

	IRR	NPV
Unlevered, before-tax (*NOIs* & *NSP*)	10.1%	$ 4,291 (with 10.0% discount rate)
Levered, before-tax (*BTCFs* & *BTER*)	16.9%	$31,831 (with 14.0% discount rate)
Levered, after-tax (*ATCFs* & *ATER*)	12.8%	$36,498 (with 9.8% discount rate)

tax rate on the income from comparable risk investments is 30 percent, the investor is actually giving up a 9.8 percent after-tax return—14 percent × (1 − 0.30)—by acquiring Centre Point. Thus, 9.8 percent is an appropriate after-tax, internal rate of return, assuming, of course, that 14 percent is an accurate measure of the investor's before-tax opportunity cost.

Effect of Taxes on Net Present Value and the Internal Rate of Return

Assuming a 9.8 percent required after-tax return on equity, the total present value of the *ATCFs* and the *ATER* is $324,258, yielding an after-tax *NPV* of $36,498 and an *IRR* of 12.8 percent. The Centre Point investment should therefore be accepted. These calculations are summarized in Exhibit 19-12.[14]

Exhibit 19-13 summarizes the effects of debt financing and income taxes on Centre Point's internal rate of return assuming the cost of debt does not vary with the amount of leverage. Note that 75 percent leverage increases the before-tax *IRR* to 16.9 percent from 10.1 percent without leverage. This result suggests the benefits of debt financing are substantial. However, as demonstrated earlier in the chapter, the use of debt financing also increases the riskiness of the investor's return on equity. Thus, it is inappropriate to apply the 10.0 percent unlevered discount rate to the levered cash flows. Assume a 4.0 percentage point risk premium is deemed appropriate for Centre Point when 75 percent leverage is employed. The levered discount rate is therefore 14 percent (10.0 + 4.0) and the levered *NPV* declines to $31,831.

What about the effect of taxes? Income taxes reduce the levered going-in *IRR* from 16.9 percent to 12.8 percent. However, if 9.8 percent is the appropriate after-tax levered discount rate, the levered *NPV* is only marginally affected by income taxes. Finally, note that although the investor's assumed tax rate on ordinary income is 30 percent, the after-tax

---

14. The *NPV* and *IRR* also can be solved for using a spreadsheet program or the cash flow (*CFj*) key of a financial calculator.

IRR is not 30 percent lower than the before-tax *IRR;* rather, the effective tax rate on the Centre Point investment is 24 percent [1 − (12.8% ÷ 16.9%)].

✓ **Concept Check**

19.8   Why is it inappropriate to discount after-tax cash flows at the investor's before-tax opportunity cost?

Why is the *effective* tax rate lower than the ordinary tax rate on taxable income from annual operations faced by the investor? First, as we shall see in Chapter 20, depreciation allows investors to defer the recognition of a portion of each annual cash flow until the property is sold. This tax deferral is valuable. Second, the effective rate of tax paid by the investor if and when the property is sold is generally less than his or her ordinary tax rate. This is, in part, because appreciation in the value of the property is taxed at favorable capital gain tax rates. The ability to defer taxes with depreciation and to have a portion of the gain at sale taxed at a capital gain tax rate both contribute to the result that the effective tax rate on commercial property investments is typically less than the tax rate on the investor's ordinary income. For many investors, their effective tax rate on commercial real estate investments is also less than the effective rate of tax they pay on alternative investments such as stocks and bonds. This is an important advantage to investors in many real estate investment opportunities.

Finally, note that the levered, after-tax *IRR* of 12.8 percent is still greater than the unlevered, before-debt *IRR* of 10.1 percent. This suggests that the positive effects of debt financing on the cash inflows and outflows more than offset the negative effect of taxes. This, of course, ignores the impact of leverage on risk.

More Detailed Cash Flow Projections

Exhibits 19-2 through 19-5 present the general form of commercial real estate pro formas. These exhibits show the major categories of revenues and expenses. However, it would be misleading to leave readers with the impression that investors regularly make investment decisions based on pro formas that contain only these major categories of revenues and expenses. Exhibit 19-14 contains an example pro forma used for the analysis of Exodus Center, a 50,000-square-foot office building. This pro forma was calculated using ARGUS Enterprise, a widely used software program for performing discounted cash flow analyses. Currently, four tenants occupy space in the Exodus Center subject to long-term leases with different maturities, lease rates, and other terms. A total of 12,000 square feet is currently vacant.

The cash flow projections in Exhibit 19-14 differ from our Centre Point pro forma in the amount of detail provided. For example, in addition to contract rent, the owner of Exodus Center is reimbursed by the tenants for a portion of the property's operating expenses. This reimbursement revenue, along with revenue from leasing roof space for a communications antennae, increases the gross income of the office building. Typical pro formas will also provide more detail on projected operating expenses, as seen in Exhibit 19-14. In addition, the components of the mortgage payment are disaggregated. Finally, ARGUS Enterprise refers to capital expenditures (*CAPX*) as leasing and capital costs and allows tenant improvements, expected leasing commissions, and other items (e.g., roof repairs) to be separately forecasted. Despite the simplifying assumptions made in our Centre Point example problem, Exhibits 19-2 through 19-5 do contain all the major categories of operating revenues and expenses.

Varying the Assumptions

As emphasized earlier, cash flow projections should be based on well-researched, realistic input assumptions. However, it is clear that the investor's point estimates (best guesses) of rental income growth, future vacancies, operating expenses, and future resale prices will prove to be wrong, either by a little or perhaps a lot. When considering a proposed acquisition, investors should recalculate *NPV*s and *IRR*s using both optimistic and pessimistic input assumptions in order to draw contrasts to the base case (i.e., most likely) scenario.

Exhibit 19-14 ARGUS Enterprise Pro Forma for Exodus Office Building

For the Years Ending	Year 1 Aug-2017	Year 2 Aug-2018	Year 3 Aug-2019	Year 4 Aug-2020	Year 5 Aug-2021	Year 6 Aug-2022
Potential gross revenue						
Base rental revenue	$ 659,088	$696,338	$ 731,988	$761,820	$783,633	$949,407
Absorption & turnover vacancy	(156,625)		(20,286)		(34,271)	(94,028)
Scheduled base rental revenue	502,463	696,338	711,702	761,820	749,362	855,379
Expense reimbursement revenue						
Real estate tax	4,071	11,083	11,593	13,096	13,546	3,497
Insurance	345	949	1,002	1,142	1,195	311
Utilities	3,952	12,551	13,046	15,121	15,337	3,832
Repairs and maintenance	2,136	6,650	6,929	8,010	8,158	2,049
Grounds & security	2,047	5,632	5,945	6,785	7,087	1,845
Total reimbursement revenue	12,551	36,865	38,515	44,154	45,323	11,535
Antennae	15,000	15,450	15,914	16,391	16,883	17,389
Total potential gross revenue	530,014	748,653	766,131	822,365	811,568	884,303
Effective gross revenue	530,014	748,653	766,131	822,365	811,568	884,303
Operating expenses						
Real estate tax	82,500	84,150	85,833	87,550	89,301	91,087
Insurance	7,000	7,210	7,426	7,649	7,879	8,115
Utilities	80,082	95,275	96,615	101,077	101,116	99,753
Repairs and maintenance	43,299	50,470	51,287	53,544	53,776	53,371
Grounds & security	41,500	42,745	44,027	45,348	46,709	48,110
Total operating expenses	254,381	279,850	285,188	295,168	298,781	300,436
Net operating income	275,633	468,803	480,943	527,197	512,787	583,867
Debt service						
Interest payments	239,034	237,014	234,762	232,322	229,680	
Principal payments	25,061	27,141	29,384	31,833	34,475	
Obligation points & fees	30,000					
Total debt service	294,155	264,155	264,156	264,155	264,155	
Leasing and capital costs						
Tenant improvements	261,000	17,562	65,670			388,545
Leasing commissions	78,300	9,217	24,343			205,840
Roof repair			55,000			
Total leasing & capital costs	339,300	26,779	145,013			594,485
Cash flow after debt service but before taxes	($357,822)	$177,869	$ 71,774	$263,042	$248,632	($10,618)

Such an exercise allows investors to determine how sensitive their estimates of *NPV* and *IRR* are to variations in important input assumptions.

Although values and rates of return can be determined by hand calculation, the computations are greatly facilitated by the use of personal computers, especially when a variety of input assumptions are considered. The use of spreadsheet programs such as Excel allows investors to quickly calculate the effect of a changed variable assumption on cash flows, values, and estimated rates of return. Numerous spreadsheet programs that facilitate the valuation and investment decision-making process are available for investors to purchase, or the analyst may custom-design an Excel spreadsheet. For complex analyses involving numerous existing leases, properties, or both, sophisticated programs such as ARGUS Enterprise (argussoftware. com) can be purchased.

cenario and "what-if" analyses both shed light on the potential risk of an investment opportunity, but each lacks the capacity to estimate the likelihood or probability of a specific outcome. This limitation is overcome by Monte Carlo simulation analysis. Simulation analysis recognizes that critical input variables, such as potential gross income, vacancies, and operating expenses, have a relevant range and a probability distribution. For example, although the investor's point estimate (best guess) is that Centre Point's potential gross income will grow at a 3 percent constant annual rate, she surely recognizes that the actual PGI growth rate in any year will vary from the 3 percent expectation. Perhaps data on past income growth rates suggest that annual PGI growth rates are normally distributed with a mean of 3 percent and a standard deviation of 2 percent. As a result of such probabilistic modeling of key input variables, a simulation model is able to generate a distribution of, say, *IRRs*—not simply a point estimate of the *IRR*. Thus, the analyst is able to answer questions such as the following: What is the probability that the *IRR* will be less than 5 percent? What is the probability that the *IRR* will be greater than 25 percent? What is the probability that the *IRR* will be between 10 and 20 percent? The ability to address such questions leads to greater insight into investment risk, which in turn leads to better property acquisition decisions.

Recent advancements in simulation software have made simulation analysis much more practical for real estate investment risk analysis. Although there are a number of vendors that provide reliable simulation software, the authors have found Crystal Ball software easy to learn and implement. www.oracle.com/us/products/applications/crystalball/overview/index.html.

Property Risk Assessment: A Simulation Approach

Summary

This chapter continues the presentation of the analytical framework for making single property real estate investment decisions that was introduced in Chapter 18. The framework has three basic components: forecasting net cash flows from the annual operation of the rental property, forecasting net cash proceeds from the eventual sale of the property, and converting these future cash flow streams into present values.

Our perspective is that of the investor in commercial real estate who has a unique set of holding period and financing requirements, and expectations about the future that may differ from those of other investors. The objective of analyzing real estate investments, therefore, is to compare the values of all property rights in real estate investment opportunities against required equity investments. The total present value of the set of property rights and cash flows to be acquired is the investment value of the equity; if this value is greater than the required cash investment, equity investors are on solid financial ground to proceed with the investment. Other important factors that are difficult to quantify may steer investors away from real estate investments.

We would be less than forthcoming if we were to leave you with the impression that the production of pro forma cash flow estimates and the calculation of net present values and internal rates of return are all that is required for successful real estate investment. Some successful investors are not well versed in discounted cash flow valuation models, and some may produce them more for the sake of appearance than as a serious step in the analysis of the property. But discounted cash flow analysis should be treated seriously. Although no one possesses a crystal ball, lenders, potential investment partners, and other market participants are increasingly likely to consider DCF analysis as fundamental to sound decision making. Put another way, individuals who are not comfortable with DCF tools and techniques are finding their job prospects in commercial real estate to be increasingly limited.

Key Terms

After-tax equity reversion (*ATER*) 515	Before-tax cash flow 507 Leverage 506	Levered cash flow 507 Unlevered cash flow 506

Test Problems

Answer the following multiple-choice questions:

1. A real estate investment is available at an initial cash outlay of $10,000 and is expected to yield cash flows of $3,343.81 per year for five years. The internal rate of return is approximately:
   a. 2 percent.
   b. 20 percent.
   c. 23 percent.
   d. 17 percent.

2. The net present value of an acquisition is equal to:
   a. The present value of expected future cash flows, plus the initial cash outlay.
   b. The present value of expected future cash flows, less the initial cash outlay.
   c. The sum of expected future cash flows, less the initial cash outlay.
   d. None of the above.

3. Present value:
   a. In excess of zero means a project is expected to yield a rate of return in excess of the discount rate employed.
   b. Is the value now of all undiscounted net benefits that are expected to be received in the future.
   c. Will always equal zero when the discount rate is the internal rate of return.
   d. Will always equal a project's purchase price when the discount rate is the internal rate of return.

4. The internal rate of return equation incorporates:
   a. Future cash outflows and inflows, but not initial cash flows.
   b. Future cash outflows and inflows, and initial cash outflow, but not initial cash inflow.
   c. Initial cash outflow and inflow, and future cash inflows, but not future cash outflows.
   d. Initial cash outflow and inflow, and future cash outflow and inflow.

5. The purchase price that will yield an investor the lowest acceptable rate of return is:
   a. The property's investment value to that investor.
   b. The property's net present value.
   c. The present value of anticipated future cash flows.
   d. Computed using the risk-free discount rate.

6. What term best describes the maximum price a buyer is willing to pay for a property?
   a. Investment value.
   b. Highest and best use value.
   c. Competitive value.
   d. Market value.

7. An income-producing property is priced at $600,000 and is expected to generate the following after-tax cash flows: Year 1: $42,000; Year 2: $44,000; Year 3: $45,000; Year 4: $50,000; and Year 5: $650,000. Would an investor with a required after-tax rate of return of 15 percent be wise to invest at the current price?
   a. No, the *NPV* is −$548,867.
   b. No, the *NPV* is −$148,867.
   c. Yes, the *NPV* is $51,133.
   d. Yes, the *NPV* is $451,133.

8. As a general rule, using financial leverage:
   a. Decreases risk to the equity investor.
   b. Increases risk to the equity investor.
   c. Has no impact on risk to the equity investor.
   d. May increase or decrease risk to the equity investor, depending on the income tax treatment of the interest expense and the equity investor's marginal income tax bracket.

9. What is the *IRR*, assuming an industrial building can be purchased for $250,000 and is expected to yield cash flows of $18,000 for each of the next five years and be sold at the end of the fifth year for $280,000?
   a. 0.09 percent
   b. 4.57 percent
   c. 9.20 percent
   d. 10.37 percent

10. Which of the following is the least true?
   a. Levered discount rates are greater than unlevered discount rates.
   b. Levered, before-tax discount rates are greater than unlevered, before-tax discount rates.
   c. After-tax discount rates are less than discount rates used to value before-tax cash flows.
   d. After-tax discount rates are greater than discount rates used to value before-tax cash flows.

Study Questions

1. List three important ways in which DCF valuation models differ from direct capitalization models.

2. Why might a commercial real estate investor borrow to help finance an investment even if he or she could afford to pay 100 percent cash?

3. Using the *CFj* key of your financial calculator, determine the *IRR* of the following series of annual cash flows: $CF_0 = -\$31,400$; $CF_1 = \$3,292$; $CF_2 = \$3,567$; $CF_3 = \$3,850$; $CF_4 = \$4,141$; and $CF_5 = \$50,659$.

4. A retail shopping center is purchased for $2.1 million. During the next four years, the property appreciates at 4 percent per year. At the time of purchase, the property is financed with a 75 percent loan-to-value ratio for 30 years at 8 percent (annual) with monthly amortization. At the end of year 4, the property is sold with 8 percent selling expenses. What is the before-tax equity reversion?

5. State, in no more than one sentence, the condition for favorable financial leverage in the calculation of *NPV*.

6. State, in no more than one sentence, the condition for favorable financial leverage in the calculation of the *IRR*.

7. An office building is purchased with the following projected cash flows:
   - *NOI* is expected to be $130,000 in year 1 with 5 percent annual increases.
   - The purchase price of the property is $720,000.
   - 100 percent equity financing is used to purchase the property.
   - The property is sold at the end of year 4 for $860,000 with selling costs of 4 percent.
   - The required unlevered rate of return is 14 percent.
   a. Calculate the unlevered internal rate of return (*IRR*).
   b. Calculate the unlevered net present value (*NPV*).

8. With a purchase price of $350,000, a small warehouse provides for an initial before-tax cash flow of $30,000, which grows by 6 percent a year. If the before-tax equity reversion after four years equals $90,000, and an initial equity investment of $175,000 is required, what is the *IRR* on the project? If the required going-in levered rate of return on the project is 10 percent, should the warehouse be purchased?

9. You are considering the acquisition of a small office building. The purchase price is $775,000. Seventy-five percent of the purchase price can be borrowed with a 30-year, 7.5 percent mortgage. Payments will be made *annually.* Up-front financing costs will total 3 percent of the loan amount. The expected before-tax cash flows from operations, assuming a five-year holding period, are as follows:

Year	BTCF
1	$48,492
2	53,768
3	59,282
4	65,043
5	71,058

The before-tax cash flow from the sale of the property is expected to be $295,050. What is the net present value of this investment, assuming a 12 percent required rate of return on levered cash flows? What is the levered internal rate of return?

10. You are considering the purchase of an apartment complex. The following assumptions are made:
- The purchase price is $1 million.
- Potential gross income (*PGI*) for the first year of operations is projected to be $171,000.
- *PGI* is expected to increase 4 percent per year.
- No vacancies are expected.
- Operating expenses are estimated at 35 percent of effective gross income. Ignore capital expenditures.
- The market value of the investment is expected to increase 4 percent per year.
- Selling expenses will be 4 percent.
- The holding period is four years.
- The appropriate unlevered rate of return to discount projected *NOI*s and the projected *NSP* is 12 percent.

- The required levered rate of return is 14 percent.
- 70 percent of the acquisition price can be borrowed with a 30-year, monthly payment mortgage.
- The annual interest rate on the mortgage will be 8 percent.
- Financing costs will equal 2 percent of the loan amount.
- There are no prepayment penalties.

a. Calculate net operating income (*NOI*) for each of the four years.
b. Calculate the net sale proceeds from the sale of the property.
c. Calculate the net present value of this investment, assuming no mortgage debt. Should you purchase? Why?
d. Calculate the internal rate of return of this investment, assuming no debt. Should you purchase? Why?
e. Calculate the monthly mortgage payment. What is the total per year?
f. Calculate the loan balance at the end of years 1, 2, 3, and 4. (*Note:* The unpaid mortgage balance at any time is equal to the present value of the remaining payments, discounted at the contract rate of interest.)
g. Calculate the amount of principal reduction achieved during each of the four years.
h. Calculate the total interest paid during each of the four years. (Remember: Debt service = Principal − Interest.)
i. Calculate the (levered) required initial equity investment.
j. Calculate the before-tax cash flow (*BTCF*) for each of the four years.
k. Calculate the before-tax equity reversion (*BTER*) from the sale of the property.
l. Calculate the (levered) net present value of this investment. Should you purchase? Why?
m. Calculate the (levered) internal rate of return of this investment. Should you purchase? Why?
n. Calculate, for the first year of operations, the

   (1) Overall (cap) rate of return.
   (2) Equity dividend rate.
   (3) Gross income multiplier.
   (4) Debt coverage ratio.

11. The expected before-tax *IRR* on a potential real estate investment is 14 percent. The expected after-tax *IRR* is 10.5 percent. What is the effective tax rate on this investment?

EXPLORE THE WEB

MIT's Commercial Real Estate Data Laboratory (CREDL)

In order for government and industry to make informed decisions about real estate public policy and business, they need accurate information about the real estate world and methods to predict and measure the results of those decisions. Reliable data and the tools to understand that data are essential for government and businesses to choose the best courses of action for business success and the greater public good. These data and tools are often nonexistent, unavailable, or difficult to interpret.

The purpose of the CREDL, developed and maintained by MIT's Center for Real Estate, is to gather this data, measure the performance of commercial real estate, and develop practical methodologies and tools to help govern business and policy decisions. CREDL also provides a public space for analysis and perspective on issues of commercial real estate, bringing together academic research and industry practices in an innovative collaboration.

Go to the CREDL website: mitcre.mit.edu/research-publications/cred. Click on the Moody's/RCA CPPI (from 2012) link. What is the Moody's/RCA Commercial Property Price Index (CPPI)? How has commercial real estate performed since 2010?

Solutions to Concept Checks

1. Investment value is very similar to market value in that it is a function of three things: (1) estimated cash flows from annual operations, (2) estimated cash proceeds from the eventual sale of the property, and (3) the discount rate applied to these future cash flows. When estimating market value, the cash flow forecasts and discount rate are based on the expectations of the *typical,* or average, investor. The calculation of investment value is based on the expectations and return requirements of a *specific* investor.

2. There is no clear answer to this. One is tempted to answer that a 10-year holding period is typically assumed because 10 years of annual cash flows is all one can comfortably fit on an 8 1/2-by-11-inch piece of paper set in landscape. A better, less cynical, answer is that 10 years is the maximum period over which investors can foresee with any accuracy changes in the economic environment, including changes in local supply and demand conditions for commercial real estate. Moreover, except for apartment properties, many commercial properties are subject to long-term leases that make the prediction of contract rental income, in the absence of lease default, possible over periods as short as 10 years. Beyond 10 years, however, the cost in effort associated with developing a detailed cash flow forecast probably exceeds the value.

3. In calculating levered cash flows, the mortgage payment is subtracted from the unlevered cash flows. Thus, levered cash flows are smaller in magnitude than unlevered cash flows.

4. The owner's claim is a residual claim because he or she only gets "paid" if the property produces enough income to cover all operating and capital expenditures, cover the mortgage payment, and cover all state and federal income taxes. The owner then gets what is "left over."

5. Three technical problems potentially associated with the use of the *IRR* as an investment decision criterion are (1) the *IRR* implicitly assumes cash flows are reinvested at the *IRR;* (2) ranking projects based on their going-in *IRR*s may produce a different ranking than the *NPV* criterion—and the *NPV* ranking is always correct; and (3) multiple *IRR* solutions are possible if the signs of the net cash inflows and outflows change from negative to positive more than once.

6. Holding all other assumptions constant, increasing the amount of leverage will increase the calculated *IRR* if the unlevered (i.e., the zero percent *LTV*) *IRR* exceeds the effective borrowing cost. Increased leverage will increase the calculated *NPV* whenever the equity discount rate equity exceeds the effective borrowing cost.

7. Leverage will increase equity returns when a property is performing well; however, the use of leverage in a poorly performing property will reduce equity returns even further than otherwise and may lead to default.

8. The appropriate after-tax discount rate should reflect the after-tax return the investor can earn on alternative taxable investments of similar risk. For example, if the investor views his or her opportunity cost of investing in a real estate project to be the 12 percent before-tax return expected on his or her current stock portfolio, what return is the taxable investor giving up on an after-tax basis? If the cash flows produced by the stock investments would be taxed at an average rate of 30 percent, then the investor is really giving up an 8.4 percent after-tax return [8.4 = 12 × (1 − 0.30)] by investing in real estate instead of stocks.

Additional Readings

Brown, R. J. *Private Real Estate Investment: Data Analysis and Decision Making,* 2nd ed. Burlington, MA: Elsevier Academic Press, 2012.

Brueggeman, William B., and Jeffrey D. Fisher. *Real Estate Finance and Investments,* 15th ed. New York: McGraw-Hill, 2015.

Collier, N. S., C. A. Collier, and D. A. Halperin. *Construction Funding: The Process of Real Estate Development, Appraisal, and Finance,* 4th ed. Hoboken, NJ: John Wiley & Sons, Inc, 2008.

Eldred, Gary W. *Investing in Real Estate,* 7th ed. Hoboken, NJ: John Wiley and Sons, Inc., 2012.

Geltner, David M., Norman G. Miller, Jim Clayton, and Piet Eichholtz. *Commercial Real Estate Analysis and Investments,* 3rd ed. Mason, OH: Cengage Learning, Inc., 2014.

Jaffe, Austin J., and C. F. Sirmans. *Fundamentals of Real Estate Investment,* 3rd ed. Upper Saddle River, NJ: Prentice Hall, 1995.

Kolbe, P. T., and, G. E. Greer. *Investment Analysis for Real Estate Decisions,* 7th ed. Chicago, IL: Dearborn Real Estate Education, 2012.

Linneman, P. *Real Estate Finance & Investments: Risk and Opportunities,* 3rd ed. Philadelphia, PA: Linneman Associates, 2012.

Sirota, D. *Essentials of Real Estate Investment,* 11th ed. Chicago, IL: Dearborn Financial Publishing, 2016.

Staiger, Roger. *Foundations of Real Estate Financial Modeling.* New York, NY, Routledge, 2015.

Sweeney, Glen, and John Gordon. *Real Estate: The Sustainable Investment: Strategies for the Next Generation.* Glen Sweeney and John Gordon, 2011.

Wiedemer, John P., Joseph E. Goeters, and J. Edward Graham. *Real Estate Investment,* 7th ed. Mason, OH: South-Western Cengage Learning, 2010.

Chapter 20

Income Taxation *and* Value

LEARNING OBJECTIVES

After reading this chapter you will be able to:

1 Incorporate income tax considerations into a discounted cash flow analysis, given appropriate assumptions.

2 Distinguish between active, passive, and portfolio income, and explain the tax treatment of each classification.

3 Calculate the after-tax cash flows from annual operations and from sale of a property, given the federal income tax treatment of mortgage financing and depreciation.

4 List and discuss the differential tax treatment of ordinary versus capital gain income and ordinary versus capital assets.

5 List the primary methods employed to defer, reduce, and/or eliminate tax liabilities.

OUTLINE

Introduction

The direct ownership of commercial real estate produces cash flows from rental operations and, typically cash flow from the eventual sale of the property. Both of these cash flow components are subject to federal and, in some cases, state income taxation. Moreover, as was noted in Chapter 18, the claims that states and the federal government have on property-level cash flows are substantial; some real estate investors face a combined state and federal tax rate that exceeds 50 percent. Consequently, the measure of investment value most relevant to investors is the present value of the expected *after-tax* cash flows from rental operations and sale.

In Chapter 19 we extended commercial property discounted cash flow analysis (DCF) to include the effects of federal income taxes. There we saw, using the example of our Centre Point office building, that the effects of federal income taxes on cash flows, discount rates, *NPV*s, and *IRR*s are substantial. However, the estimated tax liabilities incorporated into our DCF analysis in Chapter 19 were presented with minimal explanation. This chapter provides an introduction to the complex tax treatment of income-producing real estate. Our focus is on existing properties. Development entails additional tax ramifications that are beyond the scope of this chapter.

We begin by identifying the classifications of real estate for tax purposes. A general discussion of the U.S. tax system and how it treats real estate is followed by an analysis of how specific federal income tax provisions affect commercial property investments during both the rental operation phase and the disposition stage.[1] We conclude with a brief discussion of the most important tax rules that affect owner-occupied housing. Because federal income tax laws affecting real estate are extensive and complex, only abbreviated explanations of the most relevant issues are presented here. This information should be considered a starting point for learning about the tax consequences of owning real estate.

Objectives and Implementation of United States Tax Law

The most obvious objective of U.S. tax law is to raise revenues efficiently and equitably for the operations of the federal government. Congress also has designed tax law to promote certain socially desirable real estate–related activities, such as the construction and rehabilitation of housing for low-income households and the rehabilitation of historic structures.

All this is not meant to suggest that everything in the tax code has a strong economic or social rationale. Many tax provisions that apply to real estate are the result of competing political interests, and provisions favoring real estate are more likely to be passed by Congress when the influence of real estate lobbyists is particularly strong.

Tax legislation is combined into a single immense section of the federal statutory law called the Internal Revenue Code. Congress frequently revises this code, and some of these revisions have been extensive. The U.S. Treasury Department issues regulations and rulings interpreting the Internal Revenue Code. Congress also created the **Internal Revenue Service (IRS)** to collect federal taxes and to clarify and interpret regulations.

Comparing the Taxation of Individuals and Corporations

Many non-real estate corporations own commercial real estate. For example, McDonald's owns the majority of its fast food restaurants, some industrial firms own their warehouses, and banks often own their branch offices. However, the potential double taxation of income renders regular C-corporations a less desirable ownership form for entities formed primarily to own and lease income-producing real estate. Alternative ownership forms, such as limited partnerships and limited liability companies, allow owners to avoid double taxation of income produced by their rent generating investments.[2] This chapter, therefore, focuses attention on the consequences associated with using these unincorporated ownership forms to purchase income property. With these alternative ownership forms, the cash flows and tax liabilities associated with the underlying properties flow through directly to the investors/taxpayers and therefore avoid taxation at the entity level. The advantages and disadvantages of various ownership forms, including real estate investment trusts, are discussed in Chapter 17.

---

1. This chapter focuses on federal tax policies and provisions. State income taxes may also affect after-tax cash flows and returns from real estate investments. However, state income tax provisions often parallel federal provisions. Moreover, several states have no individual income tax (e.g., Florida and Texas).

2. Double taxation can occur when the corporation pays taxes on its taxable income (entity-level taxation) and then shareholders in the corporation pay taxes on dividends they receive from the corporation (investor-level taxation). With maximum federal tax rates on corporations at 35% and maximum individual federal rates now at 39.6% or higher, the tax disadvantage of the corporate form of ownership is not as clear.

Four Classes of Real Property

For purposes of federal income taxes, real estate is classified into four categories:

1. Real estate held as a **personal residence.**
2. Real estate held for sale to others: **dealer property.**
3. Real estate held for use in a trade or business activity: **trade or business property.**
4. Real estate held for investment: **investment property.**

These classifications determine, among other things, whether the real estate can be depreciated for federal income tax purposes. **Depreciation,** if permitted, allows investors to reduce the amount of taxable income they report by an amount that is intended to reflect the wear and tear that investment properties experience over time. By reducing taxable income and tax liabilities, depreciation "write-offs" increase the net cash flows taxpayers receive from real property investments. A property's tax classification may also affect the investor's tax liability when the property is sold.

Real estate used as a taxpayer's home cannot be depreciated for tax purposes. Commercial real estate, on the other hand, may be classified for tax purposes as dealer, trade or business, or investment property. Real property held for resale by a dealer is not depreciable for tax purposes because such property is viewed as inventory, not as trade or business property or property held as a long-term investment. Generally speaking, Congress allows depreciation deductions only on assets intended to be held as long-term investments rather than those held for resale. An example of an individual or firm that would typically hold real estate classified as dealer property is a homebuilder who, in the normal course of business, constructs homes for sale to homebuyers. It is important to remember that the dealer versus investor classification is *investment specific,* not *taxpayer specific.* Thus, a taxpayer could be a dealer with respect to one activity (e.g., homebuilding), but an investor with respect to one or more other activities (e.g., investing in small apartment buildings).

A commercial property investment not classified as dealer property is either a trade or business property or investment property. Consider the operator of a restaurant who owns the building in which the restaurant is located. In this case, the owner acquired the building with the intent to operate, modify, or do whatever is necessary to the structure to maximize the income from the restaurant business. For tax purposes, this real estate investment is classified as trade or business property.

What about a taxpayer who owns an apartment complex? Although this activity would seem to be an investment property, it is generally classified under U.S. tax law as a trade or business property. What about taxpayers who acquire their rental real estate by purchasing an interest in a limited liability company that, in turn, purchases the real estate? Despite the lack of active management by the passive (non-managing) investors in the limited liability company, the taxpayers involved in even these passive investments are generally considered to be operators of a trade or business activity, perhaps if for no other reason than they bear the responsibility for employing the property manager.

In short, most rental real estate is included in the trade or business category with the apparent rationale that investors in rental properties are primarily in the "business" of providing rental space to tenants. The tax treatment of trade or business property is determined according to Section 1231 of the federal tax code. Thus, trade or business real estate is often referred to as **Section 1231 property.**

✓ Concept Check

20.1 What is the primary importance of the four income tax classifications for real estate investors?

How else does the tax treatment of trade or business property differ from investment property? The sale of a trade or business property that is held for more than one year is treated as a Section 1231 transaction. Net gains from the sale of Section 1231 assets (excluding depreciation recapture income, discussed below) are taxed at capital gain tax rates—which can be significantly lower than ordinary income tax rates. In addition, net losses from the sale of Section 1231 assets are deductible without limit against other sources of income (including wages and salaries) in the year in which the losses are incurred. In contrast, losses on the sale of investment assets (e.g., undeveloped land, stocks, and bonds) may *not* be fully deductible against other income when incurred. (Taxable gains and losses from property dispositions are discussed in more detail below.)

Income Subject to Taxation

There are three types of income potentially subject to federal taxation: active income, portfolio income, and passive income. Income earned from salaries, wages, commissions, and bonuses is classified as **active income.** In contrast, income from investments in securities or unimproved land is classified as **portfolio income** and includes interest and dividend income on investments such as stocks and bonds. Dividends received from the ownership of a real estate investment trust (REIT) are also classified as portfolio income, as is interest earned on a mortgage or mortgage-backed security. Also, gains from the sale of financial securities, such as stocks and bonds, are considered portfolio income.

Passive activity income is defined to include all income generated from rental real estate investments. For example, owners of small apartment buildings that frequently find themselves doing "light" plumbing repair in the middle of the night probably do not think of themselves as "passive" investors. Nevertheless, in the context of *this* section of the tax code, their rental real estate activities are deemed to be passive in the eyes of the IRS and are therefore subject to **passive activity loss restrictions.** Unfortunately, this "passive" label is confusing because, in a *different* section of the code discussed above, virtually all income property investments are classified for depreciation purposes as trade or business properties— presumably because such investors are actively engaged in the business of providing rental space to tenants. Confused? Well, so are many tax accountants and tax attorneys.

> ✓ **Concept Check**
>
> **20.2**   How is income earned from salaries, wages, and commissions classified by the IRS? Income from investments in securities? Income generated from rental real estate investments?

www.irs.gov

Go to the IRS website and search for Publication 925 and Form 8582

What is the significance of the passive activity loss (*PAL*) restrictions for real estate investors? For individuals and partnerships, tax losses from passive activities can be used to offset positive taxable income from other passive activities, but not active or portfolio income (e.g., wages, interest, and dividends). Consider a real estate investor who owns, through three limited liability companies (LLCs), interests in two small apartment buildings and a small neighborhood shopping center. He has no other passive investment activities. Each year, the investor is allocated, by means of the LLC operating agreements, his share of the taxable gain or loss on each property. Assume in the current tax year he is allocated $3,000 and $5,000, respectively, in positive taxable income from the two apartment investments. However, his shopping center investment produced an allocated taxable loss of $10,000.

What happens? The $10,000 loss can be netted against the $8,000 in positive taxable income from his two other passive investments. However, the net $2,000 in negative taxable income from his three passive investment activities cannot be used in the current tax year to offset active or portfolio income. Is this $2,000 tax loss deduction lost forever? No, passive losses that cannot be used in a particular tax year can be carried forward indefinitely and used to offset positive passive income in future years, including passive income generated by a fully taxable sale.

It is significant that *PAL* restrictions apply even if the tax losses are caused by decreases in market rental rates, increases in vacancy rates, or increases in operating expenses or capital expenditures. Even *real* losses—that is, situations in which the before-tax cash flow (*BTCF*) on a property is also negative—are *not* deductible except against positive taxable income from other passive investment activities.

Several important exceptions exist to passive activity loss restrictions. First, regular corporations are not subject to the rule. Second, noncorporate taxpayers who actively manage residential rental investments may deduct up to $25,000 in passive activity losses against nonpassive income if their adjusted gross income (ignoring the losses) is less than $100,000.[3] "Active" management in this context requires the taxpayer to have a 10 percent interest in the property (and not be a limited partner) and be involved in the management of the property on a "substantial and continual basis."[4]

Active income is taxed at **ordinary tax rates** (see the next section). Portfolio income generated in the form of interest is also taxed at ordinary rates. However, if a stock or bond investment appreciates in nominal value during the investment holding period, the appreciation is generally taxed at a lower **capital gain tax rate.** The annual net taxable income produced by rental property operations, which is "passive" by definition, is taxed at ordinary rates. Gains from property value appreciation, however, may be eligible for favorable capital gain tax treatment.

www.taxsites.com

Tax and accounting websites directory provides great links to real estate tax sources.

Income Tax Rates

To estimate the tax implications of a flow through real estate investment, we must consider the tax rates individuals face, as well as the amount of taxable income the investment generates. In the 2016 tax year, there are seven ordinary statutory income tax rates for individuals ranging from 10 percent to 39.6 percent.[5] Exhibit 20-1 shows these rates and associated ranges of taxable income for single taxpayers in 2016. The corresponding tax rate schedule for married taxpayers (filing jointly with their spouse) is displayed in Exhibit 20-2.

All taxable income of single taxpayers equal to or below $9,275 is taxed at 10 percent. If taxable income exceeds $9,275, but does not exceed $37,650, taxes due will equal $927.5, plus 15 percent of the amount over $9,275. If taxable income exceeds $37,650, but does not exceed $91,150, the tax liability will equal $5,183.75, plus 25 percent of the

---

3. This amount is phased out at $1 for every $2 of income above $100,000. Thus, this exemption is completely phased out when adjusted gross income (*AGI*) reaches $150,000. A taxpayer with *AGI* of $120,000 could deduct up to $15,000 [$25,000 − (0.5 × $20,000)] in passive activity losses against active or portfolio income. The $100,000 amount is not indexed to inflation and has not been changed since passive activity loss restrictions were introduced by Congress in 1986.

4. Passive activity loss restrictions were further eased for some investors by the Omnibus Budget Reduction Reconciliation Act of 1993. This legislation relaxed the "automatically passive" status of rental real estate and introduced once again the opportunity to shelter salary or other income with rental losses. However, the legislation targeted this relaxation only to those in the "real estate property business," which includes nearly every type of real estate activity, including development and construction, acquisition, conversion, rental, operation, management, leasing, and brokerage. To be eligible for a waiver of the "automatically passive" rule you must (1) materially participate in the real property businesses, (2) spend more than one-half of your time for the year in those real property businesses, and (3) spend over 750 hours in total in these real property businesses.

5. The American Taxpayer Relief Act of 2012 increased the maximum statutory rate to 39.6 percent. The 2012 Act also introduced a Net Investment Income Tax (NIIT) surcharge under I.R.C. Section 1411 of 3.8 percent that applies to married households with modified adjusted gross income (AGI) in excess of $250,000, effectively raising the maximum to 43.4 percent (39.6 percent + 3.8 percent). If a taxpayer is in the 35 percent or 39.6 percent bracket on ordinary and trade or business income, he or she will be subject to the surtax. For more information, see the Tax Foundation website: taxfoundation.org/article/federal-capital-gains-tax-rates-1988-2013. "Real estate professionals" who spend substantial time working (more than 750 hours per year) in activities related to real estate, broadly defined, may be able to avoid the 3.8 percent surtax.

Exhibit 20-1 Single Taxpayers: Federal Income Tax Rate Schedule, 2016

If Taxable Income Is Over	But Not Over	Your Tax Liability Is	Of the Amount Over
$0	9,275	10%	$0
9,275	37,650	927.50 + 15%	9,275
37,650	91,150	5,183.75 + 25%	37,650
91,150	190,150	12,558.75 + 28%	91,150
190,150	413,350	46,278.75 + 33%	190,150
413,350	415,050	119,934.75 + 35%	413,350
415,050		120,529.75 + 39.6%	415,050

Note: To find updated tax rate schedules, visit the IRS website at www.irs.ustreas.gov.

Exhibit 20-2 Married Taxpayers: Federal Income Tax Rate Schedule, 2016

If Taxable Income Is Over	But Not Over	Your Tax Liability Is	Of the Amount Over
$0	18,550	10%	$0
18,550	75,300	1,855 + 15%	18,550
75,300	151,900	10,367.5 + 25%	75,300
151,900	231,450	29,517.5 + 28%	151,900
231,450	413,315	51,791.5 + 33%	231,450
413,315	466,950	111,818.5 + 35%	413,315
466,950		130,578.5 + 39.6%	466,950

Note: To find updated tax rate schedules, visit the IRS website at www.irs.ustreas.gov.

amount over $37,650. Therefore, if a single taxpayer has federal taxable income of $50,000, his or her tax liability is calculated as follows:

$$\text{Tax liability} = \$5,183.75 + [0.25 \times (\$50,000 - \$37,650)]$$
$$= \$5,183.75 + [0.25 \times \$12,350]$$
$$= \$8,271.25$$

The income ranges to which the seven rates apply are indexed annually to inflation.[6]

Estimating Tax Liabilities from Operations

In Chapters 8 and 18 we discussed the calculation of net operating income (*NOI*) from direct investments in rental property. The calculation of *NOI* involves deducting from effective gross income (*EGI*) the expenses associated with keeping the property operating and competitive in its local market. These operating expenses include property taxes, management, utilities, maintenance, and insurance. If capital expenditures (*CAPX*) are treated "above line," they also are deducted from *EGI*, resulting in the property's net operating income (*NOI*). Net operating income minus the mortgage payment is equal to the property's estimated before-tax cash flow (*BTCF*) from operations.[7]

6. If general inflation in the U.S. economy averages 3 percent per year from 2016 to 2019, the 15 percent rate would apply to taxable income of up to $41,141 [$37,650 × (1.03)³] in 2019 for a single taxpayer.

7. As discussed in Chapters 8 and 18, an alternative treatment of *CAPX* in the operating pro forma is a "below-line" treatment; that is, capital expenditures are subtracted *from NOI* to produce what may be called the property's "net cash flow." We continue to use the above-line treatment of *CAPX* here to be consistent with our treatment of *CAPX* in previous chapters.

Exhibit 20-3 Taxable Liability from Operations versus After-Tax Cash Flow

Tax Calculations	Cash Calculations
Net operating income (*NOI*)	Net operating income (*NOI*)
+ Capital expenditures (*CAPX*)	
− Depreciation (*DEP*)	
− Interest expense (*INT*)	− Interest expense (*INT*)
− Amortized financing costs (*AFC*)	− Principal amortization (*PA*)
= Taxable income (*TI*)	= Before-tax cash flow (*BTCF*)
× Ordinary Tax rate (*TR*)	− Tax liability (*TAX*)
= Tax liability (*TAX*)	= After-tax cash flow (*ATCF*)

In addition to cash flow, the ownership of income-producing real estate also generates taxable income. If the real estate is held in the form of a "regular" corporation or real estate investment trust (REIT), estimating the tax consequences is straightforward. The investor's taxable income usually is increased each year by the amount of dividend income received from the corporation or REIT.[8] However, estimating the tax effects of real estate ownership by individuals, partnerships, and limited liability corporations is more complex. This section discusses the calculation of expected annual taxable income (*TI*), the ordinary income tax liability (*TAX*), and the expected after-tax cash flow (*ATCF*) from investing in income-producing property as an individual or through a partnership, limited liability company, or S-corporation.

The general forms for calculating *TAX* and *ATCF* are displayed side by side in Exhibit 20-3. In the calculation of before-tax cash flow (*BTCF*), debt service (*DS*) is split into its two components: interest (*INT*) and principal amortization (*PA*). The amount of deductible interest in a given tax year is, generally, equal to total interest paid. The calculation of depreciation (*DEP*) and amortized, upfront, financing costs (*AFC*) are discussed in the following sections.

Cash Calculation versus Tax Calculation

As shown in Exhibit 20-3, two separate calculations are required to estimate after-tax cash flows from annual rental operations. The "cash" calculation involves a sequence of adjustments to the net operating income the investment is expected to generate. One of these adjustments is for estimated income taxes. A separate tax calculation, however, is required to estimate annual tax effects. Operating income subject to taxation differs, often significantly, from the actual (before-tax) cash flow generated by the property. As Exhibit 20-3 indicates, one difference between taxable income and before-tax cash flow is that principal amortization is subtracted from net operating income to estimate before-tax cash flow, but it is not tax deductible. Conversely, depreciation and amortized upfront financing costs (discussed below) *are* subtracted from *NOI* to find taxable income even though depreciation is a non-cash expense.

> **Concept Check**
>
> **20.3** List two cash outflows associated with property operations that are not tax deductible in the year in which they occur. List two deductible expenses that are not associated with a concurrent cash outflow.

8. A portion of the dividend received by the shareholder may be deemed by the corporation to be "return of capital" and therefore not immediately taxable, although it does reduce the shareholder's basis in the stock. Also, if a portion of the dividend reflects the investor's share of corporate-level capital gains, this portion of the dividend is taxed at the shareholder's applicable capital gain tax rate. Under the tax law in place in 2016, some "regular" dividends also qualified for taxation at capital gain rates. Capital gain taxation is discussed later in the chapter.

Operating Expenses versus Capital Improvements

As discussed in Chapters 8 and 18, operating expenses are defined as expenditures made to operate the property and keep it in good repair; they do not fundamentally alter the value of the property. Repainting the property inside or out, fixing gutters or floors, fixing leaks, plastering, and replacing broken windowpanes are examples of repairs classified as operating expenses. A capital expenditure, on the other hand, generally increases the market value of the property. Examples include the replacement of roofs, gutters, windows, and furnaces. Operating expenses are generally deductible for income tax purposes in the year in which they are paid. Capital expenditures, however, are not immediately deductible even if they represent an actual cash outflow. Rather, capital expenditures are added to the tax basis of the property and then systematically expensed through annual depreciation deductions, as explained below in the section "Depreciation Deductions." Generally, investors prefer to have cash expenditures classified for tax purposes as operating expenses rather than capital expenditures because the former are immediately deductible whereas the latter are expensed over time. Tax benefits, like other cash flow benefits, have higher present values when they are received sooner rather than later.

Why, in Exhibit 20-3, are capital expenditures *added* to net operating income in the calculation of taxable income from operations? Because with our above-line treatment of capital expenditures, *CAPX* have been subtracted from *EGI* in the calculation of *NOI*. Because *CAPX* are not tax deductible in the year in which they are paid, they must be added back in the calculation of taxable income.[9]

Costs of Mortgage Financing

The use of mortgage debt, in addition to equity capital, to finance an income property investment has four essential tax consequences. First, the periodic "price" the investor pays for borrowing—that is, the interest—is generally deductible in the year in which it is paid. However, the repayment of principal is not. Second, the annual depreciation deduction is not affected by the mix of debt and equity financing that is used because the entire acquisition price (minus the land) is depreciable. Third, mortgage funds, used for purchases or refinancings, are not taxable as income when received from the lender.

Finally, **upfront financing costs** (e.g., loan origination fees, appraisal fees) for investment properties are not fully deductible in the year in which they are paid. Instead, these costs must be amortized over the life of the loan. For example, if upfront financing costs on a 30-year loan total $3,000, the investor may deduct $100 a year when calculating taxable income from rental operations. If the loan is prepaid before the end of year 30 (perhaps because the property is sold), the remaining upfront financing costs are fully deductible in the year in which the loan obligation is extinguished. If our example loan is prepaid in year 5, then $2,600 [$3,000 − (4 × $100)] can be deducted from taxable income in year 5.

> ✓ **Concept Check**
>
> **20.4**   When does the cash flow effect associated with upfront financing costs occur? When does the tax effect occur?

---

9. Recall from Chapter 8 that investors sometimes set aside money each year in a separate account to accumulate a fund for future capital expenditures, such as replacement of roofs, kitchen equipment, and lobby or reception area furniture. These replacement reserves are not tax deductible. Therefore, if a replacement reserve is included in the calculation of *NOI,* it must be added back when calculating taxable income from operations.

www.irs.gov

How to depreciate property is explained in IRS Publication 946.

Depreciation Deductions

Why are investors in trade or business properties permitted an annual deduction (or "allowance") for depreciation even though it is not associated with an actual cash outflow during the years of operation? Because real estate depreciates or "wears out" as the capital improvements age—the roof shingles become less water resistant, the heating and air-conditioning system is less effective, the wood framing is more susceptible to water and infestation, and so on. As a result, the services and amenities provided by the improvements are less valuable, in real terms, at the end of a year than at the beginning because of this wear and tear. By allowing a depreciation expense, Congress is effectively permitting investors to deduct an estimate of this annual wear and tear as an expense associated with generating the property's rental income.

Students may be quick to point out that in many real estate markets and in many time periods, property values often *increase* over time, at least in nominal value. If properties are increasing in nominal (i.e., not adjusted for inflation) value, isn't this evidence that the properties are *not* wearing out? And if the properties are not wearing out, why should investors be allowed to take a deduction meant to approximate this aging?

The answers to these questions are found primarily in the distinction between land values and building values. Observable increases in property values may reflect an improvement in the location value of the property (due to changes in supply and demand) and, thus, the value of the land. If the increase in the value of the land exceeds the real loss in the value of the building and other improvements, the *total* value of the property may increase. In addition, increases in nominal values may occur simply because the amount of general inflation (usually measured by the consumer price index) exceeds the loss in the real value of the building and improvements. Nevertheless, the remaining economic life of the building and other improvements is decreasing over time and this "loss" of economic life is considered a legitimate cost of providing leasable space to tenants. In a sense, the depreciation allowance is meant to provide for the replacement of the depreciable asset (i.e., recovery of the initial capital costs) by the end of its economic life.

> **✓ Concept Check**
>
> **20.5** What is the "theory" behind depreciation deductions?

The size of the annual depreciation deduction is prescribed by federal law and depends on three factors: the amount of the depreciable basis, the cost recovery period, and the method of depreciation.

Depreciable Basis. The starting point for the calculation of the **depreciable basis** is the **original cost basis,** which is equal to the total acquisition price of the property (land, buildings, and personal property). To this is added any expenses directly associated with acquiring the property, such as brokerage fees (if paid by the buyer) and legal fees.[10]

The land component of the original cost basis is not depreciable because land is assumed not to wear out over time. Therefore, the portion of the total acquisition cost attributed to the land must be separated from the value of the building and any personal property. The IRS does not state how the relative values of the land and building are to be determined. Perhaps the most accurate and defensible method (to the IRS) is to have an independent real estate appraiser separately estimate the market value of each. An alternative approach is to obtain the relative values of the two components from the assessed

---

10. The original cost basis of a newly developed project equals the cost of land acquisition, plus land development costs, plus all hard and soft costs of the building and other improvements.

Commercial property owners are always looking for a way to increase cash flow and return on property investments. Unfortunately, they often fail to consider the dramatic impact depreciation can have on their taxable income because their accountants typically handle this area.

In fact, many commercial property owners may be leaving significant tax savings on the table because they are not claiming the maximum allowable

Cost Segregation Can Provide Significant Tax Savings

depreciation deductions when they and their accountants overlook the benefits of cost segregation studies. Thus, they should periodically review their depreciation schedules or consult with a specialist in the area.

Real estate investments are generally depreciated using a straight-line method over 39 years (27.5 years for residential properties). However, many personal property components of the property are eligible to be depreciated over 5, 7, or 15 years. Specialized engineering firms that focus on cost segregation—with a blend of tax, engineering, and construction knowledge—can typically reclassify between 15 and 40 percent of a building to these shorter recovery periods. By front-loading depreciation

deductions, significant tax savings can be realized.

This is not simply a matter of classifying computer equipment or office furniture in a five- or seven-year recovery period. Other items that can be reclassified include certain flooring, millwork, specialty electrical and plumbing systems, and land improvements such as asphalt paving, site lighting, and underground utilities. The list, in fact, is extensive. The good news is that the IRS is taking special pains to accommodate this opportunity if the cost segregation study is performed by qualified individuals or firms.

Source: Adapted from Jerome Kootman, "Significant Savings," *Commerical Property News,* February 16, 2006, p. 34.

values placed on the land and buildings by the local property tax assessor. If the property tax assessor concludes that the land constitutes 20 percent of the total taxable value of the property, then the owner can assume with some justification that 20 percent of the total acquisition price represents land value. As a general rule, the value of the land constitutes 10 to 30 percent of the total value of existing commercial properties.

An additional complication is that the depreciable basis may be further segregated into two components: real property (i.e., the building structure) and personal property. For example, hotel acquisitions typically include beds, tables, lobby furniture, and other items. An apartment building may include window air conditioners, refrigerators, and microwaves. Other examples of personal property include wall and floor coverings, swimming pools, and tennis courts. Generally, **personal property** is any tangible property not part of the building's core structure and, in some cases, as much as 40 percent of a property's cost can be classified as personal property.

Why is the distinction between real and personal property important? Because personal property (1) may be depreciated over fewer years than real property and (2) may be depreciated using "accelerated" methods (see below). The combination of these two effects provides larger depreciation deductions in the early years of the investment holding period, which creates an incentive on the acquisition of an existing property to allocate as much of the depreciable cost basis as possible to personal property.[11] However, a word of caution: There are no clear definitions of what constitutes personal in contrast to real property. As a general rule, the allocation of the depreciable basis should be based on each component's fair market value at the time of the acquisition. But what is the fair market value of a 10-year-old heating and air-conditioning system; 5-year-old carpeting, refrigerators, and furniture; or 20-year-old landscaping? Owners who use a **cost segregation** method for separating personal from real property often choose to hire specialized firms to do the allocations.

---

11. In addition to personal property, some property features such as grading, filling, roads, and landscaping may be depreciable as land improvements using an accelerated depreciation method over a 15-year depreciation period.

> ### Concept Check
>
> **20.6** You just purchased a small office building. Why do you have little incentive to attribute as much of the price as possible to the land? With respect to the nonland component, why do you have an incentive to attribute as much of the price as possible to personal property as opposed to real property?

Cost Recovery Period. Congressional legislation has frequently altered the period of time over which rental real estate may be depreciated for tax purposes. Currently, residential income-producing property (e.g., apartments) may be depreciated over no less than 27½ years.[12] The cost recovery period for nonresidential real property (e.g., shopping centers, industrial warehouses, hotels, and office buildings) is 39 years.[13] Personal property such as carpeting and draperies may be depreciated over 5 years, fixtures over 7 years, and landscaping and sidewalks over 15 years.

www.irs.gov

Go to the IRS site and do a search of "Depreciation."

Methods of Depreciation. Two basic methods of depreciating capital assets have been allowed: the straight-line method and a variety of "accelerated" methods. Currently, only the straight-line method is permitted for the depreciation of newly acquired or constructed real property. Straight-line depreciation is less generous to investors than accelerated methods—assuming the same cost recovery period—because accelerated methods result in greater depreciation allowances than straight-line depreciation in the early years of the depreciation schedule.

The real property depreciation allowance for a given year can be approximated by multiplying the *depreciable* basis of the real property—original cost basis minus the value of the land and personal property—times the appropriate depreciation rate. This rate is a function of the cost recovery period and the method. With a 27½-year recovery period and the straight-line method, the annual depreciation rate is:

$$Straight\text{-}line\ rate = \frac{1}{recovery\ period} = \frac{1}{27.5} = 0.03636, \text{ or } 3.636\%$$

If the real property depreciable basis is $100,000, the depreciation allowance is $3,636 (0.03636 × $100,000). With a 39-year recovery period, the annual straight-line rate is 0.02564 (i.e., 1/39) and the depreciation allowance, assuming a $100,000 depreciable basis, is $2,564.

Determining the real property depreciation allowance is complicated slightly by a tax rule known as the **midmonth convention.** Regardless of the actual date of purchase, the tax law assumes the purchase occurred on the 15th day of the month (i.e., midmonth). For

---

12. An income-producing property is considered a "residential" property for income tax purposes if at least 80 percent of the property's gross rental income is derived from the leasing of nontransient dwelling units (hotels and motels are not residential property). What about a downtown apartment building that has retail space on the first floor? So long as the rental income from the retail tenants does not exceed 20 percent of total rental income, the entire property is considered residential and may be depreciated over the shorter 27½-year recovery period.

13. From 1986 until 1993, nonresidential income property could be depreciated (straight-line) over 31½ years. Just prior to 1986, both residential and nonresidential property could be depreciated over 19 years using 175 percent declining balance depreciation. Owners who purchased property prior to 1993 can continue to use these more generous depreciation methods so long as the property is not sold and the cost recovery period has not expired.

Exhibit 20-4 Partial IRS Depreciation Table for Residential Income Property

If Recovery Year Is	Month in the First Recovery Year the Property Is Placed in Service											
	1	**2**	**3**	**4**	**5**	**6**	**7**	**8**	**9**	**10**	**11**	**12**
1	3.485	3.182	2.879	2.576	2.273	1.970	1.667	1.364	1.061	0.758	0.455	0.152
2	3.636	3.636	3.636	3.636	3.636	3.636	3.636	3.636	3.636	3.636	3.636	3.636
3	3.636	3.636	3.636	3.636	3.636	3.636	3.636	3.636	3.636	3.636	3.636	3.636
4	3.636	3.636	3.636	3.636	3.636	3.636	3.636	3.636	3.636	3.636	3.636	3.636
5	3.636	3.636	3.636	3.636	3.636	3.636	3.636	3.636	3.636	3.636	3.636	3.636
10	3.637	3.637	3.637	3.637	3.637	3.637	3.636	3.636	3.636	3.636	3.636	3.636
15	3.636	3.636	3.636	3.636	3.636	3.636	3.637	3.637	3.637	3.637	3.637	3.637
20	3.637	3.637	3.637	3.637	3.637	3.637	3.636	3.636	3.636	3.636	3.636	3.636
25	3.636	3.636	3.636	3.636	3.636	3.636	3.637	3.637	3.637	3.637	3.637	3.637
29	0.000	0.000	0.000	0.000	0.000	0.000	0.152	0.455	0.758	1.061	1.364	1.667

example, if an apartment property is purchased January 10, the depreciation rate in the first year is:

$$11.5 \text{ months} \div 12 \text{ months} \times 0.36363 = 0.03485$$

If the purchase is on April 15, the first-year rate is

$$8.5 \text{ months} \div 12 \text{ months} \times 0.0363636 = 0.02576$$

After the first year of ownership, the depreciation rate for our apartment example is the straight-line rate of 0.03636.

Despite the midmonth convention, the allowable depreciation deduction is easily calculated. Once the depreciable basis for the real property is determined, the taxpayer simply refers to the appropriate IRS table to determine the percentage of the original depreciable basis that is deductible in any given year. The midmonth convention is built into these IRS tables. A partial depreciation table for residential property is displayed in Exhibit 20-4. Each year the investor multiplies the original depreciable basis of the real property by the appropriate percentage to determine the depreciation deduction for that year.

Personal property acquired with the real property is eligible for five- and seven-year cost recovery periods and can be depreciated using 200 percent declining balance depreciation, with a switch to straight-line depreciation during the year in which it yields a larger deduction. The accelerated depreciation rate in the first year using 200 percent declining balance depreciation and a seven-year recovery period is:

$$200\% \text{ declining rate} = 2.00 \times \frac{1}{Recovery \ period} = 2.00 \times \frac{1}{7} = 0.2857$$

Thus, if the depreciable basis of seven-year personal property is $100,000, the accelerated first-year deduction is $28,570, leaving an unrecovered depreciable basis of $71,430 ($100,000 − $28,570). The accelerated rate of 0.2857 is applied to the remaining unrecovered basis to determine the depreciation allowance in a given year, although the IRS supplies taxpayers with depreciation tables similar to those shown in Exhibit 20-4 to simplify the calculations. Personal property eligible for a 15-year cost recovery period (e.g., land improvements) can be depreciated using the 150 percent declining balance method.

EXAMPLE 20-1: CALCULATING ANNUAL DEPRECIATION

On September 21, 2012, Mr. Smith purchased a small apartment building for $800,000. Of this amount, $700,000 is allocated to the value of the depreciable real property improvements. Because September is the ninth month of the year, Mr. Smith uses column 9 in Exhibit 20-4. For tax year 1, the percentage is 1.061. Therefore, Mr. Smith is allowed a deduction of $7,427 (0.01061 × $700,000). In tax years 2 through 28, the deduction will be 3.636, or 3.637, percent of $700,000, or $25,452. In tax year 29, if he has not yet disposed of the property, Mr. Smith's depreciation deduction will be $5,306 (0.00758 × $700,000). The 0.758 percent in year 29 is equal to the percent of the original depreciable basis not depreciated in years 1 through 28.

Substantial Improvements.   Capital expenditures made in years *after* the initial purchase are, effectively, treated as a separate building (if real property) or a separate improvement (if personal property). Thus, total depreciation in a given year will equal the depreciation deductions available on the original depreciable bases for real and personal property, plus the allowable deduction on subsequent capital expenditures. For example, if the roof on Mr. Smith's $800,000 apartment property is replaced for $30,000 at the end of year 10, the $30,000 roof expenditure would be depreciated on a straight-line basis over the next 27½ years. Thus, in years 11 through 27 of the investment, the total allowable depreciation deduction (*DEP*) would equal the sum of the original annual deduction ($25,452), plus the allowable deduction on the $30,000 roof replacement.

> **✓ Concept Check**
>
> **20.7**   Assume some office furniture recently purchased by the owner of a small office property can be depreciated over seven years using 200 percent declining balance depreciation. What percent of the acquisition price of the office furniture can be claimed as a depreciation deduction in year 1?

Tax Credits

Current tax law allows investors to take tax credits for the cost of renovating or rehabilitating certain older or historic structures and for the construction and rehabilitation of qualified low-income housing. It is important to understand the difference between a deduction and a credit. A credit is a dollar-for-dollar reduction of tax liability. Thus, a $1 tax credit reduces the investor's tax liability by $1. A deduction, however, benefits the taxpayer only to the extent of his or her marginal tax bracket. To illustrate, a $1 deduction for an investor in the 30 percent marginal tax bracket reduces the tax liability by $0.30 ($1 × 0.30).

www.nps.gov

Search the National Park Service site for "tax credits" to obtain extensive information.

Why do rehabilitation tax credits exist? Because our elected officials understand that without these additional tax incentives the private market will not adequately provide for the rehabilitation of older and historic structures and will underproduce housing units for low-income households. The rehabilitation investment tax credit is a subsidy feature of the tax code designed to encourage investment in the preservation of still-useful and historically significant structures.

Provided expenditures meet carefully specified criteria, the rehabilitation investment tax credit may be taken at one of two levels:

1. A one-time 10 percent credit may be taken on qualified rehabilitation expenditures on nonresidential structures placed in service before 1936.
2. A one-time 20 percent credit may be taken for rehabilitation expenditures on non-residential structures or residential structures that are rental properties, so long as the property is on the National Register of Historic Places or nominated for placement.[14]

For example, suppose a developer buys a National Register property for $200,000 and spends $500,000 in 2017 on qualified restoration and repairs approved by the Department of the Interior. The developer's 2017 tax credit is $100,000 (0.20 × $500,000).

To qualify for the 10 percent rehabilitation credit, the project must leave at least 50 percent of the building's existing external walls intact and functional. In addition, at least 75 percent of the building's internal structural framework must be kept in place. The historic property tax credit regulations are even more restrictive with respect to the use of materials, construction methods, and building redesign to preserve the historic character of the structures. Thus, redevelopers of nonresidential properties may opt for the 10 percent tax credit because of the less restrictive provisions.[15]

> ✓ **Concept Check**
>
> **20.8**   What is the difference between a tax credit and a tax deduction?

---

www.danter.com/ taxcredit

A collection of resources prepared by the Danter Company for those interested in the LIHTC program.

Low-Income Housing.   The 1986 Tax Reform Act replaced previous tax incentives on **low-income housing** with a system that entitles taxpayers who construct or rehabilitate qualified low-income housing units to benefit from tax credits. The tax credits are taken annually for 10 years. Under the Low-Income Housing Tax Credit (LIHTC) program, the present value of these tax credits is determined by several rules, but equals approximately 70 percent of the depreciable basis. Unlike tax credits for rehabilitating older property, low-income housing credits may be used to offset active and portfolio income, although limits on the maximum dollar amount of credits are applied to non-corporate taxpayers. To qualify as low-income housing, a project must set aside a certain number of units for lower-income households. The project must also meet a maximum rent restriction, follow special rules for existing housing, and obtain state credit authorization and certification for the credit from the state in which the property is (or will be) located.

www.hud.gov

Go to HUD's site and search for information on "Low Income Housing Tax Credits."

Beyond the important role the LIHTC program has played in providing housing units for low- and moderate-income households, the program has contributed significantly to the overall construction of apartment units. It is estimated, for example, that the LIHTC program accounted for over 25 percent of all multifamily housing permits during recent years. Nevertheless, critics contend the program is overly complex and not well designed to serve the needs of low-income—as opposed to moderate-income—households. Methods to expand and improve the LIHTC program continue to be debated in academic and public policy forums.

Centre Point Office Building: Taxes from Operations

In order to add the estimated income tax effects to the DCF analysis of our Centre Point office building example, assume the following: 80 percent of the $1,056,000 Centre Point acquisition price ($844,800) is allocable to depreciable real property; 20 percent ($211,200)

---

14. The National Register of Historic Places is a list of properties, areas, and districts that are unique or have some historic significance. The register is maintained by the U.S. Department of the Interior. Placement on the register requires nomination by a local historic properties committee.

15. For more information on rehabilitation tax credits, see IRS Form 3468, which is available on the IRS website (www.irs.gov).

Exhibit 20-5 Assumptions for Centre Point Office Building

- Total acquisition price: $1,056,000.
- Property consists of eight office suites, three on the first floor and five on the second.
- Contract rents: two suites at $1,800 per month, one at $3,600 per month, and five at $1,560 per month.
- Annual market rent increases: 3 percent per year.
- Vacancy and collection losses: 10 percent per year.
- Operating expenses: 40 percent of effective gross income each year.
- Capital expenditures: 5 percent of effective gross income each year.
- Expected holding period: 5 years.
- Expected selling price in year 5: Year 6 *NOI* capitalized at 8.75 percent.
- Selling expenses in year 5: 4 percent of the sale price.
- First mortgage loan: $792,000 (75 percent *LTV*).
- Annual interest rate: 6.5 percent.
- Loan term and amortization period: 30 years.
- Upfront financing costs: 3 percent of loan amount.
- Depreciable basis: 80 percent of $1,056,000 acquisition price (no personal property).
- Ordinary income tax rate: 30 percent.
- Capital gain tax rate: 15 percent.
- Depreciation recapture tax rate: 25 percent.

is allocated to nondepreciable land (for simplicity we assume no personal property); and the investor's marginal tax rate on ordinary income is 30 percent. For convenience, the complete set of assumptions for the Centre Point example is contained in Exhibit 20-5.

Following the general format displayed in Exhibit 20-3, five-year projections of taxable income and tax liability from operations are reported in Exhibit 20-6. After-tax cash flows (*ATCF*s) from operations are displayed in Exhibit 20-7. Given the assumptions in Exhibit 20-5—(*PGI*) increasing 3 percent per year, 10 percent vacancy and collection losses, operating expenses at 40 percent of (*EGI*), capital expenditures at 5 percent of *EGI*—net operating income (*NOI*) is expected to increase from $89,100 in year 1 to $100,283 in year 5. Capital expenditures (*CAPX*) are added back to net operating income

Exhibit 20-6 Centre Point Office Building: Expected Taxes from Annual Operations

	Year				
	1	**2**	**3**	**4**	**5**
Net operating income (*NOI*)	$89,100	$91,773	$94,526	$97,362	$100,283
+ Capital expenditures (*CAPX*)	8,100	8,343	8,593	8,851	9,117
− Interest (*INT*)	51,219	50,626	49,994	49,319	48,599
− Depreciation (*DEP*)	21,662	21,662	21,662	21,662	21,662
− Amortized financing costs (*AFC*)	792	792	792	792	20,592[†]
= Taxable income (*TI*)	23,527	27,036	30,672[*]	34,441[*]	18,547
× Ordinary tax rate (*TR*)	0.30	0.30	0.30	0.30	0.30
= Tax liability (*TAX*)	7,058	8,111	9,202	10,332	5,564

[†]Unamortized upfront financing costs = $23,760 − 4($792) = $20,592.

[*]Subtraction discrepancy due to rounding.

Exhibit 20-7   Centre Point Office Building: Expected After-Tax Cash Flow from Annual Operations

	Year				
	1	**2**	**3**	**4**	**5**
Net operating income (*NOI*)	$89,100	$91,773	$94,526	$97,362	$100,283
– Debt service (*DS*)	60,072	60,072	60,072	60,072	60,072
= Before-tax cash flow (*BTCF*)	29,028	31,701	34,454	37,290	40,211
– Tax liability (*TAX*)	7,058	8,111	9,202	10,332	5,564
= After-tax cash flow (*ATCF*)	21,970	23,590	25,253[*]	26,958	34,647

*Subtraction discrepancy due to rounding.

in the calculation of taxable income because they are not fully deductible when incurred, even if they represent actual cash expenditures.

The $1,056,000 Centre Point acquisition price is to be financed with a 75 percent, 30-year, 6.5 percent monthly payment loan. Total upfront financing costs will equal 3 percent of the $792,000 (0.75 × $1,056,000) loan amount, or $23,760. The total mortgage payment in each year (*DS*) is $60,072, of which $51,219 is deductible interest in year 1. The amount of deductible interest (*INT*) decreases each year as the loan balanced is amortized. The $23,760 in upfront financing costs is not immediately deductible; rather, the $23,760 is amortized over the life of the loan. This generates a $792 (*AFC*) deduction each year ($23,760 ÷ 30). If the property is sold in year 5, the unamortized financing costs of $20,592 may be deducted in full. Finally, as nonresidential property, the investment can be depreciated over 39 years using straight-line depreciation. Therefore, the annual depreciation allowance (ignoring the midmonth convention) is $21,662 ($844,800 ÷ 39). Taxable income in year 1 is expected to be $23,527; with a 30 percent ordinary tax rate, this produces an estimated tax liability of $7,058. This estimated tax liability is subtracted from the $29,028 *BTCF* to produce a projected *ATCF* of $21,970 in year 1.[16]

What Is a Tax Shelter?

Sometimes mortgage interest, depreciation, and other deductions are large enough relative to net operating income that taxable income from rental operations is negative. As discussed previously, commercial real estate investors are only able to use negative taxable income from one passive rental real estate investment to offset positive taxable income from other passive investment activities.

Suppose a property in its first year of operations after acquisition is expected to generate $20,000 in before-tax cash flow. Also assume the tax calculation yields a negative taxable income of $10,000. Given an assumed 35 percent tax rate, a *negative* $3,500 tax liability is projected. The after-tax cash flow is shown in Exhibit 20-8.

It could be argued that taxable income on a particular property is either positive or zero—if allowable deductions exceed rental income the **excess deductions** are wasted. However, if an investor can use the excess deductions from the property to offset positive

16. It should be pointed out that "year 1" in DCF projections should represent the 12 months immediately following the acquisition of the existing property. Thus, if the property is purchased and placed into service on April 1, 2017, estimated cash flows in year 1 should represent income and expenses received and incurred during the April 2017 through March 2018 time period. However, individual investors pay income taxes on a calendar year (January–December) basis. Thus, the investor's first year of ownership does not usually align perfectly with the tax year. For simplicity, the calculations presented in this chapter assume the tax year and the year of ownership directly correspond; that is, we implicitly assume that cash flows occur on a calendar year basis.

Exhibit 20-8 Taxable Liability versus After-Tax Cash Flow

= TI	$(10,000)	=	BTCF	$20,000
× TR	0.35	−	TAX	$(3,500)
= TAX	$(3,500)	=	ATCF	$23,500

taxable income from other investments, the excess deductions are not wasted because they produce additional tax savings for the investor. Thus, if the investor has $10,000 in negative taxable income from a real estate investment, $10,000 of positive taxable income from other passive investments may be sheltered; for a taxpayer in the 35 percent bracket, $3,500 is saved in taxes. Note that the additional $3,500 in tax savings occurs only if the property is purchased by the taxpayer; thus, the tax savings are directly attributable to the investment.[17]

> ✓ **Concept Check**
>
> **20.9** How can the tax liability from annual rental operations in a real estate pro forma be negative? Isn't the potential tax liability either positive or zero?

Estimating Tax Liabilities from Sale

The previous sections discuss the calculation of income taxes from rental property operations. This section focuses on the tax liability associated with the disposition of the property. The treatment of gains from property dispositions falls into two general categories:

1. "Fully taxable" sale treatment: when the seller receives full payment in the year of sale and taxable gains are fully recognized for tax purposes in the year of sale.
2. Tax-deferred arrangements: when a portion of the sale proceeds and realized taxable gain are not fully recognized until a later year, if ever.

The calculation of taxable gains from fully taxable sales is discussed first. A popular tax-deferral strategy—like-kind exchanges—is then briefly considered.

Fully Taxable Sale

When sellers of commercial properties effectively receive the full sale price in cash at closing, (minus any outstanding mortgage balance), the sale is treated as a fully taxable sale. This means the realized taxable gain must be fully recognized for tax purposes in the year of the sale, and the associated tax liability must be paid. The estimate of taxes due on sale (*TDS*) is subtracted from the before-tax equity reversion (*BTER*) to produce the projected after-tax equity reversion (*ATER*). The general form for the calculation of the *ATER* is shown in Exhibit 20-9.

Adjusted Basis. The starting point in the calculation of taxes due on sale is the **adjusted basis** (*AB*) of the property in the year of sale. The *AB* is equal to the original cost basis of the property (*OB*), plus additional real property or personal property capital expenditures

17. The alternative minimum tax (*AMT*) also may affect the tax consequences of real estate investments. Individuals must pay the higher of their regular tax liability or their minimum tax liability. Discussion of the *AMT* is beyond the scope of this chapter.

Exhibit 20-9 Calculating Cash Flow from Sale of Property

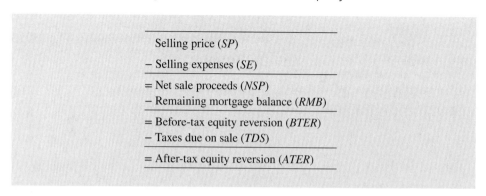

$$
\begin{aligned}
&\text{Selling price } (SP)\\
&-\text{ Selling expenses } (SE)\\
\hline
&=\text{ Net sale proceeds } (NSP)\\
&-\text{ Remaining mortgage balance } (RMB)\\
\hline
&=\text{ Before-tax equity reversion } (BTER)\\
&-\text{ Taxes due on sale } (TDS)\\
\hline
&=\text{ After-tax equity reversion } (ATER)
\end{aligned}
$$

Exhibit 20-10 Calculating the Adjusted Basis

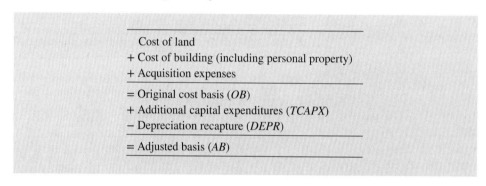

$$
\begin{aligned}
&\text{Cost of land}\\
&+\text{ Cost of building (including personal property)}\\
&+\text{ Acquisition expenses}\\
\hline
&=\text{ Original cost basis } (OB)\\
&+\text{ Additional capital expenditures } (TCAPX)\\
&-\text{ Depreciation recapture } (DEPR)\\
\hline
&=\text{ Adjusted basis } (AB)
\end{aligned}
$$

Exhibit 20-11 Calculating Taxable Gain or Loss on Sale

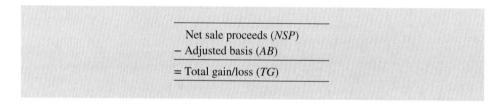

$$
\begin{aligned}
&\text{Net sale proceeds } (NSP)\\
&-\text{ Adjusted basis } (AB)\\
\hline
&=\text{ Total gain/loss } (TG)
\end{aligned}
$$

(*CAPX*), minus the cumulative amount of tax depreciation that has been taken since the property was placed in service as a rental property. We refer to cumulative depreciation at the time of sale as **depreciation recapture (DEPR).** The *OB* at acquisition is equal to the original acquisition price—land, building(s), and personal property—plus acquisition expenses (e.g., attorney fees, appraisal fee, and survey costs). Calculation of the adjusted tax basis, which is sometimes called the "book value" or the "depreciated value" of the property, is summarized in Exhibit 20-10.

Taxable Gain or Loss. For tax purposes, the total realized gain or loss on the sale of the property is equal to the net sale proceeds minus the adjusted basis. Any excess of the net sale proceeds (*NSP*) over the *AB* results in a taxable gain on sale; any deficit results in a taxable loss, as seen in Exhibit 20-11.

The difference between the before-tax equity reversion (*BTER*) in Exhibit 20-9 and the IRS's definition of the total gain (*TG* in Exhibit 20-11) should be stressed. Similar to taxable income from operations, the total amount of taxable income from sale is *not* equal to the *BTER*. Thus, multiplying the *BTER* by the capital gain tax rate to determine the taxes due on sale (*TDS*) is incorrect. Separate "tax" and "cash" calculations must be performed.

✓ **Concept Check**

> **20.10**   Why are taxes due on sale not equal to the before-tax equity reversion times the appropriate tax rate?

Types of Income Generated by a Sale.   All taxable income from investment property sales must eventually be classified as either ordinary income, depreciation recapture income, or capital gain income. The distinctions are important because capital gain income, under the tax rules in place in 2016, is subject to a maximum statutory federal tax rate of 20 percent.[18] Because the maximum statutory tax rate on ordinary income is 39.6 percent (in 2016), taxpayers can benefit greatly by having income classified as a long-term capital gain instead of ordinary income. As we shall see below, the portion of a positive gain from sale that results from tax depreciation of real property is taxed at yet a third rate—referred to as the **depreciation recapture rate.** This rate cannot exceed 25 percent. Confused? So are most taxpayers!

To qualify for the lower capital gain tax rate, the real property being sold must satisfy two criteria. First, the property must be held for more than 12 months. The taxable gain on the sale of a property purchased and sold within a single tax year is considered a short-term gain and is taxed at the seller's ordinary income tax rate. Second, even if the property is held for at least 12 months, the entire gain on sale could still be taxed at ordinary tax rates if the IRS classifies the asset as dealer property; that is, property held as inventory for sale to others, not as trade or business or investment property. The remainder of this discussion assumes the properties in question are not personal residences, were purchased at least 12 months prior to sale, and are not dealer property. The taxation of gains from the sale of a personal residence is discussed at the end of the chapter.

Taxation of Income from a Fully Taxable Sale.   As displayed in Exhibit 20-12, if the net sale proceeds exceed the undepreciated cost basis ($OB + TCAPX$), the taxable gain on the sale of depreciable real estate has two components and each is taxed at different rates.

The depreciation recapture component of the taxable gain ($DEPR$) is equal to the total amount of depreciation taken since purchase. The remainder of the taxable gain is the capital gain component ($CG = TG - DEPR$). Note that CG is the amount the property has

Exhibit 20-12   Calculating Taxes Due on Sale
Net Sale Proceeds > Original Cost Basis + Total Capital Expenditures

Net sale proceeds (NSP)
− Adjusted basis (AB)
= Taxable gain (TG)
− Depreciation recapture ($DEPR$)
= Capital gain (CG)
Capital gain tax ($CGTAX$) (maximum 20 percent statutory rate)
+ Depreciation recapture tax ($DEPRTAX$) (maximum 25 percent rate)
= Taxes due on sale (TDS)

18. As noted in footnote 5, the American Taxpayer Relief Act of 2012 introduced a Net Investment Income Tax (NIIT) surcharge under I.R.C. Section 1411 of 3.8 percent. Single filers earning more than $200,000 and joint filers earning more than $250,000 may also have to pay the 3.8 surcharge on capital gain income, effectively raising the maximum capital gain rate to 23.8 percent (20 percent + 3.8 percent).

increased in nominal value (net of selling expenses) since acquisition, relative to the original acquisition price and subsequent capital expenditures. As summarized in Exhibit 20-12, total taxes due on sale (*TDS*) are equal to the capital gain tax liability, plus the tax on accumulated depreciation (*TDS = CGTAX + DEPRTAX*). (We discuss what happens if the net sale proceeds are *less* than the original cost basis plus total capital expenditures in the section below titled "Section 1231 Property.")

But what tax rate do we apply to the depreciation and capital gain components of the total gain? As of 2016, there are several possibilities:

1. Taxpayers (not corporations) who are in the 10 percent ordinary tax bracket (see Exhibits 20-1 and 20-2) pay no tax on any long-term capital gains.
2. Taxpayers who pay ordinary federal tax rates of 25 percent to 35 percent pay a capital gain rate of 15 percent.
3. Taxpayers in the 39.6 percent tax bracket on ordinary income pay a capital gain rate of 20 percent.
4. Accumulated depreciation on real (Section 1250) property is taxed at a flat statutory rate of 25 percent, up to a maximum of the amount of the total capital gain on sale.[19]

Why the higher tax rate on the portion of the taxable gain that results from accumulated depreciation? One explanation is that this portion of the total gain did not result from appreciation in the market value of the property; rather, it resulted from prior depreciation allowances that have already produced tax savings for the investor. At sale, the IRS wants some of these prior tax savings back and, therefore, assesses a 25 percent tax rate on the (real property) depreciation recapture portion of the gain (*DEPR*) earned by most real estate investors. Investors usually come out ahead, however, because the rate at which they deducted their prior depreciation allowances usually exceeds the depreciation recapture rate.

EXAMPLE 20-2:   TAXES DUE ON SALE

Mary Lucy is selling an industrial warehouse facility for $1,650,000, from which she will net $1,600,000 in cash after deductible selling expenses. She originally purchased the property eight years ago for $1,000,000 (her original cost basis). During her ownership, Mary Lucy made no capital expenditures and claimed a total of $160,000 in depreciation deductions. Therefore, her adjusted tax basis at sale is $840,000 ($1,000,000 – $160,000). As displayed in Exhibit 20-13, her total taxable gain is $760,000. Mary Lucy will pay a tax rate of 25 percent on the $160,000 depreciation recapture portion of the gain. The capital gain component of $600,000 will be taxed at the 15 percent rate. Her total taxes due on sale will therefore be $130,000.

Although the accumulated depreciation portion of the total gain is taxed at a higher rate, Mary Lucy benefited substantially from the depreciation allowances. The depreciation she took during her ownership lowered her ordinary taxable income each year. Moreover, her depreciation deductions enabled her to realize those savings earlier, while paying only a portion of the depreciation tax savings back much later to the IRS when she sold the property.

Corporate Tax Rates.   We have emphasized numerous times that, whenever possible, commercial real estate investors avoid using a regular C corporation as their form of ownership. Limited liability companies (LLCs) and limited partnerships are preferred to corporate ownership structures because these ownership forms allow investors to obtain limited

19. The Net Investment Income Tax (NIIT) surcharge of 3.8 percent introduced by the American Taxpayer Relief Act of 2012 also applies to depreciation recapture income, effectively raising the maximum rate to 28.8 percent (25 percent + 3.8 percent). To the extent personal property is depreciated at accelerated rates, the total amount of depreciations will be the amount of depreciation that would have been taken had straight-line depreciation been used. This "excess" depreciation is tax at ordinary rates.

liability and avoid the double taxation faced by corporations. Although the maximum statutory capital gain tax rate paid by individuals is 20 percent, as of 2016, the maximum capital gain tax rate for corporations remains at 35 percent.

Section 1231 Property.   As discussed at the beginning of the chapter, virtually all developed commercial real estate is classified under current tax law as "trade or business" property. Moreover, trade or business property is classified as a Section 1231 property if it is held by the taxpayer more than one year. Our industrial property example implicitly assumes that Mary Lucy owns just one Section 1231 property. Often, however, investors have multiple Section 1231 assets that produce taxable gains and losses. If so, taxes due on sale are not separately calculated for each property and then added up. Instead, at the end of the tax year, all Section 1231 gains are netted against Section 1231 losses. If the netting process produces a net loss, the entire amount is treated as an ordinary loss that is deductible, *without limit,* against the taxpayer's other (e.g., wage and salary) income. If the netting process, however, produces a net gain, but a gain that is less than or equal to total accumulated depreciation on all Section 1231 assets, the entire net gain is taxed at the taxpayer's depreciation recapture tax rate. Finally, if the 1231 netting process produces a net gain that is positive and greater than total accumulated depreciation, then the depreciation recapture portion of the net gain is taxed at the recapture rate and the capital gain portion is taxed at the investor's capital gain tax rate, as indicated in Exhibits 20-12 and 20-13.[20]

For example, assume Gary receives $87,000 in salary income and has $20,000 of Section 1231 gains and $30,000 of Section 1231 losses in the current year. Gary has no other income, losses, or deductions affecting his adjusted gross income (*AGI*). The net Section 1231 loss of $10,000 is treated as an ordinary loss; thus, Gary's *AGI* is $77,000 ($87,000 salary − $10,000 of ordinary loss). This example illustrates one important advantage to the classification of rental property as a Section 1231 asset. Because the net Section 1231 loss is treated as ordinary income, it is fully deductible against active and portfolio income in the current year.

In sharp contrast, if taxpayers realize a loss on the sale of an investment asset (such as stocks and bonds), they may use this loss to offset positive capital gains. However, if this nettings procedure produces a net loss on investment asset dispositions, the net loss is deductible to the extent of only $3,000 per year for individual taxpayers. Therefore, if the $20,000 in Section 1231 gains and the $30,000 in losses were treated as investment property gains and losses, Gary would have a $10,000 net long-term capital loss, of which only $3,000 would be deductible against Gary's active and portfolio income in the current year.

In short, Section 1231 assets potentially provide the taxpayer with the best of both worlds: Net gains from sales in excess of accumulated depreciation are treated as capital gains, but net losses (if they occur) may be written off without limit against ordinary income.

Exhibit 20-13   Taxes Due on Sale of Mary Lucy's Industrial Property

Net sale proceeds (*NSP*)	$1,600,000
− Adjusted basis (*AB*)	840,000
= Taxable gain (*TG*)	760,000
− Depreciation recapture (*DEPR*)	160,000
= Capital gain (*CG*)	600,000
Capital gain tax (*CGTAX*) (15%)	90,000
+ Depreciation recapture tax (*DEPRTAX*) (25%)	40,000
= Taxes due on sale (*TDS*)	$130,000

20. An exception to this rule requires that net Section 1231 gains be treated as ordinary income to the extent that the taxpayer deducted net 1231 losses during the previous five years.

Centre Point Office Building: Taxes Due on Sale

For the Centre Point Office Building, the net sale proceeds (*NSP*) of the property at the end of the five-year holding period are projected to be $1,133,250. The remaining mortgage balance (*RMB*) at the end of year 5 will be $741,399. Thus, the projected before-tax equity reversion (*BTER*) is $391,851.

Total estimated capital expenditures over the projected five-year holding period are $43,004 (see Exhibit 20-6). For simplicity, we assume these capital expenditures are not depreciated during the expected holding period, but are simply added to the property's tax basis. Thus, total tax depreciation over the five-year holding period will equal the sum of the annual deductions allowed on the original cost basis ($108,308 = $21,661.54 × 5). The adjusted tax basis of the property (including land), after the fifth year of depreciation, will equal $990,696. This calculation is summarized in Exhibit 20-14.

Assuming depreciation recapture is taxed at 25 percent and the capital gain (*CG* = *TG* − *DEPR*) is taxed at 15 percent, the estimated capital gain and depreciation recapture tax liabilities are $5,137 and $27,077, respectively. Thus, taxes due on sale (*TDS*) and the after-tax equity reversion (*ATER*) are estimated to be $32,214 and $359,637, respectively. These calculations are summarized in Exhibits 20-15 and 20-16.

Exhibit 20-14 Centre Point Office Building: Adjusted Basis at Sale

Cost of land	$ 211,200
+ Cost of building	844,800
+ Acquisition expenses	0
= Original cost basis (*OB*)	1,056,000
+ Additional capital expenditures (*TCAPX*)	43,004
− Depreciation recapture (*DEPR*)	108,308
= Adjusted basis (*AB*)	$ 990,696

Exhibit 20-15 Centre Point Office Building: Taxes Due on Sale

Net sale proceeds (*NSP*)	$1,133,250
− Adjusted basis (*AB*)	990,696
= Taxable gain (*TG*)	142,554
− Depreciation recapture (*DEPR*)	108,308
= Capital gain (*CG*)	34,246
Capital gain tax (*CGTAX*) (@15%)	5,137
+ Depreciation recapture tax (*DEPRTAX*) (@25%)	27,077
= Taxes due on sale (*TDS*)	$ 32,214

Exhibit 20-16 Centre Point Office Building: Cash Flow from Sale

Net sale proceeds (*NSP*)	$1,133,250
− Remaining mortgage balance (*RMB*)	741,399
= Before-tax equity reversion (*BTER*)	391,851
− Taxes due on sale (*TDS*)	32,214
= After-tax equity reversion (*ATER*)	$ 359,637

Exhibit 20-17 Components of Taxable Gain on Sale in Year 5

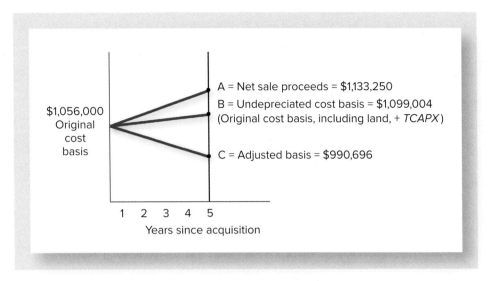

Exhibit 20-17 graphically displays the tax consequences associated with the sale of the Centre Point Office Building. The total taxable gain (*TG*) of $142,554 is equal to (A − C), where A is the estimated net sale proceeds and C is the adjusted tax basis at the end of year 5. The undepreciated basis of $1,099,004 (point B) is equal to the original cost basis of $1,056,000, plus total capital expenditures after acquisition of $43,004. The portion after acquisition of the taxable gain attributable to appreciation in the value of the property (*CG*) is $34,246 (A − B), while the portion due to depreciation recapture (*DEPR*) is $108,308 (B − C).

What would be the total taxable gain if the net sale proceeds were equal to $1,099,004, which is the original cost basis plus total capital expenditures? One might be tempted to conclude that no taxes would be due on sale if the taxpayer invested a total of $1,099,004 in the property over five years and then netted the same amount after expenses from the sale at the end of five years. However, a taxable gain of $108,308 would still be reported, an amount equal to total tax depreciation over the five years.

Net Benefits of Tax Depreciation

Tax depreciation shelters a portion of annual operating income (*NOI*) from taxation. This tax-sheltering ability, perhaps constrained by passive activity loss restrictions, reduces the annual tax liability of investors who own commercial property. However, the amount of cumulative tax depreciation (*DEPR*) is also taxed at depreciation recapture tax rates when the property is sold. Thus, the *net* benefit of tax depreciation is reduced by the present value of the increased taxes due on sale that result from depreciation recapture taxes.

Consider, for example, the Centre Point Office Building that will generate an annual depreciation deduction of $21,661.54. This deduction shelters $21,661.54 in *NOI* that would otherwise be taxed at a 30 percent rate, thereby saving the taxpayer $6,498.46 in taxes (0.30 × $21,661.54) each year for five years, or $32,492 (0.30 × $108,308) over five years.

However, when the property is sold, taxes due on sale will be $27,077 greater (0.25 × $108,308) than if the property had not been depreciated. The net benefit in present value terms of depreciation over the five-year period, assuming a 9.8 percent discount rate, is therefore:

$$Net \; benefit \; of \; depreciation = \sum_{y=1}^{5} \frac{0.30 \times (\$21,661.54)}{(1.098)^{y}} - \frac{27,077}{(1.098)^{5}}$$

$$= \$24,761 - \$16,966 = \$7,795$$

The present value of the annual tax savings is $24,761. The present value of the tax on depreciation recapture in the year of sale is $16,966. The *net* present value of deferring $108,308 in taxable income over five years is therefore $7,795.

This calculation demonstrates that the primary tax advantage of depreciation is that it provides **deferral benefits**. Income that would have been taxed at ordinary rates—$21,661.54 per year in our example—is, effectively, not taxed until the property is sold. In a sense, the IRS "loans" the investor the $32,492 (0.30 × $21,661.54 × 5) over the five-year period, and it is not repaid until the property is sold. This amounts to an interest-free loan from the IRS. And because the assumed 25 percent rate on accumulated depreciation is less than the 30 percent ordinary rate (at which the taxpayer is assumed to deduct annual depreciation), the interest rate on the loan will be negative because the investor will "pay back" in the year of sale an amount ($27,077) that is smaller than what was "borrowed" ($32,492) during the operating years. Said differently, in addition to deferring taxes to the year of sale, depreciation allows the Centre Point investor to "convert" ordinary income (taxed in this example at 30 percent) to income taxed in this example at the 25 percent depreciation recapture tax rate.

✓ **Concept Check**

20.11   What is the deferral benefit of depreciation?

Effect of Taxes on Values and Returns

The after-tax cash flows from the Centre Point Office Building are summarized in Exhibit 20-18. The initial equity investment is equal to:

$$E = \$1,056,000 - (\$792,000 - \$23,760) = \$287,760$$

where $792,000 (0.75 × $1,056,000) is the face amount of the mortgage loan and $23,760 is the amount of the upfront financing costs (0.03 × $792,000).

We are now in a position to calculate the levered, after-tax net present value (*NPV*) and internal rate of return (*IRR*) for Centre Point. Recall that in Chapter 19 we discounted the levered, before-tax, cash flows from Centre Point at a 14 percent rate because we assumed that if an investor did not purchase Centre Point, he or she could invest in an alternative project, of similar risk, and earn a 14 percent before-tax return.

Exhibit 20-18   Levered, After-Tax Cash Flows from Centre Point Office Building

Year	After-Tax Cash Flows	After-Tax Equity Reversion	Total Cash Flow	Present Value @ 9.8%
0	($287,760)		($ 287,760)	($ 287,760)
1	21,970		21,970	20,009
2	23,590		23,590	19,567
3	25,253		25,253	19,077
4	26,958		26,958	18,547
5	34,647	359,637	394,284	247,057
			Net present value =	$36,498*
			Internal rate of return =	12.8%

*Addition discrepency due to rounding

Exhibit 20-19 Effect of Debt and Taxes on the Internal Rate of Return and Net Present Value from Centre Point Office Building

	IRR	NPV
Unlevered, before-tax cash flows (*NOI*s)	10.1%	$ 4,291 (with 10.0% discount rate)
Levered, before-tax cash flows (*BTCF*s)	16.9%	$31,831 (with 14.0% discount rate)
Levered, after-tax cash flows (*ATCF*s)	12.8%	$36,498 (with 9.8% discount rate)

However, the investor is not giving up a 14 percent *after-tax* return by acquiring Centre Point; by not investing in the alternative asset, the investor would be forgoing the 14 percent before-tax return, minus the taxes that would be paid on the 14 percent return. Assuming a tax rate of 30 percent on ordinary income, the investor is giving up a 9.8 percent after-tax return [14% × (1 − 0.30)] by acquiring Centre Point. With these assumptions, the net present value of the *ATCF*s and the *ATER* is $36,498 and the going-in *IRR* is 12.8 percent. The project should therefore be accepted.[21]

Exhibit 20-19 summarizes the effects of debt financing and income taxes on the *NPV* and *IRR* associated with our Centre Point office building example. Income taxes reduce the levered going-in *IRR* from 16.9 percent to 12.8 percent. Note that the after-tax *IRR* is not simply 30 percent (the ordinary income tax rate) lower than the before-tax *IRR*. In fact, the after-tax *IRR* is just 24 percent lower than the before-tax *IRR* [1 − (12.8 ÷ 16.9)]. Twenty-four percent is the **effective tax rate**: that is, the actual percentage amount by which income taxes reduce the going-in internal rate of return. The effective tax rate of 24 percent is lower than the 30 percent ordinary tax rate primarily because of the 15 percent capital gain tax rate, the value of tax deferral, and the ability to convert (via depreciation) some ordinary income to income taxed at a 25 percent rate.

✓ **Concept Check**

20.12 The before-tax going-in *IRR* on a shopping center acquisition is 13 percent. The after-tax *IRR* is 10.4 percent. What is the effective tax rate on the investment?

If the inclusion of taxes reduces the going-in internal rate of return by 24 percent to 12.8 percent, why does the net present value *increase* slightly from $31,831 to $36,498? Because we assumed that the appropriate discount rate to apply to these after-tax cash flows is 9.8 percent, or 70 percent of the assumed 14 percent before-tax rate. Thus, although income taxes reduce the investor's cash flows from the Centre Point investment, this reduction is more than offset by the reduction in the assumed opportunity cost of invested equity.

Complications Caused by Alternative Ownership Forms

The calculated 12.8 percent after-tax internal rate of return assumes Centre Point will be purchased by an individual investor facing a 30 percent ordinary tax rate. However, the majority of commercial properties in the United States are owned by multiple investors in the form of partnerships, limited liability companies, and other direct ownership entities. As previously discussed, when individuals invest together through limited partnerships and limited liability companies, all cash flow and income tax consequences "flow through" directly to the individual investors. There is no separate entity that pays corporate income taxes and distributes net cash flows to investors in the form of dividends. However, cash

---

21. The *NPV* and *IRR* also can be solved for using the cash flow (*CF*) keys of a financial calculator or a spreadsheet program such as Microsoft Excel.

flows and taxable income are generally not passed thorough to investors based on their percentage share of total invested equity capital. As discussed in Chapter 17, the sponsor/organizer of the investment usually receives a percentage of the cash flow distributions that exceeds the percentage of equity capital suppled.

Thus, if we assume that Centre Point were going to be purchased, for example, by a limited liability company, additional assumptions would be required in order to estimate internal rates of return for the various members/investors. In particular, we would need to know what portion of the before-tax cash flows and the before-tax equity reversion to allocate to the various investors, what portion of the annual taxable incomes and the taxes due on sale to allocate, as well as the tax rates paid by each investor on ordinary and capital gain income in order to estimate investor-specific *NPV*s and *IRR*s. Although a discussion of returns to investors in flow-through ownership entities is beyond the scope of this chapter, it is important for the reader to understand that the estimate of property-level taxable income and cash flows is just the first step in determining the tax liability and returns expected by various investors in the ownership entity.

Like-Kind Exchanges

The potentially large amount of taxes due on the sale of commercial property can be a significant deterrent to fully taxable sales. A popular option for deferring capital gains taxes is the **like-kind exchange.** Section 1031 of the Internal Revenue Code allows owners of real estate, under certain circumstances, to exchange their properties for other like-kind properties and avoid paying some or all of the taxes that would ordinarily be paid in the year of the transaction. The primary motivation for a tax-deferred exchange is to alter property ownership status, yet postpone some or all capital gain and depreciation recapture taxes.[22] Additionally, an exchange may be the best way to market for-sale property in a difficult market setting.

To successfully complete a like-kind exchange, property owners must meet the following requirements:

1. The properties in an exchange must be trade or business properties or investment properties, such as land. This means dealer properties and principal residences cannot be included in the tax-deferred part of exchanges.
2. The properties in an exchange must be *like-kind* properties. To satisfy this requirement, real estate cannot be exchanged for personal property such as mortgages, bonds, stocks, farm animals, and so on. However, apartment buildings can be exchanged for office buildings, office buildings for shopping centers, shopping centers for industrial warehouses, and the like. To qualify, U.S. property must be exchanged for U.S. property.
3. Any cash or personal property received in an exchange is generally fully taxable in the year of the exchange. This non-like-kind property received is often referred to as "boot."

Although the execution of an exchange requires the assistance of a tax accountant or attorney, real estate investors need to understand how exchanges work and when they may be preferable to a fully taxable sale.

Tax Factors Affecting Homeowners

Homeowners receive preferential tax treatment under current federal income tax laws. The primary benefit is that, in most cases, homeowners do not have to report as taxable income any of the return they earn on the equity capital they have invested in their homes. The non-taxed equity return usually includes any appreciation in the value of the home that has occurred since it was purchased (i.e., the capital gain).

---

22. Like-kind exchanges postpone, but do not eliminate, capital gain taxes because the investor's tax basis in the old property becomes the starting tax basis in the new property.

Realized gains from the sale of real property must generally be recognized for federal income tax purposes in the year of sale. However, under Section 1031 of the Internal Revenue Code, real estate owners who dispose of their investment property and reinvest the net proceeds in other "like-kind" property are able to defer recognition of some or all of the capital gain and depreciation recapture income realized on the sale of the "relinquished" property.

A taxpayer who initiates a delayed tax-deferred exchange has up to 45 days after the disposition of the relinquished property to identify a "replacement" property or properties and 180 days (135 beyond the 45-day period) to complete the delayed exchange by acquiring one or more of the replacement properties. If a taxpayer is successful in completing an exchange, the realized tax liability will be deferred until the replacement property is subsequently disposed of in a fully taxable sale.

Despite the obvious appeal, taxpayers face significant compliance risk when seeking to complete the second leg of a tax-deferred exchange by identifying and purchasing a replacement property within the 45- and 180-day time limits. Moreover, the exchanger may compromise his or her bargaining position with potential sellers of replacement properties. In fact, the exchanging taxpayer may be required to pay a premium for the replacement property relative to its fair market value. If this price premium exceeds the present value of tax deferral, the use of a tax-deferred exchange will destroy, not enhance, wealth.

To evaluate the economics of tax-deferred exchanges, Ling and Petrova (2015) developed a numerical model for quantifying the value of the tax-deferral benefits. They then use regression analysis and data from the CoStar Group (www. costar.com) to examine whether investors seeking to complete a delayed exchange pay more, on average, for replacement properties than other investors.

Ling and Petrova find strong evidence that replacement exchanges in U.S. apartment and office markets are associated with significant price premiums, on average. Moreover, these average price premiums far exceed estimates of the value of tax deferral obtained via an exchange, especially if the exchanger expects to hold the replacement property for a short period of time. Thus, it appears that in the early to mid-2000s, many investors paid price premiums that offset, in whole or in part, the gain from the deferment of taxes. Like-kind exchanges decreased in popularity during the real estate downturn of 2008–2012 because falling property prices resulted in fewer gains.

Avoiding Taxes at Any Cost: The Economics of Tax-Deferred Real Estate Exchanges

Source: Excerpted from David C. Ling and Milena Petrova "The Economic Impact of Repealing or Limiting Section 1031 Like-Kind Exchanges for Real Estate Properties," July 2015. Published by www.1031taxreform.com/

www.irs.gov

For more information and examples, go to the IRS website and search for "Sale of personal residence."

As previously discussed, federal income taxes are generally due when appreciated assets such as stocks and rental properties are sold. How do homeowners avoid a similar fate? In most cases, single homeowners are permitted to exclude from taxable income up to $250,000 of the capital gain realized on the sale of property that has been used as a principal residence. The exclusion is $500,000 for married couples filing a joint income tax return. To qualify, the taxpayer must have owned and used the property as his or her principal residence for at least two years during the five-year period immediately preceding the sale. The tax exclusion is allowed each time a taxpayer sells a principal residence and meets the eligibility requirements, but generally no more often than once every two years. This capital gain exclusion promotes household mobility and wealth accumulation.

EXAMPLE 20-3: HOMEOWNER CAPITAL GAINS

Mr. and Mrs. Jones purchased a home for $170,000 in 2012 and occupied it continuously until the home was sold in 2016 for $250,000 net of selling expenses. No capital improvements were made to the home subsequent to its acquisition in 2012. Because the home was their personal residence, they were not allowed to depreciate it for tax purposes. Thus, the adjusted tax basis at the time of sale was $170,000 and the realized capital gain was $80,000. However, this gain did not have to be recognized for tax purposes because it was less than the available $500,000 exclusion. The Jones would have owed an additional $12,000 in income taxes if this $80,000 gain had been taxed at 15 percent, their regular capital gain tax rate.

Homeowners receive two significant benefits in addition to the nontaxation of their investment returns. First, homeowners are usually allowed to deduct their mortgage interest expenses on first and second homes when calculating their federal income tax liability.[23] Second, local property taxes are also deductible at the federal level. However, losses on the sale of a personal residence are not recognized.[24] In addition, discount points on a home acquisition loan are usually fully deductible in the year paid. However, discount points paid on a mortgage refinancing must be amortized over the life of the loan. Other closing costs charged by the lender, such as origination fees, credit checks, and property appraisals, are added to the tax basis. Costs associated with acquiring the property (not the mortgage) are also added to the basis. These basis additions decrease taxable gains on sale.

23. If the adjusted tax basis of a married couple's mortgage exceeds $1 million, the interest on this mortgage may not be fully deductible. For more information, see IRS Publication 936, *Home Mortgage Interest Deductions,* available on the IRS website, www.irs.gov.

24. The IRS website contains answers to frequently asked questions about the taxation of owner-occupied housing. Go to www.irs.gov and search for your topic of interest.

Summary

Federal income taxes affect real estate decisions in all of the three major phases of the ownership cycle: acquisition, operation, and disposition. The principal tax consideration during the acquisition phase involves the selection of a form of ownership that avoids the double taxation of income.

Tax shelter benefits from the direct (i.e., noncorporate) ownership of real estate are realized during the operation phase, mainly through allowances for tax depreciation. Depreciation deductions, as a noncash expense, result in lower annual taxable incomes, thus saving taxes. Current depreciation rules prescribe straight-line depreciation and a $27\frac{1}{2}$-year cost recovery period for residential rental property and a 39-year recovery period for commercial property. But current tax rules regarding passive activity losses may limit investors from fully utilizing the tax shelter benefits of depreciable real estate.

For projects involving the rehabilitation of older nonresidential structures, tax credits may be taken. If a property has historical significance, 20 percent of all qualifying rehabilitation expenditures may be taken as a tax credit, subject to passive activity loss limits. Tax credits are also available to qualified investors in low-income housing.

Real estate investors have two basic options for tax treatment when they sell property: fully taxable sale treatment and like-kind exchange. In a fully taxable sale, investors receive the entire sale proceeds from the buyer in the year of the sale, but must pay any tax liability in that year. However, real estate investors may be able to exchange their properties for like-kind real estate and defer all or some of the capital gain tax liability, so long as the exchanged properties are used in trade or business or held as investments.

Key Terms

Active income 526	Depreciation recapture rate 541	Original cost basis 531
Adjusted basis (*AB*) 539	Effective tax rate 547	Passive activity income 526
Capital gain tax rate 527	Excess deductions 538	Passive activity loss restrictions 526
Cost segregation 532	Internal Revenue Service (IRS) 524	Personal property 532
Dealer property 525	Investment property 525	Personal residence 525
Deferral benefits 546	Like-kind exchanges 548	Portfolio income 526
Depreciable basis 531	Low-income housing 536	Section 1231 property 525
Depreciation 525	Midmonth convention 533	Trade or business property 525
Depreciation recapture 540	Ordinary tax rate 527	Upfront financing costs 530

Test Problems

Answer the following multiple-choice problems:

1. Taxable income from the rental of actively managed depreciable real estate is classified as:
   a. Active income.
   b. Passive income.
   c. Portfolio income.
   d. Passive income if taxable income is negative; active income if taxable income is positive.

2. Under current federal income tax law, what is the shortest cost recovery period available to investors purchasing commercial rental property?
   a. 15 years.
   b. 19 years.
   c. 31½ years.
   d. 39 years.
   e. None of the above.

3. If an investor is a "dealer" with respect to certain real estate, that real estate is classified (by the IRS) as being held:
   a. As a personal residence.
   b. For sale to others.
   c. For use in trade or business.
   d. As an investment.
   e. None of the above.

4. When a property is sold for less than its adjusted basis, its depreciation (wear and tear) was:
   a. Estimated correctly.
   b. Underestimated.
   c. Overestimated.
   d. Determined by the owner.

5. For tax purposes, a substantial real property improvement (*CAPX*) made after the initial purchase is:
   a. Treated like a separate building.
   b. Added to the adjusted basis.
   c. Depreciated like personal property.
   d. Amortized over five years.

6. What percent of the income from residential rental property must be derived from the leasing of units occupied by tenants as housing in order for the entire depreciable basis to be depreciated using a 27½ year cost recovery period?
   a. 20 percent.
   b. 50 percent.
   c. 80 percent.
   d. 75 percent.

7. In 2012 you purchased a small office building for $450,000, which you financed with a $337,500 fixed-rate, 25-year mortgage. Upfront financing costs totaled $6,750. How much of this upfront financing expense could be written off against ordinary income in 2012?
   a. $6,750.00.
   b. $173.01.
   c. $270.00.
   d. $245.45.

8. If the investor is in the 33 percent income tax bracket, how much will a tax credit of $2,000 save the investor in taxes?
   a. $2,000.
   b. $660.
   c. $1,340.
   d. None of the above.

9. Which of the following best describes the taxation of gain and losses from the sale of Section 1231 assets?
   a. Net gains and net losses are taxed as ordinary income.
   b. Net gains and net losses are taxed as capital gain income.
   c. Net gains are taxed as ordinary income; net losses are taxed as capital gains.
   d. Net gains are taxed as capital gains; net losses are taxed as ordinary income.

10. Which of the following statements is false?
   a. Tax losses on active income can be used to offset positive portfolio income.
   b. Tax losses on portfolio income can be used to offset positive active income.
   c. A loss on the sale of a real estate stock can be used to offset a positive gain on the sale of a corporate bond.
   d. Net passive activity losses can be used to offset dividend income from a real estate stock.

Study Questions

1. Why do investors generally care whether the IRS classifies cash expenditures as operating expenses rather than capital expenditures?

2. How are the discount "points" associated with financing an income property handled for tax purposes?

   Use the following information to answer questions 3–5:

   Five years ago you purchased a small apartment complex for $1 million. You borrowed $700,000 at 7 percent for 25 years with monthly payments. The original depreciable basis was $750,000 and you have used 27½-year straight-line depreciation over the five-year holding period. Assume no capital expenditures have been made since acquisition. If you sell the property today for $1,270,000 in a fully taxable sale:

3. What will be the taxes due on sale? Assume 6 percent selling costs, 33 percent ordinary tax rate, a 15 percent capital gain tax rate, and a 25 percent recapture rate.

4. What will be the after-tax equity reversion (cash flow) from the sale?

5. Over the entire five-year holding period, how much were your taxes from rental operations reduced by the annual depreciation deductions? Ignore the increased taxes due on sale.

6. What are the four classifications of real estate holdings for tax purposes? Which classifications of property can be depreciated for tax purposes?

   Use the following information to answer questions 7–9:

   You have just purchased a small apartment complex that has a $1,000,000 depreciable basis. Assume no personal property. You are in the 28 percent ordinary tax bracket and 25 percent depreciation recapture bracket. Capital gains will be taxed at 15 percent. You discount future tax benefits from depreciation at 7 percent.

7. What is your annual depreciation deduction? Ignore the midmonth convention.

8. If you never sold the property, what would be the present value of the annual tax savings from depreciation?

9. If you sold the property at the end of five years, what would be the present value of the depreciation deductions, net of all taxes due on sale?

10. Black Acres Apartment, Inc., needs to compute taxable income (*TI*) for the preceding year and wants your assistance. The effective gross income (*EGI*) was $52,500; operating expenses were $19,000; $2,000 was put into a fund for future replacement of stoves and refrigerators; debt service was $26,662, of which $25,126 was interest; and the depreciation deduction was $17,000. Compute the taxable income from operations.

11. You are considering the purchase of a small apartment complex.
    - The purchase price, including acquisition costs, is $1 million.
    - Gross potential income in the first year is estimated at $175,000 and vacancy and collection losses are estimated to be 12 percent of gross potential income.
    - Operating expenses and capital expenditures are expected to be $36,000 and $2,000, respectively, in year 1.
    - The investor will obtain a $700,000 loan at 8 percent annual interest with annual payments for 25 years.
    - Additional upfront financing expenses will equal $25,000.
    - Assume that 25 percent of the purchase price is payment for land and that the building will be depreciated over 27½ years using straight-line depreciation. There is no personal property.
    - Your ordinary and capital gain tax rates are 35 and 15 percent, respectively.
    a. Calculate the mortgage payment, the interest deduction, the depreciation deduction, and the amortized financing costs for the first year of operations.
    b. What will be your net equity investment at "time zero"?
    c. Estimate the after-tax cash flow for the first year of operations.

12. Compute the after-tax cash flow from the sale of the following nonresidential property:
    - The purchase price was $450,000.
    - The investor obtained a $360,000 loan.
    - There were no upfront financing costs.
    - The market value of the property increased to $472,500 over the two-year holding period.
    - Selling costs are 6 percent of the sales price.
    - The investor is in the 35 percent ordinary tax bracket.
    - Capital gains will be taxed at 15 percent.
    - The balance of the loan at the time of sale is $354,276.
    - 15 percent of the initial purchase price represented the value of the land. The remaining 85 percent has been depreciated using straight-line depreciation and a 39-year cost recovery period.
    - $30,000 in capital expenditures has been incurred since acquisition; for simplicity, however, the capital expenditures have been added to the tax basis but not separately depreciated.
    a. Compute the annual depreciation deduction.

b. Compute the adjusted basis at the time of sale (after two years).
c. Compute the tax liability from sale.
d. Compute the after-tax cash flow (equity reversion) from sale.

13. A real estate investor is considering the purchase of a small office building. The following assumptions are made:
    - The purchase price is $775,000.
    - The project is a two-story office building containing a total of 34,000 leasable square feet.
    - Gross rents are expected to be $10 per square foot per year.
    - The vacancy rate is expected to be 15 percent of potential gross income per year.
    - Operating expenses are estimated at 45 percent of effective gross income.
    - 75 percent of the purchase price will be financed with a 20-year, monthly amortized, mortgage at an interest rate of 7.5 percent. There will be no upfront financing costs.
    - Of the total acquisition price, 75 percent represents depreciable real property improvements (no personal property).
    - The investor's ordinary tax rate is 30 percent and the capital gain tax rate is 15 percent.
    - Estimated capital expenditures are projected to be $10,000 per year, but for simplicity assume these expenditures will not be separately depreciated, although they will be added to the basis.

    Answer the following questions for the first year of operations:
    a. What is the equity (cash) down payment required at "time zero"?
    b. What is the annual depreciation deduction?
    c. What is the total debt service in year 1?
    d. What is the estimated net operating income?

14. A real estate investor is considering purchasing a small warehouse. Analysis has resulted in the following facts:
    - The asking price is $450,000.
    - There are 10,000 square feet of leasable area.
    - The expected rent is $5 per square foot per year; rents are expected to increase 5 percent per year. Since the property is leased to an AAA-grade tenant for 25 more years, no vacancy factor is deducted.
    - The tenant will pay all operating expenses except property taxes and insurance. These two expenses will equal 20 percent of the effective gross income (*EGI*) each year.
    - The investor can borrow 80 percent of the total cost for 20 years at an interest rate of 7 percent with monthly payments and upfront financing costs equal to 3 percent of the amount borrowed.
    - 85 percent of the total acquisition cost is depreciable over the useful life of 39 years using the straight-line method (no personal property).
    - The investor expects to sell the investment at the end of year 5.
    - The investor's ordinary income tax rate is 30 percent.
    - No capital expenditures have been made since acquisition.

    Compute the after-tax cash flows from annual rental operations over the five-year housing period.

Table 1 Reconstructed Income and Expense Statement for Question 15

Potential gross income		$105,100
Less: Vacancy at 7.04%		7,400
Effective gross income		$ 97,700
Less: Operating expenses		
Electricity	$2,000	
Water	400	
Sewer fees	30	
Heating fuel	7,600	
Payroll/contract cleaning	3,600	
Cleaning supplies	700	
Janitorial payroll	4,300	
Janitorial supplies	400	
Heating/air-conditioning	2,100	
Electrical repairs	400	
Plumbing repairs	500	
Exterior repairs	400	
Roof repairs	400	
Parking lot repairs	200	
Decorating (tenant)	1,800	
Decorating (public)	400	
Miscellaneous repairs	1,100	
Management fees	4,500	
Other administrative fees	1,000	
Landscaping maintenance	400	
Trash removal	600	
Window washing	200	
Snow removal	2,200	
Miscellaneous services	500	
Total operating expenses		35,730
Real estate taxes		15,800
Net operating income		$ 46,170

15. The property to be analyzed is a two-story, multitenant office building containing 10,000 square feet of rentable space. The building is situated on a 25,000-square-foot site that is partially landscaped and contains 35 parking spaces. The property is being offered for $500,000. The investor's ordinary and capital gain tax rates are 28 and 15 percent, respectively.

Multitenant office buildings are sometimes leased on a gross rental basis. In this case, the property owner pays all operating expenses. Income from the building is $10.51 per square foot of rentable area, for a total of $105,100 per year before vacancy losses. Office buildings in the area experience a vacancy rate of 7 percent, on average, of potential gross income.

Table 1 contains income and expense information for the property (first year pro forma). Expenses were estimated after studying the building's operating history and that of comparable buildings in the area.

A loan of $375,000 is available at 8 percent interest with a 30-year amortization schedule and annual payments.

The investor will use the straight-line depreciation method over a 39-year period. The expected purchase price of $500,000 is allocated 85 percent to building and 15 percent to the land (no personal property). This allocation is supported by the local tax assessor's records.

Rental income is expected to grow by 8 percent per year. Operating expenses are expected to grow by 4 percent per year.

The terminal capitalization rate of 10 percent is applied to expected net operating income in year 3 to determine the future sales price at the end of year 2. Selling expenses are 7 percent of the sale price. All passive activity losses (*PAL*) from the investment will be used to shelter income from passive income generators (*PIG*s), of which the investor has a "barn full." Assuming a two-year holding period, should the investor make this investment given a required levered, after-tax rate of return of 14 percent? Defend your answer with quantitative evidence from the analysis you perform.

EXPLORE THE WEB

Download the current tax rate schedule for single taxpayers from the IRS website www.irs.gov. What is the maximum statutory tax rate? Calculate the tax liability for a single taxpayer with $50,000 in taxable income. Has the tax liability increased or decreased since 2016?

Solutions to Concept Checks

1. The primary importance of the four income tax classifications is that they determine whether or not the asset can be depreciated for tax purposes.
2. Income earned from salaries, wages, and commissions is classified by the IRS as active income; income from investments in securities is classified as portfolio income; and income generated from rental real estate investments is passive activity income.
3. Capital expenditures and the principal amortization portion of the mortgage payment are not fully tax deductible in the year in which they occur even though they require cash expenditures. Depreciation and amortized financing costs

are deductible expenses not associated with a concurrent cash outflow.

4. Upfront financing costs increase the amount of cash the investor must bring to the closing table when the property is acquired, so the cash flow effect occurs at time zero. For tax purposes, however, the investor must amortize the upfront financing costs over the life of the loan, so the tax effects associated with the time zero outflow occur in small annual amounts over the investment holding period.

5. The "theory" behind depreciation deductions is that buildings, some land improvements, and personal property such as air conditioners and flooring wear out over time and this wear and tear is an unavoidable cost of providing rental space and services to tenants. Therefore, like other operating costs, it makes sense that investors are able to take a tax deduction that approximates the cost of this annual wear and tear.

6. You have little incentive to attribute value to the land because it cannot be depreciated. You also have an incentive to attribute non-land value to personal property because personal property generates larger annual depreciation deductions than real property, all else being equal.

7. The depreciation percentage is calculated as:

$$200\% \ declining \ rate = 2.0 \times \frac{1}{Recovery \ period} =$$

$$2.0 \times \frac{1}{7} = 0.2857, \ or \ 28.6\%$$

8. A $1 tax credit reduces the investor's tax *liability* by a dollar. A $1 tax deduction reduces the investor's taxable *income* by a dollar. Thus, the actual tax savings from a deduction depend on the investor's marginal tax rate (tax savings = deduction × tax rate).

9. To understand why it does make sense to show a negative tax liability if taxable income is negative, the reader must first understand that investment analysis is an *incremental* analysis. That is, investors must decide whether or not to acquire an asset, given what they already hold in their portfolios. So, if a potential real estate investment is expected to produce

negative taxable income, the excess deductions are not necessarily wasted. For example, the property owner may have positive taxable income from other rental properties. If the negative taxable income from the potential real estate investment can be used to reduce (offset) the amount of positive taxable income the investor must report for tax purposes on other passive investments, the investor's overall tax liability is reduced and the tax savings are expected to result directly from the real estate investment with negative taxable income. Thus, it generally does make sense in a pro forma to show a negative tax liability if taxable income is negative.

10. The tax consequences of a fully taxable sale are not determined by the amount of cash a sale generates. Rather, the taxable gain is a function of the relationship between the net sale proceeds and the adjusted tax basis. Moreover, the *adjusted* basis is not the original cost basis; rather, it is the original cost basis minus total depreciation. In short, the taxable income from sale is not equal to the before-tax cash flow from sale.

11. The deferral benefit of depreciation is that income from annual property operations, which would have been taxed at the investor's ordinary tax rate, is sheltered from taxation. For example, if an investor faces a 35 percent tax rate on income generated by the property, each dollar of depreciation saves the investor 35 cents in taxes. However, the investor does not get to keep the 35 cents forever if the property is sold. Why? Because each dollar of depreciation claimed as a deduction reduces the investor's adjusted tax basis at sale by a dollar. And the taxable gain on a fully taxable sale (if there is a sale) increases by a dollar for every dollar decrease in the adjusted tax basis. Thus, the dollar of property income that is not taxed during, say, year 1 of rental operations, because of the depreciation shield, is "recaptured" and taxed at sale. However, even though the investor may eventually "pay the tax man," he or she benefits from the ability to defer the tax payment until sale. An additional benefit is that the depreciation recapture tax rate is generally lower than the ordinary rate at which the depreciation was deducted.

12. The effective tax rate is 20 percent $[1 - (10.4 \div 13)]$.

Additional Readings

Cummings, J. *The Tax-Free Exchange Loophole: How Real Estate Investors Can Profit from the 1031 Exchange*. Hoboken, NJ: John Wiley and Sons, 2005.

Fishman, S. *Every Landlord's Tax Deduction Guide,* 12th ed. Berkeley, CA: Nolo Publishing, 2016.

Hoffman, W. H, J. E. Smith, and E. Willis. *South Western Federal Taxation: Individual Income Taxes 2016 Edition*. Florence, KY: Cengage Learning, 2016.

Hoven, V. *The Real Estate Investor's Tax Guide,* 5th ed. Chicago: Dearborn Publishing, 2003.

Kraemer, T. D. and T. H. Kraemer. *The Real Estate Investor's Tax Strategy Guide*. Adams Media: Avon, MA, 2009.

Ostrov, J., R. Collins, and K. Kaiser. *Tax Planning with Real Estate*. New York: Practising Law Institute, 2015.

Sonnenberg, J. *The Complete Tax Guide for Real Estate Investors: A Step-By-Step Plan to Limit Your Taxes*. Ocala, FL: Atlantic Publishing Company, 2008.

Williamson, R. *Selling Real Estate without Paying Taxes*: 2nd ed. New York: Kaplan Publishing, 2003.

The following journals provide pertinent articles on income taxation and value:

Real Estate Taxation, published quarterly by Thomson Reuters.

Real Estate Issues, published quarterly by the Counselors of Real Estate, Chicago.

PART EIGHT

Chapter 21

Enhancing Value *through* Ongoing Management

LEARNING OBJECTIVES

After reading this chapter you will be able to:

1. List five differences between the typical functions of property managers and asset managers.

2. Calculate the leasing commission to a broker, given the terms of the lease and the commission percentage.

3. Identify the optimal tenant mix in apartment properties and shopping centers.

4. List at least five elements of a typical commercial lease.

5. Describe specific steps managers must take to fulfill their fiduciary responsibility to their owners.

6. List three of the most prominent professional property manager designations.

7. Describe two functions of real estate asset managers that clearly distinguish their duties from stock and bond investment managers.

8. Describe the most recent trends in corporate real estate management.

Introduction

Chapters 18 and 19 and, indeed, much of this book deals with investment valuation; that is, how do investors evaluate the desirability of potential investment opportunities? Every investment decision involves the same two elements: the initial costs and the value of the future benefits. Making good acquisition decisions is important because, by their nature, they cannot be undone easily or costlessly.

But what about after the property is acquired? The long-term ownership of real estate puts investors in the business of providing services to users of the space; the provision of these services is extremely management intensive. Owners or their agents must repeatedly make management decisions that affect the value of the property and the investors' return on equity. Ongoing asset management is particularly important to the success of real estate investments. Unlike many publicly traded stock and bond investments, which can be bought and sold inexpensively in liquid markets, the going-in and going-out transaction costs of private commercial real estate investments are high (as a proportion of asset value). As a result, rates of return are generally maximized by holding the assets for longer periods of time, often in excess of 10 years. In addition, the majority of the return produced by investments in existing properties generally comes from net rental income, not from appreciation in the value of the property. Because of both factors—long holding periods and total returns generated primarily by the property's net operating income—commercial real estate returns are determined in no small part by how well the ongoing management function is performed.

✓ **Concept Check**

21.1   Why is ongoing asset management important in commercial real estate markets?

We classify ongoing, or continuing, management decisions into two categories: (1) those that have to do with the day-to-day operations of the property and (2) those that affect the physical, financial, or ownership structure of the property. **Property managers** are in charge of the day-to-day operations of the property. Typical functions include marketing the property to prospective tenants, selecting tenants, signing leases, collecting rent, maintaining the property, complying with all applicable landlord-tenant laws, maintaining tenant relations, and communicating with the property owner. Property management is the core function of real estate management. As we have stressed numerous times throughout the text, net operating income (*NOI*) is the fundamental determinant of property value and the activities of property managers have a significant impact on *NOI*.

The real estate industry applies the label of **asset manager** to individuals who are responsible for decisions that affect the physical, financial, or ownership structure of the property. For example, an asset manager may recommend or be responsible for decisions involving the timing and magnitude of required capital expenditures, refinancing, rehabilitation, modernization, expansion, conversion of the property to an alternative use, divestiture, or even abandonment. Asset managers may work for institutional investors such as pension funds, or for the managers of real estate syndications and real estate investment trusts (REITs). Asset managers work as liaisons between investors and their real estate investments and are involved in strategic decision making regarding the design of the investor's real estate portfolio, individual property purchases, and property dispositions. They may contract with property management firms on behalf of their investors, and make periodic reports to investors regarding the performance of their property portfolios.

Although the responsibilities of an asset manager may differ from one professional setting to the next, the asset manager often occupies a higher position in the decision-making hierarchy than property managers.

Owners as Managers

Sometimes property owners choose to perform both the property and asset manager functions themselves. This is frequently the case with smaller properties, especially those in which the owner occupies a portion of the space. Many successful real estate entrepreneurs began their careers by purchasing, renting, and managing small residential properties, such as single-family homes and duplexes. In fact, many "get rich quick in real estate" formulas marketed on late-night cable television and in hundreds of "how-to" books center around the acquisition of small residential properties that are currently being poorly managed. The get rich formulas then call for intensive management of the property, perhaps including rehabilitation or modernization of the structure. Once the owner/manager has "turned around" these underutilized (and presumably undervalued) properties, they are then held as investments or sold in the market for large profits—or at least that is the strategy. In any case, however, successful implementation of the strategy generally requires intensive management of the property.

Although some small rental properties are owner managed, most apartment, office, and retail properties employ professional property managers. In some cases, a single third-party manager performs both the property and asset management functions listed above. This is most likely to occur when the manager has been hired to oversee a single property. However, as the size of the owner's portfolio increases, it is increasingly likely that he or she will employ an asset manager, who will in turn hire one or more property managers.

We begin by discussing the management functions typically performed by property managers. We then explore the importance and contents of property management agreements and briefly tour the professional associations that support the property management industry. We then turn our attention to asset management, including the decisions to improve, alter, demolish, and reuse property. We conclude with a brief introduction to the world of corporate real estate asset management.

Functions of a Property Manager

As we argued above, the successful ownership of commercial real estate requires that space be leased to tenants at competitive rental rates. Once leased, the property and tenants must be managed—the ownership of commercial real estate is management intensive. Even if the primary goal of the investor is to maximize his or her return on investment, the ownership of commercial real estate is not a passive activity; operating a rental property is a form of business that requires ongoing management. Typical management functions are discussed below.

Marketing the Property

Leases are the engines that drive property values, but they are perishable assets. Most commercial space must therefore be marketed on a continual basis so that desirable replacement tenants can be found in a timely fashion as leases expire. The objective of the marketing plan should be to attract as many prospects as possible from the pool of possible tenants. There are many promotional tools available to managers to attract tenants, including signs, brochures, direct mail, cold calling, press releases, broadcast advertising, the Internet, and social media. With a limited budget for marketing, choosing an effective combination of promotional tools is critically important to the success of any rental property. It requires a thorough knowledge of the property for lease and a clear understanding of the market for that type of space. Increasingly, owners and managers are relying on websites and social media to market their properties. This is where the experience and ability of the property manager can produce significant benefits for the owner.

Who Should Lease the Property?   A critical question, directly related to the marketing of the property, is who should be primarily responsible for finding tenants and negotiating leases? In the case of apartment properties, the on-site manager or staff usually shows vacant apartments. Because standard form leases are used and relatively little negotiation occurs, the on-site apartment manager may handle the entire leasing process. Leasing is more complex, however, in the case of office buildings, shopping centers, industrial buildings, and other commercial space. The commercial property owner has three basic leasing options: use (1) an independent leasing broker, (2) an in-house leasing agent, or (3) the

Property Managers Take On More of an Asset Manager's Role

There's a subtle but definite shift taking place in the real estate industry. New demands and new technologies are coming together to advance the role of the property manager. Traditionally assumed to be a day-to-day role with little to no strategic responsibility, the property management function today takes on much of the aspect of asset management. This is in response to a heightened need on the part of investors and owners to capitalize on the value of their portfolios.

Today, there is significant pressure on the property management professional to put in place new or revised policies and practices to comply with vast state and federal regulations that impact the health of the real estate asset.

As a result, the skillset required to fulfill the role of the real estate management professional has changed. Included in the expanding suite of property management responsibilities are such forward-looking, strategic initiatives as establishing a property's operating policies and procedures, collaborating with property owners or boards of directors to develop ownership goals and objectives and preparing long-term financial models, just to name a few. Of course, there are still the day-to-day responsibilities traditionally associated with

property manager. Each of these alternatives has advantages and disadvantages depending on the leasing situation.

the profession, such as the collection of rents and ensuring the timely execution of such important but mundane functions as trash pickup, bill payments, and landscaping.

This expansion of responsibilities also affects the career trajectory of many property managers, providing access to the tools and processes of the formerly distinct asset management career path. Increasingly, day-to-day functions can be used as a training ground for new entrants to the field who face an unprecedented choice of career paths.

Source: Burger, Lori, "Property Managers Take On More of an Asset Manager's Role," nreionline.com/property-management/property-managers-take-more-asset-manager-s-role

© 2015 Reprinted by permission of Lori Burger.

✓ Concept Check

21.2 For nonresidential property, the owner has three primary choices when selecting the person or entity to be responsible for leasing the property. What are these choices?

The use of a leasing broker working for a local or national brokerage firm can offer the services of an organization geared solely to leasing or, as is more frequently the case, to leasing and selling commercial property. Similar to the sale of real estate, owners enter into an agreement with a brokerage firm to lease the property. As an agent, the brokerage firm has a fiduciary responsibility (discussed at length in Chapter 12) to the owner. Leasing agents working for the broker function as subagents of the listing broker. Brokers or agents that specialize in helping tenants find suitable space are often referred to as tenant representatives, or **tenant reps.**

✓ Concept Check

21.3 "Tenant reps" are licensed real estate brokers who specialize in what?

Leasing brokers are usually paid a commission when the lease is consummated. Generally, the commission is equal to a predetermined percentage of the face amount of the lease. The face amount of the lease, in turn, is equal to the total scheduled payments over the entire lease term. The percentage applied to the face value of the lease usually ranges from 3 to 5 percent. For example, if an office tenant signs a five-year lease with monthly payments of $10,000, and if the percentage commission rate is 4 percent, the leasing agent will be owed a $24,000 commission [0.04 × ($10,000 × 12 × 5)], which is typically paid when the lease is signed.

> ✓ **Concept Check**
>
> **21.4**   A tenant and owner just signed a three-year office property lease that calls for monthly payments of $6,500. The tenant was procured by a leasing agent. What commission is due the agent if the commission is specified to be 5 percent of the face value of the lease?

Leasing agents generally have but one responsibility: leasing space. Therefore, good leasing brokers are always in the market and aware of new tenants in the area, as well as the potential space needs of tenants currently signed to leases. A disadvantage is that the services of leasing agents are expensive. However, they operate in a very competitive market; therefore, what they are paid is some indication of the complexity and volatility of their job and income.

In contrast to leasing brokers, an in-house leasing agent is an employee of the property owner and is usually paid a salary plus a performance bonus. This person devotes 100 percent of his or her time to the owner's property or properties. The use of in-house leasing agents is common in the marketing of newly constructed shopping centers and, to some extent, multitenant office properties. The use of in-house agents is less likely to be observed in the marketing of existing buildings.

Finally, the owner may simply use the property manager as the leasing agent. This is frequently the case with apartment properties. The obvious advantage of this strategy is that the property manager is already familiar with the property, the tenants, and the goals of the owners. A disadvantage is that the property manager may not have sufficient expertise to negotiate complex office, industrial, and shopping center leases.

Selecting Tenants

In leasing commercial property, care must be taken to assure the prospect is willing and able to pay the rent. Tenant quality is a significant determinant of the income-producing ability of the property. Ideally, the property is of sufficient quality and desirability to allow some choice of tenants, thereby minimizing rental collection issues and other problems.

Creditworthiness.   When leasing nonresidential properties, owners would prefer to rent exclusively to credit tenants. **Credit tenants** are companies whose general debt obligations are rated "investment grade" by one or more of the U.S. rating agencies, such as Standard and Poor's and Moody's. The rationale for preferring such companies as tenants is that, if these companies have been judged to be creditworthy enough to borrow at preferential rates in the U.S. bond market, they are very unlikely to default on a lease obligation, at least in "normal" times. Certainly, credit tenants such as Microsoft and Walgreens are extremely desirable tenants, and such companies do occupy a significant amount of space in commercial properties. However, as we document in Chapter 17, the vast majority of commercial properties in the United States are small projects leased to small- and medium-size businesses that do not bring an investment-grade rating with them to the lease negotiations.

Think for a moment about your favorite neighborhood shopping center. Although the center may be "anchored" by a prominent grocery store, such as a Publix or a Kroger, the majority of the stores are likely to be local service businesses such as restaurants, dry cleaners, and barbershops. To make risk even more difficult to assess, some of these businesses may be new, or at least new to the area. Nevertheless, the previous operations and credit quality of these "in-line" lease applicants must be thoroughly investigated. The

www.nreionline.com

Online version of *National Real Estate Investor* magazine, which has numerous articles on property and corporate real estate management.

information to be verified and analyzed is usually supplied by the prospective tenant on the lease application. Financial records such as existing bank accounts and sources of income can be verified through a credit bureau. Evicting an undesirable tenant can be expensive but often can be avoided by careful screening of lease applications.

✓ **Concept Check**

21.5   What is a "credit" tenant?

Residential Properties.   Residential prospects may be asked to pay the fee for a credit check and usually are required to leave a refundable deposit to reserve the apartment unit until the credit check has been completed. When qualifying residential applicants, an applicant's past payment record, sources and amount of income, and level of indebtedness are the main concerns when evaluating rent-paying ability. Many managers are making use of tenant screening websites that provide detailed information on a prospective tenant. The manager may also contact the applicant's current landlord as well as past landlords, if possible, to collect additional information on the applicant's willingness and ability to pay rent. The ratio of prospective rent to gross monthly income is also a valuable screening tool; generally, this ratio should not exceed 30 percent. The amount of prospective rent as a percentage of the applicant's current income, however, is not a definitive measure of his or her ability to pay rent. Household size and the number of family members employed are also important factors.

All else being equal, managers prefer to lease residential units to households whose prior history indicates a probability of a long-term occupancy. This is sometimes referred to in the apartment industry as **permanence potential.** Reducing tenant turnover decreases costs for repair, cleaning, and re-leasing.

Tenant Mix.   In addition to creditworthy tenants, managers of multitenanted properties must also be concerned with tenant mix. **Tenant mix** is the synergism created by the current collection of tenants. Synergism, simply stated, means that with the right mix of tenants "the whole can be greater than the sum of its parts." In residential properties, this concept implies that managers should seek tenants with similar characteristics. This is why we frequently observe apartment complexes that cater to clienteles such as college students, young working professionals, or retirees. Mixing these groups is generally not a preferred strategy.

✓ **Concept Check**

21.6   Provide an example of a suboptimal tenant mix in an apartment complex.

The appropriate mix of tenants is often even more important in commercial properties, especially shopping centers and, to some extent, office buildings. A tenant unsuited to a location in a shopping center is not likely to attract customers for the adjoining stores. This explains why regional malls, for example, are tenanted primarily by fashion stores and gift shops. Someone shopping for a new suit at a department store is much more likely to stop at a nearby shoe store than a nearby bakery or drugstore. In contrast, neighborhood shopping centers anchored by a grocery store, which provides necessary food goods, will be occupied primarily by tenants who service the daily needs of those frequenting the grocer, for example, dry cleaners, beauty salons, liquor stores, and specialty and fast food restaurants.

The career of property manager requires strong interpersonal and analytical skills and a fair amount of negotiating prowess. This career path usually starts as an on-site assistant manager. Subsequent positions include becoming a property manager, a supervisor of several property managers, a regional manager for a large property management firm, or the owner of your own property management company. An additional attraction of a property management career is that it is a very good way to learn about many aspects of the commercial real estate industry; thus, property management can be an excellent stepping-stone to jobs in development, investments and syndication, and investment management.

Property management is growing steadily as a profession because of three significant trends. First, simultaneous growth of the population and its requirements for space has increased the total number of all types of buildings. Second, a larger percentage of real estate is investment property that requires professional management. Third, it is now widely acknowledged that property management requires specialized training and education.

Property management is a field that offers considerable opportunities for women. A survey by the Institute of Real Estate Management (IREM) found that 34 percent of its members and 49 percent of its professional designation candidates were women.

Source: Institute of Real Estate Management, *Principles of Real Estate Management,* 16th ed. (Chicago, IL: IREM, 2011, Chapter 1).

Property Management

Signing Leases

The last steps in a successful marketing and leasing program are negotiating and executing the lease. The lease is a contract between the owner (lessor) and the tenant (lessee) that transfers exclusive use and possession of the space to the tenant under the terms of the lease in return for rent or other consideration. Since the lease is the document that describes the rights and obligations of the owner and tenant, it is the primary determinant of a property's net rental income. In short, leases are the engines that drive property values.

An enforceable lease, at a minimum, must meet the usual requirements of a valid contract (discussed in Chapter 13): competent parties, mutual agreement, lawful objective, and sufficient consideration. The additional elements of a typical commercial lease are:

1. A beginning and ending date, and any provisions relating to renewal and cancellation.
2. Identification of the property owner and tenant.
3. A legal description of the leased premises.
4. The rental terms, including the amount of rent to be paid each period, the date it is due, and the place of payment and the tenant's responsibility, if any, for the payment of operating expenses.
5. Signatures of the parties to the lease.

Rent is usually paid monthly and due on the first day of the month. Commercial leases with durations longer than one year often include clauses that specify the method of adjusting rental payments over time.

If a lease does not state a specific purpose for which the property may be used, and if certain uses are not specifically disallowed by the lease, the tenant may use the property for any legal purpose. Generally, however, allowable uses are specified by the lease and a contrary use may be cause for termination of the lease by the owner.

It is not uncommon to encounter a commercial lease of 50 pages or more containing lengthy clauses that detail the duties and responsibilities of the owner and the tenant. Each clause has a specific purpose and negotiated revisions must be analyzed to determine their effect on property operations, income, and value. Clearly, the property manager must understand the purpose of each lease clause. Because of their importance and complexity, and because their terms vary significantly across property types, we devote an entire chapter (Chapter 22) to commercial leases and leasing strategy.

Exhibit 21-1 Top Third-Party Property Managers
(as of 2015)

	Square Footage of Managed Property (in millions of SF)
CBRE Group, Inc. (www.cbre.com)	3,700M
Cushman & Wakefield (www.cushmanwakefield.com)	3,029M
JLL (www.jll.com)	3,010M
Colliers International (www.colliers.com)	1,695M
Newmark Grubb Knight Frank (www.ngkf.com)	647M

Source: Data from *National Real Estate Investor Online,* www.nreionline.com

Collecting Rent

Most tenants pay their rent on time, but some will not. The property manager is responsible for the *prompt* collection of rent. Maintenance and repair expenditures, property taxes, utility bills, and other expenses of the property are paid out of rental income, and these expenses accumulate day to day. Thus, the timely collection of rental income is imperative. This undoubtedly explains why property management contracts usually tie the manager's compensation directly to rent collections.

> ✓ **Concept Check**
>
> **21.7** What is the owner's motivation for tying the property manager's compensation to the amount of rental income collected?

Managers should follow a strict and well-specified procedure for collecting overdue rent payments, as well as any applicable late fees when tenants are delinquent with their rent payments. In the event the tenant does not become current on his or her lease payments, the manager may eventually be forced to initiate eviction proceedings. Delinquency, collection, and eviction rights and procedures are always controlled by the lease and local statutes and the property manager must fully understand both the laws and the common practices that govern these matters.[1]

Complying with Landlord-Tenant Laws

State laws govern the landlord–tenant relationship and state courts are strict interpreters of commercial real estate lease agreements. So long as the lease document satisfies the requirements for a valid lease, federal and state law and the courts system are largely neutral with respect to the rights and obligations of most commercial owners and tenants. This reflects the assumption that tenants occupying office buildings, shopping centers, and industrial buildings are competent professionals fully capable of representing their position in lease negotiations.

In sharp contrast, however, federal and state legislators have been proactive in passing legislation aimed at protecting the rights and interests of households in residential rental properties. Presumably, this reflects the concern that property owners have a significant information advantage relative to potential tenants and that, left unchecked, owners would use this advantage to negotiate one-sided lease agreements.

---

1. For an expanded discussion of these issues, see Institute of Real Estate Management, *Principles of Real Estate Management,* 16th ed. (Chicago, IL: IREM, 2011), Chapter 8.

The apparent intent of state-based landlord-tenant laws is to "level the playing field" on which owners and households negotiate residential lease terms. This is accomplished by clearly spelling out the rights and obligations of both owners and tenants. For example, residential lease laws typically:

- Limit the size of the security deposit an owner can require.
- Require an owner to maintain the premises in a suitable condition for living.
- Limit the ability of an owner to enter the premises except in cases of emergency.
- Specify how many days' notice must be given before a landlord can terminate the lease.
- Permit a tenant to recover any prepaid rent and security deposit whenever a lease is terminated because of the landlord's noncompliance.

Tenants also have certain rights and obligations under these state laws. For example, a tenant must not willfully damage the premises, must use the facilities in a reasonable manner, and must comply with local housing and building codes concerning trash disposal and keeping the premises clean and safe.[2]

✓ **Concept Check**

21.8 Why do state lawmakers and courts seem more concerned about the welfare of apartment tenants than nonresidential tenants?

Maintaining Tenant Relations

Most owners of commercial real estate invested because of a profit motive—they had no burning desire to enter a service business. Nevertheless, owning and operating real estate *is* a service business and, similar to every other business, the customer must be kept satisfied. The existence of long-term leases does prevent tenants from immediately walking away if they become dissatisfied. However, leases expire and a high rate of turnover adds significantly to operating costs; tenant dissatisfaction can be very damaging to both current and future occupancy. Every communication with a tenant is an opportunity to build—or destroy—goodwill; thus, successful property managers are invariably skilled communicators who deal with tenant requests respectfully, conscientiously, and promptly.

Communicating with Owners

In addition to performing the tasks specified by the management agreement, successful property managers are skilled at communicating with the owner, or with the owner's asset manager if the property manager does not report directly to the owner. Owners, or asset managers acting on their behalf, are interested in the performance of the property, but some judgment on the part of the property manager may be involved in deciding the frequency of communications and the level of informational detail supplied to the owner. In addition to the standard reports on property performance (e.g., vacancies, turnover rates and collection losses), a good property manager will also offer his or her perspective and advice on decisions that ultimately rest with the asset manager or owner. For example, the property manager may feel strongly that a substantial rehabilitation of all or part of the premises is required to maximize the value of the property. If so, it is important that this recommendation be effectively communicated.

2. Although state landlord-tenant laws vary, some uniformity is provided by the Uniform Residential Landlord and Tenant Act (URLTA), which has been adopted by 14 states. The lease provisions required by URLTA can be found at www.law.cornell.edu/wex/landlord-tenant_law.

www.reiclub.com

Browse hundreds of articles and participate in discussion forums on real estate investment and management.

Repairing and Maintaining the Premises

Although tenants may be responsible through their lease agreements for maintaining interior walls and some of the heating and air-conditioning equipment, commercial properties are usually maintained, in large part, by the owner. Various levels of maintenance are required, depending on the type of property and the terms of the lease. The objective of maintenance and repair work, like every other aspect of property management, should be to meet the goals of the property owners, which usually center on maximization of the property's market value.

The property manager should develop a comprehensive maintenance program approved by the owner or the asset manager. This program should include a plan for replacing short-lived items, as well as anticipating nonrecurring capital expenditures, such as roof replacements and the repair and resurfacing of parking lots. A comprehensive maintenance program that includes annual and seasonal inspections forces a manager to be proactive rather than reactive in dealing with potential problems. The ability to react promptly and effectively will produce long-term savings in operating costs.

A comprehensive maintenance program also aids with tenant retention. If tenants are satisfied with their environment, they will be less likely to vacate their space when their lease terms expire. This will reduce vacancies and lease turnover costs. Tenant safety is also an issue. Owners are responsible for fire prevention, sanitation, and security. If someone is injured as a result of neglected maintenance, the economic consequences can be severe—even if liability insurance is in place. Regular maintenance reduces potential hazards and provides a safer environment for everyone on the property.

> ✓ **Concept Check**
>
> **21.9**   List two benefits of a written comprehensive maintenance program.

Maintenance and repair of the property is an ongoing process that can be separated into four principal categories:[3]

1. **Custodial maintenance** is the day-to-day cleaning and upkeep required to maintain value—and tenants.
2. **Corrective maintenance** is the ordinary repairs to a building and its equipment on a day-to-day basis. Examples include fixing a leaking roof, repairing a broken window, painting, stripping and refinishing a floor, and other routine tasks.
3. **Preventive maintenance** is a program of regular inspections and care to avert potential problems.
4. **Deferred maintenance** is ordinary custodial or corrective maintenance not performed at the time a problem is detected.

By deferring maintenance and repairs, managers can boost the short-run *NOI* of the property. However, a deteriorating building is the end result of successive decisions over a longer period of time to forgo adequate maintenance and repairs. Thus, deferred maintenance will eventually diminish the use, occupancy, and value of the property.

Maintenance as an Investment Decision.   The decision to spend on maintenance and repairs is the most frequent ongoing investment decision property owners face. Ideally, maintenance and repairs should be performed over the investment holding period to the point where the present value of the outlays for maintenance and repair equals the present value of the loss of net income and reversion value averted over the holding period. Stated differently, expenditures for maintenance and repairs should be made at a level that maximizes the owner's rate of return over the investment holding period.

---

3. See Institute of Real Estate Management, *Principles of Real Estate Management,* 16th ed. (Chicago, IL: IREM, 2011), Chapter 10.

EXAMPLE 21-1   ONGOING MAINTENANCE DECISIONS

Consider the following simple example. If a property owner spends on average $10,000 a year for 10 years on maintenance and repairs, her cash flow will be reduced annually by this amount. However, if she does not spend this amount, she will not be able to keep rents at market levels, vacancies will increase, the resale value of the property in 10 years will be lower, or all may occur. Assume that she would lose about $8,000 a year in net income and would realize a loss of $75,000 in lower property value at the time of sale. The maintenance and repair outlays represent a cost to the investor; the loss of net income and reversion value averted are the investor's gains. If the owner could earn a 10 percent return on any funds not invested in maintenance and repairs, she would conclude that the present value of the $10,000 annual maintenance and repair outlays is $61,446. This cost is less than the present value of the averted loss, or $78,073.[4]

In this example, the property is kept in a state of "normal" maintenance and repair over the investor's holding period. There would be a limit, however, to the amount that would be spent on maintenance and repair over the holding period. This limit would be reached when the present value of the cash outlays for maintenance and repair equals the present value of the loss averted.

✓ Concept Check

21.10 Investment in maintenance can be thought of as positive or negative net present value "project." What are the potential inflows associated with a maintenance expenditure? What are the outflows?

Although the above property example depicts the economics of the maintenance and repair decision, it is obvious that market imperfections and other characteristics of real estate as an investment prevent such precision in the maintenance and repair calculations and decision. Investors generally cannot accurately project the loss in net income or reversion value that is avoided over the entire investment holding period. Moreover, the length of the investment holding period is itself an uncertain variable. The time horizon involved in the maintenance and repair decision is, as a practical matter, the foreseeable short run. However, an investor can recognize how the property compares with other competing properties in the local market and can judge the level of maintenance and repair necessary to keep the property competitive in the short run.

The simple example also overlooks the requirement of larger expenditures on maintenance and repair as the building ages, to prevent a given loss in net income and reversion value. The onset of physical deterioration cannot be postponed indefinitely by maintenance and repairs, and both functional and locational obsolescence can render additional maintenance and repair expenditures infeasible. Decisions made early in the investment holding period to keep the property in good repair may not be made later when no amount of expenditure on maintenance and repair will overcome the debilitating effects of a neighborhood in transition to another land use or of a functionally obsolete heating system. A property

4. Discounting future cash flows is discussed in Chapter 14. The keystrokes for calculating the $61,446 present value of the $10,000 annual expenditure are $N = 10, I = 10, PV = ?, PMT = 10,000$, and $FV = 0$. The present value of the reduction in annual income that is averted by the maintenance program is $49,157 and the calculator keystrokes are $N = 10, I = 10, PV = ?, PMT = 8,000$, and $FV = 0$. The present value of the reduction in reversion value that is averted by the annual expenditures is $28,916 and the calculator keystrokes are $N = 10, I = 10, PV = ?, PMT = 0$, and $FV = 75,000$. Thus, the total present value of the averted loss is $78,073 ($49,157 + $28,916).

Exhibit 21-2   Contents of a Management Agreement

- Parties to the agreement
- Description of the property
- Term of the agreement
- Responsibilities of the manager
  - Financial management
  - Reports to ownership
  - General property management
- Obligations and responsibilities of the owner
  - Insurance
  - Operating and reserve fund
  - Liability
  - Legal and regulatory compliance
- Compensation for management services
- Provision for termination of agreement

Source: Institute of Real Estate Management, *Principles of Real Estate Management,* 16th ed. (Chicago, IL: IREM 2011), Chapter 5.

manager must recognize when market conditions have changed to the extent that maintenance and repair can no longer prevent loss of net operating income. This requires significant experience.

An owner whose property is in a strong market position, where fewer services can be offered to tenants for the same dollar of rental income, and where the owner will not lose tenants if the property is undermaintained, can reduce maintenance and repairs without affecting the rental income or the value of the property, at least in the short run. Such an owner faces a relatively inelastic demand for space, where the quantity of rental services demanded is not as responsive to price as it is in less desirable markets.[5]

Property Management Agreements

The above discussion of the functions of a property manager clearly indicates that the manager assumes the role of the owner in conducting the day-to-day operations of the property. Tenants often do not know who owns the property; thus, they often view the manager as the "landlord." This view is justified because the property manager can have the legal authority to advertise the property for lease, set rents, negotiate and sign leases, hire and pay employees to operate and maintain the property, collect rents, and file all necessary reports to federal, state, and local agencies. Like the broker who operates on behalf of the seller under a listing agreement, the property manager works under a **management agreement** between the property owner and the property management firm. This agreement must be carefully prepared and negotiated and must clearly establish the manager's duties, authority, and compensation.

The typical contents of a management agreement are listed in Exhibit 21-2. With respect to financial management, the agreement should carefully specify any requirements on the part of the manager to maintain separate accounts for moneys collected from tenants. The manager's authority to negotiate and execute lease contracts must be clarified, as should his or her authority to hire and fire employees and to enter into service contracts with vendors. Although the management agreement may be arranged for virtually any time period, many property managers prefer a three-year contract to provide adequate time to implement the agreed upon management plan.

---

5. Another take on the value of maintenance and repairs is that the payoff from these expenditures tends, in our opinion, to vary positively with the expected growth rate in market rents.

The management agreement establishes a relationship in which the real estate manager (agent) is authorized to act on behalf of the owner (principal). In the role of agent, the manager must exercise care in managing both money and property for the owner (fiduciary capacity). Being a fiduciary carries certain legal obligations. The manager must be loyal to the interest of the client and not engage in activities contrary to the loyalty. This means scrupulous attention to the handling of the owner's funds and not accepting any fee, commission, discount, gift, or other benefit that has not been disclosed to and approved by the owner-client. Real estate managers who achieve the Certified Property Manager (CPM) designation, obtained through the Institute of Real Estate Management, subscribe to a specific code of ethics. In addition to the fiduciary obligations noted here, the CPM Code of Ethics requires managers to hold proprietary information in confidence, to maintain accurate financial and business records for the managed property, and to protect the owner's funds. The Code also outlines the manager's duties to his or her employer, to former clients and employers, and to tenants; sets forth requirements for managing the client's property; and addresses relations with other members of the profession and compliance with laws and regulations. Ethical practices are an important part of professionalism in real estate management.

The Manager as the Owner's Agent

Source: Institute of Real Estate Management, *Principles of Real Estate Management,* 16th ed. (Chicago, IL: IREM, 2011), Chapter 5.

Owners also have responsibilities that must be detailed in the management agreement. For example, the owner is usually required to provide the manager with all essential documents such as existing leases, insurance policies, and employment and service contracts. Of course, owners must provide the manager with adequate resources to fund operating and capital expenditures as they occur.

An important characteristic of the management contract is that it creates an **agency relationship** between the manager and owner. This agency relationship empowers the manager/agent to serve as the owner's fiduciary; thus, the manager's words and actions are binding on the owner. The implications of this agency relationship are explored in more detail in the following Career Focus.

✓ Concept Check

21.11   What type of relationship is created between the owner and the manager by the property management contract?

The typical management agreement requires the manager to obtain permission from the owner or, perhaps, from the asset manager before making any structural changes to the property. In short, the authority of the property manager is usually limited to the normal operating tasks of managing real estate. Rehabilitation, modernization, and conversion of the property to another use are covered by other express grants of authority by the owner. Generally, the management agreement can be terminated when the term of the agreement expires, by notice from either the owner or the managing agent according to contract provisions, or by mutual agreement.

✓ Concept Check

21.12   The property management agreement usually conveys authority to the manager to perform what kinds of tasks?

Management Fees

The management agreement provides for a management fee, which is usually a percentage of the property's effective gross income. Typically, the percentage is lower for larger properties because of the economies of scale associated with providing property management services. The fee usually ranges from 3 to 6 percent, although higher fees are not uncommon for smaller, more-management intensive, properties. It is usually appropriate for the manager to negotiate separate fees for leasing a new building, overseeing rehabilitation or remodeling projects, or any services provided by the manager that are not part of regular management duties.

As with any fiduciary relationship, property management contracts should be written to align as closely as possible the interests of the agent (manager) with those of the principal (owner). The typical property management fee is a percentage of *gross* rental income. This would seem to create an agency problem in that the agreement does not give managers the incentives to control operating expenses while they attempt to increase rental income. For example, the manager may be tempted to overmaintain the property in an attempt to boost occupancy and gross rental income.

Basing the property management fee on net rental income, that is, *NOI* rather than effective gross income (*EGI*), would better align the interests of the owner and manager. However, this arrangement is seldom observed. One explanation for basing the management fee on *EGI* is that the amount of collected rental income is easy to verify, whereas the calculation of "net" income is complicated by the requirement to fully account for all operating and capital expenses. Moreover, the use of net income presents other problems. For example, if management compensation is based on monthly *NOI*, the manager may have an incentive to delay discretionary spending for maintenance and repairs. Such a strategy may boost *NOI* in the short run, but could be harmful to the owner's interests in the longer run. In short, although there appears to be an incentive compatibility issue associated with the use of gross rental income as the basis for the management fee, the simplicity of its calculation is a clear advantage. In addition, professional property managers are keenly aware they will not be retained by the owner when the contract expires if they have not worked hard to maximize the net income of the property. The incentive to keep the owner's business is clearly a strong one.[6]

> ### Concept Check
>
> **21.13** A prediction of "agency theory" is that owners would be better off if property management fees were based on net operating income. Why?

Professional Associations and Designations

www.irem.org

Institute of Real Estate Management (IREM).

www.boma.org

Building Owners and Managers Association International (BOMA).

www.narpm.org

National Association of Residential Property Managers.

College-level courses in property management are not widely available. Instead, most property managers learn the profession primarily by working in the industry. However, a number of professional and trade organizations exist in the field of property management. Of these, the Institute of Real Estate Management (IREM) and the Building Owners and Managers Association International (BOMA) are probably the best known. These and other groups provide both entry-level and continuing professional education for their members and work to enhance the status of professional property managers. Both of these groups offer professional designations that identify holders as having attained specific levels of competence or experience in property management.

IREM awards the certified property manager (CPM) designation to members who obtain significant property management experience and successfully complete a set of required courses in property management. The CPM designation is aimed at those who manage larger residential, office, industrial, or retail properties. IREM also offers the Accredited Resident Manager (ARM) designation for those individuals specializing in the

---

6. Readers familiar with principal-agent theory are aware that many agency problems can be solved, or at least mitigated, by repeated "games" between the principal and the agent. Each time a game is played—that is, each time a contract is signed and the parties perform—both sides reveal information about their intentions and abilities. This information can then be used by both sides to negotiate a "better" replacement contract. The problem with property management contracts is that, given their long-term nature, renegotiation does not frequently occur and therefore the contractual relationship is difficult to refine.

management of apartment buildings. The Accredited Management Organization (AMO) designation is awarded to management companies that meet the necessary requirements for certification.

BOMA provides educational programs aimed primarily at owners and managers of office buildings. BOMA awards the Real Property Administrator (RPA) designation to those who successfully complete the required course work and pass the accompanying comprehensive exam.

Asset Management

The typical functions of a property manager are summarized in the bottom portion of Exhibit 21-3. Although important, property management is but one of many asset management functions that must typically be performed during the investment holding period, as is depicted in the top portion of Exhibit 21-3. We first summarize the development of the real estate asset management profession, then briefly describe the major functions of an asset manager.

It is helpful to refer back to Exhibit 17-3 and the accompanying discussion. There we learned that most U.S. commercial real estate equity is held by noninstitutional investors, including sole proprietors, wealthy families, limited partnerships, and limited liability companies. The required asset management functions in these entities are typically carried out by the managing equity investor—that is, the general partner in a limited partnership or the managing member in an LLC. Managing equity investors may, in turn, perform the property management duties themselves (if the entity's assets are relatively small and local), use a property management subsidiary of their firm (with approval from the investors), or hire an independent third-party property management firm.

What about the U.S. commercial real estate held by institutional investors? For the most part, these institutional investors prefer to hire nationally recognized asset managers—also called investment advisers—to invest in and manage commercial real estate on their

Exhibit 21-3 Property Management—Just One Aspect of Asset Management

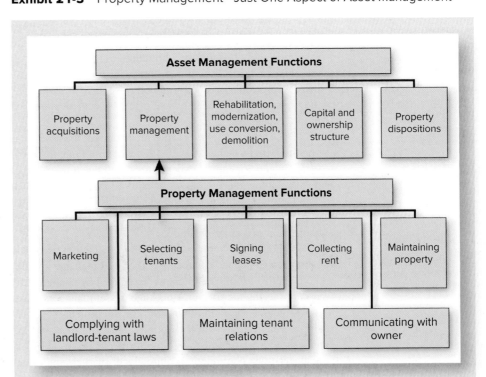

www.ifma.org

International Facilities
Management Association.

Exhibit 21-4   Top Asset Managers/Advisors of North American Assets
(as of 2014)

	Assets under Management (in $ billions)
Brookfield Asset Management	$66.1
The Blackstone Group	57.5
MetLife Real Estate Investors	41.1
Principal Real Estate Investors	34.1
JP Morgan Asset Management	32.1

behalf. Thus, the counterparts to the "managing equity investors" operating in the private entrepreneurial investment arena are "asset managers" and "investment advisers" operating in the institutional and securitized arena. The top five managers/advisers of commercial real estate assets located in North America are listed in Exhibit 21-4.

> ✓ **Concept Check**
>
> **21.14**   What kinds of functions do asset managers operating in the institutional and securitized arena perform that are similar to those operating in the private entrepreneurial investment market?

Asset Management Functions

www.realcomm.com

Link to free newsletter that addresses technology issues impacting property and asset management.

An important function performed by many asset managers is to find specific assets in which the owner/client can invest. Once assets have been identified for purchase, the manager must line up the financing, negotiate the acquisition price, and then oversee the due diligence and closing processes. These activities are required because whole assets are typically traded in the private real estate market, so investors generally end up with a controlling ownership interest in the property. These functions distinguish real estate asset managers from those who manage stock and bond portfolios for investors. Managers of stock portfolios, for example, do not have to go out and *find* assets in which to invest—thousand of stocks (and other securities) are traded on public exchanges. Nor do they have to negotiate purchase prices—securities are purchased at market value in the public exchanges.

Once commercial properties are acquired, the asset manager must monitor and control operating performance. Usually this will entail making periodic site visits, preparing long-term budgets for capital expenditures, and when necessary, appealing property tax assessments. Although decisions on whether to improve the property are required less frequently than ongoing maintenance and repair decisions, asset managers must recognize and report to owners value-enhancing opportunities for rehabilitation, remodeling, modernization, or conversion to a more profitable use.

Although most commercial mortgages cannot be costlessly prepaid if mortgage interest rates decline (see Chapter 16), the asset manager should periodically consider whether the owner's cost of capital could be reduced by changing the loan-to-value ratio or by otherwise altering the financing package. Asset managers also must be aware of opportunities to restructure the equity ownership of the project, perhaps through joint venture partnerships, joint venture buyout options, land sale-leasebacks, or complete sale-leasebacks. (These alternative financing structures are discussed in Chapter 16.) Finally, the asset manager must continually monitor local market conditions and assess whether or not to recommend the sale of the property.

Performance Evaluation and Compensation

Real estate investment managers are often compensated based on the market value of assets under management. Typical asset management fees ranged from 0.5 to 1.5 percent of the estimated value of managed assets.

Similar to the problems associated with basing a property manager's compensation on gross rental income, the policy of compensating asset managers based strictly on the value of the assets under management produces a potential agency problem. Generally, an owner's interests are best served by asset management decisions that maximize the investor's rate of return. However, if managers are compensated based on the value of the assets under management, they have an incentive to find, acquire, and *hold* assets on behalf of the investor. Such a compensation scheme offers no direct incentive for managers to *sell* properties, even if current conditions suggest they should, nor are they motivated to select for acquisition only those properties with the highest expected rates of return.

To better align the interests of owners and managers, some in the industry use performance-based compensation for asset managers, at least in part. With a performance-based management contract, a manager's fees are tied directly to the rate of return earned by investors on the portfolio of managed properties.

If some or all of the manager's compensation is based on the return performance of the assets under management, the owner and manager must agree at the outset on the appropriate benchmark for evaluation. A **benchmark** is a reference point that can be used as a standard to quantify the relative performance of an asset manager (an agent) on behalf of an investor (a principal).

✓ Concept Check

21.15 Describe the traditional compensation scheme for asset managers and the incentive problem it may create.

---

www.ncreif.com

National Council of Real Estate Investment Fiduciaries.

www.nareit.com

National Association of Real Estate Investment Trusts.

www.wilshire.com/ indexinfo/index.html

Wilshire Associates.

What return indexes can be used to evaluate the performance of the manager/adviser? If the manager has been hired by the owner to acquire and manage a portfolio of publicly traded real estate investment trusts (REITs), there are a number of potential benchmark REIT indexes from which to choose, including the various indexes and subindexes produced by FTSE NAREIT, MSCI, and Wilshire Associates. However, the majority of real estate investment advisers are employed by U.S. investors to acquire and manage portfolios of *privately* held and traded commercial real estate assets. In the private arena, benchmark return indexes are produced by the National Council of Real Estate Investment Fiduciaries (NCREIF) and MSCI.

A Closer Look at the Decision to Improve or Alter a Property

www.ftse.com/products/ indices/nareit

FTSE NAREIT U.S. real estate indicies

www.msci.com/ real-estate

MSCI is an independent provider of return indicies

Decisions to improve a property are less frequent than decisions to maintain and repair it. In contrast to maintenance and repair expenditures, which are operating expenses, the improvement (alteration) decision generally involves a capital expenditure meant to increase the value of the structure.

An improvement to the structure can involve rehabilitation, remodeling, modernization, or adaptive reuse. **Rehabilitation** is the restoration of a property to satisfactory condition without changing the floor plan, form, or style of the structure. Rehabilitation removes the effects of prolonged undermaintenance, and may involve painting, replacement of a roof, replastering, or replacement of deteriorated portions of the building.

Remodeling changes the floor plan, form, or style of a structure to correct functional or economic deficiencies. Remodeling may rearrange partitions to alter a floor plan, or it may replace obsolete electrical, plumbing, and heating systems. Remodeling may result in a conversion of the property from a use no longer suitable for the site to one that is

EXAMPLE 21-2 MEDFIRST OFFICE BUILDING

An improvement should be undertaken only if the value added to the property at least equals the cost of the improvement. Consider, as an example, the MedFirst office building. MedFirst is a small 10-year-old medical office building on a major traffic artery near downtown. Other small office buildings of fairly high quality occupy the area, and this usage is expected to continue. The building contains 7,650 square feet of rentable area. Rental rates are currently $14 per square foot.

Exhibit 21-5 provides a "before and after" valuation analysis of a $130,000 rehabilitation of the MedFirst building. Net operating income is expected to increase from $66,134 before rehabilitation to $79,726 after; this increase is the net result of higher rents, lower vacancy, a lower operating expense ratio, and lower capital expenditures. The market value of the MedFirst property is expected to be $995,844 after rehabilitation, a gain of $151,019. The gain in property value is compared with the cost of the improvements, which include material, labor, the contractor's profit, architect's fees, and an allowance for contingencies. Further, if undertaking the improvements prevented renting part or all of the structure for a period of time, the value of the lost rental income should be included as a cost. The estimated total cost of the improvements to the MedFirst building is $130,000.

The value added ($151,019) exceeds the estimated cost of improvements ($130,000) by $21,019, which is about 16 percent of the cost of improvements. The investor contemplating this rehabilitation project would undertake it only if sufficient confidence existed in the factors influencing the post-rehabilitation value and the total improvement cost.

Exhibit 21-5 Valuation of the Rehabilitation of MedFirst Office Building

	Before	After
Rent per sq. ft.	$ 14.00	$ 15.80
Net rentable area (sq. ft.)	7,650	7,650
Vacancy and collection losses	5%	3%
Operating expense ratio	30%	28%
Annual capital expenditures as a percent of effective gross income	5%	4%
Net operating income	$ 66,134	$ 79,726
Cap rate for building income	0.09	0.09
Market value of building ($NOI \div$ cap rate)	$734,825	$885,844
Site value (from market)	$110,000	$110,000
Total market value	$844,825	$995,844

Gain in value	$151,019	
Cost of improvements	$130,000	
Excess over cost	$ 21,019 (or 16%)	

competitive in the market. An **adaptive reuse** is a conversion in which the remodeling produces a creative reuse of the structure that is different from its original purpose. From an economic point of view, remodeling and rehabilitation are positive actions that add value to the property. Maintenance and repair, on the other hand, are preventive measures undertaken to prevent a loss of value.

Capital improvements can affect rents, vacancy and collection losses, operating expenses, and the reversion value of the property at the end of the investment holding

Corporate Real Estate

Many real estate professionals are employed by firms to provide in-house, site-selection, and development expertise. For example, firms such as fast-food restaurants, convenience store franchisers, supermarkets, and retailers are prospective employers for corporate real estate specialists. Site selection and development work require knowledge of a firm's product, the demographics it serves, and the linkages the firm requires to its customers and suppliers. Site-selection experts must understand urban growth patterns, transportation linkages, and market analysis. They must also be able to interpret the impact of zoning requirements, building codes, site frontage and visibility, topography, easements, drainage, utility services, and soils on a firm's site-choice decision. In addition, they need to be able to assess market values in order to negotiate reasonable purchase prices on behalf of their employer. Courses in appraisal, investment analysis, development, and urban planning will be beneficial to those who expect to pursue a career in corporate real estate.

Source: Adapted from *Real Estate Career Paths*, University of Cincinnati; business.uc. edu/centers/ real-estate/ academics/career-paths.htm

---

period. Many improvement decisions will affect rents, in some cases because after alteration the building will have more rentable area or because the quality of the services the building provides will have increased. Vacancy and collection losses also may be reduced if the improved property is more competitive in its market. Property tax payments and insurance premiums may increase if the improvements increase the value of the property. Operating expenses (e.g., utilities) may increase because the building is now larger, or decrease because of the greater efficiency of the improved property.

Abandonment, Demolition, and Reuse

Casual inspection of many urban areas will reveal abandoned buildings. Sometimes the abandoned property is left vacant. Demolition will occur only after the existing building has accumulated substantial physical deterioration and functional and locational obsolescence. In some instances, the building may be removed only after the court found it to be a hazard to public health and safety. However, the removal of relatively new buildings for a replacement use can also sometimes be observed. Such demolitions may be the result of a "taking" for a public purpose (see Chapter 4), or they may reflect profit-motivated decisions in the private sector.

The speed of reuse will depend upon the factors that affect the demand for land uses feasible at the given location and upon competition of alternative sites. At the time of reuse, the value of the site is determined by the new building, which is judged to be the highest and best use of the site. As discussed in Chapter 7, if an existing improvement already occupied the site, it no longer represented the highest and best use of the site.

Reuse of an urban site occurs when the site value under the new structure is sufficient to permit acquisition of the site and existing building at market value and to pay the cost of demolition and preparation of the site for the new structure. The reuse must yield a competitive return on the required investment.

Managing Corporate Real Estate Assets

In Chapter 17 we estimated that non-real estate corporations own in excess of $12 trillion in real estate. These real estate assets account for 25 to 40 percent of the total assets of large industrial firms. Corporate real estate includes not only specialized production and storage facilities, but also retail outlets, industrial warehouses, and office buildings that contain space suitable and attractive to a broad range of potential users.

Despite the magnitude of their real estate holdings, many non-real estate corporations have historically expended limited effort to manage these assets effectively. Instead, some corporations have largely viewed real estate as a necessary evil, which requires the significant commitment of corporate capital for relatively long periods of time to meet the needs of their principal business activities. And, although firms may carefully examine the initial acquisitions of real estate assets, many spend insufficient time thinking strategically about these assets once they have been added to the corporate balance sheet.

In recent years, however, many corporations have begun to pay increased attention to their real estate assets. Some now employ in-house corporate real estate and facilities management personnel, while others rely primarily on asset management consultants to help them rethink and restructure their real estate holdings. Many of the same firms that supply asset and investment advisory services to institutional real estate investors also supply consulting and management services to non-real estate companies. In addition, corporate real estate heads or consulting asset managers often deal with site analysis, buy versus lease decisions, acquisition and disposition, sale leaseback arrangements, property tax appeals, and a host of facility management decisions.

An important development in corporate real estate management has been the increased activity in the sale-leaseback market. Increasingly, corporations are recognizing that it is not always necessary to own a real estate asset to have control over its use. With leasing, corporate users can control and use properties without having to commit the resources necessary to own them. As a result, many corporate property owners are executing sale-leaseback transactions and then entering into net lease arrangements with the buyers of the property. With a sale-leaseback, corporate sellers can convert illiquid real estate assets into cash and the sale proceeds can then be plowed back into the main business and core assets of the company.

If corporate America is discovering the benefits of sale-leasebacks and net leases, who is taking the opposite side in these transactions? Interestingly, a broad range of investors, including pension funds, limited partnerships, and other investment opportunity funds, have come to regard net lease investments as one of the most stable and valuable property segments.

www.corenetglobal.org

Global Corporate Real Estate Network (CoreNet)—world's largest association for corporate real estate professionals.

www.calkain.com

Site of leading net lease property firm contains useful information on net lease properties and investing.

> ✓ **Concept Check**
>
> **21.16**   What is the most significant recent development in corporate real estate management?

Summary

Owners of income-producing real estate often seek the services of professional property managers. Property managers work at or near the site or sites they are managing. Property managers are responsible for negotiating leases, ensuring that tenants are satisfied, that rent is paid, and that rents reflect market conditions. Property managers work to maintain property values by skillfully selecting tenants, negotiating leases, dealing with tenant needs, accounting for income, managing operating expenses, and physically maintaining the property. Effective property managers must know their market—that is, know the competitive rental rate for their property and what concessions, if any, are being offered to tenants by direct competitors. They must be skilled at marketing their properties, understand laws regarding contractual relationships between landlords and tenants, be able to control operating expenses, and have a good understanding of property maintenance and repair issues. They are responsible to the owners, either directly or indirectly through an asset manager.

Although important, property management is just one of many asset management functions that must typically be performed during the investment holding period. For example, unlike property managers, asset managers are often charged with finding and acquiring properties on behalf of the owner/investor. Once the property is acquired, asset managers must hire and then oversee the property manager, unless the firm provides property management services. Asset managers must recognize and report to owners value-enhancing opportunities for rehabilitation, remodeling, modernization, or conversion of the property to a more profitable use. If such expenditures are undertaken, the asset manager is usually responsible for overseeing the completion of the improvements. Asset managers also may recommend changes in the capital or ownership structure, as well as recommend advantageous times to sell the property.

Key Terms

Adaptive reuse   572
Agency relationship   567
Asset manager   556
Benchmark   571
Corrective maintenance   564
Credit tenants   559

Custodial maintenance   564
Deferred maintenance   564
Management agreement   566
Permanence potential   560
Preventive maintenance   564
Property managers   556

Rehabilitation   571
Remodeling   571
Tenant mix   560
Tenant reps   558

Test Problems

Answer the following multiple-choice problems:

1. The Institute of Real Estate Management (IREM) awards which of the following designations?
   a. REM.
   b. CPM.
   c. MAI.
   d. RPA.

2. A contractual relationship in which an individual must act in the best interests of a principal when dealing with a third party is termed:
   a. An agency relationship.
   b. A lease arrangement.
   c. A tenant–landlord relationship.
   d. A joint venture contractual arrangement.

3. The requirement of a real estate property manager to act in the best interests of the landlord when dealing with a tenant is termed:
   a. An associate responsibility.
   b. Due process.
   c. A fiduciary responsibility.
   d. An implied responsibility of the employment contract.

4. Which of these is *not* typically a responsibility of a property manager?
   a. Marketing and leasing.
   b. Tenant relations.
   c. Maintenance programs.
   d. Income tax analysis.

5. Remodeling and rehabilitation:
   a. Are preventive measures undertaken to prevent a loss in value.
   b. Are most likely categorized as operating expenses.
   c. Are expected to add value to the property if undertaken.
   d. Can usually be undertaken by the property manager without consulting the owner or asset manager.

6. Both the owner and the manager may be better off if property management compensation were based on a percentage of the property's:
   a. Potential gross income.
   b. Effective gross income.

   c. Net operating income.
   d. Market value.

7. The following are necessary for a lease to be valid, *except:*
   a. Consideration.
   b. Written leases, if longer than one year, in most states.
   c. Tenant's contact phone number, or address, in the event of an emergency.
   d. Statements to the effect that the tenant agrees to lease the property for a specified period and that the owner and tenant agree to the terms of the rent.

8. The asset manager is generally NOT responsible for:
   a. Finding properties for the investor/principal.
   b. Arranging financing for properties.
   c. Making maintenance decisions.
   d. Overseeing the due-diligence of the purchase for the investor/principal.

9. Demolition of an existing property on an urban site will likely occur:
   a. After the building has been abandoned for a reasonable period of time.
   b. When the highest and best use of the property is a tax-payer use, such as a parking lot or recreational park.
   c. When the site value, assuming a new use, exceeds the value of the site under its existing use, plus the cost of demolition.
   d. When the site value, under its existing use, exceeds the cost of demolition.

10. For non-real estate corporations, which of the following is not a potential advantage of a real estate sale-leaseback?
   a. The firm can convert an illiquid asset into cash.
   b. More of the firm's capital can be invested in its core business.
   c. The firm benefits from property appreciation that occurs after the sale-leaseback.
   d. The firm may reduce its overall financing costs.

www.mhhe.com/lingarcher5e

Study Questions

1. An investor purchased a small property with an equity investment of $100,000 and an $800,000 mortgage. She has held the property for five years, and the mortgage now has a balance of $750,000. The market value of her property is estimated to be $950,000. What is her current equity investment?

2. What should be included as rehabilitation costs to be matched by value added after rehabilitation?

3. In what ways are the maintenance and repair decision and the rehabilitation decision similar? How do they differ?

4. What factors can change after rehabilitation of a property to produce a higher "after" rehabilitation value than "before" value?

5. What does the property management agreement accomplish?

6. How does routine maintenance and repair affect a property's performance?

7. Define *deferred maintenance* and list some examples.

8. How is the financial compensation for property managers usually determined? What "agency" problem does this seem to create?

9. Why is the tenant mix critically important to the performance of shopping center investments?

10. In the real estate asset management/investment advisory business, why has performance-based management replaced, or at least partially supplemented, the "traditional" scheme for compensating some asset managers?

11. In the context of asset management agreements in the private commercial real estate industry, what is a benchmark index? What is the most typical benchmark index?

12. With respect to complying with applicable landlord-tenant laws, is it easier to manage an apartment complex or an office building? Explain.

EXPLORE THE WEB

Landlord-tenant law governs the rental of commercial and residential property. It is composed primarily of state statutory and common law. A number of states have based their statutory law on the Uniform Residential Landlord and Tenant Act (URLTA). Cornell University Law School maintains a website (www.law.cornell.edu/wex/landlord-tenant_law) that contains useful information on landlord-tenant laws along with links to federal and state legislative reference materials. Visit the website and read the responsibilities of both landlords and tenants under URLTA.

Solutions to Concept Checks

1. Ongoing asset management is important in commercial real estate markets because the ownership of commercial real estate is characterized by long holding periods, which requires a prolonged period of ongoing management. Also, a significant portion of the total return on real estate investment usually comes in the form of periodic net rental income, not appreciation in property value. The maximization of periodic income requires significant management effort.

2. The owner has three basic choices for leasing nonresidential property: use an independent leasing agent/broker, use an employee, or use the property manager. Each has advantages and disadvantages.

3. Tenant reps (or representatives) are licensed real estate brokers who specialize in helping tenants find suitable rental space.

4. The leasing commission is $11,700 ($6,500 × 12 × 3) × 0.05.

5. "Credit" tenants are large companies whose publicly traded debt has been rated "investment grade" by one or more of the independent credit rating agencies.

6. An example of a suboptimal tenant mix in an apartment complex is a mixture of young families with children and retired couples without children.

7. All operating expenses for which the owner is responsible are paid out of the property's rental income. Thus, owners have an incentive to make sure the property's rental income is maximized. Tying the property manager's compensation to rent collections helps ensure that rental income is maximized.

8. State lawmakers and courts seem more concerned about the welfare of apartment tenants than commercial tenants because apartment seekers are generally in the market infrequently; thus, it is assumed that knowledgeable apartment owners and managers have a significant informational advantage over most prospective tenants. In contrast, commercial tenants are assumed to be fully capable of negotiating with commercial owners.

9. A written comprehensive maintenance program forces a manager to be proactive in planning for and dealing with required maintenance expenditures. This preparedness increases the ability of the manager to react quickly and effectively which, in turn, produces cost savings and satisfied tenants.

10. The inflows associated with an investment in maintenance are some combination of increased rents, decreased vacancies, and higher future sale prices. The outflow is the total cost of the maintenance expenditure.

11. A property management contract creates an agency relationship, which establishes a fiduciary responsibility on the part of the manager to act in the best interests of the property owner.

12. The authority of property managers is usually limited to the normal day-to-day task of operating the property. Permission of the owner or the asset manager, if the latter is a different entity than the property manager, is typically required for capital expenditures, especially those that entail significant rehabilitation, modernization, or expansion of the property.

13. Owners would seem better off if property management fees are based on net operating income because when such fees are based on gross rental income, the manager has an incentive to maximize occupancy and rental income, perhaps with insufficient regard for limiting operating expenses. In contrast, net operating income is the property's fundamental determinant of value; thus, if the manager is given an incentive to maximize it, the incentives of the owner and the manager would seem to be better aligned.

14. Asset managers perform tasks in the institutional and securitized arena that are similar to those of managing equity investors. That is, they are usually involved in decisions concerning property acquisitions, property dispositions, rehabilitation and modernization, and capital and ownership structure, in addition to day-to-day property management tasks and decisions.

15. Traditionally, asset management fees were based strictly on the market value of assets under management. This may create an incentive for managers to acquire and hold properties with insufficient regard for the purchase price and to continue to hold properties even if the interests of the owner would be best served by disposing of the asset.

16. The most significant development in corporate real estate management is the increased propensity of non-real estate firms to sell their real estate assets, redeploy the capital back into the main business of the company, and then lease the property back on a long-term basis to assure the company of its use and control.

Additional Readings

Burrell, J. *The Rental Property Manager's Toolbox: A Complete Guide Including PreWritten Forms, Agreements, Letters, and Legal Notices: With Companion CD-ROM.* Ocala, FL: Atlantic Publishing Group, 2006.

Evans, M. *Opportunities in Property Management Careers.* New York: McGraw-Hill Professional, 2007.

Income Expense Analysis: Conventional Apartments. Chicago, IL: Institute of Real Estate Management, 2015.

Income Expense Analysis: Office Buildings. Chicago, IL: Institute of Real Estate Management, 2015.

Income Expense Analysis: Shopping Centers. Chicago, IL: Institute of Real Estate Management, 2015.

Insitute of Real Estate Management. *What Property Managers Do: IREM Real Estate Management Job Analysis.* Chicago, IL: IREM, 2016.

Kyle R.C., M. S. Spodek, and F. M. Baird. *Property Management,* 6th ed. Chicago, IL: Kaplan Publishing, 2013.

McLean, A. J. *Buying and Managing Residential Real Estate,* 2nd ed. New York: McGraw-Hill Professional, 2005.

Portman, J., and M. Stewart. *Every Tenant's Legal Guide,* 8th ed. Berkeley, CA: Nolo Press, 2015.

Journal of Property Management, published bi-monthly by the Institute of Real Estate Management, provides comprehensive coverage of the real estate management industry.

Chapter 22

Leases *and* Property Types

LEARNING OBJECTIVES

After reading this chapter you will be able to:

1. Identify the essential elements of a valid commercial real estate lease.

2. Describe three common methods by which contract rents are increased over the life of a multiyear lease.

3. Explain the differences among gross, net, net-net, and triple net leases.

4. Explain the difference between lease assignment and subletting.

5. Describe four common options found in commercial leases.

6. Identify the major classes of office properties.

7. Calculate the rentable area of office space, given appropriate assumptions.

8. Identify the four major types of retail shopping centers.

Introduction

The lease is a contract between a property owner (lessor) and tenant (lessee) that transfers exclusive use and possession of space to the tenant. During the term of the lease, the owner possesses a leased fee estate with a reversion interest in the space that allows him or her to retake possession of the property at the termination or expiration of the lease.

Because the lease is the document that sets forth the rights and obligations of each party, every clause and provision can affect the property's net operating income or the riskiness of the income stream. That is why we argued in Chapter 21 that leases are the "engines that drive property values."

This chapter presents an introduction to the important world of commercial real estate leases. We begin by reviewing the essential elements of a valid lease. We then discuss important lease clauses and provisions common to all commercial leases. Because the net rent paid by commercial property tenants can be affected by a large number of lease clauses, the quoted rent often conveys limited information about the true cost or risk of a lease. We therefore discuss how to calculate the true, or effective, cost of a commercial lease. We then provide descriptions of the major property types and examine lease clauses unique or critical to the understanding and valuation of each property type.

Essential Elements of a Lease

As with any valid contract, parties to a lease must be legally competent, the objective of the lease must be legal, there must be mutual agreement between the tenant and landlord to enter into the lease agreement, and something of value (i.e., consideration) must be given or promised by both parties. The promise to pay rent constitutes the tenant's consideration. Allowing the tenant to occupy the space or property constitutes the landlord's consideration.

Valid and enforceable leases also must include the following elements:

1. The names of the landlord and tenant.
2. An adequate description of the leased premises.
3. An agreement to transfer possession of the property from the landlord to the tenant.
4. The start and end dates of the agreement.
5. A description of the rental payments.
6. The agreement must be in writing.
7. The agreement must be signed by all parties.

The start and end dates of the lease agreement and the agreed upon rental payments are both negotiated items, which we discuss in detail below. The type of description required depends upon the nature of the property, but must be precise about the physical premises being leased. For residential and small commercial properties, a street address and/or apartment number is usually adequate. Descriptions for larger multitenant office and retail properties are more detailed and may include items such as floor plans, the total square footage of the leased premises, and descriptions of parking areas.

> ✓ **Concept Check**
>
> **22.1** List five items that must appear in a lease that do not require negotiation between the owner and tenant.

**www.cityfeet.com/tools/
leasingguide/index.asp**

Guide to commercial leases, strategy, and negotiation.

Most states require the owner to give the tenant actual possession of the property. Once possession and control are conveyed, the tenant is entitled to **quiet enjoyment** of the property. This does not mean the owner must guarantee the tenant quiet neighbors; rather, it simply means that so long as the tenant complies with the lease the owner must provide the tenant with uninterrupted use of the property without any interference from the owner, the property manager, or any other person or entity that may threaten or seek to impose upon the tenant's leasehold interest in the property.

Negotiated Lease Provisions

Every clause in a commercial lease can affect the property's operating income and value. Clauses that address rent payments and the responsibilities of owners and tenants for operating expenses have a direct effect on property income. However, numerous clauses that address the operation of the property and the rights of either the tenant or the landlord can also have a significant effect on the economics of a lease and, therefore, its risk and value to both the tenant and owner. This section discusses the clauses and provisions that are typically part of a commercial lease negotiation.

Use of the Premises

If a lease does not state a specific purpose for which the property may be used or specifically forbid certain uses, the tenant may use the property for any legal purpose. Typically, however, commercial property leases contain a clause that indicates the purpose for which the space may be used. In addition to ensuring that the space is used lawfully, such clauses prevent uses that may damage the building, detract from its image and prestige, disturb or conflict with other tenants or surrounding neighbors, or expose the owner to potential legal liabilities.

Lease Term

The lease term must be clearly indicated, including the beginning and ending dates. One-year terms for apartment leases are the industry standard. For other commercial property types, however, lease lengths can vary considerably. Longer leases provide more stability for both the tenant and owner and they delay the re-leasing costs faced by tenants and owners when a tenant vacates the premises. For example, owners may face an extended period of vacancy and may incur significant search costs in their attempts to find a new tenant. With the exception of apartment projects, the owner will usually need to pay a leasing commission to the person responsible for securing a new tenant. In addition, the owner will generally need to provide a **tenant improvement (TI) allowance** to the new tenant. The TI allowance is the amount the landlord agrees to spend to build out or refurbish the space to meet the needs of the tenant's business. The owner may take care of the improvements him- or herself, pay the allowance directly to the tenant, or pay contractors on the tenant's behalf.[1]

When vacating space upon lease termination, tenants face moving costs, including the possible disruption of their business. In addition, tenants frequently make significant improvements to the space when moving in, often in excess of the TI allowance. These improvements may be lost when they vacate the premises because they have become part of the real estate (see Chapter 2). In short, both tenants and owners are negatively affected by re-leasing costs. As a result, both prefer longer-term leases, all else being the same, in order to minimize such costs.

Although longer-term leases delay re-leasing costs and provide rental rate security for both tenants and owners, a significant cost may be paid in lost flexibility. If tenants have reason to believe market rents are likely to fall in the near future, they may prefer shorter lease terms. In addition, many tenants are uncertain about what their space needs will be in the future. If tenants expect their business to grow steadily, or if their business is a risky start-up venture, shorter-term leases may be preferred. In general, the more uncertain a tenant's future space needs, the greater the value associated with flexibility.

Flexibility is also valuable to owners. For example, landlords may desire a shorter lease term if they believe market rents are likely to rise in the near future. In addition, owners often desire to alter the mix of tenants to maximize the synergies of the property. This is especially true for shopping center properties, as we discussed in Chapter 21. In short, flexibility considerations suggest shorter-term leases are more valuable to both tenants and owners. Therefore, optimal lease terms reflect the trade-offs between the desire for the flexibility inherent in short-term leases and the reduction in risk and re-leasing costs associated with longer-term leases.

---

1. Many leasing decisions are made by property or asset managers on behalf of owners. To simplify terminology, however, we will simply refer in this chapter to tenants and owners with the understanding that managers are often acting as agents for the owner.

Rental Payments

Rent for residential rental units is typically stated as a dollar amount per month. In contrast, rents for U.S. commercial properties are generally quoted on an annual cost per square foot basis; for example, $15 per square foot per year, even though rent is paid monthly.

Because of the short-term nature of most residential leases (generally one-year terms), owners have not found it necessary to include clauses that enable them to adjust rents as local and national economic conditions change. In contrast, many commercial leases have terms of 5, 10, and, in some cases, 25 years or more. Changing market conditions usually will cause market rental rates to change over such extended periods of time. These changes may result from shifts in supply and demand conditions in the local rental market (see Chapters 5 and 6), changes in property operating costs that must eventually be passed on to tenants, or from rent pressures that result from national economic factors such as inflation.

To maintain the market value of properties subject to long-term leases, commercial leases with durations longer than one year often include clauses that permit the owner to adjust rents over time and/or require the tenant to reimburse the owner for all or a portion of increased operating expenses. Clearly, the true cost of a commercial lease from the tenant's perspective is a function of both the rental rate and the proportion of operating expenses, if any, that are the responsibility of the tenant. In the remainder of this section, we discuss common methods by which rents are increased over the life of a lease. In the next section we discuss how the responsibility for the payment of operating expenses can affect the true cost and risk of a multiyear commercial lease.

Flat Rent. The simplest treatment of rent is to keep it flat for the entire lease term. For example, a five-year office lease might specify a fixed rental rate of $30 per square foot per year. The shorter the lease term, the more a **flat rent** arrangement is likely to be observed. When fixed rental rates are observed, the lease is likely to include a provision that requires the tenant to pay some or all of the property's operating expenses.

Graduated Rent. A **graduated rent** clause, also referred to as an escalation clause, provides for prespecified increases in the contract rental rate. For example, a five-year office lease might specify a rental rate of $30 per square foot per year for the first year, increasing by $2 per square foot each year for the remaining four years of the lease term. These prespecified rent increases are sometimes referred to as "step-ups" or "escalations."

Flat or graduated rent agreements that are clearly spelled out in the lease are the simplest methods of specifying rental rates over the term of a lease. The required lease payment is solely a function of time—if you know the number of months since the inception of the lease, you know the required lease payment. Thus, the simple two-dimensional graph presented in Exhibit 22-1 is able to fully capture the magnitude of required lease payments for our flat and graduated office rent examples.

Exhibit 22-1 Scheduled Rents for a Flat and Graduated Lease

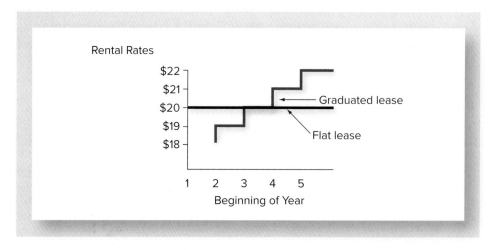

Percentage Rent. Shopping center leases often include a clause that ties total rent payments to the tenant's sales revenue. In a percentage lease, there is usually a flat or fixed component referred to as the **base rent.** In addition, the **percentage rent** clause dictates that the owner receive a prespecified percentage of tenant sales that exceed some minimum threshold amount. We will discuss percentage rent clauses in more detail below. Note, however, that total lease payments in the presence of a percentage rent clause are no longer solely a function of time. An added dimension—tenant sales—is required to determine total rent.

Responsibility for Operating Expenses

Clearly, required rent payments are an important determinant of the tenant's cost of occupancy and the owner's cash flow from the property. However, the *net* rental income generated by a lease also depends on the proportion of property-level operating expenses paid by the tenant. In a **gross lease,** the owner pays all of the property's operating expenses. Thus, owners must fully recover operating expenses in the rent. In a **net lease,** the tenant is responsible for paying a clearly defined portion of the property's operating expenses. The standard definitions of "netness" in commercial leases—net, net-net, and triple net—are displayed in Exhibit 22-2. However, in many situations these definitions are inadequate to fully describe the responsibilities of the owner and tenant under the lease, and extreme care must be taken by both sides to carefully read and negotiate the operating expense provisions of the lease.

Note that in a gross lease, the *expected* level of operating expenses over the lease term is built into the rental rate, assuming the lease was negotiated by a knowledgeable owner

Exhibit 22-2 Tenant's Responsibility for Operating Expenses

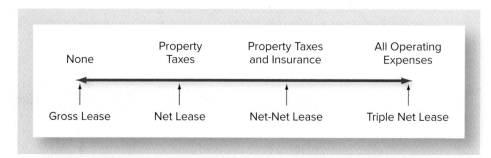

For office space design in 2016, "sense of purpose" is the new catchphrase that office-using businesses are using to attract and retain workers, including the much sought-after millennials. Versed in technology and able to work from anywhere, millennials are eschewing the stodgy ideal of a corner office; they value flexibility and demand a larger stake in the firm's purpose.

First attempts at making offices more adaptable to technology and new worker demands, such as massive cubicle farms, were really more attempts at cost-cutting than modernization. The "Best Company" firms have embraced the flexibility desired by millennials by offering many different workstations and multi-sized conference rooms that allow for both social work environments and solitary areas for head-down study. While many thought telecommuting would have more of an impact, that didn't really happen as much as expected, as millennials desire more physical connection to their career.

One of the newest methods of office flexibility involves co-working, a hybrid of a tech-type business incubator and the "rent an office" spaces offered by companies such as Regus Group Cos. Instead of having to sign a multi-year lease for a set amount of space, a company looking to open a satellite office can sign up for co-working space on a per-seat basis, with the workstations and access to shared receptionist, conference room and other typical office facilities included.

Regardless of how it's done, there's no doubt the workplace will likely look much different in the next decade, as millennials move to fill the void left by retiring baby boomers.

Modern Office Design Must Focus on Sense of Purpose

Source: Robert Carr, "Modern Office Design Must Focus on Sense of Purpose." nreionline.com/office/modern-office-design-must-focus-sense-purpose-ideal © 2016 Reprinted by permission of *National Real Estate Investor.*

and tenant in a competitive rental market. However, the owner still bears all the risk associated with *unexpected* changes in operating expenses. In contrast, tenants bear the risk associated with unexpected changes in operating expenses in a triple net lease. In some leases, the method used to share responsibility for operating expenses is a hybrid of the four basic lease types depicted in Exhibit 22-2. For example, with an **operating expense escalation clause,** only *increases* in one or more operating expenses, relative to a base year, become the responsibility of the tenant. The base year is usually the first full calendar year after the tenant moves in.

Operating expenses that are the responsibility of the tenant can be paid directly by the tenant or paid by the landlord and reimbursed by the tenant. In multitenant properties, the owner will usually pay the expenses while collecting from each tenant each month an estimate of the tenant's pro rata (or negotiated) share of the property's expenses. For example, if an office tenant occupies 6,000 square feet in a 60,000 square foot property, his or her pro rata share of expenses is 10 percent. At the end of the year, actual reimbursable expenses will be reconciled against projected expenses for the year. If the owner has collected more throughout the year than what the tenant actually owes in reimbursable expenses, the landlord generally credits the overage against what the tenant owes for the following year. However, if the landlord has collected too little from the tenant, according to the terms of the lease, the tenant will usually be required to pay the owner the amount of the deficit.

A recent trend in commercial leases is for tenants to negotiate a cap on the amount of certain operating expenses they must reimburse the landlord. Such caps are usually negotiated on operating expenses thought to be at least partially controllable by the owner, such as lawn and landscaping expenses, irrigation, painting, and general maintenance. Property-level expenses thought to be largely out of the control of the owner include property taxes, insurance, building security, and utilities. Capping the amount of some or all of the "controllable" expenses helps mitigate the risk owners will fail to act in the best interest of the tenants.

✓ **Concept Check**

22.4   Do tenants pay for expected operating expenses if they sign a gross lease?

Concessions

Once a lease has spelled out how rents are to be determined over the lease term and how owners and tenants are to share the responsibility for operating expenses, the basic economics of the lease have been established. However, lease contracts may also contain one or more **concessions** that reduce the lease cash flows. Concessions are usually offered to potential tenants to provide them with an incentive to lease space in the owner's property, but they are not reflected in the quoted rental rate.

A concession often granted to new tenants when the supply of space exceeds demand is a period of free, or perhaps reduced, rent. The owner also may commit to pay a tenant's moving expenses or penalties incurred by the tenant in breaking an existing lease.

A common concession found in office, industrial, and shopping center leases, are tenant improvement allowances, discussed above. TIs are usually stated as a per square foot amount. If a tenant is moving into an existing space that has already been finished out by a prior tenant and requires little in the way of alterations, the negotiated TI allowance may be $5 per square foot or lower. However, if a tenant is moving into newly constructed "shell" space, the owner may be required to provide a significant TI allowance to permit the tenant, or the owner on behalf of the tenant, to build out the space in an appropriate fashion. The magnitude of the tenant improvement allowance is often a heavily negotiated lease item.

Alterations and Improvements

Landlords will generally not permit tenants to make alterations or improvements to the leased premises without prior approval. This protects the landlord against value-destroying improvements, as well as damage to mechanical, electrical, heating, ventilation, and air-conditioning (HVAC) systems. To the extent the tenant is permitted to alter the leased premises, the lease should clearly state when this may be done, and under what circumstances.

The lease must also be clear about the ownership of such improvements once completed. As discussed in Chapter 2, fixtures are items of personal property permanently attached to the real property. As such, they may become the property of the owner when the lease term expires, unless the lease specifically identifies such items as the personal property of the tenant. **Trade fixtures,** in contrast, are usually paid for and installed by the tenant, and may be removed by the tenant at the termination of the lease. However, trade fixtures should be clearly identified to avoid confusion at expiration of the lease.

Assignment and Subletting

Tenants, especially those subject to long-term leases, may desire to assign or sublet all, or part, of their leased space. A lease *assignment* occurs when *all* of a tenant's rights and obligations are transferred to another party. However, the assignor remains liable for the promised rent unless relieved in writing of this responsibility by the property owner.

A **sublease** occurs when the tenant transfers a *subset* of his or her rights to another. For example, the tenant may transfer only a portion of the leased premises or transfer occupancy rights for a period of time less than the remaining lease term. Usually, the sublessee (i.e., the new tenant) pays rent to the original tenant, who in turn pays the owner the rent stipulated in the original contract. Once again, however, the original tenant remains liable for fulfilling the terms of the original lease.

Unless otherwise prohibited in the lease contract, a tenant may assign the lease or sublet. However, owners can prohibit assignment and subletting or, alternatively, clearly state the conditions under which one or both strategies may be employed.

There are numerous reasons why a tenant may wish to engage in a sublease or assignment. Perhaps the tenant has sold his or her business and no longer requires the space, or perhaps the tenant's business has grown to the point that more space is required.

Conversely, the tenant's business may have encountered financial difficulties and, as a result, he or she is seeking to reduce the firm's leased space.

Assignment and subletting can be major problems in commercial leases. Owners seek to control who occupies space in their building. Otherwise, unqualified tenants may default on sublease payments, engage in an unsafe or hazardous business, or disrupt the property's tenant mix.

✓ Concept Check

22.5 Contrast lease assignments with subletting.

Lease Options

A lease option is a clause that grants an option holder the right—but not the obligation—to do something. For example, the owner may grant a tenant who is signing a five-year lease the option to renew the lease at the end of its term for an additional five years. Lease options granted by owners to tenants reduce the expected present value of lease cash flows to the owner. Thus, in competitive rental markets, owners will require something of value from the tenant (often a higher base rent) if they grant the tenant an option. Conversely, options granted the owner that may be exercised to the detriment of the tenant generally require some form of lease concession from the owner. The existence and pricing of options in lease contracts will reflect current conditions in the rental market and the relative negotiating abilities of the two parties.

Renewal Option. **Renewal options** grant the tenant the right to renew the lease. Tenants would prefer, all else being equal, the option to renew the lease with the same terms and conditions as the original lease, including the rental rate. Owners, of course, are reluctant to agree to such renewal options for several reasons. First, market rents may increase, perhaps significantly, over the first lease term; thus, owners could be forced to renew the lease at below-market rental rates. This potential loss is not offset by the probability that tenants will renew at above-market rents if market rents decline over the first lease term. Why? Because if rents decline, tenants will not exercise the option to renew at the original contract rental rate. Therefore, this option—like all options—has a one-sided (asymmetric) payoff: If rents decline, the payoff to the owner is negative if the tenant renews at a below market rental rate; if rents rise, the payoff will be zero because the tenant will probably not exercise the option to renew. In short, from the owner's perspective this renewal option reduces the present value of the lease. Thus, owners are reluctant to grant such options unless the tenant is willing to pay for it in the form of a higher initial base rent.

As a partial compromise, owners may grant the tenant the right to renew the lease but at prevailing market rents. If the rent is reset to "market," the lease must include a formula to determine current market rent. Granting this option is expected to be less costly for the owner. However, the expected payoff to the owner on the option is still negative. Why? Because the option, if exercised, does not permit the owner to lease the space to an alternative tenant whose business might better match the owner's current marketing and leasing strategy. As previously discussed, the owner's ability to alter the tenant mix is potentially valuable, especially in retail properties and, to a lesser extent, office properties.

✓ Concept Check

22.6 Explain why option payoffs are one-sided, or asymmetric.

Cancelation Option.   Tenants may be able to negotiate the right to cancel a lease before expiration, perhaps with a termination fee. Owners may also negotiate a **cancelation option.**[2] Although not common in commercial leases, shopping center owners may seek to obtain the right to cancel a lease if the sales of a tenant do not meet or exceed a predetermined minimum amount. Similarly, shopping center tenants may negotiate the right to cancel if their sales, or those of other tenants in the center, do not reach an agreed upon threshold level.

Expansion Option.   A tenant who expects his or her business to grow may wish to negotiate an **expansion option.** A costly form of this option obligates the property owner to offer the tenant adjacent space, either at the end of the lease term or during some specified time period. Such an option is costly because the owner may have to hold space adjacent to the tenant off the market for an extended period of time to ensure that sufficient space is available should the tenant choose to exercise the expansion option. A less costly alternative for the owner is to offer a **right of first refusal,** which grants the tenant the option to lease adjacent space should it become available.

Relocation Option.   To maintain flexibility, owners of shopping centers and multitenant office buildings may negotiate **relocation options:** the right to relocate tenants within the property. In new office properties, for example, the early leasing of space to small tenants may prevent the owner from leasing larger spaces, or entire floors, to major tenants. Also, existing office and shopping center tenants may wish to expand into a contiguous area that is occupied by a small tenant. If the owner is unable to accommodate the expansion desires of larger tenants, these tenants may move to another property when their leases expire.

Most major tenants will not permit a relocation clause to enter the lease. However, smaller tenants may allow such a clause if they are guaranteed the new space will be of similar size and quality and the owner agrees to pay all reasonable moving costs.

Other Common Clauses

Access to Premises.   The lease must give owners the right to enter and inspect the leased space without violating a tenant's right to quiet enjoyment. Access to the premises allows the owner to make needed repairs and to show the space to prospective tenants near the end of the current lease term. Inspection also allows owners to monitor whether a tenant's use of the space is allowed under the terms of the lease. However, the lease should specify that, except in emergencies, the owners may inspect only at reasonable times and with sufficient prior notification.

Advertising and Signage.   Owners seek to restrict the type, location, and number of signs and graphics tenants are allowed to display on the property. Large shopping centers, for example, establish uniform graphic images and work to maintain their quality. These restrictions help keep signs and displays consistent with the building's image and the owner's marketing strategy. The location of a tenant's business name on a shopping center sign is often a heavily negotiated lease clause. Shopping center tenants may also be required by their leases to expend a certain portion of their store's sales revenues on advertising to promote their businesses.

**www.leasing
professional.com**

Downloadable complete leases and discussions of leasing strategies.

Parking.   Shopper access to parking is critical to the success of shopping centers. Thus, retail leases may require a tenant's employees to park only in designated (and less desirable) employee parking areas. Access to suitable parking also is important to office building tenants. Tenants often attempt to negotiate exclusive parking rights. The lease should be clear about tenant access to parking, both for customers and employees. The lease also must be clear about the responsibilities of owners and tenants in paying for the lighting and upkeep of the parking area.

---

2. This clause is also known as a "lease termination clause" or a "kick-out" clause.

Leasing Agents

Leasing agents are real estate sales associates or brokers who specialize in helping landlords find tenants or helping tenants find properties that fit their needs.

Some firms operate much like a traditional brokerage office—representing property owners who are searching for tenants. As agents of the property owner, the job of the leasing agent is to bring tenants to the table and help negotiate a transaction that is in the best interests of the owner—even if they claim to be objectively representing the tenant's interests as well.

Some leasing agents, often referred to as "tenant reps," work exclusively for corporate tenants. The ITRA Realty Group (www.itraglobal.com) does not believe it is possible to "negotiate from both sides of the table," so ITRA leasing affiliates, located across the country, do not represent owners. As a result, they are able to work on their client's behalf without conflict of interest and with objectivity.

Subordination and Non-Disturbance. Banks or other lenders may request—or demand—that property owners include a subordination clause in their leases. Essentially, this clause states that the lease is subordinate to any existing or future mortgages on the property. Thus, if the owner defaults on the mortgage and the lender forecloses, the lender has the right to terminate the lease and evict the tenant, even if the tenant has fulfilled all of its responsibilities under the lease. However, a subordination clause puts tenants at risk of losing their business location, which can be critical to their operations and customer relationships. In addition, they risk losing any investments they have made in leasehold improvements.

One solution is to ask the lender to enter into a non-disturbance agreement with the tenant. This agreement prohibits the lender from interfering with the tenant's use of the premises, as long as the tenant continues to pay rent and otherwise complies with the lease agreement's terms and conditions.

Effective Rent

The previous discussion reveals that the net cash flows collected by owners can be affected by a large number of lease clauses and provisions. As a result, the quoted rental rate per square foot often conveys limited information about the true cost or value of a particular lease. In addition, the significant variation often observed in commercial leases makes it difficult to compare lease alternatives, especially long-term leases.

> ### ✓ Concept Check
>
> **22.7** Why is the quoted (i.e., contract) rental rate often not a sufficient measure of the true cost of a lease?

To better measure the cost of a particular lease, it is often useful to calculate its **effective rent.** The effective rent for a monthly payment lease is the level monthly payment over the entire lease term that has the same present value as the lease. Consider, for example, a prospective 5,000 square foot, five-year office lease with a quoted rental rate of $20.00, or $1.667 a month, per square foot. The lease is a gross lease; that is, the tenant is not responsible for any of the operating expenses of the property. In addition, the tenant has negotiated eight months of free rent. Assuming the tenant could invest lease payments at a 10 percent annual rate of return, it can be shown that the effective cost of the lease, including the rent concession, is $16.72 per square foot per year.[3] Both the tenant and the owner can compare this $16.72 "true" cost/value of the lease to other lease alternatives they may have.

Broader Lease Considerations

The effective rent calculation captures many of the monetary aspects of the lease—including the time value of money—which allows leases to be compared on a more "apples-to-apples" basis. However, several important dimensions of lease desirability are not captured by the effective rent calculation.

First, the effective rent calculation is for a specific lease. Suppose the tenant in the above example expects to need the leased space, or a close substitute, for 10 years. Suppose further that a 10-year lease for highly comparable space is available and the effective rent of this alternative lease is $18.00 per square foot. If the choice between these alternatives was based solely on the effective rent, the tenant would choose the five-year lease with a $16.72 effective rent. However, in an uncertain world the tenant may be willing to pay the $1.28 per square foot premium ($18.00 − $16.72) associated with the 10-year lease in order to secure appropriate space for 10 years. We label the risk associated with the replacement of one five-year lease with another five-year lease of uncertain terms and conditions as **interlease risk.**

Interlease risk can be significantly mitigated by options embedded in the lease, such as the option to renew. If the 5-year lease above included an option to renew at the rate in effect for the first five years, the tenant's interlease risk would be significantly reduced and would decrease the tenant's incentive to choose the 10-year lease with a higher effective rent. Even the option to renew the 5-year lease at prevailing market rates in five years reduces interlease risk. In short, renewal options complicate the comparison of lease alternatives and their effects are not included in the effective rent calculation.

Two other considerations mentioned in our discussion of preferred lease terms are relevant here. First, the significant re-leasing costs faced by both tenants and landlords when a tenant vacates the premises suggest longer-term leases are preferred by both parties, all else being the same. Thus, another reason the tenant in the example might prefer the 10-year lease with a higher effective rent is that the longer lease may reduce the present value of future re-leasing costs by allowing the tenant to avoid a costly move at the end of year 5. Although longer-term leases reduce re-leasing costs and provide more rental rate security for both tenants and owners, a significant cost may be paid in terms of lost flexibility. If flexibility is deemed to be important, the tenant may rationally choose a shorter-term lease over a longer-term alternative—even if the shorter-term lease has a higher effective rent. The effects of these three broader considerations on preferred lease terms are summarized in Exhibit 22-3.

---

3. To calculate the $16.72 per square foot effective rent, the owner or tenant must first calculate the present value of the promised lease payments. In our example, this can be calculated as the present value of the lease without concessions, minus the present value of the concessions. Assuming an annual discount rate of 10 percent, the present value of the lease without concessions is $395,479.83 ($N = 60$, $I = 10\%/12$, $PV = ?$, $PMT = \$8,333.33$, and $FV = 0$). $8,333.33 = ($20.00 \times 5,000)/12$. Note that the financial calculator should be set on "Begin Mode," because lease payments are made at the beginning of the month. The present value of the eight-month rental concession is $64,769.81 ($N = 8$, $I = 10\%/12$, $PV = ?$, $PMT = \$8,333.33$, and $FV = 0$). Thus, the present value of the lease *with* concessions is $330,710. The next step is to determine the fixed monthly payment that has the same present value as the lease with concessions. This is referred to as the equivalent monthly annuity and is equal to $6,968.54 ($N = 60$, $I = 10\%/12$, $PV = 339,710$, $PMT = ?$, and $FV = 0$). Thus, the tenant is exactly indifferent between the following two lease options: (1) making payments of $6,968.54 every month for 60 months; and (2) making no payment for eight months followed by 52 monthly payments of $8,333.33. The final step in the calculation of effective rent is to convert the equivalent monthly annuity into an annual rental rate per square foot. This is known as the equivalent level rent, (*ELR*) and is equal to:

$$ELR = \frac{12 \times \$6,968.54}{5,000} = \$16.72 \; per \; sq. \, ft.$$

Exhibit 22-3 Summary of Effects of Broader Considerations on Preferred
Lease Term

	Impact on Preferred Lease Term for	
Consideration	**Tenant**	**Owner**
Interlease risk	Longer	Longer
Releasing costs	Longer	Longer
Flexibility	Shorter	Shorter

Many other nonmonetary lease clauses and terms are also not reflected in an effective rent calculation. For example, a retail tenant may choose a lease with a higher effective rent than an available alternative if the shopping center provides potential customers with easier access to parking than the alternative space. A retail tenant may also be willing to pay a higher effective rent to obtain a more prominent position on the shopping center's signs. Certainly, the exact location of a retail space or office suite within the building can have a significant effect on the rent tenants are willing to pay.

✓ **Concept Check**

22.8 Why is the effective rent of a prospective lease not a definitive measure of its desirability?

We have completed our brief tour of clauses and provisions common to many income-property leases. However, there is significant variation across property types in the type, number, and complexity of tenants and their businesses. For example, the economics that drive the apartment business are much different than the economics of the shopping center business. Even within the major categories of commercial property—multifamily, office, retail, industrial, and hospitality—there can be substantial variation in the activities and needs of tenants. Contrast, for example, the large department store tenants in a high-end mall with typical tenants occupying a small, neighborhood shopping center anchored by a grocery store. Not surprisingly, lease clauses have been developed to meet the specific needs of the tenants and owners of the various property types.

We now turn our attention to an examination of the major types of income-producing properties: residential, office, retail, industrial, and hospitality. We first define and discuss some of the major property subcategories within each of these major types. We then discuss lease clauses that are unique, or nearly so, to these property types.

Residential Rental Properties and Leases

www.nmhc.org

National Multi Housing Council, the website of a national association representing the nation's largest apartment firms, contains extensive data on the apartment industry.

The majority of residential rental units in the United States are contained in multifamily structures: that is, apartment buildings that contain five or more housing units. Multifamily structures are often classified by developmental density and architectural style. **High-rise apartment buildings** are popular in many large city centers, where the price of land is at a premium and the intensive use of land is a necessity. Buildings classified as high-rise have at least 10 to 15 stories. Larger structures may have a variety of recreational amenities, a continuously staffed front desk or all-night attendants, and retail establishments such as convenience stores and newsstands.[4]

4. In a few large metropolitan areas such as New York City, units in many high-rise apartment buildings are privately owned, although they are still typically referred to as *apartments*.

Micro-units—rental apartments about the size of a hotel room— represent a small but growing niche of the real estate multi-housing market. These miniscule living units seem ideally suited to young people who are mobile, come and (mostly) go, and live the "18-hour" lifestyle of the modern urban townscape.

So what is a micro-unit anyway? It varies,

The Rise of Micro-Unit Apartments

depending on where you are. According to a report by the Urban Land Institute (ULI), a micro-unit might be 300 sq. ft. of living space in New York City or 500 sq. ft. in Dallas. It might encompass a small studio or a one-bedroom apartment with a communal "chef kitchen" down the hall, and there may be a rooftop garden and exercise room for all to enjoy.

The attractiveness of urban living can't be stressed too much when it comes to micro-units. Besides the affordability issue of small-space living, millennials in particular are trading off space for work proximity and a flexible lifestyle. In many cases,

they're graduating from school or entering their first jobs, signing leases, and moving in with only a suitcase.

For investors and developers, the appeal is clear. Smaller units enjoy higher overall occupancy rates than mid-sized or larger units. The Urban Land Institute calculates that rental prices of these units— averaging $2.647 per sq. ft.—are up to 81 percent higher than larger units.

Source: Byron R. Carlock, "The Rise of the Micro-Unit Apartments," nreionline.com/ multifamily/rise-micro-unit-apartments-0. © 2015 Reprinted by permission of Byron R. Carlock.

Midrise apartment buildings range in height from four to nine stories and are found in both cities and suburbs. Midrise apartment buildings in city centers may provide underground parking or no parking at all, whereas their suburban counterparts usually have street-level parking available. Some buildings provide a wide range of amenities, as well as on-site management and service personnel.

Garden apartments have a relatively low density of development and are thus frequently located in suburban and nonurban areas where land is comparatively less expensive. These complexes may consist of numerous two- to three-story buildings, including a separate building containing a management office and clubhouse. Large garden style complexes are also likely to have numerous amenities such as on-site exercise facilities, spacious lawns, extensive landscaping, swimming pools, and tennis courts.

A **condominium** is a multiunit property in which the dwelling units are individually owned and the owner is responsible for the interior of the unit. The condominium arrangement also provides the owner-investor with joint ownership of the land and all common areas and elements, such as hallways, lobbies, parking areas, and recreational facilities. Similar to rental apartments, units owned as condominiums can be mid- or high-rise structures, or they can look very much like a complex of garden-style apartments. The individually owned units may be occupied by the owner or leased to a tenant. Generally, management control of the complex rests with an owners' association, which has responsibility for maintenance, taxes, insurance, water and sewage, and common-area facilities. Owner-occupied condominiums have served as a bridge from renting to the ownership of single-family detached homes for many families.

Common Lease Provisions of Residential Rental Properties

Although we have seen that almost any combination of rights and obligations can be created in a lease, some rights of a tenant cannot be removed or limited in a residential lease. These rights have been created by common law court decisions and by legal statutes to protect residential tenants who have sometimes been at the mercy of landlords. The essence of these rights is that even if a residential lease stipulated the tenant waived certain rights, the tenant can still have these rights enforced.

Most important of these nonwaivable rights is to have the property maintained in a safe and habitable condition. Another is the right to protection from unreasonable entry into the premises by the owner or property manager. Apartment owners have a greater right of entry than owners of commercial property because they are obligated to maintain the property in a safe and habitable condition. To do so, they must be able to enter the premises; however, this right is limited to *reasonable* frequency and times. Except in the case of emergencies, landlords must usually provide prior notice of entry. A final nonwaivable right permits residential tenants to cancel the lease if the premises are destroyed by fire or other hazard (a right not inherent in commercial leases).

As mentioned in Chapter 21, owners and managers must comply with all applicable landlord-tenant laws. Although such laws vary from state to state, they are intended to protect the residential tenant's interests in matters relating to the nonwaivable rights discussed above as well as other matters such as application fees, security deposits, and advance rent (e.g., the payment of the last month's rent at lease closing).

✓ Concept Check

22.9 List three nonwaivable rights that are inherent in a residential lease.

Lease Term. The most common lease term for residential rental property is one year, although shorter terms are available in some markets, such as those heavily influenced by college students.

Condition of Premises. Just prior to moving in, the tenant and property manager will usually inspect the property. The primary purpose of this joint inspection is to uncover existing incidental damage to the property so that the tenant will not be charged for it when vacating the space. The tenant becomes responsible at lease expiration for any damage not listed on the **statement of condition** signed by the tenant after the property inspection.

Utilities. Tenants are usually responsible for the payment of utilities such as gas and electricity, as well as cable TV and Internet service. Responsibility for utility payments must be clearly specified in the lease.

Rules and Regulations. Owners often distribute a set of rules and regulations, in some form or fashion, to new tenants. These rules are designed to protect the property and the rights and safety of tenants. They address issues such as pets, the use of the laundry room and other common areas, and garbage disposal. For these rules and regulations to be enforceable, they must be incorporated into the lease or listed on a separate form, signed by tenants, which indicates they have read and understand the rules.[5]

Office Properties and Leases

Although there is no definitive standard for classifying office buildings, the real estate profession commonly refers to office buildings in the following way:

1. *Class A.* These buildings usually command the highest rents because they are the most prestigious in their tenancy, location, amenities, and overall desirability. They are usually newer structures located in major metropolitan areas that have market values in excess of $10 million.
2. *Class B.* The rents in these buildings are usually less than those in Class A buildings because of a less desirable location; fewer amenities; less impressive lobbies, elevators, or appearance; or a relatively inefficient layout of the leasable space.
3. *Class C.* These buildings, which were usually once Class A or B, are older and reasonably well maintained but are below current standards for one or more reasons. Rents are set to match the rent-paying ability of lower-income tenants.

---

5. See Institute of Real Estate Management, *Principles of Real Estate Management,* 16th ed. (Chicago: IREM, 2011), Chapter 11, for an extended discussion of residential leases.

The two most important determinants of the classification of an office property are age and obsolescence. However, older buildings can be classified as Class A structures if they accommodate the current needs of potential tenants. If the space cannot be improved and updated, the class of the building is likely to decline. For example, many office buildings cannot be easily retrofitted to accommodate technological advances in computer networks and telecommunications.

According to the Institute of Real Estate Management (IREM), there are 12 fundamental criteria for classifying office buildings:

www.irem.org

The website of the Institute of Real Estate Management.

www.naiop.org

Website of the National Association of Industrial and Office properties.

Location	Lobby	Tenant services
Ease of access	Elevators	Mechanical systems
Prestige	Corridors	Management
Appearance	Office interiors	Tenant mix.[6]

Most of these factors are interdependent; for example, highly prestigious buildings are likely to have attractive appearances, an impressive lobby, and quality tenants. The prestige of a building is also a function of its location. For suburban buildings, access to major highways and linkages with places such as restaurants, high-income residential areas, and shopping facilities are extremely important.

Defining Rentable Space in Office Properties

www.boma.org

Website of the Building Owners and Managers Association International.

Because office rent is usually quoted on a dollar-per-square-foot basis, the accurate measurement of a tenant's square footage is essential. It is also important that square footage be measured in a consistent fashion in a local market so that landlords and tenants can readily compare lease alternatives. The standard for measuring office space is the one adopted by the Building Owners and Managers Association International (BOMA), although some property owners prefer their own method.

Under BOMA guidelines, the **usable area** is the square footage of the space bounded by the walls that separate one tenant's space from another.[7] Thus, the usable area is the amount of space in sole possession of the tenant. In the office floor plan depicted in Exhibit 22-4, Tenant A occupies 4,500 square feet of usable space while the three remaining tenants control 13,200 square feet. The total usable square footage on the floor is 17,700.

The **rentable area** of a tenant's leased office space is equal to the usable area, plus the tenant's prorated share of any common areas. In Exhibit 22-4, the common (shaded) area is 3,800 square feet, which includes the open areas and walkways that lead to the elevators (the X's), to the individual office suites, and to other common areas, such as restrooms and storage and utility closets. Thus, the total rentable area of the office floor is 21,500 square feet (17,700 usable plus 3,800 common).[8]

✓ **Concept Check**

22.10   What is the difference between rentable and usable areas in office leases?

How is the tenant's share of the common area calculated? First, the **rentable/usable ratio** for the entire floor is calculated by dividing the total rentable area by the total

---

6. See Institute of Real Estate Management, *Principles of Real Estate Management,* 16th ed. (Chicago: IREM, 2011), Chapter 12.

7. Technically, usable square footage is measured from the center of the demising walls (the walls between the tenants) and from the inside surface of any exterior walls and common areas walls.

8. The size of the common area does not include the square footage of the elevator shafts (in gray) or other vertical penetrations, such as staircases.

Exhibit 22-4 A Typical Office Floor Plan

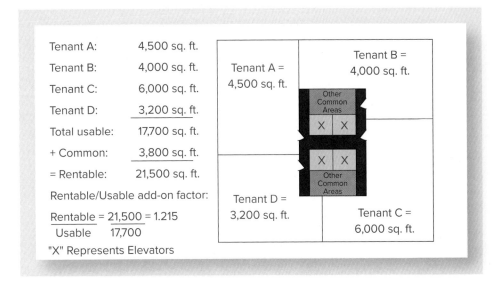

Tenant A: 4,500 sq. ft.

Tenant B: 4,000 sq. ft.

Tenant C: 6,000 sq. ft.

Tenant D: 3,200 sq. ft.

Total usable: 17,700 sq. ft.

+ Common: 3,800 sq. ft.

= Rentable: 21,500 sq. ft.

Rentable/Usable add-on factor:

$$\frac{\text{Rentable}}{\text{Usable}} = \frac{21,500}{17,700} = 1.215$$

"X" Represents Elevators

usable area. In our example, the R/U ratio, also called the **load factor,** is 1.215 (21,500 ÷ 17,700), indicating the rentable area is 21.5 percent larger than the usable area. To fully allocate the common area among the four tenants, the load factor is multiplied by each tenant's usable area. For example, Tenant A's rentable area is 5,467.5 square feet (4,500 × 1.215).[9]

Would it not be simpler to base required rental payments on usable area? Yes, but are owners able to collect more *total* rent because they quote a lower cost per square foot when using the rentable area to measure square footage? Probably not. Prospective tenants looking to rent, for example, the space now occupied by Tenant A will—or at least *should*—be aware of what it would cost on a monthly basis to rent similar space in other properties. Tenants therefore will generally not be fooled by variations in the quoted cost per square foot, so long as other owners in the market are calculating square footage in a consistent fashion.

Common Lease Provisions of Office Properties

Lease Terms.   Office leases involving major tenants may have terms as long as 25 years. However, lease terms of 5 to 10 years are more common, with terms shorter than 3 years less frequently observed because they do not provide adequate time for the owner to amortize the cost of initiating the lease, including leasing commissions and required tenant improvements. Renewal options are also frequently observed in the office sector. Tenants generally share in the payment of operating expenses, although the method typically used to share this responsibility (expense "stops") is a hybrid of the four basic lease types depicted in Exhibit 22-2.

Expense Stops.   A clause frequently found in office leases is an **expense stop.** With such a clause, the owner is directly responsible for most, if not all, property operating expenses up to a specified ("stop") amount, stated as an amount per square foot of total rentable space in a building. Expenses per square foot beyond the stop are passed through to the tenant based on each tenant's pro rata share of the building's rentable area.

---

9. In multistory office buildings, the load factor is actually based on the ratio of rentable area to usable area in the entire building.

Exhibit 22-5   The Relation between Building Operating Expenses and Tenant A's Reimbursement to the Landlord

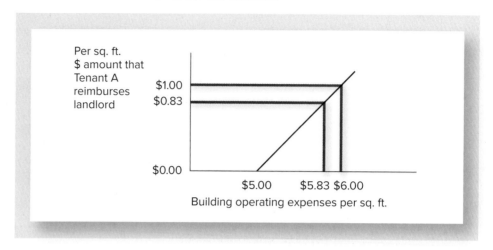

Assume, for example, an office building has 60,000 square feet of rentable area, of which Tenant A occupies 6,200 square feet. If Tenant A has a $5.00 per square foot expense stop clause, the landlord is responsible for property operating expenses up to $5.00 per square foot, which is $300,000 ($5.00 × $60,000). However, once expenses exceed $5.00 per square foot, Tenant A pays his pro rata share of the excess amount.

This relation between building expenses and Tenant A's reimbursement to the landlord is displayed in Exhibit 22-5. If total reimbursable expenses are equal to or less than $5.00 per square foot, Tenant A's expense reimbursement is equal to zero. However, if total reimbursable expenses in the current year are $350,000, or $5.83 per square foot ($350,000 ÷ 60,000), then $5,146 in operating expenses would be recoverable from Tenant A, calculated as follows:

$$\$5,146 = (\$5.83 - \$5.00) \times 6,200$$

The per square foot expense stop in office leases is often based on the property's total recoverable operating expenses in the year prior to when the tenant signed the lease. Thus, tenants in our example who sign leases in the next calendar year will likely be able to negotiate a $5.83 expense stop. Clearly, owners of multitenant properties with expense stops usually recover a larger percentage of operating expenses from older leases with lower expense stops.

✓ **Concept Check**

22.11   Whose "pain" is capped by an expense stop clause?

Retail Properties and Leases

www.icsc.org

The International Council of Shopping Centers is the global trade association of the shopping center industry.

Retail establishments are found in a variety of forms. The simplest is a freestanding retail outlet (e.g., a fast-food franchise). Many retail establishments today, however, are found in shopping centers. Shopping centers and, increasingly, freestanding establishments are often popular with individual investors and institutions that invest in commercial real estate. According to the International Council of Shopping Centers and CoStar, there are over 110,000 shopping centers of all sizes in the United States that contain more than 7 billion square feet of retail space.

Consider the various types of shopping centers:

1. **Neighborhood shopping center.** This type of center is located for the convenience of a nearby resident population. It contains retail establishments offering mostly convenience goods (e.g., groceries) and services (e.g., barbershop, video rental, and dry cleaning). These centers may be anchored by a grocery store. The gross leasable area of the anchor(s) and nonanchored tenant space is approximately 50,000 square feet, but it may be as large as 150,000 square feet. The trade area of a shopping center is the geographic area from which it draws its customers. A neighborhood center's trade area is typically within a two- to three-mile radius of the center. If it is well located, such a center can usually succeed in a trade area with a population of 1,000 to 2,500.

2. **Community shopping center.** This is a larger version of a neighborhood center. This type of center may be anchored by a discount department store and may include outlets such as clothing stores, banks, furniture stores, lawn and garden stores, fast-food operations, and professional offices (e.g., dentists). The gross leasable area (GLA) is usually three times that of a neighborhood center. A community center's trade area is usually within a three- to six-mile radius of the center.

3. **Power shopping center.** Power centers have leasable areas ranging from 250,000 to 1,000,000 square feet. The dominating feature of a power center is the high ratio of anchors to ancillary tenants. Typically, power centers contain three or more giants in hard goods retailing (e.g., toys, electronics, home furnishings). Home Depot and Wal-Mart are two prominent "big box" retailers that frequently locate their stores in power centers. These open-air centers are often located near large malls and draw shoppers from a radius of five miles or more.

4. **Regional shopping center.** Regional centers focus on general merchandise and usually have at least two anchor tenants that are major department stores (e.g., J. C. Penney's) and at least 200,000 square feet of gross leasable area devoted to nonanchor tenants. Major tenants are national chains or well-established local businesses that have high credit ratings and significant net worth. These retailers draw people from a larger area than the neighborhood or community centers, although 80 percent of their sales are typically drawn from within a 10-mile radius. Minor "in-line" tenants are located between the anchor tenants to capture customers. Often, regional centers contain several stores of one type (e.g., shoe stores). Many include small fast-food outlets arranged in food courts.

5. **Superregional malls.** These centers may have as many as five or six major tenants and hundreds of minor tenants. A typical size is 1 million square feet, but many of the larger malls exceed 2 million square feet of leasable area.

6. **Specialty shopping center.** These centers are characterized by a dominant theme or image. Many in downtown areas are located in a rehabilitated historic structure and area. A variation of specialty shopping centers is the **outlet center,** which sells name-brand goods at lower prices by eliminating the wholesale distributor.

✓ Concept Check

22.12   What is the trade area of a shopping center?

The retail tenant's primary concerns are the availability of adequate space for its business, access to their space, the volume of consumer traffic generated by the center, and the visibility of the tenant's location within the center. Additional challenges are presented by the special requirements of some tenants. For example, furniture and appliance stores require loading docks, food service providers have garbage disposal problems, and supermarkets need an abundance of close-by short-term parking.[10]

10. For more detail on the requirements of retail tenants, see Institute of Real Estate Management, *Principles of Real Estate Management,* 16th ed. (Chicago: IREM, 2011), Chapter 13.

Defining Leasable Area in Retail Properties

In retail, rents are quoted on the basis of **gross leasable area (GLA).** The GLA for a particular tenant captures the amount of space occupied and controlled by the tenant, and is therefore similar to an office tenant's usable area.[11] The GLA of the shopping center is simply the sum of the individual GLAs. The **gross floor area** of a shopping center is equal to the total GLA, plus the square footage of the common areas, which include courtyards, walkways, and escalators.

Common Lease Provisions of Retail Properties

The lease contracts between retail owners and tenants are often extremely complicated and can vary considerably across properties and tenants. Many clauses and conditions that are standard in the leases of regional mall department stores are not appropriate for a barbershop or gift store in a neighborhood shopping center. Small retail businesses often lease space for durations as short as one or two years, whereas larger tenants are often willing and able to commit to leases of much longer duration. **Anchor tenants**—the large and generally well-known retailers who draw the majority of customers to the shopping center—may sign leases with terms of 25 to 30 years, with one or more renewal options. Nonanchor tenants often make flat or indexed rental payments plus an additional payment based on some percentage of their gross sales. Tenants also typically share in paying the center's operating expenses. A review of several clauses unique to shopping center leases follows.

Percentage Rent Clause.   As mentioned previously, shopping center leases may include a clause that ties total rent payments to the tenant's sales revenue. In a percentage lease, there is usually a flat or fixed component referred to as the base rent. In addition, the percentage rent clause dictates that the property owner receive a prespecified percentage of tenant sales that exceeds some minimum threshold amount.

EXAMPLE 22-1   PERCENTAGE RENT

Assume a retail tenant is paying a base rent of $96,000 per year, or $8,000 per month. In addition, the tenant must pay additional monthly rent equal to 5 percent of gross store sales in excess of $160,000 a month. Thus, if the store produces $200,000 in gross sales in a month, total monthly rent is $10,000, calculated as follows:

$$\text{Total rent} = \text{Base rent} + \text{Percentage rent}$$
$$\$10,000 = \$8,000 + 0.05\,(\$200,000 - \$160,000)$$

The percentage rent clause gives the owner a claim on a portion of tenant sales. If monthly sales exceed the $160,000 threshold amount, the owner claims additional rent. However, if sales fall short of the $160,000 threshold, the owner collects no percentage rent, but still collects $8,000 in base rent. The payoff to the owner (and cost to the tenant) of this percentage rent clause is depicted in Exhibit 22-6. Note that the payoff on this clause to the owner is one-sided.

Percentage rent clauses are unique to retail and service tenants and offer advantages for both the owner and the tenant. For the tenant, the percentage rental offers a way of leasing space that he or she might not otherwise be willing to rent because of the uncertainty of his or her future business success. The percentage rental assures the tenant that increased rental costs will be conditional upon the success of her business.

11. The gross leasable area (GLA) may be slightly less than the tenant's "usable" area because most shopping center leases measure space from the inside of the interior walls to the outside of the exterior walls.

Exhibit 22-6 The Payoff to the Owner on a Percentage Rent Clause

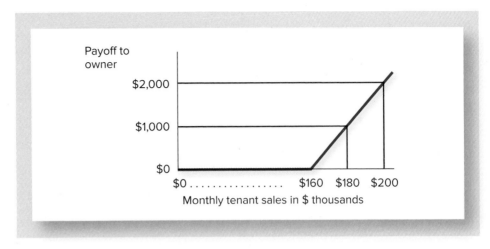

Perhaps even more important, however, is that the percentage rent clause helps to align the interests of the shopping center owner with those of the tenant. Because the owner's lease cash flows are partially determined by the success of the tenant's business, the owner has an incentive to keep the center clean and attractive, maintain adequate signage, advertise, and ensure that stores with complementary products are located nearby to help drive customers to the tenant's store. From the landlord's perspective, a percentage rental gives the owner an equity-like interest in a tenant's business. In a competitive rental market, however, tenants do not freely give away a portion of their firm's upside potential to property owners. To be induced to do so, the base rent must be lower than it would be in the absence of the percentage rent clause. Obviously, a percentage rent clause requires that the shopping center owner have access to the financial records of the tenant.[12]

✓ Concept Check

22.13 How does a percentage rent clause align the incentives of the owner and tenant?

Use Clauses. To help maintain the best mix of tenants in a shopping center, owners frequently specify the merchandise or services that can be sold by the tenant (e.g., "women's shoes" or "costume jewelry"). Conversely, large tenants may seek to restrict the way retail space close to the tenant can be used. Such clauses may be desirable in order to limit the amount of nearby competition or to help ensure adequate parking is available for potential customers. Some tenants may demand exclusives; that is, the right to be the *only* tenant in the center that provides a certain kind of merchandise or service. Owners of course seek to avoid granting such rights. During lease negotiations, tenants seek to obtain a use clause that is as broad as possible; owners, in contrast, desire narrow and restrictive use clauses. The phrase "... or any other lawful use" is not something owners are typically willing to accept.

Co-Tenancy Clause. A common clause in retail leases allows tenants to cancel the lease or pay reduced rent if key tenants in the center vacate. A large or key tenant is a big draw for traffic, especially in malls, and is often one of the major reasons a smaller tenant

---

12. With percentage leases, tenants transfer to the owners some of the risk associated with operating their business. Why do property owners accept this risk? A partial explanation is that, with multiple tenants, owners are able to diversify the risk associated with a "portfolio" of percentage rent clauses. Individual tenants, however, are often exposed to significant firm-specific risk that is difficult, with limited capital, to diversify away. Therefore, both parties can be better off if owners bear some of the tenant-specific risk in their shopping centers.

chooses to locate in a specific shopping center. A co-tenancy clause provides the tenant with some protection in the event a major tenant "goes dark."

Hours of Operation.   It is important to the success of shopping centers, both large and small, that hours of business operation are consistent across tenants. Most retail leases allow the owner to set the shopping center's hours of operation or the hours will be specified in the lease.

Common Area Maintenance.   This lease clause specifies exactly what the common areas of the shopping center are, what responsibilities the owner has to maintain and repair the common areas, and what **common area maintenance (CAM)** charges will be paid by each of the tenants. In addition to maintenance and repair costs, CAM charges typically include the cost of security personnel and alarm systems, as well as fees for the management of the common area. CAM charges, which may run from $2.00 to $5.00 per square foot per year, or more, are usually prorated among tenants based on the percentage of the center's gross leasable area (GLA) occupied by the tenant. However, important tenants may be able to negotiate better CAM terms than other tenants. For example, anchor tenants are often able to avoid reimbursing the owner for center management charges.

Other Clauses.   Retail leases commonly require the tenant to occupy the space for the entire lease term (continuous occupancy) and to keep his business operating consistently (continuous operation). For the benefit of both the tenant and the owner, retail leases also require the tenant to carry an adequate amount of liability insurance.

Industrial Properties and Leases

Industrial properties include the following:

- Large single-user buildings.
- Warehouses and self storage facilities.
- Multitenant "industrial parks."

Plants and factories are special-use properties not easily converted to other uses. Thus, they are relatively risky and are usually avoided by third-party investors, except those who specialize in the specific production processes employed at the plant (i.e., the companies that use the facilities). In contrast, warehouses and industrial parks have become popular investments in urban and suburban areas. Industrial parks are also known as business parks and research parks.

Warehouses provide space for the temporary storage of goods, such as inventory, company records, and excess raw materials. Warehouses are usually built as single-story structures with fewer design elements than most office building and shopping centers. They are relatively simple to construct, have long economic lives, and usually require less management effort than other types of commercial property.

Most new space in industrial parks is built as single-story structures that can be configured to accommodate single or multiple tenants. This industrial **flex space** is usually built without fancy lobbies or fixtures and, unlike many office properties, there are no load factors. Rents are lower than traditional office space and there is ample parking. Tenants can be firms that require large amounts of inexpensive space or firms that need their offices in the same building as their manufacturing or warehouse operations.[13]

Common Lease Provisions of Industrial Properties

Because of the highly specialized nature of many manufacturing and production processes, manufacturing tenants generally require long-term leases to assure them of possession and control of the space. This is particularly true when the tenant has invested heavily in equipment and other tenant improvements and fixtures that would be expensive to move or replicate

www.sior.com

Society of Industrial and Office Realtors.

---

13. This description of flex space draws from the Institute of Real Estate Management, *Principles of Real Estate Management,* 16th ed. (Chicago: IREM, 2011), Chapter 13.

Ever since the first shopping center leases were negotiated, owners and prospective tenants have been warring over various provisions contained within these documents. Negotiations are often time consuming and even hostile.

Brokers, tenants, owners, and lawyers cite a variety of retail lease issues—beyond rent—that are difficult to negotiate. These include provisions on the reporting of a tenant's sales; the pass-through of operating expenses; the landlord's financial contributions to tenant improvements as well as the timing of those contributions; provisions that allow tenants to cease operations without being in default; food or retail category exclusives that prohibit similar concepts within the same retail center;

the extent of any required personal guarantee on the lease; tenant rights to assign a lease; and common area maintenance costs and tenant rights to audit those charges.

Ultimately, the haggling and fine-tuning of various provisions boil down to the following factors. First, each provision has a legal and economic ramification. Second, the responsibility for operating expenses, including common area maintenance and tenant improvements, is divided between the owner and the tenant depending upon the tenant's perceived financial strength and the participants' lease negotiations skills. Third, the perceived value of the location is based upon the tenant's projected sales, which are

specific to the retail location and the supporting demographics. Last, the owner believes that the tenant will contribute positively to the retail center's drawing power, and that the tenant's income stream will contribute positively to the center's overall valuation.

Source: Adapted from Gretchen Pienta, "Got Space," CCIM Institute, July–August 2003; www.ccim.com/cire-magazine/articles/got-space/?gmSsoPc=1.

Retail Lease Negotiation

in another facility. Many warehouse properties are single-user buildings leased to tenants on a triple net basis. Most warehouse space is fairly homogenous and, unlike manufacturing and production facilities, few firm-specific tenant improvements are required. Because releasing and moving costs are relatively low and because flexibility is important, warehouse tenants do not usually seek long-term leases—three- to five-year terms are common.

Tenants in multitenant industrial park properties face many of the same leasing issues owners and tenants of multitenant office buildings and shopping centers confront. In particular, leases must be clear about the tenant's responsibility for maintenance and repair. Tenants are generally responsible for their interior space and for the maintenance of mechanical equipment. Owners are usually responsible for the maintenance of the roof and the structural components of the property. Common area maintenance is handled in much the same way as it is in shopping centers; that is, the owner maintains the common area and tenants reimburse the owner for common area maintenance costs based on their pro rata share of the space in the building or park.

Hospitality Properties

Hotels are establishments that provide transient lodging for the public as well as meals and entertainment. Motels are often located on or near a highway that are designed to serve the motor traveler. Hotels and motels serve several distinct markets including the traveler (transient market) and the visitor or conventioneer (destination market). Convention hotels cater to meetings of businesses and other organizations and are often located in or near the downtown area. Resort hotels are located near entertainment and vacation-related activities or scenic areas.

Hospitality properties have uncomplicated lease structures. Rooms are usually rented on a daily basis. In addition, hospitality properties are characterized by gross leases; even electric, water, and sewer expenses are included in the "rent."

The success of hospitality property investments is highly dependent on management. A hotel is a service business. Thus, managers should be versed in all aspects of this type of business, not just in collecting room rents and providing maintenance. Because cash flows are dependent on the management of the hospitality business, the ownership of hospitality properties by passive third-party investors is less common than with the other major property types. Instead, properties often are owned by one of the national corporate chains. Properties owned by third-party investors are typically run by hotel or motel management chains.

www.mhhe.com/lingarcher5e

Summary

The lease is the document that sets forth the rights and obligations of a tenant and property owner. Thus, from an investor's perspective, leases are the primary determinant of current and future cash flows and, as such, are the engines that drive property value. When investors are contemplating the acquisition of existing multitenant properties subject to long-term leases, their first job is to read, summarize, and value the "portfolio" of leases that will generate the property's net rental income.

Essential elements of a commercial lease include the term and the amount of rent to be paid by a tenant over the lease term. Because commercial leases often have terms of 5, 10, and, in some cases, 25 years or more, clauses that permit the owner to adjust rents over time are often included.

Although required rent payments are a fundamental determinant of lease cash flows, the *net* cash flows generated by a lease are also a function of the proportion of property-level operating expenses paid or reimbursed by the tenant. In a gross lease, the tenant makes a single rental payment to the owner, out of which the owner pays all operating expenses. In net leases, however, the tenant is responsible for paying a portion, if not all, of the operating expenses. The degree of expense "netness" must be clearly spelled out in the lease; terms such as "double net" and "triple net" are often inadequate to describe each party's responsibility for operating expenses.

Although a tenant's responsibility for rents and operating expenses establishes the basic economics of the lease, other provisions also are potentially important. For example, the owner may grant the tenant concessions that lower the value of the cash flows collected by the owner. The tenant's ability, described in the lease, to assign or sublease the space may also affect the riskiness and, therefore, the value of the lease. Options that grant the owner or the tenant the right, but not the obligation, to do something (e.g., the right to renew or cancel) can significantly affect the economics of a lease. The calculation of effective rent is designed to capture many of the monetary aspects of a lease, thereby allowing leases to be compared on a more "apples-to-apples" basis. However, the standard calculation of effective rent ignores many important considerations, such as lease options re-leasing costs, and the desire of both parties for flexibility.

Typical lease structures often vary significantly by property type. This chapter provides descriptions of the major property types and examines lease clauses that are unique or critical to the understanding and valuation of each of the major property types.

Key Terms

Anchor tenant 596

Base rent 582

Cancelation option 586

Common area maintenance (CAM) 598

Community shopping center 595

Concessions 584

Condominium 590

Effective rent 587

Expansion option 586

Expense stop 593

Flat rent 581

Flex space 598

Garden apartments 590

Graduated rent 581

Gross floor area 596

Gross leasable area (GLA) 596

Gross lease 582

High-rise apartment buildings 589

Interlease risk 588

Load factor 593

Midrise apartment buildings 590

Neighborhood shopping center 595

Net lease 582

Operating expense escalation clause 583

Outlet center 595

Percentage rent 582

Power shopping center 595

Quiet enjoyment 579

Regional shopping center 595

Relocation option 586

Renewal options 585

Rentable area 592

Rentable/usable ratio 592

Right of first refusal 586

Specialty shopping center 595

Statement of condition 591

Sublease 584

Superregional malls 595

Tenant improvement (TI) allowance 580

Trade fixtures 584

Usable area 592

Warehouses 598

Test Problems

Answer the following multiple-choice problems:

1. A lease in which the tenant pays a rent based in part on the sales of the tenant's business is known as a:
   a. Percentage lease.
   b. Participation lease.
   c. Net lease.
   d. Gross lease.

2. When the tenant pays a base rent plus some or all of the operating expenses of a property, the result is a:
   a. Gross lease.
   b. Net lease.
   c. Percentage lease.
   d. Graduated lease.

3. Existing leases:
   a. Can be ignored by potential investors when estimating investment value.
   b. Must be considered more carefully when valuing a multitenant office building than valuing an apartment complex.
   c. Are more important when estimating market value than estimating investment value.
   d. Should be assumed to have remaining terms of 10 years when estimating investment value.

4. With an expense stop clause:
   a. Operating expenses are borne by the tenant up to a specified per square foot level, above which the landlord is responsible for additional expenses.
   b. The landlord is responsible for operating expenses up to a specified level, above which increases in operating expenses become the obligation of the tenant based on the tenant's square footage.
   c. Landlords commit to a maximum tenant improvement allowance for new tenants.
   d. Tenants are reimbursed for electric bills in excess of a normal amount.

5. As a tenant, you wish to turn over all rights and responsibilities of your unexpired lease term to a new tenant. If allowed to do so by the owner, you are:
   a. Releasing your leasehold interest.
   b. Subleasing your leasehold interest.
   c. Assigning your leasehold interest.
   d. Relieving your leasehold interest.

6. Lease provisions that grant the tenant the right, but not the obligation, to do something generally result in:
   a. A lower base rent.
   b. A higher base rent.
   c. An indexed base rent.
   d. Nothing—a base rent is generally not affected by tenant options.

7. The tenant is usually responsible for paying property taxes and insurance in a:
   a. Gross lease.
   b. Net lease.
   c. Net-net lease.
   d. Triple net lease.

8. Which of the following statements regarding tenant improvements (TIs) is the least true in the context of commercial real estate leases?
   a. TIs are usually stated as a dollar per square foot amount.
   b. Tenants can generally negotiate higher TIs for existing space than for space in a newly developed project.
   c. Tenants can generally negotiate higher TIs for space in a newly developed project than for space in an existing project.
   d. The magnitude of the TIs is often a heavily negotiated lease term.

9. In shopping center leases, rents are typically quoted on the basis of what type of area occupied by the tenant?
   a. Gross leasable area.
   b. Net leasable area.
   c. Rentable area.
   d. Usable area.

10. The typical anchor tenant in a neighborhood shopping center is a:
   a. Nationally known department store.
   b. Regional department store.
   c. "Big box" retailer such as Home Depot and Circuit City.
   d. Grocery store.

Study Questions

1. Assume the owners of a midsize office building recover all operating expenses from their tenants except management and administrative expenses. The total rentable area of the office building is 100,000 square feet. The total amount of operating expenses recoverable from tenants in the current year is $700,000. Tenant B occupies 10,000 square feet of the building and has an expense stop of $5.50 per square foot. How much of the building's reimbursable operating expenses will the owners recover from Tenant B?

2. Why might a tenant prefer a lease with a higher effective rent than an alternative lease with a lower effective rent?

3. Describe the most common methods used to specify rent changes over time for a commercial lease.

4. What factors tend to make both owners and tenants prefer longer-term leases, all else being equal?

5. Assume a small office building has a total usable area of 40,000 square feet and 5,000 square feet of common area. Tenant Z occupies 6,000 square feet of usable area. What is Tenant Z's rentable area?

6. Assume a retail tenant is paying a base rent of $120,000 per year (or $10,000 per month). In addition, the tenant must pay 7 percent of gross store sales in excess of $143,000 per month as percentage rent. If the store produces $170,000 in gross sales in a month, what is the percentage rent in that month? What is the total rent due?

7. A prospective tenant has presented two lease proposals to the owner of an office building. The first alternative has a five-year term and a contract rental rate of $16.00 per square foot in the first year of the lease. The rental rate then steps up 3 percent per year over the remainder of the lease term.

So, for example, the rental rate in year 2 (months 13–24) would be $16.48. The second lease alternative is also a five-year lease with an initial contract rate of $16.00 per square foot. However, the rental rate on this lease is indexed to inflation with the adjustment made at the beginning of each year based on the actual rate of inflation in the previous year.

The owner of the office property projects that inflation will run at a rate of 3 percent per year over the five-year lease term.

a. What are the owner's projected payments over the five-year term for the two alternatives?

b. Which option is the owner likely to prefer and why?

EXPLORE THE WEB

Founded in 1957, the International Council of Shopping Centers (ICSC) is the global trade association of the shopping center industry. Its 70,000 members in the United States, Canada, and more than 100 other countries include shopping center owners, developers, managers, marketing specialists, investors, lenders, retailers, and other professionals as well as academics and public officials. Go to the ICSC website (www.icsc.org) and sample the wealth of information it contains on the shopping center industry. Then click on the *Research* tab across the top of the home page and search for "Shopping Center Facts and Stats." How many shopping centers now exist in the United States? What is the total square footage of these centers? How much employment is related to the shopping center industry?

Solutions to Concept Checks

1. Five items that must appear in a lease are (1) the names of the landlord and tenant, (2) an adequate description of the leased premises, (3) an agreement to transfer possession of the property from the landlord to the tenant, (4) the start and end dates of the agreement, and (5) a description of the rental payments.

2. The primary advantage of longer-term leases is that they delay owner and tenant re-leasing costs. The primary disadvantage is that they reduce flexibility for both the owner and tenant.

3. An escalation clause allows the owner to increase the contract rental rate to a prespecified amount at a prespecified time.

4. In competitive rental markets, owners must recover operating expenses from tenants in order to be profitable. With a gross lease, the tenant does not have to reimburse the owner for actual operating expenses because the expected level of operating expenses has already been included in the scheduled lease payments. Tenants win, and owners lose, if actual expenses are greater than expected.

5. A lease assignment conveys all of the tenant's rights and obligations to the replacement tenant; a sublease conveys only a subset of the original tenant's rights and obligations.

6. The payoffs on lease options are one-sided, or asymmetrical, because they will only be exercised if it benefits the holder of the option. If the option is not in-the-money; that is, if its exercise will not benefit the holder, it will not be exercised. Therefore, the payoff is zero.

7. The quoted, or contract, rental rate is often an insufficient measure of the true cost of a lease because from the perspective of the tenant, the cost of the lease is influenced not only by the promised rental payment, but also by the tenant's responsibility for operating expenses and the amount of concessions, including tenant improvements, that the tenant is able to negotiate. The true cost of the lease is also affected by options the tenant (or owner) may hold, such as the tenant's right to renew or cancel the lease.

8. The effective rent of a prospective lease is not a definitive measure of its desirability because it ignores broader considerations such as re-leasing costs, the desire of both parties for flexibility, and the desire of tenants and owners to avoid the risks associated with having to replace one lease with another. The effective rent calculation also ignores many other nonmonetary, but important, terms and conditions of a lease.

9. Three nonwaivable rights inherent in a residential lease are (1) the right to have the property maintained in a safe and habitable condition, (2) the right to be protected from unreasonable searches and inspections by the owner or his/her agent, and (3) the right to cancel the lease if the premises are destroyed by fire or other hazards.

10. In office leases, rentable area includes the tenant's usable area plus the tenant's pro rata share of the common areas.

11. The owner's pain is stopped or capped by an expense stop because per square foot operating expenses of the property that exceed the tenant's per square foot expense stop are passed through to the tenants. Thus, tenants begin to share the pain once reimbursable expenses, on a per square-foot basis, exceed the per square foot stop in their lease.

12. The trade area of a shopping center is the geographical area from which a shopping center generally draws its customers. Neighborhood strip centers can survive with a fairly small trade area, needing only to capture those households within a 5- to 10-minute drive of the center. In contrast, regional malls draw from a trade area that can extend for 30 to 45 minutes or more.

13. With a percentage rent clause, the owner's lease cash flows are partially determined by the success of the tenant's business. As a result, the owner has an incentive to keep the center clean and attractive, maintain adequate signage, advertise the center and its various stores, and ensure that a proper tenant mix is maintained. All of these efforts by the owners should help to increase the sales of the tenant's business.

Additional Readings

Alexander, Alan A., and Richard F. Muhlebach. *Managing and Leasing Commercial Properties.* Chicago: Institute of Real Estate Management, 2007.

Alexander, Alan A., and Richard F. Muhlebach. *The Leasing Process: Landlord and Tenant Perspectives.* Chicago: Institute of Real Estate Management, 2008.

Bogent, Daniel B. and Celeste Hammond. *Commercial Leasing: A Transactional Primer.* Durham, NC: Carolina Academic Press, 2011.

Brueggeman, William B., and Jeffrey Fisher, *Real Estate Finance and Investment,* 15th ed. New York: McGraw-Hill/Irwin, 2016.

Dillman, Rodney. *The Lease Manual*: *A Practical Guide to Negotiating Office, Retail, and Industrial Leases.* New York: American Bankers Association, 2007.

Geltner, D., N. G. Miller, Jim Clayton, and Piet Eichholtz. *Commercial Real Estate Analysis & Investment,* 3rd ed. Mason, Ohio: Thomson South-Western Publishing, 2014.

Institute of Real Estate Management. *Principles of Real Estate Management,* 16th ed. Chicago: IREM, 2011.

Institute of Real Estate Management. *Marketing and Leasing: Retail.* Chicago: IREM, 2015.

Klein, John, Allison Drucker, and Kirk Vizzier. *A Practical Guide to Green Real Estate Management.* Chicago: Institute of Real Estate Management, 2009.

Society of Industrial and Office Realtors. *Mastering Office Leasing.* Washington, DC: SIOR, 2000.

Zankel, Martin I. *Negotiating Commercial Real Estate Leases,* Fort Worth: Mesa House Publishing 2001.

www.mhhe.com/lingarcher5e

Chapter 23

Development:
The **Dynamics** *of*
Creating Value

LEARNING OBJECTIVES

After reading this chapter you will be able to:

1 List eight stages in the development process.

2 Identify major risks associated with each stage of development.

3 Describe the role of each of these in the development process: market and feasibility consultant, environmental engineer, architect, land planner, landscape architect, general contractor, and construction manager.

4 List three characteristics of the role of developer.

5 List four characteristics generally required of a developer.

OUTLINE

Introduction

Development has aptly been defined as the continual reconfiguration of the built environment to meet society's needs.[1] This definition captures the fact that development is a necessity, demanded by society to meet its needs for shelter, working space, and other permanent facilities. Developers are in many ways the quarterbacks of the real estate industry. While they are only a tiny fraction of the total industry, their role is central in creating the events that put the industry in motion. Though constrained by available resources and regulations, their decisions still have a dominating effect on what kind of real estate is available in the marketplace; what jobs are available in construction, architecture, and other related fields; and what real estate investment opportunities are available to the capital markets. Their central and visible role in the process of creating society's structures makes them both a lightning rod for social anxieties and a glamorous form of entrepreneurship.

1. Mike Miles, Gayle Berens, and Marc A. Weiss, *Real Estate Development Principles and Process,* 4th ed. (Washington, DC: Urban Land Institute, 2007), p. 1.

In this chapter, we first view the process of development and the multitude of ingredients involved at each of its several stages. But description cannot capture the dynamics of the opportunities, decisions, challenges, risks, and rewards that "come with the territory." So we use examples to illustrate how the process has played out in several interesting cases. Finally, we consider what the experience of being a developer is about and what it takes to enter the field of development.

In many ways, the subject of development is a fitting final chapter for this text because development encompasses virtually every subject covered. The developer must understand the legal nature of real property interests (Chapter 2) as well as the relevant land use regulations and regulatory processes (Chapter 4) in order to know what use is legally feasible with a parcel of land. In addition, the developer must be able to evaluate the market potential for a proposed project in order to determine its economic feasibility (Chapters 5 and 6). Also the developer must understand the relevant cash flow analysis to determine feasibility and profitability (Chapters 14, 18, and 19). Further, the developer must understand financing and investment alternatives to bring together the debt and equity capital for the project (Chapters 9 through 11, 16, and 17). If the developer is to obtain financing or expects to sell the property, the appraised value of the project is important (Chapters 7 and 8). If the developer plans to sell the property, he or she must understand the real estate transaction process (Chapters 3, 12, and 13). If the developer is creating income-producing property, it is important to understand effective property management, either for his or her own management of the property, or for assuring that the property is designed for effective management (Chapters 21 and 22). The value created in a development project is potentially influenced by any and all of these many dimensions of real estate.

The Process of Development

Development projects may arise out of a site in search of a use, a use in search of a site, or resources in search of an opportunity.[2] In each case, a specific development concept at a specific site must emerge. The ways that this happens are probably beyond cataloging. At one extreme might be a fast-food giant or a CVS, Walgreens, Wal-Mart, or other chain retailer that has evolved a dramatically successful store concept and is committed to replicating it at hundreds of locations. At the other extreme might be a landholder with a single parcel of land who, in the effort to make the land productive, conceives a new plan for use of the site. Mixed into the possibilities are experienced development organizations looking for new engagements and investors looking for high-return uses of their capital. The multitude of specific development ideas springing from these diverse situations no doubt is replete with spontaneity, false starts, amusement, and excitement. Unfortunately, it is little documented except in the "war stories" of individual developers.

We start the process of development at the point where a specific use has been chosen for a specific site. From that point forward, we can think of the process as having eight stages:

1. Establishing site control.
2. Feasibility analysis, refinement, and testing.
3. Obtaining permits.
4. Design.
5. Financing.
6. Construction.
7. Marketing and leasing.
8. Operation.

---

2. These alternatives were first articulated by James Graaskamp, the legendary professor of real estate and development at the University of Wisconsin. See, for example, *A Guide to Feasibility Analysis* (Chicago: Society of Real Estate Appraisers, 1970).

www.nmhc.org

Organization of large-scale apartment owners and developers.

www.uli.org

The Urban Land Institute, the principal development organization in the United States.

> **✓ Concept Check**
>
> **23.1** What are three basic perspectives from which development projects arise?

Establishing Site Control

Site control is the entry ticket to development. Without it, nothing else matters. The problem of site control ranges in the extreme. The dream case for a developer is owning the site outright, with no debt. This is the case when the developer is part of a family or organization owning land that, due to urban growth, has become "ripe" for more intensive use. Many railroad companies, ranches, and paper companies in California and across the "sun belt" have found themselves in this situation. An extreme example is the Irvine Ranch in Orange Country, California. With 93,000 acres on the southern perimeter of greater Los Angeles it has hosted development that ultimately will support a population of over 200,000 in one of the exemplary planned communities of the world. A much smaller example is that of a family whose farm was bisected first by Interstate 75 several decades ago, and subsequently by a major urban arterial of Gainesville, Florida. This created the only case where one owner controlled all four corners of a significant interchange on I-75, a gateway to Florida. At the other extreme of land acquisition is the legendary case of the Disney organization assembling the land for Walt Disney World. The more than 27,000 acres of the prospective site were owned by dozens of different interests. Knowing that any recognition by one of these owners as to who was seeking the land would likely result in a "hostage" situation, Disney devised elaborate blind entities to deftly and successfully acquire all of the pieces that now make up the Walt Disney World site.[3] In urban redevelopment, the problem of gaining control of multiple sites is so great that it early became one of the arguments in support of the use of the public power of eminent domain to assemble land in urban renewal programs.

www.nahb.org

The leading trade association for builders of housing.

> **✓ Concept Check**
>
> **23.2** List eight stages of the development process.

A common tool for a developer to gain control of a site is to purchase an **option** on the land that allows the developer, at a predetermined price, to choose by a certain date whether to go through with the purchase. Ideally, it allows the developer sufficient time to conduct feasibility analysis, to run soil and environmental tests, to obtain necessary zoning changes or other permits, and possibly long enough to arrange financing. The terms of an option can be very creative and will depend on the bargaining position of the two parties. It could involve giving the landowner a participation in the development in lieu of cash up front. Further, options can come in disguise, such as a contract for deed.[4] If the developer purchases the land on a contract for deed with a small down payment, then it may be easy to simply abandon the contract if the project turns out to be infeasible.

Yet another way to manage equity for land acquisition is to bring a future tenant into the development as a partner. This arrangement might be the formula that enables a new developer with few resources to enter the industry. For a tenant needing a facility, the arrangement could provide sufficient reward to justify risking involvement with the untested developer, particularly if the tenant can tolerate uncertainty in the date of

---

3. In this strategy of land assembly, Disney was following a time-honored approach in the real estate industry. The prominent New York developer, William Zeckendorf, was well known for similar methods.

4. Often called a land contract. See Chapter 9 for a discussion of a contract for deed.

completion. If the tenant will occupy a large portion of the facility to be built, the risks of the development are further reduced since market uncertainty is resolved.[5]

An important variation on joint venturing with a tenant is **build-to-suit.** The developer preleases to a financially strong, frequently national, tenant to build to the tenant's specifications. This could be, for example, a restaurant for a national fast-food chain, or a freestanding facility for a national retailer.

Still another possible solution to land acquisition is the **ground lease.** Under this arrangement, only the initial land rent must be paid out before development actually gets under way. The ground lease can offer the owner of the land an attractive arrangement since it provides a long-term, inflation-protected income (assuming that rents are reviewed and adjusted periodically) and, in case of default, gives the landowner all of the improvements. One of the most famous examples of development on a ground lease is Rockefeller Center, built during the 1930s on land then owned by Columbia University. This ultimately turned landholdings of marginal value into a fabulous source of wealth for the school.

✓ Concept Check

23.3 List four ways that a developer can finance the establishment of site control.

Feasibility Analysis, Refinement, and Testing

With a site under control the developer has time to evaluate the feasibility of the project. He or she normally will perform a financial feasibility analysis first. The feasibility study will project the expected cash flows from the project, as shown in Chapters 8 and 19. Using these cash flow projections the developer will determine whether the project works financially, as indicated by a **cash multiple** or by an NPV analysis. (See Exhibit 23-1.) Deriving the value of the project may be very informal, particularly if the cash multiple or *NPV* appears to be so high as to constitute a "slam dunk."[6] On the other hand, if the signal is marginally positive, then the developer must decide whether to retain additional market research in an effort to narrow the range of the feasibility outcomes. The additional market research also may give the developer

Exhibit 23-1 Cash Multiple versus NPV as a Feasibility Signal

We have argued that net present value (NPV) is the preferred indicator of investment performance, including for development (Chapter 19). But another signal that many developers use is a **cash multiple.** What is the cash multiple, and how does it compare to NPV?

The cash multiple is the sum of net cash flows received over the life of a project, divided by the total amount of cash paid into the project (either upfront or along the way). Thus, the cash multiple uses exactly the same cash flows as in NPV. However, it uses a zero discount rate, and *divides* by the total cash cost rather than *subtracting* it from the total inflows. This gives a simple ratio of benefit to cost, and appears to be more comfortable to many developers. So a developer may want to see an unlevered cash multiple of at least 2, for example, for a project to be considered feasible, or a substantially higher cash multiple for levered cash flows.

How does the cash multiple compare to NPV as a feasibility signal? Carefully used, since it uses the same set of cash flows, it could correlate well. But because it implicitly uses a zero discount rate, it does not directly recognize how long one must wait for the benefits, or how uncertain the benefits may be. However, if the developer is thoughtful enough to demand a higher multiple when the project is "longer" or more uncertain, then the multiple could still account for time and risk, and lead to results similar to NPV.

Since most feasibility decisions are private, little is known about exactly what cash multiples are used, or how they vary.

---

5. Whatever the option arrangement, it is important for the developer to remember that, if exercised, the option turns into a contract for sale of land, it will govern all aspects of the land purchase. Thus, the option contract needs to be as complete as any contract for sale of land in addressing issues of title examination, arrangement of financing, and other contingencies, which we discussed in Chapter 13.

6. Financial theorists have not yet determined precisely what the threshold *NPV* is for "slam dunk" classification, but developers appear to know.

useful guides to improve and refine the project concept. Obviously, the cost information of the developer also must be reasonably reliable to conduct the financial feasibility analysis, and the developer may need to order cost estimates on some aspects of the project.

If the signal is negative, then the developer must decide whether a revised plan might be feasible. If not, he or she will abandon the project, allowing any option on the land to elapse.

Even if a development appears financially feasible, it still depends on the land being free of soil problems, environmental concerns, ecological complications, seismic concerns, hydrological concerns, or anthropological or historical sensitivities. Thus, a developer commonly turns to an environmental consultant, a geologist, or other scientific experts at this point. The consultants will examine the site for underlying structural concerns, for any evidence of toxicity, wetlands, and sensitive wildlife habitat that may be protected, for example, under the Endangered Species Act. (See Industry Issues 2-1 for discussion of the Endangered Species Act.) In addition, if there is evidence of ancient ruins, the developer will need to retain an archaeologist or anthropologist to assess the presence of sensitive areas. (See Industry Issues 23-1.) Local regulatory agencies increasingly require this assessment in the form of an environmental impact statement (EIS) or environmental impact report (EIR) before issuing the necessary development permits. (See Chapter 4 for a discussion of environmental impact statements.)

> ✓ **Concept Check**
>
> **23.4**   What form of financial analysis commonly is used in a feasibility study?

If the consultant reports an underlying structural or environmental complication, the feasibility analysis must be reconsidered. The developer and consultants must determine whether the problem can be solved through either project redesign or mitigation, and whether the resulting cost affects feasibility.

If project feasibility survives structural and environmental tests, it must then make it through further hurdles. The land must have marketable title and it would be prudent for the developer to affirm this through title search at this point before significant additional investments in the project begin to occur.

Exhibit 23-2 suggests the evolutionary nature of the project planning and feasibility process. It must cycle or iterate through several dimensions, normally incorporating additional information from each dimension as the process is refined toward a decision. Market research and feasibility tests are crucial components of this process. Since they are much too complex to be treated adequately in this chapter, and since they apply to any real estate valuation or investment, we have given these subjects several separate chapters including 5, 6, 18, and 19. In the cycle depicted in Exhibit 23-2 the sophistication of the market research probably would increase with each "loop." Ultimately, however, many more of these processes will lead to "no go" than to "go."

> ✓ **Concept Check**
>
> **23.5**   Name three concerns for which a developer may retain an environmental consultant.

Obtaining Permits

Virtually all development projects require at least a site plan review. Many others will require a zoning change, possibly coupled with a parallel change in an official land use plan. Large-scale developments are likely to face some form of environmental impact or regional impact review. The cost of these reviews can reach hundreds of thousands of dollars for a large, complex development, and require a year or more to complete.

Exhibit 23-2 The Cycle of Evolving a Project*

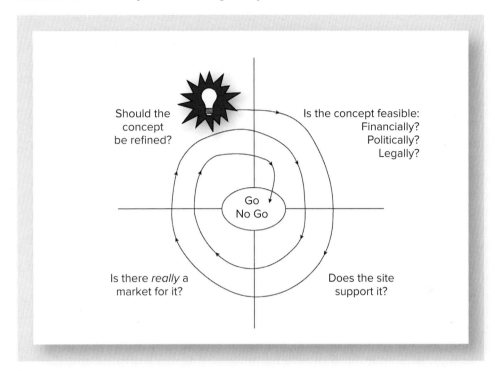

Should the concept be refined?

Is the concept feasible:
Financially?
Politically?
Legally?

Go
No Go

Is there *really* a market for it?

Does the site support it?

*This diagram borrows from one that addresses a broader perspective on development; see David Geltner, Norman G. Miller, Jim Clayton, and Piet Eichholtz, *Commercial Real Estate Analysis and Investments,* Thomson Southwestern, Mason, OH, 2007.
Source: Adapted from Gelther, David; Miller, Norman G; Clayton, Jim; Eichholtz, Piet; "Commercial Real Estate Analysis and Investments", Thomson Southwestern, Mason, OH. 2007.

✓ **Concept Check**

23.6 Even when a developer does not require a zoning change, the development project still must go through what kind of review?

If even a simple zoning change is required, the time and legal expense can be considerable and can require months, even years, with the ultimate outcome uncertain. It seems to be automatic that a developer who proposes apartments or commercial development near existing single-family neighborhoods will become the target of vigorous political resistance against the change. Even when the developer technically has all necessary permits in hand, preexisting homeowners who perceive the project as an intrusion into their neighborhood and a source of uncertain change often resort to a multitude of political maneuvers to delay and obstruct the project. They may even resort to filing lawsuits that challenge the existing zoning or permits on the slimmest of arguments. (Often a suit that fails still delays the developer enough to stop the project.) Since delay is one of the developer's biggest enemies, he or she must attempt to lay the groundwork in advance for neighborhood cooperation. This may be by providing overly generous provisions for buffering (i.e., for providing transition zones that separate surrounding land uses from the development), or by offering gifts to the neighborhood such as a "vest-pocket" park or other desirable neighborhood improvement. Being prepared for constructive negotiation with both the land use authorities and neighborhood homeowner groups is an essential component of a developer's resources.[7] (See Exhibits 23-3 and 23-4.) Probably the most dramatic failures (and successes) in the development experience

---

7. Nathan Collier, who combines successful development of multifamily projects with writing, provides excellent firsthand examples of the role of such negotiations in his compact overview of multifamily development: Nathan S. Collier, Courtland A. Collier, and Don Halperin, *Construction Funding, The Process of Real Estate Development, Appraisal and Finance,* 4th ed. (Hoboken, NJ: John Wiley & Sons, 2008).

Exhibit 23-3 Thoughts of an Experienced Developer on Land Use Negotiation

Every successful developer is a good negotiator. The path to a completed project is fraught with perils, and to succeed a developer must deftly wend his or her way through a thicket of obstructions and objections.

One of the most challenging phases of any project is the zoning/site plan process, which usually involves public hearings. The site plan process involves submitting a detailed plan—location of buildings and roads, elevations, landscaping, setbacks, utility tie ins, total square footage—showing exactly how a developer plans to use the land in accordance with an already permitted use. In theory, all the developer must show during the site planning process is that all land use regulations and ordinances have been complied with and then approval is automatic. In real life, gray areas and matters of interpretation always arise. Some requirements are as amorphous as "compatible with the surrounding neighborhood," a stipulation that is probably unconstitutionally vague. But who wants to be the developer who spends five years and a small fortune taking it to the Supreme Court? Easier just to add some buffer or agree to pay for some infrastructure improvements as long as the requested concession is financially tolerable.

With NIMBYism (not in my backyard) virtually a universal response to any development, a successful developer must be prepared to navigate the shoals of opposition. Most challenging during the zoning/site plan process, a developer often must deal with multiparty negotiations, including, at a minimum, the local government planning staff, the hearing body itself, and the citizens and interest groups attending the hearing. Each party has a different agenda, motivations, and positions. Usually people oppose a development because their homes are nearby and they perceive a negative impact on their quality of life or upon the market value of their home, which for many people is their single largest financial investment. These are all jugular emotional issues to which people react strongly. Sometimes people oppose a development for larger environmental issues. There are no magic wands a developer can wave to make opposition go away, but negotiation skills and sincere public relationship efforts can help immensely.

Source: Told by Nathan Collier, Principal, The Collier Companies, Gainesville, Florida; www.colliercompanies.com

Exhibit 23-4 A Real Story of Developer Negotiation

The "Intruder"

I once was attempting to put together a roughly 300-unit apartment development that involved a rezoning. Due to the buildup of the surrounding land, the agricultural zoning was obviously inappropriate and a rezoning was in order. But to what? The adjacent single-family neighborhood association thought single-family zoning was in their best interest and initially fought hard for that position.

A Strategy: Planned Unit Development

We began an education process through a series of meetings with the neighborhood. Our goals were to (1) present information on how extensive the permitted latitude was within the legal definition of "single-family" zoning and (2) present the alternative of a planned unit development. When the neighborhood group thought of single-family zoning, they imagined a development just like theirs: large lots, generous setbacks, expensive homes of 2,000-plus square feet. Through the use of third-party professionals (to add credibility), we were able to show how much of what they liked about their neighborhood came from the quality of the development itself and private deed restrictions and was not a legal requirement of a single-family zoning classification.

The neighborhood group quickly realized that single-family zoning classification alone would not give them the protection they desired. We then introduced the concept of a planned unit development that basically combines the rezoning and the site plan process. The land is rezoned, but it can only be developed according to the site plan submitted at the time of the rezoning. Thus, the site plan is locked into political/regulatory concrete. We offered to submit our rezoning request as a planned unit development that included several concessions: (1) setbacks several times larger than would normally be required under apartment zoning; (2) a berm; (3) extensive landscaping, much greater than the statutory minimum; (4) no buildings facing the neighborhood would be higher than two stories nor contain more than eight units, and the roofline would be "complex" (i.e., they would look like large homes); (5) all parking lot lighting would be hooded or shielded so as not to create nighttime "light pollution."

The neighborhood would benefit by knowing exactly what they were getting; the developer would benefit by achieving the approval, or even acquiescence, of the adjacent neighborhood, which virtually assures governmental approval.

Exhibit 23-4 Continued A Real Story of Developer Negotiation

So Far, Not So Good

In spite of our concessions and extensive neighborhood meetings, the day of the zoning hearing arrived without endorsement from the neighborhood association. Nonetheless, when our land use attorney inquired if we wanted a postponement, I declined. I knew that a deadline was an excellent motivator during negotiation. We continued to talk with the association, with the last meeting occurring in a crowded conference room outside the main hearing room as the zoning commission finished prior items of its agenda. Citizens, neighborhood association representatives, planning staff, and development professionals bandied about last minute proposals.

Hope?

The upside was that a majority of the neighborhood supported a core group of concessions, although it was not the same majority on every point. The downside was that enough citizens were still in opposition—most hoping for more concessions— that the neighborhood association leaders felt uncomfortable formally supporting any one proposal.

Our development professionals presented our proposal, staff had their say, and then the floor was opened for citizen comments. Requests were made not to allow any rezoning (legally unrealistic) or to have the public buy the land as a park (budget buster extraordinaire!). Requests were made for an even greater buffer or to require that buildings be limited to one story. I waited until the very end and made my presentation speaking as a member of the public.

Last Card

I pointed out that the buffer we offered matched several others in the past and there was no local precedent for a larger buffer. I mentioned that single-family zoning allowed three-story construction and that we were limiting ourselves to two stories in a neighborhood where many homes were also two stories. Also, there were no statutory requirements for the berm we were offering and our landscaping adjacent to the single-family areas vastly exceeded regulatory requirements. I mentioned that we had held a number of meetings attended by well-known and respected professionals. I then played my best card by pointing out that although the neighborhood group was not formally in agreement with us, this was in large measure due to a desire to operate by consensus as an organization. Furthermore, a majority accepted the core of our proposals. I took a bit of a gamble at this point and turned from the podium and gestured toward the president of the neighborhood association who was sitting behind me and asked "Did I state that fairly?" and was rewarded with a nod. We got the rezoning on a 5–0 vote.

Source: Told by Nathan Collier, Principal, The Collier Companies, Gainesville, Florida; www.colliercompanies.com

take place in public hearings with land use authorities whose decisions can kill a project instantly (see Industry Issues 23-1 and 23-2). These meetings frequently are dramatized by being packed standing room only with intense and resistant homeowners.

> ✓ **Concept Check**
>
> **23.7** Other than expense, what is the most common and serious threat to a typical development posed by the permitting process?

Design

When the developer has control of the property, is assured of no undiscovered legal, environmental, and ecological problems, and has the basic zoning required, it is time to turn the initial concept into a complete design. Selection of the architect is a vital step in the process, though numerous design professionals and engineers will play important subsidiary roles.

Architect. The architect can take on a range of roles. The architect can provide predesign services or schematics, which relate needed building functions to each other and to space, yielding a preliminary indication of the basic building design. From there follows the actual design, which may evolve through several stages of completeness. An increasingly important objective in this process is to create "green" buildings. (See Industry Issues 23-3.) Design development brings refinement of the interior space and exact specification of building

In 1995, developer Michael Baumann assembled investors and won approval to launch a $100 million, 600-unit apartment and commercial high-rise at the mouth of the Miami River in downtown Miami, Florida. He purchased the 2.2-acre site for $8 million. In the fall of 1998, weeks before he was to launch construction of his Brickell Pointe, archaeologists conducting a routine survey of the site detected an unusual circle formation in the bedrock surface. When experts suggested that the circle of holes might have been carved by

Ancient Tequesta Indians Win Over Modern Miami Developer

Tequesta Indians, a group that disappeared hundreds of years ago, the situation rapidly gained national attention. The focus of the national media, preservation groups, Native Americans, and an endless parade of paranormals, New Age groups, and others spiraled upward, creating an ongoing circus atmosphere at the site for weeks.

By all indications, Baumann had the right to proceed with his development. But the archaeologists involved reported that he made every effort to cooperate with them in evaluating its archaeological significance and in exploring options. He concluded, however, that redesign at that stage was infeasible. An effort to surgically remove and relocate the circle failed in mid-February 1999, and events rapidly led to legal adversarial action by the county, which sought and obtained permission from the court to

exercise eminent domain. An injunction against construction was imposed and trial was set for the following October. After a contentious summer, the county and Baumann settled on a purchase price of $26.7 million six days before trial, with Baumann offering to loan the county part of the money for the purchase. In early 2009 the Miami Circle finally was named a National Historic Landmark. It is under control of the State of Florida. The site was placed under management of HistoryMiami, a private museum society, and opened as Miami Circle, a public park, in February 2011.

Source: Adapted from Kelley, Jim; "Magic Primal", *Miami New Times*, November 16, 2000; www.miaminewtimes.com/miaminewtimes.com

Source: © JUAN CASTRO OLIVERA/AFP/Getty Images

Source: © Robert Sullivan/Getty Images

In 1985, when developer Ken McGurn sought to create the first downtown apartments in Gainesville, Florida, in over a half century, he found himself confronted by the ghost of apartments past. He needed to clear numerous dwellings from his proposed site, among which were the dilapidated shells of four Victorian structures. But a group of local citizens believed that these structures were the "apartments for workers" from an earlier era around 1900. They concluded that the structures were thus historic properties and set about to save them. The result was that McGurn's project was stopped until the issue was resolved with city authorities. Six months later he was obliged to move all four structures a little more than a half mile to four vacant lots. The move was the biggest transportation of houses in the history of the city, and drew suitable press attention. The whole undertaking cost approximately the price of a new small home at the time.

What became of the "Sad Sisters," as the structures were known locally? They remained exactly as McGurn situated them for almost 20 years—except for the effect of an additional 20 years of exposure to the elements, drug dealers, vagrants, vandals, and stray animals. In 1994, the city proposed to use them for fire department training, but a very active local historic preservationist stepped up and agreed to take them over by purchasing the lots and receiving the "Sisters" as a gift from McGurn. Unfortunately, she too was unable to implement a feasible restoration plan for them. She finally "deconstructed" the "Sad Sisters," and the salvaged pine wood has found its way into many fine homes and other structures of the area.

Gainesville Apartment Developer Haunted by the Ghost of Apartments Past

© LING.

© LING.

systems such as plumbing, electrical, and HVAC (heating, ventilation, and air conditioning). The design process finally leads to several outputs, including the contract documents, the actual detailed specifications for the building, working drawings, and rules and forms for the bidding process. Sometimes the architect assists or manages the bidding process. Other times, the architect actually manages the overall project, including the agreement between the developer and the contractor, though this role is infrequent.

Architects also can play another role earlier in the process. Often they are very effective in representing the development in public meetings with land use authorities. This is due in part to their expertise in presentations and perhaps to their comparatively favorable professional image relative to developers and attorneys.

The architect can be compensated according to several methods. Early in the development process, probably during the permitting stage, the architect may be retained on an hourly basis. In the design stage, when the project is much more narrowly defined, the compensation is likely to be based on either a percentage of the construction cost or a fixed fee plus expenses. When a percentage of cost is used, the amount will likely depend on the complexity of the project. For moderately complex designs, compensation can range between 3 and 7 percent; for simple garden apartments, it can range as low as 1 to 2 percent. Unusual projects might pay 10 percent. Obviously, a potential problem with the percentage compensation is that it rewards the architect for a more costly design. Thus, a fixed fee plus expenses may be used instead.

Selection of the architect for a development is obviously a critical step. The choice will be based on a combination of considerations, including competence and reputation, compatibility of values and goals between developer and architect, and ability of the two to communicate effectively. Since there is, in principal, inherent tension between the design function (i.e., aesthetically oriented) and the developer (i.e., cost and time oriented) communication of views and priorities is vital for a successful outcome.

Land Planner.   For land developments the developer gives the key design role to a land planner. In large projects involving multiple structures, extensive grounds, parking areas, and drainage and water retention systems, the developer will rely on a land planner to "solve" the complex land planning puzzle. The developer works closely with the land planner to evolve the basic site plan within which any structures must fit. The **land planner** in turn uses input from a number of specialists, including hydrologists, architects, marketing consultants, engineers, soils engineers, and others. Concerns of the land planner include aesthetics, optimal use and preservation of the site, traffic flows, utility systems, and drainage systems.

Landscape Architect.   The landscape architect normally serves in a more detail oriented role than the land planner. The **landscape architect** focuses on the topography, soil, and vegetation that are the context for a structure, with the goal of giving a suitable harmonious and enhancing immediate setting for the structure. This involves numerous ingredients, including grading, ground covers, shrubs, trees, flowerbeds, sign character and placement, fountains, benches, or other amenities. The landscape architect's work may also contribute to energy efficiency or drainage needs.

Engineers.   The expertise of several types of engineers must be coordinated by the architect in bringing together the final structure design. These engineers commonly work as subcontractors to the architect, but their qualifications need to be reviewed by the developer. A **soils engineer** will determine the sufficient specifications to achieve safety and stability for a structure's foundation. A **structural engineer** will determine the requisite structural skeleton to maintain the building's integrity. A **mechanical engineer** will provide specifications and design for the HVAC system and other building systems. An **electrical engineer** will design the power sources and distribution system. Finally, a **civil engineer** will design on-site utility systems, including sewers, water, streets, parking, and site grading.

Clearly, development involves extremely complex coordination, and this is one of the major challenges of the developer. It is not surprising that one knowledgeable observer has asserted that failure to achieve effective communication between developer, architect, and engineer early in the development process is the single greatest cause of project delays and cost overruns.[8]

8. Richard Peiser and Anne Frej, *Professional Real Estate Development: The ULI Guide to the Business,* 2nd ed. (Washington, DC: Urban Land Institute, 2003), p. 41.

Financing

Development has multiple phases, each with a different set of risks and different combinations of financing. We will consider financing for land acquisition, construction, and post-construction. Typically, debt financing is involved in each of these stages, but of course there must be equity capital as well. Frequently the combination of debt financing and equity is insufficient to carry the project through the construction stage. Thus, gap financing through mezzanine debt also can play an important role.

Land Acquisition Financing. Usually, a developer is reluctant or unable to commit substantial funds in the acquisition of land for development. The period before actual construction could last many months or several years, and the limited capital of a typical developer bears a very high opportunity cost because of its value in providing liquidity for current projects. But institutional lenders, such as banks, thrifts, and insurance companies, are reluctant to lend on land that generates little or no cash flow. In the rare case when an outside source provides a land loan, the total is likely to be for no more than 50 percent of the value of the land. Thus, a developer must look to other sources. We have already noted the importance of options as a solution. However, when the developer must exercise, or "go hard," on the option, more complete funding must be found. Again, the contract for deed or a purchase money mortgage from the land seller is a common solution. Others, as noted, may be to bring the land seller into the development as a joint venture partner, or to acquire use of the land through a ground lease.

But financing the land itself is not sufficient. The developer will incur significant **soft costs** before reaching the stage of construction financing, including the title examination, environmental and ecological evaluation, legal and other costs of the permitting process, and architectural and engineering fees. Thus, the developer must have equity capital. Typically, this will come mainly from outside investors through any of the business entities discussed in Chapter 17, including a subchapter S corporation or, for a large-scale development organization, through a REIT. However, the most common structure used is either a limited partnership or, increasingly, the limited liability company (LLC). Typically the financial investors will contribute funds for their share of the ownership interest, while the developer will contribute mainly expertise for a share of the venture.

Obviously, the financial investors must have confidence in the developer. Thus, the ability of the developer to raise capital depends heavily on his or her relevant track record. Investors are more likely to support a developer with more extensive experience, but it also matters what that experience is. For example, even if the developer has extensive experience in small-scale apartments, investors may be reluctant to invest with the developer in a condominium project, a large-scale apartment project, an office development, or in *any* development outside the developer's "neighborhood." Finally, investors must have confidence in the integrity of the developer since it is difficult or impossible to recover funds from a development that was never completed or from a developer who misappropriates funds.

Construction Financing.   Once the developer and architect have completed the design stage, the developer can apply for construction funding. The most common source of construction funding is a bank. Traditionally, the loan had a floating rate over prime; increasingly, it may be tied to a LIBOR rate, floating perhaps 150 to 250 basis points above LIBOR.[9] The construction loan will finance, at most, the cost of land, soft costs and **hard costs** (i.e., the direct costs of materials, labor, and subcontractors for actual construction). The loan will be disbursed to the developer in stages, frequently on the basis of either specific invoices from vendors or as the project reaches various predetermined stages of completion.

The risks of construction lending are less in a number of respects than with the land acquisition stage. Environmental risks, ecological risks, title risks, and especially the permitting risks normally will be in the past. The remaining risks are those that banks can manage effectively, and thus will underwrite. These remaining risks include the ability of the developer to manage and complete the construction process; risks of construction such as weather interruptions, materials shortages, work stoppages, strikes, or construction accidents; and, finally, rent-up following construction. Banks long have had a comparative advantage in managing construction risk because it is similar to working capital risks for any operating business. That is, monitoring the delivery and use of construction materials is similar to monitoring business inventory, while evaluating the capability of the developer to perform is not unlike evaluating other business managers in their ability to perform.

When banks are uncomfortable bearing the postconstruction risk of rent-up, they often will shed it by requiring a *take-out commitment* from a long-term lender that will pay off the construction loan, as discussed in Chapter 16. Normally, however, the construction lender tends to forgo requiring a take-out commitment if the borrower is an established developer constructing "mainstream" projects.

✓ Concept Check

23.12   What risks of development already are resolved by the time the construction lender commits to a loan?

Mezzanine Debt.   Banks seldom loan 100 percent of construction costs, except on very strong projects with strong developers. More commonly, they may fund 70 to 80 percent of project costs, or less in times of tight money. Frequently, therefore, the developer either needs or prefers to find additional capital to complete the construction stage. Equity capital is one option, but equity money requires a high yield, and funding with more equity dilutes returns to the original equity. Therefore, developers often turn to *mezzanine financing,* which can take a range of forms. While it sometimes is second mortgage debt, it often is not mortgage debt at all. Rather, ownership shares in the development entity are pledged to the mezzanine lenders as security. Thus, in the event of default, no foreclosure procedure is necessary for the mezzanine lenders to exercise their recourse. Mezzanine debt is more expensive than normal construction financing. Where construction loans might run 150 basis points to 250 basis points above the LIBOR rate, mezzanine debt will run several hundred basis points above. However, this will still be below the required yield on equity money, and, thus, more attractive to the developer.

---

9. LIBOR is the London Interbank Offering Rate, a floating interest rate among non-U.S. banks in London for U.S. dollar deposits. While the rate is floating, many lenders provide the option to buy into an interest rate swap that substitutes fixed-rate payments for the actual floating rate on the loan.

✓ **Concept Check**

> **23.13** Why might a developer need supplemental financing during the construction and leasing stages? Why would mezzanine financing be attractive?

Postconstruction Financing. The construction lender expects his or her loan to be paid off within two to three years, usually shortly after issuance of a **certificate of occupancy** from the local government certifying that the structure is safe for use. The pay off can happen either through financing arranged by the developer as the project nears completion, or through a take-out commitment arranged prior to construction funding. Normally the take-out "permanent" loan will be funded when the certificate of occupancy is issued. However, it may be funded in stages that depend on the level of leasing or occupancy starting with a relatively small **floor loan.** This, again, may necessitate "gap" or mezzanine financing. An alternative to gap financing that sometimes is used is a **subordination agreement** with the construction lender, which makes the construction loan lien inferior to the lien securing the take-out loan that follows. If the amount of the take-out loan will not pay off the construction loan completely, the developer may be able to negotiate with a friendly construction lender to subordinate the remaining portion of the loan to the take-out loan. This gets most of their money back to the construction lender while allowing the take-out lender to have a first lien position.

Another approach to postconstruction funding is the *miniperm loan.* This is a construction loan that serves as a "permanent" loan for a few years after the property is completed. The typical term might be five years from inception. The miniperm has served multiple roles in recent years. For example, if current interest rates on permanent financing are higher now than the developer believes will be available for the project in five years, then the miniperm loan is an attractive alternative to the more traditional arrangement.

There is reason to expect that permanent financing normally could be on better terms after two or three years of operating experience since the project then will be regarded as an established property. Exhibit 23-5 suggests the basis for this possibility. The life of the typical income-producing property can be divided into three phases: development and construction, lease-up, and stable operation. This is important because of risk differences between the stages. For the normal income-producing property, risks of the development and construction stage are both higher and different from the risks after completion. Quite simply, the dominating risk after construction is market risk, whereas it is not a factor at all until construction is complete. Market risk is greatest in the lease-up stage. Thus, the overall risk level of the property falls progressively from one stage to the next. It is not surprising, therefore, that a developer could get better terms with "permanent" financing for a project that has "graduated" from the lease-up stage and shows two or three years of stable operation. In this case, the miniperm could offer a cost-effective way of deferring permanent financing until more favorable terms are available due to the reduced risk of stable operations.

✓ **Concept Check**

> **23.14** Why might a developer be able to obtain more favorable "long-term" financing after a project is leased and operating than when construction has just been completed?

Exhibit 23-5   Risk Phases of an Income-Producing Property and Four Alternative Financing Sequences

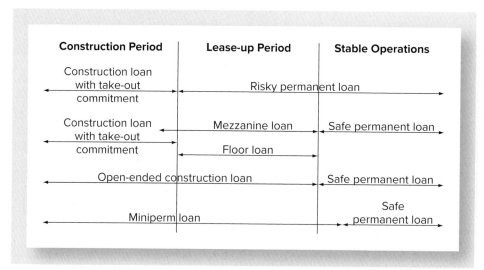

Construction

Even the smallest building project involves a multitude of separate contractors and a still larger number of steps in the process.[10] Thus, construction must be controlled and coordinated by a central authority, the **general contractor,** who in turn is responsible for subcontracting the completion of the various elements of the project. These include excavation, pouring and finishing concrete, components of the structure, building systems such as electrical, plumbing, and HVAC, landscaping, and more. While the general contractor may be fully responsible for selecting the **subcontractors** involved, it is not uncommon for the developer or architect to review, or even prearrange, some of the subcontractors where they provide especially critical aspects of the project.

The agreement with the general contractor can range on a spectrum from fixed-price bidding to a negotiated agreement at cost plus fee. Government projects usually are made through bidding to meet the requirements of the public for arm's-length competitive contracts. However, most other construction contracts are completed through negotiation. Often the arrangement will involve a maximum cost plus fee. If the cost runs higher than the maximum, the developer and general contractor split the overrun; if the cost runs less than maximum, they split the savings.

As noted before, clear understandings between developer, architect, and the general contractor are vital to keep the project on schedule and on budget. Always a construction project will require change orders in the plans because of materials changes, oversights in the planning, or new market information that dictates modification of the project. These can become extremely costly once the original contracts have been signed. Poor initial understandings lead to a high incidence of change orders.

No matter what problems arise on the construction project or what agreement exists with the general contractor, the developer bears the brunt of any failure. Therefore, the developer needs to monitor the process and be represented when decisions arise. Often a **construction manager** serves as the developer's liaison and representative on the project site. For example, the construction manager may stand in for the developer in discussions between the general contractor and architect.

---

10. One of the authors, in adding two rooms to his residence, counted approximately 25 separate subcontractors with over 100 separate tasks.

I n the construction process, a construction manager represents the developer, serving as a monitor, mediator, and advocate of the developer's goals. Because of the construction manager's need to be able to negotiate with the architect, the general contractor, subcontractors, marketing representatives, and possibly the lender, he or she must be mature and experienced enough to have credibility. Although construction managers usually play no direct role in the actual construction of a structure, they may be involved in scheduling and coordinating the design and construction processes, including the selection, hiring, and oversight of specialty trade contractors. They typically need to be very knowledgeable about, and therefore experienced with, the type of project involved.

Construction managers regularly review engineering and architectural drawings and specifications to monitor progress and ensure compliance with plans and schedules. They track and control construction costs against the project budget to avoid cost overruns. They meet regularly with the developer, trade contractors, architects, and others to monitor and coordinate all phases of the construction project. Their background may be that of an architect, contractor, or engineer.

Both the American Institute of Constructors (AIC, www.aicnet.org) and the Construction Management Association of America (CMAA, http://cmaanet.org) have established voluntary certification programs for construction managers. Requirements combine study and written examinations with verification of professional experience. Although certification is not required to work in the construction industry, voluntary certification can be valuable because it provides evidence of competence and experience.

Median annual wages of construction managers in 2015 were $87,400 according to the U.S. Bureau of Labor Statistics. From payscale.com, the middle 50 percent earned between $57,000 and $92,000. The lowest 10 percent earned less than $46,000; the highest 10 percent earned more than $120,000. According to a 2013 salary survey by the National Association of Colleges and Employers, candidates with a bachelor's degree in construction science/management received job offers averaging $57,153 a year.

Sources: Data from Bureau of Labor Statistics, *Occupational Outlook Handbook* 2010–2011 edition (Washington DCI 2011); payscale.com; NACE Salary Survey, September 2013.

Construction Manager

Construction often involves a significant number of changes; and resulting renegotiations between the architect, the general contractor, and subcontractors are very costly. As a result, an alternative arrangement has evolved known as **design-build** where the architect and general contractor are one. In complicated projects this arrangement reduces inherent design-cost conflicts that otherwise must be negotiated when plans get changed. Since the changes will be worked out within one firm, the solutions should be efficient, affording savings for the project.

Sometimes, speed of completion is exceptionally important. Then the developer may resort to a procedure called **fast-track construction.** Rather than waiting for the architect to complete the entire project design before construction, the design will be broken into sequential phases, beginning with the site design, footings and foundation, building shell, and so forth. Then construction will begin before the last phases of design are complete. While this procedure can greatly accelerate the process, the procedure has been known to result in dramatic failures where the architect discovered after construction was under way that something in an early phase is incompatible with what must follow.

✓ **Concept Check**

23.15   Explain fast-track construction and design-build. What problem does each address?

Coordination of Contracting.   The development sequence presented thus far is oversimplified in a number of ways. Commonly, several elements of the process must overlap, and several contracts may need to be negotiated simultaneously. We have noted previously that the architect normally is involved in the permitting stage, providing both initial conceptual

Is It Easy Being Green?

Why are buildings turning "green," and how far will the green building movement go? The stakes involved, as reported by the United States Green Building Council (USGBC), are startling.[*] The USGBC reports that nongreen buildings in the United States have accounted for:

- 40 percent of primary energy use.
- 72 percent of electrical consumption.
- 39 percent of CO_2 emissions.
- 13.6 percent of potable water consumption.

They claim that green buildings can dramatically reduce these impacts by:

- Lowering energy use by 24 to 50 percent.
- Lowering CO_2 emissions by 33 to 39 percent.
- Lowering water usage by 40 percent.
- Lowering solid waste by 70 percent.

What makes greening work, they claim, is that these benefits also translate to a remarkable array of financial gains.

How do we get to green? The USGBC has evolved the building certification program, Leadership in Environmental Efficiency and Design (LEED), now widely recognized. The four certification levels—certified, silver, gold, and platinum—allow points for a building on several factors, including site sustainability, water efficiency, energy efficiency, use of alternative energy sources, reuse and recycling of materials, and indoor environmental quality.

Results? By 2016 there were over 32,500 LEED certified commercial projects and USGBC claims that over 30 percent of all nonresidential construction—new and retrofit—sought LEED certification in 2015. One LEED certified project is the Toyota Motor Sales South Campus Office Development in Torrance, California, a 624,000 square foot, 40-acre office campus. The LEED measures taken in building the complex are reported to have been paid for by trimming other standard features, resulting in no net cost increase. Meanwhile the LEED measures annually save $400,000 in energy and $12,000 in water, resulting in a seven-year payback on the special equipment used. In another reported example, LEED elements in the Proximity Hotel in Greensboro, North Carolina, costing $1.5 to $2.0 million, have resulted in a 39 percent reduction in energy, 34 percent reduction in water use, and reductions of construction landfill impact by 87 percent. These resulting savings, combined with increased customer demand, are expected to achieve payback for the green building measures in four years.

The USGBC LEED program is not the only sustainability award program today. It has been joined, for example, by the Green Globes process of the Green Buildings Initiative, as well as the National Association of Home Builders Model Green Home Guidelines program, and several international programs. In addition, the Energy Star programs of the U.S. Environmental Protection Agency and the U.S. Department of Energy remain very significant.

The LEED program responded to early critics by implementing extensive changes in 2013 with a revised program called LEED v4. There is less emphasis on "glitzy" features such as bicycle racks or solar power and more emphasis on basic conservation measures such as insulation and better seals. The changes also brought a new focus on location, emphasizing the value of using existing infrastructure, valuing walkability and connectivity, and rewarding quality alternative transportation. It gives higher priority to factors related to climate change, indoor environment, and resource depletion, allowing "pilot crediting" of innovative systems, recognizing more of a building lifecycle perspective, and greatly expediting the review process.

So what is the actual environmental impact of "going green"? Research is too new and the effects too complex for a simple answer. But the evidence is evolving, and seems positive. One recent, sophisticated simulation showed a 15 to 25 percent life-cycle average reduction for a broad range of environmental impacts. Easy or not, building and development appear to be turning green.[†]

[*]Figures reported are from the website of USGBC. www.usgbc.org

[†]For details of LEED v4, refer to the USGBC website. For recent assessment of "green building" impact see, for example, S. Suh, et al., "Environmental Performance of Green Building Code and Certification Systems," *Environmental Science & Technology* 48, 2014, pp. 2551–60.

renderings and serving as a spokesman for the project. Further, the general contractor often should give input to the design process, and thus must be "on board" before the construction loan is closed. In addition, the construction lender is likely to need cost estimates from the general contractor, which depend on the design as well. Thus, the construction loan commitment may require the general contractor to be under contract. But the construction loan may require a take-out commitment by a "permanent" or long-term lender, who may require preleasing. Thus, it is possible that the developer cannot even close the land purchase (funded by the construction loan) until sufficient preleasing has occurred to satisfy the take-out lender.

Marketing and Leasing

For all but the largest of developers, the marketing and leasing of the project will be through an external broker. The developer must select the broker with care. The broker must understand the market relevant to the project. Thus, for a locally oriented, general-purpose office building, the broker needs to be familiar with, and be known in, the local business office community in order to have knowledge of prospective tenants who are approaching lease turnover, who must expand to larger facilities, and so forth. Further, the broker should not be simultaneously engaged in marketing competitive projects since this creates conflicts of interest, and dilutes the commitment of the broker. In all cases the broker must be genuinely excited about the property.

A good broker not only has valuable connections in the target market, but also has special knowledge of the market regarding what tenants want in a property. For this reason the developer is wise to bring a broker into the process during the design stage to review and advise on the evolution of the design. Not only does this increase the likelihood of achieving a marketable property, but it allows the broker to have more of a stake in the product and more reason for enthusiasm about it.

✓ Concept Check

23.16 In addition to personal and organizational capability, what are two other important requirements of a marketing agent for a development?

Developers are increasingly recognizing the value of a public relations program for a property. Community awareness can be increased through adroit "positioning" of events in the course of the development, including groundbreaking, topping out of a high-rise structure, or announcing of new tenants to the project. Sometimes developments are able to work with community charities and nonprofit organizations to host or sponsor community events. In all cases, an important part of public relations is for the developer to work closely with the press and with public land use authorities. Developers do well to recognize the needs of the press for "copy" to meet deadlines. Providing useful copy can help to foster valuable working relationships.

Similarly, the developer wants to build relationships with regulatory officials early in the process. A "no surprise" policy is advisable wherein the developer anticipates any regulatory problem or issue that may arise with the development and presents it to the regulatory officials—before third parties bring it to their attention—with a recommended solution and a demonstrated willingness to be flexible. Few features in a developer's style appear to engender more goodwill from the public and from officials than an evident willingness to explore alternative courses of action on contentious issues. This approach can be very important in public forums.

Most developments today seem to encounter the NIMBY phenomenon (not in my back yard) and perhaps the BANANA phenomenon (build absolutely nothing anywhere near anything). As noted in Exhibits 23-3 and 23-4, this usually arises from well-intended neighbors, but sometimes stems from well-organized special interest groups who are targeting the development issue merely as a step toward broader political goals. Regardless of the cause of the resistance, it is valuable to have put the project's "best foot forward" through attention to building favorable media coverage, by gaining organizational friends in the community, and by building a relationship of trust with the media and local authorities before the issues arise.

When the actual marketing for the project should begin depends on the type of property. It is not productive to launch advertising for apartments until shortly before the actual units are available. In contrast, leasing for office buildings and other facilities with long-term tenants not only can begin during the design stage, but needs to start earlier since

Ageneral contractor is the person, or firm, that executes a contract with the developer to build a project. This must be accomplished according to the plans and specifications developed by the architect and engineers, or the owner, and in line with the prevailing building codes. The general contractor solicits subcontractors who bid or negotiate to perform components of the construction project, including excavation, pouring and finishing concrete, elements of the structure, each of the separate building systems, landscaping, and many more. The

General Contractor

general contractor, therefore, is responsible for coordinating and managing people, materials, and equipment; budgets, schedules, and contracts; and the safety of employees and the general public. The general contractor must maintain the complicated sequencing and timing of all of the subcontractors, and work out solutions when the inevitable disruptions of the schedule occur. He or she is part liaison to the developer and architect, part monitor, and part enforcer.

General contractors are not salaried. The contract with the developer can range between a fixed-price bid and a cost plus fee agreement. Many general contracts involve a maximum price, as discussed in the text. If the cost exceeds the maximum price, the general contractor will share the overrun. If the cost is below, the general contractor will share the savings.

General contractors must hold a state-specific license. Normally there are no technical requirements beyond the license, but general contractors are the persons (or companies) that have gained considerable confidence in their capacity to perform. The individuals involved usually have a voluntary certification from the American Institute of Constructors (AIC, www.aicnet. org) or the Construction Management Association of America (CMAA, cmaanet. org). Virtually always the general contractor must be experienced in construction, perhaps having begun as a subcontractor in a construction specialty area. Increasingly, persons serving as general contractors have undergraduate or even graduate degrees in construction science, construction management, or civil engineering.

---

prospective commercial tenants will contract for space well in advance of their actual move. Similarly, there needs to be preselling of units in a condominium project. Further, preleasing (or preselling) is likely to be required for construction financing. For retail and some office projects, nothing really can go forward until the anchor tenants have been secured. Only then will construction funding be available, which enables closing on the land. Further, where the construction loan depends on a take-out commitment, the take-out commitment is likely to require preleasing to be well under way.

Leasing of commercial space (e.g., retail, office, or industrial) will be through a leasing agent. As explained in Chapter 21, commercial leasing is a particularly challenging and competitive specialty field; the developer wants to be assured that the broker for the project can bring these specialists to the table.

> ✓ **Concept Check**
>
> **23.17** Why must the marketing program typically begin much sooner for a nonresidential development than for a residential one?

Developers have increasingly recognized the need for sophisticated marketing of their projects. Therefore, they have turned more to outside specialists to complement in-house sales staff.

Operation

www.naiop.org

Commercial Real Estate Development Association. An important industry education, information, and advocacy organization for commercial development.

Once the project has been largely rented it is in the operating phase. Effective operational management of rental real estate is fundamental to maintaining and increasing the value of the property. The function is sufficiently important that it is the subject of two other chapters in this book: Chapter 21, "Enhancing Value through Ongoing Management," and Chapter 22, "Leases and Property Types." We defer to those chapters for discussion of the subject.

Exhibit 23-6 summarizes the phases of development. While there is, in reality, much variation, the arrows are suggestive of the order and which phases might overlap.

Exhibit 23-6 Typical Development Sequence

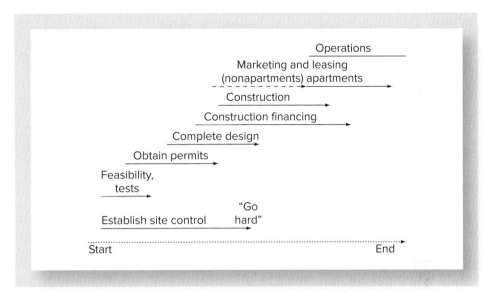

The "Numbers" of Development

Throughout the process of development, the successful developer always keeps the "numbers" in the corner of his or her eye. Even before control of the site is acquired, the developer has a concept of the project, but also will have done back-of-the-envelope calculations (nowadays, probably on a laptop) to "pencil out" the prospects. That is, the developer will not go forward on a project unless the prospective value exceeds its cost sufficiently to justify the venture. At the feasibility stage these numbers normally must be substantially refined, taking into account the unfolding specifics of the project. The developer not only creates a construction budget in the feasibility stage, but must project the initial income and operating expenses in order to compute, formally or informally, the net present value of the project.

Exhibit 23-7 presents an example of a construction budget such as might be evolved late in the feasibility process. The example is from a quality apartment project—with a total 2007 cost of about $35 million. It is fairly typical in its cost breakdown for large-scale suburban development.

The construction budget has six main components: land costs, hard costs, construction soft costs, marketing soft costs, developer's fee, and total construction financing costs. Land costs are about 12 percent of the total. They include the acquisition cost, site development in preparation for building, interest or carrying costs, and property taxes on the land. Hard costs, which are 66.3 percent of the total, are mainly the actual building construction (57.8 percent). Landscaping and hardscaping (hard surfaces on the grounds) make up another 2.6 percent of total costs, while an always important contingency reserve is 1.4 percent, representing about 2.5 percent of total hard costs.[11] This may be needed, for example, to cover change orders.

Construction soft costs are 9.4 percent of the total. Note that a huge 7.5 percent of this is a fee for utility use. Thus, permitting or impact fees are a very large component of the total cost. The architect's fee is only 0.5 percent, reflecting perhaps that the project is an adaptation of an earlier design, and relatively uncomplicated. Engineering fees are another 0.6 percent.

Other soft costs include marketing and construction financing. While marketing costs comprise 1.6 percent of the budget, construction financing is 10.2 percent and vies with land cost as the second largest item in the budget.

---

11. The hard cost contingency reserve is 1.4 percent out of 66.3 percent. Thus, reserve as a percentage of hard costs is 2.5 percent ($1.4 \div 66.3 \times 100$).

Exhibit 23-7   Construction Budget—Large Apartment Project

	% of Total
Land Costs	
Land acquisition cost	11.7%
Real estate taxes and carry costs	0.2
Total land costs	11.9%
Hard Costs	
Construction hard costs	57.8%
Permits/fees	0.4
Contingency	1.4
Telephone and TV	1.1
Security and water	0.5
Landscape and hardscape	2.6
Graphics	0.1
Pools	0.7
Other	1.7
Total hard costs	66.3%
Construction Soft Costs	
Architect	0.5%
Engineering	0.6
Geotechnical report and survey	0.1
Testing (soils, environmental assessment, etc.)	0.2
Utility use fees	7.5
Inspections	0.1
Insurance	0.1
Contingency	0.3
Subtotal construction soft costs	9.4%
Marketing Soft Costs	
Furniture, fixtures, and equipment	0.7%
Due diligence and legal fees	0.2
Closing cost	0.1
Title policy	0.2
Start-up/advertising	0.5
Subtotal marketing soft costs	1.6%*
Total soft costs	11.0%
Total—Land, Hard, and Soft Costs	89.2%
Developer's fee	1.7
Total Construction Financing Costs	10.2
Positive cash flow from operations during construction	−1.0
Total Basis in Project	**100.0%***
Construction loan (100.00%)	100.0%
Equity provided (0.00%)	0.0
Total Capital	100.0%

*Discrepancies in totals are due to rounding.

The last item is the developer's fee, fairly modest at 1.7 percent of the total budget. The project is owned by a financially strong organization that is able to obtain 100 percent construction funding. No equity is required at the outset.

There is an old saying "it is easier to ask forgiveness than it is to get permission." But the story of the Villas at Pinecrest Lakes suggests otherwise for developers. The developer of these luxury townhouse apartments in Jensen Beach, Florida was faced with conflicting regulatory restrictions for a parcel in the Pinecrest Lakes area. In accordance with Florida law, Martin County had enacted both a land use plan, which had the force of law, plus the usual local zoning restrictions. But, contrary to Florida law, the two were not consistent, and local zoning permitted the townhouses where the land use plan would not. Despite a lawsuit from the very beginning by adjacent homeowners, the County issued building permits to the developer and construction proceeded.

By 1999 five buildings were either occupied or nearing completion, and apparently were some of the nicest rental apartments in the

© JefThompson/Shutterstock

area. Then the ax fell. (Or you might say the Acts fell!) The local circuit court determined that the state-legislated land use plan prevailed, and the county's development permits were invalid. Because the developer proceeded in the face of formal legal challenge, the court finally ruled that the property had to be restored to its original condition—remove the new apartments completely. The case was appealed and finally reached the Florida Supreme Court,

where the judgment was upheld. Two years later the apartments were gone, and the developer was reported to be out something in excess of $3.3 million, after seven years of costly litigation.

Calculated Development Risk …. Miscalculated

Sources: Various news articles; Final Judgment in Case No. 96-126CA for the Circuit Court of the 19th Judicial Circuit in and for Martin County, State of Florida.

The time distribution of the main construction expenditures is shown in Exhibit 23-8. The entire construction period runs seven quarters. Thus, the first full year of operation is the third year after construction begins.

To determine project feasibility, the developer must, at a minimum, estimate net operating income (*NOI*) for the first full year of operation. Capitalizing this *NOI,* as

Exhibit 23-8   Timing of Construction Expenditures

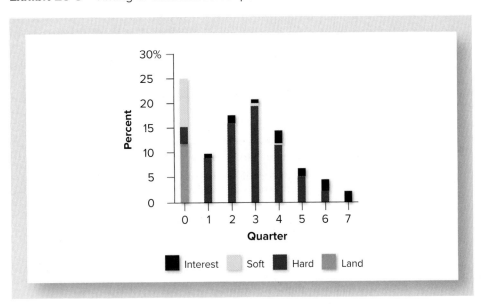

explained in Chapter 8, will indicate the prospective value of the project when finished and operating, enabling the developer to compute the difference between resulting value and total accumulated construction cost (i.e., the *NPV*) at the time of completion. The developer may take a step further, projecting *NOI* and reversion from sale over perhaps a five-year operating period, as explained in Chapter 19. This would allow for a discounted cash flow analysis for the entire project from the beginning of construction to sale, some seven years later.

What Is It Like to Be a Developer?

Successful development can result in outcomes that are satisfying in the extreme. The developer can have a dramatic and lasting positive impact on a community. Every community has its handful of individuals in the development community whose work is apparent in the character and profile of the community. In the small college city of Gainesville, Florida, for example, the work of one development organization accounts for most of the recently built structures in the downtown, and has been the force behind revitalizing an otherwise languishing central city. (See Industry Issues 23-4.) Another developer has transformed neighborhoods around the University of Florida, creating large numbers of quality apartments within walking distance of the campus and alleviating an extremely difficult housing and parking problem for students. Other local developers have contributed heavily to providing quality subdivisions for households on the threshold of housing affordability. Normally, of course, these developers enjoy financial rewards for their successes.

But there is good reason for the financial rewards. The development process depicted above is complex, uncertain, turbulent, and even hostile at times. At best, it is a competitive "sport" with about as many rules and player protections as rugby. As many developers stress, the financial path of a developer usually is best characterized by the roller coaster. Very few developers have not experienced a fall from financial highs to the point where survival is in question—more than one time in their career. As has been observed before, most developers risk losing everything they have invested in their development two or three times during the process: at the feasibility analysis stage, the permitting stage, and the marketing stage.[12]

While a superficial assessment of development may suggest that the work is for "risk seekers," a more careful assessment is that it is for risk managers, and even crisis managers. A developer also should be detail and plan oriented. It is difficult to believe that a developer has any chance of surviving the complexities, surprises, and stresses of the development process except by systematic and detailed preparation for a wide range of possible outcomes. Careful preparation also is necessary because virtually all of the problems a developer must solve are in conjunction with other persons over whom they have no control. The developer cannot expect to extract assistance or agreement from these individuals without first preparing the situation. As stated before, they must gain the confidence of a host of persons and provide the information, arguments, and incentives to make them friendly toward negotiating the solutions that the developer needs. This holds for land use authorities, neighbors of the development site, lenders, investors, and ultimately, of course, the "customers."

As if the uncertainties about other players in the development process were not enough, market cycles compound the risks. As noted in Chapter 6, cycles pervade virtually every real estate market. The precipitous decline of most real estate markets after 2006 is not a wholly new experience for seasoned real estate firms. The oscillations of the business cycle appear to be compounded in real estate by the long lead times and the scarcity of signals about immediate conditions. Thus, the developer is condemned to aim a project at a vaguely perceived, oscillating target market. Experts tend to think of real estate cycles as having four phases that might be termed trough, expansion, peak, and decline. With a minimum of perhaps two years between securing control of the land and the completion of construction,

---

12. See Peiser and Frej, *Professional Real Estate Development*, p. 4.

The Gainesville, Florida, MSA is a university, medical, and agricultural center with a population in 2011 of about 265,000. For decades the Gainesville downtown had suffered a steady exodus of businesses in response to the growing influence of I-75 to the west of the city and of the malls and power centers built near its intersections. Few new business buildings and no new residences had been constructed in the downtown for many years prior to 1980 and little remained except a variety of local and federal government facilities (marked Gov. in the photo).

Enter McGurn Investment Company, owned and operated by Ken and Linda McGurn. Working with the city, they overcame considerable obstacles to create office, retail, and restaurant space that would surround an old post office that was being converted to house the city's prized regional professional theater group, the

Hippodrome (see Hipp). That was the start of a slow but steady resurrection of Gainesville's downtown. In the years that followed, the McGurns engaged in several key projects that others would not touch, and only a lender who trusted the McGurns would finance. These included the first downtown apartments in the modern history of the city, and a dominating mixed-use project (Union Street Station, slightly right of center in the photo). Altogether, in the pivotal southeast quadrant of the downtown, shown in the photo, McGurn Investment Company has built, rehabili-

tated, or facilitated some 20 projects (indicated by asterisks). The result may be substantial asset accumulation for McGurn Investment Company, but its community effects are the most interesting story. Gainesville now is gaining something that most larger cities strive for, a vibrant 24-hour downtown.

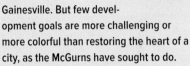
Can a Developer Affect a Community?

Other developers in other ways have had vital effects on Gainesville. But few development goals are more challenging or more colorful than restoring the heart of a city, as the McGurns have sought to do.

Who are prime developers that have impacted your city?

© LING.

Source: Told by Ken and Linda McGurn.

mcgurn.com

the likelihood of entering the market in the most desirable phase, the expansion phase, is little more than 25 percent. Further, the chance of entering a market on the decline also may be about 25 percent. While declines are unwelcome to any real estate investor, they are likely to be particularly hazardous to new development since it tends to have the highest cost structure in the market, and thus the highest break-even point.

What Does It Take to Enter Development?

It seems apparent from the demanding nature of development that playing this "quarterback" role requires exceptional capacities. Most observers note the need for strong self-assurance and a capacity to manage under stress and uncertainty. Others have identified creativity, drive, flexibility, and vision as signature characteristics of a successful developer.[13] But the requirements do not appear to stop with this immodest list. The developer also must have credibility and respect to inspire the confidence of those who are betting their work and careers on his or her capacities. James Graaskamp argued that beyond a developer's personal capacities, he or she needs to have control of something to get in the "game." Development requires money, land, knowledge, and tenants—and a would-be developer must have control of at least one of these.[14]

If Graaskamp is correct, then the path for many persons interested in entering development is through gaining knowledge. But how? Rarely, if ever, can one gain the

www.icsc.org

International Council of Shopping Centers, the principal organization of retail developers.

13. Miles, Netherton, and Schmitz, *Real Estate Development Principles and Process* 5th ed., Chapter 1.
14. As reported in Peiser and Frej, *Professional Real Estate Development*, p. 7.

knowledge necessary to have credibility as a developer without experience. As one very successful developer observed, you simply have to pay your dues to have credibility. Historically, the range of experience that serves the purpose has been remarkably diverse: brokerage, property management, income property appraisal, income property finance, construction project management, and construction lending. Some argue that construction lending is particularly valuable because a construction lender is observing the development process very closely and is in a position to ask more questions than most persons can because as the lender they have privileged access to the financial records and business plans of the developer. Attaining credentials as a developer can be accelerated by the right educational background. A degree in civil engineering, construction, and urban planning complemented with business training, or a graduate degree in real estate and development can provide background technical knowledge, and can give access to the jobs that are most effective upon which to build the right experience for entering development.

Summary

Development is the continual reconfiguration of the built environment to meet society's needs. The process of development, done successfully, not only adds great value to the land but also is subject to a myriad of challenges and risks. The development process can be described in roughly eight phases: establishing control of a site; conducting feasibility analysis, refining the development concept, and conducting tests of the site; obtaining necessary permits; design; obtaining financing; construction; marketing and leasing; and operation.

Each of these phases has its particular set of risks and challenges. In the initial stages the risks include the possibility of encountering problems with the site, including title risk, seismic problems, hydrologic problems, toxic substances, the presence of wetlands, endangered species, or archaeologically or historically sensitive matters. Risks for the project often are greatest in the permitting stage, with the threat of delay paramount. Once these risks are resolved, a construction lender is willing to loan funds for the project. The remaining risks, though still substantial, are more in the nature of management and organization, revolving around successful coordination and control of the design, contracting, and construction process. With construction completed, market risk dominates. Successful rent-up and the establishment of a stable operation bring the property risks to their lowest level.

Very different specialists are involved in each phase of the development. Early in the process, market researchers and environmental consultants can be critical. Quickly, the architect becomes important as initial schematic design and concept rendering occur, even as early as the permitting process. Attorneys may also be critical to the permitting process. Once permits are obtained, the architect and all of the design specialists take center stage. Simultaneously, construction lenders become involved and often long-term lenders as well. With design completed, the general contractor, subcontractors, and possibly a construction manager take over the process. For apartments, the marketing and leasing team takes over as soon as construction is completed; for nonresidential or condominium projects, they will have been at work well before completion, and possibly before construction gets under way. Finally, with completion of the project, a property management team steps in. The developer must be able to manage the successful completion of each stage and control the transition from one stage to the next. Errors lead to delays and cost overruns, if not failure.

Many have speculated on what is required to be a developer. Certainly it requires a capacity for risk management, a capacity to work with and engender confidence from people, and a capacity to negotiate conflicting views. Others have observed that creativity, drive, and vision are essential. Breaking into development also requires control of some critical resource such as wealth, land, potential tenants, or unique expertise. Being a developer offers the opportunity to have an exceptional impact on the community and the opportunity to accumulate exceptional wealth. However, the challenges and risks generally are commensurate with that opportunity.

Key Terms

Build-to-suit 607
Cash multiple 607
Certificate of occupancy 617
Civil engineer 614
Construction manager 618
Design-build 619
Electrical engineer 614

Fast-track construction 619
Floor loan 617
General contractor 618
Ground lease 607
Hard costs 616
Land planner 614
Landscape architect 614

Mechanical engineer 614
Option 606
Soft costs 615
Soils engineer 614
Structural engineer 614
Subcontractor 618
Subordination agreement 617

Test Problems

Answer the following multiple-choice problems:

1. The first step in the process of development is to:
   a. Establish site control.
   b. Conduct feasibility analysis.
   c. Conduct environmental tests.
   d. Retain an architect.
   e. Obtain a construction financing commitment.

2. To gain control of a site, a developer may use:
   a. An option.
   b. A ground lease.
   c. A land contract.
   d. A joint venture with a future tenant or purchaser.
   e. All of the above.

3. Which of these phases of the development process comes first?
   a. Feasibility analysis, refinement, and testing.
   b. Design.
   c. Construction financing.
   d. Contracting.
   e. Obtaining permits.

4. All of the following are usually important in facilitating the development permitting process *except:*
   a. Prior meetings with the neighbors or public.
   b. Establishing a positive relationship with the press.
   c. Demonstrating a willingness to be flexible in solving differences.
   d. Establishing the strength of your legal position early in the process.
   e. Keeping regulatory authorities informed of any "issues" you foresee, and what you propose as a solution.

5. A method of construction where the actual construction begins before the design is finished is known as:
   a. Design-build.
   b. Runaway construction.
   c. Flying design.
   d. Fast-track.
   e. Turnkey.

6. In a *land* development, the primary design professional is a:
   a. Landscape architect.
   b. Civil engineer.
   c. Land planner.
   d. Architect.
   e. Soils engineer.

7. Soft costs include all *except:*
   a. Permitting costs.
   b. Architectural and engineering fees.
   c. Construction interest.
   d. Environmental and ecological evaluation.
   e. Land improvement costs.

8. Which statement is *incorrect* concerning the typical construction loan?
   a. It is made by a bank.
   b. The interest rate floats over either the prime rate or LIBOR.
   c. The loan typically is for 80 percent or less of total construction costs.
   d. The loan extends a few years after a certificate of occupancy is issued.
   e. The loan is dispersed in stages, based on the level of completion or on actual invoices.

9. The professional responsible for determining adequate specifications for building footings and foundation is a:
   a. Landscape architect.
   b. Land planner.
   c. Civil engineer.
   d. Soils engineer.
   e. Environmental engineer.

10. When construction costs exceed the amount of the construction loan, a developer frequently will seek to cover the "gap" with:
    a. Additional equity
    b. A land contract.
    c. Mezzanine financing.
    d. Advanced rent.
    e. An option.

www.mhhe.com/lingarcher5e

Study Questions

1. Why is the permitting stage of development often the riskiest stage of the process?
2. List at least five ways that a developer may attempt to reduce the risks of the permitting process.
3. Explain what a construction manager is, and why the role could be important in development.
4. In selecting an architect, what must a developer consider about the architect besides design credentials and relevant experience?
5. Why, in some cases, must a developer begin leasing efforts even before the design is complete?
6. Compare the advantages of competitive bidding for a general contractor with negotiated cost plus fee. What is the argument for using a maximum cost with sharing of overruns or savings between developer and general contractor?
7. Explain the possible advantages of miniperm financing as opposed to traditional construction financing followed by "permanent" financing.
8. Why is property development more vulnerable to business cycle risk than investment in existing property of a similar type?

EXPLORE THE WEB

Select a city or county of interest to you. Find its official website. From there locate the planning or land use regulation page. What types of maps can you find? What information can you find on the permitting or zoning procedures for a proposed development?

Solutions to Concept Checks

1. Three basic perspectives from which development projects arise are (1) a site in search of a use, (2) a use in search of a site, and (3) capital in search of an opportunity.
2. Eight stages of the development process are to establish site control; feasibility analysis, refinement, and testing; obtaining permits; design; financing; construction; marketing and leasing; and operation.
3. A developer can finance site control by joint venturing with a primary future tenant or owner, purchasing an option, buying a contract for deed, and use of a ground lease.
4. Either a cash multiple or NPV is likely to be used for financial feasibility analysis.
5. Three concerns for which a developer might retain an environmental consultant to investigate are the presence of wetlands, presence of toxic substances, and presence of a wildlife habitat.
6. Even without the necessity of a zoning change, a developer almost always must go through a site plan review.
7. Other than expense, the most serious threat to a typical development from the permitting process is delay.
8. In the permitting stage, a developer is likely to retain an architect on an hourly basis. In the design stage, however, the architect will work under a percentage of cost contract or for a fixed fee plus expenses.
9. In selecting an architect, a developer must consider not only the architect's design capacities, but also compatibility of values and goals, and ability to communicate effectively between the two.
10. The land planner has a more macro perspective, concerned with the relationship and arrangement of all components of the project on the land. The landscape architect is responsible for the land and vegetation aesthetics that are the context for each structure.
11. Expenditures for which the developer may need equity capital include any shortfall of construction forecasting; soft costs, which include title examination, environmental and ecological evaluation; legal and other costs of the permitting process; and architectural and engineering fees.
12. By the time a construction lender commits to a loan, these risks normally should be overcome: title flaw, environmental risk, ecological risks, and, above all, the permitting risk.
13. During construction, a developer may need supplemental financing because the construction loan often covers only 70 percent of the financing needs. Mezzanine financing is cheaper than equity capital, and avoids dilution of the equity returns.
14. After a project has been completed and leased for a couple of years, most of the market risk has passed. This makes the project more valuable, facilitating financing at a lower interest rate.
15. Design-build is a construction arrangement that attempts to avoid the problem of conflict of interest between the contractor and the architect by merging the two. Fast-track is a method to improve the speed of construction, which involves beginning actual construction of the footings and cement before the rest of the design is finished.
16. In addition to having personal and organizational capacity, a marketing agent should not be engaged with a competitor and should have genuine enthusiasm for the property.
17. Marketing for a nonresidential development begins earlier because businesses plan moves over a longer period of time and must be sold on the new building beforehand. Further, a lender is likely to key the loan terms to occupancy level, which compels leasing to begin before financing.

Additional Readings

Collier, Nathan S., Courtland A. Collier, and Don A. Halperin. *Construction Funding: The Process of Real Estate Development, Appraisal and Finance,* 4th ed. Hoboken, NJ: John Wiley & Sons, 2008.

Graaskamp, James A. *A Guide to Feasibility Analysis.* Chicago, IL: Society of Real Estate Appraisers, 1970.

Kibert, Charles J. *Sustainable Construction: Green Building Design and Delivery,* 3rd ed. Hoboken, NJ: John Wiley & Sons, 2013.

McMahan, John. *Professional Property Development,* New York: McGraw-Hill, 2007.

Miles, Mike E., Laurence M. Netherton, and Adrienne Schmitz. *Real Estate Development Principles and Process,* 5th ed. Washington, DC: Urban Land Institute, 2015.

Peiser, Richard, and Daniel Hamilton. *Professional Real Estate Development: The ULI Guide to the Business,* 3rd ed. Washington, DC: Urban Land Institute, 2012.

Poorvu, William, and Jeffrey L. Cruikshank. *The Real Estate Game: The Intelligent Guide to Decision-Making and Investment.* New York: Free Press, 1999.

Stein, J., ed. *Classic Readings in Real Estate Development.* Washington, DC: Urban Land Institute, 1996.

The Urban Land Institute offers a vast array of additional publications and services related to real estate development. See ULI Bookstore, www.uli.org/Books.aspx.

Glossary

Acceleration clause Clause that makes all future payments due upon a single default of a loan. Prevents lender from having to sue for each payment once a single payment is late.

Accretion Growth in size by addition or accumulation of soil to land by gradual, natural deposits.

Accrued depreciation In cost appraisal, the identification and measurement of reductions in the current market value of a property from today's reproduction cost.

Acknowledgment Confirmation that a deed reflects the intention and action of the grantor.

Acre An important measure of land area (containing 43,560 square feet).

Active income In U.S. income tax law, taxable income earned from salaries, wages, commissions, fees, and bonuses.

Actual notice An assertion of real property interests that is open, continuous, and apparent to all who examine the property.

Ad valorem taxes Property taxes that are based on the market value of the property.

Adaptive reuse A conversion where the remodeling produces a creative reuse of the structure that is different from its original purpose.

Adjustable rate mortgage (ARM) Alternative mortgage form where the interest rate is tied to an indexed rate over the life of the loan, allowing interest rate risk to be shared by borrowers and lenders.

Adjusted basis Equal to the original cost basis, plus additional real property or personal property capital expenditures, minus the cumulative amount of tax depreciation taken since the property was placed in service.

Adjustment period The number of initial years in which an ARM remains fixed before the interest rate is allowed to be adjusted.

Adjustments Additions or subtractions from a comparable sale price or cost which are required to make the comparable property more directly comparable to the subject property.

Adverse possession Involuntary conveyance of real property rights by an individual demonstrating a use that is (1) hostile to the interests of the owner, (2) actual, (3) open and notorious, (4) continuous, and (5) exclusive.

Adverse selection Similar to an agency problem, occurs when an adviser may have an incentive to filter the investment opportunities available, keeping the more promising ones and offering the investor the less promising ones.

Affordable housing allocation A requirement that encourages or mandates a "reasonable and fair" component of new housing construction for lower-income families.

Affordable housing loans Loan purchase programs offered to primary mortgage market lenders by Fannie Mae and Freddie Mac exclusively for low- and moderate-income households.

After-tax cash flow (*ATCF*) The residual claim on the property's cash flow after the mortgage lender(s) and the state and federal government have collected their share.

After-tax equity reversion (*ATER*) The before-tax equity reversion, defined as net selling price minus the remaining mortgage balance, at the time of sale less taxes due on sale.

Agency problem Occurs when an investor (principal) relies in an uninformed manner on an adviser (agent) for advice when there may be an incentive for the adviser not to act in the best interest of the investor/principal.

Agency relationship A relationship that empowers the property manager/agent to serve as the owner's fiduciary; thus, the manager's words and actions are binding on the owner.

Age-to-life method Method of estimating improvement value that involves estimating the ratio of the effective age of an improvement to its economic life, and multiplying the resulting age-to-life ratio by the structure's reproduction cost.

Agglomeration economies The emergence of specialized resources in a locality in response to demand from multiple industries. Generally associated with large cities.

Alt-A loan A home loan for borrowers who fall short of qualifying for a standard (prime) home loan. The use of the term varies. Roughly, it refers to loans better than subprime, but below prime in borrower qualifications and loan terms. Most Alt-A loans differ from prime loans by the absence of complete documentation of borrower's income assets.

Anchor tenant The large and generally well-known retailers who draw the majority of customers to a shopping center.

Annual percentage rate An approximation of the mortgage loan's annual effective borrowing cost in the absence of early payoff. This measure includes the effect of up-front financing costs on the true cost of borrowing.

Appraisal An unbiased written estimate of the fair market value of a property.

Appraisal report The document the appraiser submits to the client and contains the appraiser's final estimate of market value, the data upon which the estimate is based, and the calculations used to arrive at the estimate.

Appraised value Estimated price or value that the "typical" investor is likely to pay for a property.

Arm's-length transaction A transaction between two parties that have no relationship with each other and who are negotiating on behalf of their own best interests. A fairly negotiated transaction and reasonably representative of market value.

Assessed value The value determined as the basis on which an owner's property tax liability is calculated, usually a percentage of market value.

Assessment lien Lien assessment by local governments to ensure that those who receive the primary benefit of neighborhood improvements will be charged their "fair share." (See *Special assessments*.)

Asset manager The representative of property owners responsible for overseeing property managers and advising owners on important strategic decisions involving properties.

Assignment The transfer of the original lessee's rights under the lease contract to another tenant. The original lessee and the new tenant may be coliable if rent payments are not made.

Assumable loan An existing loan that can be preserved by a buyer instead of being repaid by the seller when title to the mortgaged property changes hands.

Assume liability To become legally responsible for an obligation. This occurs by signing a contract, such as a financial note.

Attach To place a lien on real property.

Automated underwriting A loan underwriting approach that exploits the combination of cyber-technology and the vast lending experience imbedded in the giant loan portfolios of Freddie Mac, Fannie Mae, and other large mortgage lenders.

Automated valuation models Long-distance, electronic appraisal substitutes used to reduce the cost and time associated with loan underwriting, particularly with refinancing an existing loan. Estimate values are based on statistical techniques, exploiting the massive data resources of Fannie Mae, Freddie Mac, and large banks.

Balloon The final, large payment on a loan that is not fully amortized by date of maturity. In an interest-only loan it includes the full original balance. With a partially amortized loan it is less.

Balloon loan Loan characterized by an amortization term that is longer than the loan term. Because the loan balance will not be zero at the end of the loan term, a balloon payment is necessary to pay off the remaining loan balance in full.

Balloon mortgage Another name for a balloon loan.

Band-of-investment analysis See *mortgage-equity rate analysis.*

Bankruptcy There are three types of bankruptcy distinguished by their section in Federal Statutes: Chapter 7, liquidation; Chapter 11, court supervised "work-out"; Chapter 13, "wage-earner's proceedings." See individual entries.

Bargain-and-sale deed A deed that conveys the land itself rather than ownership interests through warranties.

Base rent Amount paid by retail tenants in percentage leases regardless of the level of the sales generated by the tenant's business.

Baseline A point of reference that runs east and west and is a feature of government rectangular survey.

Before-tax cash flows Annual net operating income less annual debt service.

Before-tax equity reversion The net sale proceeds less the outstanding balance on the mortgage loan.

Benchmark A reference point used as a standard to quantify the relative performance of a specific asset or manager acting on behalf of an investor.

Bid-rent model Model of how land users bid for location that reveals the influences on how density of land use is determined, how competing urban land uses sort out their locations, how urban land value is determined, and why land uses change over time.

Board of adjustment In local zoning law, a board of citizens, appointed by the governing body, to hear and make determinations on appeals for zoning variances. The board of adjustment is somewhat unique in that its determinations are final rather than merely recommendations to the governing body. They can be appealed only in court.

Break-even cash throwoff ratio Another name for the break-even ratio.

Break-even ratio The sum of operating expenses, capital expenditures, and debt service divided by potential gross income, this ratio measures the ability of a property to cover its obligations.

Broker license The authority granted by a state for one to own and operate a real estate brokerage business; the most complete type of real estate license.

Build-to-suit With this arrangement, the developer preleases to a financially strong tenant to build a structure to the tenant's specifications. This arrangement assures the tenant that they will have the space they require when needed and it assures the owner/builder that the space will be fully leased upon completion.

Buyer agency agreement A contract for real estate brokerage services between a buyer and a real estate agent. The broker receives compensation for successfully locating a property for the buyer to purchase.

C Corporation Corporate ownership structure that provides limited liability, but suffers from double taxation and does not enable losses to flow through to investors for current use.

Cancelation option Lease clause that gives the tenant or the owner the right, but not the obligation, to cancel the lease before expiration.

Capital expenditures Expenditures for replacements and alterations to a building (or improvement) that materially prolong its life and increase its value.

Capital gain tax rate Rate of tax applied to the portion of the taxable gain on sale that is due to appreciation in the market value of the property.

Capital market The financial sector of the economy that serves to allocate financial resources among households and firms requiring funds.

Capital structure risk The risk associated with the financing package used by the investor. In particular, increased use of mortgage debt (financial leverage) increases the riskiness of the equity investor's return.

Capitalization rate The percentage that is obtained when the income produced by a property (or a specified interest in a property) is divided by the value or sale price of the property (or the specified interest in the property). (Also see *overall capitalization rate.*)

Central place pattern A location pattern in which similar economic entities, such as a particular type of convenience service or retail establishment, tend to disperse evenly over the market region.

Certificate of occupancy Issued by the local building inspector certifying that a structure is safe to occupy.

Chain of title A set of deeds and other documents that traces the conveyance of the fee, and any interests that could limit it, down from the earliest time to the current owner.

Change date The date the interest rate on an ARM is recomputed.

Chapter 7 bankruptcy The traditional form of bankruptcy wherein the court simply liquidates the assets of the debtor and distributes the proceeds to creditors in proportion to their share of the total claims.

Chapter 11 bankruptcy A court supervised "work-out" for a troubled business.

Chapter 13 bankruptcy Similar to Chapter 11, but applies to a household, that allows the petitioner to propose a repayment plan to the court.

Checks A component of a grid system, defined as an area of 24 miles by 24 miles, used in a government rectangular survey.

Civil engineer An engineer specializing in the design and construction of public works such as roads, water systems, sewer systems, bridges, dams, and water retention systems.

Closing Event at which possession and title to real estate normally are transferred from seller to buyer.

Closing costs Sometimes called settlement costs, costs in addition to the price of a property, usually including mortgage origination fee, title insurance, attorney's fee, and prepayable items such as taxes and insurance payments collected in advance at closing and held in an escrow account until needed.

Coefficients The calculated relationships between an independent variable and a dependent variable in a regression equation. The coefficient also takes into account the influence of other independent variables and represents the marginal contribution of the explanatory variable to the predicted value.

Collateral Property pledged as security for a debt.

Commercial banks Depository institutions primarily engaged in the business of making short-term loans to businesses for inventory financing and other working capital needs.

Commingled real estate funds A collection of investment capital from various pension funds that are pooled by an investment advisor/fund manager to purchase commercial real estate properties.

Commission Payment a real estate salesperson receives for services rendered, usually expressed as a percentage of the property sale price and not usually paid until the transaction is closed.

Common area maintenance (CAM) Expenses associated with a commercial property typically include maintenance and repair costs, the cost of security personal and alarm systems, as well as fees for the management of the common area.

Community development district (CDD) lien A quasi-governmental unit with broad powers to finance, create, operate, and maintain infrastructure and related services within a private development or community. The CDD can impose taxes or assessments on the landowners, and can issue municipal, tax-exempt bonds. Its board is elected by the community landowners, and its activities are subject to full public disclosure.

Community property The automatic right of husband and wife in property acquired by their spouse during the marriage.

Community Reinvestment Act of 1977 A congressional act that encourages mortgage originators to actively lend in their communities and that requires financial institutions to evaluate the "fairness" of their lending practices.

Community shopping center A larger version of a neighborhood shopping center, this type of center is often anchored by a discount department store.

Comparable properties Properties similar to the subject property used in the sales comparison approach to calculate a single indicated value for the subject property.

Comparison activities Goods and services whose optimal location pattern is clustering.

Compounding Calculation of future values, given assumptions about the amount or amounts invested and the interest rate that is paid on the invested amounts.

Comprehensive plan A local government's general guide to a community's growth and development based on the community's goals and objectives.

Concentric ring model Model created by E. W. Burgess that offered a concentric ring model of urban form in which the center circle is the central business district. Adjacent to it is a zone of transition which contained warehousing and other industrial land uses. This was followed by a ring of lower-income residential land use, followed by a ring of middle- and upper-income land use.

Concessions Lease clauses, such as free rent, that reduce the cost of the lease to the tenant and therefore provide tenants with an incentive to lease the space from the owner.

Concurrency The requirement that public facilities and services, including roads, sewers, and schools, be available at the same time new development is completed.

Condemnation The legal procedure involved with eminent domain, the right of government to acquire private property, without the owner's consent, for public use in exchange for just compensation.

Condominium An ownership form that combines a fee simple estate for ownership of individual units and tenancy in common for ownership of common areas—describes an ownership form not a type of construction.

Condominium bylaws The official rules and regulations that govern condominium ownership.

Condominium declaration The master deed creating or establishing the condominium corporation.

Conduits Agencies and private companies that pool mortgages and sell mortgage-backed securities, using the pool of mortgages originated or purchased as the collateral for the mortgage-backed security.

Conforming conventional loan A conventional loan that meets the standards required

for purchase in the secondary market by Fannie Mae or Freddie Mac.

Consideration Anything of value given to induce another party to enter into a contract.

Constant maturity rate A common index for ARM home loans. The one-year constant maturity rate, for example, is the average of the market yield, found by survey, on any outstanding U.S. Treasury debt having exactly one year remaining to final repayment, regardless of original maturity.

Construction loans Loans used to finance the costs associated with erecting the building or buildings.

Construction manager Person hired by developers to oversee day-to-day construction activities.

Contract conditions Specific requirements that must be satisfied by or for a party to a contract. (See *contract with contingencies*.)

Contract for deed A sales arrangement in which the actual delivery of the deed conveying ownership will not occur until well after the buyer takes possession of the property. This allows the seller to finance the sale through installment payments and to have recourse to the property in case of default by the buyer/borrower.

Contract for sale The legal document between a buyer and a seller that states the purchase price and other details of the transaction, and the detailed manner in which ownership rights are to be transferred. Is generally regarded as the most important contract in real estate.

Contract rent The rent specified in the lease contract.

Contract terms The detailed requirements of a fully enforceable contract, such as the price, the downpayment, any seller financing, provisions for inspections, type evidence of title, type of deed, dates, and other details of the transaction process.

Contract with contingencies An agreement for sale that makes the sale conditional on the buyer's obtaining something such as financing or a favorable engineering report.

Convenience activities Categorization of some types of urban services and products that users seek to obtain the good or service from the closest available source.

Conventional mortgage loan Mortgage loans that do not enjoy government backing in the form of FHA insurance or a Veterans Affairs (VA) guarantee.

Cooperative A form of individual ownership of apartments, the property is owned by a corporation, of which each resident is a shareholder entitled to a proprietary lease for a particular apartment.

Corrective maintenance The ordinary repairs to a building and its equipment on a day-to-day basis.

Correlated returns Returns on one or more assets that generally move together when market conditions change.

Correlation coefficient A relative measure of the tendency of an asset's return to vary with that of another asset over time.

Correspondent relationship A business relationship in which a large lender agrees to purchase loans or to consider loan requests from a mortgage banker or mortgage broker.

Cost segregation An income tax strategy separating personal property from real property. Owners often do this because personal property can be depreciated at accelerated rates if it can be separated from the real property and other personal property.

Cost-of-funds index An index for adjustable rate mortgages based on the weighted average of interest rates paid for deposits by thrift institutions (savings and loan associations and savings banks).

Covariance An absolute measure of the tendency of an asset's return to vary with that of the returns on another asset over time.

Covenant against encumbrances A promise that the property is not encumbered with liens, easements, or other such limitations except as noted in the deed.

Covenant of quiet enjoyment A promise that the property will not be claimed by someone with a better claim to title.

Covenant of seizin A promise that the grantor truly has good title, and that he or she has the right to convey it to the buyer.

Covenants Legally binding promises for which the grantor becomes liable.

Credit scoring The statistical evaluation of borrower creditworthiness that has largely replaced the use of credit reports and the subjective examination of payment punctuality and debt balances.

Credit tenants Companies whose general debt obligations are rated "investment grade" by one or more of the U.S. rating agencies, such as Standard and Poor's and Moody's.

Credit unions Depository institutions that are restricted by their charters to serving a group of people who can show a common bond such as employees of a corporation, government unit, labor union, or trade association.

Custodial maintenance The day-to-day cleaning and upkeep required to maintain property value and tenants.

Dealer property Under U.S. income tax law, real estate held for sale to others.

Debt coverage ratio (DCR) A measure of the extent to which NOI can decline before it is insufficient to service the debt, defined as net operating income over debt service.

Debt-to-income ratio One of two common ratios used by home mortgage lenders to determine a borrower's ability to pay a debt; defined as PITI and other long-term obligations divided by the borrower's gross monthly income.

Debt yield ratio A mortgage underwriting ratio for loans on income producing property. The ratio is defined as property NOI divided by the mortgage loan amount. It indicates the rate of cash flow to the loan amount should the lender become the owner.

Declaration of covenants A document recorded in the public records together with the plat map of a subdivision. It lists the restrictive covenants for the subdivision.

Dedicate (dedication) To convey certain lands of a subdivision to the local government.

Dedicated (property) The conveyance of property from a private owner to government for public use. Common examples are the dedication of streets, parks, or other areas to local government in the course of subdivision development.

Deed A special form of written contract used to convey a permanent ownership interest in real property.

Deed of bargain and sale See *bargain-and-sale deed.*

Deed of trust An instrument used instead of a mortgage in some states. The borrower conveys a deed of trust to a trustee, who holds the deed on behalf of both borrower and lender. If the loan obligation is paid off in accordance with the note, the trustee returns the deed to the borrower. But if the borrower (trustor) defaults, the trustee exercises his power of sale to dispose of the property on behalf of the lender.

Deed restrictions Limitations imposed on the use of land and structures by clauses in a deed.

Deeds in lieu of foreclosure A legal instrument issued by defaulting borrowers that transfers all rights they have in a property to the lender. Does not necessarily convey a clean title, just whatever interest the defaulting borrower has at the time of conveyance.

Default The consequence of prolonged delinquency; the failure of a borrower to meet the terms and conditions of a note.

Defeasance clause A clause that may be contained in commercial mortgages to protect lenders from prepayments in a declining interest rate environment. With defeasance, a borrower who prepays must purchase for the lender a set of U.S. Treasury securities whose coupon payments exactly replicate the cash flows the lender will lose as a result of the prepayment of the mortgage.

Defeasance prepayment penalty See *Defeasance clause.*

Deferral benefits The gain to the taxpayer from delaying the payment of income taxes until the property is sold. This benefit is produced by the annual depreciation deduction.

Deferred maintenance Ordinary maintenance not performed at the time a problem is detected.

Deficiency judgment The legal right of lenders to file suit against borrowers when the proceeds from a foreclosure sale do not fully pay off an outstanding loan, as well as any late fees and charges.

Delivery An observable, verifiable intent that the deed is to be given by the grantor to the grantee.

Demand clause A right that permits the lender to demand prepayment of the loan.

Dependent variable The variable being "explained" in a regression equation.

Depreciable basis Generally, the value of the acquired property, also called the original cost basis, less the value of the land.

Depreciation Annual deduction that allows investors to reduce the amount of taxable income they report by an amount that is intended to reflect the wear and tear on the property over time.

Depreciation recapture The cumulative amount of depreciation that has been taken since the property was placed into service. This amount is generally taxed at the depreciation recapture tax rate when/if the property is sold.

Depreciation recapture rate The tax rate that is applied to the depreciation recapture portion of the gain on sale when/if the property is sold.

Designated agent In case a brokerage firm is agent for both a seller and a buyer, the firm sometimes designates one salesperson to serve the buyer and one to serve the seller. The two salespersons are presumed to maintain the privacy, and serve the interest of the party they represent.

Design-build An approach to building large structures where the role of architect and general contractor is merged into one.

Devised Conveyance or distribution of a decedent's real property through a will.

Direct capitalization The process of estimating the value of a property by dividing a property's annual net operating income by an overall capitalization rate.

Direct market extraction Method of estimating the appropriate capitalization rate from comparable property sales.

Discount points Upfront financing costs charged by lenders to increase the yield on a loan.

Discounting The process for equating the value of future benefits from a real estate investment to an equivalent current (present) value.

Discrimination in housing Federal and state laws prohibit discrimination in housing on the basis of race, color, religion, national origin, sex, familial status, and handicap.

Disintermediation Reference to the occurrence of conditions when the growth of deposits in banks and savings associations becomes negative, due to other, more attractive, direct investment opportunities.

Diversifiable risk Unsystematic risk that can be eliminated from a portfolio by holding securities and other investments with less than perfectly correlated returns.

Doctrine of constructive notice A common law tradition stating that if a person is capable of knowing about a claim or rule, then he or she can be bound by it.

Dominant parcel A parcel that benefits from a servient parcel in an easement appurtenant.

Dower A common law provision that grants a wife a one-third life estate in all of the real property of a decedent husband.

Dual agency A situation in which a person or firm has an agency and fiduciary relationship to both parties—seller and buyer—of a transaction.

Due diligence After a buyer and a seller have agreed on a purchase price, the buyer is provided time to verify the information that has been provided by the seller. For example, the buyer will want to verify the magnitude of certain operating expenses, the current rent charged to tenants, the lack of environmental problems, etc. This process of "kicking the tires" before final closing is the due-diligence process.

Due-on-sale clause The clause in a mortgage document that requires the borrower to pay off the loan in full if the property serving as security for the loan is sold.

Early payment mortgages Loans where the borrower makes additional payments to reduce outstanding principal more quickly than scheduled.

Earnest money A cash deposit by a buyer at the time of the offer to establish credibility of the offer, and to provide recourse to the seller if the buyer reneges.

Easement The right to use land for a specific and limited purpose. the subject, or servient parcel may give use to an adjacent, "dominant" parcel (easement appurtenant), or it may give use to persons or an organization (easement in gross).

Easement appurtenant A right of use that continues from owner to owner that involves a relationship between two parcels of land: a dominant parcel that benefits from a servient parcel.

Easement by estoppel The right of use created if a landowner gives an adjacent landowner permission to depend on her land.

Easement by prescription The acquisition of a right of easement by open, notorious, and continuous assertion of the right, hostile to the subservient land owner's interest. The amount of time required to attain the right of easement by prescription varies by state.

Easement by prior use An implied right of use that allows the owner of a landlocked parcel the right to use a previously existing path across another property for access and egress.

Easement in gross The right to use land for a specific, limited purpose unrelated to any adjacent parcel.

Easement of necessity A created implied right of use that allows the owner of a landlocked parcel the right to use a path across another property for ingress and egress.

Economic and environmental impact statements Studies of the effect that a new development will have on the economy or the environment of the region.

Economic base The set of economic activities that a city provides for the world beyond its boundaries.

Effective borrowing cost The true borrowing cost, including the effect of all upfront financing costs. Is similar to the annual percentage rate but allows for the effect of early payoff.

Effective gross income The total annual income the rental property produces after subtracting vacancy losses and adding miscellaneous income.

Effective gross income multiplier The ratio of the sale prices to the annual effective gross income of the income-producing property.

Effective rent See *equivalent level rent.*

Effective tax rate (income taxes) The percentage amount by which income taxes reduce the going-in IRR on a property acquisition or development.

Effective tax rate (property taxes) The tax liability divided by the property's market value or sale price.

Elective share Provision that gives a surviving spouse a share of most of the wealth of the decedent.

Electrical engineer An engineer specializing in the design and construction of electrical systems for production and distribution of power, and in electrical circuitry generally.

Elements of comparison The relevant characteristics used to compare and adjust the sale prices of the comparable properties in the sales comparison approach.

Eminent domain The power of government in to take private property for a public purpose by paying the owner just compensation.

Encroachment Unauthorized intrusion of a building or other improvements onto property owned by another.

Equal Credit Opportunity Act (ECOA) This act prohibits discrimination in lending practices on the basis of race, color, religion, national origin, sex, marital status, age, or because all or part of an applicant's income derives from a public assistance program.

Equitable title The right of someone to obtain full, legal title to real estate, provided the terms and conditions of the document creating equitable title (usually a contract for sale) are fulfilled.

Equity dividend rate (*EDR*) The "capitalization rate" for equity. It is derived by dividing the before-tax cash flow by the value of the invested equity capital. Sometimes referred to as the property's dividend rate/yield, also the "cash-on-cash return."

Equity of redemption A period of time allowed by courts in every state that grants delinquent mortgage borrowers the opportunity to make overdue payments and come current on the mortgage before foreclosure is complete.

Equity REITs Real estate investment trusts that invest in and operate income-producing properties.

Equivalent level rent The fixed monthly payment that has the same present value as the actual lease payments after concessions or expenses reimbursement revenue over the same term.

Errors and omission insurance A type of insurance that indemnifies professionals if they make an error in their profession or if they omit something important from their analyses.

Escrow The status of real estate transactions that are closed through the help and intercession of a third party, called an escrow agent. The deed is delivered to the escrow agent for delivery to the buyer on performance of a condition (payment of the purchase price).

Escrow account A segregated account held by brokers for the deposit of earnest money (deposit) funds. Also, a trust account of a lender used to pay for property taxes, hazard insurance, or other items on behalf of a borrower.

Escrow agent A person or company that performs the closing function for a fee; escrow agents collect all needed documents and funds for disbursement at the closing.

Escrow clause Requires a mortgage borrower to make monthly deposits into an escrow account.

Estate Interests in real property that include possession.

Estimated closing costs An estimate of all the costs to be incurred at a real estate closing. Most commonly, the estimate is provided by a lender, in accordance with the requirements of the Real Estate Settlement Procedures Act.

Evidence of title Substantiation that demonstrates that good and marketable title is being conveyed as part of a real estate transaction. Two main forms accepted are abstract with attorney's opinion, and title insurance commitment.

Exceptions and reservations clause A clause in a deed that can contain a wide variety of limits on the property interest conveyed.

Excess deductions The amount by which allowable tax deductions (including depreciation) exceed the rental income generated by the property.

Exclusionary zoning Zoning that tends to exclude lower-income groups and is prohibited.

Exclusive agency listing An agreement between a seller of property and a broker in which the seller agrees to pay a commission to the broker if anyone other than the owner finds a buyer, during the period of the agreement.

Exclusive right of sale listing An agreement between a seller of property and a broker in which the broker is assured of receiving a commission if the broker or anyone else, including the owner, finds a buyer during the period of the agreement.

Exculpatory clause Loan provision that releases the borrower from liability for fulfillment of the contract.

Expansion option Lease clause that obligates the property owner to find space for the tenant to expand the size of their leased space.

Expense stop A clause often found in commercial leases that requires landlords to pay property operating expenses up to a specified amount and tenants to pay the expenses beyond that amount. The expense stop is usually stated in a per square foot amount.

External obsolescence Losses of property value caused by forces or conditions beyond the borders of the property. The losses are deducted from a building's reproduction cost in the cost approach to estimating market value.

Externalities The unaccounted effects that a land use imposes on surrounding parcels.

Extraterritorial jurisdiction Control by a community of an area larger than the community or jurisdiction for planning and zoning purposes, granted by the state legislature, which allows local governments to plan and control urban development outside their boundaries until annexation can occur.

Fallout risk The potential loss of borrowers from the origination pipeline if mortgage interest rates decline after the loan commitment, but before the closing of the loan, which results in borrowers choosing not to close ("take down") the loan.

Fannie Mae Government-sponsored enterprise; one of the largest purchasers of residential mortgages in the secondary market.

Fast-track construction An approach to construction wherein actual construction begins before design and building specifications are complete.

Federal Housing Administration (FHA) A government-sponsored housing finance agency that operates in the primary market by providing a default insurance program, as well as other housing programs and initiatives.

Fee simple absolute An estate in land that provides the owner with a complete set of legal rights, limited only by the powers of government.

Fee simple conditional Ownership that is subject to a condition or trigger event.

Fee simple estate The complete ownership of a property; may be either absolute or conditional.

FHA mortgage insurance Government-sponsored mortgage insurance that protects lenders from any loss after foreclosure and conveyance of title to the property to the U.S. Department of Housing and Urban Development (HUD). Insurance premium is paid by the mortgage borrower.

Fiduciary relationship The special duties and obligations to a principal required of an agent, including complete loyalty, confidentiality, obedience, disclosure, accounting, care, skill, and due diligence.

Final adjusted sale price The price paid for a comparable property in the sales comparison approach, adjusted for all conditions and characteristics to approximate the subject property and the current date.

Financial intermediaries Institutions that bring together depositors and mortgage borrowers.

Financial risk The risk NOI will be less than debt service.

Fixtures Personal property that becomes real property by virtue of its permanent attachment to the realty.

Flat rent Describes a lease where the rental rate is fixed for the entire term.

Flex space Industrial space that is often built without fancy lobbies or fixtures that can be used for storage or for simple offices and that can be converted from one use to another relatively inexpensively.

Floating-rate mortgage A debt instrument whose interest rate changes over the life of the loan based on a market index such as the prime rate or LIBOR.

Floor loan In financing of large-scale building construction, a minimum level of loan that is granted until certain progress points in construction and leasing are achieved. Then the loan is increased.

Foreclosure A process to force the public sale of property to satisfy the financial obligations of a delinquent borrower to a lender. The legal purpose is to terminate ownership claims, and any subordinate liens, so that title can go to a buyer.

Form-based Zoning Codes Rather than creating a map by segregation of land uses—residential, retail, etc.—form-based zoning creates a map by segregation of development and building designs—low density, medium density, etc. Specifications for streets, public spaces, lot size, and buildings all vary in accordance with the chosen density.

Freddie Mac A government-sponsored enterprise and, along with Fannie Mae, one of the largest purchasers of residential mortgages in the secondary market.

Freehold Estate interests in real estate having unlimited duration; titled interests.

Full platform operating company This is an investment strategy that involves starting or acquiring and then operating a real estate company. The company may then acquire real estate investments, develop properties, and/or act as a general partner in a variety of investments funds. High net-worth families have been common investors in full-platform companies, while more conservative pension funds have gravitated toward safer, more passive forms of investment.

Functional obsolescence Losses in value of a building relative to its reproduction cost because the building is not consistent with modern standards or with current tastes of the market.

Funds from operations (FFO) Net (accounting) income, plus tax depreciation, plus amortization of leasing commissions and tenant improvements. Is considered a better measure of a REIT's cash flow than accounting income.

Future value The value of money in some period beyond time zero.

Garden apartments These developments have a relatively low density of development and are located in suburban and nonurban areas where land is less expensive than in urban areas.

General agent One who is empowered to represent a principal, often a business firm, in its business relationships. A general agent can contract and bind the principal within the confines of the business or employment relationship.

General contractor Usually a construction company that has responsibility for seeing that all aspects of construction are completed on time and within budget.

General lien A security interest or lien that arises out of actions unrelated to ownership of the property.

General partnerships An ownership form characterized by multiple owners, unlimited liability for each equity holder, and flow-through taxation of both taxable income and cash distributions.

General warranty deed Highest form of deed in which the grantor becomes liable for all possible covenants, or legal promises, assuring good title.

Geographical information systems (GIS) Computerized methods for analyzing data about communities using various maps and combinations or layers of maps.

Going-in cap rate The overall capitalization rate; the ratio of the first-year net operating income to the overall value (or purchase price) of the property.

Going-out cap rate The ratio of the estimated net operating income in the year following sale to the overall value of the property at the time of sale. (See *Terminal capitalization rate.*)

Government National Mortgage Association (GNMA) A federal government agency that guarantees mortgage-backed securities issued by private FHA and VA lenders.

Government-sponsored enterprises A term that refers to Fannie Mae, Freddie Mac, and several other less important government entities created by acts of Congress to promote an active secondary market for home mortgages.

Graduated rent Describes a lease that calls for prespecified increases in the contract rental rate.

Grant deed A deed containing an implied promise that the grantor actually has title and that it is not encumbered in any way, except as described in the deed. A grant deed is very similar to a warrantee deed. It is the predominant form of deed used in California.

Grantee The recipient of a conveyance of a real property interest.

Grantor The person or entity conveying the real property interest to the grantee.

Gross floor area The gross floor area of a shopping center is equal to the total gross leasable area, plus the square footage of the common areas.

Gross leasable area The standard for measuring retail space, the GLA is simply the sum of the space occupied by the tenant, and is therefore similar to the usable area of office tenants.

Gross lease Lease in which the landlord pays all operating expenses of the property.

Ground lease Leases of vacant land or of the land portion of an improved parcel of real estate.

Habendum clause Clause in a deed that defines or limits the type of interest being conveyed.

Hard costs Amounts of capital committed in development projects to materials, labor, and other tangible or nonservice inputs.

Highest and best use The use of a property found to be (1) legally permissible, (2) physically possible, (3) financially feasible, and (4) maximally productive.

High-rise apartment buildings Buildings of at least 10 to 15 stories.

Holding period Length of time an investment is held prior to sale or disposal.

Home equity loans Second mortgages, used to finance home improvements and other purchases, where homeowners can borrow against the accumulated equity in the home.

Home Mortgage Disclosure Act of 1975 An act of Congress that discourages lenders from avoiding, or redlining, certain neighborhoods in a manner related to minority composition.

Home Ownership and Equity Protection Act An act of Congress that addresses abusive, predatory practices in subprime lending and sets a trigger annual percentage rate (APR) and fee levels at which loans become subject to the law's restrictions.

Homestead exemption A provision in some states that allows specified taxpayers (usually owners of their principal full-time residences) to apply for a deduction of a certain amount from the property's assessed value in calculating the annual property tax liability.

Hospitality property Property classification that includes hotels, motels, and many types of restaurants.

Housing expense ratio A ratio used to assess the ability of a borrower to pay debt; defined as the monthly payment of principal and interest on the loan plus monthly payments into an escrow account toward property taxes and hazard insurance divided by the borrower's gross monthly income.

Hybrid ARM An adjustable rate mortgage loan that provides for an initial period of fixed interest charges, hence fixed payments, before the interest rate becomes adjustable. The fixed interest rate period typically ranges from three to ten years.

Impact fee A fee charged by a community and paid by a developer that is commensurate with the externalities created by a development. Intended to cover the development's impact on such things as roads, sewer systems, schools, and police and fire protection.

Implied easement A right of use not created by an explicit deed or explicit clause in a deed. It often is created when a subdivision map is placed in the public records.

Improvements on the land Any fixed structures such as buildings, fences, walls, and decks.

Improvements to the land The components necessary to make the land suitable for building construction or other uses and includes infrastructure, such as streets, walkways, utilities, storm water drainage systems, and other systems that may be required for land use.

Income capitalization The process of converting periodic income into a value estimate.

Independent variables Variables in a regression equation that are believed to partially explain variations in the dependent variable.

Index rate A market-determined interest rate that is the "moving part" in an adjustable interest rate.

Indicated value The final value estimate for the subject property resulting from application of one of the major approaches in the appraisal process.

Industrial property Property classification that includes warehouses and structures that house light manufacturing.

Industry economies of scale The growth of an industry within a locality that creates special resources and cost advantages for that industry.

Inflation risk The risk that general inflation in the economy will be greater than or less than expected.

Institutional-grade real estate Larger, more valuable commercial properties, generally well over $10 million, targeted by institutional investors, such as pension funds and foreign investors. These investments are generally located in the 50 to 60 largest U.S. metropolitan areas.

Insurance clause Requires the borrower/mortgagor to maintain property casualty insurance acceptable to the lender, giving the lender joint control in the use of the proceeds in case of major damage to the property.

Intangible assets Nonphysical assets such as patents and copyrights.

Intercept The base value estimate in a regression assuming that all of the explanatory variables are set equal to zero.

Interest Rent or a charge paid for the use of money. Interest may also refer to the bundle of rights held by owners of real property.

Interest rate risk The risk that changes in the general level of interest rates will affect the pricing of all securities and investments.

Interest-only amortizing mortgage A mortgage loan that is interest only for some years, perhaps ten or fifteen, after which the payment increases to an amount sufficient to fully amortize the loan in the remaining term.

Interest-only mortgage A mortgage loan that is interest only for its full term and then must be refinanced or paid off in full.

Interlease risk The risk associated with the replacement of a tenant's first lease with another lease of uncertain terms and conditions.

Intermediaries In real estate investment, third party specialists who use their expertise and knowledge to invest and manage funds on behalf of clients.

Internal rate of return (IRR) The rate of interest (discount) that equates the present value of the cash inflows to the present value of the cash outflows; that is, the rate of discount that makes the net present value equal to zero.

Internal Revenue Service (IRS) Created by Congress to collect federal income taxes and to clarify and interpret tax rules and regulations.

Internet marketing Use of the Internet to advertise real estate services, to market properties, and to provide information about specific properties. While few properties are sold exclusively through the Internet, it has become a central tool to real estate marketing today.

Intestate Conveyance of a decedent's property without a will.

Inverse condemnation A suit by a landowner to force a government to resort to eminent domain under the argument that regulation has effectively taken the full value of a property.

Investment-grade property Synonymous with institutional-grade real estate, large, relatively new and fully leased commercial properties located in major metropolitan areas, generally well over $10 million, targeted by institutional investors, such as pension funds and foreign investors.

Investment property Asset, as defined in the U.S. Internal Revenue Code, owned primarily for earning an investment return—especially capital appreciation—as opposed to an asset that is held for use in one's trade or business. Raw land and developed lots are real estate examples of investment properties.

Investment risk The possibility that future cash flows or nonmonetary costs and benefits will differ from expected values.

Investment value The value of the property to a particular investor, based on his or her specific requirements, discount rate, expectations, and so on.

Investment yield The growth in the invested dollars of an investment. Usually stated as a percentage growth or return.

Joint tenancy A form of co-ownership in which two or more owners hold equal shares and have equal rights of possession. The surviving partners divide the interests of a deceased partner.

Judicial deed A deed issued through a court-ordered proceeding.

Judicial foreclosure The process of bringing the property of delinquent borrowers to public sale that involves court action. Proceeds from the foreclosure sale are used to pay off, to the extent possible, the borrower's creditors.

Jumbo loans Nonconforming loans that exceed the maximum loan amount for purchase by Fannie Mae or Freddie Mac. Because these loans cannot be purchased by one of the GSEs, they usually carry a slightly higher interest rate.

Just compensation Payment to an owner for property taken in condemnation proceedings, usually the market value of the property taken by the government.

Land Commonly used to refer to a parcel that does not include any structures but may include some improvements to the land.

Land acquisition loans Loans to finance the purchase of raw land; perhaps the most risky of real estate loans.

Land development loans Loans to finance the installation of the on-site and off-site improvements to the land that are necessary to ready the land for construction.

Land planner In land development, lays out the basic "map" for use of the land, including location of roads, utilities, structures, water retention areas, and other elements.

Landscape architect An architect specializing in planning the arrangement of trees, other plantings, and placement of other harmonizing objects on land. Usually the focus is designing the grounds for a building or group of buildings.

Late fees Fees assessed for standard home loans when payments are received after the 15th of the month the payment is due. Also found in commercial mortgages.

Law of agency The legal rights, duties, and liabilities of principal, agent, and third parties as a result of the agency relationship between them.

Law of descent The laws and procedures controlling how a state will convey a decedent's estate among the heirs if no will exists.

Leased fee estate The bundle of rights possessed by the landlord in a leased property, made up primarily of the right to receive rental payments during the lease term and ultimately to repossess the property at the end of the lease term.

Leasehold (estate) The interest or rights of a lessee or tenant in a leased property, including the possessory interests that are a temporary conveyance of the rights of exclusion, use, and enjoyment, but not the right of disposition. The tenant receives these rights in exchange for the payment of rent.

Legal life estate A life estate created by the action of law.

Legal title Ownership of property; for real estate, a lawful claim, supported by evidence of ownership.

Lender's yield The implied discount rate, or internal rate of return, on a loan—given all of the cash inflows and outflows on the loan to the lender.

Level-payment mortgage A fully amortizing loan with equal periodic payments.

Leverage The use of mortgage debt to help finance a capital investment.

Levered cash flows The property's net rental income after subtracting any payments due the lender.

LIBOR A common index of interest rates for income producing property, the London Interbank Offering Rate is a short-term interest rate for loans among foreign banks based in London.

License The permission to use another's land for a specific and limited purpose.

Licensing laws State laws that authorize persons who meet specified qualifications to engage in a business or profession.

Lien An interest in real property that serves as security for a loan obligation. In case of default the holder of the lien is entitled to have the property sold to satisfy the debt.

Lien theory Legal theory that interprets a mortgage as a lien rather than a temporary conveyance of title.

Like-kind exchange A popular method of deferring capital gain taxes which allows owners, under certain circumstances, to exchange their properties for another and avoid paying capital gain taxes at the time of the transaction.

Limited liability company (LLC) A hybrid form of ownership that combines the corporate characteristics of limited liability with the tax characteristics of a partnership.

Limited partnership A partnership in which one party (the general partner) assumes unlimited liability in exchange for control of all material decision making. The limited partners enjoy liability that is limited to the extent of their equity contributions to the entity. All parties involved benefit from flow-through income and taxation; that is, the partnership is not taxed.

Linkages The attractions or important access needs that one land use has for other land uses.

Liquidity The ability to sell an asset quickly for fair market value.

Listing contract An agreement between an owner of real estate and a real estate broker that obligates the broker to attempt to sell the property under specified conditions and terms. It obligates the property owner to pay a commission to the broker if the broker is successful in obtaining a ready, willing, and able buyer for the property on terms specified or on terms acceptable to the seller.

Load factor Another name for the ratio of rentable to usable area in an office building. The factor is multiplied by the tenant's usable area to determine rentable area.

Loan balance The outstanding principal balance on a loan. Will always be equal to the original balance if the loan is an interest-only loan. Declines over time if the loan is self-amortizing.

Loan constant The annual debt service on a loan divided by the initial amount of the loan.

Loan underwriting Involves an analysis by the lender of the riskiness of the promised mortgage payments. Requires analysis of the potential borrower's willingness and ability to make scheduled mortgage payments.

Local economic activities Activities in a city that serve the local businesses and households.

Location quotient The ratio between the percentage of employees in a certain type of work or job classification in a community and the percentage of employees in that same type of work or job classification nationally. If the ratio exceeds 1 it indicates that the activity is a base economic activity.

Lockout provision A mortgage clause or provision prohibiting prepayment of the mortgage for a specified period of time after origination.

Low-income housing Housing targeted to households with low or moderate incomes.

Lump sum A one-time receipt or expenditure occurring in a given period.

Macroeconomic risk factors Risk factors or variables that can potentially affect the values and returns on all properties in all markets.

Management agreement The agreement that forms the basis for the relationship between the property owner and the property management firm.

Management risk Risk that a property will not be effectively managed, causing a reduction in net cash flows and returns.

Margin The "markup," typically two to three percentage points, over and above the index rate, which is charged on adjustable rate mortgages.

Market conditions The relationship between supply and demand for a particular type of real estate in a local market at a specified point in time.

Market parameters Critical summary features such as occupancy rates, rental rate growth, or sales rates, that characterize a real estate market.

Market rent The rent that could be obtained by renting a property on the open market.

Market risk factors Risk factors or variables that cannot be diversified away. Also called systematic risk factors.

Market segmentation Identification and delineation of submarkets.

Market value The price a property should sell for in a competitive market when there has been a normal offering time, no coercion, arm's-length bargaining, typical financing, and informed buyers and sellers.

Marketability study An analysis of how best to bring a product or service to the market. It considers characteristics of the product or service in relation to the needs of potential customers and which marketing channels are most likely to produce the desired results.

Marketable title Title to real property that is free of reasonable doubt.

Marketable title laws State laws intended to limit the number of years that title search must "reach back" through the title "chain."

Market-adjusted normal sale price "Normal sale price" adjusted for changes in market conditions between the date of sale and the date of appraisal of the subject property.

Maturity imbalance problem Situation faced by banks, thrifts, and other financial institutions in which long-term assets are funded with short-term liabilities.

Mechanical engineer An engineer specializing in the design and construction of heating, ventilating, and air-conditioning systems, and in other kinds of mechanical systems.

Mechanics' liens Liens that arise from construction and other improvements to real estate.

Metes and bounds Method of describing real estate in which a *mete* is a unit of measure (foot, mile) and a *bound* is a boundary marker. Essentially, a sequence of directed distances that are the boundaries of the property.

Metropolitan statistical area (MSA) An MSA is comprised of one or more urban counties, identified as a single labor market area, centered around a city with at least 50,000 in population.

Mezzanine loans A method of obtaining additional leverage on top of a traditional first mortgage. This debt is secured by the pledge of an equity interest in the borrower's partnership or business—it usually is not secured by a lien on the property.

Microeconomic risk factors Risk that is specific to a particular property or local market and that is controllable by the owner/investor. This risk can be diversified away in a portfolio.

Midmonth convention Tax rule that assumes the acquisition of an income producing property occurs on the 15th day of the month, regardless of the actual acquisition date.

Midrise apartment buildings Apartment buildings that range in height from four to nine stories.

Millage rate The dollars of tax per $1,000 of property value. For example, a millage rate of 20 means that a person owning a property having an assessed value of $100,000 would pay $20 \times 100 = \$2,000$ in tax.

Mills Units used to state the amount of property tax assessment; the number of dollars per $1,000. Twenty mills means $20 per each $1,000.

Mineral rights Rights to the subsurface, including rights to oil, gas, coal, and other substances that are mined, and can be separated from land ownership.

Miniperm loan A loan from an interim lender that provides financing for the construction period, the lease-up period, and for several years beyond the lease-up stage.

Mixed-asset portfolio A portfolio that contains a variety of types of assets; for example, stocks, bonds, and real estate.

Monthly loan constant A loan payment factor used to determine payments on a level payment, fixed rate loan.

Mortgage A lien on real property as security for a debt. A special contract by which the borrower conveys to the lender a security interest in the mortgaged property.

Mortgage assumption When buyers take over payments of mortgages of sellers and become personally liable by creating a note in their name.

Mortgage banking Full-service mortgage companies that originate, fund, and then sell the loans they originate in the secondary mortgage market, and service loans for loan investors.

Mortgage brokers An intermediary between those who demand mortgage funds and those who supply the funds. Brokers arrange mortgage loans for a fee, but do not originate or service the loans.

Mortgage insurance premium (MIP) Upfront insurance premium required by FHA-insured loans.

Mortgage joint venture A relationship between developers and others who supply all or most of the funds in the form of loans to develop properties that will be used in their business or enter their portfolios.

Mortgage menu The many types of residential loans offered by originating lenders to residential borrowers. The menu includes the cost of the various mortgage items, including the contract interest rate and number of upfront discount points and origination fees.

Mortgage REITs Real estate investment trusts that purchase mortgage obligations and effectively become real estate lenders.

Mortgagee The lender, who receives the mortgage claim.

Mortgage-equity rate analysis Estimation of an overall capitalization rate by calculating a weighted average of the capitalization rate for debt (mortgage constant) and the capitalization rate for equity (equity dividend rate). The weight is determined by the percentage that each component (debt and equity) is of the total investment.

Mortgagor The borrower or grantor of the mortgage claim.

Multifactor asset pricing model Models for determining required discount rates that assume there are several sources of macroeconomic (nondiversifiable) risk in the economy for which investors must be compensated in the form of a higher going-in internal rate of return.

Multifamily property Residential property classification that includes apartments.

Multinuclei city Phrase coined by Harris and Ullman in a landmark study that described the effects of the motor vehicle, combined with new technologies of production, that released the city from its absolute ties to the CBD.

Multiple listing service (MLS) Sharing of property sales listings by a number of real estate brokers with an agreement as to how costs and commissions are to be shared.

Multivariate regression analysis (MRA) A statistical procedure used to examine the relationship between a dependent variable and multiple independent, "explanatory," variables.

Mutual Mortgage Insurance Fund The depository for FHA insurance premiums and the source of reimbursement for lenders in the case of foreclosure losses on FHA-insured properties.

NAREIT index A value-weighted index that tracks the total return patterns of all exchange-listed REITs. Produced by the National Association of Real Estate Investment Trusts.

National Association of Realtors A principal trade or professional organization of real estate brokers. Members agree to abide by a code of ethics.

Natural vacancy rate The proportion of potential gross income not collected when the use (rental) market is in equilibrium.

NCREIF Property Index A measure of the historical performance of income properties held by pension funds and profit-sharing plans. Produced quarterly by the National Council of Real Estate Investment Fiduciaries.

Negative amortization Occurs when the loan payment is not sufficient to cover the interest cost and results in the unpaid interest being added to the original balance, causing the loan amount to increase.

Neighborhood shopping center Located for the convenience of a nearby resident population, this type of center contains retail establishments offering mostly convenience goods. Typically it is "anchored" by a supermarket.

Net asset value Equal to total market value of a REIT's underlying assets, less mortgages and other debt.

Net income multiplier (*NIM*) A cash flow multiplier calculated as the acquisition price divided by the net operating income.

Net lease Lease in which the tenant pays some or all of the operating expenses of the property in addition to rent.

Net listing Type of contract in which sellers specify the amount they will accept from the sale, with brokers keeping all proceeds in excess of that amount.

Net operating income (NOI) The type of income to a property used in direct capitalization, calculated by deducting from potential gross income vacancy and collection losses and adding other income to obtain effective gross income. From this amount all operating expenses are subtracted, including management expense and a reserve for replacements, or capital expenditures, and other nonrecurring expenses.

Net present value (NPV) The difference between the present value of the cash inflows and the present value of the cash outflows.

Net sale proceeds The expected selling price less selling expenses.

New urbanism School of planning thought that seeks to revive residential neighborhood features of the preautomobile era, including sidewalks; houses with front porches located close to streets; narrow, grid pattern streets; and supporting nonresidential services interspersed within neighborhoods.

Nonamortizing Loans that require interest payments but no regularly scheduled principal payments.

Nonbasic employment Jobs that are not involved in the production of goods or services that will be exported outside of a community. These are usually jobs involved in serving local residents. Examples are barbers, beauticians, most retail, real estate and insurance salespersons, and local bankers.

Nonconforming conventional loan A conventional loan that does not satisfy one or more underwriting standards required for purchase in the secondary market by Fannie Mae and Freddie Mac.

Nonconforming use A land use inconsistent with current zoning classification, but which is permitted to remain because it predated the current zoning. To be allowed to remain, the use must be uninterrupted, and the property structures cannot be substantially improved.

Nonjudicial foreclosure A process of bringing the property of defaulting borrowers to public sale by the lender or a trustee, outside of the court system. It must follow statutory guidelines, particularly concerning public notices of the sale.

Nonmonetary The nonfinancial costs and benefits of an investment decision.

Nonrealty items Items of personal property.

Nonrecourse loans Loans that relieve the borrower of personal liability but do not release the property as collateral for the loan.

Normal sale price The transaction price of a comparable property adjusted for nonmarket financing and non-arm's-length bargaining (conditions of sale).

Note The document (contract) defining the exact terms of a debt obligation and the liability of the borrower for the obligation.

Officer's deed Same as definition of executor's deed.

Open listing Agreement between the seller of property and a broker that provides for the broker to receive a commission if he or she sells the property. No exclusive protection is provided to the broker.

Open-end construction loan A situation in which a forward commitment has not been obtained to repay the construction loan.

Operating expense escalation clause A commercial lease clause in which increases in one or more operating expenses, relative to a base year, become the financial responsibility of the tenant.

Operating expense ratio (*OER*) A measure of annual operating costs, defined as operating expenses divided by effective gross income.

Operating expenses The expenses that are necessary to operate and maintain an income producing property.

Opportunity cost The return the investor is forgoing on an alternative investment of equal risk in order to invest in the asset under consideration. Said differently, it is the return the investor could earn on his next best alternative of similar risk.

Option The right, but not the obligation, to do something, such as buy a property, within a certain time.

Option ARM An adjustable rate mortgage loan that offered the borrower a variety of payment choices. The choices typically included a payment to fully amortize (pay off) the loan in 15 years, one to fully amortize the loan in 30 years, an interest-only payment, and a payment at an artificially low level such that unpaid interest was added to the outstanding balance each month. The loan often began with a below market interest rate for a few months.

Option contract Sets a time over which developers may buy property at a specified price.

Ordinary annuity A fixed amount of money received every period for some length of time.

Ordinary life estate Estate in which the property owner retains all rights of exclusive possession, use, and enjoyment for life while a subsequent owner holds a remainder interest that follows the life estate.

Ordinary tax rate The rate of tax applied to taxable income that is not deemed to be capital gain income or depreciation recapture income.

Original cost basis The total costs paid to acquire the property including land, building, personal property, and other acquisition costs such as lawyer fees, brokerage commissions, and so on.

Outlet center A variation of specialty shopping centers that generally sell name-brand goods at lower prices.

Overall capitalization rate The type of capitalization rate used in direct capitalization, calculated by dividing comparable properties' net operating incomes by their selling prices.

Overall caps Caps on adjustable rate mortgages that limit interest rate changes over the life of the loan.

Overall rate (of return) Another common name for the overall capitalization rate.

Overall rate of direct capitalization An overall capitalization rate estimated directly from actual transactions for comparable properties.

Ownership structure risk The effect that the chosen form of ownership can have on the risk and return ultimately earned by the investors.

Par value The remaining balance, or outstanding principal amount of a debt.

Partially amortizing A loan alternative in which the outstanding principal is partially repaid over the life of the loan, then fully retired with a larger lump sum "balloon" payment at maturity.

Passive activity income IRS classification of income that includes all income generated from trade and business activities such as rental real estate.

Passive activity loss restrictions IRS rules that, in general, allow losses from passive activities, which includes all rental properties, to be used only to offset income from other passive investments.

Patent Special type of deed that conveys title to real property owned by government to a private party.

Payment caps Protects the borrower against the shock of large payment changes; it is possible for the interest rate to increase enough that the resulting payment increase will not cover the additional interest cost.

Pension funds Retirement savings accounts that now represent a major source of equity capital in commercial real estate markets.

Percentage rent The amount of rent paid by a retail tenant in addition to the base rent. It generally is a percentage of tenant store sales above a prespecified threshold level.

Performance standard An approach to land use control that addresses concerns for urban systems such as traffic, watershed, green space, air quality or other aspects of the environment through limits to detrimental activities.

Periodic caps Provisions in adjustable rate mortgages that limit change in the contract interest rate from one change date to the next.

Periodic tenancy Any lease agreement that automatically renews each period until either party gives notice of termination.

Permanence potential The preference to lease residential units to households whose prior history indicates a probability of a long-term occupancy.

Permanent loan Long-term mortgage financing.

Personal liability Liability assumed by borrowers that allows lenders to sue them personally for fulfillment of the contract.

Personal performance (contract) A contract that requires a service or action on the part of one party. This includes leases and mortgage loans, for example, which require regular payments. Generally, these contracts are not fully assignable in that the lessee or mortgagor remains liable for the obligation.

Personal property Objects that are moveable and not permanently affixed to the land or structure, including furniture and tenant fixtures that are often purchased in conjunction with real property acquisitions.

Personal residence An owner-occupied housing unit.

Personal rights Personal freedoms derived primarily from the Bill of Rights and other amendments and clauses of the U.S. Constitution.

Physical deterioration Loss of value of a building from its reproduction cost, resulting from wear and tear over time.

Piggyback loan In home mortgage lending, a second mortgage loan created simultaneously with creation of a first mortgage loan, the latter having a loan-to-value ratio of no more than 80 percent. The "piggyback" second mortgage enables a buyer to achieve greater than 80 percent financing without incurring mortgage insurance on the first mortgage.

Pipeline risk The time between making a loan commitment and selling the loan. The mortgage banker is exposed to considerable risk during this period.

PITI The monthly payment of principal and interest on a home mortgage loan, plus monthly payments into an escrow account toward annual property taxes and hazard insurance.

Planned unit development (PUD) A development project, often involving a mixture of land uses and densities not permitted by normal zoning. It is allowed because the entire development is viewed as an integrated whole.

Plat books Register of recorded plat maps maintained by a city or county which shows boundaries, shapes, and sizes of land parcels.

Plat lot and block number An unambiguous means to provide a description of property that identifies each parcel in a surveyed map of a subdivision.

Plottage value Value added to land by assembling small parcels into larger tracts.

Police power Right of government to regulate personal activity and the use of property to protect the health, welfare, and safety of the population.

Polychlorinated biphenyls (PCBs) Cancer-causing chemicals formerly used in the manufacture of electrical connectors and equipment.

Portfolio income An IRS classification of income generated from securities such as stocks and bonds. Income directly obtained from rental real estate activities is not considered portfolio income.

Portfolio lenders Financial institutions such as banks that fund mortgage loans and then hold the loans as investments.

Portfolio perspective Viewing real estate investments in the context of an owner's other assets and overall situation.

Potential gross income The total annual income the property would produce if it were fully rented and had no collection losses.

Power of sale Mortgage provision that grants the authority to conduct foreclosure to either the lender or a trustee. Enables nonjudicial foreclosure.

Power shopping center These centers typically contain three or more giants in hard goods retailing (for example, Wal-Mart and Home Depot). The dominating feature of a power center is the high ratio of anchor tenants to smaller tenants.

Prepayment penalties Charges, designed to discourage prepayment, incurred when a mortgage is repaid before maturity.

Present value The value of future cash flows at time zero.

Preventive maintenance A program of regular inspections and care to avert potential problems.

Prime See Prime mortgage.

Prime mortgage Referring to "qualifying" home mortgages. The specific use of the term varies. Some use prime to refer to loans where the borrower has a FICO score of 660 or higher. Others also include FHA and VA mortgage loans. Still others distinguish prime by the type of lender.

Principal In brokerage, the person giving authority to an agent; in finance, the amount borrowed and owed on a loan.

Principal meridian A line of geographic reference that runs north and south in a government rectangular survey.

Private grants Conveyance of property from one private owner to another.

Private mortgage insurance (PMI) Insurance offered by private companies that reimburses the lender for capital losses in the event of default by the borrower.

Pro forma A cash flow forecast prepared to facilitate discounted cash flow analysis.

Probability distributions The distribution of all potential outcomes and their associated likelihood.

Probate State law that governs the disposition procedure of the conveyance of real property upon the death of a property owner.

Property Anything that can be owned, or possessed. It can be either a tangible asset or an intangible asset.

Property adjustments Five sale price adjustments made to comparable property transactions prices: location, physical characteristics, economic characteristics, use, and nonrealty items.

Property managers Individuals in charge of the day-to-day operations of a property.

Property rights Rights in property that include (exclusive) possession, use (enjoyment), and disposition.

Property tax lien Automatic lien placed by local governments to assure payment of property taxes.

Proprietary lease A lease of indefinite length in which the lessee pays expenses but not rent, associated with a cooperative.

Pro rata share An amount proportionate to the ownership interest of an investor.

Prorating Allocation of costs and revenues between buyer and seller of real property at closing, based on the time of ownership by each party.

Psychographics A data intensive, multivariate statistical approach for sophisticated determination of market segmentation.

Public purpose In eminent domain cases, expansion by courts of the public use concept, no longer requiring actual physical use by the condemning agency to justify condemnation.

Public use In eminent domain, requirement of actual physical use by the condemning agency to justify condemnation.

Purchase-money mortgage A mortgage created simultaneously with conveyance of ownership. Typically, where the seller lends part of the purchase price of a property to the purchaser, but also used to refer to any mortgage used to finance a purchase.

Qualified mortgage QM A class of home mortgages created by the Dodd-Frank Act aimed to assure very high ability to repay. Generally, QMs must be fully amortizing within 30 years, with limited fees. Underwriting requirements include a maximum debt-to-income ratio and carefully qualified income and assets. QMs afford the lender special protection against legal defenses in foreclosure.

Qualified residential mortgage QRM A special class of Qualified Mortgages which financial institutions will be able to securitize and sell without retaining a portion of the credit risk. With non-QRM, financial institutions will be required to retain at least five percent of credit risk if the loans are securitized and sold.

Quiet enjoyment In leasing, once the owner has conveyed possession of the property to the tenant, the owner must provide the tenant with uninterrupted use of the property without any interference that may threaten the tenant's leasehold interest in the property. In conveyance of title, the assurance that no one holds a claim to title superior to that of the grantee, and that the grantor will defend the title claim of the grantee.

Quitclaim deed Deed that conveys an individual's property rights to another but has none of the covenants of the warranty deed.

R² statistic Coefficient of multiple determination that measures how well a regression model fits the data.

Radon A naturally occurring radioactive gas found in soils in most parts of the country. In large concentrations, the gas may contribute to or cause cancer.

Range line A feature of a government rectangular survey that separates townships by east and west.

Rate lock agreement An agreement in which a loan applicant pays a nonrefundable deposit to protect against an interest rate increase before the loan is closed.

Raw land Land that does not include structures or any improvements.

Real asset Tangible objects that have value because they are useful.

Real estate The tangible assets of land and buildings; the "bundle" of rights associated with the ownership and use of the physical assets; and the industry, or business activities, related to the acquisition, operation, and disposition of the physical assets.

Real estate commission Appointed commission responsible for overseeing the implementation and administration of a state's real estate license law. It usually is empowered to grant, revoke, or suspend licenses, and otherwise discipline real estate brokers operating in the state.

Real estate investment trusts (REITs) A corporation or trust that uses the pooled capital of many investors to purchase and manage income property (equity REIT) and/or mortgage loans (mortgage REIT).

Real Estate Private Equity Funds These funds have a finite life, typically 7–10 years, with an option for the fund manager or sponsor to extend the life by an additional year or two. Because of this finite life, the fund manager is forced to eventually dispose of the assets and return the investors' capital. These funds typically have meaningful side-by-side investment by the fund sponsor/manager, aligning the manager's economic outcomes with those of the investors. The fee structures are also usually richer and more complex, allowing more features that further align interests.

Real Estate Settlement and Procedures Act (RESPA) A federal law requiring lenders to provide information on all costs associated with closing a residential loan within three business days of the loan application, to use the HUD-1 closing statement, to limit required escrow deposits, and to avoid kickbacks on loan-related services.

Real property Rights associated with ownership of land and all permanent attachments to land.

Reconciliation The process of forming a single point estimate from two or more numbers. It is used widely in the appraisal process. For example, in the sales comparison approach to develop a single indicated value from several final adjusted sale prices of comparables, and in final reconciliation to develop a final estimate of value from two or more indicated values.

Reconstructed operating statement A statement of property income and expenses formatted for the purposes of appraisal and investment analysis. Differs from typical management operating statement in the treatment of certain expenses, including management fees, mortgage payments, and vacancy and collection losses.

Recorded plat map See *Plat books.*

Recording Filing of a document with the appropriate public official or office in order to provide constructive notice to the public of a sales transaction or legal contract.

Recording statutes State laws requiring documents that convey an interest in real property to be placed in the public records in order to be binding on the public.

Recourse loans Loans in which the borrower has personal liability and the lender has legal recourse against the borrower in case of default.

Recovery fund Reserve of funds collected from real estate license fees to pay for losses to clients legally judged to have been caused by a licensed salesperson or broker. The existence of such funds varies from state to state.

Redlining Term used to describe when mortgage lenders avoid certain neighborhoods without regard to the merits of the individual loan applications.

Regional shopping center These centers are focused on apparel and discretionary merchandise, and have at least two anchor tenants that are major department stores.

Regulatory taking Under precedents of the U.S. Supreme Court, the degree of land regulation that is considered to constitute effective taking of the property. If this degree of regulation is reached, the government must compensate the property owner for loss of value.

Rehabilitation The restoration of a property to satisfactory condition without changing the floor plan, form, or style of the structure.

Reinvestment risk The risk that lenders will need to reinvest the remaining loan balance at a lower rate when borrowers prepay mortgages with above-market rates.

Release of liability A document by which a lender releases a borrower from personal liability on a note.

Reliction Receding water line that leaves dry land to be added to an adjacent landowner's property.

Relocation option Generally, a lease clause that gives the property owner the option to relocate a tenant within a shopping center or office building, provided the new space is of similar size and quality and provided the owner agrees to pay all reasonable moving costs.

Remainder estate The ownership interest subsequent to a life estate which, upon the death of the life estate owner, becomes a fee simple absolute interest.

Remodeling Actions resulting in changes to the floor plan, form, or style of a structure to correct functional or economic deficiencies.

Renewal option Lease clause that gives the tenant the right, but not the obligation, to renew the lease.

Rentable area The office tenant's usable area, plus his or her prorated share of the common areas.

Rentable/usable (R/U) ratio The ratio of total rentable area to total usable area. Will be greater than 1 in office buildings.

Repeat-sale analysis Estimation of the rate of property appreciation through statistical examination of properties that have sold twice during the sample period. Normally, the analysis is by statistical regression.

Replacement cost The cost to build a new building of equal utility to an existing building that is not an exact physical replica of the existing building.

Reproduction cost The cost to build a new building that is exactly like an existing building in every physical detail.

Rescind (rescission) The termination of a contract by cancellation. Under the Truth-in-Lending Act, a borrower's right to cancel a non-purchase loan contract within three days that is secured by his or her principal residence.

Reserve for replacements An allowance in a cash flow forecast to reflect an annual allocation for periodic replacements, releasing expenses, or tenant improvements.

Restricted appraisal report Provides a minimal discussion of the appraisal with large numbers of references to internal file documentation. If the client just wants to know what the property is worth and does not intend to provide the appraisal to anyone for use or reference, a restricted report may be sufficient.

Restrictive covenants See *deed restriction.*

Reverse mortgage An arrangement where the lender agrees to pay money to an elderly homeowner, either regularly or occasionally, and to be repaid from the homeowner's equity when he or she sells the home or obtains other financing.

Reversion The cash proceeds from sale.

Reverter An uncertain interest held by the previous owner (or heirs) associated with a conditional fee.

Right of first refusal Commercial lease clause that grants the tenant first choice to lease space in a property should it become available.

Right of prepayment The right to retire a mortgage before maturity. The right of prepayment will depend on the law of the state where the property is located and on the particular mortgage contract.

Right of survivorship The rights of surviving partners in a joint tenancy to divide the interests of a deceased partner.

Riparian rights The rights of adjacent landowners to bodies of nonnavigable waters.

Risk The possibility that actual outcomes will vary from what was expected when the asset was purchased.

Risk-adjusted discount rate The discount rate used by potential investors to value risky cash flows. Must reflect the relative riskiness of the asset/property being valued.

Risk-weighted assets The sum of an institution's portfolio assets weighted by their appropriate risk classification, used to determine regulatory capital requirements for depository institutions.

Rule of capture The owner of an oil or gas well could claim all that is pumped from it, regardless of whether the oil or gas migrated from adjacent property.

Sale-leasebacks As a method of financing needed real estate, a property owner/user simultaneously sells the property to a buyer and leases the property back from the buyer.

Salesperson license Authority granted by a state to engage in the real estate brokerage business as an employee or agent of a real estate broker.

Sandwich lease A sublet arrangement in which the initial lessee collects rent from the new lessee and pays rent to the landlord under the original lease agreement.

Savings and loan associations (S&Ls) Historically, a highly specialized home mortgage lending depository institution. Today, S&Ls range in character from mortgage lending specialists to being very similar to commercial banks.

Savings banks Historically empowered with wider investment powers than S&Ls, the two institutional forms are virtually indistinguishable today.

Second mortgage Like the first mortgage lien, a second mortgage is secured by the borrower's property that has been pledged as collateral for the loan. However, the lender holding a second mortgage is second in line behind the holder of the first mortgage to receive the sale proceeds from a foreclosure sale. Thus, the second lender is in a more risky position.

Secondary mortgage market The market where mortgage originators can divest their holdings, and existing mortgages are resold.

Section A specifically surveyed and identified square mile within the framework of the rectangular survey system.

Section 203 loan The most widely used FHA program, covering single-family home mortgages insured by the FHA under Title II, section 203 of the National Housing Act.

Section 1231 property Trade or business property held for more than one year, as classified in Section 1231 of the Internal Revenue Code.

Sector model Model of urban form proposed by Homer Hoyt that is characterized by radial corridors or wedges, particularly for higher income residential land use.

Securitized investments Investment instruments that pool investment assets, enabling investors to purchase a share in the pool of assets.

Selling expenses Costs associated with the disposition of a property.

Separate accounts An investment manager acting on behalf of multiple clients holds each client's assets in a separate account rather than as part of a commingled fund to permit customized investments for each client.

Separate property In community property states, property that the husband or wife acquired prior to the marriage, or gifts or inheritance received during the marriage.

Servient parcel A parcel that is constrained or diminished by an easement appurtenant.

Sheriff's deed Same as definition of executor's deed.

Single-factor asset pricing model A model for determining required risk-adjusted rates of return that classifies investment risk into only two categories, systematic (or macroeconomic) and property-specific (or microeconomic).

Sinking fund factor The amount that must be deposited periodically at a specified interest rate, for a specified time period, to accumulate to $1.00 at the end of the period.

Site plan Map showing the arrangement of structures, parking, streets, and other features of a development or subdivision project.

Smart growth Planning philosophy that embraces revitalization of existing communities, compact design, walkable neighborhoods, sense of place, preservation of open spaces and critical environment, community involvement in development.

Soft costs A component of construction cost including the cost of permits, legal fees, financing and insurance fees, architectural and design costs, other professional fees, and the cost of marketing.

Soils engineer An engineer specializing in the analysis of soils and soil load-bearing capacity, and in determining adequate footing and foundation requirements for a structure.

Sole proprietorship Ownership structure where all cash flow and income tax consequences flow through directly to the individual's income tax return, thereby avoiding taxation at the entity level.

Special agent A person to whom a principal has granted authority to handle a specific business transaction or to perform a specific function. Real estate brokers and salespersons are special agents.

Special assessments Property taxes levied to finance special improvements to benefit adjacent property owners. For example, property owners in a subdivision could be forced to pay for the installation of sanitary sewers.

Special warranty deed Identical to a general warranty deed except that the covenant against encumbrances applies only to the time that the grantor owned the property.

Specialty shopping center These centers are characterized by a dominant theme or image and many are located in downtown areas or rehabilitated historic structures. Outlet centers are a variation of this theme.

Specific lien An interest that derives directly from events related to a property, such as property tax and assessment liens, mortgages, and mechanics' liens.

Specific performance A legal action brought in a court of equity, compelling a party defaulting on a contract to carry out the exact requirements of the contract rather than, for example, settling for damages.

Sprawl A term applied pejoratively to many aspects of suburban development. A relatively restrictive use of the term refers to unregulated real estate development outside of central urban areas, and to "leap-frog" development.

Spread The difference between the expected yield (interest rate) on an investment and the yield (interest rate) on a riskless Treasury security with a comparable maturity.

Standard deduction The amount of deductible expenses, specified by Congress, that a taxpayer may claim in lieu of itemizing allowable personal expenditures.

Standard deviation A measure of the dispersion of a distribution around its expected value, defined as the square root of the variance.

Standard error (SE) The standard deviation of the sampling distribution of a statistic, such as an estimated mean value, or a regression coefficient.

Statement of condition A document signed by the tenant of a residential property before moving in that lists any prior damage to the unit.

Statute of Frauds Provision adopted by all states requiring that all deeds, long-term leases and mortgages must be in writing to be enforceable. Derives from the original Statute of Frauds in 1677.

Statutory redemption See *Statutory right of redemption.*

Statutory right of redemption In foreclosure, this is the right afforded the defaulting mortgagor to recover the foreclosed property for a period of time after foreclosure sale by paying the full amount of the defaulted loan plus legal costs of the foreclosure. This right is not available in all states. In states where it exists, it ranges for a few days to several years.

Structural engineer An engineer specializing in the design of buildings and other structures that are efficient for their purpose, while meeting standards of sturdiness and safety.

Subagency The agency role of a broker is extended to one or more additional brokers, who also become a fiduciary of the principal and are empowered to act on his or her behalf. The subagent shares any commission with the original broker. This agency chain can extend through multiple agents in the case of multiple-list services.

Subchapter S corporation Corporate ownership structure that is a federal tax election made with the unanimous consent of the shareholders. An S corporation possesses the same limited liability benefits for its shareholders as do C corporations but it is not a separate taxable entity.

Subcontractor Companies or individuals who provide specialized construction activities, such as installation of heating, ventilating, and air-conditioning systems, elevator systems, painting, carpet installation, and a multitude of other building components.

Subject property The property for which an appraisal of fair market value is produced.

Subject to When a buyer acquires a property having an existing mortgage loan and begins making the required payments without assuming personal responsibility for the note.

Subjective probability distribution For a set of possible outcomes of an uncertain event, an opinion or guess as to the likelihood of each possible outcome.

Sublease Occurs when the original tenant transfers a subset of his or her rights under the lease to another tenant, although the original tenant (lessee) continues to be obligated for payments.

Submarket Segment or portion of a market in which all of the properties are considered to be close substitutes by a relatively homogeneous group of potential buyers; properties that provide similar utility or satisfaction.

Subordination agreement A contract by which a party holding a superior claim agrees to make it subject to a previously inferior claim. Commonly used to reverse the priority of mortgage liens.

Subprime loans Loans made to homeowners who do not qualify for standard (prime) home loans. Subprime loans can have high fees, and costly prepayment penalties that "lock in" the borrower to a high interest rate.

Superregional malls These shopping centers have as many as five to six major tenants and hundreds of minor tenants.

Survey (of land) Process of accurately establishing the boundaries of a parcel of real estate.

Syndicate A group of persons or legal entities who come together to carry out a particular investment activity.

Systematic risk Risk that cannot be diversified away—even in a large portfolio. This type of risk results from exposure to macroeconomic risk factors.

Take-out commitment Agreement, issued by a long-term lender, to disburse the permanent loan proceeds when construction of a project has been completed according to specifications.

Tangible assets Physical things, such as automobiles, clothing, land, or buildings.

Tax assessor The local public official in charge of determining the taxable value of property in the jurisdiction as the basis for property taxation. In some states this official is called the county property appraiser.

Tax base All of the taxable properties in a jurisdiction.

Tax certificates Obligations for unpaid taxes sold by taxing jurisdictions in order to collect the amount of unpaid taxes. The property owner, in order to redeem (take back) the property, or any future purchaser of the property, must pay off the tax certificates to obtain title to the property.

Tax rate (property tax) The number of dollars of property tax divided by the taxable value of the properties. The percentage that, when multiplied by a property's taxable value, will yield the tax liability.

Taxable value The assessed value less any applicable exemptions, to determine the amount of property tax owed.

Tax-exempt properties Properties against which local jurisdictions may not levy taxes, usually including churches, synagogues, public schools, and government property.

Teaser rate The initial interest rate on an adjustable rate mortgage if it is less than the index rate plus the margin at the time of origination.

Tenancy at sufferance A tenancy that occurs when a tenant that is supposed to vacate does not, but continues to pay rent, and the landlord accepts it.

Tenancy at will A tenancy granted by landlords to tenants allowing them to remain in possession without written agreement.

Tenancy by the entireties A form of joint tenancy ownership for husband and wife.

Tenancy for years A leasehold interest for a definite period of time exceeding one year.

Tenancy in common The "normal" form of direct co-ownership, which is as close to the fee simple absolute estate as is possible, subject to the provision that one owner cannot use the property in a manner that infringes on the rights of co-owners.

Tenant improvement allowance The amount of funding the owner of commercial property must provide toward the cost of refurbishing the space to meet the tenant's needs.

Tenant mix The synergism created by the right grouping of tenants that results in the right mix of tenants that "makes the whole greater than the sum of its parts."

Tenant reps Brokers or agents that specialize in helping tenants find suitable space to lease.

Term for amortization Time period that determines the payment, and the schedule of interest and principal payments on a mortgage.

Term to maturity Term found in a balloon loan that determines when the entire remaining balance on the loan must be paid in full.

Terminal capitalization rate Rate used to convert annual net cash at the end of an expected holding period into an estimate of future sale price. (See *Going-out cap rate*.)

Terminal value The sale price at the end of the expected holding period.

Terms See *Contract terms*.

Testate Conveyance of real property upon the death of a property owner in accordance with a will.

Thrifts Depository institutions that evolved primarily to collect and invest household savings. Usually the term encompasses (former) savings and loan associations and savings banks, but not credit unions. Thrifts invested largely in home mortgage loans, and for well over a century, until about 1980, were the backbone of home mortgage finance in the United States.

Tier line A feature of a government rectangular survey that serves to number townships south or north from the base line.

Timesharing Property occupancy arrangement in which multiple individuals have use of property but, unlike traditional forms of co-ownership, the interests are at different time intervals rather than simultaneous. A timesharing arrangement may involve true co-ownership, leasehold interests, or simply permission to occupy (i.e., license).

Time value of money (TVM) techniques Standard techniques for quantifying the effects of time and risk on value.

Title abstract The compilation of all documents summarizing the chain of title into a chronological volume and then given to an attorney for final interpretation.

Title abstract with attorney's opinion Traditional evidence of title.

Title insurance Insurance paying monetary damages for loss of property from unexpected superior legal claims or for litigation to protect title. Deemed superior to the traditional abstract with opinion as evidence of title since it offers insurance, in addition.

Title insurance commitment A commitment to issue a title insurance policy. One of the two primary forms of evidence of title.

Title search The task of examining the evidence of title in the public records.

Title theory Lender receives title to the mortgaged property that ripens upon default.

Torrens certificate A rarely used means of providing evidence of title.

Township A unit within the government rectangular survey system having an area of six miles by six miles, and containing 36 fully described, one square mile sections.

Toxic waste Hazardous materials such as asbestos, fiberglass, lead paint, radon, PCBs, leaking underground storage tanks, and the like.

Trade fixtures Personal property usually paid for by the tenant that may be removed by the tenant at lease expiration.

Trade or business property Under Section 1231 of the Internal Revenue Code, real estate held for more than one year in a trade or business activity, including most income-producing property.

Transaction broker One who facilitates a real estate transaction but who is not an agent of either buyer or seller. A transaction broker is required to deal honestly and fairly with both parties and to exercise skill, care, and diligence in carrying out his or her duties.

Transaction price The prices observed on sold properties.

Transactional adjustments In an appraisal, adjustments to comparable property transaction prices that concern the nature and terms of the deal.

Trustee In mortgage lending, person who holds the deed on behalf of both the borrower and lender in a deed of trust.

Trustee's deed A deed issued by the trustee in a court-supervised disposition of property, for example by an executor and administrator of an estate, a guardian of a minor, a bankruptcy trustee, or possibly by an attorney in divorce proceedings.

Truth-in-Lending Act (TILA) A federal law requiring lenders to provide residential loan applicants with estimates of the total finance charges and the annual percentage rate (APR).

Turnkey Refers to a project where the owner or builder makes a property ready for the occupant to immediately move in and begin business.

Umbrella partnership REIT (UPREIT) An organizational structure in which a publicly traded REIT owns a fractional interest in an operating partnership, which in turn, owns all or part of individual property partnerships.

Uniform Standards of Professional Appraisal Practice (USPAP) Rules governing the appraisal process and reporting of appraisals that are developed by the Appraisal Standards Board of the Appraisal Foundation. Appraisers are obligated by law to follow these rules and guidelines.

Universal agent One to whom a principal delegates the power to act in all matters that can be delegated in place of the principal.

Unlevered cash flows The expected stream of NOIs and the expected net sale proceeds (NSP). This represents the income-producing ability of the property before subtracting the portion of the cash flows that must be paid to the lender to service or retire the debt.

Unsystematic risk The variation in portfolio returns that can be eliminated by holding securities and other investments with less than perfectly correlated returns. Results from exposure to microeconomic risk factors.

Upfront financing costs Cost incurred by the property owner to obtain mortgage financing, including loan origination fees, discount points, appraisal fees, and survey. On a rental property investment, these costs are amortized over the life of the loan for tax purposes.

Urban service area An area delineated around a community within which the local government plans to provide public services and facilities and beyond which urban development is discouraged or prohibited.

Usable area The area of an office building that is in the sole possession of the tenant.

User markets Potential occupants, both owner-occupants and tenants, or renters competing for physical location and space.

VA-guaranteed loan A government-guaranteed loan designed to help veterans obtain home mortgage loans for which they might not otherwise qualify.

Variance (statistics) A measure of the dispersion of an ex ante distribution probability around its expected value or the dispersion of historical (realized) cash flows or returns around the mean value.

Variance (zoning) A permitted deviation for a particular property from the applicable zoning requirements. To be granted only when the zoning ordinance imposes undue hardship to the property owner.

Veterans Affairs (VA) A U.S. government Department whose purpose is to help veterans readjust to civilian life.

Warehouses Provide space for the temporary storage of goods.

Warehousing The provision by commercial banks of short-term funds to mortgage banking companies to enable them to originate and fund mortgage loans until they can be sold in the secondary mortgage market.

Words of conveyance Early in the deed will be words such as "does hereby grant, bargain, sell, and convey unto. . . ." that serve to assure the grantor clearly intends to convey an interest in real property and indicates the type of deed offered by the grantor.

Yield maintenance agreement A clause in a commercial mortgage loan that requires the borrower to pay the lender a prepayment penalty if the borrower prepays the loan prior to maturity and current market interest rates are lower than the contract rate on the existing mortgage. The prepayment penalty is computed as the present value of interest income to be lost by the lender due to the early prepayment. The idea is to "make whole" the lender. Yield maintenance penalties are found strictly in loans on income-producing properties.

Zoning Regulation of land use by dividing the community into various residential, commercial, industrial and other districts. The districts are further differentiated by maximum building density.

Index

Italic page numbers indicate exhibits; **bold** page numbers indicate glossary terms; page numbers with "n" indicate footnotes.

A

abandonment
  asset management and, 573
ability to pay, 296–297
ability-to-repay standard, 298
acceleration clause, **226**
acceptance
  required for closing, 361
  required for contract for sale, 341–342, 361
access, 13
access to premises, 586
Accredited Management Organization (AMO), 569
Accredited Resident Manager (ARM), 568
accretion, **54**
accrued depreciation, 167, 179, **180**
acknowledgment, **48**–49
acquisition cost, investment value compared to, *404,* 404–405
acre, **6**
actual notice, **55**
adaptive reuse, **572**
adjustable rate mortgage (ARM), **219,** 219–221, 421–425
  adjustment periods of, 423
  considerations in choosing, 425
  example of, 421–422, *422*
  hybrid, 259–260
  index rate, 219–220
  vs. LPMs, 248
  margin, 220
  mechanics of, 421
  option, 260–261
  payment caps, 221
  rate caps, 221
  rate caps for, 423–425, *424*
  share of mortgage originations, 423, *423*
  teaser rates, 221
  teaser rates for, *421,* 421–422
adjusted funds from operations (AFFO), 477n15

adjustments, **170**
  to comparable sales data, 170–174
  property, 171
  transactional, 171
ad valorem taxes, **88**–89
adverse possession, **53,** 53n6
advertising, 586
affordable housing allocation, **74**
affordable housing loans, **299,** 299–300
after-tax cash flow *(ATCF),* **490**–491
after-tax equity reversion, **515**
agency relationship, **567**
agents. *See also* real estate agents
  designated, 311
  general, 308
  special, 308
  types of, 308
  universal, 308
agglomeration economies, **107,** 107–108
aggressive marketing, 238
agreement
  buyer agency, 309
  subordination, 617
agriculture-based economy, 102
agriculture fixtures, 23
air-conditioning, 118–119
air-conditioning system standards, 77
air space, property rights of, 21
AllianceTexas industrial community, 118
Alt-A loans, **261**–262
alterations, leased premises, 584
Amazon.com, 155
Ambler Realty Company, 79
American Housing Survey, 245
American Industrial Real Estate Association, 318
American Institute of Constructors (AIC), 619, 622
American Land Title Association, 57–58
amortization, 221n7
  alternative schedules, 420–421
  of level-payment mortgages, 418–421
  negative, 221, 238
  payments, 221–222
  term, 222
  term for, 222
amortizing mortgages, interest-only, 259
analogy
  as market analysis techniques, 134

anchor tenants, **596**
annual percentage rate (APR), 262, **414**–415
annuity
  due, future value of, 393
  future value of, *389,* 392–393
    equation for, *387,* 387–388
  present value of, *394,* 396
    equation for, *387,* 387–388
apartment building. *See also* residential properties
  high-rise, 589
  investment values of, compared to acquisition costs, *404,* 404–405
  midrise, 590
apartments, 589n4
apartment vacancy rates, *152*
Apple, 155
appraisal, 130–131, **161.** *See also* valuation
  conventional approaches to, 166–167, *167*
  conveyance of real property rights in, 171
  cost approach to, 167
  cycle of, *132*
  data analysis in, 165–166
  data collection in, 165
  Elysian Forest, planned unit development example, 135–140
  examples of, 135–150
  final notes on the process of, 151
  first analysis, 133
  identification of problem, 165
  improving one's capacity in, 151
  income approach to, 167
  informal methods of, 161
  initial collection of data, 133
  land value in, 166
  market-defining story, 132–133
  market projections and real estate cycles, 151–152
  market segmentation, 131
  Palm Grove Office Complex example, 140–142
  Plane Vista Apartments example, 142–150
  process of, 163–168, *165, 167*
  property description in, 165
  reconciliation in, 168